The SAGE Handbook of

Early Childhood Literacy

Second Edition

The SAGE Handbook of
Early Childhood
Literacy
Second Edition

Edited by
Joanne Larson
and Jackie Marsh

Los Angeles | London | New Delhi
Singapore | Washington DC

Los Angeles | London | New Delhi
Singapore | Washington DC

SAGE Publications Ltd
1 Oliver's Yard
55 City Road
London EC1Y 1SP

SAGE Publications Inc.
2455 Teller Road
Thousand Oaks, California 91320

SAGE Publications India Pvt Ltd
B 1/I 1 Mohan Cooperative Industrial Area
Mathura Road
New Delhi 110 044

SAGE Publications Asia-Pacific Pte Ltd
3 Church Street
#10-04 Samsung Hub
Singapore 049483

Typeset by: Cenveo Publisher Services
Printed in Great Britain by MPG Books Group,
Bodmin, Cornwall
Printed on paper from sustainable resources

FSC
SA-COC-1565
© 1996 Forest Stewardship Council A.C.
'The Global Benchmark for
Responsible Forest Management'

Contents

Acknowledgements   ix
International Advisory Board   xi
Notes on Contributors   xiii
Preface   xxix

PART 1   PERSPECTIVES ON EARLY CHILDHOOD LITERACY   **01**

1   The Emergence of Early Childhood Literacy   03
    Julia Gillen and Nigel Hall

2   Postcolonial Perspectives on Early Childhood Literacy   18
    Radhika Viruru

3   Gender and Early Childhood Literacy   35
    Elaine Millard and Petula Bhojwani

4   Reconceptualizing Early Childhood Literacy: The Sociocultural Influence
    and New Directions in Digital and Hybrid Media-tion   52
    Aria Razfar and Kris D. Gutiérrez

5   Play, Literacies, and the Converging Cultures of Childhood   80
    Karen E. Wohlwend

6   Policy-making in Early Childhood Literacy: Pathways to Equity
    for All Children   96
    Cecilia Rios-Aguilar

7   Disability and Early Childhood: The Importance of Creating Literacy
    Opportunities and Identities   115
    Martha Mock and Susan Hildenbrand

**PART 2   EARLY CHILDHOOD LITERACY IN FAMILIES,
COMMUNITIES, AND CULTURES ACROSS MEDIA AND MODES**   **131**

8   Researching Young Children's Out-of-School Literacy Practices   133
    Tamara Spencer, Michele Knobel, and Colin Lankshear

9   The Out-of-School Schooling of Literacy   161
     Eve Gregory and Charmian Kenner

10   Agency, Authority, and Action in Family Literacy Scholarship:
     An Analysis of the Epistemological Assumptions Operating
     in Family Literacy Scholarship   175
     *Catherine Compton-Lilly and Beth Graue with Rebecca Rogers
     and Tisha Y. Lewis*

11   Research Issues in Family Literacy   194
     Greg Brooks and Peter Hannon

12   Early Childhood Literacy and Popular Culture   207
     Jackie Marsh

13   Film and Television   223
     Muriel Robinson and Margaret Mackey

14   Critical Indigenous Literacies   251
     Debbie Reese

15   Artifactual Literacies   263
     Kate Pahl and Jennifer Rowsell

16   Space, Place and Early Childhood Literacy   279
     Sue Nichols and Helen Nixon

17   Multimodal Perspectives on Early Childhood Literacies   295
     Rosie Flewitt

PART 3   EARLY MOVES IN LITERACY   311

18   Moving into Literacy: How it all Begins   313
     Lesley Lancaster

19   Perspectives on Making Meaning: The Differential Principles
     and Means of Adults and Children   329
     Gunther Kress

20   Reading Policy: Evidence versus Power   345
     Gerald Coles

21   Becoming Biliterate   364
     Charmian Kenner and Eve Gregory

22 Early Reading Development   379
    Dominic Wyse and Usha Goswami

23 Young Children's Literary Meaning Making: A Decade of Research
    2000–2010   395
    Caitlin McMunn Dooley, Miriam Martinez, and Nancy L. Roser

24 Textbooks and Early Childhood Literacy   409
    Allan Luke, Victoria Carrington, and Cushla Kapitzke

25 Recent Trends in Research on Young Children's Authoring   423
    Deborah Wells Rowe

26 The Development of Spelling   448
    Patricia L. Scharer and Jerry Zutell

PART 4 LITERACY IN PRESCHOOL SETTINGS AND SCHOOLS   483

27 The Place of Childhoods in School Writing Programs: A Matter of Ethics   485
    Anne Haas Dyson

28 Talk and Discourse in Formal Learning Settings   501
    Joanne Larson and Shira M. Peterson

29 Effective Literacy Teaching in the Early Years of School:
    A Review of Evidence   523
    Kathy Hall

30 Creating Positive Literacy Learning Environments in Early Childhood:
    Engaging Classrooms, Creating Lifelong Readers, Writers and Thinkers   541
    Eithne Kennedy

31 Towards Knowing Well and Doing Well: Assessment and Early
    Childhood Education   561
    Sharon Murphy

32 Learning, Literacies and New Technologies: The Current Context and Future
    Possibilities   575
    Cathy Burnett and Guy Merchant

33 Critical Literacy in the Early Years: Emergence and Sustenance in an
    Age of Accountability   587
    Barbara Comber

PART 5 RESEARCHING EARLY CHILDHOOD LITERACY **603**

34 Methodologies in Research on Young Children and Literacy 605
David Bloome, Laurie Katz, Huili Hong, Patricia May-Woods
and Melissa Wilson

35 Methodologies of Early Childhood Research 633
Marjorie Faulstich Orellana and Karisa Peer

Index 653

Acknowledgements

Joanne Larson and Jackie Marsh wish to thank the editorial staff at SAGE for all their wonderful work on this second edition. We also express our gratitude to the chapter authors, old and new, who put together important and comprehensive pieces for the handbook and members of the International Advisory Board, who reviewed the chapters. Joanne Larson thanks her husband Morris, and her children Anna, Eric, and Marcus for always being there. Jackie Marsh would also like to thank her partner, Julie, and daughter, Angela, for their continuing support. Finally, we would like to acknowledge the contribution Nigel Hall made to the first edition of this book and we hope that he likes what we have done in this second edition.

International Advisory Board

Notes on Contributors

Petula Bhojwani works as an independent literacy consultant and specialises in raising boys' attainment. She has worked across the East and West Midlands, UK as a primary school literacy coordinator, regional advisor, consultant for Nottinghamshire local authority and senior lecturer in Primary Education at Birmingham City University. Her research interests are in multimodal literacies with particular attention to boys and Looked-after Children.

David Bloome is College of Education and Human Ecology (EHE) Distinguished Professor of Teaching and Learning at The Ohio State University College of Education and Human Ecology, USA. Bloome's research focuses on how people use spoken and written language for learning in classroom and non-classroom settings, and how people use language to create social relationships, to construct knowledge, and to create communities and shared histories and futures. Bloome's research focuses on children in preschool, elementary school, middle childhood, and early adolescence. Bloome's current scholarship focuses on: the social construction of intertextuality as part of the reading, writing, and learning processes; discourse analysis as a means for understanding reading, writing, and literacy events; spoken and written narrative development among young children as a foundation for learning and literacy development; and students as researchers and ethnographers of their own communities. He is the director of the Center for Video Ethnography and Discourse Analysis and the Columbus Area Writing Project.

Greg Brooks, PhD, is Emeritus Professor of Education, University of Sheffield, UK, and in 2011–12 was a member of the European Union High-Level Group of Experts. He has been engaged in educational research virtually full-time since 1977, and has published widely on the initial teaching of reading and spelling, phonics, family literacy, the assessment of schoolchildren's speaking and listening skills, intervention schemes for children and young people with poor literacy, adult literacy, and trends over time in the literacy levels of children and adults. In 1994–96 he directed the first evaluation of family literacy programmes in Britain; he subsequently directed five further evaluations in the field, and in 2008–09 took part in a national evaluation of family literacy programmes in England.

Cathy Burnett Cathy Burnett is Reader in the Department of Teacher Education at Sheffield Hallam University, UK, where she leads the Language and Literacy Research and Scholarship Group and co-leads the Teacher Education Research and Scholarship Group. Her research focuses on relationships between literacies within and beyond formal educational contexts, with a particular focus on the social practices emerging around new technologies in classrooms. She is interested in how children negotiate meaning through and around digital texts, using theories of space to explore meaning-making across on/offline contexts. Her published work has also explored the continuities and discontinuities between preservice teachers' literacy practices in different domains of their lives and considered the barriers and possibilities that teachers associate with using new texts in schools. She is co-editor of the United Kingdom Literacy Association journal, Literacy.

Victoria Carrington is a Professor of Education in the School of Education and Lifelong Learning at the University of East Anglia (UEA), UK. Before joining UEA, she held a Research South Australia (SA) Chair and was the Interim Director of the Hawke Research Institute at the University of South Australia. She has held posts at the University of Plymouth where she was Associate Dean for Research and Innovation in the Faculty of Education, the University of Queensland and the University of Tasmania. She is an editor of the international journal *Discourse: Studies in the Cultural Politics of Education* and sits on the editorial boards of a number of journals. She researches and writes extensively on the New Literacy Studies, with a particular interest in the impact of digital media on the production and distribution of text.

Gerald Coles is a full-time researcher, writer, and lecturer on literacy, learning and psychology. He is the author of *The Learning Mystique: a Critical Look at 'Learning Disabilities', Reading Lessons: the Debate over Literacy, Misreading Reading: the Bad Science that Hurts Children*, and *Reading the Naked Truth: Literacy, Legislation, and Lies*, as well as numerous articles in education, psychology and psychiatry journals. Before devoting himself to full-time research and writing, he was on the faculties of the Department of Psychiatry at Robert Wood Johnson Medical School, University of Medicine and Dentistry of New Jersey, and the Warner Graduate School of Education and Human Development at the University of Rochester, USA.

Barbara Comber is a Professor in the Faculty of Education at Queensland University of Technology, Australia. She is particularly interested in literacy education and social justice. She has conducted longitudinal ethnographic studies and collaborative action research with teachers working in high-poverty and culturally diverse communities examining the kinds of teaching that make a difference to young people's learning trajectories. She recently undertook an institutional ethnography on mandated literacy assessment and the reorganisation of teachers' work. Her current projects explore the affordances of place-based pedagogies for the development of critical and creative literacies and how teacher innovation can be sustained in high-poverty school communities.

Catherine Compton-Lilly is an Associate Professor in Curriculum and Instruction at the University of Wisconsin Madison, USA. She is the author of *Reading Families: The Literate Lives of Urban Children* (Teachers College Press, 2003), *Confronting Racism, Poverty and Power* (Heinemann, 2004), *Rereading Families* (Teachers College Press,

2007), *Reading Time* (Teachers College Press, 2012), the editor of *Breaking the Silence* (International Reading Association, 2009), and co-editor of *Bedtime Stories and Book Reports: Complexities, Concerns, and Considerations in Fostering Parent Involvement and Family Literacy* (Teachers College Press, 2010). Dr Compton-Lilly has authored articles in many literacy journals. Dr Compton-Lilly engages in longitudinal research projects that last over long periods of time. In her most recent study, she followed a group of eight inner-city students from grade 1 through grade 11. Her interests include examining how time operates as a contextual factor in children's lives as they progress through school.

Caitlin McMunn Dooley is an Associate Professor of Early Childhood Education and Director of the Doctoral Program in Early Childhood and Elementary Education at Georgia State University, USA. Her research investigates early emergent comprehension, literacy instruction and testing in elementary grades, and teacher development. Her research has been published by the International Reading Association, Literacy Research Association, and National Council of Teachers of English (NCTE), among others. Dooley has led and participated in funded research totaling more than $16.2 million. She serves as co-editor for NCTE's premier elementary-focused journal *Language Arts* (2011–2016). Dooley has received several awards, including the 2008 Jerry Johns Promising Researcher Award by the Association for Literacy Educators and Researchers. In addition to having taught elementary grades, Dooley served as a consultant to the Texas Educational Agency Student Assessment Division, the national non-profit Children's Literacy Initiative, and many urban schools and districts. Dooley earned her doctorate from the University of Texas at Austin and her undergraduate and master degrees from the University of Virginia.

Anne Haas Dyson is a former teacher of young children and, currently, a Professor of Education at the University of Illinois at Urbana-Champaign, USA. Previously she was on the faculty of the University of Georgia, Michigan State University, and the University of California, Berkeley, where she was a recipient of the campus Distinguished Teaching Award. She studies the childhood cultures and literacy learning of young schoolchildren. Among her publications are *Social Worlds of Children Learning to Write in an Urban Primary School*, which was awarded NCTE's David Russell Award for Distinguished Research, *Writing Superheroes*, and *The Brothers and Sisters Learn to Write: Popular Literacies in Childhood and School Cultures*. She recently co-authored two books with Celia Genishi, *On the Case*, on interpretive case study methods, and *Children, Language, and Literacy: Diverse Learners in Diverse Times*.

Rosie Flewitt is based in the Open University Centre for Research in Education and Education Technology (CREET), UK, where she researches and lectures in multimodal communication and young children's early experiences of literacy with print and digital technologies. She has contributed to undergraduate and postgraduate courses on Children's Literature, Childhood, Children's Perspectives in Research, and Language, Literacy and Learning in the Contemporary World. Recent research includes leading the Economic and Social Research Council (ESRC) project *Multimodal Literacies in the Early Years*

(RES-000-22-2451), and investigating the potential of iPads to enhance literacy learning and story-telling in early, primary and special education. Rosie is committed to inclusive education and has conducted two linked projects into children and parents' experiences of combining special educational services with mainstream provision.

Julia Gillen is Senior Lecturer in Digital Literacies in the Literacy Research Centre, Department of Linguistics and English Language, Lancaster University, UK. Her work is particularly concerned with learning and literacy practices of children and young people across informal and formal settings. Dr Gillen was Principal Investigator of the ESRC seminar series *Children's and Young People's Digital Literacies in Virtual Online Spaces* (RES-451-26-0731) in 2009–2010. She recently co-edited *Virtual Literacies: Interactive Spaces for Children and Young People* (with Merchant, Marsh and Davies; Routledge, 2012), *Researching Learning in Virtual Worlds* (with Peachey, Livingstone and Robbins; Springer, 2010) and *International Perspectives on Early Childhood Research: A Day in the Life* (with Cameron; Palgrave Macmillan, 2010). She is the author of *The Language of Children* (Routledge, 2003) and a co-editor of the *Journal of Early Childhood Literacy*.

Usha Goswami is Professor of Cognitive Developmental Neuroscience at the University of Cambridge and a Fellow of St John's College, Cambridge, UK. She is also Director of the Centre for Neuroscience in Education. She was previously Professor of Cognitive Developmental Psychology at the Institute of Child Health, University College London (1997–2003), and before that, University Lecturer in Experimental Psychology at the University of Cambridge (1990–1997). She received her PhD from the University of Oxford in 1987; her topic was reading and spelling by analogy. Her current research examines relations between phonology and reading; a major focus of the research is the brain basis of dyslexia. She has received a number of career awards, including the British Psychology Society's Spearman Medal (1992) and President's Award (2011), the Norman Geschwind-Rodin Prize for Dyslexia research, and Fellowships from the National Academy of Education (USA), the Leverhulme Trust, and the Alexander von Humboldt Foundation (Germany).

Beth Graue is Sorenson Professor in the Department of Curriculum and Instruction and Associate Director of Faculty, Staff and Graduate Development at the Wisconsin Center for Education Research at the University of Wisconsin–Madison, USA. A former kindergarten teacher, her research interests include kindergarten policy and practice, teacher's preparation for home–school relations, and qualitative research methods. A growing interest is public pre-kindergarten and she is studying a professional development programme designed to increase developmentally and culturally responsive practice for early mathematics.

Eve Gregory is Professor of Language and Culture and Head of the Centre for Language, Culture and Learning at Goldsmiths, University of London, UK, where she works mainly with students on MA and Doctoral degrees. Her most recent book is *Learning to Read in a New Language: Making Sense of Words and Worlds* (2008) published by SAGE. She has directed or co-directed a number of ESRC-funded projects on children's out-of-school learning and her current research is: 'Becoming literate in faith settings: Language and literacy learning in the lives of new Londoners' (2009–2013). This project examines the language and literacy learning through faith of young children of Bangladeshi Muslim, Ghanaian Pentecostal, Polish Catholic, and Tamil Hindu origin.

Kris D. Gutiérrez is Professor of Literacy and Learning Sciences and holds the Inaugural Provost's Chair at the University of Colorado, Boulder, USA. She is also Professor Emerita of Social Research Methodology in the Graduate School of Education and Information Studies at the University of California, Los Angeles, where she also served as Director of the Education Studies Minor and Director of the Center for the Study of Urban Literacies. Gutiérrez is the current President and a Fellow of the American Educational Research Association (AERA). She is also a Fellow at the National Conference on Research on Language and Literacy, and the National Education Policy Center. Her research examines learning in designed learning environments, with particular attention to students from non-dominant communities and English Learners. Her work on Third Spaces examines the affordances of syncretic approaches to literacy learning and re-mediation of functional systems of learning. Professor Gutiérrez's research has been published widely in premier academic journals and she is a co-editor of *Learning and Expanding with Activity Theory*. Additionally, Professor Gutiérrez has written a column for the *Los Angeles Times*' Reading Page. Gutiérrez was recently elected to the National Academy of Education and nominated by President Obama to be a member of the National Board for the Institute of Education Sciences. She has received numerous awards, including the 2010 AERA Hispanic Research in Elementary, Secondary, or Postsecondary Education Award and the 2010 Inaugural Award for Innovations in Research on Diversity in Teacher Education, Division K (AERA) and was the 2010 Osher Fellow at the Exploratorium Museum of Science. Previously, Gutiérrez received the AERA Distinguished Scholar Award 2007, was the 2005 recipient of the AERA Division C Sylvia Scribner Award for influencing the field of learning and instruction, and was a Fellow at the Center for Advanced Studies in the Behavioral Sciences 2006–2007.

Kathy Hall is Professsor of Education and Head of School at University College Cork. She is currently working on a co-authored book with Alicia Curtin and Vanessa Rutherford entitled *Networks of the Mind: A Critical Neurocultural Perspective on Learning* to be published by Routledge and is co-editor with Teresa Cremin, Barbara Comber and Luis Moll for *International Handbook of Research in Children's Literacy, Learning and Culture* to be published by Wiley-Blackwell. She is PI for a research project on inclusion funded by the Irish Research Council. She is supervising a range of doctoral students who are drawing on various sociocultural themes to understand such areas as literacy improvement, leadership, school choice, teacher identities, curriculum development, and transitions.

Nigel Hall is Emeritus Professor of Literacy Education, Manchester Metropolitan University, UK. Nigel Hall has interests in young children's developing knowledge of language and literacy, particularly with respect to punctuation, play and literacy, and writing. He has published extensively in all the above areas. He is also interested in literacy as a social practice, both currently and historically, and how this notion relates to primary school literacy education. He was the Director of the Punctuation Project which, supported by three ESRC awards, sought to understand how children make sense of punctuation and how teachers might best teach it. A more recent specialist interest has been in the field of child language brokering. He headed an ESRC seminar series on the topic *Children and Adolescents as Language Brokers*. He was a co-founder and joint-editor of the international research journal, the *Journal of Early Childhood Literacy*.

Peter Hannon is an Emeritus Professor in the School of Education at the University of Sheffield, UK. His main research and teaching activity is in the areas of literacy and early childhood education. He has directed projects in parental involvement in the teaching of literacy in the early school years, family literacy, preschool literacy development and in community-focused programmes for children and adults. He is the author of *Literacy, Home and School* (1995) and *Reflecting on Literacy in Education* (2000).

Susan M. Hildenbrand, EdD, has been an Assistant Professor in the Department of Undergraduate Inclusive Education at St John Fisher College, New York, USA, for the past 6 years, teaching courses on the special education process, inclusive practices, and family/school partnerships. Before working in higher education preparing preservice teachers for inclusive settings, she taught elementary special education for 10 years. Her research interests include positive classroom management strategies and co-teaching in the inclusive classroom. She lives with her husband and two children in Webster, New York.

Huili Hong is Assistant Professor in the Department of Curriculum and Instruction at East Tennessee State University Claudius G. Clemmer College of Education. Hong's programme of research is located in the area of second language learning with an emphasis on the literacy, biliteracy (or multiliteracy) development of young children. Hong's research focuses on young English language learners' literacy practices within classroom learning environments and how teachers can facilitate growth in literacy and biliteracy development, while also facilitating their academic learning and social identities that respect their current community and their social, cultural roots. Hong's current scholarship focuses on: young children's writing as an intertextual practice to construct various learning in classroom; children's speech play and playful learning, the aesthetic canon in children's playful writing; social and discursive construction of authorship among young writers; and English language learners' academic socialization.

Cushla Kapitzke is an Associate Professor in the School of Cultural and Language Studies in Education, Queensland University of Technology, Australia. Her early work as a critical literacy educator focused on the literacies afforded by new communications technologies. More recent research interests are on the sociology and politics of education generally. This work produced the edited books, *Global Knowledge Cultures* (2007), with Michael A. Peters (UIUC) and *Libr@ries: Changing Information Space and Practice* (Erlbaum, 2006) with Professor Bertram C. Bruce (UIUC). Cushla has published articles in *Educational Theory*, *Educational Philosophy and Theory*, *Teachers College Record*, and *Journal of Adolescent & Adult Literacy*.

Laurie Katz is Associate Professor in Early Childhood Education in the School of Teaching and Learning at The Ohio State University in Columbus, USA. Her research explores how the early childhood curriculum and instruction can be conceptualized to incorporate the broad diversity of children from birth to 9 years of age and their families, including children from linguistic-minority communities and children with certified disabilities. Her research topics include: the oral and written narratives of young African American children in classroom and home settings; the Students' Right to their Own Language resolution and its implementation in early childhood classrooms; and strengthening relationships between schools and families by identifying and integrating family strengths and cultural/linguistic backgrounds in the classroom.

Eithne Kennedy is a teacher educator at St. Patrick's College, Drumcondra, Dublin, where she teaches on a range of literacy courses at under-graduate and post-graduate level. Prior to joining the college faculty, she was a classroom teacher for many years in Dublin and the USA. Her doctoral research, which focused on raising literacy achievement in disadvantaged schools was awarded the International Reading Association's Outstanding Dissertation Award in 2010. As the director of the *Write to Read* research initiative, a St. Patrick's College, School and Community Literacy project, she works collaboratively with schools and communities to design and implement research-based approaches to literacy instruction aimed at raising achievement in ways that motivate and engage children as readers, writers and thinkers. She has authored and co-authored several publications in the field including policy papers on literacy, journal articles (e.g. *The Reading Teacher, RRQ*) and her first book: *Raising Literacy Achievement in High-Poverty Schools: An Evidence-Based Approach* will be published by Routledge in 2012.

Charmian Kenner is Lecturer in Educational Studies at Goldsmiths, University of London, UK. Her research focuses on bilingualism, literacy and family learning. She has led ESRC-funded studies at Goldsmiths on early biliteracy, intergenerational learning between young children and grandparents, and bilingual learning. She recently directed a research project funded by Paul Hamlyn Foundation, developing approaches to bilingual learning through partnerships between primary teachers and community language teachers. Charmian also directed the ESRC seminar series on *Complementary Schooling* (2009–2010). Her books include *Home Pages: Literacy Links for Bilingual Children* (Trentham, 2000) and *Becoming Biliterate: Young Children Learning Different Writing Systems* (Trentham, 2004). A previous ESRC seminar series led by Charmian on *Multilingual Europe* (2003–2005) resulted in an ongoing international network of researchers and the book *Multilingual Europe: Diversity and Learning* (Trentham, 2008). Publications and teaching resources developed by Charmian and colleagues at Goldsmiths can be found at: www.gold.ac.uk/clcl/multilingual-learning/

Michele Knobel is Professor of Education at Montclair State University, New Jersey, USA. She has worked in teacher education in Australia, Mexico, Canada and the USA.

Her research examines new literacy practices across a broad range of contexts. She is author, with Colin Lankshear, of *New literacies: Everyday Practices and Social Learning* (3rd edn). They have also edited *DIY Media: Creating, Sharing and Learning with New Technologies* and *A New Literacies Sampler* and *Digital Literacies: Concepts, Policies and Practices.*

Gunther Kress is Professor of Semiotics and Education at the Institute of Education, University of London, UK. His interests are in the ongoing development of Social Semiotic theory so as to understand principles of representation, meaning making and communication in contemporary social environments. The frame of application is multimodal representation and communication, with its focus on resources and forms of communication in all modes, including those of speech and writing. Conditions and environments for 'learning' in the contemporary period is one special focus of application. Some books relevant to chapter 19 are *Learning to Write* (1982/1994); *Social Semiotics* (1988, with R. Hodge); *Before Writing: Rethinking the Paths to Literacy* (1996); *Reading Images: the Grammar of Graphic Design* (1996/2006, with T. van Leeuwen); *Multimodal Discourse: the Modes and Media of Contemporary Communication* (2002, with T. van Leeuwen); *Literacy in the New Media Age* (2003); and *Multimodality. A Social Semiotic Approach to Contemporary Communication* (2010).

Lesley Lancaster is Reader in Education in the Education and Social Research Institute at Manchester Metropolitan University, UK. Her current research interests include children's early symbolic learning, writing in early childhood, distributed cognition, and multimodal analysis, with recent publications and conference papers reflecting these interests. She is on the editorial board of the *Journal of Early Childhood Literacy*, was a member of the UK Early Language and Communication Project, and Director of the ESRC-funded project Grammaticisation in Early Mark Making, and is currently writing a book, to be published by Routledge, about this study. She teaches in the field of Applied Linguistics at undergraduate and doctoral levels, and in the past she has worked as a member of a literacy advisory team, as a researcher at the National Foundation for Educational Research, and as a teacher.

Colin Lankshear has a PhD in philosophy of education and has worked in a range of academic positions in New Zealand, Australia, Canada, the USA and Mexico. He is currently an Adjunct Professor of Education at McGill University in Montreal, Canada, James Cook University in Cairns, Australia, and Mount Saint Vincent University in Halifax, Canada. His research interest is in sociocultural studies of literacy practices and new technologies. He is joint author, with Michele Knobel, of *The Handbook for Teacher Research* and *Literacies: Social Culture and Historical Perspectives.*

Joanne Larson (PhD, University of California, Los Angeles) is the Michael W. Scandling Professor of Education at the University of Rochester's Warner Graduate School of Education and Human Development, USA, and Chair of the Teaching and Curriculum Program. Her research examines how language and literacy practices mediate social and power relations in literacy events in schools and communities. She is the editor of *Literacy* *as Snake Oil: Beyond the Quick Fix* (2nd edn, Lang, 2007) and coauthor of *Making Literacy Real: Theories and Practices in Learning and Teaching* (SAGE, 2005). Larson's journal publications include research articles in *Anthropology and Education Quarterly*, *Harvard Education Review*, *Research in the Teaching of English*, *Written Communication*, *Linguistics and Education*, *Journal of Early Childhood Literacy*, and *Discourse and Society*.

Allan Luke is Professor, Faculty of Education, Queensland University of Technology, Brisbane, Australia. He is currently completing a 4-year longitudinal study of Indigenous school leadership and reform.

Margaret Mackey is a Professor in the School of Library and Information Studies at the University of Alberta, Canada. She teaches courses on reading and on multimedia literacies, as well as children's and young adult literature. She has published widely on the subject of young people's evolving literacies; her most recent book is *Narrative Pleasures in Young Adult Novels, Films, and Video Games* (Palgrave Macmillan, 2011). Currently she is working on a project to reassemble and investigate as large a collection as possible of the materials with which she became literate herself: picturebooks, novels, school textbooks, magazines, radio and television programmes, church and Sunday-school materials, museum exhibits, recorded music and audio books, and much more. She is experimenting with new digital tools for analysis and dissemination of this project

Jackie Marsh is Professor of Education at the University of Sheffield, UK. Her research focuses on the role and nature of popular culture, media and new technologies in young children's literacy development. She has conducted projects that have explored children's access to new technologies and their emergent digital literacy skills, knowledge and understanding. She has also undertaken projects in early-years settings and primary schools focused on the development of appropriate curriculum and pedagogy for the digital age. She has published widely in the field and books include: *Children, Media and Playground Cultures: Ethnographic Studies of School Playtimes* (with Willetts, Richards, Burn, and Bishop, Palgrave, in press) *Children's Virtual Play Worlds: Culture, Learning and Participation* (edited with Burke, Peter Lang, in press) and *Virtual Literacies: Interactive Spaces for Children and Young People* (edited with Merchant, Gillen, and Davies, Routledge, in press). Jackie is a co-editor of the *Journal of Early Childhood Literacy*.

Miriam Martinez is a Professor at the University of Texas in San Antonio, USA. She received her PhD from the University of Texas at Austin and is a specialist in children's literature, literary response, and integration of literature into literacy programmes. She has combined her interests in these areas in her research, publications, and teaching. Her most recent publications have included reviews of research on children's and adolescents' responses to literature and their construction of meaning in literary texts. She is a co-author of *Children's Books in Children's Hands*, a textbook in its fourth edition. She has worked extensively with schools conducting workshops on ways of promoting literature discussion in the classroom. In 2006 she was the recipient of the Arbuthnot Award from the

International Reading Association for outstanding university teacher of children's and young adults' literature. She is co-editor of the *Journal of Children's Literature*.

Patricia May-Woods is a doctoral student at the College of Education and Human Ecology in the School of Teaching and Learning at The Ohio State University, USA. May-Woods' research concerns early language and literacy development in young children, narrative inquiry, storytelling, and preschool classroom discourse. May-Woods is an Early Childhood Development faculty member at Columbus State Community College, and Early Language and Literacy Specialist for the Ohio Department of Education, Office of Early Learning and School Readiness, State Support Team. She is actively involved in local and statewide early learning projects aiming to better the quality of early educational experiences for young children. May-Woods received the Ohio Association for the Education of Young Children Teacher of Teachers Award in 2008, and was awarded the 2011 Columbus Association for the Education of Young Children (AEYC) Teacher Leadership Award.

Guy Merchant is Professor of Literacy in Education and research co-ordinator in the Department of Teacher Education at Sheffield Hallam University, UK. He has published widely on digital literacy and is particularly interested in the inter-relations between children and young people, new technology and literacy. He is research convenor for the United Kingdom Literacy Association and a member of the Association's Executive Committee and National Council. He recently co-directed the Economic and Social Research Council-funded seminar series *Children and Young People's Digital Literacies in Virtual Online Spaces* and is lead editor of the book *Virtual Literacies* (2012) that resulted from that work. He is a founding editor of the *Journal of Early Childhood Literacy*, and a member of the Editorial Board of *Literacy*. He is also active in literacy education and professional work, including writing curriculum materials and professional publications.

Elaine Millard is a visiting Research Professor at Birmingham City University, UK. From 1989-2005 she was a senior lecturer in education at the University of Sheffield, UK and an originator of its influential Masters Degree in Literacy. Elaine is Past Chair of the National Association for the Teaching of English and former editor of its research journal, *English in Education*. She has published widely in the fields of literacy and gender, creative approaches to teaching new literacies and curriculum change. Her most influential publications are *Differently Literate; Literacy and Popular Culture* (with Jackie Marsh) and *Remaking the Curriculum* (with Martin Fautley and Richard Hatcher).

Martha Mock, PhD, is an Assistant Professor at the University of Rochester, USA, with dual appointments in the Warner Graduate School of Education and the Department of Pediatrics at Strong Center for Developmental Disabilities. She has worked with and been an advocate with people with disabilities and their families for over 20 years in educational and community-based settings. She is a former special education preschool teacher and holds her Doctor of Philosophy degree in Special Education from the University of Wisconsin–Madison.

Sharon Murphy is a Professor in the Faculty of Education at York University in Toronto, Canada. Sharon taught special education in Newfoundland and later was employed in conducting educational assessments by the Newfoundland Department of Education's Learning Centre. In 1988, Sharon moved to York University where she has served as Director of the Graduate Program in the Faculty of Education, as well as Associate Dean of the Faculty of Graduate Studies. Sharon has written on assessment and literacy in a variety of venues and served a term as co-editor of *Language Arts*, a journal of the National Council of Teachers of English. She is currently working on, among other projects, an elaboration of the conceptualization of epistemic responsibility in assessment.

Sue Nichols is a Senior Lecturer in Literacy Education at the University of South Australia and a member of the Centre for Educational Research. Her research on learning has crossed diverse spaces and includes homes, schools, libraries, churches and universities. An ethnographic researcher, she has increasingly employed theories of space, mobility and networking, beginning with her chapter in *Travel Notes from the New Literacy Studies* (2006) which traced a discourse on thinking across corporate and classroom sites. She co-edited a special issue on geosemiotics in the *Journal of Early Childhood Literacy* (2011) and has co-authored a book, *Resourcing Early Learners: New Players, New Networks* (Routledge, 2012).

Helen Nixon is Associate Professor of Education in the Children and Youth Research Centre at Queensland University of Technology in Brisbane, Australia. She has published widely in the fields of English and literacy education and cultural studies and education and co-edited a special issue on geosemiotics in the *Journal of Early Childhood Literacy* (2011). Current projects funded by the Australian Research Council focus on how mandated literacy assessment changes teachers' work and how teachers negotiate the changing literacy demands of schooling in the middle years.

Marjorie Faulstich Orellana is a Professor in the Graduate School of Education and Information Studies at UCLA, USA, where she also serves as the Director of Faculty for the Teacher Education Program and co-director of the Migration Studies Group. Her interdisciplinary research examines the work that the children of immigrants do as language and culture brokers for their families, and the linguistic and literate competencies that such work cultivates. She is the author of *Translating Childhoods: Immigrant Youth, Language and Culture*, as well as articles in such journals as *Harvard Educational Review*, *Reading Research Quarterly*, *Research in the Teaching of English*, *Language Arts*, *Anthropology and Education Quarterly*, *American Anthropologist*, and *Social Problems*. She was a bilingual classroom teacher in Los Angeles from 1983 to 1993 and draws connections from ethnography to classroom practice; see for example http://centerx.gseis.ucla.edu/ xchange-repository/copy_of_fall-2010/teachers-workroom.

Kate Pahl is a Reader in Literacies in Education at the University of Sheffield, UK. She is the author, with Jennifer Rowsell, of *Literacy and Education: The New Literacy Studies in the Classroom* (2nd edn, Sage, 2012) and *Artifactual Literacies: Every Object Tells a Story* (Teachers College Press, 2010). Her research focuses on literacy in the home and the community, and most recently she has conducted a research project, with colleagues from the English programme, called 'Writing in the Home and in the Street' (Arts and Humanities Research Council (ARHC) funded). She teaches on the MA in Working with Communities as well as the EdD in Literacy and Language at the School of Education, University of Sheffield.

Karisa Peer is a PhD student in the division of Urban Schooling within the Graduate School of Education and Information Studies at UCLA, USA. She works for UCLA's National Center for Research on Evaluation, Standards, and Student Testing. Karisa has conducted research with UCLA's Civil Rights Project/Proyecto de Derechos Civiles on the impact of Arizona's 4-hour English language development (ELD) model. She has worked with the Cotsen Family Foundation to determine the degree to which the Art of Teaching mentor programme affects student performance and achievement. Her research interests include family and community literacy practices and how they shape and influence early childhood literacy practices, particularly in Latino immigrant communities. Before entering graduate school, Karisa was an early childhood programme coordinator as well as an elementary school teacher in bilingual programmes. She received a BA in Spanish and Anthropology from Middlebury College and a MA in Education from the University of San Francisco.

Shira M. Peterson, PhD, is a research associate at Children's Institute in Rochester, New York, a not-for-profit organization dedicated to strengthening children's social and emotional health. Her research focuses on supporting early educators in changing their practices with children, particularly in ways that recognize educators' 'stages of change'. Her research on teacher–child discourse, professional development, and readiness to change in the early childhood workforce has been published in journals such as *Early Childhood Research Quarterly* and *Zero to Three*, as well as several edited books. Dr Peterson is co-author of the Stage of Change Scale for Early Education and Care, and she currently offers training and consultation on responding to early educators' readiness to change.

Aria Razfar is an Associate Professor of Literacy, Language, and Culture at the University of Illinois at Chicago, USA. He is the director of Graduate Studies and the Bilingual/ESL programme in the Department of Curriculum and Instruction. His work is grounded in sociocultural and critical theories of discourse, learning, and literacy development. His research has especially contributed to the understanding of teaching and learning of non-dominant populations across the life-span, domains of knowledge, and school/non-school contexts. His work appears in major peer-reviewed journals such as *Anthropology of Education Quarterly*, *Human Development*, *Linguistics and Education*, and *Mind, Culture, and Activity*. He has served as a Principal Investigator on several projects, including the National Science Foundation (NSF) funded Center for Mathematics Education of Latinas/os (CEMELA) and the US Department of Education's Transforming Literacy, Science, and Math through Action Research (LSciMAct).

Debbie Reese is tribally enrolled at Nambe Pueblo in Northern New Mexico, USA. The publisher of *American Indians in Children's Literature*, she taught at elementary school for American Indian children in New Mexico and Oklahoma, and at public schools in Albuquerque and Pojoaque, New Mexico. After completing her PhD in Education, she cofounded the Native American House and American Indian Studies programme at the University of Illinois. She has numerous publications in books and journals in the fields of Education, Children's Literature, and Library Science.

Cecilia Rios-Aguilar is an Associate Professor at the School of Educational Studies at Claremont Graduate University, USA. Her research is multidisciplinary and uses a variety of conceptual frameworks (e.g., funds of knowledge and the forms of capital) and of statistical approaches (e.g., regression analysis, multilevel models, and social network analysis) to study the educational and occupational trajectories of under-represented students, including Latinas/os, English language learners, and immigrant and second-generation children and youth. Dr. Rios-Aguilar's applied research also includes the design and evaluation of different programmes and policies targeted to under-represented students.

Muriel Robinson is Principal and Professor of Digital Literacies at Bishop Grosseteste University College Lincoln, UK. Her interest in digital literacies grew out of PhD work looking at the ways in which children make sense of narratives in print and on television which suggested that there are many similar strategies being deployed (1997). She has worked with Margaret Mackey developing the idea of an asset model of literacy, namely a model which starts from the experiences, knowledge and skills that children have to draw on in any one situation, and has extended this model to explore the digital literacy practices of intending teachers.

Nancy L. Roser is Professor of Language and Literacy Studies, the Flawn Professor of Early Childhood, and Distinguished Teaching Professor at the University of Texas at Austin, USA. A former elementary teacher, she now teaches undergraduate elementary reading and language arts, as well as graduate courses in teaching the English Language Arts and Children's Literature. Her research interests include close inspection of children's book conversations in classrooms, the use of children's literature in literacy programmes, classroom discourse, and response to literature.

Deborah Wells Rowe is an Associate Professor in the Language, Literacy, and Culture programme at Peabody College, Vanderbilt University in Nashville, Tennessee, USA. Her research focuses on understanding how preschool and elementary children learn to read and write in classroom settings. She has conducted qualitative studies of young children's writing and book-related play, connections between drama and writing, and the multi-modal, cultural, embodied and spatial aspects of preschool literacy learning. She is currently studying how emerging bilinguals participate in writing in prekindergarten classrooms where the teachers are monolingual English speakers. In 2010, she was awarded the Dina Feitelson Research Award by the International Reading Association in recognition of her research on literacy acquisition.

Jennifer Rowsell is a Canada Research Chair in Multiliteracies at the Faculty of Education, Brock University, Canada, where she directs the Centre for Multiliteracies. Her current research projects include: an International Reading Association (IRA) Elva Knight-funded study in an urban and suburban high school where she and a teacher adopt multi-modal approaches to the teaching of English; a Social Science and Humanities Research Council (SSHRC)-funded digital reading project in an elementary school in the Toronto area; and an interview study of 30 producers who specialize in different modes of expression and representation. She has written several books, articles, and chapters in the areas of multimodality, multiliteracies, and New Literacy Studies.

Patricia L. Scharer is a Professor of Education and Human Ecology at The Ohio State University, USA. She is actively involved in two literacy projects – Literacy Collaborative, a K–6 school reform model training on-site coaches to support teacher professional development, and Reading Recovery, a research-based intervention for first-grade students experiencing difficulty learning to read and write. Dr Scharer and colleagues were awarded a $54 million federal i3 grant to scale-up Reading Recovery across the US. Dr Scharer's research interests include early literacy development, phonics and word study, and the role of children's literature to foster both literary development and literacy achievement. Her research has been published in *Reading Research Quarterly*, *Research in the Teaching of English*, *Educational Leadership*, *Language Arts*, *The Reading Teacher*, *Reading Research and Instruction*, *Journal of Reading Recovery*, *Literacy Teaching & Learning*, and the yearbooks of the National Reading Conference and the College Reading Association.

Tamara Spencer is an Assistant Professor at Montclair State University, New Jersey, USA. Her current research analyses the intersections of curricular policy and young children's literacy practices. Her publications include research articles in *Advances in Early Education and Day Care*, *Complementary Methods for Research in Education*, *Contemporary Issues in Early Childhood*, *Early Childhood Education Journal*, and *Perspectives on Urban Education*. She has taught first and second grade and worked as a literacy specialist and administrator in public schools in New York, Philadelphia, Pennsylvania, and Raleigh, North Carolina.

Radhika Viruru is a Clinical Professor in the Department of Teaching, Learning and Culture at Texas A&M University, USA, where she also serves as the Associate Department Head for Undergraduate Studies. From 2008 to 2010 she was an Associate Professor in the College of Education at Qatar University, in Doha, Qatar. Dr Viruru's interests include postcolonial theory and its application to international early childhood education. She is the author of two books on childhood and postcolonial theory (*Early Childhood Education: Postcolonial Perspectives from India*, published by SAGE, and *Childhood and Postcolonization: Power, Education and Contemporary Practice* [co-author], published by Routledge). She has recently been involved in multiple research and service projects connected to early childhood education and teacher professional development in Qatar.

Melissa Wilson teaches courses on the teaching of writing to young children and co-directs the Columbus Area Writing Project at The Ohio State University, USA, having spent 30 years teaching in elementary schools in San Antonio, Texas, and Columbus, Ohio. She has served as a coeditor of Language Arts, the elementary journal from the National

Council of Teachers of English. Her research focuses on how young children learn to write nonfiction and how they develop identities as writers. Her publications include *Success Stories from a Failing School: Teachers Living Under the Shadow of NCLB* (with Marilyn Johnston-Parsons), a chapter in the *Handbook of Research on Children's and Young Adult Literature* (with Barbara Kiefer), and an article in the Early Childhood Education Assembly (ECEA) Yearbook Perspectives and Provocation (co-authored with Laurie Katz, Caitlan Ryan and Detra Price-Dennis).

Karen E. Wohlwend is an Assistant Professor in Literacy, Culture, and Language Education at Indiana University, USA. Her current research uses action-oriented and multimodal methods of critical discourse analysis to critically examine young children's play with literacies, popular media, and digital technologies in online and classroom spaces. Wohlwend's publications include numerous articles, a recent book, *Playing Their Way into Literacies: Reading, Writing and Belonging in the Early Childhood Classroom*, and two forthcoming books: *Literacy, Play, and Globalization: Critical and Cultural Performances in Children's Converging Imaginaries* (co-authored with Carmen Medina), and *Literacy Playshop: Playing with New Literacies and Popular Media in Early Childhood Classrooms*. Awards include the International Reading Association Outstanding Dissertation Award and the American Educational Research Association Language and Social Processes Emerging Scholar Award.

Dominic Wyse is Professor of Early Childhood and Primary Education at the Institute of Education (IOE), University of London, UK. The main focus of his research is curriculum and pedagogy. Key areas of work are the teaching of English, language, literacy, and creativity. In addition to research in these areas Dominic has extensive experience in music including a position as the first Director of Music-Making at Churchill College Cambridge where he was also a Fellow. He is the lead editor of *The Routledge International Handbook of English, Language, and Literacy Teaching* (with Richard Andrews and James Hoffman) and editor of *Literacy Teaching and Education: SAGE Library of Educational Thought and Practice*. He is the lead author of *Teaching English, Language and Literacy* (3rd edn, Routledge with Russell Jones, Helen Bradford and Mary Anne Wolpert).

Jerry Zutell is Professor Emeritus and former Director of the OSU Reading Clinic at the Ohio State University, USA. He has done research and written numerous articles about assessing students' oral reading fluency, the stages of spelling development, the connections between word knowledge in spelling and reading, and instructional practices for making students better readers and spellers. Dr Zutell is the developer of the Directed Spelling Thinking Activity (DSTA) model for spelling instruction and the Theme, Context, Roots, Reference, and Review (TC3R) model for vocabulary instruction. He has served as a principal consultant on *Merriam Webster's Primary Dictionary*, and is the author of the Zaner–Bloser vocabulary series, *Word Wisdom*. Dr Zutell has recently co-authored two books for education professionals: *Instructing Students Who Have Literacy Problems* (6th edn, with Sandra McCormick) and *Essential Strategies for Word Study: Effective Methods for Improving Decoding, Spelling, and Vocabulary* (with Timothy Rasinski).

Preface

Joanne Larson and Jackie Marsh

The last several decades have been powerful ones for the study of early childhood literacy. In many countries, much more attention is being paid to the early years than previously, as politicians recognise just how vital is this period of life. Alongside increased political interest, although largely quite independent of it, has been a resurgence of research as new definitions of early childhood literacy have developed, influenced by a wide range of disciplines (see Chapter 1). There are a number of approaches, therefore, that could have been undertaken in relation to the development of this second edition of the handbook, given the current complexity and scope of the field. The handbook has 35 chapters, written by 59 authors who come from seven countries across four continents. On the whole, the chapters reflect a particular and distinctive view of early childhood literacy. The perspectives of many chapters in this book are based on a view that early childhood literacy is a global, social, historical, cultural, and political construct. Many of the chapters suggest that literacy is a social practice that is linked to cultural and linguistic practices and power relationships in specific contexts. As a social practice, literacy learning is mediated by language and accomplished in a context in which social actors position, and are positioned by, each other in verbal, non-verbal, and textual interaction.

This approach was identified for a number of reasons. The first is that the concept of early childhood literacy as a socially-situated practice is important to emphasize as a counter-balance to cognitive, individually-focused models of literacy that fail to recognize the way in which community and culture shape children's literate experiences. We believe that researchers have both a right and an obligation to think about literacy as a widespread social practice for children as well as for adults. Early childhood literacy can no longer remain the exclusive domain of educationalists and developmental psychologists. The second reason is that it is important to focus upon a broad interpretation of early childhood literacy that moves beyond the school walls, even though that can sometimes be at odds with contemporary political views of the concept. Researchers must, of course, be interested in the powerful political realities that drive education and schooling, but the extent to which so much research in literacy is driven by the agendas of schooling obscures the other realities of literacy – especially that literacy has a life outside of and beyond schooling. The third reason for the approach taken to the shaping of the handbook relates to a recognition of the ways in which literacy is changing in contemporary society. During the late twentieth century, technological developments precipitated a paradigm shift in relation to communicative practices and there was a greater focus on the ways in which people analysed and produced a range of multimodal texts. These changes have impacted greatly on children's lives and today all children, including the very young, are actively participating in their development and use. Many of the chapters in this handbook acknowledge this strong field of research in early childhood literacy and thus broaden traditional conceptions of literacy in the early years.

We have made several changes to this second edition. Given that almost 10 years have passed since the first edition, there have been significant developments in the field. We have added a number of chapters in recognition of these newer areas of research, such as multimodality, space, place and literacy, material and digital literacies. In addition, this edition addresses some gaps in the first edition, such as disability studies, policy in early childhood and indigenous literacies. We have included a chapter in the final section that surveys the range of methodologies employed in this field. This addition of a number of chapters means that it was not possible to include revised versions of all of the chapters in the previous edition of this handbook. Those chapters that did appear in the first edition and are included in this second edition have been significantly revised. The fact that we have omitted some chapters that were included in the first edition does not mean that we feel those areas are not still important or relevant, simply that we wished to broaden the scope of this edition to ensure it reflected the current breadth of early childhood literacy research and therefore this handbook supplements, rather than totally replaces, the first edition.

For the purposes of this handbook, as in the first edition, we are defining early childhood as that period from birth to 8 years old. This is a wider span than many others would accept. However, we recognise that whilst there are some variations in notions of early childhood in the Western world, there are even greater differences across the whole world. By taking a broader stance we increase inclusion, and if we extend beyond some people's preferences for what counts as 'early childhood literacy', then we also offer the opportunity to consider continuity of development across a greater period of time.

The chapters in this handbook, therefore, offer a range of critical perspectives on research and key issues in particular aspects of the field. We do not claim a comprehensive overview of early literacy research in its totality, but suggest that the chapters here represent major themes in which leading authorities in the field provide rigorous social, cultural and historical analyses of aspects of early childhood literacy. The handbook is organised around five main themes.

PART 1: PERSPECTIVES ON EARLY CHILDHOOD LITERACY

The chapters in this section examine the notion of early childhood literacy, its history as a concept, and the way research has historically and contemporaneously positioned it. They consider the social, cultural, political and economic factors that impact upon the nature, function and use of literacy in early childhood.

PART 2: EARLY CHILDHOOD LITERACY IN FAMILIES, COMMUNITIES AND CULTURES ACROSS MEDIA AND MODES

Early childhood literacy is rooted in family, community and cultural beliefs, attitudes, values and practices. In this section, the chapters centre around literacy as a social practice, exploring different ways in which families, communities and cultures construct, value and use literacy across multiple modes. In particular, these chapters explore how young children respond to these influences and develop ideas about the meanings and functions of literacy for themselves and with their families and communities.

PART 3: EARLY MOVES IN LITERACY

This cluster of chapters focuses on the processes which underpin the acquisition and development of literacy during early childhood. The emphasis in this section is on how children come to understand what literacy is, what are its purposes, and how it functions.

PART 4: LITERACY IN PRESCHOOL SETTINGS AND SCHOOLS

In most countries, but not all, schooling is the institution for controlling children's formal access to the world of written language. Schooling is often controversial, with political agendas rather than research determining the curriculum and teaching practice. In this section, the chapters explore research which has illustrated how teachers and other practitioners create settings for young children's literacy learning, and how children respond to these professional practices and values.

PART 5: RESEARCHING EARLY CHILDHOOD LITERACY

The chapters in this section explore in detail approaches to researching early childhood literacy from a largely qualitative perspective. They are designed to provide a theoretical background rather than offer practical approaches to empirical work, but in doing so provide a foundation for anyone setting out to conduct research in this field.

We hope this book will prove useful to researchers, academics working in the field, students with an academic interest in childhood literacy, and policy makers. While the main audience is likely to be those located within the discipline of education, researchers working in linguistics, cultural studies and sociology will find issues of interest. It is our intention that this handbook will provide an informative and critical introduction to key aspects of research in early childhood literacy.

PART 1

Perspectives on Early Childhood Literacy

The Emergence of Early Childhood Literacy

Julia Gillen and Nigel Hall

In this chapter we explore, rather briefly, how the approaches researchers bring to studying young children and written language have changed across time, and how in the process critical concepts have been redefined leading to the emergence of early childhood literacy as a major research focus at the beginning of the twenty-first century. We are making the claim that research into early childhood literacy is a very recent phenomenon. This may surprise many people; after all, formal research into the ways in which children have learned about written language has been going on for well over a century, and if an informal definition is adopted then it would be over many centuries, maybe even millennia. However, we want to claim that there are specific attributes of the term *early childhood literacy research* that distinguish it from the many earlier meanings that have underpinned the ways in which previous researchers have examined young children's relationships with written language.

The story of how early childhood literacy emerged as a distinctive and dynamic research area is a fairly complicated one and to do it full justice would require more space than is available to us. To keep control of our account and to contain it within the space allowed us, we have decided to focus on a small number of themes, each of which we see as significant in the emergence of early childhood literacy as now understood. There is, to start with, a crude historical direction the order of our themes; however, this becomes more difficult to sustain as we move towards the end of the twentieth century and at this point considerable overlap is unavoidable. We are conscious that in this short chapter we have to be selective about the choices made for discussion. We select mostly book-length studies for particular emphasis; for, although ideas tend to find their first output in journals or theses, they are then consolidated more comprehensively in books. Our choices are necessarily personal ones and we do not claim that we always use the most significant texts of their kind (although they may be), or that they are themselves the most influential texts, and neither do we claim that together they represent a completely coherent story. We reflect our perceptions of the changing nature of attitudes, values and influences of the particular shifting intersection among disciplines that constitutes research into learning and using written language in early childhood.

THE MOVE TOWARDS 'LITERACY' AND 'CHILDHOOD'

Psychology, written language and young children

We have chosen to start at the end of the nineteenth century. It was a time in which researchers from one discipline had begun to take a specific interest in young children's relationship with written language, although we are certainly not suggesting that it had been completely ignored before this. At this point it would be very unusual to find anyone researching literacy as, according to the *Oxford English Dictionary*, the term 'literacy' was first used in print in 1883. In the nineteenth century researchers, and anyone else, talked about reading and writing rather than literacy.

Even as the modern discipline of psychology emerged in Wundt's laboratories, it took a research interest in reading. The major theme of this early work was that reading is primarily a perceptual activity centred on sound/symbol relationships. The linking of sound and vision made reading susceptible to the interests of perceptual psychologists partly because they focussed upon individual behaviour and partly because aspects of perceptual behaviour could be measured (Catell, 1886). Another theme was acceptance of the notion that learning was unlikely to take

place unless children were 'ready' (mentally and physically). The notion of readiness in association with reading appears to have been used first by Patrick (1899), was supported by Huey (1908), and remained a dominant concept in young children's reading for the next 60 years. Huey's seminal work typifies these characteristics. A lot of it is devoted to visual perception and reading, while in the pedagogy section Huey seeks to reconcile psychological evidence relating to readiness with the contemporary practice of starting children early on reading. His answer seems in some respects to be quite contemporary: root early written language experiences in play.

It was readiness, however, that won. In 1928, two US psychologists began to explore reading readiness formally (Morphett and Washburne, 1931). They claimed that reading readiness was closely linked to mental age and, more specifically, that 'It pays to postpone beginning reading until a child has attained a mental age of six years and six months.' This position was supported by a later study that claimed, 'A mental age of seven seems to be the lowest at which a child can be expected to use phonics.' (Dolch and Bloomster, 1937). That these studies were based on ludicrous and arbitrary notions of what counted as reading (and for a stunning critical review of these studies see Coltheart, 1979) and 'satisfactory progress in reading' did not stop the educational world from falling in love with their propositions. For the next 50 years books about teaching reading repeated the readiness mantras of these four researchers. A number of consequences followed these research studies. First, an industry emerged concerned with promoting and selling reading readiness, usually with non-print-related activities and materials. Second, the limited definition of reading perpetuated a notion of learning to read as an associative activity, centred on perceptual identification and matching. Third, it supported an absolute distinction between being a reader and not being a reader.

The emphasis on measurable behaviour was abetted by the dominance at this time of behaviourism which, in its various guises, claimed to be able to control reading development through systematic reinforcement systems. By breaking down reading into narrow skills and by linking the learning of these skills to reinforcement systems children were supposed to acquire mastery of them (Skinner, 1957). Like much research into children's reading, it was based on a number of assumptions: that children's agency was insignificant, that children could learn nothing for themselves, that they were objects to be manipulated by teachers, and that that reading and writing were individual acts involving sets of discrete perceptual skills. Behaviourist theories of language learning were dealt a severe theoretical blow by Chomsky (1959) in a major review of Skinner's book, *Verbal Behavior*. On the whole, behaviourist approaches to literacy learning only survive in some areas of special education or in more experimental situations using mastery learning.

The major consequence of behaviourism and reading readiness theories was that for much of the twentieth century researchers seemed to have believed that there was simply no point in investigating, or even thinking about very young children's thinking about, understanding of and use of reading and writing; the possibility of this had been defined out of existence until they arrived in school and faced a teacher.

New disciplines and literacy

To a large extent the Second World War provided a new impetus for research into literacy, although the driving notion was 'illiteracy' and it was mostly associated with adults. It was this war with its increased requirements for more advanced skills that really brought home the significance of low literacy levels. The concept of functional literacy emerged during the war and was widely adopted in development education within mass literacy campaigns (Gray, 1956; see Akinnaso, 1991, for a personal perspective on this area) and later in adult and employment education. The notion of functional literacy for the first time forced researchers to be interested in what literacy was for and what people did with it in their everyday lives. Almost for the first time research began to consider reading as something more than simply a decoding process, and that it had a social element. It also led to the realisation that it was not only reading that needed to be considered, but also writing, although it remained true that reading received much greater attention than writing.

Another way in which the Second World War influenced research into literacy was through the emergence and consolidation of newer disciplines: cognitive psychology, the general area of information and communication studies, and psycholinguistics. These disciplines consistently revealed that communication, especially written communication, was a complex, multi-layered, and highly skilled process involving a reflective and strategic meaning-orientated approach to behaviour. While much of this work was related to adults, one book began to pull threads together and powerfully apply understandings to children learning to read. This book was Frank Smith's *Understanding Reading* (1971). It was not a research study itself, but it used a mass of evidence and theoretical work deriving from these newer disciplines. This evidence came from new studies into the cognitive perception (Neisser, 1967;

Gibson, 1969), skilled behaviour (Miller, Galanter and Pribram, 1960), communication and information theory (Pierce, 1961; Cherry, 1966; and Miller, 1967), linguistics (Chomsky, 1957 and 1965), developmental psycholinguistics (McNeill, 1966), developmental cognition (Bruner, Goodenough and Austin, 1956; Bruner, Olver and Greenfield, 1966) and those educationalists who were beginning to make use of these new disciplines (Goodman, 1968).

Smith's book immediately attracted both huge support and massive opposition and severely divided educationalists. It would not be unfair to describe this division as 'war', with such vitriol were these differences manifested. Despite this substantial opposition, Smith's book regenerated and broadened reading-related research, which swiftly flourished and began to move in directions that even Smith had not anticipated.

Smith's analysis and synthesis had a number of consequences for the emergence of early childhood literacy:

- Reading could no longer be seen simply as an associative process. It had to be recognised as a much more complex activity involving cognitive and strategic behaviour. The approach of young children to print reflected this complexity and use of strategy.
- The narrowness of research into reading was breached; the area was opened up as a topic for scrutiny and influence from a much wider set of disciplines than psychology (although this was only a beginning).
- Meaning could no longer be seen as simply sitting there in a text. It was readers who assigned meaning to print and children did this in similar ways to adults, although drawing on different experiences.

What Smith had not done in 1971 was (a) move beyond a reading-oriented understanding of print usage, and (b) follow through his own logic and consider whether children who had all these complex abilities were applying them to comprehending and making sense of print long before they moved into formal schooling. However, these newer disciplines had begun to reposition the understanding of written language as a much more dynamic and interactive process. It was these meanings that were carried forward and developed by other researchers.

The emergence of 'emergence'

At the end of the 1970s and the beginning of the 1980s the relationship between childhood and written language was changing dramatically. There had long been interest (mostly from psychologists) in how some children arrived in school able to read (Durkin, 1966; Clarke, 1976; and Forester, 1977) but such early engagement with literacy (and again it was always reading) was studied because it was believed to be unusual. Asking explicitly how young children made sense of literacy had begun with psychologists such as Reid (1966) and Downing (1979) but had extended to a crop of studies appearing in the late seventies and even continuing to the early eighties. These tended to focus on children in early schooling (Johns, 1976/7; Tovey 1976). At the same other researchers were exploring this issue in what was ultimately a more powerful way. Clay (1969), Read (1970) and Goodman (1976) became interested in the strategic behaviour of children engaging in literacy and it was their approach that led to some major shifts in the conceptualisation of early childhood and literacy. Rather than ask explicit questions of children, something that is always going to be problematic, they looked at the actual behaviours of children engaged in literacy. They saw that while many of the children's literacy behaviours were technically incorrect, they nevertheless revealed how children were strategic in approaching literacy and were working hard to develop hypotheses about how the system worked. If children aged 5 and 6 were bringing sense-making strategies to literacy, and if research from developmental psychology was demonstrating that young school-aged children were actively making sense of their worlds then how were even younger children responding to literacy? As Ferriero and Teberosky in their seminal study put it:

> It is absurd to imagine that four- or five-year-old children growing up in an urban environment that displays print everywhere (on toys, on billboards and road signs, on their clothes, on TV) do not develop any ideas about this cultural object until they find themselves sitting before a teacher.
> (1982: 12)

A number of individual case studies, by researchers studying their own children, began to focus explicitly on the period before schooling. Lass (1982) started with her child from birth, Baghban (1984) from birth to 3, Crago and Crago (1983) from 3 to 4, Payton (1984), the first British case study, across the fourth year, while Bissex (1980) followed her son during his fifth year. All showed clearly how their children were paying a lot of attention to print. Literacy was certainly beginning before schooling. At the same time researchers began reporting on broader studies involving a wider range of children (Clay, 1975; Mason, 1980; Hiebert, 1981; Harste, Burke and Woodward, 1982; Sulzby, 1985). A revolution was taking place that demanded a revaluation of literacy as something that moved beyond any conventional ability to read and write. Rather than literacy development being something that began at the start of schooling after a bout of reading readiness exercises, it was becoming a much broader continuum that had its

origins in very early childhood and drew its meaning from making sense rather than formal teaching (Hall, 1987).

The rich range of studies during the 1970s and early 1980s reflected two major moves by researchers:

- There was increasing recognition of the role that young children played in making sense of literacy: even the very youngest were strategic literacy learners who paid attention to the print world, participated in it in their own ways, and developed theories about how it worked. A new field of study appeared – emergent literacy.
- This change involved a redefinition of literacy, such that literacy began to be viewed as a much broader set of print-related behaviours than those conventionally experienced in education.

If there was a criticism that could made of much of the research of this period, it would that be that research tended to be more pragmatic than deeply theoretically based. Subsequent developments would change this. Nevertheless, early childhood literacy had begun to emerge and this shift was being greatly facilitated by research that was focusing more closely on the nature of literacy outside of schooling.

THE IMPACT OF SOCIAL AND CULTURAL PERSPECTIVES

It is at this point that any notion of maintaining a chronological sequence, however crude, breaks down, for during the last 20 years of the twentieth century a rich range of research and theoretical perspectives began to impact upon the study of young children and written language, and did so in ways that often overlapped or were inextricably intertwined. As a consequence, the following sections should in no way be viewed as discrete areas, but as aspects of a complex mixture of ideas that would, once again, redefine how young children's relationship with reading and writing could be understood.

The entry of cultural psychology

We will start with a re-entry of psychology into this story. Chronologically the work of the Russian psychologist Vygotsky belongs to the first part of the twentieth century (he died in 1934). However, after the 1962 translation of *Thought and Language* his work began to have an important influence on research into child development, language and thinking. It was however only more recently (especially Vygotsky, 1978) that his work began to influence research on literacy. The feature of Vygotsky's work that captured the interest of researchers was his recognition of the role of culture in learning, especially that individuals are inseparably connected to cultural history. This made a timely connection with the powerful emergence of sociology and anthropology into literacy research (see next sections).

Vygotsky had a particular interest in the ways in which children use many mediational tools to construct meaning (Lee and Smagorinsky, 2000), an interest shared with more semiotic theorists – see below. Vygotsky argued that language, for example, is first experienced around the child and comes to be used by the child; it is within the flow of experience of that participation in society that language is internalised and understanding develops. In interactions with their environment, including other people, Vygotsky recognised that even young children acted creatively, using their imagination. In particular, pretence play was seen by him as a very powerful opportunity for children to appropriate the symbols and tools of their culture (Vygotsky, 1967; then see Paley, 1984). He was interested in how the learning

relationship between children and their culture developed. In modern research this has primarily revolved around the dyadic exchanges that occur within what is usually termed the zone of proximal development, although Vygotsky himself never studied such exchanges as mother–child problem-solving dialogues (Van der Veer and Valsiner, 1994). Despite this, many scholars have explored naturally efficient pedagogic strategies, especially in dyads, examining how adults can structure children's routes into learning from participation and partial understanding to internalisation and expertise. Concepts such as 'scaffolding' (Wood, Bruner and Ross, 1976); 'structuring situations', 'apprenticeship' (Rogoff, 1986; 1990) and 'assisted performance' (Tharp and Gallimore, 1988) have been particularly influential. In the 1990s developments of Vygotskyan theory extended into studies that emphasised children's agency, locating literacy within a web of related cultural activities, (Gee, 1990; Göncü, 1999). The rich proliferation of such studies is reflected in following chapters.

Ethnography and literacy outside of schooling

That home circumstances made a difference to children's relationship with written language had been known to researchers for a very long time. Nevertheless, the role of the home was essentially positioned as a handmaiden to schooling. It was sociology and anthropology with their interests in cultural socialisation, the development of sociolinguistics with its interest in language as a social practice (Hymes, 1974), and the growing interest in emergent literacy that led to researchers in the 1970s and 1980s to look at literacy and homes in a different way.

Instead of trying to correlate literacy performance with crude socio-economic indicators, for the first time researchers began to ask in detail how literacy practice operated in homes and how these experiences might influence children's attitudes to and knowledge about literacy. Shirley Brice Heath (1983) brought ethnography to studying literacy in families but, significantly, looked beyond the family to the community. Across a 10-year period she examined how different community language and literacy discourses encultured children. She followed these children into schooling and explored how their early experiences interrelated with the discourses of schooling, demonstrating powerfully different effects on the children's lives in school. In the same year as Heath's book was published another anthropologist, Taylor (1983), introduced the phrase 'family literacy' after spending 3 years working with six families exploring how the children developed ideas and knowledge about literacy in their homes and how this related to their literacy experiences in schools. Neither Heath nor Taylor focussed specifically upon younger children. They did not have to as the ethnographic study of family and community literacy life included all participants in relation to each other; young children and their literacy-related behaviours now appeared in context.

Heath and Taylor were part of a significant shift in literacy studies, a shift that began to emphasise the social nature of literacy. Street (1984) after examining different theories of literacy and analysing community literacy practices in Iran concluded that Western academic models of literacy, while widespread, failed to represent the different ways in which literacy was embedded in cultural practices. Describing the Western model as treating literacy like an autonomous object, he developed the ideas of ideological 'literacies' in which different cultural and community discourses led to significantly different ways of valuing and using literacy (something also explored in Africa by Scribner and Cole, 1981, and in Alaska by Scollon and Scollon, 1981). Thus from different cultural contexts children would be bringing very different conceptions of literacy to the autonomous practices of school literacy. Tizard and Hughes (1984) examined exactly what happened when children crossed the threshold of the classroom, challenging a prevailing – and persistent – viewpoint that working-class parents necessarily contributed less to children's oral and literacy repertoires than middle-class families enjoyed.

The introduction of longitudinal approaches and ethnography to studying literacy as a social practice was very important. Uncovering the nature and significance of literacy within family and community life required diverse tools to suit different sites, and ethnography, with its focus on detailed description, the evolving of themes, the valuing of participant's perspectives, and the development of different relationships between researchers and subjects, allowed extremely detailed research to flourish. A landmark study was Wells' (1986) *The Meaning Makers*, researching children moving across different settings as they emerged from infancy, interacted with people at home then at school; following some until the end of elementary education. Significant findings included:

- Children can take the initiative in literacy-related activities from an early age, but school tended to remove responsibility from them;
- 'Listening' to books that are read to them – actually engaging in talk around and through books – is very possibly the most valuable type of early literacy activity;

- Children learn best when engaged in authentic experiences that are meaningful for them.

Considering literacy as a social practice became and remains a dominant theme in literacy studies and most frequently draws heavily, although not always directly, on ethnography. Much subsequent research concentrated on developing more theoretical accounts of literacy (for instance, Gee, 1990; Baynham, 1995, and Lankshear, 1997), or on exploring specific community literacy practices (for example, Besnier, 1995; Barton and Hamilton, 1998). Others paid more attention to children (for example, Fishman, 1988; Lofty, 1992) and some have concentrated on older children and adolescents (for example Voss, 1996; Finders, 1997, and Knobel, 1999).

How did all this work impact on the emergence of early childhood literacy?

- It demonstrated clearly that literacy cannot be divorced from language as a whole, and neither from its wider cultural context. Literacy is given meaning by the cultural discourses and practices in which it is embedded and young children are from birth witnesses to and participants in such practices.
- In uncovering young children's literacy lives in families and communities it drew attention to how young children are learning to make meaning with a much wider notion of literacy than previously considered, thus opening the way for later investigation of broader notions of authorship, young children's relationship to popular culture, and their involvement in the new technologies of communication.
- It has raised and invited powerful questions about the relationship between literacy as a social practice and literacy in schooling at a time when in many parts of the world the autonomous models of literacy was being increasingly privileged by governments.

The literacy classroom as a dynamic social space

The research shifts identified so far had been increasingly opening up literacy as a complex practice, and gradually the assumption that in classrooms the activity of teaching literacy was much less problematic came to be challenged. While earlier studies had begun to reveal that young children were strategic, active learners when faced with classroom reading demands, classrooms were still typically viewed as less dynamic situations in which children were positioned as passive consumers of literacy knowledge. Drawing on theoretical stances derived from ethnomethodology and social interactional perspectives (Garfinkel, 1967; Hymes, 1974; Goffman, 1981; Bloome and Green, 1984) a number of researchers began to problematise this instructional space. By exploring in considerable detail the activities and behaviours that made up everyday classroom life, these environments, far from being places where teachers simply taught and children simply learned, were gradually uncovered as complex communicative spaces. Children were not simply learning the academic content of lessons, but were learning (or contesting) the ways of being in classrooms. Classrooms began to be perceived as dynamic spaces that had social structures, academic structures and activity structures, and each was interlocked and interdependent (Erickson and Mohatt, 1982).

McDermott (1979) explored the discursive construction of identity and how this impacted upon performances of literacy in second-grade classrooms. With the aid of painstaking investigation of frame-by-frame video playback, McDermott demonstrated that children in the apparently chaotic bottom group were actually responding in ways that were equally strategic as the responses of children in the manifestly achieving top group. McDermott set his analysis not in the context of prior investigations into educational achievement, nor indeed in mainstream psychology, but rather in micro-sociological questioning of how people in their moment-by-moment behaviour negotiate and construct their roles and identities. This detailed, almost second-by-second examination of classroom activities became a common procedural technique in an effort to locate precisely how literacy sessions were constructed and negotiated during interactions between teachers and students, and between student and student (Green, 1987; Bloome, 1989; Heap, 1989; Floriana, 1993).

One consequence of this research was a growing focus on what it was that children brought to literacy sessions, both academically and socially, for instance recognising that child participation depended not only on the teacher's rules for participation but the child's standing and relationships with peers. These more finely focussed observations gradually changed from simple comparisons between the language and literacy of home and school in which the child's language in school was seen as somewhat impoverished. Increasingly researchers discovered that whatever the formal agendas of schooling might demand, within them children were nevertheless making rich use of their out-of-school language and literacy lives both in adolescence (Gilmore, 1986) and in early childhood (Dyson, 1989, 1993, 2002).

While the socially oriented work of the researchers in the previous two sections has been highly significant, it has also been criticised for not connecting with wider concerns of a social theory of pedagogy: 'the cross-generational production and reproduction of knowledge and power' and 'the complex fabric of texts and discourses through which social representation and reproduction is effected.' (Luke, 1992: 108) These wider perspectives on literacy emerged from the work of theorists associated with discourse studies (Lankshear and Lawler, 1987; Luke, 1988; Baker and Freebody, 1989; Edelsky, 1996) – although these have their origins in a long history of social, political and philosophical theory (Bourdieu, 1977, 1990; Foucault, 1979, 1988). Discursive approaches broaden the scope of studies into family and classroom life by examining how these social institutions are located in discourse structures and wider ideologies (Gee, 1996). Discourses are deeply embedded and largely invisible to participants within them (although not to those outside them). Some discourses have historically gained immense power and status, something that becomes unproblematic to those subscribing to their ideas and practices. This understanding of how discourses and ideologies position participants, materials and practices within early childhood, is increasingly challenged through the valuing of diversity (Cannella, 2002; Vasquez, 2004; Janks, 2010). González, Moll, and Amanti (2005) used the concept of 'funds of knowledge' to develop a powerful strategy of involving teachers to facilitate parents and their communities to come to a strength-based analysis of the resources they hold to support their children's literacy development.

Literacy as semiotic and technological practice

If there is one thing that most of the research written about so far has in common, it is that it focusses on literacy as an activity involving the use of print. To most people this long seemed an *a priori* condition of researching literacy, but one of the more recent shifts in early childhood literacy has been as a result of social semiotic theory. This theory is concerned with ways in which meaning is made in social contexts (Eco, 1979; Halliday, 1974). Conventionally literacy is an act of meaning making, whether it be in interpreting a text or generating a text, and it has always been acknowledged that there are many other forms of meaning making, e.g. through art, music, dance, etc. Historically these have always been linked generally as 'creative' areas, but specifically separated as cultural practices. Thus, for instance, there is a long history of studies of children's literacy, and a strong history of studies of children's drawings (for example, Kellog, 1969; Goodnow, 1977; Gardner, 1980), giving the impression that these activities are quite distinct. Social semiotic theory points out that as forms of meaning making they, and all other forms of meaning, have as many similarities as differences, and that it is history and ideology that assigns particular values to these differences.

Children from very early on utilise a rich range of ways to make meaning and while they might be able to distinguish between them as forms, they utilise whatever they feel is appropriate in whichever ways they want to intend a meaning (see Flewitt, this volume). One of the earliest teams of researchers to explore this area, albeit embryonically, was Harste, Woodward, and Burke (1984). They believed that young children's meaning making used exactly the same overall strategies as adults, but that their results reflected differences in experience and interest. Although focussing mostly on print-related meaning making by young children, they nevertheless viewed authoring as something that could move across communication systems and which was truly multimodal. This was taken further by Rowe (1994) in her study of preschoolers as authors. She points out that young children do not feel excessively constrained by society's distinctions between communication systems, and the belief of many that young children use a variety of graphic media because they cannot write reflects a major failure to understand how powerfully children switch between modalities as their intents shift.

The seminal text in this area is *Before Writing* (Kress, 1997). While acknowledging that children increasingly become aware of the ways in which conventions operate, Kress points out that learning is not a simply unidirectional movement in which children simply take on board a socially determined world. Children as well as adults transform the world while operating within its conventions. He argues powerfully that children's use of signs, symbols and modalities is not arbitrary but is structured and reflects strategic choices by them to represent things that are important to them. Like Haste, Burke and Woodward earlier, he argues that it is experience and interest that distinguishes their meaning making from adults, not their strategies. Young children choose what they want to represent and then select the best possible means for doing it. What is best (and often very complex) may come from different modes, means and materials, regardless of whether adult culture uses or sanctions such selections.

A number of scholars associated with Kress developed these ideas (e.g. Pahl, 1999; Lancaster, 2001; Kenner, 2004. Pahl examined meaning making in nursery school as well as the home and demonstrated how the texts young children create, while often ephemeral and 'messy', nevertheless represent a crossroads where adults' preoccupations, children's popular culture and interests, and the school and family narratives are played out. Lancaster focussed on how successfully an 18-month-old child explored in complex ways different forms of graphic representation while Kenner explored how 5-year-old bilingual children understood different graphic systems of writing, what she termed 'signs of difference'. This stress on the continuity of literacy with other semiotic systems can be linked to an emphasis on the multimodality of all communicative behaviour (Finnegan, 2002) and even the argument that in all modes symbolic representations should logically be defined 'literacies' (Lemke, 1998).

Literacy practices necessarily involve technologies. Communication technologies extend the reach of communications across space and/or time. Children's play regularly utilises pretend or actual technologies that are part of their environments (Wohlwend, 2011). For example the telephone as a medium possesses its own specific constraints and opportunities for discourse, necessitating a shift away from the 'here-and-now' characteristic of very young children's talk, to a consideration of the interlocutor's distance that is also characteristic of literacy (Gillen, 2002). In recent years engagements with digital technologies have been much studied. As discussed by Marsh (2010) and Flewitt (this volume) such research is challenged by a perhaps paradoxical social response to new technologies. Learning with those technologies long conceptualised as 'ICT' (information and communication technologies) is emphasised in education, with a commensurate hype that an early a start as possible can increase advantage. Yet simultaneously a kind of moral panic surrounds their use in early childhood, to the extent of characterising them as 'toxic' (e.g. Palmer, 2006), an anxiety that is perhaps in part a romantic nostalgia for earlier eras supposedly characterised by outdoor play and handcrafted toys. Yet, as Buckingham (2000) argued, carefully conducted research leads to a more balanced position. Studies in the UK and USA (e.g. Rideout, Vanderwater, and Wartella, 2003; Marsh

et al., 2005; Plowman, McPake, and Stephen, 2010) have subsequently shown that many young children are growing up immersed in digital technologies and new media from birth, that patterns of interaction differ and that many parents recognise that children are developing a wide range of skills, knowledge and understanding in their use. Burnett (2010) identifies three key categories of assumptions underpinning recent research on young children's literacy in connection with educational settings: of technology as deliverer of literacy, as site for interaction around texts; and medium for meaning-making. In practice, children's spontaneous interactions around digital texts can be seamlessly blended with other practices. As a technology becomes increasingly embedded in society instrumental or deterministic accounts of its influence may begin to lose their power and greater become the possibilities for recognising children's agency.

Finally it should be noted that while very young children have little social or economic power and their transformations may not significantly impact upon the wider world, as children get older this changes and as adolescents their linguistic and multimodal transformations become powerful enough to generate considerable (but ultimately futile) resistance by adults.

CONCLUSION

We are conscious that our survey has necessarily been short, is very selective and partial, and inevitably reflects the histories of the authors. We are keenly aware that nowhere have we been we able to do justice to the complexity of the perspectives included (and certainly not to those that have not been included) but know that many of the following chapters offer the opportunity to explore recent perspectives more deeply.

We began this survey at a point where the relationship between early childhood and literacy appeared relatively straightforward and unproblematic, and have explored how this relationship became more complex and problematic over time. It is clear that these changes have been dramatic and now reflect a hugely different construct of the relationship between children and written language, a perspective than can now justifiably be termed early childhood literacy. We hope we have also shown how these changes are not discrete but are situated in much wider and deeper level changes in the way research, culture, and society have been conceived. So what is now implied by the use of the phrase 'early childhood literacy'?

We would want to claim that:

- It is an all-embracing concept for a rich range of authorial and responsive practices using a variety of media and modalities, carried out by people during their early childhood.
- It is a concept that allows early childhood to be seen as a state in which people use literacy as it is appropriate, meaningful and useful to them, rather than a stage on a path to some future literate state. It is not about emergence or becoming literate; it is about being literate and allows the literacy practices and products of early childhood to be acknowledged as valid in their own right, rather than perceived as inadequate manifestations of adult literacy.
- It is a concept that allows early literacy to move way beyond the limitations and restrictions of schooling and extend into all domains of the lives of people in early childhood.
- It is a concept that has evolved out of contestation, innovation and reconceptualisation and one that has become and continues to be susceptible to the scrutiny of a wide range of theoretical and methodological positions. It is not a concept that has finished evolving, nor will it ever do so. It is a social construct and as such will never achieve fixity.

We would also want to claim that the study of early childhood literacy is in a healthy state. It is a dynamic, fresh and continuously invigorated area, as is shown by the chapters that follow. It is also unfortunately an area where much of the contemporary research has had very limited impact upon political views about pedagogic practice. We would, however, want to point out that the study of early childhood literacy is no longer constrained by pedagogic demands; it is now an area of investigation that has integrity in its own right.

REFERENCES

Akinasso, F. N. (1991) 'Literacy and individual consciousness', in E. Jennings and A. Purves (eds), *Literate Systems and Individual Lives.* Albany: SUNY Press.

Baghban, M. (1984) *Our Daughter Learns to Read and Write: A Case Study From Birth To Three.* Newark, Delaware: International Reading Association.

Baker, C. and Freebody, P. (1989) *Children's First School Books.* Oxford: Basil Blackwell.

Barton, D. and Hamilton, M. (1998) *Local Literacies: Reading and Writing in One Community.* London: Routledge.

Baynham, M. (1995) *Literacy Practices: Investigating Literacy in Social Contexts.* London: Longman.

Besnier, N. (1995) *Literacy, Emotion, and Authority: Reading and Writing on a Polynesian Atoll.* Cambridge: Cambridge University Press.

Bissex, G. (1980) *Gnys at Wrk: A Child Learns to Read and Write.* Cambridge, MA: Harvard University Press.

Bloome, D. (1989) 'Beyond access: an ethnographic study of reading and writing in a seventh grade classroom', in D. Bloome (ed.), *Classrooms and Literacy.* Norwood, NJ: Ablex Publishing Corporation. pp. 53–104.

Bloome, D. and Green, J. (1984) 'Directions in the sociolinguistic study of reading', in D. Pearson, R. Barr, M. Kamil and P. Mosenthal (eds), *Handbook of Research in Reading.* New York: Longman.

Bourdieu, P. (1977) 'The economics of linguistic exchanges', *Social Sciences Information*, 16: 645–68.

Bourdieu, P. (1990) *In Other Words: Essays Towards a Reflexive Sociology.* Stanford: Stanford University Press.

Bruner, J., Goodenough, J. and Austin, G. (1956) *A Study of Thinking*. New York: John Wiley & Sons.

Bruner, J., Olver, R. and Greenfield, P. (1966) *Studies In Cognitive Growth*. New York: John Wiley & Sons.

Buckingham, D. (2000) *After the Death of Childhood: Growing up in the Age of Electronic Media*. Cambridge: Polity Press.

Burnett, C. (2010) Technology and literacy in early childhood educational settings: A review of research. *Journal of Early Childhood Literacy*, 10(3): 247–70.

Cannella, G. (2002) *Deconstructing Early Childhood Education: Social Justice and Revolution*. New York: P. Lang.

Catell, J.M. (1886) 'The time it takes to see and name', *Mind*, 11: 63–5.

Cherry, C. (1966) *On Human Comunication*. Cambridge, MA: MIT Press.

Chomsky, N. (1957) *Syntactic Structures*. The Hague: Mouton.

Chomsky, N. (1959) 'Review of Verbal Behaviour by B. F. Skinner', *Language*, 35: 26–58.

Chomsky, N. (1965) *Aspects of a Theory of Syntax*. Cambridge, MA: MIT Press.

Clarke, M. (1976) *Young Fluent Readers*. London: Heinemann Educational Books.

Clay, M. (1969) 'Reading errors and self-correction behaviour', *British Journal of Educational Psychology*, 39: 47–56.

Clay, M. (1975) *What Did I Write?* London: Heinemann Educational Books.

Coltheart, M. (1979) 'When can children learn to read – and when should they be taught?', in T. Waller and G. Mackinnon (eds), *Reading Research: Advances In Theory And Practice*. Vol. 1. New York: Academic Press. pp.1–30.

Crago, M. and Crago, H. (1983) *Prelude to Literacy: A Pre-School Child's Encounter with Picture and Story*. Carbondale, Ill: Southern Illinois University Press.

Dolch, E. and Bloomster, M. (1937) 'Phonic readiness'. *Elementary School Journal*, 38: 201–5.

Downing, J. (1979) *Reading and Reasoning*. Edinburgh: W. and C. Black.

Durkin, D. (1966) *Children Who Read Early*. New York: Teachers College Press.

Dyson, A.H. (1989) *Multiple Worlds of Child Writers: Friends Learning to Write*. New York: Teachers College Press.

Dyson, A.H. (1993) *Social Worlds of Children Learning to Write in an Urban Primary School*. New York: Teachers College Press.

Dyson, A.H. (2002) *The Brothers and Sisters Learn to Write: Popular Literacies in Childhood and School Cultures*. New York: Teachers College Press.

Eco, U. (1979) *The Role of the Reader*. Bloomingtom: Indiana University Press.

Edelsky, C. (1996) *With Literacy and Justice for All: Rethinking the Social in Language and Education*. London: Taylor and Francis.

Erickson, F. and Mohatt, G. (1982) 'Cultural organisation of particpation structures in two classrooms of Indian students', in G. Spindler (ed.), *Doing the Ethnography of Schooling: Educational Anthropology in Action*. New York: Holt, Rinehart and Winston. pp.132–75.

Ferriero, E. and Teberosky, A. (1982) *Literacy before Schooling*. Portsmouth, N.H: Heinemann Educational Books.

Finders, M. (1997) *Just Girls: Hidden Literacies and Life in Junior High*. New York: Teachers College Press/NCTE.

Finnegan, R. (2002) *Communicating: The Multiple Modes of Human Interconnection*. London: Routledge.

Fishman, A. (1988) *Amish Literacy: What and How it Means*. Portsmouth, N.H: Heinemann Educational Books.

Floriana, A. (1993) 'Negotiating what counts: roles and relationships, texts and contexts, content and meaning', *Linguistics and Education*, 5(3 and 4): 241–75.

Forester, A. (1977) 'What teachers can learn from natural readers', *The Reading Teacher*, 31: 160–6.

Foucault, M. (1979) *Discipline and Punishment*. New York: Harper.

Foucault, M. (1988) *Technologies of the Self*. London: Tavistock.

Gardner, H. (1980) *Artful Scribbles: The Significance of Children's Drawings*. New York: Basic Books.

Garfinkel, H. (1967) *Studies in Ethnomethodology*. Englewood-Cliffs, N.J: Prentice-Hall.

Gee, J.P. (1990) *Social Linguistics and Literacies: Ideology in Discourses*. New York: Falmer Press.

Gee, J.P. (1996) *Social Linguistics and Literacies: Ideology in Discourses*. (2nd ed.) London: Falmer Press.

Gibson, E. (1969) *Principles of Perceptual Learning and Development*. New York: Appleton-Century-Crofts.

Gillen, J. (2002) 'Moves in the territory of literacy? – The telephone discourse of three- and four-year-olds', *Journal of Early Childhood Literacy* 2(1): 21–43.

Gilmore, P. (1986) 'Sub-rosa literacy: peers, play, and ownership in literacy acquisition', in B. Schiefflin and P. Gilmore (eds), *The Acquisition of Literacy: Ethnographic Perspectives*. New York: Ablex. pp.155–68.

Goffman, E. (1981) *Forms of Talk*. Oxford: Blackwell.

Göncü, A. (1999) (ed.) *Children's Engagement in the World: Sociocultural Perspectives*. Cambridge: Cambridge University Press.

González, N., Moll, L., and Amanti, C. (2005) *Funds of Knowledge: Theorizing Practice in Households, Communities, and Classrooms*. Mahwah, N.J: Lawrence Erlbaum.

Goodman, K. (1968) *The Psycholinguistic Nature of the Reading Process*. Detroit: Wayne State University Press.

Goodman, K. (1976) 'Miscue analysis: theory and reality in reading', in J. Merritt (ed.), *New Horizons in Reading*. Newark, DE: International Reading Association.

Goodnow, J. (1977) *Children Drawing*. Cambridge, MA: Harvard University Press.

Gray, W.S. (1956) *The Teaching of Reading and Writing*. Chicago: Scott Foresman.

Green, J. (1987) 'In search of meaning: a sociolinguistic perspective on lesson construction and reading', in D. Bloome (ed.), *Literacy and Schooling*. Norwood, N.J: Ablex Publishing Corporation. pp. 3–34.

Hall, N. (1987) *The Emergence of Literacy*. Sevenoaks: Hodder and Stoughton.

Halliday, M. (1974) *Language and Social Man*. London: Longman.

Harste, J., Burke, C., and Woodward, V. (1982) 'Children's language and world: initial encounters with print', in J. Langer and M. Smith-Burke (eds), *Reader Meets Author: Bridging the Gap*. Newark, DE: International Reading Association.

Harste, J., Woodward, J., and Burke, C. (1984) *Language Stories and Literacy Lessons*. Portsmouth, N.H: Heinemann Educational Books.

Heap, J. (1989) 'Sociality and cognititon in collaborative computer learning', in D. Bloome (ed.), *Classrooms and Literacy*. Norwood, N.J: Ablex Publishing Corporation. pp.135–57.

Heath, S.B. (1983) *Ways with Words: Language, Life, and Work in Communities and Classrooms*. Cambridge: Cambridge University Press.

Hiebert, E. (1981) 'Developmental patterns and inter-relationships of pre-school children's print awareness', *Reading Research Quarterly*, 16(2): 236–59.

Huey, E.B. (1908) *The Psychology and Pedagogy of Reading*. New York: Macmillan.

Hymes, D. (1974) *Foundation in Sociolinguistics*. Philadelphia: University of Pennsylvania Press.

Janks, H. (2010) *Literacy and Power*. New York: Routledge.

Johns, J. (1976/7) 'Reading is stand-up, sit-down.' *Journal of the New England Reading Association*, 12(1): 10–14.

Kellog, R. (1969) *Analyzing Children's Art*. Palo Alto, CA: National Press Books.

Kenner, C. (2004) *Becoming Biliterate: Young Children Learning Different Writing Systems*. Stoke on Trent: Trentham Books.

Knobel, M. (1999) *Everyday Literacies: Students, Discourse and Social Practice*. New York: Peter Lang.

Kress, G. (1997) *Before Writing: Rethinking the Paths to Literacy*. London: Routledge.

Lancaster, L. (2001) 'Staring at the page: the functions of gaze in a young child's interpretation of symbolic forms', *Journal of Early Childhood Literacy*, 1: 131–52.

Lankshear, C. (1997) *Changing Literacies*. Buckingham: Open University Press.

Lankshear, C. and Lawler, M. (1987) *Literacy, Schooling and Revolution*. London: Falmer Press.

Lass, B. (1982) 'Portrait of my son as an early reader', *The Reading Teacher*, 36(1): 20–8.

Lee, C. and Smagorinsky, P. (2000) 'Introduction: constructing meaning through collaborative enquiry', in C. Lee and P. Smagorinsky (eds), *Vygotskian Perspectives on Literacy Research: Constructing Meaning Through Collaborative Enquiry*. Cambridge: Cambridge University Press.

Lemke, J.L. (1998) 'Multimedia literacy demands of the scientific curriculum', *Linguistics and Education* 10(3): 247–71.

Lofty, J. (1992) *Time to Write: The Influence of Time and Culture on Learning to Write*. New York: State University of New York Press.

Luke, A. (1988) *Literacy, Textbooks and Ideology*. London: Falmer Books.

Luke, A. (1992) 'The body literate: discourse and inscription in early literacy training', *Linguistics and Education*, 4: 107–29.

McDermott, R.P. (1979) 'Kids make sense: an ethnographic account of the interactional management of success and failure in one first-grade classroom'. PhD dissertation, Stanford University.

McNeill, D. (1966) 'Developmental psycholinguistics', in F. Smith and G. Miller (eds), *The Genesis of Language*. Cambridge, MA: MIT Press.

Marsh, J. (2010) *Childhood, Culture and Creativity: A Literature Review*. Newcastle upon Tyne: Creativity, Culture and Education.

Marsh, J., Brooks, G., Hughes, J., Ritchie, L. Roberts, S., and Wright, K. (2005) *Digital Beginnings: Young Children's Use of Popular Culture, Media and New Technologies*. Sheffield: University of Sheffield.

Mason, J. (1980) 'When do children begin to read: an exploration of four-year-old children's word reading competencies', *Reading Research Quarterly*, 15(2): 203–27.

Miller, G. (1967) *The Psychology of Communication*. New York: Basic Books.

Miller, G., Galanter, E., and Pribram, K. (1960) *Plans and the Structure of Behaviour*. New York: Holt, Rinehart and Winston.

Morphett, M.V. and Washburne, C. (1931) 'When should children begin to read?', *Elementary School Journal*, 31: 496–503.

Neisser, U. (1967) *Cognitive Psychology*. New York: Appleton-Century-Crofts.

Pahl, K. (1999) *Transformations: Meaning Making in the Nursery*. Staffordshire: Trentham Books

Paley, V.G. (1984) *Boys and Girls: Superheroes in the Doll Corner*. Chicago, Ill: University of Chicago Press.

Palmer, S. (2006) *Toxic Childhood: How Modern Life is Damaging our Children ... and What We Can Do about It*. London: Orion.

Patrick, G. (1899) 'Should children under 10 learn to read and write?', *Popular Science Monthly*, 54: 382–92.

Payton, S. (1984) *Developing Awareness of Print: A Young Child's First Steps Towards Literacy*. Birmingham: Educational Review.

Pierce, J.R. (1961) *Symbols, Signals and Noise: The Nature and Process of Communication*. New York: Harper and Row.

Plowman, L., McPake, J., and Stephen, C. (2010) 'The technologisation of childhood? Young children and technology in the home', *Children & Society*, 24: 63–74.

Read, C. (1970) 'Pre-school children's knowledge of English phonology', *Harvard Educational Review*, 41(1): 1–34.

Reid, J. (1966) 'Learning to think about reading', *Educational Research*, 9: 56–62.

Rideout, V., Vandewater, E., and Wartella, E. (2003) *Zero to Six: Electronic Media in the Lives of Infants, Toddlers and Preschoolers*. Washington: Kaiser Foundation.

Rogoff, B. (1986) 'Adult assistance of children's learning', in T.E. Raphael (ed.), *The Contexts of School-Based Literacy*. New York: Random House. pp. 27–40.

Rogoff, B. (1990) *Apprenticeship in Thinking, Cognitive Development in Social Context*. New York, Oxford U.P.

Rowe, D. (1994) *Preschoolers as Authors: Literacy Learning in the Social World of the Classroom*. Cresskill, N.J: Hampton Press.

Scollon, R. and Scollon, S. (1981) *Narrative, Literacy and Face in Interethnic Communication*. Norwood, N.J: Ablex Publishing Corporation.

Scribner, S. and Cole, M. (1981) *The Psychology of Literacy*. Cambridge, MA: Harvard University Press.

Skinner, B. F. (1957) *Verbal Behavior*. New York: Appleton-Century-Crofts.

Smith, F. (1971) *Understanding Reading*. London: Holt, Rinehart and Co.

Street, B. (1984) *Literacy in Theory and Practice*. Cambridge: Cambridge University Press.

Sulzby, E. (1985) 'Kindergarteners as readers and writers', in M. Farr (ed.), *Children's Early Writing Development*. Norwood, N.J: Ablex Publishing Corporation.

Taylor, D. (1983) *Family Literacy: Young Children Learning to Read and Write*. Portsmouth, N.H: Heinemann Educational Books.

Tharp, R. and Gallimore, R. (eds) (1988) *Rousing Minds to Life: Teaching, Learning and Schooling in Social Context*. New York: Cambridge University Press.

Tizard, B. and Hughes, M. (1984) *Young Children Learning, Thinking and Talking at Home and at School*. London: Fontana.

Tovey, D. (1976) 'Children's perceptions of reading', *The Reading Teacher*, 29: 536–40.

Van der Veer, R. and Valsiner, J. (1994) 'Introduction', in R. Van der Veer and J. Valsiner (eds), *The Vygotsky Reader*. Oxford: Blackwell.

Vasquez, V. (2004) *Negotiating Critical Literacies with Young Children*. Mahwah, N.J: Lawrence Erlbaum.

Voss, M. (1996) *Hidden Literacies: Children Learning at Home and at School*. Portsmouth, N.H: Heinemann.

Vygotsky, L.S. (1962) *Thought and Language*. (Ed. and trans. by E. Haufmann and G. Vakar.) Cambridge, MA: MIT Press

Vygotsky, L.S. (1967) 'Play and its role in the mental development of the child', *Soviet Psychology*, 5(3): 6–18.

Vygotsky, L.S. (1978) *Mind in Society: the Development of Higher Psychological Processes*. (eds. M. Cole, V. John-Steiner, S. Scribner & E. Souberman) Cambridge, MA: Harvard University Press.

Wells, G. (1986) The Meaning Makers: Children Learning Language and Using Language to Learn. London: Hodder and Stoughton.

Wohlwend, K. (2011) *Playing Their Way into Literacies: Reading, Writing, and Belonging in the Early Childhood Classroom*. New York: Teachers College Press.

Wood, D.J., Bruner, J.S., and Ross, G. (1976) 'The role of tutoring in problem solving', *Journal of Child Psychology and Psychiatry*, 17: 89–100.

2

Postcolonial Perspectives on Early Childhood Literacy

Radhika Viruru

Since the last edition of this handbook was published, I have had the opportunity to live and teach at a university in the tiny Persian Gulf nation of Qatar. The government of Qatar has recently embarked upon a massive set of educational and social reforms, designed to transform its economy, which is now dependent upon its considerable natural resources, into a knowledge-based economy, which draws upon the resources and knowledge of its own people. The reform efforts in the field of education have been spearheaded by the RAND Corporation, who provide a brief history of the reforms:

> The leadership of the Arabian Gulf nation of Qatar sees education as the key to Qatar's economic and social progress. Long concerned that the country's education system was not meeting the needs of its society, the highly committed Qatari leadership approached the RAND Corporation in 2001, asking it to examine the kindergarten through grade 12 (K-12) education system in Qatar and to recommend options for building a world-class system consistent with other Qatari initiatives for social and political change, such as wider opportunities for women.
>
> (Rand Corporation, 2012).

Based on the recommendations from RAND, the Qatari government implemented a system of education which is loosely based on the American system of charter schools, within which public schools conform to a common set of standards, but retain a large degree of autonomy and individual freedom. The stated goals of the reform are to create a world-class educational system within Qatar, that will produce well-educated citizens who are capable of not just of participating but of leading the future global economy (Supreme Education Council, www.sec.gov.qa), reflecting what Tikly (2009) has described as the philosophies of new imperialism. Although the local population has for the most part enthusiastically embraced the reforms, there has been some concern in the region that the reforms are turning Qatar into a mini Western nation and represent yet another form of American imperialism (Viruru, 2011; Glasser, 2003), drawing it further away from its own culture and language. Newspapers in Saudi

Arabia, Kuwait and Jordan have described the Americanization of education in Qatar as the region's worst nightmare (Glasser, 2003). Despite such criticism however the leadership in Qatar has not backed down, and has continued to support the reforms. The re-vamped government-run schools, known as independent schools, now serve about 80,000 children in 165 schools (Rand Corporation, 2011), within which a significant portion of the instruction is done in English, and the pedagogical practices are modeled on Euro-Western models of education, such as 'child-centered' instruction (Rand Corporation, 2011).

As one might imagine, the focus has inevitably been drawn to literacy, especially among young children. There is a widely held belief that the best way to transform the economy is to transform its children. As a result, the independent schools aggressively promote literacy in English as early as in kindergarten, and parents and families are being encouraged to incorporate English into their daily lives, alongside Arabic (Kelly, Viruru, and Al-Maadadi, 2010). As part of this aggressive effort to support literacy in general, and English in particular, there has also been concern that children in Qatar are not reading enough, particularly during their leisure. UK-based Bloomsbury Publishing has now opened up a branch in Qatar as part of the government-funded Qatar Foundation and now publishes bilingual children's books, designed to encourage children to read during their leisure time. The national university recently (2009) hosted a conference on early childhood literacy, for which I was the conference chair. This conference drew national attention and publicity, with the consensus among the local media and educators being that this was a very timely discussion (Gulf Times, 2009). The conference was attended by approximately 900 local early-childhood educators who spent 2 days exploring various ways in which to promote early childhood literacy. Many of the sessions centered around 'proven' pedagogical practices that have been shown to work in Europe and the United States.

Another experience I had in Qatar that is illustrative of the complex discourses that surround literacy in the country occurred when a colleague of mine and I were asked to organize an afterschool reading program in two local elementary schools, again based on the concern that the children in the school were not reading enough for pleasure. As my colleague and I struggled to find activities for the children that were culturally appropriate, it became apparent that what the children and the school considered to be reading, and what was the national focus, were quite different. To the teachers and the children, reading was a performative activity, designed to be done precisely and correctly, with an emphasis on correct pronunciation and diction, which is very much in line with traditional Islamic educational practices (Viruru and Nasser, 2011). The indigenous definition of reading seemed to be that it was for the purpose of seeking messages about living a good life, rather than for seeking pleasure. In fact some of the families expressed concern about the children reading, as it could draw them further away from their homes and families. This was borne out by a survey that we conducted of the nearly 70 children enrolled in the program, who listed visiting relatives as a major leisure activity (Viruru and Nasser, 2011).

Current events in Qatar underline, with increased urgency, the need to gain a broader perspective on early childhood literacy. Although there is now much wider-spread recognition that literacy is a multi-faceted activity, and it has become habitual to speak of multiple literacies, much of the literature on language and young children portrays it as a process of becoming, acquiring, improving and maturing. Rarely however is attention directed towards what is lost and shut out or re-defined in this process of acquisition. In this chapter the attempt will be to both lay out a theoretical framework that supports such a view and to review the literature that takes a more complex view of the process of young children's interactions with literacy. The focus in this chapter is deliberately directed towards diverse cultural contexts, where the process of what it means to become literate is in itself being complicated by factors such as global capitalism and its continuing economic colonization of the world. This has been somewhat complicated, as much of current critical research with young children seems to focus on minority populations in North American contexts. This chapter thus will first attempt to define terms such as literacy, childhood and postcolonialism. The concept of hybridity, which is a particularly important term in postcolonial studies, is explored in depth. Vignettes from various parts of the world are then presented, such as the United States, Samoa and indigenous communities in Canada, which illustrate how early childhood literacy can assume diverse forms. The chapter concludes with a discussion of how such hybrid literacies can inform current thinking about early childhood literacy.

DEFINING TERMS

A logical starting place would be to define what one means by such terms as postcolonialism. However, as postcolonial scholars point out, it is important to recognize the power of ideas such as definitions

themselves. Cooper and Brubaker (2005) quote the words of George Orwell in this context, as having said that 'the worst thing that one can do with words is to surrender to them' (p. 59). Words such as definitions thus create the illusion that all legitimate phenomena must be defined, denying the ambiguity and complexity that characterize many human experiences. This may be particularly true in terms of the term literacy for as Cherland and Harper (2007) have said, 'the term literacy is now applied to so many areas of human endeavor that some have argued the word is fast become meaningless' (p. 12). As Brockmeier and Olsen (2009) have commented, 'it has become next to impossible to give a clear and unbounded definition of literacy: the array of phenomena referred to as literacy has become clear and unbounded itself' (p. 4). According to Cherland and Harper, there are approximately 197 different kinds of literacy listed in the Education Resources Information Center (ERIC) database, ranging from media literacy to Christian literacy to postliteracy.

Moje and O'Brien (2001) have adopted an alternative approach, focusing on the goals rather than definitions of literacy. According to these scholars, literacy research focuses on four major goals: prediction, interpretation, reform or emancipation and interruptions. When viewed from each of these goals, literacy can assume different forms, namely patterns, experience, power and turbulence respectively. Brockmeier & Olsen (2009) have said that one can no longer speak of literacy as a phenomenon; it is more appropriate to recognize it as a discourse of episteme, consisting of multiple interrelated themes. They point out that literacy is now seen as fundamental to most 'social, societal, economic and political conditions'; it is an integral part of almost every discipline within the social sciences and is also high on the agenda of major international organizations such as the United Nations and the World Bank. It is therefore more apt to view literacy as a set of discourses rather than a phenomenon. A critical part of these discourses continues to be the concept of critical literacy (Collins and Blot, 2003; Luke, 2004), which is in many ways a literacy about literacies, and that focuses on practices 'that disrupt or critique dominant knowledge-power relationships that perpetuate unequal gender, race, and class relations and instead center dialogue, debate, and dissent' (Rogers, Mosley, Kramer and The Literacy for Social Justice Teacher Research Group, 2009). Since the earlier version of this chapter was published, the literature on critical literacy has expanded exponentially, with many ethnographic and other studies on its enactment being published (Lewison, Leland, and Harste, 2008; Stevens and Bean, 2007). Within early childhood contexts, critical literacy has been linked to how 'people use language to exercise power, to enhance every day life in schools' (Vasquez, 2005: 204), emphasizing that this is not a skill that can be taught but a curriculum that needs to be lived, while working with young children (Comber, 2001, 2003). Comber (2001) has stressed that an essential part of critical literacy is the use of language to question injustice and privilege. As Vasquez (2007) has pointed out too, there is often disbelief and sometimes discomfort with the idea that young children can actually engage with issues of critical literacy, which can lead to a limiting of the spaces opened up to young children to participate in.

A key feature of literacy is that it is often defined by its other: the illiterate. As Powell (1999) has put it, the 'perpetuation of social privilege requires the establishment of criteria for measuring an individual's worth, and a crucial standard for evaluating merit is our use of oral and written language' (p. 18). Fernandez (2001) draws an interesting history of literacy, pointing out how it has inextricably been linked to issues of power and privilege. According to Fernandez, in ancient England, the dominance of the ideology of literacy can be traced to the time when Normans demanded written proof from the Anglo-Saxons of ownership of property, and employed scribes to produce false documentation disproving the Anglo-Saxon claims. As Fernandez says, 'literacy legitimates itself' (p. 34). Illiteracy has been studied in relation to many quality-of-life indicators, including but not limited to various health phenomena (Ferraz et al., 1991; Weiss, Hart, McGee, and D'Estelle, 1992) and cognitive capacities (Petersson, Reis, and Ingvar, 2001; Nitrini et al., 2004) to name but two. The unmistakable messages that emerge continue to be that illiteracy is an undesirable handicap that can only limit one's potential: illiteracy is associated with ignorance, indolence, poverty and the creation of economic havoc that the literate must fix. As Stuckey (1991) has commented, illiteracy is strongly associated with antisocial behavior: even authors such as Jonathan Kozol remarking upon the high rates of illiteracy in the prison populations in the United States. Rockhill (1993) has also commented upon the discourses which create illiterates as threats to society: illiteracy is seen as 'dangerous, a threat to liberty, to economic and technological development and to the moral well being' of civilized societies (p. 157). In contrast, as Gallego and Hollingsworth (2000) put it, students who have acquired schooled literacy are seen as having the potential to be adult citizens who are 'innovative, achievement-oriented, productive, cosmopolitical, media and politically aware, more globally (nationally and internationally) and less locally-oriented, with more liberal and human social attitudes, less likely to commit a crime, and more likely to take education and the rights and duties of citizenship seriously' (Gee, 1990, quoted in Gallego and Hollingsworth, 2000: 6). However as Hollingsworth and Gallego (2004) have suggested, acquiring academic literacy is often gained at the expense of alternative literacy forms, which are often erased in the process of acquiring formal literacy. However, one might question whether the two extremes are as irreconcilable as such statements would make them appear, for as Powell (1999) has put it, given the socially constructed nature of literacy(s), all people are literate or illiterate depending upon the social context that they are in, schooled literacy still remains a national priority for most nations. The early childhood years are often constructed as critical to children's development since they encompass the journey from illiteracy to literacy: in this chapter, alternative views to this discourse will be presented. As seen in the vignettes from Qatar presented earlier, concerns about particular kinds of illiteracy, such as disinterest in reading for pleasure, represent not only narrow definitions of what literacy is, but also seem to be directed by commercial concerns.

POSTCOLONIAL PERSPECTIVES ON LITERACY

Postcolonialism has long been a difficult term to define, and many earlier works discuss some of the issues regarding the debates of definition (Cannella and Viruru, 2004; Young, 2001). As such, that dialogue will not be revisited in this chapter. For its purposes I rely on Young's (2001) conceptualization of postcolonial studies. He has suggested that postcolonial projects have three fundamental tasks: to investigate how the culture and knowledge of the colonizers was part of the practice of colonization; to critically examine continuing global inequities and their effects; and finally to transform those 'epistemologies into new forms of cultural and political production that operate outside the protocols of metropolitan traditions and enable successful resistance to, and transformation of, the degradation and materials injustice to which disempowered peoples and societies remain subjected' (p. 69). The focus in this chapter draws the most from Young's third task, for as Young has also said, if the post in postcolonial is interpreted as 'the historical moment of the theorized introduction of new tricontinental forms and strategies of critical analysis and practice', it becomes apparent why postcolonialism continues to be a theory of hope for many (Young, 2001: 58). As this position might also suggest, postcolonial studies encompass a broad range of concerns, and as Hulme (2005) puts it, the field continues to grow. Reasons for this growth include an application of the themes of postcolonial studies to many different disciplines as well as continued historical research, which re-examines the past in light of the concerns raised by the postcolonial present. As Behdad (2005) has said, current academic research on globalization and postcolonial studies constitute a belated theoretical recognition of phenomena that have long preceded the constitution of the discourse that now recognizes them.

Similarly, the connections between postcolonialism and childhood have been argued and drawn in many previous works. As scholars of childhood have noted (Burman, 2008; Cannella and Viruru, 2004; Cannella, 1997) young children too are often referred to as beings that need to be civilized and a vital part of this civilizing process is the acquisition of (proper) language. The pertinence of this argument to the lives of young children has been argued elsewhere (Cannella and Viruru, 2004): like many colonized groups, young children have rarely been allowed to define what it means to be a child; the modern construction of childhood as a pure and magical part of one's life is seen as resembling the exotic Western fantasies that came to be called the 'Orient' (which had little to do with the realities of the people these fantasies defined as Orientals). Other common points shared by the definitions of colonized groups and young children is that children too are often seen as unruly creatures whose bodies need to be strictly controlled and their freedoms restricted; children (like other colonized groups) are often viewed as deficient but 'educable': interesting more in what they might become than what they are. One of the key ways in which children are seen as 'lacking' is that they do not use language. As Burman (2008) has commented, 'the definition and demarcation of childhood are replete with social and political meanings' (p. 67), as childhood is constantly being reconstructed, mostly in relation to what it means to be an adult.

The connections between literacy and postcolonial theory are multi-dimensional and draw from the perspectives cited above. Cherland and Harper (2007) have provided a useful summary of how postcolonial theory has been used in literacy education research. However in this chapter I would like to focus more specifically on the social construct of literacies themselves and how postcolonial theory can help us both understand and deconstruct these constructs. According to Donaldson (1998) English alphabetic writing has become such a

normal part of society, that its relationship to colonialism has been mostly obliterated. Early English writing involved the use of tools such as 'styli or brushes or pens, carefully prepared surfaces such as paper, animal skins, strips of wood, as well as inks or paints, and much more' (Ong 1982, quoted in Donaldson, 1998). According to Donaldson, this constitutes writing as a colonial technology, which existed alongside and supported other colonial technologies of power such as navigational instruments and weapons, which were key players in what some call the American Holocaust, or the obliteration of its Native peoples.

Burman (2008) speaking of early childhood literacy in particular, has said that the process of how children come to acquire language is not only one of the most theoretically 'vibrant' areas in research, but also one through which much broader questions of social development are addressed (p. 181). Burman underscores the point also that although most of the world's populations are multi-lingual, most literacy research continues to focus on mono-lingual perspectives, and continues to reify the image of the ideal situation for language development being the mother alone with her child (not even children) at home, dedicated to facilitating her child's language development. The image thus is created is that although all people in the world use language, and many of them use languages other than English (despite the erosive effects of colonialism and imperialism on the world's languages) it is only in Euro-Western mostly mono-lingual contexts that its use is properly understood and fostered. As Seed (1991) has pointed out, language has even been used as a tool to distinguish between 'civilization and barbarism': those civilizations that use written languages are considered superior to those which do not (p. 8). As Gandhi (1998) suggests, language or text, more than any other social or political product, is one of the most 'significant instigators and purveyors of colonial power' (p. 141). Simultaneously, however, postcolonial scholars have recognized the power of literacy in the adoption of an activist stance, in the pursuit of hope that Young refers to. As Huggan and Tiffin (2010) have said, while speaking of postcolonial ecocriticism, literary texts have the power to 'set out symbolic guidelines for the material transformation of the world' (p. 13) and has the power to 'write wrongs'. Similarly Sole (2005) has commented on the power of literacy to effect change: he cites the transition in South Africa, from a perspective that limited literacy (and literature in particular) to speaking about oppression to more inclusive practices that included 'popular songs, music and anonymous stories exchanged on buses and trains' as one that empowered Black South Africans to become 'makers of culture in their own right' (p. 183). Donaldson (2005) argues that it is critical in postcolonial times for oppressed groups to engage in the process of 'postcolonial appropriation' (p. 191), a term she borrows from Ashcroft et al. (1998), who define postcolonial appropriation as ways in which the colonized may appropriate some aspects of imperial culture for themselves, to define their own identities, particularly in the domains of language and textuality (p. 19).

LITERACY AND HYBRIDITY

Literacy thus occupies a contentious place both in postcolonial and early-childhood studies. From within an early-childhood framework, the acquisition of formal print literacy constitutes a point of entry into an adult world that is increasingly being defined by the ability to communicate not only in person but through multiple forms of media. As recent scholarship on childhood studies has suggested, the acquisition of formal literacy can also represent the point where more than ever, what it means to be an adult can redefine children, in the image of the adults that they are meant to be. However, as postcolonial scholars have commented, the experiences of people around the world have consistently shown that although literacy has unquestionably been used an instrument of imperialism, it has also been used to great effect as a tool for redefinition and empowerment, resulting in the emergence of hybrid perspectives, which emerge from the zone of contact between the colonizer and the colonized.

This chapter will attempt to present some examples of these hybrid perspectives. Before presenting these examples, I will briefly review some recent scholarship on hybridity itself, based particularly on the Prabhu's (2007) comprehensive discussion of hybridity in contemporary times. It is important to recognize however that hybridity too has been critiqued as belonging, if only obliquely, to essential discourses as 'they depend on a view of cultural authenticity that condemns them to a continued marginality and an eventual death' (Bourdon, 1990, quoted in Donaldson, 2005). From Donaldson's point of view hybridity is too closely allied to its demeaning ancestor, syncretism.

Prabhu (2007) traces the roots of hybridity as a colonial concept to an essentially racial beginning, as it emerged from 'real' encounters between White colonizers and natives, which were however framed by the fundamental principle that the White race was superior to all others. Prabhu believes that this history is important to an understanding of hybridity today: it can be looked at either as a product of a past encounter that continues to re-occur, albeit in different versions, around the globe, or it can be looked at as something that dramatically altered both colonizers and colonized themselves, to where hybridity itself has been redefined, bringing issues such as 'multiplicity, plurality and difference in a less specified way' to the forefront (p. 82). The allure of hybridity, according to Prabhu, lies in its claims to disrupt binary modes of thinking, to provide a space from which the subaltern might possibly speak (Spivak, 1988) and from where power can be destabilized and re-structured (p. 154). Simultaneously, Prabhu cautions that one cannot, at any point, while celebrating the emergence of the hybrid and the agency of the subaltern, forget to be cognizant of capitalism and its endorsement of hybrid 'heterogeneity, multiplicity and difference' (2007), or at least the ones that have the power to participate significantly or support global marketplaces.

Prabhu identifies two major ideas that are part of the contemporary discourses of hybridity: diaspora and creolization. Diaspora in many ways refers to an identity that is firmly tied to the concept of a home country while existing outside of it: for example, claiming identity as an Indian, links one back to the mother country and its traditions, particularly pre-colonialism. Creolization, on the other hand, releases the concept of hybridity from that sacred tie to a particular place, focusing more on the present concerns of diasporic populations that do not always refer back to the colonial encounter as well as on the alliances that have been built among them. Prabhu suggests that most theories of hybridity crystallize around these two ideas, in some form or the other. For example, the work of

Lionnet (1991), an influential postcolonial scholar, puts forward the concept of metissage, as a way to think about hybridity. She describes metissage as a site of mixture, characterized by 'indeterminacy and indecidability' (p. 6), which allows for non-hierarchical connections between traditions to emerge, and to generate literary texts (Prabhu, 2007).

The work of Edouard Glissant also offers valuable insights into how hybridity as a concept can help us better understand young children's journeys into literacies. According to Prabhu, there are three concepts in Glissant's work that are of particular interest to an understanding of hybridity: metissage, creolization and *Relation*. Metissage is seen by Glissant as encounter of retroactive understanding that creates a 'cognitive shock' but also creates the potential for revolution as it allows one to track differences; this allows for creolization, seen as an organic process in which differences continue to exist in multiple forms and become the basis for thought and action' (Prabhu, 2007). Through the concept of *Relation*, Glissant too stresses the non-logical connection between ideas in particular, stressing that 'Relation requires a constant figuring of the entire totality within which specific concepts and interactions become coherent' (Prabhu, 2007). Relation thus questions the idea of a part and a whole, suggesting that one must speak of the relationships of all things at all times, or as Prabhu puts it 'Relation requires a constant figuring of the entire totality within which specific concepts and interactions become coherent' (p. 1708). Within *Relation,* Glissant also stresses the importance of the idea of opacity, or un-understandability, which functions as a defense against essentialization and reductionism, while maintaining the importance of ethical subjectivity. Such a view of hybridity thus stresses that encounters between the oppressors and oppressed do not result in simple red-and-white-make-pink mixtures, but can lead to compounds that did not exist heretofore, and as such, cannot be understood using established modes of understanding. One of the most common remarks that my undergraduate teacher education students make about the young children they work with is that their writing and thought is often 'random': in other words lacks a logical basis. Glissant would seem to suggest that there is great value in random thought.

Hybridity thus, while perhaps born of the forcible union of the colonizer and the colonized, has evolved into a multi-faceted almost discipline of its own, that suggests many interesting possibilities for us to read encounters between young children and the world of formal literacy. I would like to present three specific examples of such encounters, relating each of them back to the theoretical perspectives presented above.

Hybrid literacies

Family literacies

The idea of family literacy is not new to the early childhood context, particularly in the United States (Reyes and Torres, 2007). In this section I would like to present examples from two different studies of family literacy programs and read their 'results' from a standpoint of hybridity, looking both at how they reveal not only the ongoing conflict between Euro-Western and other 'Native' perspectives of the world, but also at the non-hierarchical, non-logical relationships created through each one.

Family literacy programs generally refer to intergenerational programs that focus on working with families, to promote formal literacy. An assumption in setting up these programs that is often made is that the best 'results' are achieved when one focuses on early childhood literacy in the context of parenting strategies, increased parent literacy and support for children's functioning in school (St Pierre et al., 1995; Caspe, 2003). Thus many family literacy programs include early childhood care, parenting classes, bilingual education classes if needed and support for adult literacy. They have however often been criticized for approaching literacy as though it were something that families were fundamentally lacking. At best they are seen as and trying to 'fix' children and families and at worst for adopting what Reyes and Torres call a liberal 'pobrecito' (pity) kind of approach to families, which accepts differences while essentially trying to obliterate them as far as literacy is concerned.

Reyes and Torres describe their experiences in trying to modify a traditional family literacy program in the Southern United States into a decolonial program, that engaged both participants and facilitators in a dialogue about children and literacy, rather than focusing on teaching families how to practice literacy and foster it in their children. These modifications arose from the authors' own realizations that not only did their participants 'know' most of the traditional content that the program dictated (whether or not they chose to use it) but also held deeply rooted cultural beliefs that contradicted some of the core tenets of the original program. For example, while the program included a module on business practices, including, it would appear, content that suggested that participants might use their knowledge of child development and child literacy to open up a child-care business. As Reyes and Torres describe, many of the participants found this concept offensive, particularly when thinking about providing care to children within their extended families, as this was something they did for love not for money. The facilitators of the program also quickly discovered the irony of preaching about childcare and literacy to women who had raised 14 children of their own and who were now raising their great-grandchildren. Reyes and Torres found that the only ethically acceptable position to them, although it was tenuous in that they could be replaced at any time, was to engage the families in dialogue about literacy rather than present 'proven' research strategies to them. Thus the concept of family literacy, officially constituted as an instrument to help families break cycles of poverty and illiteracy, became a site of both conflict and dialogue, which at least, in this particular case, reconceptualized the very goals of the program itself.

Another example of how family literacy programs can be interpreted by diverse communities comes from my own research in an Even Start program in rural Texas (Viruru, 2009). Even Start is a federally funded family literacy program in the US, the stated purpose of which is to 'provide academic instruction to both parents and young children…in such an integrated manner that Even Start will assist in breaking the cycles of poverty and illiteracy' (United States Department of Education, 2001). Despite the many advantages that the program offers (such as free high-school classes, transportation and nutrition) many Even Start programs have trouble attracting and retaining families (Perry, 2003). Although over half of the community served by this program was African American, many of whom are poor, less than 10 per cent of the families at the center were African American, despite heavy recruitment efforts. My study presented a postcolonial reading of the interactions between the center and the African American population of the town: the center's perspective seemed to be that their purpose was to enforce the right of all children to basic essentials, such as literacy and proper nutrition. However the families who participated or otherwise interacted with the program strongly resisted this discourse of rights. Many of them objected to the idea of rights itself, as separating children from their families, by isolating them as individual rather than community beings. Important program goals such as literacy (with both parents and children expressing a preference for spoken rather than written language) and nutrition (where ideas such as importance of including all four food groups in one's daily diet were seen as an expression of privilege rather than science) were particularly contentious parts of the program. Many of the families in the study did not perceive enrollment in the program as a way of ensuring the basic rights of their children but rather as accepting colonization, and resisted its philosophy in multiple complex ways. The families who did enroll in the program tended to be Mexican-American, and took full advantage of some of the services that the program offered such as instruction in the English language, and the possibility of completing their high-school education. However, when it came to the parenting classes, which tried to teach parents ways in which to read to their children and other such literacy-related behaviors, there was a great deal of resistance, as families tried to divert the attention of the teachers towards other projects such as how to tailor dresses for their children. Thus it appeared that the families in the program used the site as a way in which to gain access to needed resources such as the English language, while trying to minimize the center's efforts to impact their child-rearing practices. The families also perceived the center's efforts to promote literacy as somewhat out of step with their own priorities: on one particular day in the parenting class, I watched the instructor reinforce the correct way of reading to a child. She went over the importance of choosing books with pictures, of holding the child on one's lap, of reading and pausing and of paying attention to the pictures. At the end of the lesson, the mothers were asked to practice these skills in front of the group. I watched the first dyad of a mother and her son go through the task as instructed and was struck more by the parenting skills that could get a toddler to sit still and listen to a story, which perhaps it had heard before, in front of a room full of other people, especially when it seemed that the mother was not that comfortable herself, than by whether the mother followed instructions correctly. The mother herself did seem uncomfortable, reading rather rapidly and in a hushed tone. Reading did not seem like anything new to them, from the way the child snuggled up to his mom and read cheek-to-cheek. At the end of the lesson I heard another parent say, 'we already know how to talk to our children … every mother knows that'.

Both these studies of family literacy programs underscore similar issues: dominant views of early childhood literacy have constructed it along somewhat scientific models, emphasizing the need for it to be 'developed' appropriately, a view that does not always fit the world view of immigrant families to the United States. In both studies the families related literacy to many other parts of their lives rather than as an isolated set of skills that had to be specifically focused on. To return to some of the ideas about postcolonialism and childhood that formed the theoretical framework for this chapter it appears that the ideologies of the programs, including a

strong emphasis on literacy as a basic right for all children, continued to be framed from a Euro-Western way of looking at the world. In my study, when the staff insisted that all children were entitled to basic rights such as a proper education, the participants read that as being told how to raise their children. What the program saw as attempting to break the cycle of poverty, the participants saw as trying to break their way of viewing the world. When the staff talked about rights, it appeared as though the participants read that as being told what was right and what was wrong. As other postcolonial scholars have pointed out, the word rights itself conjures up images that may not be comfortable to some and as such, the very usage of such a word can exclude some from the conversation. As Orford (2003) has said, ideas about human rights are often treated as though they are above social conditions and not implicated in projects of colonialism and imperialism. However, as studies such as this one show, this can be how they are enacted and perceived. Reading these studies from the viewpoints suggested by Prabhu (2007), Glissant, and Lionnet (1991), it would appear that for the participants in both family literacy programs, literacy existed within a complex system of inter-relationships, being intertwined with concepts of family, culture, knowledge and identity in ways that were quite un-understandable or opaque to outsiders. Although the participants did not altogether reject the dominant view of literacy, they insisted on bringing it within their own system of inter-relationships, to make sense of it, and give it meaning within that context.

Literacy instruction in Samoa

Duranti and Ochs' (1986) ethnographic study of literacy in a rural Western Samoan village brings out several interesting points that are suggestive of the hybrid nature of literacy acquisition in this context. Although this study was conducted over 25 years ago, it represents unique in its detailed account of the development of young children's literacy in a non-Western context. The authors found that the process of what they called transmitting literacy in school settings was made far more complex as the children were exposed not only to the complexities of written language but to a completely new set of cultural values and expectations, many of which clashed with the ways of the village in which they had been raised. Duranti and Ochs conclude that 'a global effect of literacy instruction is a change in the social identity of the child in Samoan society' (p. 214).

One interesting aspect of literacy instruction in the village was the kind of alphabet chart that was used. Duranti and Ochs found that children between the ages of 3 and 4 were sent to a local pastor's school to learn the alphabet, Arabic and Roman numbers and some passages from the Bible. The alphabet was taught mostly through the use of an alphabet chart, which the authors describe in great detail. The most striking feature of the chart was that the illustrations used on the alphabet chart represent a very clear 'Western' orientation. Although some sounds in the Samoan language were introduced by Europeans, and as such there are no 'indigenous' words that use those sounds, even the other more traditional sounds were associated with Europeanized objects. Thus the authors conclude that in this context the children are not just being taught the alphabet but also to pay attention to a world of 'objects and values' that reflect Western biases.

Duranti and Ochs also contrast the contexts and conventions of literacy use in the village, and compare them to the ones the children encounter in their schooling. Very young children in the village are socialized into what the authors call a 'disposition of attention and accommodation': they are expected to observe the activities going on around them and report on them to others. They are also expected to speak in an intelligible manner: adults do not expect simplified speech from children nor do they try to 'unravel' unintelligible speech that the children might use. Children between the ages of 3 and 4 are also expected to deliver long oral messages to other persons, using appropriate vocabulary. Children are generally not praised for such tasks. Furthermore, in the village, any kind of accomplishment, be it someone driving well on a bumpy road or making a trip to another city, is seen as a collective achievement: 'an individual's competence is defined by his audience appreciation and his merit is framed within the merit of his group' (p. 222). Thus even if someone is praised for doing something, the general response is for the praise to be returned and for the accomplishment to be generalized in to something that was not done by the person alone.

In contrast, the schooling patterns of the children reflected some very different ways of functioning as the school is organized through the Christian church and the pastors are trained in Western pedagogical methods for 4 years. Duranti and Ochs found that the kind of 'teacher talk' characteristic of Western middle-class environments was common in the school: thus simplification and clarification of terms was common, unlike in the village environment where adults rarely accommodated to what might be called the 'child-like' qualities of children's speech. Thus 3- and 4-year-old children encounter some very different definitions of what it means to be a child and what it means to use language when they enter the classroom.

In further contrast, children are also frequently praised for having accomplished literacy tasks and the praise is not reciprocated (as would be common in everyday contexts in the village). Thus when a child names an object or identifies an alphabet correctly the teacher might respond by saying 'good' or 'very good'. The child generally does not respond to such praise, not like they would in other contexts.

However as Duranti and Ochs suggest, the reasons that rural Samoans enroll their children in these schools are twofold: they want their children to be able to read the Bible and to be employable. The urban economy that surrounds the village relies heavily not only on literacy-related skills but also on the idea of individual accomplishment. Thus to earn a good income, it is essential that one learns not only the skills that are taught in the schools but also the values that undergird those skills.

This brief description of literacy acquisition in this context suggests that acquiring literacy for the children in the Samoan village is very much a process of both loss and gain, of contradiction and accommodation, of colonization and agency, and of reformulations and relationships. The connection of the local language, as well as local patterns of speech, to objects such as an alphabet chart with Western objects and the Bible creates the kind of creolization referred to by Glissant, which allows for the constitution of different realities, as children learn the skills needed for economic survival as well as cultural survival.

Acquiring Inuktitut

Crago and Allen's (1998) ethnographic study of how the Inuit children, from the Canadian Arctic, acquire their native language, Inuktitut, is also suggestive of the themes of loss and gain and interrelationships that this chapter is focusing on. It too affords unique insights into non-Western notions of literacy. There are approximately 28,000 Inuit people in the Canadian Arctic, and nearly 40 per cent of them are below the age of 15. The economy of the Inuit people used to be mostly based on hunting and gathering activities but has now changed to include more 'modern' occupations. Although most families now live in homes and apartments and most children go to school, the schooling and healthcare systems are under local Inuit control and the whole territory has an autonomous government. Crago and Allen's study provides rich detail about the language experiences of four young children (under the age of 2) and their families in one Inuit community. The study also included interview data from 20 mothers from the community.

Children in Inuit communities learn language in contexts that Crago and Allen call 'both traditional and evolving' (1998: 249). One interesting feature of many of these communities is the ways in which language is or is not used. It is common for young mothers or couples with their first child to live with their families. Care giving is also shared among family members; thus young children learn to talk in environments that include many different speakers of different age ranges. Crago and Allen found a striking difference however between the language socialization practices of the mothers aged over 45 and the younger, more 'modern' mothers. The older mothers used what the authors called a 'specific baby lexicon, a special register of affectionate talk', and they also tended to not involve children in adult conversations. What was however most striking was all the situations in which the mothers did not talk to their children: many activities that from a Western lens have been seen as 'natural' situations for conversations, were in fact conducted in silence. These included such activities as 'bedding, bathing, dressing, eating' as well as more complex ones such as 'companionship and discipline' (p. 250). The older mothers talked to their children only about a third as much as the younger mothers within the Inuit community and only a sixth as much as a comparison group of American White middle-class mothers. Most of the children of the older mothers talked more to their siblings and peers, who explicitly modeled accepted ways of behavior for them. In contrast however many of the younger mothers in Crago and Allen's study used language socialization practices that resemble more generic North American White middle-class ways. These changes appear to reflect the influence of many of the White middle-class schoolteachers who came into the community. Many younger parents model their parenting methods on the kind of classroom discourse seen in the schools.

Crago and Allen followed the children from their sample into their school and found that although the practices in their first 3 years of education, with Inuit teachers, very much reflected the cultural values of their community (for example, children were expected to attend to their peers and were allowed to model their work on that of other children), their later education reflected many discontinuities, as children were looked at much more in terms of individuals rather than as connected to their peer groups.

As Crago and Allen suggest the Inuit situation is particularly unique in that, even though it has the status of a minority language, there are strong educational and institutional policies that support its continued existence. Almost 100 per cent of the Inuit children in the studied region learn it as their first language. This however has both advantages and drawbacks, as many Inuit parents tend to take the continued existence of their language for granted and do not use it as much at home. Furthermore as many Inuit communities blend more with the larger community around them, complex processes of language shift occur. Inuit communities too are greatly impacted by electronic media, which has contributed to the restructuring of their community as well as their language. As Crago and Allen point out, all of these processes seem to reflect not only 'creative change' but loss as well and that it is important to see them as such.

CONCLUSIONS

As all of the above examples illustrate, the process of becoming 'literate' is far more complex than it might appear. Whether it be using praise in classrooms in Samoa, or instructing parents how to read to their children in rural Texas, invading the silences that have traditionally accompanied parent–child interactions in Inuit communities with talk, or encouraging children to read for pleasure in Qatar, it appears evident that around the world, young children's literacies are being modeled on Euro-Western models of what literacy is and should be. Families seem to acquiesce with these changes, mostly for economic reasons, even in relatively wealthy countries like Qatar, out of concern for the need to compete in a global economy in the future. As each one of the studies reviewed has shown, in multiple ways, language both reflects as well as creates the cultural context in which it is used: thus power over language is a particularly 'powerful' kind of power. It is therefore critically important therefore that scholars and professionals, who are interested in how children acquire language, be aware of the complex nature of this process. To look at what children acquire as they become 'literate', is, as many postcolonial scholars would point out, only part of the story. Many would also add that it is not an innocent coincidence that that is the part of the story that we attend to.

If one looks at early childhood literacy worldwide from the point of view of Moje and O'Brien's (2001) discussion of how literacy can result in patterns, experience, power and turbulence, mentioned earlier in this chapter, there seems to be an over-emphasis on guiding children to understand well defined patterns of literacy. Teachers of young children around the world are encouraged to draw upon experiences and research from Euro-Western contexts. Such constructions of literacy do not seem to make room for the diverse life experiences of children and their home environments. It is interesting that despite the recognition of the need for postcolonial appropriation (Donaldson, 2005) of language and textuality, there are few examples of how this been done successfully or at all.

REFERENCES

Ashcroft, B., Gareth, G., and Helen T. (1998). *The Empire Writes Back*. New York: Routledge.

Behdad, A. (2005). 'On globalization, again!', in A. Loomba, S. Kaul, M. Bunzl, A. Burton and J. Esty (eds), *Postcolonial Studies and Beyond*. Durham, SC: Duke University Press. pp. 62–79.

Brockmeier, J. and Olsen, D.R. (2009). 'The literacy episteme: From Innis to Derrida', in D.R. Olson and N. Torrance (eds), *The Cambridge Handbook of Literacy*. Cambridge & New York: Cambridge University Press. pp. 3–22.

Burman, E. (2008). *Deconstructing Developmental Psychology* (2nd ed.). London and New York: Routledge.

Cannella, G.S. (1997). *Deconstructing Early Childhood Education: Social Justice and Revolution*. New York: Peter Lang.

Cannella, G.S. and Viruru, R. (2004). *Childhood and (Post)colonization: Power, Education, and Contemporary Practice*. New York: Routledge

Caspe, M. (2003). 'How teachers come to understand families'. *School Community Journal*, 13(1): 10–15.

Cherland, M.R. and Harper, H. (2007). *Advocacy Research in Literacy Education: Seeking Higher Ground*. Mahwah, NJ: Erlbaum.

Collins, J. and Blot, R.K. (2003). *Literacy and Literacies: Texts, Power and Identity*. Cambridge: Cambridge University Press.

Comber, B. (2001). 'Critical inquiry or safe literacies: Who's allowed to ask which questions?', in S. Boran and B. Comber (eds), *Critiquing Whole Language and Classroom Inquiry*. Urbana, IL: National Council of Teachers of English.

Comber, B. (2003). 'Critical Literacy: what does it look like in the Early Years?', in J. Marsh (eds), *Handbook of Early Childhood Literacy*. London: Sage. pp. 355–368.

Cooper, F. and Brubaker, R. (2005). 'Identity', in F. Cooper (ed.), *Colonialism in Question: Theory, Knowledge, History*. Berkeley and Los Angeles: University of California Press. pp. 59–91.

Crago, M.B. and Allen, S.E.M. (1998). 'Acquiring Inuktitut', in O. Taylor and L. Leonard (eds), *Language Acquisition across North America: Cross-Cultural and Cross-Linguistic Perspectives*. San Diego, CA: Singular Publishing Group. pp. 245–79.

Donaldson, L.E. (1998). 'Writing the talking stick: Alphabetic literacy as colonial technology and post-colonial appropriation', *American Indian Quarterly*, 22(1/2): 46–62.

Donaldson, L.E. (2005). 'Making a joyful noise: William Appess and the search for postcolonial Method(ism)', *Interventions*, 7(2): 180–98.

Duranti, A. and Ochs, E. (1986). 'Literacy instruction in a Samoan village', in B.B. Schieffelin and P. Galimore (eds), *Acquisition of Literacy:Ethnographic Perspectives*. Ablex. pp. 213–32. [Reprinted in Ochs, E. (1998). *Culture and Language Development: Language Acquisition and Language Socialization in a Samoan Village*. London: Cambridge University Press.]

Fernandez, R. (2001). *Imagining Literacy: Rhizomes of Knowledge in American Culture and Literature*. Austin: University of Texas Press.

Ferraz M.B., Quaresma M.R., Aquino L.R., Atra, E., Tugwell, P. and Goldsmith, C.H. (1991). 'Reliability of pain scales in the assessment of literate and illiterate patients with rheumatoid arthritis', *Journal of Rheumatology*, 18(8): 1269–70.

Gallego, M. and Hollingsworth, S. (2000). 'Introduction: the idea of multiple literacies', in M. Gallego and S. Hollingsworth (eds), *What Counts as Literacy: Challenging the School Standard*. New York: Teachers College Press. pp. 1–23.

Gandhi, L. (1998). *Postcolonial Theory: A Critical Introduction*. New York; Columbia University Press.

Gee, J.P. (1990). *Social Linguistics and Literacies: Ideology in Discourses*. New York: Falmer.

Glasser, D. (2003). *Educational Reform in Qatar*. http://www.ummah.com/forum/showthread.php?13252-Educational-reform-in-Qatar

Gulf Times (2009). (http://www.gulftimes.com/site/topics/article.asp?cu_no=2&item_no=267168&version=1&template_id=36&parent_id=16

Hollingsworth, S., and Gallego, M. (2004). 'Professional development on multiple literacies in an urban professional development school'. *Journal of In-Service Education*, 30(3): 417–428.

Huggan, G. and Tiffin, H. (2010). *Postcolonial Ecocriticism: Literature, Animals and the Environment*. New York: Routledge.

Hulme, P. (2005). 'Beyond the straits: Postcolonial allegories of the globe', in A. Loomba, S. Kaul, M. Bunzl, A. Burton, and J. Esty (eds), *Postcolonial Studies and Beyond*. Durham, SC: Duke University Press. pp. 41–61.

Kelly, K., Viruru, R., and Al-Maadadi, F. (2010). 'A qualitative study of home and school practices that support the English-language development of emergent bilingual children in Qatar', paper presented at the Annual Meeting of the American Educational Research Association, Denver, Colorado, May 2010.

Lewison, M., Leland, C., and Harste, J.C. (2008). *Creating Critical Classrooms: K-8 Reading and Writing with an Edge*. New York: Lawrence Erlbaum Associates.

Lionnet, F. (1991). *Autobiographical Voices: Race, Gender, Self-Portraiture*. Ithaca, NY: Cornell.

Luke, A. (2004). 'Two takes on the critical', in B. Norton and K. Toohey (eds), *Critical Pedagogy and Language Learning*. Cambridge: Cambridge University Press.

Moje, E. and O'Brien, D. (eds) (2001). *Constructions of Literacy: Studies of Teaching And Learning in and Outside Of Secondary Schools*. Mahwah, NJ: Lawrence Erlbaum.

Nitrini, R., Caramelli, P., Herrera, E., Porto, C.S., Charchat-Fichman, H., Carthery, M. T., et al. (2004). 'Performance of illiterate and literate nondemented elderly subjects in two tests of long-term memory' *Journal of the International Neuropsychological Society*, 10: 634–8.

Orford, A. (2003). *Reading Humanitarian Intervention: Human Rights and the Use of Force in International Law*. New York: Cambridge University Press.

Perry, Y. D. (2003). Assistors to Continuous Enrollment for Women in Texas Even Start Family Literacy Programs. Unpublished doctoral dissertation, Texas A&M University.

Petersson, K.M., Reis, A., and Ingvar, M. (2001). 'Cognitive processing in literate and illiterate subjects: A review of some recent behavioral and functional neuroimaging data', *Scandinavian Journal of Pyschology*, 42: 251–67.

Powell, R. (1999). *Literacy as Moral Imperative: Facing the Challenges of a Pluralistic Society*. Lanham, MD & Cumnor Hill, UK: Rowman & Littlefield.

Prabhu, A. (2007). *Hybridity: Limits, Transformations, Prospects*. Albany: SUNY Press.

Rand Corporation (2011). http://www.rand.org/content/dam/rand/pubs/reprints/2011/RAND_RP1428.pdf

Rand Corporation (2012). http://www.rand.org/qatar.html

Reyes, L.V. and Torres, M.N. (2007). 'Decolonizing family literacy in a culture circle: Reinventing the family literacy educators' role', *Journal of Early Childhood Literacy*, 7: 73–94.

Rockhill, K. (1993). 'Gender, language and the politics of literacy', in B.V. Street (ed.), *Cross-cultural Approaches to Literacy (Cambridge Studies in Oral and Literate Culture)*. Cambridge: Cambridge University Press. pp. 156–75.

Rogers, R., Mosley, M., and Kramer, M., and The Literacy for Social Justice Teacher Research Group (2009). *Designing Socially Just Learning Communities: Critical Literacy Education across the Lifespan*. New York: Routledge.

Seed, P. (1991). 'Failing to marvel: Atahualpa's encounter with the word'. *Latin American Research Review*, 26: 7–32.

Sole, K.E. (2005). 'The deep thoughts the one in need falls into: Quotidian experience and the perspectives of poetry in postliberation South Africa', in A. Loomba, M. Bunzi, S. Kaul, A. Burton, and J. Esty (eds), *Postcolonial Studies and Beyond* Durham, SC: Duke University Press. pp. 182–205.

Spivak, G.C. (1988). 'Can the subaltern speak?', in C. Nelson and S. Grossberg (eds), *Marxism and the Interpretation of Culture*. Basingstoke: Macmillan. pp. 271–313.

St. Pierre, R., Swartz, J., Gamse, B., Murray, S., Deck, D. & Nickel, P. (1995). *National evaluation of the Even Start Family Literacy Program: Final Report*. Cambridge, MA: Abt Associates.

Stevens, L.P. and Bean, T.W. (2007). *Critical Literacy: Context, Research, and Practice in the K-12 classroom.* Thousand Oaks, CA: Sage.

Stuckey, J.E. (1991). *The Violence of Literacy.* Portsmouth, NH: Heinemann.

Tikly, L. (2009). 'Education and the new imperialism', in R. Coloma (eds), *Postcolonial Challenges in Education.* New York: Peter Lang. pp. 23–46.

United States Department of Education. *No Child Left Behind Act of 2001.* Retrieved September 8, 2002, from http://www.ed.gov/legislation.

Vasquez, V. (2005). 'Resistance, power-tricky, and colorless energy: what engagement with everyday popular culture texts can teach us about learning and literacy', in J. Marsh (ed.), *Popular Culture, New Media and Digital Literacy in Early Childhood.* New York: Routledge. pp. 153–65.

Vasquez, V. (2007). 'Using the everyday to engage in critical literacy with young children', *New England Reading Association Journal,* 43(2): 6–11.

Viruru, R. (2009). 'A postcolonial analysis of the discourse of children's rights: A case study of a family literacy program in rural Texas', paper presented at the Research Seminar on Living Rights: Theorizing Children's Rights in International Development. IUKB, Sion, Switzerland Jan 19–20, 2009.

Viruru, R. (2011). 'The impact of the New Era educational reforms on female Qatari college students: a qualitative study', paper presented at the International Congress of Qualitative Inquiry (QI2011), Urbana, IL, May 2011.

Viruru, R. and Nasser, R. (2011). 'Exploring cultural constructions of reading in the fourth grade: perspectives from Qatar', paper presented at the International Congress of Qualitative Inquiry (QI2011). Urbana, IL, May 2011.

Weiss, B.D., Hart, G., McGee, D.L., and D'Estelle, S. (1992). 'Health status of illiterate adults: relation between literacy and health status among persons with low literacy skills'. *Journal of the American Board of Family Practice,* 5(3): 257–64.

Young, R.J.C. (2001). *Postcolonialism: an Historical Introduction.* Oxford, UK: Blackwell Publishers.

3

Gender and Early Childhood Literacy

Elaine Millard and Petula Bhojwani

This chapter considers how researchers have addressed the ways in which children's gendered identity is implicated in their taking up of early literacy practices at home and in school. The print and media environment surrounding them from birth, early literacy events in the home and the formalization of literacy encounters within school, all carry messages of what it is to be an effective reader and writer. Within the simple narrative and other textual messages that are made available to the young are many accounts and implicit explanations about what a particular society considers to be appropriate ways of behaving as a male or female. It has been argued, therefore, that gender identification plays an important role not only in children's reading choices but also in their growing sense of themselves as learners and writers (Davies, 1989, 1993; Gilbert, 1989; Millard, 1994, 1997; Blair and Sanford, 2004; Dyson, 2003, 2010). This chapter examines how research has probed the ways in which literacy development

and the construction of gendered identity are interwoven to create expectations, not only of what it means to be literate, but also of what it might mean to be a gendered literate individual. In describing what has been learnt about the process of socialization into gendered literate identities, it employs a definition of gender initially adopted by feminist research into the interplay of gender and education.

Many second-wave feminists were themselves involved in education as students, researchers or teachers, documenting as a question of equal rights, the considerable divergence of the routes patterned out by contemporary educational systems for boys and girls. Their project carefully exposed embedded habits of gender differentiation which worked against the interests of both girls and women (Spender and Sarah, 1980; Stanworth, 1981). They argued that girls' talents, abilities and educational potential were severely limited by aspects of both the official and hidden curricula in schools concluding that education was a site where gender difference, imported from experiences outside the school gates, was not only confirmed by the practices of educational institutions, but even more firmly established and amplified (Delamont, 1980; Marland, 1983; Measor and Sykes, 1992; Acker, 1994; Francis, 2000; DCSF, 2009).

At the same time as researchers and teachers were focusing on the role of gender in differentiating educational opportunity, there was a growing awareness of the crucial role of literacy in education. Theorists began to re-describe literacy activities (defined previously as a set of cognitive competencies or skills acquired developmentally) as socially constructed practices, inflected by power relations and the hierarchical organization of knowledge (Freire, 1972; Heath, 1983; Street, 1996, 2003; Luke, 1988; Lankshear and McLaren, 1993; Barton and Hamilton, 1998). Literacy was understood to be constituted by specific socially derived conventions, dependent on cultural experience, rather than as a set of universal, abstract, cognitive processes arrived at through the discipline of psychology. Bakhtin's insight that an individual's knowledge of the world was constructed through the representations he or she makes of it (Bakhtin, 1981) also influenced many sociocultural studies that were concerned with bridging a gap between the person and their social world (Dyson, 1997, 1999, 2003; Hall, 2008; Wertsch, 1991). Wertsch refers to this as *mediated action* and Hall as *cultural bridging*.

Feminists had already argued that gender identity was constructed through *social practices* rather than *biological determinants*. The understanding, therefore, that literacy itself consisted of a set of social practices, rather than cognitive processes became important in explanations of the interrelationship of gendered identity and literacy development (Orellana, 1995, 1999). In their interactions with parents, carers, or teachers, children were found to be developing a sense of their own identities and potentialities as literate beings; a process which Kress has described as forming 'deep-seated dispositions in the person who is literate' (1997: 150). From a social practice perspective, children could similarly be shown to be forming ideas about which literacy activities were the most appropriate for which gender, for example, in relation to such seemingly neutral practices as sharing a book or information on screen with an adult, being supported in writing a message on a greetings card, or sending a text message on a mobile phone.

The next section of this chapter discusses the expectations and identifications which are set up for and by children through their first literacy experiences at home and in school. In giving an account of this it is important to emphasize that, although the literacy events in which children participate take place in many different settings (shops, trams, hospitals and churches, for example), the ones that have been described most often by researchers occur in homes and classrooms. Not only this, but also most of the earlier studies that focused on gendered literacy practices did so in white, middle-class, Western-nation homes. It is particularly important to keep this in mind when considering the reported outcomes of home-based research, for as Orellana has observed, 'researchers often call for attention to intersections of gender, class, race and ethnicity, but rarely explore them in practice' (1999: 65).

LITERACY IN THE HOME

At home children first encounter the range of literacy practices and resources that enable meanings to be created, transmitted and interpreted and where they are initiated as junior members into what Frank Smith (1988) memorably termed the 'literacy club'. Gunther Kress's (1997, 2010) work on multimodality is particularly useful in explaining how children come to select from the wide range of semiotic resources present in their homes. Kress demonstrates that in their early literacy exchanges children develop an awareness that 'content has a shape' and that this is part of the important things to be learned about the process of communication in a social context. By this, he suggests that children constantly draw on aspects of the materials which they find around them in designing new meanings for themselves. He further suggests that the choice of materials creates possibilities for the differentiation of gender (1997: 31, 145).

Embedded assumptions of what are appropriate play materials for boys and girls persist, as a glance in any toyshop or supermarket will show. The gender of the potential consumer is signalled quite clearly in both packaging and content. Pink and housemaking pervade many girls' toys, particularly potent in the presentation of dolls and in princess dressing-up products. Further, girls are also provided with more traditional writing and drawing materials. Boys' interests in contrast are signalled by black and red colour codes and consist of more construction and toys for action play (Millard, 2010: 308). For writing, boys are given more electronic devices for texting and imaging (DCSF: 8). Francis who studied the toys which parents reported that their children preferred, found them to be 'highly gendered, with boys' toys and resources concentrated on technology and action, and girls' on care and other stereotypically feminine interests' (2010: 36, 325). From such evidence it

may be deduced that the materials, as well as the processes, encountered in early learning and the creation of narratives in the home are saturated with inflections of gender appropriateness and children begin to characterize their own sense of identity in their use, including differential access to the materials of literacy.

Indeed, children's early literacy events in middle-class, Western-nation homes, where it is predominantly mothers who engage children in the daily practices of text sharing and message making, the very act of reading may be identified by the young as something that women do (Millard, 1997) a position which leads some boys to perceive personal reading as a passive and therefore more female-appropriate activity in school (Solsken, 1992; Millard, 1997; Maynard, 2002). Moreover, where someone other than the mother takes responsibility for children's reading, this is more often another female family member. For example, in the UK, Gregory, observing reading in extended multilingual families, found that though it was siblings who often engage younger members of the family in reading activities, it was an older sister who frequently plays the most significant role, similarly confirming the gender specificity of this activity (Gregory, 1998, 2001). In relation to the sharing of writing activities at home, a Department for Children Schools and Families (DCSF)-funded case study of an individual school reported of children in their first years of schooling: 'Some children do not see any males writing at home or at school (currently the school has no male teachers)' (DCSF, 2009: 8). Moreover, even when boys do build on their experience of writing by observing their father (such as when a young Asian boy imitated his father's practice of storing fliers by designing ones of his own (Rowsell and Pahl, 2007: 401)) their artifacts may not be understood by others as evidence of literacy skills.

Because of their experience of reading and writing in the home, most acts of literacy may become feminized in the eyes of the young observers, with the added complication that boys of all ages living in Western cultures generally appear to resist any activity that might be deemed girl-appropriate and constantly seek to define themselves as both 'not girls' and 'not feminine' (Thorne, 1993; Jordan, 1995; Millard, 1994, 1997; Smith and Wilhelm, 2002; Brozo, 2010). Moreover, parents themselves bring expectations of the kind of literacy activities which they might expect from their sons and daughters (Arthur, 2001; Weinberger, 1996; Pahl, 2001, 2002; Moss, 2001). In a study of Australian parents' construction of their children as gendered, literate subjects, Nichols (2002) concluded that a notion prevailed amongst parents that girls were developmentally more advanced in key literacy-related areas such as speech and their literacy learning as natural and unproblematic. In contrast, they considered their sons' masculinity and literacy to be in opposition, often creating parental tolerance of developmental delay and complicated by allowing agency to the boys in deciding (or not deciding) when they were ready to learn.

Prior to the interest in the gender differences found in uses of reading and writing, literacy development had been shown to be heavily dependent on access to available social and cultural capital within specific communities (Heath, 1983; Wells, 1987; Taylor and Dorsey-Gaines, 1988). This has led on to more specific enquiries into the home context for developing dispositions towards literacy, and here gender difference was shown to matter. Accessing home experience is far more demanding and complex than observation of classrooms

and therefore home experience is often deduced from discourses brought into school which make themselves known in the content of play and in the choice and production of texts (Jordan, 1995; Marsh and Millard, 2000; Millard, 1997, 2010; Dyson, 2010). Notable exceptions are ethnographic studies where the home context is either dominant (Bissex, 1980) or equally considered (Pahl, 2001).

Solsken's work (1992) provides one such in-depth study of ways in which both boys and girls develop gendered identities through their experiences of learning to read and write. From close ethnographic biographies of four children selected from a group of thirteen whom were followed from home to school for three years to record their opportunities for reading and sharing books with adults, she identified how each child's experience influenced their take up of school activities. The strength of Solsken's study lies in her focus on the children and their agency in creating literacy events as 'a self-defining social act'. Her general conclusions are more tentatively presented but she suggests that the domestic division of literacy 'labour' may lead boys to resist in school the female-defined model of literacy experienced at home, turning to play to define their sense of self. It is the construction of gendered identities as princesses and warriors, good guys and bad girls, in play, which gives rise to writing that I will turn to first, before focusing more closely on the engendering of reading and writing activities in school.

LITERACY DEVELOPED IN GENDERED PLAY

Play provides one of the earliest domains both at home and in school where narratives are shaped and take on personal meanings for identity formation. Research here has shown that children's shared cultural landscape and communicative practices outside school (Barton and Hamilton, 1998; Grugeon, 2005), allow them to draw upon 'textual toys' for pleasure, performance, and dramatic, often collaborative play (Dyson, 2003: 76). This theory has influenced studies of pre-school children, which have highlighted the centrality of media-related material objects on family practices (Marsh, 2005; Pahl, 2002, 2005, 2006). Illuminating perspectives on the interconnectedness of gender and literacy development in play have been provided, by teachers/researchers who have closely observed, and then recorded, differences in choice of activity and behaviour in nursery and primary-school settings. They show clearly how these feed into children's language and storying behaviour (Clarricoates, 1978; Davies, 1989; Paley, 1984; Pidgeon, 1993; Francis, 1998, 2010; Pahl, 1999, 2001; Howe and Parsons, 2006). Tales told from the nursery consistently report that children are sensitive to the hidden messages embedded in adult literacy practices they observe all around them and that children's constructions of appropriate roles are reinforced by adult expressions of approval or disapproval of their choice of play (Nichols, 2002). Further, Rowsell and Pahl's research has identified the ways in which these early experiences of play artifacts and multimodal literacy materials become sedimented in their own texts which are created from layers of prior identities and social practices formed at home and school (2007: 392). They suggest that texts with their 'sedimented identities' provide teachers and researchers with a lens to consider the production of text as 'a wider social practice that is active, creative and infused with identities in practice'. This is an aspect of children's literacy which will be taken up later in the chapter when we discuss the role popular culture plays in creating gendered identities.

EVIDENCE FROM CHILDREN'S WRITING

The gendered narrative preferences which have been shown to dominate children's choices in play have also been identified as powerful influences on children's early writing. In the USA, earlier research studies relied predominantly on texts produced in free-writing workshops in which school-aged children could *play* with (gendered) identities (Orellana, 1999). American writing 'workshops' inspired by the work of Graves (1983) and Calkins (1986) were also taken up in the promotion of independent or elective writing encouraged in both British and Australian schools. Researchers who analysed children's early writing described similar patterns of dominance and passivity in the content and style of children's compositions. For example, in their article *'Princesses who commit suicide'*, MacGillivray and Martinez (1998) describe how young children's stories tend to frame boys and men as heroes and girls and women as victims of violence, across age, ethnicity and gender. Maynard, researching children's writing in one UK primary school, found that, 'boys often positioned themselves as powerful and independent: girls positioned themselves as vulnerable and dependent' (2002: 89). Orellana (1999), analysing stories of Latina and Latino children, comments on radical differences in the construction of 'good girl' identities in girls' stories and the more heroically conceived 'good guys' of the boys' compositions. Another aspect frequently commented on is a contrast in the use of personal and interpersonal content in narratives. When given freedom of choice, girls are found to be interested in describing personal and domestic settings, focusing on feelings and relationship issues (Steedman, 1983; Millard, 1994), boys favour 'warrior discourses of action and adventure' (Jordan, 1995). Skaar (2009) reports finding gendered contrasts of content in older primary children's composition in both print and digital texts. He found that when groups were given access to multimodal affordances boys and girls used the 'semiotic resources' of text and image quite differently:

> Within the constraints of their digital skills and capabilities, the girls prefer semiotic resources that afford them the best opportunity to describe feelings and intimate interpersonal relations. In this case this means that they prefer to use written text. They do not choose to find pictures and symbols on the Internet to nearly the same extent as the boys do. Conversely, the boys in the study choose, to a greater degree than the girls, to use pre-coded signs (in the form of pictures and symbols) in their stories. The girls, on the other hand, tend more to code the signs themselves through the use of writing. (2009: 15)

Skaar argues therefore that boys are doing less demanding literacy thinking than girls because they use more ready-made resources to cut and paste into their texts, rather than engaging in the full process of creating meaning in words and sentences.

Millard and Marsh (2001) found similar patterns in the drawings that many children create to motivate or illustrate their written narratives. Boys and girls were shown to bring different cultural interests to their work, which were often imported directly from the popular cultural texts targeted separately at them. Clear gender differences were found in the way they related their drawings to their written narratives. Girls tended to draw stylized images of children, houses and flowers, providing decoration rather than illuminating key aspects of the story. Boys' embedded scenarios containing cartoon figures and violent action within their narratives. Millard and Marsh argue that boys' active engagement with many forms of visual meaning making often goes unremarked in research, whereas differences in the boys' and girls' choice of appropriate subject matter for writing has been well noted (Poynton, 1985; Tuck, Bayliss and Bell, 1985; White, 1986; Millard, 1994, 1997). In contrast with their more compliant sisters, much of young boys' elective writing – filled, as often it is, with violent action – can seem to teachers both disrespectful and transgressive of acceptable classroom norms. See, for example, teachers' and the researchers' strong antipathetical responses to the Australian 9-year-old boy's story 'Bloodbath EFA Bunnies' (Gilbert and Taylor, 1991: 110–13). Because of such responses to their favourite topics, boys may be given less leeway in their writing choices and as a result become disenchanted and disengaged.

Kanaris (1999) however suggests that girls may also be limited as a result of their school-focused writing interests. She argues that from their first writing experiences in school girls find themselves praised for producing what is clearly equally gendered writing in terms of both content and form and subsequently are offered limited opportunities to write in different modes or for different audiences. Further, she reported that girls were more likely to remove themselves from the action of a tale and tell their stories as the observer, remaining 'recipients or observers', whereas boys placed themselves at the centre of the action and became 'doers in a world of action' (1999: 265). Her findings mirror the active passive contrast in content of stories that was previously noted in relation to gendered play. In this light, Skaar's strictures on the limitations of boys' digital texts might be read through an alternative lens. The boys he describes are the ones who can be understood as becoming skilled in manipulating the affordances of multimodal resources and gaining greater skill in the new literacies through a choice of cutting and pasting processes. As Bearne has argued (2003) what is now at stake is an understanding of the very concept of what it is to be literate and how we asses it, suggesting that: 'perhaps "literacy" is not an adequate term to describe the texts, contexts and practices of the twenty-first century, since it privileges the written word over other forms of communication.' It is the nature of design rather than writing, that is used in the context of multimodal production by Kress and Van Leeuwen (Kress, 2003; Kress and Van Leeuwen, 2006) that is more helpful in understanding how digital literacy might be judged and competence measured so that many boys' achievements might be better accounted for. Bhojwani (2011) supports the call for a re-evaluation of the definition of school text production following her study of six to seven-year-old boys. Applying the principles and terminology identified by Kress and Van Leeuwen, she charts the ways in which the boys in her research developed composition skills and built their capacity to represent ideas. Bhojwani argues that the boys skilfully manipulated modes by combining and transferring elements from onscreen worlds and experiences to paper.

It is a question, however, of whether teachers are prepared to allow the kind of free choice of theme and modality that helps to create both interest and confidence in young writers. Pahl in her insightful book, *Transformations* (1999), argued for

an acceptance of nursery children's interests in the (gendered) narratives of popular culture. She provided clear examples of how 'much successful practice in the nursery consists of following and developing ideas from modelling and play, building on the children's trains of thought and allowing their narratives to flower' (1999: 94). Such a 'flowering' depends on a teacher's freedom to incorporate children's own interests within a literacy curriculum that offers them the freedom to choose. Pahl argues for learning contexts which encourage social play, independent text making and personal choice. Yet, in the first decade of the twenty-first century opportunities for personal blossoming in the literacy curriculum have become more limited. In the American context, Anne Haas Dyson reports that:

> Influenced by federal and state mandates for test-driven learning progress, structured literacy programs push aside time for child-initiated talk and play as they seize control of early schooling ... Such programs are particularly evident in schools serving children deemed 'low income,' who are disproportionately children of color. In these programs, writing begins as an individual task requiring diligence and independence. It does not begin as community participation allowing social and playful children to find new means for being together. (2010: 8)

In the UK, researchers and educational commentators have criticized the narrow view of literacy that was promoted through the National Curriculum and National Literacy Strategy for perpetuating a limited traditional view of English teaching that restricted children's choices and engagement with any literacy other than that which was book based (Kress, 2003; Sainsbury and Schagen, 2004). For example, Sainsbury and Schagen found a decline in reading enjoyment reported by children surveyed in at Years 4 and 6 (ages 8–11) between 1998 (before the National Literacy

Strategy was fully implemented) and 2003: a trend that was particularly marked in boys. They concluded that the drop in reading for pleasure might be connected to the prevalence of a restrictions of personal choice in current teaching practices.

This section has described how children's conceptualization of the activity of writing and their attitude towards 'doing' their own writing has been shown to influence their perceptions of themselves as writers. It has argued that what children choose to write about and the affordances they draw on in shaping content is influenced by gendered interests, which in turn are often shaped by popular culture and reflect the differences in boys' and girls' uptake of multimodal forms of communication. What emerges as a prominent factor in this process is the central role of 'new' literacies in children's lives. Popular culture informs both the gendered nature of children's preferences, whilst the affordances of the new digital literacies to which they are allowed access influence the production of their texts. The next section explores how researchers have tracked the positive uses of these influences in the classroom.

CHILDREN'S CULTURAL PREFERENCES IN WRITING

Primary-school children's familiarity with popular cultural discourses, often displayed in their drawing and writing, is suspect in many teachers' eyes because of the sexist and racist elements that are embedded in the characterizations and plot lines of their typical narratives. Anne Haas Dyson's research writing, developed over the past quarter-century (1985, 1993, 1997, 1999, 2001, 2003, 2010), has documented the processes by means of which children incorporate diverse elements of their childhood interests and cultural preoccupations into their school-focused 'work'; sometimes openly but often covertly in their hybridization of home and school discourses (2003, 2010). Dyson has described children's 'social and textual attunement to each other' which may give rise to participatory childhood cultures which carry 'traces of their sometimes choreographed efforts to textually link their social selves' and traces of 'shared topics and phrasings and even imagined worlds.' (2010: 8). Dyson writes of the importance of the teacher's mediation in the learning process so that, with guidance, ideological gaps and differences 'could become moments for collective consideration of text fairness and goodness and, also, for individual play with newly salient features' (1997: 162).

It is a course of action that is shown to be assisted by thoughtful planning, as when Jackie Marsh (1999, 2003) observed a sociodramatic role-play area set up as a Batcave in an English early-years classroom in which literacy elements, particularly opportunities for independent writing, were incorporated. Marsh's study provides a good example of Dyson's 'pedagogy of responsibility that acknowledges students' pleasures whilst assisting them in the exploration of these pleasures' (Dyson, 1997: 179). Both writers recommend that a balance can be struck between motivating interest and creating a greater understanding of how particular genres of narrative position both reader and writer.

COUNTERACTING TEXTUAL GENDER STEREOTYPES

But it is not only in popular cultural texts that gender stereotyping is located. Early research focused on gender in schools described and then developed strategies to counter the 'sexist' uses of language and stereotypical representations they uncovered in schoolbooks and basal readers which emphasized differences rather than similarities in girls' and boys' home circumstances, lived experiences and interests (Millard, 1994). In response to this imbalance, an early strategy of feminist teachers and librarians was to weed out books with derogatory, limiting and oppressive representations. Popular texts such as the stories of Enid Blyton were condemned as sexist (and racist), removed from classroom and library bookshelves and replaced with narratives which created more positive female role models. Pro-feminist texts were carefully selected to provide counter-messages of female agency and self-sufficiency on the one hand and male gentleness and/or dependency on the other. These productions, particularly those which sought to overturn female passivity, were also however, shown to conflict with children's own desires and so were often interpreted idiosyncratically by children when left to their own devices. Davies, for example, found that they interpreted the stories read to them not as narratives of liberation offering attractive lifestyles, but as traditional stories in which the counter-traditional heroine/princess had simply got it all wrong (Davies, 1989).

Rather than encouraging the tweaking of texts and careful selection of media to provide ideologically correct messages, Dyson (2010: 24) argues that teachers should focus on the language used and not the content itself in classroom enquiry so that the storylines through which cultural difference is structured and maintained can be deconstructed and understood. Her position chimes well with the postmodern emphasis on difference and complexity that has replaced older certainties about the effect of sex role, gender regimes (Kessler

et al., 1985; Millard, 2010: 306) and their textual representation. It enables strategies for early critical literacy to be developed, an approach to which I shall return at the end of this chapter. Before I do so, however, it is important to return in more detail to the question of boys' literacy, which for almost 20 years has sought to dominate the discourse on gendered achievement.

TURNING THE FOCUS TO BOYS' 'UNDER ACHIEVEMENT'

In the 1990s, much of the focus of gender research in the UK switched its an attention from girls' educational disadvantage within what had been identified as a masculinist-biased school system, to anxieties about the performance of boys, particularly in literacy-oriented subject areas. By the 1990s, girls were beginning to outperform boys in most areas of the curriculum but most particularly in English. In 1993, in the UK, The Office for Standards in Education, Children's Services and Skills (OFSTED) concluded from evidence drawn from inspectors' observations in secondary schools that boys were underachieving in all aspects of the English curriculum and expressed strong concern for the increase of the gender gap in attainment (OFSTED, 1993). A subsequent report stated: 'the wide gulf in pupils' reading performance' was judged as 'serious and unacceptable.' (OFSTED, 1996). The focus turned to earlier stages of schooling and to reading and writing targets. The need for 'explicit' teaching was presented in further reports (OFSTED, 1993, 1996, 2003, 2005) as well as attention towards schools achieving targets. The spotlight fell on literacy, and specifically on how reading and writing should be taught in order to raise standards.

This chapter has already outlined the many differences reported from classroom research into boys' and girls' responses to the stuff of literacy which had informed a wide variety of research projects. Boys' poorer performance in English was attributed initially to their relative lack of interest in reading and particularly their preference for different genres for personal reading which did not chime well with school (White, 1986; Davies and Brember, 1993; Barrs and Pidgeon, 1993; Millard, 1997; Pidgeon, 1998; Hall and Coles, 1999). It was further argued that teachers' curriculum choices also limited boys' participation and motivation in reading and writing (Alloway and Gilbert, 1997; Pahl, 1999; Millard and Marsh, 2001; Moss, 2007).

The National Literacy Strategy (NLS) was at the heart of the UK government's attempt to improve pupils' performance in literacy and altered the context in which the difference between girls' and boys' performance in reading and writing was to be both tracked and addressed. Moss (2007) argues that the stakes in performance were raised higher for schools with the introduction of national testing and the emerging importance of 'literacy'. The focus on standards became of increasingly high profile with schools' performance in the end of key-stage tests publicised through league tables. The ensuing accountability regime that underpinned the testing system, served to intensify the idea that boys had a problem with literacy as they were the main social group to attract attention.

Concerns were further fuelled and spread to other Western states by international surveys which began to show that the gaps between boys' and girls' achievements were widening in Western nation states who were being overtaken by countries in the specific rim, such as Korea. The Programme for International Student Assessment (PISA: OECD, 2000, 2003, 2006) results supported previous judgments in England (OFSTED, 1993, 1996) that boys were less interested in reading and writing activities. The Progress in International Reading Literacy Study (PIRLS) also provided evidence of an international decline in reading for enjoyment amongst boys of Western nations (PIRLS, 2003, 2007).

In response to both international and their own national findings, populist work on gender and education in Australia, the UK and America began increasingly to emphasize focusing on boys' needs alone as a priority for school improvements in literacy (see, for example, Biddulph, 1997; Hannan, 1996). Recommendations from courses to improve boys' performance in school in the UK included the use of male role models as readers and mentors, the production of boy-friendly materials, and even the use of girls as peer role models and guides. It was even suggested that boys were more 'fragile' than girls and so required better teaching (Hannan, 2000). Although many of these strategies were focused initially on teenage boys, the anxiety crept down into primary schools where girls continued to be seen to perform better than boys in all aspects of reading and writing and was therefore the place where the 'problem' was deemed to begin.

The difficulty with strategies that seek to direct attention to boys' needs in this way is that boys' education is once more framed as the dominant consideration and girls' real successes ignored (Francis, 1998: 166). It has resulted in what has been described as 'competing victims syndrome' (Alloway and Gilbert, 1997: 57) where different groups compete for attention and, more importantly, funding. Programmes directed solely at boys' under-achievement have therefore been seen as a backlash against feminism (Epstein, Elwood, Hey and Maw, 1998; Skelton and Francis, 2003).

So, over 10 years into the twenty-first century boys, as a cultural group, are still being identified as a problem, perceived as losing interest in school literacy at every phase of schooling. Despite continuing curriculum changes, the boys as 'problem' discourse continues from press, policy makers and academics, particularly in relation to the monitoring of literacy progression and gender-gap debates. Moss (2007) has argued that the many educational reform programmes aimed at boys' improvement have misdirected the debate by giving rise to questions like: 'has the teacher delivered?', 'has it been taught?', rather than, 'has the child learnt?' She recommends that attention should be focused not on the boys and their problems or even interests but on the structure of the curriculum itself. Similarly, the Australian educators, Martino and Pallotta-Charolli (2005) have strongly criticized approaches to boys' learning that focus on the provision of specifically boy-focused materials and male teachers, emphasizing instead the importance of good teaching that pays attention to each individual's needs.

The next section of this chapter turns away from what has become a creeping reification of binary and competing differences in gender that have tended to reinforce girl-focused or boy-focused approaches, to research which builds a better understandings of both identity formation and the conditions under which social justice and equity programmes may be implemented. For such approaches, we need to take the postmodern turn away from an emphasis on gender role and regimes, or sex role stereotyping and gender category maintenance towards more subtle and nuanced approaches arising from poststructuralist analysis and the associated strategies of critical literacy (Davies, 1997).

POSTMODERN ANALYSIS AND CRITICAL LITERACY

So far this chapter has shown how earlier research identification of gender difference has been crucial in raising awareness of discrimination and exclusion in language and culture and used in order to confront coercive and limiting grand narratives about male and femaleness, success and failure, agency and passivity. Early perspectives are now accepted as too simple and reductive in their understanding of gender as a series of categories that map onto simple binaries (Walkerdine, 1985, 1988; Walkerdine and Lucey, 1989; Luke and Luke, 1992). We have already suggested, in discussing developments in the teaching of writing, how in relation to the narratives of popular culture, researchers such as Anne Haas Dyson in the USA and Jackie Marsh in the UK have been able to shift an understanding of children's classroom discourse away from one-dimensional discussions of positive and gender negative stereotyping of experience, to raising more critical awareness of how their popular cultural interests can be interrogated and transformed.

For example, researchers working with popular discourses in the classroom to build on children's interests and private pleasures themselves acknowledge that the discourses carry messages that disturb adults through their perpetuation of stereotypical performance of feminine and masculine norms (Marsh and Millard, 2000, Wohlwend, 2009). Yet both Marsh

(1999, 2003, 2005) and Dyson (1999, 2003, 2010) have given accounts of classrooms where teachers enabled children to transform their understanding through sensitive interaction with each other within the guidance of a responsive teacher. Their focus on working with young children to interrogate gender role in context ties in with current postmodern understanding of the way in which the deconstruction of gender discourse can promote the development of wider possibilities for both boys and girls. A UK DCSF publication on gender policy confirms this position, stating:'Gender differences are constructed and may be reinforced in school through staff and pupils consistently associating or attributing certain behaviours and characteristics to one gender over the other and then acting accordingly' (2009: 16).

Wohlwend (2009), in challenging the marginalization of play in American kindergartens, has argued for the productive role that creative play, based on popular cultural artifacts and media entertainments, can provide when used as 'catalysts and conduits' for meaning-making through writing and drama in schools. Her own classroom based enquiry describes how a merger of new literacies and doll play provided 'important new spaces for young children to play, write, and transact identity.' She found that both boys and girls produced new narratives which frequently overturned the stereotypical gender roles attributed by the manufacturers to the dolls. She acknowledges that teachers can find commercialized toys such as the Disney Princesses, created from media projections of hyperfemininity, repugnant because of the gendered messages they bear. She argues however, that: 'by banning Barbies and Bratz from our classrooms, we take ourselves out of the conversation, ceding our influence to corporations and missing opportunities for critique and engaged learning' (2009: 80). Her recommendations therefore are that teachers and teacher-educators should be involved in researching children's interests, while at the same time questioning their own assumptions about media and gender in order to create situations in which children can engage critically with toys as texts. Her conclusions chime perfectly with the notion of the importance of understanding children's 'sedimented identities' carried in texts proposed by Rowsell and Pahl (2007).

There is no space in this chapter to describe the many different faces of postmodernism and its relevance to research. Doyle (2006) has given a very helpful survey of the leading theorists whose work informs postmodern thinking and it is his explanation, used to analyse the place of writing in the Irish curriculum that is helpful for us here:

(It is) fruitless task to attempt to encapsulate in a neatly packaged definition the phenomenon known as postmodernism, nevertheless we can say that its most readily identifiable characteristic is its questioning attitude towards, and sometimes rejection of, widely accepted beliefs and principles. Such accepted principles around the area of literacy education, for example, emphasized the 'one correct way' to teach reading – usually a phonics-based or whole language approach (depending on your standpoint). Postmodernism would reject the 'one-cap-fits-all' thinking which underlies both these approaches, and would emphasize the need to be open to a variety of approaches and methods. (2006: 131)

In his analysis, Doyle demonstrates how postmodernism works to unsettle binary oppositions linked to the maintenance of power relationships. A further importance of postmodernism in relation to thinking about children's developing literacy is that it permits researchers to understand the ways in which other binary positionings of class and race intercalate with gender to further reinforce power relations. Glenda MacNaughton (2000) for example, discusses the need to confront both the binary oppositions and the dualistic thinking which privilege race or gender or class. She writes:

> We could see gender identity and racial/ethnic identity as dynamic and mutually constitutive. Each identity is constantly in the process of forming: each identity informs and forms the other. In other words a girl is always in the process of learning what it means to be a girl, because each of us is always in the process of forming and re-forming our gender identity. (2000: 225)

Following a critical literacy path, which takes its strategies from the deconstruction and close analysis of language, she suggests that children 'could be encouraged to think critically about their own and others' culture and how each forms and informs identity. They could be encouraged to learn about the complexities of who we are rather than about superficial emblems of culture, such as particular foods and dances' (2000: 226). Her emphasis is on helping children develop the emotional skills to help them to confront racism and sexism in their everyday lives. Orellana's proposition that 'no one is locked into a single position on either end of a system of binary opposites. We can all be both good and bad, both strong and weak, both students and lovers' (1999: 80) is still pertinent in guiding discussion of the complexity of differences found in every class of children.

The most recent research considering gender issues in the early years, such as that of Wohlwend and Francis, has shown how a greater understanding children's engagements with a wide variety of texts can better inform both parents' and teachers' understanding. Children's own interests however need to be treated with a sensitive awareness of each individual's

ruling passions and the role these play in children's performance of their emergent sense of self. It is all too easy for adults to colonize young children's pleasures in order to remedy perceived 'oppressions' and in that process steal away their delight or force the activity to go underground. As Misson (1998) cautioned earlier, teachers should respect children's desired narratives and their own cultural choices. Dyson (2003, 2010) draws on Bahktin's (1981) theories of heteroglossia and hybridity to explain and welcome how school and popular texts are brought together. Millard (2006) recommends an approach to teaching this as a process of 'fusion' in which children's cultural interests are welcomed into the classroom to inform the literacy curriculum.

Current research suggests that teachers need to help their classes to unpick the multiplicity of ways in which the texts they prefer provide them with different ways of understanding the world by introducing them, little by little, to issues of discourse, knowledge and power. These are themes that have informed feminist perspectives on gender from the very beginning of their enquiries into schooling. To summarize the core message of current work in this area, it is by reading and composing and questioning texts together, and not by imposing girl- or boy-friendly initiatives, that all children can be encouraged to build an understanding of the changing nature of gender differences as they develop across cultures and time. Teachers give support more effectively by devising possibilities for learning which enable children to imagine the world in new ways, encouraging new meanings to be made, new stories to be told, no matter whether the learner in question be a girl or a boy, no matter whether the modality chosen is print or digital.

NOTE

1 For a more extensive account of the role of children's popular culture in developing literacy, see Jackie Marsh's chapter in this volume.

REFERENCES

Acker, S. (1994) *Gendered Education: Sociological Reflections on Women,Teaching and Feminism.* Buckingham: Open University Press.

Alloway, N. and Gilbert, P. (1997) 'Boys and literacy: lessons from Australia', *Gender and Education,* 9(1): 49–58.

Arthur, L. (2001) 'Popular culture and early literacy learning', *Contemporary Issues in Early Childhood,* 2(3): 295–308.

Bakhtin, M. (1981) *The Dialogic Imagination. Four Essays.* Austin: University of Texas Press.

Barrs, M. and Pidgeon, S. (eds) (1993) *Reading the Difference: Gender and Reading in the Primary School.* London: CLPE.

Barton, D. and Hamilton, M. (1998) *Local Literacies: Reading and Writing in One Community.* London: Routledge.

Bearne, E. (2003) 'Rethinking literacy: communication, representation and text', *Reading, Literacy and Language,* 37(3): 98–103.

Bhojwani, P. (2011) 'Multimodal literacies: 6–7-year-old boys remembering, redesigning and remaking meaning in home and school'. PhD thesis, University of Nottingham.

Biddulph, S. (1997) *Raising Boys: Why Boys are Different, and How to Help Them Become Happy and Well-Balanced Men.* Melbourne: Celestial Arts.

Bissex, G. (1980) *Gyns at Work: A Child Learns to Write and Read.* Cambridge: Harvard University Press.

Blair, H. and Sanford, K. (2004) 'Morphing literacy: boys reshaping their literacy practices', *Language Arts,* 81(3): 452–60.

Brozo, W. (2010) *To be a Boy to be a Reader.* 2nd revised edn. Newark, DE: International Reading Association.

Calkins, L. (1986) *The Art of Teaching Writing.* Portsmouth, NH: Heinemann.

Clarricoates, K. (1978) 'Dinosaurs in the classroom: a re-examination of some aspects of the "hidden curriculum"', *Women's Studies International Quarterly,* 1: 353–64.

Davies, B. (1989) *Frogs and Snails and Feminist Tales: Preschool Children and Gender.* London: Allen and Unwin.

Davies, B. (1993) *Shards of Glass: Children Reading and Writing Beyond Gendered Identities.* Cresskill, NJ: Hampton.

Davies, B. (1997) 'Constructing and deconstructing masculinities through critical literacy', *Gender and Education,* 9(1): 9–30.

Davies, J. and Brember, I. (1993) 'Comics or stories? Differences in the reading attitudes and habits of girls and boys in years 2, 4 and 6', *Gender and Education,* 5(3): 305–20.

DCSF (2009) *The Gender Agenda.* Nottingham: DCSF.

Delamont, S. (1980) *Sex Roles and the School.* London: Methuen.

Doyle, J. (2006) 'Postmodernism and the approach to writing in Irish primary education', *Journal of Early Childhood Literacy,* 6(2): 123–43.

Dyson, A.H. (1985) 'Three emergent writers and the school curriculum: copying and other myths', *Elementary School Journal,* 85: 497–512.

Dyson, A.H. (1993) *Social Worlds of Children Learning to Write in an Urban Primary School.* New York: Teachers College Press.

Dyson, A.H. (1997) *Writing Superheroes: Contemporary Childhood, Popular Culture, and Classroom Literacy.* New York: Teachers College Press.

Dyson, A.H. (1999) 'Coach Bombay's kids learn to write: children's appropriation of media material for school literacy', *Research in the Teaching of English,* 33: 367–402.

Dyson, A.H. (2001) 'Where are the childhoods in child-hood literacy? An exploration in outer (school) space', *Journal of Early Childhood Literacy,* 1(1): 9–40.

Dyson, A.H. (2003) *The Brothers and Sisters Learn to Write: Popular Literacies in Childhood and School Cultures.* New York: Teachers College Press.

Dyson A.H. (2010) 'Writing childhoods under construction: re-visioning 'copying' in early childhood'. *Journal of Early Childhood Literacy,* 10: 7–31.

Epstein, D., Elwood, J., Hey, V. and Maw, J. (1998) *Failing Boys: Issues in Gender and Achievement.* Buckingham: Open University Press.

Francis, B. (1998) *Power Play: Primary School Children's Construction of Gender, Power and Adult Work.* Stoke-on-Trent: Trentham.

Francis, B. (2000) *Boys and Girls Achievement Addressing the Classroom Issues.* London: Routledge Falmer.

Francis, B. (2010) 'Gender, toys and learning', *Oxford Review of Education,* 36(3): 325–44.

Freire, P. (1972) *Pedagogy of the Oppressed,* trans. M. Bergman. Harmondsworth: Penguin.

Gilbert, P. (with Rowe, K.) (1989) *Gender, Literacy and the Classroom.* Melbourne: Australian Reading Association.

Gilbert, P. and Taylor, S. (1991) *Fashioning the Feminine: Girls, Popular Culture and Schooling.* Sydney: Allen & Unwin.

Graves, D. (1983) *Writing: Teachers and Children at Work.* Exeter, NH: Heinemann.

Gregory, E. (1998) 'Siblings as mediators of literacy in linguistic minority communities', *Language and Education*, 1(12): 33–55.

Gregory, E. (2001) 'Sisters and brothers as language and literacy teachers: synergy between siblings playing and working together', *Journal of Early Childhood Literacy*, 3(1): 301–22.

Grugeon, E. (2005) 'Listening to learning outside the classroom: student teachers study playground literacies', *Literacy*, 39(1): 3–9.

Hall, K. (2008) 'Leaving middle childhood and moving into teenhood: small stories revealing identity and agency', in K. Hall, P. Murphy, and J. Soler (eds), *Pedagogy and Practice Culture and Identity.* London: Sage Publications. pp. 87–104.

Hall, C. and Coles, M. (1999) *Children's Reading Choices.* London: Routledge.

Hannan, G. (1996) *Improving Boys' Performance.* Much Wenlock, Shropshire: INSET materials.

Hannan, G. (2000) *Improving Boys' Performance.* London: Heinemann

Heath, S.B. (1983) *Ways with Words: Language, Life and Work in Communities and Classrooms.* Cambridge: Cambridge University Press.

Howe, N and Parsons, A. (2006) 'Superhero toys and boys' physically active and imaginative play', *Journal of Research in Childhood Education*, 20(4): 287–300.

Jordan, E. (1995) 'Fighting boys and fantasy play: the construction of masculinity in the early years of school', *Gender and Education*, 7(1): 68–95.

Kanaris, A. (1999) 'Gendered journeys: children's writing and the construction of gender', *Language and Education*, 13(4): 254–68.

Kessler, S., Ashenden, D.J., Connell, R.W. and Dowsett, G.W. (1985) 'Gender relations in secondary schooling', *Sociology of Education*, 58: 34–48.

Kress, G. (1997) *Before Writing: Rethinking the Paths to Literacy.* London: Routledge.

Kress, G. (2003) *Literacy in the New Media Age.* London: Routledge.

Kress, G. (2010) *Multimodality: A Social Semiotic Approach to Contemporary Communication.* Oxon: Routledge.

Kress. G. and Van Leeuwen, T. (2006) *Reading Images: The Grammar of Visual Design* (2nd ed.) London: Routledge

Lankshear, C. and McLaren, P. (1993) *Critical Literacy: Politics, Praxis, and the Postmodern.* Albany, NY: State University of New York Press.

Luke, A. (1988) *Literacy, Textbooks and Ideology.* London: Falmer.

Luke, C. and Luke, A. (1992) 'Just naming? Educational discourses and the politics of identity', in W. Pink and G. Noblitt (eds), *Futures of the Sociology of Education.* Norwood, NJ: Ablex. pp. 357–380.

MacGillivray, L. and Martinez, A. (1998) 'Princesses who commit suicide: primary children writing within and against stereotypes', *Journal of Literacy Research*, 30(10): 53–84.

MacNaughton, G. (2000) *Rethinking Gender in Early Childhood Education.* London: Chapman.

Marland, M. (1983) *Sex Differentiation and Schooling.* London: Heinemann.

Marsh, J. (1999) 'Batman and Batwoman go to school: popular culture in the literacy curriculum', *International Journal of Early Years Education*, 7(2): 117–31.

Marsh, J. (2003) 'Superhero stories: literacy, gender and popular culture', in C. Skelton and B. Francis (eds), *Boys and Girls in the Primary Classroom.* Buckingham: Open University Press. pp. 59–79.

Marsh, J. (2005) 'Ritual, performance and identity construction: young children's engagement with popular cultural and media texts', in Marsh, J. (ed.), *Popular Culture, New Media and Digital Literacy in Early Childhood.* London: Routledge Falmer. pp. 28–50.

Marsh, J. and Millard, E. (2000) *Literacy and Popular Culture: Using Children's Culture in the Classroom.* London: Chapman.

Martino, W. and Pallotta-Chiarolli, M. (2005) *'Being Normal is the Only Thing to Be': Boys and Girls' Perspectives on Gender and School.* Sydney: University of New South Wales Press.

Maynard, T. (2002) *Boys and Literacy: Exploring the Issues.* London: Routledge Falmer.

Measor, L. and Sykes, P. (1992) *Gender and Schools.* London: Cassell.

Millard, E. (1994) *Developing Readers in the Middle Years.* Buckingham: Open University Press.

Millard, E. (1997) *Differently Literate: The Schooling of Boys and Girls.* London: Falmer.

Millard, E. (2006) 'Transformative pedagogy: teachers creating a literacy of fusion', in K. Pahl and J. Rowsell (eds), *Travel Notes from the New Literacy Studies.* Clevedon, UK: Multilingual Matters. pp. 234–54.

Millard E. (2010) 'Responding to gender difference', in J. Arthur and T. Cremin (eds), *Learning to Teach in the Primary School* (2nd ed.). London: Routledge.

Millard, E. and Marsh, J. (2001) 'Words with pictures: the role of visual literacy in writing and its implication for schooling', *Reading*, 35(1): 54–61.

Misson, R. (1998) 'Theory and spice and things not nice: popular culture in the primary classroom', in M. Knobel and A. Healy (eds), *Critical Literacies in the Primary Classroom*. Newtown: Primary English Teaching Association. pp. 179–91.

Moss, G. (2001) 'Seeing with the camera: analysing children's photographs of literacy in the home' *Journal of Research in Reading*, 24(3): 279–92.

Moss, G. (2007) *Literacy and Gender*. London: Routledge.

Nichols, S. (2002) 'Parents' construction of their children as gendered, literate subjects: a critical discourse analysis', *Journal of Early Childhood Literacy*, 2(2): 123–44.

OECD (2000) Reading for Change. Reading and achievement across countries. Results from PISA 2000, available at http://www.oecd.org/dataoecd/43/54/33690904.pdf (accessed November 2011)

OECD (2003) Learning for Tomorrow's World. First Results from PISA 2003, available at, http://www.oecd.org/dataoecd/1/60/34002216.pdf (accessed January 2012)

OECD (2006) Equally Prepared for Life? How 15-year-old boys and girls perform in school http://www.oecd.org/dataoecd/59/50/42843625.pdf (accessed March 2012)

OFSTED (1993) *Access and Achievement in Urban Education*. London: OFSTED.

OFSTED (1996) *The Teaching of Reading in 45 Inner-London Primary Schools*. London: OFSTED.

OFSTED (2003) *Yes He Can – Schools Where Boys Write Well*. London: OFSTED Publications.

OFSTED (2005) *The National Literacy and Numeracy Strategies and the Primary Curriculum*. London: OFSTED.

Orellana, M.J. (1995) 'Literacy as a gendered social practice: texts, talk, tasks and take-up in two bilingual classrooms', *Reading Research Quarterly*, 30(4): 335–65.

Orellana, M.J. (1999) 'Good guys and bad girls', in M. Bucholtz, A.C. Liang and L.A. Sutton (eds), *Reinventing Identities: The Gendered Self in Discourse*. New York: Oxford University Press.

Pahl, K. (1999) *Transformations: Meaning Making in Nursery Education*. Stoke-on-Trent: Trentham.

Pahl, K. (2001) 'Texts as artefacts crossing sites: map making at home and school', *Reading, Literacy and Language*, 6(2): 120–5.

Pahl, K. (2002) 'Ephemera, mess and miscellaneous piles: texts and practices in families', *Journal of Early Childhood Literacy*, 2(2): 145–66.

Pahl, K. (2005) 'Narrative spaces and multiple identities: children's textual explorations of console games in home settings', in J. Marsh (ed.), *Popular Culture, New Media and Digital Literacy in Early Childhood*. London: Routledge Falmer. pp. 108–124.

Pahl, K. (2006) 'Children's popular culture in the home: tracing cultural practices in texts', in J. Marsh and E. Millard (eds), *Popular Literacies, Childhood and Schooling*. London: Routledge. pp. 126–45.

Paley, G. (1984) *Boys and Girls: Superheroes in the Doll's Corner*. Chicago: University of Chicago Press.

Pidgeon, S. (1993) 'Learning reading and learning gender', in M. Barrs and S. Pidgeon (eds), *Reading the Difference: Gender and Reading in the Primary School*. London: CLPE. pp. 12–18.

Pidgeon, S. (1998) 'Superhero or prince', in M. Barrs and S. Pidgeon (eds), *Boys and Reading*. London: CLPE. pp. 24–32.

PIRLS (2003) PIRLS 2001 International Report IEA's study of Reading literacy achievement in primary school 35 countriesInternational Study Center, Lynch School of Education, Boston College.

PIRLS (2007) PIRLS 2006 International Report. IEA's Progress in international reading literacy study in primary schools in 40 countries. TIMSS & PIRLS International Study Center, Lynch School of Education, Boston College.

Poynton, C. (1985) *Language and Gender: Making the Difference*. Geelong, Victoria: Deakin University Press.

Ranker, J. (2009) 'Redesigning and transforming: case study of the role of semiotic import in early composing processes.' *Journal of Early Childhood Literacy*, 9(3): 319–47.

Rowsell, J. and Pahl, K. (2007) 'Sedimented identities in texts: instances of practice', *Reading Research Quarterly*, 42(3): 388–404.

Sainsbury, S. and Schagen, I. (2004) 'Attitudes to reading at ages nine and eleven', *Journal of Research in Reading*, 27: 373–86.

Skaar, H. (2009) 'In defence of writing: a social semiotic perspective on digital media, literacy and learning', *Literacy*, 43(1): 36–42.

Skelton, C. and Francis, B. (2003) *Boys and Girls in the Primary Classroom*. Berkshire: Open University Press.

Smith, F. (1988) *Joining the Literacy Club: Further Essays into Education*. London: Heinemann.

Smith, M. and Wilhelm, J. (2002) *'Reading don't fix no Chevys': Literacy in the Lives Of Young Men*. Portsmouth, NH: Heinemann

Solsken, J. (1992) *Literacy, Gender and Work in Families and in School.* Norwood, NJ: Ablex.

Spender, D. and Sarah, E. (1980) *Learning to Lose: Sexism and Education.* London: Writers and Readers.

Stanworth, M. (1981) *Gender and Schooling: A Study of Sexual Divisions in the Schoolroom.* London: Hutchinson.

Steedman,C (1983) *The Tidy House: Little Girls Writing.* London: Virago Press

Street, B. (1996) *Social Literacies.* London: Longman.

Street, B. (2003) 'What's "new" in New Literacy Studies? Critical approaches to literacy in theory and practice', *Comparative Education,* 5(2): 77–91.

Taylor, D. and Dorsey-Gaines, C. (1988) *Growing Up Literate: Learning from Inner-City Families.* Portsmouth, NH: Heinemann.

Thorne, B. (1993) *Gender Play: Girls and Boys in School.* Buckingham: Open University Press.

Tuck, D., Bayliss, V. and Bell, M. (1985) 'Analysis of sex stereotyping in characters created by young authors', *Journal of Educational Research,* 78(4): 248–52.

Walkerdine, V. (1985) 'On the regulation of speaking and silence: subjectivity, class and gender in contemporary schooling', in V. Walkerdine, C. Urwin, and J. Steedman (eds), *Language, Gender and Childhood.* London: Routledge and Kegan Paul. pp. 203–41.

Walkerdine, V. (1988) *The Mastery of Reason.* London: Routledge.

Walkerdine, V. and Lucey, H. (1989) *Democracy in the Kitchen.* London: Virago.

Weinberger (1996) *Literacy Goes to School: The Parents' Role in Young Children's Literacy Learning.* London: Paul Chapman.

Wells, G. (1987) *The Meaning Makers: Children Learning Language and Using Language to Learn.* London: Hodder and Stoughton.

Wertsch, J. V. (1991) *Voices of the Mind: A Sociocultural Approach to Mediated Action.* London: Harvester Wheatsheaf.

White, J. (1986) 'The writing on the wall: beginning or end of a girl's career', *Women's Studies International Forum,* 9(5): 561–74.

Wohlwend, K.E. (2009) 'Damsels in discourse: girls consuming and producing identity texts through Disney princess play', *Reading Research Quarterly,* 44(1): 57–83.

4

Reconceptualizing Early Childhood Literacy: The Sociocultural Influence and New Directions in Digital and Hybrid Media-tion

Aria Razfar and Kris D. Gutiérrez

In April 2000, the US National Reading Panel (NRP) presented their analysis of more than 100,000 studies on early literacy and concluded that the five most essential components to a child's ability to read are the following: phonics, phonemic awareness, fluency, vocabulary, and comprehension. In 2002, the National Early Literacy Panel (NELP) was commissioned to examine the NRP's findings as it related to early literacy and found major limitations in the NRP report. The commission found that the report did not adequately (if at all) address the teaching implications for children under 5. Following a similar review process as the NRP, the NELP reported additional factors specific to early literacy

development such as 1) phonemic awareness, 2) ability to rapidly name random letters, numbers, objects, and colors, 3) ability to write and write one's own name, 4) phonological memory, 5) concepts about print, 6) print knowledge, 7) reading readiness, 8) oral language development, and 9) visual processing ability to match or discriminate visual symbols (NELP, 2002).

The NELP goes a long way in identifying key factors specific to early literacy and advances the findings of the NRP in important areas such as oral language development, and advocates a broader notion of 'what counts as literacy' (besides decoding text). However, we believe that the fundamental question of 'what counts as literacy in early childhood?' is not adequately addressed in the report, in part, because of the types of early literacy studies that were counted to reach this conclusion. It is clear from the conclusions that the principal unit of analysis was language form rather than the contexts of language use which suggests that most of the studies were grounded in psycholinguistic and cognitive views of literacy development. The emphasis on the social contexts of development is a fundamental premise of sociocultural and cultural historical views of early literacy, which is what we believe is missing from both reports and the programs that were subsequently funded through major federal programs such as *Reading First*. The federal *Reading First* program was borne out of the NLP and NELP findings and was commissioned to insure that every child is reading at grade level by the end of third grade. It has been spending nearly a billion dollars a year nationwide on literacy programs that are 'scientifically based' and for the most part based on traditional cognitive models of literacy; however, the recently released interim report on 18 sites across 12 states has found that while the amount of time spent on the five components of reading (phonemic awareness, phonics, vocabulary, fluency, and comprehension) as advocated by NLP has increased, there was no significant impact on reading comprehension (US Department of Education, 2008).

We believe these reports and programs suggest a narrow view of 'what counts as literacy?' and illustrate the need to incorporate a broader definition of literacy or 'literacies' that examines the complex ways in which children make meaning using multiple modalities in various contexts. This trend has continued, especially in today's discussion of the Common Core State Standards Initiative in the United States (CCSS, 2010). In the CCSS, language is defined in terms of the traditional categories of reading, writing, and speaking/listening. Because 'language' is treated as a separate category, meaning and sociocultural aspects of language across the curriculum and its significant role in learning and development are obfuscated. According to Wiggins (2011), this familiar treatment of language reproduces the status quo curriculum rather than encouraging the integration of curricula around new ways of understanding and producing oral, written, and media texts. Another limitation of the CCSS is its focus on an individual, cognitive-processing model of literacy learning. This perspective often leads to decontextualized instruction where synthesizing texts becomes the goal and the situated purpose(s) of language use is dismissed (Baynham and Prinsloo, 2009; Gutiérrez, Morales, and Martinez, 2009).

While the NRP/NELP reports and the CCSS initiative are informative and provide some useful guidelines for literacy educators, there are key elements that are missing such as children's agency, identity, diverse sociocultural and socioeconomic factors, and community based cultural resources that are crucial to their literacy development. The NELP's decision to focus on narrowly defined forms of 'conventional' literacy may keep the field of literacy research from seeing and valuing non-school early literacy practices that are more aligned with the broad, flexible, and transcultural literacy practices that will be demanded in the future (Orellana and Dwarte, 2010). Recent sociocultural studies provide useful new insights for us to re-conceptualize major questions that have been addressed by literacy scholars working from a sociocultural perspective: What are the children's literacy experiences at home and community in early childhood? What counts as literacy? What and how can schools learn from children's families and communities? How can teachers and schools understand better about the contemporary students who are sitting in their classrooms?

Razfar and Yang (2010) reviewed early literacy studies that explicitly used a sociocultural perspective in major early literacy journals from 2001 to 2009 and found six major trends and points of emphasis (Razfar and Yang, 2010; in preparation): 1) children biliteracy practices in the home (12, 18.8%); 2) popular culture and media as a meditational tool for early literacy activity (10, 15.6%); 3) technology use (10, 15.6%); 4) cross-cultural variation in language socialization (10, 15.6%); 5) critical perspectives that challenge narrow literacy policies (8, 15.6%); 6) early literacy studies that focus on different aspects of social mediation (peer assistance, multimodal tools, dialogic interactions) as a socially mediated process (14, 22%). While nearly a third of these studies (20/64, 31%) explicitly focused on technology and media, the other themes also could not avoid how the new 'generation Z' technologies mediated interactions, literacy, and learning in early childhood.

In this edition of the chapter, we have paid closer attention to sociocultural and/ or cultural–historical[1] research that focuses on the dramatic changes in information technology, digital media, online gaming, and children's access to them. Burnett and Merchant provide a comprehensive review of early literacy and technology in multiple global contexts such as the United States, Australia, and the United Kingdom. While this chapter provides an overview of the sociocultural influence in the broader literacy field, we found that it is impossible to dismiss the role of information technology; thus, we provide a

sample of this research to frame emerging directions in sociocultural theory and early literacy, especially in terms of *digital* and *hybrid mediation*. As technology blurs the boundaries of interaction, talk, and discourse, adults (practitioners, parents, and caregivers) are increasingly expected to become 'digital natives' in order to adequately mediate the learning of '*generation Z*' or the *internet generation* (Palfrey and Gasser, 2008). In previous decades, sociocultural research has provided valuable insight into children's home and community literacy practices, teachers' use of these practices to improve learning in schools, and a broader understanding of what should count as literacy. While these critical issues remain peripheral to the national discussion of early literacy development (see National Early Literacy, 2002; US Department of Education 2008), sociocultural research has continued to address these topics; in addition, it has provided a novel perspective on an emerging phenomenon in relation to early literacy development: multimodal activities with *digital* and *hybrid language* mediation.

We will explore briefly several general theoretical principles that help define a cultural historical approach to the study of early literacy development. Within this perspective, human beings interact with their worlds primarily through mediational means such as cultural artifacts or tools, and symbols, including language (Vygotsky, 1978). Language from a cultural historical or sociocultural perspective is considered the pre-eminent tool for learning and human development and is said to mediate individuals' activity in the valued practices of their communities across a lifespan (Cole, 1996; Cole and Engeström, 1993). Of significance to the focus of this chapter, a sociocultural view of learning centers attention on cultural practices, or valued activities with particular features and routines, as fundamental to understanding the nature of literacy. By focusing on the cultural activity of various communities, the influence of the organization of the valued practices of a community on the nature of learning and participation therein is made visible. Here the role of other participants and the available cultural tools in the social ecology of individuals' lives become key features of learning environments.

Following this perspective, literacy learning is a socially mediated process that cannot be understood apart from its context of development, the forms of mediation available, and the nature of participation across various cultural practices. Thus, in contrast to conceptions of literacy as the acquisition of a series of discrete skills, a sociocultural view of literacy argues that literacy learning cannot be abstracted from the cultural practices in which it is nested. Instead, there is an emphasis on the available tools or artifacts and forms of assistance present in activity (Gutiérrez, 2002).

Culture is central to this view of learning and human development and is said to mediate human activity. Here culture is not treated as an external variable – as something apart from cognition – and thus it cannot be studied directly, or in an isolated, discrete, or causal manner (Cole, 1996). Instead, a more productive approach focuses on studying how people live culturally; that is, how people participate in the quotidian activity of their communities (Moll, 2000). Of significance, a sociocultural view espouses a non-normative, non-integrated dynamic view of culture in which culture is instantiated in the practices and material conditions of everyday life. This focus on activity helps us understand that there is variation in the ways a community's members instantiate and make sense of the valued practices of their community, as well as variation in which practices individual members take up (Gutiérrez, 2002). Thus, both regularities and variation are expected in communities, as culture is not uniformly understood or practiced across the members of cultural groups (Gutiérrez and Rogoff, 2003).

This instrumental view of culture is at the core of sociocultural views of literacy and has implications for how we make sense of children's literacy practices and how we study them. Since culture is interwoven in all aspects of human development, sociocultural research necessarily foregrounds the role of culture and context in human development. Accordingly, the development of early literacy practices (and their study) is understood in relation to the contexts in which those practices are culturally, historically, and ideologically situated. From a cultural–historical view, consideration of contextual and cultural influences on language and literacy processes, of language as a lens to understand microprocesses (e.g. shifts in roles and participation over time), or of larger sociological practices and processes, allows us to understand that literacy events have a social history that links the individual to larger sociohistorical practices and processes. Thus, people's literacy practices are necessarily situated in broader social relations and historical contexts.

The concept of literacy as a social activity is illustrated by the literacy practices that people draw on when participating in literacy events (Barton, 1994). This notion of literacy as a sociocultural practice has been developed across an interdisciplinary body of work. Most notably, the work of cultural psychologists contributed new conceptions of literacy as a highly social rather than an individual accomplishment; and they promoted new methods, such as combining ethnographic and experimental studies in order to understand the relationships in indigenous forms of literacy, their practical activity, and the cognitive consequences (Scribner, 1984a, 1984b; Scribner and Cole, 1978, 1981). Within this body of work, cultural psychologists focused on social practice as a unit of analysis to conduct cross-cultural analysis (Scribner, Goody, and Cole, 1977). These cross-cultural studies linked the literacy of a cultural group to the larger societal values of the community and illustrated the complexity of the literacy practices in which children engaged outside of formal instructional contexts.

Important to the discussion in this chapter, we highlight how sociocultural theories of literacy have significantly informed our understandings of early literacy development (Bruner, 1977; Snow, 1977). Within this work, we emphasize sociocultural theories of language socialization (Ochs, 1988; Ochs and Schieffelin, 1984), as well as sociocultural studies of early literacy that have advanced our understanding of power relations *vis-à-vis* literacy practices. For example, the new literacy studies (Gee, 2001; Luke, 1994; Carrington and Luke, 2003) have illustrated that as children are socialized to particular literacy practices, they are simultaneously socialized into discourses that position them ideologically within the larger social milieu. In addition, sociocultural theories have challenged the role of formal schooling in literacy development (Nicolopoulou and Cole, 1997) and have documented how the social organization of learning of out-of-school settings can promote language and literacy development (Gutiérrez, Baquedano-Lopez, and Alvarez, 2001; Hull and Schultz, 2002; Vásquez, 2003).

More recently, especially in the last two decades, sociocultural theory's dynamic view of culture has become central to a growing body of literacy studies concerned with the education of poor children, including English language learners (Gutiérrez, Baquedano-Lopez, and Tejeda, 1999; Michaels, 1982; Moll, Saez, and Dworin, 2001; Orellana, 2001; Rueda and McIntyre, 2002; Trueba, 1999; McTavish, 2009; Taylor, Bernhard, Garg, and Cummins, 2008). Rather than only raising questions about whether children can read and write, such studies ask what children know about literacy, seeking to learn about the relationship between children's literacy and the nature of literacy practices in which they routinely engage. Of significance to this approach to studying literacy, a cultural–historical theory of learning and development challenges views that equate culture with race and ethnicity and attribute individual traits (including language use) to being a member of a particular group (Gutiérrez, 2002; Lee, 2002; Rogoff and Angelillo, 2002).

We will elaborate on these theoretical principles in our discussion of the following: 1) the historical context in which sociocultural views of early literacy development are situated; 2) emergent literacy constructivist and sociocultural perspectives; 3) sociocultural perspectives on early literacy; 4) mediation and forms of assistance in early literacy development; 5) digital and hybrid mediation; 6) language socialization and the studies of home and community early literacy practices; and 7) power relations and ideologies as mediators in early literacy practices.

HISTORICAL CONTEXT

Emergent literacy from the individual to the social

For most of the twentieth century, research on literacy as well as early literacy was dominated first by behaviorist psychology (Skinner, 1957), which conceptualized literacy development as a scripted habit formation, and then by cognitive psychology (Piaget, 1951, 1962) in which development was conceptualized as an individual and linear process. Instruction within these frameworks followed individual development; as a result, literacy practices associated with formal schooling were based on these assumptions of learning and development.

From the late 1800s to the 1920s, the research literature on reading and writing focused primarily (or almost exclusively) on the elementary school years (Teale and Sulzby, 1986). For more than 50 years, it had been widely assumed that children's literacy development began with formal schooling. From this perspective, it was believed that the mental processes necessary for reading were fundamentally intrapersonal cognitive processes that would unfold in concert with biological development (Teale and Sulzby, 1986). Thus, the process of learning to read was highly correlated with biological maturation. The idea that development precedes learning naturally lends itself to the notion of readiness. In 1925, the National Committee on Reading published the first explicit reference to the concept of reading readiness – the dominant theory of reading from the 1920s to the 1950s. In reading-readiness programs children were considered ready to read when they had met certain social, physical, and cognitive competencies (Morphett and Washburne, 1931; Morrow, 1997). Thus, literacy activities occurring in the home and community before formal schooling were not central to the process of acquiring literacy. Instead, the reading-readiness paradigm argued for literacy practices that would not interfere with the process of development. In addition, it did

not adequately recognize the social dimensions of learning and development. As a result, traditional instructional practices such as whole class instruction and emphasis on formal features of literacy, including phonics-based instruction, dominated instructional practices. In addition, the reading readiness perspective inspired many of the standardized testing batteries used to determine if a child was developmentally ready for reading. For instance, the use of word primers as a stimulus to elicit a conditioning response is an example of reading readiness research and pedagogical practices that were rooted in behaviorist psychological perspectives of human development (Gates, Bond, and Russell, 1939; Thorndike, 1921).

Emergent literacy: from social constructivism to sociocultural theory

The social turn in literacy that occurred in the past few decades was motivated by a series of events and sociocultural phenomena. When the Soviet Union launched the first satellite, Sputnik, in the 1950s, there was growing anxiety that American education was not adequately preparing the next generation. With the state of American education coming under scrutiny, researchers began to question the fundamental assumptions of prevailing educational practice, including the reading-readiness paradigm. During this period, Chomsky's classic book *Syntactic Structures* (1957) demonstrated that structural assumptions of language and cognition are incapable of accounting for the fundamental characteristics of language. Chomsky's notion of the language acquisition device (LAD) also was a major breakthrough; it illustrated that children *acquire* the rules to generate complex syntactic structures long before formal schooling. Although Chomsky's work fostered a paradigm shift in cognitive psychology and in the study of literacy and early literacy, applied linguists and linguistic anthropologists argued that Chomsky's notions did not adequately address the communicative and social dimensions of language and language learning (Hymes, 1972; Labov, 1972).

In the last half of the twentieth century, Johnson's 'War on Poverty' in the US coincided with researchers' attempts to understand 'cultural deprivation' and later to challenge deficit-model explanations for the social and educational practices of poor children, many of whom were children of color. The growing emphasis placed on the social introduced social constructivist views of learning in the field of early literacy. According to Hiebert and Raphael (1996), one of the first and most well-known early literacy movements born out of social constructivist views of learning was the *emergent literacy* perspective (e.g. Clay, 1966, 1975; Mason and Allen, 1986; Sulzby and Teale, 1991).

The emergent literacy framework, with its roots in cognitive psychology and psycholinguistics, was one of the first theories of early literacy to challenge the commonly held assumption that reading and literacy activities in general are intrapersonal and linear mental processes. The term *emergent literacy* was first used in the late 1960s to describe the behaviors of young children when they used books and writing materials in non-conventional ways (Clay, 1966). The term was used to describe the behaviors used by young children with books and when reading and writing, even though the children could not actually read and write in the conventional sense. Whereas the concept of reading readiness suggested that there was a point in time when children were ready to learn to read and write, emergent literacy suggested that

there were continuities in children's literacy development between early literacy behaviors and those displayed once children could read independently. This perspective also emphasized the importance of the relationship between reading and writing in early literacy development (Clay, 1975). Until then, it was believed that children must learn to read before they could learn to write.

This body of literature served to broaden the view of children's literacy outside of formal instruction (Mason and Allen, 1986; Sulzby and Teale, 1991). It stressed the importance of parents, caregivers, teachers, and literacy-rich environments in children's literacy development and challenged the view of reading and writing as an individual mental process that begins with formal schooling (Burns, Griffin, and Snow, 1999; Teale and Sulzby, 1986). As a result, contextual factors that lead to literacy development became a crucial dimension in the study of early literacy. The emergent literacy studies emphasized that in the period prior to formal schooling, children's literacy develops in multiple formal and informal contexts (Ferreiro and Teberosky, 1982; Stahl and Miller, 1989; Sulzby and Teale, 1991; Teale and Sulzby, 1987). Furthermore, children's contributions and participation in adult-directed activities are essential to their development.

The recognition that early literacy development is multifaceted and complex had methodological implications for how early literacy studies would be conducted. The unit of analysis in these studies focused on activity settings and situated literacy practices rather than the performance of literacy skills under controlled experimental conditions. As a result, a number of the emergent literacy studies focused on children's participation in everyday practice and utilized sustained participant observation to gain a deeper understanding of early literacy development (Mason and Allen, 1986). Ethnographic methods allowed researchers to document literacy practices and the process of literacy development as it unfolded in its natural context (both in the home and in other contexts outside of school).

These studies represent a fundamental theoretical and methodological shift from traditional experimental designs that presumed early literacy development to be an individual, discrete process (see Hiebert, 1988, for an overview of emergent literacy studies). This shift also marked a growing realization that culture is fundamental to the development of literacy, and that meaning making and cognition are interactive (with others, including artifacts) and situated in nature.

With the growing importance of culture and context in the study of early literacy came the recognition that the literacy practices of the home were essential to children's literacy development. Some of these studies examined adult–child interactions at home and made them the basis for creating similar contexts in school and other literacy projects.[2] One of the clearest indications that emergent literacy research was having widespread influence was the 1965 inauguration of Project Headstart in the US, a federally funded program designed to provide children thought to be disadvantaged by poverty with the skills they would need for formal schooling. Longitudinal studies of students enrolled in Headstart programs showed that Headstart graduates were more likely to be in college and have more educational achievement (Schweinhart, Barnes, and Weikart, 1993). Although Project Headstart illustrated the importance of home literacy practices prior to formal schooling, it

was limited in that it did not address the unique factors affecting linguistic and racial minority students. In addition, emergent literacy perspectives tended to apply a deficit view of the home–school disparity, and the problem of low achievement for linguistic and racial minorities was constructed as deficit with the home, that 'families do not read enough or lack book knowledge, that they do not value literacy or model it effectively' (Carrington and Luke, 2003: 240; Hammer, Nimmo, Cohen, Clemons Draheim, and Achenbach Johnson, 2005; Mason and Allen, 1986; also see Marvin and Mirenda, 1993; Marvin and Wright, 1997; White, 1982).

These deficit views about the literacy practices of linguistic and racial minority homes can promote narrow conceptions of literacy and culture in which literacy is considered a neutral practice. By privileging the literacy activities of formal schooling – practices that often index the values of white, middle-class communities – this work implicitly valued particular forms of literacy (Heath, 1982). Thus, the literacy activities and practices of language-minority homes were devalued in relation to the dominant literacy practices. The undervaluing of the literacy practices of non-dominant groups led to beliefs that matching home literacy practices to those valued by schools would solve the chronic underachievement of poor and non-white students. Studies drawing on sociocultural theories of human development have addressed these issues and have argued that literacy cannot be considered independent of a community's culture, history, and values (Cazden, 1979; Heath, 1982; Scribner and Cole, 1981). While emergent literacy perspectives identified the importance of literacy activity prior to school and the role of adults/caregivers in this process, early literacy researchers drawing on sociocultural theories were also able to illustrate the informal contexts in which literacy develops prior to formal schooling (Cazden, 1979; Heath, 1982; Scribner and Cole, 1978; Wells, 1985). Sociocultural theorists also recognized the importance of the adult's role in early literacy development (Bruner, 1983; Cazden, 1983; Vygotsky, 1978; Wertsch, 1978). However, one of the major differences between the emergent literacy perspective and sociocultural views of early literacy development is how adults interact with children *vis-à-vis* literacy practices (Cazden, 1991). Although adults are generally the more expert members of literacy practices, the roles of experts and novices are more fluid as we expect change in the nature of participation over time in literacy activity (Rogoff, 1990, 2003). Through active participation, children's development is mediated via available material, ideational and cultural tools. Thus, early literacy development is a multidirectional and mutually engaging process between adults and children.

STUDIES OF EARLY LITERACY: A SOCIOCULTURAL PERSPECTIVE

Although much of the work in early literacy has focused on language or reading development, it is important to acknowledge studies of the writing practices of preschool and early primary-school children, particularly those studies that illustrate the link between reading, writing, and oral language development. Of significance, sociocultural views of literacy development challenged emergent theories of writing that described stages of writing development along Piagetian lines (Ferreiro and Teberosky, 1982) and instead argued that children's writing emerges coherently but idiosyncratically (Barton, 1994; Hall,

1987; John-Steiner and Mahn, 2003). Read (1971), for example, focused on the invented spellings children use when they begin to create texts. Read argued that these spontaneous spellings serve as a window into how children begin to make sense of the conventions of written text without the help of more expert others. In general, these sociocultural studies have illustrated how writing is embedded in children's everyday practices. Carol Chomsky (1972), for example, examined children's writing as they learned to speak. Hudson (1994) provided a teacher's perspective to capture developmental change in a young child's emergent writing. Similarly, Bissex (1980) and Bissex and Bullock (1987) highlighted the logic revealed in children's early writing as children made hypotheses about language and text. These ethnographic accounts illustrate how reading, writing, and oral language develop simultaneously in formal and informal contexts and highlight the importance of studying literacy *in situ*.

Unquestionably, there has been significant interest over the last 50 years in the child as a language user and meaning maker. In the early part of the twentieth century, Lev Vygotsky (1978) was among the first to argue the social nature of learning.[3] Sociocultural perspectives across a number of disciplines have influenced the ways educational theorists think about language and literacy. Following Vygotsky, John-Steiner and Mahn (2003) have argued that the use of a social and functional approach to the study of literacy is common across this work. Specifically, John-Steiner and Mahn delineate several tenets we believe both help define this approach, and distinguish the model from other models:

1 Sociocultural studies of language and literacy employ functional vs structural models.

Of significance, there is particular focus on communicative intent and on the representational functions of language (Austin, 1962; Grice, 1975; Searle, 1969).

2   Social interaction serves as the generative context for language/literacy mastery. Here the reciprocal nature of language and context is emphasized, for example (Bruner, 1983; Wells, 1981).

3   The study of language is expanded to include meaning, use, as well as structure. Thus, the situated nature of knowledge and its relationship to specific sociohistorical contexts and practices are emphasized (Hickmann, 1987). The situatedness of language suggests that its forms must be understood in terms of context and function (Bruner, 1983; Gee, 2008).

4   Interdisciplinary methodologies, particularly ethnographic and sociological methods, generated a new field, the ethnography of communication. The focus on speech events (Searle, 1969) and the influence of culture (Scribner and Cole, 1981) contributed to a multidisciplinary foundation for the study of literacy. This line of work in particular was instrumental in new research on literacy in school contexts (Cook-Gumperz, 1986; Gilmore and Glatthorn, 1982; Schieffelin and Gilmore, 1986).

5   There is a shift in emphasis from the individual to understanding literacy practices as socially and historically situated (Goodman and Goodman, 1990; Scribner and Cole, 1981).

6   Research methodologies help explain processes and socially constructed situations. The result is an interest in activity in context (Laboratory of Comparative Human Cognition, 1983) and microgenetic approaches (Siegler and Crowley, 1991; Tudge, 1990; Wertsch and Hickmann, 1987).

These principles are elaborated in a number of edited volumes on the social origins of literacy, and their visibility signals the growing influence of this perspective. Situating their work across various contemporary contexts and communities, literacy scholars in the neo-Vygotskian tradition elaborate on many of the theoretical and methodological issues relevant to the study of early literacy development (Bloome, 1987; Candlin and Mercer, 2001; Hamilton, Barton, and Ivanic, 1994; Lee and Smagorinsky, 2000; Moll, 1990; Reyes and Halcon, 2001; Wells and Claxton, 2002).

LITERACY AS A SOCIALLY MEDIATED PROCESS; MEDIATION AND FORMS OF ASSISTANCE IN EARLY LITERACY

For researchers drawing on sociocultural theories of cognition, the individual/social dichotomy is a problematic construct in that there is a reciprocal and bilateral relationship between the social and the mental. Human beings participate in activities through the use of tools as a means to change themselves, their surroundings, as well as the tools themselves. It is important to emphasize that for Vygotsky, the pre-eminent tool that mediated human development was the use of signs, which included oral language, writing systems, and number systems. Thus, development constitutes the ability of a child to use these signs in a culturally appropriate way that is mediated by the cultural and historical context in which it is embedded. It is the more expert members of a particular practice that determine what is or is not 'appropriate' participation.

Specifically, a sociocultural understanding of learning and development focuses on the cultural resources that mediate an individual's participation and engagement in social practice. The notion of mediation becomes important to the development of a sociocultural view of literacy and, in particular, how language mediates learning and our experience. Here the notion of language as a medium has several interpretations:

Firstly, from a constructivist view of the world, all our experience is mediated, nothing is direct. Secondly, by the way they structure reality for us in social interactions, people mediate our experience;

and thirdly, texts, whether they are books, films or advertisements, mediate our experience.

(Barton, 1994: 68)

The notion of *mediation* suggests that all human actions, both external and internal, exist in relation to other material and/or symbolic objects that are culturally and historically constructed to make meaning of the world. Thus, the construction of meaning, the basis of literate practices, is always situated and embedded within human activity systems that are goal-directed and rule-governed (Wertsch, 1991). For example, the word 'ball' is reconstituted to mean 'not strike' within an activity system such as baseball (Levinson, 1992). Indeed, language is considered the tool of tools mediating human activity (Cole and Engeström, 1993).

In other words, social relations mediate individual mental processes – relations that are primarily mediated by speech, including inner speech. Although cognitive psychologists also have recognized the importance of inner speech or 'private speech' in early literacy development, cognitive psychological views of inner speech suggest that it is a self-contained, discrete activity (Piaget, 1962). In contrast, Vygotsky (1978, 1987) claimed that thought is mediated internally by meanings and externally by signs. From a sociocultural perspective, individual mental processes are contextually situated and are fundamentally social. The use of private speech as a mediator of thought demonstrates the importance of cultural tools such as language in the development of 'individual' cognition. Studies drawing on sociocultural views of early literacy development have examined the self-regulatory speech of preschool children (Berk and Spuhl, 1995; Elias and Berk, 2002; Patrick, 2000). For example, Patrick (2000) found that preschool children

(ages 4–6) increasingly used self-regulatory speech to mediate problem solving in more difficult tasks. Another study (Elias and Berk, 2002) found that children's use of self-regulatory speech is situated and mediates the development of literacy practices through participation in problem solving and sociodramatic play. Another type of inner speech, a child's *metalinguistic awareness*, or the ability to think about language and its purposes, is linked to conventional forms of literacy (Olson, 1994). Specifically, the ability to reflect upon an imagined audience and speak to the generalized other is critical to literacy (Applebee, 1978). More importantly, imagined audiences are always situated in a particular cultural context.

Vygotsky's *zone of proximal development* (hence forth ZPD or Zoped), one of the most important constructs growing out of the sociocultural tradition, has special significance to the notion of mediation and early literacy development. The ZPD emphasizes the fact that the development of a child's individual mental processes is socially mediated. Broadly defined, the Zoped is the contrast between what a child can do independently (zone of actual development or ZAD) and the child's potential development or what a child can do with the assistance of a more expert other(s) (Vygotsky, 1978). For example, two children might have the same level of actual development, but given the appropriate form of assistance, one might be able to solve many more problems than the other. Thus, while there is recognition of children's individual capabilities, their individual development is supported by their co-participation with more expert members in a particular literacy or discourse practice. In addition, how adults assist children to navigate the zone is a focal point of a number of sociocultural studies of early literacy.

However, Griffin and Cole (1984) have pointed out that most English-language interpretations have perceived the notion of the zone more narrowly than Vygotsky intended. More traditional conceptions of adult–child assistance strategies construct the child as a passive learner, where the more expert adult usually provides next-step assistance, for example, when an adult asks a question for which the answer is already known. In short, the ZPD places emphasis on what children can do *alone* in relation to what they can do with assistance.

More dynamic notions of the zone of proximal development reshape traditional conceptions where the nature of the adult–child relationship is for the most part top-down and unidirectional (Cole, 1996; Engeström, 1987; Griffin and Cole, 1984; Stone and Gutiérrez, 2007). Rogoff's (1990) notion of *apprenticeship*, for example, helps to reframe the child as an active participant in his/her literacy development. Moreover, the nature of both adult and child participation and how adults assist children in literacy activities is critical toward understanding how children effectively move through the ZPD (Bruner, 1983; Rogoff, 1990). Activity theoretical views of learning and development expand the notion of the Zoped and illustrate its complexity by documenting the role of conflict and tension inherent in learning activity and, in particular, the potentially productive role of conflict in robust learning activity (Cole, 1996; Cole and Engeström, 1993; Engeström, 1987; Gutiérrez et al., 1999).

The focus within this view is on socially supported activities, their organization, the mediational tools, the task, and the participants, and their social relationships. For example, a study of children's writing by Diaz and Flores (2001) is illustrative of this more complex understanding of the Zoped. In this work, the authors describe the importance of the teacher as sociocultural mediator in promoting the emergence of positive or productive Zopeds. Language socialization research into caregiver–child interactions also supports the view that children are actively engaged in the literacy learning process (Bruner, 1977; Ochs and Schieffelin, 1984; Snow, 1977). The role of caregivers in mediating early literacy development has been well documented by early literacy research based on sociocultural views (Bruner, 1977; Bullowa, 1979; Ochs and Schieffelin, 1984; Snow, 1977). As the more expert participant of various literacy practices, adults mediate children's early literacy development through the various assistance strategies they employ.

Of relevance to this chapter, early literacy activity is often embedded in children's play. According to Vygotsky (1978), play affords children opportunities to move beyond their daily routines and behaviors and 'contains all the developmental tendencies in a condensed form'. In particular, through imagination or imaginary play – where the boundaries are more fluid and dynamic – children can assume roles and engage in activity not afforded them in real life. Play is by nature rule governed and goal directed; however, the rules and goals are subject to manipulation by the participants, which leads to the use of higher cognitive functions. In this way, the roles and forms of participation in play serve as preparation for participation in literacy events and in development (Gillen, 2002; Hall, 1991; Nicolopoulou, 1993; Vygotsky, 1978). Thus, play serves as an important leading activity; that is, it becomes a context for reorganizing performance (Griffin and Cole, 1984). Play also affords children opportunities to use cultural symbols and practices to negotiate and navigate social relations, in particular with their peers, to drive the overall meaning-making process (Dyson, 1997). Dyson (1997) shows how enabling and less restrictive activities such as 'author's theatre' (compared with the more constraining 'author's chair') provide contexts for the development of more complex literacy tools such as negotiation of conflict, analysis of gender equity, and understanding authoritative voices as they are textually positioned (also see Dyson, 1989, 1993). The wide range of tools that are invoked and utilized through play make it an optimal activity for promoting development within and across zones of proximal development.

Another central feature of play is that it creates opportunities to interact with more expert and novice peers. Children's interaction with peers creates contexts for conflict and negotiation, which mediates the use of higher-order literacy practices (Mugny and Doise, 1978; Pellegrini, Galda, Bartini, and Charak, 1998; Pelligrini and Galda, 1990). Moreover, points of conflict are intrinsically emotional and have a strong affective component. This in turn leads to more profound reflection and higher-order cognitive functioning in children (Pelligrini, Galda, Bartini, and Charak, 1998). Semiotic mediation leads to higher-level, more abstract cognitive functioning, and embodied meaning making (Valsiner, 1997). Vygotsky showed the significance of semiotic mediation in children's development of higher cognition through the transformation of objects into symbols. For example, during imaginary play children often display the multiplicity of meaning through a single object – a stick can represent a horse, a block can stand for a telephone, etc.

Dyson (1990) described young children as 'symbol weavers' from birth. There have been a number of studies, over the last decade, which have focused on how children act as symbol weavers during imaginary play and simultaneously explore notions of self through oral narrative. As a participant observer taking on the role of playmate, Kendrick (2005) observed the narratives of a young girl as she played with her doll house. Through an analysis of the child's naturally occurring narratives, Kendrick shows how the child constructs herself, the story, and a system of values during play. The child is shown to be an active participant in their own cognitive development, in a sense authoring their own autobiographical text, instead of looking at a child's play as passive imitation of adult life. Through play, the young girl in this study gives meaning to the role of woman, possibility for her future, and social relationship in her particular family and culture.

Another study with pre-school, Cantonese speaking, English language learners shows how children during imaginary play draw on the multiple languages and symbolic tools available to them (Genishi, Stires, and Yung-Chan, 2001). This study was the result of collaboration between researchers, teachers, and staff, who all approach the learning of their kids from a sociocultural perspective. The research team designed activities that positioned the children to become problem solvers using the many symbolic tools available to them. Thus, the activities did not focus on linguistic forms (i.e. phonemic awareness) or sounding out new words in artificial contexts, but rather focused on developing their ability to solve problems in contexts they were familiar with. Children developed vocabulary as a byproduct of exploring their physical world through hands-on activities such as dramatic play, singing, and drawing. Over time, the children were empowered as they used written language to represent their thoughts and communicate with others effectively. Children in this classroom developed advanced *metalinguistic* awareness about the function and purpose of their L1 (Cantonese) and L2 (English). These studies provide vivid examples of how a sociocultural view of 'language' as symbolic mediation can help broaden our view of 'what counts as literacy?' These studies further illustrate why sociocultural and cultural historical perspectives emphasize the centrality of agency and identity in human development. When children engage in purposeful activities such as dramatic play, oral story telling, singing, and drawing, they develop 'languages' and 'literacies' as means to achieve concrete ends.

Semiotic tools include language, number systems, drawings, diagrams, maps, and all sorts of conventional signs (Vygotsky, 1981). Today, this would include internet chat, interactive online gaming, hand-held devices, the keyboard, etc. It is important to remember that these tools or 'signs' always involve a constraining dimension as well as enabling new affordances. While broomsticks and blocks were (and still are) commonly available materials for playful purposes, the digital age has fundamentally changed imaginative play in many respects especially in terms of visual images, audio stimulation, and embodied action. Instead of riding a broomstick and pretending to be a horse (an image mostly defined by the child), a child assumes to be a predetermined character – 'Mario' in Donkey Kong – climbing ladders and jumping over barrels where all of the images and actions are provided for the child. The technology itself is more than just a medium, it sometimes becomes the object of play, like the child who pretends to be talking on her cell-phone using a carrot (Wohlwend, 2009). Razfar and Yang (2010) found three major themes across sociocultural studies between 2001 and 2009: 1) multiple modalities of early literacy development through play, including play that is mediated by digital tools such as cell phones, iPods, and popular media characters; 2) studies that focus on digital media and its impact on narrative activity in the homes; and 3) studies that focus on hybrid practices using media characters and multilingual, intergenerational interactions.

Human learning and development is intimately connected to the types of mediational tools available to people both enabling and constraining the types of interactions that can occur. For example, the alphabet is considered to be one of the most dramatic cultural artifacts to affect how human beings interact with each other and the world allowing generations previously separated by time and space to interact; since the invention of the alphabet, no mediational tool has impacted literacy and meaning-making like information and media technology. Children increasingly find themselves in a semiotic world(s) that is dramatically different than the predominantly print-based one in which their parents' generation became literate. This 'new literacy' environment is broader, more dynamic, fluid, multi-layered, and multimodal. In terms of children's identity development, there are significant challenges and opportunities presented by such a dramatic shift, and sociocultural research over the last decade has aimed to examine the complexities and implications of the emerging *digital* and *hybrid* semiotic world of early literacy development.

EARLY LITERACY IN THE NEW MILLENIUM: THE INTERNET GENERATION, DIGITAL AND HYBRID *MEDIA*-TION

According to Razfar and Yang (2010), another area in which sociocultural theory has made unique contributions to our understanding of early literacy development are studies of children actively engaged in digitally mediated activities such as interactive cartoons and movies, video games, and music across various contexts. While the digital age has transformed the tools, interfaces, and the organization of some play activity, the fact remains play is still a pivotal activity for children's identity and literacy development and remains a focus of sociocultural approaches. We examined four studies that focus on how children dynamically manipulate signs and symbols during imaginary play to engage in oral narratives and explore notions of 'self.' These ethnographic studies collectively illustrate how children use multiple modalities – drawing, acting, playing, talking, and even technology to co-construct meaning with adults, develop meta-linguistic awareness, and most importantly push us to consider broader notions of what counts as literacy in early childhood.

Over the last decade, many scholars interested in the impact of technology on early literacy development have drawn on sociocultural theory (for a comprehensive review see chapter by Burnett and Merchant in this volume). While the innovations in technology have contributed to fundamental changes in early literacy, sociocultural theory has proven to be a powerful lens for understanding these changes. In this chapter, we focus on several case studies that illustrate how the concept of *mediation* helps illuminate various aspects of technology use. One of the complexities facing children in the digital age is that technology is both the object and the means of children's literacy activity. Smith (2001, 2002) illustrates early literacy development through electronic books (e-books). Children have to simultaneously become literate in the technology while pursing the content of the narrative. Wohlwend (2009) illustrated how kindergarten and first-grade children use multimodal ways to make meaning during play, combining pretend play, artifacts representing modern technologies like iPods and cellular phones, and popular media characters. While in previous generations children used broomsticks to imagine riding a horse, today they use household objects to engage in pretend play that involves technology. For example, a girl uses a carrot to pretend she is speaking on a cell-phone or kindergarten boys make an iPod using classroom materials to play with it. Technology may have changed, but the principles of learning remain constant.

These studies dispel some of the misconceptions surrounding the nature of digital media and their relationship to learning. While earlier sociocultural research heavily focused on the availability of traditional, print mediums, and the literacy events surrounding them (i.e. bedtime stories, author's chair, etc.) over the last decade there has been a number of studies that have sought to better understand how e-books have re-organized literacy events in the early years of development. In addition to traditional print-based books, children across all socioeconomic lines engage electronic picture storybooks available as CD-Rom, DVD, and free movie files available on the internet (Kim and Anderson, 2008). There are also commercial electronic storybooks available, especially targeting young children between 3 and 6 years old (De Jong and Bus, 2004). The research has shown that younger, more digitally savvy parents are more likely to draw on digital texts with their children. Kim and Anderson (2008) report on multiple ethnographic studies of mother–child book interactions in three different contexts: traditional print format, electronic CD-Rom book, and electronic video clips from internet websites provide valuable contrasts. The participants were a middle-class Korean mother and her two sons aged 3 and 7 years old who recently immigrated to Canada from South Korea. The use of electronic books was already familiar to this Korean family and they regularly read e-books in addition to traditional print books at home, almost entirely in Korean. Overall, they found that the print book interactions were longer than the e-book interactions for both children because the mother read almost every sentence on the page while the e-books were used for auditory purposes. In addition, participants had greater control of the print-based media because they can better adjust the pace of reading and intermittent explanations based on the needs of the child. When the e-books were in a more open-ended format and the participants had greater control over the page turning as opposed to automatic page-turns, the mother and child could have more quality interactions. As with any mediational tool, the question of whether children benefit more from e-book use or not depends on the context of use, the developmental history of the participants, and the different cultural factors. Perhaps it is more important to consider the benefits and limitations of each medium on a case-by-case basis rather than make sweeping generalizations. One of the intrinsic characteristics of e-books is that children become very interested in the technology itself and it is difficult to separate this from their focus on the storyline (Smith, 2002).

We use the term *hybrid mediation* to denote the intermixing of multiple signs, symbols, texts, and mediational artifacts from various oral/visual/literate genres for the purpose of embodied meaning making in novel situations and contexts. This type of re-contextualization is a valuable marker of embodied meaning making and is increasingly becoming normative for children in the digital age. It is not surprising that children are inundated with media content and popular culture materials especially in their homes and non-school community settings. Their identities, group affiliations, and 'fan identities' are highly mediated through these popularly available media outlets (Gee, 2002; Newkirk, 2006).

Given that much of the deficit model research of media (especially television) suggests that these media make children passive learners and take away more active, worthwhile activities, their learning potential is largely dismissed by adults and educational settings (Robinson and Mackey, 2003). The sociocultural research in this area has aimed to provide an asset model of media and popular culture whereby children benefit from enriched repertoires of media text. Several ethnographic studies examine how young children appropriate and recontextualize popular digital media characters in hybrid ways and how they develop advanced forms of writing as a result (Dyson, 2001a, 2003). In a single child case study of 6-year-old Noah (Dyson, 2001a), Noah regularly infuses texts from cartoons, video games, and movies from home into his school compositions with digitally based characters, plots, and visual images. These *hybrid* texts are great examples of symbolic mixing that draws from multiple genres and mediums and demonstrates the creativity of the child in authoring something novel. Similarly, Pahl's (2002) ethnographic study in three homes also showed how young children engage in playful literacy activities using texts from cards, television, video games, T-shirts, films, drawing, songs, and family narratives. For example, the children regularly created hybrid characters using Pokémon and Super Mario to make cards, TV, video game, and T-shirts. Some research has shown how drawing on media and popular culture can have potential benefits for struggling readers and those who have developed an aversion to print-based literacy (Compton-Lilly, 2006).

LANGUAGE SOCIALIZATION: STUDIES OF HOME AND COMMUNITY EARLY LITERACY PRACTICES

Human beings undergo a lifelong process of socialization whereby they continuously transform into the values of an expected social order. Sociocultural views of early literacy development emphasize that human beings are socialized to particular language practices through language itself. Language socialization is the process whereby novices gain knowledge and skills relevant to membership in a social group (Lave and Wenger, 1991; Ochs, 1991). Cross-cultural studies of language socialization have argued that adults and children actively engage each other in the meaning-making process (Geertz, 1959; Ochs and Schieffelin, 1984; Scribner and Cole, 1981; Weisner and Gallimore, 1977; Whiting and Whiting, 1975). From this perspective, language plays a fundamental, dynamic role in the construction of social languages (discourses) and identities. These identities and discourses are subject to constant fluctuation as meaning is constantly negotiated and renegotiated between various segments of society, including adults, caregivers, and children (Gee, 2001; Ochs and Schieffelin, 1986). Studies of caregiver–child interactions have helped us understand the process by which children are socialized to and through language use (Cazden, 1983; Ochs and Schieffelin, 1984). They have also

helped us reconceptualize the novice child as an agent who assumes roles as author and speaker in the meaning-making process (Larson, 1997; Ochs and Schieffelin, 1995; Rogoff, 1990; Schieffelin, 1990). They have helped us understand how children are socialized to various problem-solving practices through various language activities (Goodwin, 1990; Nelson, 1989; Rogoff, 1990). Language socialization studies have demonstrated the powerful ways in which children are socialized to various social identities such as gender, religion, learning disability, and authority (Cook, 1990; Goodwin, 1990; Gutiérrez and Stone, 1997; Mehan, 1996; Schieffelin, 1990). Further, novice members are socialized to these multiple identities through affective features of language practices (Miller, Potts, Fung, Hoogstra, and Mintz, 1990; Ochs and Schieffelin, 1989).

The continued underachievement of poor children from cultural and linguistic groups served as the impetus for language socialization studies that compared home literacy practices with those of formal schooling. Prior to the understanding that literacy is fundamentally a cultural practice, these children were labeled as having some type of developmental deficit. Language socialization studies that examined the match between formal schooling practices and the literacy practices of middle-class homes served to counter the deficit view. Cook-Gumperz (1973) argued that children who have similar literacy practices in the home and in school tend to be more successful (also see Cook-Gumperz, 1986; Scollon and Scollon, 1981). Teachers were found to rely heavily on question and language games primarily found in white, middle-class homes (Cazden, 1979). Heath's (1982) 10-year study of two communities suggested how different social and linguistic environments and literacy practices of families differentially affected how children learned questioning, storytelling, concepts of print, reading, and writing.

Recent studies have shown the impact of this cultural differential on achievement and school literacy (Compton-Lilly, 2006; Vernon-Feagans, Hammer, Miccio, and Manlove, 2001). Compton-Lilly (2006) has shown how a teacher draws on the home languages and technological literacy of an African-American 'struggling' reader to develop more traditional, school-based forms of literacies. This is only possible when the teacher values the children's funds of knowledge. Vernon-Feagans et al. (2001) demonstrated that superior narrative skills in poor African-American children are negatively related to literacy, while the narrative skills in Caucasian children in the same classrooms were positively related to achievement and school literacy. In other words, the literacy practices that African-American children come with are not valued in relation to the types of literacy practices that are valued in formal schooling. Other studies have compared the patterns of interaction and language socialization of non-white homes with the socialization patterns prevalent in school (Au, 1980; Erickson and Mohatt, 1982; Philips, 1972, 1982) to illustrate the context-specific use of speech. Philips (1972, 1982) compared the patterns of classroom interaction among Native American reservation children and among Anglo children in the same community. She found that the patterns of communication of Native American children varied systematically from one type of situation to another.

This type of emphasis on the context of interaction helped to dispel the notion that Native Americans have a developmental or linguistic deficit. In another cross-cultural study, Duranti and Ochs (1986) examined the difference in adult–child relationships and discourse in Samoan households and school settings. The different socialization practices restricted the ability of Samoan children to be full participants in formal educational contexts.

Understanding and valuing the discursive practices of the home is particularly important for the success of language minority students. Reese and Gallimore (2000) present a case study of the cultural literacy practices that mediate early literacy development of children in some Mexican and Central American immigrant families. They found that parents began to read aloud to their children as a result of the expectations placed on them by school. Nevertheless, the parents' own formal schooling and literacy experiences mediated these read-alouds. Moll et al. (1995) elaborated the concept of *funds of knowledge* to demonstrate the value of working class Latino households in transforming the teachers', parents', students' and even the researchers' views of literacy (also see Gonzalez, Moll, and Amanti, 2005). The application of this construct has been used to illustrate how the utilization of a child's complete repertoire of cultural knowledge could mediate the development of proficient, biliterate practices in both English and Spanish (Moll et al., 2001).

Over the last decade, many sociocultural theories of early literacy have dealt with linguistically and ethnically non-dominant groups, especially in the USA and UK contexts where the demographic shifts toward 'non-white' populations has been significant. Sociocultural theories of learning and cognition challenge the hegemonic position of *deficit view* for particular ethnic, socio-economic, and linguistic groups. While deficit perspectives were normative, sociocultural research highlighted alternative, non-deficit practices (Gregory, Tahera, Jessel, Kenner, and Ruby, 2007; Reyes and Torres, 2007; Morgan, 2005; Hammer et al., 2005). These studies also take into account the digitally mediated practices of these populations. Ethnographic studies of children in immigrant and non-dominant homes continue to demonstrate the sophisticated and diverse repertoire of mediational tools available to them. Children in these contexts are not only preserving their heritage languages and cultural tools, but developing new hybrid forms that merge new technologies with multiple national languages, literacies, and discourses. In some respects, these studies contain aspects of all the themes we have previously discussed (play, digital and hybrid mediation, and identity) in the context of multilingualism (Genishi et al., 2001; Gregory et al., 2007; McTavish, 2009; Taylor et al., 2008; Wollman-Bonilla, 2001). For example, researchers, teachers, and staff collaborated to build a learning environment for Cantonese-speaking pre-school students that drew on the children's meaning-making repertoire (Genishi et al., 2001). Children developed vocabulary as a byproduct of exploring their physical world through hands on activities such as dramatic play, singing, and drawing. Over time, the children were empowered as they used written language to represent their thoughts and communicate with others effectively. As a Cantonese and English bilingual herself, the teacher regularly used both languages to mediate the children's participation. In most cases teachers are not able to provide this type of mediation; however, teachers do not need to be fluent in the child's heritage language in order to value it and position them to use it for the purpose of learning. One way to do this is to draw on community members or for teachers to position themselves as

'language learners' and the student and community members as experts (McTavish, 2009; Gregory et al., 2007).

SOCIOCULTURAL THEORY, POWER RELATIONS AND EARLY LITERACY

The importance of cultural and ideological factors in children's early literacy development led to a body of work in the late 1970s and 1980s that examined the socialization practices of children in their homes. Over the last 35 years, a number of literacy researchers and practitioners who have gravitated toward sociocultural theories of learning and cognition have done so in a particular political context. For years, the cognitive psychologists and behaviorists who presented the dominant view on literacy, learning, and human development suggested that literacy was the cause of rational and abstract thinking which in turn led to modernization and the ability to properly participate in the global markets (Scollon, 2001). Thus, illiteracy, in the narrow sense, was seen as the cause of all social problems, and the relationship between literacy, power, ideologies, and the social distribution of goods became the subject of interest for early literacy research. Scollon (2001) argued that the 'benefits of literacy as well as the social problems of illiteracy are derived, not from knowledge of scripts or the lack of this knowledge, but from the ideological power struggles of those who control this knowledge and those who are excluded from participation in "literate" communities of practice'. The following studies illustrate the significance of examining early literacy development as it is embedded within social contexts of power and privilege. Although some of the studies may not be strictly considered cultural–historical

(Bernstein, 1982; Hasan, 1986), they demonstrate the importance for current and future researchers drawing on cultural–historical perspectives of early literacy to consider issues of power and privilege in then-analysis of early literacy issues. Bernstein (1982) found that different socialization practices (based on class differences) have direct implications for children's language use. The work of Bernstein and others (Bernstein, 1982; Cook-Gumperz, 1973; Hasan, 1986) shows that mother–child interactions and early language socialization practices are mediated by class and class stratification which have an effect on later literacy development. Scribner and Cole's (1981) study of the Vai community who use multiple scripts (English, Arabic, Vai) in multiple contexts of power demonstrated that social situation (usually marked by power relations) determines the use of each script. Issues of power and control are even exhibited in early childhood writing practices (Hall and Robinson, 1994).

Similarly, the new literacy studies (NLS) argue that literacy or illiteracy is highly value laden and interest driven (Gee, 2001; Lankshear and Knobel, 2003; Marsh, 2005; Street, 2001; Willett, Robinson, and Marsh, 2009). These studies aim to understand the learning and language development of children in terms of 'discourses' rather than the more limited notion of 'language'. According to Gee, 'discourses' are more integrated and comprehensive: 'A Discourse integrates ways of talking, listening, writing, reading, acting, interacting, believing, valuing, and feeling ... in the service of enacting meaningful socially situated identities and activities' (2001: 35).

Of importance here are the 'believing, valuing, and feeling' dimensions of discourse because they move beyond traditional understandings of language as a set of equally valued, abstract mental representations of the world. In addition, becoming a competent member of a particular discourse community always involves how marginally or centrally one participates in specific social situations. NLS challenged what Street (1993) and others (Nicolopoulou and Cole, 1997) have called 'autonomous models of literacy' which presume literacy practices to be discrete and neutral. Sociocultural notions like *event*, *activity*, and *practice* moved literacy studies from 'the individual' as a unit of analysis where autonomous cognitive processes are examined under controlled experimental conditions (Goody, 1968; Ong, 1982) to a broader unit of analysis, 'the social practice' (Heath, 1982; Scribner and Cole, 1981). According to Street, 'Researchers dissatisfied with the autonomous models of literacy ... have come to view literacy practices as inextricably linked to cultural and power structures in society' (1993: 7). Thus, 'ideological' models of literacy where literacy is necessarily linked to other dimensions of social life including power structures (authority and power/resistance and creativity) became the focal point of NLS. Thus, literacy practices become a site where these larger social asymmetries converge (Gee, 2001; Luke, 1996; Street, 1987).

The emergence of new technologies in recent years necessitate a critical perspective that considers children's technological use as semiotic practices embedded with values that are locally negotiated and contested by children. This work emphasizes that new technologies do not simply act upon children, but rather children also act on technology by recontexualizing meanings from multiple domains (Burnett, 2010). Scholars working from an NLS perspective have also contributed to the growing research on technology use and early literacy development (Larson and Marsh, 2005; Mavers, 2007; Wohlwend, 2009). These studies collectively show how meaning making in early childhood goes beyond the 'linguistic' in the autonomous sense. Instead, children are shown to be agents of meaning making as they engage in multi-modal literacy practices that are goal directed, socially situated, and ideologically layered.

CONCLUSION

In this chapter, we have aimed to provide the reader with an overview of the orienting principles that guide sociocultural studies of early literacy. Social constructivist views of learning and early literacy, such as the emergent literacy view, challenged the assumption that literacy learning begins with formal schooling. Sociocultural views of early literacy have also helped us understand the nature of learning as a socially mediated process, where even individual cognition is necessarily embedded within a particular social context. The understandings that language is the pre-eminent tool for development, that children are socialized to discursive practices through language, and that learning precedes development have caused a paradigm shift in the field of early literacy research. One of the major consequences, over the last 35 years, has been to move researchers and practitioners beyond the deficit views of linguistic and racial minority homes and communities. Over the last decade, the dramatic shifts in informational technologies have also promoted new types of digital and hybrid mediation. These studies have documented the complex ways in which adults and children mediate early literacy development, where the child is an active participant in his/her literacy

learning. These social relations are negotiated and renegotiated to construct multiple identities in a constantly changing social reality. Sociocultural views of early literacy have now expanded our understanding of the context of development to include larger ideological and power issues as evidenced by the new literacy studies. Sociocultural theory helps us better understand what it is to be human and how to improve the human situation *vis-à-vis* literacy practices.

NOTES

1 We use the terms 'sociocultural and 'cultural–historical' interchangeably, although we recognize their distinctions. We prefer cultural–historical as it highlights the importance of historicity.

2 See Dyson (1987) and Martinez, Cheney, McBroom, Hemmeter, and Teale (1989) for further references to emergent studies. Dyson (1987) examines the potential for traditionally 'of-task' and informal language practices to be valuable opportunities for the development of school literacy.

3 For a more detailed review of Vygotsky's work see Wertsch (1985) and Van der Veer and Valsiner (1991).

REFERENCES

Applebee, A. (1978). *The Child's Concept of Story*. Chicago: University of Chicago Press.

Au, K.H. (1980). 'Participation structures in a reading lesson with Hawaiian children: Analysis of a culturally appropriate instructional event', *Anthropology and Education Quarterly*, 1(2): 91–115.

Austin, J.L. (1962). *How to Do Things with Words*. Oxford: Clarendon.

Barton, D. (1994). *Literacy: An Introduction to the Ecology of Written Language*. Oxford: Blackwell.

Baynham, M. and Prinsloo, M. (eds) (2009). *The Future of Literacy Studies*. New York: Palgrave Macmillan.

Berk, L. and Spuhl, S. (1995). 'Maternal interaction, private speech, and task performance in preschool children', *Early Childhood Research Quarterly*, 2: 145–69.

Bernstein, B. (1982). 'Codes, modalities and the process of cultural reproduction: A model', in M.W. Apple (ed.), *Cultural and Economic Reproduction in Education: Essays on Class, Ideology, and the State*. Boston: Routledge.

Bissex, G. (1980). *Gnys at Wrk: A Child Learns to Write and Read*. Cambridge, MA: Harvard University Press.

Bissex, G. and Bullock, R. (1987). *Seeing for Ourselves: Case-study Research by Teachers of of Writing*. Portsmouth, NH: Heinneman.

Bloome, D. (1987). *Literacy and Schooling*. Norwood, NJ: Ablex.

Bruner, J. (1977). 'Early social interaction and language acquisition', in H.R. Schafer (ed.), *Studies in Mother-Infant Interaction*. London: Academic. pp. 271–89.

Bruner, J. (1983). *Child's Talk: Learning to use Language*. New York: Norton.

Bullowa, M. (1979). 'Introduction: pre linguistic communication: A field of scientific Research', in M. Bullowa (ed.), *Before Speech: The Beginnings of Interpersonal Communication*. Cambridge: Cambridge University Press. pp. 5–50.

Burnett, C. (2010). 'Technology and literacy in early childhood educational settings: A review of research', *Journal of Early Childhood Literacy*, 10(3): 247–70.

Burns, M.S., Griffin, P., and Snow, C.E. (eds) (1999). *Starting Out Right: A Guide to Promoting Children's Reading Success*. Washington, DC: National Academy Press.

Candlin, C. and Mercer, N. (2001). *English Language Teaching in its Social Context*. London: Routledge.

Carrington, V. and Luke, A. (2003). 'Reading, homes and families: From postmodern to modem?', in A. van Kleeck, S.A. Stahl, and E.B. Bauer (eds), *On Reading Books to Children: Parents and Teachers*. Mahwah, NJ: Erlbaum. pp. 231–52.

Cazden, C.B. (1979). 'Language in education: variation in the teacher-talk register', in Thirtieth Annual Georgetown University Round Table on Languages and Linguistics, Washington, DC: Center for Applied Linguistics.

Cazden, C.B. (1983). 'Peekaboo as an instructional model: Discourse development at school and at home', in B. Bain (ed.), *The Sociogenesis of Language and Human Conduct: A Multi-Disciplinary Book of Readings*. New York: Plenum Press. pp. 33–58.

Cazden, C. (1991). 'Contemporary issues and future directions: Active learners and active teachers', in J. Flood, J.M. Jensen, D. Lapp, and J.R. Squire (eds), *Handbook of Research on Teaching the English Language Arts*. New York: Macmillan. pp. 418–22.

CCSS (Common Core State Standards Initiative) (2010). *Common Core State Standards for English Language Arts*. Retrieved from http://www.corestandards.org/assets/CCSSI_ELA%20Standards.pdf

Chomsky, N. (1957). *Syntactic Structures*. The Hague: Mouton.

Chomsky, C. (1972). 'Write first, read later', *Childhood Education*, 47: 296–9.

Clay, M. (1966). 'Emergent reading behavior'. Unpublished doctoral dissertation, University of Auckland: Auckland, New Zealand.

Clay, M. (1975). *What Did I Write?* Auckland: Heinemann.

Cole, M. (1996). *Cultural Psychology*. Cambridge, MA: Harvard University Press.

Cole, M. and Engeström, Y. (1993). 'A cultural historical approach to distributed cognition', in G. Salomon (ed.), *Distributed Cognitions: Psychological and Educational Considerations*. New York: Cambridge University Press. pp. 1–46.

Compton-Lilly, C. (2006). 'Identity, childhood culture, and literacy learning: A case study', *Journal of Early Childhood Literacy*, 6(1): 57–76.

Cook, H.M. (1990). 'The role of Japanese sentence-final particle in the socialization of children', *Multilingua*, 9(4): 377–95.

Cook-Gumperz, J. (1973). 'Situated instructions: Language socialization of school aged children', in S. Ervin-Tripp and C. Mitchell-Kernan (eds), *Child Discourse*. New York: Academic. pp. 103–24.

Cook-Gumperz, J. (ed.) (1986). *The Social Construction of Literacy: Studies in International Sociolinguistics*. Cambridge, MA: Cambridge University Press.

De Jong, M. and Bus, A. G. (2004). 'The efficacy of electronic books in fostering kindergarten children's emergent story understanding', *Reading Research Quarterly*, 39(4): 378–93.

Diaz, E. and Flores, B. (2001). 'Teachers as sociocultural, sociohistorical mediator', in M. Reyes and J. Halcon (eds), *The Best for our Children: Latino/ Latino Voices on Literacy*. New York: Teachers College Press. pp. 29–47.

Duranti, A. and Ochs, E. (1986). 'Literacy instruction in a Samoan village', in B. Schieffelin and P. Gilmore (eds), *The Acquisition of Literacy: Ethnographic Perspectives*, Norwood, NJ: Ablex.

Dyson, A.H. (1987). 'The value of "time off task": Young children's spontaneous talk and deliberate text', *Harvard Educational Review*, 57(4): 396–420.

Dyson, A.H. (1989). *Multiple worlds of child writers: Friends learning to write*. New York: Teachers College Press.

Dyson, A.H. (1990). Symbol makers, symbol weavers: How children link play, pictures, and print. *Young Children*, 45(2): 50–57.

Dyson, A.H. (1993). *The Social Worlds of Children Learning to Write in an Urban Primary School*. New York: Teachers College Press.

Dyson, A.H. (1997). *Writing Superheroes: Contemporary Childhood, Popular Culture, and Literacy*. New York: Teachers College Press.

Dyson, A.H. (2001a). 'Donkey Kong in Little Bear country: A first grader's composing development in the media spotlight', *The Elementary School Journal*, 101(4): 417–33.

Dyson, A.H. (2003). "Welcome to the Jam": Popular culture, school literacy, and the making of childhoods', *Harvard Educational Review*, 73(3): 328–61.

Elias, C. and Berk, L.E. (2002). 'Self-regulation in young children: Is there a role for sociodramatic play?', *Early Childhood Research Quarterly*, 17(2): 216–38.

Engeström, E. (1987). *Learning by Expanding: An Acivity-Theoretical Approach to Developmental Research*. Helsinki: Orienta-Konsultit.

Erickson, F. and Mohatt, G. (1982). 'Cultural organization of participant structures in two classrooms of Indian students', in G.D. Spindler (ed.), *Doing the Ethnography of Schooling*. New York: Holt, Rinehart and Winston.

Ferreiro, E. and Teberosky, A. (1982). *Literacy Before Schooling*. Portsmouth, NH: Heinemann.

Gates, A., Bond, G., and Russell, H. (1939). *Methods of Determining Reading Readiness*. New York: Teachers College Press.

Gee, J.P. (2001). 'A sociocultural perspective on early literacy development', in S. Neuman and D. Dickinson (eds), *Handbook of Early Literacy Research*. New York: Guilford. pp. 30–42.

Gee, J.P. (2002). 'Identity as an analytic lens for research in education'. *Review of Research in Education*, 25: 99–125.

Gee, J.P. (2008). *Social Linguistics and Literacies: Ideology in Discourses* (3rd ed.). London: Taylor & Francis.

Geertz, H. (1959). 'The vocabulary of emotion: A study of Javanese socialization processes', *Psychiatry*, 22: 225–37.

Genishi, C., Stires, S.E., and Yung-Chan, D. (2001). 'Writing in an integrated curriculum: Prekindergarten English language learners as symbol makers', *The Elementary School Journal*, 101(4): 399–416.

Gillen, J. (2002). 'Moves in the territory of literacy? The telephone discourse of three- and four-year-olds', *Journal of Early Childhood Literacy*, 2(1): 21–43.

Gilmore, P. and Glatthorn, A.A. (1982). *Children in and out of School*. Washington, DC: Center for Applied Linguistics.

Gonzalez, N., Moll, L.C., and Amanti, C. (2005). *Funds of Knowledge: Theorizing Practices in Households and Classrooms*. Mahwah, NJ: Lawrence Erlbaum Associates.

Goodman, Y.M. and Goodman, K.S. (1990). 'Vygotsky in a whole-language perspective', in L.C. Moll (ed.), *Vygotsky and Education: Instructional Implications and Applications of Sociohistorical Psychology*. New York: Cambridge University Press. pp. 223–50.

Goodwin, M. (1990). *He-said-she-said: Talk as Social Organization among Black Children*. Bloomington, IN: Indiana University Press.

Goody, J. (1968). *Literacy in Traditional Societies*. Cambridge: Cambridge University Press.

Gregory, E., Tahera, A., Jessel, J., Kenner, C., and Ruby, M. (2007). 'Snow White in different guises: Interlingual and intercultural exchanges between grandparents and young children at home in East London', *Journal of Early Childhood Literacy*, 7(1): 5–25.

Grice, H.P. (1975). 'Logic and conversation', in P. Cole and J.L. Morgan (eds). *Syntax and Semantics: Speech Acts*. New York: Academic. pp. 41–58.

Griffin, P. and Cole, M. (1984). 'Current activity for the future: The Zo-Ped', in B. Rogoff and J. Wertsch (eds), *Children's Learning in the Zone of Proximal Development*. San Francisco: Jossey Bass. pp. 45–63.

Gutiérrez, K. (2002). 'Studying cultural practices in urban learning communities', *Human Development*, 45(4): 312–21.

Gutiérrez, K. and Rogoff, B. (2003). Cultural ways of learning: Individual traits or repertoires of practice. *Educational Researcher*, 32(5): 19–25.

Gutiérrez, K. and Stone, L. (1997). 'A cultural-historical view of learning and learning disabilities: Participating in a community of learners', *Learning Disabilities Research and Practice*, 12(2): 123–31.

Gutiérrez, K., Baquedano-Lopez, P., and Tejeda, C. (1999). 'Rethinking diversity: Hybridity and hybrid language practices in the third space', *Mind, Culture and Activity*, 6(4): 286–303.

Gutiérrez, K., Baquedano-Lopez, P., and Alvarez, H. (2001). 'Literacy as hybridity: Moving beyond bilingualism in urban classrooms', in M. de la Luz Reyes and J. Halcon (eds), *The Best for our Children: Critical Perspectives on Literacy for Latino*

Students. New York: Teachers College Press. pp. 122–41.

Gutiérrez, K.D., Morales, P.Z., and Martinez, D.C. (2009). 'Re-mediating literacy: Culture, difference, and learning for students from nondominant communities', *Review of Research in Education*, 33: 213–45.

Hall, N. (1987). *The Emergence of Literacy*. London: Arnold.

Hall, N. (1991). 'Play and the emergence of literacy', in J. Christie (ed.), *Play and Early Literacy Development*. Albany, NY: State University of New York Press. pp. 3–25.

Hall, N. and Robinson, A. (1994). 'Power and control in young children's scribbling', in M. Hamilton, D. Barton and R. Ivanic (eds), *Worlds of Literacy*. Clevedon: Multilingual Matters. pp. 121–33.

Hammer, C.S., Nimmo, D., Cohen, R., Clemons Draheim, H., and Achenbach Johnson, A. (2005). 'Book reading interactions between African American and Puerto Rican Head Start children and their mothers', *Journal of Early Childhood Literacy*, 5(3): 195–227.

Hamilton, M., Barton, D., and Ivanic, R. (eds) (1994). *Worlds of Literacy*. Clevedon: Multilingual Matters.

Hasan, R. (1986). 'The ontogenesis of ideology: An interpretation of mother-child talk', in T. Threadgold, E. Grosz, and G. Kress (eds), *Semiotics, Ideology, Language*. SASSC. Sydney: University of Sydney.

Heath, S. (1982). 'What no bedtime story means: Narrative skills at home and school', *Language in Society*, 11(2): 49–76.

Hickmann, M. (ed.) (1987). *Social and Functional Approaches to Language and Thought*. Orlando, FL: Academic.

Hiebert, E.H. (1988). 'The role of literacy experiences in early childhood programs', *The Elementary School Journal*, 89(2): 161–71.

Hiebert, E.H. and Raphael, T.E. (1996). 'Psychological perspectives on literacy and extensions to educational practice', in D.C. Berliner and R.C. Calfee (eds), *Handbook of Educational Psychology*. New York: Macmillan. pp. 550–602.

Hudson, J. (1994). 'Catherine's story: A young child learns to write', in M. Hamilton, D. Barton, and R. Ivanic (eds), *Worlds of Literacy*. Clevedon: Multilingual Matters. pp. 188–94.

Hull, G. and Schultz, K. (2002). *School's Out: Bridging Out-of-School Literacies with Classroom Practice*. New York: Teachers College Press.

Hymes, D. (1972). 'On communicative competence', in J.B. Pride and J. Holmes (eds), *Sociolinguistics*. Harmondsworth, England: Penguin Books. pp. 269–93.

John-Steiner, V. and Mahn, H. (2003). 'Sociocultural contexts for teaching and learning', in A. Reynolds, M. William, and G.E. Miller (eds), *Handbook of Psychology: Educational Psychology*. Vol. 7. New York: John Wiley and Sons. pp. 125–51.

Kendrick, M. (2005). 'Playing house: A "sideways" glance at literacy and identity in early Childhood', *Journal of Early Childhood Literacy*, 5(1): 5–28.

Kim, J. and Anderson, J. (2008). 'Mother-child shared reading with print and digital texts', *Journal of Early Childhood Literacy*, 8(2): 213–45.

Laboratory of Comparative Human Cognition (1983). 'Culture and cognitive development', in W. Kessen (ed.), *Handbook of Child Psychology*. Vol. 1. New York: Wiley.

Labov, W. (1972) 'The transformation of experience in narrative syntax', in *Language in the Inner City: Studies in the Black English Vernacular*. Philadelphia: University of Pennsylvania Press. pp. 354–96.

Lankshear, C. and Knobel, M. (2003). 'New technologies in early childhood literacy research: A review of research', *Journal of Early Childhood Literacy*, 3(1): 59–82.

Larson, J. (1997). 'Indexing instruction: The social construction of the participation framework in Kindergarten journal writing activity', *Discourse and Society*, 8(4): 501–21

Larson, J. and Marsh, J. (2005). *Making Literacy Real: Theories and Practices for Learning and Teaching*. London, UK: SAGE Publications.

Lave, J. and Wenger, E. (1991) *Situated Learning: Legitimate Peripheral Participation*. New York: Cambridge University Press.

Lee, C.D. (2002). 'Interrogating race and ethnicity as constructs in the examination of cultural processes in developmental research', *Human Development*, 45(4): 282–90.

Lee, C.D. and Smagorinsky, P. (2000) *Vygotskian Perspectives on Literacy Research: Constructing Meaning Through Collaborative Inquiry*. New York: Cambridge University Press.

Levinson, S. (1992). 'Activity types and language', in P. Drew and J. Heritage (eds), *Talk at Work: Interaction in Institutional Settings*. Cambridge: Cambridge University Press. pp. 3–66.

Luke, A. (1994). *The Social Construction of Literacy in the Primary School*. Melbourne: Macmillan.

Luke, A. (1996). 'Text and discourse in education: an introduction to critical discourse analysis', *Review of Research in Education*, 21: 3–48.

McTavish, M. (2009). '"I get my facts from the inter-net": A case study of the teaching and learning of information literacy in in-school and out-of-school contexts', *Journal of Early Childhood Literacy*, 9(1): 3–28.

Marsh, J. (ed.) (2005). *Popular Culture, New Media and Digital Literacy in Early Childhood*. London, UK: Routledge.

Martinez, M., Cheyney, M., McBroom, C, Hemmeter, A., and Teale, W. (1989). 'No-risk kindergarten literacy environments for at-risk children', in J. Allen and J. Mason (eds), *Risk Makers, Risk Takers, Risk Breakers: Reducing the Risks for Young Literacy Learners*. Portsmouth, NH: Heinemann. pp. 93–124.

Marvin, C. and Mirenda, P. (1993). 'Home literacy experiences of preschoolers enrolled in Head-Start and special education programs', *Journal of Early Intervention*, 17(4): 351–67.

Marvin, C. and Wright, O. (1997). 'Literacy socializa-tion in the homes of preschool children', *Language Speech and Hearing Services in Schools*, 28(2): 154–63.

Mason, J. and Allen, L.B. (1986). 'A review of emer-gent literacy with implications for research practice in reading', *Review of Research in Education*, 13: 3–47.

Mavers, D. (2007). 'Semiotic resourcefulness: A young child's email exchange as design', *Journal of Early Childhood Literacy*, 7(2): 155–76.

Mehan, H. (1996). 'The construction of an LD student: A case study in the politics of Representation', in M. Silverstein and G. Urban (eds), *Natural Histories Of Discourse*. Chicago: University of Chicago Press. pp. 253–76.

Michaels, S. (1982). '"Sharing time": Children's narra-tive styles and differential access to literacy', *Language in Society*, 10: 423–42.

Miller, P., Potts, R., Fung, H., Hoogstra, L., and Mintz, J. (1990). 'Narrative practices and the social con-struction of self in childhood', *American Ethnologist*, 17(2): 292–311.

Moll, L. (1990). *Vygotsky and Education*. New York: Cambridge University Press.

Moll, L. (2000). 'Inspired by Vygotsky: ethnographic experiments in education', in C.D. Lee and P. Smagorinsky (eds), *Vygotskian Perspectives on Literacy Research: Constructing Meaning through Collaborative Inquiry*. New York: Cambridge University Press. pp. 256–68.

Moll, L., Gonzalez, N., Tenery, M., Rivera, A., Rendon, P., Gonzalez, R., and Amanti, C. (1995). 'Funds of knowledge for teaching in Latino households', *Urban Education*, 29(4): 443–70.

Moll, L., Saez, R., and Dworin, J. (2001). 'Exploring biliteracy: Two student case examples of writing as a social practice', *Elementary School Journal*, 101(4): 435–49.

Morgan, A. (2005). 'Shared reading interactions between mothers and pre-school children: Case studies of three dyads from a disadvantaged community', *Journal of Early Childhood Literacy*, 5(3): 279–304.

Morphett, M.V. and Washburne, C. (1931). 'When should children begin to read?' *Elementary School Journal*, 31: 496–503.

Morrow, L. (1997). *Literacy Development in the Early Years: Helping Children Read and Write*. Boston: Allyn and Bacon.

Mugny, G. and Doise, W. (1978). 'Socio-cognitive con-flict and structure of individual and collective per-formances', *European Journal of Social Psychology*, 8: 181–92.

National Reading Panel (2000). *Report*. US Department of Health and Human Services, National Institute of Child Health and Human Development. NIH pub. No. 00-4754. Retrieved from http://www.national-readingpanel.org/Publications/summary.htm

NELP (National Early Literacy Panel) (2002). *Report*. Retrieved from http://lincs.ed.gov/publications/pdf/NELPReport09.pdf, http://www.nifl.gov/nifl/publica-tions/pdf/NELPSummary.pdf

Nelson, K. (ed.) (1989). *Narratives from the Crib*. Cambridge, MA: Harvard University Press.

Newkirk, T. (2006). 'Media and literacy: What's good?', *Educational Leadership*, 64(1): 62–6.

Nicolopoulou, A. (1993). 'Play, cognitive development, and the social world: Piaget, Vygotsky, and beyond', *Human Development*, 36(1): 1–23.

Nicolopoulou, A. and Cole, M. (1997). 'Literacy and cognition', in D.A. Wagner, L. Venezky, and B.V. Street (eds), *Literacy: An International Handbook*. New York: Garland. pp. 81–6.

Ochs, E. (1988). *Culture and Language Development: Language Acquisition and Language Socialization in a Samoan Village*. Cambridge: Cambridge University Press.

Ochs, E. (1991). 'Socialization through language and interaction: A theoretical introduction', *Issues in Applied Linguistics*, 2(2): 143–7.

Ochs, E. and Schieffelin, B. (1984). 'Language acquisition and socialization: Three developmental stories and their implications', in R. Shweder and R. Le Vine (eds). *Culture Theory: Essays on Mind, Self and Emotion*. New York: Cambridge University Press. pp. 276–320.

Ochs, E. and Schieffelin, B. (1986). 'From feelings to grammar', in B. Schieffelin, and E. Ochs (eds),

Language Socialization Across Cultures. Cambridge: Cambridge University Press. pp. 251–72.

Ochs, E. and Schieffelin, B. (1989). 'Language has a heart: The pragmatics of affect', *Text*, 9(1): 7–25.

Ochs, E. and Schieffelin, B. (1995). 'The impact of language socialization on grammatical Development', in P. Fletcher, and B. MacWhinney (eds), *The Handbook of Child Language.* Oxford: Blackwell. pp. 73–94.

Olson, D.R. (1994). *The World on Paper: The Conceptual and Cognitive Implications of Writing and Reading.* New York: Cambridge University Press.

Ong, W. (1982). *Orality and Literacy.* London: Methuen.

Orellana, M.F. (2001). 'The work kids do: Mexican and Central American children's contributions to households and schools in California', *Harvard Educational Review*, 1(3): 366–89.

Orellana, M.F. and Dwarte, J. (2010). 'A different kind of Head Start: Response to the early literacy panel report'. *Educational Researcher*, 39(4): 295–300.

Pahl, K. (2002). 'Ephemera, mess, and miscellaneous piles: Texts and practices in families', *Journal of Early Childhood Literacy*, 2(2): 145–66.

Palfrey, J. and Gasser, U. (2008). *Born Digital: Understanding the First Generation Of Digital Natives.* New York: Basic Books.

Patrick, E. (2000). 'The self-regulatory nature of preschool children's private speech in a naturalistic setting', *Applied Psycholinguistics*, 21(1): 45–61.

Pellegrini, A. and Galda, L. (1990). 'Children's play, language, and early literacy', *Topics in Language Disorders*, 10(3): 76–88.

Pellegrini, A.D., Galda, L., Bartini, M., and Charak, D. (1998). 'Oral language and literacy learning in context: The role of social relationships', *Merrill-Palmer Quarterly*, 44: 38–54.

Philips, S. (1972). 'Participation structures and communicative competence: Warm Springs children in community and classroom', in C. Cazden, P. John, and D. Hymes (eds), *Functions of Language in the Classroom.* New York: Teachers College Press.

Philips, S. (1982). *The Invisible Culture: Communication in Classroom and Community on the Warm Springs Indian Reservation.* New York: Longman.

Piaget, J. (1951). *The Child's Conception of the World.* London: Routledge and Kegan Paul.

Piaget, J. (1962). *The Language and Thought of the Child.* Tr. M. Gabain. Cleveland, OH: Meridian Books.

Razfar, A. and Yang, E. (2010). 'Sociocultural theory and early literacy development: Hybrid language practices in the digital age', *Language Arts*, 88(2): 114–124.

Razfar, A., and Yang, E. (in preparation). Sociocultural theory and early literacy development: A review of research.

Read, C. (1971). 'Pre-school children's knowledge of English phonology', in *Harvard Educational Review.* Cambridge, MA: Educational Board, Harvard University.

Reese, L., and Gallimore, R. (2000). 'Immigrant Latinos cultural model of literacy development: An evolving perspective on home-school discontinuities', *American Journal of Education*, 108(2): 103-34.

Reyes, M. and Halcon, J. (eds) (2001). *The Best for our Children: Latino/Latino Voices on Literacy.* New York: Teachers College Press.

Reyes, L.V. and Torres, M.N. (2007). 'Decolonizing family literacy in a culture circle: Reinventing the family literacy educator's role', *Journal of Early Childhood Literacy*, 7(1): 73–94.

Robinson, M. and Mackey, M. (2003). *Film and Television: Handbook of Early Childhood Literacy.* London: Sage. pp. 127–42.

Rogoff, B. (1990). *Apprenticeship in Thinking: Cognitive Development in Social Context.* New York: Oxford University Press.

Rogoff, B. (2003). *The Cultural Nature of Human Development.* New York: Oxford University Press.

Rogoff, B. and Angelillo, C. (2002). 'Investigating the coordinated functioning of multifaceted cultural practices in human development'. *Human Development*, 45(4): 211–25.

Rueda, R. and McIntyre, E. (2002). 'Toward universal literacy', in S. Stringfield and D. Land (eds.), *Educating At Risk Students: One Hundred First Yearbook of the National Society for the Study of Education.* Chicago, IL: University of Chicago Press. pp. 189–209.

Schieffelin, B. (1990). *The Give and Take of Everyday Life: Language Socialization of Kaluli Children.* New York: Cambridge University Press.

Schieffelin, B. and Gilmore, P. (1986). *The Acquisition of Literacy: Ethnographic Perspectives.* Norwood, NJ: Ablex.

Schweinhart, L., Barnes, H., and Weikart, D. (eds) (1993). *Significant Benefits: The High/Scope Perry Preschool Study Through Age 27.* Ypsilanti, MI: High/Scope Press.

Scollon, R. (2001). 'Action and text: Toward an integrated understanding of the place of text in social (inter)action', in R. Wodak and M. Meyer (eds), *Methods in Critical Discourse Analysis.* London: Sage. pp. 139–83.

Scollon, R. and Scollon, S. (1981). *Narrative and Face in Inter-Ethnic Communication.* Norwood, NJ: Ablex.

Scribner, S. (1984a). 'Literacy in three metaphors', *American Journal of Education*, 95 (1): 6–21.

Scribner, S. (1984b). 'The practice of literacy: where mind and society meet', in S.J. White and V. Teller (eds), *Annals of the New York Academy of Sciences: Discourses in Reading and Linguistics*, 433: 5–39.

Scribner, S. and Cole, M. (1978). 'Literacy without schooling: Testing for intellectual effects'. *Harvard Educational Review*, 48(4): 448–61.

Scribner, S. and Cole, M. (1981). *The Psychology of Literacy*. Cambridge, MA: Harvard University Press.

Scribner, S., Goody, J., and Cole, M. (1977). 'Writing and formal operations: A case study among the Vai', *Africa*, 47: 289–304.

Searle, J.R. (1969). *Speech Acts*. Cambridge: Cambridge University Press.

Siegler, R. and Crowley, K. (1991). 'The microgenetic method: A direct means for studying cognitive development', *American Psychologist*, 46(6): 606–20.

Skinner, B.F. (1957). *Verbal Behavior*. New York: Appleton-Century-Crofts.

Smith, C.R. (2001). 'Click and turn the page: An exploration of multiple storybook literacy', *Reading Research Quarterly*, 36(2): 152–83.

Smith, C.R. (2002). 'Click on me! An example of how a toddler used technology in play', *Journal of Early Childhood Literacy*, 2(1): 5–20.

Snow, C. (1977). 'The development of conversation between mothers and babies', *Journal of Child Language*, 4: 1–22.

Stahl, S.A. and Miller, P.D. (1989). 'Whole language and language experience approaches for beginning reading: A quantitative research synthesis', *Review of Educational Research* 59(1): 87–116.

Street, B. (1987). 'Literacy and orality as ideological constructions: Some problems in cross cultural studies' *Culture and History*. Copenhagen: Museum Tusculanum Press.

Street, B. (1993). 'Introduction: The new literacy studies', in B. Street (ed.), *Cross-cultural Approaches to Literacy*. Cambridge: Cambridge University Press. pp. 1–21.

Street, B. (ed.) (2001). *Literacy and Development: Ethnographic Perspectives*. New York: Routledge.

Stone, L. and Gutiérrez, K. (2007). 'Problem articulation and the processes of assistance: An activity theoretic view of mediation in game play', *International Journal of Educational Research*, 46(1–2): 43–56.

Sulzby, E. and Teale, W. (1991). 'Emergent literacy', in R. Barr, M.L. Kamil, P.B. Mosenthal, and P.D. Pearson (eds), *Handbook of Reading Research*. Vol. 2. New York: Longman. pp. 727–57.

Taylor, L.K., Bernhard, J.K., Garg, S., and Cummins, J. (2008). 'Affirming plural belonging: Building on students' family-based cultural and linguistic capital through multiliteracies Pedagogy', *Journal of Early Childhood Literacy*, 8(3): 269–94.

Teale, W. and Sulzby, E. (1986). *Emergent Literacy: Writing and Reading*. Norwood, NJ: Ablex.

Teale, W. and Sulzby, E. (1987). 'Literacy acquisition in early childhood: The roles of access and mediation in storybook reading', in D.A. Wagner (ed.), *The Future of Literacy in a Changing World*. New York: Pergamon. pp. 111–30.

Thorndike, E. (1921). *The Teacher's Word Book*. New York: Teachers College Press.

Trueba, H.T. (1999). 'Critical ethnography and a Vygotskian pedagogy of hope: The empowerment of Mexican immigrant children', *International Journal for Qualitative Studies in Education*, 12(6): 591–614.

Tudge, J. (1990). 'Vygotsky, the zone of proximal development, and peer collaboration: Implications for classroom practice', in L.C. Moll (ed.), *Vygotsky and Education*. Cambridge: Cambridge University Press. pp. 154–74.

US Department of Education (2008). *Reading First Impact Study: Interim Report*. Retrieved from http://ies.ed.gov/ncee/pdf/20084016.pdf

Van der Veer, R. and Valsiner, J. (1991). *Understanding Vygotsky*. London: Blackwell.

Valsiner, J. (1997). *Culture and the Development of Children's Actions: a Theory of Human Development* (2nd ed.). Chichester: John Wiley & Sons.

Vásquez, O.A. (2003). *La Clasé Magica: Imagining Optimal Possibilities in a Bilingual Community of Learners*. Mahwah, NJ: Erlbaum.

Vernon-Feagans, L., Hammer, C.S., Miccio, A., and Manlove, E. (2001). 'Early language and literacy skills in low-income African American and Hispanic children', in S. Neuman and D.K. Dickinson (eds), *Handbook for Research on Early Literacy*. New York: Guilford. pp. 192–210.

Vygotsky, L.V. (1978). *Mind in Society*. Cambridge, MA: Harvard University Press.

Vygotsky, L.V. (1981). 'The instrumental method in psychology', in J.V. Wertsch (ed.), *The Concept of Activity in Soviet Psychology*. Armonk, New York: M.E. Sharpe. pp. 134–44.

Vygotsky, L.S. (1987). *The Collected Works of L.S. Vygotsky. Vol. 1: Problems of General Psychology*, R. Rieber and A. Carton (eds). Tr. N. Minick. New York: Plenum.

Weisner, T.S. and Gallimore, R. (1977). 'My brother's keeper: Child and sibling caretaking, *Current Anthropology*, 18(2): 169–90.

Wells, G. (ed.) (1981). *Learning Through Interaction: The Study of Language Development*. Vol. 1. Cambridge: Cambridge University Press.

Wells, G. (1985). 'Pre-school literacy related activities and success in school', in D. Olson, N. Torrance, and A. Hilyard (eds), *Literacy, Language and Learning*. Cambridge: Cambridge University Press.

Wells, G. and Claxton, G. (2002). *Learning for Life in the 2lst Century*. Oxford: Blackwell.

Wertsch, J. (1978). 'Adult-child interaction and the roots of metacognition', *Quarterly Newsletter of the Institute for Comparative Human Development*, 2: 15–18.

Wertsch, J. (1985). *Vygotsky and the Social Formation of Mind*. Cambridge, MA: Harvard University Press.

Wertsch, J.V. (1991). *Voices of the Mind: A Sociocultural Approach to Mediated Action*. Cambridge, MA: Harvard University Press, Cambridge.

Wertsch, J. and Hickmann, M. (1987). 'Problem-solving in social interaction: A microgenetic Analysis', in M. Hickmann (ed.), *Social and Functional Approaches to Language and Thought*. Orlando, FL: Academic.

White, K. (1982). 'The relation between socioeconomic status and academic achievement', *Psychological Bulletin*, 91: 461–81.

Whiting, B. and Whiting, X. (1975). *Children of Six Cultures*. Cambridge, MA: Harvard University Press.

Wiggins, G. (2011). 'A diploma worth having', *Educational Leadership*, 68(6): 28–33.

Willett, R., Robinson, M. and Marsh, J. (eds) (2009). *Play, Creativity and Digital Cultures*. New York, London: Routledge.

Wohlwend, K.E. (2009). 'Early adopters: Playing new literacies and pretending new technologies in print-centric classrooms', *Journal of Early Childhood Literacy*, 9(2): 117–40.

Wollman-Bonilla, J.E. (2001). 'Family involvement in early writing instruction', *Journal of Early Childhood Literacy*, 1(2), 167–92.

5

Play, Literacies, and the Converging Cultures of Childhood

Karen E. Wohlwend

In an era where rapid and widespread change is commonplace, it is not surprising that our ideas about play, literacy, and childhood are also in transition. It is increasingly difficult to separate ways of reading, writing, playing, consuming, producing, and projecting a text that are available in proliferating and constantly-morphing technologies. Even very young children read, write, or play on hand-held interactive screens, their at-home browsings mediated by distant others across global networks. Whether in play at home, on playgrounds, in classrooms, or in virtual worlds, children are producing dynamic texts that are co-played and co-written with others. Yet, early childhood educators know this has always been the case with play. Dramatic play often requires children to stop and work out the roles and meanings of their shared narrative and materials: who will play 'Mother', what

should happen next, and whether a tattered cardboard box represents a car or a doll bed. What *has* changed is the ways that negotiated and co-played literacies weave in and out of daily living within a thick mesh of overlapping cultures that make up twenty-first century childhoods (Medina and Wohlwend, in press).

In this chapter, *culture* is defined as neither a monolithic construct nor a geographically bounded and othered group but as a glocally situated space defined by values, artifacts, and ways of doing things and being with others in a particular context (Scollon, 2001). *Play* is defined as a social and semiotic practice that facilitates pivots to imagined contexts by recontextualizing classroom reality and maintaining a 'not-real' frame (Goffman, 1974). This chapter maps changing relationships around literacy and play within converging childhood cultures – school, peer, home, consumer, and digital – by looking closely at the tangle of literacies, texts, and identities in these spaces with the aim of considering how playful literacies might proliferate pathways for learning, such as pretending which opens access to children's familiar cultural contexts, resources, and ways of knowing.

CONVERGING CULTURES

Children engage literacy in multiple, interconnected cultures – in their homes (Kendrick, 2003), communities, and online sites – engagements that require expanded repertoires for managing complex texts in a new textual landscape (Carrington, 2005). The concept of *cultural convergence* (Jenkins, Clinton, Purushotma, Robison, and Weigel, 2006) provides a way of understanding these dense sites of childhood as multiple, fluid, overlapping, blurred, and simultaneously local and global. Cultural convergence:

- merges literacy, technology, and popular media with artifacts of everyday living (e.g., toys, fast food, clothing, toothbrushes, etc.);
- fuses media narratives with material products, enacted desires, social relationships, sensory environments, and literacy practices;
- blurs consumption, production, identity, representation, and learning.

To track children's literacy practices in these convergences, many early literacy researchers have moved out of classrooms into out-of-school spaces, including digital cultures where young children are logging on to participate in social networks (Dowdall, 2009) and reading, writing, and representing selves in online worlds (Black, 2010; Marsh, 2011; Merchant, 2011).

Each cultural context circulates particular discourses – socially expected patterns of 'using language, other symbolic expressions, and "artifacts," of thinking, feeling, believing, valuing, and acting that can be used to identify oneself as a member' among a group of people (Gee, 1996: 131). In each culture, whether in schools, homes, or virtual worlds, particular ways of combining voice, gaze, and handling objects come to be expected and tacitly valued. These combinations create a web of practices that appear as natural-seeming ways of participating that act as markers of identity (e.g., insider/outsider; novice/expert) that uphold unspoken patterns of inclusion and exclusion (Scollon, 2001).

MULTIPLYING LITERACY

When cultures converge, their literacies and discourses converge as well. Children's literacy practices are situated in and distributed among convergences of schools, playgrounds, homes, neighborhoods, communities, consumer markets, technological flows, and transnational networks (Gee, 1996; New London Group, 1996; Street, 1995). Literacies are stretched and contested in these mergers, spinning off new ways of making meaning. To understand the semiotic power of these innovative practices, we must expand extant definitions of literacy and texts, looking beyond reading and writing a page of print to include video sharing, photoshopping, blogging, commenting, tweeting and retweeting, podcasting, text messaging, and other ways of participating in global social networks. This redefinition recognizes that written language makes up only one possible aspect of any literacy. Literacies are multimodal, producing texts that co-ordinate many modes, such as 'image, gaze, gesture, movement, music, speech, and sound-effect' (Kress and

Jewitt, 2003: 1). Increasingly, literacies are interactive in ways that blur the line between readers and writers and consumers and producers, generating multimodal texts that reach across networks among multiple players, co-produced with a collaborative audience (Knobel and Lankshear, 2007).

Multiple literacies encompass more than digital practices and online environments:

> the move from literacy to literacies expands the ways we think about familiar nondigital events such as play enactments, drawings, commercial toys, classroom layouts, and so on. These changes present an opportunity to rethink play as a new literacy and at the same time, revive it as a staple of early childhood curricula. We can now recognize play as a literacy for creating and coordinating a live-action text among multiple players that invests materials with pretended meanings and slips the constraints of here-and-now realities.
> (Wohlwend, 2011: 2)

GLOBALIZING PLAY

Converging cultures, literacies, and discourses challenge commonplace understandings of children's play as developmentally appropriate and innocent activity. In earlier decades, literacy play research and practice focused on classroom spaces and instructional strategies often bounded by the housekeeping corner. Teachers infused literacy into dramatic play centers by providing telephone books, grocery coupons, and other print materials for children to use as props in dramatic play scenarios (Owocki, 1999). Sociocultural perspectives showed us that children play purposefully to make sense of their cultural worlds (Göncü, 1999).

The unique ambiguity of play (Sutton-Smith, 1997) is useful for establishing child space separate from the official space of the classroom where children can temporarily suspend school rules and teacher surveillance. Play purposefully masks meanings, twists language forms, slips cultural constraints, and muddies its own definitions, producing perfect conditions for testing power and stretching the ideological limits of the surrounding culture within a deniable, and therefore, safe space. Whatever happens within a play frame is ostensibly innocuous. Play provides a seemingly innocent space where rebellious acts or threats to authority can be paradoxically expressed and denied by framing the offending action as, 'We were only playing' (Geertz, 1973).

Further, play in digital spaces involves navigating screens and projecting identities across global networks. In these immersive flows, children's play involves identity production as well as textual engagement with messages in commercial media, video games, advertised goods, and projected virtual worlds. Children in Sydney or Mexico City or London draw upon the same popular media that are produced and filmed in Hollywood, materialized in toys and goods manufactured in China, and franchised for global distribution by a single multinational corporation.

In this chapter, I reconceptualize play as an embodied literacy and situate it among young children's multiple literacies in the convergences of overlapping cultural spaces: school, home and community, peer, media, digital, and consumer cultures. Rather than a comprehensive review of the expanding and interdisciplinary literature on play, I draw upon a few key studies within each cultural frame (listed in Table 5.1) to tease out the cultural convergences and overlapping literacies to ask: What are the relationships among literacy practices, identities, and artifacts in children's play in and among cultural convergences? And where do we go from here?

Table 5.1   Selected studies across childhood cultures

Researchers/studies	Year	School	Peer	Home and community	Consumer	Digital
Kontovourki and Seigel	2009	x				
Rowe	2008	x				
Paley	2010	x	x			
Dyson	2003	x	x		x	
Wohlwend	2007	x	x		x	
Kendrick	2005		x	x		
Long, Volk, and Gregory	2007		x	x		
Edmiston	2008		x			
Marsh	2005		x	x		
Carrington	2005		x	x		
Sekeres	2009		x	x		
Carrington	2003			x		x
Lee	2009		x	x		
Vasquez	2005		x	x	x	
Grimes	2010		x		x	x
Marsh	2011			x	x	x
Black	2010				x	x
Wohlwend, Vander Zanden, Husbye, and Kuby	2011	x		x		x

PLAYING TO BE AND BELONG IN CHILDHOOD CULTURES

Playing to read and write in school cultures

Ironically in the early twenty-first century, when the ways of producing, sending, and receiving messages are expanding at a mind-numbing rate (Luke, 2007), accountability trends in the US, the UK, and elsewhere have dramatically constrained what counts as literacy in early childhood classrooms (Marsh, 2010; Stipek, 2006). For example, Early Reading First, a US federal grant program for early childhood centers, circulated a reductive model of early literacy that equated learning with mastery of a limited range of skills in oral language, phonological awareness, print awareness, and alphabetic knowledge (www2.ed.gov/programs/earlyreading/performance.html).

As governmental and administrative policy mandates focused on raising academic achievement scores measured through standardized screenings and tests, teachers faced pressure to adjust their instruction to focus on skills/tasks that closely matched the tests (e.g., letter naming, sound segmentation). In early childhood classrooms, skills practice and scripted curricula filled the schedule and squeezed out harder-to-test but richer and deeper learning in purposeful, inquiry-based reading, writing, and play (Miller and Almon, 2009; Stipek, 2006).

These restrictive conditions continue to shape many *school cultures*, the shared set of valued dispositions, practices, and artifacts that carry out 'the broad educational mission and demands for group participation inherent within classrooms' (Fernie, Madrid, and Kantor, 2011: 3). In school cultures molded in the pressure-cooker of high-stakes testing, many early childhood teachers find it difficult to defend and preserve a curricular space for play, documented regularly in US newspapers that report widespread concerns that time for play is disappearing in schools (Brown, 2009; Stewart, 2005; Weil, 2007).

A recent meta-analysis of studies on literacy play in early childhood classrooms illustrates three prevalent school culture perspectives. Roskos and colleagues (2010) categorized 30 years of literacy play research in early childhood education, mapping right, middle, and left positions onto three models of play (Smith, 2010):

- right: 'play has no important function';
- middle: 'play is one of many routes';
- left: 'play is essential for development' (Roskos, Christie, Widman, and Holding, 2010: 57–58).

The left model aligns with the view of play proponents who are concerned about the erosion of play in schools (Hirsh-Pacek, Golinkoff, Berk, and Singer, 2009; Miller and Almon, 2009) while the right 'anti-play' position drives policies that privilege direct instruction over playful exploration. The authors identified with a middle position that promotes 'blended early literacy programs' that use 'guided play' to develop early literacy skills 'such as print concepts of print and alphabet knowledge [which] can be developed through a variety of strategies, including literacy-enriched dramatic play, games, storybook reading, language experience dictation, and age-appropriate direct instruction' (p. 58). However, the meta-analysis was limited by interventionist framing which privileges quasi-experimental and experimental research designs. Only 16 studies met the authors' criteria for a viable intervention and only two of these were conducted in the last decade, so it is difficult to know how well the findings of the meta-analysis reflect the current status of classroom literacy play in the wake of governmental accountability mandates, mushrooming media franchises marketed to young children, the advent of the internet, and so on. Quantitative studies that attempt to test the effects of play (e.g., play as a variable in an experimental design to measure its efficacy as a literacy intervention) are not equipped to capture the depth of learning and nuanced relationships among children's play, reading, and writing across rapidly-changing cultures.

Qualitative studies by leading literacy play researchers including Dyson (2003, 2006, 2008), Paley (2004, 2010), and Marsh (1999, 2000) provide a way to investigate a reconceptualized literacy/play relationship within school cultures. Ethnographic research on school cultures shows that through literacy apprenticeships (Rogoff, 1995; Wohlwend, 2007) within play-friendly school cultures, teachers 'seek out opportunities to make space for play in their classrooms as a way to bring children fully into the curriculum whenever possible and to stretch who gets recognized as a successful literacy learner' (Kontovourki and Siegel, 2009: 32). For example, Rowe's (2007, 2008, 2010) studies show that play-based teacher–toddler apprenticeships in preschool classrooms develop children's understandings of the meanings of book content as well as social expectations for readers and writers. In 2-year-olds' book-to-play connections, as children move from shared meanings in read-alouds to collaborative dramatic play, they also shift their semiotic stance: 'from comprehension to reflection as children represent book meanings in the new sign system of play…' (2007: 59).

Paley's (2004, 2010) classroom research demonstrates that kindergarten children play to make meaning through their invented narratives as well as to make sense of their lived lives. Her rich portraits depict preschool children authoring stories and selves through pretense in a responsive school culture that values children's narratives. Here, play provides a conduit that allows children to import their personal literacy resources and lived histories into the classroom. Further, the collaborative nature of play enables storying with others as children engage in the shared project of making sense of the events in their individual lives. She poses the question:

> Do children make up their stories in order to play? Or do they play in order to put themselves in a story? Perhaps the secret lies in another direction. What if children play *and* invent stories because it is the way to distinguish themselves from all the other individuals, even as they reach for common ground and community?
>
> (Paley, 2010: xii)

Even without dedicated curricular space, it is probable that young children are always/already playing in school cultures, under the teacher's radar and during curricular activities such as writing workshop. For example, Kontovourki and Siegel (2009) found that kindergarten children shifted their play to comply with school culture expectations whenever the teacher approached, in order 'to leverage time for play'.

Playing to belong in peer cultures

In contrast to a top-down perspective on play that looks for a deferred benefit (e.g., play leads to increased academic achievement measured by standardized test scores), a 'sideways glance' (Schwartzman, 1976) reveals how children learn from and with each other through their literacy interactions and play transformations as they collectively imagine new social contexts, import literacy resources, and negotiate pretended identities. For example, a sideways glance reveals players' complex

positioning among selves, other players, and enacted characters:

> The metaphor captures the idea that if you look to the side of a child at play, you inevitably find other children. From this perspective, children become not only the subjects, but also the objects of their own play because they are required to simultaneously define and communicate who they are in the play event and who they are as real people in the social context ... From this perspective, a sideways glance at play as a communicative event has the potential to disclose 'a story that players tell themselves about themselves'.
>
> (Kendrick, 2005: 6)

Research from a sideways perspective asks, 'How do children mean and belong through their play?' that is, how does play create shared meanings and narratives, sustain friendships, and provide social benefits in the immediate peer culture? Corsaro (1985) defined *peer culture* as a set of 'common activities, routines, artifacts, values, concerns, and attitudes' (p. 171) developed by children for children in a particular space. Peer culture is ideologically structured

> by the possibilities and limits of the physical environment, by the socially constructed peer culture of this event (a patterned history of who plays with whom, around what themes, where, and with what materials), by the wider school culture (norms and expectations for materials use, appropriate and inappropriate behavior, etc.), and by participants explicit and implicit understandings of this way of doing everyday life in their setting.
>
> (Kantor and Fernie, 2003: 210)

Young children open and restrict access to group play in order to protect their fragile construction of negotiated meanings and play frames. Corsaro (2003) viewed this conflict as productive, resulting in negotiations that allowed children to preserve their pretense while they worked out social relationships in a multiparty space.

Dyson (2003) describes the collaborative playful composing of 6- and 7-year-old children who wrote 'from inside a particular child culture out toward school demands' (p. 5). The children in this classroom used play to imagine a pretend school family – the 'brothers and sisters' – as they appropriated 'textual toys' from popular media – bits of songs, rap, playground rhymes, sports talk – and remixed the texts to make them their own while tapping into popular appeal in ways that reconfigured and upheld classroom social relationships. Similarly in a preschool classroom, children drew upon superhero roles to assume leadership positions in peer culture and altered superhero play narratives to accommodate peers in ways that strengthened children's friendships, in part due to thoughtful negotiations by teachers (Galbraith, 2011). In one toddler classroom, teachers negotiated the peer culture interest in wrestling and rough and tumble play with school culture concern for children's physical safety, leading to innovative practices (Sanderson, 2011). In classrooms like this, teachers acknowledge and engage peer cultures so that they converge 'in ways that create a mutually supportive intersection ...' (Fernie, Madrid, and Kantor, 2011: 3). '[I]f teachers take play seriously, that is, as a way to learn more about children and their literacies, they may come to treat it as a valuable resource for child and teacher learning' (Kontovourki and Siegel, 2009: 37).

In other classrooms, peer and school cultures do not always mesh comfortably. In some classrooms, Dyson (2006, 2008, 2010) found that children's cultural resources and peer culture purposes are devalued and supplanted by a school culture focused on 'the basics'. Despite such constraints, young children did find ways to play to gain more control over literacy practices and as a source of pleasure and a resource for transforming social relationships and peer culture.

Playing to participate in home and community cultures

Through history and around the world, children have played at home, learning from siblings, parents, and grandparents, appropriating materials, gathering cultural resources, and trying out their developing repertoire of social practices as they participate in neighborhoods and communities (Göncü, 1999). Long, Volk, and Gregory (2007) explored how children learned from siblings and friends as they co-created and sustained play scenarios in ways that developed their multilingual abilities and knowledges. Three case studies in multicultural environments – an American child with Icelandic friends, Puerto Rican siblings in the Midwest United States, and Bangladeshi siblings in England – showed that children actively and intentionally pooled their cultural literacy resources and produced blended multilingual texts that enriched and supported their immediate play goals and literacy performances, whether playing *house*, *school*, or *church*. Arguing against deficit perspectives that marginalize 'children from nondominant cultures by focusing on what they do not know and what they are not able to do,' the authors found that in play, children syncretically:

> drew on multiple schemas, perspectives, and texts; negotiated with play partners; and kept an eye to the future. They understood what counted as knowledge in home, school, and community settings and practiced the use of that knowledge in their play. They rarely privileged one culture or learner over another. Reciprocity of learning and teaching did not necessarily assume the superior knowledge of older children or dominant language speakers as they alternated, sometimes moment to moment, between the roles of expert and novice.
> (Long et al., 2007: 254)

Literacy researchers who play alongside children also find that playing allows children to explore tensions and power relations among cultures and languages as they imagine 'communities to which they hope to belong' (Kendrick, 2005: 9), imaginings that allow them to expand their participation in their lived communities of practice. Kendrick acted as playmate-researcher to better understand the interplay of tensions across gender roles, imagined communities, and lived communities in a Vietnamese-Canadian 5-year-old girl's pretend play:

> Her narrativized stories convey the idea that multiple elements of her world relate to one another in the form of a story or drama.... In this way, play affords a particular 'gaze' on Leticia's subject matter; it reveals her personal interpretation about events in her social and cultural world and her participation in those events. For instance, by scripting and dramatizing her ideas of romance, motherhood, family relationships and possibilities for her future, Leticia communicates her understanding of what it means to be a woman in her particular family and culture.
>
> (Kendrick, 2005: 22)

Play enables reversals of power relations as children play into their expertise and imagine identities as more proficient literacy users. Players are on equal footing, with adults learning alongside children. In Edmiston's (2008) case study on mythic play with his son, learning was reciprocal and co-constructed as the adult followed the child's lead through fluid scenarios. As a parent, Edmiston encountered difficult dilemmas about how much violence to allow and whether to enter into war play, dilemmas that opened opportunities to imagine and play ethical selves. Drawing upon Vygotsky and Bakhtin, Edmiston theorized these productive moments as a 'workshop of life' that allowed parent and child to collaboratively confront issues of identity within the safety of pretense.

Playing to 'produse' in consumer cultures

An expanded definition of literacy that recognizes play as an embodied literacy must also acknowledge the importance of toys as texts; this recognition implicates consumer identities as well as player identities. For example, Carrington (2003) argued that Diva Starz fashion dolls are identity texts with anime-like features and pre-recorded snippets that voice 'cool girl' scripts, and position doll players as shoppers and fashionistas:

> The texts of consumer culture provide displays of available identities and lives. These texts are built around displays of style and taste, and children are being trained in particular patterns and knowledges around consumption. These texts are what they reflect – they are unashamedly commodities to be purchased and consumed, linked to the assumption of particular consumer identities.
>
> (Carrington, 2003: 94)

Dolls without pre-recorded messages also 'talk' and convey identity texts but through their accompanying film narratives as in Disney Princesses (Wohlwend, 2009) or book series such as *American Girls* (Sekeres, 2009; Marshall, 2011). These films and books provide foundational narratives that anchor multibillion dollar product franchises for multinational companies with global distribution:

> In the 20th century, the concentration of publishing for children into a small number of megacorporations, the development of synergistic marketing of multiple products of one brand, and the technological advances of the late-20th century contributed to what can be called 'branded fiction,' a genre that includes books that are one product among many that are all sold under one brand name. Within the context of branded fiction, the reader constructs the imaginary characters of the fiction through the multiple experiences of buying and living with the multiple products of a brand.
>
> (Sekeres, 2009: 399)

As children play, read, and live as the inter-texts of branded fiction, children not only consume but also produce their own meanings; they construct their own notions of characters, whether Samantha of *American*

Girls or Hannah Montana on the Disney cable network.

This kind of active meaning making is not limited to toys associated with books or other media. Children live, play, and mean in consumer cultures that flow into every aspect of everyday life. Cook (2008) points out that people do not choose to be consumers; rather we are born into 'regimes of consumption' in commercialized societies where opting out of consumption is impossible. Young children are not only targets but also participants in markets where they are key actors in shaping demand and corporate response for a range of products in franchises that include clothing, household goods, school supplies, films, video games, toys (Seiter, 1993), and even fast food toys:

> Yet, it is not a stretch to argue that there would be no McDonald's as we know it and perhaps no McDonaldization without children – that is, without living, breathing youngsters who visit there and enter into the imaginative domain created by the brand (Kincheloe, 2002). Children serve as the audience for the McDonaldland characters, the market for the Happy Meals and cross promotions, the consumers of Big Macs, the users of the Playlands and a key impetus for adult patronage of the stores.
>
> (Cook, 2008: 226)

Clearly, children are anticipated to become active economic subjects from an early age. Research tends to clump in two dichotomous perspectives on young children's participation in global media and toy markets. On one side, children are perceived as unknowing innocents who are easily exploited by marketing tactics of multinational conglomerates that determine their consumption habits (e.g., Steinberg and Kincheloe, 1997). Children are susceptible and imitative in this view, simply replaying the scripts and copying the stereotypes in their favorite films or video games (Linn, 2004). The opposing position finds more agency and power in young consumers'

buying and media understanding (Buckingham, 2000), arguing that young children remix media narratives for their own purposes and produce their own counter texts while taking pleasure in playing with media toys. However, an exploited/empowered dichotomy relies on an individuated view of the child, operating in isolation and insulated from commercial influence:

> Hence, it is important for scholars to be cognizant of the often unexamined assumption that posits children as somehow outside the realm of economic life who are then brought into it either by caring adults, like parents or teachers, or dragged in by media and marketers. That line which divides 'in' from 'out' fades every day as structures of capital help structure the imagining of the worlds into which a child enters well before its postpartum existence.
>
> (Cook, 2008: 236)

In converged consumer, home, and peer cultures, young children exercise power in shaping adult purchases of franchised goods as parents support their passion for particular media characters such as Thomas the Tank Engine. Marsh's (2005) studies involving working class families of 2-, 3-, and 4-year-old children showed that parents purchased consumer goods associated with children's favorite media. These media characters, texts, and materials form a narrative web which children use as semiotic resources for performing literate identities. For example, one child's narrative web for Disney's *Winnie the Pooh* franchise included stuffed toys, Duplo playsets, pajamas, lunchboxes, comics, and so on. The products in narrative webs enabled parent–child rituals tied to emotional security as well as literacy and identity development. Pugh's (2009) ethnographic research with 5- to 9-year-old children and their families and teachers traces the complicated classed, raced, and emotional meanings attached to use of popular media when consumption is interpreted as care, when good parenting is equated with limiting children's access to media, and when 'fitting in' with peers requires media-savvy displays. The complicated negotiations of 'economies of dignity' that merged material goods, emotions, and identities show that much more is at stake than simply buying a particular product. Parents and children across communities were equally concerned with children's consumption and desires as issues of belonging in local peer cultures and coping with the 'ratcheting up' of consumer culture. In my 3-year ethnographic study of play in classrooms, kindergartners played, wrote, and rewrote familiar Disney Princess narratives for their own films in which for example, Sleeping Beauty revived herself and fought off the dragon (Wohlwend, 2011). Drawing upon de Certeau's (1984) productive consumption, I conceptualized these kindergarten players as *produsers* (Bruns, 2008) who used microtactics to repurpose and twist the meanings of the media they consumed. Similarly, Lee (2009) found that young Korean girls twisted Disney Princess media narratives into personal texts that could reflect their own cultural and transnational experiences in the US. These kinds of micro-interactions, negotiations, and remakings pool in the marketplace, driving popularity and producing global trends and fads (e.g., Pokémon; Tobin, 2004; Vasquez, 2005) that make and break companies.

Playing to connect in digital cultures

Connectivity is the hallmark of play and literacy in online contexts. For example, playing in video games across massive networks involves reading, writing, responding, and participating in collaborations and competitions with unknown others. Online interactions produce 'thick play' and 'slippery texts' (Mackey, 2009)

with layered meanings that enable multiple interpretations. Researchers have followed children into digital space to understand whether children's play with e-books, video games, virtual worlds, and smart phones offers opportunities for more complex production and participation than available in face-to-face spaces. While there are many new technologies and apps for children to use, there are few digital cultures where children can participate in an online environment and interact with other children. Virtual worlds are a notable exception.

We know little about literacy practices in virtual worlds for young children, although the popularity of these sites continues to grow. In early 2011, Webkinz had 16 million accounts, Club Penguin 63 million, and barbiegirls 23 million (Kzero Worldswide, 2011). The studies that have been published to date suggest that the literacies that children engage in virtual worlds are severely constrained by corporate gatekeeping, Internet safety concerns, and consumer privacy policies, in Club Penguin (Marsh, 2011; Grimes, 2010), in Webkinz (Black, 2010; Wohlwend, Vander Zanden, Husbye, and Kuby, 2011), and in barbiegirls (Grimes, 2010; Wohlwend and Peppler, in press). Online worlds for young children converge home, school, consumer, and digital cultures in ways that restrict children's access to meaningful play. Black's (2010) content analysis of Webkinz, a world populated with virtual pets, reveals 'a designed culture with limitations on learning and a constrained set of literacies and social messages ... [such as] restrictions on the site's messaging systems that seriously hinder young players' ability to use in-game communication as a scaffold for their expressive literacy development' (p. 21). In a study in an after-school program, my colleagues and I found that 5- to 7-year-old children often ignored print-dense pop-up help and navigation screens intended to help guide them through the Webkinz world. Instead they relied on their knowledge of intuitive gaming conventions but this was not always enough to overcome the security barriers to online interaction (Wohlwend et al., 2011). Grimes (2010) conceptualizes children's virtual worlds as 'sites of struggle, in which children are in constant negotiation with the games' formal and informal "rule systems," which include industry trends, design choices, game rules, and government policy' (p. 203). Through her analysis of End User Licensing Agreements (EULAs) and her digital ethnographic study while playing as an avatar in six virtual worlds, Grimes found that a foregrounded concern for children's online safety in these sites justifies restrictions on child expression and peer interaction. Absent is a concern for critical interrogation of the backgrounded and abundant marketing and branding strategies endemic in these commercially sponsored worlds.

Children's playful literacies in online spaces remain important means for social interactions and meaning production, although they differ remarkably from the kinds of collaborative and negotiated play that occurs in offline spaces. Marsh's (2010, 2011) analyses of Club Penguin indicate that despite seemingly random and chaotic interactions, children used literacy practices as a 'social glue' to form a coherent social order. These practices afforded a certain agency 'as the children decided when, where, and how to use ritualistic discourse to build communities and demonstrated choice and control over their communicative practices, albeit within the constraints imposed by the producers of the virtual worlds' (2011: 131). The emergence of virtual worlds as key sites for children's digital cultures suggests the need to help children interrogate online play sites and to work toward creating and sustaining digital spaces with opportunities for creative production.

DIRECTIONS FOR TEACHING AND RESEARCH

Play is messy, situated in overlapping and conflicting contexts, and slippery, with shifts that happen moment-to-moment. But because play depends upon co-operation and shared recognition among players, there is a need to negotiate and improvise, causing the tensions between overlapping cultures to become visible and audible as players work through ambiguities in pretend identities and shared meanings. Through play, children:

- participate to take up valued roles in literate communities;
- explore literacy practices and identities in a safe 'not-real' space;
- imagine themselves and identify as literacy users;
- reflect, replay, and record their lived experiences;
- negotiate and collaborate to create shared narratives;
- access and appropriate familiar cultural resources to use with literacies;
- use literacies to create cohesive social groups;
- interpret, produse, improvise, and resemiotize a range of texts and artifacts;
- wield texts in ways that reconfigure their relative social positioning;
- connect with others around meaningful texts.

The rich playful learning summarized here from the studies in this chapter clearly indicates the literate potential of play, potential that is overlooked and unrealized in many schools. Educational policies need to recognize that by removing play from school, we are ceding instructional space for this powerful semiotic tool to corporations that by necessity focus on bottom lines, brands, and market share rather than educational goals and outcomes.

Early childhood teachers who make room for play in their classrooms should be prepared to mediate the social and cultural tensions that come with cultural convergence. Play produces complicated mixes of tactics and desires with potential to advantage some children and marginalize others. Players' collective imaginings converge cultures in ways that align with their personal goals, family histories, media passions, and school and peer expectations. A video game storyline with a popular character might be integrated into children's play for its ability to sustain a play scenario, for one fan's personal satisfaction, to improve one child's social positioning in peer culture, to align with prevailing cultural models of masculinity or femininity, and so on.

Researchers who study play need syncretic research designs able to capture the multidirectional relationships and flows of play across cultures. Here I use an activity model to illustrate how multiple lenses combine to tease out the relationships among so many overlapping cultures and potentially conflicting practices, texts, and identities. Expanded applications of cultural–historical activity theory (Engeström, 1987; Vygotsky, 1935/1978; Leont'ev, 1977) explain the complex web of relationships in the situated semiotic activity of children's play across cultures. Each culture can be conceptualized as at least one activity system with social actors wielding cultural tools to transform objects into texts, using accepted practices that fit the rules and roles of a particular community. Figure 5.1 shows a diagram of an expanded activity model that illustrates the relationships in a culture. Each box indicates an aspect of activity that can serve as

a perspective on the activity system; however all parts must be considered as influencing the activity. For example, each activity system generates a set of questions to be answered:

- who (acting with others) doing what;
- with what materials;
- in which cultural context.

Each side of the activity model triangle offers a different orientation for research. The question 'Who doing what?' focuses on social practices, uncovered through ethnographic studies such as Pugh's (2009) study in which she lived and worked among parents and children in three communities to understand how and why they engage consumer culture. Some research designs combine ethnographic data with additional methods of analysis. For example, mediated discourse analysis (Scollon, 2001) employs an ethnographic within a research design that merges activity theory with practice theory (Bourdieu, 1977) to filter social practices of importance to a culture, locating key transformational moments for microanalysis that traces actions which produce social positioning and identity work. The question 'With what materials?' focuses on the design of material resources such as the content analysis of the commercial design of virtual worlds (Black, 2010; Black and Reich, 2012). Another approach from a material orientation examines modes, which are material resources shaped and made available by cultures such as multimodal analysis of the toys that children make for themselves (Wohlwend, 2011) that draws upon social semiotic theories (Kress, 2011) and multimodal interactional discourse studies (Norris, 2004, 2006). The third question 'Which cultural context?' draws upon cultural studies, current and historical geopolitical events and markets, and critical

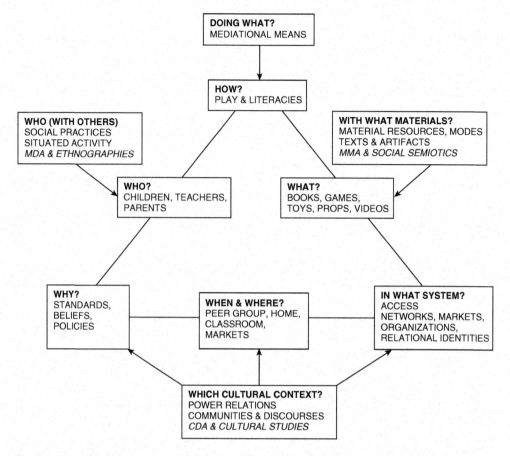

Figure 5.1   An activity model of play in a childhood culture
MDA: Mediated Discourse Analysis, CDA: Critical Discourse Analysis, MMA: Multimodal Analysis

discourse theories and analysis (Gee, 1999) to situate activity and identity building within particular discourses circulating in and around a culture.

Finally, the malleable nature of play makes it a powerful socializing tool that functions as both a means of enculturation of children and a means of cultural mediation by children as they produse played texts to make sense of increasingly complex cultural spaces. Like autonomous views of literacy (Street, 1995), the acceptance of play as an ideologically neutral practice in early childhood settings ignores its facility for social organization and cultural reproduction. An autonomous view of play

emphasizes its surface appeal that makes schoolwork more enjoyable, its amorphous nature that fabricates a simulated reality within the classroom, and its facility for producing imaginative storylines. This adult-centric view fails to consider its usefulness to children, not only as a pleasurable pastime but also as a powerful literacy for reading and writing selves and the world.

REFERENCES

Black, R. W. (2010). The language of Webkinz: Early childhood literacy in an online virtual world. *Digital Culture & Education, 2*(1), 7–24.

Black, R. W. and Reich, S. M. (2012). Culture and community in a virtual world for young children. In C. A. Steinkuehler, K. Squire, and S. Barab (Eds.), *Games, learning, and society: Learning and meaning in the digital age.* New York: Cambridge University Press.

Bourdieu, P. (1977). *Outline of a theory of practice.* Cambridge: Cambridge University Press.

Brown, E. (2009, November 21). The playtime's the thing. *Washington Post.* Retrieved from www.washingtonpost.com/wp-dyn/content/article/2009/11/20/AR2009112002391.html?utm_source=feedburner&utm_medium=feed&utm_campaign=Feed%3A+StatelineorgRss-TaxesBudget+(Stateline.org+RSS+-+Taxes+%26+Budget)

Bruns, A. (2008). *Blogs, Wikipedia, Second Life, and beyond: From production to produsage.* New York: Peter Lang.

Buckingham, D. (2000). *After the death of childhood: Growing up in the age of electronic media.* Cambridge: Polity Press.

Carrington, V. (2003). 'I'm in a bad mood. Let's go shopping': Interactive dolls, consumer culture and a 'glocalized' model of literacy. *Journal of Early Childhood Literacy,* 3(1), 83–98.

Carrington, V. (2005). New textual landscapes, information, and early literacy. In J. Marsh (Ed.), *Popular culture, new media and digital literacy in early childhood* (pp. 13–27). New York: RoutledgeFalmer.

Cook, D. (2008). The missing child in consumption theory. *Journal of Consumer Culture,* 8(2): 219–243.

Corsaro, W. A. (1985). *Friendship and peer culture in the early years.* Norwood, NJ: Ablex.

Corsaro, W. A. (2003). *We're friends right? Inside kids' culture.* Washington, DC: Joseph Henry Press.

de Certeau, M. (1984). *The practice of everyday life* (S. Rendall, Trans.). Berkeley, CA: University of California Press.

Dowdall, C. (2009). The texts of me and the texts of us: Improvisation and polished performance in social networking sites. In R. Willett, M. Robinson, and J. Marsh (Eds), *Play, creativity, and digital cultures* (pp. 73–91). New York: Routledge.

Dyson, A. H. (2003). *The brothers and sisters learn to write: Popular literacies in childhood and school cultures.* New York: Teachers College Press.

Dyson, A. H. (2006). On saying it right (write): 'Fix-its' in the foundations of learning to write', *Research in the Teaching of English,* 41(1), 8–42.

Dyson, A. H. (2008). Staying in the (curricular) lines: Practice constraints and possibilities in childhood writing. *Written Communication,* 25(1), 119–159.

Dyson, A. H. (2010). Writing childhoods under construction: Re-visioning 'copying' in early childhood. *Journal of Early Childhood Literacy,* 10(7), 8–31.

Edmiston, B. W. (2008). *Forming ethical identities in early childhood play.* London: Routledge.

Engeström, Y. (1987). *Learning by expanding: An activity-theoretical approach to developmental research.* Helskinki: Orienta-Konsultit.

Fernie, D., Madrid, S., and Kantor, R. (Eds). (2011). *Educating toddlers to teachers: Learning to see and influence the school and peer cultures of classrooms.* Cresskill, NJ: Hampton Press.

Galbraith, J. (2011). 'Welcome to our team, Shark Boy': Making superhero play visible. In D. Fernie, R. Kantor and S. Madrid (Eds), *Educating toddlers to teachers: Learning to see and influence the school and peer cultures of classrooms* (pp. 37–62). Cresskill, NJ: Hampton Press.

Gee, J. P. (1996). *Social linguistics and literacies: Ideology in discourses* (2nd edn). London: Routledge Falmer.

Gee, J. P. (1999). *An introduction to discourse analysis: Theory and method.* London: Routledge.

Geertz, C. (1973). *The interpretation of cultures: Selected essays.* New York: Basic Books.

Goffman, E. (1974). *Frame analysis: An essay on the organization of experience.* New York: Harper & Row.

Göncü, A. (Ed.) (1999). *Children's engagement in the world: Sociocultural perspectives.* Cambridge: Cambridge University Press.

Grimes, S. M. (2010). *The digital child at play: How technological, political and commercial rule systems shape children's play in virtual worlds.* Unpublished doctoral dissertation, Simon Fraser University, Burnaby, British Columbia.

Hirsh-Pasek, K., Golinkoff, R., Berk, L., and Singer, J. (2009). *A mandate for playful learning in preschool: Presenting the evidence.* New York: Oxford University Press.

Jenkins, H., Clinton, K., Purushotma, R., Robison, A., and Weigel, M. (2006). *Confronting the challenges of participatory culture: Media education for the 21st century.* An occasional paper on digital media and learning. Chicago: The John D and Catherine T MacArthur Foundation. Available from http://digitallearning.macfound.org/site/c.enJLKQNlFiG/b.2108773/apps/nl/content2.asp?content_id={CD911571-0240-4714-A93B-1D0C07C7B6C1}and notoc=1. Accessed 15 May 2007.

Kantor, R. and Fernie, D. (Eds). (2003). *Early childhood classroom processes.* Cresskill, NJ: Hampton Press.

Kendrick, M. (2003). *Converging worlds: Play, literacy, and culture*. Bern: Peter Lang.

Kendrick, M. (2005). Playing house: A 'sideways' glance at literacy and identity in early childhood. *Journal of Early Childhood Literacy, 5*(1), 1–28.

Kincheloe, J. L. (2002). *The sign of the burger: McDonald's and the culture of power*. Philadelphia: Temple University Press.

Knobel, M. and Lankshear, C. (Eds). (2007). *The new literacies sampler*. New York: Peter Lang.

Kontovourki, S. and Siegel, M. (2009). Discipline and play with/in a mandated literacy curriculum. *Language Arts, 87*(1), 30–38.

Kress, G. (2011). Discourse analysis and education: A multimodal social semiotic approach. In R. Rogers (Ed.), *Introduction to critical discourse analysis in education* (2nd edn). New York: Routledge.

Kress, G. and Jewitt, C. (2003). Introduction. In C. Jewitt and G. Kress (Eds), *Multimodal literacy* (pp. 1–18). New York: Peter Lang.

Kzero Worldswide (2011, March 4). *The Virtual Worlds Universe: Virtual worlds 2011 Q1*. www.kzero.co.uk/universe.php. Accessed 17 April 2011

Lee, L. (2009). Young American immigrant children's interpretations of popular culture: A case study of Korean girls' perspectives on royalty in Disney films. *Journal of Early Childhood Research, 7*(2), 200–215.

Leont'ev, A. N. (1977). *Activity and consciousness, philosophy in the USSR, problems of dialectical materialism*. Moscow: Progress Publishers.

Linn, S. (2004). *Consuming kids*. New York: Random House.

Long, S., Volk, D., and Gregory, E. (2007). Intentionality and expertise: Learning from observations of children at play in multilingual, multicultural contexts. *Anthropology & Education Quarterly, 38*(3), 239–259.

Luke, C. (2007). 'As seen on TV or was that my phone? New media literacy'. *Policy Futures in Education, 5*(1), 50–58.

Mackey, M. (2009). Exciting yet safe: The appeal of thick play and big worlds. In R. Willett, M. Robinson, and J. Marsh (Eds), *Play, creativity, and digital cultures* (pp. 92–107). London: Routledge.

Marsh, J. (1999). Batman and Batwoman go to school: Popular culture in the literacy curriculum. *International Journal of Early Years Education, 7*(2), 117–131.

Marsh, J. (2000). 'But I want to fly too!' Girls and superhero play in the infant classroom. *Gender and Education, 10*(2), 209–220.

Marsh, J. (2005). Ritual, performance, and identity construction: Young children's engagement with popular cultural and media texts. In J. Marsh (Ed.), *Popular culture, new media and digital literacy in early childhood* (pp. 28–50). New York: RoutledgeFalmer.

Marsh, J. (2010). *Childhood, culture and creativity: A literature review*. Sheffield, UK: Creativity, Culture and Education.

Marsh, J. (2011). Young children's literacy practices in a virtual world: Establishing an online 'interaction order'. *Reading Research Quarterly, 46*(2), 101–118.

Marshall, E. (2011). Marketing American girlhood. In E. Marshall and Ö. Sensoy (Eds), *Rethinking popular culture and media* (pp. 129–136). Milwaukee, WI: Rethinking Schools.

Medina, C. L., & Wohlwend, K. E. (In press). *Literacy, play, and globalization: Critical and cultural performances in children's converging imaginaries*. New York: Routledge.

Merchant, G. (2011, April 11). 'I oversee what the children are doing': Challenging literacy pedagogy in virtual worlds. Paper presented at the American Educational Research Association Annual Meeting, New Orleans, LA.

Miller, E. and Almon, J. (2009). *Crisis in the kindergarten: Why children need to play in school*. College Park, MD: Alliance for Childhood.

New London Group. (1996). A pedagogy of multiliteracies: Designing social futures. *Harvard Educational Review, 66*(1), 60–93.

Norris, S. (2004). *Analyzing multimodal interaction: A methodological framework*. London: Routledge.

Norris, S. (2006). Multiparty interaction: A multimodal perspective on relevance. *Discourse Studies, 8*(3), 401–421.

Owocki, G. (1999). *Literacy through play*. Portsmouth, NH: Heinemann.

Paley, V. G. (2004). *A child's work: The importance of fantasy play*. Chicago: University of Chicago Press.

Paley, V. (2010). *The boy on the beach*. Chicago: University of Chicago Press.

Pugh, A. J. (2009). *Longing and belonging: Parents, children, and consumer culture*. Berkeley, CA: University of California Press.

Rogoff, B. (1995). Observing sociocultural activity on three planes: Participatory appropriation, guided participation, and apprenticeship. In J. V. Wertsch, P. del Rio, and A. Alvarez (Eds), *Sociocultural studies of mind* (pp. 139–164). Boston, MA: Cambridge University Press.

Roskos, K. A., Christie, J. F., Widman, S., and Holding, A. (2010). Three decades in: Priming for meta-analysis in play-literacy research. *Journal of Early Childhood Literacy*, *10*(1), 55–96.

Rowe, D. W. (2007). Bringing books to life: The role of book-related dramatic play in young children's literacy learning. In K. A. Roskos and J. F. Christie (Eds), *Play and literacy in early childhood: Research from multiple perspectives* (2nd edn). New York: Lawrence Erlbaum.

Rowe, D. W. (2008). Social contracts for writing: Negotiating shared understandings about text in the preschool years. *Reading Research Quarterly*, *43*(1), 66–95.

Rowe, D. W. (2010). Directions for studying early literacy as social practice. *Language Arts*, *88*(2), 134–143.

Sanderson, M. (2011). 'Do you want to rough and tumble?' Toddler project work as an intersection of school culture and nascent peer culture. In D. Fernie, R. Kantor, and S. Madrid (Eds), *Educating toddlers to teachers: Learning to see and influence the school and peer cultures of classrooms* (pp. 15–30). Cresskill, NJ: Hampton Press.

Schwartzman, H. B. (1976). Children's play: A sideways glance at make-believe. In D. Lancy & B. A. Tindall (Eds.), *The study of play: Problems and prospects* (pp. 208–215). New York: Leisure Press.

Scollon, R. (2001). *Mediated discourse: The nexus of practice*. London: Routledge.

Seiter, E. (1993). *Sold separately: Children and parents in consumer culture*. Piscataway, NJ: Rutgers University Press.

Sekeres, D. C. (2009). The market child and branded fiction: A synergism of children's literature, consumer culture, and new literacies. *Reading Research Quarterly*, *44*(4), 399–414.

Smith, P. (2010). *Children and play*. Chichester: Wiley-Blackwell.

Steinberg, S. R. and Kincheloe, J. L. (Eds). (1997). *Kinderculture: The corporate construction of childhood*. Boulder, CO: Westview Press.

Stewart, T. L. (2005, November 4). For kindergartners, playtime is over: Full-day schedules, emphasis on learning create 'new 1st grade'. *Dallas Morning News*. p. 6B.

Stipek, D. (2006). No child left behind comes to preschool. *Elementary School Journal*, *106*(5), 455–465.

Street, B. V. (1995). *Social literacies: Critical approaches to literary development*. Singapore: Pearson Education Asia.

Sutton-Smith, B. (1997). *The ambiguity of play*. Cambridge, MA: Harvard University Press.

Tobin, J. (2004). *Pikachu's global adventure: The rise and fall of Pokémon*. Durham, NC: Duke University Press.

Vasquez, V. M. (2005). Resistance, power-tricky, and colorless energy: What engagement with everyday popular culture texts can teach us about learning, and literacy. In J. Marsh (Ed.), *Popular culture, new media and digital literacy in early childhood* (pp. 201–218). New York: Routledge Falmer.

Vygotsky, L. (1935/1978). *Mind in society* (A. Luria, M. Lopez-Morillas, and M. Cole, Trans.). Cambridge, MA: Harvard University Press.

Weil, E. (2007, June 3). When should a kid start kindergarten? *New York Times Magazine*. Retrieved from www.nytimes.com/2007/06/03/magazine/03 kindergarten-t.html?pagewanted=all.

Wohlwend, K. E. (2007). *Kindergarten as nexus of practice: A mediated discourse analysis of reading, writing, play, and design practices in an early literacy apprenticeship*. Unpublished doctoral dissertation, University of Iowa, Iowa City.

Wohlwend, K. E. (2009). Damsels in discourse: Girls consuming and producing gendered identity texts through Disney Princess play. *Reading Research Quarterly*, *44*(1), 57–83.

Wohlwend, K. E. (2011). *Playing their way into literacies: Reading, writing, and belonging in the early childhood classroom*. New York: Teachers College Press.

Wohlwend, K. E. and Peppler, K. A. (In press). Designing with pink technologies and Barbie transmedia. In F. McArdle and G. M. Boldt (Eds), *Education, the arts, and changing childhoods*. London: Routledge.

Wohlwend, K. E., Vander Zanden, S., Husbye, N. E., and Kuby, C. R. (2011). Navigating discourses in place in the world of Webkinz. *Journal of Early Childhood Literacy*, *11*(2), 141–163.

6

Policy-Making in Early Childhood Literacy: Pathways to Equity for all Children

Cecilia Rios-Aguilar

INTRODUCTION

Literacy, when narrowly defined as a set of limited and predictable skills, has been found to be one of the most important foundations for success in school and life (August and Shanahan, 2006; Snow, Barnes, Chandler, Goodman, and Hemphill, 1991; Snow, Burns, and Griffin, 1998). In addition to the contributions of this particular line of research, educators, practitioners, and the public in general are increasingly recognizing the critical importance of developing such literacy skills from birth and not from the start of formal schooling. As a result, there has been a strong interest in developing policies, programs, and curriculum initiatives that that enhance efficiency in the allocation of public resources, and presumably too, provide equality of educational opportunities for all young children (see Heckman, 2006). Indeed, for

decades, several countries[1] (e.g., Australia, Colombia, Canada, France, Germany, India, Ireland, Sweden, Turkey, and the UK) and most states in the US have adopted some type of early childhood program with a literacy component (for a comprehensive review of these programs see Reynolds, Wang, and Walberg, 2003). Even in the current climate of fiscal challenges and constraints, most early childhood initiatives continue to be strongly supported by the public (Raden and McCabe, 2004). The argument is that there exist benefits and savings generated by (certain) early childhood programs, and if these can be scaled up, public investment in such programs will benefit not only the children and their families, but also the society who funds them. As more children reach their full potential as active contributors to the economy, the government will see long-term savings in the form of lower welfare payments, higher tax revenues, and lower criminal justice system costs (Karoly et al., 1998; Karoly, Kilburn, and Cannon, 2005).

As argued by Shannon (1998), recent political debates and a certain line of scholarship, have linked a particular kind of literacy with economic self-realization, but have failed to build on the literacy (broadly conceived) skills of children living in poverty. Indeed, some researchers and policy-makers have continuously claimed that there exists a *literacy crisis* (or gap) in the US, particularly in early childhood. Such crisis, purportedly, exists mainly because 'children from low-income communities are entering kindergarten without the basic early literacy skills for lifelong success' (Jumpstart, 2009: 1). The solution to the literacy 'tragedy',[2] according to some, is efficient and cost-effective investments that begin before a child even reaches kindergarten. Unfortunately, research studies (e.g., *Preventing Reading Difficulties in Young Children* (Snow, Burns, and Griffin, 1998), *From Neurons to Neighborhoods* (Shonkoff and Phillips, 2000), and *Eager to Learn* (Bowman, Donovan, and Burns, 2000), combined with federal and state policies (e.g., Good Start, Grow Smart, Early Reading First, Head Start, English-only laws), and program recommendations (e.g., reading aloud to children, and improved access to books) that are consistent with the literacy crisis perspective, offer simplistic and reductionist understandings of literacy and literacy pedagogy. Indeed, the main goal of this particular approach is to get children 'ready' to achieve high scores on subsequent high-stakes test of reading and writing (McGee and Richgels, 2003). Embedded in the aforementioned research, policies and programs are conceptions of literacy that clearly privilege certain kinds of decontextualized and school-like literacy behaviors and knowledge over more contextualized and functional knowledge about literacy that *all* children possess (McGee and Richgels, 2003; Woods and Henderson, 2008). In addition, children (and their families and communities) who are considered 'risky' (i.e., come from poor backgrounds, are from racially/ethnically under-represented groups, and are not fully proficient in dominant languages) are seen as a monolithic population that is in need of being rescued (González, Moll, and Amanti, 2005).

As stated earlier, early childhood development in general, and early childhood literacy in particular, have been placed at the forefront of most research agendas and policy debates in many different fields, including economics, education, anthropology, and psychology. More specifically, a certain group of researchers who understand literacy as a set of skills that should serve schools and the economy, have been concerned as to how well children are reading and writing since literacy has been associated with other numerous social and economic outcomes, namely higher academic achievement (Campbell and Ramey, 1994), lower delinquency and antisocial behaviors (Yoshikawa, 1995), and higher-paying jobs and life success (Schweinhart, Barnes, and Weikart, 1993; Currie, 2001). As a result of these associations, early childhood is regarded, by those who define literacy in such narrow ways, as the single best investment for enabling children to develop skills that will likely benefit them for a lifetime (Cunha and Heckman, 2009; Dickinson and Neuman, 2006; Heckman, 2004, 2006; Heckman, Stixrud, and Urzua, 2006). In this chapter, I review various studies on early childhood and early childhood literacy in light of recent policy discussions from an economics and human capital perspective. Most importantly, I claim that policies in early childhood literacy should have equity, as opposed to efficiency, as the primary criteria in mind. In addition, I argue that research studies and language policies need to broaden their conceptualizations of literacy, and to examine the multiple contexts in which various literacies take place and how these influence children's language development. A critical examination of existing policies in early childhood education within the economics literature is imperative to better understand the faulty logic underlying such policies. Most importantly, this critique will show how existing policies deny poor and working class students (and their families and communities) access to codes of power and forms of knowledge and opportunities to use multiple literacies they practice in their daily lives.

According to prominent economist James Heckman, a strong advocate for investments in early childhood, four key concepts need to be considered when designing *efficient* and sound policies in this area: (1) the process of skill formation is affected by an interaction between genetics and individual experience, (2) the mastery of skills that are essential for economic success and the development of their underlying neural pathways follow hierarchical rules, (3) cognitive, linguistic, social, and emotional competencies are interdependent, and (4) although adaptation continues throughout life, human abilities are formed in a predictable sequence of sensitive periods (see Heckman (2006: 1900) for more specific details on each of these concepts). Heckman (2006), as well as many other researchers (e.g., Brooks-Gunn, Cunha, Duncan, Heckman and Sojourner, 2006; Cunha and Heckman, 2009) have also argued that family environments are

major predictors of cognitive and non-cognitive abilities. More specifically, this line of research claims that 'environments' (clearly referring only to two-parent homes or intact families) that do *not* stimulate young children and that fail to nurture (certain type of) skills at early ages place children at an early disadvantage. Empirical evidence, from this perspective, indicates that disadvantage arises from lack of stimulation rather than by facing challenging contexts such as poverty, limited parental education, significant social deprivation or neglect, and exposure to interpersonal violence (Cunha and Heckman, 2009).

Most recent policies related to early childhood development have been designed and implemented taking into consideration Heckman's *model of skill formation*. According to this policy perspective, there is no equity-efficiency tradeoff when investing in young children. In other words, this means that 'early interventions promote fairness and social justice and at the same time promote productivity in the economy and society at large' (Heckman, 2006: 1902). The argument is basically the following: investments in early childhood are efficient because the rate of return of such investments is higher than any other type of intervention (e.g., reduced class size, public job training, and tuition subsidies), and they are also equitable because they can (to a certain degree) compensate for, what researchers (including Heckman) label as, *deficient* early family environments.

Similarly, policies directed to improve early childhood literacy skills of children, particularly those targeted to under-represented groups, are often based on *quick fixes* and *one-size-fit-all* type of interventions. As such, there seems to be a long-lasting false hope in current policy-making that the perceived *literacy crisis* will be solved by pursuing the goal of a certain type of literacy for all children by the end of 3 years of schooling (Woods and Henderson, 2008). As Comber and Nichols (2004) argue, promoting a specific kind of literacy in some early childhood contexts has been assumed to be the most efficient way to promote future educational success, as well as to assure a productive workforce for the contemporary global economy. However, existing evidence of such efforts reveal that decontextualized approaches to literacy learning do *not* have lasting effects. Most importantly, the findings indicate that a whole range of issues, including gender, ethnicity, language and accent, poverty and location along with other social, cultural and contextual factors impact students' literacy learning in complex ways (Woods, 2004). Therefore, ignoring understandings of literacy as a set of rich and complex social practices (Barton and Hamilton, 2000; Street, 1993, 1999) narrows and marginalizes access to literacy for at least some groups of students. As a result, researchers, educators, and policy-makers may end up designing programs and policies that lead to inequitable literacy and educational pathways.

Given the current state of policy-making in early childhood literacy, it is necessary to examine, from a critical perspective, the definitions, assumptions, and methods used to promote certain policies. For this reason, this chapter will carefully examine some of the assumptions embedded in Heckman's model of skill formation. I will utilize existing research on immigrant students and English Language Learners (ELLs) to explain how the model may be biased towards a rigid and uniform understanding of what literacy and learning mean for under-represented students (and their families and communities). Then, I discuss an approach – anthropological–ecological – and datasets – Panel Study of Income Dynamics (PSID) and the Child Development Supplement (CDS) – that needs to be incorporated into future research and policy-making if the goal is to promote equity (and efficiency) for all young children.

The chapter is organized as follows. First a philosophical discussion of the fashionable efficiency–equity tradeoff is offered. I rely on the literature in economics to suggest that in order to design sound policies in early childhood literacy, there is a need to define the notions of equity and efficiency. Immediately after, Heckman's model of skill formation is presented. Next, I offer a critique of some aspects of Heckman's model. Existing research on ELL and immigrant students is utilized to elaborate the critique. Finally, the chapter presents an alternative approach and a longitudinal dataset that can be used to examine the literacy development of various sub-groups of students. The chapter concludes by arguing for equitable policies in early childhood literacy and in subsequent levels of education.

EQUITY–EFFICIENCY TRADEOFF

According to Osberg (1995), Arthur Okun (1975) is generally recognized to have made popular the notion that a great tradeoff between equity and efficiency exists. To put it simply, a tradeoff exists when the implementation of a program or policy designed to increase one result may decrease in the other (Le Grand, 1990). For example, broad-access educational programs widely thought to improve equality in educational opportunity and thus equity, are blamed (by some) for concurrently damaging educational excellence, thus damaging efficiency (Le Grand, 1990). As a result of the efficiency–equity tradeoff ideology, policy-makers in several fields, including economics and education, have argued that in the process of allocating scarce resources to competing ends, the tradeoff between equity and efficiency is just another one of the many tough choices that economically rational individuals have to make and live with (Osberg, 1995).

Recent analyses of education data (see Freeman, Machin, and Viarengo, 2010) suggest the existence of a different type of tradeoff in educational outcomes: a *virtuous* one. In their analyses of eighth-grade math scores from several countries, Freeman et al. (2010) found that countries with the highest test scores have low inequality in scores, whereas countries with low test scores have high inequality. This evidence, according to the authors, supports policy interventions that aim primarily at helping students in the lower part of the distribution, such as early-childhood education programs focused on disadvantaged children. Similarly, Heckman (2004, 2006) argues that there is no efficiency–equity tradeoff when investing in early-childhood programs. Specifically, Heckman claims that investing in disadvantaged children should not be an argument of fairness (or equity), but a productivity (or efficiency) one. Furthermore, Heckman argues that the efficiency argument is more powerful than the equity argument, in part because the gains from such investment can be quantified and are quite substantial. Heckman and Masterov (2007) conclude that, on productivity grounds, it makes perfect sense to invest in young children from disadvantaged environments. These children, according to empirical evidence they present, are more likely to end in environments conducive to crime, have out-of-wedlock births and drop out of school. Thus, 'early interventions that, partially, remediate the effects of adverse

environments can reverse some of the harm of disadvantage and have a high economic return. They benefit not only the children themselves, but also their children, as well as society at large' (Heckman and Masterov, 2007: 2).

The efficiency argument is clearly illustrated in Figure 6.1. The figure shows the rates of return to human capital investment in disadvantaged children. An optimal investment program, from the point of view of economic efficiency, equates returns across all stages of the life cycle to the opportunity cost. The figure shows that, at current levels of funding, we overinvest in most schooling and post-schooling programs and under-invest in preschool programs for disadvantaged students.

The problem with the aforementioned tradeoff arguments is that equity and efficiency are rarely defined precisely, and the mechanisms that link them are often only vaguely specified (Osberg, 1995). Furthermore, the central question that is hardly ever asked in educational policy-making is whether (or not) the equity–efficiency tradeoff actually makes sense. Le Grand (1990) argues that the notion of an efficiency–equity tradeoff is,

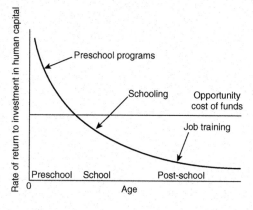

Figure 6.1   Rates of return to human capital investment

Note: figure obtained from Heckman et al. (2006)

indeed, deceitful. He makes three important philosophical points to consider. First, he claims, there are two types of tradeoff to which the concept could refer: a value and a production tradeoff. A value tradeoff refers specifically to the values of an individual making an assessment of different alternatives. A production tradeoff can be defined as the capacity of a program (or economic or social organization) to deliver different combinations of objectives. The difference between the two is critical to consider when making educational policies because they are distinct, not only conceptually, but also in the methods of establishing their existence and magnitude. In practice, Le Grand (1990) argues, that it is the production tradeoff that typically matters. Second, at least according to one general definition of efficiency – one that refers to society's ability to attain its primary objectives – the notion of a tradeoff between equity and efficiency literally does not make sense, for tradeoffs can only exist between primary objectives, of which efficiency is not one. In other words, Le Grand (1990) states that efficiency is a secondary goal or objective that can only acquire meaning with reference to primary objectives, such as equity. Equity and efficiency, then, do not have the same status. Third, even if efficiency is understood as a primary objective (i.e., in terms of economic growth or of Pareto-optimality[3]), there are serious problems in understanding what is precisely being traded-off against what (in either value or production terms). A final point that Le Grand (1990) makes is that it is typical in economics to treat efficiency, in contrast to equity, as a concept that is relatively unproblematic. However, as clearly elaborated in Le Grand's article (1990), 'the interpretation of efficiency is as much a complex and value-laden business as the interpretation of equity, a fact that complicates even more the interpretation of the trade-off between them' (p. 566).

Having these considerations in mind, I argue that making policies in early childhood should be a matter of equity, not exclusively of efficiency. In other words, as Le Grand (1990) states, the *elusive* idea that efficiency is the ultimate goal needs to be questioned, particularly when designing and implementing policies for certain groups of under-represented students, including immigrant and ELL students. In addition, policy-makers must carefully define both equity and efficiency when evaluating alternative policies and programs.

The following section of this chapter concentrates on discussing in more detail some of the values and assumptions embedded in Heckman's *model of skill formation*. It is important to keep in mind that it is not my intention to elaborate on each of the key components of the model because of the scope of this chapter and because of my limited knowledge on certain areas (e.g., genetics, psychology, linguistics, econometrics, and neuroscience). Instead, I will use existing research on the literacy practices among immigrant and ELL students (González et al., 2005; Moll, Saez, and Dworin, 2001; Reyes, 2006; Reyes and Azuara, 2008; Rios-Aguilar and Gándara, 2013; Rios-Aguilar, González Canché, and Sabetghadam, 2012) to highlight the need for: (1) alternative notions and conceptual frameworks; (2) consistent research methodologies; and (3) alternative policies that aim at improving equity in educational opportunities for all students.

THE PROCESS OF SKILL FORMATION

The main premise in Heckman's model is that skill formation is a life-cycle process.

It starts before the child is born, and goes on throughout most of the adult life. Families and schools have a role in this process. The multiple skills and multiple abilities acquired during early years are critical in explaining schooling and occupational success. Therefore, investing in early-childhood programs makes sense from efficiency and equity perspectives (Carneiro and Heckman, 2003).

The following 13 points summarize the model of skill formation proposed by Heckman in several of the vast number of published articles:

(1) Life-cycle skill formation is a dynamic process where early inputs greatly affect the productivity of later inputs in the life-cycle of children. Skill begets skill; motivation begets motivation. Early failure begets later failure.
(2) Many major economic and social problems can be traced to low levels of skill and ability in the population.
(3) Abilities are multiple in nature.
(4) Much public policy discussion focuses on cognitive ability and especially IQ.
(5) Non-cognitive skills are also important for success in life.
(6) Motivation, perseverance and tenacity feed into performance in society at large and even affect scores on achievement tests.
(7) Early family environments are major predictors of both cognitive and non-cognitive ability.
(8) The previous point is a major source of concern because family environments in the US have deteriorated over the past 40 years.
(9) Experiments support the non-experimental evidence that adverse family environments promote adult failure.
(10) If we intervene early enough, we can affect both cognitive and non-cognitive abilities.
(11) Early interventions promote schooling, reduce crime, promote workforce productivity and reduce teenage pregnancy.
(12) These interventions have high benefit–cost ratios and rates of return.
(13) Early interventions targeted toward disadvantaged children have much higher returns than later interventions, such as reduced pupil–teacher ratios, public job training, convict rehabilitation programs, tuition subsidies or expenditure on police.

Not only have prominent economists made this type of argument, but also other organizations and fields such as the National Scientific Council, the National Research Council and the Institute of Medicine have concluded that that 'virtually every aspect of early human development, from the brain's evolving circuitry to the child's capacity for empathy, is affected by the environments and experiences that are encountered in a cumulative fashion, beginning in the prenatal period and extending throughout the early childhood years' (Knudsen, Heckman, Cameron, and Shonkoff, 2006: 10155). It is not the scope of this paper to review in detail all the components of the model of skill formation. For that reason, I will elaborate on some components of the model using a concrete example that is linked to literacy: the process of language acquisition.

Language acquisition: an illustration of Heckman's argument

Knudsen et al. (2006) use the example of language acquisition to exemplify how the model of skill formation works. Here is a sketch of their argument. According to many researchers (e.g., Doupe and Kuhl, 1999; Newport, Bavelier, and Neville, 2001), language acquisition in humans is a well-studied example of a complex cognitive ability that is shaped by early experience. More interestingly, Knudsen et al. (2006) claim that:

> all children at birth are capable of learning any of the world's languages. As they experience a particular language they become expert in analyzing, interpreting and producing its distinctive sounds, and individuals who are exposed to multiple languages during the early years of life learn to speak each with equal facility (p. 10157–58).

Furthermore, they state that social factors play an important role in regulating the process of language acquisition, and that learning a second language as an adult necessitates far greater effort than learning it as a child, and the result is never as complete. Consequently, they argue, language acquisition demonstrates both the *hierarchical nature of learning* – early skills influence the ability to master later skills – and the *phenomenon of sensitive periods* in development – times early in life when specific abilities can be mastered and shaped more readily than later.

The empirical evidence used to support their argument is the following:

> Statistically, language proficiency decreases progressively as language learning is delayed beyond 7 years, and reaches adult levels by the end of adolescence. People who have never experienced language throughout their childhood are apparently incapable of acquiring a facility with language at a later age, despite intense training. Not all aspects of language learning are subject to sensitive periods. For example, proficiency with phonetic comprehension and production, grammar and syntax is learned most effectively early in life, whereas semantics and vocabulary are learned with similar facility throughout life (Knudsen et al., 2006: 10159).

Figure 6.2 illustrates what Knudsen et al. (2006) understand by *sensitive* (or critical) *periods* in language acquisition. Interestingly, the data used in the study they cite (see Johnson and Newport (1989) for details of the study) focuses on the second-language acquisition experiences of 46 Korean and Chinese speakers who arrived in the United States at different points in time.

The example presented by Heckman regarding language acquisition serves as a basis to examine some of the assumptions and biases embedded in the model of skill formation. In what follows, I discuss some aspects of this model and how existing research on literacy practices contradicts some of Heckman's assertions.

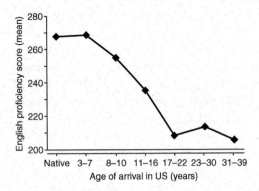

Figure 6.2   Sensitive period for language acquisition

Note: figure obtained from Knudsen et al. (2006). Copyright (2006) National Academy of Sciences, USA.

A critique of Heckman's model of skill formation

Heckman's model has played a predominant role when designing, implementing, and assessing policies in early childhood education (including those specifically related to early childhood literacy). In this section, I offer a critique of two components of the model of skill formation – notions of literacy and the sequentialism perspective on language acquisition. It is expected that the reflections offered in this section may help researchers, educators, and policymakers in re-conceptualizing and re-designing policies in early childhood literacy. In particular, those policies targeted to under-represented students whose literacy needs often are framed within larger discussions without taking into consideration particular community and family resources to use as a foundation for new literacy policies and programs.

THE NEED FOR COMPREHENSIVE CONCEPTUALIZATIONS: LITERACY AND BILITERACY

The first point that needs to be discussed is related to important terminology and conceptualizations that are currently used by policy-makers. First, it should be noted that embedded in Heckman's argument and, particularly, in the example of language acquisition, is a narrow conception of literacy. Most interestingly, in reviewing critically Heckman's work, there is no mention of the various literacy practices in which young children and their families (not only parents) actually engage. In fact, the model only pays attention to the development of certain skills – sound recognition, phonemic awareness, word identification, and letter-sound correspondence. Not only the conception of literacy is simplistic, but also the evidence provided is questionable, particularly because research on phonological awareness has been unclear about when, where, and how exactly these skills develop regardless of context (Reyes and Azuara, 2008). For decades, many researchers (e.g., Larson and Rios-Aguilar, 2007; Mandel Morrow, Rueda and Lapp, 2010; Woods and Henderson, 2008) have urged policy-makers not to focus exclusively on this narrow set of skills, but on a myriad literacy practices in which children and families engage every day. Indeed, literacy research that provides examples which document and analyze the multiple literacy practices of all families, including those that the model characterizes as adverse family environments, is certainly vast. Literacy practices occur in many settings, contexts, and activities. These practices are diverse in function, form, and purpose. In addition to personal and family literacy practices, some researchers (e.g., Cushman, 1998) have highlighted the considerable literacy and language-based components that develop as part of being involved in a variety of community activities. Other researchers (e.g., Gee, Hull, and Lankshear, 1996; Hull, 1997) have examined the role of literacy in the context of work.

As stated earlier, the need for policies and research to broaden the conception of literacy is clearly not an innovative idea. What should be kept in mind, as we continue designing and implementing policies in early childhood literacy, is the following: How to incorporate multiple literacies into models that attempt to explain children's language development; how to study the power of the multiple contexts in which literacy practices take place; how to design interventions that incorporate multiple literacies; and how to assess the effectiveness of these interventions. As Schultz and Hull (2002) and Cole (1995) claim, categorizing the different literacy practices into, for example, school- and non-school-based literacy practices is not productive. These contexts are not perfectly separated or bounded. Therefore, it is critical to attempt to account for movement from one context to another, instead of thinking of literacy practices from a purely hierarchical perspective. In sum, researchers and policy-makers should not oversimplify the power of contexts when studying and analyzing literacy practices.

In addition to highlighting the need to broaden the understanding of literacy, there is a great necessity to reconsider the utilization of labels such as English Learner, English Language Learner, or Limited English Proficient students, particularly in the field of early childhood literacy. English (as is the case of other dominant languages in other countries) seems to play a powerful role in early childhood literacy. There is no doubt that researchers recognize the value of acquiring multiple languages. Even Heckman's model acknowledges the fact that all children can learn any language in the world. In fact, the benefits of bilingualism are well documented in the literature. Work by Diaz and Klinger (1991), Hakuta (1986), and others, has established that bilingualism and biliteracy enhance cognitive and metalinguistic abilities (Reyes and Azuara, 2008). Unfortunately, due to many complexities, only very few studies explore biliteracy, and even fewer focus on examining biliteracy development among low-income families (for examples of this scholarship see Dworin, 2003; Reyes and Azuara, 2008, and Zentella, 2005). Findings from these studies indicate that *all* children should not be classified as being only one type (i.e., ELL), instead they should be considered (to some degree) *biliterate* in two languages. Alternatively, researchers (i.e., Gutiérrez, Zepeda, and Castro, 2010) have suggested the use of the term Dual Language Learner (DLL) to refer to 'young learners who are acquiring two languages simultaneously or who are developing their primary language as they learn a second language' (Gutiérrez et al., 2010: 334). Furthermore, the scant evidence suggests that, even across biliterate students from similar backgrounds, there is a diverse range of language and literacy experiences and competencies developed in their particular contexts. Consequently, as argued by Reyes and Azuara (2008), models that focus on examining the diverse pathways to emergent biliteracy in early childhood must be developed. As clearly articulated by García, Kleifgen, and Falchi (2008), if policies ignore the bilingualism that students can and must develop through schooling, they perpetuate inequities in the educational trajectories of underrepresented students. Finally, in order to move the field forward, researchers must also pay attention to the ways in which we measure and/or assess biliteracy. As argued by Proctor and Silverman (2011), with so many bilingual and biliterate children entering US schools, there is an urgent necessity to create new, cutting-edge and valid measures and analytic procedures that more thoroughly explore bilingualism and biliteracy and their relevance to the academic trajectories of bilingual children.

Non-sequential approaches to literacy and biliteracy development

Literacy, as previously argued, is an important tool and is a functional and embedded part of many kinds of activity settings (Reese and Gallimore, 2000). In every setting, there are different activities, participants, purposes, and styles of interaction. For example, literacy practices are embedded in domestic chores, entertainment, work, school, religious activities, and communication for diverse social purposes (Rios-Aguilar, 2010). Consequently, learning to be literate begins early for children in every household that engages in some or all of these diverse activities. Just as language learning begins before a child utters a word, so too does literacy begin to emerge before children can actually read or write in conventional terms (Mason and Allen, 1986). For more than 30 years, researchers have claimed that listening, speaking, reading, and writing abilities (as aspects of language, both oral and written) develop concurrently and interrelatedly, rather than sequentially (Teale, 1986). Moreover, as argued by Yaden (2008), the emergence of literacy is characterized by 'spurts, plateaus, and regressions ... development typically is not smoothly uniform and cumulative, but asynchronous and nonlinear' (Yaden, 2008: 10).

Some components of Heckman's model seem to contradict what extensive research on literacy (and biliteracy) development has found. More surprising is the fact that none of the articles published by Heckman and colleagues cite the work of prominent researchers (e.g., Vygotsky, 1978; Moll et al., 2001; Goodman, 1986; Rowe, 2006) who have examined how children learn language through interactions with people in their immediate context (Reyes and Azuara, 2008; Reyes, in press). This voluminous body of work needs to be taken into consideration when attempting to understand how children actually make sense of language and how they use it in real-life situations. Unfortunately, not only does Heckman's model fail to recognize existing research, but existing educational laws and policies at the federal and state level in the US, such as No Child Left Behind (NCLB) and the 'English-only' policies of certain states (e.g., Arizona, California, and Massachusetts) also advocate for reductionist perspectives of literacy and for a deficit perspective of children and their families. Sadly, the consequences of the implementation of such restrictive language policies severely affect the education that under-represented students actually receive. That is, teaching practices often suffer as educators strive to find alternative ways to implement top-down national and local educational policies that are plainly misguided (Gándara and Hopkins, 2010; García et al., 2008). Most likely, it is the conflicting nature of research, policy, and teaching practices responsible for much of the failure in school of these students and not the students' language and culture.

As argued by Gutiérrez et al. (2010), the field of early childhood literacy is in great need of research that examines: (1) how children exposed to two languages from an early age develop in relation to their specific individual differences and sociocultural contexts, including different types of educational interventions; (2) how early literacy skills in the first language influence literacy development in English, and how the development of academic literacy unfolds; and (3) the effects of specific instructional and pedagogical practices and approaches with a different language of instruction on children's first- and second-language development. Furthermore, future policies should promote robust literacy and learning programs and practices rather than seeking magic solutions to improve the educational (and occupational) opportunities of all children. Now, it is important to state that conducting research on early childhood literacy and biliteracy development is a complex and difficult task. In the following sections, I briefly discuss a conceptual framework and datasets that can help in moving the field of early childhood literacy forward, and that can assist policy-makers in re-conceptualizing and re-designing policies.

PROPOSED FRAMEWORKS AND METHODOLOGIES IN EARLY CHILDHOOD LITERACY AND BILITERACY

An integrated and multidisciplinary approach to biliteracy

The approach integrates three frameworks, namely (1) an anthropological ecologically-oriented approach;[4] (2) funds of knowledge, emphasizing how social interactions and the household environment promote language and literacy learning in young children; and (3) language and literacy research of English language learners (see Goodman, 1984; McCardle and Hoff, 2006) that focuses on children's early literacy development and the mediating factors impacting its development. It is important to point out that these theoretical frameworks have usually been applied individually, and not collectively. Hence, this approach is novel both in attempting to integrate these various frameworks and in applying them to the study the literacy development of immigrant and biliterate children.

There is need to highlight that the main unit of analysis of this approach is the household. The household has been a staple of anthropological analysis for good reason: it is the smallest unit of social organization and its activities of production, consumption, exchange, and reproduction are central to its survival. From an *anthropological–ecological* perspective households are viewed as variously embedded in other structures, and understood in terms of livelihood systems (Wilk, 1996). Seen this way households are not fixed objects, but instead are sites where labor and resources are allocated and consumed, and through which knowledge and power can transcend these flows (Carr, 2005). This focus on the embedded nature of households and livelihoods draws our attention to questions of access to resources: to the material conditions of households, to the stocks and flows which are necessary to maintain them, to the ways in which they use and allocate labor, and to the funds of knowledge (González et al., 2005) they contain. This approach also underlines the kinds of vulnerabilities each of these domains entail. While literature on livelihoods and vulnerabilities has emerged largely in the context of work on food security in developing countries (e.g., Blaikie, 1994; de Haan, Drinkwater, Rakodi, and Westley, 2002), this literature has been expanded to other contexts (de Haan et al., 2002; Park, Greenberg, Nell, Marsh, and Mjahed, 2003). The anthropological–ecological framework focuses on households' vulnerabilities to analyze the various levels in which external and

internal factors might impact the literacy experiences in which immigrant young children (from different backgrounds) participate at home with family and other extended members.

While the broad term 'vulnerability' has been treated as a symptom of poverty, such portrayals do little to reveal the underlying causes. Vulnerability is a socially constructed phenomenon. Household vulnerability can be analyzed on various levels and separated into external and internal factors that compromise its capacity to absorb and recover from the particular risks and shocks (Ellis and Mdoe, 2003; Nelson, 2005). Coping strategies differ from everyday livelihood strategies (although they may become daily livelihood activities) in that they may require substantial tradeoffs, increase risk, and constrain long-term responses and adaptation, and are undertaken under duress as short-term responses to a crisis (Corbett, 1988). The adoption of the household vulnerability and resources approach has the potential to inform the current debate on what *school readiness* means in the context of immigrant children and their families, especially in relation to literacy development. In contrast to deficit models which assume that poverty and lack of economic resources produce deficiencies before a child even begins school, this framework assumes that children are impacted by both vulnerabilities and access to funds of knowledge.

The proposed ecological framework is also valuable because it integrates insights from anthropology, biology, educational linguistics, and psychology that 'enable an appreciation of the interdisciplinary nature of literacy and language studies' (Pahl, 2008: 306). Reyes and Azuara (2008) argue that an ecological approach helps researchers to examine the complex interrelationships among the different factors within these environments (e.g., languages used, their speakers, their interpretations of text) that influence young emergent bilinguals' biliteracy development.

Methodological approaches to research on early childhood literacy

Not only does the field of early childhood literacy need to use alternative conceptual frameworks to study literacy development, but also there is a need to design studies that are consistent with those approaches. Instead of proposing either qualitative or quantitative approaches, I urge scholars to think more critically and to incorporate multidisciplinary perspectives to design research studies that are dynamic, innovative, and flexible. And, most importantly, researchers must look for ways to influence policy-making processes and key actors in the decision-making process. This is certainly not an easy task. Therefore, I am not proposing one single model or approach that works. Instead, I briefly describe one dataset that is, in my opinion, underutilized and that can be used to answer important research questions related to the development of literacy among young children from diverse backgrounds. This dataset contains multiple activities in which children and families engage, and it can be used to broaden the conception of literacy.

The Panel Study of Income Dynamics and the Child Development Supplement

The Panel Study of Income Dynamics (PSID) is a longitudinal study of a representative sample of US individuals and the families in which they reside. Since 1968, the PSID has collected data on family composition changes, housing and food expenditures, marriage and fertility histories, employment, income, time spent in housework, health, consumption, wealth, pensions and savings, and philanthropic giving. The sample size has grown from 4800 families in 1968 to more than 7000 families in 2001. At the conclusion of 2003 data collection (a new data collection is made available every other year), the PSID will have collected information about more than 65,000 individuals spanning as much as 36 years of their lives. One of the main advantages of the PSID is that it has maintained the comparability of the data throughout time. Indeed, over the years, the general design and content of certain variables have remained largely unchanged.

The Child Development Supplement (CDS) is one research component of the PSID. In 1997, the PSID supplemented its main data collection with additional information on PSID parents and their 0–12-year-old children. The objective of this study is to provide researchers with a comprehensive, nationally representative, and longitudinal database of children and their families with which to study the dynamic process of early human capital formation. Out of the 2705 families selected for CDS-I, 2394 families (88%) participated, providing information on 3563 children. In 2002–2003, CDS re-contacted families in CDS-I who remained active in the PSID panel as of 2001. CDS-II successfully re-interviewed 2017 families (91%) who provided data on 2908 children/adolescents aged 5–18 years. One of the main advantages of utilizing the CDS information is the availability of children's time-diary data. Time diaries (TD) are a chronological report by the child's primary caretaker, and in some instances, by the child him- or herself about the child's activities over a specified recent 24-hour period, beginning at midnight (who the reporter is depends on the age of the child). In the TD data, respondents were asked to provide the detailed time and nature of the activity in which children participated during specific assigned days. For each activity, respondents provided the following details: (1) time the activity began and ended; (2) whether the child was watching TV or a video; (3) where the child was doing the activity; (5) who was participating in the activity with the child; (6) who else was with the child, but was not directly involved in the activity; and (7) what else was the child doing with the primary activity. The TD data contained in the CDS is very extensive. There are approximately 600 activities in which children participate with their families (broadly conceived) that can be aggregated into 11 major categories: work and other income-producing activities; household activities; childcare; obtaining goods and services; personal needs and care; home computer and related activities; educational and professional training; organizational activities; entertainment/social activities; sports and active leisure; and passive leisure. There is also available TD data for examining the activities done at preschool.

While there are clear limitations to the sample and survey and TD data collected in the PSID and CDS, there is enormous potential to examine the literacy development of young children with this dataset, particularly when the multiple data are used strategically (see for example Villena and Rios-Aguilar, 2010). For instance, researchers can combine PSID, CDS, and TD data with US census data to investigate the composition of households and how certain aspects of households, including vulnerabilities and funds of knowledge, mediate children's literacy, educational, and occupational pathways. There is opportunity to study many issues from a longitudinal perspective, which is one of the most important features of the data.

In addition, the CDS and TD data allow researchers to broaden their conceptions of literacy and to examine the myriad literacy practices in which all children and families engage. Indeed, embedded in the 600 different types of activities that are coded in the TD data, there exists a wealth of resources that are related and/or mediate children's literacy development. Ignoring these literacy practices may perpetuate inequities in the educational and occupational attainment of all children. It is important to mention that analyses of CDS and PSID data can inform future research and policy-making in the US. In other countries, there also exist longitudinal datasets (e.g., 1970 British Cohort, National Longitudinal Study of Children and Youth in Canada and Growing Up in Australia: The Longitudinal Study of Australian Children) that have also the potential to influence future scholarship and language policies.

CONCLUSION

As previously stated, there is a growing awareness of the importance of the early years. Many early childhood programs (including those with literacy components) internationally have been designed and implemented as a result of viewing these investments as efficient and equitable (from an economic perspective). In addition, there is agreement that a persistent literacy achievement gap during the schooling trajectory between children living in poverty and/or children from diverse backgrounds, and those of more economically advantaged and mainstream communities exist (McGill-Franzen, 2010). Most recently, the National Institute for Literacy in the US convened an expert panel – the National Early Literacy Panel (NELP) – to identify and synthesize the relevant research on the early precursors to school success in literacy. The primary goal of NELP was to promote practices that support early literacy development. Unfortunately, as argued by Gutiérrez et al. (2010) and Pearson and Hiebert (2010), the report has several limitations. For instance, it does not provide insights or recommendations for improving instruction. In addition, the data is not disaggregated enough to learn about what works for certain sub-groups of students. Most interesting is the fact that NELP's report (as well as other previous reports) does not provide a policy perspective that can inform policy-makers, researchers, and educators. In fact, Pearson and Hiebert (2010) claim that the report 'simply reinforces practices that have already been widely implemented without resounding success' (p. 287). My contention is that scientific reports, whether at the intent of scientists or not, have a long history of constructing difference in ways that maintain the power dynamics already at play within the social structure. Such a history should not be forgotten, especially when current policies in the field of early childhood argue that the economic growth of the US depends on the literacy and educational capacities developed by children (and their families) who come from diverse backgrounds. Furthermore, the *literacy crisis* discourse tends to take a modern-day fairy-tale approach to the experiences of under-represented students, their families and communities. The discourse not only neglects the resources embedded in all households, but also disregards the historical and social context in which literacy takes place, and replaces complexity with a simpler, normalized approach (based on efficiency models) that focuses almost exclusively on the so-called

happy ending – less crime and teenage pregnancy rates and more economic growth.

This chapter provides a critical perspective of the field of early-childhood literacy policy. Specifically, the chapter demonstrates that, despite the shortcomings in existing surveys and datasets, researchers can still do much to consider the complexity of literacy practices in all households using existing data. Even slight changes in how these data are accounted for in analyses can result in big differences in terms of how we think about the literacy development of young children. Differing levels of disaggregation and consideration of between and within group differences and similarities can provide important insights into diverse literacy pathways issues even if the findings are not statistically significant. In their book, *The cult of statistical significance: How the standard error costs us jobs, justice, and lives,* Ziliak and McCloskey (2011) claim: 'for the past eighty years it appears that some of the sciences have made a mistake by basing decisions on statistical "significance" … which should be a tiny part of an inquiry concerned with the size and importance of relationships' (pp. 2–3). They explain that, especially in the life, human, and social sciences, the emphasis on statistical significance has come at the expense of broader philosophical inquiry such that, instead of asking *whether or why* certain phenomena are occurring, researchers and policy-makers have begun instead exploring on *how much* of the phenomena are occurring. This is largely the case in the study of early childhood literacy.

Is there an alternative to *the literacy crisis* and to *the model of skill formation?* I am hesitant to offer an alternative metaphor through which researchers, practitioners, and policy-makers can better understand the literacy development of young children. However, I argue that any such model and future research should be flexible and include elements that address issues of power, language, intentionality, stratification, race, ethnicity, and class. Furthermore, I argue that researchers and policy-makers need to make an effort to (re-)conceptualize and (re-)design policies in the field of early childhood literacy. The efforts must be oriented towards providing equal opportunities for all children to succeed in school and in life. In addition, educators, researchers, and policy-makers must also pay considerable attention to educational policies at different levels: basic, secondary, and post-secondary. These policies also have implications for the literacy development and educational trajectories of under-represented students. In other words, while starting early and investing resources in early childhood literacy is important, we must not forget that children will attend schools and will continue to learn languages in multiple ways. Their family and community contexts will interact with what happens inside classrooms and educational institutions. All these interactions will influence students' literacy pathways and, simultaneously, their academic opportunities and trajectories. We need to design *equitable policies* in the field of early childhood literacy that do not over-emphasize efficiency at the expense of young children.

NOTES

1 See Spence Boocock (1995) and Kamerman (2000) for detailed reviews of early childhood programs in several countries, including the US.

2 The literacy tragedy as defined by several organizations such as the National Right to Read Foundation.

REFERENCES

August, D. and Shanahan, T. (2006). *Developing literacy in second-language learners: Report of the National Literacy Panel on language-minority children and youth*. Mahwah, NJ: Erlbaum.

Barton, D. and Hamilton, M. (2000). 'Literacy practices'. In D. Barton, M. Hamilton, and R. Ivanic (Eds), *Situated literacies: Reading and writing in context* (pp. 7–15). New York: Routledge.

Blaikie P. M. (Ed.) (1994). *At risk: Natural hazards, people's vulnerability, and disasters*. New York/London: Routledge.

Bowman, B., Donovan, S., and Burns, S. (Eds) (2000). *Eager to learn: Educating our preschoolers*. National Research Council. Washington, D.C.: National Academy Press.

Brooks-Gunn, J., Cunha, F., Duncan, G., Heckman, J., and Sojourner, A. (2006). *Infant Health and Development Program*. Northwestern University. A re-analysis of the IHDP program. Unpublished manuscript.

Campbell, F. A. and Ramey, C. T. (1994). 'Effects of early intervention on intellectual and academic achievement: A follow-up study from low-income families'. *Child Development*, 65, 684–698.

Carneiro, P. and Heckman, J. (2003). 'Human Capital Policy'. In J. J. Heckman, B. Krueger, and B. Friedman (Eds), *Inequality in America: What role for human capital policies?* (pp. 77–237). Cambridge, MA: MIT Press.

Carr, M. (2005). 'The leading edge of learning: Recognising children's self-making narratives'. *European Early Childhood Education Research Journal*, 13(2), 41–50.

Cole, M. (1995). 'The supra-individual envelope of development: Activity and practice, situation and context'. In J. J. Goodnow, P. J. Miller, and F. Kessel (Eds), *Cultural practices as contexts for development* (pp. 105–118). San Francisco: Jossey-Bass.

Comber, B. and Nichols, S. (2004). 'Getting the big picture: Regulating knowledge in the early childhood literacy curriculum'. *Journal of Early Childhood Literacy*, 4(1), 43–63.

Corbett, J. (1988). 'Famine and household coping strategies'. *World Development*, 16(9), 1099–1112.

Cunha, F. and Heckman, J. (2009). 'The economics and psychology of inequality and human development'. *Journal of the European Economic Association*, 7(2–3), 320–364.

Currie, J. (2001). 'Early childhood education programs'. *The Journal of Economic Perspectives*, 15, 213–238.

Cushman, E. (1998). *The struggle and the tools: Oral and literate strategies in an inner city community.* Albany, NY: State University Press of New York.

de Haan, A., Drinkwater, M., Rakodi, C., and Westley, K. (2002). 'Methods for understanding urban poverty and livelihoods'. Retrieved from www.liveli hoods.org/info/docs/urb_pov2.pdf

Diaz, R. M. and Klinger, C. (1991). 'Towards an explanatory model of the interaction between bilingualism and cognitive development'. In E. Bialystok (Ed.), *Language processing in bilingual children* (pp. 167–192). Cambridge, UK: Cambridge University Press.

Dickinson, D. and Neuman, S. B. (Eds) (2006). *Handbook of early literacy research.* New York, NY: Guilford Press.

Doupe, A. J. and Kuhl, P. K. (1999). 'Birdsong and human speech: common themes and mechanisms'. *Annual Review of Neuroscience, 22,* 567–631.

Dworin, J. E. (2003). 'Insights into biliteracy development: Toward a bidirectional theory of bilingual pedagogy'. *Journal of Hispanic Higher Education, 2*(2), 171–186.

Ellis, F. and, Mdoe, N. (2003). 'Livelihoods and rural poverty reduction in Tanzania'. *World Development, 31*(8), 1367–1384.

Freeman, R., Machin, S., and Viarengo, M. (2010). *Variation in educational outcomes and policies across countries and of schools within countries.* National Bureau of Economic Research (Working paper no. 16903).

Gándara, P. and Hopkins, M. (2010). *Forbidden languages: English learners and restrictive language policies.* New York: Teachers College Press.

García, O., Kleifgen, J. A., and Falchi, L. (2008). 'From English language learners to emergent bilinguals'. In *Equity matters: Research review No. 1.* New York: Teachers College, Columbia University.

Gee, J. P., Hull, G., and Lankshear, C. (1996). *The new work order: Behind the language of the new capitalism.* Boulder, CO: Westview.

González, N., Moll, L., and Amanti, C. (2005). *Funds of knowledge: Theorizing practices in households, communities, and classrooms.* Mahwah, NJ: Lawrence Erlbaum Associates.

Goodman, Y. (1984). 'The development of initial literacy'. In H. Goelman, A. Oberg, and F. Smith (Eds), *Awakening to literacy* (pp. 102–109). Exeter, NH: Heinemann.

Goodman, Y. (1986). 'Children coming to know literacy'. In W. Teale and E. Sulzby (Eds), *Emergent literacy: Writing and reading* (pp. 1–14). Norwood, NJ: Ablex.

Gutiérrez, K. D., Zepeda, M., and Castro, D. C. (2010). 'Advancing early literacy learning for all children: Implications of the NELP report for dual-language learners'. *Educational Researcher, 39,* 334–339.

Hakuta, K. (1986). *Mirror of language: The debate on bilingualism.* New York: Basic.

Heckman, J. (2004). 'Lessons from the technology of skill formation'. *Annals of the New York Academy of Sciences, 1038,* 1–22.

Heckman, J. (2006). 'Skill formation and the economics of investing in disadvantaged children. *Science', 312,* 1900–1902.

Heckman, J. and Masterov, D. (2007). 'The productivity argument for investing in young children'. *Review of Agricultural Economics, 29*(3), 446–493.

Heckman, J., Stixrud, J., and Urzua, S. (2006). 'The effect of cognitive and non-cognitive abilities on labor market outcomes and social behavior'. *Journal of Labor Economics, 24,* 411–482.

Hull, G. (1997). *Changing work, changing workers: Critical perspectives on language, literacy and skills.* Albany, NY: State University of New York Press.

Johnson, J. S. and Newport, E. L. (1989). 'Critical period effects in second language learning: the influence of maturational state on the acquisition of ESL'. *Cognitive Psychology, 21,* 60–99.

Jumpstart (2009). *America's early childhood.* Washington DC: Jumpstart. Retrieved from: www.jstart.org/site/DocServer/America_s_Early_Child hood_Literacy_Gap.pdf?docID=3923

Kamerman, S. (2000). 'Early childhood education and care: An overview of the developments in OECD countries'. *International Journal of Education Research, 33,* 7–30.

Karoly, L., Greenwood, P., Everingham, S., Houbé, J., Kilburn, R., Rydell, P., Sanders, M., and Chiesa, J. (1998). *Investing in our children: What we know and don't know about the costs and benefits of early childhood interventions,* Santa Monica, California: RAND Corporation.

Karoly, L., Kilburn, R., and Cannon, J. (2005). *Early childhood interventions: Proven results, future promise,* Santa Monica, California: RAND Corporation.

Knudsen, E., Cameron, J., Heckman, J., and Shonkoff, J. (2006). 'Economic, neurobiological, and behavioral perspectives on building America's future workforce'. *Proceedings of the National Academy of Sciences, 103*(27), 10155–10162.

Larson, J. and Rios-Aguilar, C. (2007). 'Speaking truth to policy'. *Language Arts, 84*(5), 458–460.

Le Grand, J. (1990). 'Equity versus efficiency: The elusive trade-off'. *Ethics, 100*(3), 554–568.

Mason, J., and Allen, J. (1986). *A review of emergent literacy with implications for research and practice in reading.* Unpublished manuscript.

McCardle, P. and Hoff, E. (eds) (2006). *Cross-linguistic experiments in infant word form recognition.* United Kingdom: Multilingual Matters Ltd.

McGee, L. and Richgels, D. (2003). *Designing early literacy programs: Strategies for at-risk preschool and kindergarten children.* New York: Guilford Press.

McGill-Franzen, A. (ed.) (2010). Special issue on the National Early Literacy Panel report. *Educational Researcher, 39*(4), 275–278. http://www.aera.net/Publications/Journals/EducationalResearcher/ERIssuesandArchives/Volume39Number4May2010/tabid/12739/Default.aspx.

Mandel Morrow, L., Rueda, R., and Lapp, D. (Eds). (2010). *Handbook of research on literacy and diversity.* New York: Guilford Publications.

Moll, L., Saez, R., and Dworin, J. (2001). 'Exploring biliteracy: Two student case examples of writing as a social practice'. *The Elementary School Journal, 101*(4), 435–449.

Nelson, D. (2005). *The public and private sides of persistent vulnerability to drought: An applied model for public planning in Ceare, Brazil.* Unpublished Doctoral Dissertation. University of Arizona.

Newport, E. L., Bavelier, D., and Neville, H. J. (2001). 'Critical thinking about critical periods: Perspectives on a critical period for language acquisition'. In E. Dupoux (Ed.), *Language, brain and cognitive development,* (pp. 481–502). Cambridge, MA: MIT Press.

Osberg, L. (1995, March). 'The equity/efficiency trade-off in retrospect'. Keynote address to conference on Economic Growth and Income Inequality. Laurentian University, Sudbury, Ontario.

Pahl, S. (2008). 'The ecology of literacy and language: Discourses, identities and practices in homes, schools and communities'. In A. Creese, P. Martin, and N.H. Hornberger (Eds), *Encyclopedia of language and education: Vol. 9. Ecology of language* (pp. 305–315). Berlin, Germany: Springer.

Park, T., Greenberg, J., Nell, E. J., Marsh, S., and Mjahed, M. (2003). 'Research on urbanization in the developing world: New directions'. *Journal of Political Ecology, 10,* 69–94.

Pearson, D. and Hiebert, E. (2010). 'National Reports in literacy: Building a scientific base for practice and policy'. *Educational Researcher, 39,* 286–294.

Proctor, P. and Silverman, R. (2011). 'Confounds in assessing the associations between biliteracy and English language proficiency'. *Educational Researcher, 40*(2), 62–64.

Raden, A. and McCabe, L. (2004). *Researching universal prekindergarten: Thoughts on critical questions and research domains from policy makers, child advocates and researchers.* New York: Foundation for Child Development.

Reese, L. J. and Gallimore, R. (2000). 'Immigrant Latinos' cultural model of literacy development: An evolving perspective on home-school discontinuities'. *American Journal of Education, 108*(2), 103–134.

Reyes, I. (in press). 'Biliteracy among children and youth'. *Reading Research Quarterly.*

Reyes, I. (2006). 'Exploring connections between emergent biliteracy and bilingualism'. *Journal of Early Childhood Literacy, 6*(3), 264–292.

Reyes, I. and Azuara, P. (2008). 'Emergent biliteracy in young Mexican immigrant children'. *Reading Research Quarterly, 43*(4), 374–498.

Reynolds, A. J., Wang, M. C., and Walberg, H. J. (Eds. (2003). *Early childhood programs for a new century.* Washington, DC: CWLA Press.

Rios-Aguilar, C., & Gándara, P. (2013). 'Horne v. Flores and the future of language policy: Special Issue'. *Teachers College Record.*

Rios-Aguilar, C., González-Canché, M., & Sabetghadam, S. (2012). 'Examining the impact of restrictive language policies: The Arizona 4-hour English language development block'. *Language Policy, 11*(1), 47–80.

Rios-Aguilar, C. (2010). 'Measuring funds of knowledge: Contributions to Latina/o students' academic and non-academic outcomes'. *Teachers College Record, 112*(8), 2209–2257.

Rowe, D. (2006). *Expanding the agenda for early literacy research: The potentials of reframing early literacy learning as social practice.* Paper presented at the annual meeting of the American Educational Research Association, San Francisco, CA.

Schultz, K. and Hull, G. (2002). 'Locating literacy in theory in out-of-school contexts'. In G. Hull and K. Schultz (Eds), *School's out! Bridging out-of-school literacies with classroom practice* (pp. 11–31). New York: Teachers College Press.

Schweinhart, L. J., Barnes, H., and Weikart, D. (1993). *Significant benefits: The high/scope Perry preschool study through age 27.* Monograph of the High/Scope Educational Research Foundation, 10, Ypsilanti, Michigan: High-Scope Educational Research Foundation.

Shannon, P. (1998). *Reading poverty.* Wesport, CT: Heinemann.

Shonkoff, J. and Phillips, D. (Eds) (2000). *From neurons to neighborhoods: The science of early childhood development.* Washington, DC: National Academy Press.

Snow, C., Barnes, W., Chandler, J., Goodman, I., and Hemphill, L. (1991). *Unfulfilled expectations: Home and school influences on literacy.* Cambridge, MA: Harvard University Press.

Snow, C., Burns, M., and Griffin, P. (Eds) (1998). *Preventing reading difficulties in young children.* Washington, DC: National Academy Press.

Spence Boocock, S. (1995). 'Early childhood programs in other nations: Goals and outcomes'. *The Future of Children: Long-Term Outcomes of Early Childhood Programs, 5*(3), 94–114.

Street, B. (1993). 'Introduction: The new literacy studies'. In B. Street (Ed.), *Cross-cultural approaches to literacy* (pp. 1–21). New York: Cambridge University Press.

Street, B. (1999). 'The meaning of literacy'. In D. Wagner, R. Venezky, and B. Street (Eds), *Literacy: An international handbook* (pp. 34–40). Boulder, CO: Westview.

Teale, W. (1986). 'Home background and young children's literacy development'. In W. H. Teale and E. Sulzby (Eds). *Emergent literacy: Writing and reading.* Norwood, NJ: Ablex.

Villena, B. and Rios-Aguilar, C. (2010). *Estimating direct effects of parental time-investment in children's cognitive and non-cognitive outcomes.* Paper presented at the Panel Study of Income Dynamics Workshop, Ann Arbor, MI.

Vygotsky, L. (1978). *Mind and society: The development of higher psychological processes.* (M. Cole, V. John-Steiner, S. Scribner, and E. Souberman Eds). Cambridge, MA: Harvard University Press.

Wilk, R. (1996). *Economies and cultures: Foundation of economic anthropology.* Boulder, CO: Westview Press.

Woods, A. (2004). *The contexts and purposes of school literacy pedagogy: Failing in the early years.* Unpublished Doctorate of Philosophy, University of Queensland, Brisbane, Australia.

Woods, A. and Henderson, R. (2008). 'The early intervention solution: Enabling or constraining literacy learning'. *Journal of Early Childhood Literacy, 8*(3), 251–268.

Yaden, D. B., Jr (2008). *Some considerations on the nature and determinants of developmental change in the acquisition and growth of early literacy from developmental science.* Paper presented at the Martha King Colloquium Series, Ohio State University, Columbus.

Yoshikawa, H. (1995). 'Long-term effects of early childhood programs on social outcomes and delinquency'. *The Future of Children: Long-Term Outcomes of Early Childhood Programs, 5*(3), 51–75.

Zentella, A.C. (Ed.) (2005). *Building on strength: Language and literacy in Latino families and communities.* New York: Teachers College Press.

Ziliak, S. T. and McCloskey, D. (2011). *The cult of statistical significance: How the standard error costs us jobs, justice, and lives.* Ann Arbor: University of Michigan Press.

7

Disability and Early Childhood: The Importance of Creating Literacy Opportunities and Identities

Martha Mock and Susan Hildenbrand

INTRODUCTION

Over the last decade researchers in the fields of early childhood literacy and early childhood intervention have begun to interact meaningfully. Although the focus tends to be on the programmatic or intervention aspects of literacy engagement, there is a noticeable absence of discussion related to literacy and literacy identity as a readily accepted construct in the early childhood disability world (Browder, Wakeman, Spooner, Ahlgrim-Delzell, and Algozzine, 2006). Rightfully so, interventionists, parents, and early childhood teachers are focused on diagnosis, eligibility for services, service delivery (e.g., physical therapy, speech language pathology) (Marvin, 1994), challenging behaviors, assessing developmental delays, as well as everyday

survival. With this focus has come inattention in research related to literacy identity and how this interfaces with disability. Myths about students labeled with disabilities, particularly significant disabilities, include an inability to learn to read, to understand literacy concepts, to learn over extended periods of time, and to appreciate being literate; all of which prohibit them from gaining citizenship in the classroom (Kliewer, Biklen, and Kasa-Hendrickson, 2006; Kliewer et al., 2004). These myths and negative stereotypes about students labeled with disabilities have led to an inattentiveness to fostering literacy identity; students labeled with disabilities are often deemed invisible by the adults who are responsible for their literacy development, and this 'invisibility translates into an absence of opportunities to encounter activities that foster literacy' (Kliewer et al., 2006, p. 172).

In this chapter we begin with a discussion about disability and citizenship in the literacy classroom for students labeled with disabilities.[1] This is followed by an examination of a system of literacy instruction that is based on mastery of a succession of skills and traditional means of assessment that does not allow the true literacy abilities of students labeled with disabilities to be recognized and acknowledged. Then, we present an overview of the current literature in the area of literacy and early childhood disability intervention. In addition we discuss how best practices relate to literacy and disability as recommended by the National Association for the Education of Young Children (NAEYC), the Division for Early Childhood (DEC), and the International Reading Association (IRA). We then provide an interpretation of one literacy framework situated within the construct of disability, make recommendations for future research to the field of early childhood, and argue that literacy must not be an afterthought in the field of disability, as it situates students labeled with disabilities on a lifelong trajectory that signifies a lack of access to literacy in the broadest sense, which continues to perpetuate the irrational myths about students labeled with disabilities.

DISABILITY AND CITIZENSHIP

In the traditional realm of literacy development, students labeled with disabilities have been perceived as non-literate and incapable of attaining the skills necessary to become fully literate citizens in the classroom. This is attributed mainly to the denial of entrance into literate rich environments that promote access to literacy and acknowledgement of non-traditional literacy skills and abilities. If a young child does not have access to the skills required to become literate due to exclusion, they will never be considerate a full citizen in any literate community. According to Kliewer et al. (2006), 'among children segregated from the cultural locations of educational privilege, opportunities to develop as literate citizens have historically been curtailed, circumscribed, suppressed, or wholly outlawed by those in control of the formal institutions of education' (p. 163).

Unfortunately, 'children with construed significant developmental disabilities are today primarily considered to be naturally illiterate – cerebrally unable...' (Kliewer et al., 2004, p. 377). Lack of understanding of multiple modes of literacy and responses that do not mirror traditional literacy models and typical developmental milestones add to the practice of segregating students labeled with disabilities into classrooms where best practices are not implemented and expectations for literacy are lowered or non-existent.

THEMES OF 'LITERATE DISCONNECTION'

When observing and analyzing the citizenship of children labeled with disabilities in an early childhood classroom, Kliewer et al. (2006) posit that children experience literate disconnection and 'subjugated, seemingly voiceless positions' (p. 166) in the form of four main themes: 1) rendering literate possibility invisible; 2) representing disability as a static construct; 3) having literate accomplishment censured and dismissed; and 4) proving literate competence. Each theme supports the overarching belief that 'the degenerate and the defective could not function as full and literate citizens of society' (Kliewer et al., 2006, p. 168). These themes of literate disconnection identified by Kliewer and other authors are perpetuated by the lack of access and focus on quality literacy instruction and the lack of the acknowledgement of literacy competence based on traditional measures of assessment (Basil and Reyes, 2003; Browder et al., 2006, 2009; Kliewer, 1998; Kliewer and Biklen, 2001; Kliewer et al., 2004, 2006; Mirenda, 2003).

The first theme, rendering literate possibility invisible, centers around the misconception that offering traditional, research-supported instructional literacy strategies is unnecessary and fruitless for children labeled with significant disabilities, due to '...established beliefs about competence or incompetence and specifically with a narrative of pessimism that accompanies the construct of disability' (Kliewer et al., 2006, p. 175). Tragically, this obstruction and absence of instruction in best practices frequently occurs in the actions of special education practitioners who exert tremendous influence over the day-to-day opportunities or lack of opportunities in literacy instruction (Kliewer et al., 2006).

The second theme, representing disability as a static construct, feeds into the stereotype that students with disabilities are 'spiritually and intellectually enfossilized, unable to grow toward citizenship, literate or otherwise' (Kliewer et al., 2006 p. 168). Therefore, students labeled with disabilities are herded into segregated, non-rigorous classroom settings that do not place any importance on literacy instruction, and these programs may in fact be devoid of any literacy instruction at all. As Kliewer et al. (2006) state, 'Professionals widely subscribe to the notion of the individual with disabilities as organically unable to grow as a citizen and so divert the labeled person into programs absent of expectations of literacy', and in response, these students 'commonly live down to the expectations that surround them' (p. 177). However, ironically, 'it is in the opportunity of literate citizenship, so often overtly denied, that we find literate accomplishment among people with disabilities' (Kliewer et al., 2006, p. 177).

Literate accomplishment, censured and dismissed, is the third theme of literacy disconnection associated with students labeled with disabilities, as identified by Kliewer and colleagues (2006). In many instances in which the literacy accomplishments of students labeled with disabilities do not mirror traditional benchmarks of achievement and success, they have been discussed and documented, but 'the response from professional authorities has been to censure and dismiss these documented accomplishments' (Kliewer et al., 2006, p. 177). For students labeled with disabilities, it is an overwhelming belief that they are somehow incapable of *real* literacy, including imagination, transcendence, and critical reasoning, so they can obviously never become full, participating citizens in any literate community of learners. As Kliewer and colleagues (2006) caution, 'Such censure and dismissal actively denigrate explorations of the possibility that people presumed to be hopelessly subliterate might find through literacy a profound way into community connectedness' (p. 182).

The final theme, proving literate competence, unfairly places the burden of proof regarding the right to literate citizenship squarely on the shoulders of those on the cultural margins (Kliewer et al., 2006). At times the demonstration of *being literate* is extremely difficult for students labeled with disabilities to exhibit in the traditional manner, thereby making a shift in the minds of current professionals an insurmountable task; 'the criteria of proof and manner in which they were met were determined by those who held authority without consulting the needs or interests of the person whose capacities were suspect' (Kliewer et al., 2006, p. 169).

This denial of literacy framed by the four themes of literate disconnection is insidious and 'hegemonic; a part of an ideology or control imposed on the marginalization by those who lay claim to the center' (Kliewer et al., 2006, p. 186). Unfortunately, literacy citizenship appears to be reserved for those whose valued citizenship is fundamentally presumed, which excludes children labeled with disabilities who are not members of the privileged majority (Kliewer et al., 2006).

We will return to this powerful discussion of access to literacy and literacy environments at the end of this chapter. Now we provide a review of current research studies focused on literacy, early childhood intervention and disability.

LITERACY INTERVENTION AND EARLY CHILDHOOD DISABILITY RESEARCH

In the first section of this chapter we have guided the reader to reconsider the construct of disability and who has access to literacy; in this section we present an overview of the current literature available on the topics of interventions for young children labeled with disabilities. Disability intersects with the research in early childhood in three areas: children at-risk, specific types of disabilities, and early childhood intervention. The fourth area we have chosen to include in this review of the current literature, is research of students labeled with significant disabilities;

while much of this literature focuses on older children, there are concepts and ideas we believe valuable and applicable to young children labeled with disabilities. We begin first with a cursory discussion of the relevant concepts found in the early childhood at-risk literature.

CHILDREN WHO ARE LABELED AT-RISK

Research on children labeled at-risk for literacy delays is readily available and provides numerous suggestions for how to address the needs of students labeled at-risk, as well as those of their family (Gettinger and Stoiber, 2008; Gonzalez and Uhing, 2008; Justice and Pullen, 2003; Missall, McConnell, and Cadigan, 2006; Powell, Diamond, and Koehler, 2009). Strategies typically include a type of home-based intervention or parent training, professional development for the teachers and direct interventions with young children measured with traditional literacy assessment; such as the Exemplary Model of Early Reading Growth and Excellence (EMERGE) (Gettinger and Stoiber, 2008). In addition, specific strategies such as adult–child shared storybook reading, literacy enriched play settings, and teacher-directed structured phonological awareness curricula (Justice and Pullen, 2003) have been studied with the at-risk population. While these studies may offer useful models or strategies, the researchers do not address issues related to disability and how that impacts the various levels or types of intervention (home, school, individual child). The constructs of disability and at-risk tend to be used to define two separate groups of students. In the US, students labeled with disabilities have met the federal criteria for having a disability

(Individuals with Disabilities Education Improvement Act; IDEA, 2004), where as students labeled at-risk are a more loosely defined group of students who may qualify based on income, family structure, low-test scores, or perceived risk of developing a disability label. We have chosen to include in this chapter a brief summary of one model that addresses children labeled at-risk, which also includes the element of the potential to develop a label of disability or developmental.

The EMERGE program developed by Gettinger and Stoiber (2008) utilized the Response to Intervention approach, commonly known as RTI in schools. RTI was designed to reduce the number of students being referred to special education, and to address any identified skill deficits quickly through a tiered approach to intervention (i.e., whole group, small group, individual instruction) (Fuchs and Fuchs, 2006). EMERGE focuses on four goals:

> 1 to develop and implement a multi-tiered instructional model ... 2 to implement screening and progress monitoring procedures to identify children who require more intensified intervention than what is provided through instructional and environmental enhancements in the regular classroom ... 3 to create high-quality, literacy-rich learning environments that support the development of young children's early literacy and language skills and promote positive learning behaviors ... 4 to provide intensive and continuous professional development and ongoing literacy coaching that is grounded in scientifically based knowledge of early literacy development ... (p. 200).

To implement the above four goals the authors utilized scientifically based early literacy curricula, screening and progress monitoring of the children, in literacy-rich classrooms where they provided 'ongoing professional development, literacy coaching and collaborative planning' (p. 200). Family involvement was also a key component of the initiative. Utilizing these essential components in addition to a multi-tiered approach designed around RTI (i.e., whole-group enrichment curricula and strategies, small-group instruction and then individual instruction) the researchers found significant benefits to the children ($n = 188$) who participated in EMERGE classrooms through an increase in their literacy development skills as measured by formal assessments (measuring vocabulary, alphabet knowledge, alliteration, rhyming, story retelling, picture naming, print awareness, and name writing) as compared to the students ($n = 154$) who participated in control classrooms (Gettinger and Stoiber, 2008). While students labeled at-risk benefited from the literacy environments and interventions in the EMERGE classrooms, it is unclear how students labeled with disabilities who may have possessed more significant disabilities or communication challenges fared.

For further reading in the area of at-risk (including disability) also see the following authors: Baroody and Diamond (2010); Dodici, Draper, and Peterson (2003); Justice and Pullen (2003); Lonigan, Anthony, Bloomfield, Dyer, and Samwel (1999); Missall et al. (2006); Powell et al. (2010); Spencer and Slocoum (2010); and Van Der Heyden, Snyder, Broussard, and Ramsdell (2008).

EARLY CHILDHOOD INTERVENTION

Numerous strategies and literacy interventions have been developed and studied with students labeled with disabilities. There is one body of literature that is disability specific, meaning that all participants in the study were labeled with the same disability. Autism, hearing impairment, specific language impairment, and deaf–blindness are four specific disability areas in which literacy research and interventions for young children have been conducted (see the following studies: Al Otaiba, Puranik, Ziolkowski, and Montgomery, 2009; Arm, Most, and Simon, 2008; Bedrosian, Lasker, Speidel, and Politsch, 2003; DesJardin and Ambrose, 2010; Kaderavek and Sulzby, 2000; Kluth and Chandler-Olcott, 2007; Kluth and Darmondy-Latham; 2003; Koppenhaver and Erickson, 2003; McKenzi, 2009; Whalon, Al Otaib, and Delano, 2009). The utilization of disability-specific strategies may be necessary in some instances to ensure individual types of learning styles and needs are met, but this should not mean that students labeled with these specific types of disabilities are solely limited to specific teaching strategies and learning outcomes. While the authors acknowledge the significant contributions that this area of literature possesses in terms of value to students, teachers, practitioners, and parents, the purpose of the following section in this chapter is to offer evidence in support of access to literacy and literacy instruction for young children labeled with disabilities more generally.

The next section focuses on reviewing the current literature in two areas, *child-focused* interventions and strategies and *adult-focused* interventions and strategies. Studies described in both sections focus on the outcome of increasing a young child's engagement and participation in literacy. We defined *child-focused* as studies that selected an intervention with the primary purpose of instructing or impacting the child's literacy practice, and *adult-focused* as studies that selected an intervention with the primary purpose of instructing or impacting the adult's literacy practices with a child or children.

Child-focused interventions and strategies

There are four types of child-focused interventions and strategies: play-based (at home and school), daily routines (at home and school), technology, and curriculum content.

Play-based

Play-based strategies in literacy instruction are numerous. Utilizing play within preschool, day care and home settings for young children labeled with disabilities is essential to support their emergent and early literacy practices (Hanline, 2001). Hanline (2001) provides specific strategies for teachers and parents, such as exposure to books and other printed materials, repeated interaction with writing materials (e.g., markers, crayons, chalk, paint), activities that promote vocabulary development (e.g., read-aloud), and experiences that promote auditory processing and phonological awareness (e.g., songs, poems, rhymes, finger plays). Types of play should include: block and micro-symbolic play (i.e., cars, animals, people), macro-symbolic play (i.e., role playing, housekeeping activities), and fluid construction activities (i.e., paint, glue, water, sand). All of these types of play with infants, toddlers, and young children involve language and materials that effectively lend themselves to emergent literacy skills. Making these connections explicit for family members, teachers and day-care providers is necessary to ensure that young children labeled with disabilities have full access to developmentally appropriate learning opportunities.

Daily routines

Use of daily activities such as bathing and washing up, dressing, feeding, shopping, and riding in the car or on a bus are all activities to comment and expand upon for young children (Bingham and Pennington, 2007). Promoting such early literacy enrichment experiences with a focus on the progression of oral language development including self-talk, parallel talk, and expansion or modeling of more complex language and grammar can occur during daily activities in a young child's life. Also, including print concepts and phonemic awareness as a part of reading at home and reading stories at preschool is suggested. Presenting concepts consistently in the home across all other child settings also facilitates language and literacy development and helps to reinforce a young child's literacy identity (Bingham and Pennington, 2007).

Marinelli (2001) argues that utilizing specific strategies in early-childhood classrooms and in the home can also increase definitional skills in young children. According to Marinelli (2001) definitional skills are related to language development and literacy, therefore focusing specific attention on developing definitional skills within the context of a young child's day is fundamental.

While the above play-based and routine-based strategies reviewed above may seem commonplace in the world of literacy, for many years the field of disability ignored such strategies in favor of more specialized, specific disability intervention strategies.

Technology

Within the significant disabilities literature, researchers have developed specific interventions and strategies in which students labeled with significant disabilities use augmentative and alternative communication (AAC) devices (Bedrosian et al., 2003; Soto, Yu, and Henneberry, 2007; Waller et al., 2001). This means that students utilize simple or complex devices or tools to communicate (i.e., small computers or computer pads, voice output devices, picture cards). According to Snow (1983; Snow, Tabors, and Dickinson, 2001) a strong link exists between oral narratives and development of literacy skills. Therefore, due to the limited narrative opportunities available to students who use AAC devices, Soto and colleagues (2007) believed that developing additional interventions was essential to increasing their overall literacy skills and abilities. In this particular study, an 8-year-old who uses an AAC device to communicate participated to develop increased narrative skills. The program developed by Soto and colleagues consisted of three narrative experiences; storybook reading and retelling, generation of personal stories, and fictional story generation. The consistent use of the strategies allowed the participant to improve her ability to tell stories, and to participate in conversation successfully. In addition she showed an increase in her use of complex vocabulary and relevant story elements (Soto et al., 2007). Studies such as this designed to increase access to specific instructional strategies and activities around specific elements of literacy continue to be essential in moving the fields of disability and early-childhood literacy forward together.

In addition, Douglas, Ayres, Langone, Bell, and Meade (2009) developed eText supports (voice and text-to-speech, text highlighting, video summaries) as a means of literacy instruction and engagement for children labeled with disabilities. With the growth of technology within both the classroom and home, technology strategies continue to impact Universal Design for Learning (Dixon, 2008).

Skouge, Rao, and Boisvert (2007) promote shared reading experiences through the use of multimedia and technology. They present numerous suggestions made for young children labeled with specific disabilities as well as for new immigrants and bilingual families. Recorded books (both audio and video), utilizing software such as Apple iMovie and Microsoft movie maker are a few of the suggestions made. The authors also identify ways to incorporate technology alongside other authentic literacy experiences, such as reading storybooks and writing stories.

Curriculum and content exposure and learning

Browder et al., 2009 developed a conceptual foundation for literacy for students labeled with significant disabilities, stating that, 'A conceptual model of literacy also should set the expectation that every student receive the opportunity to learn to read' (p. 271). Browder and colleagues (2009) also argue that curricular content must be chronologically age appropriate; this is frequently *not* the case within upper grades for students labeled with significant disabilities. The purpose of the development of their conceptual model is twofold for students labeled with significant disabilities, 'to increase access to literature, and … to increase independence as a reader' (p. 271). They also argue for their framework to be utilized in further research.

Adult-focused interventions and strategies

We have chosen to include adult-focused interventions and strategies that highlight four areas: changing teachers' perceptions of students, coaching and professional development, curriculum training and student assessment, and family involvement.

Changing teachers' perceptions of students

In a study conducted by Kliewer and Landis (1999), they question the understanding that a teacher's role is to develop individualized instruction that divides children into groups, and separates them by functional skill level. In their qualitative study they explored the perceptions of primary school teachers and their understanding of curricular individualization for their students who were labeled with moderate and severe disabilities. Through this study they discovered that when teachers understood disability and literacy from a local knowledge versus institutional perspective, they were better able to support students labeled with disabilities. Institutional understandings of both disability (i.e., deficit-model thinking) and literacy (i.e., reading-readiness models of thinking) significantly impacted teachers' abilities to implement meaningful literacy instruction. Institutional understandings of disability and literacy affected the teachers' beliefs and attitudes, thereby affecting the young children's access to literacy activities and curriculum. Kliewer and Landis (1999) state, 'the teacher's responsibility is to support the child, as necessary, in order to connect him or her to the surrounding classroom's literate community' (p. 97). When teachers understood this was the expectation and their role, they were better able to meet the literacy needs of the preschool and primary students labeled with disabilities.

Coaching and professional development

In a study conducted by Hsieh, Hemmeter, McCollum, and Ostrosky (2009), five preschool teachers received coaching to increase their use of emergent literacy evidence-based practices in their classrooms. The chosen instructional areas were oral language, alphabetic code, and

print knowledge. Teachers received training, observations and then subsequent
training to assist in maintaining and implementing the specific strategies to improve
their instructional abilities. While all
teachers eventually reached the criterion
goal for use of the specific strategies, the
authors continue by stating, 'Despite the
effectiveness of the intervention for all the
teachers, the extent to which the five teachers eventually used the three clusters of
strategies varied considerably, as did the
time needed to reach criterion ...' (Hsieh
et al., 2009, p. 244).

Curriculum training and student assessment
Browder, Ahlgrim-Delzell, Courtade,
Gibbs, and Flowers (2008) adapted current
successful reading strategies for use with
students labeled with severe intellectual
disabilities and autism. In addition, the
researchers developed a curriculum for use
in this study as well as modification to
assessment tools was necessary to measure
student gains. Many standardized instruments that measure literacy skills and gains
assume verbal abilities (Browder et al.,
2008). Some students labeled with severe
intellectual disabilities in this study were
non-verbal communicators, thereby necessitating the modification to the assessment
tool. The 23 students who participated in
this randomized control group study (12
control, 11 treatment) were selected by
seven special education teachers who
agreed to participate in this yearlong study.
Teachers received training on shared stories and task analysis of engaging students
in reading and comprehension tasks, and
classroom observations of teacher instruction and feedback were both included as
part of the training. Students in the control
group received more traditional site-word
instruction with a commercially designed
curriculum. Students who received the

newly developed curriculum did show significant improvements on the Early Literacy
Skills Assessment and in the area of phonemic awareness.

Pierce, Summer, and O'deKirk (2009)
developed an authentic assessment strategy
and tool for individualizing and informing
practice with young children who are
labeled with disabilities. The tool, the
Bridge, was developed by the same authors
in 2005 and was grounded in the Division
for Early Childhood Recommended
Practices (Sandall, Hemmeter, Smith, and
McLean, 2005) discussed later in this
chapter. In addition to being informed by
the DEC Recommended Practices, the
Bridge was adapted from the Teacher
Rating of Language and Literacy
(Dickinson, McCabe, and Sprague, 2001).
The foundation of this authentic assessment is observation by preschool teachers,
care providers and family members.
Portfolios, writing and literacy samples are
also used to assess young children's
progress in the area of literacy. The tool
also guides adults in how to modify or shift
their own interactions and strategies based
upon the child's progress.

Family involvement and literacy
Bruns and Pierce (2007) advocate for an
approach to literacy that includes family
involvement, increasing family literacy
skills, through programs like Even Start
Family Literacy program (Even Start, n.d.)
or other adult learning programs, as well
as classroom teachers selecting already
published early literacy programs to
improve literacy. The authors of the article
provide specific family involvement strategies such as family journals, parent–
teacher communication, and after-school
programs. While family involvement and
issues of culture (Cheatham and Santos,
2005; Cheatham, Santos, and Ro, 2007) as

a strategy for child-focused intervention has been a focus in special education for decades, it was not until recently that literacy because a focus of family involvement (Marvin, 1994).

The above section of this chapter highlighted child and adult interventions through which students labeled with disabilities will become readers and literate citizens in their classrooms, homes and communities. Both types of interventions create student access to information within their world to be valued community members. In the next section, we highlight three professional organizations and present the organizational stance of each membership body on disability and early childhood literacy.

DISABILITY AND EARLY CHILDHOOD LITERACY: PERSPECTIVES OF PROFESSIONAL ORGANIZATIONS

The Division for Early Childhood (DEC) is a division of the Council for Exceptional Children in the US and is an international association of approximately 3800 professionals, practitioners, and parents focused on early childhood and disability. In 2005 the *DEC recommended practices* was revised (Sandall et al., 2005). The recommended practices are evidence- and research-based practices designed to inform the field about best practices to address the needs of young children labeled with disabilities. The direct practices are divided into five areas: assessment, child-focused practices, family-based practices, interdisciplinary models, and technology applications. The purpose of these practices is to guide and prepare interventionists, teachers, and family members who interact and support the learning of young children labeled with disabilities. While there are general suggestions about types of materials and loose guidelines about types of curricula, no guidance is provided about how to broadly construct, infuse and channel literacy and early literacy within the home, child-care, or preschool environments.

However, DEC has been a leader in the disability field through the development of position statements focused on cultural and linguistic diversity as well as fostering diverse family values, including language; all important components in a young child's developing literacy identity. DEC also endorsed the 1998 (NAEYC) joint position statement on *Learning to read and write: developmentally appropriate practices for young children*, which is discussed later in this section. In addition, DEC has begun to address literacy with the publication of multiple early literacy articles published each year in the DEC practitioner journal *Young Exceptional Children*. These three efforts demonstrate an increased commitment by DEC as a professional organization to early literacy development within the field of disability.

The National Association for the Education of Young Children (NAEYC) in the US is a professional organization comprised of approximately 80,000 educators, administrators and parents interested in the high-quality education of young children. In addition to the joint statement on the inclusion of young children labeled with disabilities developed by NAEYC and DEC (DEC/NAEYC, 2009), NAEYC and the International Reading Association (IRA) professionals developed a joint position statement on *Learning to read and write: developmentally appropriate practices for young children* (NAEYC, 1998). As previously stated, DEC, as well as numerous other professional organizations, endorsed this position on early literacy development. Within this position statement one particular point is relevant to young children labeled with disabilities, 'Among many early childhood teachers, a maturationist view of young children's development persists despite much evidence to the contrary' (NAEYC, 1998: 2). As previously discussed, the readiness view of literacy for children labeled with disabilities continues well beyond the early childhood years into later elementary, middle and even into high school.

In line with the previously mentioned professional organizations, the authors believe that in order for young children labeled with disabilities to create literacy identities, they need access to *environments*, *relationships*, and *communication*.

Environments

Young children labeled with disabilities need access to environments where literacy activities are occurring through *curriculum content*; including exposure to engaging, developmentally appropriate curriculum and literacy content is essential (Bingham and Pennington, 2007; Hanline, 2001; Katims and Pierce, 1995). Young children labeled with disabilities also need access to *physical space*; classrooms where literacy is a core focus of the educational space (Neuman, Copple, and Bredekamp, 2000); classrooms with literacy-rich environments including posters with writing, white boards, labels for materials, developmentally appropriate and challenging books, and plentiful writing materials. For students labeled with disabilities accessing the physical environment through adapted materials, audio and visual books is also important. Literacy-rich environments also include writing centers, multiple adult read-aloud opportunities, and access to high-quality children's literature (Katims and Pierce, 1995). There are now multiple ways for children to hear read-alouds in addition to adults; utilizing media such as books on CDs, on-line audio books accessed through a computer or on iPods, and iPads. These additional methods of accessing text and stories should not be limited to students labeled with disabilities. Attention to Universal Design for Learning principles within classrooms and other early childhood settings and daycare (Dixon, 2008) is another way in which opening access to classroom spaces to all children may be fostered.

In addition to considering what content curriculum exists within the environment and how the physical space is organized, the location of the space where young children labeled with disabilities spend their time is fundamental. In the field of early intervention and special education the concept of having young children labeled with disabilities located in the same places their peers without disability labels spend time is called *natural learning environments* (McWilliam, Casey, and Sims, 2009; O'Brien, 2001; Sandall et al., 2005). Natural environments include places like preschool, day care, family day care, and community settings (i.e., stores, libraries, parks). While this idea may seem commonplace, young children labeled with disabilities are still frequently segregated (Odom, 2002) into specialized settings that are believed to be *better* for them.

Relationships

Accessing adults, same-age peers and family members who develop meaningful and strengths-based relationships with young children labeled with disabilities is a second point of essential literacy access. *Adults* who believe in the abilities of young children labeled with disabilities and who presume competence (Jorgensen,

McSheehan, and Sonnenmeier, 2007), and who are focused on a strengths-based model of education are crucial to the development of a child's literacy identity. Also fundamental is access to adults who possess attitudes that encourage meaningful literacy engagement as well as those who possess skills to support both peer and parental relationships (Sandall et al., 2005). In addition, access to same-age peers or siblings who can read and write and participate in literacy activities is vital. Peers and siblings are able to support one another in literacy learning. Finally, access to family members who provide literacy support to young children labeled with disabilities within the context of everyday home life (McWilliam et al., 2009; Sandall et al., 2005) is foundational in building a young child's literacy identity.

Communication

Access to a means of expressing communication, a means of understanding communication, and people to communicate with are also essential to the development of a young child labeled with a disability. As previously mentioned, assumptions about a young child's ability to communicate or understand language are frequently made. Assisting in the development of a comprehensive communication system for young children labeled with significant disabilities is a vital step in accessing literacy. For some students, augmentative and alternative means of communication (AAC) are more easily achieved in our technology-rich society (i.e., iPads, Dynavox®).

As previously cited, Soto and colleagues (2007) view developing ways for children labeled with significant disabilities to express their thoughts and needs as an essential step to achieving literacy engagement. In addition, having access to adults who are utilizing supportive strategies of engagement with content, materials (Katims and Pierce 1995), and peers assists in the development of literacy identity.

WHO IS ON THE LADDER TO LITERACY?

When examining the research surrounding the development of competent literacy skills, the image of a 'normative ladder to literacy' is frequently presented and accepted (Kliewer and Biklen, 2001; Kliewer et al., 2004; Rowe, 2010). This normative ladder to literacy is described as a linear, subskill model where 'each rung of the ladder constitutes increasingly complex, normative subskills, with the first or earliest rungs primarily associated with letter and phonemic abilities, as identified in school-based reading program. Only later are the rungs associated with understanding and meaning of text' (Kliewer et al., 2004, p. 378). It is also believed that within this literacy framework, cognitive mastery is required prior to taking the next step of the ladder (Kliewer and Biklen, 2001). However, allowing only for this prescribed mastery and progression of skills has 'bound and constrained what we currently know about preschool literacy' (Rowe, 2010). Unfortunately, children labeled with disabilities often find it difficult to master these skills in the prescribed order so they are considered naturally illiterate and an intellectual improbability, and students labeled with disabilities are ultimately resigned to remain on the lower rungs. Kliewer and Biklen (2001) state:

> The metaphor of incremental ascension to the privileged height of competent reader supports the removal of these students to other locations. It is, so the logic goes, in their own interest. They are steered to stepladders with fewer rungs, which

leads to functional or life skills. Literacy as a process of critical thinking, interaction, or abstract communication is never considered.' (p. 2)

Therefore, children labeled with disabilities remain isolated, segregated, and deemed unable among their typically developing peers when inclusion actually allows for success in literacy to occur and citizenship to commence.

INCLUSION: THE FUNDAMENTAL KEY TO LITERATE CITIZENSHIP

Within the current framework of literacy instruction, separating children from literacy is 'not a logical consequence of the child's lack of cognitive ability; rather, it is a moral choice made when particular student-constructed meanings are misunderstood and devalued' (Kliewer, 1998, p. 168). However, inclusive education appears to be fundamental to the literate citizenship of children labeled with significant disabilities (Kliewer et al., 2004). 'In its rejection of the status quo of segregated schooling, inclusion immersed students in the wonderfully chaotic patterns, semiotic systems, and narrative forms of the early childhood literate community' (Kliewer et al., 2004, p. 398). Recent research into emergent literacy has revealed that not only are best practices in literacy imperative for all learners, a community of literacy learners is also necessary for any growth in literacy to occur (Rowe, 2010). Social and cultural perspectives (Lave and Wenger, 1991) suggest that children become literate from the vantage point of the social positions that they occupy and the types of participation that this social position allows. Consequently, when students labeled with disabilities are prohibited from entry into literate classrooms, they are denied the opportunity to be

'drawn into the literacy practices of their communities ... [and] begin to learn what textual intentions, procedures, and reading/writing processes are valued for use in specific kinds of literacy. At the same time, they take up positions in the power structure of the community, try on identities as particular kinds of readers and writers, and take up or contest social rules and expectations for their participation' (Rowe, 2010, p. 137)

This full participation does not always occur naturally, and 'physical presence alone will not lead to the benefits for all learners' (Chandler-Olcott and Kluth, 2009 p. 556).

A teacher's belief in the commitment to each student's ability to become literate and gain full citizenship in the inclusive classroom is also critical for entry into the literate community for students labeled with disabilities. This acceptance of students labeled with disabilities into early childhood education settings also has benefits to the students without disability labels in the classroom (Chandler-Olcott and Kluth, 2009). As Chandler-Olcott and Kluth (2009) suggest about inclusive literacy classrooms, 'Often overlooked in situations like this is the intellectual benefit for all learners or acquiring and refining a repertoire of representational tools' (p. 550).

NEED FOR FUTURE RESEARCH

While the readiness model still persists in preschool and kindergarten, the authors assert it persists to an even greater extent when disability is present. Children labeled with disabilities are held to an unrealistic and higher standard for a longer period of time, thereby fostering a consistent lack of access to curriculum. Therefore, designing research studies utilizing literacy frameworks (rather than sole intervention models) is necessary. Literacy must not be an afterthought for young children labeled with disabilities, but a primary area of focus. We suggest the following four areas as points for this inquiry:

1   Analysis of decision making that leads to disallowing children labeled with disabilities access to rich literacy environments;
2   Analysis of decision making that leads to the lack of pursuit of the teaching of reading and other literacy skills;
3   Application of current best practices in early childhood literacy to expand and include children labeled with disabilities;
4   Promoting a literacy identity for young children with disabilities, by consistently positioning and constructing them as capable of literacy interactions.

'A community that excludes *even one* of its members, is *no* community at all.'
                              –Dan Wilkins (2004)

NOTE

1   The authors choose to use 'students labeled with disabilities' rather than 'students with disabilities' as we believe disability to be a socially constructed entity and not a truth.

REFERENCES

Al Otaiba, S., Puranik, C., Ziolkowski, R., and Montgomery, T. (2009). Effectiveness of early phonological awareness interventions for students with speech and language impairments. *The Journal of Special Education*, *43*(2), 107–128.

Arm, D., Most, T., and Simon, A. (2008). Early literacy of kindergartners with hearing impairment: The role of mother–child collaborative writing. *Topics in Early Childhood Special Education*, *28*(1), 31–41.

Baroody, A. and Diamond, K. (2010). Links among home literacy environment, literacy interest, and emergent literacy skills in preschoolers at risk for reading difficulties. *Topics in Early Childhood Education*, 22 December, 2010, DOI: 10.1177/0271121410392803.

Basil, C. and Reyes, S. (2003). Acquisition of literacy skills by children with severe disability. *Child Language Teaching and Therapy*, *19*(1), 27–48.

Bedrosian, J., Lasker, J., Speidel, K., and Politsch, A. (2003). Enhancing the written narrative skills of an AAC student with autism: Evidence based research issues. *Topics in Language Disorders*, *23*(4), 305–324.

Bingham, A. and Pennington, J. (2007). As easy as ABC: Facilitative early literacy enrichment experiences. *Young Exceptional Children*, *10*(2), 17–29.

Browder, D., Wakeman, S., Spooner, F., Ahlgrim-Delzell, L., and Algozzine, B. (2006). Research on reading instruction for individuals with significant cognitive disabilities. *Exceptional Children*, *72*(4), 392–408.

Browder, D., Ahlgrim-Delzell, L., Courtade, G., Gibbs, S., and Flowers, C. (2008). Evaluation of the effectiveness of an early literacy program for students with significant developmental disabilities. *Exceptional Children*, *75*(1), 33–52.

Browder, D., Gibbs, S., Alhgrim-Delzell, L., Courtade, G., Mraz, M., and Flowers, C. (2009). Literacy for students with severe developmental disabilities. *Remedial and Special Education*, *30*(5), 269–282.

Bruns, D. and Pierce, C. (2007). Let's read together: Tools for early literacy development for all young children. *Young Exceptional Children*, *10*(2), 2–10.

Chandler-Olcott , K. and Kluth, P. (2009). Why everyone benefits from including students with autism in literacy classrooms. *The Reading Teacher*, *62*(7), 548–557.

Cheatham, G. and Santos, R.M. (2005). A-B-Cs of bridging home and school expectations: For children and families of diverse backgrounds. *Young Exceptional Children*, *8*(3), 3–10.

Cheatham, G., Santos, R.M., and Ro, Y. (2007). Home language acquisition and retention for young children with special needs. *Young Exceptional Children*, *11*(1), 27–38.

DEC/NAEYC (Division for Early Childhood and National Association for the Education of Young Children). (2009). *Early childhood inclusion: A joint position statement of the Division for Early Childhood and the National Association for the Education of Young Children*. Retrieved from www.dec-sped.org/About_DEC/Position_Statements_and_Concept_Papers/Inclusion

DesJardin, J. and Ambrose, S. (2010). The importance of the home literacy environment for developing literacy skills in young children who are deaf or hard of hearing. *Young Exceptional Children*, *13*(5), 28–44.

Dickinson, D., McCabe, A., and Sprague, K. (2001). Teacher rating of oral language and literacy

(TROLL). Retrieved from www.ciera.org/library/reports/inquiry-3/3-016/3-016.pdf

Dixon, S. (2008). Language is everywhere! Universally designed strategies to nurture oral and written language. *Young Exceptional Children*, *11*(4), 2–12.

Dodici, B., Draper, D., and Peterson, C. (2003). 'Early parent–child interactions and early literacy development. *Topics in Early Childhood Special Education*, *23*(3), 124–136.

Douglas, K., Ayres, K., Langone, J., Bell, V., and Meade, C. (2009). Expanding literacy for learners with intellectual disabilities: The role of supported eText. *Journal of Special Education Technology*, *24*(3), 35–44.

Even Start (n.d.). *National Even Start Association providing a national voice and vision for Even Start family literacy programs website*. Retrieved from www.evenstartnetwork.net

Fuchs, D. and Fuchs, L. (2006). Introduction to response to intervention: What, why, and how valid is it? *Reading Research Quarterly*, *41*(1), 93–99.

Gettinger, M. and Stoiber, K. (2008). Applying a response-to-intervention model for early literacy development in low-income children. *Topics in Early Childhood Special Education*, *27*(4), 198–213.

Gonzalez, J. and Uhing, B. (2008). Home literacy environments and young Hispanic children's English and Spanish oral language: A communality analysis. *Journal of Early Intervention*, *30*(2), 116–139.

Hanline, M. F. (2001). Supporting emergent literacy in play-based activities. *Young Exceptional Children*, *4*(4), 10–15.

Hsieh, W.Y., Hemmeter, M.L., McCollum, J., and Ostrosky, M. (2009). Using coaching to increase preschool teachers' use of emergent literacy teaching strategies. *Early Childhood Research Quarterly*, *24*, 229–247.

IDEA (Individuals with Disabilities Improvement Education Act) (2004). P.L. 108-446, 20 U.S.C §§ 1400 *et seq.*

Jorgensen, C., McSheehan, M., and Sonnenmeier, R. (2007). Presumed competence reflected in the educational programs of students with IDD before and after the Beyond Access professional development intervention. *Journal of Intellectual and Developmental Disability*, *32*(4), 248–262.

Justice, L. and Pullen, P. (2003). Promising interventions for promoting emergent literacy skills: Three evidence-based approaches. *Topics in Early Childhood Special Education*, *23*(3), 99–113.

Kaderavek, J. and Sulzby, E. (2000). Narrative production by children with and without specific language impairment: Oral narratives and emergent readings.

Journal of Speech, Language and Hearing Research, *43*(1), 34–49.

Katims, D. and Pierce, P. (1995). Literacy-rich environments and the transition of young children with special needs. *Topics in Early Childhood Special Education*, *15*(2), 219–234.

Kliewer, C. (1998). Citizenship in the literate community: An ethnography of children with Down syndrome and the written word. *Exceptional Children*, *64*, 167–180.

Kliewer, C. and Biklen, D. (2001). 'School's not really a place for reading': A research synthesis of literate lives of students with severe disabilities. *Journal of the Association for Persons with Severe Handicaps*, *26*(1), 1–12.

Kliewer, C. and Landis, D. (1999). Individualizing literacy instruction for young children with moderate to severe disabilities. *Exceptional Children*, *66*(1), 85–100.

Kliewer, C., Fitzgerald, L., Meyer-Mork, J., Hartman, P., English-Sand, P., and Rascher, D. (2004). Citizenship for all in the literate community: An ethnography of young children with significant disabilities in inclusive early childhood settings. *Harvard Educational Review*, *74*(4), 373–403.

Kliewer, C., Biklen, D., and Kasa-Hendrickson, C. (2006). Who may be literate? Disability and resistance of the cultural denial of competence. *American Educational Research Journal*, *43*(2), 163–192.

Kluth, P. and Chandler-Olcott, K. (2007). *A land we can share: Teaching literacy to students with autism*. Baltimore, MD: Paul H. Brookes.

Kluth, P. and Darmondy-Latham, J. (2003). Beyond sight words: Literacy opportunities for students with autism. *The Reading Teacher*, *56*(6), 532–535.

Koppenhaver, D. and Erickson, K. (2003). Natural emergent literacy supports for preschoolers with autism and severe communication impairments. *Topics in Language Disorders*, *23*(4), 283–292.

Lave, J. and Wenger, E. (1991). *Situated learning: Legitimate peripheral participation*. Cambridge, United Kingdom: Cambridge University Press.

Lonigan, C., Anthony, J., Bloomfield, B., Dyer, S., and Samwel, C. (1999). Effects of two shared-reading interventions on emergent literacy skills of at-risk preschoolers. *Journal of Early Intervention*, *22*(4), 306–322.

McKenzi, A.R. (2009). Emergent literacy supports for students who are deaf-blind or have visual and multiple impairments: A multiple-case study. *Journal of Visual Impairments and Blindness*, *103*(5), 291–302.

McWilliam, R.A., Casey, A., and Sims, J. (2009). The Routines-Based Interview: A method for gathering information and assessing needs. *Infants & Young Children, 22*(3), 224–233.

Marinelli, S. (2001). What does 'apple' mean? *Young Exceptional Children, 4*(2), 2–11.

Marvin, C. (1994). Home literacy experiences of preschool children with single and multiple disabilities. *Topics in Early Childhood Special Education, 14*(4), 436–454.

Mirenda, P. (2003). 'He's not really a reader…': Perspectives on supporting literacy development in individuals with autism. *Topics in Language Disorders, 23*(4), 271–282.

Missall, K., McConnell, S., and Cadigan, K. (2006). Early literacy development: Skill growth and relations between variables for preschool children. *Journal of Early Intervention, 29*(1), 1–21.

NAEYC (National Association for the Education of Young Children) (1998). Learning to read and write: developmentally appropriate practices for young children. *Young Children, 53*(4), 30–46.

Neuman, S., Copple, C., and Bredekamp, S. (2000). *Learning to read and write: Developmentally appropriate practices for young children.* Washington, DC: National Association for the Education of Young Children.

O'Brien, M. (2001). Inclusive child care for infants and toddlers: A natural environment for all children. In M.J. Guralnick, *Early childhood inclusion: Focus on change,* (pp. 229–251). Baltimore, MD: Paul H. Brookes.

Odom, S. (Ed.) (2002). *Widening the circle: Including children with disabilities in preschool programs.* New York: Teachers College Press.

Pierce, P., Summer, G., and O'deKirk, M. (2009). The Bridge: An authentic literacy assessment strategy for individualizing and informing practice with young children with disabilities. *Young Exceptional Children, 12*(3), 2–14.

Powell, D., Diamond, K., and Koehler, M. (2009). Use of a case-based hypermedia resource in an early literacy coaching intervention with pre-kindergarten teachers. *Topics in Early Childhood Special Education, 29*(4), 239–249.

Rowe, D.W. (2010). Directions for studying early literacy as social practice. *Language Arts, 88*(2), 134–143.

Sandall, S., Hemmeter, M.L., Smith, B., and McLean, M. (2005). *DEC Recommended Practices: A comprehensive guide for practical application early intervention/early childhood special education.* Frederick, CO: Sopris West.

Skouge, J., Rao, K., and Boisvert, P. (2007). Promoting early literacy for diverse learners using audio and video technology. *Early Childhood Education Journal, 35*(1), 5–11.

Snow, C.E. (1983). Literacy and language: Relationships during the preschool years, *Harvard Educational Review 53,* 165–189. Reprinted in S. Beck and L.N. Oláh (Eds), *Perspectives on language and literacy: Beyond the here and now,* (pp. 161–186). Harvard Educational Review Reprint Series.

Snow, C.E., Tabors, P., and Dickinson, D. (2001). Language development in the preschool years. In D.K. Dickinson and P.O. Tabors (Eds), *Beginning literacy with language,* (pp. 1–26), Baltimore, MD: Paul H. Brookes Publishing.

Soto, G., Yu, B., and Henneberry, S. (2007). Supporting the development of narrative skills of an eight-year old child who uses an augmentative and alternative communication device. *Child Language Teaching and Therapy, 23*(1), 27–45.

Spencer, T. and Slocoum, T. (2010). The effect of a narrative intervention on story retelling and personal story generation skills of preschoolers with risk factors and narrative language delays. *Journal of Early Intervention, 32*(3), 178–199.

Van Der Heyden, A., Snyder, P., Broussard, C., and Ramsdell, K. (2008). Measuring response to early literacy intervention with preschoolers at risk. *Topics in Early Childhood Education, 27*(4), 232–249.

Waller, A., O'Mara, D., Tait, L, Booth, L., Brophy-Arnott, B., and Hood, H. (2001). Using written stories to support the use of narrative in conversational interactions: Case study. *Augmentative and Alternative Communication, 17*(4), 221–232.

Whalon, K., Al Otaib, S., and Delano, M. (2009). Evidence-based reading instruction for individuals with autism spectrum disorders. *Focus on Autism and Other Developmental Disabilities, 24*(1), 3–16.

Wilkins, D. (2004). *The ninth degree.* Retrieved from http://www.everyoneisincluded.us/inclusionquotes 06.html

Early Childhood Literacy in Families, Communities, and Cultures across Media and Modes

Researching Young Children's Out-of-School Literacy Practices

Tamara Spencer, Michele Knobel, and Colin Lankshear

INTRODUCTION

'Out-of-school literacies' means different things to different people, and has been enlisted in diverse types of research during the past three or so decades to serve a range of educational purposes. In this chapter we outline some of the positions that have been adopted to date and provide examples of the research done under these. Most of the chapter, however, will be devoted to our preferred conception of young children's 'out-of-school literacies'.

Two broad distinctions delineate the main positions available on out-of-school literacy research. One distinction is between views that include out-of-school literacies as *any* literacy practice – including school-like or school-centric literacies – occurring in contexts outside formal school settings, and views that omit school literacies from consideration. Those taking the former

position will be prepared to include, for example, caregiver or intergenerational story-reading to young children, name writing, print awareness, decoding food product and other brand-related labels, completing school homework, drawing and colouring, oral book-like storytelling, among others (cf. Cairney, 2002; Wasik, 2004; Weigel, Martin, and Bennett, 2006). Those who take the second position, however, adopt the view that one defining feature of an out-of-school literacy is that it is *not* generally recognised as a characteristic or valued school literacy (cf. Hull and Schultz, 2002; Marsh, 2005a). Indeed, from this perspective, out-of-school literacies will typically be literacies that are *not* – or up until recently have not been – permitted or tolerated (and are not necessarily even practised as 'literacies') in school. Ten years ago, efforts to legitimate aspects of popular culture-based or social group-based literacies within the life of the school were seen by some as attempts to 'smuggle' out-of-school literacies into – or endorse them within – classroom curriculum and pedagogy. Somewhat ironically now, popular culture and other 'new' forms of literacy practice are being drawn on in many classrooms as resources for shoring up *traditional* literacy teaching practices in schools (cf. critiques in Knobel and Lankshear, 2010; Wohlwend, 2010). At the same time, deeply contextualised qualitative studies of what young children are doing with literacy in their everyday lives outside school continue to identify significant gaps between what children are already able to do with literacy and what is assumed about them as literacy learners in school. As such, while specific talk of 'out-of-school' literacies is somewhat on the wane due to the blurring of demarcations between 'home' and 'school', the area itself remains deeply important to literacy research.

The second broad distinction relates to age. Some researchers recognise out-of-school literacy practices engaged in by people of any age. Others, however, confine their interest in out-of-school literacies to practices engaged in by persons during their formal preschool/kindergarten to end of high-school years. This raises some interesting questions. In some ways it seems odd to think of someone who does not attend school as practicing 'out-of-school' literacies: at least, in the case of adults beyond compulsory education. It may not be so odd, however, to think of the concept applying to very young children who are becoming initiated into emergent literacy behaviours and other forms of primary socialisation that will have an impact one way or another on their school literacy achievement. The issue is clouded by the emergence of concepts such as 'lifelong learning', which entails people of all

ages 'going back to school' in some sense (whether school *per se*, a higher education institution, work-based training programmes, ongoing professional development, adult education of one form or another, and so on). The issue is clouded still further by the existence of a set of concepts that nest around the border between school and the wider world. These concepts include community literacies, literacy via popular culture resources, intergenerational literacy, family literacy, and so on (see related chapters in this volume). There is usually an implication here that school literacy is the *real* one on which other literacies depend for their recognition and in relation to which they are regarded as 'unofficial' and less important or valid (if not actually *antagonistic*), or to which they relate in a *service* capacity in order to help enhance school literacy performance.

These two distinctions provide four broad positions that are available so far as defining and distinguishing 'out-of-school literacy practice' are concerned (see Table 8.1). In the table, we define 'school age' as spanning formal preschool or kindergarten through to the end of high school. Over the past 10 years, formal preschooling has become an established norm in most English-speaking countries, with many young children (4–5 years old) required by law to attend half-day or full-day preschools, which warrants their inclusion in this grouping.

Our main interest in this chapter lies with research falling within the third quadrant – the study of school-aged children and their 'not-school' literacies. As we argue later, despite positive moves in this direction, this approach to investigating children's out-of-school literacies still holds significant promise for directly informing effective pedagogical practice,

Table 8.1   Four available research positions within out-of-school literacy studies

	Any literacy	*Not 'school' literacies*
School age range	Quadrant 1: Any literacy practice engaged in by a school-age individual in a setting outside the school	Quadrant 3: Any literacy practice engaged in by school-age individuals in settings outside the school that is *not* a formally recognised literacy practice within school pedagogy and curriculum
Any age	Quadrant 2: Any literacy practice engaged in by persons of any age within non-school (i.e., non-formal education) settings	Quadrant 4: Any literacy practice engaged in by persons of any age within non-school (formal education) settings that is *not* a recognised literacy belonging to a formal education curriculum or pedagogy

for challenging commonly held but detrimental assumptions and stereotypes regarding traditionally marginalised school children and their out-of-school lives, and for helping to shape more equitable literacy education policies. Before discussing this particular body of research, however, it is useful to consider briefly the other three quadrants in our matrix.

Quadrant 1: Any literacy, any school age range

Quadrant 1 above describes research studies focusing on what children do outside school that contributes directly to them developing (or not developing) sound and efficacious understandings – largely defined by school conceptions – of how written, spoken, and visual texts 'operate' (much of what is referred to as 'family literacy studies' falls into this category). Interestingly, in the 10 years that have elapsed since this chapter was first written, there have been noticeable and widespread shifts in expectations regarding young children's literacy proficiencies within pre-school and kindergarten settings. Indeed, a number of relatively recent curricular policies and initiatives in a range of countries

have pushed early childhood literacy development to the centre stage of educational reform moves (e.g., Early Years Literacy in Australia; Early Reading First and Reading First in the United States). The Early Reading First Policy in the US, for example, provides substantial funding for young children to '*enter* kindergarten with the necessary cognitive, language, and early literacy skills for success in school' (Roskos and Vukelich, 2006: 295; our emphasis). While the US seems to be leading the way in policy-driven curriculum in early literacy education settings, similar moves are underway within other countries like England, Australia, New Zealand, and elsewhere (e.g., Comber and Nichols, 2004; Duncan, 2004; Soler and Openshaw, 2007) in the form of standardised literacy testing for young children and the development of national curriculum packages and performance standards upon entry into primary school. The kinds of literacy proficiencies promoted for young children under these policies and initiatives are, for the most part, heavily shaped by school-centric definitions of literacy proficiency (Spencer, Falchi, and Ghiso, 2011). This, in turn, has generated a large body of research that focusses on young children and their *preparation* for reading and writing effectively in school. This research falls most often into Quadrant 1.

Studies found in Quadrant 1 are most often framed theoretically by psycholinguistics, developmental psychology and cultural psychology (especially, by appropriations from Vygotsky). Key concepts include: 'emergent literacy', 'literacy development', 'disadvantage', 'connection' and 'disconnection', 'collaborative home–school partnerships' – and, increasingly, 'intergenerational and sibling roles', 'meaning construction', 'diversity' and 'literacy processes'. At least three types of purposes characterise this body of research: (1) to document (and sometimes to evaluate, but rarely to intervene in) caregiver–child or child–child interactions with texts in order to identify children's emerging understandings of the functions and purposes of print (e.g., Gregory, Arju, Jessel, Kenner, and Mahera, 2007; Kenner, 2000; Kim and Anderson, 2008; Mui and Anderson, 2008; Smith, 2001, 2005; Rodriguez, 2004); (2) to compare young children's prior-to-school literacy development with their in-school literacy performance in order to better understand transitions from informal literacy learning at home to formal literacy learning at school (Arthur, Beecher, and Jones Diaz, 2001; Evans and Shaw, 2008); and (3) studies that respond to what are seen as the limitations of emergent literacy studies that 'do not fully take account of social and cultural variations that exist in young children's literacy learning trajectories' at home and school (Jones Diaz, Arthur, Becher, and McNaught, 2000: 231). Studies falling into Quadrant 1 often do not involve the researcher in conducting detailed observations in homes. Instead, they rely on parent reporting of home-based literacy practices via interviews or surveys, recordings of literacy events made by children and/or their caregivers, parent-completed inventories, diaries and/or checklists, formal texts produced in relation to family/home literacy initiatives, and so on (cf. Anderson, Anderson, Friedrich, and Kim, 2010; Bloome, Katz, Solsken, Willett, and Wilson-Keenan, 2000; Nichols, Nixon, and Rowsell, 2009; Parke, Drury, Kenner, and Robertson, 2002; Reese and Gallimore, 2000; Wasik, 2004). These studies generally tend to be investigatory or evaluative in nature, rather than interventionist. That is, they aim at documenting the extent to which young children are developing literacy skills and understandings they will need for school (e.g., correct letter name and sound identification, awareness of print, displaying reading readiness indicators).

Quadrant 2: Any literacy, any age

Quadrant 2 describes studies investigating literacy learning or competent performance regardless of age or non-school location. In the past, theories used to frame these evaluative studies have included, among others: psycholinguistics, cultural psychology, and emergent literacy theory. Recently, sociocultural theories of literacy as a practice within the context of after-school or family literacy programmes, or theories of multimodal literacies have been popular, too. Key concepts characterising this research include: 'transformation', 'disadvantage', 'communities of learners', 'social context', 'power', and 'discourse'. These studies may be: (1) *exploratory* (e.g., documenting pregnant teenagers' literacy levels, documenting lower-income families' story-reading practices); (2) *comparative* (e.g., comparing parents and grandparents reading to young children, comparing the home reading practices of diverse families along lines of class and/or ethnicity); or (3) *evaluative* (e.g., evaluating the effectiveness of a storybook reading programme that targets single mothers). Studies falling within this quadrant mainly have some family- or community-based intervention programme development in mind – and are often concerned with evaluating the efficacy of an existing family literacy intervention programme (Dail, McGee, and Edwards, 2009; Anderson and Morrison, 2007; Johnson, 2009; Purcell-Gates, 2000; St Pierre, Riciutti, and Rimdzius, 2005). Most family and community literacy programme studies and evaluations aim at helping parents deliver effective literacy instruction at home (Powell, Okagaki, and Bojczyk, 2004; Sénéchal and Young, 2008; Saint-Laurent and Giasson, 2005). Data mainly are collected by means of families videorecording literacy events at home, teacher and parent interviews, observing programme participant demonstrations of a new skill or process, or by documenting programmes in action via ethnographic means. As with studies in Quadrant 1, criteria used to analyse or evaluate home literacies and literacy interventions tend to be drawn from school-focussed definitions of literacy. These programmes and evaluative studies have a tendency to be rather 'adult-centric' in orientation, too; studying, for example, 'how parents and other adults prepare (or do not prepare) preschool-age children for later school literacy work' (Orellana, Reynolds, Dorner, and Meza, 2003: 18)

Interventions developed or evaluated in the course of these studies generally target families with parents who are judged to be struggling with standard literacy themselves. They range widely. Some interventions train parents to engage in talk about texts with their children that is 'lexically rich, includes extended discourses, and is somewhat distanced from the here and now' (Jordan, Snow, and Porche, 2000: 526; see also Tran, McNaughton, and Parr, 2011) or to 'develop [literacy-related] practices that fit into their family routines' (e.g., Dail et al., 2009). Others equip mothers of young babies with free books and instructional materials (e.g., Hardman and Jones, 1999), or provide reading-related materials to families (e.g., Dail et al., 2009). Others challenge the 'non-neutrality' of literacy instruction and remediation at school by examining a range of discourses and language uses operating in the homes and schools of traditionally marginalised children (e.g., Dudley-Marling and Lucas, 2009; Genishi and Dyson, 2009; Rogers, Tyson, and Marshall, 2000).

Quadrant 4: Non-schooled literacies, any age

Studies falling within Quadrant 4 focus largely on everyday literacy practices of adults and include work- and community-based activity and learning (cf. Gee, Hull, and Lankshear, 1996; Gee, 2011). This body of research 'explores the functions of literacy' (Hull and Schultz, 2001: 597) in a wide range of practical contexts in order to better understand the 'literacy requirements and literacy-related social practices of a variety of workplaces' and adult literacy programmes, and draws attention to ways in which literacy education in schools – including universities – does not always equip adults with the kinds of literacy know-how required by the world of work (2001: 597). Theories and methodologies drawn on by these studies include: cultural psychology (e.g., Scribner and Cole, 1981; Cole, 1996), feminist theory (cf. Gowen, 1992; Heller, 1997), the New Literacy Studies (e.g., Gee, 1996, 2011;

Street, 1984; 2005), linguistic anthropology (e.g., Scollon and Scollon, 2001), sociolinguistics (e.g., conversation analysis, language variation studies, critical discourse analysis), post-structuralist feminist theories (e.g., Walkerdine, 1990; Thomas, 2007), and social semiotics and multimodality (e.g., Kress, 2003). Key concepts include: 'discourse' – including different orders of discourse such as 'dominant discourse' and 'marginal discourse' – 'identity', 'social context', 'social practice', 'language/literacy practice', and 'literacies'. Data are generated by means of detailed interviews and ethnographic-type observations of participants' literacy uses and literacy-related activities.

These studies set in place a research tradition that typically addresses literacies not formally recognised in school-like or workplace settings yet nonetheless require relatively high degrees of literate competence in order to operate in everyday work, community and home contexts. These 'alternative' literacies include profession-related literacies, like those practiced by taxi drivers (e.g., Breier, Taetsane, and Sait, 1996), nurses (e.g., Cook-Gumperz and Hanna, 1997), factory workers (e.g., Hull, 1997; Kleifgen, 2001), or farm hands (e.g., Gibson, 1996); religion-based literacies such as those practiced by individuals (cf. Guerra and Farr, 2002), the Amish in the US (e.g., Fishman, 1988), or within a community of Seventh Day Adventists in Australia (e.g., Kapitzke, 1995); literacies within economically-depressed urban areas, along with those needed for local revitalisation projects (e.g., Barton and Hamilton, 1998; Kell, 2006); within indigenous communities (e.g., de la Piedra, 2009); within prisons or related programmes (e.g., Wilson, 2000; Vasudevan, 2010); literacy practices within low-income or unemployed households (e.g., Stein and

Slominsky, 2006); digitally networked and other popular culture and technology-related literacies of adults (e.g., Delgado-Gaitan, 2005; Mackey, 2007); and so on.

RESEARCHING STUDENTS' OUT-OF-SCHOOL LITERACIES

Studies of out-of-school literacy falling within Quadrant 3 focus on literacies that are defined *against* the grain of schooled literacies. These are variously referred to as 'everyday' (Prinsloo and Breier, 1996), 'local' (Barton and Hamilton, 1998), 'ordinary' (Lyons, 2007; see also Barton and Papen, 2010), 'alternative' (Cook-Gumperz and Keller-Cohen, 1993), 'hidden' (Finders, 1997), 'in-between' (Sarroub, 2002), 'vernacular' (Camitta, 1993; Barton, 2007) literacies, and so on. These studies begin with the assumption that regardless of what standardised tests or school scores might suggest, most school students are well able to practice and engage competently in literacies outside school. Much of the driving force behind them has been to advocate for a range of students and their rich literate social practices in reaction to narrow, school-based and 'schooled' literacies that privilege particular and normative language and literacy uses – and to teacher-made claims that there is a 'lack of literacy' in poor/working-class/non-white homes. Such teacher views and the privileged literacies associated with them work to further disadvantage already-marginalised children and social groups within a society (cf. Gee, 2011; Heath, 1983; Hicks, 2002; Taylor and Dorsey-Gaines, 1988). Research falling within our third quadrant is generally concerned with comparing the in-school and out-of-school literacy competencies and experiences of diverse pre-schoolers and school students. They aim to reveal congruencies and breaches between what children and young people are *already* able to do with literacy outside formal school contexts and what they are *expected* to do and be as 'literate' subjects within school settings.

Out-of-school studies of preschoolers' and students' literacies are not, however, interested in *privileging* non-school literacies over school literacies. This research approach recognises the very real impact and importance of students being able to navigate and produce polished and successful school literacies. Hence, it neither relies on home literacy practices as barometers of school success nor takes school literacy as a benchmark for evaluating students' out-of-school practices. Moreover, a focus on out-of-school literacies does not limit these literacies to home or community settings alone. Out-of-school literacies – particularly those associated with popular youth culture and digital communication and production – can be and are brought into classrooms (cf. Alvermann, 2010; Mahiri, 2003; Gee, 2007; Hill and Vasudevan, 2007), just as school literacies can be and are brought into homes and communities (Black, 2008, 2010; Volk and de Acosta, 2001).

The concept of 'practice' in the sense of 'a recurrent, goal-directed sequence of activities using a particular technology and particular systems of knowledge' (Scribner and Cole, 1981: 236), is integral to studying out-of-school (and in-school) literacies. A concern with literacy *practice* always takes into account knowing *and* doing, and calls into play the notion of *literacies* as a way of describing how people negotiate and construct patterned and socially recognisable ways of knowing, using language, and 'doing' to achieve different social and cultural purposes within different social and cultural contexts (Gee, 2011; Lankshear and Knobel, 2011).

Studies of students' out-of-school literacies pursue a diverse range of purposes. These include:

- examination of identity constructions and practices along lines of race (Fisher, 2003), class (Jones, 2006), gender (Finders, 1997; Schultz, 1996, 2002), and gender orientation (Blackburn, 2003, 2005)
- mapping multilingual negotiations of identity and cultural, religious and school discourses (Sarroub, 2002; Skilton-Sylvester, 2002)
- documenting the literacy practices of students belonging to marginal groups or youth deemed 'at risk' of failing school (e.g., Moje, 2000; Schultz, 2002).
- investigating differential literacy education outcomes for a range of often-silenced or overlooked children – such as those from white, working class homes, from marginal ethnic groups, migrant communities, or those excluded from school, etc. (Campano and Carpenter, 2005; Davies, 2006; Heath, 1983; Hicks, 2002; Lam, 2010; Pahl, 2002)
- alerting teachers to the literacies in which students are already proficient but that may not have been accommodated in class (Alvermann, 2010; Heath, 1983; Volk and de Acosta, 2001)
- undertaking exploratory studies that simply want to know what students do and "be" with literacy outside school settings (de la Piedra, 2009; Guzzetti and Gamboa, 2004; Knobel, 1999; Stein and Slominsky, 2006). This includes looking closely at how preschoolers and students are making use of a range of digital technologies in their everyday, out-of-school lives (Black, 2008, 2010; Lankshear and Knobel, 2011; Leander and Mills, 2007; Marsh, 2005b; Thomas, 2007).

Such studies often pursue multiple purposes.

This body of research differs from the studies in Quadrants 1 and 2 by emphasising contextualised documentation and analysis of everyday literacy practices that are not constrained by 'school-centric' views or standards of what constitutes 'effective' literacy.

Some researchers might argue that studies of children's literacy in after-school programmes should be included within this set of studies (e.g., Hull and Schultz, 2001). We do not engage with such studies here because of the often formalised nature and context of such programmes and they thus fall outside the scope of our interest here. Moreover, literacy research into after-school programmes tends to focus on older students and thus is not directly relevant to our purposes here (useful introductions to such studies can, for example, be found in Alvermann, 2001; Hill and Vasudevan, 2007; Hull and Schultz, 2002; Hull and Stornaiuolo, 2010). Moreover, a number of researchers have looked closely at the ways in which students have drawn on popular culture resources and knowledge to create texts at school for predominately teacher-generated purposes (e.g., Dyson, 2003; Vasquez, 2005; Wohlwend, 2009). This is an important body of work that also lies outside the scope of this particular chapter. It has not been easy drawing a boundary around what to include and exclude for our purposes here. Since this chapter was first written, sociocultural framings of out-of-school literacies have broadened well beyond the edges of the New Literacy Studies (which is what we took as our original reference point) to include theories from human geography (e.g., Leander and Sheehy, 2004), media studies theories (e.g., Marsh, 2005a), and postcolonial and globalisation theories (e.g., Lam, 2010), among others. This has certainly complicated the criteria for judging what kinds of studies belong in our corpus for the purposes of this chapter. As such, we have moved with the times and cast as wide a net as possible within the parameters we've established with respect to what constitutes 'out-of-school' literacies.

The remainder of this chapter deals with research that focusses on the contextualised study of young children's out-of-school literacies. This field of study has a stronger foothold within the educational research landscape than it did when this chapter was first written 10 years ago, and we believe this still-growing body of work reflects recognition that contextualised studies of young children's out-of-school literacies *do* have significant and enduring potential for enhancing understanding of the rich literate lives of young children and their literacy practices and learning experiences. We pay particular attention to research that focusses on children in the 'early school years' age range, approximately preschool-aged children to third grade (i.e., 4–8 years of age). In short, in order to be able to make claims about young children and their *out-of-school* literacy practices, the children studied need to be engaged in attending some kind of formalised, school or school-like institution; to put this another way, in order to be able to make claims about out-of-school literacy practices, a comparative base of 'in-school' literacy practices needs to be acknowledged (even if only tacitly). A few studies on which we focus examine toddler-aged children (Davidson, 2009; Marsh, 2004; Robinson and Turnbull, 2005), but take as their principal frame of reference children who spend at least part of each week in formal preschool or school settings. In keeping with conventions within the early childhood field, we typically will refer to this group as 'children' or 'young children' rather than 'students', but understand it to include those children who regularly attend some kind of formalised, school-like institution.

Researching young children's out-of-school literacies

In 2002, Hull and Schultz published the first comprehensive review of out-of-school literacy research. They located close to 50 out-of-school studies from the US, England, Wales, Australia, Mexico, and South Africa. Only one of the studies listed by Hull and Schultz dealt with children 8 years old or younger. This was Shirley Brice Heath's classic ethnography of three communities and their literacy practices (Heath, 1982, 1983). Our own review of the literature at the time indicated that out-of-school literacy practices involving children from birth to age 8 was a sorely under-researched area (Knobel and Lankshear, 2003). We found a total of four studies that were conducted from a sociocultural theoretical orientation and which focussed on children's out-of-school literacy practices.

To locate the most recent English-language research into the out-of-school literacy lives of young children, we searched EBSCO, Academic Premier, Education Research Complete, JSTOR, and Google Scholar to find empirical, published (in books or journals) research studies dating from 2003 to 2011, the time elapsed since the first edition of this chapter. Key descriptors included: 'out-of-school + literacy', 'literacies', 'new literacies', 'vernacular literacies' and 'everyday literacies', 'popular culture + new media', 'technology + literacy', 'digital games + literacy', and 'bilingualism + bicultural literacies'. Queries also contained the search terms 'early childhood' or 'preschool' to focus search returns on children in preschool through to 8 years of age. In addition, we identified key international English-language education and literacy journals that published early childhood research and literacy studies (i.e., *Reading Research Quarterly*, *Literacy*, *Journal of Early Childhood Literacy Research*, *Contemporary Issues in Early Childhood*, *Early Childhood Education Journal*, *Language Arts*). These journals

were hand-searched to find additional studies missed by our original database searches. Only studies that included an explicit focus on out-of-school contexts were selected; consequently, studies conducted entirely within preschool, school and after-school programme settings were excluded. This process identified nine 'new' studies, making a total of 13 studies in all when we include the four from the first edition of this chapter, that fall into Quadrant 3 of our typology (i.e., Davidson, 2009; Heath, 1983; Hicks, 2002; McTavish, 2009; Marsh, 2004, 2010; Mavers, 2007; Pahl, 2002, 2005; Perry and Moses, 2011; Robinson and Turnbull, 2005; Shegar and Weninger, 2010; Volk and de Acosta, 2001).

These studies all used qualitative research methods such as those drawn from ethnography and case study, although some were part of larger studies that included both quantitative and qualitative dimensions (e.g., McTavish, 2009; Marsh, 2010). Data collection methods included audio and video recordings, interviews, observations, field notes, and collection of artifacts and photographs. Data were collected from a range of settings, including homes, churches, playgrounds, and schools (the latter for comparative purposes). Data analysis methods included conversation analysis, inductive coding strategies, social semiotic analysis, and theme analysis, among others. Studies were conducted in England, Canada, Singapore, Australia, and the US. The number of participants in each study ranged from 1 to 26, and focus participants ranged in age from 2 to 8 years old (with the exception of Heath's study. Heath (1982) conducted a 10+ year ethnography and research participants comprised members of several families from three communities of different social and economic classes). Across these studies, male and female genders were more or less evenly included. The duration of data collection ranged from one study of two children using a computer to conduct research work for 30 minutes (Davidson, 2009) through to studies of young children's out-of-school literacy practices lasting years.

In the section that follows, we analyse and discuss this corpus of studies. Our analysis suggested three general thematic categories:

(1) studies that situate young children's out-of-school literacies within family and community relationships and document a host of rich language and literacy practices not always seen by teachers as congruent with school literacies. These studies also demonstrate the ways in which children take up and use literacy practices as they learn to be members of their communities or social groups (Heath, 1982; Hicks, 2002; Robinson and Turnbull, 2005; McTavish, 2009; Volk and de Acosta, 2001);

(2) studies that focus on young children's play and their growing understandings of how literacies and digital technologies (in particular) 'work' (Marsh, 2004, 2010; Pahl, 2005); and

(3) instances when 'non-school' texts like television shows, video games, or internet sites etc. – along with attendant social practices – present new meaning making and textual opportunities for young children (Davidson, 2009; Mavers, 2007; Pahl, 2002; Perry and Moses, 2011; Shegar and Weninger, 2010).

These three distinctions are largely heuristic in nature and there is certainly a good deal of overlap between each. Nonetheless, these three categories are useful for drawing attention to interesting similarities among these studies, and for identifying possible trends in early childhood out-of-school literacies research.

(1) Young children's social relationships and their out-of school literacies

In this set of studies (Heath, 1982; Hicks, 2002; Robinson and Turnbull, 2005; McTavish, 2009; Volk and de Acosta, 2001), the researchers ground their inquiries within sociocultural contexts and provide ethnographic accounts that position young children's literacy practices as fully embedded in home, familial, and community or social life. To do so, they provide extensive descriptions of children acquiring and practicing literacies that inevitably overlap with older family or community members' literacy practices. A key theme found in these five studies is 'the ways in which material relations and attachments with others shape early practices of reading' (Hicks, 2002: 41). Findings from this set of studies suggest that understanding children's literacy practices and abilities at home (and at school) cannot discount the importance of family and class values and family and other social relationships. Attention is drawn to ways children's socially-valued out-of-school literacy practices are taken up, made room for, or excluded in classrooms. In all five studies, the researchers aim at disrupting discourses in which 'underprivileged children' are viewed as 'lacking' knowledge or needed language and literacy skills, a viewpoint that all too often permeates current early childhood education policies and initiatives.

Shirley Brice Heath's (1982) 10-year ethnography of three southern, US communities – Maintown, Roadville, Trackton – aims at informing teachers' literacy pedagogy by documenting the ways of speaking, reading, writing and listening in each of these communities. The middle-class community of Maintown participated in language practices overtly valued and used in school (e.g., knowing fairytales and being able to write fictional stories, asking a question whose answer is known to both the asker and the respondent) and which prepared children for operating relatively seamlessly between home and school. Children in Roadville – a white, working-class community – engaged in literacy events that valued factual information over fiction. Invented stories were regarded as 'lies', and bedtime story reading with parents emphasised factual or literal engagement with the text. Roadville students did well in school until the teacher began expecting more abstract and creative work which they were unable to produce successfully. Children in Trackton – an African-American working class community – were taught to be independent and to hold their own in oral engagements with others. They played with words, invented rhymes, crafted elaborate oral narratives, and engaged in witty repartee and teasing word play with adults and peers. Few of these complex literacies were included in the Grade 1 curriculum and Trackton children were confused by school literacy practices such as 'Once upon a time' stories, item identification worksheets, unfamiliar question forms, and 'what-explanations' (p. 69).

Deborah Hicks' (2002) 3-year ethnographic case study of two white, working-class children living in a large US city focusses on Laurie and Jake. Laurie is a vibrant young girl whose out-of-school life at 5 years old was filled with imaginary travel to exotic places, mythical beasts, and the desire for a prince (in the form of a loving father) to rescue her family. By the middle of Grade 1, however, Laurie had fallen seriously behind her classmates in reading and writing and required remedial intervention at school. She became increasingly disaffected with school while being medicated for an attention deficit disorder and dealing with her sometimes turbulent home-life. At home, 5-year-old Jake moved freely and confidently between a range of literacy-related activities that involved learning by doing ('rather than by talking about parts of a task'; p. 99), linking texts

to three-dimensional objects (e.g., car racing magazines with his model cars), working collaboratively with his father in building or fixing things, being read to by his grandmother, reading or recalling facts from information texts (e.g., on US presidents), and the like. In Grades 1 and 2, however, Hicks watched as Jake increasingly tuned out of lessons – especially reading lessons – and became more and more angrily frustrated with the lock-stepped, seat-bound nature of the school's reading programme and the tasks required of him.

An 8-year-old, Indo-Canadian boy – Rajan – is at the heart of Marianne McTavish's (2009) 3-month-long case study of in-school and out-of-school information literacy practices. Rajan lives in a working-class area with his parents, brother and grandparents. Punjabi is the primary language spoken at home. Data were collected in Rajan's home and yard, his neighbourhood, and at the local park, as well as at school. Rajan regularly engaged with family members around a range of information texts associated with their shared passion for sport (especially soccer) and world events. This included discussing sport, watching televised games together, looking up information on the internet using the family computer, contributing to a collaboratively written flowchart recording that season's wins and losses, watching English and Punjabi news broadcasts, and so on. In short, Rajan's out-of-school information literacy practices were a seamless part of larger shared interests and social practices. In-school data were collected during a classroom focus on information texts. Here, 'information' was often sets of decontextualised facts that Rajan had trouble recalling, and information literacy focussed heavily on the structure of information texts (e.g., defining terms like 'glossary', 'index'). The single computer in the classroom was rarely used. McTavish argues for the importance of knowing and understanding the dynamic ways in which information literacy connects with learning, doing, and being outside of school.

Muriel Robinson and Bernardo Turnbull (2005) conducted a 6-year ethnographic case study of one child, Verónica, and her literacy practices at home. Their findings challenge assumptions that popular culture texts and artifacts harm children's literacy development. The researchers used an 'asset model' approach (p. 52) to examine the skills, competencies and knowledge children acquire when they make sense of print and media texts while simultaneously being enculturated into 'traditional' conceptions of text. The wide range of texts that Verónica experienced served to inform her social interactions and furnished opportunities for 're-interpreting the world' (p. 65). As a 2-year-old, she displayed interest in traditional reading- and writing-like behaviour; however, her symbolic repertoire extended beyond this to include audio-visual texts and toys. For example, Verónica developed an intense interest in dinosaurs and did not distinguish between the textual resources she called upon (e.g. television, books, computer games) in her 'asset bank' (p. 68) as she explored this topic. Family members engaged in literacy events with movies, billboards, books, and images of dinosaurs, thereby creating communicative and literate practices that Verónica felt vested and expert in as a participant. In sum, Verónica's understandings of the content (e.g., dinosaurs) and texts (e.g., television shows) intertwined with the social relationships and interests that governed her early childhood years. Robinson and Turnbull argue that children approach a broad range of texts in a 'truly porous' (p. 69) fashion, and suggest that

children's literacy learning involves 'ongoing negotiations of meaning' across a range of textual and meaning-making resources (p. 70).

Dinah Volk and Martha de Acosta (2001) conducted yearlong ethnographic case studies of three Puerto Rican children (two aged 6 years, one aged 5 years) and their everyday lives in a working class area of a large city in the US mid-west. All three were 'Spanish-dominant' and belonged to Protestant churches. All attended the same bilingual preschool. Among other things, Volk and de Acosta found the literacies promoted at church entailed memorisation, repetition, group oral recitation and reading the Bible. Nevertheless, Volk and de Acosta suggest that far from encouraging rote learning and passivity, church literacy practices served to enroll these children as '[a]ctive participants with more competent others' in learning 'the language and behaviors valued in many classrooms' (p. 218). Indeed, Volk and de Acosta found that what counted as literacy at home and at church was 'primarily social interactions with familiar texts containing significant and useful knowledge' (p. 219). In contrast, what counted as literacy in school 'was a progression from social to individual interactions with print' (pp. 219–220). Thus, literacy events at home and at church tended to be much more collaborative than at school, despite the kindergarten teacher's overt interest in group learning and shared meaning-making.

All five studies focus on children's literacies within their everyday practices and in conjunction with an array of community, familial, and school relationships. Heath's study confronted taken-for-granted assumptions that children from working-class families did not engage in rich literacy experiences at home or in their communities. While it has been close to 30 years since Heath's groundbreaking study, her call for educators to rethink the ways of speaking, reading, writing and listening valued most in class, and to make greater efforts to accommodate different ways of being literate – such as those demonstrated by the Roadville and Trackton children – remains relevant and pressing. Hicks' study highlights what happens when rich home literacy practices are out of kilter with school literacy practices, and what can be lost when teachers overlook the literacies young children *do* bring with them to school. Volk and de Acosta used their study findings to critique research that focusses *solely* on parent-child interactions, and which misses 'the complexity and richness' of wider support networks and literacy practices occurring within the everyday lives of young children (p. 216). They called on teachers to recognise children's out-of-school literacies as significant resources to draw on in classroom-based teaching. Robinson and Turnbull's 'asset model' and case study points to the range of textual knowledge children acquire simply through participating in socially-shared literacy practices. These researchers emphasise the osmotic relationship between the various literacy practices in a child's life and the knowledge a child can acquire from making meaning across an array of resources. Collectively, these studies remind educators to think carefully about literacy practices within the out-of-school lives of young children and how to build on these in ways that help to maximise literacy success in school for all children.

(2) Out-of-school literacies and play

This set of studies (Marsh, 2004, 2010; Pahl, 2005) emphasises the relationship between play and the out-of-school literacy practices of children. The relationship between play and literacy development has been examined extensively from cognitive, ecological, and sociocultural perspectives (Marsh, 2010). However, in most of this literature, 'play' is viewed as a space that can be enhanced by literacy activities or as a time when adults might intervene to further support 'literacy-rich play' (Morrow and Schickedanz, 2006; Neuman and Roskos, 1992). This orientation towards play largely restricts 'what counts' to whatever is valuable in the service of school-like literacy behaviours. The studies presented in this section take an alternative view and focus instead on children engaging in play as a social and cultural practice. That is, Marsh (2004, 2010) and Pahl (2005) consider the literacy tools, skills and understandings young children develop and choose to use when provided with an imaginative space in which to wonder, speculate, and 'try on' different social practices and identities.

Jackie Marsh's investigation of children's 'techno-literacies' (2004) stands as a forerunner in drawing academic attention to young children's digital literacy practices. Although Marsh's study focussed on children younger than 4 years old, we have included it here because of her specific focus on 'emergent literacy' which is a key theoretical and curricular element in many early childhood settings. In her study, Marsh argued that emergent literacy perspectives within early childhood studies needed to be reworked to include digital technology and multimodal meaning-making, as well as considerations of how young children take charge of their own learning through play. Marsh's study of toddlers' emergent techno-literacies involved working-class families with children aged 2.5–3 years old in a Sure Start region – defined by the location of the UK government's 'early years' intervention programmes. Survey responses (from

44 families), along with interviews and home visits (involving 26 families), identified a broad range of literacy practices within participating families. Although television- and movie-watching dominated these young children's everyday literacy practices, parents reported that their children engaged in a range of playful actions while watching television, including talking to the characters or about the programme, playing with objects to hand, dancing, and/or singing. In addition, children regularly re-enacted narratives seen on television, often relating a show to their own lived experiences. In addition, 32 families reported owning a computer and/or a gaming device, and Marsh found that young children were learning – with the help of older family members – a range of game narrative navigation skills and acquiring increased dexterity and game know-how even when 'pretend playing' a game.

In subsequent research, Marsh (2010) examined children's use of commercial 'virtual worlds', which are steeped in socially- and literacy-rich playful practices. Marsh focussed on 13 children, aged 5–7 years and all from working-class families, who indicated within the context of a larger study they used online virtual worlds (e.g., *Club Penguin*, *Barbie Girls*, *Nicktropolis*). She found that 'play' of various kinds attracted these children to virtual worlds. This included playing programmed in-world games (e.g., mini puzzle games, hide-and-seek), as well as the world itself affording a rich space for 'fantasy play, socio-dramatic play, ritualised play, games with rules, and what might be called "rough and tumble play"' (p. 30). Play regularly involved literacy as a key component of games and world use (e.g., sending private messages to others, text-based chatting with others, reading in-world newspapers and letters, reading in-world library

books and other instructions on game play and world navigation). Marsh argues that many virtual world literacy practices resonate with valued school literacy practices (e.g., word recognition skills, scanning text in order to retrieve appropriate information, familiarity with different text structures, spelling skills, using texts to collaborate with others) and virtual world play should be seen as a worthwhile practice.

Drawing on data from a larger, 3-year linguistic ethnography of children's communicative practices, Kate Pahl (2005) examines the ways in which three 5–6-year-old boys used console video games to develop new textual practices and narrative structures, and to engage in complex identity work. She found that all three boys treated the 'figured worlds' of video games as 'cultural resources' for improvisation and play. Text making, in addition to playing the actual games, included recontextualising games as drawings on paper (which often added elements not found in the game), as sociodramatic play grounded in some aspect of the game(s), such as 'pretend fighting', and in talk about or while playing games. Through their text making, the boys explored a range of narrative forms and structures, and recursive, narrative selves (e.g., as the in-game 'fighting man', the skilful player, the in-game victim, the narrator, the child himself; p. 142). Pahl explains how this 'reconceptualisation' of console game playing has much to offer in-school writing practices, including new narrative forms that focus on space, levels, and settings, as well as new understandings of the knowledge and textual practices children bring with them to school.

This set of studies uses detailed, situated empirical data to examine the relationship between children's play – a longstanding cornerstone of early childhood research and pedagogy – and their out-of-school literacy practices. The studies draw attention to literacy practices that might otherwise be overlooked or dismissed within early childhood studies, and underscore the importance of taking seriously young children's very real and often sophisticated uses of digital technologies. Our review of the research literature suggests that this is an important contribution to the field, and one where there remains much room for further research. Marsh's studies provide important new theoretical and methodological positions from which to examine the relationship between popular culture, new literacies, and young children's out-of-school literacy development. Pahl reminds us that console or video game play is rarely one single, well-bounded thing for young children; it provides rich meaning-making resources and identities for all kinds of imaginative and valuable play and learning. In sum, this body of work emphasises the importance of paying close attention to how children make sense of their worlds and how they play with and around digital media in ways that feed directly into their literacy practices and learning.

(3) New textual and meaning-making practices and opportunities

'New' is always a tricky descriptor to use – it can invoke a break from the old, a sense of chronological development, a new-for-now orientation, and so on. In the present case, 'new' refers to research that identifies ways in which young children are making and sharing meanings and generating texts that have not yet been documented well. It may be because they are indeed 'new' ways in a never-before-seen sense, or because they have flown under the research radar. The body of research in this section (Davidson, 2009; Mavers,

2007; Pahl, 2002; Perry and Moses, 2011; Shegar and Weninger, 2010) focusses on texts and literacy practices not typically recognised in school as having value (e.g., television shows, video games, trading cards, free-ranging internet use, interest-driven research) in order to better understand the knowledge and proficiencies children amass when participating in social practices, and how social practices using 'non-school texts' inform both out-of-school and in-school literacy knowledge and development.

Christina Davidson's (2009) ethnomethodological study focusses on two young Australian siblings and their internet use at home (p. 40). Denny (almost 3 years old) and Matthew (6.5 years), together with their father (with some input from their mother), were searching for information about lizards using Google, Wikipedia and a reference book about reptiles. Davidson demonstrates the 'seamless ways in which the two children moved between texts and technologies as they accomplished various social activities; whether it was talking about a computer image, doing a Google search, finding the name of a lizard in a book, or keying in a name to do a Google search' (p. 50). The children's searches were accompanied by rich social interaction among the children and their parents as they were collaboratively 'generating, communicating and negotiating meaningful content' using different texts and previous experiences (p. 50). Davidson argues that distinctions between 'old' and 'new' literacies simply do not exist for young children who are 'powerful users of technologies' and other meaning-making resources at home (p. 50). She calls for educators to also blur the lines between 'old' and 'new' literacies, and make space for sustained social interactions in the classroom as children generate and negotiate meaningful content and participate in real-beyond-school social practices.

Diane Mavers (2007) used social semiotic analysis to interpret the ways in which one young girl – Kathleen (aged 6 years) – used printed text resourcefully within a specific social context. This context comprised an exchange of four emails between Kathleen and her uncle (each sent two messages) over the course of 4 days. Mavers argues that young children are especially resourceful when it comes to making meaning with whatever they have to hand. She also argues that alphabetic writing is usefully understood as a semiotic – rather than simply a linguistic – resource. In the case of Kathleen's emails, Mavers scrutinises Kathleen's opening informal greeting, the absence of capitalisation and minimal use of punctuation, spacing between words, her spelling, and how the latter causes some confusion on the uncle's part (he read 'baeg' as 'bag' instead of 'badge') – quickly repaired in a brief second message from Kathleen that mixes spoken and written conventions. Mavers discusses how these things combined demonstrate Kathleen's understanding of the ways in which written language can be 'designed' to address specific needs within particular social contexts. She urges educators to view children's writing practices as indicators of important existing 'literate capacities' and understandings (p. 172), rather than as not-yet-adult writing practices.

Over 18 months, Pahl (2002) documented three boys' text production practices at home. Two boys had been excluded from school. All were from single-parent (mother) families. Two boys were Indian or Anglo-Indian, and one was Turkish. Sol (6 years) drew Pokémon characters and scenes, built Pokémon figures from modelling clay, and created his own Pokémon trading cards, inventing new characters in the process. Fatih (5 years) used resources from Pokémon, Nintendo's *Super Mario* video games, his mother's prayer practices, and 'his own internal landscape of birds and chickens' in his drawings and narratives (p. 152). Edward (8 years) drew detailed images of trains (his great-grandfather helped build Indian railways) and his grandmother's farm in Wales. Family-oriented resources, like narratives about farm life, trains and other experiences, were key to Edward's meaning-making rather than popular cultural resources. For Pahl, localised, fleeting texts – 'ephemeral' and shortlived (made from anything to hand) – demonstrate literate understandings and resourceful improvisations in relation to text production and meaning making more so than conventionally recognised texts. Pahl calls for researchers to pay closer attention to 'children's meaning making in the home as intimately connected with the space in which it is produced' (p. 164) to better understand the complexities of young children's meaning-making practices.

As part of a larger study, Kristen Perry and Annie Moses' (2011) 18-month ethnography examined television viewing and the language and literacy practices of three Sudanese refugee families – and four focal children (in kindergarten or first grade) from across these families – in the US. The families all spoke Arabic at home, but were quite different from each other in terms of educational background and current occupations. Perry and Moses found television viewing – whether engaged or intermittent – along with talking about shows, drawing characters from shows, playing television-related computer games, reading websites connected to shows, or browsing library books about shows, provided children (and their parents) with resources for making connections with their Sudanese culture and heritage (e.g., DVDs of music videos or soap-opera-style dramas from different African countries), religious practices, and their new US context (including American history, politics and pop culture). Television also provided children with opportunities to engage in meaningful English language and print literacy skills, such as reading text captions on the TV screen, reading DVD covers, writing stories based on shows, or playing television-related computer games. Perry and Moses argue that television was an important language and literacy learning resource in these families, especially for the four focal children, and that these children's multimedia interests and engagements can be used to further their literacy development at school.

Five bilingual boys (aged 5–6 years) in Singapore and their home literacy practices form the core of Chitra Shegar and Csilla Weninger's (2010) ethnography. The boys were observed for 30 hours each during a 9-month period across a range of activities, including drawing, watching television or DVDs, using the computer, and reading books in English or Tamil. Shegar and Weninger found that prior textual experiences enabled the boys to engage more fully with texts to hand (e.g., discussing a dinosaur storybook included spoken references to information gleaned from watching movies such as *Walking with Dinosaurs* and *Jurassic Park*). Popular culture intertextuality proved to be a resource for creating new texts, too (e.g., collages of cartoon characters cut from cereal boxes), as well as for developing links between different text types and content (e.g., links between Superman movies and newspaper reports of the death of Superman actor, Christopher Reeves). They also identified 'thematic' intertextuality

(e.g., 'magic' things, 'scary' things) that the boys drew on and that spurred them to engage with new texts. The researchers emphasise how children's pop-culture intertextual practices can scaffold literacy learning at school, although typically children's popular culture knowledge in school settings accrues only social and not intellectual capital.

In this collection of studies, the researchers describe a diverse range of meaning-making practices in young children's out-of-school lives in ways that challenge the still-dominant text-centric nature of literacy learning in most early-childhood classrooms. The researchers show how even very young children can draw on popular culture and other media, ephemeral text-making practices, shared family interests, digital media and affordances, and the like, to express and explore a range of ideas and interests. These studies show how many young children are currently practising well-formed and effective literacies in out-of-school settings – rather than simply developing 'emergent' literacy skills in readiness for 'developmentally' sequenced learning at school. They also show how young children are availing themselves of all kinds of 'new' opportunities to create and share texts with others (e.g., email exchanges, researching lizards, generating new texts by building on popular culture and media resources). Out-of-school literacy practices are clearly understood by the children in these studies to be part and parcel of their everyday social interactions and practices, rather than stand-alone, one-off acts of meaning making (the latter characterises many of the school literacy experiences for these children as reported by the researchers).

In addition, this set of studies speaks to the ways in which these 'new' (new in the sense of being new hybrid forms altogether, as well as new-to-the-child) textual spaces and opportunities are taken up for social purposes. Davidson's and Mavers' studies focus attention on how children's computer use is often thoroughly social, and can involve negotiated, collaborative meaning making that extends well beyond the computer screen. In the case of the studies by Perry and Moses, Shegar and Weninger, and Pahl, television, popular culture and text production steeped in family interests and experiences provide an entrance point – linguistically, intellectually and socially – to (potential) in-school literacy success for diverse children. This stands in contrast with the in-school experiences of many of the children in these studies which are often built around narrow conceptions of literacy competence as the ability to encode and decode printed texts.

DISCUSSION

Our summaries have not done justice to the detailed descriptions and analyses of the young children and their literacy practices presented in these studies. They do, however, indicate the significant contributions such studies can make to understanding the rich and complex literacy practices in which children engage within their everyday lives, and notably, to understanding children often regarded officially as 'literacy failures', or as *not having* 'literacy' at home. These studies demonstrate ways in which literacy practices are always deeply *social*: embedded in and constituting an array of familial, community and school relationships and socially recognised practices.

Our personal interest in and commitment to the kinds of studies falling within Quadrant 3 of our matrix stem from their potential to challenge narrow *scholastic*

conceptions of literacies that become a basis for allocating and withholding school success in inequitable ways. These studies collectively alert teachers to young children's existing understandings of and facility with literacies within a range of social practices, and concretely suggest how best to build on these understandings and capabilities in classrooms. This is especially important with regard to studies documenting everyday literacy practices of marginalised children – whether this marginalisation is in terms of class, academic performance, gender, behaviour, religion, home language, ethnicity, and so on. Out-of-school studies of young children's literacy practices can also alert researchers and educators to the complexities associated with becoming 'school literate' and fluent in *school* discourses.

Three trends

It is possible to see across the body of studies surveyed in this chapter at least three interesting trends with respect to research: (1) an increased theoretical hybridity, (2) greater explicit recognition of the role of popular culture and digital technologies in young children's literacy practices, and (3) a blurring of in-school and out-of-school distinctions. Each of these is discussed in turn below.

(1) Theoretical hybridity

Interestingly, the bulk of the studies published within the past 8 or so years evidences moves towards drawing on theories found beyond what traditionally has shaped out-of-school literacies research. Hull and Schultz (2001: 576), for example, identify three broad theoretical orientations – and mixes – that characterised the studies found in their exhaustive review of out-of-school literacies research: ethnography of communication, Vygotskian perspectives and activity theory, and the New Literacy Studies. In our corpus, we find these three orientations, along with theoretical insights from conversation analysis (Davidson, 2009), social semiotics (Marsh, 2004; Mavers, 2007), play theory (Marsh, 2010; Pahl, 2005), social identity theories (Marsh, 2010; Pahl, 2005), media theories (Marsh, 2004, 2010; Perry and Moses, 2011), new literacies studies (Davidson, 2009), and literary theory (Shegar and Weninger, 2010). Admittedly, our corpus of studies remains insufficient numbers-wise for extrapolating to larger bodies of work, but at least within the field of early childhood and out-of-school literacy studies it appears there is a shift towards tailoring theoretical frameworks for studies that enable researchers to best explain what is happening in their data, rather than using pre-established theoretical frameworks. This shift certainly matches trends in related areas of research. Kress and Street (2006) discuss the usefulness of complementary theories – like those of the New Literacy Studies and social semiotics (including multimodality) – in helping to more fully explain the complexities of current literacy practices. They also point to 'a growing move, … an increasing awareness that the complexity and the fluidity of the world – of which representation is but a part – demands the joining of intellectual, theoretical resources, demands the fashioning of new [analytic] tools from the old' (p. x; see also Pahl and Rowsell, 2006). Similarly, in our own work (Lankshear and Knobel, 2011), we've pointed to the importance of developing new 'converging' or hybrid theories for framing sociocultural studies of literacies – especially when these entail digital technologies of one kind or another. Hybrid theoretical framings enable researchers to foreground

concepts and elements, such as 'identity', 'social practice', 'space', 'play', 'learning', 'meaning making', and the like, that have not always been included, or sufficiently explained or defined analytically in previous out-of-school literacy studies. The diversity of the hybrid or tailored theoretical framings found in the studies falling into our Quadrant 3 certainly seems to speak to a growing recognition of the complexities of young children's literacies and social practices.

(2) Literacies, popular culture and digital technologies

A comprehensive survey of the English-language research literature we conducted in 2002 (Lankshear and Knobel, 2003) focussed on young children (birth to 8 years) and their engagement with digital technologies, and found this to be a much under-studied area. Eight years later, a similar review by Burnett (2010) found that while young children and digital technology has received some academic attention, little of this has been directed at understanding new technologies in children's out-of-school lives, or to social practices associated with young children's digital technology use. The bulk of the research surveyed by Burnett was shaped by psycholinguistic theories of reading and most often took the form of quantitative studies of technology as a 'deliverer of literacy' (p. 254). That being said, a hallmark of the out-of-school studies described in this chapter – especially those published since 2004 – is their inclusion of young children's engagement in a range of digitally-mediated practices. Marsh's 2004 study of very young children's engagement with a broad range of media in the home was among the first – if not *the* first – publications to report on the important literacy learning and use opportunities afforded by family-assisted video game playing by very young children. Admittedly, in line with Burnett's findings, our corpus includes only two studies that explicitly target children's contextualised use of digital technologies within their homes (Marsh, 2010; Pahl, 2005). Nonetheless, both studies draw important attention to the need to rethink existing conceptions of 'emergent' literacy proficiencies to take account of the quite complex literacies young children are already practising when they participate in virtual worlds or video game playing.

What is perhaps most interesting about our corpus of studies is the way in which children's engagement with digital technologies is included as a matter of course within their detailed, descriptive accounts. This parallels large-scale studies that show young children across all socioeconomic classes in developed countries independently, and with support, using computer software and the internet, DVD players, and playing video games etc. on a regular basis and for extended periods of time (cf. Marsh et al., 2005; Blanchard and Moore, 2010). In our corpus, researchers find that using digital technologies is rarely anything out of the ordinary, and that their use is typically in the service of some interest or shared undertaking. So, for example, Davidson (2009) finds that, for at least two young children, reading information found online is just one strategy among many (such as referring to hardcopy books, a parent) on which they can draw to learn more about lizards. In doing so, she underscores how it is the interaction around these multiplicity of sources in which knowledge is co-constructed and shared. Lizards, rather than texts per se, are the centre of these children's attention. Similarly, Verónica (Robinson and Turnbull, 2005) makes no distinction between dinosaur-themed video games,

hardcopy books, or television shows in her passion for learning more about dinosaurs. McTavish (2009) explains how Rajan's computer and video game use is fully embedded in a dynamic range of family and friendship interests and relationships. Six-year-old Kathleen in Mavers' (2007) study uses email to correspond with an uncle – where sharing the news about a significant swimming achievement was her driving purpose, and her choice of mode matched her older brothers' and her parents' modes of engaging with others. Similar examples abound in our article set. None of the researchers found the children in their studies drawing distinctions between reading and writing with printed or digital texts, and many found seamless movement between different modes based on immediate purpose, a larger set of situated social interactions, or on key moves within a given social practice (e.g. navigating a virtual world, playing a video game, updating a sports results spreadsheet). This directly challenges research studies and curriculum plans that assume a single text, such as a reading skills website or a CD-ROM book, can 'deliver literacy' effectively to young children as part of a learning programme. The 'everyday-ness' of practices involving digital technologies and networks in young children's out-of-school lives also underscores the importance of recognising such technologies and networks as important, not to be under-estimated – but not parcelled-off – elements of children's out-of-school literacy practices.

It's fair to argue that the study of young children's technology use owes much to the earlier and ongoing study of young children's engagement with and use of popular culture as a resource for meaning making. Marsh's (2005a) edited collection, *Popular Culture, New Media and Digital Literacy in Early Childhood*, for example, presented a timely compilation of studies highlighting young children's complex literacy practices. Prior to this, much of the research on young children and their engagement with popular culture and digital technologies tended to emphasise threats new media posed to children's 'appropriate development' (see critiques of this in Blanchard and Moore, 2010; Copple and Bredekamp, 2009; Marsh, 2010). When young children's computer use was examined more positively in the early 2000s, research tended to focus on using digital technologies to teach, practice, or explore traditional print-centric elements such as alphabetic principles or phonemic awareness (Blanchard and Moore, 2010; Davidson, 2009; Wohlwend, 2010). The studies surveyed in this chapter certainly suggest a strong trend towards more detailed and nuanced understandings of young children's use of popular culture and digital media in their 'everyday' literacy practices, and increased focus on meaning-making rather than text-consumption or 'learning to read'.

(3) Blurred in-school and out-of-school distinctions

As already signalled, many of the more recent studies we surveyed threw into question the possibility of a clear divide between in-school and out-of-school literacies. McTavish (2009), for example, documents how Rajan and three friends' interest in street racing video games sparked collaboratively writing a script called 'Chopper 4 life'. They began working on the script at home, then brought it to school where all four worked on it during free moments (admittedly, this text didn't catch the teacher's attention and didn't become part of their formal schoolwork). During a curriculum focus on information texts at school, Rajan also used a range of resources

at home – the internet, religious texts, his grandparents – to produce a detailed poster on the importance of gurus in his family's religious life outside school. He proudly brought this poster to school to share with the class (although it was only allotted a brief show-and-tell presentation, then set aside and forgotten by his teacher). In Perry and Moses' study (2011), some families visited their local library and borrowed CD-ROM books for children to use at home to work on key reading skills needed for school. The young children in Volk and de Acosta's study (2001) were helped with their school homework by older siblings, who drew on their own understandings of how school texts work to explain how a task was to be completed. Indeed, we found drawing boundaries around the set of studies that fell into our Quadrant 3 difficult at times – especially when it came to studies documenting literacy practices in more or less 'unregulated' school spaces, such as playgrounds. The blurring of in-school and out-of-school literacies in many studies in our corpus certainly resonates with larger trends in sociocultural studies of literacy practices. Leander (e.g., 2003, 2007) was among the first to challenge too-neat distinctions between in-school and out-of-school literacies, arguing that different settings do not necessarily coincide with different literacies (e.g., he observed children at school working on their personal blogs, shopping, instant messaging others in class, and then completing school work at home, etc.). This insight reminds us all over again of just how complex even very young children's literacy practices are, and just how important discursive understandings of literacies are and their 'embeddedness' in a range of social practices (each entailing socially recognised ways of doing, knowing and being) when it comes to even beginning to think about teaching literacies effectively in schools.

The need for more

Given the enduring value of the kinds of studies found in our Quadrant 3, we continue to wonder why there remains a relative absence of ethnographic-type investigations of young children's everyday literacy practices (cf. similar puzzlement in Blanchard and Moore, 2010; Burnett, 2010). Perhaps the answer lies in difficulties regularly encountered in researching young children's practices. Hicks, for example, recounts problems associated with interviewing kindergarten children: 'A few children expressed their response to our request that they reflect on their kindergarten learning experiences by breaking out into song and dance. Others sat stiffly, responding as though they were on a television talk show' (2002: 107). Another difficulty lies in the need for accessing young children in their home settings, which is increasingly difficult to arrange without strong pre-existing social ties between the researcher and the researched. We also speculate that the absence of research in this area is in part a function of early-years education as currently construed by policy and funding arrangements, and which has long been dominated by developmental psychology and attention to measuring literacy skill growth (Genishi and Dyson, 2009). Within the US at least, heavy-handed emphasis on 'literacy skills' and 'scientifically proven' (i.e., by quantitative research) literacy teaching methods leaves little space for well-informed perspectives (Spencer, 2011) that posit children as active agents of their own literacy learning and practices outside school contexts (this may also explain why the bulk of the 13 studies in Quadrant 3 were conducted and published in contexts outside the US).

That said, there *has* been an increase in research published in this chapter's focus area in the past 10 years, especially in terms of studies examining the ways in which young children make effective use of popular culture, new media, and digital technologies in their out-of-school literacy practices. We like to think this indicates something of a critical response by researchers to the increasingly constricted and test-based conceptions of literacy evident in schools in the US, England, Australia, Canada and elsewhere; that researchers are turning to detailed and contextualised accounts of young children's literacies in order to challenge what counts as literacy 'success' and 'failure' at school. Certainly, studies by practitioner researchers like Cook (2005) seem to suggest that some teachers are indeed taking seriously shifts in young children's meaning-making practices in their classrooms. Cook's study was sparked by a paradox in her own life as a teacher and a parent: 'How do I, as a teacher, tell parents to read to their children when I cannot find time to do it myself? There is a dichotomy between what my "teacher voice" tells parents to do and what I am, in fact, doing as a parent' (p. 421). Cook examined the mismatch between her own children's preferences at home – for video games, short-hand notes, television viewing – and those she should 'value' as a teacher of literacy. In doing so, she discovered the importance of taking children's out-of-school literacy practices seriously, and how it is possible to 'discover' new literacies when the child's lead is followed. Studies like Cook's suggest it is indeed possible for teachers to bring out-of-school literacy practice into the classrooms without such practices being reified and narrowed in line with curriculum directives, or without such practices simply being relegated to show-and-tell spaces in classrooms. So, while there is certainly a need for more ethnographic or case study investigations of young children's literacy practices in their out-of-school lives, there is also a pressing need for research that documents teachers who are successfully able to leverage out-of-school literacies with respect to helping all students in their classes maximise their literacy success in school within the skills-focussed, lockstepped literacy curriculum found in too many schools.

CONCLUSION

Small-scale, out-of-school literacy studies investigations grounded in young children's everyday lives cannot be generalised to wider populations. This, however, is not to deny their theoretical and pedagogical value beyond the scope of each study; quite the reverse. Out-of-school literacy studies have enormous value in their *resonances* with other researchers' findings, with teachers' in-class experiences with a diverse range of young children, and with families' experiences of school–home relationships.

Patterns and similarities across diverse out-of-school literacy studies sound a call to action for researchers and educators alike to pay close attention to children's out-of-school lives. This will help educators build on students' literacy strengths in meaningful and ultimately successful ways – a particularly necessary stance in a time when recent policies are most concerned with 'effective' measures to teach early literacy. Invariably, these efforts have attended to 'traditional' literacy development with little recursivity between children's literate lives across home and school

contexts. Indeed, resonances across the studies surveyed in this chapter call for young children's practices to be taken seriously in their own right, and afford educators at all levels important insights into how young children are able to draw on a range of literacy understandings to get things done effectively in their social worlds.

ACKNOWLEDGEMENT

Tamara Spencer, Michele Knobel, and Colin Lankshear would like to thank Rosanna Appio for her research and writing assistance with Chapter 8, 'Researching young children's out-of-school literacy practices.'

REFERENCES

Alvermann, D. (2001) 'Reading adolescents' reading identities: looking back to see ahead', *Journal of Adolescent and Adult Literacy*, 44(8): 676–95.

Alvermann, D. (ed.) (2010) *Adolescents' Online Literacies: Connecting Classrooms, Digital Media and Popular Culture*. New York: Peter Lang.

Anderson, J. and Morrison, F. (2007) 'A great program … for me as a gramma: caregivers evaluate a family literacy initiative', *Canadian Journal of Education*, 30(1): 68–89.

Anderson, J., Anderson, A., Friedrich, N., and Kim, J. (2010) 'Taking stock of family literacy: some contemporary perspectives', *Journal of Early Childhood Literacy*, 10(1): 33–53.

Arthur, L., Beecher, B., and Jones Diaz, C. (2001) 'Early literacy: congruence and incongruence between home and early childhood settings', in M. Kalantzis (ed.), *Languages of Learning: Changing Communication and Changing Literacy Teaching*. Melbourne: Common Ground. pp. 65–73.

Barton, D. (2007) *Literacy: an Introduction to the Ecology of Written Language* (2nd ed.) Oxford: Blackwell.

Barton, D. and Hamilton, M. (1998) *Local Literacies: Reading and Writing in One Community*. London: Routledge.

Barton, D. and Papen, U. (2010) *The Anthropology of Writing: Understanding Textually-Mediated Social Worlds.* London: Continuum.

Black, R. (2008) *Adolescents and Online Fan Fiction.* New York: Peter Lang.

Black, R. (2010) 'The language of Webkinz: early childhood literacy in an online virtual world', *Digital Culture & Education,* 2(1): 7–24.

Blackburn, M. (2003) 'Exploring literacy performances and power dynamics at The Loft: queer youth reading the world and word', *Research in the Teaching of English,* 37(4): 467–90.

Blackburn, M. (2005) 'Agency in borderland discourses: examining language use in a community center with Black queer youth', *Teachers College Record,* 107(1): 89–113.

Blanchard, J. and Moore, T. (2010) *The Digital World of Young Children: Impact on Emergent Literacy. White paper prepared for the Pearson Foundation.* Arizona State University, College of Teacher Education and Leadership, USA.

Bloome, D., Katz, L., Solsken, J., Willett, J., and Wilson-Keenan, J. (2000) 'Interpellations of family/community and classroom literacy practices', *The Journal of Educational Research,* 93(3): 155–64.

Breier, M., Taetsane, M., and Sait, L. (1996) 'Taking literacy for a ride: – reading and writing in the taxi industry', in M. Prinsloo and M. Breier (eds), *The Social Uses of Literacy: Theory and Practice in Contemporary South Africa.* Bertsham, South Africa: Sached and Benjamins. pp. 213–34.

Burnett, C. (2010) 'Technology and literacy in early childhood educational settings: a review of research', *Journal of Early Childhood Literacy,* 10(3): 247–70.

Cairney, T. (2002) 'Bridging home and school literacy: In search of transformative approaches to curriculum', *Early Childhood Development and Care.* 172(2): 153–172.

Camitta, M. (1993) 'Vernacular writing: varieties of literacy among Philadelphia high school students', in B. Street (ed.), *Cross-Cultural Approaches to Literacy.* Cambridge: Cambridge University Press. pp. 228–46.

Campano, G. and Carpenter, M. (2005) 'The second class: providing spaces in the margins', *Language Arts,* 82(3): 186–94.

Cole, M. (1996) *Cultural Psychology: a Once and Future Discipline.* Cambridge, MA: Harvard University Press.

Comber, B. and Nichols, N. (2004) 'Getting the big picture: regulating knowledge in the early childhood literacy curriculum', *Journal of Early Childhood Literacy,* 4(1): 43–63.

Cook, S. J. (2005) 'Behind closed doors: discovering the literacies in our children's everyday lives', *Language Arts,* 82(6): 420–30.

Cook-Gumperz, J. and Hanna, K. (1997) 'Nurses' work, women's work: some recent issues of professional literacy and practice', in G. Hull (ed.), *Changing Work, Changing Workers: Critical Perspectives on Language, Literacy, and Skills.* Albany, NY: State University of New York Press. pp. 316–34.

Cook-Gumperz, J. and Keller-Cohen, D. (1993) 'Alternative literacies in school and beyond: multiple literacies of speaking and writing', *Anthropology and Education Quarterly,* 24(4): 283–7.

Copple, C. and Bredekamp, S. (eds) (2009) *Developmentally Appropriate Practice in Early Childhood Programs Serving Children from Birth through Age 8* (3rd ed.) Washington, D.C.: National Association for the Education of Young Children.

Dail, A. R., McGee, L. M., and Edwards, P. A. (2009) 'The role of community book club in changing literacy practices', *Literacy Teaching and Learning,* 13(1, 2): 25–56.

Davidson, C. (2009) 'Young children's engagement with digital texts and literacies in the home: pressing matters for the teaching of English in the early years of schooling', *English Teaching: Practice & Critique,* 8(3): 36–54.

Davies, J. (2006) 'Escaping the borderlands: an exploration of the internet as a cultural space for teenaged wiccan girls', in K. Pahl and J. Rowsell (eds), *Travel Notes from the New Literacy Studies: Instances of Practice.* Clevedon, UK: Multilingual Matters. pp. 72–94.

de la Piedra, M. T. (2009) 'Hybrid literacies: the case of a Quechua community in the Andes', *Anthropology and Education Quarterly,* 40(2): 110–28.

Delgado-Gaitan, C. (2005) 'Family narratives in multiple literacies', *Anthropology and Education Quarterly,* 36(3): 265–72.

Dudley-Marling, C. and Lucas, K. (2009) 'Pathologizing the language and culture of poor children', *Language Arts,* 86: 362–70.

Duncan, J. (2004) 'Misplacing the teacher?: New Zealand early childhood teachers and early childhood education policy reforms, 1984–96', *Contemporary Issues in Early Childhood,* 5(2): 160–77.

Dyson, A. H. (2003) *The Brothers and Sisters Learn to Write: Popular Literacies in Childhood and School Cultures.* New York: Teachers College Press.

Evans, M. A. and Shaw, D. (2008) 'Home grown for reading: parental contributions to young children's emergent literacy and word recognition', *Canadian Psychology/Psychologie Canadienne,* 49(2): 89–95.

Finders, M. (1997) *Just Girls: Hidden Literacies and Life in Junior High*. New York: Teachers College Press.

Fisher, M. (2003) 'Open mics and open minds: spoken word poetry in African diaspora participatory literacy communities', *Harvard Educational Review*, 73(3): 362–89.

Fishman, A. (1988) *Amish Literacy: What and How it Means*. Portsmouth, NH: Heinemann.

Gee, J. (1996) *Social Linguistics and Literacies: Ideology in Discourses*. New York: Routledge.

Gee, J. (2007) *Good Video Games and Good Learning*. New York: Peter Lang.

Gee, J. (2011) *Social Linguistics and Literacies: Ideology in Discourses* (4th ed.) New York: Routledge.

Gee, J., Hull, G., and Lankshear, C. (1996) *The New Work Order: Behind the Language of the New Capitalism*. Sydney: Allen and Unwin.

Genishi, C. and Dyson, A. H. (2009) *Children, Language, and Literacy: Diverse Learners in Diverse Times*. New York: Teachers College Press.

Gibson, D. (1996) 'Literacy, knowledge, gender and power in the workplace on three farms in the Western Cape', in M. Prinsloo and M. Breier (eds), *The Social Uses of Literacy: Theory and Practice in Contemporary South Africa*. Bertsham, South Africa: Sached and Benjamins. pp. 49–64.

Gowen, S. (1992) *The Politics of Workplace Literacy: a Case Study*. New York: Teachers College Press.

Gregory, E., Arju, T., Jessel, J., Kenner, C., and Mahera, R. (2007) 'Snow White in disguise: interlingual and intercultural exchanges between grandparents and young children at home in East London', *Journal of Early Childhood Literacy*, 7(1): 5–25.

Guerra, J. and Farr, M. (2002) 'Writing on the margins: the spiritual and autobiographical discourse of two *Mexicanas* in Chicago', in G. Hull and K. Schultz (eds), *School's Out! Bridging Out-of-School Literacies with Classroom Practice*. New York: Teachers College Press. pp. 96–123.

Guzzetti, B. and Gamboa, M. (2004) 'Zines for social justice: adolescent girls writing on their own', *Reading Research Quarterly*, 39(4): 408–36.

Hardman, M. and Jones, L. (1999) 'Sharing books with babies: evaluation of an early literacy intervention', *Educational Review*, 51(3): 221–9.

Heath, S. (1982) 'What no bedtime story means: narrative skills at home and school', *Language and Society*, 11: 49–76.

Heath, S. (1983) *Ways with Words: Language, Life and Work in Community and Classrooms*. Cambridge, MA: Cambridge University Press.

Heller, C. (1997) *Until We Are Strong Together: Women Writers in the Tenderloin*. New York: Teachers College Press.

Hicks, D. (2002) *Reading Lives: Working-Class Children and Literacy Learning*. New York: Teachers College Press.

Hill, M. and Vasudevan, L. (eds) (2007) *Media, Learning, and Sites of Possibility*. New York: Peter Lang.

Hull, G. (ed.) (1997) *Changing Work, Changing Workers: Critical Perspectives on Language, Literacy, and Skills*. Albany, NY: State University of New York Press.

Hull, G. and Schultz, K. (2001) 'Literacy and learning out of school: a review of theory and research', *Review of Educational Research*, 71(4): 575–611.

Hull, G. and Schultz, K. (2002) 'Negotiating the boundaries between school and non-school literacies', in G. Hull and K. Schultz (eds), *School's Out! Bridging Out-of-School Literacies with Classroom Practice*. New York: Teachers College Press. pp. 1–10.

Hull, G. and Stornaiuolo, A. (2010) 'Literate arts in a global world: reframing social networking as cosmopolitan practice', *Journal of Adolescent and Adult Literacy*, 54(2): 85–95.

Johnson, L. R. (2009) 'Challenging "best practices" in family literacy and parent education programs: the development and enactment of mothering knowledge among Puerto Rican and Latina mothers in Chicago', *Anthropology and Education Quarterly*, 40(3): 257–76.

Jones, S. (2006) 'Language with an attitude: white girls performing class', *Language Arts*, 84(2): 114–24.

Jones Diaz, C., Arthur, L., Beecher, B., and McNaught, M. (2000) 'Multiple literacies in early childhood: what do families and communities think about their children's early literacy learning?', *Australian Journal of Language and Literacy*, 23(3): 230–44.

Jordan, G., Snow, C., and Porche, M. (2000) 'Project EASE: the effect of a family literacy project on kindergarten students' early literacy skills', *Reading Research Quarterly*, 35(4): 524–48.

Kapitzke, C. (1995) *Literacy and Religion: the Textual Politics and Practice of Seventh-Day Adventism*. Amsterdam: Benjamins.

Kell, C. (2006) 'Crossing the margins: literacy, semiotics and the recontextualisation of meanings', in K. Pahl and J. Rowsell (eds), *Travel Notes from the New Literacy Studies*. Clevedon, UK: Multilingual Matters. pp. 147–70.

Kenner, C. (2000) 'Biliteracy in a monolingual school system? English and Gujarati in South London', *Language, Culture and Curriculum*, 13(1): 13–30.

Kim, J. and Anderson, J. (2008) 'Mother-child shared reading with print and electronic books', *Journal of Early Childhood Literacy*, 8(2): 213–45.

Kleifgen, J. A. (2001) 'Assembling talk: social alignments in the workplace', *Research on Language and Social Interaction*, 34(3): 279–308.

Knobel, M. (1999) *Everyday Literacies: Students, Discourse and Social Practices.* New York: Peter Lang.

Knobel, M. and Lankshear, C. (2003) 'Researching young children's out-of-school literacy practices', in N. Hall, J. Larsen and J. Marsh (eds), *Handbook of Early Childhood Literacy.* London: Sage Publications. pp. 51–65.

Knobel, M. and Lankshear, C. (eds) (2010) *DIY Media: Creating, Sharing and Learning with New Technologies.* New York: Peter Lang.

Kress, G. (2003) *Literacy in the New Media Age.* London: Routledge Falmer.

Kress, G. and Street, B. (2006) 'Foreword', in K. Pahl and J. Rowsell (eds), *Travel Notes from the New Literacy Studies: Instances of Practices.* Clevedon, UK: Multilingual Matters. pp. 8–10.

Lam, W. S. E. (2010) 'Multiliteracies on instant messaging in negotiating local, translocal, and transnational affiliations: a case of an adolescent immigrant', *Reading Research Quarterly*, 44(4): 377–97.

Lankshear, C. and Knobel, M. (2003) 'New technologies in early childhood literacy research: a review of research', *Journal of Early Childhood Literacy*, 3(1): 59–82.

Lankshear, C. and Knobel, M. (2011) *New Literacies: Everyday Practices and Social Learning* (3rd ed.) Maidenhead, UK: Open University Press.

Leander, K. (2003) 'Writing travelers' tales on new literacyscapes', *Reading Research Quarterly*, 38(3): 392–5.

Leander, K. (2007) '"You won't be needing your laptops today": wired bodies in the wireless classroom', in M. Knobel and C. Lankshear (eds), *A New Literacies Sampler.* New York: Peter Lang. pp. 25–48.

Leander, K. and Mills, S. (2007) 'The transnational development of an online role player game by youth: tracing the flows of literacy, an online game imaginary, and digital resources', in M. Blackburn and C. T. Clark (eds), *Literacy Research for Political Action.* New York: Peter Lang. pp. 177–98.

Leander, K. and Sheehy, M. (eds) (2004) *Spatializing Literacy Research and Practice.* New York: Peter Lang.

Lyons, M. (ed.) (2007) *Ordinary Writings, Personal Narratives: Writing Practices in 19th and Early 20th Century Europe.* Bern: Peter Lang.

Mackey, M. (2007) *Mapping Recreational Literacies.* New York: Peter Lang.

Mahiri, J. (ed.) (2003) *What They Don't Learn in School: Literacy in the Lives of Urban Youth.* New York: Peter Lang.

Marsh, J. (2004) 'The techno-literacy practices of young children', *Journal of Early Childhood Research*, 2(1): 51–66.

Marsh, J. (ed.) (2005a) *Popular Culture, New Media and Digital Literacy in Early Childhood.* London and New York: Routledge, Taylor & Francis.

Marsh, J. (2005b) 'Ritual, performance and identity construction: young children's engagement with popular cultural and media texts', in J. Marsh (ed.), *Popular Culture, New Media and Digital Literacy in Early Childhood.* London and New York: Routledge, Taylor & Francis. pp. 28–50.

Marsh J. (2010) 'Young children's play in online virtual worlds', *Journal of Early Childhood Research*, 8(23): 23–39.

Marsh, J., Brooks, G., Hughes, J., Ritchie, L., Roberts, S., and Wright, K. (2005) 'Digital beginnings: young children's use of popular culture, media and new technologies', Report of the Young Children's Use of Popular Culture, Media and New Technologies Study, funded by BBC Worldwide and the Esmée Fairbairn Foundation, Literacy Research Centre, University of Sheffield, UK.

Mavers, D. (2007) 'Semiotic resourcefulness: a young child's email exchange as design', *Journal of Early Childhood Literacy*, 7(2): 155–76.

McTavish, M. (2009) '"I get my facts from the Internet": a case study of the teaching and learning of information literacy in in-school and out-of-school contexts', *Journal of Early Childhood Literacy*, 9(1): 3–28.

Moje, E. (2000) '"To be part of the story": the literacy practices of gangsta adolescents', *Teachers College Record*, 102(3): 651–90.

Morrow, L. and Schickedanz, J. (2006) 'The relationships between sociodramatic play and literacy development', in D. Dickinson and S. Neuman (eds), *Handbook of Early Literacy Research.* Vol. 2. New York: The Guilford Press. pp. 269–80.

Mui, S. and Anderson, J. (2008) 'At home with the Johars: another look at family literacy', *The Reading Teacher*, 62(3): 234–43.

Neuman, S. B. and Roskos, K. (1992) 'Literacy objects as cultural tools: effects on children's literacy behaviors in play', *Reading Research Quarterly*, 27(3): 203–25.

Nichols, S., Nixon, H., and Rowsell, J. (2009) 'The "good" parent in relation to early childhood literacy:

symbolic terrain and lived practice', *Literacy: Special Issue on Identity*, 43(2): 65–74.

Orellana, M. F., Reynolds, J., Dorner, L., and Meza, M. (2003) 'In other words: translating or "para-phrasing" literacy practice in immigrant households', *Reading Research Quarterly*, 38(1): 12–34.

Pahl, K. (2002) 'Ephemera, mess and miscellaneous piles: texts and practices in families', *Journal of Early Childhood Literacy*, 2(2): 145–66.

Pahl, K. (2005) 'Narrative spaces and multiple identities: children's textual explorations of console games in home settings', in J. Marsh (ed.), *Popular Culture, New Media and Digital Literacy in Early Childhood*. London and New York: Routledge, Taylor & Francis. pp. 126–45.

Pahl, K. and Rowsell, J. (eds) (2006) *Travel Notes from the New Literacy Studies: Instances of Practices*. Clevedon, UK: Multilingual Matters.

Parke, T., Drury, R., Kenner, C., and Robertson, L. (2002) 'Revealing invisible worlds: connecting the mainstream with bilingual children's home and community learning', *Journal of Early Childhood Literacy*, 2(2): 195–220.

Perry, K. and Moses, A. (2011) 'Television, language, and literacy practices in Sudanese refugee families: "I learned how to spell English on Channel 18"', *Research in the Teaching of English*, 45(3): 278–305.

Powell, D., Okagaki, L., and Bojczyk, K. (2004) 'Evaluating parent participation and outcomes in family literacy programs: cultural diversity considerations', in B. H. Wasik (ed.), *Handbook of Family Literacy*. Mahwah, NJ: Lawrence Erlbaum Associates, Inc. pp. 551–66.

Prinsloo, M. and Breier, M. (1996) 'Introduction', in M. Prinsloo and M. Breier (eds), *The Social Uses of Literacy: Theory and Practice in Contemporary South Africa*. Bertsham, South Africa: Sached and Benjamins. pp. 11–30.

Purcell-Gates, V. (2000) 'Family literacy', in M.L. Kamil, P.B. Mosenthall, P.D. Pearson, and R. Carr (eds), *Handbook of Reading Research*. Vol. 3. Mahwah, NJ: Lawrence Erlbaum. pp. 853–70.

Reese, L. and Gallimore, R. (2000) 'Immigrant Latinos' cultural model of literacy development: an evolving perspective on home-school discontinuities', *American Journal of Education*, 108(2): 103–34.

Robinson, M. and Turnbull, B. (2005) 'Verónica: an asset model of becoming literate', in J. Marsh (ed.), *Popular Culture, New Media and Digital Literacy in Early Childhood*. London and New York: Routledge, Taylor & Francis. pp. 51–72.

Rodriguez, M. V. (2004) 'Language and literacy practices in Dominican families in New York City', *Early Child Development and Care*, 176(2): 171–82.

Rogers, T., Tyson, C., and Marshall, E. (2000) 'Living dialogues in one neighbourhood: moving towards understanding across discourses and practices of literacy and schooling', *Journal of Literacy Research*, 32(1): 1–24.

Roskos, K. and Vukelich, C. (2006) 'Early literacy policy and pedagogy', in S. B. Neuman and D. K. Dickinson (eds), *Handbook of Early Literacy Research*. Vol. 2. New York: The Guilford Press. pp. 295–310.

Saint-Laurent, L. and Giasson, J. (2005) 'Effects of a family literacy program adapting parental intervention to first graders' evolution of reading and writing abilities', *Journal of Early Childhood Literacy*, 5(3): 253–78.

Sarroub, L. (2002) 'In-betweenness: religion and conflicting visions of literacy', *Reading Research Quarterly*, 37(2): 130–49.

Scollon, R. and Scollon, S. W. (2001) *Intercultural Communication: A Discourse Approach* (2nd ed.) Malden, MA: Blackwell Publishers Inc.

Schultz, K. (1996) 'Between school and work: the literacies of urban adolescent females', *Anthropology and Education Quarterly*, 27: 517–44.

Schultz, K. (2002) 'Looking across space and time: reconceptualizing literacy learning in and out of school', *Research in the Teaching of English*, 36(3): 356–90.

Scribner, S. and Cole, M. (1981) *The Psychology of Literacy*. Cambridge, MA: Harvard University Press.

Sénéchal, M. and Young, L. (2008) 'The effect of family literacy interventions on children's acquisition of reading from Kindergarten to Grade 3: a meta-analytic review', *Review of Educational Research*, 78(4): 880–907.

Shegar, C. and Weninger, C. (2010) 'Intertextuality in preschoolers' engagement with popular culture: implications for literacy development', *Language and Education*, 24(5): 431–47.

Skilton-Sylvester, E. (2002) 'Literate at home but not at school: a Cambodian girl's journey from playwright to struggling writer', in G. Hull and K. Schultz (eds), *School's Out! Bridging Out-of-School Literacies with Classroom Practice*. New York: Teachers College Press. pp. 61–95.

Smith, C. (2001) 'Click and turn the page: an exploration of multiple storybook literacy', *Reading Research Quarterly*, 36–(2): 152–83.

Smith, C. (2005) 'The CD-ROM game: a toddler engaged in computer-based dramatic play', in J. Marsh (ed.), *Popular Culture, New Media and*

Digital Literacy in Early Childhood. London and New York: Routledge, Taylor & Francis. pp. 108–25.

Soler, J. and Openshaw, R. (2007) '"To be or not to be?": the politics of teaching phonics in England and New Zealand', *Journal of Early Childhood Literacy*, 7(3): 333–52.

Spencer, T. (2011) 'Learning to read in the wake of reform: young children's experiences with scientifically based reading curriculum', *Perspectives on Urban Education*, 8(2): 41–50.

Spencer, T., Falchi, L., and Ghiso, M. P. (2011) 'Linguistically diverse children and educators (re) forming early literacy policy', *Early Childhood Education Journal*, 39(2): 115–23.

Stein, P. and Slominsky, L. (2006) 'An eye on the text and an eye on the future: multimodal literacy in three Johannesburg families', in K. Pahl and J. Rowsell (eds), *Travel Notes from the New Literacy Studies: Instances of Practice*. Clevedon, UK: Multilingual Matters. pp. 118–46.

St Pierre, R. G., Ricciuti, A. E., and Rimdzius, T. A. (2005) 'Effects of a family literacy program on low-literate children and their parents: findings from an evaluation of the Even Start family literacy program', *Developmental Psychology*, 41(6): 953–70.

Street, B. (1984) *Literacy in Theory and Practice.* Cambridge, UK: Cambridge University Press.

Street, B. (2005) 'Recent applications of the new literacy studies in educational contexts', *Research in the Teaching of English*, 39(4): 417–23.

Taylor, D. and Dorsey-Gaines, C. (1988) *Growing up Literate: Learning from Inner-City Families.* Portsmouth, NH: Heinemann.

Thomas, A. (2007) *Youth Online: Identity and Literacy in the Digital Age.* New York: Peter Lang.

Tran, T. B., McNaughton, S., and Parr, J. (2011) 'Family literacy practices and the promise of optimization', in C. Rubie-Davies (ed.), *Educational Psychology: Concepts, Research and Challenges.* New York: Routledge. pp. 229–48.

Vasquez, V. (2005) 'Resistance, power-tricky, and colorless energy: what engagement with everyday popular culture texts can teach us about learning and literacy', in J. Marsh (ed.), *Popular Culture, New Media and Digital Literacy in Early Childhood.* London: Routledge, Taylor & Francis. pp. 201–18.

Vasudevan, L. (2010) 'Education remix: new media, literacies, and the emerging digital geographies', *Digital Culture and Education,* 2. Retrieved 23 May 2011, from www.digitalcultureandeducation.com/uncategorized/vasudevan_2010_html/

Volk, D. and de Acosta, M. (2001) '"Many differing ladders, many ways to climb…": literacy events in the bilingual classroom, homes, and community of three Puerto Rican kindergartners', *Journal of Early Childhood Literacy*, 1(2): 193–223.

Walkerdine, V. (1990) *Schoolgirl Fictions.* New York: Verso.

Wasik, B. (ed.) (2004) *Handbook of Family Literacy.* Mahwah, NJ: Lawrence Erlbaum Associates, Inc.

Weigel, D. J., Martin, S. S., and Bennett, K. K. (2006) 'Contributions of the home literacy environment to preschool-aged children's emerging literacy and language skills', *Early Child Development and Care*, 176(3, 4): 357–78.

Wilson, A. (2000) 'There is no escape from third-space theory: borderland discourse and the "in-between" literacies of prisons', in D. Barton, M. Hamilton and R. Ivanič (eds), *Situated Literacies: Reading and Writing in Context.* London: Routledge. pp. 54–69.

Wohlwend, K. E. (2009) 'Damsels in discourse: girls consuming and producing identity texts through Disney Princess play', *Reading Research Quarterly*, 44(1): 57–83.

Wohlwend, K. E. (2010) 'A is for avatar: young children in literacy 2.0 worlds and literacy 1.0 schools', *Language Arts*, 88(2): 144–52.

9

The Out-of-School Schooling of Literacy

Eve Gregory and Charmian Kenner

Across generations, families have always ensured that young children have access to important cultural practices, and one way of doing so has been through formal classes. Such classes have been particularly crucial to the lives of new immigrant families who are anxious both to preserve the language, literacy, and religion of their heritage and to give young children extra tuition in the language and literacy of the new country. Out-of-school schooling thus encompasses a range of different 'community' classes: religious or liturgical, mother-tongue language and literacy classes and Saturday classes in the host language, often covering a range of subjects across the curriculum. This chapter assesses the value of such classes, in terms of cognitive, linguistic and social benefits accruing to young children in their early years in school. It then goes on to review studies describing a range of community classes in different countries, contrasting them with the learning taking place in mainstream schools.

THE OUT-OF-SCHOOL SCHOOLING OF LITERACY

Six year old Maruf talks avidly about his Qur'anic class:

> Maruf: There are eighty-three children.
> AW (researcher): Eighty-three children in your Arabic class! And when do you go to that?
> Maruf: Seven o'clock to nine o'clock.
> AW: On?
> Maruf: A night.
> AW: Every night?
> Maruf: Monday to Friday.
> AW: Monday to Friday! You go for two hours every night! Aren't you tired?
> Maruf: I don't feel tired.
> AW: And are you the youngest then?
> Maruf: Yes and I'm on the Qur'an.
> AW: You're on the Qur'an now?
> Maruf: I'm on the last one.

Maruf explains that he is reading the last primer before starting the Qur'an. He goes on to explain more about the structure of his classes:

> AW: How many teachers are there for eighty-three children?
> Maruf: There's two.

AW: Only two? Who are they?
Maruf: One is the Qur'an...you know, all the Qur'an...he can say it without looking.
AW: He can? What's his name?
Maruf: I don't know. And one is...he can...he knows all the meanings.
AW: Does he? Does he tell you the meanings?
Maruf: Yes he does.
AW: So do you just read the Qur'an for two hours? Is that what you do?
Maruf: Yes, but I don't sometimes, I talk sometimes.
AW: You don't!
Maruf: I do.

(Gregory and Williams, 2000: 168–9)

The breadth of Maruf's learning reflects that of many young children working in classes established by their local communities throughout the world. This chapter examines existing research studies that describe this 'out-of-school schooling' in which young children engage. It deals only with formal classes taking place outside mainstream school hours, not the more informal ways in which families and communities might foster literacy at home. The classes described are often known as 'community classes' which acts as a blanket term to cover mother-tongue or national standard heritage language classes, religious or liturgical classes or supplementary classes or Saturday schools that may be in either the mother-tongue or host language (or a combination of both) and cover a range of curriculum areas. A variety of terms are used for these classes in different countries. For example, in the UK, they are usually called 'supplementary schools', or 'complementary schools' (Lytra and Martin, 2010), whilst other terms such as 'heritage language schools' or 'community-based schools' are common in the US.

In different sections, the chapter addresses the following questions: What benefits might accrue to children spending many hours, like Maruf in the excerpt above, participating in this learning? How and why were these classes set up by different communities? What is their scope and what particular classes exist, taking the UK as an example? What is the nature of learning taking place? How different is it from mainstream school learning? Finally, how should mainstream teachers conceptualise this learning?

Bilingualism and biliteracy: a theoretical framework

'He who knows no other language does not truly know his own'.
(Goethe quoted by Vygotsky, in John-Steiner, 1985: 368)

Any discussion on mother-tongue classes needs to be situated in the literature relating to the advantages and/or disadvantages of bilingualism and biliteracy as well as that recognising the inextricable link between language and culture (Vygotsky, 1962; Sapir, 1970). A considerable body of evidence has been collected since the 1960s pointing to the advanced development of specific types of linguistic and cognitive skills of bilinguals given certain conditions (summarised in Gregory and Kelly, 1992; Gregory, 1994a, 1994b). Linguistic skills are expressed in a greater metalinguistic and analytic competence where attention can be focused on isolated components (Feldman and Shen, 1971; Ianco-Worrall, 1972; Ben-Zeev, 1977; Swain and Cummins, 1979; Bain and Yu, 1980; Hakuta, 1986; and Arnberg, 1987). Cognitive advantages are most obvious in areas such as conservation of measurement, classification according to shape, colour or size or manipulating and recognising visual patterns (Peal and Lambert, 1962; Liedtke and Nelson, 1968; Ben-Zeev, 1977). Bilingualism is also found to enhance children's development of executive control, which means they can selectively attend to the most relevant aspects of a task when there are competing stimuli (Bialystok, 2010). The crucial question relating to the topic of this chapter is: What are the conditions whereby these advantages accrue?

As early as the 1930s, when Western European research was pointing unambiguously to the negative effects of bilingualism (Jesperson, 1923; Saer, 1924; Goodenough, 1926), a very different direction was taken by Vygotsky (1935, trans. 1962). Vygotsky's thesis was that bilingualism enabled a child 'to see his language as one particular system among many, to view its phenomena under more general categories ... [which] leads to awareness of his linguistic operations' (1962: 110). It is through gaining control over two languages involving different lexical, syntactic and semantic systems, as well as possibly two different scripts, or, put simply, through learning that there are two ways of saying the same thing, that the individual gains an added analytical awareness, which, argued Vygotsky, contributes to a more conscious understanding of linguistic patterns in general. Later research studies in the West supported Vygotsky's thesis that this awareness is particularly enhanced through literacy learning in two languages (Verhoeven, 1987; Wagner, 1993; Gregory, 1996; Kenner, 2000a; Rosowsky, 2001). The skills of young children who are becoming biliterate are examined later in Chapter 21 of this volume (Kenner and Gregory).

The key to gaining access to this consciousness is the effective mastery of two or more languages, whereby learning a second language is 'added' to the development of the first (Cummins, 1979, 1992). In contrast, for children learning in 'subtractive' contexts, where their first language is 'submerged' (Skutnabb-Kangas, 1984) and seen merely as an obstacle to be overcome, no cognitive or linguistic advantages

are likely to accrue. Additionally, it is now widely argued that second language learning runs parallel with first language competence and that acquisition of a second language is, indeed, dependent upon the level of development in the first language (John-Steiner, 1985). This thesis has been termed the 'linguistic interdependence principle' which simply states that first and second language skills are interdependent.

A number of research studies also support the view of a common underlying cognitive proficiency across languages (Vygotsky, 1962; Cummins, 1981; Hamers and Blanc, 1989) which states that young children are capable of transferring cognitive functioning in their first language at home and in their community classes to their second language in school (Gregory, 1994b; Kenner, 2000b) as well as vice versa. Problems are likely to arise when no transfer is possible because a child has not acquired a certain cognitive functioning in the first language when beginning a second in school (Skutnabb-Kangas, 1984). A recognition of the principle of additive enrichment and common underlying proficiency would provide strong support for the benefits of community language and literacy classes in young children's lives. Not only will young children become proficiently bilingual and biliterate, strong evidence suggests that mother-tongue proficiency will enhance second language learning and cognitive skills more generally in their mainstream schools.

Community classes: a historical perspective

Aumie (aged 78) tells his childhood memories of Hebrew classes in London's East End:

We would go five times a week. So you'd come home from school... and then by five o'clock, we

would be in Hebrew classes until 7, and, as far as I was concerned, by 8 o'clock I was back in the Synagogue choir for rehearsals twice a week ... You would learn phonetically, the twenty-four letters of the Hebrew alphabet ... we would learn letter by letter and then build up the words... Learning Hebrew phonetically like this we were soon able to read quite quickly. We would read mechanically without understanding the words ...
(Gregory and Williams, 2000: 89)

Here we take the example of the UK to demonstrate how community class teaching and learning has developed over time. There is a long history of such schooling; some studies are autobiographical (Rosen, 1999) or recount the memories of older citizens such as Aumie above. By the end of the nineteenth century, we know that 30–40 'chevras' or religious associations had been established in the East End of London, which took over pastoral care of the poor as well as religious teaching (Fishman, 1979: 78). An important function of the chevras was to teach Hebrew and to prepare children (mostly boys) for their bar mitzvah. By 1891, there were some 200 of these classes in the East End with 2000 boys on their roll (Gregory and Williams, 2000: 55). The children attended in the morning before school, during their lunch break or after school. Their accommodation was sparse – usually one or two rooms of a small house – and materials consisted largely of religious and sacred texts to be learned. These classes were entirely separate from the mainstream school, although evidence is available that some state schools recognised the religious and cultural practices of their communities through holidays and the school kitchen, etc. (Gregory and Williams, 2000).

During the first half of the twentieth century, community classes remained largely invisible to the wider host society. However, in 1976 came the publication of a highly controversial draft directive from Europe. The Draft Directive on the Education of Migrant Children proposed the right of all migrant children in European Union states to tuition in their mother-tongue. Although the directive was almost totally rejected by most local education authorities in the UK, it led to the setting up of the National Council for Mother Tongue Teaching (NCMTT), an active body campaigning for the recognition of mother-tongue teaching in mainstream schools. For a short period during the 1980s and, following the MOTET (Mother-Tongue to English Teaching Project) set up by the DES (Department of Education and Science), mother-tongue teaching even entered mainstream primary classrooms in Bradford (Fitzpatrick, 1987) and Bedford (Tosi, 1984). Although these innovative bilingual education projects provided evidence that young children could operate as well in English in addition to performing better in maths and in their mother-tongue than the control group, they were short-lived. Their death knell struck in 1985 with the publication of a major government report, the Swann Report, which stated clearly that the place for mother-tongue teaching lay firmly outside school and within the communities themselves (DES, 1985). Any mother-tongue teaching in school should comprise only 'emergency support' until competence in English had been achieved. From that time on, community classes largely retreated underground to become invisible.

Nevertheless, throughout the UK and particularly in London's East End, community classes have continued to thrive until the present day. The East End Community School set up in 1977 by Mohammed Nurul Hoque and Anwara Hussein is one such class in Tower Hamlets. Aiming to teach both English and Bengali language and literature (especially poetry), maths, Arabic, general science, history, geography, singing, needlework, knitting, and other crafts and art; it expanded from 13 to 63 students in just 18 months. The school has long hours; 4.30–6.30 every evening, 10am–5pm on Saturdays and special activities on Sundays, which bear witness to its popularity. Ros, an Oxford graduate tells fondly of her memories of this school:

> We were very lucky – although we didn't think so at the time. We had the East End Community School organised by Nurul Hoque and Anwara Hussein. They are very well known in the community and I think they've done wonders for people of my generation. I have fluent Bengali with GCSE grade A and I owe it to them ... it was incredibly tiring because it was straight after school and we had to go and then we'd miss things like Neighbours ... it was Monday to Friday like 4 till half past 6. We'd have Arabic on Friday and Saturday. It was more Bengali-based, which is why our Bengali is so much better than our Arabic.
>
> (Gregory and Williams, 2000: 132)

The scope of community class attendance

Maruf's description of his community class opening this chapter came as a surprise to his mainstream class teacher. She was unaware of the importance of Qur'anic class learning in his life, since he did not talk about it in school and, like many community classes, it remained invisible to both the mainstream school and the wider host community.

In recent years, awareness has grown regarding the prevalence and importance of community classes in the UK. National associations have been set up for several well-represented languages, including Chinese and Arabic. A database produced under the auspices of the Our Languages project (Our Languages, 2011), funded by the UK Government, contains details of over 500 community classes or schools in the UK. However, this is likely to represent only a fraction of existing provision made by communities for their children's learning. The Languages Review, a government report on languages in education, commented that:

> Supplementary schools are run by almost every ethnic community group in England including African Caribbean, Afghan, Somali, Greek, Jewish, Turkish, Russian and Iranian. They offer children support in national curriculum subjects, as well as the opportunity to learn their community's mother tongues and to understand more about their ethnic or national culture and heritage.
>
> (DfES, 2007)

The London Borough of Tower Hamlets, for example, where Maruf lived, supports over 90 classes in languages ranging from Bengali and Arabic to Somali, Urdu, Cantonese, Vietnamese and Lithuanian, attended by around 5000 children overall. The Borough has developed curricula, assessment and teacher training for community languages.

The Our Languages project (Our Languages, 2011) stimulated such initiatives on a national scale, fostering collaboration between the community and mainstream sectors through case studies of successful school partnerships, increasing entries for accreditation in community languages (now possible in a wide range of languages through the new Asset Languages system), and providing training for community teachers so that they could progress towards mainstream qualifications.

Community classes also exist to a significant extent in other countries. In the US for example, Chinese, Vietnamese, Khmer, Russian, Korean, and South Asian communities around the country have established their own after-school, church or temple, or Saturday schools. Similar networks are found in Canada and Australia (Brinton et al., 2008).

Benefits of community class attendance

A recent study on the effect of supplementary schools on children's attainment in England (Maylor et al., 2010) examined both language classes and those supporting mainstream curriculum subjects such as English, maths and science. A survey was conducted of 1136 supplementary schools across the country and over 300 responded. Case studies highlighted 'immense dedication and commitment' amongst staff, and many parents reported an improvement in the skills, knowledge and examination results of their children since attending supplementary school. Possible reasons for this included smaller class sizes in which teachers were able to adapt topics to their pupils' interests and explore a range of teaching and learning strategies. Children could develop increased self-confidence and positive learner identities, rooted in a better understanding of their cultural backgrounds. Supplementary schools were also characterised by good teacher–parent relationships, which supported children's learning.

A further level of detail is provided by ethnographic studies of the teaching and learning that takes place in community classes. Recent findings include how children develop multilingual practices in complementary settings around the UK (Creese et al., 2006); the enrichment of learning for 5-year-olds who attend literacy classes in Urdu and Arabic (Robertson, 2007); the ways in which children can transfer knowledge between their languages in complementary Saturday classes in Bradford, northern England (Conteh and Begum, 2008); the contribution to educational achievement of Chinese schools (Chen, 2007; Francis et al., 2010) and Portuguese schools (Barradas, 2007); and

how children negotiate their bilingual identities in complementary school (Souza, 2010).

Faith settings are of particular importance to migrant communities when settling in a new country. A study of children's language and literacy learning in four such settings in London (Bangladeshi Muslim, Tamil Hindu, Polish Catholic and Ghanaian Pentecostal) has revealed how practice and performance around key texts contribute to children's high-level thinking about abstract concepts as well as their development of rich vocabulary in both their heritage language and English. Learning is enhanced by taking place through multimodal approaches including song, dance, gesture and chant, as well as repetition, recitation, echoing and memorisation (Gregory et al., 2013, in press).

Such studies reveal not only the scope of community class learning in young children's lives but also the significant impact such learning might have on their work in mainstream classes. We discuss more closely the nature of this learning in the following section.

Other worlds of learning

The class takes place in a neighbour's front room. About 30 children of all ages ... line the walls like a human square, seated with their raiel (a beautifully carved wooden stand upon which to place the Qur'an or the initial primers) in front of them. There is a loud hum as they all chant their individual practice piece. Their elderly teacher whom the children affectionately call 'nanna' (grandfather) holds a bamboo cane which he uses only lightly as if symbolically. 'These children need discipline, or they will climb the sky!' ... Like many of the children, he (Louthfur) rocks to and fro to the sound of the voices. Children do this because they are encouraged to develop a harmonious voice; they are told Allah listens to his servants and is pleased if time is taken to make the verse sound meaningful. The old man's wife takes children who have already started the Qur'an into a separate room so she can hear the recitations clearly. She comments,

'English is important for this life. But Arabic is required for the life hereafter which is eternal! Therefore, it must be given the greatest importance ... Or else, how can our children know?'
(Rashid in Gregory, 1996: 41)

During the last two decades of the twentieth century, ethnographic studies began to provide teachers and researchers entry into the worlds of community classes. Few such studies existed before 1990 although longitudinal work conducted in Liberia (Scribner and Cole, 1981), Iran (Street, 1984) and Morocco (Wagner et al., 1986) was beginning to indicate the existence of multiple language and literacy practices taking place in both adults' and young children's lives. This section examines briefly ethnographic studies inviting outsiders into the community classes of young children in three contexts: Anglo-American children in a north-eastern US state, Samoan American children in California, and Bangladeshi British children in Spitalfields, East London. We extract patterns of similarity and difference in these studies as well as with mainstream classrooms.

Both Heath (1983) and Anderson and Stokes (1984) stressed the importance of Bible reading in the lives of different communities in the US, but did not follow the children into their religious classes. Taking up these findings, Zinsser (1986) provides a finely-tuned analysis of the classes of 4- and 5-year-old pre-primary children attending two fundamentalist (evangelical) Sunday Schools (termed Bible classes) in an Anglo-American community. Teachers in these classes were non-professionals, largely mothers of children attending the Sunday School. Important to members of this Church was the belief that the Bible was the actual word of God to be taken literally, word for word, rather than more freely, as in other Protestant Churches. Through their Bible classes, argues Zinsser,

young children learned and were taught a great deal about literacy. The teaching of Biblical texts itself was highly structured and followed tight routines and rituals. Children learned through listening carefully:

Teacher: Does everybody have their listening ears on today?
(Children place their hands on their ears and turn them as though turning knobs)
(Zinsser, 1986: 60),

by memorisation:

Teacher: Every time you have a problem, the Lord can help remind you of memory verses – of verses in the Bible. And that is how you can make the devil run away from you (1986: 61),

by singing:

The B-I-B-L-E
Yes, that's the book for me!
I stand alone on the word of God
The Bible! (holding Bible aloft) (1986: 62),

and by answering questions directly from the Bible:

Teacher: What have we been learning about?
Children: (chorus) God!
Teacher: God and his son Jesus (1986: 63).

Crucially, however, children were being taught more than reciting from the Bible and Bible stories. They were becoming familiar with books and as a source of important textual material; they were learning about the role of turn-taking in learning to read as well as forms of questions and answers and contextualisation cues. In a wider sense, they were being taught the importance of the Bible as a source of divine inspiration and knowledge:

Mother: (to daughter) Does David have his Bible?
Daughter: (who is carrying her Bible) He'd better!
Mother: Rachel, go back and look. It was right on top of Mommy's Bible.
(Zinsser, 1986: 57)

These Bible classes form a very special type of 'community class' in which young children are being 'schooled' not just in literacy particularly and learning more generally, but in becoming worthy and valuable citizens of their community. Mother-tongue teaching is not, however, an issue here. This is taken up in different ways in the two ethnographic studies described below.

For the Bangladeshi British community in East London, mother-tongue learning is seen as crucial to cultural and identity maintenance. The War of Independence with West Pakistan in 1971 heralded a new beginning for Bangladesh, since victory elevated the language to national status. Pride in Bengali poetry and literature is reflected in the numerous bookshops in Brick Lane (centre of the community in East London). On a more practical level, literacy in Bengali is the means of maintaining contact between children in Britain and their relatives back home. Literacy is also crucial to have access to any form of literature from the heritage country, since the Bangladeshi British community speak Sylheti, a dialect of Bengali without a written form.

Unlike the Bible classes in the congregationalist church, Bengali lessons are focused primarily on the learning of language and literacy; sometimes, indeed, they cover other curriculum areas such as maths and history. They are also held in a variety of different premises, ranging from purpose-built schools to families' living rooms. The particular class referred to below is long-established and well-organised:

> Situated behind Petticoat Lane Market, this Bengali school is funded through the voluntary sector. It comprises two mobile rooms, the walls bare except for a few information posters made by the children. The room I enter has several rows of desks at which children sit quietly – some writing, others practising words under their breath. At the beginning, the teacher sits in front of the room, then starts to walk around. The children who are mumbling are practising the previous day's work and as the teacher passes around, the voice of the child he is listening to is momentarily amplified so that the teacher can correct if necessary before moving on to the next. Later the children read, some at a fast pace whilst others read with careful deliberation. When the teacher reaches the child I have come to observe, she reads confidently and eloquently and the few mistakes she makes are firmly corrected. Parts that are not understood are explained briefly in Sylheti … and the lesson continues in this way to the end.
> (N. Rashid, Unpublished fieldnotes, 1996)

The younger children learn by individual tuition whereby teachers follow the pattern of 'demonstration/practice/test':

> Teacher: K, KO, GO
> Nazma: (repeats)
> Teacher: Go on, read it.
> Nazma: (mutters quietly)
> Teacher: Read it loudly
> Nazma: (quietly says the alphabet)
> Teacher: Say it again.
> Nazma: (repeats the letters)
> Teacher: Not like that, like this (stresses the different inflections of the letters)
> Nazma: (quietly repeats)
> Teacher: Good. What next?
> Nazma: (continues)
> Teacher: Which one is 'Dho'?
> Nazma: This one.
> Teacher: Then carry on. No, say it like this 'Pho'
> (Gregory, 1996: 35–6)

Interestingly, the primers used in Bengali classes are mostly imported from Bangladesh, assume a linguistic and cultural familiarity with the text and illustrations by the children and make no allowances for those who may never have left the UK. The children's parents are generally comfortable with these, since they may well have used the books for their own literacy learning. Nevertheless, Figure 9.1 shows how strange both illustration and text might be for young Bangladeshi British children.

কে কোথায় আছে বল। আব্বার হাতে কি? তিনি কোথা থেকে এলেন?
কাক তাড়াবে কে? কেন? ছেলেমেয়েদের নাম কি?

আম্মা আর আব্বা।
আনু আর আবু।
আমার নাম আনু।
আমার নাম আবু।

উঠানে ধান।
কাক এল।

Figure 9.1   Illustration and text from Bengali primer

The text rhymes in Bengali and reads: 'The day has gone; Put the ducks and chickens in the house; Give grandmother her medicine. In auntie's hand there is some rice-pudding; Which is very sweet to eat; Inside there are different sweet-cakes' (the Bengali text goes on to name a few). Both illustration and text assume knowledge not just of the language, but cultural practices (food, etc.), simple village life and the extended family living together and caring for each other. All of these might be unknown in the host country but provide a link with the family's heritage.

Community classes may well combine religious practices with formal tuition of the heritage language. Where children are already second- or even third-generation immigrants, it is important to realise that this may no longer be the mother-tongue. This is the situation described by Duranti et al. (1995) in their detailed analysis of *Change and tradition in literacy instruction in a Samoan American community*. Currently more than 90,000 ethnic Samoans live in California, most born and raised there. Local communities view the setting up of a Samoan church as a priority, an important component of which is the religious school, where, like in a Samoan village, very young children are introduced to the Samoan alphabet and numbers. The study presented draws its data from the Samoan Congregational Church in Los Angeles, a church which, like others in the community, provides daily contact to all generations for the preservation of what Samoan parents and grandparents refer to as the 'Samoan way of life'. Crucially, the learning of literacy is set within cultural events such as weddings, funerals and other rites of passage for which special clothes are worn and traditional oratory can be heard. Children sing Christian songs in both languages with traditional Samoan

body movements. In this manner, English code interfaces with Samoan expressive gesture, although the Church service is almost entirely in Samoan.

In their classes, children aged 5 and younger are expected to recite and master the very same *Pi Tautau* (letter, sound, number and word chart) used in pastors' schools throughout the Samoan islands. At first glance, this is what the children seem to achieve, through the method of word-by-word repetition after the teacher. However, the researchers go on to point out ways in which the learning reveals important discontinuities with its village counterpart. Crucially, unlike mother-tongue Samoan speakers, American Samoan children have only rudimentary knowledge of Samoan when they begin learning to read the language. Additionally, some of their teachers might not be fluent in the language themselves. A consequence of this is that some children are able to correct the teacher – a practice that would be unthinkable in Samoa. As a result of this linguistic insecurity by both children and teachers, only the actual *Pi Tautau* recitation takes place in Samoan. Both the introduction and any explanations are given in English. Thus, whereas in Samoa the *Pi Tautau* is used only to teach *reading,* in California it is used to teach the *language* as well.

Paradoxically, then, reading the *Pi Tautau* serves a dual function as both an initiator into the traditional religious and linguistic heritage of the Samoan people and as an object of westernisation. In California, the practice is seen as a powerful symbol of Samoan culture; in village Samoa, it would be viewed as predominantly an Anglophile practice. In California, reading the *Pi Tautau* is seen as part of a wider effort to bolster Samoan identity. Yet its westernisation is revealed through both the objects depicted in the chart (Coca Cola bottles and ocean liners) and the methods of teaching. Also, the didactic methods customary in Samoa are complemented by an individualised child-centred approach whereby peers help each other. This study, therefore, reveals the syncretism of practices taking place in community classes where children and their families have two 'homes'. By the mid-twenty-first century, this situation will be common for many children throughout the world. *Pi Tautau* may, therefore, be indicative of many community classes throughout the world as immigrants blend different worlds, syncretising new and old identities in their children's learning.

Although the community classes outlined above take place in different parts of the world and are quite different in the language and culture they are promoting, they share certain key features. First, all implicitly teach not just a language, literacy or religion, but a whole way of life. Importantly, in the last two examples, this way of life cannot directly replicate that of the country of origin, but will *syncretise* the new and the old. Bangladeshi British teachers need to give children individual attention, whereas they would traditionally engage in whole-class teaching, since classes usually have pupils from a variety of ages and stages. Learning, then, takes place through observation of older classmates. Samoan American teachers use English to explain the text and are also adopting more child-centred approaches. Second, all the above studies refer to the classroom as a safe 'haven'; a meeting-place where 'members' share common practices and expectations. Third, teachers in all these classes have high expectations for their pupils, never doubting their ability to succeed. Finally, in all these classes, learning takes place within a very definite and familiar structure, using languages, routines and rituals that have been passed down across generations. Parents will not feel lost and excluded when they enter these classrooms but will immediately feel a part of the learning taking place.

CONCLUSION

The argument is gaining ground that people with access to different languages, cultural and religious practices have not just funds of knowledge but a range of choices that are inaccessible to monolinguals. In recent years, recognition has finally been given to the importance of indigenous languages in countries colonised or conquered by those more powerful:

> Millions of new urban settlers around the world are determined to preserve their original languages in addition to acquiring the languages of their new countries. In the contemporary world, with greater intensity of people movement and with rapid changes in communication, it has become much easier for people to maintain and develop cultural and family ties across diasporas. That, in turn, is playing an important part in the formation of new global cultures.
> (Gurnah, 2000: 234)

For example, initial literacy programmes in indigenous languages have been integrated into mainstream classrooms in Mexico, Bolivia, Guatemala, Peru and New Zealand. In Mexico, initial literacy text-books have been translated into 36 languages – each reflecting families in traditional dress and engaged in appropriate work practices (SEP, 1993). In New Zealand (Aotearoa in Māori), there has been a resurgence of *te reo* and *nga tikanga* (Māori language and culture) (May and Hill, 2005).

In his work on transnational media and Turkish migrants in Europe, Robbins (2001) argues for the use of satellite TV as providing people with different 'cultural spaces' within which they can both think and have experiences. In similar ways, community classes may provide young children with different cultural and linguistic spaces where they can develop cognitive, cultural and linguistic flexibility with which to tackle the world. It is this capacity to operate across cultures, to think across and through different rituals, routines and languages that should give children confidence to deal with their future worlds.

REFERENCES

Anderson, A.B. and Stokes, S.J. (1984) 'Social and institutional influences on the development and practice of literacy', in H. Goelman, A. Oberg, and F. Smith (eds), *Awakening to Literacy*. Portsmouth, NH: Heinemann Educational.

Arnberg, L. (1987) *Raising Children Bilingually: The Pre-School Years*. Cleveland: Multilingual Matters.

Bain, B. and Yu, A. (1980) 'Cognitive consequences of raising children bilingually: One parent, one language', *Canadian Journal of Psychology*, 34: 304–13.

Barradas, O. (2007) 'Learning Portuguese: A tale of two worlds', in J. Conteh, P. Martin, and L. Robertson (eds), *Multilingual Learning: Stories from Schools and Communities in Britain*. Stoke-on-Trent: Trentham Books. pp. 87–102.

Ben-Zeev, S. (1977) 'The influence of bilingualism on cognitive strategy and cognitive development', *Child Development*, 48: 1009–18.

Bialystok, E. (2010). 'Global–local and trail-making tasks by monolingual and bilingual children: Beyond inhibition', *Developmental Psychology, 46:* 93–105.

Brinton, D., Kagan, O., and Bauckus, S. (eds) (2008) *Heritage Language Education: A New Field Emerging*. New York: Routledge.

Chen, Y. (2007) 'Contributing to success: Chinese parents and the community school', in J. Conteh, P. Martin, and L. Robertson (eds), *Multilingual Learning: Stories from Schools and Communities in Britain*. Stoke-on-Trent: Trentham Books. pp. 63–85.

Conteh, J. and Begum, S. (2008) 'Bilingual teachers as agents of social change: Linking the community and the mainstream', in C. Kenner and T. Hickey (eds),

Multilingual Europe: Diversity and Learning. Stoke-on-Trent: Trentham Books. pp. 104–8.

Creese, A., Bhatt, A., Bhojani, N., and Martin, P. (2006) 'Multicultural, heritage and learner identities in complementary schools', *Language and Education*, 20(1): 23–43.

Cummins, J. (1979) 'Linguistic interdependence and the educational development of bilingual children', *Review of Educational Research*, 49: 222–51.

Cummins, J. (1981) *Bilingualism and Minority Language Teaching*. Ontario: Ontario Institute for Studies in Education.

Cummins, J. (1992) 'Heritage language teaching in Canadian schools', *Journal of Curriculum Studies*, 24(3): 281–6.

DES (Department of Education and Science) (1985) *An Education for all: The Report of the Committee of Inquiry into Education for Children of Ethnic Minority Groups (The Swann Report)*. London: HMSO.

DfES (Department for Education and Skills) (2007) *Languages Review*. Annesley: DfES.

Duranti, A., Ochs, E., and Ta'ase, E.K. (1995) 'Change and tradition in literacy instruction in a Samoan American community', *Educational Foundations*, Fall: 57–75.

Feldman, C. and Shen, M. (1971) 'Some language-related cognitive advantages of bilingual five year olds', *Journal of Genetic Psychology*, 118: 235–44.

Fishman, J. (1979) *The Streets of East London*. London: Duckworth.

Fitzpatrick, F. (1987) *The Open Door*. Clevedon: Multilingual Matters.

Francis, B., Archer, L., and Mau, A. (2010) 'Chinese complementary school pupils' social and educational subjectivities', in V. Lytra and P. Martin (eds), *Sites of Multilingualism: Complementary Schools in Britain Today*. Stoke-on-Trent: Trentham Books. pp. 85–96.

Goodenough, F. (1926) 'Racial differences in the intelligence of schoolchildren', *Journal of Experimental Psychology*, 9: 388–97.

Gregory, E. (1994a) 'Non-native speakers and the National Curriculum' in G. Blenkin and V. Kelly (eds), *The National Curriculum and Early Learning*. London: Paul Chapman Publishing.

Gregory, E. (1994b) 'Cultural assumptions and early years pedagogy: The effect of the home culture on minority children's interpretation of reading in school', *Language, Culture and Curriculum*, 7(2): 111–24.

Gregory, E. (1996) *Making Sense of a New World: Learning to Read in a Second Language*. London: Paul Chapman Publishing.

Gregory, E. and Kelly, C. (1992) 'Bilingualism and assessment', in G. Blenkin and V. Kelly (eds) *Assessment in Early Childhood Education*. London: Paul Chapman Publishing.

Gregory, E. and Williams, A. (2000) *City Literacies: Learning to Read Across Generations and Cultures*. London: Routledge.

Gregory, E., Choudhury, H., Ilankuberan, A., Kwapong, A., and Woodham, M. (2013, in press) 'Practise, performance and perfection: Learning sacred texts in four faith communities in London', *International Journal of the Sociology of Language in Education*.

Gurnah, A. (2000) 'Languages and literacies for autonomy', in M. Martin-Jones and K. Jones (eds) *Multilingual Literacies*. Amsterdam: John Benjamins.

Hakuta, K. (1986) *Mirror of Language: The Debate on Bilingualism*. New York: Basic Books.

Hamers, J.F. and Blanc, M.H. (1989) *Bilinguality and Bilingualism*. Cambridge: Cambridge University Press.

Heath, S.B. (1983) *Ways with Words: Language and Life in Communities and Classrooms*. Cambridge: Cambridge University Press.

Ianco-Worrall, A. (1972) 'Bilingualism and cognitive development', *Child Development*, 43: 1390–400.

Jesperson, O. (1923) *Language*. London: George Allen and Unwin.

John-Steiner, V. (1985) 'The road to competence in an alien land: A Vygotskian perspective on bilingualism' in J.V. Wertsch (ed.), *Culture, Communication and Cognition, Vygotskian Perspectives*. Cambridge: Cambridge University Press.

Kenner, C. (2000a) *Home Pages*. Stoke-on-Trent: Trentham Books.

Kenner, C. (2000b) 'Children writing in a multilingual nursery', in M. Martin-Jones and K. Jones (eds), *Multilingual Literacies*. Amsterdam: John Benjamins.

Liedtke, W.W. and Nelson, L.D. (1968) 'Concept formation and bilingualism', *Alberta Journal of Education Research*, 14: 225–32.

Lytra, V. and Martin, P. (eds) (2010) *Sites of Multilingualism: Complementary Schools in Britain Today*. Stoke-on-Trent: Trentham Books.

May, S. and Hill, R. (2005) 'Māori-medium education: Current issues and challenges' *International Journal of Bilingual Education and Bilingualism*, 8(5): 377–403.

Maylor, U., Glass, K., Issa, T., Kuyok, A., Minty, S., Rose, A., and Ross, A. (2010) *Impact of Supplementary Schools on Pupils' Attainment: An Investigation into What Factors Contribute to Educational Improvements*. London: DCSF.

Our Languages (2011) www.ourlanguages.org.uk, accessed 15 July 2011.

Peal, E. and Lambert, W.E. (1962) 'The relation of bilingualism and intelligence', *Psychological Monographs: General and Applied*, 76(546): 1–23.

Robbins, K. (2001) 'Beyond imagined community? Transnational media and Turkish migrants in Europe'. Inaugual lecture, Goldsmiths College, London.

Robertson, L. (2007) 'The story of bilingual children learning to read', in J. Conteh, P. Martin, and L. Helavaara Robertson (eds), *Multilingual Learning: Stories from Schools and Communities in Britain*. Stoke-on-Trent: TrenthamBooks. pp. 41–61.

Rosen, H. (1999) *Are You Still Circumcised?* London: Five Leaves Publications.

Rosowsky, A. (2001) Decoding as a cultural practice and its effects on the reading process of bilingual pupils. *Language and Education*, 15(1): 56–70.

Saer, D.J. (1924) 'An inquiry into the effect of bilingualism upon the intelligence of young children', *Journal of Experimental Psychology*, 6: 232–40 and 266–74.

Sapir, E. (1970) *Culture, Language and Personality*. Berkeley: University of California Press.

Scribner, S. and Cole, M. (1981) *The Psychology of Literacy*. Cambridge, MA: Harvard University Press.

SEP (Secretaria de Educacion Publica) (1993) *Maaya T'aan (Primer ciclo)*. Mexico: Comision National de los libros de texto gratuitos.

Skutnabb-Kangas, T. (1984) *Bilingualism or Not? – The Education of Minorities*. Clevedon: Multilingual Matters.

Souza, A. (2010) 'Language choice and identity negotiations in a Brazilian Portuguese community school', in V. Lytra and P. Martin(eds) *Sites of Multilingualism: Complementary Schools in Britain Today*. Stoke-on-Trent: Trentham Books. pp. 97–107.

Street, B. (1984) *Literacy in Theory and Practice*. Cambridge: Cambridge University Press.

Swain, M. and Cummins, J. (1979) 'Bilingualism, cognitive functioning and education', *Language Teaching and Linguistics Abstracts*, 12(1): 4–18.

Tosi, A. (1984) *Immigration and Bilingual Education*. Oxford: Pergamon.

Verhoeven, L. (1987) *Ethnic Minority Children Acquiring Literacy*. Dordrecht: Foris.

Vygotsky, L. (1962 translation) *Thought and Language*. Cambridge, MA: MIT Press.

Wagner, D.A. (1993) *Literacy, Culture and Development: Becoming Literate in Morocco*. Cambridge: Cambridge University Press.

Wagner, D.A., Messick, B., and Spratt, J. (1986) 'Studying literacy in Morocco', in B.B. Schieffelin and D. Gilmore (eds), *The Acquisition of Literacy: Ethnographic Perspectives*. Norwood, NJ: Ablex.

Zinsser, C. (1986) 'For the Bible tells me so: Teaching children in a fundamentalist church', in B. Schieffelin and D. Gilmore (eds), *The Acquisition of Literacy: Ethnographic Perspectives*. Norwood, NJ: Ablex.

10

Agency, Authority, and Action in Family Literacy Scholarship: An Analysis of the Epistemological Assumptions Operating in Family Literacy Scholarship

Catherine Compton-Lilly and Beth Graue
with Rebecca Rogers and Tisha Y. Lewis

Much has been written about what children and families bring to schools. This literature has helped us understand the diverse resources that families embody in their children and the degree to which schools take up these resources in their practice. This view of families as competent and supportive of their children's learning rests on assumptions that stand in contrast to scholarship that assumes a deficit perspective about diverse families. These assumptions have profound effects on the questions that are possible, the methods used, and the implications derived. In this chapter, we explore the ways that family literacy researchers have created their knowledge through the epistemological frameworks enacted in their research. Specifically, we ask what assumptions relate to the effects people can have on the world, the nature of knowledge, and the course of educational change. Recognizing the epistemological assumptions that frame family literacy research is significant for several reasons. First, it has the potential to invite family literacy scholars to reflect on the assumptions that are implicit in our work. Second, this analysis reveals the ways in which multiple and sometimes competing epistemologies coexist in the same research studies. Third, it reveals general patterns within research strands and across the field as well as opportunities for disrupting these patterns. Fourth, this analysis highlights increasing attention to the complexities that complicate simple explanations that correlate home practices with later literacy learning. Finally, we reveal some of the strengths and weaknesses that are inherent in both quantitative and qualitative approaches to family literacy.

We recognize that undertaking a review in this way is itself an epistemological stance, one that is critically interpretive. From this perspective, knowledge, including scholarship, is constructed by researchers within frameworks that privilege particular groups. Rather than explaining what is known, we work to understand *how* knowledge comes to be when scholars ask certain questions, with specific tools. We hope to identify who and what is privileged in the process and what results these stances have for practice.

To assist us in this task, we draw on the work of Holland, Lachicotte, Skinner, and Cain (1998). Their framework provides tools that recognize individuals as creative and strategic agents who act within sets of material and cultural forces that shape opportunities and action. Their ideas represent an asset-based viewpoint that straddles structural notions of power and individual choice and interest. A key idea in this work is agency or the generative capacities of people to act. Holland et al. speak of agency when they note that 'human collectives and individuals often move themselves – led by hope, desperation, or even playfulness, but certainly by no rational plan – from one set of socially and culturally formed subjectivities to another' (1998: 7). Agency is fueled by improvisations that people bring to unique and often unexpected situations. All people possess agency although it 'may be frail, especially among those with little power, but it happens daily and mundanely, and

it deserves our attention' (Holland et al., 1998: 5). In this chapter, we focus on the degree and types of agency that are ascribed to family members and the educators who work with families.

However, agency does not operate outside of power. 'People do not act only as agents. They also have the capacity to act as "instruments" of other agents, and to be "patients," to be the recipients of the acts of others' (Holland et al., 1998: 44). In Holland et al.'s account people are always 'malleable, changeable, and subject to discursive powers' (1995: 5). They construct and are constructed by 'figured worlds' (1995: 52); the historical, social, and culturally constructed spaces in which people sense the worlds they inhabit. Within these figured worlds 'particular characters and actors are recognized, significance is assigned to certain acts, and particular outcomes are valued over others' (1995: 52) – thus authority operates. In this paper, we examine how family literacy scholarship assigns and recognizes authority.

Holland et al.'s (1995) figured worlds also present visions of actions that might be taken. In our analyses of family literacy scholarship, these actions include what scholars believe could and should be done in classrooms and research communities. As Holland et al. explain, 'People tell others who they are, but even more important, they tell themselves and then try to act as though they are who they say they are' (1995: 3). We argue that these ideas apply in the world of research where scholars enact performances within their epistemologically themed figured worlds.

CONSIDERING EPISTEMOLOGIES

Epistemologies enable the 'rules and standards of reason that organize perceptions, ways of responding to the world, and the conceptions of "self"' (Popkewitz, 1998: x). They make certain things visible, valued, and real. For example, objectivist perspectives characterize the world as comprised of things that can be objectively known through measurement and description. Objectivist accounts present researchers as describing reality through observation and measurement. A major focus of these objectivist accounts is discovering causal mechanisms by monitoring the effects of particular practices on learning. Individual and contextual factors not part of a study's design are viewed as irrelevant.

Subjectivist accounts challenge the idea that participants act in predictable ways. These accounts highlight the multiple, evolving actions that participants use as they meet the challenges they encounter in their daily lives. In lieu of a notion of linear progress, subjectivists focus on the idiosyncratic and local actions that reflect specific situations and histories. These discontinuities and complexities complicate simple models of agency in which particular acts lead to predictable outcomes. Subjectivist conceptions of agency propose that any given act may result in an infinite number of outcomes.

A third option provides a melding of the objectivism and subjectivism. Constructionist research portrays the world as built through human interaction. In contrast to the objectivist who approaches an already existing world that is to be measured, constructionists focus on the ways that individuals and groups construct meaning within local social, cultural, political, and historical contexts. For constructionists, the world is there but is given meaning through human interaction.

Our point in this paper is that scholars bring epistemological assumptions to their work that impact the ways they characterize and respond to families, design instructional experiences, and understand and assess development and change. In this critical vein, we focus specifically on epistemological beliefs related to agency, authority, and scholarly and pedagogical action.

The specifically political nature of epistemology has been noted by scholars who read race into the assumptions brought to research. Scheurich and Young argue 'epistemological racism' (1994: 4) is rooted in deeply seated and historically grounded assumptions about the world. Epistemologies 'arise out of the social history of a particular social group' and 'no epistemology is context free' (1994: 8). The historic dominance of the White culture has resulted in the denial of epistemologies grounded in alternative social histories, including those rooted in African and indigenous cultures. Scheurich and Young noted that White scholars are generally comfortable with White epistemologies affecting the nature of the university, definitions of legitimate scholarship, methodologies deemed worthy, and assumptions brought to research contexts.

In a similar vein, Gillborn (2005) explored the relationship between educational policy and White supremacy. He argued that White educators and scholars were often unaware of the performances of White supremacy in which they and others engaged. These acts involved the enactment of accepted identities continuously strengthened and legitimized 'through countless acts of reiteration and reinforcement' (2005: 490), that simultaneously denied other ways of being and acting. Research that examines diversity provides a particularly rich site for examining epistemological beliefs. Epistemological awareness is particularly significant for scholars who generally work with diverse families. As Hall (2001) explained, questions related to multiculturalism 'undermine and unsettle all of the existing totalities'

(2001: 5) by recognizing the existence of multiple ways of understanding the world.

While some have argued that episte-mologies can be sorted across a continuum ranging from objectivist to subjectivist (Crotty, 1998), tensions can exist among the epistemological stances embedded in particular studies or educational practices. Ultimately it is by grappling with episte-mological pluralism that we can begin to identify the strengths and limits offered by various epistemological stances and to rec-ognize how 'different approaches raise different questions, different models of inquiry, and different outcomes' (Caper, 2001: 8). In this chapter, we do not catego-rize the texts we analyzed according to particular epistemologies. Instead, we identify the discernable epistemologies that operate in these texts. Like Caper, we argue that these patterns have much to tell us about ourselves as scholars and about the state of family literacy scholarship.

METHODOLOGY

We draw on a recently completed integra-tive review of family literacy scholarship (Compton-Lilly, Rogers, and Lewis, 2012). While the full review included multiple analyses including a qualitative review of over 200 reviews of family literacy and an analysis of comprehensive edited volumes across time, in this review, we focus on citation coding patterns from 272 articles, book chapters, and reports that included reviews of family literacy scholarship. We developed a citation-coding scheme to identify family literacy scholars and researchers who were extensively cited in reviews of family literacy. We analyzed both reviews that extended over two paragraphs (213 reviews) and brief reviews (59 reviews) – generally two paragraphs or

less – to identify major researchers who consistently appeared as major citations. This analytic process was developed and refined as we crafted the following coding system to identify major citations. The following codes were entered on the refer-ence page for each article, book chapter, or report.

L (List) – The study was referenced only on a list with other references.
S (Sentence) – The study was discussed in –one to three sentences and was not a major reference.
P (Paragraph) – The study was discussed in –one or two paragraphs or four or more sentences.
C (Central) – The study was discussed in –one or two paragraphs and was central to the paper and its argument.

We created a chart of all the studies that were coded at the paragraph or central (C) level. Through our analysis of over 1000 citations, we identified scholars and texts whose work was cited extensively.

In the current chapter, we draw on two data sets based on this citation coding analysis. The first analysis involves the work of the 18 most cited researchers that were major citations in at least nine of the 272 reviews we analyzed (see Table 10.1). We focused only on the work of frequently cited scholars who worked directly in the field of family literacy – addressing empirical, theoretical, or policy issues related to family literacy. We did not examine the work of highly cited theorists (i.e., Bourdieu, Bronfenbrenner, Freire, Vygotsky) or scholars who worked in related fields (i.e., Durkin, Lareau, Michaels, Street, Sulzby, Teale), as this review focuses specifically on epistemo-logical assumptions within the field of family literacy.

While this analysis identified scholars and studies that have been widely recog-nized in the field, all of these scholars published their first major work prior

Table 10.1   Eighteen most cited scholars in reviews of family literacy

Number of citations	Dates of works cited	Researcher	Methods/theory
46	1982–1995	Shirley Brice Heath	Qualitative ethnography
41	1981–1997	Denny Taylor	Qualitative ethnography
34	1988–2000	Victoria Purcell-Gates	Qualitative ethnography
33	1990–2005	Luis Moll	Qualitative ethnography
24	1977–2001	Catherine Snow	Quantitative Causal/predictive
23	1992–1998	Trevor Cairney	Family literacy theory
22	1992–2003	Vivian Gadsden	Qualitative Family literacy theory
21	1987–1997	Elsa Auerbach	Family literacy theory
18	1996–2002	Monique Sénéchal	Quantitative Causal/predictive
17	1987–2001	Concha Delgado-Gaitan	Qualitative
17	1988–2001	Grover J. Whitehurst	Quantitative Causal/predictive
12	1991–2004	Robert G. St. Pierre	Quantitative Program effects
11	1994–2003	Linda Baker	Qualitative Program development
11	1991–2000	Barbara D. DeBaryshe	Quantitative Causal/predictive
10	1987–1999	Peter Hannon	Qualitative reviews
10	1988–2001	Adriana G. Bus	Quantitative Causal/predictive
10	1990–1999	Jeanne Paratore	Family literacy theory
9	1993–1997	Christine Marvin	Quantitative

to 1997. Thus this analysis does not identify or examine the work of scholars who appeared as major citations during the past 15 years. Consequentially, we also analyzed the work of the six most cited scholars who first appeared as major citations in 1997 or later (see Table 10.2). While these studies were only cited in four to six of the 272 reviews, this second analysis highlights recent trends related to authority, agency, and pedagogical action.

In most cases, the most cited publication from each scholar was selected for analysis. If more than one publication had the same number of citations, one of these articles was selected for review. When the most frequently cited text was unavailable, we utilized the scholar's next most cited text.

We used critical discourse analysis in our examination of the texts of the most cited publications. Rogers (2004) describes critical discourse analysis as a valuable tool for revealing the contradictions embedded in practices and policies. Specifically, critical discourse analysis brings a critical lens to the relationships between language and discourse 'in the construction and representation of this social world' (Rogers, 2004: 3). In the current analysis, we grappled with the ways the language used by family literacy scholars illuminated epistemological assumptions related to research participants, sources of authority, and pedagogical and scholarly actions proposed by family literacy scholars.

To explore agency, we examined the ways researchers identified and positioned research participants (e.g., respondents, participants, contributors). Specifically, we identified the types of activities (e.g., procedural, cognitive, intellectual) that were attributed to research participants and whether participants were recognized as

Table 10.2   Recent family literacy scholars

Author	Number of major citations	Top cited text	Text type
Mary Ann Evans	6	Evans, M.A., Shaw, D., and Bell, M. (2000). 'Home literacy activities and their influence in early literacy skills', *Canadian Journal of Experimental Psychology*, 54(2): 65–75.	Quantitative research study
Stephen R. Burgess	6	Burgess, S., Hecht, S., and Lonigan, C. (2002). 'Relations of the home literacy environment (HLE) the development of reading related abilities: A one year longitudinal study', *Reading Research Quarterly*, 37(4): 408–26.	Quantitative research study
Eve Gregory	5	Gregory, E. and Williams, A. (2000). *City Literacies: Learning to Read across Generations and Cultures*. London: Routledge.	Qualitative research study
Olivia N. Saracho	5	Saracho, O.N. (2000). 'Literacy development in the family context', *Early Childhood Development & Care*, 165, 107–14.	Research review
Fumiyo Tao	4	Tao, F., Gamse, B., and Tarr, H. (1998). 'National evaluation of Even Start family literacy programs, 1994–1997', Final Report. Washington, DC: US Department of Education, Planning and Evaluation Service.	Research review
Kate Pahl	4	Pahl, K. (2004). 'Narratives, artifacts and cultural identities', *Linguistics and Education*, 15(4): 339–58.	Qualitative research study

contributing valuable assets and insights to research projects. Finally, we examined the ways teachers were positioned within research studies and the degree of reciprocity that was recognized among participants, teachers, and researchers.

We also examined discourses that referenced the sources of authority recognized by researchers. Discourse analysis revealed whether researchers established their claims by citing the findings of other studies, highlighting the strength of research methodologies, or by reporting of correlations. For example, correlations and the strength of relationships among variables were established through language that ranged from 'confirming' to 'tending to support.' Some researchers located authority with institutions and mainstream ways of making sense of the world. Other researchers recognized the role they played in the crafting of research findings and challenged the notion that their findings are either universal or comprehensive.

Next, critical discourse analysis was applied to the descriptions of pedagogical and scholarly action proposed by researchers. These prescriptions were sometimes very specific, in terms of a particular instructional practice, or they were sometimes broad, attending to the relevance of local contexts and the contingencies that diversity brings to working with families and in communities. To analyze these data, we attended to a range of directive language including prescriptive words/phrases such as 'must', 'is central', and provided 'clear guidelines' as opposed to more guarded language such as 'only if,' and 'has a potential.' The current state of family literacy scholarship is the product of intertwined social, cultural, and epistemological factors. This critical discourse analysis reveals how epistemological stances function in family literacy scholarship and provide insights into the ways diversity is conceptualized, positioned and addressed.

EPISTEMOLOGIES AND THE MOST FREQUENTLY CITED SCHOLARS

Agency in family literacy scholarship

In this section, we draw upon position papers, reports, and empirical studies conducted by the most cited scholars to consider the types of agency attributed to research participants. Family literacy, from an objectivist perspective, is the study of the activities and practices that families enact in producing literate children. The research in this tradition focuses on predicting outcomes and designing interventions to enhance experience. From a subjectivist perspective family family literacy practices involve power between home and school that marginalizes the experiences and resources of those outside a mainstream group. The epistemological differences between these two stances are signaled by their labels – for the objectivist, literacy is a singular noun representing a normative view, while the subjectivist notion is inherently multiple, representing multiple views and experiences related to being literate.

Constructionist views of family literacy focus on the ways that individuals and groups construct meanings of literacy and the roles of families.

In the documents we analyzed, the agency attributed to participants was discernable in descriptions of participants within the research project as well as in the ways literacy practices and processes were conceptualized. These depictions were signaled by the verbs used to describe their contributions and the degree of reciprocity recognized among participants and between participants and researchers.

In some studies, participants were positioned as having little agency, with no identity outside of the research project. For example, in a 1993 survey study, research participants are described as 'respondents' using phrases such as 'Respondents were asked…' (Marvin and Mirenda, 1993: 361) or 'children in the SpEd group were identified' (Marvin and Mirenda, 1993: 354–5). This pattern continued in other studies 'Children's degree of exposure to joint reading was measured….' (DeBaryshe, 1995: 5); 'children's receptive vocabulary was assessed…' (Senechal, LeFevre, Hudson, and Lawson, 1996: 523). These authors position respondents as reactive objects of investigation whose existence was framed by the actions of the researchers. Other researchers named the actors involved in research studies, but still positioned them as objects of study that could be measured or assessed.

Participants were also positioned in passive ways through the use of verbs that denoted low-level cognitive processes: 'parents were asked to recognize…' (Senechal et al., 1996: 521); 'caretakers completing the survey…' (DeBaryshe, 1995: 12); 'The respondent answered…' (Senechal et al., 1996: 524); 'parents indicated…' (Senechal et al., 1996: 533).

In a few cases, strong language passively positioned participants. Senechal et al. noted that 'children were required...' (1996: 527) to engage in particular activities and noted twice that 'data were taken' (DeBaryshe, 1995: 5, 12) to 'represent' families.

Ascribed agency within literacy practices could also be discerned in research reports. Children in particular were often positioned as the recipients of processes that acted on them rather than as active meaning constructors: 'Reading books aloud exposes children...' (Bus, van Ijzendoorn, and Pellegrini, 1995: 2); and 'preschool children learn vocabulary from shared reading events' (Senechal et al., 1996: 521).

While this linguistic analysis highlights subtle positionings, it is important to recognize that within reports, the author's epistemological understandings were sometimes internally inconsistent. For example, while above DeBaryshe (1995) is quoted as measuring children's exposure to joint reading, in the conclusion of the paper, she notes that mothers may also engage in more sophisticated processes stating, 'perhaps mothers who believe in the importance of reading attribute the same characteristics to their children.' (DeBaryshe, 1995: 17).

Constructionist perspectives on family literacy depict active constructors of meaning interacting in local settings. For example, Taylor and Dorsey-Gaines described participants as '*active members in a print community in which literacy is used for a wide variety of social, technical, and aesthetic purposes*' (1988: 200, italics in the original) and described successful students who were 'able to maintain the shift between home and school and sustain both worlds' (1988: 209). They quoted one student, Jerry, who stated, 'I am a producer. I can produce' (1988: 195).

Moll and his colleagues (Moll, Amanti, Neff, and Gonzalez, 1992) also described participants as active and engaged in their own learning. As they explained, 'children in the households are not passive bystanders, as they seem in the classrooms, but active participants in a broad range of activities' (1992: 134). Through the research process, they became 'active learners' and strategically used their 'social contacts outside the classroom to access new knowledge for the development of their studies' (1992: 138). Taylor and Dorsey-Gaines described parents as 'sharing,' 'creating', and 'valuing' (1988: 194). Baker, Serpell, and Sonnenschein (1995) described children participating in food preparation, interacting with food labels, and attending to environmental print and Hannon noted that 'Children learn a great deal before they even get to school' (1995: 36).

Auerbach (1989) critiqued family literacy models that involved the transmission of school practices to families. She described these programs as 'teaching parents', 'providing parents', 'assisting parents,' 'training parents,' and 'giving parents' (Auerbach, 1989: 168–9). In each of these constructions, parents are positioned as the recipients of the actions rather than as actors. In contrast, other researchers treat subjects as living active people, giving them pseudonyms to convey an identity.

The research of Moll et al. (1992) offered an additional insight relative to agency. Specifically, they situated teachers as change agents. While they noted that in their previous work they had 'relied on the researchers to present their findings to the teachers and to figure out the relevance of that information for teaching' (p. 134), in this 1992 article, they presented 'teacher–researcher collaborations' (1992: 135) in which teachers were directly involved in data collection and analysis.

While references to collaborative meetings as 'training workshops' (1992: 135) suggested that the researchers retained their authority and expertise, teacher knowledge and capacity were recognized as means to change. As they noted, 'It is the teacher, not the anthropologist, who is ultimately the bridge between the students' world, theirs and the family's funds of knowledge, and the classroom experience' (1992: 137). Teachers were positioned as agential in the sense that their actions mattered; however, those actions were contingent on the information they learned about families and gained through training.

While the constructionist perspectives examined in the current analysis tended to ascribe more agential competencies to research participants, this was not consistently true within some studies. For example, Hannon (1995) noted that even parents with minimal literacy skills 'may still be able to help by encouraging their children, talking about stories, responding to the sense of what children read, and providing opportunities for children's reading to develop' (Hannon, 1995: 36). Cairney (1995) reported that 'parents, in turn, can also be given the opportunity to observe and understand the definitions of literacy that schools support and which ultimately empower individuals to take their places in society' (1995: 521). The language used by Hannon and Cairney recognizes parental agency but in both cases this agency is marked by contingencies. Low-literate parents 'may' be able to help their children (Hannon, 1995) and parents must be 'given' opportunities (Cairney, 1995). Thus the agency is not inherent in the parents' capabilities but dependant on situations that allow agency and provide the assistance of others.

In a book entitled *Literacy for Empowerment*, Delgado-Gaitan (1990)

voiced multiple discourses in reference to parent empowerment, the strengths of families, the role of advocates, and the need for parent training. She argued that schools must 'incorporate the parents and the culture of the home as an integral part of the school instructional plan' (Delgado-Gaitan, 1990: 1) and noted that 'Spanish-speaking parents assisted their children in the education process' and 'socialized each other to maximize their potential in dealing with school' (Delgado-Gaitan, 1990: 4-5). However, throughout the text Delgado-Gaitan (1990) highlighted a parent training program and the role of advocates – people who could assist parents in their efforts to help their children.

While presented as a means to empowerment, tensions related to advocacy and training are apparent. When parents asked school officials for help in dealing with disciplinary problems, they were also provided with presentations on AIDS and child abuse. These 'awareness building sessions helped 'parents to become acquainted with their needs'' (Delgado-Gaitan, 1990: 144), raising questions about who defines and names the needs of families. Likewise, when parents resolved to organize as a group, the researcher provided advice on how to proceed, noting that 'most Spanish-speaking parents did not have much experience with schools and therefore could not participate actively in them' (1990: 144). Finally, Delgado-Gaitan advocated that 'state level policy needs to mandate training for teachers to provide education to families' (1990: 168). While mandated training was certainly helpful to some families, this transmission model challenges notions of empowerment by suggesting that educators must provide parents with training.

Furthermore, Delgado-Gaitan (1990) noted the role of advocates, including herself, who supported parents, provided resources, and shared information. While these are laudable claims, the underlying message is that parents could act on behalf of their children only with institutional support. In sum, Delgado-Gaitan's project (1990) highlights the complexities that operate at the intersection of supporting and empowering families and raises questions about who is empowered: teachers, advocates, or parents? These types of studies are typical of the critical constructionist perspective that interrogates the role of power in literacy while recognizing the material resources that limit access to that power.

Some researchers highlight the evolving, changing, and flexible networks and situations in which participants act and interact. These networks involve children and parents as active and engaged contributors. Moll and his colleagues note that networks are 'flexible, adaptive, and active' (1992: 133). These networks are also described as reciprocal with social relationships supporting both parents and children. Auerbach (1989) also documented a two-way support system between child and parent that was particularly significant in immigrant families. Baker and her colleagues described bidirectional influences between children and parents as 'children's behaviors influence those of their parents which in turn influence future behaviors of the children' (1995: 250). Similarly, Gadsden reported 'reciprocal learning relationships between parent and child' (1994: 73).

While some researchers described active reciprocity among family members, Taylor and Dorsey-Gaines described participants and researchers 'learning from one another' (1988: xiv). They describe the critical role that families play in helping researchers to confront existing 'images from the mass media' (1988: xiv) and 'deal on a daily basis with our own ethnocentrism and mental baggage' (1988: xv). As Hannon (1995) noted 'A recurring theme in the recent literature is that parents must be viewed as equal partners and that there must be a reciprocal relationship' between parents, educators, and researchers. He described literacy as a relative construct noting that 'what matters is the individual's ability to cope with the demands they experience in society' (Hannon, 1995: 7).

Finally, agency also occurs as parents choose not to do things. For example, Auerbach noted that parents in her study 'often intentionally avoided "doing literacy" with their children in the ways they had been taught in schools in order to avoid replicating what they remembered as negative experiences' (1989: 173). Rather than passive recipients, Auerbach maintained that 'for less literate parents it is precisely this attitude of advocacy and critical examination of school practices that may be their most powerful tool in shaping their children's school achievement' (Auerbach, 1989: 175). Gadsden argued that the success of a family literacy program depended to a large measure on 'whether family members themselves were key actors in determining their roles in their own literacy development, and not simply defined as the product or recipients of an effort' (1994: 69).

In some cases, more recent scholarship attributed increased agency to participants. Although 'asked' low level questions and being 'required' to complete prescribed tasks, Tao, Gamse, and Tarr (1998) describe parents who could 'of course, obtain child and adult services on their own' (Tao et al., 1998: 1) and explained 'gains for Even Start families may not be due alone to participation in the project' (1998: 2). However, these examples of agential language were presented alongside less empowering references to 'increasing the ability of participating parents to be their child's "first and best teacher,"' (1998: 1) and 'training parents' (1998: 5).

Recent descriptions of 'syncretism' (Gregory and Williams, 2000: 13) highlight the blending of literacy practices across multiple contexts 'resulting in a form of reinterpretation that is both new and dynamic' (2000: 13). Similarly, Pahl (2004) explores how members of immigrant families used artifacts alongside texts and oral narratives. Specifically, she examined artifacts created by children alongside the stories told by the children and their parents. These texts positioned children and parents as active meaning makers who drew upon multiple modalities while recognizing how 'the telling of stories can be passed across generations, and can be closely associated with artifacts, which then trigger the retelling of narratives once more' (2004: 356).

Authority in family literacy scholarship

Objectivist epistemologies locate authority within science and with scientists – highlighting the importance of unbiased and proven methods as well as the expertise of the researcher. Subjectivist versions recognize multiple forms of authority accepting shifting perspectives, negotiated meanings, and fragmented understandings. Constructionist researchers frame authority as a mutually constitutive of the relationships of individuals and groups in context. In the family literacy scholarship, some researchers referenced the research itself as being authoritative.

In objectivist studies, correlational language was often used to support research findings; this perspective prizes the co-occurrence of characteristics and activities or the use of one characteristic as the proxy of another:

'... environmental factors that appeared to be correlated with reading acquisition' (Marvin and Mirenda, 1993: 351);
'... maternal reading interaction style served as the measure of home practices' (DeBaryshe, 1995: 10);
'... have correlated strongly with eventual success in reading' (Paratore, Melzi, and Krol-Sinclair, 1999: 2).

Correlational language was also present in some constructionist studies. Purcell-Gates (1996) noted 'The children's scores on the written language knowledge measures, with the exception of intentionality, were positively related to the years they had experienced formal literacy instruction' (1996: 422) and that knowledge about the conventions of written language 'appeared to be learned more by children in homes in which print was used to a greater degree' (1996: 422).

Claims of causality, which were stronger than correlational claims, were only encountered in a few quantitative studies:

'Our analysis provides a clear and affirmative answer to the question of whether or not storybook reading is one of the most important activities for developing the knowledge required for eventual success in reading' (Bus et al., 1995: 15);
'The purpose of this study was to test a causal model of the determinants and outcomes of parent-child book reading practices. As expected ... were predictive .... These results are consistent ...' (DeBaryshe, 1995: 17).

Researchers often expressed authority and expertise through the language they used. Researchers 'constructed,' 'conducted,' 'implemented,' and 'tested' studies. These verbs connote expertise and authority, and researchers are positioned as qualified and capable of creating sophisticated and laudable research projects. For example, Marvin and Mirenda 'implemented an intensive emergent literacy program with preschoolers' (1993: 353) and Bus et al. conducted a meta-analysis 'to test empirical evidence regarding the importance of joint book reading' (1995: 1).

Both quantitative and qualitative researchers often used the pronoun 'we' to position themselves. The verbs used in conjunction with 'we' by quantitative researchers included various tenses of expect, exclude, eliminate, establish, ask, use, replace, select, and measure. Each of these verbs suggests methodological actions that affect the research study and entail scientific language related to research design. Qualitative researchers tended to use the pronoun 'we' in conjunction with develop, explore, know, and believe. Paratore et al. state, 'We have worked from the belief …' (1999: 5).

Notably, the verbs used by qualitative researchers generally reflect analytic processes (e.g., develop, explore, know, and believe) rather than methodological actions. For example, Purcell-Gates 'reported', 'accompanied families,' and 'noted' various literacy practices (1996: 412). Rather than focusing on crafting a research project via acts such as excluding, eliminating, selecting, and measuring, Purcell-Gates' language served description via participant observation. She documented literacy practices in a particular community. Taylor and Dorsey-Gaines used the pronoun 'we' to ask 'what have we learned' and 'how can we (as researchers, educators, and policy makers) use the information we have gained' (1988: xviii). They also use the direct object 'us', placing themselves in the subordinate position asking 'how have the families helped us' and 'what have the families taught us' (1988: xviii).

At times the researcher operated as an omniscient and unidentified force. As Marvin and Mirenda noted, 'the data were analyzed' (1993: 354) and as Senechal et al. explained, the 'books were obtained …' (1996: 523). Purcell-Gates reports that 'codes were derived directly from the data' (1996: 415) while Saracho notes that 'several categories emerged from the analysis of the data' (2000: 110). Agents in these statements are implied but not identified. At other times, researchers relied on an assumedly shared sense of logic with their readers; Bus et al. presented with phrases such as 'it seems reasonable to assume …' (1995: 3).

A number of studies located the authority within the studies themselves. Nuanced terms are used – ranging from language that indicates correlation to less forceful and more tentative language; we have used italics and bold text to draw attention to the language used by these scholars:

'… the results give **straightforward support** for family literacy programs' (Bus et al., 1995: 15);

'There were a number of **potentially important** differences' (Marvin and Mirenda, 1993: 363);

'Our results were **highly consistent** …' (DeBaryshe, 1995: 9);

'Overall, **it appears** …' (Marvin and Mirenda, 1993: 359, 360);

'… the results also **tend to support** …' (Bus et al., 1995: 17);

'The results from this study **are promising**' (Saracho, 2000: 113).

From 'straightforward support' to results that 'tend to support', each of these statements places a degree of authority in the research study and the methods entailed. One report, authored by Catherine Snow and her colleagues, used particularly strong language to present the findings of that report conducted by the Committee on the

Prevention of Reading Disabilities in Young Children and carried out at the request of the US Department of Education's Office of Special Education Programs and its Office of Educational Research and Improvement. Their language includes the following:

'It is *imperative* …' (Snow, Burns, and Griffin, 1998: 10);
'A *critical component* is …' (Snow et al., 1998: 10);
'Teachers *need to be* knowledgeable about …' (Snow et al., 1998: 10);
'Schools *have the responsibility* …' (Snow et al., 1998: 10);
'… *should be taught* …' (Snow et al., 1998: 11).

Some verbs, including 'found' and 'revealed', suggest that research studies enable researchers to see truths that were previously invisible. This language suggests objectivist models that trust science to reveal the truths about the world:

'No significant differences were found' (Marvin and Mirenda, 1993: 361);
'I found, for the most part, only slightly different distributions and proportions …' (Purcell-Gates, 1996: 419);
'Our study revealed …' (Baker et al., 1995: 248);
'We found, as a result of this investigation,…' (Auerbach, 1989: 167);
'In our own work, we, too, have found and reported evidence …' (Paratore et al., 1999: 7).

Scholars across epistemologies referenced the work of other researchers and drew on the findings of others to support their claims:

'Sulzby's (1958) emergent reading scale suggests …' (Bus et al., 1995: 2);
'Many other researchers have echoed Auerbach's viewpoint' (Paratore et al., 1999: 3);
'… we were influenced by Lareau's (1989) study …' (Paratore et al., 1999: 4).

Scholars, particularly those who presented position papers or reviews of scholarship,

referred to general bodies of knowledge to support their arguments. They reference collective knowledge within the field:

'Several rigorously designed studies have found …' (St Pierre and Layzer, 1996: para 9);
'Cognitive studies of reading have identified phonological processing as crucial to skillful reading' (Snow et al., 1998: 24);
'A body of ethnographic and linguistic research has emerged over the last 20 years …' (Purcell-Gates, 1996: 406);
'Several earlier influential studies have documented …' (Purcell-Gates, 1996: 406).

Both objectivist and constructionist perspectives located the validity of their research on the strength of the research instruments they employed. 'The survey was found to have high face validity by two university professors who specialize in the study of reading development and early reading practices' (Marvin and Mirenda, 1993: 353). Likewise, Moll and his colleagues noted 'Qualitative research offers a range of methodological alternatives that can fathom the array of cultural and intellectual resources available to students and teachers within these households' (1992: 132). Purcell-Gates noted that graduate students 'coded the fieldnotes, after training and practice with the principal researcher' (1996: 416) and that the 'reliability of coding for literacy event type and for participant structure was assessed by recoding each field note by a second coder and calculating the degree of agreement' (1996: 417).

In some cases researcher authority is shared with others. Moll and his colleagues describe the formation of study groups that involve teachers. They describe these as 'collaborative ventures between teachers and researchers' in which they discuss 'developing understanding of households and classrooms' (1992: 132).

Authority can also be located within larger institutions and involve accepted practices and beliefs. Auerbach (1989) draws on Heath: 'Since authority is vested in those belonging to the mainstream culture, the literacy practices of the mainstream become the norm and have higher status in school contexts.' (1989: 173). Likewise, Hannon (1995) recognized 'the *constructed* nature of school literacy' (Hannon, 1995: 11, italics in the original) and noted that 'many teachers were persuaded that *some* form of parental involvement in the teaching of reading was worthwhile even if they were unclear about the distinctions between "home reading", "parent listening", "paired reading", and "shared reading"' (Hannon, 1995: 25). These challenges to dominant notions of parent involvement in literacy beg the question asked by Gadsden: 'who decides what the purposes [of family literacy] should be' (1994: 58).

Finally, in some cases, researchers recognize the role they play in crafting research accounts. Bridging constructionist and subjectivist epistemologies Taylor and Dorsey-Gaines referenced 'the descriptions we have constructed' (1988: 194) and noted 'the text that we have created is neither fact nor fiction' (1988: 202). They place themselves within the realm of the study, 'we were also trying to understand ourselves, true and false, personal perceptions and deceptions, the ethnocentrism of our own mental baggage' (1988: 202).

Some researchers situate authority within scientific findings and in the strength of methods that were used. Others locate authority and knowledge within families and communities. Taking a critical subjectivist perspective, Auerbach describes this as 'an alternative formulation' (1989: 175) of family literacy that highlights

multiple and local ways of being and becoming literate. She critiques the field, noting that authority has not consistently been placed in people and their experiences, 'existing models of family literacy programs seemed not to be informed by ethnographic research or substantiated by what we learned from the students themselves' (1989: 167).

While more recent reports continue to reference the work of other scholars, the strength of their research designs, and the correlations they identify as supporting their research claims, some newer objectivist studies, tended to use more guarded language to present their claims:

'... it is not sufficient simply to measure pre/post "gains" on test scores, employment income, or parenting skills' (Tao et al., 1998: 1);
'It appears from all these measures ...' (Tao et al., 1998: 3).

In addition, researchers in general tended to highlight the complexities of literacy learning and the multiple variables that could and should be considered. For example, Evans, Shaw, and Bell (2000) noted, 'existing research into these home literacy activities has frequently failed to take child individual differences into consideration, or has failed to partial out socio-economic status, or has not used standardized methods of reading achievement' (2000: 66). Burgess, Hecht, and Lonigan (2002), note the 'complexity of the relationships between the HLE [home literacy environment] and developmental and educational outcomes' and lament that many 'studies can be characterized as relatively simplistic univariate approaches that are likely to generate an incomplete and distorted picture of causal pathways' (2002: 412). They argue that 'researchers have noted the need for more research that begins to unravel the complex relations between the HLE and language and literacy outcomes' (2002: 412).

Rather than focusing on simple correlations between home literacy activities and school success, these studies focus on interrelationships among multiple dimensions of literacy practices, home literacy environments, and parental involvement in reading and coaching children. This approach recognizes the multiple dimensions of home literacy activities and focuses on the unique contributions of various practices. In addition, Burgess and his colleagues (2002) distinguish between sharing literacy practices with parents and helping parents to understand why particular experiences are important and identifying the factors that affect parents' proclivity to enact these practices across time. These studies are solidly objectivist in orientation, portraying family literacy as multiply determined but examinable through isolation of effects.

There were also differences between the recent examples of constructionist work and the examples presented earlier. Gregory and Williams (2000) explicitly located research participants within the temporal and spatial locations of generations. They noted the different political contexts that existed before and after World War II and various educational reforms that have operated across time. As they explained, these differences affected not only people's educational options and experiences, but also the ways educators came to understand the relationships between poverty and literacy learning. Similarly, Pahl (2004) focused on the narratives told by immigrant families. As she reported, 'Narratives can act as timescale-oriented bridges between local experience and longer globally connected events' (2004: 342). Both of these researchers highlighted the location of participants within complex historical and political contexts.

Pedagogical and scholarly action

The research we reviewed often asserted implications for instructional practice or future scholarly work. While objectivist epistemologies often led to clearly defined actions based on identified causal relationships, subjectivist perspectives often resulted in general, and often redundant, guidelines for working with families.

Based on their meta-analysis of existing studies, Bus et al. (1995) advocated for reading books to children noting that 'book reading is a part of a whole range of characteristics which are all indicative of a literate environment, and that book reading is a central aspect' (1995: 16). Marvin and Mirenda (1993) asserted that 'Home environments for children with special needs should provide greater access to writing materials on a more regular basis' (1993: 365). Snow and her colleagues created 'clear guidelines for helping children become successful readers' (Snow et al., 1998: 2) with recommendations that described 'high quality reading instruction' (Snow et al., 1998: 5). These claims are specific and based on purported relations among variables.

In other cases, researchers make similarly specific practice implications based on observational data. Hannon encouraged practitioners to address the 'neglect of writing' (1995: 145) in family literacy programs. Based on the challenges faced by Spanish-speaking families, Delgado-Gaitan (1990) advocated that schools provide translation services for written documents and parent meetings. She maintained that Spanish-speaking parents must be included in decision-making processes and teachers must be provided with training that would support their work with Spanish-speaking families. In addition, Delgado-Gaitan argues that teachers need 'training' (1990: 168) that will enable them to advocate for parents.

Other researchers offer more guarded recommendations. Some suggested that the effects of particular practices are always contingent on local contexts. DeBaryshe warned that parent–child literacy programs 'will be successful only if the goals or techniques of the reading program mesh with parents' preexisting beliefs' (1995: 18). Drawing on his work with family literacy programs, Hannon (1995) reminded readers 'to avoid an uncritical formulation of what are problems and what are solutions. Literacy does have a potential for both oppression and liberation' (Hannon, 1995: 12).

Some qualitative scholars report remarkably similar implications for educators. Consider the following set of general recommendations (our emphasis):

'... it is more effective to encourage parental involvement that is consistent with **existing beliefs about how children learn to read** than to try to change parents' beliefs' (Baker et al., 1995: 249);

'The primary purpose of this work is to develop deep innovations in teaching that draw upon the **knowledge and skills found in local households'** (Moll et al., 1992: 132);

[The need to focus on] 'the ways in which school and home learning can build on and complement each other' and 'instruction needs to be **congruent with the children's previous experience'** (Purcell-Gates, 1996: 427).

Each recommendation highlighted the knowledges that children and families brought to literacy while encouraging educators and researchers to recognize and build on those knowledges. These studies were informed by subjectivist insights related to multiplicity, diversity, emergence, change, and recursivity. They rely on descriptions of local communities challenging the assumption that the solution lies in the implementation of specific practices by practitioners. These studies provide few concrete implications for change, beyond the generally and often repeated claims presented above that implore researchers and educators to build on the strengths of families. This lack of explicit direction is in line with subjectivist logic, which eschews authority through prediction.

In contrast, correlational studies are much more likely to fuse particular practices related literacy achievement and can be implemented in classrooms. Objectivist perspectives tend to offer possible actions and perhaps solutions. Recognizing that storybook reading, or explicit instruction in literacy correlates with later academic success, has clear implications. Actions are identified and thus provide clear prescriptions for action.

Scholars also differ in terms of where they locate the potential for change. Moll and his colleagues (1992) strive to confront teachers' assumptions while building new insights and possibilities. Likewise Taylor and Dorsey-Gaines concluded, 'If we are to teach, we must first examine our own assumptions about families and children' (1988: 203). However, while highlighting the complexity and contingencies that accompany working with families, these implications place responsibility for change on teachers and as Hannon maintained, 'teachers cannot possibly adopt all the ways of involving parents' (1995: 32); he argued that they must choose features from various models and studies.

In addition to making recommendations for changes in classrooms and programs, some scholars make recommendations related to future research. In some cases, the recommendations for research focus on what researchers can/should do to build knowledge. For example, Hannon describes the need to 'run further experiments' (Hannon, 1995: 141). Marvin and Mirenda (1993) note 'Future studies examining the literacy practices used in Head Start and ECSE classrooms are warranted' (Marvin and Mirenda, 1993: 365). Snow et al. identify among their goals translating 'research findings into advice and guidance for parents, educators, publishers, and others' and conveying this 'advice to the targeted audiences...' (1998: 1–2).

In other cases, guidelines for scholarship are more democratically stated, including practitioners whose input is necessary for relevant research. Gadsden maintains that 'investigators should (re)assume leadership in developing the field, sharing leadership and responsibility with practitioners' (1994: 80). Hannon notes that researchers 'must search for this [ideal] program dialogically with the people' (Hannon, 1995: 11). Discursively, the location of actors in future research reveals epistemological assumptions about where knowledge exists and who has the authority to act upon it.

Recently, Gregory and Williams (2000) proposed an alternative to mismatch models in which the student differences were viewed as obstacles. This approach encouraged teachers to support children in comparing and contrasting the various literacy and language practices that they encountered at home and at school arguing that '*difference* complements mainstream school literacy rather than opposes it' (2000: 11). Subjectivist assumptions are discernable in this view including the recognition of multiple literacies that are enacted within specific power-laden contexts.

DISCUSSION AND IMPLICATIONS

This epistemological analysis reveals insights about the figured worlds (Holland et al., 1998) of family literacy scholars. Scholars attribute various degrees and types of agency to family members and the educators who work with them. In some accounts participants are presented as respondents who act on the requests of researchers; in other accounts they are described as agentful and as teaching researchers about their worlds. As highlighted in constructionist accounts, figured worlds also involve authority and power, which are described and acknowledged in various ways. Finally, figured world analysis reveals that actions of researchers are grounded in the epistemological assumptions that they bring to their work. The recommendations that researchers make are not simply based on research findings but on the ways that research findings inhabit the figured worlds of scholars.

First, our analysis of family literacy scholarship invites family literacy scholars to reflect on the assumptions that are implicit in their work. Our reading highlights the contingent nature of knowledge construction. It shows that 'if you believe ... then you can know ....' Recognizing that our knowledge and therefore our action is enabled and constrained by our assumptions about the world is itself a subjectivist perspective, one that situates knowledge in multiple domains and within multiple histories. The distinctly political and historical nature of knowledge is made visible from this perspective, helping us see how researchers are positioned as knowers and how the field of family literacy is conceptualized and described. While this reading complicates the field, our responsibilities, and the implications of our work, it is worth exploring. It provides a window on to the mechanisms that generate our knowledge and our relevance for the practice of literacy.

Second, this analysis reveals general patterns within research strands and across the field as well as opportunities for disrupting these patterns. For example, it highlights the ways multiple, and sometimes competing, epistemologies often coexist in the same research studies. The constructionist perspective, which merges objectivist and subjectivist viewpoints, allows us to meld what might seem to be contradictory epistemological assumptions to strategically craft family literacy initiatives, programs, and classroom practices that recognize the contexts in which families operate, the local hopes and dreams of families, and institutional demands that accompany school success.

Third, this analysis highlights increasing attention to the complexities that complicate analyses of literacy in families. Consistent with constructionist approaches, the contexts in which literacy practices take place are increasingly highlighted by researchers who privilege both objectivist and subjectivist epistemological stances.

Finally, we reveal some of the strengths and weaknesses that are inherent in various approaches to family literacy. Once we accept that virtually all scholarly and practical efforts, in both diversity scholarship and family literacy scholarship, reflect multiple epistemological stances, we can begin to harness these ways of thinking to serve families and children who operate in local contexts. By recognizing both idealized visions of linear scientific development and idiosyncratic and local visions of literacy learning, we can begin to collaborate with families to identify what structured, hierarchical and scientifically-based experiences will serve children well in schools while also examining which

cultural, linguistic, classed, and gendered practices from outside of school should be recognized and nurtured. While objectivist visions of literacy learning tend to highlight official benchmarks and ways of being literate, educational experiences based on subjectivist stances often require individual children and families to bear the effects of attending to local practices within larger institutions that do not necessarily value their ways of being literate.

A constructionist perspective creates possibilities for researchers, practitioners, and family members to collaboratively design productive literacy experiences for children that strategically allow children to become literate. As Luke maintained, educators must 'set aside issues of truth for the moment' and 'form a provisional political coalition' (1995: 94) that addresses not only the possibilities presented by subjectivist visions of diversity but also the objectivist expectations that accompany existing school structures.

REFERENCES

Auerbach, E. (1989). 'Toward a socio-contextual approach to family literacy', *Harvard Educational Review*, 59: 165–87.

Baker, L., Serpell, R., and Sonnenschein, S. (1995). 'Opportunities for literacy learning in the homes of preschoolers', in L.M. Morrow, *Family Literacy Connections in Schools and Communities*, pp. 236–52. Newark, DE: International Reading Association.

Burgess, S., Hecht, S., and Lonigan, C. (2002). 'Relations of the home literacy environment (HLE) the development of reading related abilities: A one-year longitudinal study', *Reading Research Quarterly*, 37(4): 408–26.

Bus, A.G., van Ijzendoorn, M.H., and Pellegrini, A.D. (1995). 'Joint book reading makes for success in learning to read: A meta analysis of intergenerational transmission of literacy', *Review of Educational Research*, 65: 1–21.

Cairney, T.H. (1995). 'Developing parent partnerships in secondary literacy learning', *Journal of Reading*, 38(7): 520–6.

Caper, C. (2001). 'Epistemological pluralism and Laible's epistemology of love: What is the conversation?' Presented at American Educational Research Association, Seattle, Washington, April 2001.

Compton-Lilly, C., Rogers, B., and Lewis, T. (2012). 'Analyzing diversity epistemology: An integrative critical review of family literacy scholarship', *Reading Research Quarterly*, 47(1): 33–60.

Crotty, M. (1998). *The Foundations of Social Research*. Los Angeles: Sage Publications.

DeBaryshe, B.D. (1995). 'Maternal belief systems: Lincoln in the home reading process', *Journal of Applied Developmental Psychology*, 16(1): 1–20.

Delgado-Gaitan, C. (1990). *Literacy for Empowerment*. New York: Falmer Press.

Evans, M.A., Shaw, D., and Bell, M. (2000). 'Home literacy activities and their influence in early literacy skills', *Canadian Journal of Experimental Psychology*, 54(2): 65–75.

Gadsden, V.L. (1994). 'Understanding family literacy: Conceptual issues facing the field', *Teachers College Record*, 96(1): 58–66.

Gillborn, D. (2005). 'Educational policy as an act of white supremacy: Whiteness, critical race theory and educational reform', *Journal of Education Policy*, 20(4): 485–505.

Gregory, E. and Williams, A. (2000). *City Literacies: Learning to Read across Generations and Cultures*. London: Routledge.

Hall, S. (2001) 'The multicultural question', Pavis Papers in Social and Cultural Research, no. 4., Milton Keynes: The Pavis Centre for Social and Cultural Research, The Open University.

Hannon, P. (1995). *Literacy, Home, and School: Research and Practice in Teaching Literacy with Parents*. London: Falmer Press.

Holland, D., Lachicotte, W., Skinner, D., and Cain, C. (1998). *Identity and Agency in Cultural Worlds*. Cambridge, MA: Harvard University Press.

Luke, A. (1995). 'Getting our hands dirty: Provisional politics in post modern conditions', in R. Smith, and P. Wexler (eds), *After Postmodernism: Education, Politics, and Identity*. Washington, DC: Falmer Press, pp. 83–97.

Marvin, C. and Mirenda, P. (1993). 'Home literacy experiences of preschoolers enrolled in Head Start and special education programs', *Journal of Early Intervention*, 17(4): 351–67.

Moll, L., Amanti, C., Neff, D., and Gonzalez, N. (1992). 'Funds of knowledge for teaching: Using a qualitative approach to connect homes and classrooms', *Theory into Practice*, 31(2): 132–41.

Pahl, K. (2004). 'Narratives, artifacts and cultural identities', *Linguistics and Education*, (15)4: 339–58.

Paratore, J.R., Melzi, G., and Krol-Sinclair, B. (1999). *What Should We Expect of Family Literacy?* Newark, DE: International Reading Association.

Popkewitz, T. (1998). *Struggling for the Soul: The Politics of Schooling and the Construction of the Teacher*. New York: Teachers College Press.

Purcell-Gates, V. (1996). 'Stories, coupons and the TV guide', *Reading Research Quarterly*, 31: 406–28.

Rogers, R. (ed.) (2004). *An introduction to critical discourse analysis*. New York: Routledge.

Saracho, O.N. (2000). 'Literacy development in the family context', *Early Childhood Development and Care*, 165: 107–14.

Scheurich, J.J. and Young, M.D. (1994). 'Coloring epistemologies: Are our research epistemologies racially biased?', *Educational Researcher*, 26(4): 4–16.

Senechal, M., LeFevre, J., Hudson, E., and Lawson, P.L. (1996). 'Knowledge of storybooks as a predictor of young children's vocabulary', *Journal of Educational Psychology*, 88: 520–36.

Snow, C., Burns, M.S., and Griffin, P.G. (1998) *Preventing Reading Difficulties with Young Children*. Washington, DC: National Academy Press.

St Pierre, R. and Layzer, J. (1996). 'Informing approaches to serving families in family literacy programs: Lessons from other family intervention programs', in R. St Pierre and J. Layzer (eds), *Family Literacy: Directions in Research and Implications for Practice*. New York: Abt Associates.

Tao, F., Gamse, B., and Tarr, H. (1998). 'National evaluation of Even Start family literacy programs, 1994–1997', Final Report. Washington, DC: US Department of Education, Planning and Evaluation Service.

Taylor, D. and Dorsey-Gaines, C. (1988). *Growing Up Literate*. Portsmouth, New Hampshire: Heinemann.

11

Research Issues in Family Literacy

Greg Brooks and Peter Hannon

INTRODUCTION

'Family literacy research has become indispensable for a full understanding of how young children learn literacy, and how they may be taught or helped to acquire it' (Hannon, 2003: 99). That was how Peter Hannon opened the chapter titled 'Family literacy programmes' in the first edition of this Handbook. In it he concentrated on the context and rationale for such programmes, and on research issues in the field. Since his chapter appeared there has been extensive further research and publication, including a detailed history and analysis of family literacy in England (Brooks et al., 2012, which should be read alongside this chapter, especially for initiatives which clearly were family literacy programmes before Taylor, 1983 coined the term), and several powerful reviews of the field worldwide: Erion (2006), Nye et al. (2006), Brooks et al. (2008), Mol et al. (2008), Sénéchal and Young (2008),

Carpentieri et al. (2011), Steensel et al. (2011) and Manz, Hughes, Barnabas, Bracaliello and Ginsburg-Block (2010)

Given the widespread acceptance and adoption of family literacy programmes, we considered it would be redundant to re-state the arguments for establishing family literacy programmes, and have instead concentrated, as the chapter title indicates, on research issues in the field. Several of these (deficit approaches, targeting of programmes, gender, bilingualism, training and professional development, and policy relevance and policy research) already featured in the earlier chapter. While there is evidence of effectiveness, do the benefits last? And research gaps are new. All have been singled out because, to us, they seem currently to have high theoretical or practical interest. As a set they constitute a large field of educational activity in which can be found, in some form or other, many issues of interest to early childhood literacy researchers.

The field has grown hugely since its inception. The idea of programmes or interventions to extend or change family literacy practices had ephemeral precursors in Britain (and no doubt elsewhere) from the 1950s, but the first sustained programmes began in Turkey in 1983, in the USA in the late 1980s, and in England and Wales in 1994: see Bekman (1998) on the Turkish Early Enrichment Project, Nash (1987) on the University of Massachusetts English Family Literacy Project, and Brooks et al. (1996) and Poulson et al. (1997) on the Basic Skills Agency's first programmes in England and Wales.

Deficit approaches

Right from the start of family literacy programmes in English-speaking countries it has often been noted that programmes developed by early childhood educators tend to emphasise taking school literacy into families (Cairney, 2002), rather than the engagement of schools in the families' literacy. Some adult educators do the same but many take a more sceptical view of the value of school literacy (which has often been problematic in their students' lives) and a more positive view of the strengths of parents and families in relation to everyday life and literacy. There have been critiques (by Auerbach, 1989, 1995, 1997; Grant, 1997; Taylor, 1997) of what is termed a 'deficit approach' in family literacy programmes. Families may be heavily engaged in literacy practices and have many literacy skills, but these may not be the practices and skills valued by schools. Further, it is probable that there are family literacy programmes which proceed on ignorant, and even offensive, assumptions concerning what certain families do *not* do or what they are supposed to be *incapable* of doing. They are also ignoring research

which has shown more generally the extent of families' knowledge undervalued by schools (Moll et al., 1992). Such assumptions, as well as being educationally unsound, have political consequences in 'explaining' the situation of poor families in terms of their literacy being less than, rather than simply different from, that of the powerful in society whose hegemonic definition of what counts as literacy goes unchallenged.

This issue may not, however, be quite as straightforward as stated and it is one that could benefit from further research – both conceptual and empirical. The term 'deficit approach' is not entirely helpful for there is a sense in which there is nothing wrong with deficits – with learners acknowledging they have them or with teachers seeking to address them. None of us would ever engage in any conscious learning if we did not feel we had some deficit we wanted to make up. Problems arise if differences (e.g. in literacy practices) are uncritically viewed as deficits, if deficits are imputed to learners without their assent, if deficits are exaggerated, or if deficits are seen as *all* that learners have (i.e. their cultural strengths are devalued). These problems can arise in any form of literacy education – indeed in any form of education – but they are more exposed in the case of family literacy programmes, within which the cultural values and practices of homes and schools are brought together.

The challenge for family literacy educators is to value what families bring to programmes, but not to the extent of simply reflecting back families' existing literacy practices (for it is patronising to suppose families need help with their existing literacy practices). Somehow they must offer families access to some different or additional literacy practices, but through collaboration and negotiation rather than imposition. If educators fail either to facilitate families' entry into powerful literacy practices or to empower them to challenge those practices, they will simply perpetuate families' continued exclusion from whatever benefits participation in those practices confers. Some family literacy programmes have taken up this challenge (e.g. several cited in Taylor, 1997) but their efforts are documented rather than rigorously evaluated. Using and valuing what families already know in order to teach them what they do not know is a subtle process that can easily go wrong. Research can help by elucidating teaching possibilities and pitfalls.

Targeting of programmes

A recurrent idea in family literacy discourse, related to 'deficit' thinking, is that there are families in which parents have literacy difficulties and in which it is supposed the children are consequently destined to have low literacy achievement, at least by school measures. The policy and professional literature in family literacy, if not the research literature, abounds with claims that there is a 'cycle of underachievement' which can be broken, but only by targeting parents' and children's literacy at the same time and in the same programmes. Conspicuous advocates of this view in the USA have included Nickse (1990) and Darling (1993), and in the UK the former Adult Literacy and Basic Skills Unit (1993a). It leads directly to the idea that targeting intergenerational family literacy programmes on families where parents have literacy difficulties will have a major impact on literacy levels in society.

Despite a certain common-sense appeal this idea suffers from two main problems. First, it would entail a scale of provision

and participation that is most unlikely to occur. For every child from a poor background to arrive at school ready to learn to read and write (possibly already having made a start) would require every family in such circumstances to attend a family literacy programme. Manifestly, this would require much larger programmes and many more families coming forward for them than happens currently; and any form of compulsion (e.g. making social security benefits contingent on attendance) would certainly be counter-productive, being yet a further imposition on poor families. Turkey (population about 71 million) has the largest family literacy programme in the world – about 70,000 families are served per year – and even there the scale would need to be at least one order of magnitude larger to approach universal coverage.

Second, the idea is poorly supported by research evidence. It is actually two propositions wrapped together: (a) that parents with literacy difficulties will have low-achieving children; and (b) that low-achieving children have parents with literacy difficulties. Both have to be true for the 'cycle of underachievement' claim to be accepted as an explanation for literacy inequalities in society (and for targeted family literacy programmes to be seen as the remedy).

There have been two attempts in Britain to conduct research into the literacy of parents and children in representative samples large enough to permit statistical analyses (Adult Literacy and Basic Skills Unit, 1993b; Bynner and Parsons, 2005). In the first, ALBSU commissioned research from City University, London, into a sample of 1,761 families, with 2,617 children, drawn from the National Child Development Study sample, a lifetime cohort study of (originally) all the people born in Britain in a week of April 1958. Parents were asked in interviews whether, since leaving school, they had had any problems with reading, writing, or spelling. Children's reading was tested by the Peabody Individual Achievement Test. The focus of the study was the link between parents' reported literacy difficulties and their children's literacy test attainment.

The study found that most of the children whose parents reported literacy difficulties had poor reading scores – but since there were only 27 children with parents who reported literacy difficulties this provided only very weak support for the idea that intergenerational programmes might be beneficial. Moreover, Hannon (2000b) re-interpreted the ALBSU data and showed that they contradicted the converse idea, namely that the great majority of children with low reading scores would have parents who reported literacy difficulties – on the contrary, the great majority of children with low reading scores did not have such parents.

More recently, Bynner and Parsons (2005) reported preliminary findings from the age 34 sweep of the British Cohort Study 1970, a lifetime cohort study following (originally) all the people born in Britain in a week in April 1970. In 2004, the cohort members were re-contacted and both their own and their children's literacy was tested. Correlating the two sets of scores again showed that 'the average scores for children of parents with the poorest grasp of literacy … were markedly lower.' However, the logic of this finding is once more reversed: what needs to be shown is what proportion of low-scoring children had parents with low literacy scores. This analysis has yet to be done, either by Bynner and Parsons themselves or by anyone else, since Bynner and Parsons presented their new data in such

a way as to make re-analysis impossible. Meanwhile the new data appear to provide no firmer support for the theory of intergenerational transfer and for intergenerational programmes than the data from the 1990s. It follows that targeting family literacy programmes only on those families where parents acknowledge that they have literacy difficulties can make no more than a modest contribution to reducing literacy inequalities amongst young children.

Gender

Much of the family literacy literature consistently refers to 'parents' in programmes when generally it would be more accurate to talk of 'mothers'. This is not to say that fathers or male carers are never involved in programmes, only that the numbers are generally low, typically well under 10% in centre-based programmes, as comprehensively demonstrated for Britain by Goldman (2005, especially pp.71–72). Morgan et al. (2009) have, however, shown that there can be extensive involvement of fathers at home that is easily overlooked. Using the word 'parent' is inclusive and helps maximise the number of fathers who are involved (if programmes referred only to mothers the gendered nature of parental involvement would be reinforced, and it is likely that there would be even fewer fathers). Sticking to 'parent', however, must not blind us to the highly gendered nature of parental involvement. Many programmes are sensitive to this issue and have made serious efforts to include men, in some cases adopting this as a primary goal (Haggart, 2000; Lloyd, 2001; Millard, 2001; Karther, 2002). A small-scale programme in England some years ago for family literacy and numeracy in prisons almost exclusively recruited fathers (Basic Skills Agency, undated), not surprisingly since over 90% of the prison population are men. In Turkey, where it would be culturally unacceptable for women and men to attend the same classes, the Mother-Child Education Foundation has developed fathers' programmes, which are extensive and well-attended, though not nearly as widespread as those for mothers.

There are at least three research challenges here. First, given that far fewer' fathers than mothers attend family literacy programmes, it would be helpful to understand more about the gendered nature of family literacy practices and how they vary in different economic and family circumstances (e.g. as men in industrialised countries respond to increased literacy demands in the workplace). Both quantitative and qualitative studies could make a contribution. It would be interesting to know whether men's lower involvement is an artefact of school-based programmes where employment and cultural expectations reduce fathers' attendance; they may be more involved, if less visibly so, in home-based programmes. Second, research could usefully distinguish different kinds of family structure and the different roles that men and women now perform within them as parents, step-parents, grandparents, foster parents, carers. Third, it would be helpful to have detailed evaluations of those programmes that have made special efforts to involve men. To be really helpful such studies would need to go beyond documentation of interesting cases to a quantitative evaluation of key issues such as take-up and outcomes.

Bilingualism

More research is needed into programmes for bilingual or multilingual families. There have been valuable reports either of research or concerning programme design by Auerbach (1989, 2002), Delgado-Gaitan (1990), Hirst (1998), Brooks et al. (1999), Blackledge (2000), Kenner (2000), Cairney (2002) and Rodriguez-Brown (2003, 2004), and most recently a national evaluation of family literacy programmes has provided useful data on native and non-native English-speaking families in England (Swain et al., 2009) – see below. These reports point out how such families can be different (e.g. in relation to the gendering of parenting, expectations of children) but also how they can often be similar (e.g. in parents' aspirations for their children). What also emerges is how families are perceived by educators (who may grossly underestimate the cultural resources of homes). However, much of the literature concerning family literacy programmes concerns monolingual, English-speaking families. As we move further into the 21st century and take an international perspective it becomes ever clearer that bilingualism and multilingualism, rather than monolingualism, will be the norm.

Some of the issues to be investigated are very complex. For example, the first language of some families may not have a written form or, if it has, it may not be much used by family members. Parents' literacy can appear limited in comparison with what is familiar in industrialised countries. Parents' aspirations for their own and their children's literacy may or may not accord with the assumptions of programme designers and national policy-makers. Different cultures, different concepts of childhood and different pedagogies may require their own programmes and desired outcomes. Research still needs to catch up with global realities.

Evidence of effectiveness

All previous reviews of the benefits of family literacy programmes for children, and for parents' ability to support their children's learning, have been superseded by Carpentieri et al. (2011), a comprehensive report funded by and submitted to the European Commission. It was based primarily on six previous meta-analyses; Table 11.1 presents those studies' average effect sizes for impact on children's literacy.

Thus the evidence on the whole shows that family literacy programmes benefit children's literacy development, as measured within the programmes. Carpentieri et al. (2011) also found strong evidence of benefit to parents' ability to support their children's learning. However, they did not review evidence on benefit to parents' own literacy skills, but in any case the evidence base for benefit to parents' literacy skills is surprisingly meagre. We know of only six studies giving data on parents' literacy skills. Three conducted in England and Wales (Basic Skills Agency, undated; Brooks et al., 1996, 1999) showed positive effects, but all had one-group pre-test/post-test designs; two with stronger designs, the Even Start In-Depth study in the USA (St Pierre et al., 1995, 1996; Gamse et al., 1997) and Parent Empowerment through Family Literacy in Malta (Camilleri, 2004; Camilleri et al., 2005) showed no benefit; and a recent national evaluation in England (Swain et al., 2009 and forthcoming) showed only very small average amounts of benefit. This is hardly a convincing haul of evidence; programme evaluators need to put much more

Table 11.1 Average effect sizes for children's literacy from six meta-analyses of family literacy studies

Study	Effect size
Steensel et al. (2011)	0.18
Manz et al. (in press)	0.33
Nye et al. (2006)	0.42
Erion (2006)	0.55
Mol et al. (2008)	0.59
Sénéchal and Young (2008)	0.68

effort into gathering performance data from parents.

Do the benefits last?

The only follow-up studies known to us come from Britain and Turkey. The Basic Skills Agency's Family Literacy Demonstration Programmes (one of the three programmes mentioned in the previous paragraph as having found positive effects on parents' literacy during the programmes) were the subject of three follow-ups, 3 months, 9 months and 2½-3 years after the end of the programmes: Brooks et al. (1996, 1997) showed that the children had maintained their gains, and that the parents had gone from strength to strength.

The evidence from the Turkish Early Enrichment Project (TEEP) is much longer-term and very impressive (Kağıtçıbaşı et al., 2009). TEEP was conducted in 1983–85 with 4- to 6-year-old children from disadvantaged backgrounds; the research programme compared them with similar children from non-participating families. Data showing benefits to the children and to their mothers' child-rearing practices were gathered at the end of the programmes, and the children were studied again seven years later, at the end of their primary schooling – again showing positive results. Most recently, 131 of the original 255 people studied as children were re-contacted 19 years on, in 2003–04, at (on average) age 25.7. Participants still showed significant benefits relative to non-participants; in particular, 45% of the study group were attending or had attended university, versus 30% of the comparison group.

Research gaps

Also noticeable in the family literacy literature are four questions it does not address at all. To the best of our knowledge, there have never been any studies

1) comparing the progress made by parents or children in two different family literacy programmes;
2) comparing the progress made by children who attend family literacy classes with that made by children who attend other forms of preschool;
3) comparing the progress made by parents in family literacy programmes with that made by adult literacy learners in stand-alone adult literacy programmes; or
4) investigating family literacy programmes that take account of literacy in this digital age.

The first of these gaps can only be addressed by consciously and deliberately setting up such studies. The best design for them would be randomised control trials, so that it would be as certain as possible that any difference in outcomes was due to the programmes and not to any pre-existing and uncontrolled differences between the groups of participants receiving the different programmes. This is not meant to underplay the difficulties of persuading both providers and participating parents to go along with random assignment to one programme or another. However, if such a study ever proves possible, the data-gathering should cover not only reading but also writing, attitudes to literacy, the parents' self-confidence, and benefits to the children's skills.

The second gap in the research base concerns children: do children who attend family literacy classes benefit more than they would in other forms of preschool? This gap could be filled in either or both of two ways: using tests with children in family literacy programmes which have also been used with children in other forms of preschool provision, or mounting an RCT. We currently know of no evidence under either heading, and both present problems.

Using tests with children in family literacy programmes which have also been used with children in other forms of preschool provision would be an indirect and easier approach, but less convincing. It is obvious that the only identical factors in the two sets of programmes would be the tests, and that a host of other variables would be completely uncontrolled, for example, content of the teaching, quality of implementation of the programme, length of course, numbers of boys and girls in the two types of programme, etc. This approach would therefore provide weak evidence, given the non-comparability of the samples and programmes.

The evidence would be much more direct and convincing (but more difficult to collect) if it came from one or more studies in which as many variables as possible were controlled other than the one of interest, namely whether the children were attending family literacy or stand-alone preschool provision. This approach would ideally require a specific, well-designed and large RCT. Parents would agree that their children should receive the preschool element of a family literacy programme immediately, but that they themselves should be allocated randomly to receive their part of it either simultaneously with their children or at the next opportunity (say, the following term). Both groups of children would be given the relevant tests both pre and post, and the research questions would concern whether either group made more progress than the other. Only within such a design could it be assumed that the two groups of children differed only in whether or not they were participating in a family literacy or stand-alone preschool programme, and any differences in outcome could then be attributed with some confidence to that single variable (given sufficiently comparable levels of teaching content and quality and of learner attendance, etc., in the two groups; such factors would need to be measured while the study was in progress). Such a study would need to be large, especially since it would have to be a cluster trial – perhaps a minimum of 44 classes and a minimum post-test sample of 308 children. Desirable though such an RCT would be, we are confident that no such study has yet been attempted, and we know of no plans to mount one, or even the extensive pilot work that should precede it. In fact, a proposal for such a study in England was refused funding in 2009.

The third gap could be filled, as with children, in either or both of two ways, using tests with parents in family literacy programmes which have also been used with adults in stand-alone adult literacy programmes, or mounting an RCT.

There is at least one instance in the United States of family literacy courses where a standard adult literacy test was administered to the parents. St Pierre et al. (1995, 1996; see also Gamse et al., 1997) reported on the national evaluation of Even Start conducted in 1991–93. Many thousands of parents were administered the Comprehensive Adult Student Assessment System (CASAS): they made gains, but no greater on average than those in general adult literacy programmes.

In Britain, there is also one instance of this sort. In the national evaluation of family literacy programmes in England carried out in 2007–08, Swain et al. (2009 and forthcoming) used reading and writing tests which had previously been used in various adult literacy projects, and Tables 11.2 and 11.3 present all the relevant results for reading and writing respectively.

From these figures it would seem that parents in the Learning Literacy Together family literacy evaluation whose first language was not English made excellent progress in reading which was better than

Table 11.2   Reading test gains for adult literacy learners in England

Name of study	Reference(s)	Language status	Sample size	Average gain	Effect size
Effective Practice in Reading	Brooks et al. (2007)	mainly L1	179	6.5	0.65
The Learner Study	Rhys Warner et al. (2008); Vorhaus et al.	L1	186	4.0	0.40
	(2009); Brooks and Pilling (forthcoming)	L2	123	6.1	0.61
Progress for Adult Literacy Learners	Burton et al. (2010)	mainly L1	74	5.9	0.59
Improving Literacy at Work	Wolf and Evans (2011)	L1	153	0.6	0.06
		L2	108	3.5	0.35
Learning Literacy Together	Swain et al. (forthcoming)	L1	295	−1.5	−0.15
		L2	73	9.3	0.93

Notes: 1) L1 = native speakers of English; L2 = non-native speakers of English
2) The gains are expressed in standardised score points; the test has a range of 0–100, mean of 50 and standard deviation of 10.
3) The figures for Improving Literacy at Work are not directly stated in Wolf and Evans (2011) but were supplied, on request, by a colleague of theirs.
4) The effect sizes were calculated by dividing the average gain by the standard deviation of the test.
5) All gains except those for L1 learners in the Improving Literacy at Work and Learning Literacy Together studies were statistically significant.

Table 11.3   Writing test gains for adult literacy learners in England

Name of study	Reference(s)	Language status	Sample size	Average gain
Effective Practice in Writing	Grief et al. (2007)	mainly L1	199	1.5
The Learner Study	Rhys Warner et al. (2008); Vorhaus et al. (2009); Brooks and Pilling (forthcoming)	L1 L2	96 115	0.7 1.2
Progress for Adult Literacy Learners	Burton et al. (2010)	mainly L1	17	2.4
Learning Literacy Together	Swain et al. (forthcoming)	L1	99	1.4
		L2	18	0.3

Notes: 1) L1 = native speakers of English; L2 = non-native speakers of English
  2) The gains are expressed in raw score points; the test has a maximum score of 29.
  3) Because the test is not standardised and there were no control or comparison groups, effect sizes could not be calculated.
  4) All gains except those for L1 learners in the Learner Study and L2 learners in the Learning Literacy Together study were statistically significant.

that made by native or non-native speakers in any of the other studies, and that native-speaking parents in Learning Literacy Together made reasonable progress in writing compared to other studies; however, no inference can be drawn from the result for native-speaking parents on reading in Learning Literacy Together because the full data show a clear ceiling effect, such that this group had no real opportunity to show improvement. (This ceiling effect does, however, show that most of the native-speaking parents in this study were already quite competent readers, and therefore not strictly speaking in the target population for family literacy programmes.)

However, it is obvious that the only identical factors in these two sets of studies (and in Even Start) were the tests, and that a host of other variables were completely uncontrolled, for example, content of the teaching, quality of implementation of the programme, length of course, numbers of men and women in the two types of programme, their ages and how many of them had young children, etc. The figures above are therefore weak evidence, given the non-comparability of the samples and programmes.

The evidence would again be much more convincing if it came from one or more RCTs in which the variable of interest would be whether the parents were attending family literacy or stand-alone adult literacy courses. The RCT would be the mirror-image of that with children just described. Parents would agree to receive the adult literacy element of a family literacy programme immediately, but for their children to be allocated randomly to receive their part of it either simultaneously with them or at the next opportunity. Both groups of parents would take the relevant tests both pre and post, and the research questions would concern whether either group made more progress, or showed more change in attitudes, etc., than the other. Only within such a design could it be assumed that the two groups of parents differed only in whether or not they were participating in a family literacy or an adult literacy programme, and any differences in outcome could then be attributed with some confidence to that single variable (given sufficiently comparable levels of teaching content and quality and of learner attendance, etc., in the two groups; such factors would need to be measured while the study was in progress). Other considerations, including the need for the trial to be large, would be the same as for the child study. Again, we are confident that no such study has yet been attempted, and we know of no current plans to mount one.

Finally, we also know of no studies so far which have taken account of the use of information and communication technologies within family literacy programmes. This gap could be remedied either as part of attempts to remedy those already mentioned, or as a free-standing project. In either case, there seem to be no such studies under way or planned.

What all this points to strongly is the need both to gather more and better data on family literacy programmes, and to strengthen the programmes themselves.

Training and professional development

If early childhood educators are to play a full part in family literacy programmes they need appropriate training and professional development opportunities. Working with adults demands a different awareness and set of skills than does working with groups of children. Nutbrown et al. (1991) proposed a framework for pre-service and in-service provision within which early childhood educators could become better equipped to meet the demands of family literacy programmes, and urged research into key issues. Since then there appears to have been very little progress either in the provision of training and professional development or in associated research. Potentially, there are as many issues worth researching in training and professional

development in relation to family literacy work as there are in relation to wider aspects of early childhood and adult education. There is the issue, for example, of whether family literacy teachers/tutors should be reflective practitioners or technicians implementing – and obediently following – prescriptions of programme designers (Hannon, 2000a). Another issue is the role of organisations providing or accrediting training who may use the opportunity to impose their particular models of family literacy. Research can enable a more open and critical approach to programme development and to related professional development.

Policy relevance and policy research

It is by no means clear what role family literacy programmes should play in relation to mainstream, compulsory early childhood education. It could be argued that all education should take a family approach; alternatively that family literacy programmes can never be more than an adjunct to mainstream provision, perhaps only in areas of disadvantage. Research has a role to play here, not only in providing evidence – particularly about take-up and effectiveness – to inform family literacy policies but also in examining and critiquing those policies. One area where there is scope to do this concerns the claims made for family literacy programmes. Some of these seem rather extravagant. In the USA, the National Center for Family Literacy (1994) has claimed that family literacy programmes enable 'at-risk families with little hope to reverse the cycle of under-education and poverty', bringing about changes that 'pave the way for school success, and thereafter life success' (p.1). Brizius and Foster (1993) have claimed family literacy 'provides disadvantaged children with educational opportunities that can enable them to lift themselves out of poverty and dependency' (p.11). Although it is to be hoped that family literacy programmes can make a useful contribution to these goals, promising more than the research evidence warrants may store up trouble for the future.

CONCLUSION

Family literacy programmes have, over the past three decades, come to occupy an important role in early childhood literacy education. The effectiveness of programmes for children and for parents' ability to help their children is reasonably well established, but there remain significant unanswered questions about benefits for parents, the extent and duration of effects, and whether family literacy programmes provide greater benefits than stand-alone preschool or adult literacy provision. There are also other areas to be developed, relating for example to implied deficits, gender, bilingualism, professional development, and policy. These are to be expected in any field of education but may be more exposed in family literacy programmes. All of them can be illuminated by future research.

REFERENCES

Adult Literacy and Basic Skills Unit (ALBSU) (1993a) *Family Literacy News, No. 1*. London: Adult Literacy and Basic Skills Unit.

Adult Literacy and Basic Skills Unit (ALBSU) (1993b) *Parents and their children: the intergenerational effect of poor basic skills*. London: Adult Literacy and Basic Skills Unit.

Auerbach, E.R. (1989) Toward a social-contextual approach to family literacy. *Harvard Educational Review*, 59 (2), 165–81.

Auerbach, E.R. (1995) Which way for family literacy: intervention or empowerment? In Morrow, L.M. (ed.) *Family Literacy: Connections in Schools and*

Communities (pp.11–27). Newark, DE: International Reading Association.

Auerbach, E.R. (1997) Reading between the lines. In Taylor, D. (ed.), *Many Families, Many Literacies: An International Declaration of Principles* (pp.71–82). Portsmouth, NH: Heinemann.

Auerbach, E. (ed.) (2002) *Community Partnerships*. Alexandria, VA: TESOL.

Bekman, S. (1998) *A fair chance: an evaluation of the mother-child education program*, Istanbul: Mother-Child Education Foundation Publications.

Blackledge, A. (2000) *Literacy, power and social justice*. Stoke-on-Trent: Trentham.

Brizius, J.A., and Foster, S.A. (1993) *Generation to generation: realizing the promise of family literacy*. Ypsilanti, MI: High/Scope Press.

Brooks, G. and Pilling, M. (forthcoming) *The impact of Skills for Life on adult literacy, language and numeracy learners. Final report on analysis of new quantitative data*. London: National Research and Development Centre for Adult Literacy and Numeracy.

Brooks, G., Gorman, T., Harman, D. and Wilkin, A. (1996) *Family literacy works: the NFER evaluation of the Basic Skills Agency's family literacy demonstration programmes*. London: Basic Skills Agency.

Brooks, G., Gorman, T., Harman, J., Hutchison, D., Kinder, K., Moor, H. and Wilkin, A. (1997) *Family literacy lasts: the NFER follow-up study of the Basic Skills Agency's demonstration programmes*. London: Basic Skills Agency.

Brooks, G., Harman, J., Hutchison, D., Kendall, S., and Wilkin, A. (1999) *Family literacy for new groups: the NFER evaluation of family literacy with linguistic minorities, Year 4 and Year 7*. London: Basic Skills Agency.

Brooks, G., Burton, M., Cole, P. and Szczerbiński, M. (2007) *Effective teaching and learning: reading*. London: National Research and Development Centre for Adult Literacy and Numeracy. http://www.nrdc.org.uk/publications_details.asp?ID=90

Brooks, G., Pahl, K., Pollard, A. and Rees, F. (2008). *Effective and inclusive practices in family literacy, language and numeracy: a review of programmes and practice in the UK and internationally*. Reading, UK: CfBT Education Trust. http://www.cfbt.com/evidenceforeducation/our_research/evidence_for_youth/family_learning.aspx

Brooks, G., Hannon, P. and Bird, V. (2012) Family literacy in England', in Wasik, B. and Van Horn, B. (eds) *Handbook of Family Literacy* (2nd ed.). (pp. 325–338). New York and London: Routledge.

Burton, M., Davey, J., Lewis, M., Ritchie, L. and Brooks, G. (2010) *Progress for adult literacy learners*.

London: National Research and Development Centre for Adult Literacy and Numeracy. http://www.nrdc.org.uk/publications_details.asp?ID=175#

Bynner, J. and Parsons, S. (2005) New light on literacy and numeracy. *Reflect (Journal of the National Research and Development Centre for adult literacy and numeracy)*, no.4 (October), 32–3.

Cairney, T. (2002) Bridging home and school literacy: in search of transformative approaches to curriculum. *Early Child Development and Care*, 172 (2), 153–72.

Camilleri, J. (2004) Literacy as a family affair: an evaluation of effectiveness of local and trans-national family literacy programmes. Unpublished M.Ed. dissertation, University of Sheffield School of Education.

Camilleri, J., Spiteri, S. and Wolfendale, S. (2005) Parent empowerment for family literacy: a European initiative. *Literacy*, 39 (2), 74–80.

Carpentieri, J., Fairfax-Cholmeley, K., Litster, J. and Vorhaus, J. (2011) *Family literacy in Europe: using parental support initiatives to enhance early literacy development*. London: National Research and Development Centre for Adult Literacy and Numeracy.

Darling, S. (1993) Focus on family literacy: the national perspective. *NCFL Newsletter*, 5 (1), p. 3.

Delgado-Gaitan, C. (1990) *Literacy for Empowerment: the Role of Parents in Children's Education*. London: Falmer Press.

Erion, J. (2006) Parent Tutoring: A Meta-Analysis. *Education and Treatment of Children*, 29 (1), 28.

Gamse, B., Conger, D., Elson, D. and McCarthy, M. (1997) *Follow-up study of families in the even start in-depth study: final report*. Cambridge, MA: Abt Associates Inc.

Goldman, R. (2005) *Fathers' involvement in their children's education*. London: National Family and Parenting Institute.

Grant, A. (1997) 'Debating intergenerational family literacy: myths, critiques, and counterperspectives', in Taylor, D. (ed.), *Many Families, Many Literacies: An International Declaration of Principles* (pp. 216–225). Portsmouth, NH: Heinemann.

Grief, S., Meyer, B. and Burgess, A. (2007) *Effective teaching and learning: writing*. London: National Research and Development Centre for Adult Literacy and Numeracy. http://www.nrdc.org.uk/publications_details.asp?ID=88

Haggart, J. (2000) *Learning legacies: a guide to family learning*. Leicester: National Institute of Adult and Continuing Education.

Hannon, P. (2000a) *Reflecting on Literacy in Education*. London and New York: Routledge Falmer.

Hannon, P. (2000b) Rhetoric and research in family literacy. *British Educational Research Journal*, 26 (1), 121–38.

Hannon, P. (2003) Family literacy programmes. In Hall, N., Larson, J., and Marsh, J. (eds), *Handbook of Early Childhood Literacy* (pp. 99–111). London/Thousand Oaks CA: SAGE.

Hirst, K. (1998) Pre-school literacy experiences of children in Punjabi, Urdu and Gujerati speaking families in England. *British Educational Research Journal*, 24 (4), 415–29.

Kağıtçıbaşı, Ç., Sunar, D., Bekman, S., Baydar, N., and Cemalcilar, Z. (2009) Continuing effects of early enrichment in adult life: The Turkish Early Enrichment Project 22 years later. *Journal of Applied Developmental Psychology*, 30 (5), 764–79.

Karther, D. (2002) Fathers with low literacy and their children. *The Reading Teacher*, 56 (2), 184–93.

Kenner, C. (2000) *Home Pages: Literacy Links for Bilingual Children*. Stoke-on-Trent: Trentham.

Lloyd, T. (2001) *What works with fathers?* London: Working With Men.

Manz, P.H., Hughes, C., Barnabas, E., Bracaliello, C. and Ginsburg-Block, M. (2010) A descriptive review and meta-analysis of family-based emergent literacy interventions: To what extent is the research applicable to low-income, ethnic-minority or linguistically-diverse young children? *Early Childhood Research Quarterly*, 25 (4), 409–31.

Millard, E. (2001) *It's a man thing! Evaluation report of CEDC's Fathers and Reading project*. Coventry: Community Education Development Centre.

Mol, S.E., Bus, A.G., De Jong, M.T. and Smeets, D.J.H. (2008) Added value of dialogic parent-child book readings: A meta-analysis. *Early Education and Development*, 19, 7–26.

Moll, L., Amanti, C., Neff, D., and Gonzalez, N. (1992) Funds of knowledge for teaching: using a qualitative approach to connect homes and classrooms. *Theory Into Practice*, 31 (2), 132–41.

Morgan, A., Nutbrown, C. and Hannon, P. (2009) Fathers' involvement in young children's literacy development: implications for family literacy programmes. *British Educational Research Journal*, 35 (2), 167–85.

Nash, A. (1987) *English family literacy: an annotated bibliography*. Boston: English Family Literacy Project, University of Massachusetts.

National Center for Family Literacy (NCFL) (1994) Communicating the power of family literacy. *NCFL Newsletter*, 6 (1), p: 1.

Nickse, R.S. (1990) *Family and intergenerational literacy programs: an update of 'Noises of Literacy'*. Columbus, OH: ERIC Clearinghouse on Adult,

Career and Vocational Education, Ohio State University.

Nutbrown, C., Hannon, P. and Weinberger, J. (1991) Training teachers to work with parents to promote early literacy development. *International Journal of Early Childhood*, 23 (2), 1–10.

Nye, C., Turner, H. and Schwartz, J. (2006) Approaches to parent involvement for improving the academic performance of elementary school age children, 14 (11), 06. Accessed at http://www.campbellcollaboration.org/lib/download/63/

Poulson, L., Macleod, F., Bennett, N. and Wray, D. (1997) *Family literacy: Practice in Local Programmes*. London: Basic Skills Agency.

Rhys Warner, J., Vorhaus, J., Appleby, Y., Bathmaker, A-M., Brooks, G., Cole, P., Pilling, M. and Pearce, L. (2008) *The Learner Study: the impact of the Skills for Life strategy on adult literacy, language and numeracy learners. Summary report*. London: National Research and Development Centre for Adult Literacy and Numeracy. http://www.nrdc.org.uk/publications_details.asp?ID=158

Rodriguez-Brown, F.V. (2003) Family literacy in English language learning communities: issues related to program development, implementation, and practice. In DeBruin-Parecki, A. and Krol-Sinclair, B. (eds), *Family Literacy: From Theory to Practice* (pp. 126–46). Newark DE: International Reading Association.

Rodriguez-Brown, F.V. (2004) Project FLAME: a parent support family literacy model. In Wasik, B.H. (ed.), *Handbook of Family Literacy*. Mahwah NJ: Lawrence Erlbaum.

Sénéchal, M. and Young, L. (2008) The Effect of Family Literacy Interventions on Children's Acquisition of Reading From Kindergarten to Grade 3: A Meta-Analytic Review. *Review of Educational Research*, 78 (4), 880–907.

Steensel, R. van, McElvany, N., Kurvers, J. and Herppich, S. (2011). How effective are family literacy programs? Results of a meta-analysis. *Review of Educational Research*, 81 (1), 69–96.

St. Pierre, R., Swartz, J., Gamse, B., Murray, S., Deck, D. and Nickel, P. (1995) *National evaluation of the Even Start family literacy program*. Washington, DC: U.S. Department of Education, Office of Policy and Planning.

St. Pierre, R.G., Swartz, J.P., Murray, S. and Deck, D. (1996) *Improving Family Literacy: Findings From the National Even Start Evaluation*, Cambridge MA: Abt Associates Inc.

Swain, J., Welby, S., Brooks, G., Bosley, S, Frumkin, L., Fairfax-Cholmeley, K., Pérez, A. and Cara, O. (2009). *Learning literacy together: the impact and effectiveness of family literacy on parents, children, families and schools. Executive summary – October 2009*. Coventry: Learning and Skills Improvement Service. http://www.nrdc.org.uk/publications_details.asp?ID=162

Swain, J., Welby, S., Brooks, G., Bosley, S, Frumkin, L., Fairfax-Cholmeley, K., Pérez, A. and Cara, O. (forthcoming). *Learning literacy together: the impact and effectiveness of family literacy on parents, children, families and schools. Full report*. London: National Research and Development Centre for Adult Literacy and Numeracy.

Taylor, D. (1983) *Family Literacy: Young Children Learning to Read and Write*. Exeter, NH: Heinemann.

Taylor, D. (ed.) (1997) *Many Families, Many Literacies: An International Declaration of Principles*. Portsmouth, NH: Heinemann.

Vorhaus, J., Howard, U., Brooks, G., Bathmaker, A-M., and Appleby, Y. (2009) The impact of the, "Skills for Life" infrastructure on learners: a summary of methods and findings. In Reder, S. and Bynner, J. (eds), *Tracking Adult Literacy and Numeracy Skills: findings from longitudinal research* (pp. 200–21). New York and Abingdon, UK: Routledge.

Wolf, A. and Evans, K. (2011) *Improving Literacy at Work*. London and New York: Routledge.

12

Early Childhood Literacy and Popular Culture

Jackie Marsh

Schooling across centuries and continents has celebrated particular versions of 'high' culture in the hope of leading the populace to 'the best that has been thought and known in the world' (Matthew Arnold, *Culture and Anarchy*, 1869). As Steedman suggests, schools have historically seen themselves as places 'where working-class children might be compensated for belonging to working-class families' (Steedman, 1985: 156). This is no less true of schooling for young children as it is for the education of their older counterparts. This chapter focuses on research that has challenged this hegemonic construction of the literacy curriculum, research which has thrust issues relating to the study of the popular firmly onto the educational agenda.

The chapter begins with an exploration of the concept of popular culture itself and discusses the relationship between literacy and popular culture. The role of popular culture in the literacy practices undertaken in the home is then identified, before the chapter moves on to discuss research which has focused on the use of popular culture in nurseries/ kindergartens and schools. In the final part of the chapter, ways in which future research agendas might be shaped by contemporary issues and concerns are discussed. What is not addressed in these pages is the question of the need for a focus on popular culture in the first place. For such a discussion, see Williams (1965) and Willis (1990) who remind us that schools should not exist to compensate children for their cultural experiences, but should, in fact, recognise and build on them. As many children's cultural experiences are located firmly within the realm of the popular, it is necessary to turn first to a critical examination of this concept.

POPULAR CULTURE AND LITERACY

Definitions of popular culture are as varied and contradictory as those of culture itself (Jenks, 1993). The strict dichotomy between high and low culture which has been posited for many years can no longer be sustained. There is much evidence that texts which have long been assumed to represent 'high' culture actually began their days within the popular realm, as is the case with the work of Shakespeare, for example (Levine, 1991). However, it is clear that there are inherent divisions and cultural hierarchies and, therefore, it is possible to identify those texts and artefacts which may be seen as popular:

> Popular culture refers to the beliefs and practices, and the objects through which they are organized, that are widely shared among a population. This includes folk beliefs, practices and the objects rooted in local traditions, and mass beliefs, practices and objects generated in political and commercial centers. It includes elite cultural forms that have been popularized as well as popular forms that have been elevated to the museum tradition.
>
> (Mukerji and Schudson, 1991: 3)

Such a postmodern construction of the term allows us to recognise that popular cultural forms are constantly changing and are bound by socio-cultural contexts. Children's popular cultural pursuits are obviously inflected by local concerns and contexts and thus there can be no comprehensive account of the texts that might be involved in children's popular cultural practices. For some children in majority world cultures, or in economically disadvantaged communities in minority world countries, artefacts of popular culture may be few in number, might be adaptations of cultural products aimed at adults, or locally produced and fashioned from the materials to hand – paper, stone, wood, metal and so on, having little to do with manufactured, globalised narratives derived from television or film. This is not the case, of course, in all majority world or economically disadvantaged communities and Ritzer's critique of the 'McDonalization' of global cultures (Ritzer, 1996) is an incisive

account of how multinational industries have ruthlessly expanded global operations, discounting localised practices and cultural knowledge and values. The notion of 'mediascapes' is significant in this respect. Appadurai (1996) developed a framework for exploring disjunctures between economy, culture and politics in a globalised economy and identified five global cultural flows which he termed ethnoscapes, mediascapes, technoscapes, financescapes and ideoscapes. The term 'mediascapes' refers to the global distribution of electronic media and images of the world created by media. These inter-relate to create narratives in which commodities and ideology are combined in complex ways, and Appadurai argues that these mediascapes offer scripts for imagined lives. Globalised mediascapes are thus incorporated into children's play and their everyday lives. However, children demonstrate agency in the ways in which global narratives are taken up. Lee (2009), for example, analysed the responses of 10 Korean girls, aged 5–8, to Disney films. She found that the girls consistently reframed the texts to focus on their own cultural understandings, rooted in their experience in Korean immigrant families in the USA.

Children's popular culture includes a wide range of cultural objects. Figure 12.1 outlines some of the texts and artefacts that may be included in any exploration of the term. This is not, of course, an exhaustive list. As suggested earlier, access to and use of the texts and artefacts which are contained within this web are obviously dependent on culture, economic capital and social context.

Manufacturers and media industries have been swift to exploit the possibilities afforded by the inter-relationships between these texts. Narratives are developed across

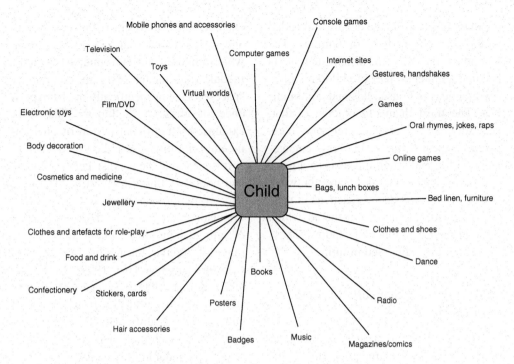

Figure 12.1 Texts and artefacts in children's popular culture

computer games, television programmes, toys, cards, stickers, fast food gifts and so on and many children are able to play with, watch, listen to, eat, wear and sleep on texts and artefacts which are linked to their favourite characters and media texts. This 'transmedia intertextuality' (Kinder, 1991: 3) contributes to the development of peer culture and means that children can engage in specific narratives even if they own only a relatively minor part of the system, for example stickers and cards (Marsh and Millard, 2000).

The inter-textual web of children's popular culture has become more complex over the years, with an ever-increasing range of text and practices. As we are now immersed in the new media age, it is clear that children's cultural interests are strongly embedded in new technologies. The digital turn in children's popular

culture has been reflected in research and scholarship into this area, which now includes studies of children's online popular practices and their relationships with the toys and artefacts of offline life (Burke and Marsh, in press). In this chapter, research which has explored young children's engagement with popular cultural texts, both digital and non-digital, will be reviewed in relation to the home and school domains as separate spaces, although it is acknowledged that there is much overlap.

POPULAR CULTURE IN THE HOME

There are four key themes which emerge from a review of studies which have explored children's literacy practices within the home. The first is the extent to which popular cultural texts are deeply embedded within the literacy lives of families. The second is the way in which such texts become an integral part of children's literacy practices in households and communities. The third theme to emerge is that, generally, in the research reported here, parents appear to view children's engagement with popular cultural texts in a positive light. Finally, the dissonance between home and nursery/school practices in relation to popular culture is a thread which runs through a number of studies. These themes will be addressed in turn.

The range of popular cultural texts in the home

There is evidence to suggest that popular cultural texts are an integral part of the literacy environment in many homes. Although not a specific focus of most studies located within domestic sites, research which has documented the literacy texts and practices situated in young children's homes has demonstrated that, within this sphere, children and parents encounter a range of cultural and media texts.

Early studies of home literacy practices indicated that family members generally engage with a range of texts which include TV guides, junk mail and food labels (Cairney, Lowe, Munsie, Ruge, and Buchanan, 1996; Purcell-Gates, 1996; Weinberger, 1996). As interest in children's literacy practices that are mediated through new technologies has grown in recent years, studies have outlined how young children are surrounded by digital texts in the home, such as computer games, console games and television and film (Blanchard and Moore, 2010; Marsh, Brooks, Hughes, Ritchie, and Roberts, 2005, Plowman, Stephen, and McPake, 2010; Wolfe and Flewitt, 2010). Yamada-Rice (2011) has

extended this analysis to the community and her research indicates the extent to which children are surrounded by multimodal, multimedia texts in community spaces, focusing specifically on the experience of children in Japan. This work extends the traditional notion of environmental print to visual and digital texts.

It is clear that the pervasiveness of media and popular cultural texts in many homes and communities crosses cultural and linguistic boundaries and there is evidence of bilingual families owning and using a range of popular and media texts in more than one language (Xu, 1999; Rodriguez, 1999; Kenner, 2000). Savage (2012), in a study of six 5–7-year-olds from a range of cultural backgrounds who lived in Qatar, noted that the children had access to wide range of popular cultural texts, both digital and non-digital, texts which were written in a variety of languages.

Children's popular cultural literacy practices in the home

The second theme to emerge from a consideration of the literature relating to popular culture in the home is that children draw readily from these texts and artefacts in their home-based literacy practices. Numerous studies have demonstrated how children engage in a range of literacy practices in the home which involve popular cultural texts such as comics, books based on television characters and environmental print linked to media texts (stickers, labels, video labels, computer game boxes and so on) (Marsh and Thomspon, 2001; Marsh et al., 2005; Pahl, 2005). More recent research has extended traditional definitions of literacy to identify the ways in which other aspects of popular culture, such as toys and artefacts, contribute to children's multimodal, communicative practices in the home (see Pahl and Rowsell, 2010; this volume).

Given the extent to which children's cultural practices are now embedded within digital media, there has been a significant body of work conducted over the past 10 years which has demonstrated the significance of popular digital texts within children's home literacy practices. In the UK, Marsh et al. (2005) conducted a survey of 1852 parents of children aged from birth to six in 10 Local Authorities in England in which young children's use of popular culture, media and new technologies was identified. The 'Digital Beginnings' study concluded that many young children were competent users of technologies from an early age and that they engaged with a wide range of digital texts such as computer games, console games, television and film and mobile phones. Subsequent studies of young children's use of technology in the UK have confirmed this immersion in the digital landscapes of contemporary society (Plowman et al. 2010; Wolfe and Flewitt, 2010). This work resonates with studies conducted in the USA, which indicated that children under the age of 6 are immersed in technology from birth (Rideout and Hamel, 2006; Rideout, Vandewater and Wartella, 2003). Young children's communicative practices using these digital technologies range from searching the Internet for information using Google (Davidson, 2009) playing online games and using virtual worlds (Marsh, 2010a, 2011), using technologies such as mobile phones (Marsh et al., 2005) and iPads (Savage, 2012) to write, to engaging in Skype conversations with family members (Savage, 2012), often from birth (see Mackey and Robinson, this volume).

Bilingual children access and use a range of digital texts that are multilingual in nature. For example, Kenner (2000) outlines the literacy practices of three bilingual children in their London homes. 3-year-old Billy's favourite literacy item, his mother noted, was a Thai karaoke video that displayed the words of the songs in Thai script across the screen, which Billy enjoyed watching and singing along to. Meera, also aged 3, copied Gujerati script from magazines, encouraged by her father. 4-year-old Mohammed used a song tape to learn Arabic letters and loved to identify the names of different makes of cars when out in the community. Savage (2012), in an analysis of the home literacy practices of six multilingual 5–7-year-olds in Qatar, identified the way in which the children enjoyed English texts related to their popular cultural interests, such as Disney princesses, Barbie and Spiderman, but also notes that the children accessed texts which were connected to their heritage culture. For example, two Japanese girls, Momo and Akari, both enjoyed playing with Hello Kitty artefacts, which reflected their Asian heritage. Momo also stated that she enjoyed reading a comic book about Doraemon, a popular cartoon cat character in Japan.

It is important to note that in home engagement in literacy, children move seamlessly across the popular/traditional cultural boundaries. Shegar and Weninger (2010) report on an ethnographic study of the home literacy practices of five preschool boys in Singapore. They identified that the boys engaged with a wide range of cultural texts and noted the presence of 'thematic intertextuality' (2010: 442), in which children were interested in texts that apparently seemed unconnected, but which had themes that interested the children. Sina, for example, was fond of magic and enjoyed the magical aspects of text ranging from Sabrina and the Powerpuff

Girls to Cinderella and Aladdin; Sarad relished the scariness of texts such as Spiderman and Steve Jackson's *Sorcery!*. They note that these thematic intertextual practices moved across both popular cultural and more traditional texts.

In many countries, popular cultural and media texts often form the majority of young children's first encounters with spoken and written English. In a number of studies, children's engagement with popular culture in the home has been linked to the development of English as an additional language. Xu (1999) documented the home literacy practices of six Chinese-American children aged between 5 and 6. She found that children often read, along-side their parents, the TV guides in order to find out about their favourite programmes. All of the children watched television for at least 1 hour per day. For the children in Xu's study, popular culture was an important means of developing an understanding and use of English as an additional language. Orellana (1994) also identified, in an analysis of three Spanish-speaking children's superhero play, that watching popular television programmes helped to develop the children's American-English. In Li's (2006) study of three bilingual 6- and 7-year-old children in Canada, some of the children chose to speak English at home because of their orientation to media texts. For example, Kevin chose not to speak Cantonese to his family and his father suggested that it was because he enjoyed watching English cartoons and playing video games. There are complex issues relating to cultural imperialism and hegemonic constructions of cultural identities within media texts which need to be traced in this process. This process need not been detrimental to children's identities, however. Savage (2012) noticed in her study that engagement with popular cultural texts in the home enabled children to develop skills in their heritage languages in ways which were not possible at school. This suggests that popular culture has a role to play in young children's acquisition of language and, for bilingual children, it can provide a means of creating cultural and linguistic shared spaces between home, school and community (Kenner, 2000; Savage, 2012).

Parental attitudes

Despite the unease of a number of early years educators concerning the influence of popular culture on young children (see Levin and Rosenquest, 2001; Palmer, 2006), it would appear that many parents view things rather differently. Makin et al. (1999) interviewed 60 parents across 79 early years settings in Australia. The researchers noted that, in discussions with Aboriginal parents and other groups of parents who spoke languages other than English, the use of technology such as TV, video and computer games was highly valued by them as a means of acquiring English as an additional language (Makin et al., 1999: 130). In a number of studies in which parents have been interviewed on this topic, there is evidence that many parents not only provide popular cultural and media resources for their children and recognise their role in promoting early literacy development, but are positive about the place of such texts in their children's lives (Weinberger, 1996; Xu, 1999; Marsh and Thompson, 2001; Arthur, 2001a, 2001b; Marsh et al., 2005).

The approval of popular cultural texts by parents is not universal, of course. Plowman et al.'s (2010) case studies of young children's use of technology in the home identified that that patterns of inter-action differed across families due to a range of factors, which included parents' attitudes towards and experiences of technology. Some parents expressed anxieties about children's use of technologies, including concerns about the possibility of over-use. In an Australian study (Fox, Diezmann, and Grieshaber, 2011) three teachers and 10 parents of children in the preparatory year of schooling (the year before formal schooling begins) were interviewed about their views of technology. It was found that teachers were optimistic about the use of technology, but the mothers were opposed to its use home. It is of interest that eight of the 10 mothers had experienced university, three at postgraduate level. It may be that issues of social class were pertinent here, as in other studies, middle-class parents have been more likely to comment on the potentially adverse effects of technology (Marsh et al., 2005).

Parents are not offered informed guidance on young children's engagement with popular culture and new technologies and they are frequently subject to reductive discourses in this respect. Nichols, Nixon, and Rowsell (2009) report on a geosemiotic study of the kinds of texts on parenting that parents had access to in three sites: two in and around Adelaide, South Australia and a third site in Princeton, NJ, USA. They report on two key types of texts that were presented to parents – those from the commercial world (such as adverts for electronic toys) and those that were produced by health or education workers to promote parental engagement in learning. Nichols et al. suggest that:

The commercial and institutional texts that together constitute a symbolic world of parents and early learning each, in different ways, present a reductive view of parenting practice as it relates to children's learning. Toy advertisements present a world in which the child's interaction with an object produces the simultaneous experience of

fun and learning and the most important parent identity is as consumer. The promise held out is that merely the provision of this book, toy or baby computer is sufficient parental involvement for learning to occur. Missing from this discourse is the social context of relationships in the family. Health and educational providers, on the other hand, emphasise social relations and make parent–child interaction central. Missing from this discourse is overt parent power, and recognition of the in-practice simultaneity of parents' literacy work with other kinds of work as well as their continual negotiation of multiple subject positions as parents.

(Nichols et al., 2009: 73)

This points to the need for early years educators to be aware of competing discourses in relation to parenting and to offer opportunities for parents to reflect on how they already support children's digital literacy practices and help them identify ways in which they might want to develop this further in order to foster enjoyment and intergenerational learning.

Home–school differences

Congruency between home and educational sites is an important concept if institutions are to build upon the richness of children's media literacy backgrounds. In a study of 79 early childhood education sites in Australia, in which the research team interviewed two staff members at each site and conducted focus group interviews with 60 parents, Makin et al. (1999) found that literacy practices embedded within technology and popular culture were pervasive in homes, yet few early years settings incorporated such resources into the curriculum. Although 71 percent of parents identified technology and popular culture as important to their child's literacy development, only 13 percent of staff acknowledged such practices occurred within the home, with many staff expressing concerns about these literacy events, in particular the viewing of television. This disparity between home and school practices was also identified in the Digital Beginnings study (Marsh et al., 2005).

Whilst this work was conducted some years ago, more recent research indicates that these patterns persist. This is clearly the case in Karen Wohlwend's (2009a) account of children from print-centric early years classrooms in the US, who longed to play with the new technologies and media that were part of their everyday experiences outside of school. She details how one child, thwarted by the limitations of the toys on offer in the classroom, drew his own mobile phone:

> He gave an oblong piece of paper rounded corners and penciled a 3 by 3 array of squares below a much larger square to represent a numeric pad and an LCD screen. Additional phone features (receiver, compact size) were emphasized by adding play actions: he held the opened paper flat in the palm of his hand, raised his hand to his ear, talked into the paper for a few seconds, then snapped it shut with one hand, and tucked it into his pocket.
>
> (Wohlwend, 2009a: 125)

The 5- to 7-year-old 'early adopters' in Wohlwend's study used paper and pencil to create mobile phones, iPods and video games in order to bring their own cultural worlds into the early years classroom in the face of technological neglect.

In a UK study investigating 4- and 5-year-old children's perceptions of reading, Levy (2011) identified that the 12 young children she studied were developing broad constructions of reading literacy within their home settings, which involved engagement with multimodal screen and paper-based texts. Yet, as the children moved into their Reception year at school, definitions of reading became dominated by a 'schooled' discourse that focused on the need to decode printed text in reading

scheme books. Many of the children subsequently lost confidence in themselves as readers, because their out-of-school literacy identities did not match those of school. In a similar manner, Johnson (2010) reports that even when children might have access to new technologies in the classroom, it might not lead to enthusiastic engagement. She conducted a survey in which 38 6- and 7-year-old children in Australia completed a 10-item rating scale on Internet use at home and school. Her findings indicate that:

> For the current sample, inverse relationships between home and school Internet use suggest that young children who frequently use and enjoy the Internet at home avoid using the Internet at school, particularly with respect to email but with the exception of playing games.
>
> (Johnson, 2010: 290)

It may be the case that these children found the socio-cultural practices surrounding the use of computers in these two domains very different, thus impacting on their engagement. In a review of the relationship between home and school literacy practices, Marsh (2010b) characterised the differences as outlined in Table 12.1.

Despite this apparent chasm between home and school literacy practices, there has been a range of work that has identified what happens when popular cultural texts and practices do permeate the classroom walls, which is reviewed in the next section.

POPULAR CULTURE, LITERACY AND SCHOOLING

In 1985, Carolyn Steedman outlined how Amarjit, a Punjabi girl living in a northern UK town, created a song using the materials she had to hand which were, in this

Table 12.1 Differences in home and school literacy practices

Literacy as experienced in many homes	Literacy as experienced in many early years settings and schools
• On-screen reading extensive	• On-screen reading minimal
• Multimodal	• Focused on written word and image
• Non-linear reading pathways	• Linear reading pathways
• Fluidity/ crossing of boundaries	• Limited to written page
• Multiple authorship/ unknown authorship	• Known, primarily single authorship
• Always linked to production	• Analysis and production separate
• Embedded in communities of practice/ affinity groups	• Individualistic
• Shaped by mediascapes	• Little reference to mediascapes
• Child constituted as social reader	• Child constituted as individual reader
• Reading integral part of identity construction/ performance	• Reading constructs school reader identities (successful or unsuccessful in relation to school practices)

case, a reading primer and her own voice. Steedman notes that:

> 'An act of transformation like this can be seen as an act of play, in the same way as reading and writing are play, a way of manipulating the symbols of a social and emotional world, and of abstracting meaning from a particular reality.'
>
> (Steedman, 1985: 138).

Nowhere has children's playful transformation and reconceptualisation of media texts been traced more powerfully than in Anne Haas Dyson's work. Dyson's corpus of work (e.g., 1994, 1996, 1997, 2003, 2006, 2010, this volume) has been central to the development of our understanding of the ways in which children transgress the restrictions of the 'null curriculum' in early childhood classrooms. Her writing demonstrates how children take up media and popular cultural texts in their creation of an 'unofficial curriculum' (Dyson, 1997) in which they negotiate teacher-mandated tasks but reconstruct them in order that their own interests and desires are woven into the daily fabric of classroom life. Dyson's extensive work on popular culture has focused specifically on the writing curriculum, but much of what she has to say about the potential of media texts can

be applied more widely across the literacy curriculum.

In an early study, Dyson (1994) observed a second-grade classroom class in San Francisco for a period of 3 months. The data reported on in her paper focuses on observations relating to the use of 'Author's Theater', in which children wrote stories which were then performed by peers of their choosing. In the study, Dyson illustrates how the children's media stories generated power struggles in which class, race and gender were used as markers of identity and agency and informed how the children's stories were developed and performed. In a book which provides more extensive details of the research undertaken in this school (Dyson, 1997), she describes how further data were collected by means of extensive observations of children in their second- and third-grade classrooms and through the collection of their written texts, audiotapes of the Author's Theater and the recording of conversations with the children and their teacher. These rich data provided further information about the way in which children constructed their unofficial social worlds and how popular culture informed that construction. In choosing which of

their classmates were to act out their stories, children played with notions of exclusivity and inclusivity and were negotiating
their social worlds as much as they were
creating written ones. In this study, Dyson
outlines the attraction of superhero stories
for young children and indicates how they
are both liberating (in providing a forum
in which children's knowledge can be
drawn upon) and limiting (in providing
a forum in which stereotyped roles are
rife). The worlds created by children were
unofficial in the sense that the popular
material was not introduced by Kristin,
the teacher involved in the study, although
she obviously sanctioned its use. Despite
the lack of official recognition of popular texts in mandated curricula, children
throughout Dyson's studies have imaginatively exploited this rich source of semiotic
material as they create media-saturated
'figured worlds' (Holland, Lachiotte,
Skinner and Cain, 1998) within the realm
of the classroom.

Children use this cultural agency to
refashion media discourses in a playful
and inventive manner. Dyson (1999: 379–
80) outlines five ways in which media was
appropriated by children for use in schooled
texts in one of her studies in which children drew from sports in their writing.
First, media was used to inform the *content*
of texts, such as the use of the names of
particular sports teams. Second, *communicative forms* from media were adopted and
adapted, such as the format of games
results. Third *graphic conventions*, such as
symbols of teams, found their way into
children's texts. Fourth, *voiced utterances,*
that is, particular lines spoken by narrators or characters, were embedded in the
writing of some children in the class.
Finally, children utilised media *ideologies,*
for example as they drew on the relationship between gender and power as it is

frequently reflected in the discourses of
sports.

These five categories can be traced in
the ways in which children appropriate
media texts in a range of other studies
outlined in this chapter and indicate the
extent to which media discourses permeate
children's meaning-making. This process
of requisition serves to validate children's
own cultural resources and, in addition,
it enables them to negotiate and navigate
peer relationships, the theme of Dyson's
2003 study of another elementary classroom in which children used popular texts
as cultural capital in order to gain entry
into the social worlds of their peers. This
work exemplifies Seiter's (1993) notion
of popular culture as the 'lingua franca'
of playgrounds, which offers a means for
children from disparate linguistic, cultural and economic backgrounds to forge
common links and develop dialogic
communities of practice. In more recent
work, Dyson (2006, 2008a, 2008b, 2010,
this volume) has juxtaposed the rich range
of writing practices that emerge from children's social and cultural engagements
with the normative expectations of a standardised curriculum and she has exposed
the way in which the latter devalues and
dismisses the former, with significant
impacts on children's literate identities.

A number of theories have informed
work examining the relationship between
literacy and popular culture. Marsh (2008)
outlines four key theoretical models which
have informed the use of children's cultural texts, practices and artefacts in the
classroom in order to promote creativity.
The first is a utilitarian model, which indicates that children's cultural practices can
be leveraged in the classroom in order
to ensure that children are orientated to
schooled literacy practices by becoming
more motivated to engage in reading and

writing tasks that are focused on their cultural interests. The second model is the 'cultural capital' model which draws from Bourdieu's (1977) work to suggest that by incorporating popular cultural texts into the classroom, we are recognising children's cultural capital and thereby lessening the potential for symbolic violence to occur. Symbolic violence is the consequence of a dominant class imposing its own cultural values and interests on a dominated group, who then accept this situation without question. Historically, schools have privileged canonical texts at the expense of working-class children's textual pleasures, but in this second model, popular culture can offer a bridge between home and school cultures. The third model draws on critical theory to suggest that popular cultural texts have integral value and can be studied in their own right, as part of a critical literacy curriculum in which texts of all kinds, both popular and canonical, are subject to critical analysis. The final model draws on third space/recontextualisation theories to suggest that the classroom can offer a space which blends both home and school cultures. By enabling pupils to draw on out-of-school discourses in the classroom, new kinds of knowledge can be created. The kinds of vernacular, localised knowledge children develop in out-of-school practices combine with the more formal structures of curriculum knowledge and this recontextualisation produces new knowledge which crystallises experiences across home and school. Some studies of the use of children's popular culture in classrooms draw on one or more of these models, others are located within one particular paradigm. What work in this field has gradually moved to acknowledge over the years is that institutional spaces for learning can offer creative and enabling environments

for work that embrace children's culture, but this is achieved only through careful consideration of the ways in which children's own identities and agency can be valued in the process. An example of this process can be found in Parry's (2010) account of film-making in a primary classroom, in which children were encouraged to draw on their home experiences of viewing films in the production of their own filmic texts. She relates how this enabled one child, Connor, who was otherwise disengaged from school, to explore aspects of his own identity and to value his own cultural interests. This required a sensitive approach from the teacher in which the child's passion for film was recognised and sensitively drawn upon to inform classroom practice.

In recent years, studies of the relationship between popular culture and the literacy curriculum have focused on media and new technologies (see Wohlwend, this volume). The digital turn in the study of children's popular cultural practices, which mirrors somewhat the changes of interest in New Literacy Studies generally (Mills, 2010) has led to a series of projects examining the inclusion of digital literacy texts and practices in the early childhood curriculum. Reviews of this area of work can be found in Burnett and Merchant (this volume), Levy and Marsh (2010) and Levy, Yamada-Rice, and Marsh (in press) and therefore the issues need not be explored here. It is worth noting, however, that there have been a number of highly favourable outcomes in terms of pupil engagement and achievement reported from projects which utilise digital technology and/or popular culture for creative production in the classroom. The focus on integrating media and new technologies into the literacy curriculum has had a discernible impact. For example, in the 'Digital Beginnings' project (Marsh et al., 2005), nine early years settings introduced aspects of popular culture, media and new technologies into the communication, language and literacy curriculum. Activities included making electronic and digital books, watching and analysing moving image stories and creating presentations using electronic software. One of the aims of the study was to examine the impact of these action research projects on the motivation and engagement of children in curriculum activities related to communication, language and literacy. In order to identify this, practitioners undertook three observations of 14 children prior to the project and three observations of the same children during the project, using *The Leuven Involvement Scale for Young Children* (Laevers, 1994). Outcomes indicated that children's levels of engagement in activities were higher when the curriculum incorporated their interests in popular culture, media and new technologies (Marsh et al., 2005). Similar findings were identified in the Home School Knowledge Exchange Project in the UK (Feiler et al., 2007). Activities were developed in four primary schools, two in Bristol and two in Cardiff, which aimed to draw on the practices and experiences of home in the classroom. For example, children brought to school, in a shoebox, artefacts that were important to them, including those related to popular culture, which were then used to support literacy. Quantitative findings with regard to the impact of the project on reading were inconclusive, but qualitative findings suggest that the project had a positive impact on children's confidence and self-esteem and teachers' pedagogical practice. Similarly, projects in which film analysis was embedded into the primary writing curriculum led to increased attainment in standardised assessment tests (Marsh and Bearne, 2008).

Research with older children and teenagers has demonstrated how the use of popular culture in the classroom can be embedded within a critical approach to pedagogy, which involves the examination of the sources, uses and effects of power within a text (Alvermann, Moon, and Hagood, 1999; Heron-Hruby and Alvermann, 2009). Critical literacy approaches to the use and creation of popular texts have also been adopted in early years classrooms (Comber and Simpson, 2001; Vasquez, 2004). As Comber's chapter in this volume suggests, work in this area demonstrates how children's lived experiences develop their capacity to explore critically the texts they encounter in a range of contexts, skills which can be drawn upon in enlightened and imaginative ways in classrooms. The work reviewed by Comber demonstrates that, although we can enhance children's critical literacy skills, they do not begin this process as empty ciphers; they enter classrooms with a wealth of understanding about the popular cultural world around them. Misson (1998) also reminds us that we must approach this work with an understanding of the pleasures such texts bring to children and seek to respect this pleasure, not destroy it. Recent studies in this area (e.g., Saltmarsh, 2009; Savage, 2012; Vasquez, 2010; Vasquez and Felderman, 2012; Wohlwend, 2009b, 2011) examine the complexities of children's interactions with popular cultural and explore identity, agency and resistance in relation to issues of stereotyping and commercialism in these texts.

CONCLUSION

From the research reviewed within this chapter, it can be seen that much is known about the way in which popular culture penetrates children's home literacy practices and the means by which it can inform the early childhood literacy curriculum. Nevertheless, there is clearly still much work to be done in the field. In particular, there needs to be much more detailed research undertaken that helps to identify what children's popular cultural interests are across a range of cultural and social contexts. For example, the majority of the large-scale surveys of young children's engagement with popular and media texts have been undertaken in the UK (Marsh et al., 2005; Plowman et al., 2010) and the United States (Rideout and Hamel, 2006; Rideout et al., 2003) and there is a need to conduct similar surveys in other countries in order to determine the large-scale patterns in this area. At the other extreme, other than the studies of Flewitt (see this volume), Pahl (2002), Savage (2012) and Yamada-Rice, (2011), there are few ethnographic studies of young children's engagement with popular cultural texts in homes and communities and it would be valuable to extend this work to include longitudinal studies of developments in children's use of these texts over time.

As was suggested previously, due to the increasing use of new technologies in the popular cultural practices of children, there has been some innovative work in recent years which has sought to embed digital literacy practices into the curriculum, as suggested in this chapter (see Burnett and Merchant, this volume). Research agendas that extend this area of investigation so that we might develop further understanding about the ways in which educators might assess children's learning in this area need to be developed. Further, whilst some studies focus on culturally diverse classrooms and families, as outlined in this chapter, there is a need for more detailed research on the emergent digital literacy practices of Black, Asian

and Latino children in order that a broad understanding is developed of all children's engagement in literacy in the digital age. This is also the case in relation to children who are often placed on the margins of research early childhood literacy, such as children with disabilities, looked after children and children from Traveller communities. Finally, it is clear that the popular cultural worlds of young children are increasingly merging online and offline worlds. Children play with friends they know online and they also encounter toys and artefacts relating to particular narratives in both online and offline environments (Black, 2010; Burke and Marsh, in press; Marsh, 2010a, 2011; Wohlwend, Vander Zanden, Husbye, and Kuby, 2011). For this generation, the boundaries between online and offline are more permeable that an any other time in history. It will be important to trace what this means for children's understanding of modality and for their literacy practices in both home and school domains in the years ahead.

REFERENCES

Alvermann, D., Moon, J.S., and Hagood, M.C. (1999) *Popular Culture in the Classroom: Teaching and Researching Critical Media Literacy*. Newark, DE: IRA/NRC.

Appadurai, A. (1996) *Modernity at Large: Cultural Dimensions of Globalization*. Minneapolis: University of Minnesota Press.

Arnold, M. (1869) *Culture and Anarchy: An Essay in Political and Social Criticism*. London: Smith, Elder & Co.

Arthur, L. (2001a) 'Popular culture and early literacy learning', *Contemporary Issues in Early Childhood*, 2(3): 295–308.

Arthur, L. (2001b) 'Young children as critical consumers', *Australian Journal of Language and Literacy*, 24(3): 182–94.

Black, R.W. (2010) 'The language of Webkinz: Early childhood literacy in an online virtual world', *Digital Culture & Education*, 2(1): 7–24.

Blanchard, J. and Moore, T. (2010). 'The digital world of young children: Impact on emergent literacy', Pearson Foundation White Chapter. Retrieved 20 March 2010 from http://www.pearsonfoundation.org/downloads/EmergentLiteracy-White Paper.pdf

Bourdieu, P. (1977) *Outline of a Theory of Practice.* Cambridge: Cambridge University Press.

Burke, A. and Marsh, J. (eds) (in press) *Children's Virtual Play Worlds: Culture, Learning and Participation.* New York: Peter Lang.

Cairney, T.H., Lowe, K., Munsie, L., Ruge, J., and Buchanan, J. (1996) *Developing Partnerships: The Home, School and Community Interface.* Vols 1–3. Canberra: DEET. www.nepean.uws.edu.au/uws/uwsn/admin/research/pvc_research/html/dev_partner.html Accessed on 2 July 2000.

Comber, B. and Simpson, A. (eds) (2001) *Negotiating Critical Literacies in Classrooms.* Mahwah, NJ: Erlbaum.

Davidson, C. (2009) 'Young children's engagement with digital texts and literacies in the home: Pressing matters for the teaching of English in the early years of schooling', *English Teaching: Practice and Critique*, 8(3): 36–54.

Dyson, A.H. (1994) 'The Ninjas, the X-Men, and the Ladies: Playing with power and identity in an urban primary school', *Teachers College Record*, 96(2): 219–39.

Dyson, A.H. (1996) 'Cultural constellations and childhood identities: On Greek gods, cartoon heroes, and the social lives of schoolchildren', *Harvard Educational Review*, 66(3): 471–95.

Dyson, A.H. (1997) *Writing Superheroes: Contemporary Childhood, Popular Culture, and Classroom Literacy.* New York: Teachers College Press.

Dyson, A.H. (1999) 'Coach Bombay's kids learn to write: Children's appropriation of media material for school literacy', *Research in the Teaching of English*, 33: 367–402.

Dyson, A.H. (2003) *The Brothers and Sisters Learn to Write.* New York: Teachers College.

Dyson, A.H. (2006) 'On saying it right (write): "Fix-its" in the foundations of learning to write', *Research in the Teaching of English*, 41: 8–44.

Dyson, A.H. (2008a) 'Staying in the (curricular) lines: Practice constraints and possibilities in childhood writing', *Written Communication*, 25: 119–57.

Dyson, A.H. (2008b) 'The Pine Cone Wars: Studying writing in a community of children', *Language Arts*, 85: 305–15.

Dyson, A.H. (2010) 'Writing childhoods under construction: Revisioning "copying" in early childhood', *Journal of Early Childhood Literacy*, 10: 7–31.

Feiler, A., Andrews, J., Greenhough, P., Hughes, M., Johnson, D., Scanlan, M., and Yee, W.C. (2007) *Improving Primary Literacy: Linking Home and School.* London: Routledge.

Fox, J.L., Diezmann, C.M., and Grieshaber, S.J. (2011) 'Teachers' and parents' perspectives of digital technology in the lives of young children', in S. Howard (ed.), AARE Annual Conference 2010, 28 November to 2 December 2010, Melbourne, Australia. http://eprints.qut.edu.au/41179/

Heron-Hruby, A. and Alvermann, D.E. (2009) 'Implications of adolescents' popular culture use for school literacy', in K.D. Wood and W.E. Blanton (eds), *Literacy Instruction for Adolescents: Research-Based Practices.* New York: Guilford. pp. 210–27.

Holland, D., Lachicotte, W., Skinner, D., and Cain, C. (1998) *Identity and Agency in Cultural Worlds.* Cambridge, Mass: Harvard University Press.

Jenks, C. (1993) *Culture.* London: Routledge.

Johnson, G.M. (2010) 'Young children's Internet use at home and school: Patterns and profiles', *Journal of Early Childhood Research*, 8: 282–93. doi: 10.1177/1476718X10379783

Kenner, C. (2000) *Home Pages: Literacy Links for Bilingual Children.* Staffordshire: Trentham Books.

Kinder, M. (1991) *Playing with Power in Movies: Television and Video Games from Muppet Babies to Teenage Mutant Ninja Turtles.* Berkeley: University of California Press.

Laevers, F. (1994). *Defining and Assessing Quality in Early Childhood Education.* Leuven: Leuven University Press.

Lee, L. (2009) 'Young American immigrant children's interpretations of popular culture: A case study of Korean girls' perspectives on royalty in Disney films', *Journal of Early Childhood Research*, 7: 200–15.

Levin, D.E. and Rosenquest, B. (2001) 'The increasing role of electronic toys in the lives of infants and toddlers: Should we be concerned?', *Contemporary Issues in Early Childhood*, 2(2): 242–47.

Levine, S. (1991) 'William Shakespeare and the American people: A study in cultural transformation', in C. Mukerji and M. Schudson (eds), *Rethinking Popular Culture: Contemporary Perspectives in Cultural Studies.* Berkeley: University of California Press.

Levy, R. (2011) *Young Children Reading at Home and at School.* London: Sage.

Levy, R. and Marsh, J. (2010) 'Literacy and ICT in the early years', in D. Lapp and D. Fisher (eds), *Handbook of Research on Teaching the English Language Arts.* New York: Routledge. pp. 168–74.

Levy, R., Yamada-Rice, D., and Marsh, J. (in press) 'Digital literacies in the primary classroom', in K. Hall, T. Cremin, B. Comber, and L. Moll (eds), *International Handbook of Research in Children's Literacy, Learning and Culture.* Oxford: Wiley-Blackwell.

Li, G. (2006). 'Biliteracy and trilingual practices in the home context: Case studies of Chinese-Canadian children', *Journal of Early Childhood Literacy,* 6(3): 355–81.

Makin, L., Hayden, J., Holland, A., Arthur, L., Beecher, B., Jones Diaz, C., and McNaught, M. (1999) *Mapping Literacy Practices in Early Childhood Services,* Sydney: NSW Department of Education and Training and NSW Department of Community Services.

Marsh, J. (2008) 'Popular culture in the language arts classroom', in J. Flood, S.B. Heath and D. Lapp (eds), *Handbook of Research on Teaching the Visual and Creative Arts.* Vol II. New York: Erlbaum/Taylor & Francis Group. pp. 529–36.

Marsh, J. (2010a) 'Young children's play in online virtual worlds', *Journal of Early Childhood Research,* 8(1): 23–39.

Marsh, J. (2010b) 'The relationship between home and school literacy practices', in D. Wyse, R. Andrews, and J. Hoffman (eds), *The International Handbook of English, Language and Literacy Teaching.* London: Routledge. pp. 305–16.

Marsh, J. (2011) 'Young children's literacy practices in a virtual world: Establishing an online interaction order', *Reading Research Quarterly,* 46(2): 101–18. doi: 10.1598/RRQ.46.2.1.

Marsh, J. and Bearne, E. (2008) *Moving Literacy On: Evaluation of the BFI Training Project for Lead Practitioners on Moving Image Education.* Leicester: UKLA.

Marsh, J. and Millard, E. (2000) *Literacy and Popular Culture: Using Children's Culture in the Classroom.* London: Paul Chapman.

Marsh, J. and Thompson, P. (2001) 'Parental involvement in literacy development: Using media texts', *Journal of Research in Reading,* 24(3): 266–78.

Marsh, J., Brooks, G., Hughes, J., Ritchie, L., and Roberts, S. (2005). *Digital Beginnings: Young Children's Use of Popular Culture, Media and New Technologies.* Sheffield, UK: University of Sheffield. Retrieved January 2009, at www.digitalbeginnings. shef.ac.uk/

Mills, K. (2010) 'A review of the "digital turn" in the new literacy studies', *Review of Educational*

Research, 80(2): 246–71. doi: 10.3102/ 0034654310364401.

Misson, R. (1998) 'Theory and spice, and things not nice: popular culture in the primary classroom', in M. Knobel and A. Healy (eds), *Critical Literacies in the Primary Classroom.* Newtown, NSW: PETA. pp. 53–62.

Mukerji, C. and Schudson, M. (1991) *Rethinking Popular Culture: Contemporary Perspectives in Cultural Studies.* Berkeley: University of California Press.

Nichols, S., Nixon, H., and Rowsell, J. (2009) 'The "good" parent in relation to early childhood literacy: Symbolic terrain and lived practice', *Literacy,* 43(2): 65–74.

Orellana, M.F. (1994) 'Appropriating the voice of the superheroes: Three preschoolers' bilingual language uses in play', *Early Childhood Research Quarterly,* 9: 171–93.

Pahl, K. (2002) 'Ephemera, mess and miscellaneous piles: Texts and practices in families', *Journal of Early Childhood Literacy,* 2(2): 145–66.

Pahl, K. (2005). 'Children's popular culture in the home: Tracing cultural practices in texts', in J. Marsh and E. Millard (eds), *Popular Literacies, Childhood and Schooling.* London: Routledge/Falmer. pp. 29–53.

Pahl, K. and Roswell, J. (2010) *Artifactual Literacies – Every Object Tells a Story.* London: Teachers College Press.

Palmer, S. (2006) *Toxic Childhood.* London: Orion Press.

Parry, B. (2010) 'Helping children tell the stories in their heads', in C. Bazalgette (ed.), *Teaching Media in Primary Schools.* London: Sage.

Plowman, L., Stephen, C., and McPake, J. (2010) *Growing Up With Technology: Young Children Learning in a Digital World.* London: Routledge.

Rideout, V. and Hamel, E. (2006) *The Media Family: Electronic Media in the Lives of Infants, Toddlers Preschoolers and their Parents.* California: Kaiser Family Foundation. Retrieved 13th May 2012 from: http://www.kff.org/entmedia/ upload/7500.pdf

Rideout, V.J., Vandewater, E.A., and Wartella, E.A. (2003). *Zero to Six: Electronic Media in the Lives of Infants, Toddlers and Preschoolers.* Washington: Kaiser Foundation.

Purcell-Gates, V. (1996) 'Stories, coupons and the TV guide: Relationships between home literacy experiences and emergent literacy experiences', *Reading Research Quarterly,* 31(4): 406–28.

Ritzer, G. (1996) *The McDonaldization of Society.* (revised edn). Thousand Oaks, California: Pine Forge Press/Sage.

Rodriguez, M.V. (1999) 'Home literacy experiences of three young Dominican children in New York City', *Educators for Urban Minorities*, 1(1): 19–31.

Saltmarsh, S. (2009) 'Becoming economic subjects: Agency, consumption and popular culture in early childhood', *Discourse: Studies in the Cultural Politics of Education*, 30(1): 47–59. doi:10.1080/01596300802643082.

Savage, M. (2012) 'Home literacy and agency: An ethnographic approach to studying the home literacy practices of six multiliterate children in Qatar'. Unpublished EdD Thesis, University of Sheffield.

Seiter, E. (1993) *Sold Separately: Children and Parents in Consumer Culture.* New York: Rutgers University Press.

Shegar, C. and Weninger, C. (2010) 'Intertextuality in preschoolers' engagement with popular culture: Implications for literacy development', *Language and Education*, 24(5): 431–47. http://dx.doi.org/10.1080/09500782.2010.486861.

Steedman, C. (1985) '"Listen, how the caged bird sings": Amarjit's song', in C. Steedman, V. Walkerdine, C. Urwin (eds), *Language, Gender and Childhood*. London: Routledge & Kegan Paul.

Vasquez, V. (2004) *Negotiating Critical Literacies with Young Children.* Mahwah, NJ: Lawrence Erlbaum.

Vasquez, V. (2010) *Getting Beyond I Like the Book: Creating Spaces for Critical Literacy Across the Curriculum.* Newark, DE: IRA.

Vasquez, V. and Felderman, C. (2012) *Technology and Critical Literacy in Early Childhood.* New York: Routledge Press.

Weinberger, J. (1996) *Literacy Goes to School: the Parents' Role in Young Children's Literacy Learning.* London: Paul Chapman.

Williams, R. (1965) *The Long Revolution.* Harmonsworth: Penguin.

Willis, P. (1990) *Common Culture.* Buckingham: Open University Press.

Wohlwend, K. (2009a) 'Early adopters: Playing new literacies and pretending new technologies in print-centric classrooms', *Journal of Early Childhood Literacy*, 9(2): 117–40.

Wohlwend, K.E. (2009b) 'Damsels in discourse: Girls consuming and producing gendered identity texts through Disney Princess play', *Reading Research Quarterly*, 44(1): 57–83.

Wohlwend, K.E. (2011). *Playing Their Way into Literacies: Reading, Writing, and Belonging in the Early Childhood Classroom.* New York: Teachers College Press.

Wohlwend, K.E., Vander Zanden, S., Husbye, N.E., and Kuby, C.R. (2011) 'Navigating discourses in place in the world of Webkinz', *Journal of Early Childhood Literacy*, 11(2): 141–163.

Wolfe, S. and Flewitt, R.S. (2010) 'New technologies, new multimodal literacy practices and young children's metacognitive development', *Cambridge Journal of Education*, 40(4): 387–99.

Xu, S.H. (1999) 'Young Chinese ESL children's home literacy experiences', *Reading Horizons*, 40(1): 47–64.

Yamada-Rice, D. (2011) 'New media, evolving multimodal literacy practices and the potential impact of increased use of the visual mode in the urban environment on young children's learning', *Literacy*, 45(1): 32–43. doi: 10.1111/j.1741-4369.2011.00578.x.

13

Film and Television

Muriel Robinson and
Margaret Mackey

Twenty-first-century children in most areas of the world become literate in a context that includes many forms of televisual text as part of their daily environment. In this chapter we will explore current evidence which illuminates our understanding of the relationship between televisual texts and children's literacy development, and of the complexities of the exchanges between print and televisual forms. The *Oxford English Dictionary* defines 'televisual' as relating exclusively to television, but we will expand that definition to include television and also the other formats that provide moving image and sound. In the first edition of this chapter, that list included film, video, and DVD; now it must be expanded to include computer screens that offer streaming video, YouTube clips, animated websites, and Skype exchanges with known interlocutors. We must also take account of the small screens of mobile phones that may offer a variety of animated games or a collection of home videos. It is probably important to pay particular attention to the intimacy of Facetime exchanges,

live video interactions between two smartphones that may offer contingent and highly personal salience for an infant communicator, especially as the mobile screen is often held close to the child's face, within the focal range of all but the very youngest of babies. DVDs produced especially for infants and marketed to their parents as educational are also much more prominent than they were a decade ago, and have sparked some detailed studies that have begun to fill some of the gaps we identified in the research literature on our first foray into this territory.

Literacy occurs as a set of situated practices (Barton and Hamilton, 1998); that is, we read as part of a social world in real contexts, and our literate behaviours are influenced by and influence the world we are in. One impact of televisual texts, and television in particular, has been to reposition children both in the world and in their relation to texts. Children now approach all their texts as multiliterate interpreters (New London Group, 1996). Their plural understanding of literacy inflects all their dealings with text. The past decade has expanded the repertoire of relatively abstract understanding that children glean from their screen encounters. Those who wish to explore children's literary understanding must take account of *all* the kinds of text that contribute to children's growing relationship with literacy. Another highly significant development in the situated literacies of today's young people is the fact that just as children may learn some facts about reading through their early efforts at writing, a considerable proportion of today's children are much more likely to participate in the production as well as the reception of moving images, with consequent impact on their capacity to make sense of the package of moving image and audio.

The complexities of the relationship between print and televisual texts are insufficiently understood. Ten years ago, we were concerned that too much research was being conducted within parameters that simply did not make enough space for complex analysis. The situation has improved greatly over the past decade, but there is still room for research to catch up with contemporary media affordances. We also need more research that acknowledges that there might be a role for infants simply to enjoy video texts; because of the difficulty of gauging babies' responses, most of the contemporary research that we located stresses infant learning as a form of measurable outcome, and pays little or no attention to televisual texts as a source of pleasure for babies and toddlers.

THE NEW REALITIES OF DOMESTIC MEDIA

Although there is now much more detailed and subtle research into infants' and toddlers' relationship with the televisual, research necessarily operates in a time lag, and it is difficult for scholars to keep up with the accelerating changes in small-screen technologies. An American survey from late 2011 provides one perspective on the speed of change. Common Sense Media reported that many US children, aged 0–8, are making various uses of mobile devices:

> Half (52 percent) of all children now have access to one of the newer mobile devices at home: either a smartphone (41 percent), a video iPod (21 percent), or an iPad or other tablet device (8 percent).
>
> More than a quarter (29 percent) of all parents have downloaded 'apps' (applications used on mobile devices) for their children to use. And more than a third (38 percent) of children have ever used one of these newer mobile devices, including 10 percent of 0–1-year-olds, 39 percent of 2–4-year-olds, and 52 percent of 5–8-year-olds. . . .
>
> Computer use is pervasive among very young children, with half (53 percent) of all 2–4-year-olds having ever used a computer. . . . Even among 2- to 4-year-olds, 12 percent use a computer every day, with another 24 percent doing so at least once a week.
>
> (Rideout, 2011: 9)

Ten years ago, we might have omitted those computer statistics, striking though they are. Today, however, children commonly gain access via their computer screens to moving images that must be considered televisual by our criteria above. And to these statistics for mobile apps and computers must be added the figures for watching television and DVDs.

In a typical day, 47 percent of babies and toddlers ages 0 through 1 watch TV or DVDs, and those who watch spend an average of nearly 2 hours (1:54) doing so. This is an average of :53 among all children in this age group, compared to an average of :23 a day reading or being read to (Rideout, 2011: 11).

According to this survey, 30 percent of 0–1-year-olds have a television in their bedroom, as do 44 percent of 2–4-year-olds (Rideout, 2011: 11). An earlier report, based on 19 percent of all toddlers having a TV set in their bedrooms, suggested that 38 percent of them could turn it on by themselves and 40 percent knew how to change channels with the remote control (Courage and Setliff, 2010: 221).

Television sets in the nursery are a phenomenon with cultural impact, but there are social and economic implications as well, and not necessarily the ones we might expect. In upper income homes in the USA, only 20 percent of children aged 0–8 years old have a TV in their bedroom; however, in lower-income households, 64 percent of children are thus equipped (Rideout, 2011: 12). According to this survey, 37 percent of American infants in their first year watch television or videos every day and 73 percent of children aged between 2 and 4 do so.

This survey reflects the media lives of very young children in one country, but it is plausible to assume that conditions in many other Western countries are not wildly different. The penetration of television into children's bedrooms may vary, as may the ubiquity of mobile phones, or the market dominance of baby videos, but there is no doubt that young children in much of the world are being exposed to very much more screen time than ever before.

We found little research on the impact of YouTube on young children, but the global usage figures are staggering and involve a high level of participation. According to *The New Yorker* in early 2012, 'Today, it has eight hundred million unique users a month, and generates more than three billion views a day. Forty-eight hours of new video are uploaded to the site every minute' (Seabrook, 2012: 26). Some of these video hours feature young children, and it is very probable that many more young children participate by viewing. We need to know more about what these junior viewers may be learning about the televisual world through exposure to amateur and unscripted video featuring families like or very unlike their own. It seems plausible that it is a different lesson from that learned through the viewing of highly crafted programming.

Facebook and other social media sites offer yet another portal, and many young children will be accustomed to seeing home video featured on their own or their parents' sites, among a range of imported video clips. Again, much more needs to be known.

TELEVISUAL IMAGES AND THE YOUNGEST CHILDREN: NEW RESEARCH

In the past, it has been noteworthy how much existing research into children and television assumed a deficit model in which television is perceived as interfering with other activities and displacing more 'valuable' activities. Much research ran the risk of being blinded by its own assumptions into confusing causation and correlation, or of attempting to single out 'effects' of particular kinds of television programmes without attending to the complexity of the child viewer's situation. In 1986: 2, Hodge and Tripp were moved to suggest 'the problem, we will argue, is that these "experts" have been trying to answer the wrong questions in the wrong order, with theories and methods that have been overly partial and inadequate.'

Much earlier research was often also unhelpful in terms of exploring the complexity of children's experiences of the moving image because it focused on one medium, usually television or video (with video often being treated as television, in that there were rarely opportunities for the children to pause or rewind or even view repeatedly). Yet the figures from the 2011 American survey indicate that many children are moving among a variety of media formats at a very young age indeed. In such circumstances, their experience and understanding rapidly becomes more sophisticated than many singularly-focused laboratory experiments can properly assess.

At the same time, it is important to recognize that not all deficits relate to the televisual. The National Literacy Trust in a disquieting 2011 survey of British children suggested a serious decrease in child book ownership: 'In 2005, 1 in 10 of the children and young people we surveyed said they did not have a book of their own at home; while in 2011 the figure stands at a startling 1 child in 3' (Clark et al., 2011: 3).

But a deficit model approach only makes room for some of what we understand about children's media experience. Before we explore the more recent research, we will investigate the potential of an 'asset model' rather than a 'deficit model' of televiewing.

SOME REAL-WORLD EXAMPLES: AN ASSET MODEL

Tyner has coined a useful phrase, talking of 'an asset model' of someone's media experience: 'An asset model for media teaching assumes that mass media and popular culture content can work as a benefit to literacy instead of as a social deficit' (1998: 7). She argues that we may increase our understanding by exploring what assets a person brings to bear on a literacy event.

Tyner does not develop this model further, but we find it a useful concept to help us explore the interrelationship between print and televisual literacies. Ten years ago, we offered a few examples to demonstrate the complexity of the links:

- Verónica, from Mexico City, develops a deep interest in dinosaurs when she is just 2. The first sign is a request to own two very small remaindered books. Watching videos of the BBC's 'Walking with Dinosaurs' leads to the moment 6 months later when the family drive past a huge billboard for the Disney film *Dinosaur*. Verónica's assets are sufficient for her to ask if this is a poster for a film about dinosaurs, and if so, whether she can go and see it. She negotiates with her parents that they will take her but that if she doesn't like it she can leave. She watches the whole film and this viewing is the spur for a continued interest in all things to do with Aladar in particular and dinosaurs in general, still alive 2 years after the first interest, and registered through the use of many different media.
- Philip, a Canadian 6-year-old, is a passionate ice hockey fan. His first successful reading experience comes when he shows his grandmother his hockey sticker book and recognizes players of the Toronto Maple Leafs by deciphering the distinctive shapes of their names on their jerseys. He has cheered for them on television, and played them on his PlayStation game; his mediated experience supplies a strong emotional core to his reading repertoire.
- Batanai, aged 5, lives in a mixed suburb of Harare. He is an ardent viewer of 'Thomas the Tank Engine' which appears weekly on Zimbabwean television. He owns only one 'Thomas' book, and certainly does not have any access to accoutrements such as pyjamas or nightlights, but he is able to hold his own with vigour and enthusiasm in discussions about Thomas with British and Canadian visitors. Reinforced as an expert on the topic, he continues his engagement with these popular stories.

Today we would add two very young children to this list:

- Alice, a Canadian baby, is 2 months old when she first starts attending carefully to Facetime conversations with her aunt and grandparents, who are known to her in face-to-face contact as well. Photographs show her sitting bolt upright and engaging with the image and voice, then peering round the back of the phone as if to locate the complete person whose face and voice are coming through the screen. By the time she is 6 months old, she responds to a Facetime game of peek-a-boo with her aunt with many giggles; and an ordinary voice-only telephone conversation puzzles her and causes her to look for the picture.

- Kieran, a British boy of 22 months, knows how to open games on his grandmother's mobile phone, adjust for audio and screen size, and make the requisite responses to the game's demands. When he tires of playing, he shifts to Grandma's stash of images, expertly sorting through the thumbnails of the still photographs in order to locate and play the videos of himself which are his favourites.

Our two new examples are both Western children, but mobile technology is ubiquitous in many parts of the world (see Appendix, Table 13.A.1 for a detailed international breakdown of ownership figures for mobile phones). Just as television is a global commonplace, so the mobile phone is just about everywhere. As smart technology becomes cheaper, an ever broader range of children will have greater access to the kind of personally contingent and salient participatory experience that Alice and Kieran already take for granted in their mediated lives.

Rather than worrying about this broad range of media experience as a kind of interference with the virtues of print literacy, it makes much more sense to explore the values of the enriched repertoires which these children are all enabled to bring to bear on their encounters with print, and *vice versa*. Their media experiences are undeniably assets in their literate lives, not only in relation to print but also in terms of more broadly conceived literacies.

But the deficit model is a concept with slippery rhetorical attributes that responds to different pressures over time. As access and attitudes shift, for example, it is now possible to see the marketers of infant DVDs begin to express the idea that parents should buy video texts for their babies in order to *counter* presumed deficits:

> A survey of the screen media market for children under 2 found that educational claims were nearly ubiquitous on baby products, and that marketers may be capitalizing on parental anxieties about normal child development and a presumed deficit when it comes to teaching their children the skills they need to be ready for school.
> (Wartella et al., 2010: 120)

The social, cultural, and economic context within which very young children make their way as media users is both complex and mutable; the changes within a single decade of domestic media use are extensive and sometimes contradictory.

It is difficult to express the complexities of the situation in which contemporary literacies are rooted without oversimplifying things. However, in Figure 13.1 we schematically indicate the major elements in the literacy engagement of a contemporary child: the child, the text, the community, and the broader environment. The ingredients in each quadrant should be read from the centre outwards and summarize the behaviours involved for each element. The questions on the spokes represent some important issues that arise in the overlap between the main players in this engagement. Around the outer perimeter we have indicated the wide range of texts we believe to be part of a child's experience of literacy in the modern world, many of which are dealt with more extensively in other chapters in this book but which need to be seen as a totality even where the discussion, as here, emphasizes televisual and printed texts.

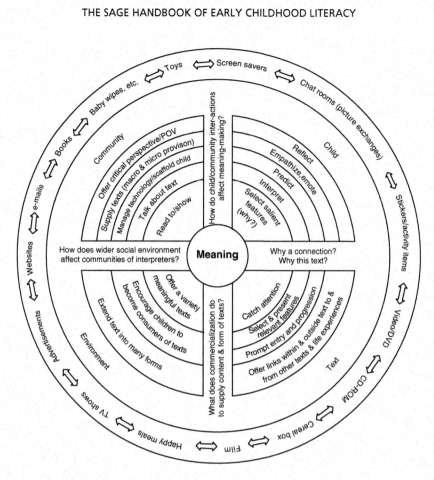

Figure 13.1   Literacy engagement of a contemporary child

In addition to learning how to interpret specific conventions of particular televisual texts, children also learn what programmes or films speak to their needs in a particular context. Meaning, as Livingstone (1990) reminds us, is negotiated between text and interpreter. Both are important and we ignore either at the risk of an impoverished understanding.

We developed this diagram 10 years ago without any anticipation of the way that a Skype or Facetime conversation or a home-loaded YouTube video might affect it. Without a doubt, such texts involve the child in new relationships with community and environment. Many children today,

more tomorrow, will learn about interpreting televisual texts in situations where the community and environment are known to them both in real life and also as part of their mediated world. Increasingly the adults and older siblings in their family will be watching televisual content sent to them through links on Facebook pages or recommended in other ways so that even individual viewing has a social element; they may well be in a context where others are engaging in shared response to programming through such media and are more likely than ever to be aware of such shared reader response. Our diagram presciently demonstrates why such a profoundly social development needs to be actively considered in the next round of research into infant understanding of the televisual.

THE CIVICS OF EARLY LITERACY: THE CHILD AND THE WIDER SOCIAL ENVIRONMENT

Social theories of literacy explore the situated practices that comprise literate engagements in particular contexts. Such approaches open up many complexities in how we observe and understand literacy, increasing our attention to the political, economic, social and cultural aspects of our interactions with texts. In Figure 13.1 we refer to the role of the environment in providing meaningful texts in many forms and in encouraging children to engage with them. In this section we look at how this happens and what impact it may have on children's developing understanding of literacies. This approach leads us to ask about the impact of commercialization on supply, content and form, questions which are only partly satisfactorily answered by the existing research (though the situation is much better than a decade ago) and which deserve fuller investigation.

Few, if any, contemporary children live in circumstances that actively exclude media exposure, yet some research is reluctant to acknowledge this reality. Livingstone points out how, for much modern sociology, the child is represented as living a *non-mediated* childhood: this is 'a carefree child playing hopscotch with friends in a nearby park, not a child with music on the headphones watching television in her bedroom' (1998: 438). The emergent literacies of small children often do not feature very significantly within the framework of

social theories of literacy. Kalantzis and Cope describe literacy teaching as 'always … a civic act' (2000: 140), but it is unusual to consider early literates as young citizens (though David Buckingham has made some interesting steps in this direction, [see, for example, Buckingham, 2000, 2011; de Block and Buckingham, 2010]). Small children are often not regarded as political, economic, social or cultural agents in their own right. Frequently we consider their main literate activity as *being read to*, a phrase that emphasizes passivity. Children's learning about literacy is still more often perceived as developmental or cognitive; they will achieve agency one day but for the present they are simply learning how to 'belong to the club' (Smith, 1983), in specific, observable, and non-political ways. Such a perspective denies the complexity of children's agency as they learn to place themselves within the world of multiple literacy demands. The new salience of the fact that it is easier for a relatively uncoordinated baby to push a button or press a space-bar than turn a book page means that very young children may gain forms of control over some of the non-print media accessible to them at an ever younger age. The consequent change in their first steps into agency over their mediated experiences needs to be taken seriously by those who are interested in the literacy of the very young.

Television plays a constituent role in the development of literacies in a variety of ways. Its address incorporates small children into the economic world from which we often assume they are naturally shielded. National variations in the quantity and address of advertising permitted on children's television also help to establish civic differences. Kenway and Bullen remind us of the complex relationship between Western consumer children and those children who produce the goods: 'Without doubt, the consuming child of the West is the beneficiary of labouring children of such countries as Indonesia, China and Pakistan' (2001: 37).

But the picture is not completely one-sided with TV as a purely Western phenomenon. Children all over the world watch television. The tables in the appendix provide a detailed breakdown of ownership figures for both colour and black-and-white television. The ubiquity of television is a significant social factor around the world, as these figures demonstrate. The global penetration of the mobile phone opens doors to other kinds of infant access to media, although, of course, the capacities of mobile telephones vary widely. With widespread domestic ownership, as manifested in the appendix, it is clear that small children everywhere are learning to make sense of televisual text.

Small children are, in fact, busy making sense of the whole world and responding to the different ways in which they are addressed. Even though adults may not explicitly notice the role of the toddler consumer, children use the information they are given and respond to the different ways they are spoken to.

Implicitly, scholars of early literacy do take note of the way that little children are integrated into society as consumers. We read descriptions of how children develop scripts that outline an expected sequence of events, and what to expect on a trip to McDonald's is sometimes presented as a neutral specimen of such scripts (for example, see Neuman, 1995: 21). Similarly, McDonald's golden arches are presented as an early exemplar of the interpretable symbol (Harste, Woodward, and Burke, 1984: 27). But televisual texts play a more complex role in children's lives than simply

developing their economic roles. Television locates children in an economic world, it provides information about the social world, it locates them as fully fledged participants in popular culture, and it also provides some forms of explicit instruction on literate behaviours – perhaps the most researched aspect of television experience for children. Programmes such as 'Sesame Street', 'The Teletubbies', 'Blue's Clues', and 'Reading Rainbow' are intensively studied both by those making the programmes and by outsiders (see, for example, Fisch et al., 1999, and Sell et al., 1995, on 'Sesame Street'; Anderson et al., 2000, on 'Blue's Clues'; Wood and Duke, 1997, on 'Reading Rainbow'; and Marsh, 2000, and Howard and Roberts, 2003, on 'The Teletubbies'). 'Sesame Street' in particular takes account of small children as international citizens with its production of many different national inserts for the programme.

Similarly the baby DVDs created by Disney for the 'Baby Einstein' label, for example, are beginning to attract the attention of researchers (see, for example, Anderson and Hanson, 2010; Courage and Setliff, 2010; Troseth, 2010; Wartella et al., 2010; Courage and Howe, 2010; Vandewater et al., 2010; Barr et al., 2007; Krcmar, 2011). Many of these studies and others like them focus on how much children can learn about their own worlds through watching televisual images; the idea of a deficit reappears in many of these works as the theory of the 'video deficit,' which posits that children find it difficult to transfer and apply information gleaned from a televisual image to affect their behaviour in the real world. Rather less attention appears to be paid to how young children learn to interpret screened images as a form of literacy, in other words how they learn to make sense of televisual images *within* the 2-D context of the DVD universe. Yet babies can learn to follow the pages of a book with every indication of attention and we do not ask them to demonstrate their awareness of a very hungry caterpillar in 'real life'. It seems possible that the focus on the degree to which infants can *apply* their newly acquired video knowledge may deal with only part of their developing awareness.

Louise Rosenblatt, as early as 1938, observed an equivalent focus on the informational elements of reading. She drew a distinction between efferent and aesthetic reading that may be helpful in helping us to consider new research into young children's viewing. Efferent reading calls upon the reader to 'narrow his attention to building up the meanings, the ideas, the directions to be retained; attention focuses on accumulating what is to be carried away at the end of the reading' (2005: 73). Aesthetic reading, by contrast, focuses on 'what is being created *during* the actual reading' (2005: 73). Readers, according to Rosenblatt, 'lend our sensations, our emotions, our sense of being alive, to the new experience' (2005: 75) that is evoked by the text. To what extent infants and toddlers can contribute this kind of attention to a televisual text is not entirely clear; our purpose is not to make any claims but to point out that the issue of simple infant pleasure in such texts is barely explored at all in the research we uncovered.

Efferent viewing, on the other hand, is much more extensively investigated. Researchers explore whether toddlers can learn new words from a televisual text, or can intuit where a researcher has hidden a toy in the next room when all the information comes through a video image. (See, for example, Strouse and Troseth, 2008; Krcmar, 2011, 2010; Barr et al., 2007; and many more.)

Viewing in real life, of course, is usually rather more casual in intent. Televisual images are presented to children in a variety of social contexts. In some households the television is on all the time as a matter of course and children must also learn strategies for ignoring it. In other households, there are strict rules and limits on viewing. Today, we must also always remember that access to screens does not stop with television sets; both commercial and domestic televisual content is also available through the increasingly available smartphones and iPads. Chiong and Shuler describe what they label a '*pass-back effect*' that occurs when an adult 'passes their own mobile device to a child' (2010: 7). Their report considers the role of apps in the lives of young children but does not pay much attention to the attractions of family photographs and videos or to how young children might view professionally-produced television on mobile devices.

Public discussion of the role of these screens in the lives of young children is contradictory. Courage and Howe outline two broadly divergent perspectives, and point out that both viewpoints are short on scientific backing:

One message comes from the influential American Academy of Pediatrics (AAP (1999, 2001) who issued strong public statements in which they recommended that children under 2 years of age not watch any television or video material at all, a position recently endorsed in a policy brief from the government of Australia (Get up and grow, 2009). Although no direct scientific evidence was provided to support the declaration by either of these groups, the implication clearly was that the time spent viewing video was time lost from play, language and social interactions that are viewed as essential to optimizing early brain growth and cognitive development. Perhaps as a result of the lack of clear and convincing evidence many parents have apparently ignored the recommendation . . .

An alternative message to parents comes largely from those within the media industry itself.

They contend that infant-directed video material can provide an opportunity to enhance early learning through educational content that focuses on themes such as language, shape, color, music, reading, and number that are embedded in an engaging and perceptually salient video format. This assertion is also provided without any direct evidence beyond parent testimonials. (2010: 101–2)

'In part,' say Courage and Howe,

the lack of definitive answers about the impact of baby video material on infant and toddler development lies in the fact that 'viewing television' is not a simple unitary activity and that getting to the heart of the matter requires systematic answers to a series of rather complex questions. These in turn, depend on factors related to the infant (e.g., age, cognitive level, temperament), the family and viewing contexts (e.g., parental education, co-viewing style, whether the material is foreground or background for the baby), and the material itself (e.g., adult- or child-directed, comprehensibility, production techniques used). (2010: 103)

We would draw on Rosenblatt to suggest that research also needs to take account of viewing stance; is the child trying to learn something or to engage with the experience of the moment with no other outcomes entailed or expected?

But Courage and Howe's list is a testimonial to progress in attempts to understand the viewing of very young children. Such sophisticated questions as they raise about baby viewing experiences were not really being asked 10 years ago, let alone answered. A special issue of *Developmental Review* in 2010 provides a good overview of the way in which research on these topics has blossomed over the past decade. Anderson and Hanson, in their contribution to this special issue, say the impetus to conduct such research arises out of some of the confusion around the topic. Their declaration entails a rejection of a deficit model approach as an *a priori* assumption. Like other contributors to this issue, they want to find out rather than simply assume.

This paper is motivated in part by the popularity of baby videos combined with the failure of many research studies to find learning from them. It is also motivated by the long debate over television and its impact on older children including the claim that television is a mindless activity. (2010: 240)

COMMUNITIES OF INTERPRETERS: CHILD–COMMUNITY INTERACTIONS AND MEANING MAKING

As well as being situated in a broadly defined social world, children are active members of a range of particular communities, all of which are themselves influenced by change in the wider environment, as well as being forces for change in turn. A significant factor for any user of media is the network of communities of interpreters we draw on when making meaning. Fish (1980) first set out the principle of interpretive communities as a way of describing the interactions by which we make meanings and assign intentions to texts as a collaborative act. We have extended the idea to describe the ways in which each of us belongs to a series of communities with whom we have a dialectic relationship, from which emerges our understanding of any text (Robinson, 1997). For young children, the communities of interpreters are particularly significant since one of the roles of the more experienced reader is to mediate the text to the child. As shown in Figure 13.1, the child relies on the community to read and show texts in the first instance, but also for talk about text, for help with the technology, for supply of texts and for a critical perspective and point of view. As we explore the ways in which this interaction happens, it is important also to ask, as we do in Figure 13.1, about the impact of such interactions on the meaning-making process.

A major change in the last decade involves the appearance of the personally salient community, not only as a collective support group for interpretation but also as the *subjects* of much video content. A baby who Facetimes with a relation does not do so alone, and both the adult at the baby's end of the conversation *and* the adult on the screen are scaffolding the infant's responses. The exchange is tailored to the baby's reactions and communicative efforts. The relationship between video and real-world understanding is radically shifted by such exchanges, especially when the interlocutor on the screen is well known to the child (a commonplace example of such exchanges may involve a parent at each end of the conversation and it is hard to imagine how the salience of such a conversation could be greater for the infant). The smartphone exchange (and to a lesser extent the video content stored on the cell phone itself or on a YouTube or Facebook entry) offers the infant an introduction to mediated life that engages with some of the most important people and settings of the child's daily routines. It is a potent combination that cries out for further study. At the same time, babies are exposed to more and more DVD material that is deliberately crafted to attract their attention through visual and audio cues and repetitions, enhancing their awareness of non-family video potential.

The Facetime exchange is just about impossible for a very young child to organize alone, so the scaffolding of adult company is normally part of the scenario. In contrast, although the makers of baby DVDs stress the importance of parents co-viewing with their child, such information as exists suggests that parents are more likely to seize the opportunity of baby viewing time to get on with household tasks (Courage and Setliff, 2010: 232).

THE CONTINUUM OF TEXTS: BOUNDARIES AND DIRECTIONALITY

We are increasingly aware that a simple opposition between printed books and televisual texts is an inadequate model of the complexities of textual interrelations which exist in the world today. The outer perimeter of Figure 13.1, as explained above, represents this complexity, but can only do so imperfectly: as Livingstone and Bovill point out, research on what are collectively known as new media 'involves studying a moving target' (1999: 1, 6). This chapter was originally intended to focus on television and literacy but to do so would present an artificial picture of the realities of reading today even for very young children.

Children retain access to 'old' forms of televisual experience: film, TV, DVD versions of both. Today they add forms that seem new to the adults in their lives but, of course, are simply part of the daily mix for the children themselves: specially produced DVDs, live video conversation, stored digital images and audio, interactive animations and games, video clips on the computer screen, and so forth.

At one level, it may not much matter which of these formats a child is watching, but in terms of the phenomenological detail of the experience there are substantial differences. Conventions designed for the big screen (pan shots, for example) 'read' differently on the small screen; close-ups designed for the intimacy of television viewing may appear differently if shown on a large screen by a digital projector (see Willems, 2000), or the tiny screen of a mobile phone. Even a brief analysis of each format reveals substantial differences in the quality of experience.

Film seen in a cinema is an 'event', with attendant rituals (sitting in separate seats in the dark, eating or at least smelling pop-corn), and usually involving planning and anticipation. The scale of the screen, the loudness of the surround sound, and the need for a certain level of social decorum all feature in the experience. In contrast, television is familiar and domestic, although this distinction has been blurred by the increasing tendency to buy very large screens and surround-sound equipment for domestic use. In December 2011 the Sharp Corporation increased its sales esti-mate of 60 and 70 inch screens to forecast that they would reach their North American target of one million sets sold through USA sales alone by March 2012 (www. hdtvtest.co.uk/news/sharp-big-screen-tv-usa-201112141569.htm, accessed 10 February 2012). In the main, whatever the size of the screen, television viewing occurs on a daily basis alongside many other mundane activities. Viewers may opt in and out of the experience as they choose. Children often attend to television in very partial ways, using sound as a cue for visual atten-tion, for example. Bickham et al. speak of the child as 'making continuous decisions about attention based on partial informa-tion' (2001: 105). With so many new ways of retrieving or rewinding televisual texts, however, viewers need not worry so much about seizing the moment. We know too little about the consequent impact on forms of attention.

Another highly salient quality of tele-vision is its 'flow' (Williams, 1974: 86), its ongoing continuity. A televiewing expe-rience may vary substantially according to whether it is a specially selected pro-gramme or a mere tuning into whatever happens to be onscreen at the moment. The flow includes station breaks, advertise-ments, previews of upcoming shows, as well as the programmes themselves, and viewers learn early that a discontinuous

form of viewing is often appropriate. However, 'flow' as described by Williams is based on a version of television hardly recognizable today. Routinely families will manage their viewing through devices and website provision allowing them to timeshift at will and to access almost any programme on demand. At the other extreme, increasingly there are specialist channels for children's programming which run continuously for several hours a day. It would be interesting to understand how these changes to the nature of televi-sion have affected children's experiences; are they more likely to be left to view spe-cialist children's channels unattended? Do they also learn to watch on demand at an early age? We did not find any studies on this topic.

In our first version of this chapter, we discussed video and DVD as different in format. As we rewrite, video has become almost a distant memory and DVD itself has become old technology, with online and downloadable material vying with DVD for consumer attention. Nevertheless, DVD remains a significant presence in children's lives. Watching a DVD is a domestic experience and the large-scale elements of movies are reduced to the smaller screen and more modest speakers of domestic equipment; often the DVD also represents a reformatting of material designed for film or television. At the same time, while the experience of watching a DVD resembles television viewing in many ways, it is not exactly the same, even in a world where increasingly TV is itself available on demand. Crucially, of course, the DVD is both skippable and repeatable. The viewer is much more in charge of the experience than with either film or television; and a DVD actually shares some qualities with a book in terms of ready accessibility and repeatability.

The browsability of a DVD, as with a book, offers random access. DVDs also offer the potential to watch the same scene with different soundtracks, so even a very young viewer can alternate between the diegetic soundtrack of the story itself and an explanatory commentary. DVDs first introduced the deleted scenes and outtakes that are now a feature of many children's intellectual understanding of the construction of story. Even an animated cartoon such as *Toy Story* or *Monsters, Inc.* will now include simulations of outtakes, and all but the very youngest viewers are expected to get the joke.

Children do still encounter a form of video through home movie production, though increasingly the video camera will be one of many features on a digital camera or mobile phone. Home video offers a route to a different kind of understanding of televisual experience, but its scale and impact are different according to how it is stored and reproduced; the intimacy of the mobile phone screen compensates to some degree for the smallness of scale, as compared to a computer. Children who live with a mobile phone equipped with a video camera may have access to a kind of do-it-yourself form of action replay of their own lives: 4-month-old Joseph reacts with apparent pleasure to video of his swimming lessons with his father, replayed on his mother's mobile phone. And the online conversation has different qualities of accessibility and scale according to whether it is screened through Skype on the computer or through Facetime on the small screen.

Some children will possess a broader range of such televisual experiences than others. Many contemporary Western children will be familiar with several of the items on the list; many non-Western children will have experience of at least one or two. The contents of these different formats may also vary. Children's viewing may include any or all of the following categories:

- story (real world or cartoon);
- information;
- a loose blend of the two (a child-oriented programme such as 'Sesame Street' or 'Baby Einstein' or an adult programme such as a cookery or a home makeover programme);
- recreational non-narrative such as sports;
- persuasive material (mainly in advertisements but also in other forms);
- music with associated visuals;
- domestic recordings, still and moving, with and without audio, with and without the capacity for being replayed instantly to the participants;
- live conversation with people elsewhere with associated visuals;
- interactive games with moving images that respond to the child's input.

All of these formats and many of these content areas 'leak'. Material that appears on television or film reappears in the child's world in many other ways: in books related to the televisual production, in toys and commodities, in environmental print of many different kinds. If film and television had no other impact on print literacy than to serve as a repertoire of background information, their role would still be significant.

Table 13.1 below represents a quick environmental scan of two websites: amazon.com and Google. The increase in numbers since we conducted a similar scan 10 years ago is exponential, and some of the totals are scarcely credible (and of course they are all suspect in that we did not vet carefully for duplications and the like). But however rough-and-ready our methodology, our table tells us something about the universe that today's young children take very much for granted.

Contemporary children grow up within the context of a multimedia bath of

Table 13.1   Three sets of texts with televisual connections

	Baby Einstein[1]	Sesame Street[1]	General Disney texts[1]
Total listings on amazon.com	3567	16,760	195,083
DVDs	284	352	11,118
Children's books	328	1546	3011
Toys and games	652	2641	34,462
Software/computer games	2	97	1621
Children's music	245	727	6462
Websites[2]	14,100,000	10,200,000	864,000,000

1 www.amazon.com, accessed 22 January 2012
2 www.google.com, accessed 22 January 2012

symbol systems. While adults readily differentiate print from audio from television from computer text, small children start from scratch and may observe these texts quite differently. It is striking how much of the research about television/film and print literacy works on the assumption that these operations represent discrete categories, when, as we see above, much of children's early textual experience washes across media boundaries. A noteworthy exception is the study by Livingstone and Bovill, which starts from a recognition that 'In their everyday lives children and young people weave together a huge diversity of activities. This interconnection across activities may be more or less *ad hoc*, but it may also be deliberate, as in the intertextual integration of content themes across diverse media forms.' (1999: 13).

Adults often see texts as operating in a single direction: first you have the original and then all the spin-offs. Child consumers of these texts often do not perceive such a singular directionality, and deal happily with a set of coexisting plurals.

Some elements transfer directly across media. In the simplest cases, as shown above, it is a straightforward reworking of familiar content. But access to a variety of media texts enables other kinds of transfers involving cognitive developments, such as the need to sort out the relationship between size and distance (see Abelman, 1989), or the development of story schemata (see Neuman, 1995; Tobin, 2000). Other aspects of literate processing of texts in different media are distinct: pace is determined by the producer in television and film (though video and DVD restore some control to the user) but it is negotiable in print, for example (though it may be a site of contestation between children and the adults reading to them) (see Wright et al., 1984, for a discussion of pace and attention in television).

A BROADER VIEW: WHERE TEXTS AND YOUNG CHILDREN CONNECT

In our view, the most useful research into the interrelationship between televisual and print literacies is that which takes account of the complexities outlined above. This is where, in Figure 13.1, the child and the text interact and we are led to ask about the nature of the connection and the reasons why particular texts resonate for particular children. Unfortunately, many of the studies that explore contemporary multiliteracies do not deal with the youngest children, and many studies that do focus on learning more than pleasure.

Those researchers who do take a holistic approach to the literacies of the youngest children often produce findings that confirm that children are aware of the complexities that surround them. As Sipe expresses it: 'it would seem that the children know that stories do not merely *lean* on other stories; stories are so *porous* to each other that they can be combined, stitched, woven together, and fused into more all-encompassing imbrications and palimpsests.' (2000: 85).

This observation is based on his analysis of children aged 5, 6, and 7, and their responses to the stories read to them at school. His young subjects make use of textual repertoires based in a variety of media, and televisual texts clearly fuel their developing understanding.

Dyson (1994, 1997, 1999, 2000; Genishi and Dyson, 2009) has worked for years with children aged between 6 and 9, and her full, rich reports of their literate lives are perhaps the most powerful contemporary testimony to how children make sense of the world through the use of an enormous variety of textual filters. Dyson's explorations of children's own written and drawn creations and their ongoing conversations provide deeper and more complex insights into their textual understandings than any amount of testing of the 'learning' of details could ever do, as the much fuller account of Dyson's work given by Marsh in this volume attests.

Marsh herself has been indefatigable in attending to the media lives of the very young (Marsh, 2000, 2008, 2010, 2011). She too undertakes complex explorations of how media experience for the very young is embedded in a social context.

PROCESSING ISSUES: DEALING WITH THE TEXT

It is often assumed that words are abstract entities made up of the straight and rounded lines of individual letters, and requiring intense training to decode, while moving images can be interpreted by the application of intuitive knowledge about the real world. Such assumptions do not acknowledge the true complexity of the situation, and in Figure 13.1 we have attempted to represent the need to consider the role of the child in processing the text and the need to examine the text to see how it prompts the child to engage with it and to make connections with other texts and with the world. Small children have much to learn before they can make sense of moving images.

The elements of print decoding are amply dealt with elsewhere in this book, so here we will concentrate on what is needed to interpret moving images, and the connections to print literacy. A primary requirement is to learn that the images represent three-dimensional 'reality'. Children who have access to home video images develop this understanding in a different way from those children whose viewing is confined to externally provided texts. Children who have access to one or many toys related to televisual texts with which they are familiar will also operate within a different ontological framework from those who only ever see the characters portrayed as moving images in the two dimensions of the screen. Little research explores these complex contingencies of what and how small children learn about comprehending moving images.

The grammar of cut, camera angle, zoom, and edit is not intuitively clear to young children. These elements of the moving image provide spatial and temporal information that young viewers must learn how to process into their final interpretation. Viewers must also learn to coordinate the language of soundtrack (musical underlining or foreshadowing, sound effects, dialogue) with the content of the images that run in parallel – not to mention the more complex processing challenge when the soundtrack for one scene continues to underlie a change of visual images. Much evidence suggests that small children actually make use of the audio-track to help them decide when to expend visual attention on the screen (see, for example, Rolandelli et al., 1991; Calvert and Scott, 1989; Calvert, 2001). As with print processing, comprehension of these features must reach a level of automaticity before it can be relied on not to interfere with the creation of meaning; the interpretation of moving images, like the interpretation of print, calls for an ability to orchestrate many sources of information within the limits of a finite capacity for attention.

There is rather more research on the subject of modality, of how children develop an understanding of the relationship of a particular set of moving images to reality. Early on, children distinguish between cartoons and images of real people. Their grasp of the fictionality of live-action drama and of the relationship to daily life of the news and documentaries is more subtly developed (Hodge and Tripp, 1986; Flavell et al., 1990; Howard, 1994, 1996; Chandler, 1997). Comparable work with print fiction (Lewis, 2001) shows that the idea of fiction in print is also a complex conceptual development. It is, of course, rather more difficult with print to operate a default position that all images are real until proven otherwise. Television, with its moving images of real people, is often misleadingly close to our own daily

experience and children must learn the ontological implications of the framing mechanisms. This task is complicated by the modality variations of the daily television schedule in particular, as news, advertisements, cartoons, game shows, and dramatic representations mingle on the screen. Film, video and DVD, in contrast, are usually framed apart from real life in various formal and pragmatic ways and need rather less sorting out. Mobile interactive formats function in a wide variety of contexts; their very portability is probably the main framing element.

In addition to developing generic understandings of conventions, modality, and the framing of different formats, children learn to make local decisions about how to attend to any given programme. Bickham et al., in an attempt to resolve the active and passive models of television viewing into a single and more useful picture, describe a viewer as engaged in moment-to-moment decisions:

> As sampling occurs, the viewer gains information from the features observed. Animation, character voices, and production style can notify the viewer of content type, age of intended audience, and other program-specific information. The viewer, now more knowledgeable about the show's content, can consider specific cognitive and motivational questions: Is this a program I recognize? Is it a program for people like me? Can I understand it? Does it meet my current viewing goals? Will it be fun to watch? Positive answers to these questions lead to further attention. This attention, however, is constantly re-evaluated: Am I understanding this? How much mental energy is required to continue to understand? Is this memorable enough to merit my investment of energy? Transitions in the program elicit a requestioning of the current attentional state based on the cognitive and motivational goals of the child viewer. (2001: 108)

Television is based on a flow of programming but it is a flow designed to take interruptions into account, and thus more resembles magazine reading with a series of relatively short items loosely linked together – spatially in the case of a print magazine, temporally on television. Child viewers learn to manage their own attention in the context of this flow.

CONVENTIONS OF INTERPRETATION

We would argue that one reason why the research we have been citing fails in many cases to illuminate our understandings of the ways in which children in the early years become literate across a range of media is that the questions which would allow such an understanding to be developed have rarely been asked. One starting point for future work would be to consider conventions of interpretation in different media and how these might be learned. Rabinowitz (1987) has produced a useful list of grouped protocols for interpretation which could be used in this way and which informed the development of our diagram. He bases them on conventional nineteenth- and twentieth-century narrative prose and calls them, somewhat misleadingly, 'rules of reading'. It is instructive to apply his 'rules' to the processes of televisual interpretation, for they have a generic utility that draws out surprising parallels.

Rabinowitz's first rules are the *rules of notice*. How do you decide what to pay attention to? In print, there are numerous conventions for attracting notice: something mentioned in a sentence that opens or closes a paragraph, for example, receives extra attention; a single-sentence paragraph receives even more. Chapter titles, punctuation, repetition, question and answer may all draw attention.

What are the televisual parallels? Obviously camera angles, zooms, and close-ups are features that attract and direct attention, perhaps even more peremptorily than their print counterparts. The grammar of these televisual rules of notice is no more intuitive than the print version; viewers, like readers, have to learn how to interpret these pointers. Clearly the audiotrack also has an important role to play in establishing what to notice.

Rules of signification are applied after rules of notice. When we have decided what to pay attention to, we must then decide how to attend to it. Is a narrator reliable? Is a character trustworthy? Is a particular account of a situation merely a set-up to delude unwary readers? What is going on that the author or director is *not* drawing our attention to?

With televisual texts, one element of signification that we probably need to take account of is the trustworthiness of the camera angle. What is happening outside the range of the viewfinder? Other ingredients are extraneous to the internal world of the story but highly relevant to our interpretive operation: for example, if we recognize a well-known actor we are likely to attend to that character rather differently, at least initially, expecting her to play an important part in the story. A significant character can be 'slid into' a print story rather more unobtrusively in many cases.

Rabinowitz's third category involves the *rules of configuration*. These protocols help us to assemble the elements of the story into a workable whole. An event early in the story will likely have consequences later on. Rabinowitz's account of this convention is that in a story we can expect that *something* will happen but that *not anything* can happen once the parameters of the story are laid down. Genre expectations feed into how we put plot elements together. Whether our expectations are met or shattered, they still play a part in how we construct the story.

Of all the protocols, the rules of configuration are the most straightforward and apply the most universally across media. If a character forgets her keys in the early stages of a story, we are entitled to expect some later outcome of that event and our anticipation of such a development plays a part in how we compose the story. Whether this happens televisually or in print is not a major consideration.

The final set of protocols is the *rules of coherence*, which we generally apply after we have finished the story. These enable us to make the best possible sense of the story as a whole. We tidy loose ends, decide where particular details fit into the story as a whole, reinterpret events and characters – and also gaps and/or excesses – so they make metaphoric or thematic sense.

Partly because they are retrospectively applied, there is likely to be a stronger social element in the assessment of the rules of coherence. It is rather more likely that a televisual text will be experienced socially in the first place, and discussions about coherence often follow quickly: witness the cinema-goers discussing the film as they leave the theatre or the television viewers commenting on the latest episode of a favourite programme on the playground next morning. Occasionally a print story will create its own powerful community that operates on a relatively immediate basis. For example, the drive to acquire and read the newest 'Harry Potter' title was at least partly related to the urge to participate in the first conversations after the story was finished; a strong social imperative is mingled with the private experience of the text.

Rabinowitz does not explore the activities of readers to validate his categories of rules, and there is not space here to extend this discussion to detail how these rules might be understood in print and televisual literacy; but one of us has made substantial use of his interpretive schema and found it to apply usefully both to print and also to texts in other media (see Mackey, 2002, 2007). It would be valuable to extend and develop this work with a wider group of younger children.

A common metaphor for the reading process is orchestration (Chittenden et al., 2001: 73). In terms of reading televisual media, the metaphor holds good. The selection of what is relevant and helpful may be more complex where the text has many potential channels through which to offer information. So a televisual text, with its range of points of view, movement, multiple voices, background music, sound effects and even subtitles, offers a rich experience from which to select. But as Lewis (2001) has shown, the polysemic world of picturebooks offers a challenge of similar kind to the beginning reader: do they choose between competing stories in *Come Away from the Water, Shirley* (Burningham, 1977), or attempt to synthesize the two? Across all media, to use Margaret Meek's (1988) famous phrase, texts teach what readers learn.

Research into very young children has tended to work at a relatively simplistic level with regard to television. Thus we know that young children are more likely to pay attention to a programme if there is sound and vision than to vision alone (Hollenbeck and Slaby, 1979), but not much about how young children construe meaning from the range of sources which is offered. It seems that some codes are learned very young; Verónica at three and a half chose to tell us that some of the music in *Dinosaur* was *muy feo* (very ugly or nasty) and that this meant something bad was going to happen. More systematic research into such phenomena might add to our understanding of the interactions between the processes of becoming literate in a range of media more helpfully than the more limited research currently available.

MAPPING THE TERRITORY

In this chapter we have attempted to show what we already know from research about the complex interrelationships of print and televisual literacies and how children become expert meaning makers of all kinds of texts. Although there is a huge corpus of research into certain aspects of this territory, there are still too many areas which seem to us to be central but which have been neglected by research. There is a tendency to study what is easily measurable rather than to start, as Dyson and Marsh do, by observing what children are doing and trying to understand the significance of their behaviour and what it shows about how the key lessons of cross-media literacy are learned. Other very valuable work focuses on either televisual or print texts rather than on the interaction between the two; we need more research into the interconnections among different literacies.

In Figure 13.1 we set out a series of issues concerning the interaction between the four quadrants of our diagram. Throughout the chapter we have attempted to show what evidence is available to answer such questions with regard to young children. To summarize, we believe that if we are to understand fully how children under seven learn to be literate across a range of printed and televisual texts, we need to ask not simply separate questions about the ways the child learns to process information, the ways in which the texts themselves invite interpretation, and the roles of the community and the wider environment in developing children as literate members of society. We have begun to suggest the questions which allow the *interaction* of child, text, community and environment to be problematized and have argued that much existing research

fails to address these crossover questions sufficiently.

We have argued that the earlier corpus of research based on a deficit model is fundamentally flawed, since it sets up oppositions between print and television which cannot be justified. We have suggested that a more helpful way forward might be an asset model, which looks at what children actually do and how their understandings are extended by encounters with a wide range of texts, mediated by the interpretive communities to which they belong and by the broader social contexts in which they live. More current research does address this complexity in more fruitful ways but we have argued that its efferent focus on learning effects has excluded consideration of the child viewer's aesthetic reaction. We still need more researchers who are attempting to answer the questions we identified in Figure 13.1. We have suggested that one constructive way forward would be to build on Rabinowitz's 'rules of reading' reinterpreted as conventions of interpretation. What is clear is that, despite the huge corpus of work which purports to explore the nature of children's literacy development, we still have few real answers as to how the four quadrants of our diagram – child, text, community and environment – work together as young children become literate. As the media world of even the youngest children becomes ever more complex, more multifaceted research is urgently needed.

NOTE

The authors would like to thank Jody Mendenhall and Shelagh Genuis, both of the University of Alberta, Canada, for their contributions to the 2012 and 2002 literature searches that underpin this chapter.

APPENDIX

Table 13.A.1　Percentage of households with mobile telephone, 2006–2011

Country	2006	2007	2008	2009	2010	2011
Algeria	55.7	68.0	80.0	93.8	96.1	96.9
Argentina	41.8	50.3	57.8	64.5	69.5	73.6
Australia	85.9	87.8	89.4	90.7	91.7	92.6
Austria	90.6	91.9	92.5	99.0	99.6	99.7
Azerbaijan	59.8	70.6	81.7	85.5	88.0	89.9
Bahrain	89.3	91.0	92.1	92.9	93.5	93.8
Belarus	52.0	61.4	68.6	74.0	78.7	82.0
Belgium	90.0	91.6	92.9	93.7	94.3	94.6
Bolivia	48.1	57.0	66.1	73.6	79.5	83.7
Bosnia-Herzegovina	63.2	71.0	74.8	76.4	77.3	78.0
Brazil	26.2	31.7	37.6	41.2	44.5	47.7
Bulgaria	64.0	66.6	70.1	73.5	76.2	78.6
Cameroon	41.2	47.9	54.6	59.7	63.7	66.9
Canada	67.7	71.4	73.2	77.2	78.3	80.6
Chile	75.3	78.8	81.7	83.7	85.4	86.7
China	73.8	80.5	84.9	87.8	89.8	91.2
Colombia	63.7	75.7	83.8	87.2	90.5	92.3
Costa Rica	56.4	60.4	69.2	69.5	69.7	69.9
Croatia	85.4	89.9	92.8	94.7	96.0	96.7
Czech Republic 98.4	99.0	99.3	99.4	99.4	99.4	
Denmark	94.0	95.0	95.0	98.0	97.0	97.0
Dominican Republic	56.4	68.6	75.9	80.4	82.5	84.0
Ecuador	63.8	66.8	69.9	73.7	80.1	87.7
Egypt	30.2	35.5	40.5	45.0	49.1	52.7
Estonia	83.0	87.0	90.0	92.3	93.9	94.9
Finland	95.5	97.0	97.3	97.5	97.8	98.0
France	74.3	76.9	78.9	80.4	81.7	82.9
Georgia	68.5	76.8	81.6	84.4	86.8	88.6
Germany	80.6	81.8	86.3	86.7	87.2	87.6
Greece	79.5	82.2	85.0	87.3	89.2	90.8
Guatemala	39.7	44.4	47.5	49.6	51.2	52.3
Hong Kong, China	97.1	98.3	99.0	99.3	99.4	99.5
Hungary	84.4	86.4	88.0	90.4	91.9	92.8
India	21.9	26.3	30.2	33.6	37.3	41.1
Indonesia	27.3	33.7	39.3	44.7	49.4	53.4
Iran	32.8	37.0	40.7	43.5	45.3	46.6
Ireland	90.0	91.1	92.2	93.2	94.2	95.2
Israel	87.2	89.3	90.7	91.8	92.7	93.5
Italy	83.9	85.8	87.3	87.8	88.5	89.4
Japan	88.0	90.5	90.2	92.7	94.4	95.6
Jordan	67.7	84.1	93.7	97.1	98.8	99.5

(Continued)

Table 13.A.1 (Continued)

Country	2006	2007	2008	2009	2010	2011
Kazakhstan	66.0	73.5	78.0	81.4	84.2	86.4
Kenya	41.7	52.2	61.5	67.7	72.4	76.1
Kuwait	92.1	93.4	94.3	95.0	95.7	96.2
Latvia	85.0	90.4	93.4	95.6	97.1	98.2
Lithuania	77.0	77.5	81.9	87.0	89.5	91.0
Macedonia	71.0	77.9	78.5	82.4	84.9	86.5
Malaysia	79.1	84.6	89.4	92.6	94.5	95.4
Mexico	47.0	55.2	58.5	61.9	65.1	68.0
Montenegro	85.7	87.0	89.0	92.2	94.5	95.7
Morocco	59.1	76.9	81.2	83.6	85.1	86.4
Netherlands	92.0	92.9	93.7	94.3	94.8	95.1
New Zealand	77.0	78.5	79.9	81.3	82.6	83.7
Nigeria	28.5	41.8	49.7	56.0	60.5	63.9
Norway	95.0	97.0	97.9	98.6	99.0	99.3
Pakistan	13.8	19.5	24.2	27.8	31.5	34.4
Peru	28.1	42.9	51.6	59.1	65.2	69.6
Philippines	56.6	63.1	70.1	75.7	79.3	81.8
Poland	73.1	79.3	83.5	86.5	88.7	90.4
Portugal	85.6	87.2	87.0	87.4	88.1	89.0
Qatar	89.3	91.0	92.4	93.3	94.0	94.5
Romania	76.7	82.4	86.6	90.2	92.7	94.3
Russia	71.9	80.4	86.6	90.9	93.9	96.1
Saudi Arabia	90.2	91.9	94.0	95.1	96.1	96.7
Serbia	64.4	67.6	72.3	73.2	74.1	74.9
Singapore	98.2	98.9	99.4	99.7	99.8	99.9
Slovakia	85.4	88.5	88.5	87.2	88.5	88.7
Slovenia	86.3	88.5	89.7	90.6	91.3	91.9
South Africa	67.5	72.9	80.1	84.8	87.8	90.1
South Korea	97.2	97.7	98.1	98.4	98.8	99.1
Spain	89.1	90.9	92.1	93.5	94.6	95.5
Sweden	95.0	96.2	97.3	98.0	98.5	98.9
Switzerland	87.5	88.9	90.3	91.5	92.6	93.4
Taiwan	94.8	96.5	97.8	98.8	99.6	100.0
Thailand	70.7	74.2	77.2	80.0	82.0	83.8
Tunisia	64.0	70.8	75.9	79.6	82.6	84.7
Turkey	80.0	86.1	87.2	87.6	88.1	88.5
Turkmenistan	5.0	6.4	7.7	8.9	10.0	11.1
Ukraine	30.9	53.9	76.8	80.5	84.2	87.4
United Arab Emirates	94.0	96.2	97.6	98.5	99.1	99.3
UK	79.2	78.4	79.0	81.0	82.5	83.8
Uruguay	48.9	57.7	64.9	70.9	74.9	78.5
USA	90.5	94.1	96.1	97.3	97.8	98.1
Uzbekistan	8.7	10.9	13.1	14.9	16.7	18.3
Venezuela	39.1	40.2	41.3	42.3	43.2	44.1
Vietnam	12.0	17.3	22.4	27.5	32.2	36.2

Source: Possession of Mobile Telephone: Euromonitor International from national statistics
Date Exported (GMT): 25/01/2012 02:54:46 © Euromonitor International

Table 13.A.2 Percentage of households with colour television, 2006–2011

Country	2006	2007	2008	2009	2010	2011
Algeria	90.8	91.8	92.7	93.6	94.3	94.8
Argentina	94.9	95.4	95.9	96.3	96.7	97.1
Australia	98.9	99.0	99.1	99.2	99.3	99.3
Austria	95.0	97.0	96.8	96.6	96.6	96.6
Azerbaijan	84.3	87.2	90.1	91.9	93.2	94.2
Bahrain	98.3	98.6	98.9	99.2	99.3	99.5
Belarus	93.6	94.1	94.6	95.0	95.3	95.6
Belgium	96.0	96.1	96.1	96.2	96.2	96.3
Bolivia	64.7	66.5	68.7	69.9	70.7	71.4
Bosnia-Herzegovina	91.1	91.4	91.9	92.2	92.6	92.8
Brazil	93.0	94.5	95.1	95.3	95.4	95.6
Bulgaria	87.6	88.9	90.0	90.9	91.7	92.4
Cameroon	25.1	30.7	31.9	32.9	33.8	34.5
Canada	99.0	98.9	98.8	98.9	99.0	99.0
Chile	93.0	93.9	94.6	95.3	95.9	96.3
China	93.2	95.3	96.1	96.5	96.6	96.8
Colombia	81.6	85.4	88.5	90.4	91.5	92.3
Costa Rica	93.7	94.9	95.8	95.9	95.8	95.9
Croatia	94.9	96.2	97.4	99.0	99.6	99.8
Czech Republic	97.5	97.9	98.2	98.4	98.7	98.9
Denmark	98.0	98.0	98.0	98.0	98.0	98.0
Dominican Republic	76.6	77.4	78.1	78.8	79.4	79.9
Ecuador	78.9	81.1	83.3	82.7	85.1	85.4
Egypt	82.0	85.4	88.2	90.1	91.4	92.4
Estonia	95.0	96.0	96.9	97.4	97.7	98.0
Finland	95.0	95.1	95.1	95.2	95.2	95.2
France	97.0	97.3	97.1	97.0	97.0	97.0
Georgia	89.3	89.8	90.3	90.8	91.2	91.5
Germany	95.2	95.9	94.1	95.9	97.6	98.6
Greece	98.7	98.7	98.7	98.7	98.7	98.7
Guatemala	68.6	69.8	70.9	72.0	72.9	73.7
Hong Kong, China	99.5	99.5	99.5	99.5	99.6	99.6
Hungary	99.0	99.4	99.6	99.7	99.8	99.9
India	45.9	50.2	55.0	60.2	63.6	65.9
Indonesia	68.1	68.7	69.3	69.8	70.4	70.9
Iran	88.1	88.4	88.7	88.9	89.1	89.3
Ireland	98.0	98.1	98.1	98.2	98.2	98.2
Israel	91.2	90.5	90.1	89.9	89.8	89.9
Italy	96.2	96.4	96.6	96.8	96.9	97.0
Japan	99.5	99.7	99.4	99.4	99.4	99.5
Jordan	89.7	91.1	92.2	93.1	94.0	94.7
Kazakhstan	93.1	94.0	94.7	95.3	95.7	96.1
Kenya	24.2	26.5	28.6	30.4	32.0	33.4

(Continued)

Table 13.A.2 (*Continued*)

Country	2006	2007	2008	2009	2010	2011
Kuwait	98.8	98.8	98.8	98.9	98.9	98.9
Latvia	94.8	95.3	95.8	96.2	96.5	96.7
Lithuania	96.0	97.0	98.0	98.3	98.4	98.5
Macedonia	96.3	96.5	96.5	96.9	97.1	97.1
Malaysia	96.1	96.9	97.7	98.1	98.4	98.6
Mexico	93.4	93.3	93.2	93.3	93.5	93.8
Montenegro	99.6	97.7	97.8	98.7	98.1	98.4
Morocco	76.5	75.9	76.2	77.1	78.1	79.1
Netherlands	98.7	98.8	99.0	99.1	99.3	99.4
New Zealand	98.5	98.6	98.6	98.6	98.7	98.7
Nigeria	33.3	34.3	39.3	41.3	42.8	44.0
Norway	95.0	95.3	95.6	95.8	96.0	96.1
Pakistan	55.7	55.7	55.7	55.8	56.0	56.1
Peru	57.3	61.0	64.0	66.2	67.9	69.5
Philippines	69.3	70.4	71.1	71.7	72.4	72.9
Poland	96.9	97.1	97.5	97.8	98.0	98.1
Portugal	99.5	99.4	99.3	99.3	99.3	99.3
Qatar	97.7	97.8	97.9	97.9	98.0	98.0
Romania	88.0	90.7	92.6	93.9	94.8	95.7
Russia	93.9	5.1	96.1	96.8	97.3	97.6
Saudi Arabia	97.5	97.7	97.9	98.0	98.1	98.3
Serbia	96.0	96.0	96.1	97.1	97.5	97.8
Singapore	99.4	99.4	99.4	99.4	99.5	99.5
Slovakia	97.9	98.7	99.0	99.2	99.3	99.4
Slovenia	96.6	96.5	97.1	97.4	97.6	97.8
South Africa	64.4	66.6	68.9	71.1	73.0	74.7
South Korea	96.5	96.5	96.6	96.6	96.7	96.7
Spain	99.6	99.5	99.7	99.6	99.5	99.5
Sweden	97.3	97.5	97.7	97.9	98.0	98.1
Switzerland	94.4	94.5	94.6	94.6	94.7	94.8
Taiwan	99.6	99.4	99.4	99.6	99.7	99.7
Thailand	92.0	92.1	92.3	92.5	92.7	92.9
Tunisia	78.1	80.5	82.9	84.7	86.1	87.5
Turkey	93.4	93.8	94.2	94.6	94.9	95.1
Turkmenistan	73.9	74.7	75.2	75.6	76.0	76.3
Ukraine	88.7	91.3	93.9	94.5	95.0	95.5
United Arab Emirates	99.8	99.8	99.8	99.9	99.9	99.9
UK	99.0	99.0	99.0	99.0	99.0	99.0
Uruguay	90.7	90.6	90.6	90.6	90.6	90.6
USA	98.6	98.8	98.9	99.0	99.1	99.2
Uzbekistan	80.2	81.0	81.6	82.0	82.4	82.7
Venezuela	89.7	90.8	91.7	92.4	93.0	93.6
Vietnam	78.2	82.6	86.9	89.7	91.8	93.6

Source: Possession of Colour TV Set: Euromonitor International from national statistics
Date Exported (GMT): 25/01/2012 02:54:46 © Euromonitor International

Table 13.A.3   Percentage of households with black and white television, 2006–2011

Country	2006	2007	2008	2009	2010	2011
Algeria	13.1	11.9	10.8	10.0	9.3	8.6
Argentina	1.3	1.1	0.9	0.7	0.5	0.4
Australia	1.5	1.2	1.0	0.8	0.6	0.5
Austria	1.1	1.0	0.9	0.8	0.8	0.7
Azerbaijan	22.7	22.2	19.0	18.4	17.4	15.8
Bahrain	0.5	0.3	0.2	0.2	0.1	0.1
Belarus	9.8	8.0	6.4	5.1	4.0	3.1
Belgium	2.6	2.3	1.9	1.7	1.4	1.2
Bolivia	15.8	14.6	13.4	12.3	11.3	10.3
Bosnia-Herzegovina	5.2	3.8	2.8	2.0	1.5	1.0
Brazil	2.0	1.4	0.9	0.4	0.2	0.1
Bulgaria	10.5	9.1	8.0	6.9	6.1	5.3
Cameroon	13.8	12.3	11.1	10.0	8.9	8.0
Canada	3.0	2.6	2.3	2.0	1.8	1.5
Chile	4.0	2.8	1.9	1.3	0.9	0.6
China	11.5	9.1	6.9	5.3	4.2	3.3
Colombia	3.4	2.7	2.0	1.5	1.1	0.8
Costa Rica	4.4	3.6	2.9	2.5	2.0	1.7
Croatia	6.0	4.4	3.2	2.3	1.7	1.2
Czech Republic	4.5	3.8	3.1	2.4	1.9	1.6
Denmark	1.6	1.5	1.3	1.2	1.1	1.0
Dominican Republic	5.4	4.5	3.7	3.1	2.6	2.1
Ecuador	16.3	14.3	12.1	10.1	8.1	6.5
Egypt	16.1	12.2	8.1	5.6	4.0	2.9
Estonia	4.4	3.4	2.5	1.8	1.4	1.0
Finland	2.1	1.7	1.4	1.1	0.9	0.7
France	1.3	1.1	0.9	0.7	0.6	0.5
Georgia	11.3	9.4	8.0	6.7	5.6	4.7
Germany	0.8	0.7	0.7	0.6	0.6	0.6
Greece	2.3	2.0	1.8	1.6	1.5	1.3
Guatemala	5.6	4.6	3.8	3.1	2.6	2.2
Hong Kong, China	1.1	0.9	0.7	0.5	0.4	0.3
Hungary	3.1	2.4	1.8	1.4	1.1	0.8
India	18.3	16.2	14.6	13.3	12.1	11.0
Indonesia	15.8	13.9	12.3	10.8	9.5	8.3
Iran	3.0	2.7	2.5	2.2	2.0	1.8
Ireland	0.1	0.1	0.1	0.0	0.0	0.0
Israel	3.3	2.7	2.2	1.8	1.5	1.2
Italy	2.3	2.0	1.8	1.6	1.5	1.3
Japan		0.7	0.5	0.3	0.2	0.2
Jordan	17.4	15.9	14.6	13.3	12.2	11.2
Kazakhstan	26.1	24.4	22.7	21.1	19.6	18.2
Kenya	7.8	7.1	6.5	5.9	5.5	5.0

(Continued)

Table 13.A.3 (*Continued*)

Country	2006	2007	2008	2009	2010	2011
Kuwait	0.2	0.1	0.1	0.1	0.0	0.0
Latvia	5.3	4.4	3.6	3.0	2.5	2.1
Lithuania	7.0	5.0	3.0	2.2	1.7	1.3
Macedonia	3.8	4.8	3.2	2.7	2.3	2.0
Malaysia	0.6	0.5	0.4	0.3	0.2	0.2
Mexico	9.9	8.2	6.8	5.6	4.6	3.8
Montenegro	8.1	6.6	5.5	4.5	3.8	3.2
Morocco	18.0	15.7	13.9	12.3	10.7	9.2
Netherlands	4.4	3.9	3.4	3.0	2.6	2.3
New Zealand	1.7	1.3	1.0	0.8	0.6	0.5
Nigeria	8.2	6.8	6.0	5.3	4.6	4.1
Norway	1.9	1.7	1.6	1.5	1.4	1.3
Pakistan	8.4	7.7	7.1	6.6	6.1	5.4
Peru	24.8	15.5	2.2	10.4	8.8	7.5
Philippines	14.6	12.7	11.0	9.5	8.3	7.2
Poland	1.1	0.8	0.6	0.4	0.3	0.2
Portugal	4.4	3.8	3.3	2.9	2.6	2.2
Qatar	0.4	0.3	0.2	0.2	0.1	0.1
Romania	9.3	6.1	2.4	0.6	0.1	0.0
Russia	7.2	6.0	5.0	4.3	3.7	3.2
Saudi Arabia	0.8	0.6	0.4	0.3	0.2	0.2
Serbia	8.0	6.6	5.4	4.5	3.7	3.1
Singapore	0.5	0.4	0.3	0.2	0.1	0.1
Slovakia	3.2	2.8	2.4	2.1	1.8	1.6
Slovenia	2.8	4.7	5.6	5.5	4.9	4.2
South Africa	4.0	3.4	2.8	2.3	1.9	1.5
South Korea	1.2	0.9	0.7	0.6	0.5	0.4
Spain	2.2	2.0	1.7	1.5	1.4	1.2
Sweden	2.2	1.7	1.4	1.1	0.8	0.7
Switzerland	1.9	1.8	1.8	1.7	1.6	1.6
Taiwan	1.5	1.2	0.9	0.7	0.5	0.4
Thailand	1.5	1.2	0.9	0.6	0.4	0.3
Tunisia	18.6	17.3	16.1	14.9	13.9	12.9
Turkey	10.7	9.3	7.9	6.8	5.7	4.8
Turkmenistan	22.7	20.3	18.1	16.1	14.4	12.9
Ukraine	11.9	9.1	6.3	5.0	4.1	3.4
United Arab Emirates	0.3	0.2	0.1	0.1	0.1	0.0
UK	0.4	0.3	0.3	0.2	0.2	0.2
Uruguay	1.7	1.5	1.2	0.9	0.8	0.6
USA	2.4	2.1	1.8	1.6	1.4	1.2
Uzbekistan	23.9	21.9	20.0	18.2	16.7	15.2
Venezuela	7.5	6.3	5.3	4.6	4.0	3.5
Vietnam	10.2	8.7	7.4	6.3	5.4	4.6

Source: Possession of Black and White TV Set: Euromonitor International from national statistics Date Exported (GMT): 25/01/2012 02:54:46 © Euromonitor International

REFERENCES

Abelman, R. (1989) 'From here to eternity: children's acquisition of understanding of projective size on television', *Human Communication Research*, 15(3): 463–81.

Anderson, D.R. and Hanson, K.F. (2010) 'From blooming, buzzing confusion to media literacy: the early development of television viewing', *Developmental Review*, 30: 239–55.

Anderson, D.R., Bryant, J., Wilder, A., Santomero, A., Williams, M., and Crawley, A.M. (2000) 'Researching *Blue's Clues*: viewing behavior and impact', Research Synthesis Essay, *Media Psychology*, 2: 179–94.

Barr, R., Muentenor, P., Garcia, A., Fujimoto, M., and Chavez, V. (2007) 'The effect of repetition on imitation from television during infancy', *Developmental Psychobiology*, 49(2): 196–207.

Barton, D. and Hamilton, M. (1998) *Local Literacies: Reading and Writing in One Community*. London: Routledge.

Bickham, D.S., Wright, J.C., and Huston, A.C. (2001) 'Attention, comprehension, and the educational influences of television', in D.G. Singer and J.L. Singer (eds), *Handbook of Children and the Media*. Thousand Oaks, CA: Sage. pp. 101–19.

Buckingham, D. (2000) *The Making of Citizens: Young People, News and Politics*. London: Routledge.

Buckingham, D. (2011) *The Material Child*. Cambridge: Polity.

Burningham, J. (1977) *Come Away from the Water, Shirley*. New York: Crowell.

Calvert, S.L. (2001) 'Impact of televised songs on children's and young adults' memory of educational content', *Media Psychology*, 3: 325–42.

Calvert, S.L. and Scott, M.C. (1989) 'Sound effects for children's temporal integration of fast-paced television content', *Journal of Broadcasting and Electronic Media*, 33(3): 233–46.

Chiong, C. and Shuler, C. (2010) *Learning: Is There an App for That? Investigations of Young Children's Usage and Learning with Mobile Devices and Apps*. New York: Joan Ganz Cooney Center at Sesame Workshop.

Chittenden, E. and Salinger, T. with Bussis, A.M. (2001) *Inquiry into Meaning: an Investigation of Learning to Read*, rev. edn. New York: Teachers College Press.

Clark, C., Woodley, J., and Lewis, F. (2011) *The Gift of Reading in 2011: Children and Young People's Access to Books and Attitudes towards Reading*. London: National Literacy Trust.

Chandler, D. (1997) 'Children's understanding of what is "real" on television: a review of the literature', *Journal of Educational Media*, 23 (1): 67–82.

Courage, M.L. and Howe, M.L. (2010) 'To watch or not to watch: infants and toddlers in a brave new electronic world', *Developmental Review*, 30: 101–15.

Courage, M.L. and Setliff, A.E. (2010) 'When babies watch television: attention-getting, attention-holding, and the implications for learning from video material', *Developmental Review*, 30: 220–38.

de Block, L. and Buckingham, D. (2010) *Global Children, Global Media: Migration, Media and Childhood*, Basingstoke: Palgrave Macmillan.

Dyson, A.H. (1994) The Ninjas, the X-Men, and the Ladies: Playing with Power and Identity in an Urban Primary School. National Center for the Study of Writing, Technical Report no. 70.

Dyson, A.H. (1997) *Writing Superheroes: Contemporary Childhood, Popular Culture, and Classroom Literacy*. New York: Teachers College Press.

Dyson, A.H. (1999) 'Coach Bombay's kids learn to write: children's appropriation of media material for school literacy', *Research in the Teaching of English*, 33: 367–402.

Dyson, A.H. (2000) 'On reframing children's words: the perils, promises, and pleasures of writing children', *Research in the Teaching of English*, 34: 352–67.

Fisch, S.M., Truglio, R.T., and Cole, C.F. (1999) 'The impact of *Sesame Street* on preschool children: a review and synthesis of 30 years' research', Research Synthesis Essay, *Media Psychology*, 1: 165–90.

Fish, S. (1980) *Is There a Text in This Class? The Authority of Interpretive Communities*. Cambridge, MA: Harvard University Press.

Flavell, J.H., Flavell, E.R., Green, F.L., and Korfmacher, J.E. (1990) 'Do young children think of television images as pictures or real objects?', *Journal of Broadcasting and Electronic Media*, 34(4): 399–419.

Genishi, C. and Dyson, A. H. (2009) *Children, Language, and Literacy: Diverse Learners in Diverse Times*. (Language and Literacy Series) New York: Teachers' College Press.

Harste, J.C., Woodward, V.A., and Burke, C.L. (1984) *Language Stories and Literacy Lessons*. Portsmouth, NH: Heinemann.

Hodge, B. and Tripp, D. (1986) *Children and Television*. Cambridge: Polity.

Hollenbeck, A.R. and Slaby, R.G. (1979) 'Infant visual and vocal responses to television', *Child Development*, 50(1): 41–5.

Howard, S. (1994) '"Real bunnies don't stand on two legs": five-, six- and seven-year-old children's perceptions of television's "reality"', *Australian Journal of Early Childhood*, 19(4): 35–43.

Howard, S. (1996) '"Bananas can't talk": young children judging the reality of Big Bird, Bugs and the Bananas', *Australian Journal of Early Childhood*. 21 (4): 25–30.

Howard, S. and Roberts, S. (2003) 'Winning hearts and minds: television and the very young audience', *Contemporary Issues in Early Childhood*, 3: 325–37. *International Marketing Data and Statistics 2000*. London: Euromonitor.

Kalantzis, M. and Cope, B. (2000) 'Changing the role of schools', in B. Cope and M. Kalantzis (eds), *Multiliteracies: Literacy Learning and the Design of Social Futures*. New London Group. London: Routledge.

Kenway, J. and Bullen, E. (2001) *Consuming Children: Education–Entertainment–Advertising*. Buckingham: Open University Press.

Krcmar, M. (2010) 'Can social meaningfulness and repeat exposure help infants and toddlers overcome the video deficit?', *Media Psychology*, 13(1): 31–53.

Krcmar, M. (2011) 'Word learning in very young children from infant-directed DVDs', *Journal of Communication*, 61(4): 780–94.

Lewis, D. (2001) *Reading Contemporary Picturebooks: Picturing Text*. London: Routledge/Falmer.

Livingstone, S. (1990) *Making Sense of Television: the Psychology of Audience Interpretation*, London: Routledge.

Livingstone, S. (1998) 'Mediated childhoods: a comparative approach to young people's changing media environment in Europe', *European Journal of Communication*, 13(4): 435–56.

Livingstone, S. and Bovill, M. (1999) *Young People, New Media*. London: LSE.

Mackey, M. (2002) *Literacies across Media: Playing the Text*. London: Routledge Falmer.

Mackey, M. (2007) *Mapping Recreational Literacies: Contemporary Adults at Play*. New York: Peter Lang

Marsh, J. (2000) 'Teletubby tales: popular culture in the early years language and literacy curriculum', *Contemporary Issues in Early Childhood*, 1(2): 119–33.

Marsh, J. (2008) 'Popular culture in the language arts classroom', in J. Flood, S.B. Heath and D. Lapp (eds), *Handbook of Research in the Visual and Creative Arts, Volume II*, New York: Macmillan/International Reading Association.

Marsh, J. (2010) 'Young children's play in online virtual worlds', *Journal of Early Childhood Research*, 7(3): 1–17.

Marsh, J. (2011) 'Young children's literacy practices in a virtual world: Establishing an online interaction order', *Reading Research Quarterly*, 46(2): 101–18.

Meek, M. (1988) *How Texts Teach What Readers Learn*. Stroud: Thimble.

Neuman, S.B. (1995) *Literacy in the Television Age: the Myth of the TV Effect*, (2nd ed.) Norwood, NJ: Ablex.

New London Group (1996) 'A pedagogy of multiliteracies: designing social futures', *Harvard Educational Review*, 66: 60–91.

Rabinowitz, P.J. (1987) *Before Reading: Narrative Conventions and the Politics of Interpretation*. Ithaca, NY: Cornell University Press.

Rideout, V. (2011) *Zero to Eight: Children's Media Use in America*. San Francisco: Common Sense Media.

Robinson, M. (1997) *Children Reading Print and Television*. London: Falmer.

Rolandelli, D.R., Wright, J.C., Huston, A.C., and Eakins, D. (1991) 'Children's auditory and visual processing of narrated and nonnarrated television programming', *Journal of Experimental Child Psychology*, 51: 90–122.

Rosenblatt, L. (2005) *Making Meaning with Texts: Selected Essays*. Portsmouth, NH: Heinemann.

Seabrook, J. (2012) 'Streaming dreams', *The New Yorker* 16 January, 24–30.

Sell, M.A., Ray, G.E., and Lovelace, L. (1995) 'Preschool children's comprehension of a *Sesame Street* video tape: the effects of repeated viewing and previewing instructions', *Educational Technology Research and Development*, 43(3): 49–60.

Sipe, L.R. (2000) '"Those two gingerbread boys could be brothers": how children use intertextual connections during storybook readalouds', *Children's Literature in Education*, 31(2): 73–90.

Smith, F. (1983) *Essays into Literacy*. Exeter, NH: Heinemann.

Strouse, G.A. and Troseth, G.L. (2008) '"Don't try this at home": toddlers' imitation of new skills from people on video', *Journal of Experimental Child Psychology*, 101: 262–80.

Tobin, J. (2000) *'Good Guys Don't Wear Hats': Children's Talk about the Media*. New York: Teachers College Press.

Troseth, G.L. (2010) 'Is it life or is it Memorex? Video as a representation of reality', *Developmental Review* 30: 155–75.

Tyner, K. (1998) *Literacy in a Digital World: Teaching and Learning in the Age of Information*. Mahwah, NJ: Erlbaum.

Vandewater, E.A., Barr, R., Park, S.E., and Lee, S.-J. (2010) 'A US study of transfer of learning from video to books in toddlers', *Journal of Children & Media*, 4(4): 450–67.

Wartella, E., Richert, R.A., and Robb, M.B. (2010) 'Babies, television and videos: how did we get here?', *Developmental Review*, 30: 116–27.

Willems, M. (2000) 'Video and its paradoxes', in Russell Jackson (ed.), *The Cambridge Companion to Shakespeare on Film*. Cambridge: Cambridge University Press.

Williams, R. (1974) *Television: Technology and Cultural Form*. London: Fontana/Collins.

Wood, J.M. and Duke, N.K. (1997) 'Inside "Reading Rainbow": a spectrum of strategies for promoting literacy', *Language Arts*, 74: 95–106.

Wright, J.C., Huston, A.C., Ross, R.P., Calvert, S.L., Rolandelli, D., Weeks, L.A., Raeissi, P., and Potts, R. (1984) 'Pace and continuity of television programs: effects on children's attention and comprehension', *Developmental Psychology*, 20(4): 653–66.

14

Critical Indigenous Literacies

Debbie Reese

What are critical Indigenous literacies? What does one mean by 'Indigenous'? What does one mean by 'literacies'? Why is literacy pluralized, and why is 'critical' necessary? What does it mean to be literate? As the set of questions demonstrate, there is a lot to unpack in the title of this chapter: 'Critical Indigenous literacies.' Unpacking it means going beyond the discipline of education into American Indian and Indigenous studies and situating the chapter in an historical and political context.[1]

The Civil Rights movement of the 1960s led to the development of multicultural education. In the 1980s and 1990s, critical multiculturalists pointed to its weaknesses. Taxel (1995: 155) described a trend toward addressing 'the interests, concerns, and experiences of individuals and groups considered outside of the sociopolitical and cultural mainstream of American society.' It was, in effect, an effort to move beyond an additive approach to teaching children about people who were different from white, middle-class Americans. It was, and is, an important pedagogical shift, but

beneath it was an erroneous assumption that everyone in America was seeking 'the American dream.' Generally speaking, American Indians have sought to protect tribal sovereignty. Conceptualizing education and literacy as a means by which all people, including those who are deemed 'multicultural' to acquire the social and cultural capital of the dominant culture does not reflect interests of Indigenous peoples. American Indian scholars assert that the multicultural framework that grew out of the Civil Rights movement obscures our status as citizens of sovereign nations and prevents the nation building work that is necessary for the well-being of our youth and nations (Cook-Lynn, 2005). Nation building means maintaining and reclaiming ways of being Native that include exerting jurisdictional control over our intellectual property (stories), teaching and using our languages, and working towards reclaiming and using artifacts taken from us by anthropologists and pothunters (Coffey and Tsosie, 2001).

Because of treaties and federal Indian law, Native peoples in the US have rights to self-government, land, resources, and practice of our religions that other ethnic groups do not (Champagne, 2005). Native people have dual citizenship in their specific Native nation and the US, too. These fundamental ideas are at the heart of Native Nations, but relatively unknown to most people from dominant groups. Crossing disciplinary boundaries – from education and social sciences to American Indian studies – creates the space necessary to answer the questions posed above. In order to discuss Indigenous literacies, I will use American Indians as a case example of indigeneity and begin by unpacking and challenging commonly held ideas about who American Indians are. Doing that means situating this chapter in a framework unfamiliar to most Americans who do not know that American Indians are citizens of sovereign nations, and as such, are not simply another group identified as a 'people of color' (Cook-Lynn, 2007). It may be helpful to view the chapter as akin to the critical literacy defined by Luke and Freebody (1997), wherein Indigenous scholars bring our critical perspectives to bear on the topic, and reject externally imposed notions of literacy and education in favor of our own agendas.

In *Indigenizing the Academy* (2004), Mihesuah and Wilson describe a four-point framework for the process of indigenizing the universities and colleges from which educational theorizing and practice emanate. The four points are introduced here briefly and will be woven into the remainder of the chapter. First, indigenizing means 'to carve a space where Indigenous values and knowledge are respected' (Mihesuah and Wilson, 2004: 2). Histories of the United States, for adult and child readers, are replete with references to Indigenous people as 'primitive' and/or 'pagan.' The task for colonizers was to 'Christianize and civilize' Indigenous peoples. A critical Indigenous literacy challenges those characterizations, and it asserts that Indigenous values and knowledge were neither primitive nor pagan. Rather, they are worthy of the same respect accorded to Western epistemologies. Second, indigenizing means to create an environment that supports research and methodologies useful to Indigenous nations or community building. Creating this environment requires an aggressive displacement of stereotypes and biased ideology about American Indians, and, it requires an intellectual climate that embraces studies that seek to work with Indigenous nations so that Native nations and youth are empowered as Indigenous entities and individuals who take pride in their identity as citizens of a tribal nation (Cook-Lynn, 2005).

Doing this, however, is an unsettling and radical change that decenters the master narrative, the knowledge-for-knowledge-sake orientation of the academy, and, the audience for, and purpose of, the research itself (Deloria, 1969; Cook-Lynn, 1998). This leads to Mihesuah and Wilson's third point: supporting one another as institutional foundations are shaken. This support means, for some, creating space for the letting go of emotionally laden ideas and practices embedded in the master narrative. The fourth point is to compel institutional responsiveness to Indigenous issues, concerns, and communities. It means moving away from studies that position Indigenous peoples as subjects of study, to speaking with us in order to design studies that are centered on needs that we identify rather than ones outsiders may be invested in studying. It means stepping away from critical pedagogies that 'retain the deep structures of Western thought' and inadvertently function as homogenizing agents (Grande, 2004: 3).

Grande argues that to be truly democratic and emancipatory, critical theorists must engage the work of Native scholars and our conceptualization of sovereignty, thereby developing a 'red pedagogy' that will better serve Native people. In his critique of critical race theory (CRT), Brayboy argues that for American Indians, it is colonization, not racism, which is endemic in society. He writes: 'By colonization, I mean that European American thought, knowledge, and power structures dominate present-day society in the United States' (Brayboy, 2005: 430). In practice, this domination means that Indigenous knowledge is dismissed. That dismissal includes Native stories, which Brayboy argues '...are not separate from theory; they make up theory and are, therefore, real and legitimate sources of data and ways of being' (Brayboy, 2005: 430). Indigenous critical theory, as described by Byrd (2008: para 4) is, 'a contentious, oppositional discourse that confronts imperialism and colonialism' and that it is a 'diagnostic way of reading and interpreting colonial logics that underpin cultural, intellectual, and political discourses. The work of these Indigenous scholars demonstrates an invigorated and concerted effort to indigenize the education of all children.

This indigenization is vital, not in an abstract or theoretical way, but in the on-the-ground lives of Indigenous peoples. Calls for change go back to the 1800s. In 1829, William Apes, a Pequot man raised by whites, wrote that he was afraid of his own people because of 'the many stories I had heard of their cruelty toward the whites' and that if the whites 'had told me how cruel they had been to the "poor Indian," I should have apprehended as much harm from them' (Apes and

O'Connell, 1829: 11). Less than a hundred years later, Native parents in Chicago wrote to the mayor, objecting to what their children were being taught in Chicago schools. In part, they wrote 'We do not know if school histories are pro-British, but we do know that they are unjust to the life of our people – the American Indian. They call all white victories, battles, and all Indian victories, massacres', and the parents asked that history be taught in a balanced way (Costo and Henry, 1927). Apes and the Chicago parents were engaged in what we know today as critical literacy. They expressed concern with good reason. Studies document that stereotypical imagery is having a negative effect on the well-being of Native youth (Faircloth and Tippeconic, 2010; Fryberg, Markus, Oyserman and Stone, 2008).

Of Warrior Chiefs and Indian Princesses: The Psychological Consequences of American Indian Mascots, (Fryberg, Markus, Oyserman and Stone, 2008) examines the effects of specific representations of American Indians on the self-concept of Native and non-Native students. Situating their study in four theoretical frameworks (stereotype accessibility, stereotype threat, social representation, and social identity theory), the researchers carried out a series of studies in which Native and non-Native high school and college students were shown a set of images that included Chief Wahoo, the mascot of the Cleveland Indians baseball team, and Pocahontas from the Disney feature film. As a red-faced, bulbous nosed caricature of an American Indian, Chief Wahoo is a negative image. Attractive and spirited, Pocahontas is a positive image. Fryberg and her colleagues found that exposure to the series of images had a negative impact on American Indian students' feelings of personal and community worth and self-efficacy. One might expect that the positive image would have a positive impact, but that was not the case. Fryberg et al. suggest that the negative effects may be due to the absence of *contemporary positive* images of American Indians in American society (emphasis mine). They write, 'American Indian mascots and other common American Indian representations do not cue associations that are relevant or useful for students' identity construction' (Fryberg et al., 2008: 216). In another study, Fryberg and Oyserman (2011) studied the impact of images of American Indian mascots on European Americans and found that the images had a *positive* effect on their self-esteem. Fryberg and Oyserman found that through this imagery, European Americans can symbolically connect to a romanticized past yet incur no social cost for doing so. In effect, they bask in the reflected glory of a romanticized American Indian past. They do this, however, at a cost to Native youth who drop out of school at alarming rates. Their latter study points to the need for change in the way that all children – Native and non-Native – are taught about American Indians.

Beaulieu (2000) asserts that, historically, educators have defined successful educational programs for Native students as ones that 'enable students to leave their communities' and that this measure of success 'alienates the students from their homes and communities' and contributes to dropout rates. In 2010, a major study of dropout and graduation rates among American Indians was published as part of the Civil Rights Project at UCLA. Faircloth and Tippeconnic (2010) used data generated by the 2005 National Center for Education Statistics, looking specifically at statistics from seven states with the highest percentage of American Indian and Alaska Native students, and from five states in the

northwestern part of the US. They found that less than half of Native students in the 12 states graduate from high school, and that graduation rates have gotten worse over time. Their study reports that Native students drop out, or 'are pushed out' (2010: 4) due to a variety of factors including lack of student engagement, a perceived lack of empathy among teachers, and irrelevant curriculum. These findings confirm those reported earlier by Dehyle (1992).

Incorporating sovereignty, Indigenous literacies, languages, and children's books that accurately reflect Indigenous lives can address the factors Faircloth and Tippecconnic discuss. With tribal sovereignty, Native nation building, and studies pertinent to literacy of Indigenous youth as my framework, I turn to education.

IN THE BEGINNING

Generally, leading texts about literacy in the United States focus on the colonial period and efforts to teach children to read and write using texts like *The New England Primer*. A prime example is *Literacy in the United States* (Kaestle, Damon-Moore, Stedman, and Tinsley, 1993). If, however, the narrative is a complete one that reflects 'We the People' of the United States, it will begin prior to the colonial period, with the literacies of the Indigenous peoples of the land that came to be known as the United States. 'Literacies' and 'peoples' are deliberately pluralized because, contrary to popular belief, there was no 'Indian' tribe. Instead, there were hundreds of distinct tribal nations, each with its own name, territory, governance, language, stories, and ways of educating its children to be literate members of its nation. Though a great many people believe that Indigenous peoples were primitive, that notion prevails only if we privilege the Western alphabet with its structured grammar and printed page. If the mark of a literate civilization is its ability to communicate with its citizens, then we must be open to alternatives to a formalistic European literacy.

Ancestors of today's Pueblo peoples lived in well-ordered communities like Chaco Canyon as long ago as 850 AD. They created petroglyphs in rocks, pictographs on stone and plaster, and designs on their pottery and basketry that constituted a writing system by which they conveyed and affirmed complex meanings and beliefs amongst group members (Ragsdale, 1997). The same is true for *waniyetu wowapi*, or winter counts that are tribal histories recorded by Plains tribes on animal hides. Drawn by and cared for by Keepers, Thornton (2002) writes that scholars have studied more than 150 different Lakota winter counts that provide wide-ranging detailed histories that note, for example, that 'Dakota and Omaha made peace' in 1791 and 'Little Beaver's house burned' in 1809 (Thornton, 2002: 730).

Among the Haudenosaunee, the Friendship Belt and the Two Row Wampum record two of the most important treaties between them and Europeans (Muller, 2007). The Friendship Belt represents the Covenant Chain alliance that was established in 1677 between the Haudenosaunee and the English, and is predated by the Two Row Wampum which is the oldest treaty between the two nations. In her study, Haas (2007) describes diplomatic agreements recorded on wampum belts as 'hypertext technologies' that 'extended human memories of inherited knowledges through interconnected, nonlinear designs and associate storage and retrieval methods' (2007: 78).

Low (2006) documents mnemonic Cheyenne ledger art of the 1860s that was rooted in other media (bark, stone, hide) and used as a way to preserve tribal narratives. They are, she writes, a communal activity in which several individuals create them. This communal production reflects a Native way of being, grounded in community rather than the individualistic orientation seen in European and American societies. The emphasis on community is also seen in stories and their telling in the oral tradition that is a central to Native cultures. Amongst Alaska Natives, stories are primarily told by women, who use a *yaaruin*, or, storyknife traditionally made of wood, bone, or ivory to draw illustrations on the ground or in the snow as they tell or sing a story (Rivers, 2002). As noted earlier, stories were told with the purpose of passing teachings and knowledge from one generation to the next.

Basso's (1996) study of landscape and language among the Western Apache nation contains many Apache stories including ones that document major shifts in local climatic patterns and related changes in the landscape itself. Tribal member Charles Henry told Basso creation stories as well as stories of place names and social conduct. Basso's reflections on landscape and language in history and story amongst the Apache and around the world led Basso to coin an especially insightful phrase that is the title for his book: *Wisdom Sits in Places*. The stories human beings tell about those places are the wisdoms that are the guiding foundation for societies. That the Apaches have not yet (as of Basso's study) produced a tribal historian – as conceptualized by Anglo-American standards – does not, and should not, detract from a well-established manner of transmitting Apache knowledge that has worked for the Apaches for hundreds of years.

Not recognizing or acknowledging any of these forms of literacy or teachings allowed colonizing nations to characterize Indigenous peoples as uncivilized and in need of European or Western systems of education delivered through Christian education.

TO 'CHRISTIANIZE AND CIVILIZE'

Indigenous leaders and scholars regard formalized systems of education imposed on us as weapons of colonization that would 'Christianize and civilize' us as they worked to dispossess Native nations of our lands and cultures (Grande, 2000; Lomawaima and McCarty, 2006; Begaye, 2007). Most Puritan missionaries in the 1600s thought the Indians were 'totally devoid of civilization' (Szasz, 2007: 106). John Eliot is credited with establishing 14 'Praying Towns' in New England between 1651 and 1674, each of which had a school. By 1661, Elliot had learned the Massachusett language from Massachusett Indians who spoke it and English, and had published the first Bible in an Indian language. Used in the schools, it served the dual purpose of Christianizing and civilizing Massachusett students (Szasz, 2007). The goal of Eleazor Wheelock's school on the east coast in the 1760s was to 'save the Indians from themselves and to save the English from the Indians' (Axtell, 1981: 97). Little changed in the next 200 years when the first federally run boarding school opened in 1879. Established by a military officer named Richard Henry Pratt, Carlisle Indian Industrial School's motto was to 'Kill the Indian, save the man.'

Government boarding schools have been the subject of a great deal of scholarship in the last few decades. Lomawaima (1995) cites McBeth's 1983 study as the first one that incorporated voices and opinions of Native alumni of boarding schools. It was preceded by several noteworthy autobiographical accounts. The first is *The Middle Five* (1900) by Francis LaFlesche. Published in 1900, it is an autobiography of his childhood at a Presbyterian mission school in the 1880s. La Flesche was Omaha. His book was used in the schools, as stated in a letter by Clara D. True, a teacher in Santa Clara Pueblo, New Mexico. A more contemporary account is *Indian School Days* (1988) by Basil Johnston, an Anishinaabe man who attended a Jesuit boarding school in northern Ontario in the 1930s. Since then, numerous research texts have been published. They include *Education for Extinction: American Indians and the Boarding School Experience 1875–1928* (Adams, 1995), *Boarding School Seasons: American Indian Families 1900–1940* (Child, 1998), *Education Beyond the Mesas* (Gilbert, 2010), and *They Called it Prairie Light: The Story of Chilocco Indian School* (Lomawaima, 1995). In the schools, children were forbidden from speaking their own language. Many report being punished for speaking their own language. The school curriculum was developed around preparing students to be service and domestic workers.

INDIGENOUS LANGUAGES

Prior to European arrival, Indigenous peoples of the Americas spoke several hundred different languages. In the mid-1990s, studies indicated that 90% of the 175 Native languages that survived the boarding school assimilation period had no child speakers (Johansen, 2004), and more than a third had fewer than 100 people who could speak the language (Beaulieu, 2000). Indigenous language loss is attributed to assimilationist educational policies. Today there is a range of Indigenous language use. Studies show that participants deeply value their language, and in their homes, children hear elders speak a variety of one or more Indigenous languages along with English and Spanish. Amongst the communities studied, use of Indigenous language was strongest within the Navajo community but that overall, the most vibrant use of Indigenous language was in ceremonial and cultural contexts. Students viewed English as necessary, but also as a language of colonization. Many felt insecure for not being fluent in their Native language, while others reported feeling shame for that fluency – a shame they linked to English-only policies (Begaye, 2007; McCarty, Romero-Little, Warhol, and Zepeda, 2009).

Language revitalization programs take many forms, including community-based programs that bring together educators, parents, and other community stakeholders in language immersion settings that incorporate tribally specific curriculum (McCarty et al., 2009). At Cochiti Pueblo in New Mexico, the Tribal Council launched a program in the summer of 1996. All instruction was oral; no written texts were used. In 1995, the Piegan Institute (an adults-only program begun in the mid-1980s) launched *Nizipuhwahsin* (Real Speak) for a small group of pre-school children. Its goal is to produce proficient speakers of Blackfeet through programs for children in grades K–8. LaPier and Farr (2006) write that their students are top-performing students in both, Blackfeet and mainstream academics. In Fort Defiance, Arizona, Dine (Navajo) parents and teachers established Tsehootsooi Dine Bi'olta' (The Navajo School at the Meadow between the Rocks) for children in K–7 grades (Johnson and Legatz, 2006). Similar programs are in Alaska (Williams, 2006) and Hawaii (Wilson, 2006).

THE PLACE OF CHILDREN'S LITERATURE

Teachers committed to a 'We the People' framework that includes Indigenous peoples can use works of children's literature that are Nation building in orientation. By that, I mean works of children's literature that are:

(1) tribally specific rather than overly broad (about a specific tribal nation rather than 'American Indian');
(2) well researched and written by authors who are Indigenous; and
(3) unbiased in use of language and portrayal of conflicts.

For Indigenous children, Native Nation-building children's literature provides them with a reflection of their experiences as Indigenous peoples and for children who are not Indigenous, these texts provide a window into a culture that is unfamiliar to them (Bishop, 1993). Along with those three criteria, teachers must not lose sight of early childhood practices that emphasize a 'here-and-now' approach to instruction. Applying the 'here-and-now' approach to instruction about American Indians requires teachers to develop lessons that provide children with information about Native peoples in the community or nearby locales, and what they do in today's society. These books are also helpful in deconstructing stereotypical images found in popular and classic children's books such as *Thanksgiving Day* (Rockwell, 1999), *The Berenstain Bears Go to Camp* (Berenstain, 1982), *Brother Eagle, Sister*

Sky (Jeffers, 1991) and *Little House on the Prairie* (Wilder, 1935).

WHAT LIES AHEAD

Optimizing the literacies of Indigenous children will require educators to step away from genocidal and well-intentioned efforts to rescue us from the legacies of a tragic history and towards a 'space of engagement' (Grande, 2008: 234) that begins with educators entering that space of engagement with knowledge of the significance of sovereignty to Native nations, a genuine commitment to work alongside us in our chosen Native nation-building educational activities, and skills to select texts that are Nation-building in orientation. This orientation to Indigenous literacies will generate parent- and community-based early childhood education programs that are culturally, linguistically, and developmentally appropriate, but rigorous research is necessary. Demmert, McCardle, Mele-McCarthy, and Leos (2006) call for an increase in the number of American Indian researchers, an increase in community-based participatory research, studies that compare the effectiveness of culture-based programs to existing ones, and a focus on early childhood development. Increasingly, Indigenous populations around the world are developing documents such as *Protocols for Producing Indigenous Australian Writing* (ACA, 2007) and tribal protocols like the ones developed by the Hopi Cultural Preservation Office (Hopi Nation, n.d.). Indigenous nations, with the support of the United Nations and its Declaration of the Rights of Indigenous Peoples, are working to protect our intellectual property, resources, and our status as sovereign nations. Even with hundreds of years of colonialism, our persistence is evident.

Our sovereignty is at stake, and we will persevere.

NOTE

1 I use 'American Indian' because of the legal standing of that phrase in US law. In the US, there is no agreement regarding the use of 'American Indian' or 'Native American'. Best practice is to use the name of a specific tribal nation. In Canada, 'First Nations' and 'aboriginal' are used; in Australia, 'aborigines' is used. Aotearoa New Zealand, the Pacific Island nations, and Central and South America all have Indigenous populations with specific names. Given the depth and breadth of Indigenous peoples, it is not appropriate to discuss them as a single entity. This chapter will offer principles within an American Indian framework that may be applied to other Indigenous populations.

APPENDIX A

Contemporary Native children's literature

Rather than rely solely on children books marketed as American Indian myths, legends, or folktales, teachers can select picture books that tell stories of Native children of the present day. Board books, picture books, and non-fiction photo essays are available that portray the richness of a Native child's life are excellent options.

Boozhoo Means Hello (Himanga, 2002) is a bilingual board book that features photographs of Native toddlers at play. In some of the photographs, the tribally-specific décor of the classroom is visible. Each page features a few words in Ojibwe and English, and there is a pronunciation guide on the last page.

The question/answer format of *Where Did You Get Your Moccasins* (Wheeler, 1986) is familiar to anyone who has been at a kindergarten show-and-tell. In this story, Jody brings his moccasins to school and tells his classmates about how they were made for him by his Kookum (grand-mother). The children are shown sitting on the floor amidst low bookshelves of books, thereby situating the story in the present day.

Alphabet books with an 'I is for Indian' page are no longer being published. Teachers looking for an Indigenous alphabet book will find much to appreciate in *Lii Yiiboo Nayaapiwak lii Swer/Owls See Clearly at Night* (Flett, 2010). The bold, tribally specific illustrations and text are preceded by an introduction about the peoples that are called Metis and their language, Michif.

Jingle Dancer (Smith, 2000) is about Jenna, a young Muscogee Creek girl who plans to do the jingle dance for the first time at an upcoming pow wow. To prepare for it, she watches a video of her grandmother doing the dance, and she visits Native relatives in her neighborhood who help her prepare her regalia (jingle dress, moccasins, fan). Smith beautifully captures the work and joy of a Native family and community goes through when a young person dances for the first time. Given its plot, the book affirms that work and joy for the young Native reader, and its modern day setting tells non-Native readers that Jenna, Muscogee Creek people (and by extension, American Indians) did not vanish; instead, they learn that we are part of today's society and that Native families like Jenna's live in houses on tree-lined streets and that we wear the same kinds of everyday clothes (jeans) they and their parents (business suits) do. Throughout the book, illustrations of the inside of Jenna's home mirror Native homes. The Native artwork on the walls and the trunk in the corner where Jenna's grandmother stores their traditional clothing are material items that mark this as a Native residence where Native ways of being are the norm.

Making good choices: traditional stories

Human beings – regardless of location, race, nation, or religion – tell stories. We use stories about religious beliefs, customs, history, lifestyle, language, values, and the people and places we hold sacred to preserve and pass on our culture(s) from one generation to the next. These stories are rooted in the oral or storytelling tradition, and they have life and purpose. Many, like Creation (Book I of Genesis), are sacred to those who tell them. Like the stories in the Bible, Native stories are sacred to the Native people who tell them. Our stories have life and purpose. Yet, they are not treated with the same respect given to stories rooted in the world religions. Instead of being shelved in Religion, for example, Native stories are more likely to be found in Folklore. One Native writer who addresses this double standard is Joseph Bruchac (Abenaki). He writes that 'rather than being "mere myths," with "myth" being used in the pejorative sense of "untruth," those ancient traditional tales were a distillation of the deep knowledge held by the many Native American nations about the workings of the world around them' (1996, ix). In *Yellow Woman and a Beauty of the Spirit,* acclaimed Acoma Pueblo writer Leslie Marmon Silko writes that story is the medium by which the Pueblo people transmit their 'entire culture, a worldview complete with proven strategies for survival' (Silko 1996, 30). In her discussion of hunting stories, she says:

These accounts contained information of critical importance about the behavior and migration patterns of mule deer. Hunting stories carefully described key landmarks and locations of fresh water. Thus, a deer-hunt story might also serve as a map. Lost travelers and lost pinon-nut gatherers have been saved by sighting a rock formation they recognize only because they once heard a hunting story describing this rock formation. (1996: 32)

Silko's words tell us why most of the retellings of Native stories on the market are unacceptable. The stories are about survival. They are not timeless, quaint, or exotic stories to the people they belong to. Nonetheless, many award-winning books are 'based on' Native stories, marketed, and used by teachers as though they are Native stories. Two examples from the 1970s are Gerald McDermott's *Arrow to the Sun* and Paul Goble's *The Girl Who Loved Wild Horses*. Neither one provides tribally specific information. McDermott's book is especially troubling for its multiple misrepresentations of Pueblo Indians (Reese, 2007). However, given the centrality of story to Native communities, teachers can thoughtfully incorporate them by selecting books whose design situates the stories in a specific context. Some examples follow.

Muskrat Will Be Swimming (Savageau, 1996) features Jeannie, a little girl whose classmates call 'Lake Rat' because she lives in a shanty town by the lake. Each day on her way to school, Jeannie passes by the fancy houses of her classmates, and though she tries to tell them about the wonderful things she sees at the lake, they still tease her. One evening her grandfather notices her moping. They got for a walk, and he tells her about his own childhood and names he was called. Together, they talk about what a 'Lake Rat' might be. Jeannie suggests it could be a muskrat. Her grandfather tells her their creation story, which features a muskrat who brought earth from the bottom of the lake, placing it on Turtle's back, forming the land for human beings to live on. Literally and figuratively, Jeannie carries some of that earth with her after that. It reminds her of who she is.

In *The Story of the Milky Way: A Cherokee Tale* (Bruchac and Ross, 1995), the story opens and closes with a present-day family in which the grandfather tells two children the Cherokee story of the Milky Way. Through this technique, readers learn by way of the story and illustrations, that Native people are part of today's society and that they tell stories specific to their identities.

One look at the art in *Coyote and the Winnowing Birds: Iisaw Niqw Tsaayantotaqam Tsiroot: A Traditional Hopi Tale* (Sekaquaptewa, 1994) tells the reader that Native children are part of today's society, and that they produce art that looks much like that created by the reader. The illustrations for the entire story are done by Hopi children who use pencil and markers to depict eagles, mesas, coyote, and scenes from the story. The book is bilingual in its use of English and Hopi on each page. Immediately following the story are pages of information about the Hopi alphabet and pronunciation guides. The final pages include a Hopi to English glossary, and an English to Hopi one as well.

Many Native stories are meant to be told at a specific time of year or for a specific reason (much like stories about Santa Claus). The opening pages of *Beaver Steals Fire* (Confederated Salish and Kootenai Tribes, 2005) convey that contextual information to the reader.

REFERENCES

Apes, W. and O'Connell, B. (1829). *A Son of the Forest and Other Writings*. Amherst: University of Massachusetts Press.

ACA (Australia Council for the Arts) (2007). *Writing Protocols for Producing Indigenous Australian Writing*. Surry Hills: Australia Council for the Arts.

Adams, D.W. (1995). *Education for Extinction: American Indians and the Boarding School*

Experience, 1875–1928. Lawrence: University Press of Kansas.

Axtell, J. (1981). 'Dr. Wheelock's little red school', in J. Axtell (ed.), *The European and the Indian: Essays in the Ethnohistory of Colonial North America*. Oxford, England: Oxford University Press. pp. 87–109.

Basso, K.H. (1996). *Wisdom Sits in Places: Landscape and Language Among the Western Apache*. Albuquerque: University of New Mexico Press.

Beaulieu, D.L. (2000). 'Comprehensive reform and American Indian education', *Journal of American Indian Education*, 39(2): 29–38.

Begaye, T. (2007). 'Native teacher understanding of culture as a concept for curricular inclusion', *Wicazo Sa Review*, 22(1): 35–52.

Berenstain, S. and Berenstain, J. (1982). *The Berenstain Bears go to Camp*. New York: Random House.

Bishop, R.S. (1993). 'Multicultural literature for children: Making informed choices', in V.J. Harris (ed.), *Teaching Multicultural Literature in Grades K–8*. Norwood, MA: Christopher-Gordon. pp. 37–54.

Bruchac, J. and Ross, G. (1995). *The Story of the Milky Way: A Cherokee Tale*. New York: Dial Books for Young Readers.

Bruchac, J. (1996). *Roots of Survival*. Golden:, Fulcrum Publishing.

Brayboy, B.M.K.J. (2005). 'Toward a tribal critical race theory in education', *The Urban Review*, 37(5): 425–446.

Byrd, J. (2008). 'How the West was not one', *KRiTiK*. Champaign, IL: Unit for Criticism and Interpretive Theory at the University of Illinois, Urbana-Champaign. http://unitcrit.blogspot.com/2008/04/how-west-was-not-one.html

Champagne, D. (2005). 'From sovereignty to minority: As American as apple pie', *Wicazo Sa Review*, 20(2): 21–36.

Child, B.J. (1998). *Boarding School Seasons: American Indian Families, 1900–1940*. Lincoln: University of Nebraska Press.

Coffey, W. and Tsosie, R. (2001). 'Rethinking the tribal sovereignty doctrine: Cultural sovereignty and the collective future of Indian nations', *Stanford Law and Policy Review*, 12(2): 191–221.

Confederated Salish and Kootenai Tribes. (2005). *Beaver Steals Fire: A Salish Coyote Story*. Lincoln: University of Nebraska Press.

Cook-Lynn, E. (1998). 'American Indian intellectualism and the new Indian story', in D.A. Mihesuah (ed.), *Natives and Academics: Researching and Writing About American Indians*. Lincoln: University of Nebraska Press. pp. 111–138.

Cook-Lynn, E. (2005). 'Keynote address: Indian studies—How it looks back at us after twenty years', *Wicazo Sa Review*, 20(1): 179–187.

Cook-Lynn, E. (2007). 'Scandal', *Wicazo Sa Review*, 22(1): 85–89.

Costo, R. and Henry, J. (1927). *Textbooks and the American Indian*. San Francisco: Indian Historian Press.

Deloria, Jr., V. (1969). *Custer Died for Your Sins*. New York City: Macmillan.

Dehyle, D. (1992). 'Constructing failure and maintaining cultural identity: Navajo and Ute school leavers', *Journal of American Indian Education*, 31(2): 24–47.

Demmert, W., McCardle, P., Mele-McCarthy, J., and Leos, K. (2006). 'Preparing Native American children for academic success: A blueprint for research', *Journal of American Indian Education*, 45(3): 92–106.

Faircloth, S.C. and Tippeconnic III, J.W. (2010). *The Dropout/Graduation Crisis Among American Indian and Alaska Native Students: Failure to Respond Places the Future of Native Peoples at Risk*. Los Angeles, CA: The Civil Rights Project/Proyecto Derechos Civiles at UCLA.

Flett, J. (2010). *Owls See Clearly at Night: A Michif Alphabet/Lii Yiiboo Miyo-Waapamik Lii Swer: L'alfabet di Michif*. Vancouver: Simply Read Books.

Fond du Lac Head Start Program. (2002). *Boozhoo: Come Play With Us*. Minneapolis: Fond du Lac Band of Lake Superior Chippewa.

Fryberg, S.A., Markus, H.R., Oyserman, D., and Stone, J.M. (2008). 'Of warrior chiefs and Indian princesses: The psychological consequences of American Indian mascots', *Basic and Applied Social Psychology*, 30(3): 208–218.

Fryberg, S.A. and Oyserman, D. (2011). 'Feeling good about Chief Wahoo: Basking in the reflected glory of American Indians', Unpublished manuscript, University of Arizona.

Gilbert, M.S. (2010). *Education Beyond the Mesas: Hopi Students at Sherman Institute, 1902–1929*. Lincoln: University of Nebraska Press.

Goble. P. (1978). *The Girl Who Loved Wild Horses*. Scarsdale: Bradbury Press.

Grande, S. (2000). 'American Indian identity and intellectualism: The quest for a new red pedagogy'. *Qualitative Studies in Education*, 13: 415–426.

Grande, S. (2004). *Red Pedagogy: Native American Social and Political Thought*. Lanham: Rowman & Littlefield.

Grande, S. (2008). 'Red pedagogy: The un-methodology', in N.K. Denzin, Y.S. Lincoln, and L.T. Smith (eds), *Handbook of Critical and Indigenous Methodologies*. Los Angeles, CA: Sage.

Haas, A.M. (2007). 'Wampum as hypertext: An American Indian intellectual tradition of multimedia theory and practice', *Studies in American Indian Literatures*, 19(4): 77–100.

Hopi Nation. Hopi Cultural Preservation Office Policy and Research. www.nau.edu/~hcpo-p/index.html.

Himanga, D. (2002). *Boozhoo Means Hello*. Cloquet, MN: Fond du Lac Band of Lake Superior Chippewa.

Jeffers, S. (1991). *Brother Eagle, Sister Sky: A Message from Chief Seattle*. New York: Dial Books.

Johansen, B.E. (2004). 'Back from the (nearly) dead: Reviving indigenous languages across North America', *The American Indian Quarterly*, 28(3/4): 566–82.

Johnson, F.T. and Legatz, J. (2006). 'Tsehootsooi Dine Bi'olta', *Journal of American Indian Education*, 45(2): 26–33.

Johnston, B. (1988). *Indian School Days*. Norman: University of Oklahoma Press.

Kaestle, C.F., Damon-Moore, H., Stedman, L.C., and Tinsley, K. (1993). *Literacy in the United States*. New Haven, CT: Yale University Press.

LaFlesche, F. (1900). *The Middle Five*. Lincoln: University of Nebraska Press.

LaPier, R. and Farr, W. (2006). 'An important gift: Blackfeet language and history', *Journal of American Indian Education*, 45(2): 34–7.

Leitich Smith, C. (2000). *Jingle Dancer*. New York: Morrow Junior Books.

Lomawaima, K.T. (1995). 'Educating Native Americans', in J.A. Banks and C.A. McGee Banks (ed.), *Handbook of Research on Multicultural Education*. New York: MacMillan Publishing.

Lomawaima, K.T. and McCarty, T.L. (2006). *'To Remain an Indian': Lessons in Democracy from a Century of Native American Education*. New York: Teachers College Press.

Low, D. (2006). 'Composite indigenous genre Cheyenne ledger art as literature', *Studies in American Indian Literatures*, 13(2): 83–104.

Luke, A. and Freebody, P. (1997). 'Critical literacy and the question of normativity', in *Constructing Critical Literacies*. Creskill, NJ: Hampton. pp. 1–18.

McCarty, T.L., Romero-Little, M.E., Warhol, L., and Zepeda, O. (2009). 'Indigenous youth as language policy makers', *Journal of Language, Identity, and Education*, 8(5): 291–306.

McDermott, G. (1974). *Arrow to the Sun*. New York: Viking Press.

Mihesuah, D.A. and Wilson, A.C. (eds) (2004). *Indigenizing the Academy: Transforming Scholarship and Empowering Communities*. Lincoln, NE: University of Nebraska Press.

Muller, K.V. (2007). 'The two 'mystery' belts of Grand River: A biography of the Two Row Wampum and the friendship belt', *The American Indian Quarterly*, 31(1): 129–64.

Ragsdale, J.W., Jr (1997). 'Anasazi jurisprudence', *American Indian Law Review*, 22(2): 393–444.

Reese, D. (2007). 'Proceed with caution: Using Native American folktales in the classroom', *Language Arts*, 84(3): 245–56.

Rivers, N. (2002). 'Story knife'. Smithsonian Institution. http://alaska.si.edu/record.asp?id=222.

Rockwell, A. (1999). *Thanksgiving Day*. New York: HarperCollins Publishers.

Savageau, C. (1996). *Muskrat Will Be Swimming*. Flagstaff: Northland Publishers.

Sekaquaptewa, E. (1994). *Coyote and the Winnowing Birds = Lisaw Niqw Tsaayantotaqam Tsiroot: A Traditional Hopi Tale*. Santa Fe: Clear Light Publishers.

Silko, L.M. (1996). *Yellow Woman and a Beauty of the Spirit*. New York: Simon & Schuster.

Szasz, M.C. (2007). *Indian Education in the American Colonies: 1607–1783*. Albuquerque: University of New Mexico Press.

Taxel, J. (1995). 'Cultural Politics and Writing for Young People', in *Battling Dragons: Conflict and Controversy in Children's Literature*, Portsmouth, NH: Heinemann. 155–69.

Thornton, R. (2002). 'A Rosebud Reservation Winter Count, circa 1751–1752 to 1886–1887', *Ethnohistory*, 49(4): 723–35.

Wilder, L.I. (1935). *Little House on the Prairie*. New York: Harper & Brothers.

Wheeler, B. (1986). *Where Did You Get Your Moccasins?* Winnipeg: Pemmican Publications.

Williams, B. (2006). 'Yupik language programs at Lower Kuskokwim School District, Bethel, Alaska', *Journal of American Indian Education*, 45(2): 37–41.

Wilson, W.H. (2006). 'Nawahi Hawaiian Laboratory School', *Journal of American Indian Education*, 45(2): 42–4.

15

Artifactual Literacies

Kate Pahl and Jennifer Rowsell

My favourite object is probably a tiny little baby
  gro, this big.
When I had my little girl, she was only two
  pounds
so her babygro fit her Barbie doll now, (ohh)
despite the fact she is now fourteen
and I can't believe she ever was that small
but it reminds me of her
(a class teacher describing her special object on
  first day of the *My Family My Story* project, from
  Pahl and Rowsell, 2010)

This quote comes from a research study called *My Family, My Story* and it highlights a core theme in the chapter, which is the artifactually mediated cultural worlds of children (Pahl and Rowsell, 2010). We draw on research in homes and communities to present a picture of early childhood literacy that connects narratives and stories to treasured objects. We argue that children's literacy experiences often connect to everyday objects and the meaning-making systems that they offer. We will elaborate on this research and theoretical principles to discuss the following: (1) the turn to out-of-school and home literacies; (2) the importance of valuing children's objects; (3) a review of research on artifactual literacies; (4) an artifactual literacies approach to literacy; (5) design literacies meets artifactual literacies; and (6) a case study of artifactual literacies in action.

Much, if not all, of the literacy practices as experienced by young children happen outside school contexts, and most happen in the home. It is important that the field of early childhood literacy, therefore, adequately represents the experiences of children at home and acknowledges the diversity of home literacy practices. Early childhood literacy is constructed in the home and school, and while the 'home' field is now much more discursively represented in the field, 'schooled literacy practices' (Street and Street, 1991) continues to hold sway for many educators.

THE OUT-OF-SCHOOL AND HOME LITERACIES TURN

Early literacy starts in the home. Children are born, and grow up, in the main, in environments where they live, with a caregiver, parent, siblings, grandparents, and other relatives (Gregory, Long, and Volk, 2004).

Their early experiences of literacy and language are meshed with their own embodied and tacit experiences of care-giving and receiving. These experiences are cultural (Rogoff, 2003) and shaped by language (Heath, 1983; Moll et al, 1992). Out of these early experiences comes an engagement with literacies of many kinds including written scripts, oral recitation, digital media, and everyday writing. Street described literacy as being *ideological*, that is, shaped by the community's social practices. He used the word *autonomous* to describe how literacy was seen as a set of skills in schools and institutions (Street, 1984). This view of literacy was developed in a number of different studies (Barton and Hamilton, 1998; Gregory and Williams, 2000). Pahl looked at how children engaged in a number of different practices, not just ones that looked like literacy, at home. The children in Pahl's study used different tools to express meaning, such as a bead map, or a drawing of the Welsh Valley Farm (Pahl, 2002). These tools were used as *representational resources* to create meanings (Kress, 1997). This type of research demonstrated the importance of literacy being connected to language and cultural practices and drew attention to the way in which children experience literacy in much wider ways than previously realized, while questioning the autonomy of school as the main place where literacy was experienced. Multimodal research understood that children use a variety of modes to express meaning which has helped to redefine literacy (Kress, 1997; Pahl, 2003).

VALUING CHILDREN'S OBJECTS

An artifactual literacies approach draws on the concept of literacy as situated and multimodal, but unites this with a focus on material culture, particularly in home settings. As a field of practice and research, material cultural studies offer a particularly rich vein to inform schooling. Schooling is already a materially situated social practice, but it is often separated in content from home. When people tell stories of their lives, they create opportunities for space and place to be evoked and within these spaces, objects exist. People tell different stories about the same object. When a study of narrative is put together with material cultural studies, literacy becomes materially situated. Rachel Hurdley found that people told different stories at different times about the same objects on their mantelpieces (Hurdley, 2006). Daniel Miller found that stories about objects opened a window into people's emotional and social landscapes (Miller, 2008). Shalini Shankar argued that objects did not need to be present to be important – a new car could be indexed in everyday talk as an important object even if not present (Shankar, 2006).

Jackie Marsh (2003) highlighted the extent of the objects within children's worlds, as their popular cultural icons are distributed across a range of products and objects including packed lunch boxes, duvets, curtains, toys and home objects such as mugs and cutlery. This distribution reflects the way in which children experience their ruling passions (Barton and Hamilton, 1998) as culturally mediated through objects. Recently a number of studies (e.g., McRae, 2008) have looked at the power of objects in children's cultural worlds. McCrae (2008) argues that some objects are seen as 'safe' and 'permissable' especially within classroom settings, and some objects are more 'dangerous' for example, Bratz dolls signal different kinds of cultural worlds, possibly those less congruent with the acceptable boundaries of childhood and constructions of early literacy and language within early childhood that are allowable (Marsh, 2003; this volume). These objects open up meaning-making worlds for children. Wohlwend (2009; this volume) has shown how play with objects, notably Barbie, can open up textually mediated worlds in new ways, and how the literacy and language practices that spread from this activity are rich and diverse.

We start by reviewing the literature on the use of artifacts in classrooms and homes to make meaning. We define the term 'artifacts' and show how, in our work, we have linked it to literacy. We consider its potential as a methodology within early childhood literacy for supporting meaning making. We then move to the *production* of artifactual worlds. There is an added dimension to documenting material worlds and that is to research the origins, the production of objects such as Barbies and how production orients practice and meaning making.

A central argument of the chapter is that children's commercial, technological, and hand-made artifacts provide an invaluable lens into their meaning making. In their afterword to *Travel Notes from the New Literacy Studies*, Deborah Brandt and Katie Clinton drew attention to local–global connections and how 'our interactions with technologies provide the resources for meaning making' (Brandt and Clinton, 2006: 256). Using Bruno Latour's translation model (1996), Brandt and Clinton open up a space of analysis to look at 'how we act by mediating the actions of other mediators' (Brandt and Clinton, 2006: 254). Brandt and Clinton used this model to inform their argument that multimodality provides a language for talking about technologies 'as active and ideological

social agents toward which readers and writers orient' (Brandt and Clinton, 2006: 254). We build on Brandt and Clinton's argument by examining and celebrating children's material worlds as orienting their understandings of, and pathways into meaning making. Children's artifactual worlds and the producers of children's material culture situate children to ways of seeing and mediating their worlds. Here we present new directions for artifactual literacies and highlight where we think the field is going to go next.

A REVIEW OF THE LITERATURE ON ARTIFACTUAL LITERACIES

Here, we review the literature that led us to develop the concept of artifactual literacies. We focus on literacy initially but also widen the term to use 'literacies' to signal the way in which literacy is multiple and multimodal (Flewitt, 2008). A theory of multimodality allows for ideas to be represented visually as well as in writing. The concept of multimodality grew out of semiotics – the study of signs – and the importance of seeing all sign making, or semiosis, as composed of an ensemble of modes (Kress and Van Leeuwen, 1996). Children's texts include drawings as well as writing. Texts can be multimodal and have material qualities, as they contain words and images and these both work together to create meaning (Kress, 1997; Kress and Van Leeuwen, 1996). Scholars have taken up the challenge of multimodal literacy and have illustrated in their research how meaning makers learn quite naturally through a variety of modes, sometimes in isolation and sometimes combined (Flewitt, 2008; Kress, 1997; Jewitt and Kress, 2003; Lancaster, 2003; Stein, 2003).

Meaning makers infuse the texts they write with their identities, and passions. In our work we have called this infusion *sedimentation*, and we have come up with the idea of 'sedimented identities in texts' to describe how students bring their own ways of being, doing, and feeling – their acquired dispositions – into writing (Rowsell and Pahl, 2007). The texts that children create have sedimented within them embedded shards of everyday experiences, and these experiences can be found in drawings, talk, and writing.

The process of sedimentation of social practices into modes is one that can be observed happening over time. Literacy practices unfold in material settings and are linked to the habitus. Ethnography is a way of doing research that combines thick description of everyday practice with a close account of cultures, peoples, and places (Heath and Street, 2008). It is situated, involving a longitudinal and considered study that attends to reflexivity, positionality, and multiple sources of data. Through extended study, ethnography provides a window onto meaning makers and their intentions.

When we combined ethnography with multimodality, we realized that a new theory was needed, a theory of artifactual literacies. Artifactual literacies combines a focus on texts as multimodal together with a situated account of literacies as material and artifactual within home, school, and community settings. What has been helpful in making multimodal literacy real has been to bring together multimodality as an account of the material, physical qualities of texts, together with an account of how these texts came into being or were being used, through ethnography (e.g., Kell, 2006; Stein, 2003). Meaning makers engage with text making, bringing identities with them. Looking simultaneously at the multimodal using an ethnographic perspective necessitates a close study of people, spaces, and artifacts (Green and Bloome, 1997). However, doing so involves a consideration of such disciplines as cultural geography, material cultural studies, visual sociology, and visual and sensory ethnography (e.g., Back, 2007; Christiansen and O'Brien, 2003; Miller, 2008; Pink, 2007, 2009). These disciplines can help to unravel the complexities of understanding artifacts and their link to everyday life in a situated, sensory, and visual way. A cross-disciplinary account of literacy that includes material cultural studies as well as New Literacy Studies opens up the reach of our understanding of young children's early literacy in and out of school contexts. The nature of literacy today is more variegated and multi-faceted than ever, and as a discipline, needs to look across other disciplines to understand contemporary meaning making.

We have therefore benefited from understanding literacy as sensory (Pink, 2009), material (Miller, 2010) and entangled with objects and other forms of inscriptions (Ingold, 2007). These scholars enabled us to take the leap into seeing the artifactual as sensory, tactile, and felt in everyday life and how objects can serve as a link to literacy.

Artifactual literacies can be levered for the public good (Kinloch, 2010; Lewis, 2011; McLean, 2011). It can shift the relationship between literacy and power. Some students have more access to literate forms of communication, and thus inhabit literacy more easily than others. We also draw on the work of Barbara Comber and others to recognize the importance of bringing unheard voices into literacy, for, by interrogating how literacy is situated, inequality can be challenged through critical literacies (Comber, 2010; Rogers,

Mosley and Kramer, and the Literacy for Social Justice Teacher Research Group, 2009). Artifactual literacy as an approach provides educators with a critical way of teaching literacy through a connection to lived lives and everyday experiences.

THE EVERYDAY IN THE ARTIFACTUAL

The everyday can be strange and complex when it is not your own space or everyday world. We draw our definition of the 'everyday' from Bourdieu's notion of the everyday as realized in 'practice' (1990) but also as culturally significant, from Williams' concept of 'culture is ordinary' (Williams, 1961, 2001). Everyday practice is important for educators to take on board. We have found the word *habitus* useful to describe lived experience, the acquired dispositions that shape everyday practice (Bourdieu, 1990). We can include in the habitus such as the following: everyday routines, household chores, household interactions, household literacy practices, calendars on the wall, routinized experiences, religious practices, rites of passage, parenting practices, cooking, and sharing experiences. Bourdieu (1990) described the habitus as a system of acquired dispositions, which, over time, coheres into practice and is inherited and passed down the generations. Bringing an alertness to the meanings created in everyday spaces requires an ethnographic perspective that can inform artifactual literacies. It is a holistic vision. The work of Luis Moll and colleagues has been helpful in articulating the funds of knowledge learners bring from their home worlds into the classroom (Gonzalez, Moll, and Amanti, 2005).

Identity is a key aspect of the work in artifactual literacies, in that artifacts and identities are intertwined. Identities reside on a sea of stuff and of experiences. These experiences are intertwined with material culture. Material culture is portable and travels with us. We have particularly noted the importance of objects for the identities of migrating families. Museums can be important spaces in which to validate their identities and articulate new identities. By placing home objects in museums, new kinds of stories can be told, and new identities recognized. Communities carry with them a host of artifacts, and if we pay attention to these artifacts, new voices can be listened to (Clifford, 1997; Macdonald, 2003; Bennett, 2005; Pahl and Pollard, 2010).

What these different ideas provide is a way of looking at early literacy education that is wider than writing and reading (literacy) but also wider than drawing, gesture, oral storytelling, and three dimensional representation (multimodality). This way of working lets in the everyday, in that it acknowledges the material culture that students inhabit out of school. It accounts for the timescales and rhythms of the everyday, in that artifacts can be interrogated and understood in relation to the timescales associated with them.

ARTIFACTUAL LITERACIES AS AN APPROACH TO EARLY CHILDHOOD LITERACY

In our work, we use the term artifact and object interchangeably, but we focus principally on the idea of the artifact. The notion of artifact can be defined as a thing or object that:

- has physical features that makes it distinct such as color or texture;
- is created, found, carried, put on display, hidden, evoked in language, or worn;

- embodies people, stories, thoughts, communities, identities, and experiences;
- is valued or made by a meaning-maker in a particular context.

Artifacts bring in everyday life. They are material, and they represent culture. They can link literacy, multimodality, and material culture together, by focusing the lens on meaning making that is situated and material. Artifacts open up stories and give opportunities for telling stories. Every object can tell a story: many objects carry many stories within them. These stories are repeated in interaction and remain continually told and re-told to visitors, changing in the process. Artifacts can connect worlds, as they travel between worlds. When a child connects to literacy and is asked to write a story, this is the end of a long process of meaning making that could begin in a different setting, in the everyday. For example, a child could love toy cars and be obsessed with collecting them. This interest spills into a story about cars. In school this could then be told or written as a narrative text and/or crafted as a digital story.

Artifactual literacy opens a new world that celebrates different sorts of values – the handmade (Whitty, Rose, Baisley, Comeau, and Thompson, 2008), the sensory (Pink, 2009), the storied (Hurdley, 2006), and the material (Miller, 2008). In letting new kinds of disciplines into literacy, literacy looks different. This artifactual approach offers a challenge for curriculum makers to listen to unheard voices. To conceptualize artifactual literacy requires an understanding of literacy as a situated social practice together with literacy as *materially* situated. This then brings in the everyday world of objects and stories to create meaning.

Artifacts are sensory. They carry color and smell and shape and these sensory properties also affect meaning. The habitus, the ways of being in everyday life, can be also described as sensory and embodied (Bourdieu, 1990). An understanding of habitus and artifacts within habitus moves the sensory world into centre stage. Practices involve the sensory and require situated understanding of the world that resides in everyday place-making (Pink, 2009). Acquired dispositions that move across generations, such as ways of speaking, gesture, smell, and touch are themselves embodied. A sensory response to artifacts is important when working in material culture. Elliot Eisner talks about 'somatic knowledge' as embodied responses to the world (Eisner, 2002). Artifacts smell, they can be felt, heard, listened to, and looked at. Paying attention to meaning through artifacts involves recognizing embodied understandings as responses.

Objects uncover people and epistemologies. Not having respect for an object undermines a way of understanding the world, cutting off from an important line of enquiry. An embodied appreciation of space and place provides a richer and more situated understanding of objects together with an 'in the world' appreciation of experiences such as food and visual media (Pink, 2009). This links to the theory by Lanigan and others which has focused on a semiotic phenomenology, that is, a way of understanding experience that is located in the body and is somatic (Lanigan, 1988). What these ideas provide is a way of looking at literacy education that is wider than writing and reading (literacy), but also is wider than drawing, gesture, oral storytelling and three-dimensional representation (multimodality). This way of working acknowledges the material culture that students inhabit out of school.

Objects are linked to timescales and are also tied to particular places and spaces. These spaces can be intercultural and transnational, and can cross linguistic and cultural boundaries. For example, in a discussion of the enduring value of gold in her family, Ruksana, a British Asian woman, also talked of how she liked to spray her elephants gold, these elephants were a pair of polystyrene elephants that she had decorated and put in her living room, to reflect an aesthetic she liked. However, she also talked of the enduring value of gold as a core family symbol of inheritance and support. Gold was described jokingly as being like 'bling' by another family member. The meanings around gold shifted and were reproduced in different ways in different cultural contexts (Pahl and Pollard, 2008).

Children draw on their artifactual experiences as a resource for meaning making. Artifacts are objects to grow with. Many students have a favorite stuffed toy they recall from early childhood, that they still treasure. Children can identify the stages of childhood through their objects. Here is Sam, age 8, talking about his objects (see Pahl, 2003, 2005):

> I've always been changing my subject. When I was a baby I liked wheels, then I liked Thomas the Tank Engine, then I liked Robots, I liked Space then I liked Pokémon through seven and a little bit of eight, then I'm into Warhammer now I've moved on from the rest of my – I was getting bigger all those eight life years.
> (Interview, 20 November 2001)

Artifacts lever power different in classroom settings. For example, in a project which involved asking parents and children to work jointly to fill shoeboxes to represent the children's identities called 'All about me', conducted with 5–6 year-olds in Bristol, UK, the project team found out that the object boxes opened up new worlds in new ways,

> It was noticeable that some of their boxes contained some very personal items – a first babygro, a page from the local paper in which the child had featured in an article on a children's bereavement service, a book called 'You Are Special', presented to the child at nursery school.
> (Greenhough et al., 2005: 99)

The project enabled the children to bring their home identities into school but also had a powerful role in inspiring writing. Some of the writing was strong and let in new emotional spaces (Scanlan, 2010). Artifacts are entangled within identities and can be evoked and re-animated within narratives. Artifacts can open up new worlds of experience. Talking about artifacts provides ways into narratives that are not always accessible in other ways. They can be used to encourage children to respect diversity, to find points of commonality across communities and can be used as important starting points for literacy learning. Artifacts are also key ingredients for family stories, that provide meaning and direction for lives lived in communities. Collective and social memories are helped and brought into new spaces through family stories and artifacts (Connerton, 1989; Brooke, 2003).

Sometimes we may not recognize the meaning-making potential of artifacts. For instance, commercial artifacts such as Sponge Bob toys, Dora the Explorer stuffed dolls, Toy Story bedspreads, console games; there are so many media-driven objects that children value and that play a role in their narratives. These objects orient their story-telling, their conceptions of characterization, humour, aesthetics, and notions of design. Children have passion for media and popular culture texts and as educators we need to respect and, most importantly, understand their passion for these artifacts. Hence, we take an equal account of production and reception logic of artifacts as a window into early childhood literacy.

We argue for the power of artifacts to lever in experiences from outside school and to unite children who might have disparate experiences, creating listening opportunities between children and adults. Artifacts mediate experience in gentler ways. Artifacts sit between human and material worlds and in this way, they are the liminal, in-between, border spaces that allow complex identities to feel comfortable. We now turn to a further field we have identified: that of the artifactual nature of children's worlds as expressed in the designs of the texts they engage in, thus further shifting the artifactual nature of their literacies.

DESIGN LITERACIES MEETS ARTIFACTUAL LITERACIES

In the field of early childhood literacy, there has been powerful work by scholars such as Jackie Marsh (2010) and Karen Wohlwend (2009) prompting us to acknowledge commercial artifacts as key objects or artifacts which signal important meaning-making practices by children. Marsh (2010) investigated children's use of virtual worlds that offer a range of opportunities. Marsh developed a mixed-methods study of multimodal resources in the home tied to commercial juggernauts such as Club Penguin and Barbie Girls. Marsh demonstrated how home sites enable children to create and dress avatars and decorate avatar homes and care for pets. Similarly, Wohlwend (2009) shows how gender identity messages circulate through toys and artifacts that surround young children as consumers. Anne Haas Dyson (2003) argued that literacy educators need to take account of children's

engagement with the diversity of literacies in order to successfully make sense of print and text making in contemporary communicational landscapes. From such work, there is an acknowledgement that we need to stretch beyond a sole gaze on schooling, even home cultures, to look at how designers and marketplace producers design virtual worlds, toys, and immersive worlds for young children (Sheridan-Rabideau and Rowsell, 2010; Rowsell, 2012).

Toys, action figures, lunch boxes, t-shirts, dolls, and other objects occupy a treasured place in children's lives and we should examine their role and what they can tell us about children's learning. To examine material worlds, we take account of where objects are situated, how objects are used *and* we account for their production. Sometimes valued objects or artifacts are hand-made or handed-down, but more often than not, valued artifacts are store-bought and commercially oriented. We described earlier the concept of an Ariadne's thread running between commercial artifacts and media and technology producers. We harness our work applying artifactual literacies in our research (Pahl and Rowsell, 2010) to an account of marketplace producers' logic of text production (Sheridan-Rabideau and Rowsell, 2010).

ARTIFACTUAL LITERACIES AS A TRIGGER FOR HOME MEANING MAKING

In this small vignette of practice, we describe the way in which artifactual literacies are found in the home. In an ethnographic study on writing in the home, an understanding of literacy as artifactual was derived from the dataset. This case study is taken from a year-long study of four 8–13-year-old girls' meaning-making practices in two homes ('Writing in the Home and in the Street' funded by the Arts and Humanities Research Council, UK). In this example Kate describes meaning-making practices in one of the homes, which is inhabited by Anita, and her husband, Abdul, and their three daughters, who were 12, 8, and 2. Anita's home is suffused with artifacts. Within these objects, literacy appears but it is often embedded within artifacts.

This home helped develop an understanding of artifactual literacies as they occur naturalistically. As an ethnographer, Kate records her perceptions and fieldnotes using the first person. Here is an extract from an account of the home:

> When I walk in, the things on the floor and on the seating area vary. Sometimes there are toys and small books strewn about the floor of the back living room. As part of the ethnography, I asked the older girls to record these objects (see figure 15.1).
>
> There are to be found fragments of script within the toys and artifacts. For example a board book

for the youngest child, aged two was inscribed with Arabic letters. The family members attend mosque school, as British Muslims, and their literacies were multilingual. Writing was both fixed and fluid in the home, instantiated in artifacts. For example, I encountered an 'Etch-a-Sketch' in which the youngest writes on where the script is wholly artifactual and ephemeral. These objects are relatively fluid, in that they move about, and are sometimes visible, and sometimes are tidied away when the youngest is asleep and the mother does the housework. A computer is placed in the corner, on which the older girls (8 and 12) do their homework and write stories and emails to me, and the mother sends orders for garden products.

This computer is fixed. However, many of the artifactual literacies in the household are fluid. The literacy practices in this household are embedded within the artifacts that surround them. For example, here is a purse-making episode, described by Lucy, 12:

> Lucy: Here, I have made a purse
> And I can put my money and cards in it
> And I have put lots of stickers
> And three D stickers as well on
> And I have put all my favourite things on this side
> And I have put some things I hate and some things I like on this side

Figure 15.1   Artifactual Literacies in a home

I have got little gems and stars
And little animals and food on
And little signs that say keep out top secret (film;
4 August 2010)

For Lucy's sister, who is 2, her experience of literacy is mediated through artifacts. She experiences the textiles and embroidery that the family constantly engages in. This piece of embroidery, for example, was stitched by her older sister and was an example of the many craft activities the family produced (See Figure 15.2 below).

Lucy's aunt explained in an email how the family's meaning making was imbued with their family heritage in relation to textiles:

> The textile side of our heritage comes from the women in the family. We have older relatives that do appliqué, crochet, embroidery, sewing, and knitting (from the girl's mother's side their grandmothers sister and cousin and from their father side his two cousins who live close by). My younger sister loves craft type of activities and buys the girls a lot of resources to do sewing and fabric work especially on birthdays, Christmas, and Eid
> (Written text from the girls' aunt, e-mail, August 2010)

An artifactual literacies approach can take account of these craft productions, and notice the material nature of the inscriptions that are produced within the home. These productions are located in the everyday, handmade world of artifactual literacies. They can be transported across to school settings, in projects such as the shoebox project,

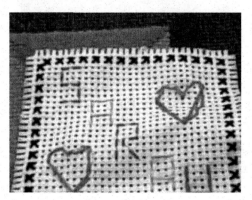

Figure 15.2   Embroidery

or using a home literacies lens to look at writing. They open up cultural worlds and act as a lever for articulating and represent diverse family ecologies (Lee, 2008).

NEW DIRECTIONS IN ARTIFACTUAL LITERACIES

Here, we highlight the directions we think the field of artifactual literacies is going, and point to some ways forward. We also consider the problematics of this methodology and highlight some research that we think could usefully further the field yet more. We begin by considering artifactual critical literacies, then literacies in relation to place and space and then examine how artifactual literacies can be levered for the public good in early literacy.

Artifactual critical literacies

Critical literacy education is in-place; that is, it accounts for place and space in its methodology. Comber (2010) has used a place-based approach combined with critical literacy to look at the ways in which children's literacies of place can effect social change. This work also involves artifacts.

Critical literacy is about mobilizing that platform using texts; artifactual critical literacy is about mobilizing that platform through artifacts. Artifacts open up worlds that bring in new identities. For example, a further step would then be to interrogate the artifacts in relation to institutes of power. Artifacts could be discussed from the point of view of:

- value – does value matter in the case of this artifact? If not, why not?;
- timescale – what is the timescale of the artifact? Is it intergenerational?;
- space – what spaces has the artifact inhabited, and how has it traveled?;

- production – is the artifact found or newly made? How was it made?;
- mode – what modality is most salient and why?;
- relation to institutions of power – who controls the artifact and its attendant communities?

By asking questions of artifacts in relation to the way they are made, the timescales, and the modality of their making, and linking this interrogation to a design literacies perspective (Sheridan-Rabideau and Rowsell, 2010), it is possible to open up meaning-making spaces for young children which privilege their worlds, be it Barbie, Pokémon, Club Penguin or their grandmother's biscuit tin. For example, a discussion of the role of a Pokémon card in a young person's life could incorporate the various manifestations of Pokémon (cards, games, TV series, dolls, etc.) as well as the ways in which these cards have accompanied the child through life and the role of Pokémon cards at home and at school, and their different uses across domains of practice. This then could extend critical literacy work with young children, drawing, for example on the work of Larson and Marsh (2005) on critical literacy in the classroom.

Place-based artifactual literacies

This way of working moves out of the spaces of the classroom into the connective spaces of community. Barbara Comber (2010) worked with teachers within the tradition of critical literacy in order to focus on place-based pedagogies, to develop what she describes, from Gruenewald, as a 'critical pedagogy of place' (2003: 45). This focuses outwards, from schools into the complex and contradictory spaces of communities, with a focus on social justice and visions of change. Children published writing and art to articulate a vision for the communities they inhabited. Students

mapped their communities and created multimodal texts that presented alternative visions of what their school, the surrounding areas and play spaces could look like (Comber, 2010).

The perspective from which a community is viewed affects the sense of its space. Children grow up and observe their neighborhoods and communities. Their visions of place and space might not be the same as adults as they encounter their social worlds from a different perspective (Orellana, 1999). We argue that children's experiences of neighborhood means that place, too, is always shifting, as artifacts and experience are rolled up into new life trajectories and experiences. Children walk through the neighborhood, and as they grow older, their experience of place shifts. From looking at the world when sitting in a stroller, a child then walks holding an adult's hands through the mall, experiencing the place-shaped literacies around them. Tim Ingold (2007) talks about 'entangled' pathways; that is, he focuses on the making of routes in the sensory experiences of place. Sarah Pink (2009) has described ways in which places can be sensed through participation in practices such as walking, eating, and sharing chores and routines. Place is experienced bodily and the mapping of place through visual methods, such as video camera and photography, and audio methods of recording can call up memories of place that can be collectively shared in classrooms.

ARTIFACTUAL LITERACIES FOR THE PUBLIC GOOD

What happens if artifacts are united with a critical literacies perspective? Critical literacies is about accounting for power. Power resides within texts, but also can be discussed and accounted for during the

making of texts and in the uniting of perspectives to collectively create social
change. It accounts for different ways of
conceptualizing identities, communities,
and texts. Critical literacy education is also
in-place. It means accounting for communities. By walking through a community,
looking at visual signs and experiencing
a community fully, a deeper engagement
with space and place is let in. Within
these spaces are artifacts, embedded in
public and private spaces. Recent work
in spatial literacies include work drawing on the work of Soja (2010) who
describes space as a site for creating more
equality, or, conversely, the inequalities
that are set up through space can be
challenged. Massey (2005) talks about the
'thrown togetherness' of neighbourhoods.
Young children inhabit spaces that are
riven with power imbalances. Their worlds
can be interrogated using artifactual
critical literacies.

By describing our work as being linked
to the public good, that is, using an artifactual literacies approach to create spaces
for children that are equitable we can make
explicit and frame the work in a particular
way. This perspective draws on work by
Morrell (2008) and Kinloch (2010) in
working with older children to identify key
artifacts in neighborhoods and make sense
of them in relation to sites and distribution
of power. For example, in an early childhood context, community walk-arounds
can identify where children locate their
meaning making and sense of place. They
can then draw on these place-making methodologies in their writing (Comber, 2010).
An artifactual literacies approach can
lever home experiences, the messy, everyday handmade world of home literacies
and popular culture and open up equitable
meaning making spaces in the classroom
(see Nichols and Nixon, chapter 16 this

volume; Wohlwend, chapter 5 this volume;
Marsh, chapter 12 this volume).

MERGING ARTIFACTUAL LITERACIES WITH DESIGN LITERACIES AS A HEURISTIC FOR EARLY CHILDHOOD LITERACY

What happens when commercially produced artifacts are viewed as valuable
heuristics into children's meaning-making?
The power of Dora or Scooby Doo lie
in their stories, narratives, designs, and
most importantly, children's remixing of
their narratives in their everyday meaning-
making. Karen Wohlwend (2009) shows
how gender identity messages circulate
through toys and artifacts that surround
young children as consumers. Through
close analysis of commercial texts and
products, Wohlwend examines the close
connection between commercialized products and children's meaning-making. From
another perspective, Helen Nixon focuses
on commercial providers as key networks
of information about parenting and children's development and literacy learning
(Nixon, 2011). There will be increasing
research focus on commercialized literacy
and communicational and artifactual media
as key learning tools for children's literacy
development. Combining artifactual literacy as an approach to early childhood literacy with design literacies as accounting
for commercial designers' role in learning
will (and should) be a key factor for future
research in early literacy.

We have signaled this merging of a field
as taking greater prominence as we move
further into the twenty-first century. An
artifactual-design literacies approach creates a niche field devoted not only to the
technologies of choice by children and
tweens, but also to an acknowledgement

that commercial providers have a voice and play a role in educating young children.

PROBLEMS AND QUESTIONS

In this section we highlight some problems and questions we have identified associated with the field of artifactual literacies. First, we have a challenge in the form of global warming. How can an artifactual-literacies approach work to create sustainability for our children? We have begun to theorize links across from rural literacies and sustainable literacies (Brooke, 2003; Comber, 2010; Pahl and Rowsell, 2012) that then recognize the artifactual nature of the natural world, for example, garden making as collaborative text, which can then unite an artifactual literacies approach with place making (Pahl and Rowsell, 2012)

We would also like artifactual literacies to lever power in the direction of new migrants, and those who are fleeing hostility. Artifactual literacies can also evoke timescales that are long and short, and they can bridge spaces. Artifacts can signal migratory spaces and can be represented in multiple languages and modalities (Pahl, Pollard, and Rafiq, 2009). In that way, they signal the presence of the dispossessed and migratory and signal epistemological realities that are sometimes hidden.

CONCLUSION

Artifacts position learners differently. Artifacts open up modalities and subjectivities. To extend their argument, Brandt and Clinton talk about how the autonomous model that Brian Street (1993) identified in his work as a universalized, reified notion of what literacy is and should be dictates the kinds of thinking and reasoning that occurs when reading and writing. If there is a print-based, universalized, autonomous model, then it follows that print-bearing texts have the power and the technologies of print are more important than human-mediated actions used to understand and reason with them. However, Latour (1996) and his model of mediation resists the temptation to define technologies acting on something or someone and, instead, views meaning making as more fluid and emergent based on social interaction. As a result, Brandt and Clinton put affordances forward as a more ideological way of seeing how we think and reason with things and technologies. In their words: 'if we think of literacy technologies as having affordances and if we think of people mediating these affordances, then we have a model for thinking about both human and non-human action' (Brandt and Clinton, 2006: 255). This is a key notion running throughout the chapter: we think and reason through objects and correspondingly, they shape what it means to be literate. We can also celebrate the diversity of cultural spaces outside school in a way that lets in new kinds of identities, through script, toys, and handmade objects.

This kind of work can then question the settled nature of objects within kindergarten and nursery settings to allow new identities to reside within these spaces and be heard. The writing that stems from artifactual literacies connects to the everyday world of the habitus, it is linked in with the sensory, embodied world of objects and can draw on a wider range of modalities in the meaning-making process. Artifactual literacies in the early years is therefore both a methodology for encouraging writing, a way of understanding the production of meaning making and a window into children's popular cultural worlds that acknowledges the materiality of these worlds. We would like to celebrate artifactual literacies as an approach that lets in diversity and challenges normative scripts for family life; rather it listens to young children's passions and embedded worlds, and makes them visible.

REFERENCES

Back, L. (2007). *The Art of Listening*. Oxford: Berg.

Barton, D. and Hamilton, M. (1998). *Local Literacies: Reading and Writing in One Community*. London: Routledge.

Bennett, T. (2005). 'Civic laboratories: Museums, cultural objecthood and the governance of the social', *Cultural Studies*, 19(5): 521–47.

Bourdieu, P. (1990). *The Logic of Practice*. Tr. R. Nice. Cambridge: Polity Press.

Brandt, D. and Clinton, K. (2006). *Afterword to Travel Notes to the New Literacy Studies*. Clevedon, UK: Multilingual Matters.

Brooke, R.E. (ed.) (2003). *Rural Voices: Place-Conscious Education and the Teaching of Writing*. New York: Teachers College Press.

Christiansen, P. and O'Brien, M. (eds) (2003). *Children in the City: Home, Neighbourhood and Community*. London: Routledge.

Clifford, J. (1997). *Routes, Travel and Translation in the Late Twentieth Century*. Cambridge, MA: Harvard University Press.

Comber, B. (2010). 'Critical literacies in place: Teachers who work for just and sustainable communities', in: J. Lavia and M. Moore (eds), *Cross-Cultural Perspectives in Policy and Practice: Decolonizing Community Contexts*. London: Routledge. pp. 46–57.

Connerton, P. (1989). *How Societies Remember*. Cambridge: Cambridge University Press.

Dyson, A.H. (2003). *The Brothers and Sisters Learn to Write: Popular Literacies in Childhood and School Cultures*. New York: Teachers College Press.

Eisner, E.W. (2002). *The Arts and the Creation of Mind*. New Haven: Yale University Press.

Flewitt, R. (2008) 'Multimodal literacies', in J. Marsh and E. Hallet (eds), *Desirable Literacies: Approaches to Language and Literacy in the Early Years*. London: Sage. pp. 122–39.

Gonzalez, N., Moll, L., and Amanti, C. (eds) (2005). *Funds of Knowledge: Theorizing Practices in Households, Communities and Classrooms*. Rahway, NJ: Lawrence Erlbaum Ass.

Green, J. and Bloome, D. (1997). 'Ethnography and ethnographers of and in education: A situated perspective', in J. Flood, S. Heath, and D. Lapp (eds), *A Handbook for Literacy Educators: Research on Teaching the Communicative and Visual Arts*. New York: Macmillan. pp. 1–12.

Greenhough, P., Scanlan, M., Feiler, A., Johnson, D., Yee, W.C., Andrews, J., Price, A., Smithson, M., and Hughes, M. (2005). 'Boxing clever: using shoeboxes to support home–school knowledge exchange', *Literacy*, 39(2): 97–103.

Gregory, E and Williams, A. (2000). *City Literacies: Learning to read across generations and cultures*. London: Routledge.

Gregory, E., Long, S., and Volk, D. (eds) (2004). *Many Pathways to Literacy: Young Children Learning with Siblings, Grandparents, Peers, Communities*. London: Routledge.

Gruenewald, D. (2003). 'The best of both worlds: A critical pedagogy of place', *Educational Researcher*, 32(3): 3–12.

Heath, S.B. (1983). *Ways with Words: Language, Life and Work in Communities and Classrooms*. Cambridge: Cambridge University Press.

Heath, S.B. and Street, B.V. (with Mills, M.) (2008). *On Ethnography: Approaches to Language and Literacy Research*. New York: Teachers College Press/NCRLL.

Hurdley, R. (2006). 'Dismantling mantelpieces: Narrating identities and materializing culture in the home', *Sociology*, 40(4): 71733.

Ingold, T. (2007). *Lines: A Brief History*. London: Routledge.

Jewitt, C. and Kress, G. (eds) (2003). *Multimodal Literacy*. London: Peter Lang.

Kell, C. (2006). 'Crossing the margins: Literacy, semiotics and the recontextualisation of meanings', in: K. Pahl and J. Rowsell (eds) (2006). *Travel Notes from the New Literacy Studies: Instances of Practice*. Clevedon, UK: Multilingual Matters. pp. 147–72.

Kinloch, V. (2010). *Harlem on our Minds: Place, Race, and the Literacies of Urban Youth*. New York: Teachers College Press.

Kress, G. (1997). *Before Writing: Rethinking the Paths to Literacy*. London: Routledge.

Kress, G. and Van Leeuwen, T. (1996). *Reading Images: The Grammar of Visual Design*. London: Routledge.

Lancaster, L. (2003). 'Beginning at the beginning: How a young child constructs time multimodally', in G. Kress and C. Jewitt (eds), *Multimodal Literacy*. London: Peter Lang. pp. 107–22.

Lanigan, R.L. (1988). *Phenomenology of Communication: Merleau-Ponty's Thematic in Communcology and Semiology*. Pittsburgh, PA: Duquesne University Press.

Larson, J. and Marsh, J. (2005). *Making Literacy Real: Theories and Practices for Learning and Teaching*. London: Sage.

Latour, B. (1996). *Aramis, or the Love of Technology*. Cambridge, MA: Harvard University Press.

Lee, C.D. (2008). 'The centrality of culture to the scientific study of learning and development: How an ecological framework in education research facilitates civic responsibility', *Educational Researcher*, 37: 267.

Lewis, T. (2011). 'Intergenerational meaning-making between a mother and son in digital spaces', in C. Compton-Lilly and S. Greene (eds), *Bedtime Stories and Book Reports: Connecting Parent Involvement and Family Literacy*. New York: Teachers College Press. pp. 85–94.

Macdonald, S. (2003). 'Museums, national, postnational and transcultural identities', *Museum and Society*, 1(1): 1–16.

MacRae, C. (2008). 'Representing space: Katie's horse and the recalcitrant object', *Contemporary Issues in Early Childhood*, 9(4): 275–86.

Marsh, J. (2003). 'Early childhood literacy and popular culture', in N. Hall, J. Larson, and J. Marsh (eds), *Handbook of Early Childhood Literacy*. London, New Dehli, Thousand Oaks, CA: Sage. pp. 112–25.

Marsh, J. (2010). 'Young children's play in online virtual worlds', *Journal of Early Childhood Research*, 8(1): 23–39.

Massey, D. (2005). *For Space*. London: Sage.

McLean, C. (2011). 'Cultural dialogue as identity-work', in S. Abrams and J. Rowsell (eds), *Rethinking Identity and Literacy Education in the 21st Century*. Teachers College Record Annual Yearbook. New York: Teachers College Press.

Miller, D. (2008). *The Comfort of Things*. Cambridge, MA: Polity Press.

Miller, D. (2010). *Stuff*. London: Routledge.

Moll, L., Amanti, C., Neff, D., and Gonzalez, N. (1992). Funds of knowledge for teaching: Using a qualitative approach to connect homes and classrooms. *Theory Into Practice*, 31: 132–141.

Morrell, E. (2008). *Critical Literacy and Urban Youth: Pedagogies of Access, Dissent and Liberation*. London and New York: Routledge.

Nixon, H. (2011). 'From bricks to clicks: Hybrid commercial spaces in the landscape of early literacy and learning', *Journal of Early Childhood Literacy*, 11(2): 114–140.

Orellana, M.F. (1999). 'Space and place in an urban landscape: Learning from children's views of their social worlds', *Visual Sociology*, 14: 23–88.

Pahl, K. (2002). 'Ephemera, mess and miscellaneous piles: texts and practices in families', *Journal of Early Childhood Literacy*, 2(2): 145–65.

Pahl, K. (2003). 'Children's text making at home: Transforming meaning across modes', in C. Jewitt and G. Kress (eds), *Multimodal Literacy*. New York: Peter Lang. pp. 139–54.

Pahl, K. (2005). 'Children's popular culture in the home: Tracing cultural practices in texts', in J. Marsh and E. Millard (eds), *Popular Literacies, Childhood and Schooling*. London: Routledge/Falmer. pp. 29–53.

Pahl, K. and Pollard, A. (2008). '"Bling – the Asians introduced that to the country": Gold and its value within a group of families of South Asian origin in Yorkshire', *Visual Communication*, 7(2): 170–82.

Pahl, K. and Pollard, A. (2010). 'The case of the disappearing object: Narratives and artefacts in homes and a museum exhibition from Pakistani heritage families in South Yorkshire', *Museum and Society*, 8(1): 1–17.

Pahl, K. and Rowsell, J. (2010). *Artfactual Literacies: Every Object Tells a Story*. New York: Teachers College Press.

Pahl, K. and Rowsell, J. (2012). *Literacy and Education: Understanding the New Literacy Studies in the Classroom*. 2nd edn. London: Sage.

Pahl, K. with Pollard, A., and Rafiq, Z. (2009). 'Changing identities, changing spaces: The Ferham families exhibition in Rotherham', *Moving Worlds*, 9(2): 80–103.

Pink, S. (2007). *Doing Visual Ethnography*. 2nd edn. London: Sage.

Pink, S. (2009). *Doing Sensory Ethnography*. London: Sage.

Rogers, R., Mosley, M., Kramer, M.A., and the Literacy for Social Justice Teacher Research Group (2009). *Designing Socially Just Learning Communities*. London: Routledge.

Rogoff, B. (2003). *The Cultural Nature of Human Development*. Cambridge: Cambridge University Press.

Rowsell, J. (2012). *Working With Multimodality: Learning in a Digital Age*. London: Routledge.

Rowsell, J. and Pahl, K. (2007). 'Sedimented identities in texts: Instances of practice', *Reading Research Quarterly*, 42(3): 388–401.

Scanlan, M. (2010) 'Opening the box: Literacy, artefacts and identity', *Literacy*, 44(1): 28–36.

Shankar, S. (2006) 'Metaconsumptive practices and the circulation of objectifications', *Journal of Material Culture*, 11(3): 293–317.

Sheridan-Rabideau, M.P. and Rowsell, J. (2010). *Design Literacies: Learning and Innovation in the Digital Age*. London: Routledge.

Soja, E. (2010). *Seeking Spatial Justice*. Minneapolis: University of Minnesota Press.

Stein, P. (2003). 'The Olifantsvlei Fresh Stories project: Multimodality, creativity and fixing in the semiotic chain', in C. Jewitt and G. Kress (eds), *Multimodal Literacy*. New York: Peter Lang. pp. 123–38.

Street, B.V. (1984). *Literacy in Theory and Practice*. Cambridge: Cambridge University Press.

Street, B.V. (ed.) (1993). *Cross-Cultural Approaches to Literacy*. Cambridge: Cambridge University Press.

Street, B.V. and Street, J. (1991). 'The schooling of literacy', in D. Barton and R. Ivanic (eds), *Writing in the Community*. London: Sage. pp. 143–66.

Whitty, P., Rose, S., with Baisley, D., Comeau, L., and Thompson, A. (2008). 'Honouring educators' co-construction of picture books', *Child Study*, 33(2): 21–3.

Williams, R. (1961). *The Long Revolution*. London: Penguin.

Williams, R. (2001). 'Culture is ordinary', reprinted in J. Higgins (ed.), *The Raymond Williams Reader*. London: Blackwell. ['Culture is ordinary' was first published in N. MacKenzie (ed.) (1958). *Convictions*. Macgibbon and Gee.]

Wohlwend, K. (2009). 'Damsels in discourse: Girls consuming and producing identity texts through Disney princess play', *Reading Research Quarterly*, 44(1): 57–83.

16

Space, Place and Early Childhood Literacy

Sue Nichols and Helen Nixon

INTRODUCTION

This chapter examines the changing landscape of literacy in the early years and considers how the diverse spaces and places in which early literacy learning is promoted and takes place can be conceptualised and researched. Ethnographic researchers have for some time emphasised the situatedness of literacy practices, arguing that they are produced and learned in the context of particular social and located relationships (e.g., Barton and Hamilton 1998; Barton, Hamilton and Ivanic 2000; Heath, 1983; Street, 1984; see also Leander and Sheehy, 2004, for studies that disrupt what they call a 'folk' notion of how literacies are 'situated'). They study literacy and identity in and across the settings that constitute people's lifeworlds in what Barton (1994) has described as an 'ecology' of literate practices across home, school and community contexts. Early literacy research in this tradition has focussed largely on the

home, and has paid attention to factors such as the social class, linguistic heritage and cultural practices of immediate and extended families. However, studies that focus centrally on the material and spatial aspects of contexts as contributors to the process of early literacy learning have been comparatively rare.

The 'spatial turn' (Soja 2010: 13) in social research owes much to the conceptual work of Lefebvre (1971/1991) who argued that space is socially produced. Lefebvre identified and challenged two dominant ways of thinking about space, both of which downplayed the social dimension of human life: the concept of physical space (the geographical perspective) and the concept of mental space (the philosophical perspective). He argued not only that there is such a thing as social space, but that both physical and mental spaces are also socially produced. The social production of physical space is easiest to understand in relation to the architectural environment, such as a school building, which is clearly designed by humans in order to encompass human activity. Lefebvre argued that even what is believed to be pure nature is, in contemporary conditions, socially produced, for example by an agreement not to exploit the natural resources in a wilderness.

As a critical social theorist, Lefebvre was interested in power and in the ways that social space can be shaped to control social subjects. His comments on spatial practice are particularly resonant in relation to the role of space in systems of schooling: 'Spatial practice ... embraces production and reproduction, and the particular locations and spatial sets characteristic of each social formation. Spatial practice ensures continuity and some degree of coherence. ... this cohesion implies a guaranteed level of *competence* and a specific level of *performance*' (1971/1991: 33). Later in this chapter, we will discuss examples of spatial practice in the early childhood classroom which illustrate how the child's competence and performance are spatially and materially regulated.

Critical spatial theory has challenged social researchers to research in spatially sensitive ways. This involves attending to space as physical (materially present), as mental (conceptualised) and as social (culturally experienced). What has been called 'place-based' research takes a similarly expanded view, challenging limited views of space as separate from human action. Gieryn for instance defines place in terms of three features: geographic location, material form, and investment with meaning and value. In relation to material form he writes: 'Social processes (difference, power, inequality, collective action) happen through the material forms that we design, build, use, and protest' (2000; 465).

Applied to literacy, this perspective encourages us to ask: What are the material forms through which the social processes of literacy are enacted and how have these been designed?

In educational research, the field of policy sociology has drawn on the work of Lefebvre, and social geographers Harvey, Massey and Soja, to develop 'sophisticated understandings of the competing rationalities underlying educational policy change, social inequality and cultural practices' (Gulson and Symes, 2007: 98; see special issues of *Discourse: Studies in the Cultural Politics of Education*, 2011, 32(2), and *Critical Studies in Education*, 2011, 52(3)). However, the language of spatiality in educational research has most often been employed metaphorically, lending weight to the argument that space and place are as yet 'under-examined and under-theorized components of educational studies, development and critique' (Gulson and Symes, 2007 100). In particular, 'space' has often been employed as a metaphor for non-material qualities and processes much as the term 'landscape' is used in the first sentence of this chapter. The notion of a 'space for talk' is one of the ways in which the metaphor is employed: McIntyre, Kyle, and Moore for instance describe teachers 'creating a space for children to construct new understandings through talk' (2006: 60) and also discuss how the research meetings 'provided a space to discuss instructional practices' (2000: 45). Opportunity, possibility and permission are notions that are part of this understanding of space, as when Rogers and Mosley 'report an instance of "racial literacy" in which teachers "opened a space for themselves as white people to critique the unfair practices of other white people" (2006: 483). Understanding space in this metaphorical way usefully directs attention to aspects of power, control and agency; however, it does not necessarily translate into, or mesh in any straightforward way with, an understanding of space as specific material environments in which embodied participation occurs. In conceptualising space and place in relation to children's literacy participation, we argue for a 'semiotics of materiality' (Law, 2003). That is to say, we are focusing on space conceptualised in relation to material places, rather than as a more abstract construct.

Of course, this raises the question of the status of cyberspace. In considering the status of the virtual in a spatially sensitive conceptualisation of early childhood literacy, we take heed from studies which show that 'Internet media [are] continuous with and embedded in other social spaces' (Miller and Slater, 2001). Virtual spaces are constructed using strategies of representation that present them as having elements of geographic space (Gieryn, 2000). But more than this, the virtual is experienced by embodied human actors located in physical space who have to coordinate their interactions with material objects (keypads, screens) in order to accomplish actions in the virtual realm (Wohlwend, Vander Zanden, Husbye, and Kuby, 2011).

In this chapter, we focus on studies that can contribute to a 'semiotics of materiality' of early childhood literacy through focussing on space and place as dimensions of children's literacy development, learning and resourcing. This is not to critique other understandings of space but to add another layer to our understanding of early childhood literacy participation and learning. The first three sections of the chapter are devoted to studies that investigate the material and spatial aspects of the literacy environments of the home, the neighbourhood and institutionalised education and care settings. In the final

section, we explore how these spaces are connected by considering literacy learning as something that is accomplished *across* spaces and *in interaction with* ideas, signs and resources that flow into and out of specific places.

DOMESTIC SPACES AND EARLY CHILDHOOD LITERACY

The home has long been accepted as an important setting for later learning. However, despite the common use of spatial metaphors in depicting the home as an important 'site' or 'environment' for learning in the early years, rarely do studies investigate the home as a socially configured and material space. Rather, research has tended to rely on statistical analysis of scientifically validated 'inventories',[1] sometimes supplemented by interviews or focus groups with parents, to correlate aspects of the 'home environment' with children's learning and development. The field of early childhood literacy has been no exception in this regard.

Research conducted by Weigel, Martin, and Bennett (2005, 2006) is typical of an approach that backgrounds features of the home as a domestic space for literacy learning. Although this study is based on the ecological theory of Brofenbrenner (1979), and argues the importance and *interdependence* of the home and other early childhood care *environments*, the spatial and material qualities of these environments are not investigated. For example, drawing on earlier studies, Weigel et al. (2006) identify three key aspects of the 'home literacy environment' that have been considered influential: *parental demographic characteristics* (e.g., level of education, household income, literacy levels); *parental literacy habits* that expose children to models of literacy (time spent reading, writing, watching television); and *parent–child literacy activities* such as shared book reading and language activities (how often parents read to children and visit the library with them, the number of picture books in the home for children's use) (2006: 195–8). Statistical analyses of data generated from inventories about such characteristics lead researchers to categorise and compare home literacy environments as being more or less 'rich in direct and indirect literacy opportunities for children' (Weigel et al., 2006: 209). However, despite their emphasis on the home as an environment, studies like this tend to ignore or downplay reports of parents that comment on the material obstacles or spatial challenges to fostering literacy learning in the home such as 'lack of *reading materials* and a quiet *place*' (2006: 201, italics added).

Despite the limitations of studies of the home literacy environment that have relied on parent-completed inventories of the variables described above, some studies have also reported on qualitative data about the *spatial arrangements* of the home and *literacy-related material objects* found within it. Weinberger (1996), for example, noted specific details about the kinds of literacy-related objects that children aged 3–6 years had access to and how they were sourced. She notes that some children 'had access to drawing and writing materials, games and TV', and that 'books in the home were usually bought from the post office, newsagent or supermarket' (1996: 54). While this study did not specifically focus on how the home was configured or used as a space, the author noted how literacy materials, particularly books, were organised and placed in the home. She points out that, in most homes, 'most books were stored on shelves'

(1996: 90). However for the children aged 3 years whose books were kept in the toybox rather than on shelves, five of the total of 60 children from 42 families 'had literacy difficulties' (1996: 90). In another study by Wilkinson (2003), case studies of the at-home reading practices of four children aged from 22 months to 34 months were produced on the basis of interviews with parents, three of which took place in the home. Wilkinson too describes, but does not comment on, the physical arrangement of books in homes. For example, in each of the three homes she visited books were described as 'lined up carefully' (2003: 282) by the children's mothers; 'carefully lined up on the floor' (2003: 283); and 'organized ... [in a book shelf] into doing books, story books and information books' (2003: 285). Such findings hint at the potential value of inquiring more closely into the material features and spatial arrangements of the home in relation to the opportunities these provide for children's literacy learning and whether and how these possibilities are taken up.

Many early childhood researchers over time have noted the range of popular cultural objects and texts that exist in the home (see Marsh, chapter 12 this volume). Most recently, the widespread take up of personal computers and digital devices has renewed researchers' attention to the home as a *space* for early literacy development that accompanies children's participation in popular media cultures. This is especially the case in studies that assume that literacy practices in the home are complex, varied and multimodal. As has been noted by social geographers, a cultural shift to the digital age has coincided with increased parental supervision of, and constraints on, children's play inside and outside the spaces of the home (e.g., Valentine and Holloway, 2001). One the one hand, concerns have been expressed about the so-called 'digital bedroom' and children's engagement with popular media in that largely unregulated domestic space. Parents who prefer to 'supervise' children's interactions with television and digital media report that they pay attention to how they arrange the living areas or 'public' spaces of the home to include these devices. On the other hand, the case has been made that confinement to the home – whether due to children's preference for playing with media, or parents' religious and cultural beliefs or fears for children's safety – can also benefit children's literacy development. In their study of one Mexican immigrant home, for example, Reyes and Azuara (2008) found that parents responded to constraints on family income and living space by providing plenty of literacy materials within the home and allowed their free use in places that other parents might actively discourage. As the authors point out, this made literacy-related activities and inscriptions very visible in the domestic space because 'the living rooms walls become canvases on which drawings and letters are printed. Children scribbled in their [writing] pads and on couches and the walls' (2008: 386).

More recently, Rainbird and Rowsell (2011) draw on interviews with parents in four US homes to consider some of the specific ways in which parents consciously design, furnish and resource spaces of the home to foster children's literacy learning. They found that these (mostly middle-class) parents used space and objects to mark out specific areas of the home that were considered desirable places for children to play in and to interact with books, writing materials and media either during independent play or while participating in activities with adults. At the same time, the arrangement, furnishing and use of these domestic spaces – as with all spaces – have powerful semiotic and ideological dimensions (Scollon and Scollon, 2003) that index particular orientations towards and values about childhood, family life, literacy and learning, and so on. Parents and children both shape and are shaped by the social relations and practices that are possible in these spaces (Lefebvre, 1971/1991; Massey, 2000). In the Rainbird and Rowsell (2011) study, parents variously described these domestic spaces of the home as 'book nooks', toy areas, computer areas, and play and media spaces. However, despite such distinctions being made in parent interviews, the authors also noted that 'there is fluidity to the home space whereby borders between designated learning spaces and family spaces become blurred' (2011: 220). This theme of the mobility and flows – rather than fixity and stasis – of material objects and concepts about early literacy learning within the home, but also into and out of the home, is central to the larger study of parents' information-seeking about early learning in which these cases are situated (Nichols, 2011; Nichols, Nixon, and Rowsell; 2009, Nixon, 2011). We return to the topic of flows between spaces later in the chapter.

Marsh (e.g., 2004, 2006, and chapter 12 this volume; Marsh, Brooks, Hughes, Ritchie, and Roberts, 2005) has been at the forefront of studies into early childhood literacy and children's use of popular culture in the home, including digital media (see Spencer, Knobel, and Lankshear, chapter 8 this volume). Along with other researchers (see review in Leander, Phillips, and Taylor, 2010), Marsh has drawn attention to the limitations of thinking about the home as a social space of learning that is completely separated from the outside world. With regard to literacy, researchers have long noted the intersections between literacy learning and children's encounters with signs, symbols and texts inside and outside the home, including those originating in popular and consumer culture. However, the flow of images and signs into the home, facilitated by the advent of television and the rise of consumer culture post World War Two (Kline, 1993; Luke, 1990; Seiter, 1995), has arguably increased in pace and volume since the advent of digital media and the intensification of forms of economic and cultural globalisation (Marsh 2006). In this process, young children and their families have become significant markets as potential consumers of products and services for the home, including those specifically promoted as 'educational' (Nixon, 1998; Scanlon and Buckingham, 2004; Seiter, 1995). As Mackey and Robinson (first edition) point out: 'the salience and virtues of environmental print suddenly acquire a price tag, and the infant is inculcated into a world where literacy includes the concept of brand recognition' (p. 134). That is, logos and brands on objects and in advertising media have become common materials for early reading experiences and storytelling.

At the same time, the corporate world of the brand has scaled up attempts to convince parents that the contemporary home has an important function to play in children's educational success by being fashioned as a *learning space*. There now operates a huge industry designed to sell products and services that claim to assist parents to make over domestic spaces in the home into 'learning environments' filled with material objects and resources designed to make literacy, numeracy and science learning fun, exciting and challenging for their children. In the process, parents and children are constructed as

co-consumers (Cook, 2008) of the play-tables, activity centres, storage boxes, wall charts, posters, educational activity books and toys, toy laptops and other 'electronic learning aids' that supposedly ensure that the home operates as a space that is full of early learning educational resources and opportunities (Scanlon and Buckingham, 2004; Marsh, 2010; Nixon, 2011).

COMMUNITY SPACES AND EARLY CHILDHOOD LITERACY

Within the body of work of researchers who have taken space and place seriously as dimensions of children's literacy learning are studies that investigate the literacy environments of children's neighbourhoods. One of the most comprehensive studies was undertaken by Neuman and Celano (2001, 2006). The study compared four neighbourhoods of different socio-economic status in terms of the opportunities they offered for children and their families to engage in literacy-related activities such as purchasing or borrowing reading materials, reading signs and posters, and finding safe and comfortable places to sit and read. Their method involved walking through a block of each neighbourhood and systematically noting every store and stand likely to sell reading materials, every sign and its condition (readability), public spaces where reading could be undertaken, and relevant institutional sites (libraries, child care centres, etc). They found that neighbourhoods showed 'major and striking differences at almost all levels' in terms of access to literacy resources and opportunities (Neuman and Celano, 2001: 15).

Graffiti is one of the indicators of a print-poor environment in Neuman and Celano's inventory (2001) because it is often written over other signs, obscuring them. The logic here is that environmental print has to be clearly legible to be decoded. An interesting counterpoint to this work is that of Orellana and Hernandez (1999) who earlier utilised a 'literacy walk' method with child participants focusing on an inner city neighbourhood. The researchers began the activity with a teacherly interaction routine, pointing to signs and asking the children what they said or what language they were in, but were met with little enthusiasm. This changed when the children came across some graffiti that had been inscribed into the cement when it had been wet. The children identified this as 'rayados' or 'scratching' and the work of local gang members. They were able to identify which gang the members came from by pointing to key letters in the graffiti. They also spontaneously pointed out the difference between these inscriptions and those nearby that had been stamped into the pavement by the city council, referring to their authors respectively as 'cholos' (gang members) and 'senores' ('misters' or officials).

A community child's perspective can reveal the presence of different value systems in relation to the reading of environmental print. Successfully decoding graffiti has real practical utility for urban children because it can assist them to more safely navigate their neighbourhoods:

'[I]nner-city children's lives and futures depend on their proper reading of gang symbols. They may be quite sophisticated at interpreting graffiti even as they have little [to] say about signs that are placed in their community by outsiders' (Orellana and Hernandez, 1999: 618).

In the same study (Orellana and Hernandez, 1999), the local market emerged as another significant place for children to encounter environmental print. The significance of commercial settings for young children's developing awareness of the semiotic character of their environments is supported by other research. Marsh (2006) has highlighted advertising as a significant element of the 'mediascape' which children inhabit:

'... the media industry have been quick to exploit this particular third space (Soja, 1996) through marketing strategies which mean that shop windows, buses, bus stops and billboards are awash with images and logos from popular media narratives.' (2006: 27).

As we have discussed earlier, many children's homes are part of this medias cape – settings where images, texts and objects reference both popular and 'educational' narratives. As Marsh points out, this positions children to be competent readers of the semiotics of the marketplace.

In one study, children in more and less commercialised neighbourhoods participated in the research. Chan and McNeal (2007) surveyed urban and rural Chinese children with the aim of gauging their propensity to value different sources of information. One of the greatest differences was that urban children were much more likely to see shops as places where one would find useful information about products. The authors comment that 'retail shops in rural areas ... do not target the rural children ... most of the street ads were selling medicines and agricultural insecticides' (Chan and McNeal, 2007: 113). Thus both the amount of environmental print and its salience to children's interests was much greater in the city than the villages. Yamada-Rice's (2011) preliminary work, in which she compares the written and visual modes in samples taken from the streets of London and Tokyo, is an interesting development in studies of texts in the environment and what might be involved in young children's culturally-based meaning-making as they encounter these texts.

Their community environments can offer children opportunities to appreciate the cultural power of symbols. Reading symbols is a significant dimension of literacy in the world outside school. An example is given by Jimenez and Smith (2008) in their exploration of the multi-dimensional nature of Mexican children's literacy exposure. The writers point to a particular symbol which is ubiquitous in public spaces including on metro signs, on currency and on murals and so is part of children's textual landscape. This symbol, an eagle clutching a serpent in its beak while perched on a cactus, signifies the 'valor of the Aztecs ... [and] confirm[s] the prophetic directive of the Aztecs' patron deity, Huitzilopochtli, who ordained that their future city should be built on the site where the eagle clutched the serpent' (2008: 33). Each of the symbolic elements – the cactus, eagle and serpent – were also elements in Mesoamerican pictographic script. Thus children in this community learn the significance of symbols in organising the movement of people (e.g., the metro), signifying the presence and importance of social institutions (current) and connecting the past with the present and future.

So far, we have focused on urban landscapes and their semiotic characteristics. The concept of reading the landscape takes on a different character when considering the situation of children growing up on the land. The indigenous communities that are the original inhabitants of 'developed' nations raise their children in the hope of their effective participation in both traditional and western cultural and educational practices. In an ethnographic study of Australian aboriginal families living in a remote community, Hanlen (2002) discovered the importance of being able to produce and interpret texts of and on the landscape. These included carving symbols on rocks and trees, making inscriptions in the soil, using stencils to mark stone, reading animal tracks, navigating using landmarks and astronomical signs as well as creating representations of the land in the modalities of painting, song and dance. The use of body painting also transforms indigenous people into embodied texts with specific significance in relation to cultural practices. These forms of literacy are deeply imbued with the meaning of place, particularly of the land for which the tribal group are custodians. The knowledge of how to produce and interpret these texts 'requires many years of contextualised education and practise in relation to social practices' (Hanlen, 2002: 1155). For young children, as with mainstream literacy, their understandings and skills are at an emergent stage.

INSTITUTIONAL SPACES AND EARLY CHILDHOOD LITERACY

Lawn (1999) defined the classroom as 'a hardware and a software' where hardware refers to 'the material structure (spaces, walls, furniture, tools)' and software to 'the working procedures, series of ideas and knowledge systems operating within it' (1999: 78). In our review of the use of the term 'space' in early childhood education literature, we noticed that it has been more often applied to the soft side. For instance, 'space' sometimes refers to conversational space, or the arena of talk which is regulated by the teacher and in which (s)he exercises power to allow or disallow particular voices or viewpoints. An example of this is McIntyre et al.'s report on students' group discussions in which they argue that 'creat[ing] a space for children to talk' (2006: 44) is a means of 'promot[ing] collaborative work and the sharing of ideas' (2006: 60). The term 'space' takes on a particular inflection when used in a social justice context as when Rogers and Mosely state that 'racial literacy can create spaces for white, working class children to step into texts to identify, problematize, and, most importantly, reconstruct whiteness' (2006: 483). Here they are referring to how a teacher in a second-grade classroom uses literary and other texts and guided discussion to raise children's awareness of racism.

In this review, we have focused on studies which include both the 'hard' and the 'soft' aspects of the educational context. Early childhood is a particularly interesting domain from this perspective since there is considerable variation between different kinds of educational and care settings as well as across country and cultural contexts. A playgroup is different from a Reception classroom (Miller and Smith, 2004) and a kindergarten in France is different from a kindergarten in the UK (David, Gouch, and Jago, 2001). Included in our discussion are studies which incorporate analysis of some dimensions of the material space of the setting in question, for instance, by looking at where literacy resources are placed and how they are handled (Nichols, 2004) or, by considering how instructional approaches involved the shaping of children's bodies (Kamler, Maclean, Reid and Simpson, 1994).

One lens for examining the impact of institutional spaces is to look at children's transition from preschool to school environments. These studies demonstrate the interwoven nature of the hard and soft dimensions of educational contexts and how each impacts on the meaning and practice of language and literacy. One of the key differences between these two contexts is in the provision of space for mobility and play. In their in-depth study of children's first month of school, Kamler and colleagues noted that the Reception teacher gave great emphasis on children learning physical self-regulation in the early weeks, implying the difference from preschool by stating 'It can't be the sort of environment where people are running around free and easy' (1992: 43). The researchers describe in detail how the teacher's talk and non-verbal communication explicitly directs the placement of children's bodies in relation to classroom furniture in order to position them to undertake a literacy task (drawing):

> Standing up with your piece of paper. Stand up with your piece of paper in your hand. Now this is tricky, this is very tricky, because I know how children like to run, but I don't want you to run I want you to walk as *quietly as you possibly can shh*, and stand **behind** a chair. Am I standing **behind** this chair? ... No, I am standing in front of it. This is **behind** the chair. I want you to go to a chair and stand behind a chair. (1992: 103)

Like many other Reception classrooms, this one did not have an adjoining outdoor play area, art area, dress-up clothes or dolls, thus reducing the kinds of play that were possible. The children in one longitudinal case study of transition (Comber and Nichols, 2004; Hill, 2004; Nichols, 2003, 2004) commented on the difference between their preschool and their Reception classroom. Five-year-old Toby spoke for his peers:

> Toby (to researcher): We want to go back to kindy, don't we Harrison?
> Harrison: Yes!
> Researcher: Why's that?
> Toby: It's bigger. It's *much* bigger. Isn't it Harrison?
> Harrison: Yes.

Toby: And you don't have to do work there. Only
play.
Other boy: More toys.
Toby: We have to work *all* the time here.
(2004: 108)

Here the restriction in space is associated
with the restriction of opportunities to play
and both are associated with an emphasis
on work. Work is what is done when sitting at a table. Even though Toby's preschool had been designated an Early
Learning Centre (ELC) and incorporated
many objectives into its curriculum, the
children there had not experienced their
learning as work. Work in that setting was
only spoken of in relation to adults' occupations and children's role play of adult
work in created settings. The ELC had
been a transformable space in which temporary new designs such as a cafe, stage
or castle could be constructed and provide
a focus for experiential learning (Hill,
2004).

Individual accountability is one of the
key lessons of transition to school and one
which is taught both explicitly and through
the management of space and bodies.
The aforementioned study illustrates this
through the case of Rose who is required
to change her orientation from collaborative to individual text production as she
becomes socialised into the Reception
classroom (Nichols, 2008). An observation
of Rose and her friend Henry in kindergarten shows the embodied nature of their
joint text production:

Their heads close together, their gaze encom-
passed both picture planes, while bodies, sounds
and images wove the story together. The same
visual images and symbols crossed their pages:
wavy ghost shapes and dotted lines tracing
the ghosts' movements through the imagined
space. Four hands moved between the two
sheets, often in rhythm with their owner's production of sound effects (i.e. stuttering sounds
accompanied the marking of the dotted lines).
(2004: 25)

The integration of physical movement
and sociality into children's text making
is one of the key ways in which literacy development and play are mutually
supportive. Another example is given by
Wohlwend (2009) in her study of a preschool setting. Here two boys are shown
reproducing the experience of a video
game through the medium of paper and
crayon:

Kirby's counter attack began with a circling gesture that mimicked swirling tornadic action. First
circling the orange crayon above the paper before
touching down, Kirby rapidly moved his crayon in
overlapping circles on paper, emphasizing and
concretizing the violent, messy, and spiraling
nature of tornadoes as he laid down loops of
orange crayon. (2009: 129)

In Rowe's (2008) study of a preschool
writing centre, she discussed three 'contracts' governing text production that
children are required to learn as part of
their socialisation into literacy. These are:
the 'boundary contract' which requires
that 'edges of a piece of paper should
be seen as a physical boundary for marks
and, therefore, for the text' (2008: 82);
the representational contract which pre-
serves the distinction between drawing
and writing; and the ownership contract
which requires children to take possession of and responsibility for their own
texts.

All three of these contracts are contra-
vened by collaborative text production of
the kind reported by both Wohlwend (2009)
and Nichols (2008). Returning to the case
of Rose, her experience of the Reception
class shows the significance of the change
in the material and spatial context in teaching her to observe these contracts. In the
early weeks of school, Rose realises that
the situation has changed. During a period
in which the children are set a writing task
(draw something and write the letter it

starts with), she is observed in the following interaction:

> Rose leans over towards the child on the other side of her. She reaches over and draws something on this girl's page.
> Girl: 'Now look what you did!'
> Rose puts her hand over her mouth.
> Mrs S. tells the class if anyone moves around they'll be sent to buddy class.
>
> (Nichols, 2008: 26)

This example shows how firmly the relative positioning of child, table and piece of paper is established from the onset of formal literacy training. Rose's attempted initiation of collaboration (as her actions can be read from the perspective of her preschool experience) is in the classroom context a multiple transgression: spatial, textual and social. The teacher's caution threatens to remove transgressive children from the classroom space altogether.

One way in which institutional space operates to regulate children in the service of the curricular agenda is through the production of visibility or, to put it another way, through reducing access to places for children to carry out their own agendas unseen by authority. In her historical study of the kindergarten movement, Tyler (1993) explains that settings were designed to facilitate adult observation of children, in some cases through the use of one-way mirrors. Design features such as the scaling of furniture and the division of the room into different zones of activity enabled judgements about individual children's levels of physical, social and cognitive development.

In the school setting, children are made visible through the construction of talk and activity routines. Kamler et al. (1994) refer to the common practice of sitting children in a circle for 'morning talk': 'A child whose turn it is must either speak or refuse to speak ... All eyes are on her, and in the circle there are no obstructions to hide behind, and no distractions' (Kamler et al., 1994: 138). The authors note the impact of the dominance of collective interaction and work routines on children's peer conversations: 'Peer discourse happens in the spaces left by the classroom discourse; it is built in spaces where the teacher's gaze is absent.' (Kamler et al., 1994: 202). Here space has both a hard and a soft meaning. The teacher's adult height and her use of adult-sized furniture, along with the absence of physical barriers in the room, mean that there are no physical spaces for children to be unseen and unheard by the teacher. At the same time, the adult's control of the activity structure and topic means there is little opportunity for peer dialogue to be incorporated into the official curriculum.

CONNECTING SPACES IN EARLY CHILDHOOD LITERACY

At the outset of this chapter we noted conceptualisations of the internet as providing 'spaces' for play and learning. We return to this theme here because of the ways in which digital media can be seen to *connect* spaces in early childhood literacy. Carrington (2005), for example, has used the term 'textual landscape' to capture the idea that children actively interact with and within the social spaces and text-saturated environments that digital technologies create or enable children to create. In this process there is a level of *flow and connectedness* between offline and online spaces and practices, and local and global spaces. The corporate world has been quick to capitalise on this situation with advertisers of early learning products and services designed for young children and their parents now as likely to reach into the home via the email box as the post box, and as likely to connect people to spaces outside the home as close as the corner store as to more distant spaces or global repositories like online stores. Further, advertisers are keen to promote the idea that, because 'learning happens everywhere' – that is, in all available spaces – then parents need support to learn how to make the home, the bedroom, the car and the shopping mall *productive* spaces for early learning and, to this end, online spaces are promoted as key places where such support can be sourced (Nixon, 2011).

Researchers remain cautious about how fluid the situation actually is when it comes to the literate practices that children are encouraged to engage in within institutionalised educational settings. Indeed, while studies of technology and literacy in homes and early childhood settings note that there is *movement* between children's literate practices in the worlds of the home and the classroom, they also note *tensions* between these worlds (see review in Burnett, 2010, and Spencer, Knobel, and Lankshear, chapter 8 this volume). As illustrated in McTavish's (2009) case study of an 8-year-old's information literacy practices in school and out of school, some children 'may sustain separate literate lives within and beyond school' (2009: 250). She found that whereas home-based practices might often be 'associated with networked multimodal texts embedded in meaningful, social contexts', a child's school-based literate practices may be 'book-based, individual, and print orientated' (2009: 250) and therefore quite different.

The notion that children inhabit multiple social worlds has been an important contribution to understandings of literacy development and particularly in highlighting the difference that children's out-of-school

experiences can make to their encounters with the official curriculum (Dickie and McDonald, 2011; Dyson, 1993). Such a view has been important in challenging any simple binary of 'the home' and 'the school' that represents their relation as one of either alignment or disjuncture. It has also encouraged educators to build connections between children's experiences in and out of school, in ways that acknowledge that significant learning happens in home and community contexts. This understanding has contributed to the transformation of education environments, through the incorporation of 'outside world' spaces, particularly into preschool and kindergarten settings. Educators can go to considerable trouble in their attempts to replicate aspects of these social settings in their kindergartens and classrooms as in this example of a shoe store set-up:

> ... a 'SALE' sign was prominently displayed over a shelf of marked-down items; a 'MASTER CARD' sign with logo was displayed on the check-out counter and a Master Card credit card was in each customer's wallet; the shoes were divided into children's, women's, and men's and appropriately labeled; the storage room was labeled 'STORAGE ROOM' with a 'NO CUSTOMERS BEYOND THIS POINT' sign nearby.
>
> (Vukelich, 1994: 158)

Such insertions create new forms of hybrid space in educational settings, just as in domestic settings adults may create spaces that insert school-like literacy practices into home life (and, indeed, children can do this in their play (cf. Parke, Drury, Kenner, and Robertson, 2002). The actions that go on in these inserted spaces take from their meta-contexts (school or home) elements of that institution's agenda, as when the textual practices of children in a school 'shop' are documented by a teacher and used as evidence of literacy learning. This can translate into limited versions of connecting the classroom with other settings that children inhabit. For instance, lifting logos (such as Doritos and McDonalds) from material objects and places (such as a packet on a supermarket shelf) and transporting them into the classroom as a piece of text strips the practice of reading a logo of its social meaning. In one study, researchers used a test in which a logo was presented 'correctly' (i.e., with original spelling) and then in four different 'incorrect versions', e.g., 'Cheerios' (correct); 'Jeerios, Queerios, Cheerioz, Cheeriot' (incorrect) (Blair and Savage, 2006). Thus a concept that arose from an appreciation of the significance of local settings can be translated into a decontextualised curricular approach, effectively taking the environment out of environmental print.

CONCLUSION

In this chapter we have noted that there is further scope for theories of space as socially constituted to contribute to the field of early childhood literacy. However, we have tried to emphasise the importance of continued attention to the material dimensions of social space. We have reviewed studies in early childhood literacy that have done this, to a greater or lesser extent, in order to suggest the potential gains for educational researchers and practitioners from adopting a 'material semiotic' approach to space and place (see also Pahl and Rowsell, chapter 15 this volume). In order for such gains to be achieved, it will be important for educators to foster their curiosity and powers of observation in relation to the places and spaces in which children encounter and learn to participate in language and literacy practices. Adopting critical spatial theory as a lens challenges researchers in early childhood

education to look at familiar scenes in unfamiliar ways. Soja writes: '[T]his strategic foregrounding of the spatial flexes interpretive muscles that have not been well developed or widely applied in the past. This in turn raises new possibilities for discovering hidden insights, alternative theories and revised modes of understanding.' (2010: 17).

This may mean looking with fresh eyes at educational settings as material spaces as well as visiting key places in children's neighbourhoods to consider the kinds of textual practices that may occur in these places or may be constrained by them. When knowledge of out-of-school spaces is produced via unreflective assumptions about children's lives outside of school, rather than knowledge produced through inquiry and dialogue, there are limitations to what can be incorporated into a broader understanding of literacy learning and a literacy curriculum likely to socially inclusive. We hope that encountering the work of researchers who bring a spatially sensitive approach to early childhood literacy will encourage further exploration of the range of material features of, and relationships in and between, these environments and how this may impact on children's learning.

NOTE

1 Examples include the Home Observation for Measurement of the Environment Inventory (HOME) (Caldwell and Bradley, 1984) and the Home Screening Questionnaire (Frankenberg and Coons, 1986).

REFERENCES

Barton, D. (1994). *Literacy: An Introduction to the Ecology of the Written Language.* Cambridge, MA: Blackwell.

Barton, D. and Hamilton, M. (1998). *Local literacies*. London: Routledge.

Barton, D., Hamilton, M., and Ivanic, R. (eds) (2000). *Situated Literacies*. London and New York: Routledge.

Blair, R. and Savage, R. (2006) 'Name writing but not environmental print recognition is related to letter-sound knowledge and phonological awareness in pre-readers', *Reading and Writing*, 19(9): 991–1016.

Bronfenbrenner, U. (1979). *The Ecology of Human Development: Experiments by Nature and Design*. Cambridge, MA: Harvard University Press.

Burnett, C. (2010). 'Technology and literacy in early childhood settings: A review of research', *Journal of Early Childhood Literacy*, 10(3): 247–70.

Caldwell, B. and Bradley, R. (1984). *Home Observation for Measurement of the Environment (HOME)*. Revised Edition. Little Rock: University of Arkansas.

Carrington, V. (2005). 'New textual landscapes, information, new childhood', in J. Marsh (ed.), *Popular Culture: Media and Digital Literacies in Early Childhood*. London: Sage. pp. 13–27.

Chan, K. and McNeal, J. (2007). 'Chinese children's perception of personal and commercial communication: An urban-rural comparison', *Asian Journal of Communication*, 17(1): 97–116.

Cook, D. (2008). 'The missing child in consumption theory', *Journal of Consumer Culture*, 8(2): 219–43.

Comber, B. and Nichols, S. (2004). 'Getting the big picture: Regulating knowledge in the early childhood literacy curriculum', *Journal of Early Childhood Literacy*, 4(1): 43–63.

David, T., Gouch, K., and Jago, M. (2001). 'Cultural constructions of childhood and early literacy', *Literacy* 35(2): 47–53.

Dickie, J. and McDonald, G. (2011). 'Literacy in church and family sites through the eyes of Samoan children in New Zealand', *Literacy*, 45(1): 25–31.

Dyson, A. H. (1993) *Social Worlds of Children Learning to Write in an Urban Primary School*. New York: Teachers College Press.

Frankenberg, W. K. and Coons, C. E. (1986). 'Home Screening Questionnaire: Its validity in assessing home environment', *Journal of Pediatrics*, 108(4): 624–6.

Gieryn, T. (2000). 'A place for space in sociology', *Annual Review of Sociology*, 26: 463–96.

Gulson, K. and Symes, C. (2007). 'Knowing one's place: Space, theory, education', *Critical Studies in Education*, 48(1): 97–110.

Hanlen, W. (2002) 'Indigenous literacy: Learning from the centre not the margin', *International Journal of Learning*, 9: 1152–65.

Heath, S. B. (1983). *Ways with Words: Language Life and Work in Communities and Classrooms*. Cambridge and New York: Cambridge University Press.

Hill, S. (2004). 'Privileged literacy in preschool', *Australian Journal of Language and Literacy*, 27(2): 159–71.

Jimenez, R. T. and Smith, P. H. (2008) 'Mesoamerican literacies: Indigenous writing systems and contemporary possibilities', *Reading Research Quarterly*, 43(1): 28–47.

Kamler, B., Maclean, R., Reid, J., and Simpson, A. (1994). *Shaping up Nicely: The Formation of Schoolgirls and Schoolboys in the First Month of School*. Canberra: Department of Employment Education & Training.

Kline, S. (1993). *Out of the Garden: Toys and Children's Culture in the Age of TV Marketing*. London: Verso.

Law, J. (2003). *Materialities, Spatialities, Globalities*. Lancaster: Centre for Science Studies, Lancaster University.

Lawn, M. (1999). Designing teaching: the classroom as a technology. In I. Grosvenor, M. Lawn & K. Rousmaniere (Eds.), *Silences and Images: The social history of the classroom*. New York: Peter Lang.

Leander, K. and Sheehy, M. (2004). *Spatializing Literacy Research and Practice*. New York: Peter Lang.

Leander, K., Phillips, N., and Taylor, K. (2010). 'The changing social spaces of learning: Mapping new mobilities', *Review of Research in Education*, 34(1): 329–94.

Lefebvre, H. (1971 tr. 1991). *The Production of Space*. Tr. D. Nicholson-Smith. Oxford: Basil Blackwell.

Luke, C. (1990). *Constructing the Child Viewer: An Historical Study of the Discourse on Television and Children, 1950–1980*. New York: Praeger Press.

Marsh, J. (2004). 'The techno-literacy practices of young children', *Journal of Early Childhood Research*, 2(1): 51–66.

Marsh, J. (2006). 'Global, local/public, private: Young children's engagement in digital literacy practices in the home', in K. Pahl and J. Rowsell (eds), *Travel Notes from the New Literacy Studies*. Clevedon UK: Multilingual Matters Ltd. pp. 19–38.

Marsh, J. (2010). 'Young children's play in online virtual worlds', *Journal of Early Childhood Research*, 8(1): 2339.

Marsh, J., Brooks, G., Hughes, J., Ritchie, L., and Roberts, S. (2005). *Digital Beginnings: Young Children's Use of Popular Culture, Media and New Technologies*. Sheffield: University of Sheffield. Available online at: www.digitalbeginnings.shef.ac.uk/ (accessed 8 July 2011).

Massey, D. (2000). 'The conceptualisation of place', in D. Massey and P. Jess (eds), *A Place in the World? Places, Cultures and Globalization*. New York: Oxford University Press. pp. 45–85.

McIntyre, M., Kyle, D., and Moore, G. (2006). 'A primary-grade teacher's guidance toward small-group dialogue', *Reading Research Quarterly*, 41(1): 36–66.

McTavish, M. (2009). '"I get my facts from the Internet": A case study of the teaching and learning of information literacy in in-school and out-of-school contexts', *Journal of Early Childhood Literacy*, 9(1): 3–28.

Miller, L. and Smith, A. P. (2004). Practitioners' beliefs and children's experiences of literacy in four early years settings', *Early Years*, 24(2): 121–33.

Neuman, S. and Celano, D. (2001). 'Access to print in low-income and middle-income communities: An ecological study of four neighbourhoods', *Reading Research Quarterly*, 36(1): 8–26.

Neuman, S. and Celano, D. (2006). 'The knowledge gap: Implications of leveling the playing field for low-income and middle-income children', *Reading Research Quarterly*, 41(2): 176–201.

Nichols, S. (2003). 'Reading the social world', in J. Barnett and B. Comber (eds), *Look Again: Longitudinal Case Studies of Children Learning Literacy*. Rozelle, NSW: Primary English Teaching Association.

Nichols, S. (2004). 'Literacy learning and children's social agendas in the school entry classroom', *Australian Journal of Literacy and Language*, 27(2): 101–13.

Nichols, S. (2008). 'Ghosts, houses and the psycho brother: A young girl working on gendered and schooled identities through text production', *Redress*, 17(2): 22–30.

Nichols, S. (2011). 'Young children's literacy in the activity space of the library: A geo-semiotic investigation', *Journal of Early Childhood Literacy*, 11(2): 164–89.

Nichols, S., Nixon, H., and Rowsell, J. (2009). 'The "good" parent in relation to early childhood literacy: Symbolic terrain and lived practice', *Literacy*, 43(2): 65–74.

Nixon, H. (1998). 'Fun and games are serious business', in J. Sefton-Green (ed.), *Digital Diversions: Youth Culture in the Age of Multimedia*. London: University College London Press. pp. 21–42.

Nixon, H. (2011). '"From bricks to clicks": Hybrid commercial spaces in the landscape of early literacy and learning', *Journal of Early Childhood Literacy*, 11(2): 114–40.

Orellana, M. F. and Hernandez, A. (1999). 'Talking the walk: Children reading urban environmental print', *The Reading Teacher*, 52(6): 612–19.

Parke, T., Drury, R., Kenner, C., and Robertson, L. H. (2002). 'Revealing invisible worlds: Connecting the mainstream with bilingual children's home and community learning', *Journal of Early Childhood Literacy*, 2(2): 195–220.

Rainbird, S. and Rowsell, J. (2011). '"Literacy nooks": Geosemiotics and domains of literacy in home spaces', *Journal of Early Childhood Literacy*, 11(2): 214–31.

Reyes, I. and Azuara, P. (2008). 'Emergent biliteracy in young Mexican immigrant children', *Reading Research Quarterly*, 43(4): 374–98.

Rogers, R. and Mosley, M. (2006). 'Racial literacy in a second-grade classroom: Critical race theory, whiteness studies, and literacy', *Research Reading Research Quarterly*, 41(4): 462–95.

Rowe, D. (2008). 'Social contracts for writing: Negotiating shared understandings about text in the preschool years', *Reading Research Quarterly*, 43(1): 66–95.

Scanlon, M. and Buckingham, D. (2004). 'Home learning and the educational marketplace', *Oxford Review of Education*, 30(2): 287–303.

Scollon, R. and Scollon, S. (2003). *Discourses in Place: Language in the Material World*. London: Routledge.

Seiter, E. (1995). *Sold Separately: Parents and Children in Consumer Culture*. New Brunswick, NJ: Rutgers University Press.

Street, B. (1984). *Literacy in Theory and Practice*. Cambridge: Cambridge University Press.

Tyler, D. (1993). 'Making better children', in D. Meredyth and D. Tyler (eds), *Child and Citizen*. Nathan Qld: Griffith University Press. pp. 35–60.

Valentine, G. and Holloway, S. (2001). 'On-line dangers? Geographies of parents' fears for children's safety in cyberspace', *Professional Geographer*, 53: 71–83.

Vukelich, C. (1994). 'Effects of play interventions on young children's reading of environmental print', *Early Childhood Research Quarterly*, 9: 153–70.

Weigel, D., Martin, S., and Bennett, K. (2005). 'Ecological influences of the home and the child-care center on preschool-age children's literacy development', *Reading Research Quarterly*, 40: 204–33.

Weigel, D., Martin, S., and Bennett, K. (2006). 'Mothers' literacy beliefs: Connections with the home literacy environment and pre-school children's literacy development', *Journal of Early Childhood Literacy*, 6(2): 191–211.

Weinberger, J. (1996). 'A longitudinal study of children's early literacy experiences at home and later literacy development at home and school', *Journal of Research in Reading*, 19(1): 14–24.

Wilkinson, K. (2003). 'Children's favorite books', *Journal of Early Childhood Literacy*, 3(3): 275–301.

Wohlwend, K. (2009). 'Early adopters: Playing new literacies and pretending new technologies in print-centric classrooms', *Journal of Early Childhood Literacy*, 9(2): 117–40.

Wohlwend, K., Vander Zanden, S., Husbye, N., and Kuby, C. (2011). 'Navigating discourses in place in the world of Webkinz', *Journal of Early Childhood Literacy*, 11(2): 141–63.

Yamada-Rice, D. (2011). 'New media, evolving multimodal literacy practices and the potential impact of increased use of the visual mode in the urban environment on young children's learning', *Literacy*, 45(1): 32–43.

17

Multimodal Perspectives on Early Childhood Literacies

Rosie Flewitt

INTRODUCTION

As young children in today's world go about their everyday lives, what are their experiences of literacy? How have the literacy practices they encounter changed as a result of the 'digital age', and are print-based definitions still adequate for theorising early literacy? These are profound and unresolved questions that are driving forward the development of diverse strands of current educational theory, and in this chapter, I consider how multimodal perspectives can offer fresh insights into contemporary early literacy learning.

Multimodality offers a new framework for analyzing and responding to a changing communicative landscape, but communication through multiple modes is by no means a new phenomenon. Throughout the history of human culture, mankind has used gesture, gaze, body movements, and images in the mediation of knowledge, skills, identities, and social practices. From early cave paintings and engravings on tools, visual sources of information have been used as a key resource for conveying information (Lewis-Williams, 2002), and using multiple symbol systems has been part of human practice for thousands of years. Yet in literacy education, the uniquely human characteristic of language has been prioritised as the most important meaning-making system. In comparatively recent years, the assumption that language is *always* central to meaning-making has begun to be challenged, in part due to the emergence of new communicative practices associated with the widespread use of screen-based texts and interactive digital media in everyday literacy practices. With digital texts, meanings are often constructed and interpreted through complex combinations of still and moving images, icons, words, screen layout, colours, and sounds, and these changes raise fundamental questions about what 'becoming literate' involves in a multimedia world.

I begin this chapter by introducing multimodality, and outline the particular insights it can offer to sociocultural learning theory. Taking a view of literacy as socially framed active engagement with a range of texts rather than as a simple process of 'decoding' and 'encoding' written language, I review recent studies of early childhood literacy that have adopted a multimodal approach, and give detailed examples from my own research to illustrate how multimodal investigation can contribute subtle yet profound insights into early childhood literacy, shedding new light on old assumptions about meaning-making and symbolic representation, and on new literacy practices with digital technologies.

WHAT IS MULTIMODALITY?

The term 'multimodality' describes approaches to representation which assume that communication and meaning making are about more than just language. Multimodality takes into account the many different modes in printed and on-screen texts (such as image, layout, colour, sound, and language) and also the different modes that people use as they engage in face-to-face interaction (such as gesture, gaze, movement, artefacts, and language). Although some linguistic studies in the past have paid attention to features of communication other than language, such as intonation, facial expression, and gestures, these features have tended to be investigated separately (e.g., Streeck, 1993; Kendon, 2004) or have been assumed to be secondary to language. Furthermore, linguistic research has tended to categorise modes other than language in terms of what they are not, rather than what they are, with umbrella terms such as 'para-linguistic' or 'non-verbal' (e.g., Cruttenden, 1997).

These terms reflect an underlying assumption that language is the most complex and most powerful communicative mode. Multimodality offers a fundamentally different perspective on communication. Rather than examining modes in isolation, multimodal studies consider how multiple modes work together to create meanings in a 'multimodal ensemble' (Kress, Jewitt, Ogborn, and Tsatsarelis, 2001), and 'step away from the notion that language always plays a central role in interaction, without denying that it often does' (Norris, 2004: 2). This significant shift in perspective offers radically new insights into understandings of communicative and learning processes.

Multimodality is a comparatively recent field of enquiry in education research which initially evolved out of Michael Halliday's theory of social semiotics[1] (Halliday, 1973, 1978). Halliday's work drew attention to the interdependent relationship between language and social context, and to how communicative events are shaped by both linguistic and social processes. He insisted that 'language is as it is because of its function in the social structure' (1973: 65). According to Halliday's theory, the meaning of any utterance depends on an understanding of the range of utterances which are possible in a given social context. This means that when analyzing texts, researchers using social semiotic theory ask themselves questions such as 'Out of the range of possible utterances, why did the speaker/ writer choose that grammatical structure and those particular words in that particular social context?' This aspect of choice in text-making is also central to multimodality, but rather than focusing exclusively on the linguistic mode, multimodal analysis leads to questions such as 'Why did the participant choose words to express meaning X, gestures to express Y and gaze to express Z, and what does that tell us about the inter-relationships between modes, the social relationships between participants and the social setting in which the exchange took place?'

Such considerations in turn lead to questions about the *affordances* of different modes. Young children encounter and use many different modes as they make sense of the world, such as gaze, gesture, music, dance, drawing and talk, and the material properties of different modes offer different possibilities and constraints for communication and learning in different social contexts (Hull and Nelson, 2005). The concept of affordances derives from the work of the psychologist James Gibson (1977), who used the term to refer to the 'action possibilities' that are latent in the environment, and which human beings may or may not perceive or be able to use. In multimodal research, the term affordance is used to describe how different modes offer different potentials for meaning-making, depending on the materiality of the mode, the perceptions and abilities of social actors and the social context in which they are used (Flewitt, 2005; Hull and Nelson, 2005). For instance, gesture can be a precise yet transient and silent mode of expression. In some contexts these attributes lead to gesture being used as a preferred mode, often in combination with gaze exchange, such as sign language for the hearing impaired, or amongst backstage theatre staff where silence is required, or children playing hide-and-seek games. Gesture is also often combined with talk in expert/learner apprenticeship situations, where the 'expert' indicates relevant structure in the environment that is the focus of joint work (Goodwin, 2007). However, in different social contexts, gesture might not be so highly valued a communicative mode, such as a child's response to a teacher's

question in a classroom context. These situated uses of particular modes show how, in addition to the materiality of each mode, the affordances of modes are shaped partially by social practices, and by the values attributed to them by a given society or social group. This latter point was illustrated by Shirley Brice Heath's seminal study *Ways with Words* (Heath, 1983), where the high value placed on oral literacy in some home environments contrasted with the higher value that schools placed on the written mode. The privileging of one mode over others, such as western societies' tendency to esteem written language above other communicative modes in its educational institutions, reflects the dynamics of power at play in societies and in cultures. With this clear focus on the material and social affordances of modes, multimodality can offer original and telling insights into sociocultural learning theory.

MULTIMODAL INTERPRETATIONS OF SOCIOCULTURAL LEARNING THEORY

As discussed, a social semiotic approach to multimodality takes into account the close relationship between social context and the meaning potentials of diverse communicative modes. Similarly, in sociocultural theory (Vygotsky, 1978, 1986; Wertsch, 1991, 2007), mental processes are viewed as social in origin, motivated by emotion and mediated through action and interaction using cultural artefacts and symbolic representations (including language) that have evolved over time. Wertsch (1991: 15) illustrates this notion of 'mediated action' with the example of an engineer using computer imaging to design the body of a car. Wertsch suggests it makes no sense to try to isolate the mental action of the individual (the engineer) from the mechanism that is mediating that action (in this case, the computer), as the action and the mediational means are both central to psychological processing. According to this theory, the mediation of knowledge and skills is always dependent upon the materiality of the artefactual and linguistic tools and resources used in the process of meaning making, and those tools and resources evolve in social activity and social practices. For example, for centuries humans have used pens, pencils and paper to write with, and printed maps to find their way around, whereas in comparatively recent times, people have begun to write increasingly with keyboard or touchscreen technologies, and to find their way around with global positioning systems (GPS). Through socialisation in the culture(s) in which they live, individuals learn how to appropriate the tools and practices for meaning making that characterise that culture. As tools and the processes of their use change over time, so they in turn shape socioculturally-situated cognitive development.

Although Vygotsky recognised the role of diverse symbolic representations in meaning-making, including both material artefacts and language as mediational tools, his work and that of subsequent neo-Vygotskian theorists tended to prioritise language as the principle means through which meanings are negotiated. For example, Mercer (2000, 2010; Mercer and Littleton, 2007) has investigated how young primary-aged children use language to combine their thoughts and to 'think together' in order to get things done. Alexander (2000) has shown how patterns of classroom talk and interaction are tied to culture and history, and are deeply habituated in teachers' pedagogical practice, and

in this volume, Razfar and Gutièrrez (citing Cole and Engestrom, 1993) prioritise language as 'the tool of tools mediating human activity' in their discussion of sociocultural research into early childhood literacy.

More recently, academics working in the field of multimodality have extended this line of sociocultural enquiry to investigate not only how language is used as a cultural and psychological tool, but also how embodied modes (gaze, gesture, orientation, movement and talk, etc.) and material resources are integral to meaning making, how modes are interdependent and how their use changes over time as societies and communities continuously develop. As Kress (1997: 13) observes: 'As children are drawn into cultures, "what is to hand", becomes more and more that which the culture values and therefore makes readily available.' By extending the boundaries of enquiry beyond language, multimodal studies constitute a growing body of rich research into how young children learn to mediate meaning through multiple modes (including language) and in diverse media, giving new insights into how literacy practices are changing in an increasingly digitised communicative landscape.

Furthermore, the advent of compact and affordable digital video recorders has made new tools available to education researchers, who have begun to use video data not only to investigate early literacy development with new and traditional technologies, but also to re-examine how multiple modes are integral to meaning-making in face-to-face interaction, revealing how young children appropriate a range of cultural tools and resources as they become fully-fledged participants in a symbolic world that requires mastery of a broad repertoire of representational systems and practices.

MULTIMODAL LITERACIES IN THE EARLY YEARS

The 1980s witnessed a significant shift in literacy research with the development of the concept of literacy as embedded in social and cultural values and practices (Heath, 1983; Taylor, 1983; Street, 1984; Dyson, 2001). In early literacy the notion of 'emergent literacy', which originated in the work of New Zealander Marie Clay (1966), began attracting followers throughout the 1980s (see Gillen and Hall, this volume). Research conducted from this perspective, combined with a view of literacy as social practice, has shown that children gain a wealth of knowledge about different literacy materials as they go about their everyday lives. Within family and community networks (Gregory, Long, and Volk, 2004), children encounter many different kinds of literacies (Hall, 1998; Kress, 2000), in diverse 'literacy eco-systems' (Kenner, 2005).

Recent studies have begun to register further shifts in our perceptions of what early literacy is in contemporary society, partially in response to the ways that digital technologies have fundamentally changed the kinds of texts that can be produced and interpreted in the construction and exchange of knowledge. Kress (2003: 1) argues that it 'is no longer possible to think about literacy in isolation from a vast array of social, technological and economic factors', and he identifies two related characteristics of contemporary literacy practices: a shift from the centuries-long dominance of the medium of the book to the increasing use of the medium of the screen, from printed to digital texts; and from the dominance of writing to the salience of screen design and the juxtaposition of images, words, sound effects, graphs, charts, music, animation, etc.

In an increasingly complex digitised world, researchers have developed a pluralistic view of 'literacy' and have coined new terms such as 'digital literacies' (Carrington and Robinson, 2009), 'new literacies' (Baker, 2010) and 'multiple literacies' (New London Group, 2000), which take into account how meanings are made through combinations of diverse modes, including linguistic, visual, audio, gestural, and spatial. These studies view literacy development as engagement in a range of complex activities that unfold in a network of social practices, where becoming literate is a social process that is shaped by a child's search for meaning in multiple communicative contexts. This contrasts sharply with conventional understandings of the term 'literacy' as the acquisition of a set of transferable, decoding and encoding skills needed for reading and writing, and throws doubt on the relevance of a 'simple' view of literacy that has held sway in recent policy and curriculum guidance.

What then will be the effects of technological changes on young children's experiences of literacy, and how can early years educators help them to prepare for the forms and purposes literacy will take in their future lives?

The need for a re-conceptualisation of early literacy

In their review of early literacy research and new technologies, Lankshear and Knobel (2003) observe that there has been a distinct divide in approaches between a view of literacy as associated primarily with printed texts, and a view of literacy as involving multimodal texts, with very few studies falling into the latter category. Bearne (2009) argues that existing literacy definitions fail to account for the variety of semiotic resources found in the contemporary texts that children create and read. Citing examples from 7-year-old children's uses of multiple modes in their creations of a PowerPoint presentation, a spoken narrative, and a picturebook, Bearne illustrates how the children skilfully drew on the affordances offered by multiple modes in diverse media for rhetorical effect. She concludes that a robust theoretical framework that encompasses multiple modes is needed, along with deliberate teaching to foster and develop young children's multimodal text production.

However, despite contemporary changes to everyday literacy practices and the potential offered by multimodal perspectives, the reading and creation of multimodal texts has continued to be largely unrecognised in many early years curricula. In the UK and USA there has been a focus on language 'basics' and the acquisition of skills associated with reading print above other forms of reading (Alexander, 2010; Bearne, 2009; Dyson, 2008). This approach bears little resemblance to the contemporary literacy practices that young children encounter in their daily lives (Plowman, Stephen, and McPake, 2010a, 2010b; Wolfe and Flewitt, 2010). By contrast, in New Zealand, the early childhood curriculum *Te Whāriki* (Ministry of Education, 1996) identifies communicative competence in young children as including 'an increasingly elaborate repertoire' of non-verbal forms of communication, e.g., the language of images, art, dance, drama, mathematics, movement, rhythm and music' (1996: 72), in addition to verbal language. In Australia, the *Early Years Learning Framework* recognises the multimodal and sometimes digital nature of texts, and encourages educators to engage children in analysis of the

ways in which diverse texts are constructed to reflect different perspectives (Arthur, 2010).

Growing up in a world of digital literacy practices

Around the turn of the new millennium, research began to evidence how new technologies were becoming integral to children's literacy experiences. New terms were coined to describe this process of change, such as 'digital natives' (Prensky, 2001), 'the Net Generation' (Tapscott, 1998) and 'early adopters' (see Wohlwend, 2009) referring to the first generation to grow up surrounded by digital media and connections to the Internet. However, at the level of education practice, research has consistently found that many practitioners are reticent about engaging with information and communications technology (ICT) and popular culture, and they need help to reflect on how they can extend their repertoire of pedagogical actions to support literacy learning with new technologies (Marsh, 2006; Plowman, Stephen, and McPake, 2010b; Wolfe and Flewitt, 2010). Carrington (2005) equates this reticence with Freud's notion of 'das Unheimliche' (the uncanny) and suggests that while many young children are familiar with the social and technical processes of reading, producing and disseminating digital texts, these practices are unsettling for many educators and policy-makers in their roles as representatives of the social institution of school.

There are, however, small pockets of change which build on earlier research that highlighted how young children's explorations of texts in both 'old' and 'new' media are multimodal and social. These earlier studies include, for example, Kress' (1997) observations of young children extending and enhancing meanings by making homes out of cushions and blankets, drawing cars, cutting them out, adding logos and driving them round while making engine noises, and Harste, Woodward, and Burke's (1984) observations of pre-school children's inventiveness in their production of multimodal symbol systems. More recently, Marsh (2005) has shown how popular culture shapes early literacy, and Hill and Mulhearn (2007) have worked with teacher-researchers to develop an inquiry-based multiliteracies curriculum that incorporates children's use of multiple modes in their meaning making across a range of technologies. In a similar vein, Ryan, Scott, and Walsh (2010) discuss how teachers can set about improving their expertise as analysts and critics of texts to guide their planning and teaching of literacy in this 'new' text world. Even if early education settings remain print-centric, research evidence has shown that young children use their imagination to include new technologies in their play. In a 3-year ethnographic study of children's literacy play in kindergarten and primary classrooms, Wohlwend (2009) observed how 5–7-year-olds transformed paper and pencil resources into pretend mobile phones and video games, and used these to strengthen their literate identities and the cohesiveness of their play groups. These studies constitute a growing body of research which has begun to highlight the need to broaden traditional concepts of reading and writing, to acknowledge the multimodal nature of young children's interaction with diverse texts and to develop pedagogy that links homes and early years schooling (see also Marsh et al., 2005; Plowman, Stephen, and McPake, 2010a; Wolfe and Flewitt, 2010).

One example of the small but growing body of research in this field is a study[2] funded by the Economic and Social Research Council (ESRC), which investigated 3- and 4-year-old children's early literacy experiences as they engaged with a range of printed and digital technologies at home and in a nursery (Flewitt, 2011; Wolfe and Flewitt, 2010). This study investigated contemporary literacy learning through detailed analysis of young children's uses of multiple modes in different media. For example, two twin girls, Jane and Elizabeth, were observed and video recorded at home as they played a computer game called 'Match It', where players were required to 'turn over' cards in rotation, memorise them and make matching pairs of objects (rhyming pairs, objects beginning with the same letter, etc.). On the screen, each object was identified by an image, in writing (a word in a speech bubble) and by a computer 'voice-over'. As was frequently observed in this household, the girls' mother participated in the activity with her daughters, this time sitting quietly behind them to offer help when needed. In interview, the mother commented how she tried to make the most of the motivational value of computer-based activities. Throughout the activity, both girls and the mother focused on the screen, the girls' concentration was intense and their interaction around the screen was characterised by highly collaborative dialogue negotiated through multiple modes, particularly talk, gaze direction and actions, which were all used to articulate their thinking processes. For example, Elizabeth clicked on the image of an 'ice-cream', saying the word aloud as she scanned the screen for its correct 'pair'. Jane, standing beside her, with her gaze also fixed on the screen, whispered the initial sound 'I' and her sister lighted on the 'iron' with a triumphant declaration 'iron and ice-cream'. Occasionally, the mother intervened to give strategic help, such as sounding out initial letters and recognising rhyming words. She also supported their navigation of the activity by drawing attention to salient aspects, for example 'Click on the rabbit opens the Matching Pairs game', by silently pointing to relevant items on the screen, and helping the girls overcome immediate problems by leaning forwards and, cupping her hand over their hands, silently directing their control of the mouse.

For these girls, learning to read on screen involved the interpretation of often complex and subtle cues offered by layout, images, icons and sounds. For example, they identified the PLAY icon with confidence and recognised the cue for action which was signified very subtly by a change in colour of the cuff on the hand pointer, from purple to red. Overall, they displayed a clear ability to decode the on-screen signs and symbols and to understand how they interrelated to produce meaning. Reading on screen therefore involved acting and interacting with diverse modes, and with increasing practice, they gained confidence in controlling the technical challenges presented by the medium, such as manipulating the mouse to move on-screen features and recognising which modes to attend to at different times. Later in the study, both girls were observed in the nursery setting learning how to type their names to log on to the computer – a procedure that tested their abilities to match upper and lower case letters with the symbols on the keyboard. Although initially supported by a teacher, they later returned to the computer to rehearse the skills that would allow them independent access to games (see Wolfe and Flewitt, 2010).

Research into the potentials and challenges of new technologies for young children's literacy learning is itself in its infancy, and much work remains to be done if we are to understand better how digital practices relate to other dimensions of children's literacy learning and how young children learn to negotiate the diverse modes and media which characterise contemporary literacy (see Burnett, 2010; Flewitt, 2011; Lankshear and Knobel, 2003).

Exploring meanings across modes with more traditional media

Multimodal studies of early literacy have shown how exploring concepts in multiple modes can enrich young children's understandings, and can equally enrich adults' insights into those understandings. With a focus on the visual mode, Albers, Frederick, and Cowan (2009) illustrate how close analysis of graphic, structural and semantic information in third-grade children's drawings reveals the subtleties of their understandings of gender, which reflect both personal and societal discourses. Lancaster shows how 2-year-old children's complex abstract reasoning is rooted in their physical and emotional engagement with the world (2001), and how the mark-making practices of children aged under 3 demonstrate their emerging understanding of the grammatical features and structures that are typical of writing systems in their cultures (2007).

Expressing meanings across modes is not a simple process of transferral, as meanings are re-shaped by the affordances of each mode. In multimodal studies, moving meanings across modes is referred to as *transduction*. Kress describes transduction as 'a process in which something which has been configured or shaped in one or more modes is reconfigured, reshaped according to the affordances of a quite different mode' (Kress, 2003: 47). In the process of transduction, meanings are explored in different ways by sign-makers and these changes can reveal subtle insights into children's understandings. In line with Kress and Van Leeuwen's proposal that 'our ability to match concepts with an appropriate signifier is based on our physical experience of the relevant phenomena' (2001: 75), Haggerty and Mitchell (2010) discuss how kindergarten children's interests and physical activities can act as a mainstay of support which the mode of talk can be mapped onto, and they show how children's spatial, motor and kinaesthetic understandings can be 'transduced' into verbal understandings and vice versa.

One example of how practitioners can draw on multiple modes to support early literacy learning is shown in the following extract from an ethnographic study of inclusive practices in early years education in England, funded by Rix, Thompson, Rothenberg Foundation (Flewitt, Nind, and Payler, 2009). In this study, detailed multimodal analysis of video recordings offered a framework for unraveling how the physical layout of resources, the actions of staff members and their fine-tuned and multimodal responses to children contributed to the inclusion of a 4-year-old girl with learning difficulties, Mandy, in the literacy practices of an inclusive preschool playgroup (Flewitt, Nind, and Payler, 2009). The brief data extract shown in Table 17.1 is taken from a whole-class book-reading activity, where the children were sitting on the floor in a circle around the teacher, with Mandy in a specially adapted supportive chair beside the teacher.

A quick glance down the columns of this multimodal representation of the first 30 seconds of the book-reading shows how the teacher achieved shared attention within the learning space through the second-by-second, responsive fine tuning of her body orientation, gaze direction, body movements and talk. She used gaze constantly to check all the children were attending, and, by moving her gaze from them to the book, she directed their gaze to the object of attention (Lines 2, 6, 12). To focus Mandy's attention on the literacy activity, the teacher used body movements to signal the book as the learning object (Line 7), supplemented by gaze direction and touch (Line 9) and a few quietly spoken single words (Lines 11 and 14). The multimodal representation format in Table 17.1 illustrates how breaking down communicative events into their constituent modal parts unpicks the detail of how diverse modes are integral to everyday communication and meaning making. In this teaching/learning episode, if only the words had been recorded and transcribed, then readers of the research, and indeed the researchers themselves, would not have been able to understand the multimodal complexity of how the interaction unfolded – and why it worked so effectively to include Mandy. The multimodal approach adopted in this study revealed how some practitioners inadvertently excluded Mandy from literacy activities by giving conflicting messages in different modes, whilst others, as illustrated above, enabled her active participation in literacy events through their sensitive and coordinated multimodal responses to her meaning-making (Flewitt, Nind, and Payler, 2009; Nind, Flewitt, and Payler, 2010).

Multimodality and bridging the gap between formal and informal literacy practices

Ethnographic studies of literacy as rooted in social practice have begun to reveal the

Table 17.1   Multimodal transcript of 30 seconds of shared book reading

Participant	Body orientation	Speech/ vocalisation	Gaze	Body movement
1 Teacher	Towards circle of children	Right Mr Wolf and the three bears	From children to book	Holding up closed book
2 Teacher		and it's written by	Glance to circle of children, then back to book	Points to name on book cover
3 Teacher		Jan	Raises gaze to children	Still pointing to name on book cover
4 Child	Towards centre of circle	I'm hungry	To teacher	Moves hands to hold her stomach
5 Teacher	Towards child	Are you hungry? I think we all are	To child	
6 Teacher	Towards circle of children	Jan Fearnley	Around the circle of children, back to book	Pointing to author's name on cover
7 Teacher	Twists towards Mandy	Mandy	Fixed on Mandy	Inclines head towards Mandy to gain her attention while pointing at name on cover
8 Mandy	Towards circle of children		To toy she is holding	Mouthing toy and turning it with hands
9 Teacher	Towards Mandy		To Mandy	Gently touches Mandy's arm, then moves hand back to book
10 Mandy	Towards circle of children		To teacher's hand on her arm, follows teacher's hand as it moves to book, so gaze rests on book	
11 Teacher	Towards Mandy	Ok?	To Mandy	Opens book and begins to turn book's pages
12 Teacher	Turning towards circle of children		Glance around circle of children then fixed gaze at book	
13 Mandy	Towards circle of children		To toy	Turning toy in her hands
14 Teacher	Towards Mandy	Look	Glance from book to Mandy	Turning pages of book
15 Mandy	Towards teacher		To book	Holding toy still

complexities of how fledgling literacy learners are inducted into literacy practices in different social settings, and how they express their meanings through the inter-relationship between multiple modes. Using Bourdieu's concept of *habitus*

(1977, 1990), Pahl (2009) illustrates how 6–7-year-old children's ways of being at home and in the classroom are reflected in the multimodal artefacts they create, and in their talk about those artefacts. The children in this study were making 'panorama boxes' out of shoe boxes to represent an environment such as the ocean or jungle. Talking with them about their creations, Pahl found that traces of each child's social history were sedimented in the boxes. This was particularly apparent when the children improvised and did something different from what might have been expected: the meanings were not immediately apparent in the artefacts themselves, and could easily have been dismissed as insignificant or a misunderstanding of the task, but gained significance through the children's talk about the multimodal texts they had created.

This notion of improvisation and divergence from school literacy practices is reflected in Mavers' analysis of a series of informal e-mail exchanges between a 6-year-old girl and her uncle (Mavers, 2007), where the girl is both strategic and resourceful in the semiotic choices she makes. The girl selects and combines particular lexical and syntactic choices which do not reflect her knowledge of formal writing (such as the use of capitals and spaces between letters), but which evidence her subtle understandings of the less formal writing practices used in personal e-mail exchanges. Mavers' study suggests that writing can be conceptualised as a process of design that involves multiple decisions beyond the linguistic that draw on the affordances of the material and social resources offered by multiple modes.

Young children's 'unofficial' uses of multiple modes in classroom contexts also lend rich insights into their interests and understandings, and Björkvall and Engblom (2010) propose that rather than disregarding children's divergence from formal literacy tasks when working with ICT, teachers could seek ways to connect unofficial computer activities to 'official'

ones in classrooms where contemporary technologies are present. Levy (2009) reaches a similar conclusion in her study of how the multiple modes available in digital technologies, particularly computers, can help 3–6-year-old children learn how to use and make sense of print, within a context that is meaningful, motivating and free from issues of proficiency grading. Yet Levy's findings also revealed that as the children progressed through their first year in primary school, many lost confidence in themselves as readers as they began to conform to the perceived definition of reading as the need to decode printed text. Similarly, Lee and O'Rourke (2006) found that young children's explorations of multiple modes available in computer software was a natural extension of their interests and often helped them to make important connections between concrete and abstract experiences as well as engaging in the design and redesign processes which are crucial to developing multiliteracies. Early and Yeung (2009) observed how a Canadian teacher's innovative pedagogical approach using multimodal processes and practices increased children's French language awareness and proficiency, in both oral and written modes. The multimodal nature of the tasks offered something for all learners and provided multiple points of entry into the language, which in turn improved the chances of success in language learning which led to an increased desire to continue to learn French.

These studies all build on Roskos and Christie's reflections on the links between play and literacy, where they conclude that playfulness can serve literacy by providing meaningful contexts that promote literacy activity, skills and strategies, and help children build connections between oral and written modes (Roskos and Christie, 2001), and where they call for new theoretical approaches to explore the contribution that play makes to early literacy development (Roskos and Christie, 2011).

CONCLUSION

Many everyday literacy practices in the developed world are now influenced in some way by digital technologies, and individuals need to develop competence in and critical awareness of how knowledge is negotiated through multiple modes in diverse media. As Kress (2010) points out, in contemporary communicative landscapes it can no longer be assumed that language does all the significant semiotic work.

In this chapter, I have considered how multimodal perspectives can offer a new framework for understanding literacy, informed by children's diverse cultural and linguistic experiences and by their uses of a range of symbolic conventions. Multimodal research has given fresh insights into early literacy learning with 'traditional' resources, and has also begun to unravel the complexities of young children's emergent literacy practices in a digital age, revealing the fundamental role of new technologies in young children's early literacy learning, identity formation and construction of themselves as knowledgeable beings. This body of research draws attention to the need for policy makers and practitioners to acknowledge the rapid changes that are taking place in contemporary communicative practices and to be sensitive to how these practices traverse both formal and informal learning spaces. It also highlights the need for further research into how children engage with a range of texts in diverse settings as they endeavour to make sense of the literacy systems they encounter in their social and cultural worlds, and to recognise how these are valued by others.

NOTES

1 In semiotic theory, a sign has two components, the signifier (e.g., a word, image, sound) and the signified (the thing being represented). For many years the relationship between the signified (e.g., a chair) and the signifier (the word 'chair' or a painting of a chair) was considered to be arbitrary (Saussure, 1974). This suggested that people play a fairly passive role in the selection of signs. Social semiosis refutes this passivity, and puts a greater emphasis on the active, choice-making role of the sign maker. From this perspective, sign makers usually, if not always, have at their disposal a range of *semiotic resources*, and they choose from this range a single mode or a combination of modes that they feel will best suit the circumstance they are in and the purpose of whatever it is they want to communicate.

2 Rosie Flewitt, *Multimodal Literacies in the Early Years* ESRC RES-000-22-2451.

REFERENCES

Albers, P., Frederick, T., and Cowan, K. (2009) 'An analysis of the visual texts of 3rd grade children', *Journal of Early Childhood Literacy*, 9(2): 234–60.

Alexander, R. (2000) *Culture and Pedagogy: International Comparisons in Primary Education*. Oxford: Blackwell Publishing.

Alexander, R. (ed.) (2010) *Children, their World, their Education: Final Report and Recommendations of the Cambridge Primary Review*. Abingdon: Routledge.

Arthur, L. (2010) 'The (draft) English National Curriculum: an early childhood perspective', *Curriculum Perspectives*, 30(3): 56–8.

Baker, E.A. (2010) *The New Literacies: Multiple Perspectives on Research and Practice*. London: The Guilford Press.

Bearne, E. (2009) 'Multimodality, literacy and texts, developing a discourse', *Journal of Early Childhood Literacy*, 9(2): 156–87.

Björkvall, A. and Engblom, C. (2010) 'Young children's exploration of semiotic resources during unofficial computer activities in the classroom', *Journal of Early Childhood Literacy*, 10(3): 271–93.

Bourdieu, P. (1977) *Outline of a Theory of Practice*. Tr. R. Nice. Cambridge: Cambridge University Press.

Bourdieu, P. (1990) *The Logic of Practice*. Tr. R. Nice. Cambridge: Polity Press.

Burnett, C. (2010) 'Technology and literacy in early childhood settings: A review of research', *Journal of Early Childhood Literacy*, 10(3): 247–70.

Carrington, V. (2005) 'The uncanny, digital texts and literacy', *Language and Education*, 19(6): 467–82.

Carrington, V. and Robinson, M. (2009) *Digital Literacies: Social Learning and Classroom Practices*. London, England: Sage.

Clay, M. (1966) 'Emergent reading behavior' Unpublished doctoral dissertation, University of Auckland, New Zealand.

Cole, M. and Engestrom, Y. (1993) 'A cultural historical approach to distributed cognition', in G. Salomon (ed.), *Distributed Cognitions: Psychological and Educational Considerations*. New York: Cambridge University Press. pp. 1–46.

Cruttenden, A. (1997) *Intonation*. Cambridge, MA: Cambridge University Press.

Dyson, A.H. (2001) 'Where are the childhoods in childhood literacy? An exploration in outer (school) space', *Journal of Early Childhood Literacy*, 1(1): 9–39.

Dyson, A.H. (2008) 'Staying in the (curricular) lines: practice constraints and possibilities in childhood writing', *Written Communication*, 25(1): 119–59.

Early, M. and Yeung, C. (2009) 'Producing multimodal picture books and dramatic performances in a core French classroom: an exploratory case study', *The Canadian Modern Language Review*, 66(2): 299–322.

Flewitt, R.S. (2005) 'Is every child's voice heard? Researching the different ways 3-year-old children communicate and make meaning at home and in a preschool playgroup', *Early Years: International Journal of Research and Development*, 25(3): 207–22.

Flewitt, R.S. (2011) 'Bringing ethnography to a multimodal investigation of early literacy in a digital age', *Qualitative Research Special Issue: Multimodality and ethnography: working at the intersection* (Issue Editors, B. Dicks, R.S. Flewitt, L. Lancaster, and K. Pahl) 3: 293–310.

Flewitt, R.S., Nind, M., and Payler, J. (2009) '"If she's left with books she'll just eat them": considering inclusive multimodal literacy practices', *Journal of Early Childhood Literacy*, 9(2): 211–33.

Gibson, J. (1977) 'The theory of affordances', in R. Shaw and J. Bransford (eds), *Perceiving, Acting and Knowing: Toward an Ecological Psychology*. Hillsdale, NJ: Lawrence Erlbaum. pp. 67–82.

Goodwin, C. (2007) 'Participation, stance and affect in the organization of activities', *Discourse Society*, 18(1): 53–73.

Gregory, E., Long, S., and Volk, D. (2004) *Many Pathways to Literacy: Young Children Learning with Siblings, Grandparents, Peers and Communities*. New York and London: RoutledgeFalmer.

Haggerty, M. and Mitchell, L. (2010) 'Exploring curriculum implications of multimodal literacy in a New Zealand early childhood setting', *European Early Childhood Education Research Journal*, 18(3): 327–39.

Hall, K. (1998) 'Critical literacy and the case for it in the early years of school', in *Language, Culture and Curriculum*, 11(2): 183–94.

Halliday, M.A.K. (1973) *Explorations in the Functions of Language*. London: Edward Arnold.

Halliday, M.A.K. (1978) *Language as Social Semiotic: The Social Interpretation of Language and Meaning*. London: Edward Arnold.

Harste, J.C., Woodward, V., and Burke, C. (1984) *Language Stories and Literacy Lessons*. Portsmouth, NH: Heinemann.

Heath, S.B. (1983) *Ways with Words: Language, Life and Word in Communities and Classrooms*. Cambridge: Cambridge University Press.

Hill, S. and Mulhearn, G. (2007) 'Children of the new millennium: research and professional learning into practice', *Australian Research in Early Childhood Education*, 14(1): 57–67.

Hull, G. and Nelson, M. (2005) 'Locating the semiotic power of multimodality', *Written Communication*, 22(2): 224–61.

Jewitt, C. and Kress, G. (eds) (2003) *Multimodal Literacy*. New York: Peter Lang.

Kendon, A. (2004) *Gesture: Visible Action as Utterance*. Cambridge: Cambridge University Press.

Kenner, C. (2005) 'Bilingual families as literacy eco-systems', *Early Years*, 25(3): 283–98.

Kress, G.R. (1997) *Before Writing: Rethinking the Paths to Literacy*. London: Routledge.

Kress, G.R. (2000) '"You've just got to learn how to see": curriculum subjects, young people and schooled engagement with the world', *Linguistics and Education*, 11(4): 401–15.

Kress, G.R. (2003) *Literacy in the Media Age*. London: Routledge.

Kress, G.R. (2010) *Multimodality: a Social Semiotic Approach to Contemporary Communication*. London: Routledge.

Kress, G.R. and van Leeuwen, T. (2001) *Multimodal Discourse: The Modes and Media of Contemporary Communication*. London: Edward Arnold.

Kress, G., Jewitt, C., Ogborn, J., and Tsatsarelis, C. (2001) *Multimodal Teaching and Learning: The Rhetorics of the Science Classroom*. London: Continuum Books.

Lancaster, L. (2001) 'Staring at the page: the functions of gaze in a young child's interpretation of symbolic forms', *Journal of Early Childhood Literacy*, 1(2): 131–52.

Lancaster, L. (2007) 'Representing the ways of the world: how graphic signs are constructed by children under three', *Journal of Early Childhood Literacy*, 7: 2.

Lankshear, C. and Knobel, M. (2003) 'New technologies in early childhood literacy research: a review of research', *Journal of Early Childhood Literacy*, 3(1): 59–82.

Lee, L. and O'Rourke, M. (2006) 'Information and communication technologies: transforming views of literacies in early childhood settings', *Early Years*, 26(1): 49–62.

Levy, R. (2009) '"You have to understand words ... but not read them": young children becoming readers in a digital age', *Journal of Research in Reading*, 32(1): 75–91.

Lewis-Williams, D. (2002) *The Mind in the Cave: Consciousness and the Origins of Art*. London: Thames and Hudson.

Marsh, J. (eds) (2005) *Popular Culture, New Media and Digital Literacy in Early Childhood*. Abingdon: RoutledgeFalmer.

Marsh, J. (2006) 'Popular culture in the literacy curriculum: A Bourdieuian analysis', *Reading Research Quarterly*, 41(2): 160–74.

Marsh, J., Brooks, G., Hughes, J., Ritchie, L., and Roberts, S. (2005) *Digital Beginnings: Young Children's Use of Popular Culture, Media and New Technologies*. Sheffield, UK: University of Sheffield.

Mavers, D. (2007) 'Semiotic resourcefulness: a young child's e-mail exchange as design,' *Journal of Early Childhood Literacy*, 7(2): 153–74.

Mercer, N. (2000) *Words and Minds: How we use Language to Think Together*. London: Routledge.

Mercer, N. (2010) http://thinkingtogether.educ.cam.ac.uk/ Accessed 22 April 2010.

Mercer, N. and Littleton, K. (2007) *Dialogue and the Development of Children's Thinking*. London: Routledge.

Ministry of Education (1996) *Te Whāriki. He Whāriki Mātauranga mōngā Mokopuna o Aotearoa: Early Childhood Curriculum* Wellington: Learning Media.

New London Group (2000) 'A pedagogy of multiliteracies designing social futures', in B. Cope and M. Kalantzis (eds), *Multiliteracies: Literacy Learning and the Design of Social Futures*. London: Routledge. pp. 9–38.

Nind, M., Flewitt, R., and Payler, J. (2010) 'The social experience of early childhood for children with learning disabilities: inclusion, competence and agency', *British Journal of Sociology of Education*, 31(6): 653–70.

Norris, S. (2004) *Analyzing Multimodal Interaction*. London and New York: Routledge.

Pahl, K. (2009) 'Interactions, intersections and improvisations: studying the multimodal texts and classroom talk of six- to seven-year olds', *Journal of Early Childhood Literacy*, 9(2): 188–210.

Plowman, L., Stephen, C., and McPake, J. (2010a) *Growing Up With Technology: Young Children Learning in a Digital World*. London: Routledge.

Plowman, L., Stephen, C., and McPake, J. (2010b) 'Supporting young children's learning with technology at home and in preschool', *Research Papers in Education*, 25(1): 93–113.

Prensky, M. (2001) 'Digital natives, digital immigrants', *On the Horizon*, 9(5): 1–6.

Roskos, K. and Christie, J. (2001) 'Examining the play-literacy interface : A critical review and future directions', *Journal of Early Childhood Literacy*, 1(1): 59–89.

Roskos, K. and Christie, J. (2011) 'Mindbrain and play-literacy connections', *Journal of Early Childhood Literacy*, 11(1): 73–94.

Ryan, J., Scott, A., and Walsh, M. (2010) 'Pedagogy in the multimodal classroom: an analysis of the challenges and opportunities for teachers', *Teachers and Teaching: Theory and Practice*, 16(4): 477–89.

Saussure, F. de (1974) *Course in General Linguistics*. (Edited by Charles Bally and Albert Sechehaye) New York: McGraw Hill.

Streeck, J. (1993) 'Gesture as communication: its coordination with gaze and speech', *Communication Monographs*, 60(4): 275–99.

Street, B. (1984) *Literacy in Theory and Practice*. Cambridge: Cambridge University Press.

Tapscott, D. (1998) *Growing Up Digital: The Rise of the Net Generation*. New York: McGraw Hill.

Taylor, D. (1983) *Family Literacy: Young Children Learning to Read and Write*. Portsmouth, NH: Heinemann.

Vygotsky, L.S. (1978) *Mind in Society: the Development of Higher Psychological Processes,*. Cambridge, MA: Harvard University Press.

Vygotsky, L.S. (1986) *Thought and Language*. Cambridge, MA: MIT Press.

Wertsch, J.V. (1991) *Voices of the Mind: A Sociocultural Approach to Mediated Action*. Cambridge, MA: Harvard University Press.

Wertsch, J.V. (2007) 'Mediation.', in H. Daniels, M. Cole, and J.V. Wertsch (eds), *The Cambridge Companion to Vygotsky*. New York: Cambridge University Press. pp. 178–92.

Wohlwend, K. (2009) 'Early adopters: Playing new literacies and pretending new technologies in print-centric classrooms', *Journal of Early Childhood Literacy*, 9(2): 117–40.

Wolfe, S. and Flewitt, R.S. (2010) 'New technologies, new multimodal literacy practices and young children's metacognitive development', *Cambridge Journal of Education*, 40(4): 387–99.

PART 3

Early Moves in Literacy

18

Moving into Literacy:
How it all Begins

Lesley Lancaster

INTRODUCTION

There is very little research into the development of literacy much before the age of 3. There are a number of studies of its development between the ages of 3 and 5 or 6 (Torrey, 1973; Clark, 1976; Bissex, 1980; Luria, 1983; Ferreiro and Teberosky, 1982; Kress, 1997, 2000), and although there are references to earlier stages of literacy in some of these, there are only two studies that deal specifically with the earliest stages of writing and use of notation by children of this age (Lancaster and Roberts, 2006; Tolchinsky, 2003). This is perhaps unsurprising since very young children are not likely to be literate in the commonly understood sense of the term, and therefore, so the argument might go, there is not a great deal of evidence to consider. However, this does leave a significant gap in the account of children's development of literacy. It would be surprising if, from an apparent position of no

serious engagement with print at all, children are suddenly able to explode into the type of rampant, creative, independent and reasoned relationship with the medium, which is described in most of the studies cited above. It appears as if much groundwork has been laid before. However, there are both theoretical and practical reasons why this has not invited a great deal of attention in educational circles.

The influence of Jean Piaget on educational thinking about children's cognitive development has been considerable over the years. Critiques of aspects of his work have been accepted for some time now (Donaldson, 1978; Deloache and Brown, 1987; Feldman, 1987; Thelen and Smith, 1994), but the legacy has persisted. Two claims of Piaget can be held to partial account for the lack of attention to early literate activity. First, there is the suggestion that learning happens in fairly discrete stages, with the very earliest involving little more than reflexive responses to the external environment. In other words, children have to reach the right stage before they are able to cope with the physical, cognitive and symbolic demands of reading and writing. Secondly, there is the view that a common process of development pervades all areas of cognition, rather than there being different domains of cognition and learning with individual developmental spectrums. Accordingly, young children would not be able to recognise features of literacy as part of a unique symbolic system, distinguishable from other such systems.

A second factor influencing the investigation of early literacy comes from the study of the development of writing itself, and in particular its relationship to speech. A traditional view holds that writing is predominately a transcription of speech (Havelock, 1976; Gelb, 1952); that it developed in order to enable talk to be written down. It would therefore be quite reasonable to suggest that until children have reached a fair level of proficiency with spoken language, they are not going to have the requisite skills to understand or produce written language: they cannot read or write down talk if they are not yet producing it. The marks that children do make prior to being able to make this connection are frequently described as 'scribble', with its rather unhelpful association with marks that are purposeless, illegible or meaningless. Within the literature, it tends to refer specifically to a period of development prior to there being any real connection being made between letter forms and spoken meaning: Sulzby (1986) refers to the way in which children of 5 or 6 who are aware of 'conventional spelling', will revert to the use of 'lower-order forms like scribbling' (1986: 70) in certain situations. The suggestion here is that where the connection between speech and writing is not made, these features of children's

'written' productions have 'lower-order' communicative intention and representational purpose.

The third reason why this early stage of literacy has not been researched to the same extent as literacy beyond infancy is a practical one. Once children reach the age of 3, most receive some form of formal education within the nursery education system. The population of children under the age of 2 however, is much more widely located, with children attending children's centres and playgroups, as well as being looked after at home or by childminders. Access, in other words, is more difficult. It is also problematic to work with children this young without the co-operation and help of someone the child knows and trusts. Whilst this can have many benefits, it does add practical and organisational difficulties to research. The other side of this is that the relative ease of working with children in institutional settings also contributes to what Street (1995) calls the 'pedagogisation' of literacy: the reduction of reading and writing to social practices predominately associated with schooled learning. This contributes to the exclusion of the literacy practices of infants and children who are not yet part of the formal educational system from serious consideration.

In spite of the sparsity of research studies concerned exclusively with children's development of literacy before the age of 3, studies from disciplines like art education show that these children are capable of a range of representational behaviour (Cox, 2005; Anning, 2003; Wolf and Perry, 1988). Far from this being a quiescent period, children of this age avidly explore graphic systems, much as do children later on. In this chapter, I shall look at evidence that they are able to systematically explore graphic systems as a way of representing significant features of their personal, social and cultural experiences, long before any direct connection with language is made. I shall show that they are capable of recognising unique features of different domains of representation: writing, drawing and number, and I shall look at how even the very earliest marks made by children reflect intention and meaning. Finally, I shall discuss the view that they are already actively acquiring parallel systems of representation within these domains between the ages of 12 and 24 months. In other words they are already actively producing and interpreting different levels and genres of written language and different means of representing them.

PREAMBLE

In certain very obvious senses, it can be said that literacy begins at the beginning. At the start of the twenty-first century, most children are born into cultures that are in one way or another driven or affected by a complex array of literacy practices. The social and material evidence of their operation is pervasive, although it goes without saying that individual exposure to this is variable, both within and across cultures and communities. And long before they might be expected to understand much about it, babies and toddlers are on the receiving end of a kind of intense semiotic acculturation, which includes writing of many kinds in many forms. Clothes, bed covers, eating and drinking utensils, toys, videos, games, story books: a host of merchandise covered in pictures, logos, numbers and print of all kinds, representing characters and objects from media events of the moment. These are part of a huge industry producing an array of items which are directed at the families of very young children and ultimately, of

course, at young children themselves. Marsh in this volume (Figure 12.1) demonstrates the extent of the modes and media involved.

Initially, it is the adults who respond to the particular characters, narratives and images signified by these various objects. However, their cultural significance is mediated through talking, showing, shaking, touching, and the countless other ways in which adults communicate with babies about significant things. The baby's first response is likely to be to their material qualities, and its exploration to involve senses like vision, touch and taste. However, the fact that, initially at least, a baby finds putting an object in its mouth an effective mode of exploration, does not preclude it being responsive to its other signifying features. Nor does it preclude it from directing the focus of its attention to objects and images not in the least designed to be interesting or attractive to an infant. Very young children are notorious for finding unpredictable things salient. I recall my son, as a young baby, screaming when being moved from one part of the room to another so that he could watch the movement of what I considered to be a really interesting mobile. I eventually realised that in his original spot, he was watching the movement of the leaves of a tree, reflected through a sunny window as flickering shadows onto the ceiling. I had interrupted some serious semiotic work.

Even the best-intentioned adults have a tendency to disrupt this kind of intense engagement which young children have with seemingly unimportant or irrelevant objects and activities often, of course, for their own protection and safety. My mother remembers an incident that happened when she was probably less than a year old. She was crawling along a beach when she spotted what she considered to be the most brightly coloured and desirable object she had ever seen. She crawled towards it with delight and anticipation, and was just about to grab it when a hand came down and snatched it away from her grasp. The object, she realised much later, was a Swan Vestas matchbox, with its highly coloured images and lettering. Eighty years later, she could still recollect the feeling of devastating loss and disappointment!

These examples illustrate some important things about how very young children engage with visual and graphic representations of meaning. In both cases, the activity is independently constructed; it is purposeful and compelling, involving, potentially at least, a commitment of time and effort to find out more. In the case of the matchbox, the compulsion was also a physical and bodily one: to hold and scrutinise the desired object. Watching shifting patterns of shadowy images, on the other hand, requires prolonged visual concentration. It also requires considerable intellectual engagement with what amounts to a fluctuating sequence of abstract images. This kind of intense desire to find out more, the need to be physically involved and the extended concentration and interest in things at an abstract level, are also the qualities which very young children require to start engaging with all the cultural paraphernalia and attendant semiotic systems which surround them; including, of course, systems of writing. Whether they are just generally aware and responsive to all of this, or whether they start to sort out how these systems work as soon as they are aware of them, is central to a consideration of how literacy develops.

INTENTIONALITY

In part, the answer to this question lies in the extent to which we accept that the marks and signs that children produce prior to being able to operate with conventional systems of inscription are intentional; in other words, the extent to which these signs are produced with the purpose of conveying a specific meaning, albeit using unconventional systems and notations. Goodman (1986) is unequivocal in her assertion that whatever and however marks are produced, they are always 'a serious expression of meaning'. Lancaster and Roberts studied children under the age of 3 mark-making at home with parents or carers, and examined the extent to which they used system and regularity in their mark-making, based on categories derived from everyday experience. The children in the study consistently communicated what they intended their marks to mean, either in advance of making them, or subsequent to their production. They often resolved the problem of relying on personal rather than conventional systems of notation by combining deictic language and gesture to instantiate meaning: for example simultaneously stating 'that's x', and putting a finger on the relevant item on the page. Rowe (2008a), looking at 2-year-olds interacting with adults at a writing table in a preschool, similarly found children to be purposeful in the signs they made. Here too, the children used a combination of strategies to convey meaning. Whereas adults invariably used talk when referring to the content and meaning of signs, the children, who were still developing as language users, would often use subtle combinations of gaze, gesture, talk and action to communicate their graphic intentions. Cox (2005) observed the range of representational purposes and meanings in the drawing activity of children in a nursery classroom. She concluded that such representation is part of broader, intentional meaning-making activity, in which children actively define reality and bring shape and order to their experience, rather than passively reflect what is 'seen'. The problem lies not in children's lack of intentionality in the signs that they make, but in the difficulty that adults have in interpreting them.

RECOGNISING DIFFERENT DOMAINS

Harste et al. (1984) claim that by the time that they reach the age of 3, children are quite insistent about there being a distinction between drawing and writing. Evidence comes from the marks that children make, and their function and purpose. Although there is not necessarily a consistency between the forms of marks used to represent these different modes, nevertheless, whatever form is chosen is used consistently and systematically within the constraints of the particular sign or text being produced. A number of factors can be significant in how this choice of marks is made, including the dominant writing script in their communities (Harris and Hatano, 1999). Useful evidence comes from the productions of slightly older children who have access to more than one writing script from an early age. Gregory and Williams (2000) shows the skill and proficiency with which such children move between two very different writing systems that use marks in quite different ways, Bengali and English. Kenner (2002 and in this volume), in her study of young children learning to write in two different writing systems at the same time, demonstrates that at 5 and 6, children are able to clearly articulate distinctions between the semiotic principles operating for the different systems they are using. This includes being able to point out that there is a distinction between a logographic system like Chinese and a pictorial system.

In other words, the decisions that children make about which system is which, and how they are constructed, are consistent, rational and well informed. As has already been suggested, it looks as if in order to have the capacity to reach such a sophisticated conceptual level by the time they are 5 or 6, children will have been engaged in serious analyses of the systems of representation around them for some time. In contrast with Piagetian thinking about this, they will have recognised different domains of cognition and learning and made a start on working out their distinctive features long before they reach the age of 3.

Karmiloff-Smith (1992) found that by the time they are 4, children readily discriminate between drawing, writing and number, as well as between drawing and writing. They apply clearly differentiated constraints to the three modes of notation: drawings are not acceptable as either number or writing; single elements are acceptable as number, but not as writing, as are repeated identical elements; linkage between elements is accepted for writing, but not for number; and a limited number of elements is accepted in a written string, but not for numbers. Clearly this involves sophisticated analyses and a considerable degree of understanding of the salient features of the different modes of notation. It is unlikely that the ability to recognise notational properties is something which happens suddenly in late infancy, particularly in view of evidence which suggests that babies as young as 4 months old can distinguish between different number arrays (Treiber and Wilcox, 1984), and by 6 months, can detect numerical correspondence between auditory and visual inputs (Starkey et al., 1985). It also seems unlikely that such useful insights are dispensed with, and much more likely that children's learning about domains of symbolic representation is a continuous, developing and expanding process, which starts very early on in their lives.

Whilst children under 3 might not be able to verbally articulate the differences between writing, drawing and number in the same way that a 4-year-old can, this does not mean that they are not aware of them; the problem lies in the difficulty of gaining access to what it is they know and how they come to know it. Deloache et al. (1979) show that already at 5 months old, children are able to recognise relatively abstract pictures of objects. Karmiloff-Smith notes that by the time they are 10–18 months, children readily differentiate between drawing and writing in their productions. They are 'adamant' she says, about the distinction between a mark that is a drawing and one that is writing. However, the relationship between process and product has to be taken fully into account when considering the intentions of children this young. The mark on its own is likely to be ambiguous without the context of its production, since toddlers go about the *processes* of drawing and writing differently, even though the outcome might be largely undifferentiated. So, for example, they tend to lift the pen from the page much more frequently when pretending to write than when pretending to draw. As has already been mentioned, children of this age also use multiple modes of communication to help ascribe meaning to their notations: language and gesture, for example, can be used to ascribe identity to otherwise undifferentiated marks, along the lines of, 'This mark I am pointing to is writing because I say it is writing, this one is a cat because I say it is a cat' (Lancaster, 2001). However, children of this age also have the capacity to distinguish between writing-like and drawing-like marks in the types of notation that they

use. Chan and Nunes (1998) reported that Chinese-speaking 3-year-olds tended to use circles and whorls when representing drawing, and lines and dots for writing. Lancaster (2007: 131–9) shows that children under the age of 3 differentiate between iconic and non-iconic marks according to the overall meaning and purpose of the signs and texts that they are producing. For example, 2-year-old Ruby, when representing the character Belle from Disney's *Beauty and the Beast*, produces two quite different texts in one marking episode, with each using a distinct form of notation; both systems of marking are driven by the representational purpose of the text. In one case, marks are used iconically to produce the kinds of outcomes more generally associated with drawing systems, and in the other, the marks are used in the more arbitrary, non-iconic way associated with writing systems. In the former case, she uses a range of marks to represent Belle's physical attributes – face, limbs, dress, and so on; in the latter she uses simple zigzags to foreground Belle's locative relationship to a line representing 'the castle'. In neither case was she using anything like a conventional drawing or writing system, but she was already making a distinction in the notation in ways that were relevant to the development of these systems.

INTERACTION

The interactions between very young children, adults, and older children collaborating in this kind of symbolic activity are a vital part of the process of producing graphic signs for young children (Halliday, 1975; Trevarthen, 1990). Communicative processes, and processes of physical and material production are often an integral part of the outcome. The final production has to be understood by taking into account the circumstances that gave rise to it, given that conventional symbols are not yet being used. Central to this is the interpersonal engagement that surrounds the process of sign production. Rowe shows how social interaction between adults and 2-year-old children provide a starting point for the negotiation of what she describes as 'social contracts for writing'. These are social and cultural rules involving the material features of written texts, ways in which writing is used to represent meaning, differences between writing and other semiotic systems, and relations between people and texts (2008b). The textual intentions of individual children are often jointly negotiated with adults during face-to-face interactions. Dunst and Gorman (2009) suggest that interaction between adults, infants and toddlers is associated with a more sustained and complex engagement with mark-making. Flewitt (2005) examined the differences between adult and child interactions in a playgroup and in the home. At home, the children had opportunities for extended exchanges concerning past shared experiences; however, this type of exchange was lacking in the playgroup. Lancaster and Roberts (2006) found that adult–child interactions of this kind were central to extended, sustained episodes of mark-making and text production, and the development of children's understanding of how writing and other notational systems operate.

EXPANDING WAYS OF MEANING IN DIFFERENT DOMAINS

If children are able to distinguish between writing, drawing and number before they are 2, then it follows that this is based on their experience and perceptions of how each of these domains individually represent meaning. However, this is far from being a straightforward thing to sort out since the domains also have features in common, at least in certain circumstances, and frequently operate multimodally, as well as being presented in a range of different media. So writing can be represented graphically, two-dimensionally on a page, using a simple tool like a pencil, as can drawing and numbers; numbers can also be represented by writing, writing and numbers can be incorporated into drawings; but then writing can also be read aloud, numbers can be represented three-dimensionally by an abacus, quantity and spatial organisation can be incorporated into written meanings, drawings can be made to move in cartoons, and so on.

If one starts to consider the sheer range of possibilities which each domain of symbolic representation presents to young children in the twenty-first century, then it is not difficult to reach the conclusion that to view them as principally pedagogical practices is to significantly misrepresent the nature of the task facing children, as well as the complex nature of symbolic systems involved. Indeed Teale (1986) concludes that for preschool children, 90 per cent of their reading and writing experiences occur as part of the daily lives of their families and communities, rather than as being seen and acknowledged as literacy activities per se. As Goodman (1986) points out, children know that most things in their lives are organised systematically, and this insight is applied to the complexities of symbolic representation as they present in the course of daily routines and interactions. Pahl (1999) shows how they interpret things according to the information and resources to which they have access at the time, and according to what is currently salient to their thinking. She cites the example of a child in a nursery copying every feature of an adult's rendition of his name, including mistakes and superfluous dots; the same child could also produce his own version quite independently. Pahl's explanation is that to the child, these tasks are quite different: the first he constructed as a design task, whilst the second 'required subjective decisions about what constituted his name' (1999: 63). In other words, to see this task as a process with a single outcome is to entirely misunderstand the complexity of the child's understanding of the ways in which meanings can be represented graphically.

This range of representational possibilities includes both traditional and digital technologies. The digital domain is an essentially multimodal one, with different modes operating interdependently in the creation of meaning. Davies (2011) makes a distinction between *digital* literacies, where digital media are used to produce text, and *new* literacies, which describe new collaborative reading and writing practices that are emerging in the new communicative 'spaces' afforded by digital media. Children under the age of 3 participate in both these literacies which, according to Marsh (2006, 2004) incorporate a range of 'techno-social' practices such as email, text messages, internet, and chat rooms. Marsh looked at the communicative practices of children between 30 months and 5 years of age, and found that even the youngest children participated in these practices in the home with parents and older siblings. They were able to observe the increasingly central role that was played by new and digital literacies in social interaction, and in the management and retrieval of information in family life. Wohlwend and Handsfield (2010) discuss the construction of young children as pre-

cocious users of digital technologies through an analysis of a parent-produced YouTube video of a 2-year-old operating a computer to browse on-line nursery rhymes. Wolfe and Flewitt (2010) however, point to the limited opportunities for the use of electronic resources in nursery settings, compared to the diversity of opportunities in the home.

CONSTRUCTING SIGNS

Both writing and drawing suffer from being dominated by pedagogical concerns and by being frequently reduced to a single endpoint: in the case of writing, correctly making links between sounds and letters, and in the case of drawing, the achievement of realistic picturing. Wolf and Perry (1988) suggest that in fact, drawing involves a wide repertoire of visual languages. In investigating how young children develop drawing skills, they identify three broad areas of development: the invention of drawing systems; the construction of distinctions between different graphic genres (between maps, drawings and diagrams, for example); and the evolution of specific renditions of visual images. Here, their definition of 'drawing' also included features of the process of production. Looking at the creations of children between 12 and 15 months, they identified the appearance and use of a series of distinguishable systems. Cox (2005: 120) similarly describes the creative but systematic use of graphic schema. Children combined marks such as vertical and horizontal lines, zigzags, grids, arcs, core and radials in different ways to created different meanings and achieve their representational purposes.

Significant analogies can be drawn here with features of writing development. Wolf and Perry describe one of the earliest of these systems, evident at between 12 and 14 months, as 'object-based representations', where drawing materials and tools are substituted for the referents which the child has in mind. So the pen might be rolled up in the paper to signify the object 'hot dog', rather than being used to make marks which represent it graphically. Kress (1997) describes a range of creative constructions devised by children moving into literacy, which could be similarly characterised. Rowe (1994) also shows how immediate and transformative children can be at this stage: turning a paper plate into a note by pencilling across it, giving it to someone, and then throwing it into the air to demonstrate how it flies. Labbo (1996) shows how children use the computer screen to similarly explore symbols and objects. These children are slightly older, between 3 and 5, but they are still using the same multimodal strategies as the younger children, though arguably at a more developed level. The system is also broadly the same whether it is being considered as drawing or writing. As Kress points out, the principles deployed in the learning of writing are much the same as for other sign systems, 'employing the strategy of using the best, most apt available form for the expression of a particular meaning.' (1997: 17). This is central to all children's early representations of symbolic meaning. What is clear is that children under 3 are able to construct graphic signs that are fully meaningful in their own right; and whilst neither drawing nor writing in conventional terms, they are already drawing on the symbolic principles which determine these systems.

Another system which Wolf and Perry identify as appearing at about the same age is that of 'gestural representations', where gestures are incorporated into the process of signifying meanings. They give the example of a child saying 'bunny' and hopping a marker across the page, making a trail of dotted footprints. Vygotsky (1978) suggests that gesture is also linked to the development of written signs in much the same way, and many of his examples are very similar in structure and concept to those cited by Wolf and Perry. Lancaster (1999) describes a child of 23 months using gesture to 'read' writing. Looking at a line of print on a title page, she moves her pointing hand rhythmically back and forth along the line, saying in unison with the movement, 'says writing David's, writing David's'. The gesture models the movement of her older brother's hand as he writes. These signs, with their precise integration of language and gestural action, comprise the most useful and appropriate forms available to these children at these times to express these meanings. Lancaster and Roberts found that this process of 'enactment' tended to be commonly used in the representation of action by under-3s where verbal structures would be used in conventional written forms, and appeared to be a solution to the problem of depicting movement through time within a spatial medium. For example, one child produced a graphic sign on a page representing water and a fish, then followed this by running up the room and back announcing that 'it is swimming'.

The third system of drawing activity identified by Wolf and Perry, they describe as 'point-plot representations'. At around 20 months, children start to make 'planful' use of graphic properties. They are able to record the number and location of an object's features by linking the graphic properties of the marks with the spatial features represented on the surface of the paper. So, a human body might be represented by a line above another line, and two lines at the bottom: top half, bottom half, and feet. This 'planful' linking of marks, properties of marks, and spatial organisation is also well documented in the development of children's writing between 3 and school age, and is discussed in detail in a number of the studies referred to at the start of this chapter. Marks are made and placed systematically to express ideas and concepts. Ferreiro and Teberosky (1982) describe how a child might make a very large mark because it signifies a big animal, or conversely a small one because it signifies a small animal; and a mark might be placed adjacent to another mark because it signifies something which is part of, or owned by the object or person represented by that mark. Luria (1983) shows how children also ascribe meaning to otherwise very similar marks by how they are located on the page.

Thelen and Smith (1994) point out that the facility to organise and classify space symbolically is clearly evident by the time children are 18 months old. Lancaster (1999) shows the same kind of systematic organisation of marks and space at 23 months. The child in this study is making a card for her mother, with the support and collaboration of her father. The page she is working on is organised so that the same mark can be used to represent different things according to how it is placed on the page: for example, one side of the page has 'cat' marks and the other 'drawing' marks; 'writing' marks are placed at the very bottom of the page, as close to the edge as possible. These constraints reveal that she already understands significant things about symbolic practice and representative domains. A graphic mark can be used to represent different systems (drawing and writing) and objects (cats); these have different relationships to the surrounding space,

with drawing and object marks being less constrained and linear in their relationship than writing. Anning (2003), Kress (1997), Matthews (1994), and Pahl (1999) have also observed the keen interest which very young children have in organising space, including the ways in which they physically inhabit it, and the ways in which this experience informs their perception of symbolic space. Space is of itself a significant meaning-making resource (see Kress and van Leeuwen, 1996), which young children use to very good effect.

In my example, principles of spatial organisation are used to structure a simple narrative based around a cat, involving a sequence of possessive 'events' where activity is implied by this ownership: cat's tree; cat's house; cat's treehouse. For very young children, ownership tends to involve a physical relationship with an object or person: holding, touching or being very close to what is desired. Tomasello (1992) reports on how such social encounters and relationships are reflected in the ways in which children construct a linguistic system. He notes that by 17 months, a child is able to express possession by saying the one 'next' to the other, as in 'mummy sock'. So, both physical experience and language provide vital tools in dealing with the difficult problem of how to represent a narrative with a temporal organisation involving a sequence of different events, on the fixed and two-dimensional space of the page, in a consistent and repeatable way. The principle of adjacency, of locating a mark representing someone, close to the mark representing the thing that they own, is one approach adopted by the child in this study. This suggests the beginnings of an insight into two significant and distinct features of writing: generic structure and grammatical organisation. Lancaster (2012) identifies the use of generic structures in the textual productions of children under 3 as playing a crucial role in the development of an understanding of the principles of symbolic reference that underlie written and other notational systems. According to Deacon (1997), learning any kind of symbol system requires an approach that allows attention to seemingly obvious associations to be set aside, in order that the larger scale logic of relationships between symbols can be noticed. In terms of writing, this means that learning about the details of notational structures is initially secondary to understanding its superordinate structures. Lancaster and Roberts (2006) provide evidence of 2-year-old children using consistent organisational principles in their productions, according to the representational purpose of the medium. These tended to be typical of diagrammatic genres that combine modes of writing and visual display, and included inventories of people attending a specified social event, and settings and mappings of places where events were located or set, sometimes including routes from one element to the next. Whilst the children had their own individual take on these representations, common principles were deployed: inventories, for example, deployed linear sequences of near identical marks or lines, with each representing one attendee at an event. No iconicity was required in the notation used, as the purpose of these texts was to register the attendance of a particular group of people, rather than to record their individual attributes.

MAKING MARKS

Consistent reference has been made throughout this chapter to the marks which children under the age of 3 make, and the systematic ways in which they are generated and presented. Reference has also been made to the way in which they are frequently described as 'scribble', with all the negative connotations associated with the term. None of the evidence discussed so far suggests that this characterisation is likely to be an accurate one. The fact that children's earliest marks are seen as falling short of intentionally representing alphabets, or images which closely resemble real objects, has often meant that they have been regarded as simply part of a stage to be passed through, on the way to the real thing. However, whilst there is limited research on how young children construe the material structure of written notations, what there is provides evidence of their systematic engagement with its basic elements.

Dissanayake (1992) says that children of this age require the physical trace of a marker in order to remain interested in what they are doing. If the marker fails to leave a mark, they lose interest in the activity. The related actions and movements are not in themselves enough: the visual sign is after all an essential characteristic of writing and of artistic practices, and children are surrounded by evidence of these in every possible medium. A significant distinction between these modes, however, is that in the case of print, its signifying status remains fixed in spite of local variation: letters of the alphabet, logograms and ideograms are identifiable as such whether they are handwritten, printed or typed, and in spite of variations in handwriting, print type, size or location (see Goodman, 1976). It is most unlikely that children's early ability to discriminate between drawing and writing does not include a level of understanding about this defining feature of systems of written notation.

According to Kellogg (1970), there are 20 distinct kinds of markings which have been identified in the graphic productions of children 2 years old and younger. On the basis of the overall direction of the movement of the hand making them, these can be grouped into six categories: vertical, horizontal, diagonal, circular, alternating, and no line movement; the category 'alternating' includes wavy lines and zigzags; 'no line movement' refers to dots. These categories also include single line markings and multiple line versions: so vertical, horizontal and diagonal lines can be represented singly or multiply. The alternating lines include a 'roving' line which meanders and one which doubles back on itself, creating enclosed areas. One might surmise, though, that this is more likely to be the case when they are 'drawing' than when they are 'writing'. Fein (1993) has identified similar categories of markings, and her evidence also shows interesting individual variation within categories. So, for example, a meander (Kellog's 'zigzag' within the 'alternating' category) can be made with either a rounded or a sharp turning point. In this case the mark remains fixed in spite of local variation, presaging systems of print: handwriting of a sort. Baghban (1984) shows evidence of this range of marks being used in the productions of her daughter between the ages of 18 and 24 months. Both Kellogg and Fein show how these marks continue to be used and to develop in complexity as children get older, and Kellogg points out that the different categories of mark evolve into the construction of both written forms and forms used for artistic expression and design.

Whilst the marks themselves do not constitute a recognisable system of written notation, nevertheless, qualities intrinsic to them can be incorporated into the structure of the 'point-plot organisation' which I have described. In an example discussed previously (Lancaster, 1999) a single type of mark, a zigzag, is used throughout the making of the card. The use of a constant category of mark means that it is its placement that is the variable factor which signifies distinctions of meaning. Variation to qualities of the mark itself has the potential to introduce a further level of distinction. An extended zigzag, going from the top to the bottom of the page, is assigned the ascription 'tree'; with its length and span, it also resembles a tree. Acknowledging the resemblance, the little girl adds 'branches' at the top; this time the zigzag is curved in an wide arch going from the 'tree' into the middle of the page, maintaining a link between representation and resemblance. The 'writing' at the bottom of the page also has a structural a resemblance to that which it represents, being a linear sequence of small zigzags. These intentional and systematic variations to the graphic device itself suggest the operation of a basic morphology. Tolchinsky says that the properties of notational systems provide crucial clues to why they are such potent communicative and cognitive tools. She suggests that their potency arises from the amount of cognitive work that is put into play when forming, using, and interpreting external representations (2003: 4). This is a strong argument in support of constructing the evidence discussed in this chapter as confirmation of young children's ability to start engaging with this work long before they encounter any formal instruction in the operation of writing and other notated systems.

CONTINUOUS DEVELOPMENT

The evidence already discussed in this chapter suggests that children between the ages of 1 and 2 have the capacity to distinguish confidently between writing and drawing, and to recognise and produce certain features, qualities and marks, characteristic of both these modes; even well before this age, they have the capacity to recognise many of these features. One construction which has been put on the relationship between these modes is that writing evolves from drawing, both developmentally and historically. Martlew and Sorsby (1995) suggest that children's ability to draw writing provides evidence of this. However, the boundaries between writing and drawing are far from being fixed and absolute, and children move comfortably around them, using whatever is most salient and useful to interpret and communicate what is needful. In doing this, they are not only using elements which are characteristic of each mode, but also those which they have in common; and at this stage in life, they will commonly experience texts where writing and pictures operate in tandem. To draw writing is as reasonable as to write about a drawing, and would seem to demonstrate a sound understanding of the semiotic functions which are distinct to each mode, as well as those which are common to both.

A parallel can be drawn with interpretations of early writing systems, which suggest that they evolved through a highly pictographic stage to become increasingly abstract systems. However, evidence from the very earliest systems suggest that this is not the case (Schmandt-Besserat, 2007, 1978), and that graphic marking has always been used for different purposes, with drawing and writing having different representational functions, then as now. Writing developed to communicate information by graphic means (Harris, 2000; Gaur, 2000; Olson, 1994), whereas drawing developed for the purposes of aesthetic expression, even though the two modes might have drawn on similar types and methods of marking. It is likely that young children's recognition of the distinction between the modes is also based on an understanding of this fundamental difference in function. Kenner's (2002) example of a young Chinese boy, who dismisses a fellow pupil's idea that an oval shape could represent a mouth in Chinese on the basis that in Chinese you have to write, 'not draw pictures', demonstrates this point nicely. However, this still leaves open questions about development in each domain: what happens to these very early representational methods and structures which children construct and operate. Wolf and Perry claim that children's early drawing systems are frequently regarded as being simply preparatory. Luria makes a similar point with respect to early writing systems, describing them as 'primitive techniques' that are 'similar to what we call writing' and which 'served as necessary stages along the way' (1988: 237). In other words, the outcomes of all that intense semiotic exploration simply wither away. The conclusions which Wolf and Perry draw about children's early drawing systems however, suggest a much more likely developmental path. Each of the systems which they develop and use is not so much a stage on the way to realism, as a system which continues to evolve and to remain useful; nothing is wasted. Mackay (2002) demonstrates a similar path for the early use of bodily modes like gesture in communicating graphic meaning, with it continuing to have a significant communicative role to play in the interpretative strategies of much older children. At the same time, new systems are acquired, as and when they are needed: what Pariser calls 'a kitbag of graphic strategies' (1999: 104).

Important parallels can again be drawn. The ways in which infants and young children set about the interpretation and production of writing suggests that like drawing, writing is also a multiply constituted mode. By the time they are 2, children have been grappling with different generic structures, ways of displaying and representing meanings and information, spatial organisation, systems of marking, notational systems, morphological distinctions, and the movement between the interpretation and expression of writing. Each of these constituents of early writing continues to be used and to evolve. To reduce writing to the making of correct links between letters and sounds is to misrepresent both the nature of writing and children's ways of constructing it. This is not to underestimate the significance of this feature of writing, but to make the point that this is one of many. Children discover a great many things about writing as a system before they reach the point of needing to investigate its relationship to speech. Development, in other words, is continuous.

As stated at the beginning of this chapter, this continues to be a field in which there is little research, in spite of its considerable significance in relation to understanding the whole continuum of writing literacy development, and to providing appropriate support for children throughout their earliest years. Furthermore, research into the learning and teaching of writing per se continues to lag significantly behind the innumerable studies produced about the teaching of reading. Two aspects of the work discussed present particularly important and timely opportunities for further research. First, the centrality of interactions between very young children and adults to intentional mark and sign-making activity, and their deep entrenchment in social and cultural worlds has potentially far-reaching implications for our understanding of the early cognition of symbolic systems, and a consequential bearing on educational practice; and second, the radical changes to the literacy landscape induced by digital technology will impact not just on future experiences of young children, but on their activity and practice from early infancy in ways that are currently little understood. Far from this being a stage of limited semiotic activity, restricted by a lack of cognitive, social and linguistic development, it is a time when children are actively and independently interested and involved in representational matters in ways that should be central to research in the field.

REFERENCES

Anning, A. (2003) 'Pathways to the graphicacy club: the crossroad of home and pre-school', *Journal of Early Childhood Literacy*, 3(1): 5–35.

Baghban, M. (1984) *Our Daughter Learns to Read and Write: a Case Study from Birth to Three*. Newark: International Reading Association.

Bissex, G.L. (1980) *Gnys at Wrk: A Child Learns to Read and Write*. Cambridge: Harvard University Press.

Chan, L. and Nunes, T. (1998) 'Children's understanding of the formal and functional characteristics of Written Chinese', *Applied Psycholinguistics*, 19: 115–31.

Clark, M.M. (1976) *Young Fluent Readers*. London: Heinemann Educational Books.

Cox, S. (2005) 'Intention and meaning in young children's drawing', *JADE* 24(2): 115–25.

Davies, J. (2011) Literacy in a Digital Age. www.open. ac.uk/blogs/literacy-in-a-digital-age. Accessed June 2011.

Deacon, T.W. (1997) *The Symbolic Species*. New York: Norton.

Deloache, J. and Brown, A. (1987) 'The early emergence of planning skills in children', in J. Bruner and H. Haste (eds), *Making Sense: The Child's Construction of the World*. London: Methuen.

Deloache, J., Strauss, M. and Maynard, J. (1979) 'Picture perception in infancy', *Infant Behavior and Development*, 2: 77–89.

Dissanayake, E. (1992) *Homo Aestheticus: Where Art Comes from and Why*. New York: Free Press.

Donaldson, M. (1978) *Children's Minds*. London: Collins.

Dunst, C.J. and Gorman, E. (2009) 'Development of infant and toddler mark making and scribbling'. *CELL Reviews*, 2(2): 1–6.

Feldman, C.F. (1987) 'Thought from language: the linguistic construction of cognitive representations', in J. Bruner and H. Haste (eds), *Making Sense: The Child's Construction of the World*. London: Methuen.

Fein, S. (1993) *First Drawings: Genesis of Visual Thinking*. Pleasant Hill: Exelrod Press.

Ferreiro, E. and Teberosky, A. (1982) *Literacy before Schooling*. Exeter, NH: Heinemann Educational Books.

Flewitt, R. (2005) 'Is every child's voice heard? Researching the different ways 3-year-old children communicate and make meaning at home and in a pre-school playgroup', *Early Years*, 25(3): 207–22.

Gaur, A. (2000) *Literacy and the Politics of Writing*. Bristol: Intellect Books.

Gelb, I.J. (1952) *The Study of Writing: the Foundations of Grammatology*. London: Routledge and Kegan Paul.

Goodman, N. (1976) *Languages of Art*. Indianapolis: Hacket Publishing Company.

Goodman, Y. (1986) 'Children coming to know literacy', in W.H. Teale and E. Sulzby (eds), *Emergent Literacy: Writing and Reading*. New Jersey: Ablex Publishing Company.

Gregory, E. and Williams, A. (2000) *City Literacies: Learning to Read across Generations and Cultures*. London: Routledge.

Halliday, M.A.K. (1975) *Learning How to Mean: Explorations in the Development of Language*. London: Edward Arnold.

Harris, R. (2000) *Rethinking Writing*. London: The Athlone Press.

Harris, M. and Hatano, G. (eds) (1999) *Learning to Read and Write; a Cross-linguistic Perspective*. Cambridge: Cambridge University Press.

Harste, J.C., Woodward, V.A. and Burke, C.L. (1984) *Language Stories and Literacy Lessons*. Portsmouth: Heinemann.

Havelock, E.A. (1976) *Origins of Western Literacy*. Toronto: OISE Press.

Karmiloff-Smith, A. (1992) *Beyond Modularity: A Developmental Perspective on Cognitive Science*. Cambridge, MA: The MIT Press.

Kellogg, R. (1970) *Analyzing Children's Art*. Palo Alto: National Press Books.

Kenner, C. (2002) 'Signs of difference: how children learn to write in different script systems: an ESRC-funded project', paper presented at Manchester Metropolitan University, 13 June 2002.

Kress, G. (1997) *Before Writing: Rethinking the Paths to Literacy*. London: Routledge.

Kress, G. (2000) *Early Spelling: Between Convention and Creativity*. London: Routledge.

Kress, G. and van Leeuwen, T. (1996) *Reading Images: The Grammar of Visual Design*. London: Routledge.

Labbo, L. (1996) 'A semiotic analysis of young children's symbol making in a classroom computer center', *Reading Research Quarterly*, 31(4): 356–85.

Lancaster, L. (1999) 'Exploring the need to mean: a multimodal analysis of a child's use of semiotic resources in the mediation of symbolic meanings'. Unpublished PhD thesis, University of London.

Lancaster, L. (2001) 'Staring at the page: the function of gaze in a young child's interpretation of symbolic forms', *Journal of Childhood Literacy*, 1(2): 131–52.

Lancaster, L. (2007) 'Representing the ways of the world: how children under three start to use syntax in graphic signs', *Journal of Early Childhood Literacy*, 7(2): 123–51.

Lancaster, L. (2012, forthcoming) *Mapping Meaning: The Early Construction of Written Genres*. Under review for '*Written Communication*'.

Lancaster, L. and Roberts, R. (2006) *Grammaticisation in Early Mark Making: A Multimodal Investigation*. Economic and Social Research Council, End of Award Report: RES-000-22-0599

Luria, A. (1983) 'The development of writing in the child', in M. Martlew (ed.), *The Psychology of Written Language: Developmental and Educational Perspectives*. Chichester: John Wiley & Sons.

Mackay, M. (2002) '"The most thinking book": attention, performance and the picturebook', in E. Bearne and M. Styles (eds), *Art, Narrative and Childhood*. Stoke on Trent: Trentham.

Marsh, J. (2004) 'The techno practices of young children', *Journal of Early Childhood Research*, 2(1): 51–66.

Marsh, J. (2006) 'Global, local/public, private: young children's engagement in digital literacy practices in the home', in K. Pahl and J. Rowsell, *Travel Notes from the New Literacy Studies*. Clevedon: Multilingual Matters.

Martlew, M. and Sorsby, A. (1995) 'The precursors of writing: graphic representation in preschool children', *Learning and Instruction*, 5: 1–19.

Matthews, J. (1994) *Helping Children to Draw and Paint in Early Childhood: Children and Visual Representation.* London: Hodder and Stoughton.

Olson, D. (1994) *The World on Paper.* Cambridge: Cambridge University Press.

Pahl, K. (1999) *Transformations: Meaning Making in a Nursery.* London: Trentham Books.

Pariser, D. (1999) 'Children of Kronos: what two artists and two cultures did with their childhood art', *The Journal of Aesthetic Education,* 33(1): 62–72.

Rowe, D. (1994) *Preschoolers as Authors: Literacy Learning in the Social World of the Classroom.* New Jersey: Hampton Press.

Rowe, D. (2008a) 'The social construction of intentionality: two year olds and adults participation at a preschool writing center'. *Research in the Teaching of English,* 42(4): 387–434.

Rowe, D. (2008b) 'Social contracts for writing: negotiating shared understandings about text in the pre-school years', *Reading Research Quarterly,* 43(1): 66–95.

Schmandt-Besserat, D. (1978) 'The earliest precursors of writing', *Scientific American,* 238(6): 38–47.

Schmandt-Besserat, D. (2007) *When Writing Met Art.* Austin: University of Texas Press.

Starkey, P., Gelman, R. and Spelke, E.S. (1985) 'Detection of number or numerousness by human infants', *Science,* 222: 179–181.

Street, B.V. (1995) *Social Literacies: Critical Approaches to Literacy in Development, Ethnography and Education* London: Longman.

Sulzby, E. (1986) 'Writing and reading: signs of oral and written language organisation in the young child', in W.H. Teale and E. Sulzby (eds), *Emergent Literacy: Writing and Reading.* New Jersey: Ablex Publishing Company.

Teale, W.H. (1986) 'Home background and young children's literacy development', in W.H. Teale and E. Sulzby (eds), *Emergent Literacy: Writing and Reading.* New Jersey: Ablex Publishing Company.

Thelen, E. and Smith, L.B. (1994) *A Dynamic Systems Approach to the Development of Cognition and Action.* Cambridge, MA: The MIT Press.

Tolchinsky, L. (2003) *The Cradle of Culture and What Children Know about Writing and Numbers Before Being Taught.* New York: Psychology Press.

Tomasello, M (1992) *First Verbs: A Case Study of Early Grammatical Development.* Cambridge: Cambridge University Press.

Torrey, J.W. (1973) 'Learning to read without a teacher: a case study', in F. Smith (ed.), *Psycholinguistics and Reading.* New York: Holt, Rinehart and Winston.

Treiber, F. and Wilcox, S. (1984) 'Discrimination of number by infants', *Infant Behavior and Development,* 7: 93–100.

Trevarthen, C. (1990) 'Growth and education in the hemispheres', in C. Trevarthen (ed.) *Brain Circuits and Functions of the Mind.* Cambridge: Cambridge University Press.

Vygotsky, L.S. (1978) *Mind in Society.* Cambridge: Harvard University Press.

Wolf, D. and Perry, M.D. (1988) 'From endpoints to repertoires: some new conclusions about drawing development', *Journal of Aesthetic Education,* 22(1): 17–34.

Wolfe, S. and Flewitt, R.S. (2010) 'New technologies, new multimodal literacy practices and young children's metacognitive development', *Cambridge Journal of Education,* 40(4): 387–99.

Wohlwend, K.E. and Handsfield, L.J. (2010) 'Twinkle, twitter little stars: tensions and flows in interpreting social constructions of the techno-toddler'. Paper presented at National Reading Conference, Fortworth, Texas, December 3–6.

19

Perspectives on Making Meaning: The Differential Principles and Means of Adults and Children

Gunther Kress

Children come into the world with an absolute interest in meaning. To them, knowing what the world means is of more than academic interest. Yet even if they are born into a 'literate society', the technology of the script systems of their parents' cultures is just one part of the vast web of meanings that makes up the world they will need to understand and learn to deal with. Nor is it a particularly focal part for them; it certainly has none of the overwhelming significance that it has for many of the adults around them; it is as important or less than many other aspects of their world. It is there to be dealt with like so much else, and that is that.

This is a fundamental difference in orientation and perspective of child and adult toward the issue of meaning, and to writing and reading specifically, one that it is crucial to recognize if we, the adults, wish to facilitate the entry of the young into full use of that resource. Whether it is in an attempt to understand the paths that children take into the world of writing, or to develop pedagogies – formal or informal – around the learning of writing and reading, an understanding of the child's perspective is a *sine qua non* for the success of any attempts in that direction.

From these two perspectives, the issue of (meaning and) meaning making looks different in several respects. Adults, having been 'socialized', are oriented toward convention – the frame of rules which their societies have erected to regulate social action. Children are oriented to 'truth', to that which the evidence of their senses tells them is incontrovertibly the case. Convention hovers close to 'law'; what conforms to convention is 'correct', and what does not conform is therefore to be avoided. So an orientation to convention leads to a focus on correctness, while an orientation to truth leads to a focus on accuracy. As far as making meaning is concerned, adults focus on what their cultures provide and their societies have taught them to regard as the proper means for making meaning. Language as speech is one such ready-made means, and in 'literate societies', language as writing is the most valued. Children focus on that which best serves the purpose, given what is to hand for making the meaning that they wish to make.

Last, but by no means least, there is a deep difference in perspective on how meaning is made. The adult's focus is on the correct use of culturally ready-made resources, in accord with convention. In that approach the means for making meaning seem to pre-exist the meanings to be made, as 'signs' which come with (clear, often strict) instructions for their use. Dictionaries and grammars enshrine the sense both of ready-made signs and of correct rules of use. Children make their means for making meaning, according to two distinct needs. On the one hand, they make signs to express that which they wish to represent – to make it real *as a sign*, to *realize* a meaning: to give material reality to a meaning. On the other hand that which they wish to represent is governed by their *interest* at the moment of making the sign. This 'interest' works in at least two ways: first, to select that which is to be represented, and then to select those aspects of the thing to be represented which are the focus of their interest at the moment of making the sign. Their 'interest' selects and then focuses on that which is criterial for the maker of the sign about that which is to be represented in the moment of representation.

The material sign-making stuff – the signifier – is chosen so as to best represent that which is to be meant – the (immaterial) signified. It is chosen according to its aptness for the purpose. To choose an actual example that I have used on several occasions, if the meaning to be realized – the signified – is to be of 'car', and the child's interest in 'car' at that moment regards wheels as criterial, then aptness to represent wheels will select the signifier stuff, to be joined with the signified 'car'. Wheels can be signified aptly by the 'signifier stuff' of 'circles': several circles-as-wheels can be the 'signifier stuff' to signify 'car'.

Children's early meaning making is governed by the very fact that they do not use ready-made signifiers: and so their meaning making is led both by that which is to hand, and by that which is apt for the purpose of meeting this interest.

Neither the adults' nor the children's views are accidental. The adults' view is the outcome of ceaseless social-cultural-semiotic theoretical work over the history of their society; the dominant theory itself is always shaped by the highest-level social and political arrangements, and reflects the ideologies of those who form and sustain such arrangements. The adults' view derives from and is buttressed by such theory, appearing in the guise of 'common sense'. The children's view is the result of their need to understand that which is everywhere yet to be understood – and what is to be understood includes the adults' views of things. It is no wonder that adults see a path ready-made that children should take 'towards' literacy; and it is no wonder that this path makes no real sense to children, for in most ways it does not match their interest, which shapes how they see their world.

I need to make it clear that I am not talking about the reality of adult meaning making; I am talking about assumptions, perceptions, both common-sense and theoretical *perspectives*, and not about actual *practices*. The process of meaning making is the same for adults as it is for children: all use the means which are available and which seem most apt to make the meanings that their interests lead them to make. Both transform the means for making meaning. The difference lies in the fact that adults have already learned so much more than children have: they have learned what they should regard as the 'apt means' as much as 'correct' ways for making meaning; and they have learned to believe that their actions do not transform the means they use in making meaning. They have learned to accept a perspective that tells them that – with some exceptions – they must remain within convention. When they do not do so, as is often the case, they nevertheless feel that there were rules that they have transgressed, rules which they should have observed. Children, in their turn, increasingly learn to pick up adults' concerns with correctness, and some will come to strive for that in their practices of making meaning.

Here is the contrast between adults' views (*not* practices) and the views and practices of children:

- convention versus truth;
- correctness versus accuracy;
- culturally made means used conventionally versus apt use of that which is to hand for the purpose;
- language as writing versus whatever is to hand that is apt for the purpose.

These distinct principles exist together with a difference in approach to meaning making which can be characterized as *the use of ready-made signs in line with convention* versus *signs-to-be-made, with interest governing sign-making*.

From these principles flow differing dispositions to practice. I focus on each of the principles in turn and draw out some consequences of the distinctive dispositions towards representation and communication of children and adults, and explore some of the implications for views on learning through the use of examples. The recognition of the differences in principle is needed as the basis on which to build changed practices. There already exists a strong body of work that looks newly at children's making of meaning and at questions of learning, knowing and the making of meaning through many more means than those of speech or writing alone. I will make reference to this work where it becomes relevant, including some work that goes outside the age range envisaged in this handbook, and including some work with a strictly theoretical focus. Inevitably all this work constitutes a challenge to dominant notions of literacy, of learning, as much as it does to theories of (making of) meaning much more widely.

Such thinking and such work is not new. Many of these insights have been developed by researchers and practitioners working in this field over a considerable period. What is the case is that their effect on mainstream theory has been relatively limited, and their effect on practice and application less than it might or should have been. The early work of Charles Read (1968) stands in that line, as does some of the work of Marie Clay later (1975); though in her case the insights of the work have had profound effects in practical ways, as in the project of Reading Recovery. There is the work of Ann Haas Dyson (1986) and of Glenda Bissex (1980). Barr's article '*Maps of play*' (1988) extended the boundaries of thinking about meaning making and representation in the field of literacy and learning. Of course some of the theoretical work of Vygotsky (1978), on which Barr for instance draws, as of Piaget (1990), points in this direction. However, for both these theorists, language remained in its central 'place' – even though Vygotsky had a strong interest in representations other than language. Nodelman (1988) is laden with insight and inspiration. Yet the 'truth' of convention had remained more or less unchallenged. This work is diverse in terms of its origin and location in disciplines – from education, psychology, linguistics, literary theory – and that, in part, may account for the fact that its impact has been less than one might have expected, given the plausibility of the accounts provided.

That is one difference with a growing – and by now already considerable – body of research and writing which attempts to provide material for that rethinking, retheorizing, and reorientation, a considerable amount of which is focused on quite young children. Examples are Marsh (2003), Marsh and Larson (2005); Pahl (1999); Pahl and Rowsell (2006); Mavers (2003, 2010); Lancaster (2001, 2003); Stein (2003), to name a few. This work takes (different kinds of) ethnographic approaches and some of it 'fuses' that with a social semiotic theory of multimodal representation and communication as one starting point (see Hodge and Kress, 1988; Kress and van Leeuwen, 2001; Kress, 1997, 2010, 2011) In such work all modes – speech and writing included – are accorded the role that they actually have in specific representational practices. Here I provide a theoretical framing for some of that work. One unifying aspect – even if in different ways, with differing emphases – is a *semiotic* framework (rather than say, a *linguistic* or *psychological* one), and an interest in dealing with speech and writing in a multimodal environment, where there are many culturally shaped resources – modes – for making meaning.

THE MEANS FOR MAKING MEANING: WRITING AND SPEECH IN THE FULL ENVIRONMENT OF COMMUNICATION

The first difference, in principle, focuses on the means for making meaning: language as (speech or) writing versus whatever is to hand that is apt for the purpose. For the adult the resource that is, almost inevitably, in focus is language, in nearly all environments and for nearly all purposes; and language as writing is most highly valued. For the child there is, initially, no resource that is necessarily focal. Anything that is to hand that will 'make a mark' and is apt for the purpose will be drawn into the making of a sign: speech, of course, but other kinds and uses of sound as well, whether banging a saucepan, or using the voice in imitating some other sound; making a 'graphic' mark on a surface as in drawing, scratching, 'smearing' with food, building, making models, using blankets, boxes, bits of paper or cardboard, coat-hangers, in fact any material thing at all that turns out to be suited for the realization of the meanings to be meant and 'made material'. And whereas for the adult both the means for making meaning and even the meanings themselves seem to pre-exist their use in meaning making – a sense in which everything we do or say is a cliché – for the child the potentials for materializing and making meanings are in principle unbounded.

This immediately leads to a difference in how the resources and their use are seen. Adults simply 'know' that there are rules of use (even if they would not be able to articulate them), while for most of the materials that children press into service to make their meanings there are no rules; and if there were, children either would not know them or would not necessarily observe them if they did. However, at this point we already have the question of 'orientation'. Children are very attentive to what the potentials of the materials are for making the meanings that they want to make. Lack of knowledge of convention or absence of rules is replaced by and substituted for by acute observation. There are no rules that say what a cardboard box of a certain size might be made to mean. However, the acutely observant and evaluating eye and hand of the child can determine that it can become a boat, or a room, or a car; its qualities as container give it a potential for meaning which is open to use in transformations of various kinds. The adult's reliance on convention is replaced by an acutely analytic assessment of the meaning potentials of the material object. The analytic assessment is founded on principles of meaning (making) of a rigorous kind – a seriousness of 'reading' of the object for its sign-making potential.

Two things emerge from that: to the adult there appears to be a fixed set of resources, with convention to guide their use in action; for the child there is no limitation – other than what is to hand – and aptness for purpose guides use.

Let me then take as an example the notion of 'car'. I say 'notion' because as will become clear in a moment, there is no stable 'concept' or meaning of 'car'. The car that I had described just above was the car as represented by a 3-year-old. Its focus and meaning was 'car-as-wheels'. We might notice that this graphically realized car has no lexical equivalent in either speech or writing. If we wanted to represent it in either one, we would be forced into a quite lengthy description: it is not a car-with-wheels, but a car-as-wheels. Speech or writing, as much as drawing, have, in that respect as in others, different 'affordances': you can do certain things with the graphic mode of image that

you cannot do (so easily) with the written, and vice versa. But the interest of the sign maker shifts, both from occasion to occasion and, with constant experience, through age. Age, in the case of children, is often described by the term *development*, though it might be better to see it as the process whereby they increasingly 'work themselves into' the meanings of their social group – as socialization.

The car in Figure 19.1 was made by the child who made the 'circles car', but some 3 years later. This car represents a very different meaning: the extremely sleek, aerodynamic arrow shape speaks of speed and power; the high level of sheen (on the original surface) is achieved by intense pressure in thickly applying the crayon; the red colour, in the original has a small black trimming. All these express a specific interest and meaning of 'car', one that is a long way from the 'wheels-car' of 3 years earlier. The meanings are difficult to reproduce in the mode of writing: it is quite simply the case that they are meanings best expressed in this graphic mode (or graphic modes, if we take colour to be a mode). The 'car' has been cut out with great precision from the sheet of paper on which it had been drawn, so that it is no longer a *representation on a page*, it is now an *object in the world*. As such it can participate in actions *in* the world in ways that words do not or can not. But the fact that we cannot easily provide a gloss on the meaning here in either speech or writing is not to say that the meaning is vague, ambiguous or imprecise; far from it. The problem is no other than that of providing an image representation of a spoken or written text.

It is clear that precise meanings are being made, with apt means, the means that are to hand. By comparison the lexical item, the word 'car', is imprecise; it applies

Figure 19.1   Arrow car

to both these cars and yet covers the meaning of neither. Words, it turns out, are quite vague, maybe too vague – unless heavily modified – to convey the meanings that are here conveyed.

A third car is different again. Figure 19.2 shows a further example of 'car'. It differs in meaning yet again: power is very much in focus, but this time it is power in the service of violence: the violence of the powerful engine spewing flames, of the wheels kicking up dirt and gravel, producing sparks and flames on the road; as well as the violence of the weaponry attached to the car, and of the rocket just fired. The agent in control of all this power is shown, so that we have a more complex sign 'the power that the driver of this car has at his command'. This drawing has also been cut out: but this time it is not so much the car as object in the world, but as the picture of a car which can be transported away from the page. The cutting-out is far less careful; clearly the aim has not been to produce an object in the world: no effort is expended on the object as such, it is a *drawing* of a car in motion, not the production of an object. As a drawing it can be moved, it has become transportable, not as object in the world but rather as 'image of the object'.

Again we might reflect on the task of representing this cut-out drawing in words, and realize that what would result would be an entirely different representation: it would either be a description of this image; or it would be a re-presentation of this image, where what is here shown as a *display* would become a representation of events and actions related by words in sequence, a simple *narrative*. That is, it would be a representation in which time and sequence of actions would dominate: 'There is a car, travelling at great speed along a road, the driver has just fired a

Figure 19.2   Rocket car

rocket, its engines are belching flames and smoke, etc.'

The translation, whichever one we chose, would not be the original, of course. It would be different: it would not be more accurate, more precise, more clear. It would be different; and it would not do what the original does. This is important to realize: the graphic representation is precise; it is complex in its meanings; it is neither ambiguous nor vague. It is meaning made with apt and available means. It is ontologically different to the written or spoken representation that might have stood in its place.

I will discuss another car, made by the same child as the others, at the same time as the previous one. It is three-dimensional, made from lego blocks. It looks like a car which – more even than the last – has been influenced by a number of models: above all both by (super-fast) speedboats and space vehicles. But in this it shows us the flexibility and the openness of the

potentials for making meaning which exist outside of the conventionally given means. Three-dimensionality makes new demands and also opens up new possibilities for meaning. It demands symmetry, for instance, in a way the graphic representations do not. An unbalanced three-dimensional 'car' would not function; it would lean over or topple, apart from its aesthetically displeasing shape.

In all these examples we are touching on the issue of meaning to be made and on the meaning potentials of the means for making meaning. What is clear is that 'word' is quite limited compared to the means employed here. What is also clear is that these representations are complex: they belong to and draw on the cultural world of their makers; they display clear principles of meaning; and they function very differently to words, whether in speech or in writing. Above all, in each instance the representations realize the varying interests of their makers, and do so by using means aptly, so that the signifier stuff in its arrangement realizes the meanings that were meant to be meant. Nor are the signs, in any way, arbitrary conjunctions of form and meaning.

WHAT THE CULTURE PROVIDES, AND WHAT IS TO HAND

In the examples just discussed, the ready-made means that culture provides are words, in speech or in writing: the word 'car' as well as words to modify it, 'a *sleek red* car', 'a *fast heavily armed* car', and so on. The child maker of the meaning 'car' made his own means of making meaning, graphic means, and in the case of the three-dimensional model, Lego blocks. The use of the Lego blocks is the use of culturally made means, though whether they are used conventionally in this case – whether a 'car' of this exact kind has been made before – must be very much in question. In the case of the drawn cars there is no doubt that these are means made by the child. The issue of *culturally made means used conventionally* versus *apt use of that which is to hand for the purpose* is a difficult one in the case of children. On the one hand, culture has many ready-made means for them – 'toys', by and large, of various kinds. The set of objects that provides the means for the child to assemble a farmyard with animals, machinery, buildings, fences, is a resource for making meanings. And quite clearly the resource comes as a set of signs with rules for their use attached. I am not here talking of any 'instructions' that might come with a box of toys, but talking rather of the inbuilt structure that says that the roof goes on the house; that the fences surround the garden and the fields; that the machinery is stored in the barn; and so on.

On the other hand, however, children are notoriously eager to go beyond and against the set of signs and the rules coded with them, and they extend both the inventory of object signs, and with equal facility the rules that regulate the larger structures that are made. In so far as they do so, they transform the ready-made signs into quite new signs, and create quite new rules which may have little affinity with the rules as they were. So nearly any toy at all can be brought into the farmyard structure, for instance. As with all other signs that they make, the relevant point for them is 'aptness' for purpose: it is their interest which determines what is to be criterial. If a female doll is, by adult judgement, far too large to fit into the arrangement of a farm-yard, the fact that there might have been a need for a farmer's wife easily overrules the here irrelevant matter of size. The doll is what is to hand; it is female and a female figure is what is needed, so this criterial feature becomes the basis for the making of the new sign. The principles of sign making persist, and are not threatened.

What emerges from examples such as these is that in all cases, the notion of the *culturally made means used conventionally* is not or is barely tenable. Even the signs that seem to be there, ready-made for some pre-determined use, are treated as material from which to make new signs. Children's semiotic actions, that is, their work in making meaning, are always and inevitable transformative of the materials used.

Nevertheless, the use of ready-made materials brings some constraints – perhaps less for children than for adults or older children – deriving from the histories of prior use of the material, which both endows the materials with the meanings of past action, and in doing so suggests, more or less strongly, constraints on the extent of transformations for present use. Yet the childish gaze falls on many materials that do not bear such constraining meanings, but where we can nevertheless clearly see the principle of the *apt use of that which is to hand for the purpose* of making meaning.

Take my next example, a 'helmet' (Figure 19.3). It is made from a very strong shiny cardboard box, which had contained barbecue briquets. It has some holes cut into it, to allow the wearer to peer out; it has its bottom knocked out, so that it will fit over the wearer's head. What is important here – as in other meaning making – is that purpose and intent, *interest,* precede the making of the sign. There is an intent to make a helmet, because a helmet is needed for a game involving 'fighting with swords'; the child's interest lights on the solidity and sheen of the material. The material that

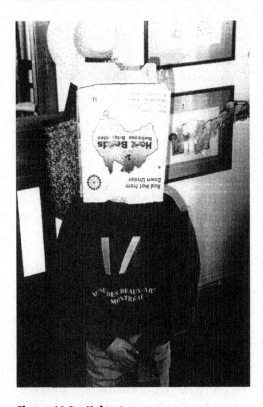

Figure 19.3   Helmet

is to hand becomes the material signifier for the signified 'helmet', and so the sign *helmet* is made. It is important to be aware of the steps involved in the making of this sign here, because what might appear as fairly random action is actually the result of a complex process of design. What is produced is not just one sign, but the complex set of signs of a game and all its essential elements. The game itself is designed, as are its individual elements. The material to serve as the signifier stuff for the sign 'helmet' is selected for its aptness in relation both to that one sign, this *object*-sign, and to its function in the larger design made here, in which it has its place.

With the notion of *design* we have moved a considerable distance from randomness in the selection of apt signifier materials: design implies intent in relation to specific imagined features and tasks of the meaning to be made, whether that meaning is expressed as the complex sign of a verbal text, or the complex sign of the objects and relations of a game. The application of meaning-making principles is the same, though the materials, the means for making meaning, are not linguistic.

In design, as in all sign making, the process of transformation is crucial. Some existent material is selected as the means for realizing a meaning, and in its fusion with the meaning to be expressed, the material changes in its potential to mean; a new sign is produced: the semiotic resources have been transformed.

CHILDREN'S PRINCIPLES OF MAKING MEANING: THE TRUTH OF CONVENTION AND THE TRUTH OF EXPERIENCE.

As adults we know (or might accept at least provisionally) that 'truth' is a semiotic construct. Children take a different view. Social truths derive from the exertion of power sustained over time, and individuals meet that truth in the guise of 'convention', 'common sense', of what is 'just natural', or quite simply 'true'. Children do not initially have access to this 'truth'. Instead they are reliant on the evidence of their senses to tell them the 'truth' about the world. 'Spelling', to move the discussion closer to language and literacy, is a very good case in point. 'Spelling' is 'knowing how to write words correctly'; it is very much the 'truth' of convention. We need not detain ourselves long on arguing this issue. In my examples here I refer to spelling in Standard (British) English; other dialects of English and other languages have different 'truths'. Here I look briefly at the spellings of a child, where the 'truth' is what his senses perceive, and what his attempt at interpretation tells him as the meaning of the world that is spelled (Figure 19.4).

Let me focus on two aspects of this example in turn. Take first 'spelling', this time as transcription of sounds into letters. We notice that James spells *their* as *there*, *little* as *littel*, and *nothing* as *nofing*; he also spells *can't* as *con't*, though in this case instead of *spelling* incorrectly, he might just have been 'mis-writing' the letter *a* as an *o*. In the case of *nofing*, however, the *f* is definitely what he will hear in his (north) London dialect. And there is nothing that would make it plausible for him to use the letter sequence *t h* as a means of transcribing what he hears as an *f*. In the case of *littel*, speakers of his dialect insert the 'weak' vowel 'schwa' between two consonants (t and l) in these contexts, rather than treating the *l* as a semi-vowel. The spelling of *there* is an instance where he is unaware of the truth of convention, which separates two lexical

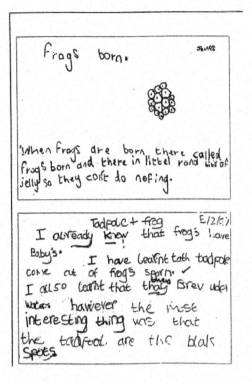

Figure 19.4   Frogs born

items which are identical in speech by a difference in orthography. Another 6-year-old from the same dialect area spells *breathe* as *brev*, following the same truth as James, and she spells *under* as *uda*, because in this dialect the *n* before the voiced dental plosive has just about disappeared through nasalizing the preceding vowel. For both children this is the truth of the evidence of their ears: and both, as do all children who have no hearing difficulties, transcribe the sounds of the speech they hear with razor-sharp accuracy – given the severely limited means of the letters of the alphabet; they are acute analysts of the sounds of speech.

But there are other truths as well: and most strikingly these are the truths of meanings that are made here. The phrase 'frog's spawn' is obviously not known to James, but that does not mean that he does not need to know what it means. In this case he is asked to perform a semantic 'transcription' rather than the phonetic one just exemplified. He takes the route that seems most promising: 'this topic is about the life-cycle of frogs', he seems to say to himself, 'so clearly this phrase is about frogs (being) born'. This too is the truth of evidence – not the evidence of his ears, but the evidence of his rigorous logic. The 6-year-old girl (from a different school in north London) who wrote *brev* faced the same problem as James, she too did not know the meaning of 'frogspawn', though she took a different route to understanding this phrase. She wrote *I have learnt that tadpole come out of frog's sporn*. This 'truth' is in part phonological and therefore conventional, in that she seems to know that word-initial consonant clusters such as *sp* (as in *sporn*) are permitted in English, but that *sb* is not (a problem that James did not have to deal with, as in his 'spelling' he had separated the *s* and the *b* in frog*s b*orn). In part the resolution lies in syntax. English has many noun phrases such as *X's Y*: – 'mum's bag', 'dog's dinner', – and this knowledge leads to her transcription and spelling. It is the 'truth' of a part of the syntax of her language that she knows already. From the point of view of the adult it is a paradoxical solution: the truth of convention used to tell the truth of experience.

In the cases here the truth of experience is modified somewhat: the act of perception is never neutral, it is always an act which transforms that which is perceived, apprehended, transformed in the light of existing knowledge. In the case of these 6-year-olds, perception is already shaped by considerable cultural knowing, though the principle of 'truth to experience' remains. But these examples also belong to the same principles of meaning making that I discussed in relation to the 'car' examples: a bit of the world around the child is drawn into the designs of the child, whether in articulation (the signs made outwardly) or in interpretation (the signs made inwardly). There is no difference in the principles of meaning making: a bit of the world around the child is focused on and becomes the material which serves to make a new sign in conjunction with that which is to be meant – in the last case a 'syntactic truth' and a 'semantic truth'.

The principles of meaning making, of the construction of signs, are shared by all these examples, whether in speech, writing, or in three-dimensional making. We cannot hope to understand children's meaning making if ignore these principles and focus on (in any case too narrow conceptions of) language alone, the mode in which convention rules most strongly as far as common sense and reality both are concerned. Of course, the same principles of sign making apply to language as apply elsewhere; most of the time, however, they are somewhat harder to trace. In the last example that I wish to discuss here I want to bring together the two principles which are not as yet not directly discussed: *correctness* versus *accuracy*; and *the use of ready-made signs in line with convention* versus *signs-to-be-made with interest governing both sign making and sign use*. In fact both have been implicitly there in all of the previous discussion, but here I want to focus on them explicitly.

Take my last example, Figure 19.5. The written text, in 'translation', is:

Flowers
I pick the flowers
From my garden I turn around
And stop to see the
Yellow rose I go to pick one
A thorn gets stuck in my finger

Flawase

I Pike bhe Flawase

From my gadin i tone areawd
and Sbop to See bhe

Yolow roSe I go to Pike wine
a thone gest Stik in my figir

Figure 19.5   Flawase

Appearances seemingly to the contrary, I want to say that this child poet is oriented toward the truth of experience, attempting to transcribe as fully as she can that which she wishes to realize. For a start, being a poem, aesthetic principles – transcribing and realizing beauty – come first: from the beautifully handwritten and displayed graphic aspects of the poem, to the attempt at a 'heightened' diction achieved through the graphic representation of phonic means. The sounds which are suggested here are not simply the sounds of speech in the ordinary mode, but the sounds of a heightened diction. Lengthening is suggested in the spelling of *flawase*, to be pronounced slowly; similarly with *pike*, where the final *e* is meant to produce a lengthening of the medial vowel (as she will have been told by her teacher with words like *care*, *sore*, *nine*, and so on). The *i* sound in *gadin*, not lengthened here by a word-final *e*, but 'raised' to a clear *i* sound

rather than the lower, lax sound of the weak vowel, as in the usual pronunciation of 'garden' with a final 'schwa'. In the *areawd* the child strives, with the tripthong (e a oo – ar*eaw*d) to ensure that the reader who reads this aloud is forced into great deliberateness and care in pronuncing the word. All these – to give just some of the instances here – are attempts to produce and transcribe (or to produce in transcription) all the marks of 'poetic diction'. It is the truth of accuracy to poetic form and requirement which is striven for here.

The elements of the visual image – in the original they are in colour – parallel the verbal signs: from the intense neon-yellow of the rose, to the (only slightly more pronounced) dense spacing of the thorns on this rose; the beautifully drawn petals of the rose; the clinical precision of the drawing of the injured finger; and the flowers in the vase. All these speak of the same register: the aesthetic. Correctness is absolutely not the issue here; accuracy in terms of the (here, aesthetic) interest of the sign maker is. And even though ready-made signs are available for use, the child poetess takes the effort to make the signs that correspond to her interest. Clearly the *signs-to-be-made* are made *with the interest of the sign maker* governing both sign making and sign use.

We might ask at this point, 'What sets this off from adult sign making?' My response would be: on the one hand, the *general* processes of sign making are the same for both; on the other hand, the adult would never stray so far from convention in the way child has done. But above all, and linked to all this, the child focuses in a profoundly distinct way on 'that which is to be transcribed'. For the adult 'that which is to be transcribed' has already become shaped by convention: by lexis, syntax and orthography. The adult's interest are unlikely to match the precision of the child's interest. It would not encompass the aesthetic concerns of the child in the precision with which they are represented/transcribed here. A poet might; and we know that poets use alliteration as a meaning-making device; but for a poet it is a device within the bounds of convention.

For the child and for the adult that which is perceived differ profoundly, and so the child's and the adult's senses of what is to be recorded and transcribed differ. As well as that, the means, the resources, the forms of transcription available to the child differ entirely from those which convention provides, and which adults would use.

THE CONTEST OF PRINCIPLES AND MEANS: A NEED FOR A THEORETICAL RE-ORIENTATION

In 'moving into' – in working their way into – the technologies of representation, transcription and recording of their cultures, their meanings, children are faced with a dual task. As my last example has shown, they must 'reduce' that which they wish to transcribe, and in order to do that they must in effect change their criteria of seeing and valuation. If their society says that the aesthetic dimension is not important, is irrelevant, or is not wanted, or is wanted only in rare moments, or is possible only for selected individuals, and is in any case only ever to be handled in specific ways, then that is what children will have to learn. They must learn to represent through and with the means that their society says to them are the appropriate means for representing. That means forgoing the use of the many means that they have used for making meaning, and it

means forgoing the adherence to the principle of aptness for purpose – at least ostensibly.

All sign making, adult as much as childish, is founded on the principle of aptness of the material/formal means for realization of the immaterial/conceptual means. But at the moment, that is not acknowledged. Children must therefore abjure the theory of meaning which they have held implicitly and acted on explicitly in all their meaning making, and exchange it for the implausible theory to which adults subscribe. They have to learn to give up public practice of one kind of truth and learn the public confession of another, the truth of convention. They have to give up adherence to accuracy, and learn to live with correctness. That is a slow and difficult path; it is a path of disillusionment, of ever mounting cynicism; and it is the path that schooling still lays out for them.

In the meantime the theories held by the adults – whether the adults in the school or those who have the power to frame what will happen in and around the school – have ceased to be serviceable. The truth of convention – that is, of knowledge as the product of social power – was serviceable in the Western nation-states of the nineteenth century and of the early part of the twentieth. It produced allegiance to authority and it reduced both the scope and the desire for individual variation and (to some extent) the reality of that as well. In the information-based and consumption-led societies of the early part of this century, this theory has lots its link to the present social world. Its lack of fit with that world is now everywhere visible to those who care to take a moment to look: there is a lack of registration between the two. Children bear the brunt of that, and society the cost.

RETHINKING REPRESENTATION, MEANING, AND LEARNING

As I indicated at the beginning, there is now a growing – and to some extent already considerable – body of research and writing which attempts to provide material for that rethinking, retheorizing, and reorientation, and a considerable amount of this is focused on the quite young. It takes the social semiotic theory of multimodal representation as a starting point, even if at the moment in quite different ways. In that work speech and writing are accorded their place in the multimodal representational environment characteristic of the present period; but so are other modes. Kress (1997, 2000); Kenner (2000, 2003); Pahl (1999); Moss (2001, 2003); Kress and Jewitt (2003), as well as a special edition of the journal *Reading: Literacy and Language* (Bearne and Kress, 2001), all attest to the many and varied modes which appear in children's making of meaning. In Lancaster (2003) a multimodal approach is used to describe both communication/representation and 'attention' in the joint 'reading' of a picturebook by a father and his 2-year-old daughter. The work of Mavers (2003) applies multimodal social semiotic theory to the work of children in primary schools. The implications of multimodal ways of thinking and describing have had a particular effect in the work of South African educators (Stein, 2003) for whom the rich variety of cultures present in that new nation, with their differing orientations to and valuations of representation, present a particular theoretical and pedagogical problem.

The implications of the approach sketched here are far-reaching. They affect still largely dominant conceptions of language: as central, whether as writing or as speech; as a full means of representation

and communication; and as definitive of human rationality. In the approach sketched here it can be seen that rationality, affect and emotion reside in all making of meaning. It becomes apparent that writing or speech are never 'full' means for representation, that they are always partial. And so the question arises in what ways *all* modes, speech and writing no less than image, or gesture, or body movement, or three-dimensional objects, are partial, and what their potentials are and their limitations. But in asking that question, we are shifting our conception of meaning making decisively in the direction of the real – and never unconstrained – agency of every maker of signs. Making meaning is now seen, from a social/political perspective, as a question of rhetoric: 'What are the best means to represent that which I wish to communicate here, now, for this audience?'. And from a semiotic point of view it is seen as a question of design: 'What are the means that I have available to me, and how do I deploy them in the most apt fashion to realize the design that I have here, arising out of my interest in this environment?' These are requirements that go beyond 'competence', and they incorporate the aims of 'critique'; because now I need to have full awareness of the potentials of the resources I use in relation to that with which I wish make my representation as a successful message in this social environment.

The aim of 'competence in use' related to an era of stability; its goal was to ensure reliable performance and continued stability. The aim of 'critique' related to an era of the challenge of stable systems, and its goal was to 'bring into crisis' that which was no longer seen as adequate, just, equitable. We are no longer in a period of stability; stable systems are difficult to find. We are in an era of radical instability, so that new aims are essential: the fostering of a disposition in which I feel capable of shaping my designs, in environments which I understand, with resources whose potentials, limitations, and relations to my audience here, now, I fully understand. The new goal is to allow me to act meaningfully in an unstable environment. This requires a disposition to the making of meaning which goes entirely beyond 'competence', and incorporates its aims and those of 'critique' in a constantly transformative response to the communicational demands of my environment.

Such a conception places the maker of meaning at the centre, aware of the cultural and social shape of the resources for representing, aware of the social shape of the environments of communication and of its constraints, and yet meaningfully agentive and always innovative. That might serve as the basis of new theories of learning, as much as of representation and communication.

REFERENCES

Barr, M. (1988) 'Maps of play', in M. Meek and C. Mills (eds), *Language and Literacy in the Primary School*. Lewes: Falmer.

Bearne, E. and Kress, G.R. (eds) (2001) *Reading: Literacy and Language*, 35 (3).

Bissex, G.L. (1980) *Gnys at Work: a Child Learns to Write and Read*. Cambridge, MA: Harvard University Press.

Clay, M. (1975) *What Did I Write? Beginning Writing Behaviour*. London: Heinemann.

Dyson, A.H. (1986) 'The imaginary worlds of childhood: a multimedia presentation', *Language Arts*, 63(8): 799–808.

Hodge, R.I.V. and Kress, G.R. (1988) *Social Semiotics*. Cambridge: Polity.

Kenner, C. (2000) *Homepages*. Stoke-on-Trent: Trentham.

Kenner, C. (2003) 'Embodied knowledges: young children's engagement with the act of writing', in G.R. Kress and C. Jewitt (eds), *Multimodal Literacy*. New York: Lang.

Kress, G.R. (1997) *Before Writing: Rethinking the Paths to Literacy*. London: Routledge.

Kress, G.R. (2000) *Early Spelling: Between Convention and Creativity*. London: Routledge.

Kress, G.R. (2010) *Multimodality. A Social Semiotic Approach to Contemporary Communication*. London: RoutledgeFalmer.

Kress, G.R. (2011) '"Partnerships in research": multimodality and ethnography', *Qualitative Research*, 11: 239–60.

Kress, G.R. and Jewitt, C. (eds) (2003) *Multimodal Literacy*. New York: Peter Lang.

Kress, G.R. and van Leeuwen, T. (2001) *Multimodal Discourse: the Modes and Media of Contemporary Communication*. London: Arnold.

Lancaster, L. (2001) 'Staring at the page: the functions of gaze in a young child's interpretation of symbolic forms', *Journal of Early Childhood Literacy*, 1(2): 131–52.

Lancaster, L. (2003) 'Beginning at the beginning: how a young child constructs time multimodally', in G.R. Kress and C. Jewitt (eds), *Multimodal Literacy*. New York: Lang.

Marsh, J. (2003) 'One way traffic? Connections between literacy practices in the home and in the nursery', *British Journal of Educational Research*, 29(3): 369–82.

Marsh, J. and Larson, J. (2005) *Making Literacy Real. Theories and Practices for Learning and Teaching*. London: Sage.

Mavers, D. (2003) 'Communicating meanings through image: composition, spatial arrangement and links in student mind maps', in G.R. Kress and C. Jewitt (eds), *Multimodal Literacy*. New York: Lang.

Mavers, D. (2010) *Children's Drawing and Writing: The Remarkable in the Unremarkable* New York: Routledge Falmer.

Moss, G. (2001) 'To work or play: junior age non-fiction as objects of design', *Reading Literacy and Language*, 35(3): 106–10.

Moss, G. (2003) 'Putting the text back into practice: junior-age non-fiction as objects of design', in G.R. Kress and C. Jewitt (eds), *Multimodal Literacy*. New York: Lang.

Nodelman, P. (1988) *Words about Pictures: the Narrative Art of Children's Picture Books*. London: University of Georgia Press.

Pahl, K. (1999) *Transformations: Meaning Making in a Nursery School*. Stoke-on-Trent: Trentham.

Pahl, K. and Rowsell, J. (2006) *Travel Notes from the New Literacy Studies: Instances of Practice*. London: Multilingual Matters.

Piaget, J. (1990) *The Child's Conception of the World*. London: Rowman and Littlefield.

Read, C. (1968) *Children's Creative Spelling*. London: Routledge and Kegan Paul.

Stein, P. (2003) 'The Olifantsvlei fresh stories project: multimodality, creativity and fixing in the semiotic chain', in G.R. Kress and C. Jewitt (eds), *Multimodal Literacy*. New York: Lang.

Vygotsky, L.S. (1978) *Mind in Society: the Development of Higher Psychological Processes*. Cambridge, MA: Harvard University Press.

20

Reading Policy: Evidence versus Power

Gerald Coles

In an ideal world, a teacher could read about and apply to classroom teaching many of the valuable, research-supported ideas in this *Handbook of Early Childhood Literacy*. However, classrooms exist in a world so far from ideal in which, in recent years, many recommendations in this Handbook have been legally, forcefully, and unscrupulously branded as contrary to 'scientifically-based reading instruction.' A teacher emphasizing meaning-making, teaching according to constructivist principles, promoting critical literacy, or criticizing reading textbooks is likely to be censured by administrative superiors or worse.

The problem has been glaring in the United States but also runs deep in other nations. What had become an international movement of educators 'from all around the world – Mexico, Venezuela, Argentina, Uruguay, Canada, Egypt, Puerto Rico, Taiwan' began to be attacked and vilified, starting in the 1990s, and by 2000, in the name of scientific, back-to-basics reading instruction, the entire whole-language movement was in jeopardy (Stice, Bertrand, and Manning, 2006: 88).

In Australia, for example, politicians and the media drummed-up a 'sense of moral panic around literacy instruction' that targeted 'a simplistic and demonised version of "whole-language."' The attack, threatening 'to derail significant advances in theoretical and practical understandings' of literacy, applauding a 'scientific paradigm,' maintained that the literacy future of students was threatened unless 'scientific instruction' prevailed (Gannon and Sawyer, 2007).

At first glance, 'scientifically-based reading instruction' sounds good and seems unassailable. After all, why teach reading with methods that are not scientifically-based when a scientific alternative is available? And if scientifically-based reading instruction has been uncovered, why not legally compel all teachers to use it?

This had been exactly the thinking and actions of key members of George W. Bush's administration who promoted the 'Reading First' legislation that was central in No Child Left Behind (NCLB). While the Barack Obama administration formally put NCLB on hold, legal promotion and enforcement of 'scientific reading education' has continued with the Common Core Standards devised in the Obama administration. Regardless of how deficient 'scientific reading instruction' actually is in substance, as I will explain, teachers have been compelled to employ it in their classrooms and to eschew alternatives, particularly the *bête noire* of 'science-based' proponents, whole-language. The following discussion focuses on the United States, but, as I suggested above, parallels can be found in many other nations.

While 'scientifically-based reading education' sounds like something new, containing no-nonsense research, in fact it's a new name for a character in an old story. In 1875, for example, school superintendent Francis W. Parker was attempting to counter scripted, skills-heavy, thinking-lite reading education in the schools of Quincy, Massachusetts. Denouncing conventional schooling for subjecting children to 'dull, wearisome hours of listless activity' that destroyed their 'imagination, curiosity, and love for mental activity,' Parker promoted literacy education that actively involved children in their own learning by engaging them imaginatively, practically and creatively. Just as children learned to speak in contexts that emphasized meaning, so too would they learn written language, Parker insisted (Curti, 1935).

In recent years, a reprise of Parker's 'Quincy method' was the reform of the 1960s known as 'open education,' which also targeted stultifying schooling. As educator Roland Barth (1972) explained,

it aimed to create education on the belief that by providing 'children with sufficient materials which involve looking at words, talking, listening, writing, and reading, they will somehow evolve their own best individualized reading program and will learn to read.' Open education was short-lived because advocates of conventional education attacked these and similar educational alternatives, arguing that research demonstrated that students in these classrooms had significantly lower academic achievement than students in traditional classrooms. Retrospective studies have repudiated this claim, determining that the research offered no clear conclusions about the superiority of one form of instruction over the other. Nevertheless, the baseless 'scientific' claims were sufficient to force schools using open classrooms to revert, in the words of educator James Rothenberg, back to 'traditional methods [and] authoritarian classroom control' (1989: 76).

Alongside the 1960s effort to introduce classroom structural changes grew the 'Great Debate', so named in 1967 by educator Jeanne Chall, who amplified Rudolf Flesch's 1950s defense of phonics teaching. By contrasting phonics with look–say (erroneously conceptualized as 'meaning–emphasis' instruction), not only did she declare phonics the winner, but went far beyond that by advocating extensive top-down, tightly controlled teaching be used up through high school. All this in the name of scientific facts which, in fact, did not exist (Coles, 1998: 44–7).

In the late 1960s whole-language emerged. It too was critical of look–say, although whole-language opponents, such as Chall, consistently conflated the two. Whole-language conceives of learning to read as a meaning-making process using predictable, meaningful texts and, despite relentless claims to the contrary, does include instruction of sound–symbol associations when needed. Children are involved in choosing and reading interesting storybooks, rather than reading assigned textbooks (basal readers) filled with vapid stories. Students are more involved in decisions about what to read, certainly more than students in skills-heavy classrooms directed by pre-packaged programs. For whole-language, writing and reading are essential interactive processes, with word skills taught as needed.

Whole-language rapidly captured the attention of many teachers, who began using it in their classrooms (sometimes, unfortunately, with only minimal understanding of the fundamental principles of whole-language). Once again, conventional education and its 'schooled to order' agenda, in the words of historian David Nasaw (1981), faced a threat. Consequently, as whole-language struggled to enter and gain legitimacy in classrooms through the 1970s and 1980s, it immediately faced claims that it was ineffective, as judged by reading test results. Research actually showed that it was at least as effective as conventional reading instruction and often more so, an issue I will discuss more fully below, but as with Open Education, an objective examination of the scientific research was never part of the attack on whole-language.

For proponents of pre-packaged, skills-heavy, teacher-managed instruction, any alternative was anathema. For example, in 1985, *Becoming a Nation of Readers* claimed that for beginning reading, the centerpiece of 'verified practices' was phonics instruction: 'The issue is no longer … whether children should be taught phonics. The issues now are specific ones of just how it should be done' (Commission on Reading, 1985). In 1986, Secretary of Education William J. Bennett's report, *First Lessons*, recommended including explicit phonic instruction in early reading because it was supported by available knowledge about the basic processes of reading. As educator Ira Shor (1992) documented, the drummed-up literacy crisis and back-to-basics campaign used concepts such as excellence, standards, accountability, and research, apolitical terms that cloaked the attack's formidable core of a conservative political makeup centered not on phonics versus no-phonics but on the very experience and purposes of schooling.

With the threat to conventional literacy education rising and whole-language use increasing – even though whole-language instruction, was far, far from being a dominant force in classrooms – a Republican policy paper, *Illiteracy: An Incurable Disease or Educational Malpractice?* appeared in 1989 and acquired political power through a provision in the 1990 Adult Literacy Act. Henceforth, phonics was added to a list of instructional methods eligible for federal funds, which the chair of the Republican Policy Committee hailed as a great victory, stating, 'Research shows phonics is the most effective way to teach people to read' (Rothman, 1990: 1). In fact, the paper supported no such conclusion, but at the level of federal power, the facts did not matter.

The counter-attack was threatened in 1994 when there was an effort to include a statement in a Congressional education bill that 'learning basic skills ... before engaging in more complex' literacy activities was a 'disproven theory.' Opponents of this viewpoint immediately launched a campaign that caused Congressional supporters of the bill to worry that they might appear to be anti-phonics and, therefore, anti-education, and the statement was subsequently dropped from the final legislative version. (Coles, 1998: chapter 1). Again, politics, not research, won the day.

NEUROPSYCHOLOGY, READING AND POLITICS: BLOOD BROTHERS

Through the 1980s and early 1990s, a phenomenon developed that had a profound influence on reading education. Brain research that previously had focused on a subset of poor readers – purportedly the 'learning disabled' – and claimed to have found connections between brain activity (dysfunctions) and failure to learn to read, suddenly began claiming that the brain 'glitches' identified in this research offered an understanding of how all children learn to read and how they must be taught.

In a 1996 article on reading disabilities published in *Scientific American*, Yale University researcher Sally Shaywitz asserted: 'Over the past two decades, a coherent model of dyslexia has emerged that is based on phonological processing. This phonological model is consistent both with the clinical symptoms of dyslexia and with what neuroscientists know about brain organization and function' (1996: 99).

Claims of finding 'evidence for aberrant auditory anatomy' that created phonological deficits that lead to reading disabilities were made by other reading disabilities researchers. For example, Albert Galaburda and colleagues (Galaburda, Menard, and Rosen, 1994), studying the brains of deceased individuals said to have been reading disabled, had for over a decade been reporting to have found abnormalities in a region of the brain that processed arriving sounds as part of the auditory processing system.

In my various writings during these years I thoroughly examined and debunked each of these claims. An example is a

Shaywitz et al. (1998) study, widely reported in the media, which became part of 'evidence' for skills-emphasis teaching in all beginning reading. A close look at this representative study is worthwhile to get an idea of the extent to which this work contributes to an understanding of literacy acquisition.

A 'BRAIN GLITCH'

Studying 29 'dyslexic' readers (14 men and 15 women, ages 16–54 years), Shaywitz and her colleagues (1998) used functional magnetic resonance imagery (MRI), a technology that provides information about the structure and function of the brain, while the subjects engaged in a sequence of reading and reading-related tasks. Whether or not the adults actually met criteria for being diagnosed as 'dyslexic' cannot be determined because, except for their IQ score range, we are told nothing else about them. For the sake of the primary focus of my appraisal, however, I will accept this categorization.

The study used a sequence of five tasks, beginning with one that required no ability with written language (asking subjects to decide whether or not lines matched: \\V versus \V\).

The second task asked subjects to match patterns of upper- and lower-case letters (bbBb versus bbBb). This required letter, but not phonological, knowledge.

The third task asked the subjects if letters rhymed ('Do T and V rhyme?'). This added 'a phonological processing demand', requiring knowing and comparing the sounds of the letters.

The fourth task asked the subjects if non-words rhymed ('Do leat and bête rhyme?'). This task required 'analysis of more complex structures'.

The fifth and last task required that the subjects know complex sound–symbol relationships and the meaning of words ('Are corn and rice in the same category?'), requiring both phonological and semantic knowledge and processing.

Clearly, this study is not simply about the brain and reading, but is *a priori* linked to skills-emphasis theory and pedagogy, of which phonological awareness is the centerpiece. That is, using this viewpoint, the researchers contrived a study around their conception of what is causal in beginning reading, namely, phonological awareness. In addition, assuming that this study actually enables one to draw conclusions about 'reading' begs the question, because the attenuated reading-related tasks that were used, while providing activities for potentially useful functional MRI information about language, cannot be thought to represent 'reading'. At best, they pertain to delimited skills. Alternative definitions of 'reading' certainly would have led to the creation of very different 'reading' tasks – perhaps even one in which the subjects actually 'read' sentences! (For other definitions see, for example, Ruddell, Ruddell, and Singer, 1994.) The study was also infused with an assumption that a neuropsychological deficit (or, as Shaywitz has described it, 'a brain glitch') can cause reading problems in otherwise normal children (Kolata, 1998).

When we look at the results, we see how the researchers' presumptions influenced interpretation of the data. Shaywitz and her colleagues found group differences in brain patterns while the subjects were engaged in the various tasks. The good readers showed 'a systematic increase in activation' in the brain areas studied, when going from the second (matching letter patterns) to the fourth (determining if nonwords rhyme) task. That is, there was an increase in brain activation as the tasks increased demands for applying phonological awareness abilities. In contrast, the dyslexics showed a fairly steady level of brain activation, rather than an increase, in response to these tasks. Generally speaking, the brain activation for these tasks was higher for the good readers than for the dyslexics, although one area of the brain showed the reverse pattern.

Examining the activation in the brain hemispheres, the researchers found that for good readers the activation was greater in the left, and for dyslexics it was greater in the right. This pattern held across all tasks.

Shaywitz and her colleagues concluded that 'for dyslexic readers, these brain activation patterns provide evidence of an imperfectly functioning system for segmenting words into their phonological constituents'. This malfunctioning was 'evident' to the researchers when they asked the dyslexics to respond to increasing demands on phonological analysis. The dyslexic readers demonstrated 'a functional disruption' in the rear area of the brain in which visual and sound identification and associations are made during reading. These findings, according to the researchers, added 'neurological support' to evidence obtained through studies at the behavioral and cognitive levels that pointed 'to the critical role of phonological analysis and its impairment in dyslexia' (1998: 2640).

The problem with these interpretations is that functional MRI data themselves do not carry an imprint of their meaning, that is, they do not point to a cause of the specific brain activation. The specific activation linked to responses generated by the five tasks tells us nothing about the processes that produced the activation. The specific activation facts would actually make possible various reasonable explanations, and given the limited data in this study, they would all have equal legitimacy.

For example, the study disregarded problem-solving approaches, learning experiences, personal meanings, emotions, motivation, and confidence, to name but a few potential influences that could have affected the group outcomes. Studies have shown that during tasks of this kind, altering any one of these background and processing factors could result in altered patterns of brain functioning (Coles, 1987). Furthermore, since there were initial ability differences between the groups, why would anyone assume that the brain activity for the two groups would be the same when doing these tasks?

CZECHLEXIA?

A similar study by Shaywitz and colleagues (2002) also used functional MRI to identify brain areas that were active when good and poor readers did non-word and real-word tasks. Normal readers showed more activation in the back of their brain, while the dyslexic group showed more activation in the front and side regions.

Continuing to be guided by the assumption that 'converging evidence indicates a functional disruption in the neural systems for reading in adults with dyslexia' (Shaywitz et al., 2002: 101), a press release (NIH–NICHD, 2002) stated, 'Children who are poor readers appear to have a disruption in the part of their brain involved in reading phonetically.' The study does not provide the means for supporting these conclusions however, because it is only one more investigation containing methodological confusion of correlation and causation. That is, as was true for the

previous Shaywitz study, the fact that there is a difference in the brain activation between good and poor readers does not mean that the brain activation is the cause of the respective reading abilities. Rather, we know only that the activation is correlated with reading ability.

Consider the following experiment. If two groups of normal people were asked to read a Czechoslovakian text, and if only one group could read Czechoslovakian, who would expect the brain activation of the two groups to be the same? And would anyone think that differences in brain activity revealed dysfunctions (Czechlexia), not differences? This failure to distinguish between correlation and causation fosters the single-minded interpretation of the data represented by this and similar studies. We do know from the study that the brain activity of good and poor readers differs when they do reading tasks, but that is all we know. Certainly nothing can be concluded about the cause of the reading problems or extracted to help guide teachers in the best way to teach reading.

ADD MEDIA POWER

Corporate media power worked in tandem with political power in that what has passed through the gates of the former has been story after story justifying lockstep reading instruction, while voices not supporting this instruction have rarely been heard. For example, a New York Times website search reveals that the aforementioned leading advocate for skill-heavy reading instruction, Sally Shaywitz, appeared in approximately 15 articles from the 1990s to 2011. In these, she was featured either as a lead researcher for a new discovery about the brain and reading acquisition or as an important commentator on someone else's research on the topic. In addition, several summary sections on reading, appearing in the Science or Education sections of the paper, include citations and summaries of her research and views often cite and offer brief summaries of her book on dyslexia.

In contrast, during the same time period Kenneth Goodman, whose constructivist theory of reading launched the whole-language movement and arguably is the most important reading educator of the last 50 years, has been in five *New York Times* articles. Early on it seemed that Goodman's work would receive the newspaper's attention. A 1975 article, 'Approach to reading rethought,' offered a full overview of Goodman's 'miscues' research and constructivist learning, and a 1988 article, 'Go away, Dick and Jane,' also provided an accurate rendition of whole-language, even though it pitted the approach against whole-word teaching, not against phonics-heavy instruction. However, as whole-language gained strength in classrooms, Goodman essentially disappeared from the pages of the *Times,* turning up very briefly in one article in 1996 and two in 1997.

Increasingly, media criticisms of whole-language and praise of intensive skills instruction appeared in tandem with efforts to pass legislation at state and federal levels that would mandate publisher-scripted, skills-heavy beginning reading instruction. For example, in the month prior to passage of the federal 1998 *Reading Excellence Act* (H.R. 2514), a *Time* article advised that 'phonics must be systematic and explicit if the full benefit is to be derived from it. To deprive children of that benefit is destructive.' *US News & World Reports* (Toch, 1997) stressed the need to teach 'language sounds and the relationship of sounds to letters' before exposing children to literature 'to promote comprehension.' An article in *The Atlantic Monthly* (Lemann, 1997) observed: 'No independent scientific researchers trumpet whole-language's virtues' (implying that there existed independent scientific researchers who were trumpeting attacks on whole-language). *Newsweek* (Wingert and Kantrowitz, 1997) assured readers that 'the reading instruction methods' beneficial to all children are known as 'linguistics (sound to letters) and phonics (letters to sound),' methods that make 'kids sound out words.' Doing so makes the 'association between symbol and sound virtually automatic,' thereby enabling children to concentrate on the meaning of words.

This media drum roll helped garner support for the *Reading Excellence Act,* however, no major media source looked behind the act to examine how it was drafted. Had that happened it would have been discovered that the bill was created not by independent 'scientific researchers' but by House education committee staff member Bob Sweet, who had no professional training or experience either in reading or education. Sweet had led the Moral Majority in New Hampshire, helped Ronald Reagan win the primary in that state, and 'was rewarded by Reagan with powerful federal jobs in education and social policy, where he pursued the goals of the educational New Right – Christian private schools, public school prayer and fundamentalist values.' Sweet also was an advocate of creationism and favored abolishing the US Department of Education and reducing spending on education (*Boston Sunday Globe*, 1990). And he was a big phonics guy.

The bill's impact on literacy education lay in its explicit definition of reading, reading instruction, and 'reliable' research – all of which emphasized lockstep skills. At the forefront of the definition was 'the ability to use phonics skills, that is, knowledge of letters and sounds, to decode printed words quickly and effortlessly, both silently and aloud.' Instructional practices were defined as those based on 'replicable, reliable research,' a term that at first glance might seem reasonable. However, when examining who was asked to testify during the committee hearings and which research the House and Senate committees thought 'replicable and reliable,' one can see that the phrase referred only to research believed to demonstrate the need for early, direct instruction of skills. Instructional practices were to be derived from 'scientifically based reading instruction,' a term appearing 29 times in the text of the act. As Ken Goodman observed, the term was code for a particular paradigm of research and views of reading, one that dismissed whole-language research as unscientific but regarded as scientific the body of studies that emphasized the need for early, direct, systematic, and explicit instruction of skills (Goodman, 1998).

The bipartisanship of this legislation needs to be underscored to understand both the history of the political maneuvers that promoted skills-heavy instruction and beat back all competitors, and to grasp the challenges for future activism on behalf of the right to assess and choose instructional alternatives. The *Reading Excellence Act*, while contrived by arch-right-wing Republicans, passed with the Democrats controlling the Senate committee on education and with a Democratic president. Yet neither questioned nor offered any opposition to this narrow, lockstep pedagogy.

Neither did the Democrats attempt to understand or exercise any power over the ersatz research and political machinations

being brewed at the National Institute of Child and Human Development (NICHD), a branch of the National Department of Health and Human Services. During the later years of the Clinton administration and through the George W. Bush administration, G. Reid Lyon, head of the reading branch of NICHD, became the principal orchestrator of a campaign to enforce skills-heavy instruction in every American school. As the *Wall Street Journal* reported, he and George W. Bush 'had a long and fruitful, if little-noticed relationship ... As president, Mr Bush [turned] to his phonics mentor to expand the [Texas school] program nationally. Mr Lyon [was Bush's] reading guru ... reading czar may be more accurate' (Davis, 2001). Lyon provided vast funds for 41 reading research institutes at universities across the country that rolled out studies promoting skills-heavy instruction. These institutes also provided the expert testimony to Congressional committees that were considering education bills that embraced skills-first instruction.

Officially, these research sites across the country were 'deployed to identify what it takes to learn to read, to delineate the factors that impede robust reading development, and to determine how best to prevent and remediate reading failure' (Lyon, 1999: 88). Unofficially, they were forging facts to fit a foregone conclusion.

Yet as valuable as these institutes were as ideological foundries, imposing lockstep reading education in the nation's classrooms required more and that turned out to be the National Reading Panel report (2000), the identified gold standard by which all reading instruction could be measured and upon which federal reading legislation embracing 'scientific reading instruction' could be erected.

THE NATIONAL READING PANEL REPORT OR FOOL'S GOLD

A careful reading of the Report shows that it was fool's gold. It is beyond the scope of this chapter to provide a full analysis of the Report's multitude of deficiencies and distortions. To obtain that the reader should see my book *Reading the Naked Truth: Literacy, Legislation, and Lies* (Coles, 2003), which provides a thorough examination of the Report. Here I will provide a few examples, demonstrating that scientific evidence had nothing to do with imposition of Reading First instruction throughout the nation's schools.

Seemingly, a national report on 'reading' would, among other things, first want to provide a clear definition of the term. Yet although the term was used liberally throughout the Report, its definition was ever-changing. Reading in one place might mean reading real or nonsense words and somewhere else it meant reading aloud smoothly and rapidly. Most importantly, seldom did it mean comprehending text, a process most people would define as key in reading. The predominant definition of reading was reading at the word level, with a special stress on decoding skills. A reader's use of context, syntax, and other written language information gleaned from a sentence or the broader text containing the word was noticeably absent from the Report's explanation. The Report's definition of 'reading' focused on how readers develop skill at reading words by alphabetic processing, rather than on how readers use meaningful textual contexts to derive meaning. Consequently, bias towards arriving at particular research 'facts' about reading were inherent in the Report's predominant definition and embedded assumptions about 'reading.'

'COMPARED WITH WHAT?'

The Report claims to have eliminated studies containing substantial methodological problems, yet an examination of the studies selected reveals the contrary, an example of which is the 'compared with what?' problem. Imagine an experiment in which a control group of first graders is instructed in muffin making and compared with an experimental group trained in phonemic awareness skills. At the end of the training period, reading tests show that the experimental group did better, leading the experimenters to conclude that the study demonstrates the superiority of phonemic awareness training in beginning reading. Later, the National Reading Panel calculates the effect size and reports it as large. Had this actually happened, the preposterous conclusions would be evident to any reader. Yet the kind of incongruous comparison I have described is exactly what is contained in many of the studies used in the Report, that is, studies using control groups that provide no proper contrast for judging the value of the instruction used by the experimental group, and certainly no comparison with the implicit and explicit enemy of the Panel, constructivist literacy learning.

An example is a study in which kindergarten and first-grade students were placed either in one of two skills-training groups or in a control group. One of the training groups learned to blend phonemes and to segment them in words. A second group learned these skills and practiced applying them in reading. The control group just listened to stories. The Report explained 'that at the end of the training period, the two skills treatment groups outperformed the control group on measures of phonemic awareness and reading.

Between the two training groups, the second achieved higher reading scores.'

The first 'compared with what?' problem is in the experimental-control comparison that pitted instruction against no instruction (that is, just listening to a story and answering questions about it). Consequently, concluding that the experimental groups did better on phonemic awareness and reading is not especially informative. Furthermore, the classroom instruction used a basal reading series – important information not mentioned in the Report, and the root of the second 'compared with what?' problem. Because the study did not include another kind of reading instruction, a constructivist one, for example, the Report could not maintain, as it did, that the study showed that the special and separate skills training will benefit a beginning reading program. The most we can conclude is that in beginning reading instruction, if a basal program like this one is used, adding phonemic skills training could help mollify the program's deficiencies.

This 'compared with what?' problem is one of several methodological issues in the studies that were ignored as the Panel ran away from what an accurate reading of its studies would have concluded:

- Skills-emphasis instruction is not superior to teaching skills as needed;
- Skills-emphasis instruction has no greater benefits, compared with other instruction, in comprehension beyond first or second grade;
- Skills-emphasis instruction does not help 'disabled' or 'at-risk' readers overcome their problems and become normal readers.

The second conclusion, evident to anyone who actually studied the Report, is especially pertinent because, as I will discuss below, that's exactly what a formal federal follow-up study concluded several years later (after millions of children had been damaged by this form of instruction).

WHOLE-LANGUAGE

What about the chief target of the Report, whole-language? The Report concluded that 'students taught systematic phonics outperformed students who were taught a variety of nonsystematic or non-phonics programs', including whole-language approaches (National Reading Panel, 2000: 2–134). The following is an overview of the handful of studies upon which this claim was based.

Study one: 'Better reading growth'

One study (Wilson and Norman, 1998) compared whole-language and phonics/skill-based second-grade classroom instruction. In the former, skills were taught as needed, using the contexts of story reading and writing to teach a skill, but when poor readers needed particular skills, the teacher did teach them in isolation. In the phonics/skills classrooms, skills were taught through direct instruction, independently of story reading.

At the end of second grade, the children in both classrooms had comparable scores on tests of word recognition in isolation and in context and comparable scores in passage comprehension. There were 'few overall differences' between the two teaching groups, the study's researchers concluded. The students did differ on one word identification test (a cloze test, in which a student identified deleted words in sentences), and this one favored the whole-language group! Surprisingly, although the phonics/skills approach emphasized letter-sound information, students taught with this approach did not use this information 'significantly more for word identification than did students taught in a whole-language approach.' These results are especially revealing because a chief argument for explicit phonics programs is that they give beginning readers a boost in word identification, an argument not supported here. The actual data from the study, then, contradict the Report's conclusions there was 'better reading growth' in skills-emphasis over whole-language classrooms.

Study two: Whole-language = no loss in student achievement

The next study (Klesius, Griffith, and Zielonka, 1991) also compared the effectiveness of direct instruction of phonics skills in traditional classrooms with a whole-language approach that emphasized meaning and comprehension and taught phonics less explicitly, relying more on the process of self-discovery of alphabetic principles through writing and reading.

At the end of the school year, these first graders, many of whom were from low-income families, showed no significant differences in measures of reading comprehension, vocabulary, phonemic awareness, decoding, spelling, and writing. Contrary to what one would surmise from just reading the Report, the study also confirmed that 'children in a whole-language program' can 'learn the alphabet principle through extensive writing and extensive exposure to print.'

Moreover, the researchers concluded that the comparable results indicated that skills-emphasis, scripted programs were not necessary: 'with little in-service, teachers could make a transition to whole-language without loss in student achievement. It appears to be possible for teachers to abandon teachers' manuals which include a detailed scope and sequence of skills as well as detailed lesson plans' (1991: 59). This judgment was not quoted in the Report.

Beyond the similar test outcomes and their implications for choosing among instructional approaches, the researchers were disappointed to find that neither instructional approach was significant for closing the gap between the students with low and high incoming reading skills. This outcome raises an important issue that has been minimized in the debate over beginning literacy instruction and totally ignored in the Report: focusing on instruction exclusively and neglecting a more comprehensive policy toward the hardships faced by poor children is likely to produce disappointing results regardless of the educational approach employed.

Study three: Comparable outcomes

First graders in a class using a skills-emphasis basal reading program that included little writing were compared with other students in a whole-language class that taught phonics 'indirectly through the examination of words with similar spelling (e.g., words beginning with the same consonant or ending with the same phonogram)' and in 'daily writing activities' (Griffith, Klesius, and Kromey, 1992: 87).

At the end of the school year, no group differences were found in tests of word recognition, reading comprehension, or spelling phonetically predictable words and nonsense words. This similar success occurred, the researchers noted, even though 'children in the whole-language instruction classroom did not receive direct phonic instruction; overall they appeared able to use letter-sound correspondence information to decode words at a level equal to that of the children who had received direct instruction in phonics sounds.' Moreover, 'the children in the whole-language classroom could read non-sense words at a level equal to that of children' in the skills-emphasis classroom (1992: 90) The researchers regarded this as especially telling because the nonsense words test was aimed solely at testing phonics skills. None of these observations were in the Report.

Beyond the similarities, the researchers noted one important difference: The children in the whole-language classroom 'engaged daily in multiple writing experiences' and consequently 'wrote more words and used more unique words in their compositions than did the children in the traditional classroom.' Furthermore, the children in the whole -language classrooms wrote more fluently. The trade-off appears to have been that they were 'less concerned about spelling words correctly.' However, test results showed that at that point in their literacy development, their spelling was not worse than that of children in skills-emphasis classrooms. Nothing about researchers' observations about writing in whole-language classes is mentioned in the Report.

Unfortunately, these comparable outcomes still meant that both kinds of classes continued to have underachieving readers, again indicating that instructional policy needs to be part of a larger policy approach. Although the researchers did not provide any information about the children's backgrounds beyond saying that they live in a 'rural school district,' we may assume that, as is common in rural areas, at least some of the children were poor, had limited access to preschool education, had limited access to books, and had life stressors that might have impeded learning.

Study four: The Foorman study

In 1998 a study by Barbara Foorman and colleagues (Foorman, Francis, Fletcher, Schatschneider, and Mehta, 1998) became the hit of the media and proponents of skills-emphasis teaching who saw it as the premier study demonstrating the superiority of direct instruction over whole-language. Following publication of the 'Foorman study,' as it was called, I obtained the original data – thanks largely to the Freedom of Information Act – and conducted an in-depth analysis of the results of the two approaches. First- and second-grade classroom data showed that both teaching approaches produced about the same achievement outcomes in reading comprehension, but neither approach had a satisfactory impact for students: that is, poor readers remained poor readers.

This conclusion did not address the question of whether the classes the researchers identified as whole-language actually met that description. Given the limited information the published study provided about the classes, there is no way of determining the extent to which the 'whole-language' class was that. Regardless, it is clear that direct instruction emphasizing skills did not produce superior reading comprehension. I also did a reanalysis of the results of measures of letter identification, word identification and reading pseudowords (dif, giz, blif, etc.) and found that, as was true for reading comprehension results, overall test performances for both groups were comparable.

Study five: Variables influencing students' growth

Concerned that 'the current movement toward whole-language is also a movement away from phonics,' a whole-language program was modified to include a daily 15-minute period of total-class systematic, intensive, and direct phonics instruction and compared with instruction using a basal reading program that also included the direct teaching of phonics (Eldredge, 1991: 35). The students in the study were first graders from low socioeconomic families, and in a school with the largest student turnover in the district. The researchers emphasized that although the 'modified whole-language approach used in this study differed markedly from generally accepted whole-language approaches,' the whole-language classrooms spent the majority of time on activities common in whole-language teaching (1991: 26). Unlike the whole-language teaching, the basal instruction tended not to integrate all the language arts, even though the children did write stories each day. At the end of the school year, the students in the modified whole-language program 'made greater vocabulary gains, comprehension gains and total reading gains than students involved in the basal program (1991: 33).

Because the modified whole-language approach used a variety of practices and the study did not include a whole-language classroom that taught phonics skills 'as needed,' it is hard to identify the phonics program as the key difference affecting the outcome measures, although this is exactly what the Report did. Integrating the language arts; organizing literacy learning around themes and units of study that emerged from the children's backgrounds, interests, and ideas; including writing as soon as the children entered school; using stories that contained natural language and predictable language patterns, encouraging children to share readings and writings – all this carried no weight in the Report, which calculated that the large statistical effect in comprehension in the modified

whole-language class was due to the phonics program! Also ignored was the observation of the researcher himself, who noted that a 'major weakness of this study' was that the 'variables influencing students' growth' were 'difficult to define, identify, and control' (1991: 31).

Studies six and seven: These are not whole-language

Another study in the Report (Evans and Carr, 1985) was cited as including whole-language teaching, when in fact it did not! Rather, the researchers themselves called it 'language experience' instruction (instruction based primarily on stories derived from children's experiences and dictated by them), although it was not exactly that either. The children in these classes first dictated words to a teacher, then constructed their own bank of sight words drawn from stories, and they needed to master 150 sight words 'before [they were] to be involved in any group instruction using basal or published materials' (1985: 331). There is no information about what the teachers in the classrooms did with these basals and other materials. The instruction was compared with a basal reading program that included skills workbooks and phonics drills. Given the paucity of information about the 'language experience' group and its use of a basal reading program, it is not clear what was proven in this study. Whatever it might have been, it was not about whole-language and the Panel had no basis for including it in the Report.

Similarly, another study the Report described as evaluating whole-language did not (Santa and Hoien, 1999). One group used an individual tutoring program that included book reading, word study, writing, and 'systematic, explicit instruction' on phonemic analysis (1999: 58). Other 'at-risk' children were taught in small groups in which they read books but did no writing and had no skills instruction. This control group the Report labeled 'whole-language.'

Outcome measures showed better results for the first group, meaning that individual tutoring was superior to group instruction, teaching word skills was more effective than not teaching them, and writing was more effective than no writing. The Report concluded that the experimental group demonstrated a larger effect in reading comprehension over whole-language, a misleading conclusion, to say the least.

Study eight: Omitting what didn't support the report's conclusions

A study by Penny Freppon (1991) compared reading outcomes for first-grade children taught with either skills-based or literature-based/whole-language instruction. The Report focused on only a single test, which assessed the children's oral reading, and found that the groups had comparable rates of accurate word identification. Therefore, in the 'oral reading' column in the Report's appendix that outlines research results, the effect size is listed as zero.

What is not known from reading the Report alone is that Freppon's study went beyond this single outcome by looking closely at both the way in which the children processed written language while reading and what conceptions of reading they held. She found that even though the literature-based/whole-language instruction did not explicitly teach skills, the children in both forms of instruction 'were knowledgeable about the importance of decoding' and 'successfully used it in

reading' (1991: 159). There was no evidence that whole-language instruction diminished children's sense of the value of this aspect of reading. This finding accords with other research that found that as children learn to read, they problem-solve and, by doing so, attain increased ability to understand causal and reciprocal relationships. As part of this problem solving, they grasp that a key problem to be solved in learning to read is the mastery of connections between graphemes and phonemes.

The similar group knowledge of decoding did not mean that each group used the strategy in the same way: the skills-emphasis group used it as a primary one, while the whole-language group used it to a lesser degree because that group employed a greater variety of strategies, such as rereading, using context, and skipping words. An unexpected finding was that even though the whole-language children 'attempted to sound out words less often,' when they did attempt it, they 'achieved a higher success rate of correctly sounding out words.' Their rate was 53 per cent compared with 32 per cent for the skills-emphasis children.

These findings also indicate that a study's particular definition of reading is likely to produce particular kinds of reading processes. The implicit definition of reading in whole-language instruction made decoding a key, not the key, in orchestrating this reading process. For the skills group, the grapheme-phoneme task loomed larger both as a strategy and as the meaning of reading and was more *the* key than *a* key. In the skills classroom, reading for meaning was included but was 'incidental' to word skills instruction (1991: 144).

The literature-based instruction evoked different thinking and memory use.

Decoding skills were included, but more attention was drawn to meaning, with the teacher encouraging the children to think about what was going on in the story. In interviews with the children, the litera-ture-based group expressed greater 'under-standings of the use of multiple strategies in reading' and 'associated reading with language' (whether something makes sense or sounds like a sentence), whereas the skills-emphasis group 'expressed under-standing of sounding out as a primary reading strategy' and 'associated reading with getting words correct' (1991: 152). Almost all of the children in the literature group 'said that understanding the story or both understanding and getting words right is more important in reading.' In contrast, only half the children in the skills group chose these explanations; nearly all the remaining half chose 'getting words right' as most important (1991: 153).

Asked about 'the characteristics of good readers,' the skills group emphasized 'knowing and learning words and sounding out words.' In contrast, the literature-based group discussed characteristics such as 'reading a lot' and 'understanding the story.' The skills group included 'paying attention to the teacher' and 'knowing their place in the book,' characteristics that were not mentioned by the literature group (1991: 153). These findings suggest that skills-emphasis teaching tends to encour-age conformity and dependence, whereas literature emphasis teaching tends to encour-age independence and self-confidence.

The Freppon study also suggests an extremely important conclusion: instruc-tion itself contributes to the construction of the reading process to a considerable degree, and different instruction produces different reading processes. Furthermore, it suggests that the entire model of reading underpinning the Report is false. That is,

there is no preordained reading process, and skills-emphasis teaching cannot be said to work better than other instructional approaches because it is better configured to fundamental cognitive processes. Skills-emphasis teaching configures cognition, and in doing so it helps create cognitive processes specifically adequate for accom-plishing tasks and reaching goals in that pedagogy. This is very different from assuming that reading achievement goals are invariable, that pre-established cogni-tive processes must be evoked, and that the best way to do so is with skills-based instruction. These findings also put in seri-ous doubt the theory that children have a limited working memory requiring a youngster to focus on only one kind of beginning reading strategy. It appears that children can successfully orchestrate sev-eral strategies in working memory while not diminishing their ability to identify words and comprehend stories.

Although there is no evidence in this study that children in the literature group have an advantage in standardized test achievement, there is evidence that they were becoming competent in more read-ing abilities and were acquiring a deeper meaning and apprehension of reading than were the children in the skills-emphasis classes. Finally, this research has useful implications for the questions about which instructional approach is better. This study suggests that the answer depends on the criteria for 'better.' By conventional stand-ardized test measures, both groups were comparable and, depending on the criteria, both work. But what is considered 'better' and 'what works' for skills-emphasis instruc-tion would be unacceptably limited and insufficient for educators and parents who have a different view of what constitutes good reading and a good reader, e.g., 'read-ing a lot' and 'understanding the story.'

Studies six and seven: Produced better reading growth

Two studies remain to be mentioned, both of which the Report identified as including whole-language instruction. One study found no differences in reading achievement outcomes at the end of first grade between the 'whole-language' teaching and *Distar*, a phonics program (Traweek and Berninger, 1997). The other study (Stuart, 1999), said to assess whole-language teaching, was done with children in Britain who were learning English as a second language, the vast majority of whom were Sylheti speakers, with three Canton speakers, and four speakers of other languages. This isolated research contains too many differences in student characteristics to be relevant to the Report's purposes, even though the Report apparently thought it to be.

These are the entire studies the Report used to draw conclusions when pitting whole-language against skills instruction, and supposedly supported the Report's conclusion that 'phonics produced better reading growth' than 'whole-language approaches' and that 'students taught systematic phonics outperformed students who were taught' with 'whole-language approaches' (National Reading Panel, 2000: 2–134). Clearly, the Panel either did not adequately read the actual research reports or purposely misrepresented the studies content and conclusions.

POWER, NOT EVIDENCE, WINS THE DAY

This review of the research reveals that the ascendancy of skills-heavy, scripted, publisher-directed pedagogy has had nothing to do with evidence. Had the latter been the criterion, at the very least the National Reading Panel Report, the premier document supposedly supporting 'scientifically-based reading instruction,' would have had to conclude that teachers could choose a reading approach among those reviewed. Or, had the Panel actually paid attention to the evidence supposedly in front of them, they would have recommended the use of whole-language because, as the Freppon study suggests, whole-language promotes a number of important dimensions of reading, such as a better grasp of the purpose of reading, and a fuller orchestration of various reading strategies. Furthermore, by not addressing the 'compared with what?' and other issues in the bulk of the research reviewed, the Panel would have had to acknowledge that their research base offered little upon which to draw any conclusion about skills-emphasis instruction.

Another example of why evidence matters so little and what teachers are up against is the process that rolled the *No Child Left Behind Act* (NCLB) of 2001, of which Reading First was a key component, into law. Proposed by President Bush, it had bipartisan support that included the very liberal Senator Edward Kennedy. In the House, 194 Democrats voted for it, only 10 voted against it. In the Senate only two Democrats voted against it.

Furthermore, it is important to underscore that at the time Reading First/NCLB was moving through Congress, the Democrats controlled the Senate, thanks to Vermont Republican Jim Jeffords, who left the party in 2001 to become an independent, thereby tipping the one-seat party difference to the Democrats. With this tip, Senator Kennedy became chair of the Senate Health, Education, Labor and Pensions Committee. The Committee, of course, then had a Democratic majority, among whom was Hillary Clinton. This was the opportunity, thought educational activists such as myself, who oppose scripted skills-heavy reading education, to garner Democratic support, or at least to have our viewpoints expressed at a Congressional hearing.

At the time I was on several educational listservs sympathetic to whole-language pedagogy and a campaign was organized to assure that the committee would not hear just one side of the issue pertaining to the Reading First legislature. Many educators emailed or wrote to all Democratic members and some Republican members of the Senate committee, explaining their position on reading education, often citing their own experience and published research, and suggesting educators whom the committee should invite to testify.

I wrote to every committee member, explaining the issues, recommending invitees, and with my letter I included copies of two of my books and a few of my articles. I did not expect the members to read them, but I thought the materials would demonstrate my status as an authority on the reading issues the committee was considering.

What happened? The hearings came and went, with no testimony from any opponent of the proposed Reading First legislation. During this time I heard back from no committee members, nor did I receive as little as an acknowledgement of my letter and the materials I had sent. Several months after the hearings were completed I did receive a perfunctory 'thank you, constituent, for your input' letter from Hillary Clinton's office. To this day I retain the image of Ted Kennedy standing behind a seated George W. Bush, who was signing into law the *No Child Left Behind Act* of 2001 of which Reading First was an instructional cornerstone.

To the surprise of no one who paid attention to the actual evidence, the predictable occurred. A 2008 examination of Reading First instruction concluded that students taught with 'scientifically based reading instruction' did not score better on reading comprehension tests than did students not taught with this instruction (Gamse, Bloom, Kemple, and Jacob, 2008). Also not surprising, defenders of 'scientific-reading instruction,' particularly those who were members of the Panel, nonetheless recommended that the problem might have been improper implementation, thereby recalling Einstein's well-known definition of insanity; doing the same thing over and over again and expecting different results.

Adding to the recognition of the failure of Reading First instruction was the uncovering of fraud and financial conflicts of interests among those who administered the program at the federal level. Schools receiving Reading First funds were being forced to purchase the products of commercial publishers and testing companies to which the Reading First administrators were financially tied (Manzo, 2007). This was an old story, something I and others began documenting a decade ago when associations were revealed between the Bush family and the McGraw's of McGraw-Hill, which became the leading publisher of Reading First materials (Metcalf, 2002).

With the Obama administration and Arne Duncan as Secretary of Education, Reading First is officially in deep freeze, but 'scientific reading instruction' continues in full force through the 'Common Core Standards,' which is shaping classroom instruction. Its grade-by-grade curriculum and testing standards reflect skills-heavy building-blocks reading instruction – exactly the same promoted through the National Reading Panel (www.corestandards.org). Despite the continued lack of evidence supporting this instruction and based solely on political power, this pedagogy continues to pervade classrooms, dominate teachers and misshape students' learning. Whatever hope there might have been for a policy change with the Obama administration vanished with Duncan, who has long promoted 'scientific reading instruction' (Schmidt, 2002).

In an International Reading Association Panel on 'National Literacy Policies,' Kenneth Goodman (2010) observed:

> In the context of 21st century America, everything that we as educators have learned about literacy through our research and the theory we have built from that work is less valued than conceptions of literacy that serve the political and economic purposes of those who have the power to control the decision-making.'

Will this change? I write this at a time the 'Occupy Wall Street' movement is growing and educators are becoming a part of it, particularly through a 'Save Our Schools' movement (www.saveourschools-march.org), whose endorsers include educators who have opposed 'scientific reading instruction.' One aim of this movement is to enable 'teacher and student access to a wide-range of instructional programs and technologies.' Only through power can this be achieved, only through opposition to power will teachers be able to use the many valuable ideas in this Handbook.

REFERENCES

Boston Sunday Globe (1990). 'An injustice to juveniles', 25 February.

Barth, R. (1972). Open Education and the American School. New York: Agathon. p. 37.

Bennett, W.J. (1986). A Report on Elementary Education in America. Washington, DC: US Department of Education.

Coles, G. (1987). The Learning Mystique: a Critical Look at 'Learning Disabilities'. New York: Pantheon.

Coles, G. (1998). Reading Lessons: The Debate over Literacy. New York: Hill and Wang.

Coles, G. (2003). Reading the Naked Truth: Literacy, Legislation and Lies. Portsmouth, NH: Heinemann.

Commission on Reading, National Academy of Education (1985). Becoming a Nation of Readers. Washington, DC: US Department of Education.

Curti, M. (1935). The Social Ideas of American Educators. New York: Charles Scribner's Sons.

Davis, B. (2001). 'Phonics mavin is at center of Bush's education push,' Wall Street Journal, 23 April. A24.

Eldredge, L. (1991). 'An experiment with a modified whole language approach in first-grade classrooms', Reading Research and Instruction, 30: 21–38.

Evans, M. and Carr, T. (1985). 'Cognitive abilities, conditions of learning, and the early development of reading skill', Reading Research Quarterly, 20: 327–50.

Fiske, E. B. (1975, July 9). "About Education; Approach to Reading Rethought," New York Times, 37.

Foorman, B., Francis, D., Fletcher, J., Schatschneider, C., and Mehta, P. (1998). 'The role of instruction in learning to read: preventing reading failure in at-risk children', Journal of Educational Psychology, 90: 37–55.

Freppon, P. (1991). 'Children's concepts of the nature and purpose of·reading in different instructional settings', Journal of Reading Behavior, 23: 139–63.

Galaburda, A.M., Menard, M.T., and Rosen, G.D. (1994). 'Evidence for aberrant auditory anatomy in developmental dyslexia', Proceedings of the National Academy of Science, 91: 8010–13.

Gamse, B.C., Bloom, H.S., Kemple, J.J., and Jacob, R.T. (2008). Reading First Impact Study: Interim Report (NCEE 2008-4016). Washington, DC: National Center for Education Evaluation and Regional Assistance, Institute of Education Sciences, US Department of Education.

Gannon, S. and Sawyer W. (2007). 'Whole language and moral panic in Australia', International Journal of Progressive Education, 3: 31–57.

Goodman, K. (1998). 'Comments on the Reading Excellence Act', Reading Online www.readingonline. org.

Goodman, K. (2010). 'Whose knowledge is worth what?', National Literacy Policies: The View from the Classroom. www.readinghalloffame.org/node/287.

Griffith, P.J., Klesius, J., and Kromey, J. (1992). 'The effect of phonemic awareness on the literacy development of first grade children in a traditional or a whole language classroom', Journal of Research in Childhood Education, 6: 85–92.

Klesius, J., Griffith, P., and Zielonka, P. (1991). 'A whole language and traditional instruction comparison: overall effectiveness and development of the alphabetic principle', *Reading Research and Instruction*, 30: 47–61.

Kolata, G. (1998) 'Scientists track the process of reading through the brain', *New York Times*, 3 March: F3.

Lemann, N. (1997). 'The Reading Wars', *Atlantic Monthly*, November: 78.

Lyon, G.R. (1999). 'In celebration of science in the study of reading development, reading difficulties, and reading instruction. The NICHD Perspective', *Issues in Education: Contributions from Educational Psychology*. 5: 85–115.

Manzo, K. (2007). 'House panel grills witnesses on Reading First', *Education Week*, April 24: 26.

Metcalf, S. (2002). 'Reading between the lines', *The Nation*, 28 January. www.thenation.com/article/reading-between-lines.

Nasaw, D. (1981). *Schooled to Order: A Social History of Public Schooling in the United States*. USA: Oxford University Press.

National Reading Panel (2000). *Report of the National Reading Panel: Teaching Children to Read. Reports of the Subgroups*. Washington, DC: National Institutes of Child Health and Human Development.

NIH–NICHD (2002) 'Children's reading disability attributed to brain impairment', Press Release, 2 August, http://www.nichd.nih.gov/news/releases/disability.cfm

Rothenberg, J. (1989). 'The open classroom reconsidered', *Elementary School Journal*, 90: 69–86.

Rothman, R. (1990). 'From a 'Great Debate' to a full-scale war', *Education Week*, 21 March:1–11.

Ruddell, R.B., Ruddell, M.R., and Singer, H. (eds) (1994) *Theoretical Models and Processes of Reading*. 4th edn. Newark, DE: International Reading Association.

Salmans, S. (1988, November 6) "New Directions; Go Away, Dick and Jane," *New York Times*, 29.

Santa, C. and Hoien, T. (1999). 'An assessment of early steps: a program for early intervention of reading problems', *Reading Research Quarterly*, 34: 54–79.

Schmidt, G.N. (2002, October 29) "Duncan Boosts Controversial Science Claim About Early Reading Instruction," Substance News.

Shaywitz, S.E. (1996). 'Dyslexia', *Scientific American*, November: 98–104.

Shaywitz, S.E., Shaywitz, B.A., Pugh, K.R., Fulbright, R.K., Constable, R.T., Mencl, W.E., Shankweiler, P., Liberman, A.M., Skudlarski, P., Fletcher, J.M., Katz, L., Marchione, K.E., Lacadie, C., Gatenby, C., and Gore, J.C. (1998) 'Functional disruption in the organization of the brain for reading in dyslexia', *Proceedings of the National Academy of Sciences*, 95: 2636–41.

Shaywitz, B.A., Shaywitz, S.E., Pugh, K.R., Mencl, W.E., Fulbright, R.K., Skudlarski, P., Constable, R.T., Marchione, K.E., Fletcher, J.M., Lyon, G.R., and Gore, J.C. (2002) 'Disruption of posterior brain systems for reading in children with developmental dyslexia', *Biological Psychiatry*, 52: 101–10.

Shor, I. (1992). *Culture Wars: Schools and Society in the Conservative Restoration*. Chicago: University of Chicago Press.

Stice, C.F., Bertrand, N.P. and Manning, M. (2007). 'A brief history of whole language and the winter workshops: from miscue analysis to liberatory pedagogy', in M. Taylor, *Whole Language Teaching, Whole-Hearted Practice: Looking Back, Looking Forward*. New York: Peter Lang.

Stuart, M. (1999). 'Getting reading for reading: early phoneme awareness and phonics teaching improves reading and spelling in inner-city second language learners', *British Journal of Educational Psychology*, 69: 587–605.

Toch, T. (1997). 'The reading wars continue.' *US News & World Report*, 27 October: 77.

Traweek, K. and Berninger, V. (1997). 'Comparisons of beginning literacy programs: alternative paths in the same learning outcome', *Learning Disability Quarterly*, 20: 160–8.

Wilson, K. and Norman, C. (1998). 'Differences in word recognition based on approach to reading instruction', *Alberta Journal of Educational Research*, 44: 221–30.

Wingert, P. and Kantrowitz, B. (1997). 'Why Andy couldn't read,' *Newsweek*, 27 October: 56–64

21

Becoming Biliterate

Charmian Kenner and Eve Gregory

More children in the world are bilingual than monolingual, and more children are being educated bilingually or in a second language than only in their mother tongue, according to Tucker (1996). This may seem an unusual statistic from the point of view of Anglo-centric countries, where mainstream schooling tends to be monolingual in English and bilingualism is perceived as outside the norm, but children in many other countries are indeed learning to read and write in more than one language and often in more than one script. Datta (2007) describes how in India, for example, children in every region learn three languages in school. These include a regional or local language such as Bengali in Calcutta, and Hindi as the national language, as well as English. Each of these is written in a different script, and Datta herself had become literate in all three languages simultaneously via home tuition from her mother before entering school at age 7 (Datta, 2007: 2).

Thus it clearly is possible for very young children to become multiliterate, and in many settings internationally this is seen as a normal part of literacy development. This chapter will focus on minority-language children whose development is taking place in majority-language contexts, since young learners in these situations face particular challenges. In England, North America and Australasia, for example, where English is seen as the dominant world language, there is relatively little support for children to develop a minority-language literacy such as Bengali or Spanish. However, families and communities persist in their efforts to accomplish this goal (see Gregory and Kenner, chapter 21 this volume) and evidence for the cognitive and cultural advantages of bilingualism and biliteracy (Gregory and Kenner, chapter 21 this volume) suggests that mainstream education should broaden in these directions.

We will begin by looking at the ways in which young children may encounter writing in different languages through literacy practices at home and in their communities. We will then discuss the processes involved in becoming biliterate, looking particularly at how children transfer cultural and linguistic knowledge between their literacies. Finally, the chapter will consider research on promoting biliteracy in mainstream classroom contexts.

EARLY ENCOUNTERS WITH BILITERACY

It is only recently that researchers have begun to investigate young children's participation in literacy events in bilingual homes, and to reflect on the implications for early learning. In this section we outline several aspects arising from this research: children's understanding of the purposes of writing and reading, the varying nature of multiliterate experience, and children's awareness of different scripts.

Purposes for reading and writing

The propensity for young children to take note of family literacy events was recorded by Minns (1990), who researched the literacy lives of 4-year-olds growing up in the English Midlands. The parents of Gurdeep, for example, commented that even when he was a baby 'you'd be reading or writing and he'd be out there sitting in that corner and quickly he would pick it up' (Minns, 1990: 7). He would be the first to want to open birthday cards and wedding invitations, which would be read out to him, and would try to copy his parents when he saw them writing in Panjabi and English.

Children in Kenner's study of a multilingual nursery in South London (Kenner, 2000) showed a similar desire to participate as readers and writers, as shown in the following example:

> Danny, a four-year-old who had recently arrived with his mother from Ecuador, attended the primary school nursery class where he was beginning to learn to read in English. Meanwhile, Danny was engaged in a variety of Spanish-based literacy activities at home.
>
> When his mother wrote letters to Ecuador in Spanish, Danny would sit beside her and dictate what he wanted her to include. At the same time, he would rapidly cover pages with emergent writing to make his own letter.
>
> Another important source of literacy knowledge for Danny was the Bible. He and his mother read the Bible together in Spanish regularly and Danny would open the book himself to read again, saying for example 'Papá Dios nos da las flores' ('Our Father God gives us the flowers').
>
> Danny's uncle had given him a storybook called 'El Rey León' (based on the Disney film 'The Lion King'), with an accompanying audiotape. Danny derived considerable enjoyment from simultaneously listening to the tape and looking at the book. He entered into the spirit of the story, enunciating the words with resonance, and knew when to turn the page. He could also perform the song from the tape, strumming along on an imaginary guitar.
>
> (discussed in Kenner, 2000: 13–14)

Thus even before attending the more formal lessons provided at community language schools (also known as complementary schools or heritage language schools), children are likely to be involved in writing and reading in their immediate environment. Bilingual family literacy practices tend to be based around key social purposes, as identified by ethnographic researchers Martin-Jones and Bhatt (1998) in their work on the experience of Gujarati-speaking families in the English Midlands. For these families, the main reasons for using Gujarati literacy included:

- keeping in touch with relatives living abroad,
- maintaining links with the wider community in Britain,
- religious observance,
- supporting cultural interests.

From the description of Danny's home activities in Spanish, we can see that he is involved from an early age with writing to family abroad and with religious literacy. Cultural interests are also a significant reason for wanting to read, although with this particular text Danny is being introduced to the global media-associated culture of Disney rather than the more traditional literary heritage of Ecuador.

The varying nature of multiliterate experience

The purposes for writing and reading in bilingual families involve both continuity and change. Some communities, such as the Mainland Chinese families described by An (2000) are expecting to return to their home country after a few years' stay abroad, and parents concentrate on maintaining children's literacy in their home language, with fairly intensive home teaching taking place from the age of 6 or so. In other cases, parents and grandparents will be maintaining religious or other cultural practices as discussed above, but the family's intention to stay in a new country will also give rise to further literacy needs. Most of the 30 Pakistani-origin families with children aged 2, 3 or 4 years old interviewed by Hirst (1998) in an English inner-city area wanted their children to become competent in four languages: English for everyday life and education, Urdu to write to relatives, Panjabi (spoken) to use with the family, and Arabic to participate in the Muslim religion.

Hirst documented the print-rich environments of the children growing up in these families, who were from a range of socio-economic backgrounds. 27 of the 30 children were said to be given opportunities to share books and stories at home, and more than half of the children owned between 4 and 12 books. The children participated in many family literacy events, from writing greetings cards to religious worship. Often books were in English and greetings cards, for example, were written in English as well as Urdu.

Increasingly, migration creates the phenomenon of 'transnational' families, who are continually crossing borders and therefore need to be skilled in more than one language and literacy. De la Piedra (2011) describes how Mexican-origin mothers and daughters living in the El Paso area read and wrote together in both English and Spanish. Most children attended dual-language education programmes, so homework was tackled bilingually. Meanwhile, parents and children gave each other two-way support as they engaged in digital literacy practices such as internet chat, connecting the family with relatives across the border. Mothers could provide help with Spanish, whilst daughters were proficient at using new technologies.

It is evident that many minority-language families make considerable efforts to help their children become biliterate or multiliterate. A study of 3–6-year-olds from British Bangladeshi families in East London highlighted the key role played by grandparents in maintaining language and literacy with young children, through joint activities ranging from reciting Bengali poetry to cooking and gardening (Kenner et al., 2007). Hancock (2006) interviewed Chinese mothers bringing up their children in Scotland and noted the variety of teaching approaches they used. As well as ensuring that children practised Chinese characters in order to improve memorisation and handwriting skills, some parents used imaginative descriptions to encourage visualisation such as 'draw two eyes' or 'add a moustache', or focused attention on the meaning of radicals that formed part of semantically-related characters (such as the radical for 'rain' that occurs in both 'raincoat' and 'umbrella').

In settings where parents feel unconfident about their knowledge in English, researchers have found that older siblings take on the role of teacher, particularly in helping younger children to learn to read (Rashid and Gregory, 1997; Volk, 1999; Obied, 2009). With an awareness of literacy practices from both mainstream and community language schools, siblings are well-placed to combine these practices in their teaching. Thus a range of interactions around literacy may occur through young bilingual children's participation in home and community events with a variety of family members (Gregory et al., 2004).

Although English literacy will figure to a greater or lesser extent in the lives of most bilingual families living in an English-dominant society, new technologies have revitalised the possibility of maintaining other languages and literacies. As well as the internet resources mentioned above, many more cable and satellite channels are now available in minority languages and these are being tuned into enthusiastically in homes around the world, as shown by research such as that of Cruickshank (2004) with Lebanese-origin families in Australia. Visits to bilingual children's homes in London (Kenner, 2005) gave a window onto this highly varied world, in which a family might be watching 'Who Wants to be a Millionaire?' in English one moment and then switch to the news on Arabic satellite TV. Print in the family's other writing system, such as Arabic or Chinese, was thus present on screen as well as in dictionaries on the shelf or posters and calendars on the wall, and young children re-worked material from popular culture to create their own multilingual texts.

Children's awareness of different scripts

There is evidence that very young children take note of the symbols being used for writing and reading as well as the overall purpose of each literacy event. Saxena (1994: 100) provides us with a case study of a Panjabi Hindu family living in Southall, west London. The 4-year-old son encounters a variety of languages and a variety of scripts during a typical day. Although teaching only occurs in English at his primary school, as he enters the building he sees bilingual signs in the Gurmukhi and Devanagari scripts, designed for the multilingual school community. The Gurmukhi script is usually used for Panjabi and the Devanagari script for Hindi, although as Saxena points out, both languages can be written in both scripts. When the child gets home from school in the afternoon, his grandmother sends him to the local shop with a shopping list written in Hindi/Devanagari, and the shopkeeper records the goods sold in the same language and script.

During the day, the 4-year-old can also observe his parents and grandparents reading and writing; for example, his mother reads Hindi film magazines and novels, and together with his grandmother writes to relatives in India in Panjabi–Hindi mixed code using Devanagari script. The family also uses English for a number of purposes, such as when the father reads a newspaper in the morning or the grandfather reads his grandson a storybook in English brought home from primary school. The complexity of this multiliteracy environment is not lost on the little boy; Saxena states that he can already distinguish between the Gurmukhi and Devanagari scripts and the Roman script in which English is written.

Similarly, Kenner's (2000) case study of 4-year-old Meera, from a Gujarati-speaking family, shows how a young child who had been receiving no formal instruction in her home language literacy still recognised the difference between that script and English.

Meera stated clearly that she wished to work with Gujarati – 'I want my Gujarati' – and began to produce her own emergent 'Gujarati' symbols, using her mother's writing as a resource.

THE PROCESSES INVOLVED IN BECOMING BILITERATE

It is clear from the above discussion that children growing up in bilingual or multilingual homes tend to have access to a variety of texts and literacy practices involving different languages. This experience is supplemented by their school learning, whether at community-run classes (as discussed by Gregory and Kenner, chapter 21 this volume) or in mainstream school. What do children make of these inputs and what factors come into play which can aid or hinder the development of biliteracy? This section looks at research on children's learning about different writing systems and different cultural worlds, and then considers to what extent children can transfer aspects of knowledge between their literacies.

Knowledge about different writing systems

One part of the process of becoming biliterate involves producing the symbols which make up different writing systems and recognising what they stand for. Research with young children shows that they are capable of differentiating two or more script systems and of beginning to distinguish the principles on which these are based. Datta (2007: 86) gives an example of a 5-year-old, Raki, who spontaneously produced three types of script in one text, demonstrating her knowledge of letters from the Bengali, Arabic and English

alphabets. Raki was also experimenting with ways of forming words by combining consonants and vowels in Bengali.

Kenner (2004a) followed 6-year-olds in London learning to write in Chinese, Arabic or Spanish as well as English, and found that children understand the form-meaning relationship in their different writing systems. In this project, the participant bilingual children were asked to conduct 'peer-teaching sessions' – teaching their mainstream primary school classmates how to write in their home language system. Tala, who was attending Arabic Saturday school, showed that she understood how each Arabic letter has four different forms: as well as the main form in which it appears in the alphabet, there are initial, medial and final forms which must be used when the letter appears joined to others at the beginning, in the middle or at the end of a word respectively. Tala explained to her primary school peers which letters she used from the Arabic alphabet chart to construct her name, and how they looked different 'because I joined them up'. Pointing to the letter which began her name, she said 'There's a T in Arabic like this ...' and as she demonstrated how to join this letter to the following one, she stated 'and now I change it, because Arabic is magic'.

Yazan, who attended the same community language school as Tala, was clear about the directionality of books in Arabic as compared to English. When showing his Arabic textbook to his primary school class, Yazan pointed to the front cover. Recognising that his audience would have expected this to be the back of the book, he stated 'Not the end'. He then turned to the back cover, emphasising 'This is the end', and reinforced the concept by returning to the front and stating 'This is the first'.

The principles mentioned so far had been directly taught to Tala and Yazan at Arabic school, but children in the study also showed that they were making their own deductions about how writing systems worked. For example, teachers at the Chinese community school were not observed to discuss the conceptual basis of the Chinese writing system as compared to English. Yet in a peer teaching session, Ming compared the three characters which represented his full Chinese name (Lai Sei Ming) on the front of his Chinese school exercise book to his name as written in English school, 'Ming'. He remarked 'That one's got three words and the English one's got four' (i.e., four letters). Later he said 'Ming is four, seven if it's together', referring to the seven letters needed for his full name in English, 'Ming Lai'. Here Ming was distinguishing between the characters used to represent whole words in Chinese, and the alphabetic letters which form the building blocks of English.

These young children also demonstrated that they were able to produce complex symbols with care and accuracy, often from memory. This ability has surprised teachers from mainstream schools, who would be expecting emergent writing – as yet relatively unsophisticated – from children of this age. An extract from Selina's exercise book (see Fig. 21.1) in her first year of Chinese school, when she was aged 5, shows how she was learning the particular sequence of strokes with which to build up a character, and then practising the whole character numerous times. Children were required to pay great attention to the detail of each stroke, so that the character could not be confused with another similar one, and to ensure that the character was harmoniously balanced in the centre of each square.

Knowledge about different cultural worlds

Children's engagement with their different writing systems occurs in particular cultural contexts – such as home, community school or place of worship – and is thus part of the meanings they encounter as they represent and experience their complex bilingual worlds. Their engagement with the overall purpose and content of text also opens out a variety of cultural knowledge. The Welsh Language Board (1999) includes the following aspects in its list of advantages arising from bilingual education: 'twice the enjoyment of reading and writing' and 'access to two cultures and worlds of experience'.

An example comes from Gurdeep, the 4-year-old mentioned above who was growing up in the English Midlands. Minns (1990) commented on the literary worlds which were opened up for Gurdeep by reading the sacred Sikh text, the Guru Granth Saheb, with his mother and by hearing her tell folk tales in Panjabi with their clear moral messages. Meanwhile, Gurdeep also experienced children's stories in English written out of a different cultural tradition, both in his primary school class and when his father read him books borrowed from the local library. Gregory et al. (2007) show how a child can syncretise cultural meanings from different versions of a classic tale, for example when reading 'Snow White' (already familiar in English) in a Bengali storybook with the support of a grandparent.

Datta (2007) emphasises how children's knowledge is strongly based in the oral, written and media discourses encountered at home and in their communities, the content and the style of which influence children's learning. She quotes a student teacher who began to investigate the

Figure 21.1   From Selina's first-year exercise book: learning the stroke sequence to build up a character (in the right-hand column) and practising the whole character

multilingual literacy worlds of 8-year-old English-Gujarati bilinguals in her primary school class and concluded 'it appears that their linguistic and literary learning is mostly embedded in cultural and religious experiences' (Datta, 2007: 38). If young children's home-based literacy experience is very different from that offered in mainstream school, teachers may need to cater specifically for this difference, as will be discussed below.

Transfer between literacies

Concepts and ideas which bilingual children develop in one language can interact with those developed in another, as explained by Cummins (1991). Some examples of how this could happen with literacies are given by Baker (2011: 322): once children understand that letters stand for sounds, or that words can be guessed from the storyline, these principles can be applied when reading or writing in another language.

Several researchers have found evidence for this kind of transfer. Verhoeven (1994) studied the early biliteracy learning of Turkish children in the Netherlands and found that word decoding skills and reading comprehension skills developed in Turkish predicted corresponding skills when Dutch was acquired later. Transfer can also occur when literacies have different orthographies: Wagner (1994) found a positive interaction between the learning of French and Arabic in Morocco.

The process of creating and interpreting textual meanings can be enriched through multilingual experience. When Sneddon (2000) studied children from a Gujarati and Urdu-speaking Muslim community in north-east London, she found that children who had opportunities to develop their language through using the cultural and leisure facilities of the local Gujarati community centre had a higher level of linguistic vitality in Gujarati than those who did not have this opportunity. This led to children being more creative story tellers in both Gujarati and English. Meanwhile, the children were becoming literate in Urdu for religious purposes, via community classes in which they answered complex questions on textual comprehension, with discussion taking place in English and Gujarati as well as Urdu. Sneddon suggests that this negotiation of meanings between three languages may provide strategies which can also be used when reading in the English mainstream classroom. Dual language books are also a potentially powerful source of knowledge for bilingual children; Sneddon (2009) explores the many ways in which young children, reading with parents or friends, can build understanding and develop meta-linguistic skills by studying a parallel text.

With regard to early writing, researchers have observed that young bilingual children have the propensity to write in more than one language within the same text, combining the resources available from their different literacies. Mor-Sommerfeld (2002) gives examples of children writing stories and messages in both Hebrew and English, switching from one language to the other and finding inventive ways to deal with the different directionalities of each script. She gives this process the apt name of 'language mosaic'. Kenner (2004b) noted that 6-year-old Brian, growing up in London with Spanish as his home language, combined Spanish and English literacy resources within one phrase in order to write a caption for his drawing of a flying bear (see Fig. 21.2). For the Spanish phrase 'un oso que vuele' ('a bear that flies') Brian wrote '1osokwle'. The number '1' represented 'un' ('un' can mean both 'a' and '1' in Spanish) – thus Brian was making use of the number system as a resource here too. The word 'oso' was familiar to Brian and he could write it spontaneously. He then called upon his knowledge of the English alphabet (the letter-name K and the sound of /w/) to give a good representation of the sounds he needed at this point. The final part 'le' is the rather more standard ending to the word 'vuele'.

As well as the possibility of transferring understandings across the variety of writing systems already mentioned in this section, logographic systems such as Chinese can be combined with alphabetic systems in order to represent meaning. Selina, one of the children in Kenner's study, produced drawings of her mother and sister accompanied by both Chinese and English writing. In an increasingly multilingual world, this kind of linguistic creativity is likely to stand children in good stead later on in life.

Figure 21.2   Brian's drawing and caption of 'un oso que vuele' ('a bear which flies')

Combining linguistic codes and switching between them can also be a strategy used by children to aid their learning. Gort (2006) studied 6-year-olds in a Spanish/English two-way bilingual education programme in the northeastern USA, and observed how they used words or phrases from one language as a scaffold when learning the other. By working cross-linguistically and bi-directionally on encoding, spelling, punctuation and editing, children developed the two linguistic systems alongside each other. Such approaches have been described by García (2009) as 'translanguaging'. Gutiérrez et al. (2011) argue for the creation of 'polylingual and polycultural learning ecologies' in early childhood settings, to facilitate these synergies in children's thinking.

Cognitive and cultural challenges involved in biliteracy learning

Children meet various challenges when they learn a second or third written language, especially if the new literacy is not immediately connected with their home language and culture. These challenges may be phonological, syntactic, semantic and textual, and young learners will have particular advantages and disadvantages when they set out to deal with them.

It is often found that bilingual children are more confident about decoding words than about answering comprehension questions on a whole text, for example. Rosowsky (2001) discovered that bilingual learners may be more accurate than monolingual peers when reading aloud, and he suggests that decoding skills are reinforced by the teaching of this aspect in community classes. However, overall comprehension of a passage involves grammatical and cultural knowledge which is less easily available in a second language, and here the monolingual children in Rosowsky's study tended to do better.

Within the area of phonology, some aspects will also be easier for bilingual learners than others. Gregory (2008: 127) points out that in a first language, children will be familiar with the usual patterns of sounds: for example, sounds which tend to occur in clusters, or tend to start or end words. In a second language, children have less experience from which to build this understanding.

Thus it is possible to analyse the likely strengths and difficulties which second language learners will have in the areas of phonological, syntactical, lexical, semantic and bibliographic knowledge respectively. The following list shows examples based on a fuller discussion by Gregory (2008, Chapter 5).

Grapho-phonic knowledge

Strengths: Concept of matching symbols to sounds can transfer.

Difficulties: Hard to distinguish/pronounce sounds not used in own language.

Syntactic knowledge

Strengths: Awareness that different grammatical structures exist.

Difficulties: Don't yet have a 'feel' for grammar in the new language.

Lexical knowledge

Strengths: Awareness that words have different forms and properties.

Difficulties: May not know collocation (e.g., 'grind' goes with 'corn').

Semantic knowledge

Strengths: Awareness that different cultural experiences will exist.

Difficulties: Cultural content will be unfamiliar, so hard to predict text.

Bibliographic knowledge

Strengths: Experience of different kinds of texts.

Difficulties: Format and style of English storybook may be unfamiliar.

In the final section of this chapter, we discuss how teachers can help bilingual children to build on their strengths and increase their knowledge base in both or all of their literacies.

THE TASK FOR EDUCATORS

Throughout the chapter, we have highlighted a number of areas which educators of bilingual children need to keep in mind in order to support the development of biliteracy. Now we consider research evidence on tackling the cognitive and cultural challenges just described, and bring together examples of successful classroom practice regarding biliteracy work with minority-language children in mainstream schools, identifying the common factors involved.

Building new knowledge bases

Second-language researchers have emphasised that a clearly organised approach is necessary to ensure children become more deeply acquainted with the structure and content of a new literacy. Gregory (2008) lays out the varied activities that can be undertaken to introduce emergent bilinguals to the unfamiliar aspects of another written language. For example, with regard to building lexical knowledge, teachers can provide experiences which will highlight certain words so that these become meaningful and memorable for children. Words can also be introduced in lexical sets, grouped around a theme, which again makes it easier to store and recall them.

Gibbons (2002) explains how literacy learning in a new language needs to be scaffolded effectively, by providing models of language use for different purposes and contexts and enabling children to make this language part of their repertoire. For example, when teaching children to write stories in a second language, the different elements of story structure should be clearly set out. Young writers can be encouraged to jointly construct text with peers and the teacher, so that explicit discussion about language can take place. Good practice for the teaching of literacy in English as a second or additional language is also characterised by being strongly based in speaking and listening, and by integrating work at word, sentence and text level to create meaningful literacy experiences (Flynn, 2007).

Building on knowledge that children already have

Cummins (2006) emphasises the importance of selecting culturally relevant texts and drawing on children's own experience, and also of encouraging the use of home languages to build concepts and negotiate meaning. Several authors show how work which connects with home language experience can be a springboard for children's development in a second literacy. McWilliam (1998) suggests asking children to compare the use of vocabulary in their different languages, to highlight awareness of specific meanings and word classes. Datta (2007) gives striking examples of how to connect with children's rich imaginative worlds that arise from texts and events encountered in homes and communities. These experiences can then become a starting point for writing in English. The young writer of a ghost story could draw on knowledge of ghost stories from Bangladesh, whilst the writer of poetry could draw on the rich imagery and use of metaphor in Bollywood film songs, or ideas from the Buddhist tradition about peace and harmony. Meanwhile, through this 'intercultural literate community approach' (Datta, 2007: 39) children can also be introduced to the metaphors and imaginative devices used in English literature.

Gregory (2008, Chapters 6 and 7) argues that both an 'inside-out' approach (starting from the known) and an 'outside-in' approach (introducing the unknown) are needed when teaching reading. These two approaches complement each other in order to fully develop bilingual children's literacy capabilities in their second language.

Developing literacy in children's home languages

In majority-language contexts, the balance of power is heavily in favour of the dominant language and literacy. Few opportunities are offered for children to study their home literacy: as discussed by Gregory and Kenner (chapter 9 this volume), such opportunities are almost always in voluntary-run, under-funded out-of-school classes. As a result, children tend to focus more strongly on the dominant literacy, and this may limit development of their full potential as biliterates.

A number of researchers have therefore devised and implemented action-research projects to develop children's literacy in the minority language alongside the majority language. Such research has demonstrated that when children have the opportunity to work with their home languages and literacies in supportive mainstream classroom environments, their development of the majority language also benefits. The projects described below share certain key factors, including the integration of bilingual work into the curriculum, parental involvement, and an increase in the status of the minority literacy.

Kenner (2000) found that bringing home texts such as newspapers, videos and calendars in different languages into a south London nursery class, supported by parents writing in the classroom, was successful in stimulating literacy work by both bilingual and monolingual children. A partnership project with parents in a primary school in France, in which aspects of different languages and cultures were presented to the whole class, was similarly effective in raising the profile of families from minority language backgrounds (Young and Hélot, 2008).

The importance of relevant cultural themes for literacy work is highlighted by Masny and Ghahremani-Ghajar (1999), who found that Somali children in a Canadian elementary school who were thought by their teachers to be illiterate began to demonstrate literacy skills when the teacher-researcher brought in books such as the Qur'an. The same teacher drew on Somali themes for language work and invited participation from parents in spoken Somali. With this approach of 'weaving multiple literacies', children began to make progress in their learning.

By producing diverse types of dual language text (written, spoken, visual, musical, dramatic, or combinations of these in multi-modal form), children can construct positive multilingual identities and develop literacy more rapidly in both languages. Cummins (2006) gives examples of these 'identity texts', created by young children at a Canadian elementary school and made publicly available on the school's Dual Language Showcase website, thus enabling the young authors to share their work with relatives and friends locally and worldwide.

Multilingual computer-based texts show considerable potential for biliteracy work. They are linguistically flexible and motivating, enabling children to manipulate different scripts and realize ideas on screen. Edwards (2009: 109) describes how an 'Urdu club' with computer access in a multilingual English primary school aided literacy development for children. Meanwhile, parents used the resources to produce dual-language books and other teaching materials, gaining the status of expert within the school. Anderson (2001) found that producing web pages helped secondary school pupils in London extend their writing in both English and Bengali; this approach could be adapted for young children, who are keen to experience web page authorship.

Bilingual education

Whilst identifying the above projects as ways of supporting bilingual children's literacy learning in mainstream English classrooms, we would emphasise that biliteracy development would be greatly enhanced if dual-language education was more widely available. Verhoeven (1999) points out that literacy in two languages can be acquired either successively or simultaneously. Since ethnographic studies have shown that literacy in the mother tongue may help to enhance community and cultural identity, 'both cognitive and anthropological arguments speak in favor of a biliteracy curriculum' (Verhoeven, 1999: 147). Given the importance of raising the status of minority literacies in order to promote additive bilingualism (see Gregory and Kenner, chapter 21 this volume), this biliteracy curriculum is most likely to be successful if it is participated in by all children rather than by bilingual pupils only. Thomas and Collier's longitudinal assessment of the effects of different types of bilingual education in the United States (2002) showed that the most effective were two-way immersion programmes involving children from both Spanish-speaking and non-Spanish-speaking backgrounds.

Bilingual education in the United States also takes place in languages including Korean, Cantonese, Arabic, French, Japanese, Navajo, Portuguese and Russian (García, 2005). However, such programmes have had to close in Arizona and California, where laws have been passed to prohibit bilingual schooling (Dworin and Moll, 2006). Educators in English-dominant countries therefore need to continually campaign to support biliteracy in a political environment hostile to other languages (Manyak, 2006). Bilingual education also needs to be developed in close consultation with parents and communities through a critical empowerment approach, as shown by the case study of a successful Samoan/English bilingual programme in a New Zealand primary school (Tuafuti and McCaffery, 2005), in order to address the imbalance in power relationships between majority and minority languages.

Biliteracy futures

Children's early learning experiences lay the foundations for later development, and for this reason it is particularly important that educators should pay attention to young children's biliterate development in the mainstream classroom. Otherwise children may feel that the domains in which their home literacy can be used are highly restricted, and even if community classes are on offer, their motivation to attend and learn can be diminished. Hardman (1998) found that in a Cambodian community in the United States, children had pride and confidence in their family's spoken language, but little interest in writing Cambodian. Hardman comments 'Possibly, because there is no room for L1 literacy in the children's school, there is no room for it anywhere in their lives' (1998: 72).

Emergent biliteracy can be successful when children are supported in developing both languages in different genres and for different functions, as demonstrated by a bicultural programme in Arizona (Reyes, 2006). Access to a wide variety of print materials in the home language can therefore aid children in finding their individual paths to biliteracy. Tse (2001) interviewed 10 adults who had grown up in the United States, to find out how they had developed relatively high levels of literacy in their home languages of Spanish, Cantonese and Japanese respectively. One important common factor was reading for pleasure, which could involve novels, magazines, newspapers and comic books for example. Tse notes the results of a survey which showed the lack of Spanish-speaking materials in elementary school libraries even where schools had populations of over 90% Spanish-speaking children, and she argues that more books in minority languages should be provided by the mainstream.

CONCLUSION

Parents can give key support in developing biliteracy, as demonstrated in a recent guide to effective learning strategies at home (Wang, 2011), and complementary schools also play an important role (Conteh et al., 2007; Lytra and Martin, 2010). However, parents' and children's perceptions of their heritage languages are hugely influenced by attitudes in the wider society, so a concerted effort between schools, families and community organizations is vital (Li, 2006). As explained earlier in this chapter, for young children who live bilingually or trilingually, there are many links between their experiences as well as differences. When schools address the child as a whole person and give status to the minority literacy as a valued part of mainstream education, these links are strengthened with all-round benefits for self-esteem and learning.

REFERENCES

An, R. (2000) 'Learning to read and write at home: the experience of Chinese families in Britain', in M. Martin-Jones and K. Jones (eds), *Multilingual Literacies*. Amsterdam: John Benjamins. pp. 71–90.

Anderson, J. (2001) 'Web publishing in non-Roman scripts: effects on the writing process', *Language and Education*, 15(4): 229–49.

Baker, C. (2011) *Foundations of Bilingual Education and Bilingualism*. (5th edn). Clevedon, Avon: Multilingual Matters.

Conteh, J., Martin, P., and Helavaara Robertson, L. (eds) (2007) *Multilingual Learning: Stories from Schools and Communities in Britain*. Stoke-on-Trent: Trentham.

Cruickshank, K. (2004) 'Literacy in multilingual contexts: Change in teenagers' reading and writing', *Language and Education*, 18(6): 459–73.

Cummins, J. (1991) 'Interdependence of first and second language proficiency in bilingual children', in E. Bialystok (ed.), *Language Processing in Bilingual Children*. Cambridge: Cambridge University Press. pp. 70–89.

Cummins, J. (2006) 'Identity texts: The imaginative construction of self through multiliteracies pedagogy', in O. García, T. Skutnabb-Kangas, and M. Torres-Guzmán (eds), *Imagining Multilingual Schools: Languages in Education and Globalisation*. Clevedon, Avon: Multilingual Matters. pp. 51–68.

Datta, M. (2007) *Bilinguality and Literacy: Principles and Practice*. (2nd edn). London: Continuum.

de la Piedra, M. (2011) '"Tanto necesitamos de aquí como necesitamos de allá": *leer juntas* among Mexican transnational mothers and daughters', *Language and Education*, 25(1): 65–78.

Dworin, J. and Moll, L. (2006) 'Guest editors' introduction: special issue on biliteracy', *Journal of Early Childhood Literacy*, 6(3): 234–40.

Edwards, V. (2009) *Learning to be Literate: Multilingual Perspectives*. Clevedon, Avon: Multilingual Matters.

Flynn, N. (2007) 'Good practice for pupils learning English as an additional language: Lessons from effective literacy teachers in inner-city primary schools', *Journal of Early Childhood Literacy*, 7(2): 177–98.

García, E. (2005) *Teaching and Learning in Two Languages*. New York: Teachers College Press.

García, O. (2009) *Bilingual Education in the 21st Century: A Global Perspective*. Oxford: Wiley/Blackwell.

Gibbons, P. (2002) *Scaffolding Language, Scaffolding Learning: Teaching Second Language Learners in the Mainstream Classroom*. Portsmouth, NH: Heinemann.

Gort, M. (2006) 'Strategic code-switching, interliteracy, and other phenomena of emergent bilingual writing: Lessons from first grade dual language classrooms', *Journal of Early Childhood Literacy*, 6(3): 323–54.

Gregory, E. (2008) *Learning to Read in a New Language*. London: Sage.

Gregory, E., Long, S., and Volk, D. (eds) (2004) *Many Pathways to Literacy*. London: Routledge.

Gregory, E., Arju, T., Jessel, J., Kenner, C., and Ruby, M. (2007) 'Snow White in different guises: Interlingual and intercultural exchanges between grandparents and young children at home in East London', *Journal of Early Childhood Literacy*, 7(1): 5–25.

Gutiérrez, K., Bien, A., Selland, M., and Pierce, D. (2011) 'Polylingual and polycultural learning ecologies: Mediating emergent academic literacies for dual language learners', *Journal of Early Childhood Literacy*, 11(2): 232–61.

Hancock, A. (2006) 'Attitudes and approaches to literacy in Scottish Chinese families', *Language and Education*, 20(5): 355–73.

Hardman, J. (1998) 'Literacy and bilingualism in a Cambodian community in the USA', in A. Durgunoglu and L. Verhoeven (eds), *Literacy Development in a Multilingual Context: Cross-Cultural Perspectives*. New Jersey: Lawrence Erlbaum Associates. pp. 51–81.

Hirst, K. (1998) 'Pre-school literacy experiences of children in Punjabi, Urdu and Gujerati speaking families in England', *British Educational Research Journal*, 24(4): 415–29.

Kenner, C. (2000) *Home Pages: Literacy Links for Bilingual Children*. Stoke-on-Trent: Trentham Books.

Kenner, C. (2004a) *Becoming Biliterate: Young Children Learning Different Writing Systems*. Stoke-on-Trent: Trentham Books.

Kenner, C. (2004b) 'Living in simultaneous worlds: Difference and integration in bilingual script-learning', *International Journal of Bilingual Education and Bilingualism*, 7(1): 43–61.

Kenner, C. (2005) 'Bilingual children's uses of popular culture in text-making', in J. Marsh (ed.), *Popular Culture, Media and Digital Literacies in Early Childhood*. London: RoutledgeFalmer. pp. 73–87.

Kenner, C., Ruby, M., Gregory, E., Jessel, J., and Arju, T. (2007) 'Intergenerational learning between children and grandparents in East London', *Journal of Early Childhood Research*, 5(2): 219–43.

Li, G. (2006) 'Biliteracy and trilingual practices in the home context: Case studies of Chinese-Canadian children', *Journal of Early Childhood Literacy*, 6(3): 355–81.

Lytra, V. and Martin, P. (eds) (2010) *Sites of Multilingualism: Complementary Schools in Britain Today*. Stoke-on-Trent: Trentham Books.

Manyak, P. (2006) 'Fostering biliteracy in a monolingual milieu: Reflections on two counter-hegemonic English immersion classes', *Journal of Early Childhood Literacy*, 6(3): 241–66.

Martin-Jones, M. and Bhatt, A. (1998) 'Multilingual literacies in the lives of young Gujaratis in Leicester', in A. Durgunoglu and L. Verhoeven (eds), *Literacy Development in a Multilingual Context: Cross-Cultural Perspectives*. New Jersey: Lawrence Erlbaum Associates. pp. 37–50.

Masny, D. and Ghahremani-Ghajar, S. (1999) 'Weaving multiple literacies: Somali children and their teachers in the context of school culture', *Language, Culture and Curriculum*, 12(1): 72–93.

McWilliam, N. (1998) *What's in a Word? Vocabulary Development in Multilingual Classrooms*. Stoke-on-Trent: Trentham Books.

Minns, H. (1990) *Read It To Me Now!* London: Virago.

Mor-Sommerfeld, A. (2002) 'Language mosaic: Developing literacy in a second-new language – a new perspective' *Reading, Literacy and Language*, 36(3): 99–105.

Obied, V. (2009) 'How do siblings shape the language environment in bilingual families?', *International Journal of Bilingual Education and Bilingualism*, 12(6): 705–20.

Rashid, N. and Gregory, E. (1997) 'Learning to read, reading to learn: The importance of siblings in the language development of young bilingual children', in E. Gregory (ed.), *One Child, Many Worlds: Early Learning in Multicultural Communities*. London: David Fulton. pp. 107–21.

Reyes, I. (2006) 'Exploring connections between emergent biliteracy and bilingualism', *Journal of Early Childhood Literacy*, 6(3): 267–92.

Rosowsky, A. (2001) 'Decoding as a cultural practice and its effects on the reading process of bilingual pupils', *Language and Education*, 15(1): 56–70.

Saxena, M. (1994) 'Literacies amongst the Panjabis in Southall (Britain)', in J. Maybin (ed.), *Language and Literacy in Social Practice*. Clevedon: Multilingual Matters. pp. 96–116.

Sneddon, R. (2000) 'Language and literacy: children's experiences in multilingual environments', *International Journal of Bilingual Education and Bilingualism*, 3(4): 265–82.

Sneddon, R. (2009) *Bilingual Books, Biliterate Children: Learning to Read through Dual Language Books*. Stoke-on-Trent: Trentham Books.

Thomas W. and Collier, V. (2002) *A National Study of School Effectiveness for Language Minority Students' Long-term Achievement*. Final report: Project 1.1. Santa Cruz, CA: Center for Research on Education, Diversity and Excellence, University of California.

Tse, L. (2001) 'Heritage language literacy: A study of US biliterates', *Language, Culture and Curriculum*, 14(3): 256–68.

Tuafuti, P. and McCaffery, J. (2005) 'Family and community empowerment through bilingual education', *International Journal of Bilingual Education and Bilingualism*, 8(5): 480–503.

Tucker, R. (1996) 'Some thoughts concerning innovative language education programmes', *Journal of Multilingual and Multicultural Development*, 17(2–4): 315–20.

Verhoeven, L. (1994) 'Transfer in bilingual development', *Language Learning*, 44(3): 381–415.

Verhoeven, L. (1999) 'Second language reading', in D. Wagner, R. Venezky, and B. Street (eds), *Literacy: An International Handbook*. Oxford: Westview Press. pp. 143–7.

Volk, D. (1999) 'The teaching and the enjoyment and being together: Sibling teaching in the family of a Puerto Rican kindergartner', *Early Childhood Research Quarterly*, 14(1): 5–34.

Wang, X. (2011) *Learning to Read and Write in the Multilingual Family*. Clevedon: Multilingual Matters.

Wagner, D.A. (1994) *Literacy, Culture and Development: Becoming literate in Morocco*. Cambridge: Cambridge University Press.

Welsh Language Board (1999) *Two Languages: Twice the Choice*. Cardiff: Welsh Language Board.

Young, A. and Hélot, C. (2008) 'Parent-teacher partnerships: Co-constructing knowledge about languages and cultures in a French primary school', in C. Kenner and T. Hickey (eds), *Multilingual Europe: Diversity and Learning*. Stoke-on-Trent: Trentham Books. pp. 89–95.

22

Early Reading Development

Dominic Wyse and Usha Goswami

Written language is one of the supreme achievements of human beings. It has enabled our ability to communicate over distances, to record history, to analyse at new depths, and to create new artistic forms. It is a cultural invention that in turn has had profound cultural and social effects. The creation of alphabetic written language was a highly significant development. All alphabets were originally derived from the Semitic syllabaries of the second millennium. The developments from both Greek script and the Roman alphabet can be seen in the use of the Latinised form of the first two letters of the Greek alphabet in the word itself, 'alphabet'. Alpha was derived from the Semitic 'aleph' and 'beta' from 'beth' (Goody and Watt, 1963). Historically, the alphabet has been at the heart of some of the most enduring debates about the development of written communication, for example whether the alphabet simply emerged from logographic or pictographic forms. In Harris' (1986) examination of the origins of writing, he called this particular idea of emergence an evolutionary fallacy, arguing instead that the alphabet was 'the great invention' because its graphic signs have almost no limitations for human communication. The continuing development of writing, for example through internet and electronic text forms, is further testament to written language's extraordinary capacity to adapt to, and be part of, cultural change.

A more recent debate inspired by the alphabet, and its links with speech, has been its place in reading teaching. From the 1960s onwards this debate became polarised between those who thought that reading was best taught *bottom-up* (put simply, teaching from phonemes and letters to texts) and those who thought that reading was best taught *top-down* (from texts to letters and phonemes). Currently this debate is complemented by interactive models that combine bottom-up and top-down approaches. Bottom-up approaches to the teaching of reading have a very long history. Until the early 1800s the teaching of reading and the teaching of spelling in England were indistinguishable. Therefore, evidence on reading teaching at this time can be found in the hundreds of different spelling textbooks that were published. Michael (1984) argued, on the basis of an analysis of the spelling books that reading teaching was for most teachers a bottom-up approach. As early as 1610 this was clear, for example: 'Therefore let the scholler, being thus traded (i.e. schooled) from letters to syllables of one Consonant: from syllables of one Consonant, to syllables of many Consonants: from syllables of many Consonants, to words of many syllables; proceede to sentences' (1984: 57). Michael suggests that the approach was a consequence of the prevailing view that complex things could only be learned by children if they were first broken down into their component parts (a theory that still informs some current opinions of how children learn to read). In his chapter that examines the growth of whole-word methods, Michael also identifies what he sees as the first published reference to whole-word teaching. Charles Hoole, in his translation of the preface to Comenius' *Orbis Sensualium Pictus* (1659) said, 'reading cannot but be learned; and indeed too, which thing is to be noted, without using any ordinary tedious spelling, that most troublesome torture of wits, which may be wholly avoyded by this Method [the whole word method]' (1984: 60).

Our chapter explores the development of reading from the perspective of evidence across languages, and considers the possible implications for the teaching of reading in English and for literacy policy. The first section of the chapter examines reading development from a cognitive perspective in relation to phonological awareness. Next, we consider the development of phonological awareness and reading in a wider socio-cultural educational context, including attention to teaching and learning in the context of educational policy-making. We conclude by identifying some of the key messages from research and suggest that reading teaching might be improved through policy-making that takes account of interdisciplinary evidence.

The main methodological orientation that underpins our approach to this chapter is interdisciplinarity. In a broad sense, interdisciplinarity has been used to refer to a range of practices, from borrowing and solving problems across disciplines to the actual emergence of an interdiscipline. But central to the interdisciplinary methodology that informs our understanding is integration, the combining of theoretical perspectives from different fields of knowledge. The process of integration that is key in interdisciplinarity entails a step in which the disciplinary perspectives are seen in a new configuration. The substantive areas of this methodological orientation are cognitive, psycholinguistic, socio-cultural and educational. In part the reasons for selecting these disciplinary areas above others relate to our experience and interests, but we also think that their integration offers the potential for a significant contribution to enduring issues.

PHONOLOGICAL AWARENESS IN DIFFERENT LANGUAGES

As Port (2007) has noted, to a literate adult 'it seems intuitively obvious that speech presents itself to our consciousness in the form of letter-like symbolic units … when we hear someone say "tomato", we seem to hear it as a sequence of consonant and vowel sound units' (Port, 2007: 143–4). However, Port goes on to note '… there is virtually no evidence that supports [this] traditional view of linguistic representation'. Classically, these letter-like symbolic units have been called 'phonemes'. Conceptually, phonemes are the smallest elements of sound that change a word's meaning (as in 'cat' versus 'cap'). Obviously, a pre-literate child who has represented 'cat' and 'cap' as distinctive but complex auditory patterns can distinguish between these two words when listening, and can use them appropriately when speaking. Many children can also learn which sequences of letters are used systematically to represent these auditory patterns when they are taught the alphabet. However, other children will struggle. This is because the sound elements that are symbolised by the alphabet do not have an acoustic correlate in the speech stream.

Take our example of the spoken words 'cat' and 'cap'. Both words comprise a single syllable, both words sound very similar at the beginning, but they sound different at the end. We can either say that these words do not rhyme, or we can say that they differ in terms of their final 'phoneme'. In the written form of these words, the alphabet uses the change from T to P to signal this difference in sound structure (or 'phonology'). However, whereas the sound symbolised by the letter P has one acoustic form in the spoken word 'cap', it has a different acoustic form in the spoken word 'spoon'. Beginning readers may well try to write the word 'spoon' as SBN, and acoustically this makes sense. In order to acquire literacy, children have to overlook some acoustic differences between their phonological templates, and highlight some acoustic similarities. Across languages, children become able to reflect upon the units of sound that comprise spoken words as their language skills develop, and this process of reflection is called 'phonological awareness'. Phonological awareness follows a sequential developmental path. Within a particular language, the ease with which children will learn about phonemes and

acquire grapheme-phoneme recoding skills (or 'phonic' knowledge) depends on their pre-reading levels of 'phonological awareness'.

What is the form of the 'prosodic templates' that infants are acquiring? For English, the dominant template is a rhythmic pattern comprising two syllables, with stronger stress on the first syllable. Examples are 'mummy', 'daddy', 'baby' and 'bottle'. Indeed, child phonologists have pointed out that the words that we use with infants and young children are often adapted to fit this phonological template. We say 'doggie' instead of 'dog', and 'milkie' instead of 'milk'. Young children also seem to find it easier to produce this rhythmic pattern, for example saying 'nana' for 'banana'. The dominant prosodic templates differ in different languages. For example, the dominant prosodic pattern in French is to lengthen the final syllable. Whereas in English the main stress in a word like 'elephant' is on the first syllable, in French the main stress in 'elefant' is on the final syllable. Even very young infants are aware of these prosodic differences between languages. Nevertheless, mothers and fathers across languages use a special prosodic register, called infant-directed speech, to highlight these rhythmic cues for their babies. Infant-directed speech uses auditory features like exaggerated rhythm and intonation, heightened pitch and increased duration. This prosodic exaggeration seems to serve a language-learning function, helping infants in different languages to extract individual words from the speech stream on the basis of pitch and rhythmic cues (e.g., Echols, 1996).

Prosodic variation works at the syllable level of speech, and is not often marked in the written form (although it is in some languages, like Spanish). Nevertheless, the syllable is the primary perceptual linguistic unit across languages. As phonological awareness develops, children first become aware of syllables. Children can reflect on syllables as phonological units by the age of 3–4 years. For example, they can count the number of syllables in spoken words (deciding that 'butterfly' has three syllables, and 'bottle' has two syllables, see Liberman, Shankweiler, Fischer, and Carter, 1974), and they can decide whether words share syllables or not (deciding that 'hammer' and 'hammock' share the first syllable, see Treiman and Zukowski, 1991). Soon after, children become aware of intra-syllabic units called 'onsets' and 'rimes'. The onset in any syllable is the sound pattern before the vowel. The onset in 'swing' would be the sound corresponding to the letters SW, and the onset in 'string' would be the sound corresponding to the letters STR. For monosyllabic words, rimes and rhymes are the same level of linguistic structure. A word like 'cap' rhymes with a word like 'tap', and the shared (rime) sound unit is the sound corresponding to the letters AP. However, 'capture' does not rhyme with 'caption'. Although the rime of the first syllable is the same in both words, the rime of the second syllable differs. Instead, 'capture' rhymes with 'rapture', because these two words share their phonological structure after the first onset (linguists call this shared phonological unit a 'super-rime', see Davis, 1989). For our purposes, it is enough that any spoken syllable can be divided into two units, onset and rime, by segmenting at the vowel. Children are able to reflect on the onsets and rimes that comprise spoken syllables by the age of 4–5 years (e.g., Bradley and Bryant, 1983; Ho and Bryant, 1997). They are aware of rhyme even earlier (e.g., Chukovsky, 1963; Bryant, Bradley, MacLean, and Crossland, 1989).

Across languages, therefore, pre-reading children are aware of the phonological structure of syllables at the onset-rime level. Cross-language divergence comes only when the development of phoneme awareness is studied.

PHONOLOGICAL COMPLEXITY

The rate of development of phoneme awareness varies markedly across languages. Two factors appear to be particularly important in explaining this cross-language variation: the phonological complexity of syllable structures in different languages, and the spelling (orthographic) consistency of the written form of the language. Most languages in the world have syllables with a simple phonological structure. In these languages, the dominant syllable type is consonant-vowel or CV. In languages like Italian, Finnish and Spanish, most words are made up of syllables with this pattern, for example 'Mamma', 'ragazza' (*Italian*, girl) and 'casa' (*Italian*, house). In spoken English, the dominant monosyllable type is CVC. English has lots of words like 'girl', 'house', 'cat' and 'dog', which follow a CVC phonological pattern ('girl' has a CVC pattern as the vowel is the single sound made by the letters IR). In fact, 43 per cent of monosyllables correspond to this pattern (De Cara and Goswami, 2002). English also has many CCVC monosyllables ('skip', 'pram', 'black'; 15 per cent of monosyllables), CVCC monosyllables ('past', 'bump', 'build'; 21 per cent of monosyllables), and CCVCC monosyllables ('crust', 'stamp', 5 per cent of monosyllables). The CV syllable only represents 5 per cent of English monosyllables ('see', 'go', 'do'). So English is rather different from many languages in terms of the phonological complexity of its syllable structure. English has syllables that are comprised of a number of phonemes (e.g., 'stamp' has five phonemes, 'past' has four phonemes). English is not unique, as languages like German, Welsh and Czech also have complex syllables. Note that when the dominant syllable type for the language is CV, a child who is aware of onsets and rimes is also in effect aware of phonemes. A CV syllable has a single-phoneme onset and a single-phoneme rime (e.g., 's-ee', 't-oo', 's-igh'). Note that for English, a CV phonological structure does not necessarily correspond to a CV spelling pattern. So phonological complexity is one cross-language factor that affects the development of phonemic awareness when the alphabet is taught.

ORTHOGRAPHIC CONSISTENCY

Orthographic (spelling) consistency is the other cross-language factor that affects the development of phonological awareness. In many alphabetic languages, there is 1:1 consistency between letters and sounds. The same letter always corresponds to the same sound, or phoneme. Examples of highly consistent writing systems are Finnish, Italian, Spanish, German, Czech and Welsh. Furthermore, some languages have a smaller number of phonemes than others. Finnish has 21 phonemes, and when loan words are considered (i.e., words adopted from other languages, like the word 'pizza' from Italian), it has 25 phonemes. A language like English has 44 phonemes. In other alphabetic languages, there is a 1:many correspondence between letters and sounds. The same letter can correspond to more than one sound. Examples are French, Danish, English and Portuguese. Indeed, for the

English orthography the same letter may correspond to four or more sounds. For example, the letter A makes a different sound in CAP, FATHER, SAW, MAKE and BARE. Although most inconsistency occurs with vowels, it also occurs with consonants (consider G in MAGIC versus BAG, or C in CAKE versus CIRCLE). In fact, the degree of orthographic inconsistency in English is much higher than in other orthographies (Berndt, Reggia, and Mitchum, 1987; Ziegler, Stone, and Jacobs, 1997). So children learning to read in English have to face two barriers that make learning to recode words to sound 'bottom-up' more challenging. They have to learn orthographic patterns for complex syllables that contain lots of different phonemes, and they have to learn these phonemes even though the target sounds that they are learning can be represented by lots of different letters. As phonemes do not have acoustic correlates in the speech stream, the degree of orthographic inconsistency in English is especially problematic.

ACQUIRING READING IN LANGUAGES USING THE ALPHABET

Perhaps unsurprisingly, therefore, English children learn to recode letters to sound fairly slowly in comparison to children who are learning to read other languages. The term 'phonological recoding' is frequently used to refer to the efficient and automatic mapping of print to sound (see Share, 1995). Phonological recoding is a critical component of reading development across languages. In orthographically consistent languages with simple syllable structures, phonological recoding is taught very efficiently via systematic phonics instruction. Children are taught the sound made by each letter, they are taught to blend these sounds together, and they learn to recode words to sound. Children learning to read languages with complex syllable structures also acquire phonological recoding skills rapidly once tuition in phonics begins, as long as these languages have high orthographic consistency. As Landerl notes, in most consistent orthographies 'reading is typically taught via a straightforward phonics teaching regime ... [with] heavy emphasis on teaching of letter-sound correspondences' (2000: 240). Given its high utility in other languages, should we then endorse Rose's (2006) claim for English that for English, too, synthetic phonics offers 'the vast majority of beginners the best route to becoming skilled readers' (Rose, 2006: 19)? In our view, the experimental data do not support this claim.

Experimental data suggest instead that phonological recoding in English occurs at more than one linguistic level or 'psycholinguistic grain size'. To become an efficient reader of English, the data suggest that children acquire orthography–phonology connections at the psycholinguistic level of whole words and at the psycholinguistic level of onsets and rimes *as well as* at the psycholinguistic level of the phoneme. One experimental marker of the acquisition of the whole-word grain size is the *pseudohomophone* effect. A pseudohomophone is an item that sounds like a real word, but is not a real word, for example FAIK. If children are faster and more accurate at recoding an item like FAIK to sound than a matched nonword item like DAIK, this is indicative of accessing whole-word phonology. Goswami, Ziegler, Dalton, and Schneider (2001) demonstrated that pseudohomophone effects were stronger for English children than for German children. They gave English and German children with reading ages of 7, 8

and 9 years two types of nonword to read, items like DAIK and items like FAIK. The children were matched for their ability to read the real words that were used as a basis for the pseudohomophones. The two types of nonword were matched within-language for orthographic familiarity. Goswami et al. (2001) found that while German children read aloud items like DAIK as fast and as accurately as items like FAIK, English children were significantly more accurate at reading aloud the pseudohomophones (FAIK) than the control items (DAIK). However, the opposite happened when the children had to make a 'lexical decision' about whether items like FAIK and DAIK were real words or not. When recoding to sound was not involved, the English children performed better. They found it easy to reject items like FAIK very quickly, whereas the German children struggled. Goswami et al. (2001) suggested that this was because the English children had learned about specific orthography–phonology connections at the word level. They knew that orthographic patterns like FAIK were not real words. The German children, who could recode any item to sound very efficiently by using grapheme–phoneme recoding, had not developed these kinds of psycholinguistic units.

An experimental marker for the acquisition of psycholinguistic units at the grain size of the rime is switching costs in nonword reading. Nonwords like DAKE are analogous in spelling at the rime level to many real words (e.g., MAKE, CAKE, BAKE, LAKE). Nonwords like DAIK, which require exactly the same recoding to sound, have no analogies at the rime level – the spelling pattern AIK is not used in English. Goswami, Ziegler, Dalton, and Schneider (2003) devised lists of these two types of nonwords for English versus

German. One list contained familiar ortho-graphic patterns for rimes (DAKE, MURN), while the second did not (DAIK, MIRN). Children who have developed psycholinguistic units for rimes via learn-ing to read real words should find the lists that contained DAKE-type nonwords easy to read aloud, as they can apply a 'rhyme analogy' strategy. They can also, of course, use a synthetic phonics strategy, applying grapheme–phoneme relations (here involv-ing the 'magic e' for DAKE). However, the DAIK-type nonwords can *only* be recoded to sound by using a synthetic phonics strat-egy. Two predictions follow. The first is that if children show an advantage (greater accuracy) in reading nonwords like DAKE than in reading nonwords like DAIK, they must have developed psycholinguistic units at the grain size of the rime. The second is that if the two types of nonword are mixed together in a list (e.g., DAIK, MURN …), then it should slow children down, and perhaps make them more inaccurate as well, because they might try to alternate between a rhyme analogy recoding strat-egy and a synthetic phonics recoding strategy. 7-, 8- and 9-year-old readers in English and German were again tested. The data revealed that blocking word lists by grain size increased recoding accuracy for the English children but not for the German children. Furthermore, switching costs for mixed lists were found for the English children but not for the German children. Goswami et al. (2003) argued that the German children were already relying exclusively on synthetic phonics strategies – that is, they were recoding words to sound at the smallest psycholin-guistic grain size of the phoneme.

One way of thinking about such data is to suggest that children who learn to read English are developing 'phonological recoding' strategies at more than one psycholinguistic grain size. Indeed, Brown and Deavers (1999) suggested that children learning to read in English developed both 'small unit' and 'large unit' strategies in parallel. In our view, these data show that the brain naturally develops this combina-tion of strategies because of the nature of the orthography that it is learning to read, and the complex phonology that this orthography represents. The 'strategies' are not explicit and are not used purposely by children; rather the brain has devel-oped these internal psycholinguistic units on the basis of incremental reading experi-ence of English words. The brain is then naturally faster and more efficient for some kinds of words than for others, and this can be explored using methods from cognitive psychology, such as nonword reading stud-ies. However, 'psycholinguistic grain size theory' (Ziegler and Goswami, 2005) also raises important questions about learning and teaching. For example, do we best teach young children the efficient and automatic mapping of print to sound in English using only one grain size, as in a synthetic phonics approach, or do we try to teach children about rimes and about whole words as well?

PSYCHOLINGUISTIC GRAIN SIZE THEORY: IMPLICATIONS FOR LEARNING

With respect to learning, we can use exist-ing data sets to show that children learning to read English acquire phonological recod-ing skills more slowly than children learn-ing to read in other alphabetic languages. For example, a large-scale and carefully controlled cross-language reading study reported by Seymour, Aro, and Erskine (2003) involved participating scientists from 14 European Community countries, who developed matched sets of items of simple real words (BALL, BOY) and nonwords (DEM, FIP) for use across these 14 languages. The items were given to children from each country during their first year of reading instruction (for further details, see Seymour et al., 2003). All participating schools followed a reading instructional programme based on grapheme–phoneme level phonics (the schools contributing the English data were in Scotland). The results of this cross-language study are shown in Table 22.1.

The data show a clear relationship between orthographic consistency and the speed of acquiring efficient and automatic mapping of print to sound. Children who were learning to read languages with consistent spelling systems (such as Greek, Finnish, German, Italian and Spanish) performed at almost ceiling levels, for both word and nonword reading, by the middle of first grade (irrespective of age). English-speaking children performed extremely poorly in their first year of

learning to read (reading 34 per cent of real word items correctly, and 29 per cent of nonword items). Danish children (71 per cent correct), Portuguese children (73 per cent correct), and French children (79 per cent correct) also showed lower levels of accuracy than Greek and Finnish children during the first year of acquisition. This would be expected given the reduced orthographic consistency of these languages. Smaller experimental studies comparing fewer languages have obtained very similar results. For example, when French, Spanish and English are compared, then Spanish children reach ceiling levels much faster than French children, who in turn are faster than English children (Goswami, Gombert, and de Barrera, 1998). When English and German are compared, the German children outperform the English children until the age of around 9–10 years (Frith, Wimmer, and Landerl, 1998).

However, it might be objected that there are many socio-cultural differences across languages which have not been taken into account by cross-language psychology studies such as these. For example, there are likely to be differences in school systems, school curricula, teaching methods and demographic distributions between different countries, and such differences cannot be controlled systematically in experimental cross-language studies.

One way to get around these inherent problems with cross-language studies is to compare beginning reading skills in children who live in the same communities but are learning to read in different languages. English and Welsh provide a good example. Particularly in North Wales, English and Welsh are often spoken and read within the same communities, and there may be two primary schools in such communities, one for Welsh-speakers and one

Table 22.1   Data (% correct) from the large-scale study of reading skills at the end of grade 1 in 14 European languages (adapted from Tables 5 and 6 of Seymour, Aro, and Erskine, 2003)

Language	Familiar real words	Nonwords
Greek	98	92
Finnish	98	95
German	98	94
Austrian German	97	92
Italian	95	89
Spanish	95	89
Swedish	95	88
Dutch	95	82
Icelandic	94	86
Norwegian	92	91
French	79	85
Portuguese	73	77
Danish	71	54
Scottish English	34	29

for English-speakers. These schools will serve the same geographical catchment area, they will be administered by the same local educational authorities, and they will follow similar curricula and teaching approaches. The difference will be in the language of instruction. Both English and Welsh have complex syllable structures, but whereas English has a highly inconsistent orthography, Welsh has a highly consistent orthography. A series of studies by Hanley and his colleagues (Hanley, Masterson, Spencer, and Evans, 2004; Spencer and Hanley, 2003; see also Ellis and Hooper, 2001) have demonstrated that English-speaking children's reading skills develop at the same slow pace in Wales as is found everywhere else. In contrast, Welsh-speaking children learn more like Finnish children. In Hanley's studies, the Welsh-speaking children read more than twice as many words accurately as the English-speaking children after the same amount of reading instruction. After 3 years of reading instruction, the English children 'caught up'. Again, this mirrors the results found in the other cross-language studies that have been discussed. The slow rate of learning of the English children is only temporary. After around 3 or 4 years of reading instruction, they are indistinguishable in reading achievement from children who have learned to read orthographically consistent languages.

Psycholinguistic grain size theory accounts for the developmental sequence of phonological awareness across languages, and for initial differences in learning spelling–sound correspondences. In spite of differences in the phonological and orthographic structure of words in different languages, the developmental sequence for phonological awareness is the same: early sensitivity to larger phonological units and subsequent awareness of smaller

phonological units, i.e., syllables, onset-rimes, onset-nucleus-coda, phoneme. For the smallest units (phonemes), orthographic structure affects the speed of learning, with advantages for children learning more transparent orthographies.

The first part of this chapter has mainly addressed children's phonological awareness and understanding of spelling sound correspondences. However although these are important aspects of reading development there are a considerable range of other factors that have to be taken account of when considering how children's development can be supported through teaching. The second half of the chapter addresses some of these factors.

FROM GRAINSIZE IN LEARNING TO CONTEXTS FOR TEACHING

Children naturally encounter written language and the alphabetic code through engagement with texts. These texts are often only single words, for example the child's name, or short phrases, for example packaging and signs, but children are also likely to encounter written language in books. The context that surrounds the reading of a book, often a story book, is of prime importance to scholars working in the socio-cultural educational tradition. One aspect of this is the nature of the text itself. For example, the controlled vocabulary of a reading scheme book or basal reader will lead to a rather different experience for the child than an encounter with a 'trade' book written by an author with the intent of engaging young readers (Levy, 2009). This is one of the reasons that Meek argued that *Texts Teach What Readers Learn* (Meek, 1988).

An important aspect of children's encounters with texts is the extent to which children are motivated and interested to engage with them. Evidence about the nature of young children's interest in language and literacy learning has come from ethnographic case studies of individual children (e.g., Bissex, 1980) but also from studies of early-years settings (Harste, Woodward, and Burke, 1984) which have revealed the creative ways that young children engage with language and literacy. Research has also shown the disparities that exist between literacy in formal educational settings and home literacy, including children's motivation for different kinds of texts than those preferred in formal educational settings (Marsh, 2003; Wells, 1986). Wigfield and Guthrie (1997) found that children's reading motivation predicted the amount and breadth of their reading. They also found that intrinsic motivation predicted more strongly amount and breadth than extrinsic motivation. The implications from a range of studies point to the importance of encouraging children's motivation, for example by providing texts that are likely to interest them. However, there is of course a dilemma in relation to intrinsic motivation. When does encouragement to read by teachers become extrinsic motivation? This implies a subtle balanced between the *requirement* to read, and *encouragement* to read.

Once appropriate texts have been selected by the teacher in order to motivate children and to best support their development of reading (taking due account of children's interests) there is a need to understand the nature of the 'interaction' between text and reader. Rosenblatt (1985) theorised the idea of *transaction* to explain what happens between reader and text. Reading is a two-way process that includes the processes of decoding and literal interpretation that flow from text to reader, but also the reader bringing their experiences,

knowledge and understandings that flow from reader to textual interpretation. As Rosenblatt says, 'we need to see the reading act as an event involving a particular individual and a particular text, happening at a particular time, under particular circumstances, in a particular social and cultural setting, and as part of the ongoing life of the individual and the group' (1985: 100). Rosenblatt argued that her notion of the transaction was not the same as the separation of text and reader that is a feature of some cognitive views of transaction, including information processing models, because of the decontextualisation of processes that she felt was a feature of such models.

The idea of reading embedded in a social and cultural setting is also of central concern to scholars in the *new literacies* tradition. Prior to the 1970s the word 'literacy' was not typically used in relation to schooling in the countries of the West; reading and writing were the preferred terms. But increasingly politicians and policy-makers began to talk about crises in relation to levels of literacy. At the same time sociocultural work on the study of language was increasingly focusing on literacy (Lanksheare and Knobel, 2006). A classic line of thinking in the new literacies tradition was portrayed by the New London Group's (NLG) concept of *multiliteracies*. In particular the NLG recommended a new pedagogy based on *situated practice*, *overt instruction* (of a nontraditional kind to include a metalanguage of *design*) *critical framing*, and *transformed practice*. Their position was built on the idea that traditional pedagogy represents 'page-bound, official, standard ... formalized, monolingual, monocultural, and rule governed forms of language' (New London Group, 1996: 61). The NLG's contribution to understanding of literacy pedagogy was in three main areas: 1) a necessary emphasis on cultural and linguistic diversity; 2) the recognition of local diversity interacting with global connectedness; and 3) the idea of *situated practice* that included the important concept of a community of learners. The NLG were critical of what they called 'mere literacy' that they claim involves a focus on language only, based on rules and correct usage that leads to 'more or less authoritarian pedagogy' (1996: 64).

Working in the *new literacies* tradition, Street (2003) argued that there was an important additional distinction to be made between *autonomous* and *ideological* models of literacy. Autonomous models assume that the improvement of literacy, for example in economically disadvantaged groups of people, will automatically lead to societal and material advancement. Ideological models require consideration of the social and economic conditions that led to disadvantage in the first place. Street also makes a distinction between literacy *events* and literacy *practices*. A literacy event takes place when written language is integral to the participants' interactions. Literacy practices account for literacy events but also add the social models of literacy that are brought to bear by participants. Literacy practices in this sense share some of the features of Rosenblatt's (1985) transactions.

READING PEDAGOGY AND POLICY

For teachers the socio-cultural context for texts and transactions is the professional one. It is in the professional context where the pedagogies that teachers might adopt, including reading teaching, are mediated by policy, and the early-years curriculum is an area that continues to be strongly

affected by policy. Policy in many countries in the last 20 years has increasingly located reading within drives to improve literacy. But where policy makers have often reduced the complexities of reading to a limited focus on literacy, socio-cultural educational work has provided critiques of such foci.

In spite of the promising lines of research and theory on the place of phonological awareness and alphabetic knowledge in learning to read, and the appropriate context for such learning, educational policy in many countries fails to adequately reflect such developments. In particular policy seems to favour simple and narrow forms of instruction in favour of approaches that build on the kind of research and theory reviewed in this chapter. Typically the complexities of grainsize and the contexts for text transactions are reduced to a debate about a bottom-up approach such as synthetic phonics. Brief examples from the US, Australia and England illustrate this.

In the United States the National Reading Panel (NRP) (National Institute of Child Health and Human Development, 2000) concluded that reading teaching should not focus too much on the teaching of letter-sound relations at the expense of the application of this knowledge in the context of reading texts. Also that phonics should not become the dominant component in a reading program, so educators 'must keep the end in mind and insure that children understand the purpose of learning letter-sounds' (2000: 2–96). The importance of the cautions about phonics becoming a dominant component are given added weight if we consider the findings of Camilli, Vargas, and Yurecko (2003). Camilli et al. replicated the meta-analysis from the NRP phonics instruction report and found a smaller but still significant effect for systematic phonics ($d = 0.24$)

than the NRP but also found an effect for systematic language activities ($d = 0.29$) and an effect for individual tutoring ($d = 0.40$). Hence the effect for individual tutoring was larger than the effect for systematic phonics and that the effect for systematic language activities was slightly larger but comparable with that for systematic phonics. These findings resulted in their conclusion that 'systematic phonics instruction when combined with language activities and individual tutoring may *triple* the effect of phonics alone'. (Camilli et al. 2003).

Unfortunately the conclusions of the NRP and Camilli et al. seem not have been sufficiently reflected in policy on reading pedagogy in the US. Policy on the teaching of reading became strongly influenced by federal government through the legislation of *No Child Left Behind*. Phonics instruction frequently received more attention than other important aspects of reading pedagogy sometimes *in extremis* (Cummins, 2007). Allington (2010) argues that federal education policy adopted a narrow, ideologically defined notion of 'scientifically-based reliable, replicable' reading research (SBRR). This determined the kind of reading pedagogy that states had to implement in order to receive federal funding. However, as shown in this chapter, scientifically-based reliable and replicable reading research is much broader than synthetic phonics. To date there is no compelling evidence that reading standards have improved as a result of the No Child Left Behind (NCLB) legislation and the narrow definition of SBRR. In fact, there is some evidence of NCLB leading to more limited reading curricula and to decreased curricular and instructional coherence (Allington, 2010)

The difficulties of maintaining research informed reading pedagogy in the context of policy formation and implementation are also revealed in Australia. The Commonwealth government in Australia carried out a review of research on literacy, influenced by the work of the NRP, but effectively restricted its focus to the teaching of reading. Although the report recommended that 'teachers [should] provide an integrated approach to reading that supports the development of oral language, vocabulary, grammar, reading fluency, comprehension and the literacies of new technologies'. (Australian Government DEST, 2005: 14) and 'no one approach of itself can address the complex nature of reading difficulties. An integrated approach requires that teachers have a thorough understanding of a range of effective strategies, as well as knowing when and why to apply them' (Australian Government DEST, 2005). Sawyer (2010) argues that the synthetic phonics approach was foregrounded and particularly favoured by the report. Of particular concern to Sawyer was the use of the study by Johnston and Watson (2005) as the basis for the suggestion in the report that the case for synthetic phonics was clearly proven, whereas the research showing the significance of balanced reading instruction was 'assertion'.

In 2006, concerns expressed by many in education that England's *National Literacy Strategy* (NLS) approach to reading teaching (implemented from 1997 to 2010) was not working (ironically from both synthetic phonics advocates and from those committed to a more balanced approach to the teaching of reading) led to a government-commissioned review into the teaching of early reading in England. It was hoped that this might result in a more rigorous analysis of research evidence as the basis for policy concerning how to improve reading teaching. This unfortunately was not the case. The outcome of the review was the decision to prescribe synthetic phonics as the sole method for teaching reading, something that caused controversy (Ellis, 2007; Gouch and Lambirth, 2008; Kershner and Howard, 2006; Lewis and Ellis, 2006; Wyse and Styles, 2007). As Wyse and Goswami (2008) pointed out, the report did not draw sufficiently upon the large amount of high-quality research evidence available about the teaching of reading and phonological awareness.

Wyse, Andrews, and Hoffman (2010) summarise what they see as a pattern in the kinds of policy responses to the teaching of reading described above. First, a dubious characterisation by politicians that education is failing, followed by 'decisive' action giving a reason for greater centralisation as the government 'takes responsibility' for improving performance; then the inevitable increase in a battery of measures to gauge progress and the impact of curricular interventions ('high-stakes testing'); a gradual seeping in of pedagogical control as well as curricular control, leading to loss of teacher autonomy and agency. Such control eventually becomes unworkable, uninspiring, and ceases to provide the results it is intended to deliver; and so a reaction sets in, freeing up teachers to have more agency within what and how they teach; allowing more space for creativity across the whole English and language curriculum; making the curriculum more closely related to the outside world. Perry, Amadeo, Fletcher, and Walker's (2010) work confirms the gap between evidence and policy making, the politicisation of decisions on pedagogy, the speed of policy change, and the role of the media in exacerbating some of these problems. Moss and Huxford (2007) suggested that a focus by researchers on understanding the contexts of policy enactment, more than 'finding new content for policy to convey'

(2007: 72), would be a helpful way forward, yet in spite of some researchers' direct engagement with government on policy implementation and their understanding of the contexts of policy enactment, the problems with politicisation and lack of attention to the full range of evidence remain, suggesting different problems such as increasing political control of education (see Wyse, 2011).

CONCLUSION

Scientifically based and reliable research on how to teach the reading of English supports the direct teaching of all relevant psycholinguistic grain sizes. Larger units are important, and for all psycholinguistic grain sizes children need to see how the decoding of letters is related to the comprehension and understanding of text. Wyse and Goswami (2008) and Wyse (2010) review evidence from experimental trials comparing different teaching approaches to examine the empirical case for the approach they call contextualised phonics teaching.

While new literacy theory accurately identifies the risks of politically motivated authoritarian pedagogy there is a need for development of this idea and its consequences. New literacy theory could be enhanced through an interdisciplinary analysis of socio-cultural *and* psychological/cognitive work. This would entail more rigorous attention to the links between teaching at the micro level, for example the alphabetic code, and teaching at the macro level, for example the transactions between readers and texts. The benefits of this approach are enhanced theory, a stronger empirical case to challenge narrowly-focused visions of literacy, and a rationale for innovative research-based practice.

Street (2003) argued that 'The next stage of work in this area is to move beyond [these] theoretical critiques and to develop positive proposals for interventions in teaching, curriculum, measurement criteria, and teacher education in both the formal and informal sectors, based upon these principles' (2003: 82). An example of such practice from Queensland Australia was given by Street, but since that paper was written, government policy in Australia appears to have changed. Currently, there are movements away from the theory of new literacy studies as an influence on policy and practice (see Sawyer, 2010). This is part of a continuing trend internationally, seen particularly in the US, the UK, Australia and New Zealand, to more instrumental or autonomous forms of literacy.

Over the past 20 years research evidence has accumulated to show the important role of phonological awareness in learning to read. One of the implications of this research has been greater emphasis on the teaching of phonics as part of early reading teaching. It has also been theorised that this emphasis in teaching should differ according to the language that is being learned. Supporting children's development of phonological awareness, and teaching them about the alphabetic code, is one important part of reading teaching. However, teachers have to engage with a number of other important aspects if they are to support children's development as readers most effectively. One of these aspects concerns texts, and the contexts and ways in which children engage with texts. But the teaching of reading also has to be understood in the wider pedagogical context that requires the teaching of English, language *and* literacy. The pedagogical context is subject to influences from research but also from the political domain of educational policy that increasingly affects the ways in which teachers can teach. No matter how good the research and scholarship on the development of reading is, it will not be realised in practice unless educational policy-making attends to the full range of rigorous scholarly work.

REFERENCES

Allington, R. (2010). 'Recent federal education policy in the United States', in D. Wyse, R. Andrews, and J. Hoffman (eds), *The Routledge International Handbook of English, Language and Literacy Teaching*. (pp. 496–507). London: Routledge.

Australian Government DEST (Department of Education Science and Training) (2005). *Teaching Reading. Report and Recommendations. National Enquiry into the Teaching of Literacy.* Barton, Australia: Department of Education, Science and Training.

Berndt, R.S., Reggia, J.A., and Mitchum, C.C. (1987). 'Empirically derived probabilities for grapheme-to-phoneme correspondences in English', *Behavior Research Methods, Instruments, & Computers*, 19: 1–9.

Bissex, G. (1980). *Gnys at Wrk: A Child Learns to Read and Write.* Cambridge, MA: Harvard University Press.

Bradley, L. and Bryant, P.E. (1983). 'Categorising sounds and learning to read: A causal connection', *Nature*, 310: 419–21.

Brown, G.D.A. and Deavers, R.P. (1999). 'Units of analysis in nonword reading: Evidence from children and adults', *Journal of Experimental Child Psychology*, 73(3): 208–42.

Bryant, P.E., Bradley, L., MacLean, M., and Crossland, J. (1989). 'Nursery rhymes, phonological skills and reading', *Journal of Child Language*, 16: 407–28.

Camilli, G., Vargas, S., and Yurecko, M. (2003). 'Teaching children to read: The fragile link between science and federal education policy', *Education Policy Analysis Archives*, 11(15). Retrieved 1 March 2006, from http://epaa.asu.edu/epaa/v11n15/

Chukovsky, K. (1963). *From Two to Five.* Berkeley, CA: University of California Press.

Cummins, J. (2007). 'Pedagogies for the poor? Realigning reading instruction for low-income students with scientifically based reading instruction', *Educational Researcher*, 36(9): 564–72.

Davis, S. (1989). 'On a non-argument for the rhyme', *Journal of Linguistics*, 25(1): 211–17.

De Cara, B., and Goswami, U. (2002). 'Statistical analysis of similarity relations among spoken words: Evidence for the special status of rimes in English', *Behavioural Research Methods and Instrumentation*, 34(3): 416–23.

Echols, C. (1996). 'A role for stress in early speech segmentation', in J.L. Morgan and K. Demuth (eds), *Bootstrapping from Speech to Grammar in Early Acquisition*. (pp. 151–70). Mahwah, NJ: Lawrence Erlbaum Associates.

Ellis, S. (2007). 'Policy and research: Lessons from the Clackmannanshire synthetic phonics initiative', *Journal of Early Childhood Literacy*, 7(3): 281–97.

Ellis, N.C. and Hooper, A.M. (2001). 'Why learning to read is easier in Welsh than in English: Orthographic transparency effects evinced with frequency-matched tests', *Applied Psycholinguistics*, 22: 571–99.

Frith, U., Wimmer, H., and Landerl, K. (1998). 'Differences in phonological recoding in German- and English-speaking children', *Scientific Studies of Reading*, 2(1): 31–54.

Goody, J., and Watt, I. (1963). The consequences of literacy', *Comparative Studies in Society and History*, 5(3): 304–45.

Goswami, U., Gombert, J.E., and de Barrera, L.F. (1998). 'Children's orthographic representations and linguistic transparency: Nonsense word reading in English, French, and Spanish', *Applied Psycholinguistics*, 19(1): 19–52.

Goswami, U., Ziegler, J.C., Dalton, L., and Schneider, W. (2001). 'Pseudohomophone effects and phonological recoding procedures in reading development in English and German', *Journal of Memory & Language*, 45(4): 648–64.

Goswami, U., Ziegler, J.C., Dalton, L., and Schneider, W. (2003). 'Nonword reading across orthographies: How flexible is the choice of reading units?' *Applied Psycholinguistics*, 24: 235–47.

Gouch, K. and Lambirth, A. (2008). *Understanding Phonics and the Teaching of Reading: Critical Perspectives*. Maidenhead: McGraw-Hill/Open University Press.

Hanley, J.R., Masterson, J., Spencer, L.H., and Evans, D. (2004). 'How long do the advantages of learning a transparent orthography last? An investigation of the reading skills and reading impairment of Welsh children at 10 years of age', *Quarterly Journal of Experimental Psychology*, 57(8): 1393–410.

Harris, R. (1986). *The Origin of Writing*. London: Duckworth.

Harste, J.C., Woodward, V.A., and Burke, C.L. (1984). *Language Stories and Literacy Lessons*. Portsmouth, NH: Heinemann Educational Books.

Ho, C.S.-H. and Bryant, P. (1997). 'Phonological skills are important in learning to read Chinese', *Developmental Psychology*, 33: 946–51.

Johnston, R. and Watson, J. (2005). The Effects of Synthetic Phonics Teaching of Reading and Spelling attainment: A Seven Year Longitudinal Study. Retrieved 10 December, 2006, from http://www.scotland.gov.uk/Resource/Doc/36496/0023582.pdf

Kershner, R. and Howard, J. (2006). *The Psychology of Education Review*, 30(2): 1–60.

Landerl, K. (2000). 'Influences of orthographic consistency and reading instruction on the development of nonword reading skills', *European Journal of Psychology of Education*, 15: 239–57.

Lanksheare, C. and Knobel, M. (2006). *New Literacies: Everyday Practices and Classroom Learning*. Maidenhead: Open University Press.

Levy, R. (2009). 'Children's perceptions of reading and the use of reading scheme texts', *Cambridge Journal of Education*, 39(3): 361–77.

Lewis, M. and Ellis, S. (eds). (2006). *Phonics: Practice Research and Policy*. London: Paul Chapman Publishing.

Liberman, I.Y., Shankweiler, D., Fischer, F.W., and Carter, B. (1974). 'Explicit syllable and phoneme segmentation in the young child', *Journal of Experimental Child Psychology*, 18: 201–12.

Marsh, J. (2003). 'One way traffic? Connections between literacy practices at home and in the nursery', *British Educational Research Journal*, 29(3) 370–82.

Meek, M. (1988). *How Texts Teach what Readers Learn*. Stroud: Thimble Press.

Michael, I. (1984). 'Early evidence for whole word methods', in G. Brooks and A.K. Pugh (eds), *Studies in the History of Reading*. Reading: Centre for the Teaching of Reading, University of Reading.

Moss, G. and Huxford, L. (2007). 'Exploring literacy policy making from the inside out', in L. Saunders (ed.), *Educational Research and Policy-Making: Exploring the Border Country between Research and Policy*. London: Routledge.

National Institute of Child Health and Human Development (NICHD) (2000). *Report of the National Reading Panel. Teaching Children to Read: An Evidence-Based Assessment of the Scientific Research Literature on Reading and its Implications for Reading Instruction: Reports of the Subgroups*.

(NIH Publication no. 00-4754). Washington, DC: US Government Printing Office.

New London Group (1996). 'A pedagogy of multiliteracies: Designing social futures', *Harvard Educational Review*, 66(1): 60–93.

Perry, P., Amadeo, C., Fletcher, M., and Walker, E. (2010). *Instinct or Reason: How Education Policy is Made and How we Might Make it Better*. Reading: CfBT Education Trust.

Port, R. (2007). 'How are words stored in memory? Beyond phones and phonemes', *New Ideas in Psychology*, 25: 143–70.

Rose, J. (2006). *Independent Review of the Teaching of Early Reading*. Nottingham: DfES Publications.

Rosenblatt, L. (1985). 'Viewpoints: Transaction versus interaction: A terminological rescue operation', *Research in the Teaching of English*, 19(1): 96–107.

Sawyer, W. (2010). 'English teaching in Australia and New Zealand', in D. Wyse, R. Andrews, and J. Hoffman (eds), *The Routledge International Handbook of English, Language and Literacy Teaching*, (pp. 508–517). London: Routledge.

Seymour, P.H.K., Aro, M., and Erskine, J.M. (2003). 'Foundation literacy acquisition in European orthographies', *British Journal of Psychology*, 94: 143–74.

Share, D.L. (1995). 'Phonological recoding and self-teaching: Sine qua non of reading acquisition', *Cognition*, 55(2): 151–218.

Spencer, L.H. and Hanley, J.R. (2003). 'Effects of orthographic transparency on reading and phoneme awareness in children learning to read in Wales', *British Journal of Psychology*, 94(1): 1–28.

Street, B. (2003). 'What's "new" in new literacy studies? Critical approaches to literacy in theory and practice', *Current Issues in Comparative Education*, 5(2): 1–14.

Treiman, R. and Zukowski, A. (1991). 'Levels of phonological awareness', in S. Brady and D. Shankweiler (eds), *Phonological Processes in Literacy*. Hillsdale, NJ: Erlbaum.

Wells, G. (1986). *The Meaning Makers: Children Learning Language and Using Language to Learn*. London: Hodder and Stoughton.

Wigfield, A. and Guthrie, J. (1997). 'Relations of children's motivation for reading to the amount and breadth of their reading', *Journal of Educational Psychology*, 89(3): 420–32.

Wyse, D. (2010). 'Contextualised phonics teaching', in K. Hall, U. Goswami, C. Harrison, S. Ellis, and J. Soler (eds), *Interdisciplinary Perspectives on Learning to Read: Culture, Cognition and Pedagogy*. London: Routledge.

Wyse, D. (2011). 'The control of language or the language of control? Primary teachers' knowledge in the context of policy', in S. Ellis and E. McCarthy (eds), *Applied Linguistics and the Primary School*. Cambridge: Cambridge University Press.

Wyse, D. and Goswami, U. (2008). 'Synthetic phonics and the teaching of reading', *British Educational Research Journal*, 34(6): 691–710.

Wyse, D. and Styles, M. (2007). 'Synthetic phonics and the teaching of reading: The debate surrounding England's "Rose report"', *Literacy*, 41(1): 35–42.

Wyse, D., Andrews, R., and Hoffman, J. (eds). (2010). *The Routledge International Handbook of English, Language, and Literacy Teaching*. London: Routledge.

Ziegler, J.C. and Goswami, U. (2005). 'Reading acquisition, developmental dyslexia, and skilled reading across languages: A psycholinguistic grain size theory', *Psychological Bulletin*, 131(1): 3–29.

Ziegler, J.C., Stone, G.O., and Jacobs, A.M. (1997). 'What is the pronunciation for -ough and the spelling for u/? A database for computing feedforward and feedback consistency in English', *Behavior Research Methods, Instruments & Computers*, 29(4): 600–18.

23

Young Children's Literary Meaning Making: A Decade of Research 2000–2010

Caitlin McMunn Dooley, Miriam Martinez, and Nancy L. Roser

Literary meaning making is a gateway through which many young children in western cultures enter the world of literacy. In this chapter we review research from the past decade (2000–2010) that provides insights into how young children from preschool to approximately age 8 construct meaning as they read, listen, and respond to literature. This research suggests that the opportunity to participate in literary meaning making is one of the most important experiences contributing to a child's literacy development (e.g., Dooley, 2010; Dooley, Matthews, Matthews, and Champion, 2009; Sipe, 2008; Wohlwend, 2009). Unlike constrained skills, such as the identification of letter-sound relationships or alphabetic knowledge that become less predictive of literacy development as a child becomes an increasingly proficient reader, literary meaning making is unconstrained across a lifetime of reading development (Alexander, 2005/2006; Paris, 2005).

As we define it here, literary meaning making involves constructing meaning in diverse genres including fiction, nonfiction, or poetry. Through interactions with these genres – interactions often guided by proficient adult readers, children have the opportunity to become increasingly proficient in their interactions with authentic texts. These genres are demonstrated in a vast range of reading material, including books, electronic texts, and other digital media. However, for the purposes of this chapter, we focus on book-related (e-book and paper books) interactions to build upon the first edition. In the first edition of this chapter, we reviewed research and inquiries from approximately 1978 to 2000 that shed light on the emergence of young children's literary meaning making with books from ages 4 to 8. In this second edition, we review research findings from the past decade that have extended our understanding of how young construct literary meaning. While meaning making can occur in multiple contexts and with a variety of texts, we bounded our inquiry to include book-related interactions in school contexts to maintain the focus of the chapter and complement other chapters in this handbook. We organize our review using a framework often used in syntheses of research on response to literature – studies focusing on the reader, the text, and the context.

CHANGING THEORIES

Foundational to understanding literary meaning making, Rosenblatt's (1938/1965; 1978/1994) transactional theory of reading made explicit how readers transact with texts to create meaning. Rosenblatt proposed that each reader approaches texts with unique qualities, knowledge, and purposes, and strives to construct meanings with texts that may or may not adhere to an author's intention. Rosenblatt suggested that readers seek meanings that are socially compatible – or, in other words, seem to adhere to some constellation of socially constructed meanings; however, no two readers will create exactly the same meaning. While reader-response theory continues to provide the framework for current research on literary meaning making, in the past decade additional theoretical lenses have been used to explore literary response including Vygotsky's (1978) sociocultural theory and critical perspectives on literacy, discourse, gender, class, and race.

THE READER

The extensive research of Sipe and his colleagues (Sipe, 2001, 2006; Sipe and Bauer, 2001; Sipe and Brightman, 2005, 2006, 2008, 2009) conducted over the past decade and synthesized in Sipe's book *Storytime: Young Children's Literary Understanding in the Classroom* (2008), has revealed the potential complexity of young children's literary meaning making in the context of picturebooks. Analyzing the responses of children ages 5 through 8 (kindergarten through grade 2), Sipe (2008) identified five distinct types of responses contributed by his subjects: 1 analytical, 2 intertextual, 3 personal, 4 transparent, and 5 performative. Analytical responses, which accounted for 73 per cent of his subjects' responses, provide particularly important insights into children's literary meaning making. According to Sipe (2008), children's analytical responses included those in which they 'discussed the structure and meaning of the verbal text, the illustration sequence; the ways in which the verbal text and pictures related to each other; conventional visual semiotic codes; and the traditional elements of narrative ... as well as narrative techniques' (2008: 85). Character and plot are building blocks of narrative, and Sipe's subjects explored both of these story elements in group storybook discussion. The children worked to understand not only external facets of character but more importantly internal facets such as feelings, thoughts, and motivations. They also spent time working to understand plots and causal relationships within stories. Perhaps of particular significance were those instances in which the children assumed a structural perspective on stories, stepping back from the particular story being shared to offer insights about elements found across stories (e.g., the common use of three in fairy tales). The children also offered thematic and quasi-thematic statements about stories, most typically in response to a teacher's invitation to talk about the message of a story.

While analytical responses accounted for the greatest percentage of responses in Sipe's research, his subjects also engaged in other kinds of literary meaning-making during storybook read-alouds. In their *intertextual* responses, children's focus shifted away from the story being read aloud to a focus on the relationship of the target text to other texts. While these intertextual responses appeared to serve the children in a variety of ways (e.g., making predictions, interpreting character feelings and motivations), some of the intertextual responses served as a means of synthesizing across texts as children attempted to make generalizations and draw conclusions about sets of stories, a type of intertextual response that served as a particularly 'powerful interpretive strategy' (Sipe, 2008: 136).

Sipe described three additional types of response contributed by his subjects that give insights into young children's narrative meaning making. In their *personal responses*, the children linked story characters and events to their own experiences, questioned stories based on their personal experiences, and made text-to-life connections in which they attempted to use stories to better understand life, a type of response that has been associated with the meaning making of older respondents (e.g., McGinley and Kamberelis, 1996). Sipe found *transparent responses* to be relatively rare, but when they occurred, these responses revealed the depth of engagement in story worlds of which young children are capable. Included in this category of response were instances in which children talked to characters in

stories or appeared to become a character and speak in role. Sipe argued that responses of this nature suggested that the children had 'surrendered to the "power of text" (Scholes, 1985) and had a "lived-through experience" (Rosenblatt, 1978/1994)' (Sipe, 2008: 169).

Performative responses were ones in which the text served as a platform for children's creativity as children entered the story world and changed it for their own purposes. This type of response may be akin to the kind of story-based response associated with children's play in dramatic play centers. Sipe (2006) added one further aspect of response that he called *resistance*. Children expressed opposition to texts because of conflicts between their known stories and the stories presented, objections to the author's craft, and evocation of painful realities.

CHILDREN FROM DIVERSE CULTURES

Only in the past decade have researchers started to consider cultural factors that may impact young children's literary meaning making. In a case study focused on a 7-year-old bilingual child's participation in literature discussions, Martinez-Roldán (2003) found that the opportunity to share personal narratives related to stories enabled the child to draw on her funds of knowledge in making narrative meaning. The researcher argued that opportunities to share personal stories may be especially important for children from non-dominant cultures.

Copenhaver-Johnson, Bowman, and Johnson (2007) reported on the responses of 6- and 7-year-old children to books related to race and power. The children were white and African-American. Because the teachers in this investigation believed the classroom had to be a safe place if meaningful conversations about race and power were to occur, they deliberately took a back seat in conversations. Across time they found that in class conversations the children slowly moved away from entrenched cultural notions and began to question positions of white privilege. In conjunction with the research of López-Robertson (2010) and Martinez-Roldán and López-Robertson (1999/2000), the research of Copenhaver-Johnson and her colleagues suggests that even young children are able to assume a critical stance in response to literature.

THE TEXT

The picture storybook remains a mainstay of literature for young children. Nonetheless, there is now a much greater array of genres and texts for children from which to choose. Palinscar and Duke suggest that the 'explosion of texts' (2004: 183) now accessible via the web, the availability of hypertext and hypermedia, and a renewed attention to non-fiction in the early grades have greatly expanded the types of texts available for young children. Concomitantly, in both the design of investigations and the analysis of data, researchers of the past decade appear to have been more attuned to the textual context in which young children respond to literature. Together these studies reveal insights into how children's literary meaning making may be shaped by the text.

MEANING MAKING IN DIVERSE LITERARY FORMATS

The picturebook format

Picturebooks play a prominent role in the literacy lives of many young children.

This literary format is distinctive in that the story (or information) is conveyed through both the verbal and visual sign systems, and research reveals that young children draw on both systems in their literary meaning making. Walsh (2008) described a project which children (all second-language learners) in kindergarten and year one (first grade) engaged in discussions around picture books. They 'read the pictures' as visual texts, developing in the complexity of their responses over the 2 years. The children's responses demonstrated aesthetic and analytic approaches to 'reading pictures' that, in turn, enhanced their understanding of the picture books. In addition, researchers have learned about the wide variety of visuals that appeal to children as they make meaning.

In an investigation of literature discussion in a classroom with 6- and 7-year-olds, Sipe and Brightman (2005) found that illustrations and other visual features such as endpapers were a rich source of information for narrative meaning making during read-alouds. The children drew on pictorial information to make inferences about setting, to better understand various facets of character, and to make and confirm predictions about plot. Sipe's (2008) research has also revealed that young children respond to features of illustration craft including artistic medium and illustrational conventions and codes that convey meaning (e.g., color to convey emotion or line to convey movement).

Similarly, Azripe and Styles (2002) describe the process children go though to make meaning with visual images. They present the question, Is this how [the child] normally and naturally reads images, or have I just taught her how to do it by asking her to look? While there is some chance that children would have attended to visuals on their own, the authors believe that simply by being asked 'What do you see?' they (and the children's teachers) may have prompted children to attend to visual images more closely.

Chapter book format

While not all children under the age of 8 are introduced to the more complex literary format of the chapter book, some do encounter chapter books, most often through read-alouds. Martinez and Roser (2008) conducted three case studies focused on how children used their literary response journals to negotiate the demands of a chapter book read aloud by the classroom teacher. While the three first graders in their study used their journals in somewhat different ways, each appeared to continue to live inside the story world as they wrote in response to the book. The children wrote primarily about the key literary elements of plot and character. Their character responses focused largely on inner facets of character such as character conflicts and feelings and on character relationships. In addition, as they wrote in their journals, the children relied primarily on the strategies of recreating and speculating, strategies with the potential for supporting story understanding.

Diverse genres

Discussing the importance of genre knowledge in reading of proficient readers, Langer (1990) noted that readers 'seek to identify the genre from the moment reading begins and [their] early hypotheses...help shape how they read and the meanings they create' (1990: 232). Increasingly, researchers exploring young children's literary meaning making have attended to genre. Some have chosen to investigate children's responses within particular genres while others have looked at responses across genres.

Shine and Roser (1999) compared the responses of preschoolers to four different genres of picturebook – fantasy, realistic fiction, narrative non-fiction, and poetic stories. The children assumed distinct stances to each of the different genres. They assumed an 'imagining' stance to fantasy, a 'recognizing' stance to realistic fiction, a 'knowing' stance to narrative non-fiction, and an 'appropriating' stance to poetic stories. They further found that genre played a role in the children's selective attention to literary elements and the interpretive strategies they utilized in constructing meaning. The research of Shine and Roser suggests that even very young children are sensitive to differences in genre. In a related study, Elster and Hanauer (2002) looked at elementary aged children's discussions of two literary genres – poetry and stories – and found that the children focused more on features of craft and genre during discussions of poetry than during discussions of stories. By contrast, in discussions of stories the children focused more on what Elster and Hanauer termed text internal meaning (characters and events) and on illustrations.

Postmodern picturebooks

Postmodern picturebooks have proliferated across the past decade. Stories in this challenging sub-genre are often comprised of multi-stranded narratives (from different characters' perspectives and/or from different points in time) and often have non-linear plots. The narrators of postmodern stories frequently address readers directly and comment on their own narration. Intertextuality and parody are also common to postmodern literature (Goldstone and Labbo, 2004). This sub-genre of children's literature presents unique opportunities for gaining insights into children's narrative meaning making because of its complexity.

A number of researchers have investigated young children's encounters with postmodern picturebooks (e.g., Arizpe, 2001; Pantaleo, 2002, 2004). The youngest children studied (ages 6 and 7) responded to Anthony Browne's *Voices in the Park* (2001) (Pantaleo, 2004). Browne's picture storybook presents four intertextual narratives from the perspective of four visitors to a city park. The trajectory of events is non-linear and non-sequential, and the perspectives narrated present a critical view of economic and other social boundaries that segregate the characters. One of nine books used over 10 weeks in Pantaleo's study, *Voices in the Park* was shared with a first grade class over seven read-aloud sessions. Pantaleo found that the children strived to make intratextual connections or 'text-within-the-same-text connections' (2004: 220). In large part, the children did not notice or comment on the parodies or allusions within the text (e.g., the human mother's wolf-shaped shadow; the beggar dressed as Santa Claus). They engaged in interpreting the synergy between images and text presented in the book, often beginning a read-aloud session by searching the images for 'secrets' or visual jokes before allowing Pantaleo to begin reading. Pantaleo (2002) also inspected the responses of 6- and 7-year-olds to a postmodern version of *The Three Pigs* (Wiesner, 2001). She reported that the children were aware of and talked about metafictive devices such as the nonlinear and nonsequential organization and format of the book and the multiple layers of meaning and multiple narratives in both text and illustrations. Pantaleo observed that *The Three Pigs* (like other postmodern

picturebooks) requires readers to have heightened engagement in meaning construction and that her subjects 'rose to the occasion' (2002: 81) as they co-authored the book.

Arizpe (2001) studied the responses of children (ages 8 and 9) to Anthony Browne's *The Tunnel* (1990/1997). This book presents vivid images and scant text to tell a story of Rose, a bookish girl, who crawled through a tunnel to follow her brother, only to find him turned to stone. When she hugs him and her tears fall upon him, he is brought back to life. Arizpe (2001) shared the book with 72 children from three schools in London and Cambridge, UK. She found that the children searched for narrative structure among the pictures. In addition, their familiarity with the text (after repeated readings) increased the depth and dimension of their responses. In analyzing children's responses to the visual images in the book, Arizpe found that children searched for meaning or reference for any perceived symbol. In other words, they sought to interpret visual referents, even unconventional referents, as they searched for narrative structure. The children also used background knowledge of the fairytale genre to piece together the events created through image into a fairy tale. This macro-structural genre knowledge enabled their literary meaning making.

Pantaleo suggested that the 'synergy among the various metafictive devices in *Voices in the Park* creates an overarching indeterminacy in the text and positions the readers in a co-authoring role' (2004: 226). Her point is well taken with respect to postmodern and multimodal texts. As children, and other readers, search for converging meanings among multiple modes and intertextual narratives, they are positioned more and more as active meaning makers.

Mulitmodal (including postmodern) texts necessitate an expansion of interpretive repertoires. Serafini (2010) suggests that these dynamic texts require new research and pedagogy to explore how to broaden the methods and perspectives to guide young readers to stitch together meaning. Children's literary meaning making with postmodern picture books may be important windows to understanding how they navigate the intricacies of multimodal texts.

Informational texts

Informational texts have received much attention in recent years, perhaps in response to Duke's eye-opening study that revealed the paucity of such texts, especially in classrooms serving low-income communities (Duke, 2000). Mallett (2004, 2010) provides important guides for early-grades teachers as they incorporate non-fiction in their classrooms. Yet there are relatively few investigations of young children's responses to informational books.

In the few investigations of young children's meaning making with non-fiction, researchers point out how adept children are at using these texts to explore their worlds. In one qualitative investigation, Mallett (2003) described how children in a Reception class (ages 4–5) investigated babies through real-world observation and non-fiction texts, culminating in each child making his/her own book about babies. Heller (2006) documented the responses of four first graders (ages 6–7) to informational books. The children were participants in a classroom book club. Heller's analysis of oral and written responses revealed that the children expressed both aesthetic and efferent responses to the informational books shared in book club. Many of the children's aesthetic responses were expressed non-verbally through body language, laughter, facial expressions, and gestures. The children responded verbally by telling both personal and fictional narratives and by 'talking facts' (2006: 365) (e.g., retelling, sharing intertextual connections, thinking critically, posing questions).

Likewise, Tower (2002) investigated the responses of 4- and 5-year-olds to non-narrative informational picturebooks during small group read-alouds and during group emergent readings of the books. As the children participated in discussions, they interacted with the books largely by identifying and describing objects and events, by connecting information to their own lives, and by drawing conclusions based on information in the books as well as their own knowledge of the world. Of particular note was the children's reliance on illustration information in their meaning making. While the children did draw on information presented through text, in large part, their discussions drew heavily on information presented through illustrations. Tower concluded that 'the children in this study responded to the texts they heard in ways that indicate they were attuned to particular characteristics of those texts that marked genre and purpose' (2002: 79).

E-texts

The newest text-types available to young children are e-texts, such as e-books available on computers, digital reading devices, and other platforms. Digital texts can transform reading, and thus meaning making, because of their capacity to integrate multiple modes by which a reader can construct meaning (Korat and Shamir, 2006). Meaning making is enhanced by electronic texts and media, especially when the media converge on shared concepts or narratives (Bus and Neuman, 2009; Walsh, 2006). Most relevant to young children's literary meaning making, CD-ROM talking books have been investigated as potentially beneficial texts for reader response. Labbo and Kuhn (2000) investigated a young child's understanding of story after interacting with a CD-ROM storybook and found that the multimodal features could become 'inconsiderate' to young readers. These features distracted children when they were incongruent or incidental to the story. Their findings echo Bus and Neuman's (2009) recommendation that digital texts present stories in coherent ways so that children can retell the story and respond to the text as a story. They warn that the 'extra' games and animations that accompany 'Living Books' sometimes fragment the story simply through gadgetry and cause children to become passive witnesses to these text-like novelties rather than engage them in the story world.

More recently, Larson (2010) studied how 17 children in a second-grade classroom (7- and 8-year-olds) responded to reading using a Kindle digital reading device. She focused her analysis on observations of two girls who partnered to read *Friendship According to Humphrey* by Betty G. Birney (2006) for 40 minutes daily. Larson found that both girls enjoyed using the digital devices to read and the digital note-taking devices prompted their responses to reading. Larson categorized their responses as: 1 understanding of story (e.g., retelling); 2 personal meaning making; 3 questioning; 4 answering questions posed in the text; and 5 response to literary features/literary evaluation. While both girls engaged in all types of responses, most of their responses were in categories 1 (understanding the story) and 2 (personal meaning making). Both girls reported that they enjoyed reading the Kindle e-book more than hard-copy books, though neither liked the 'text-to-speech' feature because of the computer-like voice.

Perhaps because of their newness, technologies related to early childhood literacy development are vastly under-researched (Marsh, 2004). The studies of digital tools that do exist rarely focus on interpretive forms of meaning making. Yet, this is truly a 'great frontier' for research on literary meaning making given the integral relationship between technology and literacy (Marsh and Singleton, 2009). Technological tools like e-books, computers, cell phones, and other devices are changing the face of what 'books' and 'stories' look like at a pace faster than ever before. Along with these changes, researchers are trying to understand how (and perhaps whether) digital integration of modalities (image, print, sound, voice, etc.) presents a new frontier for theory development. Certainly picture books are the original 'integrated' text – pairing image and print to convey meaning. Yet, contemporary texts increasingly contain hypertext, video, music, graphic design, and images. Walsh (2006, 2007) detailed the differences between print-based and multimodal texts, suggesting that visual images and design elements (such as positioning, frames, menus, and links) within multimodal texts create a vastly different experience for readers as they make meaning. As Serafini (2010) observed, 'readers in today's world need new skills and strategies for constructing meaning in transaction with these multimodal texts as they are encountered during the social practices of interpretation and representation' (2010: 87).

THE (SCHOOL) CONTEXT

Researchers investigate meaning making in many contexts – including homes, communities, places of worship, and schools. We focus on school contexts in this section to explain how teachers and playful school environments can support young children's literary meaning making.

Teacher support

Researchers across the past decade have looked closely at ways in which teachers' language, strategies, and pedagogies shape and support children's literary meaning making. Maloch and her colleagues (2008) studied the interactions of two teachers and their 8- and 9-year-old students over the course of a 6-week fantasy unit. Focusing on the talk that occurred, the researchers identified three discursive moves that the teachers made to support students' understandings: 1 evoking and reframing shared experiences with texts; 2 revoicing students' contributions as a way of focusing and deepening insights; and 3 strengthening familiarity with the literary genre by moving student talk between abstractions and specifics (and back again).

Because of their length and potential complexity, chapter books are likely to present distinctive challenges to young readers. In their study of how one first-grade teacher helped children navigate their first experience with a chapter book, Fuhrken, McDonnold, Martinez, and Roser, (2005) identified a number of different moves the teacher used to support the children's meaning making: 1 encouraging a speculative stance; 2 emphasizing important content; 3 inviting into the story world; 4 modeling responsive reading; and 5 threading across content. In addition, the researchers described how the teacher helped the children focus on character (traits, intentions, needs and behaviors) as a way to both engage with the text and sort out the plot. The researchers argued that 'the "care-actors" in stories cause us to care about what happens to them… and while we linger – reflecting on their traits, mulling their relationships, gauging their development, or even weighing their goals – we find ourselves reading more deeply' (Roser, Martinez, Fuhrken, and McDonnold, 2007: 548).

Elster and Hanauer (2002) described the ways in which 10 teachers shared poetry and stories with their students (ages 5–9). While the teachers used many common strategies to engage children across the two genres, the sharing of poetry was overall a more participatory experience. In particular, the teachers in this study promoted involvement with poetry by reading expressively, by rereading poems, and by inviting children to read along or act out poems. They observed that the immediate rereading of poems served as a means of promoting children's participation in the poetry reading and of highlighting the form or meaning of words within the poem. In addition, the teachers invited open ended, aesthetically-oriented discussions of poems, as well as discussion of language forms (e.g., rhythm, rhyme, imagery).

In his research, Sipe (2008) found that the language of instruction impacted children's meaning making. He reported that the teachers in whose classroom he collected data tended to use literary terminology with their students (e.g., endpages, double-page spread). The children in these classrooms picked up and used this same terminology which, in turn, focused their attention on these textual features. In effect, because their teachers introduced the language of literature in book discussions, the children in Sipe's studies appeared to more readily examine picturebooks with an eye toward craft.

Multicultural children's literature has long been of primary importance to early childhood educators. Souto-Manning (2009) described how multicultural literature, and children's responses to that literature, can be transformative to learning and enable culturally responsive pedagogy. Souto-Manning's teacher research study of her own first-grade class demonstrates how children's literary meaning making, their connections to texts and inquiry of multiple perspectives presented across texts, perpetuated their critical examination of their own classroom. This group of 19 students recognized similarities in their own pull-out programs (for ESOL (English for speakers of other languages), special education, gifted and talented, reading support) segregated them by race much like books about the civil rights movement showed segregated spaces. Their literary meaning making moved them, along with their teacher, to advocate for a 'push in' model in which resource teachers would visit their classroom and serve any child in need. Souto-Manning's study presents the transformative possibilities of young children's deep literary meaning making,

Similarly, Quintero (2009) observes that a 'problem-posing method of critical literacy encourages students to experience and make conscious the transformations that often occur through the reading of and reflection on literature' (2009: 84). She encourages teachers to explore multicultural texts with their students, revealing and discussing cultural inaccuracies, investigating controversial topics, and discovering relevance to their own lives and languages.

Quintero describes lessons in which student teachers integrated literature into 'problem-posing' curricular framework to encourage children's reflections and engagements (aesthetic and efferent) by way of centers, discussions, demonstrations, interactive read alouds, writing, and other activities.

May (2011) elicits the notion of 'animating' to explain how a teacher of 8–10-year-olds shared multicultural non-fiction literature in a culturally responsive way. This 2-year ethnographic study of a southwest US classroom of mostly Mexican-American children concluded that when teachers read aloud or repeat and paraphrase others' words, they are animating those words. The teacher in this classroom used multiple opportunities to ask questions, add related information, elicit personal narratives, and restate children's questions and statements to assist in the creation of meaning making. In each interaction, the teacher reinforced the students' position as sense makers.

Play as pedagogy

Studies of literary meaning making that span into younger ages (especially age 4 and younger) emphasize the need for pretend play as a 'nexus of practice' (Wohlwend, 2008a) for reading, writing, and responding. Thus, we would be remiss if we did not emphasize play as pedagogy here. However, many advocates of play resist the notion that the object of play would be something as academic as literary meaning making (Roskos, Christie, Widman, and Holding, 2010). Nonetheless, we agree with Wohlwend (2008a, 2008b, 2009) that playful interactions allow children to piece together the modes that make story lives live. Play allows for literate performances (Sipe, 2000, 2006) that translate image, gaze, gesture, movement, music, speech, and sound-effect into stories that often mimic stories read and told (Adomat, 2010; Siegel, 2006). Morrow and Gambrell (2004) suggest that preschool children practice 'creative storytelling' with props, chalk talks, recorded stories, electronic storybooks, flannel boards, music and sound effects. In these ways, children enact what Langer (1995) would have called 'being in' the story world.

CONCLUSION

Research over the past decade has revealed young children's potential for engaging in complex literary meaning making across a range of text types, especially with the support of adult mediators who step into the role of literary curator (Eeds and Peterson, 1991). Yet ironically changes in policy over the past decade have too often impeded the ability for teachers and children to engage in deep literary discussions (Rosenblatt, 2002). These policies require 'covering' standards that risk fragmenting knowledge into minute details that lack context and interdisciplinary connections. These policies require multiple-choice tests that focus on low-level skills and ignore the importance of personal meaning making.

In addition, emphasis on and frequent use of reading assessments in the early grades has grown exponentially in the past 25 years (Paris and Hoffman, 2004). Though more than 100 tests are available to test more than 200 early literacy skills, Meisels and Piker (2000) found that only 14 per cent of the tests showed evidence of moderate to good reliability. Most standardized tests for K-3 disregard literary meaning making as a measurable outcome.

Even tests of comprehension are difficult to find at these early grade levels. New tests of narrative comprehension (e.g., Paris and Paris, 2003) provide one example of how literary meaning making might be integrated into an assessable format. Not surprisingly, early grade teachers find informal measures that they design and embed in curricula to be much more informative than standardized measures (Paris and Hoffman, 2004), yet they also report feeling much pressure to 'teach to the test' which means teaching low-level skills.

The next decade promises advances in research, pedagogy, and practice. We also hope for improved understandings of the effects of early development on young children's progress as meaning makers; improved performance assessments that teachers can use to gauge instruction and student progress; improved access to various text types for children in schools and homes, especially for low-income communities; and improved understandings about how families and teachers might construct experiences that best facilitate children's literary meaning making, through talk and other modalities; improved digital tools that elicit young children's literary meaning making; and improved research and pedagogy, especially for children who are learning English as a second language or have disabilities.

REFERENCES

Adomat, D. S. (2010). 'Dramatic interpretations: Performative responses of young children to picturebook read alouds', *Children's Literature in Education*, 41(3): 207–21. doi:10/1598/RT.62.8.1

Alexander, P. A. (2005/2006). 'The path to competence: A lifespan developmental perspective on reading', *Journal of Literacy Research*, 37, 413–36. doi:10.1207/s15548430jlr3704_1

Arizpe, E. (2001). '"Letting the story out": Visual encounters with Anthony Browne's *The Tunnel*. *Reading: Literacy and Language*, 35(3): 115–19. doi:10.1111/1467-9345.00173

Azripe, E. and Styles, M. (2002). *Children Reading Pictures: Interpreting Visual Texts*. London: Routledge-Falmer.

Bus, A. G. and Neuman, S. B. (2009). *Multimedia and Literacy Development: Improving Achievement for Young Learners*. New York: Routledge.

Copenhaver-Johnson, J., Bowman, J., and Johnson, A. (2007). 'Santa stories: Children's inquiry about race during picturebook read-alouds', *Language Arts*, 84(3): 234–44.

Dooley, C. M. (2010). 'Young children's approaches to books: The emergence of comprehension', *The Reading Teacher*, 64(2): 120–30. doi:10.1598/RT.64.2.4

Dooley, C. M., Matthews, M. W., Matthews, L., and Champion, R. N. (2009). 'Emergent comprehension: The role of intentions during early print experiences', *National Reading Conference Yearbook*, 58: 261–76.

Duke, N. K. (2000). '3.6 minutes per day: The scarcity of informational texts in first grade', *Reading Research Quarterly*, 35: 202–24. doi:10.1598/RRQ.35.2.1

Eeds, M. and Peterson, R. (1991). 'Teacher as curator: Learning to talk about literature', *The Reading Teacher*, 45: 118–26.

Elster, C. A. and Hanauer, D. I. (2002). Voicing texts, voices around texts: Reading poems in elementary school classrooms', *Research in the Teaching of English*, 37(1): 89–134. doi: 10.2307/j50000352

Goldstone, B. P. and Labbo, L. (2004). 'The postmodern picture book: A new subgenre', *Language Arts*, 81:196–204.

Heller, M. F. (2006). 'Telling stories and talking facts: First graders' engagements in a nonfiction book club', *The Reading Teacher*, 60: 358–69. doi:10.1598/RT.60.4.5

Korat, O. and Shamir, A. (2006). 'The educational electronic book as a tool for supporting children's emergent literacy in low versus middle SES groups', *Computers & Education*, 50: 110–24. doi:10.1016/j.compedu.2006.04.002

Labbo, L. D. and Kuhn, M. R. (2000). 'Weaving chains of affect and cognition: A young child's understanding of CD-ROM talking books', *Journal of Literacy Research*, 32(2): 187–210. doi:10.1080/10862960009548073

Langer, J. A. (1990). 'The process of understanding: Reading for literary and informative purposes', *Research in the Teaching of English*, 24: 229–60.

Langer, J. A. (1995). *Envisioning Literature: Literary Understanding and Literature Instruction*. Newark, DE: International Reading Association and Teachers College Press.

Larson, L. (2010). 'Digital readers: The next chapter in e-book reading and response', *The Reading Teacher*, 64(1): 15–22. doi:10.1598/RT.64.1.2

López-Robertson, J. (2010). '"Lo agarraron y lo echaron p'tras": Discusing critical social issues with young Latinas/Discutiendo críticas y temas sociales con niñas latinas', *Columbian Applied Linguistics Journal*, 12(2): 43–54.

Mallett, M. (2003). 'Making early non-fiction exciting', *Literacy Today*, September: 26.

Mallett, M. (2004). *Early Years Non-fiction*. New York: Routledge.

Mallett, M. (2010). *Choosing and Using Fiction and Non-fiction 3-11*. New York: Routledge.

Maloch, B., Roser, N., Martinez, M., Harmon, J., Burke, A., Duncan, D., Russell, K., and Zapata, A. (2008). 'An investigation of learning to reading and write fantasy', in Y. Kim, V. J. Risko, D. L. Compton, D. K. Dickinson, M. K. Hundley, R. T. Jiménez, K. M. Leander, and D. W. Rowe (eds), *57th Yearbook of the National Reading Conference*. Oak Creek, WI: National Reading Conference. pp. 256–70.

Marsh, J. (2004). 'The techno-literacy practices of young children', *Journal of Early Childhood Research*, 2: 51–66. doi:10.1177/1476718X0421003

Marsh, J. and Singleton, C. (2009). 'Editorial: Literacy and technology: Questions of relationship', *Journal of Research in Reading*, 32: 1–5. doi:10.1111/j.1467-9817.2008.01377.x

Martinez, M. and Roser, N. L. (2008). 'Writing to understand lengthy text: How first graders use response journals to support their understanding of a challenging chapter book', *Literacy Research and Instruction*, 47: 195–210. doi:10.1080/19388070802062781

Martinez-Roldán, C. (2003). 'Building worlds and identities: A case study of the role of narratives in bilingual literature discussion', *Research in the Teaching of English*, 37(4): 494–526.

Martínez-Roldán, C. and López-Robertson, J. (1999/2000). 'Initiating literature circles in a first-grade bilingual classroom', *The Reading Teacher*, 53(4): 270–281.

May, L. (2011). 'Animating talk and texts: Culturally relevant teacher read-alouds of informational texts', *Journal of Literacy Research*, 43: 3–38. doi:10.1177/1086296X10397869

McGinley, W. and Kamberelis, G. (1996). '*Maniac Magee* and *Ragtime Tumpie*: Children negotiating self and world through reading and writing', *Research in the Teaching of English*, 30: 75–113.

Meisels, S. J. and Piker, R. A. (2000). *An Analysis of Early Literacy Assessments Used for Instruction* (Tech. Rep. No. 3-002). Ann Arbor, MI: University of Michigan, Center for the Improvement of Early Reading Achievement.

Morrow, L. M. and Gambrell, L. B. (2004). *Using Children's Literature in Preschool: Comprehending and Enjoying Books*. Newark, DL: International Reading Association.

Palinscar, A. S. and Duke, N. K. (2004). 'The role of text and text-reader interactions in young children's reading development and achievement', *Elementary School Journal*, 105(2): 183–97. doi:0013-5984/2004/10502-0004

Pantaleo, S. (2002). 'Grade 1 students meet David Wiesner's *The Three Pigs*', *Journal of Children's Literature*, 28: 72–84.

Pantaleo, S. (2004). 'Young children interpret the metafictive in Anthony Browne's *Voices in the Park*', *Journal of Early Childhood Literacy*, 4: 211–33. doi:10.1177/1468798404044516

Paris, S. G. (2005). 'Reinterpreting the development of reading skills', *Reading Research Quarterly*, 40: 184–202. doi:10.1598/RRQ.40.2.3

Paris, S. G. and Hoffman, J. V. (2004). 'Reading assessments in kindergarten through third grade: Findings from the Center for the Improvement of Early Reading Achievement', *Elementary School Journal*, 105(2): 199–217. doi:0013-5984/2004/10502-0005$05.00

Paris, S. and Paris, S. G. (2003). 'Assessing narrative comprehension in young children', *Reading Research Quarterly*, 38: 36–76. doi:10.1598/RRQ.38.1.3

Quintero, E. P. (2009). *Critical Literacy in Early Childhood Education: Artful Story and the Integrated Curriculum*. New York: Peter Lang.

Rosenblatt, L. (1938/1965). *Literature as Exploration*. New York: D. Appleton-Century.

Rosenblatt, L. (1978/1994). *The Reader, the Text, the Poem: The Transactional Theory of the Literary Work*. Carbondale, IL: Southern Illinois University Press.

Rosenblatt, L. (2002). *Acceptance Speech for the Distinguished Scholar Lifetime Achievement Award*. Speech presented at the National Reading Conference. Miami, FL.

Roser, N. L., Martinez, M., McDonnold, K., and Fuhrken, C. (2005). 'Young children learn to read chapter books', in Maloch, B., Hoffman, J. V., Schallert, D. L., and Fairbanks, C. M. (eds), *54th Yearbook of the National Reading Conference*. Oak Creek, WI: National Reading Conference. pp. 301–17.

Roser, N., Martinez, M., Fuhrken, C., and McDonnold, K. (2007). 'Characters as guides to meaning', *The Reading Teacher*, 60(5): 548–59. doi:10.1598/RT.60.6.5

Roskos, K. A., Christie, J. F., Widman, S., and Holding, A. (2010). 'Three decades in: Priming for meta-analysis in play-literacy research', *Journal of Early Childood Literacy*, 10: 55–96. doi:10.1177/1468798409357580

Scholes, R. (1985). *Textual Power: Literary Theory and the Teaching of English*. New Haven, CN: Yale University Press.

Serafini, F. (2010). 'Reading multimodal texts: Perceptual, structural, and ideological perspectives', *Children's Literature in Education*, 41: 85–104. doi:10.1007/10583-010-9100-5

Shine, S. and Roser, N. (1999). 'The role of genre in preschoolers' response to picture Books', *Research in the Teaching of English*, 34(2): 197–254. doi:10.2307/j50000352

Siegel, M. (2006). 'Rereading the signs: Multimodal transformations in the field of literacy education', *Language Arts*, 84(1): 65–77.

Sipe, L. R. (2000). 'The construction of literary understanding by first and second graders in oral response to picture storybook read-alouds', *Reading Research Quarterly*, 35(2): 252–75.

Sipe, L. R. (2001). 'A palimpsest of stories: Young children's intertextual links during readalouds of fairytale variants', *Reading Research and Instruction*, 40: 333–52.

Sipe, L. R. (2006). 'Young children's resistance to stories', *The Reading Teacher*, 60(11): 6–13. doi:10.1598/RT.60.11

Sipe, L. R. (2008). *Storytime: Young Children's Literary Understanding in the Classroom*. New York: Teachers College Press.

Sipe, L. R. and Bauer, J. (2001). 'Urban kindergartners' literary understanding of picture storybooks', *The New Advocate*, 14: 329–42.

Sipe, L. R. and Brightman, A. (2005). 'Young children's visual meaning-making during readalouds of picture storybooks', *National Reading Conference Yearbook*, 54: 349–61.

Sipe, L. R. and Brightman, A. (2006). 'Teacher scaffolding of first-graders' literary understanding during readalouds of fairytale variants', *National Reading Conference Yearbook*, 55: 276–92.

Sipe, L. R. and Brightman, A. (2008). 'First graders' "signature" responses during picturebook read-alouds', *Journal of Children's Literature Studies*, 5(2): 18–36.

Sipe, L. R. and Brightman, A. (2009). 'Young children's interpretations of page breaks in contemporary picturebooks', *Journal of Literacy Research*, 41: 1–36. doi:10.1080/10862960802695214

Souto-Manning, M. (2009). 'Negotiating culturally responsive pedagogy through multicultural children's literature: Towards critical democratic literacy practices in a first grade classroom', *Journal of Early Childhood Literacy*, 9: 50–74. doi:10.1177/1468798408101105

Tower, C. (2002). '"It's a snake, you guys!": The power of text characteristics on children's responses to information books', *Research in the Teaching of English*, 37: 55–88.

Vygotsky, L. (1978). *Mind in Society: The Development of Higher Psychological Processes* (Trans. M. Cole). Cambridge, MA: Harvard University Press. (First published in 1969 by MIT Press).

Walsh, M. (2003). '"Reading" pictures: What do they reveal? Young children's reading of visual texts', *Reading Language and Literacy*, November: 123–8.

Walsh, M. (2006). 'The "textual shift": Examining the reading process with print, visual, and multimodal texts', *Australian Journal of Language and Literacy*, 29(1): 24–37.

Walsh, M. (2007). 'Reading digital texts', *Australian Journal of Language and Literacy*, 30(1): 40–53.

Walsh, M. (2008). Worlds have collided and modes have merged: Classroom evidence of changed literacy practices. *Literacy*, 42(2), 101–108.

Wohlwend, K. E. (2008a). 'Kindergarten as nexus of practice: A mediated discourse analysis of reading, writing, play, and design in early literacy apprenticeship', *Reading Research Quarterly*, 43(3): 332–4. doi:dx.doi.org/10.1598/RRQ.43.4.1

Wohlwend, K. (2008b). 'Play as a literacy of possibilities: Expanding meanings in practices, materials, and spaces', *Language Arts*, 86(2): 127–636.

Wohlwend, K. E. (2009). 'Damsels in discourse: Girls consuming and producing identity texts through Disney princess play', *Reading Research Quarterly*, 44(1): 57–83. doi:dx.doi.org/10.1598/RRQ.44.1.3

Children's literature cited

Birney, B. G. (2006). *Friendship According to Humphrey*. New York: Puffin.

Browne, A. (1990/1997). *The Tunnel*. London: Walker Books Ltd.

Browne, A. (2001). *Voices in the Park*. New York: DK Publishing.

Wiesner, D. (2001). *The Three Pigs*. New York: Clarion.

24

Textbooks and Early Childhood Literacy

Allan Luke, Victoria Carrington, and Cushla Kapitzke

TEXTS AS ARTEFACTS OF CHILDHOOD

If childhood is a social construction, then its social practices are contingent upon and undertaken with historically evolving cultural technologies and artefacts. These technologies include the domestic implements of infant care and childrearing. They include the core technologies of modern childhood: toys and books. In the current political economy of childhood toys and books, in traditional and digital forms, have a special place, having evolved into linked and co-marketed pedagogic commodities. They are the cultural artefacts that parents, families and care-givers purchase with income that is surplus to basic requirements for food, shelter, and health. They are the aesthetic and didactic objects of children's work and desire. They are the nexus of everyday discourse and interaction by children and adults.

Particularly in light of the emergence of digital technology, it is worth recalling that the centrality of the book and the textbook in childhood is a recent phenomenon. Walter Ong (1958: 150) observed that the book was a 'pedagogical juggernaut' which 'made knowledge something a corporation could traffic in, impersonal and abstract.' Since the Protestant Reformation and the emergence of state-sponsored schooling in the fifteenth and sixteenth centuries, Anglo-European childhood involved institutional training in schools and churches with print (cf. Elson, 1964). Indeed, the orientation towards common core text study was characteristic of Confucian educational traditions, predating Western developments and spreading throughout East Asia (Nozaki, Openshaw and Luke, 2005). Nonetheless, and despite longstanding Muslim, Hebraic and alterior Judeo-Christian traditions of hermeneutic training and exegetic study by youth (Kapitzke,

1995), what counts as the textbook and its centrality in formal schooling continues to be defined by modernist Western/Northern educational theory and practice. Current educational policies focus on standardization of text (and affiliated assessment, pedagogical approach and/or professional commodity) as a key strategy for improving achievement and, purportedly, more equitable educational outcomes.

Throughout the history of schooling, formal education of children entailed formal pedagogical interaction with an official school text: the textbook. The textbook is a print or digital artefact comprised of written, visual and multisemiotic text designed for pedagogical purposes. That is, textbooks are didactic in form and content, authored and authorized for the selection, construction and transmission of valued knowledges and practices to apprentice readers. As such the forms and contents, ideologies and discourses of textbooks constitute an official and authorized version of cultural knowledge and literate practice.

In the current 'political economy of textbook publishing' (Apple and Christian-Smith, 1991), school-based early childhood literacy still involves primers, basal readers, and, more generally, reading instructional series including graded or levelled storybooks for children in the initial years of schooling. This current situation has been linked to varying forms and kinds of political control of early reading instruction via policy imperatives around systems 'accountability' (Willis and Harris, 2000). Sixty years ago, the development of print materials reached its zenith in the large-scale deployment, adoption and sales of reading series and adjunct materials by publishers like Scott-Foresman, Ginn, Harcourt-Brace, Macmillan and others. These textbooks have evolved to include home study and readings for an expanded educational marketplace.

Changes in current cultures and economies of childhood are marked by two major developments. First, there is an increased targeting by multinational publishers of middle and upper socioeconomic classes concerned about their children's early literacy and numeracy. Second, there is an accelerated uptake of digital technology, mass media, and linked children's toys and consumables among these same classes of child/parent consumers. So while current policies have focused educators on the role of standardized texts and tests in the remaking of school literacy, our concern here is what has been a major move in the economy and production of textbooks that has gone relatively unremarked amongst educational researchers: the articulation of new technologies, popular culture and textbooks in home and out-of-school pedagogy.

What follows is an historical introduction to ideology and political economy of the school textbook, describing its design principles and current policy uses. We then expand the definition of textbooks on two axes. First, an overview of 'graded' children's and infants' literature and reading materials that are commercially marketed for home, preschool and childcare reading events is developed. We then turn to consumer and popular texts in print and digital formats as home and public pedagogies.

TEXTBOOKS AND THE PRODUCTION OF THE MODERN READING CHILD

Childhood and the 'reading child' have been objects of pedagogical discourses and practices for over five centuries (Aries, 1962). The development of a formalized, transportable and replicable technology for the construction of the child through literature was realized in the earliest Reformation textbooks. One of the earliest, most successful reading textbooks for children was written by the German churchman, Johann Comenius. His Latin primer, *Orbis Sensualium Pictus* (*The Visible World in Pictures*), was printed in 1658 and subsequently used across England, Europe and America for 200 years (Venezky, 1992). Comenius' text was different from other incunabular pediatric and pedagogical literature because of its illustrations, which were included to assist reading comprehension. Typical of Protestant Reformation primers, readership and identity were tied to religious belief and the German state. The technology of the printing press coupled with religious zeal in Protestant Germany to generate new discourses and practices for and about children. In stated purpose, reading and writing linked the lives and identities of children – which were often brutally short – to issues of eternity. Pragmatically, however, textual practices developed as modalities of social and cultural control. These textbooks prescribed for children how and what one could read, in what lingua francas, for what cultural and religious, social and economic purposes. The mandating of basic early childhood literacy teaching, the development of secular reading textbooks and a school inspectorate to monitor and control classroom practices with the book were linked institutional strategies used by Luther and colleagues (Luke, 1989).

Residual traces of Comenius' influence on the design and format of textbooks remained until the second half of the twentieth century. Textbook production and use in this premodern era was ad hoc and particularistic. Written and published by individuals, textbooks were also brought to school by individual students. Some teachers kept small, eclectic collections in their classrooms, but these were used with individuals and small groups, rather than with whole classes. In the US, spelling was taught from a range of texts, which might include Noah Webster's *Spelling Book* (c. 1783), or Dilworth (c. 1740) and Perry's (c. 1777) common spellers. Other significant textbooks in the development of literacy acquisition and public schooling during this era included McGuffey's *Eclectic Readers* (c. 1836) and Latin primers such as Kennedy's *The Public School Latin Primer* (c. 1866) and Arnold's *Latin Prose Composition* (c. 1839). Whilst these texts each had their own curriculum and instructional method, they had continuing influences on reading and writing instruction for more than a 100 years until the 1950s with the demise of Latin grammar as a required curriculum subject (Westbury, 1990).

The historical development of the early literacy textbook was strongly tied to religious and moral training, affiliated with Protestant state ideology, and featured overt attacks on other belief systems – a case in point is Webster's *Spelling Book* depiction of the Roman Catholic Pope.

With the eighteenth and nineteenth century spread of empire, textbooks and early literacy training became ideal vehicles for the inculcation of colonial values and allegiance to the crown (Pennycook, 1998). Hence, books like the *Irish Readers* (c. 1830), the *Royal Readers* (c. 1890), and the *Ontario Readers* (c. 1880) all presented strong colonial themes of empire and race, national and linguistic hegemony. Dutch, French, Portuguese, Spanish and German colonial administrations also imported curricula and textbooks. Prior to the emergence of cheap, accessible and widely distributed books in the early twentieth century, for many rural and urban communities in the US, Canada, Australia and New Zealand, early school textbooks and affiliated religious texts (e.g., the Bible, hymnals, prayer books, *Paradise Lost*) were the only available print materials in many colonial homes, and were the staples of family and communal readings. In this regard, before the advent of mass commercial print culture, the influence of the textbook on moral and ideological formation was profound by virtue of its near-universal availability and relative exclusivity. Further, home-based early childhood literacy events and those of the schools often shared religious and colonial literary contents (Luke and Kapitzke, 1994; Kapitzke, 1999).

Development of the basal reading series by American educational psychologists in the early twentieth century has, to this day, profoundly shaped what counts as literacy, literacy instruction and reading in early childhood. Historical studies by Shannon (1989) and Luke (1988) document the emergence during the early and mid-twentieth century of the commercially structured, 'scientifically' designed and mass marketed reading textbooks in the US. The prototype of the contemporary reading series was William S. Gray and May Hill Arbuthnot's *Dick and Jane* (c. 1925) series, which dominated early literacy instruction in the US, Canada and other parts of the English-speaking world for over a half-century.

A continuing focal point of public and scholarly debate is the matter of overt moral and cultural content of early childhood reading materials. Since the *Dick and Jane* prototypes, questions about textbook ideological representation have been recurrent. These include critiques of the representation of gender relations in early readers, the exclusion of minoritized identities and cultures in children's literature, and, indeed, the construction of particular White and middle-class versions of childhood as the norm (Baker and Freebody, 1987). In this way, content analyses have called attention to the degree and extent to which textbooks construct, rather than represent, worlds of childhood, prescribing national, regional and local forms of cultural identity and social action (see articles in Apple and Christian-Smith, 1991; Chen, 2002; Nozaki, Openshaw, and Luke, 2005).

In contrast with Protestant and colonialist traditions, the designers of modern textbooks consistently have focused on literacy instruction qua scientific method rather than ideological and moral training. This view of the textbook as codification of pedagogic method is the dominant paradigm of American educational science, more specifically, of the field of reading psychology.

But what is distinctive is not only the particular scientific definition of reading of any textbook per se. In the case of *Dick and Jane*, the books were premised on then contemporary models of word recognition, while current legislated approaches in the US and UK have moved towards direct instruction in phonics. More profound was the pedagogic logic of the modern textbook: 1) that narrative reading text could be designed on the basis of psychological theories of instruction and skill (whether behaviorist, cognitive or psycholinguistic) and not on literary content or religious values per se; 2) that a whole suite of 'teacher-proofed' curricular commodities including guidebooks, student workbooks, adjunct visual and instructional materials, and tests could be delivered as a total 'curriculum'; and 3) that standardized tests could be developed on comparable design principles to assess teacher and system efficacy at delivery of the whole package. This sets the grounds not only for a redefinition of literacy pedagogy as the object of science (and not moral or literary training), a move formalized in the current US and UK policy environments, but also for transnational corporate production and marketing and, indeed 'snake oil sales' (Larson, 2002).

To this day, then, the early reading textbook is a key design/artefact – in its aesthetic and representational form (as marketed and consumed curriculum commodity) and via its educational and sociocultural functions (as mandated 'skill', interactional tool and ideological message system). It is a powerful economic phenomenon in its own right: a multinational product that can be adapted, translated, and niche-marketed in a range of national and regional markets; a comprehensive suite of educational commodities with a pedagogic reach that extends far beyond children's narrative reading text; a scientifically 'tested' and 'proven' product. Current market research estimates the overall US Prep–12 print textbook market as over $8 billion (Simba Information, 2010); the 45 million tests conducted each year in the US under the No Child Left Behind policy framework are estimated to have an annual market value of $517 million to the private sector (Jackson and Bassett, 2005). Further, many US or UK reading series are editorially altered for local adoption across English-speaking markets.

In the UK and US, the textbook is a central policy tool for a regulatory system that aims at standardization and quality assurance of classroom literacy events. While the Reformation textbook was a response to the demands of mass schooling in the newly invented secular nation-state, the modern reading series was the response of educational sciences and large publishing houses to the demands of modernist, urban society *par excellence*. As an embodiment of pedagogic method (phonics, word recognition, whole language, etc.), it promises discipline, standardization and accountability in the mass delivery of literacy skills. As an educational commodity, large-scale adoption across state systems guarantees efficient economies of scale, interstate and transnational export potential, and, increasingly, viable economies of scope for the development of further editions, adjunct and affiliated products in other areas of educational demand and consumption.

There is some recent evidence of the enlistment of many of these approaches to textbook development, with their attendant epistemological and curricular assumptions, in the educational systems of rapidly industrializing and globalizing states in Asia, the Pacific and Africa (e.g., Suaysuwan and Kapitzke, 2005). In some instances, as in Korea, this has entailed a direct and explicit textual translation of the values, ideologies and semiotic codes of American reading series (Lee, 2004). The role of the state in the political economy of the textbook, of course, depends upon nation or region specific regulation and policy. In the case of many developing countries, the state has retained the responsibility not only for adoption and monitoring of textbook form and content, but often for their production and distribution. In the North and West, the political economy of textbook production, adoption and implementation tends to be more complex, linking government policy, assessment and accountability systems, and the establishment of regional and state markets for multinational educational commodities. The current debates over literacy and reading in the US and UK are cases in point.

The implementation of national literacy-in-education policies in the US, UK, Australia and New Zealand have again focused policy and academic debate on methods, reviving simmering debates over the place of phonics, direct instruction, literature study and standardized achievement tests as principal measures for assessing school and program efficacy. These debates begin from the baseline assumptions of the technocratic model. The first assumption is that the best methods for teaching literacy and the best textbook packages can be determined by reference to an evidence-base wholly reliant on classical psychological experimental design and achievement tests. The second assumption is that the optimal instructional method can be coded, broadcast and implemented across large educational jurisdictions through the mandating of preferred textbooks and affiliated instructional sequences – with ongoing controversies over the US federal government's moves to provide support only for those reading programs (e.g., Open Court) based on 'scientific evidence' (Cunningham, 2001; Garan, 2001).

THE CROSSOVER OF TEXTBOOKS INTO HOME READING

Goodman, Shannon, Freeman, and Murphy (1988) used the term 'basalisation' to refer to the textbook development practices described above. Typically, this involves the attachment of a teachers' guide to direct the pragmatic use of texts – the 'running metatextual commentary' (Luke, de Castell, and Luke, 1989) on the children's narrative; and control of the 'level' of the text, usually through the application of a conventional readability scheme that places limits on vocabulary, lexical density and syntactic complexity. Texts are leveled and 'graded' for the incremental introduction of digraph and diphthong combinations, basic grammatical structures, punctuation and orthographic patterns, and core word recognition patterns for sequenced skill outcomes.

These and other linguistic, semiotic and physical characteristics of the textbook have evolved in relation to the sociolinguistic and cultural context where they are most likely to be read and used: the classroom. There are ongoing debates among early childhood educators about how, when, and with which techniques children should receive formal and informal instruction in literacy, whether this should occur in schools or homes, under whose professional jurisdiction, and so forth. There has been an international push to extend and formalize aspects of early literacy experience into earlier years of schooling, and home and childcare settings. In part, this reflects the policy focus on early intervention, widespread concern about home school transitions for children from lower socioeconomic, cultural and linguistic minority groups, and an affiliated movement for family literacy, home reading activities preparatory to formal schooling. At the same time, the market in both print materials and educational toys amongst middle class parents who seek to accelerate their children's skill and intellectual development has expanded.

The early twentieth century architects of the literacy textbook worked in an era in which the sales of *Dick and Jane* readers to schools would have been the largest market available. In the early to mid-twentieth century, working families still relied greatly on public and school libraries for access to books. To this day funding cutbacks in public libraries have their most direct effects on those communities without the surplus income to purchase books. Yet few publishers could have imagined the market possibilities for early reading instructional materials into homes. The use of books in home and community settings for formal and informal introductions to literacy practices now constitutes a significant and growing proportion of the trade publishing industry.

By recent accounts, the children's literature market is now a multi-billion dollar transnational enterprise. According to Cummins (2001), the average American book price of all children's and young adult titles is $US8.41 for paperbacks and $17.57 for hardbound texts, rising on average 5.7 per cent per year in cost. The Publishers Association described the UK children's book market as having end purchaser sales of £473m in 2010. This industry includes, of course, best-selling children's books, with over 10 million copies of Beatrix Potter books in print, such early childhood classics as Mercer Mayer's *Just Me and My Dad*, with almost 5 million copies in print, Dr Seuss, Sesame Street reading materials and other books.

In recent years there has been an extension of textbooks into the home reading environment, beginning with the movement of 'graded' texts into trade markets. Trade journals like the *School Library Journal* have long categorized 'children's and young adult titles' sales by age/grade, for example, 'preschool to grade 4', 'grade 5 and up'. But more recently, marketing has involved increased 'basalisation' and branding by level. Series like the best-selling *I Can Read* series and many Golden Books have long branded reading ages through readability formulae. But in the UK and many other countries, popular bookstore chains like WH Smith list, shelve and market books by official National Literacy Strategy levels. Textbook-style design features are crossing over into the general trade children's literature field, and home reading is being brought into alignment with the official categories and practices of school literacy events.

In its most overt form, this involves crossover product development and marketing by multinationals like McGraw-Hill. McGraw-Hill's *Imagine It!* Reading series has been closely aligned to the US Common Core State Standards. Beginning from an enhanced market-share position in early childhood textbooks, McGraw-Hill has expanded its range of affiliated products into the home market. Graded readers for use in the home are sold on the McGraw-Hill Children's Publishing website that also features 'Fun Free Stuff!', along with sample lessons, helpful tips, and activities for parents:

SRA *Imagine It!* Is a comprehensive Reading and Language Arts program that will teach your children to read, write and think independently ("http://www.imagineitreading.com/CA/ENG_US/at_home.php"www.imagineitreading.com/CA/ENG_US/at_home.php).

In this marketing text, the push is on for parents to better align their home reading practices with those of the reading series through the purchase of textbook-like commodities. But this doesn't stop with reading and literature per se. In the same catalogue, grades 1 and 2 test preparation materials are marketed to parents: 'Test preparation material from the nation's #1 school testing company!' is said to '… offer… children the preparation they need to achieve success on standardized tests'. All of this occurs under the umbrella of official endorsement of a co-marketed product by the federal government and various scientific 'experts'.

Textbooks for the teaching of reading – and their affiliated worksheets, flashcards and standardized tests – are no longer the focus of formal instruction solely in schools. Textbook design and marketing principles have been extended into the non-school market, making for a de facto institutionalization and domestication of home reading – among those social classes with sufficient surplus income – by state literacy policy. This involves both the leveling and scientific grading of texts, their marketing in relation to official school levels, badged products which are based on product recognition and loyalty (e.g., SRA), print and multimedia that are derived from school series, activities and texts officially adopted for school use. The modern textbook thus is extending into the home, into 'family literacy', 'early intervention' and new constructions of early childhood, abetted by a multinational political economy of text production. These developments mark the confluence of state intervention in the shaping of what counts as literacy, the standardization of school reading practices, and the expansion of consumer markets by multinational publishers (Beder, Varney, and Gosden, 2009). This confluence functions to align parental aspirations for children with policy conceptions of the literate learner as a skilled, measurable, performance-oriented entity. As a governmental strategy, it mobilizes citizens – namely, parents and children – as technically competent textual users and 'economized' human capital for the global knowledge economy.

THE MOVE FROM HOME READING TO MASS MEDIA AND NEW TECHNOLOGIES

While there has undeniably been a standardization of state mandated practices around literacy extending from teacher education to classroom literacy textbooks and into reading pedagogies (the UK's Literacy Strategy alongside OFSTED (Office for Standards in Education, Children's Services and Skills) inspections and accreditation of university provision and classroom audits is a prime example) during the same period, there has been a diversification of what we would consider to be instructional literacy texts in homes and communities. This expansion of the format and scope of the reading 'textbook' and pedagogies into informal educational settings has more recently been complicated further by the emergence of a child-focused mass consumer market and the impact of digital media. It is no longer only formal literacy texts or the school-like texts created for the family market described above making their way into homes and family literacy practices. In addition to these more obvious literacy textbooks, the textual artefacts of mass media consumer culture have become deeply entrenched in contemporary family life and now are pedagogic literacy teaching tools in their own right.

A decade ago there was still a clear delineation between mass-market early literacy instruction texts aimed at aspirational parents and the texts that could be associated more directly with a globalized mass media culture. However, the increased disaggregation of the consumer and media market in the ensuing years has led to the emergence of an entire niche market of artefacts, media and consumer items focused specifically around children. These include texts – online social networking and games sites, virtual worlds, magazines, television programming – that position children as consumers in their own right and often as active participants in globalized information and cultural flows. There is a large and growing body of research and scholarship chronicling the pedagogic power of popular cultural texts (Marsh, 2000; Marsh and Millard, 2000) alongside the emergence of new textual practices around digital media and the various technologies associated with it. This work takes account of the complexities of literate practices in contemporary multimodal textual landscapes (Bearne, 2005; Kress, 2003; Kress and van Leeuwen, 2001; Marsh, 2005; Sadin, 2007), the emergence of new models of childhood to accompany these emergent practices and cultural formations (Bullen and Kenway, 2001; Dowdall, 2009; Holloway and Valentine, 2003; Ito, Baumer, Bittanti, boyd, Cody, Herr-Stephenson, et al., 2009; Jenkins et al., 2006) and the implications of these shifts for classroom practice (Burnett, 2009; Davies and Merchant, 2009; Lankshear and Knobel, 2006). The argument is therefore well established that while not replacing print-based textbooks and textual practices, these emerging multimodal practices respond to, and bring with them, new cultural, economic and political contexts, and consequently have implications for literate identities and constructions of 'child' and 'childhood'.

A key shift that has accompanied the advent of digital technologies and media is the reconceptualization of children as creators and distributors of text and other content rather than as receivers of text via school and home-based textbooks and adult mediation (Jenkins et al., 2006). The word produser has moved into circulation in media and cultural studies fields in order to describe the new relationship that young people are carving out with technology, audiences and the various media to which they now have access (Bruns, 2009). This is a new model of childhood that inserts children as agentive individuals within global flows of information and technology and the identities and skill sets that attach have implications for the role and form of textbooks in literacy instruction. As is the case with the older forms of instructional textbook provided for children, these identities and skills are never neutral and not always optimal.

Leaving aside issues of access, there is a large and growing diversity in the types of pedagogic experiences with text that are available to children both online and off. Online virtual worlds for children are an interesting emergent example of this diversification in action and its implications for young children as they learn to be literate across various forms of text. Media and gaming industry analysts predict that by 2011 more than 50 per cent of all children between the ages of 6 and 12 will be regular visitors to online virtual worlds. This is, of course, the precise age group that is the particular focus of the traditional literacy textbooks of schooling. Currently, worlds like Habbo, Neopets and Club Penguin have 124 million, 50 million and 22 million registered users, respectively. This makes these sites a significant cultural and social influence for contemporary children. And, following in the footsteps of the children's literature and text market described earlier, they are also highly profitable business ventures. According to some analysts, the most popular half-dozen children's virtual worlds, including Club Penguin, Neopets and BarbieGirls, generated around $US300 million in 2009.

One of the fastest growing virtual worlds for children, with registrations already passing 15 million, is Mattell's BarbieGirls™. BarbieGirls™ is a beautifully constructed Barbie-themed virtual world where players, predominantly young girls, create an avatar and play games, chat, earn currency, buy clothing and personal features (such as eyes and hairstyles for their avatars) and furnish their loft-style apartments. To facilitate these interactive and shopping activities, the virtual world incorporates a range of text across a series of in-world activity zones that include bedrooms, clothing shops, cinema, furniture stores, pet stores, mall and theme park. These texts include orienting information; a range of safety and consumer information; game instructions; chat-bubble advice and encouragement from in-game characters; billboards, both animated and static; email and chat; word search games; and videos. Across this set of texts and sites there are opportunities to read and interpret texts in a variety of genres and a range of levels and limited, monitored opportunities to create email and chat texts. However, while the safety and consumer information presented on the outskirts of the site requires high levels of comprehension and the ability to process quite complex and lengthy onscreen text, the game instructions and conversational texts with which players come into regular contact as they navigate the various games and shopping opportunities make lesser demands on decoding, comprehension and critical analysis capacities (Carrington and Hodgetts, 2010; see also Marsh (2011) for an analysis of young children engaging with Club Penguin). There is a large volume of text across this online site as it creates a 'virtual' world.

In a print-based publication concerned with textbooks and early childhood literacy, it is possible to write online sites and texts off as 'not textbooks' and not 'real' literacy. However, like the classroom-based text of traditional reading instruction, these texts are highly pedagogic and play an important role in the construction of young people's identities as literates and as citizens. BarbieGirls™ is just one of the many and varied online sites with

which young children may engage on a daily basis, yet it is a powerful one: in its straddling of popular culture, mass media and digital technologies, it is a timely illustration of the pedagogic reach of these new informal texts. The textual demands of the site are low but at the same time, the texts are highly gendered, and work to construct young girls as 'natural consumers' (Rappaport, 2001). While the formal texts of school instruction work to construct a state-authorized literate citizen, these powerful informal instructional texts are constructing other identities, practices and skill sets around text. It is also increasingly clear that online social networking sites and virtual worlds are highly significant cultural sites for young people in contemporary cultures (Boyd, 2007) where a range of social and cultural practices are developed and practiced.

Our point here is that these are now sites where children encounter a large volume of text and develop dispositions and practices in relation to citizenship and literacy. Where discussions of the pedagogic texts of early literacy would once have been limited to religious or school based textbooks, texts from mass media and popular culture now claim the authority to instruct children in how to participate in childhood and how to be a particular type of literate citizen. In his analysis of 'unschooled learning', Mahiri (2001) argued that the official curriculum and the institutionalized school are at risk of being superseded. Commenting more recently in relation to digital media, Jenkins et al. (2006) fears for the future of young people who do not access the 'hidden curriculum' of participation and learning in online communities of practice. Where earlier generations of children were socialized into textual practices primarily within the boundaries of family, school, religious organization and community, media culture now provides a key apprenticeship into practices with text and literate identities, and provides many of the social and cultural markers of engagement and successful participation. This makes these texts key sites and technologies of literacy instruction.

FROM TEXTBOOKS TO PEDAGOGIC TEXTS

Ong's (1958) print-based 'pedagogical juggernaut' rolls on. Aided by current policy settings that emphasize accountability via standardized testing, the modern textbook continues to assert a dominant influence on early childhood literacy. More than a corpus of valued knowledges, official ideologies and beliefs, the reading series acts as a codification of instructional approach, of educational science and as a way of steering from a distance teachers' and children's interactions with literacy. As we have shown here, textbooks, primers, basal readers, and the common 'graded' or 'leveled' texts designed for pedagogical and literary uses in the home remain a central part of childhood in print-based economies and cultures.

The political economy of text publishing is actively seeking out new products, new markets and new niches for children, parents and teachers as text consumers. If there is an axiom that arises from the commodification of school-knowledge and literacy, it is that publishers and their affiliated knowledge and entertainment corporations necessarily establish, constitute and build new consumer wants, new communities and new target groups of youth and parents. Emergent information technologies have helped to shape and accelerate these developments.

At the same time, traditional print-based industries have expanded, consisting of interesting blends of smaller 'start-up' publishers and large multinational affiliates of larger media/entertainment corporations. The cross-over effects we have described are not just from textbooks to children's literature, but also involve the co-development, co-marketing and development of toys and parenting products, movies and websites, videogames and other mass media products (Cope and Kalantzis, 2001). On bestseller lists we find children's literature and reading series with spin-off connections to movies and cartoons. In this way, narrative literature acts to directly market products, from Arthur stuffed figures to Bob the Builder tool-kits. Band-aids, cereals and household products also are spun off from these characters and themes. Movie and videogames producers routinely purchase the rights of best-selling children's books to produce other textual products based on these characters and stories. While its hegemony in the school-based production of the literate subject remains unrivalled, the textbook has lost any monopoly on children's moral, intellectual and psychological development that it might once have had. In information societies and economies of signs, the textbook has become one of an array of textual products that are changing the face of early childhood literacy practices.

In ways that early analysts and critics from Ong (1958) to Elson (1964) couldn't have foreseen, the textbook is morphing into new shapes, both as a textual genre and as a commodity, an object of media cross-over and textual/semiotic convergence (Kalmbach, 1997). Exploded diagrams and 'callouts' in textbooks illustrate this process of intertextual transference and hybridity. Callouts, copied from technical illustrations of the 'model kit' and 'repair manual' genre, are the captions of visual/verbal display in exploded diagrams. Each callout assembles an arrangement of descriptive and contextual details that complement and extend the visual image. This shift to visual display in school textbooks is to be expected as designers, authors and illustrators – who themselves were reared on Sesame Street, MTV, video and computer games – enter the publishing industry.

The advent and spread of a globalized but differentiated consumer culture based on the commodification and consumption of texts has already had a visible impact on the reshaping of the experiences and discourses of childhood (Lee, 2001), and of children's early literacy texts and literate practices. In the semiotic economies of 'developed' and advanced capitalist societies, the production and consumption of text and discourse have become key economic and cultural foci. Early childhood in home and school, mass media and shopping mall is being reframed as a training ground for early literacy. At the same time, these sites have become focal points for the commodification of childhood. At once, the literacy textbook is reasserting its traditional authority over the shaping of what counts as literacy in the school, while it inexorably seeks out new niches, new crossovers, new forms and new markets.

REFERENCES

Apple, M. W. and Christian-Smith, L. C. (eds) (1991). *The Politics of the Textbook*. New York: Routledge.

Aries, P. (1962). *Centuries of Childhood: A Social History of Family Life*. Tr. R. Baldick. New York: Alfred Knopf.

Baker, C. D. and Freebody, P. (1987). *Children's First Schoolbooks*. Oxford: Basil Blackwell.

Bearne, E. (2005). 'Multimodal texts: What they are and how children use them', in J. Evans (ed.), *Literacy Moves on: Popular Culture, New Technologies and Critical Literacy in the Elementary Classroom*. New York: Heinemann.

Beder, S., Varney, W., and Gosden, R. (2009). *This Little Kiddy Went to Market: The Corporate Capture of Childhood*. Sydney: UNSW Press.

Boyd, D. (2007). 'Why youth (heart) social network sites: The role of networked publics in teenage social life', in D. Buckingham (ed.), *Youth, Identity and Digital Media*. MacArthur Foundation Series on Digital Learning. Cambridge, MA: MIT Press.

Bruns, A. (2009) 'From prosumer to produser: Understanding user-led content creation', presented at Transforming Audiences 2009, 3–4 September 2009, London.

Bullen, E. and Kenway, J. (2001). *Consuming Children: Education-Entertainment-Advertising*. London: Open University Press.

Burnett, C. (2009). 'Personal digital literacies versus classroom literacies: Investigating per-service teachers' digital lives in and beyond the classroom', in V. Carrington and M. Robinson (eds), *Digital Literacies: Social Learning and Classroom Practices*. London: Sage. pp. 115–30.

Carrington, V. and Hodgetts, K. (2010). 'Literacy-lite in BarbieGirls', *British Journal of Sociology of Education*, 31(6): 671–82.

Chen, J. (2002). 'Reforming textbooks, reshaping school knowledge: Taiwan's textbook deregulation in the 1990s', *Pedagogy, Culture and Society*, 10(1): 39–72.

Cope, B. and Kalantzis, D. (eds) (2001). *Print and Electronic Text Convergence*. Altona: Common Ground Publishing.

Cummins, J. (2001). 'Average book prices '01: Dead trees and wooden nickels', *School Library Journal*, 1 March 2001, retrieved from http://www.schoollibraryjournal.com/article/CA83276.html

Cunningham, J. (2001). 'The National Reading Panel report', *Reading Research Quarterly*, 36(3): 326–35.

Davies, J. and Merchant, G. (2009). 'Negotiating the blogosphere: Educational possibilities', in V. Carrington and M. Robinson (eds), *Digital Literacies: Social Learning and Classroom Practices*. London: Sage. pp. 81–94.

Dowdall, C. (2009). 'Masters and critics: Children as producers of online digital texts', in V. Carrington and M. Robinson (eds), *Digital Literacies: Social Learning and Classroom Practice*. London: Sage. pp. 28–43.

Elson, R. M. (1964). *Guardians of Tradition: American Schoolbooks of the Nineteenth Century*. Lincoln, NE: University of Nebraska Press.

Garan, E. (2001). 'Beyond the smoke and mirrors: A critique of the National Reading Panel report on phonics', *Phi Delta Kappan*, 82(7): 500–6.

Goodman, K., Shannon, P., Freeman, Y., and Murphy, S. (1988). *Report Card on Basal Readers*. Katonah, NY: Richard C. Owen.

Holloway, S. and Valentine, G. (2003). *Cyberkids: Children in the Information Age*. London: Routledge.

Ito, M., Baumer, S., Bittanti, M., boyd, d., Cody, R., Herr-Stephenson, B., Horst, A., Lange, P., Mahendran, D., Katynka, Z., Martinez, C., Pascoe, J., Perkel, D., Robinson, L., Sims, C., and Tripp, L. (2009). *Hanging Out, Messing Around and Geeking Out: Kids Living and Learning with New Media*. Cambridge, MA: MIT Press.

Jackson, J. M. and Bassett, E. (2005). *The State of the K-12 State Assessment Market*. Boston: Eduventures.

Jenkins, H., Clinton, K., Purushotma, R., Robison, A., and Weigel, M. (2006). 'Confronting the challenges of participatory culture: Media education for the 21st century', an occasional paper on digital media and learning. The John D and Catherine T MacArthur Foundation. Available: http://digitallearning.macfound.org/site/c.enJLKQNlFiG/b.2108773/apps/nl/content2.asp?content_id={CD911571-0240-4714-A93B-1D0C07C7B6C1}&notoc=1

Kalmbach, J. R. (1997). *The Computer and the Page: Publishing, Technology, and the Classroom*. Norwood, NJ: Ablex.

Kapitzke, C. (1995). *Literacy and Religion*. Amsterdam: John Benjamins.

Kapitzke, C. (1999). 'Literacy and religion: The word, the holy word and the world', in D. A. Wagner, R. L. Venezky and B. V. Street (eds), *Literacy: An International Handbook*. Boulder, CO: Westview Press. pp. 113–18.

Kress, G. (2003) *Literacy in the New Media Age*. London: Routledge.

Kress, G. and van Leeuwen, T. (2001). *Multimodal Discourse: the Modes of Contemporary Communication*. London: Arnold.

Lankshear, C. and Knobel, M. (2006) *New Literacies: Everyday Practices and Classroom Learning*. London: Open University Press.

Larson, J. (ed.) (2002). *Literacy as Snake Oil: Beyond the Quick Fix*. New York: Peter Lang.

Lee, N. (2001). *Childhood and Society: Growing Up in an Age of Uncertainty*. Philadelphia, PA: Open University Press.

Lee, G. (2004) 'Culture of children's reading education and the United States', *Childhood Education*. 80(5): 261–265.

Lee, I. (2005). 'The representation of new times in Korean language textbooks', in Y. Nozaki, R. Openshaw, and A. Luke (eds), *Struggles over Difference: Curriculum, Texts and Pedagogy in the Asia-Pacific*. Albany, NY: State University of New York Press.

Luke, A. (1988). *Literacy, Textbooks, and Ideology: Postwar Literacy Instruction and the Mythology of Dick and Jane*. London: Falmer Press.

Luke, C. (1989). *Pedagogy, Printing, and Protestantism: The Discourse on Childhood*. Albany, NY: State University of New York Press.

Luke, A. and Kapitzke, C. (1994). 'Pedagogy and paradox: Teaching interpretation in a religious community', in H. Parret (ed.), *Pretending to Communicate*. Berlin/New York: de Gruyter. pp. 124–40.

Luke, C., de Castell, S., and Luke, A. (1989). 'Beyond criticism: The authority of the school textbook', in S. de Castell, A. Luke, and C. Luke (eds), *Language, Authority and Criticism*. London: Falmer Press. pp. 245–60.

Mahiri, J. (2001). 'Pop culture pedagogy and the end(s) of school', *Journal of Adolescent and Adult Literacy*, 44(4): 382–5.

Marsh, J. (2000). 'Teletubby tales: Popular culture in the early years language and literacy curriculum', *Contemporary Issues in Early Childhood*, 1(2): 119–33.

Marsh, J. (ed.) (2005). *Popular Culture: Media and Digital Literacies in Early Childhood*. London: Sage.

Marsh, J. (2011). 'Young children's literacy practices in a virtual world: Establishing an online interaction order', *Reading Research Quarterly*, 46(2): 101–18. doi:10.1598/RRQ.46.2.1

Marsh, J. and Millard, E. (2000). *Literacy and Popular Culture*. London: Paul Chapman.

Nozaki, Y., Openshaw, R., and Luke, A. (eds) (2005). *Struggles over Difference: Curriculum, Texts and Pedagogies in the Asia-Pacific*. Albany, NY: State University of New York Press.

Ong, W. (1958). *Ramus: Method and the Decay of Discourse*. Cambridge, MA: Harvard University Press.

Pennycook, A. (1998). *English and the Discourses of Colonialism*. London: Routledge.

Rappaport, E. (2001). *Shopping for Pleasure: Women in the Making of London's West End*. Princeton, NJ: Princeton University Press.

Sadin, E. (2007). *Signs of the Times: Communication and Information: An Analysis of New Urban Spaces*. Boston: Springer.

Shannon, P. (1989). *Broken Promises: Reading Instruction in Twentieth Century America*. South Hadley, MA: Bergin & Garvey.

Simba Information (2010) 'Publishing for the PreK–12 Market, 2008–2011', accessed 10 October 2010 from: http://www.reportsandreports.com/reports/26656-publishing-for-the-prek-12-market-2010-2011.html

Suaysuwan, N. and Kapitzke, C. (2005). 'Thai English language textbooks, 1960–2000: Postwar, industrial, and global changes', in Y. Nozaki, R. Openshaw, and A. Luke (eds), *Struggles over Difference: Curriculum, Texts and Pedagogy in the Asia-Pacific*.

Albany, NY: State University of New York Press. pp. 79–97.

Venezky, R. L. (1992). 'Textbooks in school and society', in P. W. Jackson (ed.), *Handbook of Research on Curriculum*. New York: Macmillan. pp. 436–59.

Westbury, I. (1990). 'Textbooks, textbook publishers, and the quality of schooling', in D. L. Elliott and A. Woodward (eds), *Textbooks and Schooling in the United States* pp. 1–22. Chicago, IL: University of Chicago Press.

Willis, A. I. and Harris, V. (2000). 'Political acts: Literacy learning and teaching', *Reading Research Quarterly* 35(1): 72–88.

25

Recent Trends in Research on Young Children's Authoring

Deborah Wells Rowe

My goal in this chapter is to identify the growing edge of twenty-first century research on early childhood authoring. For the purposes of this review, I have selected studies that investigate young children's writing, often in conjunction with oral, visual, and embodied modes of representing meanings. Building from earlier reviews of the topics, theoretical vantage points, and analytic methods used to explore early childhood writing (Rowe, 2003, 2009; Yaden, Rowe, and MacGillivray, 2000), this chapter focuses on the shifts and changes that constitute our field's forward movement. As such, this chapter is both historical and forward-looking. While research is sometimes described as hierarchical, with new insights building incrementally from existing ones, it is also the case that researchers follow 'lines of flight' (Deleuze and Guattari, 1987) that break established patterns and take our understandings in new directions. In this review, I identify 10 trends representing substantial changes in theory, method, focus, or research intensity during in the last decade. Where appropriate, I connect current research to earlier lines of work from the 1970s, 1980s, and 1990s.

To this end, the review is organized around three major theoretical stances that undergird the most active lines of research on childhood authoring. First, I discuss current trends in studies focused on cognitive and sociocognitive features of composing, especially the processes involved in building genre knowledge, name writing, and spelling. The next section reviews work focused on exploring sociocultural features of composing including local literacy practices in homes and classrooms, and the composing processes of emerging bilinguals/biliterates. Finally, I turn to a rapidly expanding body of research conducted from a social semiotic perspective, with special attention to the lines of work related to multimodal composing processes, play, and digital literacies.

SCOPE OF THE REVIEW

For the period from 2000 to mid-year 2011, I conducted a systematic literature search for studies relating to early childhood authoring. I used electronic databases to search for studies of young children's writing (birth through age 8) and augmented this method with hand searches of 22 English-language journals that publish research on literacy or early childhood learning (i.e., *Applied Psycholinguistics, Australian Journal of Early Childhood, Developmental Psychology, Early Childhood Education Journal, Early Childhood Research Quarterly, Elementary School Journal, Journal of Early Childhood Literacy, Journal of Literacy Research, Journal of Research in Reading, Language Arts, Language and Education, International Journal of Early Childhood, International Journal of Education & the Arts, Learning & Instruction, Reading and Writing Quarterly, Reading, Literacy and Language, Reading Research Quarterly, Reading Teacher, Research in the Teaching of English, Written Language & Literacy, Yearbook of the National Reading Conference, Young Children*). Research monographs published during this period were also included.

Using these procedures, I located 180 research reports related to young children's authoring published from 2000 to mid-2011. To identify current and emerging trends, I categorized studies by research focus and theoretical frame, and compared them to 90 studies conducted between 1990 and 2000 previously identified with similar procedures (Rowe, 2009). For this chapter, I focus on the field's forward movement as signaled by shifts in theoretical perspectives, research questions, research approaches, or overall research intensity.

COGNITIVE AND SOCIOCOGNITIVE PERSPECTIVES ON CHILDHOOD AUTHORING

Much of the existing research on young children's authoring has focused on describing patterns in children's written texts and, from those patterns, inferring the nature of children's hypotheses about print. In general, this work has taken a constructivist view of young children's authoring. That is, children are seen as building their own understandings about the nature of the writing system (Ferreiro, 1990). They do so by constructing and testing hypotheses about print (Clay, 1991; Ferreiro and Teberosky, 1982; Harste, Woodward, and Burke, 1984; Rowe, 1994; Teale and Sulzby, 1986a) rather than learning through direct imitation of print in the environment. It is because young children's hypotheses are thought to be 'true constructions' (Besse, 1996; Ferreiro, 1990; Ferreiro, Pontecorvo, and Zucchermaglio, 1996; Goodman, 1990; Kamii, Long, and Manning, 2001; Schickedanz, 1990; Sulzby, 1986) and do not entirely mirror adult views of writing that their products often look so unconventional to adult eyes. The writing behaviors that precede and develop into conventional literacy have been termed 'emergent literacy' (Teale and Sulzby, 1986b).

Researchers working from an emergent literacy perspective, then, have defined early authoring attempts in terms of children's mental processes rather than the conventionality of their textual products (Harste et al., 1984). This stance has opened the door for extensive analysis of children's texts and the hypotheses about print presumed to guide authoring. Research attention in the 1970s, 1980s, and 1990s focused on describing patterns and developmental progressions in various features of children's unconventional texts. Researchers focused on describing textual patterns related to the forms (i.e., types of marks) children use for writing, speech-print links, depiction of word units, directionality, spatial arrangement of marks, differences between marks used for writing and drawing, spelling patterns, and genre-specific text features. As detailed below, some descriptive research has continued into the twenty-first century, especially in the line of work aimed at more fully exploring children's knowledge and use of the features of different genres.

Trend 1: Moving from generic to genre-specific descriptions of child authoring

Emergent literacy researchers have produced an extensive body of observational and cross-sectional research tracking the trajectory of children's textual forms across time as they grow older. Overall, there is little debate that, in general, children's writing becomes more conventional over time. With regard to writing forms, recent descriptive research (Kenner, 2000; Kenner and Kress, 2003) generally confirms patterns observed during previous decades (e.g., Clay, 1975; Dyson, 1985; Ferreiro and Teberosky, 1982; Harste et al., 1984). Writing begins with scribbles that are largely undifferentiated and over time moves in a general trajectory toward forms that have more writing-like characteristics including linearity, conventional directional patterns, and individual units (Yang and Noel, 2006). Recent research also confirms that children experiment with spatial arrangement of text on the page (Kenner, 2000; Yang and Noel, 2006). Cross-linguistic research (Kenner and Kress, 2003; Pine, 1992) supports seminal observations (Harste et al., 1984) that

young children produce graphic forms and exhibit visual noticing behaviors that reflect the writing systems of their cultures.

While a considerable database has been created to describe the expected forms and general progression of children's marks, Kress (1994) has argued that learning to write is not a generic process, but instead involves learning the demands and potentials of different genres. Further, genre features are multimodal, including not only language registers and text structures, but also types and uses of images and ways of visually formatting text and graphics (Kress, 1994; Pappas, Varelas, Gill, Ortiz, and Keblawe-Shamah, 2009).

In the last decade, researchers have actively explored children's genre knowledge. There is considerable evidence that preschoolers construct texts that reflect syntactic, semantic, and spatial features of genres such as stories, science reports, arguments, lists, labels, signs, poems, letters, and e-mails (Donovan, 2001; Mavers, 2007; Pantaleo, 2009; Pappas et al., 2009; Riley and Reedy, 2005; Wolf, 2006; Wollman-Bonilla, 2000, 2003). Pappas and her colleagues (2009) for example, reported that first- through third-graders were able to use appropriate scientific registers (e.g., generic nouns and technical terms) and visual techniques common in science writing (e.g., diagrams and magnified image insets), though not always in same ways demonstrated in published texts.

Overall, research shows that by 6–7 years of age, young writers can demonstrate considerable knowledge of micro-level features of story and information genres including cohesion, tense, vocabulary, word order, spatial arrangement, and use of images (Donovan, 2001; Pappas et al., 2009). Researchers have shown that children's ability to produce genre-appropriate meanings outstrips their ability to record them in writing (Donovan, 2001), and children's stories, generally, are more conventional than information pieces such as science reports (Kamberelis and Bovino, 1999). Genre knowledge, like other aspects of children's authoring, appears to develop early, become more complex with age (Donovan, 2001; Smolkin and Donovan, 2004), and to be expressed differently depending on the complexity of the task (Borzone de Manrique and Signorini, 1998). Further, as might be expected, children's knowledge and control of specific genre features develops as they have intensive formal or informal opportunities to read and write in the genre (Mavers, 2007; Pantaleo, 2009; Pappas et al., 2009).

Researchers working from sociocultural perspectives have extended the scope of genre research by investigating its cultural basis and embedded power structures. Bloome, Katz, and Champion (2003) demonstrated that African-American preschoolers' written narratives often reflected community storytelling patterns, rather than school-based story structures. They argue that school preferences for hierarchical narrative structures have the potential to marginalize children who use other genre structures rooted in out-of-school experiences. As children gain experience in school, some appear to build genre knowledge by appropriating cultural forms of writing and reworking them to create hybrids that fit specific school tasks and audiences (Dyson, 2001; Solsken, Willett, and Wilson-Keenan, 2000; Wollman-Bonilla, 2000).

Trend 2: Exploring name writing–reading connections

Because name writing is the cultural context in which many young children are first invited to write, and because of children's intense personal connection to their names, name writing has been an area of historical interest for early writing researchers. It was young children's rendering of their names on psychological test booklets that serendipitously caught Hildreth's (1936) eye and led to publication of one of the first descriptive studies of emergent writing. Confirming Hildreth's seminal work, recent research shows that children's name writing progresses from unorganized scribbles to marks that are progressively more writing-like. When compared to their attempts to write other messages, preschoolers' names are more conventional in form. Children move toward conventionality more quickly in name writing than when writing other words (Levin, Both-DeVries, Aram, and Bus, 2005), suggesting that children may approach name writing in ways that are different from other writing tasks. Treiman and her colleagues (Treiman, Kessler, and Bourassa, 2001) confirm that young writers often rely on familiar letters from their names when composing messages, as evidenced by kindergarteners' tendency to overuse letters from their own first names when attempting to spell other words. They conclude that name writing has an important connection to early spelling, and that spellings that look random, may be related, instead, to the frequency of exposure to the letters in the child's name.

Recently, however, researchers have extended work begun by Bloodgood (1999) exploring the correlations between name writing and subskills thought to be related to reading achievement (Bloodgood, 1999; Haney, Bissonnette, and Behnken, 2003; Martens, 1999; Welsch, Sullivan, and Justice, 2003). These studies explore whether, in learning to write their names, children may also be forming foundational understandings like phonological awareness and the alphabetic principle. Results of correlational studies show that name writing is related to alphabet knowledge and general understandings about print such as letter identification and concept of word (Bloodgood, 1999; Welsch et al., 2003). Findings are mixed as to whether name writing is related to phonological awareness (Haney et al., 2003; Welsch et al., 2003). Based on the observation that many young children write their names wholly or partly conventionally while using random letters to spell other words, Levin and her colleagues (Levin et al., 2005) suggest that name writing is a special case where children learn their names as a whole – a hypothesis that explains findings of some studies that conventional name writing is not consistently related to phonological awareness or understanding of the alphabet principle.

Trend 3: Retheorizing developmental spelling trajectories

Young children's spelling patterns have remained an active area of interest in the last decade, continuing the line of research begun in the 1970s by Read's (1971) seminal work on young writers' unconventional spellings. Following Read, studies in this tradition have analyzed patterns in children's unconventional spellings as an index of their hypotheses about print. This research approach has resulted in an extensive body of work supporting the theory that spelling development in alphabetic languages occurs in a fairly predictable way, with children constructing a series of qualitatively different hypotheses about how speech is represented in print (Fresch, 2001; Henderson and Beers, 1980; Hughes and Searle, 1991; Korkeamaki and Dreher, 2000; Mayer and Moskos, 1998). In this work, children's spelling development is characterized as a hierarchical progression of qualitatively different ways of thinking that build progressively on one another. In general, this line of research shows that children progress from spellings where there is no link between letters and sounds to spellings where letters are used to represent some or all of a word's sounds. Next, children begin to use orthographic rules and visual strategies. In a final stage, conventional spelling becomes well established.

This theoretical conception of spelling development has fueled continuing research focused on the features of language to which children attend as they invent spellings. Researchers working across a variety of languages have shown that preschool and early-grades spellers attend to both phonemes and syllables, and that the language grain size depends on developmental stage, task demands, and the characteristics of the language and its orthography (Winskel and Widjaja, 2007). Young writers sometimes use a letter-name strategy to spell words that contain beginning or ending syllables corresponding to the name of an alphabet letter (e.g., YD for 'wind') (Martins and Silva, 2001). The importance of phonological awareness and the child's own speech-based, phonological representations of words has been further demonstrated by findings that children create spellings based on the dialect spoken at home, even when words are dictated to them in the standard dialect (Jalil and Liow, 2008). Other studies (Lehtonen and Bryant, 2005) show that as children become more competent spellers, they make use of morphology as well as phonological cues. Attention to morphology may be related to language characteristics such as the extent to which the orthography's spelling rules are morphologically based.

Thus, despite many differences in method (data collection techniques, instructional contexts, and different oral and signed languages), many older and more recent studies support a developmental progression of learning to spell in English and in other alphabetic languages such as Spanish and Greek (Defior, Jiménez-Fernández, and Serrano, 2009; Loizidou-Ieridou, Masterson, and Hanley, 2010), with the specific nature of the language's orthographic system affecting the pace and sequence with which spelling patterns are learned.

Recently, however, some researchers have presented data challenging a strict stage-like progression of spelling development, beginning with observations that a range of spelling abilities may be displayed at any one time, especially as children transition between stages (Gentry, 2000; Korkeamaki and Dreher, 2000). Further challenges to stage theory come from studies drawing on data that goes beyond spelling errors. Sharp and her colleagues (Sharp, Sinatra, and Reynolds, 2008) have used fine-grained microgenetic analyses of children's self-reported explanations about spelling strategies along with evidence from spelling errors, to conclude that a stage theory does not fully explain observed patterns in children's spellings. Their data show that children use multiple strategies to spell a word, and that they may employ both more and less sophisticated strategies. Though children's use of less sophisticated strategies declines over time, children do not drop these strategies from their repertoires. Share and colleagues propose that this observed pattern in the developmental progression of children's spelling abilities is better described by an overlapping wave model.

A second challenge to spelling stage theory comes from studies using experimental designs to investigate children's responses to morphology instruction. Though stage theory would predict that children could only profitably use morphological strategies later in their spelling development (Bear and Templeton, 1998), an experimental study by Devonshire and Fluck (2010) shows that instruction in morphological strategies can improve the spelling of English-speaking 5–11-year-olds, and that students simultaneously use more and less sophisticated strategies to spell words. Both findings run counter to stage theory predictions. The authors suggest that while children's spelling development does reflect an overall progression toward more sophisticated strategies, students may not necessarily think in qualitatively different ways from one phase to the next. Together, these results present significant challenges to stage models of spelling development, and represent the growing edge of research in this area.

Trend 4: Exploring spelling–reading connections

As in name-writing research, researchers recently have begun to explore connections between spelling and reading in English and other languages. While in previous decades spelling was primarily of interest as part of the writing process, researchers are now exploring the possibility that as children construct spellings, they learn and practice important skills that are also foundational to reading. Both correlational and experimental designs provide evidence of important spelling–reading connections. For example, studies with primary grades students have shown significant positive correlations between phonological awareness and spelling for Dutch children (Verhagen, Aarnoutse, and Van Leeuwe, 2010) and for both phonological awareness and the alphabetic principle for hearing-impaired French-speaking students (Sirois, Boisclair, and Giasson, 2008). Similarly, for monolingual, Spanish speaking, kindergarteners writing level was strongly and positively correlated to scores on phonological awareness tasks, with writing level explaining most of the variance in response types on these tasks (Vernon, Calderón, and Castro, 2004). In an experimental study with English-speaking kindergarteners, Ouellette and Sénéchal (2008) found that invented spelling training led to positive gains in phonological awareness, orthographic awareness, and word reading. Overall, these studies suggest that invented spelling provides an important venue for learning phonological awareness and for integrating a variety of skills that are required for reading (Ouellette and Sénéchal, 2008). Further, experience inventing spellings appears to act as a self-teaching mechanism in orthographic learning (Shahar-Yames and Share, 2008), and is more effective than reading words alone.

SOCIOCULTURAL PERSPECTIVES ON CHILDHOOD AUTHORING

The research reviewed thus far has viewed authoring as an 'in head' phenomenon, albeit one that is shaped by people and social situations. In the last decade, researchers interested in social and cultural aspects of authoring have challenged this notion of authoring as an individual mental act, suggesting, instead, that authoring occurs *between* people as they negotiate authoring processes, meanings, and textual forms as part of their everyday activities. As Barton and Hamilton (2000) argue: 'Literacy becomes a community resource, realised in social relationships rather than a property of individuals' (2000: 13). They note that at a micro-level, literacy events are often accomplished jointly by a number of participants with the resulting literacy practices moving beyond the individuals' understandings and meanings. At a macro-level, communities create social rules and hold taken-for-granted assumptions about who can use and produce particular literacies under what circumstances (Barton and Hamilton, 2000; Santa Barbara Classroom Discourse Group, 1992).

From this perspective, authoring is seen as social practice – the accepted and valued ways of 'doing' authoring (or art or talk) in a particular community (Barton and Hamilton, 1998; Lave and Wenger, 1991; Lemke, 1995). While literacy practices are, in part, defined by observable behaviors involving print, they also involve values, attitudes, feelings and social relationships (Barton and Hamilton, 2000; Street, 1995). Authoring practices include definitions of text, the ways community members talk about authoring, ideological views of literacy, and participants' socially constructed identities. Embedded in literacy practices are power relations that determine the use and distribution of texts and who has access to various positions in authoring events. Social practices are ideological in that they support the power of one social group to dominate another (Lemke, 1995).

In the last decade, researchers working from sociocultural perspectives have built an active line of research that reframes the constructive work of composing as local, ideological, and positioned. In these studies it matters where, when, and with whom research is conducted. Rather than searching for universals or attempting to construct portraits of generic child writers, researchers working from sociocultural perspectives seek, instead, to understand how particular writers engage in the local writing practices of specific classrooms and communities. An important question in this line of research is how children's hypotheses, texts, and authoring processes are shaped by cultural practices around writing in their communities or classrooms, and also how children's participation as authors helps shape community practices. Researchers' desire to understand sociocultural features of childhood authoring is evident in three recent research trends: exploring family literacy practices, the process of learning to write through participation in local literacy events, and the ways children learn about authoring in multilingual environments.

Trend 5: Exploring how authoring is shaped by family literacy practices

When writing is seen as a socially situated act, young children's hypotheses and writing strategies are assumed to be rooted in the literacy practices of local communities. At home, children learn to write through social participation in everyday writing events. Because adult family members and siblings are important participants in children's home writing experiences, family literacy interactions are key to understanding young children's authoring (Aram, 2010). As a result, the culture- and class-based nature of young children's writing is an expanding area of investigation for researchers working within sociocultural frames. Perhaps because of the difficulty of conducting research in children's homes, or because of the field's focus on schooled literacy, only a few researchers (e.g., Hicks, 2002; Reyes, 2006) have directly investigated how young children experience writing at home or in their communities. However, a number of researchers have conducted depth interviews of parents (e.g., Compton-Lilly, 2003; Lynch, 2008; Meier, 2000) or observed children's use of community- and

home-based writing practices in classroom settings (e.g., Bloome et al., 2003; Dyson, 2003). Additionally, some researchers have observed family responses to standard writing tasks (Aram, 2010) as a means of understanding patterns of family interaction around writing.

These studies demonstrate that, by participating in home writing events, children learn a variety of writing attitudes, definitions, and purposes that serve as resources for organizing their first writing attempts. From interviews of low-income families in the United States, Lynch (2008) found that parents of 4-year-olds engaged in more reading than writing activities with their child. When parents reported writing with their child, activities were usually confined to writing the alphabet or spelling words. Almost no parents in this sample invited their young children to write stories or other connected messages. In contrast, other patterns of parent–child writing have been observed in classic and more recent case studies (Baghban, 1984; Bissex, 1980; Martens, 1996; Neumann, Hood, and Neumann, 2009) conducted by literacy-researcher parents with their own children. In these homes, parents engaged their preschoolers in noticing print in the environment, talked with their child about his/her unconventional writing, and engaged in a variety of joint writing events (Neumann et al., 2009).

An Israeli study found that children get a fairly consistent message about writing from interactions with adults at home. Aram (2010) found that middle-socioeconomic status (SES) mothers and fathers living in the same household tend to interact in similar ways as they engage their child in writing words and that family guidance styles are associated with different kinds of child outcomes on measures of emergent writing. Other studies suggest that parents, children, and teachers may hold differing views of 'good' writing and of appropriate writing experiences for young children. Meier (2000) found that parents and children from a Spanish/ English bilingual community in the US valued conventional forms of writing and alphabet practice over more open-ended emergent literacy activities planned by teachers. Social class may also affect children's experiences with writing. Working in Israel, Korat and Levin (2002) found that low-SES and high-SES mothers held different beliefs and engaged in different kinds of interactions with their children around spelling. At the same time, Wollman-Bonilla's (2001) analysis of parent entries in family message journals demonstrates that, at home, children may experience a wider variety of genres and more flexible uses of writing than in their school writing. Further, as children launch into writing, they may use it for culturally-based purposes appropriated from their homes and communities. A number of researchers have shown how children use home-based popular culture texts along with oral and literate traditions as resources for writing in classroom settings (Bloome et al., 2003; Dyson, 2001, 2003).

Despite the importance of understanding culture- and class-based variation in children's writing experiences, it is also important to note that broad categories describing social class, ethnicity, and home language are not necessarily good predictors of individual children's home literacy experiences. Researchers have observed considerable variation in the writing practices of low income and minority homes (Purcell-Gates, 1996; Taylor and Dorsey-Gaines, 1988; Teale, 1986). Families who share similar ethnic or social class backgrounds may not share the same literacy values, beliefs, and writing practices.

Trend 6: Exploring the sociocultural construction of children's authoring practices

In the last decade, researchers have begun to turn the cultural lens inward to examine school writing practices. Though a good deal of the existing research on early writing has been conducted with white, middle-class children, or in mainstream preschool contexts, the cultural basis for mainstream writing practices has been less frequently analyzed than when children belong to 'other' writing communities. As early writing is reframed as a cultural practice, researchers are beginning to highlight the cultural basis for school literacy (Meier, 2000; Wilson, 2000). Rowe (2008a), for example, highlighted the connections between middle-class child-rearing practices and teacher interactions around writing in an emergent literacy preschool. Overall, this line of work challenges a view of writing that normalizes middle-class and schooled practices, and reveals ways that children from diverse backgrounds may be silenced, or marginalized when their writing does not match expected mainstream patterns (Bloome et al., 2003).

Researchers have also investigated *what* children learn about writing as they participate in the temporary cultures of classroom writing communities (Larson and Maier, 2000; Manyak, 2001). For example, studying 2-year-olds' and teachers' interactions at a classroom writing table, Rowe (2008b) identified the social contracts, or socially negotiated understandings, about writing that children were forming through participation in classroom writing practices.

Through close analysis of classroom talk and actions, some literacy researchers (Manyak, 2001; Rowe, 2008a) have explored *how* preschool and elementary children learn these culturally situated literacies through participation in authoring events. The focus of this work is on understanding how social participation gives children access to roles and knowledge needed to become members of the classroom writing community (Larson and Maier, 2000). Shifts between roles as experts and novices (Manyak, 2001), and as teacher, author, co-author, and overhearer, allow the social distribution of knowledge about writing, and give children access to central roles in writing events well before they can take them up independently (Larson and Maier, 2000; Rowe, 2008a).

While this work highlights the powerful role adults play in guiding children's participation in some kinds of learning-to-write events (Rowe, 2008a), researchers working from sociocultural perspectives have also studied the agency of child authors and their influence in shaping classroom literacy practices. From interviews of 5–7-year-olds in the United Kingdom, Fisher (2010) found that during classroom writing events, children made choices of available tools, resources, and relations to support their writing, and in so doing took up particular kinds of roles. Rowe and Neitzel (2010) found that 2-year-olds' participation in preschool writing events was shaped by patterns of personal interest – a finding also supported by research conducted from social semiotic perspectives (Kress, 1997; Rowsell and Pahl, 2007). Therefore, learning to write involves much more than adding new skills to children's cognitive repertoires. It requires that children take on new cultural identities and affects their sense of self in profound ways (Compton-Lilly, 2006; Dyson, 2001, 2003; Manyak, 2001; Rowe, Fitch, and Bass, 2001). In classrooms where young children select their own topics, writing involves assuming a 'social voice' (Dyson, 2001) and positions them in particular ways in relation to their peers, the ongoing dialogue in their classroom, and to the texts and practices of the larger society (Compton-Lilly, 2006; Dyson, 2001, 2003; Van Sluys, 2003). Dyson's (2003) research with first graders has demonstrated that young writers use texts to construct social affiliations with their peers, as well as to accept and resist the ways they are positioned by others. Overall, this line of research reveals that young children's writing functions as much to establish 'who I am in relation to you' as to serve other communicative purposes (Van Sluys, 2003).

Authoring as an ideological practice

In the studies just described, literacy researchers were interested in describing the situated and distributed nature of authoring practices. Others working from a sociocultural perspective have studied the ideological nature of literacy practices; that is, they have focused on the ways that a group's common-sense views of literacy create and maintain power over others (Lemke, 1995; Sheridan, Street, and Bloome, 2000), and are framed by relations of status and dominance within larger political contexts. Not only are children's authoring roles embedded within hierarchies of social relationships, but the 'stuff' of authoring is also ideologically loaded. When children construct written texts, they are doing more than selecting words. They are manipulating ideological symbols of power (or weakness) (Dyson, 2000) and displaying an (often implicit) interdependence between meanings and the social and political positions they occupy (Lemke, 1995). When young children write, they appropriate cultural materials as a means of cultural production (Dyson, 2001).

From this perspective, authoring is co-constructed in local interactions and as part of larger social and political ideologies. Children's participation in authoring practices must be read against the structuring processes of race, gender, and class in the larger society (Dyson, 2000). Dyson's (1997, 2001, 2003, 2008) research in culturally diverse American classrooms has been particularly influential in opening young children's authoring practices to ideological analysis. Her work demonstrates how young authors use texts to construct social affiliations with their peers, as well as to accept and resist the ways they are positioned by others. Overall, Dyson has found that children not only flexibly reframe cultural materials, but also recast existing social relationships and social practices. Dyson's analyses demonstrate that childhood authoring involves assuming a 'social voice' (2001) that positions children in particular ways in relation to the ongoing dialogue in their classroom community and in relation to the texts and practices of the larger society. Social and symbolic flexibility and recontextualization processes are key authoring processes used by child authors as they move across symbolic, social, and ideological boundaries (Dyson, 2000, 2001).

Ideological analyses have highlighted the intercultural (Lemke, 1995) nature of classroom authoring events. Because children are simultaneously positioned in the overlapping communities of official and peer culture (Dyson, 2008; Rowe, Fitch, and Bass, 2001; Rowe and Leander, 2005), the same authoring activities often have very different meanings for children's positions as students in the official world and as friends in the peer world.

Overall, in the last decade an increasing number of studies of childhood authoring have concerned themselves with understanding authoring as part of the social and cultural practices of homes and schools. Studies have focused on the ways local beliefs, values and practices shape what and how young children learn about authoring. At the same time, some researchers have begun to focus on the role of child agency as children make choices about social participation. Authoring is neither generic nor politically neutral. Therefore, researchers have focused on the ways child authors take up, adapt, or resist positions in existing systems of power relations. Negotiating their places in these cultural systems is a key part of authoring.

Trend 7: Learning to write in multiple languages

The globalizing economy of the twenty-first century has led not only to increased cultural diversity among students, but also to increased linguistic diversity. While the majority of studies on child authoring has, to date, been conducted with monolingual speakers, there is a strong and growing line of research focusing on the authoring practices of young children who are learning to write in multiple languages. Researchers (Moll, Saez, and Dworin, 2001; Reyes and Azuara, 2008) working in this area have noted that young children experience a variety of multilingual contexts, ranging from those where neither of the child's languages is marked as lower status, to those where children are only supported in learning English as a new language and no support is provided for learning to author texts in their home language. In the last decade, most research related to young children's multilingual authoring experiences has been conducted in bilingual settings where children are simultaneously supported in learning to write in two or more languages. Studies of emergent biliterates have focused on what young children learn about writing and how the cultural and linguistic practices of home and school affect literacy learning. A primary conclusion of this work is that children who are learning English as another language do not constitute a monolithic group. Studies of young writers show that some children have support from parents and community members in speaking and writing both their first language (L1) and English at home (Moll et al., 2001; Reyes, 2006) while other children live in close-knit communities where English is rarely spoken or written (Qian and Pan, 2006).

Researchers taking a social semiotic perspective have been interested in young emerging biliterates' understandings of the visual characteristics of the scripts of their two languages. Kenner, Kress, and their colleagues (Kenner, 2000; Kenner and Kress, 2003; Kenner, Kress, Al-Khatib, Kam, and Tsai, 2004) have studied how children approach writing when they are learning English along with either Spanish, Arabic, or Chinese. They found that, despite differences in the orthographic rules (i.e., alphabetic, logographic) and scripts used for each language, young children were able to recognize and explore the principles used to organize both scripts. Children coped well with simultaneously learning different writing systems, challenging the notion that young are confused by differences in languages. Kenner and Kress (2003) suggest that children's metalinguistic awareness of print features may be enhanced by their biliterate experiences, and note that children explore and talk about socially salient features of scripts

such as the importance of precise strokes in Chinese, and the special ways letters are joined together in Arabic. Overall, they conclude that from bi-scriptal experience, children learn different ways of designing symbols and using graphic space on the page, and that children recognize the differences in visual characteristics and the actions used to produce their two languages.

Researchers working from a sociocultural perspective have also focused on describing children's biliterate strategies and interactions at home and school. Both Gort (2006) and Reyes (2006) found that literacy learning is bidirectional, with children using both languages as resources for writing and strategically transferring both emergent and mature literacy understandings between languages. For young children learning to write in two languages simultaneously, the majority of writing-related behaviors (e.g., speech/print match, alphabetic principle) are applied cross-linguistically. As noted in research on oral language learning, young emerging biliterates strategically codeswitch (Gort, 2006; Reyes, 2006) to create hybrid written texts that generally follow the language practices valued in their classrooms and homes. Additionally the writing of emergent bilinguals is characterized by interliteracy, the temporary application of L1 syntax, phonology, semantics, and print conventions to L2 writing (Gort, 2006). As with monolingual children, writing in both L1 and L2 is meaning driven (Moll et al., 2001) and choices of which language to use in writing are related to children's identities in relation to different audiences and writing purposes (Kennedy, 2006; Reyes, 2006).

With regard to the social construction of biliterate practices, researchers (Moll et al.,

2001; Reyes, 2006; Reyes and Azuara, 2008) have demonstrated that children develop concepts about writing from an early age through active social participation in bilingual/biliterate events in their communities and schools. Children's literacy knowledge is highly variable and fluid, since it is situated and influenced by family- and context-specific patterns of language and literacy use involving the child's two languages (Moll et al., 2001; Reyes and Azuara, 2008). Overall, current research suggests that the process of learning to write in multiple languages is not only influenced by the child's cognitive strategies but also by family and community literacy events in which the child participates.

SOCIAL SEMIOTIC PERSPECTIVES ON CHILDHOOD AUTHORING

Trend 8: Exploring multimodal features of children's authoring

The most dramatic research trend in the last decade has been the increase in the number of studies focusing on multimodal features of young children's authoring. Kress states: 'multimodality is an absolute fact of children's semiotic practices' (1997: 137). Authoring for young children involves language, vocalization, gesture, gaze, bodily action, and graphic production (Lancaster, 2001).

While observations of children's tendencies to combine writing with other semiotic systems such as talk, drawing, gesture, and dramatic play were present in the seminal work of Harste et al., (1984) and Dyson (1986), and have received continued attention throughout the 1990s (e.g., Dyson, 2003; Rowe, 1994; Siegel, 1995), studies of multimodal authoring comprise the most heavily studied research strand during the last decade. In all, for the years of 2000 through 2009, I located 29 studies of multimodality in early childhood authoring as compared to only eight in the period from 1990 to 1999 (cf., Rowe, 2008c). In the most recent decade, the 29 studies were distributed as follows: three focused on boundaries between drawing and writing, five on multimodality in play, five on multimodal authoring in digital literacy contexts, and the remaining 16 on multimodality in traditional, paper-based composing events at school or home.

While it is possible that young, children's authoring processes have become more multimodal in the last decade because of the affordances of twenty-first century digital composing tools, I doubt this is the main reason for the field's increased interest in multimodality. After all, from the beginning, emergent literacy researchers (e.g., Dyson, 1997; Harste et al., 1984; Kenner et al., 2004; Rowe, 1987) have described the irrepressibly multimodal nature of young children's authoring regardless of the materials or composing tools made available. While some of these researchers have considered multimodal authoring worthy of study in its own right, others have focused on children's understanding of the boundaries between writing and drawing. Underlying this line of research is an implicit view of mature authoring as monomodal and print-centered (Levin and Bus, 2003; Robins and Treiman, 2009; Yang and Noel, 2006). The number of studies focused on modal boundaries remained almost constant across the decades under consideration (i.e., two studies in the 1990s and three in the 2000s), while studies focusing on the features and processes used to construct multimodal texts more than doubled.

A careful reading of recent research suggests that shifts in researchers' views of literacy to sociocultural and social semiotic perspectives (Kress, 1994, 1997; Kress and Van Leeuwen, 2006; New London Group, 1996) were spurred on by an increasing awareness of the importance of multimodality in twenty-first century digital technologies. Additionally, for early literacy researchers, limiting the focus of research to children's writing is to ignore a large part of young children's meaning-making. These influences have worked together to bring multimodal authoring to the forefront of researcher attention as an acceptable and desirable practice. Multimodal authoring is no longer seen as a childish practice to be put aside as soon as children can write. In the current environment, young children's penchant for 'symbol weaving' (Dyson, 1986) is increasingly being normalized and valued as part of dominant literacy practices (Harste, 2000; Kress, 1997).

Modal boundaries for writing and drawing

Perhaps, because adults often assume that very young children's unconventional marks are drawing rather than writing, one line of seminal work in this area has focused on establishing whether preschoolers distinguish writing from drawing (e.g., Ferreiro and Teberosky, 1982; Harste et al., 1984). Several current studies specifically addressed writing–drawing relationships. Lancaster's (2007) study of 1- and 2-year-olds found that these youngest preschoolers did not distinguish between writing and drawing, but instead made use of the structural features of both systems. Rowe (2008b), on the other hand, found that most 2-year-olds used different marks to distinguish drawing from writing within a composing event, though across events they did not use consistent types of mark

for writing and drawing. For older preschoolers, both seminal and more recent research has supported the conclusion that, by age 3, many children have different action plans for writing and drawing and are developing an understanding of differences in the two modes of representation (Brenneman, Massey, Machado, and Gelman, 1996; Landsmann, 1996). However, this conclusion has recently been called into question. Levin and Bus' study of 2–4-year-olds found that even after children begin to produce writing-like forms, they may be 'drawing print' (2003: 891). While the question as to what understandings children have about writing and drawing, and whether drawing precedes writing remains open to further investigation, recent research (Robins and Treiman, 2009) confirms that parents talk to their children in ways that highlight connections between speaking and writing (e.g., 'What does this [written text] say?') and differentiate writing from drawing. This work suggests that adult talk may provide information that children need to understand conventional differences between drawing and writing.

Multimodal composing

Almost all researchers observing young children's authoring have commented on their tendencies to combine writing with other semiotic systems such as talk, drawing, gesture, and dramatic play. Researchers working from semiotic perspectives (Kendrick and McKay, 2004; Lancaster, 2007; Pahl, 2001, 2002; Siegel, Kontovourki, Schmier, and Enriquez, 2008) are currently expanding the line of research exploring the connections between writing and other sign systems (e.g., art, oral language, gesture, gaze, movement, music) with an eye toward more fully understanding the multimodal nature of children's texts and authoring processes. While adults and older children are more likely to have adopted dominant views of writing as separate from other forms of communication, very young children have less cultural experience and so are less constrained by boundaries between sign systems (Kress, 1997). Authoring for young children involves language, vocalization, gesture, gaze, bodily action, and graphic production (Lancaster, 2001, 2006; Wright, 2007).

Both seminal and more recent studies document children's flexible interweaving of semiotic systems (Berghoff and Hamilton, 2000). Researchers have also begun to investigate children's interweaving of linguistic (i.e., print) and visual resources (i.e., font, color, and layout) as they compose on computers (Marsh, 2006; Mavers, 2007; Siegel, 2006; Siegel et al., 2008). From a semiotic perspective, meaning-making can be considered a process of design (Mavers, 2007; Ranker, 2007, 2009; Siegel et al., 2008) in which multimodal authoring practices allow children to draw on meanings formed in a variety of sign systems and to gain access to authoring events using non-linguistic forms of communication (Harste, 2000). Several researchers have described transmediation (Genishi, Stires, and Yung-Chan, 2001; Rowe, Fitch, and Bass, 2003; Siegel et al., 2008) or transduction (Kress, 1997; Marsh, 2006) – movement of meanings across sign systems – as an important part of multimodal authoring activities. Multimodal authoring appears to be particularly important for beginning writers, those whose strength is not language, or who are learning English as another language (Genishi et al., 2001; Ranker, 2009; Rowe et al., 2001).

When researchers broaden the semiotic boundaries of authoring, another outcome is an increased focus on the embodied and material nature of authoring practices. Young children perform their early writings with gesture, facial expression, and pantomime (Lancaster, 2007; Wright, 2007). Embodied practices such as gaze and body posture carry important meanings, and are closely monitored by adults who interact with young authors (Lancaster, 2001). The arrangement of their bodies in classroom space helps to position young authors as particular kinds of students and authors (Siegel et al., 2008). Multimodal authoring practices are also strongly influenced by the physical materials that are available in the environment (Pahl and Rowsell, 2010; Rowe, 2008a, 2008b). As Kress (1997) points out, the materiality of the objects is important in that children are adopting and adapting culturally significant elements of complex signs when they combine paper, writing tools, and objects from their environment, with gesture, talk, and drama.

Overall, it is clear that, very early, children begin to wrestle with the characteristic visual arrays and meaning potentials of a variety of sign systems. Throughout the early years, children's texts and writing performances are decidedly multimodal. Though some research continues to cast children's multimodal writing as a step along the way toward more mature, print-only texts, semiotic perspectives reframe children's multimodal texts and writing performances in relation to more expansive views that celebrate and normalize composing with multiple sign systems (Dyson, 2004; Harste et al., 1984; Siegel, 1995) and that connect multimodal composing to the increasing multimodality of children's twenty-first-century textual experiences (Kress and Van Leeuwen, 2006; Mavers, 2007; New London Group, 1996; Wright, 2007). This trend suggests that childhood writing will increasingly be studied as one facet of a more complex multimodal design process in which pictures, gestures, music, and movement join reading and writing as 'basic' resources for composing (Dyson, 2004; Siegel, 2006).

Trend 9: Play as a multimodal literacy

A ninth trend addresses the re-emergence of play as an important context for authoring research. In the 1990s an active line of research investigated children's reading and writing activities during play. Naturalistic studies of children's spontaneous dramatic play show that children often write as part of the literate roles they take on in play (Neuman and Roskos, 1991). This observation led researchers to design a number of studies where literacy materials and props were added to dramatic play centers with the goal of providing more opportunities for literacy-related play, including writing. Results show that writing and reading activities increase in literacy-enriched play centers (Christie and Enz, 1992; Morrow, 1991; Morrow and Rand, 1991; Neuman and Roskos, 1991, 1992, 1993; Vukelich, 1991), and that adult scaffolding further increases literacy-related play in these centers (Morrow and Rand, 1991; Vukelich, 1991). While this line of research showed that dramatic play could offer children opportunities for authoring practice, only a few researchers pursued this line of study after 2000.

However, recently, a new line of literacy-play research has appeared, this time influenced by social semiotic perspectives on multimodality. Wohlwend (2008) argues that play is a multimodal form of literacy in its own right. Play requires the fast-paced blending of forms and modalities needed by authors in twenty-first-century literacy events. Through play, children try

out conventional uses of different modalities, explore the multimodal potentials of materials, negotiate social spaces for interaction, and laminate other time-spaces to the present one (Wohlwend, 2008, 2009). Both Kontovourki and Siegel (2009) and Lysaker, Wheat, and Benson (2010) make similar arguments after observing children's flexible shifts between academic and playful engagement in classroom writing activities. Kontovourki and Siegel argue that play allows children to make spaces for their childhood practices, interests, and ways of making meaning, and functions as an important multimodal literacy. Their study shows that children use play as a context for trying on literate identities, for redefining themselves as authors, and for making connections to texts and experiences that go beyond the page. Children's multimodal, 'played' texts are more complex than the traces left on the page, allowing children to engage as both authors and characters in the developing stories.

Trend 10: Young authors composing in a digital world

As literacy research, in general, experiences a digital turn, early literacy researchers have begun to explore young children's participation in digital literacy practices. Several studies (Hill, 2010; Marsh, Brooks, Hughes, Ritchie, Roberts, and Wright, 2007; Rideout, Vandewater, and Wartella, 2003; Yamada-Rice, 2010) have used survey or observational methods to gauge young children's access and engagement with digital media and composing tools outside of school, finding that many preschool and early-grades children have daily opportunities to interact with and within the environments created by digital technologies.

When studying child authoring, researchers have focused on ways the content and processes of authoring are influenced by digital environments. A number of researchers have reported that young authors appropriate and transform themes, characters, and story lines from popular culture texts encountered through television, movies, video games, and on-line sources and use them in their written and multimodal texts (Dyson, 1997, 2002; Marsh et al., 2005; Pahl, 2002; Ranker, 2007, 2009; Wohlwend, 2009). Dyson (2001) has found that first graders creatively and flexibly borrow from media sources available to them outside of school, adapting them to the social structures and purposes of school writing (Dyson, 2003). Similarly, Wohlwend (2009) found that kindergarteners adopt and adapt themes from popular media and use them as resources for designing play scenarios and as the basis for written texts. Ranker (2007) found that multimodal composing involves intertextuality and redesign of media content and genre features. Overall, studies of young children's use of digital content and themes in multimodal composing and play contexts, show that young authors use digital content as resources for interaction, expression, learning about the world, and to take up positions in the formal world of the classroom and the informal world of peer culture. Their products are highly multimodal and intertextual, combining a variety of sign systems and materials and creatively redesigning media content and structures for new purposes. With opportunities to negotiate the meanings of their texts with others, they can also adopt a critical stance (Dyson, 2001; Hill, 2010).

A second focus has been children's use of digital communication and composing tools. Wohlwend (2009) found that when children had no school access to the digital tools they used at home (e.g., cell phones, video games), they still found ways to incorporate these tools into their composing at school. In her study, kindergarteners collaboratively played out interactive video game scenarios with paper and markers, and used available art and construction materials to fashion pretend cell phones for their play. In the same way children play at writing grocery lists in literacy-enriched play centers (Neuman and Roskos, 1991), she found that children play at digital literacy by inventing material representations of their preferred digital tools and creating shared social spaces where digital literacy practices can be imaginatively played out.

Increasingly, researchers have directly studied young children's composing processes with digital tools. These studies vary from those that focus on composing with print-centered digital tools, to those that investigate children's composing with tools that foreground visual and auditory modes of representation. Mavers (2007), for example, investigated a 6-year-old's composing processes when sending e-mail to a relative – a print-centered activity. She found that the child's texts involved careful decisions about how to use and integrate a variety of sign systems including words, grammar, punctuation, spacing, font, color, and that the child's e-mail messages were shaped by the affordances of the computer environment, her own interests, and her social relationships with her audience. Kontovourki and Siegel (2009) also observed kindergarteners composing on computers, but in a school setting. Though the curriculum remained print-centered, children composed using the visual meaning-making resources offered by a computer drawing program. These researchers found that the digital environment offered open-ended opportunities for playful exploration of a variety of modalities and offered different kinds of opportunities for students to position themselves as accomplished authors. Bjorkvall and Engbloom (2010) conducted case studies of three Swedish 7- and 8-year-olds in schools where every child worked with computers in all subjects, and where children had access to a much wider array of digital tools and resources than in the previous studies. In this digitally-rich school environment, the researchers found that children brought considerable expertise to authoring events. They engaged in multimodal digital play that resulted in texts where meanings were expressed both through writing and visual modes.

While much of the literacy-focused research on digital composing has retained a strong focus on the role of print, some researchers have begun to investigate children's composing practices in situations where print plays a support role and where the goal is the production of texts where visual modes are foregrounded. For example, working with 5–8-year-olds, Hill (2010) reported a case study of children composing movie versions of fairy tales. While children read a variety of fairy tale storybooks, used print to write out scripts, and used drawing to create storyboards, these traditional page-based forms of literacy were used in service of designing movies where visual features were highlighted and where print played only a minor role. Marsh (2006) also studied children's design processes during a movie-making activity. The 3- and 4-year-olds in

her study created short animated films using webcams and editing software on laptop computers. These very young composers demonstrated emergent understandings of the differing affordances of paper-based and digital moving image-based stories, realizing that stories changed in important ways when moved from paper to the screen. Together, these studies of children's visual literacy practices represent a growing line of research in which the production of images is no longer seen as the precursor to literacy, but as an important form of literacy in its own right.

Overall, each of these studies provides a glimpse into the ways that digital tools can open up opportunities for expression as children experiment with the many visual modalities and textual options for composing. While digital composing frequently involves page- and screen-based writing and reading, print skills comprise only part of what children know and learn as they compose in digital environments. This research highlights the importance of studying the variety of digital modalities and text types available to children, and how digital tools bound products and authoring processes, as paper and pencil did in the last century.

Collectively, these investigations show the importance of digital literacies for young authors and represent the leading edge of a line of research that will undoubtedly become even more important in decades to come. As Dyson (2003) suggests, children are textual scavengers who creatively and profitably make use of attractive and engaging digital media content and tools as they author their own multimodal texts. As young children have increased exposure to digital content and increased access to digital composing tools, research on young children's emerging techno-literacies

(Bjorkvall and Engbloom, 2010) will also become increasingly important for the field of early literacy research.

CODA: THE POTENTIALS OF EXISTING PATHS AND LINES OF FLIGHT FOR RESEARCH ON EARLY CHILDHOOD AUTHORING

In the last decade, research on early childhood authoring has experienced a resurgence of interest generated by both new connections between existing socio-cognitive theories of writing and reading and by lines of flight (Deleuze and Guattari, 1987) moving the field beyond traditional notions of print literacy to connect childhood authoring to twenty-first-century technologies and broader semiotic notions of multimodal sign making, and social and cultural practice. For early literacy researchers working from cognitive and sociocognitive perspectives, the past decade has seen the linkage of research on emergent writing and reading, forging new kinds of connections in lines of research that have previously been conducted in parallel. Correlational and experimental research studying reading/writing connections have the potential to help both teachers and students see the strategic interconnections between reading and writing processes, and to encourage educators to give writing a more prominent place in early grades classrooms.

Researchers working from sociocultural perspectives are well along the way to developing theories and methods that allow them to unpack the social, cultural, and ideological features of the local literacy events in which children learn about authoring. As the field has moved toward views of authoring that are more situated, it has become increasingly challenging to see commonalities across studies that are so rich in particulars. The challenge for researchers is to situate their research reports in the lifeworlds of children, while at the same time making clear to readers what kinds of insights might travel beyond the local contexts studied. Researchers need to push past thick description to consider how observed patterns relate to or challenge framing theories and models of child authoring. The field needs not only rich description, but also richly developed theories carefully grounded in data.

Finally, as adults become engaged with twenty-first-century literacies that require flexible design and creative reframing of multimodal resources, young children's play looks more like our own work. The last decade has launched a line of research on children's emergent techno-literacies (Bjorkvall and Engbloom, 2010) and techno-composing. This work promises to be increasingly important if we are to understand children's real world authoring practices on the page, on the screen, and through play. While in the past young children's authoring processes were considered temporary approximations of mature authoring, we may now find young authors leading the way toward new literacy practices for the twenty-first century.

REFERENCES

Aram, D. (2010). 'Writing with young children: A comparison of paternal and maternal guidance', *Journal of Research in Reading*, 33(1): 4–19.

Baghban, M. (1984). *Our Daughter Learns to Read and Write. A Case Study from Birth to Three*. Newark, DE: International Reading Association.

Barton, D. and Hamilton, M. (1998). *Local Literacies. Reading and Writing in One Community*. London: Routledge.

Barton, D. and Hamilton, M. (2000). 'Literacy practices', in D. Barton, M. Hamilton, and R. Ivanic (eds), *Situated Literacies. Reading and Writing in Context*. London: Routledge. pp. 7–15.

Bear, D. and Templeton, S. (1998). 'Explorations in spelling: Foundations for learning and teaching phonics, spelling, and vocabulary', *Reading Teacher*, 52: 222–42.

Berghoff, B. and Hamilton, S. (2000). 'Inquiry and multiple ways of knowing in a first grade', in B. Berghoff, K. Egawa, J. C. Harste, and B. Hoonan (eds), *Beyond Reading and Writing: Inquiry Curriculum and Multiple Ways of Knowing*. Urbana, IL: National Council of Teachers of English.

Besse, J. M. (1996). 'An approach to writing in kindergarten', in M. Orsolini, B. Burge, and L. B. Resnick (eds), *Children's Early Text Construction*. Mahwah, NJ: Lawrence Erlbaum. pp. 127–44.

Bissex, G. (1980). *GNYS AT WRK: A Child Learns to Read and Write*. Cambridge, MA: Harvard University Press.

Bjorkvall, A. and Engbloom, C. (2010). 'Young children's exploration of semiotic resources during unofficial computer activities in the classroom', *Journal of Early Childhood Literacy*, 10(3): 271–93.

Bloodgood, J. (1999). 'What's in a name? Children's name writing and name acquisition', *Reading Research Quarterly*, 34: 342–67.

Bloome, D., Katz, L., and Champion, T. (2003). 'Young children's narratives and ideologies of language in classrooms', *Reading & Writing Quarterly*, 19: 2005–223.

Borzone de Manrique, A. M. and Signorini, A. (1998). 'Emergent writing forms in Spanish', *Reading and Writing: An Interdisciplinary Journal*, 10: 499–517.

Brenneman, K., Massey, C., Machado, S., & Gelman, R. (1996). 'Young children's plans for writing and drawing'. *Cognitive Development*, 11, 397–419.

Christie, J. and Enz, B. J. (1992). 'The effects of literacy play interventions on preschoolers' play patterns and literacy development', *Early Education and Development*, 3: 205–20.

Clay, M. (1975). *What Did I Write?* Auckland, New Zealand: Heinemann.

Clay, M. (1991). *Becoming Literate. The Construction of Inner Control*. Portsmouth, NH: Heinemann.

Compton-Lilly, C. (2003). *Reading Families. The Literate Lives of Urban Children*. New York: Teachers College Press.

Compton-Lilly, C. (2006). 'Identity, childhood culture, and literacy learning: A case study', *Journal of Early Childhood Literacy*, 6(1): 57–76.

Defior, S., Jiménez-Fernández, G., and Serrano, F. (2009). 'Complexity and lexicality effects on the acquisition of Spanish spelling', *Learning & Instruction*, 19: 55–65.

Deleuze, G. and Guattari, F. (1987). *A Thousand Plateaus: Capitalism and Schizophrenia*. Tr. B. Massumi. Minnesota: University of Minnessota Press.

Devonshire, V. and Fluck, M. (2010). 'Spelling development: Fine-tuning strategy-use and capitalising on the connections between words', *Learning & Instruction*, 20: 361–71.

Donovan, C. A. (2001). 'Children's development and control of written story and informational genres. Insights from one elementary school', *Research in the Teaching of English*, 35: 394–447.

Dyson, A. (1985). 'Individual differences in emerging writing', in M. Farr (ed.), *Advances in Writing Research, Volume One: Children's Early Writing Development*. Norwood, NJ: Ablex.

Dyson, A. (1986). 'Transitions and tensions: Interrelationships between drawing, talking, and dictating of young children', *Research in the Teaching of English*, 20: 279–409.

Dyson, A. (1997). *Writing Superheroes. Contemporary Childhood, Popular Culture, and Classroom Literacy*. New York: Teachers College Press.

Dyson, A. (2000). 'On reframing children's words: The perils, promises, and pleasures of writing children', *Research in the Teaching of English*, 34(3): 352–67.

Dyson, A. (2001). 'Donkey Kong in Little Bear country: A first grader's composing development in the media spotlight', *Elementary School Journal*, 101(4): 417–33.

Dyson, A. (2002). 'Writing and children's symbolic repertoires: Development unhinged', in S. B. Neuman and D. Dickinson (eds), *Handbook of Early Literacy Research*. New York: Guilford Press. pp. 126–41.

Dyson, A. (2003). *The Brothers and Sisters Learn to Write. Popular Literacies and School Cultures*. New York: Teachers College Press.

Dyson, A. (2004). 'Diversity as a "handful": Toward retheorizing the basics', *Research in the Teaching of English*, 39(2): 210–14.

Dyson, A. (2008). 'The Pine Cone wars: Studying writing in a community of children', *Language Arts*, 85(4): 305–15.

Ferreiro, E. (1990). 'Literacy development: Psychogenesis', in Y. Goodman (ed.), *How Children Construct Literacy. Piagetian Perspectives*. Newark, DE: International Reading Association. pp. 12–25.

Ferreiro, E. and Teberosky, A. (1982). *Literacy Before Schooling*. Portsmouth, NH: Heinemann.

Ferreiro, E., Pontecorvo, C., and Zucchermaglio, C. (1996). 'PIZZA or PIZA? How children interpret the doubling of letters in writing', in C. Pontecorvo, M. Orsolini, B. Burge, and L. B. Resnick (eds), *Children's Early Text Construction*. Mahwah, NJ: Lawrence Erlbaum. pp. 145–63.

Fisher, R. (2010). 'Young writers' construction of agency', *Journal of Early Childhood Literacy*, 10(4): 410–29.

Fresch, M. J. (2001). 'Journal entries as a window on spelling knowledge', *Reading Teacher*, 54(5): 500–13.

Genishi, C., Stires, S. E., and Yung-Chan, D. (2001). 'Writing in an integrated curriculum: Prekindergarten English language learners as symbol makers', *The Elementary School Journal*, 101(4): 399–416.

Gentry, J. R. (2000). 'A retrospective on invented spelling and a look forward', *Reading Teacher*, 54(3): 318–32.

Goodman, Y. (ed.). (1990). *How Children Construct Literacy. Piagetian Perspectives*. Newark, DE: International Reading Association.

Gort, M. (2006). 'Strategic codeswitching, interliteracy, and other personal of emergent bilingual writing: Lessons from first grade dual language classrooms', *Journal of Early Childhood Literacy*, 6(3): 323–454.

Haney, M. R., Bissonnette, V., and Behnken, K. L. (2003). 'The relationship among name writing and early literacy skills in kindergarten children', *Child Study Journal*, 33(2): 99–114.

Harste, J. C. (2000). 'Six points of departure', in B. Berghoff, K. Egawa, J. C. Harste, and B. Hoonan (eds), *Beyond Reading and Writing: Inquiry Curriculum and Multiple Ways of Knowing*. Urbana, IL: National Council of Teachers of English. pp. 1–16.

Harste, J. C., Woodward, V. A., and Burke, C. L. (1984). *Language Stories and Literacy Lessons*. Portsmouth, NH: Heinemann.

Henderson, E. and Beers, J. (1980). *Developmental and Cognitive Aspects of Learning to Spell: A Reflection of Word Knowledge*. Newark, DE: International Reading Association.

Hicks, D. (2002). *Reading Lives. Working Class Children and Literacy Learning*. New York: Teachers College Press.

Hildreth, G. (1936). 'Developmental sequences in name writing', *Child Development*, 7: 291–303.

Hill, S. (2010). 'The millennium generation: Teacher-researchers exploring new forms of literacy', *Journal of Early Childhood Literacy*, 10(3): 314–40.

Hughes, M. and Searle, D. (1991). 'A longitudinal study of the growth of spelling abilities within the contex of the development of literacy', in J. Zutell, S. McCormick, L. Caton, and P. O'Keefe (eds), *Learner Factors/Teacher Factors: Issues in Literacy Research and Instruction. Fortieth Yearbook of the National Reading Conference*. Chicago: National Reading Conference.

Jalil, S. B. and Liow, S. J. R. (2008). 'How does home language influence early spellings? Phonologically plausible errors of diglossic Malay children', *Applied Psycholinguistics*, 29(4): 535–52.

Kamberelis, G. and Bovino, T. D. (1999). 'Cultural artifacts as scaffolds for genre development', *Reading Research Quarterly*, 34(2): 138–70.

Kamii, C., Long, R. and Manning, M. (2001). 'Kindergarteners' development toward "invented" spelling and a glottographic theory', *Linguistics and Education*, 12: 195–210.

Kendrick, M. and McKay, R. (2004). 'Drawings as an alternate way of understanding young children's constructions of literacy', *Journal of Early Childhood Literacy*, 4(1): 109–28.

Kennedy, E. (2006). 'Literacy development of linguistically diverse first graders in a mainstream English classroom: Connecting speaking and writing', *Journal of Early Childhood Literacy*, 6(2): 163–89.

Kenner, C. (2000). 'Symbols make text: A social semiotic analysis of writing in a multilingual nursery', *Written Language and Literacy*, 3(2): 235–66.

Kenner, C. and Kress, G. (2003). 'The multisemiotic resources of biliterate children', *Journal of Early Childhood Literacy*, 3(2): 179–202.

Kenner, C., Kress, G., Al-Khatib, H., Kam, R., and Tsai, K.-C. (2004). 'Finding the keys to biliteracy: How young children interpret different writing systems', *Language and Education*, 18(2): 124–44.

Kontovourki, S. and Siegel, M. (2009). 'Discipline and play with/in a mandated literacy curriculum', *Language Arts*, 87(1): 30–8.

Korat, O. and Levin, I. (2002). 'Spelling acquisition in two societal groups: Mother child interaction, maternal beliefs and child's spelling', *Journal of Literacy Research*, 34(2): 209–36.

Korkeamaki, R.-L. and Dreher, M. J. (2000). 'Finnish kindergarteners' literacy development in contextualized literacy episodes: A focus on spelling', *Journal of Literacy Research*, 32(3): 349–93.

Kress, G. (1994). *Learning to Write* (2nd ed.). London: Routledge.

Kress, G. (1997). *Before Writing: Rethinking the Paths to Literacy*. London: Routledge.

Kress, G. and Van Leeuwen, T. (2006). *Reading Images: The Grammar of Visual Design*. London: Routledge.

Lancaster, L. (2001). 'Staring at the page: The function of gaze in a young child's interpretation of symbolic forms', *Journal of Early Childhood Literacy*, 1(2): 131–52.

Lancaster, L. (2006). 'Grammaticisation in early mark making: A multimodal investigation', *ESRC End of Award Report*. Cheshire, UK: Manchester Metropolitan University.

Lancaster, L. (2007). 'Representing the ways of the world: How children under three start to use syntax in graphic signs', *Journal of Early Childhood Literacy*, 7(3): 123–54.

Landsmann, L. T. (1996). Three accounts of literacy and the role of environment. In C. Pontecorvo, M. Orsolini, B. Burge & L. Resnick (eds), *Children's early text construction* (pp. 101–126). Mahwah, NJ: Lawrence Erlbaum.

Larson, J. and Maier, M. (2000). 'Co-authoring classroom texts: Shifting participant roles in writing activity', *Research in the Teaching of English*, 34(4): 468–97.

Lave, J. and Wenger, E. (1991). *Situated Learning. Legitimate Peripheral Participation*. Cambridge: Cambridge University Press.

Lehtonen, A. and Bryant, P. (2005). 'Active players or just passive bystanders? The role of morphemes in spelling development in a transparent orthography', *Applied Psycholinguistics*, 26: 137–55.

Lemke, J. (1995). *Textual Politics*. London: Taylor & Francis.

Levin, I. and Bus, A. G. (2003). 'How is emergent writing based on drawing? Analyses of children's products and their sorting by children and mothers', *Developmental Psychology*, 39(5): 891–905.

Levin, I., Both-DeVries, A., Aram, D., and Bus, A. G. (2005). 'Writing starts with own name writing: From scribbling to conventional spelling in Israeli and Dutch children', *Applied Psycholinguistics*, 26: 463–77.

Loizidou-Ieridou, N., Masterson, J., and Hanley, J. R. (2010). 'Spelling development in 6–11-year-old Greek-speaking Cypriot children', *Journal of Research in Reading*, 33(4): 247–62.

Lynch, J. (2008). 'Engagement with print: Low-income families and Head Start children', *Journal of Early Childhood Literacy*, 8(2): 151–75.

Lysaker, J., Wheat, J., and Benson, E. (2010). 'Children's spontaneous play in writer's workshop', *Journal of Early Childhood Literacy*, 10(2): 209–29.

Manyak, P. (2001). 'Participation, hybridity, and carnival: A situated analysis of a dynamic literacy practice in a primary-grade English immersion class', *Journal of Literacy Research*, 33: 423–65.

Marsh, J. (2006). 'Emergent media literacy: Digital animation in early childhood', *Language and Education*, 20(6): 493–506.

Marsh, J., Brooks, G., Hughes, J., Ritchie, L., Roberts, S., and Wright, K. (2005). *Digital Beginnings: Young Children's Use of Popular Culture, Media and New Technologies*. Sheffield: University of Sheffield.

Martens, P. A. (1996). *I Already Know How to Read. A Child's View of Literacy*. Portsmouth, NH: Heinemann.

Martens, P. A. (1999). '"Mommy, how do you write 'Sarah'?": The role of name writing in one child's literacy', *Journal of Research in Childhood Education*, 14(1): 5–15.

Martins, M. A. and Silva, C. (2001). 'Letter names, phonological awareness, and the phonetization of writing', *European Journal of Psychology of Education*, 16(4): 605–17.

Mavers, D. (2007). 'Semiotic resourcefulness: A young child's email exchange as design' *Journal of Early Childhood Literacy*, 7(2): 155–76.

Mayer, C. and Moskos, E. (1998). 'Deaf children learning to spell', *Research in the Teaching of English*, 33: 158–80.

Meier, D. R. (2000). *Scribble Scrabble. Learning to Read and Write. Success with Diverse Teachers, Children, and Families*. New York: Teachers College Press.

Moll, L. C., Saez, R., and Dworin, J. (2001). 'Exploring biliteracy: Two student case examples of writing as social practice', *The Elementary School Journal*, 101(4): 435–49.

Morrow, L. M. (1991). 'Relationships among physical design of play centers, teachers' on literacy in play, and children's literacy behaviors during play', in S. McCormick and J. Zutell (eds), *Learner Factors/Teacher Factors: Issues in Literacy Research and Instruction. Thirty-Eighth Yearbook of the National Reading Conference*. Chicago: National Reading Conference. pp. 77–86.

Morrow, L. M. and Rand, M. (1991). 'Promoting literacy during play by designing early childhood classroom environments', *Reading Research and Instruction*, 35: 85–101.

Neuman, S. B. and Roskos, K. (1991). 'The influence of literacy-enriched play centers on preschoolers' conceptions of the functions of print', in J. Christie (ed.), *Play and Early Literacy Development*. Albany, NY: State University of New York Press. pp. 167–87.

Neuman, S. B. and Roskos, K. (1992). 'Literacy objects as cultural tools: Effects on children's literacy behaviors in play', *Reading Research Quarterly*, 27: 203–25.

Neuman, S. B. and Roskos, K. (1993). 'Access to print for children of poverty: Differential effects of adult mediation and literacy-enriched play settings on environmental and functional print tasks', *American Educational Research Journal*, 30: 95–122.

Neumann, M. M., Hood, M., and Neumann, D. L. (2009). 'The scaffolding of emergent literacy skills in the home environment: A case study', *Early Childhood Education Journal*, 36: 313–19.

New London Group (1996). 'A pedagogy of multiliteracies: Designing social futures', *Harvard Educational Review*, 66(1): 60–92.

Ouellette, G. and Sénéchal, M. (2008). 'Pathways to literacy: A study of invented spelling and its role in learning to read', *Child Development*, 79(4): 899–913.

Pahl, K. (2001). 'Texts as artefacts crossing sites: Map making at home and school', *Reading, Literacy, & Language*, 35(3): 120–5.

Pahl, K. (2002). 'Ephemera, mess and miscellaneous piles: Texts and practices in families', *Journal of Early Childhood Literacy*, 2(2): 145–66.

Pahl, K. and Rowsell, J. (2010). *Artifactual Literacies. Every Object Tells a Story*. New York: Teachers College Press.

Pantaleo, S. (2009). 'An ecological perspective on the socially embedded nature of reading and writing', *Journal of Early Childhood Literacy*, 9(1): 75–99.

Pappas, C. C., Varelas, M., Gill, S. R., Ortiz, I., and Keblawe-Shamah, N. (2009). 'Multimodal books in science-literacy units: Language and visual images for meaning-making', *Language Arts*, 86(2): 201–11.

Pine, N. (1992). 'Early traces of literate behavior: Graphical knowledge demonstrated by three-year-olds in the United States and China', *LACUS Forum*, 18: 77–90.

Purcell-Gates, V. (1996). 'Stories, coupons, and the *TV Guide*: Relationships between home literacy experiences and emergent literacy knowledge', *Reading Research Quarterly*, 31(4): 406–28.

Qian, G. and Pan, J. (2006). 'Susanna's way of becoming literate: A case study of literacy acquisition by a young girl from a Chinese immigrant family', *Reading Horizons*, 47(1): 75–96.

Ranker, J. (2007). 'Designing meaning with multiple media sources: A case study of an eight-year-old student's writing processes', *Research in the Teaching of English*, 41(4): 402–34.

Ranker, J. (2009). 'Redesigning and transforming: A case study of the role of semiotic import in early composing processes', *Journal of Early Childhood Literacy*, 9(3): 319–47.

Read, C. (1971). 'Preschool children's knowledge of English phonology', *Harvard Educational Review*, 41: 1–34.

Reyes, I. (2006). 'Exploring connections between emergent biliteracy and bilingualism', *Journal of Early Childhood Literacy*, 6(3): 267–92.

Reyes, I. and Azuara, P. (2008). 'Emergent biliteracy in young Mexican immigrant children', *Reading Research Quarterly*, 43(4): 374–98.

Rideout, V. J., Vandewater, E. A., and Wartella, E. A. (2003). *Zero to Six: Electronic Media in the Lives of Infants, Toddlers, and Preschoolers*. Washington: Henry J. Kaiser Family Foundation.

Riley, J. and Reedy, D. (2005). 'Developing young children's thinking through learning to write argument', *Journal of Early Childhood Literacy*, 5(1): 29–51.

Robins, S. and Treiman, R. (2009). 'Talking about writing: What we can learn from conversations between parents and their young children', *Applied Psycholinguistics*, 30, 463–84.

Rowe, D. W. (1987). 'Literacy learning as an intertextual process', in J. E. Readence and R. S. Baldwin (eds), *Research in Literacy: Merging Perspectives. Thirty-Sixth Yearbook of the National Reading Conference*. Rochester: National Reading Conference. pp. 101–12.

Rowe, D. W. (1994). *Preschoolers as Authors: Literacy Learning in the Social World of the Classroom*. Cresskill, NJ: Hampton Press.

Rowe, D. W. (2003). 'The nature of young children's authoring', in N. Hall, J. Larson, and J. Marsh (eds), *Handbook of Early Childhood Literacy*. London: Sage. pp. 258–70.

Rowe, D. W. (2008a). 'The social construction of intentionality: Two-year-olds' and adults' participation at a preschool writing center', *Research in the Teaching of English*, 42(4): 387–434.

Rowe, D. W. (2008b). 'Social contracts for writing: Negotiating shared understandings about text in the preschool years', *Reading Research Quarterly*, 43(1): 66–95.

Rowe, D. W. (2008c). 'Development of writing abilities in childhood', in C. Bazerman (ed.), *Handbook of Research on Writing*. Mahwah, NJ: Lawrence Erlbaum. pp. 401–19.

Rowe, D. W. (2009). 'Early written communication', in R. Beard, D. Myhill, J. Riley, and M. Nystrand (eds), *SAGE Handbook of Writing Development*. Los Angeles: Sage. pp. 213–31.

Rowe, D. W. and Leander, K. (2005). 'Analyzing the production of third space in classroom literacy events', in B. Maloch, J. V. Hoffman, D. L. Schallert, C. M. Fairbanks, and J. Worthy (eds), *54th Yearbook of the National Reading Conference*. Oak Creek, WI: National Reading Conference. pp. 318–33.

Rowe, D. W. and Neitzel, C. (2010). 'Interest and agency in two- and three-year-olds' participation in emergent writing', *Reading Research Quarterly*, 45(2): 169–95.

Rowe, D. W., Fitch, J. D., and Bass, A. S. (2001). 'Power, identity, and instructional stance in the writers' workshop', *Language Arts*, 78: 426–34.

Rowe, D. W., Fitch, J. F., and Bass, A. (2003). 'Toy stories as opportunities for imagination and reflection in writers' workshop', *Language Arts*, 80(5): 363–74.

Rowsell, J. and Pahl, K. (2007). 'Sedimented identities in texts: Instances of practice', *Reading Research Quarterly*, 42(3): 388–404.

Santa Barbara Classroom Discourse Group (1992). 'Constructing literacy in classrooms: Literate action as social accomplishment', in H. H. Marshall (ed.), *Redefining Student Learning: Roots of Educational Change*. Norwood, NJ: Ablex. pp. 119–50.

Schickedanz, J. A. (1990). *Adam's Righting Revolutions: One Child's Literacy Development from Infancy through Grade One*. Portsmouth, NH: Heinemann.

Shahar-Yames, D. and Share, D. L. (2008). 'Spelling as a self-teaching mechanism in orthographic learning', *Journal of Research in Reading*, 31(1): 22–39.

Sharp, A. C., Sinatra, G. M., and Reynolds, R. E. (2008). 'The development of children's orthographic knowledge: A microgenetic perspective', *Reading Research Quarterly*, 43(3): 206–26.

Sheridan, D., Street, B., and Bloome, D. (2000). *Writing Ourselves: Mass Observations and Literacy Practices*. Cresskill, NJ: Hampton Press.

Siegel, M. (1995). 'More than words: The generative power of transmediation for learning', *Canadian Journal of Education*, 20(4): 455–75.

Siegel, M. (2006). 'Rereading the signs Multimodal transformations in the field of literacy education', *Language Arts*, 84(1): 65–77.

Siegel, M., Kontovourki, S., Schmier, S., and Enriquez, G. (2008). 'Literacy in motion: A case study of a shape-shifting kindergarterner' *Language Arts*, 86(2): 89–98.

Sirois, P., Boisclair, A., and Giasson, J. (2008). 'Understanding of the alphabetic principle through invented spelling among hearing-impaired children learning to read and write: Experimentation with a pedagogical approach', *Journal of Research in Reading*, 31(4): 339–58.

Smolkin, L. B. and Donovan, C. A. (2004). 'Developing conscious understanding of genre: The relationship between implicit and explicit knowledge during the five-to-seven shift', in J. Worthy, B. Maloch, J. V. Hoffman, D. L. Schallert, and C. M. Fairbanks (eds), *53rd Yearbook of the National Reading Conference*. Oak Creek, WI: National Reading Conference. pp. 385–99.

Solsken, J., Willett, J., and Wilson-Keenan, J.-A. (2000). 'Cultivating hybrid texts in multicultural classrooms: Promise and challenge', *Research in the Teaching of English*, 35(2): 179–212.

Street, B. V. (1995). *Social Literacies. Critical Approaches to Literacy Development, Ethnography and Education*. London: Longman.

Sulzby, E. (1986). 'Writing and reading: Signs of oral and written language organization in the young child', in W. Teale and E. Sulzby (eds), *Emergent Literacy*. Norwood, NJ: Ablex. pp. 50–89.

Taylor, D. and Dorsey-Gaines, D. (1988). *Growing up Literate. Learning from Inner-City Families*. Portsmouth, NH: Heinemann.

Teale, W. (1986). 'Home background and young children's literacy development', in W. Teale and E. Sulzby (eds), *Emergent Literacy*. Norwood, NJ: Ablex. pp. 173–206.

Teale, W. and Sulzby, E. (eds). (1986a). *Emergent Literacy*. Norwood, NJ: Ablex.

Teale, W. and Sulzby, E. (1986b). 'Introduction. Emergent literacy as a perspective for examining how young children become writers and readers', in W. Teale and E. Sulzby (eds), *Emergent Literacy*. Norwood, NJ: Ablex. pp. 7–25.

Treiman, R., Kessler, B., and Bourassa, D. (2001). 'Children's own names influence their spelling', *Applied Psycholinguistics*, 22: 555–70.

Van Sluys, K. (2003). 'Writing and identity construction: A young author's life in transition', *Language Arts*, 80(3): 176–84.

Verhagen, W. G. M., Aarnoutse, C. A. J., and Van Leeuwe, J. F. J. (2010). 'Spelling and word recognition in grades 1 and 2: Relations to phonological awareness and naming speed in Dutch children', *Applied Psycholinguistics*, 31: 59–80.

Vernon, S., Calderón, G., and Castro, L. (2004). 'The relationship between phonological awareness and writing in Spanish-speaking kindergarteners', *Written Language and Literacy*, 7(1): 101–18.

Vukelich, C. (1991). 'Materials and modeling: Promoting literacy during play', in J. Christie (ed.), *Play and Early Literacy Development*. Albany: State University of New York Press. pp. 215–31.

Welsch, J. G., Sullivan, A., and Justice, L. M. (2003). 'That's my letter!: What preschoolers' name writing representations tell us about emergent literacy knowledge', *Journal of Literacy Research*, 35(2): 757–76.

Wilson, C. (2000). *Telling a Different Story. Teaching and Literacy in an Urban Preschool*. New York: Teachers College Press.

Winskel, H. and Widjaja, V. (2007). 'Phonological awareness, letter knowledge, and literacy development in Indonesian beginner readers and spellers', *Applied Psycholinguistics*, 28: 23–45.

Wohlwend, K. (2008). 'Play as a literacy of possibilities: Expanding meanings in practices, materials, and spaces', *Language Arts*, 86(2): 127–36.

Wohlwend, K. (2009). 'Early adopters: Playing new literacies and pretending new technologies in print-centric classrooms', *Journal of Early Childhood Literacy*, 9(2): 117–40.

Wolf, S. A. (2006). 'The mermaid's purse: Looking closely at young children's art and poetry', *Language Arts*, 84(1): 10–20.

Wollman-Bonilla, J. E. (2000). 'Teaching science writing to first graders: Genre learning and recontextualization', *Research in the Teaching of English*, 35: 35–65.

Wollman-Bonilla, J. E. (2001). 'Family involvement in early writing instruction', *Journal of Early Childhood Literacy*, 1: 167–92.

Wollman-Bonilla, J. E. (2003). 'E-mail as genre: A beginning writer learns the conventions', *Language Arts*, 81(2): 126–34.

Wright, S. (2007). 'Young children's meaning-making through drawing and 'telling'. Analogies to filmic textual features', *Australian Journal of Early Childhood*, 32(4): 37–48.

Yaden, D., Rowe, D. W., and MacGillivray, L. (2000). 'Emergent literacy. A matter (polyphony) of perspectives', in M. Kamil, P. Mosenthal, P. D. Pearson, and R. Barr (eds), *Handbook of Reading Research*. Vol. III. Mahwah, NJ: Lawrence Erlbaum. pp. 425–54.

Yamada-Rice, D. (2010) 'Beyond words: An enquiry into children's home visual communication practices', *Journal of Early Childhood Literacy*, 10(3): 341–363.

Yang, H. C. and Noel, A. M. (2006). 'The developmental characteristics of four- and five-year-old pre-schoolers' drawing: An analysis of scribbles, placement patterns, emergent writing, and name writing in archived spontaneous drawing samples', *Journal of Early Childhood Literacy*, 6(2): 145–62.

26

The Development of Spelling

Patricia L. Scharer and Jerry Zutell

In *The Barnhart Dictionary of Etymology* (Barnhart, 1988), the verb **to spell** is defined first as to 'name the letters of.' Along with the related noun form, **spell**, meaning 'words supposed to have magical powers, incantation, charm,' **to spell** is related to an older root, '… in part probably developed from Old English *spellian* to tell, declare, relate, speak,' (1988: 1044) and occurs in compound form in **Gospel**, the good **story** of Christ's life on earth. Spelling is clearly an important aspect of effective written communication, of our ability to tell our stories well. (Ironically, given the definition of the noun form, English spelling often also has the reputation of being mysterious and/or mystifying. Good spellers may be considered *charmed* in their ability to master the system, though the system itself is rarely thought of as *charming*!)

The perspective guiding this chapter is that spelling represents the development of the child's gradual understanding and control over a complex system, universal in its general structure but also very specific to the child's spoken and written

language environment. Understanding how children go about figuring out the specific characteristics of their language system as readers and writers can provide insights into their socio-cognitive processes, literacy development, and the ways children learn over time in response to their instructional contexts. Exploring the relationships between reading, writing, and spelling is a significant part of literacy scholarship (Pollo, Kessler, and Treiman, 2009; Ritchey, 2008). Further, spelling can have a permanence that contrasts with the transience of the reading event. The speller reveals his understanding and mastery of the language's writing system through both correct and approximate attempts. Thus, spelling has been perceived as an important indicator of literacy competence and a record of school performance that is available for both examination and criticism by parents and the general public as well as by educators.

This chapter will review research and scholarship about how young children through age 8 unravel some of the mysteries of how their language is represented in print. Specifically, we will deal with how words are represented through spelling systems and how students understand this relationship as manifested in their writing and spelling attempts and the change in those attempts over time. The chapter will be organized into four sections. The first section will provide an introductory discussion of how writing systems map spoken language to written forms. The second section will deal with how young children acquire basic and broad concepts about the relationship between written and spoken language. Then we will review research on learning to spell as a developmental process as well as discuss differing perspectives and critiques of stage theories. The chapter will close by addressing significant instructional issues including the debate surrounding invented (temporary) spellings and recent approaches to assessment and instruction.

HISTORY AND THE NATURE OF WRITING SYSTEMS

Before exploring how children gain control of their spelling system, it is important to review some basic principles about the nature of writing systems and of how orthographies represent linguistic units in print. Coulmas asserts that 'a conventional relation between graphical sign and linguistic unit is crucial for writing.' (1989: 27). He defines the process by which graphical signs with concrete references came to be associated with linguistic signs for those objects as 'phonetization' (1989: 26). Once the primary value of the written sign became a sound it was transformed from icon to symbol. Young children must come to understand this essential characteristic.

Each language uses a particular system for mapping pronunciations of significant units to a system of written symbols. In theory, writing systems can be divided into two general classes: 1 those whose symbols represent units of sound, which combine to form pronunciations of linguistic units, and 2 those whose symbols cue meanings, which are then mapped to particular pronunciations. The first class can be further divided into alphabetic systems, which map symbols to sounds at the phonemic level, and syllabic systems in which each symbol represents a spoken syllable. Examples of alphabetic systems include most western European systems, e.g., English, French, Spanish. Korean Han'gul is an often-cited example of a syllabic system, and Chinese, a meaning-based system. Alphabetic systems have the advantage of using a small number of symbols to represent a very large number of pronunciations, but at the cost of a high level of abstractness. The Chinese system is said to be less abstract, but requires the learning of a large number of distinct characters. Syllabic systems fall between these extremes.

In reality, well-developed systems tend to be multi-layered in representing relationships, with trade-offs between the demands of sound, visual pattern, meaning, and historical influences. Letter combinations represent meanings as well as sounds, and spellings sometimes preserve meanings when variations in pronunciations are predictable from the phonological context. For example, the English morpheme **s**, meaning plural, is spelled the same in **cats** and **ribs** though the pronunciation is /s/ in the first word and /z/ in the second. A further consideration is that the development of most writing systems has been greatly affected by historical, social, and political factors along with linguistic ones. Once writing systems were initially established for a language, both the oral language and written language evolved over time, somewhat independently, but also in connection with each other. These developmental changes have had a direct impact on the relationship between spellings and pronunciations. In some cases, a relatively slow rate of orthographic change (once print had been relatively standardized) has interacted with a greater change in pronunciation over time and place to add considerable complexity to the relationship between spelling and sound.

English is a particularly noteworthy example in this respect. (See Henderson [1990] and Venezky [1999] for fuller historical treatments.) While English began as a Germanic language, and is typically categorized as such, the Norman Conquest led to the eventual blending of Anglo-Saxon and Norman French into a new language. Many new spelling conventions were adopted from French as well; other changes are believed to have been made by scribes in order to make handwriting clearer, sometimes at the expense of phonological accuracy. For example, the replacement of **u** by **o** in **ton** and **woman** was supposedly motivated by the desire to break the confusion of a succession of a large number of vertical strokes (Venezky, 1999). As the need to represent new ideas increased, Latin and Greek elements (prefixes, roots, and suffixes) were used to build new word forms. The sound–letter relationships in such multi-syllabic words are further complicated by the English pattern of distributing stress unequally across syllables depending on the number of syllables per word as in the following set of words from the same root: **oppose**, **opposite**, and **opposition**. In such cases, spelling tends to preserve and make visible connections that may not be as apparent in pronunciation.

During the Age of Discovery, contact with new peoples and other European languages in new environments led to a large number of adoptions and adaptations of foreign words that did not always correspond to typical English letter–sound relationships. Contrast, for example, the borrowings of **vanilla** and **tortilla** from Spanish. Note, too, the various pronunciations of **ch** in **child** (Anglo-Saxon), **chef** (French) and **chorus** (Greek) but the /ch/ sound in **cello** (Italian). The spread of English-speaking peoples to new parts of the word and the military, political, and commercial prominence of British and later American institutions and culture have led to the development of varieties of English across the globe.

The result is a set of orthographies in which contentions between phonetic, visual, semantic, and etymological demands are resolved at the expense of simple, straightforward, sound–letter relationships (Cummings, 1988). It would seem that the demands of such a system on a beginning learner would be higher than on those learning one with simpler, more phonetically transparent and regular relationships.

Similarly, though the Chinese system has often been simplistically described as logographic, the vast majority of Chinese characters are compounds with both meaning and phonetic elements that combine to specify a distinct morphemic-syllabic unit. A compound Chinese character consists of two elements – a classifier that conveys something about the meaning of the overall character and a phonetic element that provides information about its pronunciation. Coulmas (1989) gives the example of the phonetic element, pronounced **tang**, which, when combined with the classifier for water, yields the compound character meaning 'pond' (1989: 101).

However, an important difference between Chinese and alphabetic systems is that in Chinese the phonetic and meaning elements occur in *separate parts* of the character. In alphabetic and syllabic systems the meaning and pronunciation are conveyed simultaneously by the combination of symbols. The English spelling **m-a-n** cannot be broken into distinct parts representing the pronunciation on the one hand, and the meaning (adult masculine human) on the other. Further, the phonetic element in the Chinese character cannot be parsed into subunits that map to individual phonemes in the character's pronunciation, which is the basis of alphabetic systems. Thus, while both kinds of systems provide information about sound and sense, they do so in very different ways. Some scholars hypothesize that such differences in how information is presented may lead to differences in how it is processed. For example, preliminary findings suggest that Chinese readers attend to phonetic information later during word reading processes than do readers of alphabetic scripts (Ju and Jackson, 1995).

HOW CHILDREN ACQUIRE EARLY WRITTEN LANGUAGE UNDERSTANDINGS

The brief analysis above points to the complexity of the task children face as they learn about their writing system and its unique characteristics. Researchers studying preschool children for the past 40 years have sought to document, describe, and analyze the processes through which children become conventional spellers. The distinction made by Coulmas (1989) between three tiers (writing system, script, and orthography) is a useful way to consider the levels of understanding required

for children to become conventional spellers. At one level, learners must grasp the general principles underlying a writing system as it relates to oral language (e.g., consistency in directionality). At another, they must become familiar with the features of the specific kind of script (e.g., letters or characters) that accompanies the language they speak. In addition, they must master the specific rules and patterns of that orthography, both in terms of internal visual rules and how pronunciations and meanings of oral linguistic units are mapped to particular written forms. To illustrate, though English has 52 letters, not all letters are used in the same way orthographically; for example, English words never start with **ck** or end with a **q**. Furthermore, English in the US and English in the UK have varying spelling patterns (such as **theater/theatre** or **honor/ honour**).

Given these layers of understandings, it is no small task for children to learn the complexities of their writing system and its accompanying script and orthography. This includes learning many aspects of how print 'works' in their language. Children must learn that written symbols are different from objects or pictures, that there are specific features of their script (Bourassa and Treiman, 2001), that the writing system has a consistency, and also that there are complex characteristics of the writing system such as directionality and concept of word (Hughes and Searle, 2000; Craig, 2006).

In this section we argue that although these aspects are often individually described in developmental ways based upon studies of children of various ages, there is also reciprocity between these understandings such that what children learn about one may support the development of a more complex understanding of another. Sulzby (1996) writes that 'each child acquires the abilities to read and to write within a culture in which both oral and written language are being acquired simultaneously and that the two together comprise 'language'' (1996: 28).

Goswami (1992) argues that children's emerging knowledge of phonological and orthographic concepts interact, each refining the other as the child's understanding becomes more complete. Because of the nature of a literate society, children experience both print and oral language simultaneously as they begin to understand how oral language carries messages and also the specific characteristics and organization of the script that they see around them. This 'common ground' (Clay, 2006: 11) between oral and written language is further documented by Ehri and Rosenthal (2007) who studied second- and fifth-grade students' vocabulary development and concluded that students 'learned the pronunciations and meanings of new vocabulary words better when they were exposed to their spellings than when they only spoke the words' (2006: 403–4).

Thus, learning to spell must be discussed within the context of learning much more than the relationship between symbols and sounds but rather how symbols map on to language in a manner that begins with approximations and moves to conventions. Goswami's (1992, 1994, 2001) work on children's phonological awareness focuses on the relationships between learning about print and the oral aspects of language including children's abilities to recognize, categorize, and manipulate spoken language in the absence of print. This work emphasizes that children's phonological awareness, as well as their understandings of the match between written and spoken forms, is in the process of development. Students' abilities to represent

spoken language will be affected by their current phonological understandings. For example, in her 2001 review of the research on early phonological development, Goswami suggests that there is a developmental progression from phonological awareness of larger to smaller units. Her findings suggest that: 1 syllables are natural units of analysis for English speakers; 2 onsets and rimes are particularly salient for young learners as their phonology becomes more segmented; 3 children are able to use onset and rime as the basis for analogy at a young age; 4 phonological awareness of onset and rime predict later success in reading and spelling; and 5 phonemic awareness develops through instruction in alphabetic orthography. At the beginning stages of language development, phonological processing is, for the most part, holistic. As vocabularies expand 'there is considerable developmental pressure to represent these words in the brain in a way that will distinguish them from other words and allow the child to recognize them accurately and quickly during speech comprehension ...' (2001: 113). To distinguish between these similarly sounding words both quickly and accurately, child linguists argue that children must begin to represent the sequences of sounds that constitute each known word in their brains. They must represent the 'segmental phonology' of the words they know.

From another perspective, children must understand the concepts relative to wordness in both oral and written contexts. The concept of word operates primarily in literate societies and, in some ways, is defined by the writing system (Coulmas, 1989). For adults, the definition of a spoken word may seem simple; but, for children, it is an understanding that takes many years of experiences with oral and written language to refine. Papandropoulou and Sinclair (1974) approached their study of young children (ages 4–10) with a Piagetian lens and found that the youngest children did not differentiate between words and things; they typically described words as either objects or actions (**strawberry** is a word because it grows in the garden or **pencil** is a word because it writes). For these children, the length of the word was relative to the size or location of the object (**train** is a long word because it goes and goes). Later, between the ages of 5 and 7, children described words as 'what you use to say about something' (1974: 244) but limited this definition to comments (proposing full sentences as words) or labels of objects, explaining that **the** is not a word because you need something else like **the truck** to be a word. By the ages of 6–8, however, words are seen as part of a larger more meaningful expression (bits of a story). This development of a concept of word is both gradual and complex. 'Gradually words become detached from the objects and events they refer to, and it is only fairly late in cognitive development that they are regarded as meaningful elements inside a systematic frame of linguistic representation' (Papandropoulou and Sinclair, 1974: 249).

Clay (1975) also describes children's simultaneous learning across various aspects of written language arguing that '[t]he individual child's progress in mastering the complexity of the writing system seems to involve letters, words, and word groups all at the one time, at first in approximate, specific and what seem to be primitive ways and later with considerable skill' (1975: 19). Children begin to learn the general characteristics of the script accompanying their writing system as they begin to draw, scribble, or write mock letters loosely reflecting conventional print

(Clay, 2005; 2010). For Portecorvo and Orsolini (1996), the distinction between drawing and writing is the first phase of writing development followed by a time when 'children explore the graphic and syntactical regularities of the notation system' (1996: 15). In a manner that parallels the drawings of the cave dwellers, pictures carry the meanings of young children who, when asked to look at the story, may attend only to the picture (Clay, 1975). Pictures are broad and interpretive; but the symbols children must learn representing spoken language units are narrow and specific.

Harste, Burke, and Woodward (1982) asked 4-year-old children from a variety of international backgrounds to write everything they could write. Children's writing samples were clearly influenced by their environments as the English-speaking child wrote in cursive-like scribbles; the Israeli child's sample looked much like the Hebrew alphabet; and the Arab child pointed out that the researchers wouldn't be able to read her sample since Arabic has more dots than English. None of these children wrote a recognizable word or could read their message, yet their samples reflected an initial understanding of the nature of three different orthographies. Harste and his colleagues argued that these children were creating hypotheses about how written language works that were constantly being challenged and revised as they learned more and more about 'how the grapho-phonemic, syntactic, and semantic systems of language operate in relation to one another and in relation to those things known about the world' (1982: 65).

As children learn the specific visual qualities of the system, their attempts reveal an element of experimentation as they explore the various ways to make letter forms. They often repeat pictures, letter-like shapes, or individual words to make longer messages, a phenomenon that Clay (1975) calls the Recurring Principle. Children often learn the letters of their names first; these letters are a key feature of later writings (Bloodgood, 1999). According to Ferreiro and Teberosky (1982), a child's name is tremendously important and 'in many cases, the child's own name functions as the first stable form endowed with meaning' (1982: 213). It is this meaning that anchors the child's understanding that a specific written form consistently represents a particular meaning, a concept critical to further development. Both-de Vries and Bus (2008, 2010) studied Dutch preschool children who could write strings of conventional letters but few correct spellings and found that 'children's control for writing their own proper name influenced spellings of unpracticed words' (2008: 37). Slightly older children, however, use more than the letters of their names. Adults around them had taught the children other names 'thereby stimulating children to use other letters in their invented spellings' (2008: 52).

As children gain control over their name, they may repeat one or more letters of their name reorganized into a new pattern, employing what Clay calls the Generating Principle to create messages with more complex letter arrangements. A longitudinal case study by Martens (1999) documented the importance of learning to write her name in one child's literacy development from ages 2 to 5. Similarly, extensive use of letters found in children's names was documented in Bloodgood's (1999) research, as data analysis revealed that the letters in children's names accounted for nearly half of the random letter writing done by 4- and 5-year-old children as they used the same letters over and over to write

their messages. This finding is further supported by a rigorous study of children in Brazil and the United States completed by Pollo et al. (2009).

As children become more familiar with letter forms and their names, they also begin to develop hypotheses about how these forms are linked to sounds in the stream of speech, to oral words. Kamii and Manning (1999) reviewed findings in this area, beginning with Ferreiro and her colleagues' delineation of four levels of writing revealed when analyzing children's spellings in Spanish: 1 letter strings, made up of similar letters, but of different lengths (see discussion of Clay's work, above); 2 letter strings with a fairly fixed range of length, with more letter-like forms included and some differentiation of letters used and/or their order to indicate word differences; 3 use of one character per syllable, but usually no phonetic connection between the letter and the sounds in the syllable (though, within this level, some children begin to use a vowel for each syllable); and 4 evidence of considerable knowledge of grapho-phono correspondences. Kamii, Long, Manning, and Manning (1990) found that English-speaking children generally followed the same levels as the Spanish-speaking children in the Ferreiro studies, with some important differences. At the third level, Spanish-speaking children focus on syllables, using a vowel for each; English-speaking children at this level focus on consonants. They suggest that these differences are likely due to differences in the phonologies of the two languages. In a follow-up study, Kamii and Manning (1999) asked students to write related word pairs in which one word had more syllables than the other (e.g. **ham/hamster**). They found that some students at the second level began to differentiate between the two words by using longer strings for the words with more syllables, though the letters might be totally different. Other students within this level used the same letters for similar parts in the words, though still using letter strings without grapho-phono correspondences. So, while children's writings may appear somewhat random to adults, closer analysis reveals a developing system of organization and relationships even at this early stage.

While children are developing a conceptual understanding about spoken words as abstract or arbitrary labels distinct from the objects themselves, basic regularities inherent in print, and general features particular to their own scripts, they are also beginning to make links between oral and written words in more systematic ways. Morris (1993) and his colleagues (Morris, Bloodgood, Lomax, and Perney, 2003) have demonstrated that the ability to match spoken words in reading with written words in text is a crucial event in learning to read and write. In two longitudinal studies of emergent readers they documented the pivotal nature of this critical element and concluded that beginning consonant knowledge facilitates children's matching of oral and written words, which then further facilitates phonemic segmentation, a skill supporting word recognition. Uhry's (1999) results were consistent with these findings. Likewise, Hughes and Searle (1991, 1997) found that to 'develop as fully Phonemic spellers, the children had to establish a stable voice-print match, demonstrated by pointing accurately to words as they read memorized text' (1991: 167).

Such connections between reading and spelling reflect fairly recent lines of research. For most of the 20th century, scholars and educators focused on the differences in spelling and reading rather than the connections between them. This focus was reflected in the clear separation between reading/phonics instruction and spelling practice, often done at very different parts of day with separate, unconnected instructional materials used for each (Read and Hodges, 1982). More recently, however, research and scholarship has focused on the important similarities and connections between the word processing required for reading, writing, vocabulary, and spelling. For example, Ehri and Rosenthal (2007) found that linking the spellings and meanings of vocabulary words facilitates learning and conclude that isolated vocabulary instruction of the past based on oral discussion is insufficient. 'Teachers need to show the spellings of new vocabulary words when they discuss their meanings.' (2007: 389).

Frith (1985) proposed a model in which 'phonemic awareness in reading develops as a consequence of spelling experience' (Goswami, 1994: 292). In fact, Morris and Perney (1984) found that a developmental spelling measure administered at the beginning and middle of first grade (ages 6–7 years) was a strong predictor of sight word acquisition by the end of the year. This finding is not surprising in light of the fact that a considerable body of research has now demonstrated strong positive relationships between phonemic awareness, spelling, and success in learning to read (e.g., Ehri, 1987; Griffith, 1991; Tangel and Blachman, 1992).

Developmentally sensitive measures, like the one Morris used, capture changes in phoneme awareness as children move from Pre-phonetic to Semi-phonetic to Letter Name spellings and beyond (Richgels, 2001). Based on findings from the studies cited above (Morris, 1993; Morris et al., 2003), Morris has proposed an interactive, sequential process of early literacy learning in which knowledge of beginning consonants (as demonstrated by the child's early spelling attempts) provides a textual anchor for examining word form in greater detail. As the ability to match spoken and oral work accurately stabilizes, supportive text provides the opportunity for matching word pronunciations to letter sequences. Phonemic awareness is thus extended and is reflected in more sophisticated invented spellings. Words are initially learned and successfully identified mostly in supportive contexts with partial letter cues (in the pattern of first; first and last; first, last, and middle). As the specifics of the alphabetic principles are internalized, words are more fully processed, and a stable and expanding sight vocabulary gradually emerges.

Research by Stellakis and Kondyli (2004) documented strong reciprocity between spelling, writing and reading in Greek kindergarten classrooms. The authors concluded that student spelling achievement is supported by increased opportunities to write messages even before conventional spellings are prevalent. The effectiveness of an interactive writing approach was studied by Craig (2006) and compared to a skill-sequenced program of metalinguistic games. The treatment was designed 'to maximize the children's involvement during writing and to build on children's developmental spellings' (2006: 716). For 16 weeks, this group negotiated a message with their teacher and the children wrote the message on individual white boards. Children in the treatment group scored the same as the metalinguistic games group on phonological awareness and spelling achievement but scored higher on word identification, passage comprehension, and word reading development. Similarly, based on a longitudinal study of K–6 children's spelling

development, Hughes and Searle (2000) argue that writing, 'the second 'R'' (2000: 203), 'challenges children to use their knowledge of print to express their thoughts on paper' (2000: 203).

Several other studies suggest that connections between reading, writing, and spelling remain strong beyond beginning stages. In a study of children's ability to notice and report letters in reading specially taught words, Invernizzi (1992) found that the ability to recall the presence or absence of specific letters was clearly related to stage of spelling development and dependent on the complexity of the feature to which the letter belonged. For example, spellers at Within Word Pattern and beyond were very good at recalling the presence of e-markers while Letter Name spellers only performed at chance on this feature. Bear (1992) compared first graders' developmental spellings to the fluency of their oral readings and found that spelling measures could account for three-fifths of the variance in reading rate. Letter Name spellings were significantly and negatively correlated with fluency, while performance on selected Within Word Pattern features was strongly associated with fluency measures. In both cross-sectional and longitudinal studies, Zutell (1992; Zutell and Fresch, 1991; Zutell and Rasinski, 1989) found that reading and developmental spelling measures were highly correlated for third- and fifth-grade students, with factor analysis strongly supporting a single factor solution which Zutell labeled underlying word knowledge.

A significant finding of these lines of research is that children's written productions that may appear random in nature actually reveal complex thinking on several dimensions, indicating that children's initial, inchoate understandings are moving toward increasingly refined hypotheses about orthography even before they make clear letter–sound connections. Such studies begin to describe the complex and inventive nature of the development of print concepts that happen simultaneously, sequentially, and reciprocally as young children become increasingly proficient with reading and writing tasks.

HOW CHILDREN ACQUIRE PROFICIENCY AS SPELLERS: DEVELOPMENTAL PERSPECTIVES

Current understandings of spelling development in English, once children grasp the Alphabetic Principle, are highly indebted to the seminal work of Charles Read (1971, 1975, 1986). Read's initial study focused on the spelling attempts of preschool children. He discovered that children from different settings and without formal instruction often produced similar misspellings. Most remarkably, his analysis demonstrated that such errors were neither random nor the result of auditory/phonological immaturity or deficit. Many were, in fact, quite logical, given the knowledge base the children were operating with (knowledge of the names of the letters, but little sight-word knowledge) and the complex way English spelling maps phonological relationships to print. For example, Read pointed out that the spelling of /dr/ blends with initial **J** or **G** and the spelling of /tr/ blends with initial **H** or **CH** was not due to 'mishearing' or 'mispronunciation' but to the ambiguity created by the fact that the pronunciation of the first element in each is affricated in the environment of the /r/; that is, it shares a feature of articulation with the related sound and the letters associated with it. The first phoneme in **drag** *does* sound like and is articulated like the

first phoneme in **jet**. In similar fashion, Read found that children often misspell short vowel sounds in particular ways (for example, **E** for 'short i', as in **set** for **sit**, **A** for 'short e' as in **bag** for **beg**, **I** for 'short o' as in **mip** for **mop**). Due to the Great Vowel Shift, a major historical change in the pronunciation of English long vowels, short vowels and long vowels are not paired in spelling as they are in sound. Read argued that children were using a Letter Name strategy; that is, they were matching the phonemes heard in words with letters whose names also include those phonemes. Since short vowels are not used as the names of letters in English, children classified those sounds as similar to the closest long vowel letter name. The vowel sound in **beg** *is* more similar to the name of the letter **A** than it is to the name of the letter **E**. Thus Read argued that children were not memorizing spellings but constructing or *inventing* their own plausible system based on abstract phonological relationships. They were recognizing relationships that adults had learned to ignore in the course of becoming literate (Read, 1971, 1975).

While Read's initial study was conducted with a limited number of children, the importance of Read's observations and analyses cannot be overestimated. His later work and that of other spelling scholars confirmed and extended those early findings. As a result of his work, the study of children's spellings gained in respect and attention. Researchers applied his techniques and insights in case studies of young children (e.g., Bissex, 1980; Gentry, 1982) and in studies of children in the early grades of formal instruction, generally confirming, often refining and elaborating on our understandings of children's understandings (Beers and Henderson, 1977; Treiman, 1993).

The late Edmund Henderson had been collecting and categorizing young children's spellings over several years before Read's work was published. He recognized Read's work as the 'Rosetta Stone' of spelling research in that it provided the key to deciphering and understanding the mental processes underlying children's attempts (Henderson and Beers, 1980). Over the last 40 years Henderson, his students and colleagues, and their students and colleagues have pursued a line of research focusing on the developmental and conceptual nature of children's understandings and learning, extending their investigations on the one hand to younger and/or less knowledgeable children, not yet fully using the Letter Name strategies that Read described, and, on the other, to mature students grappling with the complexities of the derivational and etymological aspects of English orthographies (Henderson and Beers, 1980; Morris, 1989a, 1989b; Templeton and Bear, 1992; Templeton and Morris, 2000). (See Zutell, 2008, for a historical review). They proposed a stage-like or phase-like quality to spelling development in which attempts change over time, both in terms of how words are misspelled and in terms of which features (e.g., consonant blends, long vowel markers) and word types are spelled correctly. Patterns of development are affected by the child's knowledge base, strategies, and the complexity and familiarity of the features and words under examination (Gentry, 1978; Henderson, 1990; Schlagal, 1992).

Henderson (1990) suggested the following early levels of development: 1 *Pre-phonetic*, characterized by letter strings that represent concepts and ideas, but without a discernible match between letters and sounds (see above for a closer analysis of patterns of attempts at this stage);

2 *Semi-phonetic*, characterized in the early part by the use of single letters to represent beginning or particularly salient sounds in the word; over time children include letters for both beginning and ending sounds, with long vowels generally represented before short ones; 3 *Letter Name* (now often labeled *Phonetic* or *Alphabetic*), characterized by the ability to consistently match first-to-last in spoken words with left-to-right in the written forms, generally representing each phoneme in a word, regularly with the logic Read described; it is at this stage that students begin to develop a working sight vocabulary for reading that also supports developing knowledge of and hypotheses about visual and meaning-based features (Ehri, 1992; Morris, 1992); 4 *Within Word Pattern* (also called *Transitional*), characterized by correct spelling of well-known words, single consonants and many blend and consonant digraph patterns, and by good control of short vowel patterns. At this stage children begin to include visual features like vowel markers and other silent letter patterns into their spellings, though they may only gradually do so with accuracy on a regular basis; they are also more likely to use analogy strategies as they are able to process letters in 'chunks' rather than individually. Because of the particular complexity of English visual patterns and their relationships to sound and meaning, full control of these elements may require several years of experience and study. (See also Goswami, 1994, 1999.)

Henderson also suggested two higher-level stages: *Syllable Juncture*, in which students grapple with patterns for combining syllables, including consonant doubling and e-drop patterns, and *Derivational Constancy*, in which students deal with the morphological patterns in English multi-syllabic words whose pronunciations often obscure the links in meaning and spelling among words in the same root-word families (e.g., **cave-cavity-excavation**). The distinct and sequential nature of these stages have been called into question (Ehri, 1992; Gentry, 2000), and current descriptions view these as aspects or phases of later development that may parallel and/or overlap with each other and the later part of the Within Word Pattern stage (Bear, Invernizzi, Templeton, and Johnston, 2011).

Other scholars have made significant contributions paralleling and complementing this line of research. One area that has received considerable attention is children's understanding of morphological markers and their complex representation in oral and written form. As noted above, English orthography tends to preserve the same spelling in such markers when pronunciation changes predictably in different phonological environments. For example, the spellings of **-s, -es** for plural and third person singular remain stable when the phonological environment requires /z/ or /^z/ in pronunciation (e.g., **desks, swims, dresses**). Studies have generally found that young spellers (6–8 years old) become aware of and gain control over this feature relatively early (Beers and Beers, 1992; Read, 1975). In a similar vein, Treiman (e.g., Treiman and Cassar, 1996) found that in highly focused conditions young children show sensitivity to morphology in their spellings of identical sounds depending on their relationships to morphemic units. For example, nasal omission, a misspelling Read had initially noted, was more likely to occur in **brand** (one morpheme) than in **tuned** (two morphemes with the second phoneme in the final blend functioning as a morpheme).

Further evidence of the relationship between morphological awareness and children's spellings in grades 2 and 4 was found by Deacon, Kirby, and Casselman-Bell (2009). In their study, morphological awareness made a significant contribution to spelling (8 per cent) after controlling for a number of variables (verbal and nonverbal intelligence, phonological awareness, verbal short-term memory, and rapid automatized naming).

Bryant, Nunes, and Bindman (1999, 2000) report a detailed 3-year study of the acquisition of the past-tense morpheme with children who began the study at ages 6, 7, and 8. In English, the **-ed** spelling is maintained in regular verbs whether the pronunciation is /t/, /d/, or /^d/ (e.g., **skipped, trimmed, wanted**). On the other hand, 'strong' or irregular English verbs tend to vary the vowel while maintaining the direct phoneme-grapheme match for the past tense morpheme. (e.g., **sleep-slept, find-found**). The situation is further complicated by the fact that the same final consonant blend pronunciations exist in words unrelated to past tense (**soft, blind**). Bryant et al.'s findings support a stage/phase model for past tense morphology that includes; 1 a *Pre-phonetic* stage in which endings are not represented in a consistent way; 2 a *Phonetic* stage in which all endings are spelled phonetically, including those for regular past tense verbs; 3 a stage of *Generalizations and Overgeneralizations* in which the **-ed** ending is applied to both strong verbs (**sleped** for **slept)** and single morpheme words (**sofed** for **soft)**; 4 a *Generalizations Only* stage in which strong verbs may be spelled with **-ed**, but single morpheme words are spelled conventionally; and 5 a *Correct* stage in which strong verb endings are again spelled phonetically. They also found that children's movement through the stages is strongly related to their specific sensitivity to grammatical distinctions. Bryant et al. conclude that 'children's linguistic awareness contributes to their progress in learning to read and spell in different and possibly separable ways' (2000: 273).

The work of Bryant, Nunes, and Bindman on morphological development fits well with other stage/phase models. Yet Pacton and Deacon (2008) are cautious about attributing student spellings *exclusively* to the use of morphological rules. In their review of studies of children's use of morphological information in English and French, they suggest that children may well use other sources of information like letter patterns, statistical regularities and co-occurrences, and analogies in combination with morphological information.

Recently, other researchers have posited a *continuous* model of development in which '… children can use a variety of sources of knowledge from a very early age …' (Bosse, Valdois, and Tainturier (2003: 694). This work falls into two categories: 1 studies of overt use of conscious strategies and 2 research on implicit and incidental learning.

Rittle-Johnson and Siegler (1999) have proposed an overlapping waves model in which '… abundant variability, adaptive choice, and gradual change are fundamental features of cognition at all points of development.' (1999: 332). In their longitudinal study of students during first and second grade, they recorded student overt behaviors during spelling and their retrospective reports about the strategies they used. They also introduced a 'prohibited' condition in which students were discouraged from using back-up strategies and more or less forced to use only retrieval to produce their spellings. They argue that the correlations between 'prohibited' and 'allowed' spellings are likely to provide a truer picture of word difficulty than simply calculating correct responses and that differences in rates of correctness is a measure of the effectiveness of student use of back-up strategies.

Rittle-Johnson and Siegler (1999) describe six strategies that students used: retrieval, sounding-out, retrieval/sounding-out, drawing analogies, relying on rules, and visualization. Almost all students used more than one strategy, the most prevalent ones being retrieval, sounding-out, and a combination of the two. In first grade, just less than one-quarter of the students used one or more of the other three strategies. By second grade, the percentages increased considerably for these other three, especially for relying on rules. However, the percentages of spellings in which these three strategies were actually used were only 6 per cent (Grade 1) and 16 per cent (Grade 2). The correlations between errors in the prohibited condition and the use of back-up strategies were quite high, as predicted, and the effectiveness of the strategies varied considerably, with retrieval being the most effective (86 per cent in Grade 1, 96 per cent in Grade 2) and sounding-out being the least effective (15 per cent in Grade 1, 34 per cent in Grade 2). Even when spellings with sounding-out were coded more liberally, only 50 per cent of those for first graders and 68 per cent for second graders were coded as fully phonemic. (Note that this coding did not seem to have taken into account all the predictable misspellings that Read and others have described.) Remarkably, Rittle-Johnson and Siegler take these equivocal results as strong support for their overlapping wave model and in contradiction to stage/phase explanations.

In order to create a more fine-grained understanding of developmental processes,

Sharp, Sinatra, and Reynolds (2008) combined Rittle-Johnson and Siegler's methodology with classic feature/error analysis and a microgenetic design characterized by repeated observations, trial-by-trial analysis, and ongoing documentation. In their study they examined and analyzed the responses of 31 first-grade at-risk students to six spelling inventories in three sessions over a 5-month period beginning in mid-year.

Sharp et al. describe nine categories that students used: complete retrieval, partial retrieval, sounding out, rule use, analogy, visual checking, guessing, copying, and chunking. (Note that the first six are very similar, though not identical, to those described by Rittle-Johnson and Siegler, while the last three are additional.) As evidence of variability in strategy use, they report that students used more than one strategy on 89 per cent of words spelled. Complete retrieval and rule use increased over time, while the use of guessing decreased. Whereas Rittle-Johnson and Siegler found that the use of multiple strategies increased with word difficulty, the students in this study more or less 'gave up' on the more difficult words, using fewer strategies on them. As spelling features were more accurately represented, the use of more effective strategies increased and the use of less effective strategies decreased. Students who performed better on the initial screening progressed at a faster rate than low performers. While both groups increased, the number of strategies used from the first through the third sessions/ trials, lower performers used less sophisticated strategies like guessing; higher performers rarely guessed and added more effective strategies like analogy, chunking, and visual checking to their repertoires (2008: 221).

Sharp et al. conclude that their data and analyses are consistent with the three requirements of the overlapping wave model: variability, adaptability, and gradual change. However, they acknowledge that their findings do not contradict those of either stage/phase theorists or incrementalists (gradual and continuous change). Rather, they believe that both perspectives provide key insights and that spelling proceeds in both phases and degrees. (In her case study of six third-graders Young (2008) reached similar conclusions.)

Certainly collecting and analyzing data on students' conscious understandings of orthographic features and how they apply them to figure out specific spellings can be quite informative about the nature of spelling development and can be useful in guiding instruction. In fact, researchers and educators from a stage/phase tradition have encouraged and engaged in such discussions with students (e.g., Fresch, 2000; Rasinski and Zutell, 2010). Both Rittle-Johnson and Siegler and Sharp et al. present innovative techniques in the designs of their studies that may be very useful to other researchers. However, it is much bolder to assert the validity of a wave model of development either in opposition to or reciprocally with a stages/phases perspective on development. Several limitations and questionable aspects of their methodologies leave this conclusion in doubt.

First, the classification of strategies is suspect. Retrieval, especially quick and easy retrieval, is not a strategy in the same sense as the others the authors propose. Retrieval is a form of *knowledge* that comes to mind once words are learned (whether perfectly or imperfectly). It involves very different processes than, say, sounding out a word or applying a rule or analogy. When retrieval is subtracted from the total, the count of the use of multiple strategies diminishes considerably. (Sharp et al.

recognize this problem, but still consider retrieval a strategy, specifically because they wanted to replicate that aspect of Rittle-Johnson and Siegler's design.)

Similarly, guessing is a *lack of strategy* rather than a viable one. Students typically report guessing when either they are not consciously aware of how they generated a spelling or when they are frustrated by the difficulty of the task, are fatigued or distracted. Notably, Sharp et al. add this category, possibly because the match between the at-risk students and the word lists they used created many instances of spelling at frustration level. This is supported in their data by the low percentage of correct spellings across the three sessions and by the fact that guessing diminished considerably as spellers became more knowledgeable and skilled.

Further, rule use, analogy, and chunking may well be seen as a series of strategies consistent with the movement from Letter Name into the Within Word Pattern stage/phase of development rather than as distinct and non-stage based. For this kind of analysis, what is important is not that a student uses an analogy rather than a rule, but the complexity/frequency of the instance in which the strategy is used. For example, it is very different to draw an analogy between two words with the same beginning letter than two with complex letter combinations. As for chunking, use of the high frequency and straightforward *-ing* chunk predictably occurs earlier than use of the *-tion* chunk, while in terms of a general strategy, they might be counted in the same category. Similarly, spellers may persistently report sounding out as a strategy at various stages, but their actual behaviors and the resultant spellings are likely to be very different at the Semiphonetic, Letter Name, and Within Word Pattern stages/phases and beyond.

As students begin to receive formal instruction in word learning, especially in heavily phonics-based programs, they may well take on the language of rules and strategies before they are able to apply these effectively. From a developmental phase/stage perspective, *how well* a speller uses a strategy is more revealing and important than a verbal report or researcher inference about the existence of its use – hence the informative and instructionally useful description of a speller as 'using but confusing' a particular orthographic feature (Invernizzi, Abouzeid, and Gill, 1994).

In summary, the methodologies introduced by overlapping wave researchers have the potential to provide significant additions to our understanding of children's word learning. That students' thinking about words and their consciously applied strategies should be considered along with and in interaction with their actual productions is a point well taken. However, the conceptual flaws in the characterization of strategies and the examination of their use, so essential to the supporting research for this model, cast serious doubt as to its reasonableness as an explanation for spelling development, whether as an alternative to, or in reciprocal relationship with, a stage/phase perspective.

Research on implicit/incidental word learning is generally grounded in connectionist models and techniques. Findings from this literature suggest that young children are acquiring graphotactic information (e.g., that double consonants do not appear at the beginnings of words) and are sensitive to word frequency from early development. In recent experiments student responses have been investigated in the context of more tightly controlled stimuli and situations. In many such studies, responses items might be contrasted when words are controlled for frequency, length, and/or regularity using distributional statistics for both across and within-word patterns.

For example, Caravolas, Kessler, Hulme, and Snowling (2005) studied the vowel spellings of British children taught using a phonics program emphasizing letter sounds in kindergarten then first grade. They used a specified word list and regression analysis to estimate the contribution of unconditional consistency (likelihood of a vowel spelling given its pronunciation), conditional consistency (likelihood of the spelling given following letters, i.e., the rime elements), word frequency, sound-letter knowledge and letter-name knowledge to correct spellings. They found that the children were sensitive to unconditional consistency and word frequency, but not yet to conditional consistency. In other words, at this level, students are still focused on individual sound–letter relationships, not the vowel and what comes after it.

Bosse et al. (2003) explored whether French children in grades one through five could spell pseudo-words by analogy to reference words. In the first of three experiments, only children in grades three through five showed statistically significant use of analogy. Since few first- and second-graders could spell the reference words correctly, the researchers conducted a second experiment in which first- and second-graders were specifically taught the reference words beforehand. A significant analogy effect was found only among students in second grade. Notably, the first-graders failed to learn the reference words well even with instruction. In the third experiment, a group of first-graders were trained extensively on the reference words as part of their classroom instruction. By the end of the training they spelled the

reference words more accurately than a control group, produced more target spellings on neighbor pseudo-words than on control pseudo-words, and had a higher rate of analogies than did the control group. The authors conclude that even young students can use analogy to spell words if they have accurate spelling knowledge of the reference words.

While the authors of these studies see their results as evidence of continuous and implicit learning and, in the second case especially, as in contradiction to stage/phase models, these findings can also be interpreted as consistent with current stage/phase perspectives. Kindergarten and first grade students are likely to be in either the Semi-Phonetic or Phonetic stage/phase of development, and so are still moving left-to-right across words, not chunking or attending to the vowel in the context of what follows. What is striking in the second study is not that young students can use analogies, but how much effort the researchers had to make to get them to that point, by which time they may well have been transitioning to early Within Word Pattern.

The authors of these studies often contrast their positions on development with older, less detailed and more rigid formulations of stage/phase theory (i.e., Frith, 1985), while recent interpretations (e.g., Bear et al., 2011) allow for more gradual transitions between and overlapping across stages. On the other hand, applying stage/phase-based analyses and grouping techniques might well prove to be a useful way to gain greater insights from the data collected in highly controlled experimental conditions. In any case, findings and explanations from these varying perspectives may well be seen as complimentary rather than contrastive. Both perspectives support a model of learning to spell that includes constructive processes in which children use their growing linguistic knowledge to generate implicit and explicit hypotheses and refine them over time as their base of knowledge and print experience expands.

The knowledge base, concepts, and techniques developed in the spirit of a developmental perspective have also been extended to address differences between normal functioning and low ability readers/spellers. Boder (1973) had suggested three categories: *dysphonetic*, *dyseidetic*, and *mixed* spellers. But re-analysis of her findings in light of Read's descriptions of logical spellings called into question the true number of dysphonetic spellings in her data (Henderson, 1992). Further, with the growing recognition of the importance of instructional level in spelling assessment and instruction (Morris, Nelson, and Perney, 1986; Morris, Blanton, Blanton, Nowacek, and Perney, 1995; Schlagal, 1992), studies have compared low-functioning spellers at their instructional level with younger spellers at the same level of ability rather than with average spellers in the same grade. Under these conditions, differences between groups are greatly reduced in comparison to earlier studies (Invernizzi and Worthy, 1989). This finding suggests that *delay in learning* and a need for more processing time (Abouzeid, 1992), rather than *differences in processing*, is a more viable explanation of disabled spellers' difficulties. (See also Bourassa, Treiman, and Kessler, 2006.) It may also explain the finding from Graham's (2000) review indicating that good spellers are more successful than poor spellers in transferring knowledge from instructed spellings to uninstructed ones and are also more likely to make gains in their spelling ability from their reading. This may be because poor spellers are often instructed at grade

rather than instructional level, and so do not form the strong and detailed memories for words that effective, appropriately leveled instruction makes possible.

SPELLING IN OTHER ALPHABETIC LANGUAGES

Read's discovery and explanation of invented spellings for English-speaking learners and the elaboration of stages/phases of development have naturally raised questions about the applicability of such concepts to learning to spell in other languages. Early studies in other languages used similar techniques for describing error patterns and developmental trends. For example, investigations of children's spelling patterns for Spanish (Temple, 1978; Valle-Arroyo, 1990), French (Gill, 1980), Portuguese (Pinheiro, 1995) and Greek (Porpodas, 1989) suggested a movement away from strictly phonetic strategies to increasing use of strategies based on orthographic and morpho-graphemic knowledge. Investigations of children's spellings in Portuguese (Nunes-Carraher, 1985, as reported Bryant et al., 1999) and in French (Fayol, Thevenin, Jarousse, and Totereau, 1999) found patterns for the development of morphological markers parallel to those found by Bryant et al. (1999) discussed above.

In the current literature, investigations of the units of analysis children use in their reading and spelling are often referred to as 'grain sizes.' These include individual phonemes, onsets and rimes (coda), syllables, morphemes and full words. In different languages different grain sizes seem to have more prominence, having varying effects on children's early spellings.

For example, in a more recent study, Cardoso-Martins, Correa, Lemos, and

Napoleao (2006) fitted the spellings of 4- to 7-year-old Portuguese learners to both Ehri's and Ferriero's developmental models. They concluded that Ehri's partial alphabetic phase provided a more accurate and parsimonious explanation of student spelling behaviors than Ferriero's syllabic stage, suggesting more commonality across alphabetic languages.

According to Kim (2010) Korean is considered an alphabetic syllabary in which letters are composed in a syllabic block. The author analyzed the spellings of 5-year-old Korean children instructed in a whole word approach, but with control of syllable types moving from simple to complex. The author found that students did use a phonological transcription strategy despite not having any specific instruction in phonological awareness or alphabet knowledge. Errors on phonologically opaque words were 'legal' in the sense that children used spellings that would be accepted phonologically. As Kim points out, letter names and sounds are extremely consistent in Korean, and this may well have supported their use as units. Correspondingly, alphabetic knowledge was significantly correlated to spelling even when vocabulary and phonological awareness were controlled for.

Yet, Rickard Liow and Lee (2004) examined the spellings of 6–8-year-olds in Malay, which they describe as a semi-syllabic or shallow alphabetic-syllabic script. After grouping students according to their spelling accuracy, they analyzed the children's error patterns. They found that even the lowest group was able to preserve stem syllables rather than individual phonemes and concluded that their spellings were based on syllables and morphemes, in correspondence to classroom instruction. On the other hand, in their study of the spellings of students in first, then second grade, in Indonesian (which they describe as a dialect of Malay), Winskel and Widjaja (2007) concluded that the phoneme is the prominent unit of phonological analysis with the syllable playing a significant part, especially in longer, multisyllabic and heavily affixed words. They conclude that their results highlight '... the variable nature of grain size used by beginners, which is dependent on the developmental stage, the demands of the task administered, and the characteristics of language and its orthography' (2007: 23). Given the mixed results of various studies, we would agree, though we would add the focus of literacy instruction as another important variable.

ENGLISH AS 'OUTLIER'

There has also been a consistent finding for both word recognition and spelling in other languages across a wide variety of recent research reports and reviews of the research literature (e.g., Caravolas, 2006; Share, 2008). In English-speaking countries, literacy instruction often begins earlier and is more intensively focused on phonological awareness and print knowledge, while in many European countries, literacy instruction often begins later (for example, as early as 5 years old for English versus as late as 7 in Scandinavian countries [Share, 2008]). Yet after their first year of instruction, non-English students receiving instruction later score higher on measures of word recognition, regular, pseudo-word recognition, and spelling than their English-speaking counterparts at a similar age, often reaching close to ceiling levels on the measures by the end of the first year of formal instruction. English-speaking students typically do not reach the same level of competence until approximately third grade, by then sometimes having 5 years of instruction on print conventions. In a study across 14 nations Seymour, Aro, and Erskine (2003) (as reported in Share, 2008) found the average accuracy across all nations for decoding real words at the end of first grade at 87 per cent, but English word reading at 34 per cent. Similarly, accuracy for nonwords averaged 82 per cent across all nations with English being 29 per cent.

These comparative findings also seem to hold true when item difficulty is closely matched across languages (Caravolas, 2006) and when comparing differences within students simultaneously learning English and a more transparent orthography. Additionally, mastery of phonemic awareness and phonemic segmentation is more challenging and prolonged for young children learning English orthography than for European children whose instruction begins later (e.g., Goswami, Ziegler and Richardson, 2005).

Currently, the accepted explanation for this phenomenon is the orthographic depth hypothesis (for reviews see Caravolas, 2006 and Share, 2008). Writing systems vary in the consistency and transparency of their letter–sound (reading) and sound–letter (spelling) correspondences. Shallow systems are highly consistent and transparent for both sets of correspondences. Some systems fall in between and/ or may be shallow for letter–sound relationships, but less consistent or predictable for sound–letter relationships. Czech, Finnish, and Turkish, for example, are often cited as having shallow, transparent, orthographies for both reading and spelling, while French, German, Dutch, and Greek are examples of orthographies that are consistent for letter–sound relationships, but less predictable for spelling (Caravolas, 2006). English, on the other hand, is widely considered to be '… the most complex of all the world's alphabetic orthographies' (Share, 2008: 584, note 1), with complex and often unpredictable correspondences for both reading and spelling, so much so that Share has described English as an 'outlier' orthography (2008: 584). For historical reasons, this is particularly the case for the high-frequency English words that make up a large proportion of words students learn in beginning literacy instruction. English is a very 'deep' orthography, especially for young learners.

According to the orthographic depth hypothesis, shallow orthographies are easier to learn because they provide frequent, positive examples of the alphabetic principle. English, being a very deep orthography, does not provide such a consistent match. Students learning to read and spell in English must sort through a large number of counterexamples along with positive ones in order to figure out how letters and sounds go together, creating a temporary state of ambivalence or confusion.

Students learning a transparent orthography are able to spell most words and pseudo-words correctly after the end of a formal year of instruction because once the concept of phonemic awareness is understood and letter-names and/or letter-sounds are learned, spelling is a straightforward application of that knowledge. Several authors suggest that, even in orthographies that are less transparent for spelling, but consistent for reading, encounters with consistent letter–sound relationships and regular accurate reading provides an advantage for spelling accuracy as well (e.g., Wimmer and Landerl, 1997, as reported in Caravolas, 2006).

Many of the current studies of reading and spelling in other languages also explore factors that predict spelling. The strongest predictors of spelling in alphabetic languages are letter name/sound knowledge and phonological awareness, often measured at the phonemic level (e.g., Leppänen, Niemi, Aunola, and Nurmi, 2006). This has led to the general conclusion that while patterns of development across languages may be different depending upon the level of transparency and other salient linguistic factors (e.g., the prominence of syllables and/or morphemes in a language and its orthographic structure), the basic processes are quite similar. Several scholars have suggested that there is a general pattern in which phonemic awareness predicts invented or phonological spellings, which then predict early reading. In transparent orthographies, by the end of first grade or 1 year of formal instruction, as student scores approach ceiling on phonological measures like phonemic segmentation, then word and nonword reading accuracy predicts spelling rather than the other way around, though phonological measures tend to be important for spelling accuracy longer than for reading. Again, English seems to be somewhat exceptional in that the relationship between phonemic awareness and both literacy skills lasts well into third grade.

In a study with a slightly different approach, Furnes and Samuelsson (2011) explored the relationships between rapid automatic naming (RAN) as well as phonological awareness (PA) and reading and spelling, comparing Australian/US with Scandinavian students in a longitudinal study from kindergarten through second grade. While they concluded that the patterns of relationships were quite similar across languages, RAN was more related to reading and PA to spelling. In a Dutch study (Verhagen, Aarnoutse, and van Leeuwe, 2010), naming speed, in particular, was found to be significantly related to both word recognition speed and spelling accuracy at the end of Grade 2. The authors contend that, '… naming speed appears to predict the speed and accuracy with which a child can access underlying orthographic representations for both word recognition and spelling accuracy purposes' (2010: 76). (For English, see Savage, Pillay, and Melidona, 2008.)

How, then, do these now numerous, rather complex, and sometimes conflicting studies and findings across alphabetic and syllabic orthographies contribute to a developmental perspective on spelling? Students' error patterns do differ across languages according to the structure and demands of these orthographies. Clearly development will be paced differently in different orthographies depending on a variety of factors, including the linguistic structure of the language, the transparency of the orthography, and the focus of programs used to deliver spelling instruction. Orthographies vary considerably in their transparency, but are typically less transparent – thus more difficult – for spelling than for word reading, though in many languages children control unambiguous sound–letter relationships fairly early and easily after formal literacy instruction has begun. English, being to a large extent an 'outlier' in degree of complexity for both reading and spelling, leads to particularly unique patterns of errors for students.

Still, important commonalities do seem to exist, even across more and less transparent orthographies. Early spelling begins with phonological units and moves towards more linguistically abstract and complex ones. The relationship between reading and spelling is mutually supportive; in particular, early spelling development predicts early reading, while later reading development provides the word knowledge and experience to support later steps in learning to spell. Across languages the factors that most directly affect spelling, letter name/sound knowledge, phonological awareness, reading ability, processing speed, and sensitivity to syntactic and morphological patterns predict ability in very similar ways.

SPELLING INSTRUCTION: FROM MEMORIZATION TO CONCEPTUALIZATION

Early instructional methods for alphabetic systems, dating back to Greco-Roman times, emphasized memorization of letters that were then applied to the spelling and pronunciation of words. This technique was commonly called the ABCDery method (Otto, 1973). Early American spelling instruction emphasized lengthy recitations and memorization; spelling research focused on the identification of practice and study techniques for learning letter combinations and words. This perspective was motivated by a characterization of English spelling as highly irregular and by a behaviorist, stimulus-response view of the learning process (Templeton and Morris, 2000).

At the beginning of the twentieth century, however, research shifted to analyzing the characteristics of words relative to their spelling difficulty, resulting in 'demon' lists of challenging words. Teachers were encouraged to help students learn these words by visualizing (Lee and Lee, 1941) and taking tests leading to mastery. Research focused on developing frequency counts of words in reading and writing (high frequency words as deserving the most attention), tracking student errors in terms of control of letter–sound matches, and discovering effective practice techniques and time plans to enhance memorization.

High-frequency words were taught by having children copy sentences with words commonly used in children's writing and complete dictation exercises in hopes that children would become accustomed to spelling correctly (Scharer, 1992).

By the middle of the twentieth century, grade-level consumable spelling books were a common mode of formal spelling instruction requiring that young children cycle through a different set of words each week by completing various workbook exercises culminating in a final test on Friday. These materials, however, were criticized because students were often required to study words they already knew or were too difficult for them to learn developmentally, and the activities did not help children to learn orthographic patterns or to transfer spelling lessons to their writing (Gill and Scharer, 1996; Zutell, 1994).

More recently, two lines of research have significantly influenced early spelling instruction. First, research has begun to document a positive correlation between a young child's ability to perform tasks of phonological awareness (an awareness of aspects of spoken language such as words, syllables, rhymes, and individual phonemes), phonemic awareness (a conscious awareness that words are made up of phonemes that can be both isolated and manipulated), and later achievement in both reading and spelling (Adams, 1990; Ball and Blachman, 1991; Ehri, 1980; Goswami, 1999; Griffith, 1991; National Reading Panel, 2000; Richgels, 2001). For example, as reported in Goswami (1999), Bradley and Bryant (1983) studied the impact of phonological training on children (ages 4–5) with poor phonological awareness. Two years of training for the experimental group focused on onset and rime through picture sorts of rhyming words and manipulation of plastic alphabet letters to create new rhyming words. One control group was taught semantic classification; the other was unseen. After training, children in the experimental group were 8 months ahead of the semantic classification group in reading and a full year ahead in spelling; experimental scores were 1 year ahead of the unseen control group in reading and 2 years ahead in spelling.

Further, based upon their meta-analysis, the US National Reading Panel (2000) concluded that phonemic awareness training interventions of 20 hours or less supported kindergarten children as spellers. But, while promising, this analysis was unable to determine specific teaching techniques that were most effective and engaging for both teachers and students or to document positive effects for disabled spellers. Recommendations regarding instruction are further complicated by studies documenting the reciprocity between the development of phonological and phonemic awareness and learning to read and write (Adams, 1990; Goswami, 2001; Silva and Alves-Martins, 2002). Wood (2004), for example, reexamined data from the 1998 longitudinal study by Wood and Terrell to see if preschool children with differences in letter knowledge also differed in phonological awareness and found no significant differences in either phonological awareness or literacy attainment. 'These results suggest that phonological awareness development may not be dependent upon exposure to alphabetic tuition as suggested by Morais (1991), and this lack of difference in phonological awareness would explain why there was little difference between the two groups on literacy attainment overall' (Wood, 2004: 9). Silva and Alves-Martins (2002) found that either 2 weeks of phonological awareness

training or guided discussions of children's invented spellings enabled young children to move from presyllabic writing to syllabic writing.

These studies highlight the complexity of children's learning as spellers and challenge the position of linear skill-based instructional programs emphasizing instruction to control of one dimension (such as phonemic awareness or letter knowledge) before learning about another. In fact, McGee and Richgels (2000) write with concern that recommendations for phonological or phonemic awareness training in classroom contexts may result in scripted programs 'so divorced from actually reading and writing of authentic texts for real purposes as to be counterproductive for those students who already have phonemic awareness, or are on their way to acquiring it in other, more functional and contextualized ways' (2000: 212). Consequently, educators are challenged to determine an appropriate curricular sequence, emphasis, and instructional balance between attention to phonological awareness, phonemic awareness, reading instruction, and writing instruction to support children's literacy development

A second influential line of research is the four decades of developmental spelling studies, which have also led to innovative ideas about instruction. The issue of correctness in writing, for example, takes on a new perspective as invented spellings are viewed as windows into a child's thought processes, and assessment targets children's developmental stages in ways that can effectively influence instruction (Richgels, 2001). Looking at each child developmentally calls into question practices of having the same grade-level curriculum for every child in the class in favor of providing instruction based upon the needs of groups and individuals.

Thus, developmental research calls for teachers to identify students' appropriate levels using spelling assessments and plan instruction to meet the range of needs identified. This instruction places new demands upon teachers' expertise when compared to whole class instruction using published spelling programs (basals). These three issues – invented spelling, spelling assessment, and meeting the needs of low achieving spellers – are addressed below.

Invented spelling

Although issues relative to invented spelling often focus on the early years of school, spellers of all ages use invented spelling any time they approximate an unknown word while writing. Fifty years ago, writing, for young children, meant copying sentences; independent writing was not encouraged until children's conventional spellings matched the messages they wrote to ensure accuracy. More recently, however, instructional recommendations have focused on encouraging young children to create and write messages using the knowledge they have of the system, no matter how incomplete (Scharer and Pinnell, 2008). Consequently, preschool and kindergarten children find writing materials in play centers (Morrow, 1990), opportunities for journal writing, and teachers who encourage and celebrate their early writing attempts (Clay, 2010).

Concerns that children will not learn conventional spellings if allowed to write words unconventionally have been countered with arguments describing the advantages of encouraging young children to see themselves as writers and to write stories and messages each day (Clarke, 1988; Morris, 1981; Read, 1986). Adams' review of research, for example, concluded that 'the process of inventing spellings is essentially a process of phonics...The evidence that invented spelling activity simultaneously develops phonemic awareness and promotes understanding of the alphabetic principle is extremely promising' (1990: 387). Additional studies indicate that students encouraged to invent spellings seem to write longer, higher quality texts and are more successful at spelling unfamiliar words correctly (Gettinger, 1993; Griffith, Klesius, and Kromrey, 1992).

The benefits of invented spelling, however, are not limited to spelling and writing. Research by Ouellette and Sénéchal (2008) compared three groups of kindergarten children for 4 weeks. One group used invented spellings and received appropriate feedback from their teacher; the other two groups were trained in phonological awareness or drew pictures. The invented spelling group demonstrated more advanced spellings and learned to read more words in a learn-to-read task than the other two groups. The authors conclude that 'invented spelling coupled with feedback helps children hone and integrate a host of important skills that are potentially involved in learning to read' (2008: 908).

A key component of the arguments surrounding invented spelling focuses on the role of instruction, reflecting concerns that children will not learn the conventions of print without a daily spelling program. Although whole language supporters such as Wilde (1990) have documented the spelling gains of students who read widely and write daily without formal spelling instruction, Richgels (1995) argues that children need both: 1 the opportunity to learn about grapho-phonemic relationships through both wide reading and many opportunities to write their own messages and 2 planned instruction modeling conventional spellings and teaching orthographic features based upon student needs.

Such instruction, however, need not focus on worksheets or isolated drills. During interactive writing lessons, for example, the teacher models conventional spellings and teaches specific orthographic features as the teacher and children craft their message together; work together to write the message word by word, by saying the word slowly and writing the sounds that are heard; share the pen such that children write the letters they know; and reread the message to ensure accurate representation of the text (McCarrier, Pinnell, and Fountas, 2000). Sipe argues for an 'active role for the teacher' (2001: 267) who supports young spellers by teaching them to say words slowly and to write down what they hear. Sipe also recommended that teachers help children who find this difficult by using sound boxes, one for each phoneme, an instructional technique used in the writing portion of a Reading Recovery lesson adapted from the work of the Russian psychologist, Elkonin (Clay, 2005).

'What can you show us?' is another instructional context for kindergarten children to develop both phonemic awareness and early concepts about letters, sounds, and words (Richgels, Poremba, and McGee, 1996) by asking children to examine a text with enlarged print (such as a poem, big book, or language experience chart) and demonstrate what they know about the text. Such instruction teaches concepts such as letter or word identification, letter–sound correspondences, rhyming words, or other text features. Spelling instruction in these contexts is placed securely within the contexts of reading and writing meaningful texts.

An important point, however, is that attention to early concepts must be addressed instructionally as it is not sufficient to assume that all children will learn them incidentally. Morris (1993) compared two different approaches to kindergarten instruction – one with a language experience approach and one emphasizing oral language and play. By May, 84 per cent of the children in the kindergarten classroom using a language experience approach were successful with the concept of word task; only 50 per cent of the children in the classroom emphasizing oral language and play understood the concept of word. Similarly, 71 per cent of the students in the language experience classrooms could segment words into phonemes but only 18 per cent of the students in the language/play classroom could successfully perform the same task. This study highlights the importance of teaching young children concepts about words, which will then facilitate phonemic segmentation, letter–sound relationships, and word recognition through activities such as shared writing, language experience stories, shared reading, and helping children to write their own texts.

Bear et al.(2000/2011) encourage teachers to find out what children are 'using but confusing,' demonstrating partial, yet incomplete knowledge of spelling concepts and to target their instruction accordingly. For example, children who represent each word with letter-like shapes demonstrating little grapho-phonemic relationships are not yet ready for formal spelling instruction but can benefit from rhyming games, shared readings of poems, songs, and stories, sorting activities with pictures, and attention to learning the letters of their names. Based on his series of studies on concept of word, Morris (1993) concluded that formal spelling instruction should be delayed until the child has a firm concept of word to avoid both confusion and frustration.

Spellers who begin to demonstrate the accurate use of initial and final consonants and some evidence of short vowel understandings can benefit from studying CVC word patterns through word sorts, word hunts, word families, and rhyming words (Ganske, 2000). Johnston encourages teachers to carefully consider when to teach word families arguing that 'well-timed instruction with word families can help children solidify tentative understandings, sort out current confusions, and move along to new understandings in the most efficient manner' (1999: 67). Clay (2001), however, cautions that emphasizing word families may limit children's writing development as this can 'create misconceptions such as "all words belong to word families"' (2001: 24). As children develop a concept of word and begin to move beyond the sounds of letter names that they hear, they may begin to demonstrate some knowledge of silent letters that signals for instruction featuring more complex word sorts with VCe or CVVC patterns. Including words that do not exactly fit the pattern in word sorts supports the development of a more flexible understanding about how words work. The teacher's role, then, is to build the instructional program by organizing instruction to teach spelling features and concepts based upon students' developmental levels.

Such instruction, however, contrasts sharply with the widespread use of basal spellers, typically one book for each grade level with a specific sequence of word lists and features. Such materials have been criticized for a one-size-fits-all approach that does not meet the needs of many children in a particular grade. Ness (2010) for example, assessed the developmental levels

in one third-grade classroom and found that the group to be so diverse as to span four levels: letter name, within word, syllable juncture, and derivational constancy. Ritchey (2008) studied kindergarten students and also found a wide range of proficiency in the ability to spell both nonsense and real words. Because of such diversity, Schlagal (2002) argues for both the limitations of singular, grade level spelling materials and the challenges faced by teachers attempting to respond to a range of individual needs. He proposes that teachers use the resources found in a range of spelling basals, with their organized, progressively more difficult lists, to plan instruction for small groups of children with similar abilities, thereby matching instruction with ability to scaffold learning.

Spelling assessment

Planning instruction based upon each student's needs first, however, requires that teachers have appropriate tools for determining students' knowledge (Al Otaiba and Hosp, 2010). At the preschool level, for example, Puranik and Apel (2010) studied three groups of preschoolers as they spelled 12 CVC and VC words using letter tiles, orally, or by writing. They analyzed children's attempts using a seven-point scale to provide greater depth of information than whether or not the spelling was correct. The researchers found that spelling ability was related to letter writing ability but only until the children could write 19 or more letters after which, they spelled equally well across the three treatments.

The line of developmental spelling research from the University of Virginia has yielded spelling assessments such as Schlagal's (1989) Qualitative Inventory of Word Knowledge (QIWK), spelling inventories for primary and intermediate learners by Bear et al. (2000/2011), and Ganske's (2000) Developmental Spelling Analysis (DSA). Each of these assessments provides lists of carefully selected words that gradually increase in both familiarity and feature difficulty. The words on each list are initially analyzed as either correct or incorrect but then more closely analyzed in terms of word features. Analysis of children's spelling attempts on these assessments enables teachers to determine each child's developmental level and gain preliminary information about the orthographic features the child controls. Also informed by developmental spelling research, Fresch (2001) used a longitudinal case study of a child from kindergarten to fourth grade to demonstrate the effectiveness of analyzing journal entries to inform instruction. The teacher's analysis provided a 'window on children's current operating knowledge' (2001: 513) which both guides instruction and documents growth.

In an effort to design a spelling assessment more sensitive than typical lists scored by percentage of accuracy, Masterson and Apel (2010) designed an assessment called the Spelling Sensitivity Score and then studied spelling knowledge from kindergarten to grade 5. The authors concluded that their tool would benefit teachers interested in matching instruction to student needs; the tool would also enable researchers to more clearly study underlying sources of linguistic knowledge.

Low-achieving spellers

A recently study by Graham et al. (2008) revealed that 42 per cent of the K–3 teachers surveyed made little or no accommodation for students struggling as spellers. The most frequent adaptations, when made, were one-to-one help or a modification in teaching procedures, but 66 per cent of these adaptations were made by only 25 per cent of the teachers surveyed. Williams and Hufnagel (2005) found that the whole-class instruction provided in one kindergarten classroom was targeted beyond the low-achieving student resulting in limited transfer of instructional principles to those students' spellings. Thus, young spellers who struggle may continue to have difficulty, unable to catch up with higher achieving peers.

Key to resolving this issue seems to be two-fold – helping teachers to better understand their students as spellers and also to manage classroom time and organization ensuring opportunities for appropriate small group instruction (Carpenter, Gehsmann, Smith, Bear, and Templeton, 2009). Although spelling research focusing on struggling spellers is limited, there are early studies which are promising and focus on providing instruction at the child's level. In a yearlong study using spelling materials matching students' developmental levels, Morris and his colleagues found that low-achieving students using materials at the appropriate level scored higher than low spellers taught with more difficult materials (Morris et al., 1995). Later, Brown, Morris and Fields (2005) documented the progress of students in the third author's second-grade classroom while implementing a developmental spelling program with a focus on managing small groups. By the end of the year, the 'low-achieving spellers in September nearly "caught up" with their average-achieving classmates' (2005: 165). When teachers selected words for study which were appropriate for each group, students experienced success and accelerated learning.

FUTURE DIRECTIONS

Recent research has provided significant information about how young children learn to spell. However, further studies are needed to clarify questions related to process, development, and instruction.

Recent studies have combined error analysis with student report data. While we have not always agreed with the conclusions of these studies (e.g., Sharp et al., 2008), we think these two methodologies can be complimentary and mutually supportive in providing more detailed accounts of learner processing. Technological advances, such as electronic tablets and unobtrusive cameras, have the potential for recording time sequences in spelling that may well reveal points of ease or the need for conscious decision-making, providing a finer grained analysis.

While there has been an expanding literature on developmental differences and similarities within and across alphabetic systems, this enterprise has just recently gained momentum. Future studies should continue to distinguish those aspects of learning about printed language that are more or less universal and those particular to specific types of orthographies. Many of the current studies focus on controlling the frequency, regularity, or wordness of spelling items with less detailed analysis of error patterns or student thinking. We would hope that the fine-grained techniques used in recent English spelling studies might be applied to spelling in other languages as well.

Although a review of bilingual and second language spelling development was beyond the scope of this chapter, we recognize that studies are also needed about how children's learning is affected by their exposure to one or more systems simultaneously. With the increased globalization of society, many students are learning to speak and write in two languages at the same time – in their native language and a second language in which they will be expected to function in a literate manner. It is also important to distinguish between situations in which the second language is learned as a foreign language (i.e., situations in which the primary mode of oral and written communication at home, school, and community is the native language) and contexts in which the second language is the principal means of communication in school and the larger community (e.g., for immigrant populations). These would be rich, though complex, contexts in which to more carefully explore developmental issues.

Other important questions relate to differences between normally developing and disabled readers/spellers. Preliminary studies suggest that differences may be more related to amount of time for learning and/or inappropriate instruction than to differences in perceptual/cognitive processing and/or abilities. Further research may help to resolve this discussion. Increasingly advanced technology available for the study of brain activity during language and literacy processing may yield significant insights about brain function with important instructional implications for students experiencing learning difficulties.

A large proportion of spelling studies done thus far have focused on children as they begin formal schooling; a small number of recent studies have been done with younger students. This emerging line of research has documented that important concepts about spelling are formed early and are developing during preschool and the early years of formal education. Studies are needed to examine the implications of instruction for 3- to 5-year-old children by identifying appropriate assessment tools, sensitive to young children's needs; by exploring instructional practices in preschool settings that foster accelerated development; and by examining appropriate practices to provide early intervention for children at-risk. Such studies could contribute to current questions about the relationship between development and instruction; that is, how does instruction foster or impede spelling development?

A theme throughout this review has been that learning to spell is a complex task, as children learn to understand oral language and its functions, develop concepts about the visual aspects of print, and learn the specific relationships between oral and written language unique to their orthographic system. The line of research followed by Morris and his colleagues (1981, 1989a, 1989b, 1992, 1993; Morris et al., 2003) exploring the relationship between a learner's concept of word and spelling has begun to provide insights into the relationships between complex factors. More research is needed to identify how learning about the orthographic system through reading and writing relate to one another over time.

Correlational and experimental studies on phonological and phonemic awareness and their relationship to spelling development have been gaining interest in the research community. But many of these studies have been criticized for limitations in their design. In a review of experimental methodology on interventions to develop phonological awareness, Troia (1999) reviewed 39 studies and found that most had serious methodological flaws. In fact, only seven of the studies met two-thirds or more of the evaluative criteria; all had at least one fatal flaw. Such reviews point to the challenges of designing valid and reliable research to inform the field about

early spelling teaching and learning. Experimental studies often focus on single aspects of oral or written language in fragmented, isolated ways leaving important questions about the application of findings to complex classroom contexts. New and creative methodologies are required, building on the experimental research of the past, to inform future classroom instruction.

Lines of early spelling research have typically focused on children and their learning processes. However, given the critical role of teachers in helping children to become conventional spellers, research must also focus on teachers and what they need to know and do in classrooms of diverse learners. At one time, instructional materials and professional development activities provided teachers with rather scripted, dogmatic (and sometimes erroneous) information about the nature of the orthographic system. Later, attention to spelling was limited, in preference to a focus on more holistic methods of literacy instruction. Currently there is renewed interest in providing teachers with accurate and useful information about the nature of the writing system and developmental processes. Models of spelling instruction based on developmental research recognize the range of abilities found in classrooms and reject one-size-fits-all, grade-level programs. Such models require that teachers have a new level of knowledge about: how spelling systems work, how children learn, how to assess students' knowledge, and how to organize classrooms to facilitate learning for diverse learners. More research is needed to study student achievement in classrooms where teachers are working to meet the needs of individual spellers. At this time, however, it appears that only a small minority of teachers are moving in this direction;

struggling spellers are particularly at risk. Teacher education programs might increase their efforts to develop, implement, and document innovative preservice and inservice programs that provide teachers with the knowledge, skills and dispositions they need to make such effective instruction a reality in their classrooms. Additional studies of the support needed for teachers to implement more complex spelling programs than whole-group basals would clearly inform the field.

Finally, new tools available in classrooms such as electronic tablets, applications, and 'smart boards' are growing both in popularity and use for spelling instruction. The quality of instruction relative to children's use of such devices, however, has yet to be studied.

REFERENCES

Abouzeid, M.P. (1992). 'Stages of word knowledge in reading disabled children', in S. Templeton and D.R. Bear (eds), *Development of Orthographic Knowledge and the Foundations of Literacy: A Memorial Festschrift for Edmund H. Henderson*. Hillsdale, NJ: Lawrence Erlbaum Associates. pp. 279–306.

Adams, M.J. (1990). *Beginning to Read: Thinking and Learning about Print*. Cambridge, MA: MIT Press.

Al Otaiba, S. and Hosp, J.L. (2010). 'Spell it out: The need for detailed spelling assessment to inform instruction', *Assessment for Effective Intervention*, 36: 3–6.

Ball, E.W. and Blachman, B.A. (1991). 'Does phoneme awareness training in kindergarten make a difference in early word recognition and developmental spelling?', *Reading Research Quarterly*, 24(1): 49–66.

Barnhart, R.K. (ed.) (1988). *The Barnhart Dictionary of Etymology: The Core Vocabulary of Standard English – Produced by American Scholarship*. New York: H.W. Wilson.

Bear, D.R. (1992). 'The prosody of oral reading and stages of word knowledge', in S. Templeton and D.R. Bear (eds), *Development of Orthographic Knowledge and the Foundations of*

Literacy: A Memorial Festschrift for Edmund H. Henderson. Hillsdale, NJ: Lawrence Erlbaum Associates. pp. 137–90.

Bear, D.R., Invernizzi, M., Templeton, S., and Johnston, F. (2000/2011). *Words Their Way: Word Study for Phonics, Vocabulary, and Spelling Instruction*. Boston, MA: Allyn & Bacon, Inc.

Beers, C.S. and Beers, J.W. (1992). 'Children's spelling of English inflectional morphology', in S. Templeton and D.R. Bear (eds), *Development of Orthographic Knowledge and the Foundations of Literacy: A Memorial Festschrift for Edmund H. Henderson*. Hillsdale, NJ: Lawrence Erlbaum Associates. pp. 231–52.

Beers, J.W. and Henderson, E.H. (1977). 'A study of developing orthographic concepts among first graders', *Research in the Teaching of English*, 2: 133–48.

Bissex, G. (1980). *GYNS AT WRK: A Child Learns to Write and Read*. Cambridge, MA: Harvard University Press.

Bloodgood, J.W. (1999). 'What's in a name? Children's name writing and literacy acquisition', *Reading Research Quarterly*, 34(3): 342–67.

Boder, E. (1973). 'Developmental dyslexia: A developmental approach based on three atypical reading-spelling patterns', *Developmental Medicine and Child Neurology*, 15: 663–87.

Bosse, M., Valdois, S., and Tainturier, M. (2003). 'Analogy without priming in early spelling development', *Reading & Writing*, 16(7): 693–716.

Both-de Vries, A.C., and Bus, A.G. (2008). 'Name writing: A first step to phonetic writing?', *Literacy Teaching and Learning*, 12(2): 37–55.

Both-de Vries, A.C. and Bus, A.G. (2010). 'The proper name as a starting point for basic reading skills', *Reading and Writing*, 23(2): 173–87.

Bourassa, D.C. and Treiman, R. (2001). 'Spelling development and disability: The importance of linguistic factors', *Language, Speech, and Hearing Services in Schools*, 32: 172–81.

Bourassa, D.C., Treiman, R., and Kessler, B. (2006). 'Use of morphology in spelling by children with dyslexia and typically developing children', *Memory & Cognition*, 34: 703–14.

Bradley, L. and Bryant, P.E. (1983). 'Categorising sounds and learning to read: a causal connection', *Nature*, 3(10): 419–21.

Brown, K.J., Morris, D., and Fields, M.K. (2005). 'Intervention after grade 1: Serving increased numbers of struggling readers effectively', *Journal of Literacy Research*, 37: 61–94.

Bryant, P., Nunes, T., and Bindman, M. (1999). 'Morphemes and spelling', in T. Nunes (ed.), *Learning to Read: An Integrated View from Research and Practice*. Dordrecht, The Netherlands: Kluwer Academic Publishers. pp. 15–41.

Bryant, P., Nunes, T., and Bindman, M. (2000). 'The relations between children's linguistic awareness and spelling: The case of the apostrophe', *Reading and Writing*, 12, 253–76.

Caravolas, M. (2006). 'Learning to spell in different languages: How orthographic variables might affect early literacy', in R.M. Joshi and P.G. Aaron (eds), *Handbook of Orthography and Literacy*. Mahwah, NJ: Erlbaum. pp. 497–511.

Caravolas, M., Kessler, B., Hulme, C., and Snowling, M. (2005). 'Effects of orthographic consistency, frequency, and letter knowledge on children's vowel spelling development', *Journal of Experimental Child Psychology*, 92(4): 307–21.

Cardoso-Martins, C., Correa, M., Lemos, L., and Napoleao, R.F. (2006). 'Is there a syllabic stage in spelling development? Evidence from Portuguese-speaking children', *Journal of Educational Psychology*, 98: 628–41.

Carpenter, K., Gehsmann, K., Smith, R., Bear, D., and Templeton, S. (2009). 'Learning together: Putting word study instruction into practice', *The California Reader*, 42(3): 4–18.

Clarke, L.K. (1988). 'Invented versus tradition spelling in first graders' writings: Effects on learning to spell and read', *Research in the Teaching of English*, 22: 281–309.

Clay, M. (1975). *What did I Write?* Portsmouth, NH: Heinemann.

Clay, M. (2001). *Change over Time in Children's Literacy Development*. Portsmouth, NH: Heinemann.

Clay, M. (2005). *Literacy Lessons Designed for Individuals: Teaching Procedures*. Auckland, New Zealand: Heinemann.

Clay, M. (2006). *Change over Time in Children's Literacy Development*. Portsmouth, NH: Heinemann.

Clay, M. (2010). *How Very Young Children Explore Writing*. Portsmouth, NH: Heinemann.

Coulmas, F. (1989). *The Writing Systems of the World*. New York: Basil Blackwell.

Craig, S. A. (2006). 'The effects of an adapted interactive writing intervention on kindergarten children's phonological awareness, spelling, and early reading development', *Journal of Educational Psychology*, 98(4): 714–31.

Cummings, D.W. (1988). *American English Spelling: An Informal Description*. Baltimore, MD: John Hopkins University Press.

Deacon, H., Kirby, J.R., and Casselman-Bell, M. (2009). 'How robust is the contribution of morphological awareness to general spelling outcomes?', *Reading Psychology*, 30: 301–18.

Ehri, L.C. (1980). 'The development of orthographic images', in U. Frith (ed.), *Cognitive Processes in Spelling*. New York: Academic Press. pp. 311–38.

Ehri, L.C. (1987). 'Learning to spell and read words', *Journal of Reading Behavior*, 19: 5–31.

Ehri, L.C. (1992). 'Review and commentary: Stage of spelling development', in S. Templeton and D.R. Bear (eds), *Development of Orthographic Knowledge and the Foundations of Literacy: A Memorial Festschrift for Edmund H. Henderson*. Hillsdale, NJ: Lawrence Erlbaum Associates. pp. 307–32.

Ehri, L.C. and Rosenthal, J. (2007). 'Spellings of words: A neglected facilitator of vocabulary learning', *Journal of Literacy Research*, 39(4): 389–409.

Fayol, M., Thevenin, M.G., Jarousse, J.P., and Totereau, C. (1999). 'From learning to teaching to learning French written morphology' in T. Nunes (ed.), *Learning to Read: An Integrated View from Research and Practice*. Dordrecht, The Netherlands: Kluwer Academic Publishers. pp. 43–64.

Ferreiro, E. and Teberosky, A. (1982). *Literacy before Schooling*. Portsmouth, NH: Heinemann.

Fresch, M.J. (2000). 'What we learned from Josh: Sorting out word sorting', *Language Arts*, 77(3): 232–40.

Fresch, M.J. (2001). 'Journal entries as a window on spelling knowledge', *The Reading Teacher*, 54(5): 500–13.

Frith, U. (1985). 'Beneath the surface of developmental dyslexia', in K. Patterson, M. Coltheart, and J. Marshall (eds), *Surface Dyslexia*. Cambridge: Academic Press. pp. 301–30.

Furnes, B. and Samuelsson, S. (2011). 'Phonological awareness and rapid automatized naming predicting early development in reading and spelling: Results from a cross-linguistic longitudinal study', *Learning and Individual Differences*, 21(1): 85–95.

Ganske, K. (2000). *Word Journeys: Assessment-Guided Phonics, Spelling, and Vocabulary Instruction*. New York: Guilford Press.

Gentry, J.R. (1978). 'Early spelling strategies', *Elementary School Journal*, 79: 88–92.

Gentry, J.R. (1982). 'An analysis of developmental spelling in GNYS AT WRK', *The Reading Teacher*, 36: 192–200.

Gentry, J.R. (2000). 'A retrospective on invented spelling and a look forward', *The Reading Teacher*, 54(3): 318–32.

Gettinger, M. (1993). 'Effects of invented spelling and direct instruction on spelling performance of second-grade boys', *Journal of Applied Behavior Analysis*, 3: 281–91.

Gill, C.E. (1980). 'An analysis of spelling errors in French'. Unpublished doctoral dissertation. University of Virginia.

Gill, C.H. and Scharer, P.L. (1996). 'Why do they get it on Friday and misspell it on Monday'? Teachers inquiring about their students as spellers', *Language Arts*, 73: 89–96.

Goswami, U. (1992). 'Annotation: Phonological factors in spelling development', *The Journal of Child Psychology & Psychiatry*, 33(6): 967–75.

Goswami, U. (1994). 'Development of reading and spelling skills', in M. Rutter and D.F. Hay (eds), *Development Through Life: A Handbook for Clinicians*. London: Blackwell Scientific Publications. pp. 284–302.

Goswami, U. (1999). 'Integrating orthographic and phonological knowledge as reading develops: Onsets, rimes, and analogies in children's reading', in R. Klein and P. McMullen (eds), *Converging Methods for Understanding Reading and Dyslexia*. Cambridge, MA: MIT Press. pp. 57–75.

Goswami, U. (2001). 'Early phonological development', in S.B. Neuman and D.K. Dickinson (eds), *Handbook of Early Literacy Research*. New York: The Guilford Press. pp. 111–25.

Goswami, U., Ziegler, J.C., and Richardson, U. (2005). 'The effects of spelling consistency on phonological awareness: A comparison of English and German', *Journal of Experimental Child Psychology*, 92(4) 345–65.

Graham, S. (2000). 'Should the natural learning approach replace spelling instruction?', *Journal of Educational Psychology*, 92: 235–47.

Graham, S., Morphy, P., Harris, K., Fink-Chorzempa, B., Saddler, B., Moran, S., and Mason, L. (2008). 'Teaching spelling in the primary grades: A national survey of instructional practices and adaptations', *American Educational Research Journal*, 45(3): 796–825.

Griffith, P.L. (1991). 'Phonemic awareness helps first graders invent spellings and third graders remember correct spellings', *Journal of Reading Behavior*, 23(2): 215–33.

Griffith, P.L., Klesius, J.P., and Kromrey, J.D. (1992). 'The effect of phonemic awareness on the literacy development of first grade children in a traditional or a whole language classroom', *Journal of Research in Childhood Education*, 6(2): 85–92.

Harste, J.C., Burke, C.L., and Woodward, V.A. (1982). 'Children's language and world: Initial encounters with print', in J.A. Langer and M.T. Smith-Burke (eds), *Reader Meets Author/Bridging the Gap: A Psycholinguistic and Sociolinguistic Perspective*. Newark, DE: International Reading Association. pp. 105–31.

Henderson, E.H. (1990). *Teaching Spelling* 2nd edn. Boston: Houghton Mifflin.

Henderson, E.H. (1992). 'The interface of lexical competence and knowledge of written words', in S. Templeton and D.R. Bear (eds), *Development of Orthographic Knowledge and the Foundations of Literacy: A Memorial Festschrift for Edmund H. Henderson*. Hillsdale, NJ: Lawrence Erlbaum Associates. pp. 1–30.

Henderson, E.H. and Beers, J.W. (eds) (1980). *Developmental and Cognitive Aspects of Learning To Spell: A Reflection of Word Knowledge*. Newark, DE: International Reading Association.

Hughes, M. and Searle, D. (1991). 'A longitudinal study of the growth of spelling abilities within the context of the development of literacy', in J. Zutell and S. McCormick (eds), *Learner Factors/Teacher Factors: Issues in Literacy Research and Instruction*. Chicago: National Reading Conference. pp. 159–68.

Hughes, M. and Searle, D. (1997). *The Violent E and Other Tricky Sounds: Learning to Spelling from Kindergarten through Grade 6*. York, ME: Stenhouse.

Hughes, M. and Searle, D. (2000). 'Spelling and "the Second 'R'"', *Language Arts*, 77(3): 203–8.

Invernizzi, M. (1992). 'The vowel and what follows: A phonological frame of orthographic analysis', in S. Templeton and D.R. Bear (eds), *Development of Orthographic Knowledge and the Foundations of Literacy: A Memorial Festschrift for Edmund H. Henderson*. Hillsdale, NJ: Lawrence Erlbaum Associates. pp. 105–36.

Invernizzi, M.A. and Worthy, M.J. (1989). 'An orthographic comparison of the spelling errors of learning disabled and normal children across four grade levels of spelling achievement', *Reading Psychology*, 10(2): 173–88.

Invernizzi, M., Abouzeid, M., and Gill, T. (1994). 'Using students' invented spellings as a guide for spelling instruction that emphasizes word study', *Elementary School Journal*, 95(2), 155–67.

Johnston, F.R. (1999). 'The timing and teaching of word families', *The Reading Teacher*, 53(1): 64–75.

Ju, D. and Jackson, N.E. (1995). 'Graphic and phonological processing in Chinese character identification'. *Journal of Reading Behavior*, 27(3): 299–313.

Kamii, C. and Manning, M. (1999). 'Before "invented" spelling: kindergartners' awareness that writing is related to the sounds of speech', *Journal of Research in Childhood Education*, 14(1): 16–25.

Kamii, C., Long, R., Manning, M., and Manning, G. (1990). 'Spelling in kindergarten: A constructivist analysis comparing Spanish-speaking and English-speaking children', *Journal of Research in Childhood Education*, 4(2): 91–7.

Kim, Y. (2010). 'Componential skills in early spelling development in Korean', *Scientific Studies of Reading*, 14(2): 137–58.

Lee, D.M. and Lee, J.M. (1941). 'The spelling load is too heavy', in J.S. Hudson, N.V. Lind, and W. Jacob Jr (eds), *Language Arts in the Elementary School*. Washington, DC: National Education Association of the United States. Dept. of Elementary School Principals. pp. 484–7.

Leppänen, U., Niemi, P., Aunola, K., and Nurmi, J. (2006). 'Development of reading and spelling Finnish from preschool to grade 1 and grade 2', *Scientific Studies of Reading*, 101: 3–30.

Martens, P.A. (1999). '"Mommy, how do you write 'Sarah'?": The role of name writing in one child's literacy', *Journal of Research in Childhood Education*, 14(1): 5–15.

Masterson, J.J. and Apel, K. (2010). 'The spelling sensitivity score: Noting developmental changes in spelling knowledge', *Assessment for Effective Intervention*, 36(1): 35–45.

McCarrier, A., Pinnell, G.S., and Fountas, I.C. (2000). *Interactive Writing: How Language and Literacy Come Together, K-2*. Portsmouth, NH: Heinemann.

McGee, L.M. and Richgels, D.J. (2000). *Literacy's Beginnings: Supporting Young Readers and Writers*. 3rd edn. Needham Heights, MA: Allyn & Bacon.

Morais, J. (1991). 'Constraints on the development of phonemic awareness', in S. Brady and D. Shankweiler (eds), *Phonological Processes in Literacy. A Tribute to Isabelle Liberman*. Hillsdale, NJ: Lawrence Erlbaum Associates.

Morris, D. (1981). 'Concept of word: A developmental phenomenon in the beginning reading and writing processes', *Language Arts*, 58(6): 659–68.

Morris, D. (ed.) (1989a). *Reading Psychology: An International Quarterly*, 10(2).

Morris, D. (ed.) (1989b). *Reading Psychology: An International Quarterly*, 10(3).

Morris, D. (1992). 'Concept of word: A pivotal understanding in the learning-to-read process', in S. Templeton and D. Bear (eds), *Development of Orthographic Knowledge and the Foundations of Literacy: A Memorial Festschrift of Edmund H. Henderson*. Hillsdale, NJ: Lawrence Erlbaum Associates. pp. 53–78.

Morris, D. (1993). 'The relationship between children's concept of word in text and phoneme awareness in learning to read: A longitudinal study', *Research in the Teaching of English*, 27(2): 133–54.

Morris, D. and Perney, J. (1984). 'Development spelling as a predictor of first-grade reading achievement', *Elementary School Journal*, 84(4): 440–57.

Morris, D., Nelson, L., and Perney, J. (1986). 'Exploring the concept of "spelling instructional level" through the analysis of error-types', *Elementary School Journal*, 66(2): 28–41.

Morris, D., Blanton, L., Blanton, W.E., Nowacek, J., and Perney, J. (1995). 'Teaching low-achieving spellers at their "instructional level"', *Elementary School Journal*, 96(3): 163–78.

Morris, D., Bloodgood, J., Lomax, R., and Perney, J. (2003). 'Developmental steps in learning to read: A longitudinal study in kindergarten and first grade'. *Reading Research Quarterly*, 38(3): 302–28.

Morrow, L.M. (1990). 'Preparing the classroom environment to promote literacy during play', *Early Childhood Research Quarterly*, 5: 537–54.

National Reading Panel (2000). *Report of the National Reading Panel: Teaching Children to Read: An Evidence-Based Assessment of the Scientific Research Literature on Reading and its Implications for Reading Instruction: Report of the Subgroups*. Washington, DC: US Department of Health and Human Services.

Ness, M.K. (2010). 'Examining one class of third-grade spellers: The diagnostic potential of students' spelling', *Reading Horizons*, 50(2): 113–30.

Otto, H.J. (1973). 'Historical roots of contemporary elementary education', in J.I. Goodlad and H.G. Shane (eds), *The Elementary School in the United States*. Chicago: University of Chicago Press. pp. 36–58.

Ouellette, G. and Sénéchal, M. (2008). 'Pathways to Literacy: A study of invented spelling and its role in learning to read' *Child Development*, 79(4): 899–913.

Pacton, S. and Deacon, S. H. (2008). 'The timing and mechanisms of children's use of morphological information in spelling: A review of evidence from

English and French'. *Cognitive Development*, 23(3): 339–59.

Papandropoulou, I. and Sinclair, H. (1974). 'What is a word? Experimental study of children's ideas on grammar', *Human Development*, 17: 241–58.

Pinheiro, A.M.V. (1995). 'Reading and spelling development in Brazilian Portuguese', *Reading and Writing: An Interdisciplinary Journal*, 7: 111–38.

Pollo, T.C., Kessler, B., and Treiman, R. (2009). 'Statistical patterns in children's early writing', *Journal of Experimental Child Psychology*, 104: 410–26.

Porpodas, C.D. (1989). 'The phonological factor in reading and spelling of Greek', in P.G. Aaron and R.M. Joshi (eds), *Reading and Writing Disorders in Different Orthographic Systems*. Dordrecht/Boston/London: Kluwer Academic Publishers. pp. 177–88.

Portecorvo, C. and Orsolini, M. (1996). 'Writing and written language in children's development', in C. Pontecorvo, M. Orsolini, B. Burge, and L.B. Resnick (eds), *Children's Early Text Construction*. Mahwah, NJ: Lawrence Erlbaum. pp. 3–23.

Puranik, C. and Apel, K. (2010). 'Effect of assessment task and letter writing ability on preschool children's spelling performance', *Assessment for Effective Intervention*, 36(1): 46–56.

Rasinski, T. and Zutell, J. (2010). *Essential Strategies for Word Study: Effective Methods for Improving Decoding, Spelling, and Vocabulary*. New York: Scholastic.

Read, C. (1971). 'Pre-school children's knowledge of English phonology', *Harvard Educational Review*, 41(1): 1–34.

Read, C. (1975). 'Children's categorization of speech sounds in English', *Monographs of the National Council of Teachers of English*. (No. 17).

Read, C. (1986). *Children's Creative Spelling*. London: Routledge & Kegan Paul.

Read, C. and Hodges, R. (1982). 'Spelling', in H. Mitzel (ed.), *Encyclopedia of Educational Research*. 5th edn. New York: Macmillan. pp. 1758–67.

Richgels, D.J. (1995). 'Invented spelling ability and printed word learning in kindergarten', *Reading Research Quarterly*, 30(1): 96–109.

Richgels, D.J. (2001). 'Invented spelling, phonemic awareness, and reading and writing instruction', in S.B. Neuman and D.K. Dickinson (eds), *Handbook of Early Literacy Research*. New York: The Guilford Press. pp. 142–55.

Richgels, D.J., Poremba, K.J., and McGee, L.M. (1996). 'Kindergarteners talk about print: Phonemic awareness in meaningful contexts', *The Reading Teacher*, 49(8): 632–42.

Rickard Liow, S.J., and Lee, L.C. (2004). 'Metalinguistic awareness and semi-syllabic scripts: Children's spelling errors in Malay', *Reading and Writing*, 17(1/2): 7–26.

Ritchey, K.D. (2008). 'The building blocks of writing: Learning to write letters and spell words', *Reading and Writing*, 21: 27–47.

Rittle-Johnson, B.R. and Siegler, R.S. (1999). 'Learning to spell: Variability, choice and change in children's strategy use', *Child Development*, 70(2): 332–48.

Savage, R., Pillay, V., and Melidona, S. (2008). 'Rapid serial naming is a unique predictor of spelling in children', *Journal of Learning Disabilities*. 41(3): 235–50.

Seymour, P.H.K., Aro, M., and Erskine, J.M. (2003). 'Foundation literacy acquisition in European orthographies', *British Journal of Psychology*, 94: 143–74.

Scharer, P.L. (1992). 'From memorization to conceptualization: History informing the teaching and learning of spelling', *Journal of Language Experience*, 11(1): 43–58.

Scharer, P.L. and Pinnell, G.S. (eds) (2008). *Guiding K-3 Writers to Independence: The New Essentials*. New York: Scholastic.

Share, D.L. (2008). 'On the Anglocentricities of current reading research and practice: The perils of overreliance on an "outlier" orthography', *Psychological Bulletin*, 134(4): 584–615.

Sharp, A.C., Sinatra, G.M, and Reynolds, R.E. (2008). 'The development of children's orthographic knowledge: A microgenetic perspective', *Reading Research Quarterly*, 43(3): 206–26.

Schlagal, R. (1989). Constancy and change in spelling development. *Reading Psychology*, 10(3), 207–229.

Schlagal, R.C. (1992). 'Patterns of orthographic development into the intermediate grades', in S. Templeton and D. Bear (eds), *Development of Orthographic Knowledge and the Foundations of Literacy: A Memorial Festschrift of Edmund H. Henderson*. Hillsdale, NJ: Lawrence Erlbaum Associates. pp. 31–52.

Schlagal, R. (2002). 'Classroom spelling instruction: History, research, and practice', *Reading Research and Instruction*, 42(1): 44–57.

Silva, C. and Alves-Martins, M. (2002). 'Phonological skills and writing of presyllabic children', *Reading Research Quarterly*, 37(4): 466–83.

Sipe, L.R. (2001). 'Invention, convention and intervention: Invented spelling and the teacher's role', *The Reading Teacher*, 55(3): 264–73.

Stellakis, N. and Kondyli, M. (2004). 'The emergence of writing: Children's writing during the pre-alphabetic spelling phase', *Educational Studies in Language and Literature*, 4: 129–50.

Sulzby, E. (1996). 'Roles of oral and written language as children approach conventional literacy', in C. Pontecorvo, M. Orsolini, B. Burge, and L.B. Resnick (eds), *Children's Early Text Construction*. Mahwah, NJ: Lawrence Erlbaum. pp. 25–46.

Tangel, D.M. and Blachman, B.A. (1992). 'Effects of phoneme awareness instruction on kindergarten children's invented spelling', *Journal of Reading Behavior*, 24: 233–61.

Temple, C. (1978). 'An Analysis of Spelling Errors in Spanish'. Doctoral dissertation, University of Virginia.

Templeton, S. and Bear, D. (eds) (1992) *Development of Orthographic Knowledge and the Foundations of Literacy: A Memorial Festschrift of Edmund H. Henderson*. Hillsdale, NJ: Lawrence Erlbaum Associates.

Templeton, C. and Morris, D. (2000). 'Spelling', in M.L. Kamil, P.B. Mosenthal, P.D. Pearson, and R. Barr (eds), *Handbook of Reading Research*. Vol. 3. Mahwah, NJ: Lawrence Erlbaum. pp. 525–43.

Treiman, R. (1993). *Beginning to Spell: A Study of First-Grade Children*. New York: Oxford University Press.

Treiman, R. and Cassar, M. (1996). 'Effects of morphology on children's spelling of final consonant clusters', *Journal of Experimental Child Psychology*, 63: 141–70.

Troia, G.A. (1999). 'Phonological awareness intervention research: A critical review of the experimental methodology', *Reading Research Quarterly*, 34(1): 28–52.

Uhry, J.K. (1999). 'Invented spelling in kindergarten: The relationship with finger-point reading', *Reading and Writing: An Interdisciplinary Journal*, 11: 441–64.

Valle-Arroyo, F. (1990). 'Spelling errors in Spanish', *Reading and writing: An Interdisciplinary Journal*, 2: 83–98.

Venezky, R.L. (1999). *The American Way of Spelling: The Structure and Origin of American English Orthography*. New York: The Guilford Press.

Verhagen, W., Aarnoutse, C., and van Leeuwe, J. (2010). 'Spelling and word recognition in grades 1 and 2: Relations to phonological awareness and naming speed in Dutch children', *Applied Psycholinguistics*, 31: 59–80.

Wilde, S. (1990). 'A proposal for a new spelling curriculum', *The Elementary School Journal*, 90(3): 275–89.

Williams, C. and Hufnagel, K. (2005). 'The impact of word study instruction on kindergarten children's journal writing', *Research in the Teaching of English*, 39(3): 233–70.

Wimmer, H. and Landerl, K. (1997). 'How learning to spell German differs from learning to spell English', in C.A. Perfetti, L. Reiben, and M. Fayol (eds), *Learning to Spell: Research, Theory, and Practice Across Languages*. Mahwah, NJ: Lawrence Erlbaum. pp. 81–96.

Winskel, H. and Widjaja, V. (2007). 'Phonological awareness, letter knowledge and literacy development in Indonesian beginner readers and spellers', *Applied Psycholinguistics*, 28(1): 23–45.

Wood, C. (2004). 'Do levels of pre-school alphabetic tuition affect the development of phonological awareness and early literacy?', *Educational Psychology*, 24(1): 3–11.

Young, K. (2008). Don't just look, listen: uncovering children's cognitive strategies during spelling-related activities. *Education 3–13*, 36(2): 127–138.

Zutell, J. (1992). 'An integrated view of word knowledge: Correlational studies of the relationships between spelling, reading, and conceptual development', in S. Templeton and D. Bear (eds), *Development of Orthographic Knowledge and the Foundations of Literacy: A Memorial Festschrift of Edmund H. Henderson*. Hillsdale, NJ: Lawrence Erlbaum Associates. pp. 213–30.

Zutell, J. (1994). 'Spelling instruction', in A.C. Purves, L. Papa, and S. Jordan (eds), *Encyclopedia of English Studies and Language Arts*. Vol. 2. New York: Scholastic. pp. 1098–100.

Zutell, J. (2008). 'Changing perspectives on word knowledge: Spelling and vocabulary', in M.J. Fresch (ed.), *An Essential History of Current Reading Practices*. Newark, DE: International Reading Association. pp. 186–206.

Zutell, J. and Fresch, M.J. (1991). 'A longitudinal study of reading and spelling connections for third and fifth grade students', paper presented at the 36th annual convention of the International Reading Association, May 1991, Las Vegas, NV.

Zutell, J. and Rasinski, T. (1989). 'Reading and spelling connections in third and fifth grade students', *Reading Psychology*, 10(2): 137–55.

PART 4

Literacy in Preschool Settings and Schools

The Place of Childhoods in School Writing Programs: A Matter of Ethics

Anne Haas Dyson

In an essay on childhood and poetry, Pablo Neruda recounted a childhood event that captured the essence of his experiences as a writer, indeed, I would say, as a participant in a community of others:

> One time ... in the backyard of our house in Temuco ... I came upon a hole in one of the boards of the fence ... All of a sudden a hand appeared a tiny hand of a boy about my own age. By the time I came close again, the hand was gone, and in its place there was a marvelous [toy] white sheep ... I went into the house and brought out a treasure of my own: a pinecone, opened, full of odor and resin, which I adored. I set it down in the same spot and went off with the sheep.
> (Neruda, 2004: 132).

A never-to-be-known child on the other side of his fence made an offering; Neruda felt compelled to respond. He shared a corner of this precarious planet with an unseen other; he was obligated to respond. The exchange of toy sheep and pine cone became, for him, a metaphor for the poems

he would push through publishers' fences to unknown others with whom he felt a shared humanity.

Written communication is an act of responsiveness to others with whom we share some actual or virtual place (Bakhtin, 1981). In literacy events, people respond in some way to each other, given their social memberships, cultural norms, and the occasion at hand. As Tomasello (2009) argues, human beings are given to such responsiveness; our biologically-gifted engagement with others is shaped by social institutions and cultural norms. And these, as it happens, are experienced by young children not only in relationships with adults but also in relationships with other children (Corsaro, 2011).

Imagine, for example, writing time in Mrs Bee's kindergarten in a small urban area in the upper Midwest of the United States. The children are from a low-income neighborhood and are all, like Mrs Bee herself, African American.

Mrs Bee has worked all year long to teach her children to write, just as she is directed in her mandated curricular guidebooks. The children are to express themselves as individuals, crafting their *own true* experiences on paper. They are not to climb into other people's true stories, nor take them for their own use. Mrs Bee, though, has not been entirely successful at preventing this.

On this May day, I, the adult friend and observer of Mrs Bee's children, am sitting by 5-year-old Jamal. Coretta comes over to our table. She wants to read me her story. On the first page of that story is a picture of a car in front of a big building with double doors; on the second, three girls stand in front of that building. These are stick-figure girls with chin-length curved lines on either side of their heads (marking them as Coretta's just-a-quick-sketch girls, with no elaborate hair dos or high heels). Coretta's written text is about liking to go to the mall and about her plan to take her friends on a mall trip.

'What about me?' says the observant Jamal. 'I'm your friend.' Moreover, he continues, *he* is the one driving the car to the mall. 'For real.' Coretta, who is standing, leans over, puts her paper on the table, and, in full view of Jamal, begins drawing another stick figure, one with no hair hanging down, just a line across the top of the head. (In truth, Jamal has dreadlocks.)

'You're gonna add him,' I say, quite interested in the turn of events.

'I *have* to,' says Coretta softly.

'I *have* to,' said Coretta, but, in the official world, she did not have to. Mrs Bee was not telling her to fix her piece; *Jamal* was. 'I *have* to,' said Coretta, but she did not have to. She could have responded by positioning herself as a good student; that is, she could have said 'You make your story how you want it; this is my story,' but she did not. She could have responded as a girl; that is, she could have said 'Only us girls are going to the mall,' but she did not. Coretta made a choice as an individual – an individual who felt obligated to a friend and was now negotiating a kind of textual play. And Coretta *was* playing – she was pretending to go to the mall, and Jamal wanted to play too.

Jamal and Coretta bring us deep into their unofficial peer world, where children did not act as isolated individuals, but, rather, had responsibilities to each other. If Coretta was to be a good friend in an ethical sense, she *had* to respond to Jamal. As her friend, Jamal had every right to expect to be included in Coretta's imagined trip with her *friends*.

In the view of the philosopher Kwame Appiah, ethics has to do with what we should do as an individual because we share communities, indeed, identities, with particular others. We feel a sense of obligation, and of purpose, through our membership in communities, be they large ethnic ones, or smaller ones involving family or friends. To draw on the language philosopher Bakhtin, our ethics are enacted through responsiveness to others. The Bakhtinian scholars Clark and Holquist explain that ethics are not 'abstract principles but [rather] the pattern of the actual deeds I perform in the event that is my life. My self is that which through such performance answers other selves and the world from the unique place and time I occupy in existence' (1984: 64).

Through language use, the self enters into relationships with others and, in the process, negotiates both a social encounter and a sense of how she or he belongs in the world. Am I a friend? Jamal asks Coretta.

If so, I should be in the text, and the play, too.

This chapter focuses on the ethics that govern official writing programs for the young and those enacted in the unofficial or peer lives of children themselves. Undergirded by both childhood studies (Corsaro, 2011; Qvortrup, 2005) and dialogic theory (Bakhtin, 1981), I consider, first, the ideologies of language and childhoods that play themselves out in many official writing programs designed to teach 'the basics' of written communication. In these official worlds, there are expectations for what a 'good' child writer should do or, more accurately, should be.

Then I turn to the unofficial worlds of childhoods, where there are also expectations for others' behavior. These expectations are not necessarily isomorphic with those of official worlds. In fact, like Pablo Neruda, children may feel obligated to respond to peers and friends with whom they share a place in their known worlds.

I illustrate this potential ethical gap primarily with data from Mrs Bee's kindergarten, gathered during a recent project on the ideologies about childhood and language that undergird efforts to teach writing 'basics' to young children. My interest was in highly test-regulated schools serving children labeled 'at risk' of school failure simply by their very existence – that is, because of family income, minority status, and/or a home language other than the local 'standard' English. Through this project, then, I met Mrs Bee and, at another school, Mrs Kay, who taught first grade.

In both their districts, the writing program blended an emphasis on conventional 'basics' (e.g., knowing letter names and sounds, using standard 'grammar') with an emphasis on the writing process and the production of real 'life stories,' to quote Mrs Kay. Children in both rooms could begin their composing by drawing, but they were under pressure to move as quickly as possible into the use of written symbols.

Over the course of at least an academic year in each site, I used ethnographic methods to probe institutional expectations of the 'proper' child writer. I observed and audiotaped classroom lessons and child talk; I collected all official child products and amassed documents with curricular objectives, assessment benchmarks, and mandated guidebooks. (Research methods are provided in Dyson, 2008a, and forthcoming.)

The governing ethics of both official and unofficial worlds were evident, first, in teachers' and children's objections to perceived ethical violations – to perceptions that someone was not being, for example, 'fair,' 'good,' or 'nice' in their composing. As will become clear, these violations often flowed from how writing was socially organized. For example, if writing is organized as a task for expressing individual truths, then one can be accused of taking someone else's ideas and of inventing false truths. If writing is organized as a socially playful task, then the violations differ; as Jamal has already suggested, a writer can be accused of not being inclusive – of not letting somebody play – or, more broadly, of not being responsive.

In this chapter's consideration of ethics and school writing programs, I turn mainly to Mrs Bee's room for illustrative vignettes because her children were newer to this business of schooling and to the expectations of their school writing program. Moreover, Mrs Bee, a conscientious and caring teacher, was new to the mandated writing program and tried hard to implement it as expected. Indeed, initially she was monitored regularly by program consultants to make sure that she was enacting the program as required.

Like Jamal and Coretta, young children cross-culturally are drawn to other children and to play, albeit in situated, particular ways. This desire for social companionship does not automatically disappear when children cross the threshold into school. Indeed, through this chapter, I am arguing that the studied school writing programs, and restrictive programs across the globe, can be viewed as disregarding and, moreover, marginalizing childhoods themselves.

THE PLACE OF THE CHILD SELF IN OFFICIAL WRITING CURRICULA

Throughout the world, learning to write is most often a matter of learning the 'basic' conventions of letter forms, spelling, and sentence structure. Because of local educational traditions, testing regimes, and economic circumstances, including a paucity of teachers, space, and supplies, learning to write may not entail composition at all; rather, children may copy, fill-in-the-blank, and write teacher-dictated text (e.g., Dewayani, 2011; Lisanza, 2011; Prinsloo, 2004; Sahni, 2001). In US schools serving children deemed 'at risk,' the 'basics' are considered especially important (Genishi and Dyson, 2009; Hirsh-Pasek, Golinkoff, Berk, and Singer, 2009). But even in situations where progressive writing pedagogies ostensibly occur, uniformity of mandated lessons and testing regimes may squeeze children's intentions out of the official world (Dyson, 2008a; Newkirk, 2009; Salvio and Boldt, 2009).

In such curricula, the dominant ideology of child selves is a particularly 'unattractive' version of individualism, to borrow

from Appiah (2005: 15); in this ideology, individuality and sociability are competing goals. One must apply oneself and do one's work; one must not play around with one's seatmates. For example, in conventional basics instruction (e.g., Moats, 2004), the successful child moves to the head of the class by quickly mastering the grammatical and orthographic rules of writing conventions and, thereby, learning the best means for written expression.

In these instructional contexts, the key participant mode is a pedagogical one between teachers and children (as individuals and as a collective). Children rely on their teachers' ears and eyes for identifying 'errors' or, to use common classroom vernacular, 'fix-its' (Dyson, 2006). Such errors tend to embody a homogeneous and hierarchical notion of language. These hierarchical 'fix-its' are related to tested skills; they merit no rationale beyond an explanation of the rule itself, since violated rules are viewed as holding across literacy practices. So, for example, when assuming grammatical agency in English, 'my friend and I' always beat 'me and my friend,' no matter who, when, or where 'me' and 'my friend' might be. There are no situational variations, no sociocultural vernaculars, no developmentally insightful 'errors' (e.g., Moats, 2004). Similarly, the official relationship among children themselves is also hierarchical (i.e., children are differentially skillful).

In mandated writing process or workshop approaches for early schooling (e.g., Calkins and Mermelstein, 2003), young children are viewed as learning to express themselves, not only by learning to edit for rules, but also by going inward: the good child 'thinks' and then selects a potential topic from their repertoire of 'real' experiences. There may be structured times when children are to share their plans with each other or provide editorial critiques to a partner. But, often, the ultimate goal is for the individual to quite literally produce texts, and thereby selves, in which 'you [the author] matter most' (Appiah, 2005: 15).

Critics have long questioned the individualistic ideology seemingly embedded in writing pedagogy, including writing workshop approaches (e.g., Smith and Stock, 2003; Tobin, 1995; see related critiques by Boldt, 2009; Cooper, 2009; Newkirk, 2009). As Tobin (1995) argues, self-expression should not be confused with free expression; its discursive renderings are taught, a point he illustrates through vignettes from his studies of Japanese and American preschools. Just as children are guided to become cultural members through their families (DeLoache and Gottlieb, 2000; Ochs and Schieffelin, 2001), they are guided to learn the social structures, content, and conventions considered appropriate in their classrooms (Cazden, 2001). And, I add, they are taught 'ethics,' the rights and obligations they have as classroom members and, more particularly, as 'writers.' To examine the ethics of this version of individualism, below I bring readers into Mrs Bee's room.

'A real story about you' (the you that is not Spiderman)

From the beginning of the school year, Mrs Bee was conscientious about the mandated curriculum and, given that, she identified two interrelated ethical problems – the children took other people's ideas, and, hence, they did not tell their own truths. In September of the school year, Mrs Bee had modeled a personal story about having gone skiing. She had acted out her story, trudging up an imagined hill,

skiing down and then – oops – falling right on her bottom. The children laughed at this story; they seemed to *love* it. When they were sent to their work tables, many children imagined themselves having similar adventures. But this was a problem, as Mrs Bee explained to her children:

> A lot of you copied *my* story [about snow skiing]. That is not good. That's illegal. You can't copy my story … You have to have your own story, your own thoughts, your *own* idea … I know there are many things that you guys like to do and have already done.

Mrs Bee was approaching her children as individuals with ethical obligations as writers. Writers are obligated to keep their distance and refrain from taking what is not theirs. Undergirding that concern, though, was another stressed by her program. Consistent with current writing pedagogy in the US, the children were to value their individual experiences, to see them as the source of writing material. Thus, Mrs Bee referred to the real things that 'you guys like to do and have already done.' Good writers draw on their true selves – their true experiences – and then express those true selves in a text evaluated by the teacher.

Contributing to these ethical violations was children's shared attraction to characters and plots lines from popular media. Sponge Bob, Hannah Montana, and Spiderman were, in fact, part of many children's everyday experiences. They watched them on the television, they conversed about them and, during writing, many enjoyed drawing them in the midst of varied adventures. But this posed the ethical problem of truth.

It is not unusual for children's interest in popular media to be dismissed in school and, moreover, in official writing. Children's use of such media resources can be seen as vulgar, violent, evidence of crass consumerism, or a just plain silly waste of time (Marsh, 2003; Newkirk, 2009). In Mrs Bee's room, though, the main problem was that of truth. There were to be no unruly to-be-continued worlds of impossible doings. Children *could* write, for example, about wanting to see a superhero movie, about getting a Spiderman toy or game for a birthday present, or even about wanting such a toy from Santa (an allowed popular figure). In other words, the commoditization of childhood pleasures was just fine. What was not fine was entering into an imagined world in which the child could become Spiderman or some other awesome figure. They could not, for example, fly through the air on paper.

In the excerpt below, from early in the school year, Mrs Bee explained the situation to her children:

Mrs Bee: I don't want you dreaming up something about Superman, Batman, and all those folk. Because they're not really real ... You can't say anything about Spiderman 'cause you don't know who that is.
Children: I do! I do! (voices ring out)
Mrs Bee: No you don't.
Children: M:: m. ('Yes I do,' the children are saying, quite assertively.)
Mrs Bee: Do you know the real Spiderman?
Children: Yes!
Mrs Bee: No, you don't. Spiderman is not a real person. He's just a character.

Mrs Bee went on to explain that Spiderman flies through the air with strings attached; he may look like he's flying, but he is not. After Mrs Bee finished, the children talked among themselves about Spiderman. 'Want me to tell you where Spiderman work at?' Cici asked her tablemates. 'My mama said Pizza Hut ...'

Soon the children began their composing, and the ethical problems of truth and 'illegal' copying arose again, as will

be seen when the spotlight moves to unofficial worlds and their participant modes.

Potential problems with the 'truth'

The notion of being 'truthful,' and its link to valuing one's 'real' life, is problematic. In part, this is because cross-culturally, a major aspect of children's *real* life is *pretend play* (although its substance and perceived value varies [Lancy, 2007; Montgomery, 2009]). In that play, children may imagine themselves into others' experiences – appropriating, improvising on, even mocking their words and deeds.

In addition, a 'story' worth telling may be one that dramatizes an experiential germ of a story and thus transforms it into an engaging, if not literally true, one. Performative storytelling (involving, for example, image-creating metaphors or exaggerated plot action) is not confined to any one categorized cultural group. Nonetheless, a performative telling of a 'true story' – which is definitely not true – is one aspect of the African American storytelling heritage. In such an event, the teller's tale may emphasize an encounter with social or physical adversity (Smitherman, 1986). For their part, Mrs Bee's children did tell exaggerated (and amusing) stories, as will soon be illustrated.

Finally, one might ask, *is* writing about going inside the self in search of an inner authenticity? Or is it, as Bakhtin (1986) and Volosinov (1986) argued, about the self as articulated in response to the other? In the child collective, an ethics of responsiveness emerges. Below I draw on dialogic views of language and ethnographic views of child cultures to gain insight into the potential place of child selves in *un*official writing.

THE PLACE OF CHILD SELVES IN UNOFFICIAL CURRICULA

As earlier noted, in official worlds, children are positioned as individuals in hierarchical relationships with each other; this positioning is based on relative placement on a graded list of skills. They are to take individual ownership, to refrain from copying others, and to be truthful to their own experiences. And yet, whatever the curricular demands, young children do not just do as they are told.

Children's agency, and their relationships with other children, is central to the concept of childhood cultures. These cultures entail the communicative and often playful social practices that children produce as they respond to the adult-introduced social practices that comprise, and constrain, their everyday experiences in time and space (Corsaro, 2011; James, Jenks, and Prout, 1998). Playgrounds are spaces where children are relatively free to organize their own activities; they are prime sites for the study of childhood cultures (e.g., Beresin, 2010; Corsaro, 1985; Opie and Opie, 1959; Opie, 1993).

Classrooms are spaces where children are not so free. Nonetheless, children's unofficial or peer cultures have been documented by ethnographers working in preschools and elementary schools (e.g., Corsaro, 2011; Thorne, 1993, 2005). The unofficial cultures that are enacted during writing times *are* supported by official resources, like writing tools, seatmates, and, of course, guidance on written language itself. However, unofficial worlds are steeped in social relationships, shared experiential knowledge (like media figures and local pleasures), and common practices (like storytelling and pretend play) that can provide avenues into composing.

For this to happen, children need at least some time and space for interactions during writing. For example, in Dewayani's (2011) study of Indonesian street children focused, in part, on nongovernmental organisation-sponsored early childhood classrooms, writing lessons for 6-year-olds involved children copying text from the board and, also, writing their teachers' dictations. In a relaxed and open-ended drawing time, children did play on paper, remixing popular and folk material (e.g., traditional ghosts who carried 'BlackBerry' phones). However, this action was never linked to multimodal composing. Composing itself thus allowed no space for the guiding energy of children at play.

When such energy is generated, children's interest in each other's activity helps situate their writing within, and contributes to the maintenance and development of, peer cultures. In so doing, unofficial worlds may align with the ideology of responsiveness or a dialogic ideology of child selves. That is, children may feel obligated to respond to children with whom they feel some shared connection (e.g., small children, peers, boys or girls, children of a particular ethnic culture or language community).

Thus, new kinds of ethics appear. These ethics do not have to do with the unencumbered self but with the responsive self, who is subject to issues of inclusion, reciprocity, and the ideologies implicit in the representation of others. These ethics are enacted through what can be called relational fix-it's, illustrated by Jamal's call for inclusion in Coretta's mall adventure and, in fact, by her care in representing him as male. Related examples have appeared in many qualitative studies of classroom writing over the years (e.g., Christianakis, 2010; Dyson, 1985, 1993; Gallas, 1992; Kontovourki and Siegel,

2009; Wohlwend, 2008). The cultures – and the children – thus depicted are not idyllic; these are *our* children after all, and, depending on school demographics, their social dynamics intersect with societal complexities, like ethnic culture, gender, race, language, and class.

These new ethical concerns imply participation modes involving relations among children themselves. These modes leave in their wake intertextually-linked child products that share topics, words, even sentences; that is, what remains are choreographies of texts – the graphic remnants of social moves among writing children and their peers. Below, I sample these relations and the resultant textual choreography. I emphasize not the modes themselves (discussed elsewhere [Dyson, 2010]), but the ethical issues they entailed and the ways in which these conflicted with official ethics during composing time.

'Me too': Collegiality and writing

In Mrs Bee's and Mrs Kay's rooms, the diverse participation modes among the children varied in complexity (Dyson, 2010). They included, for example, a *collegial interest* in each other's symbol-making, a deliberate effort to *coordinate* actions and 'write about' a common topic, and *complementary* actions, in which children not only shared a topic but also separated their roles as social players and, thus, as composers. Birthday party play involved this mode of relating. If I as author invite you to a pretend party, then you as author should write that you are coming to my pretend party. There were even *collaborative improvisations*, in which children's ongoing writing actions were directly responsive to others, as when a group of children reconfigured a playground chase game as textual play (e.g., when Manny

wrote how the girls would lose, Tionna wrote that they were 'tofe girls'). (These latter, complex relations took place primarily in Mrs Kay's first grade [for one extended illustration, see Dyson, 2008b].) In both rooms, though, informal collegiality was a foundational mode for all other modes.

Indeed, collegiality was a pervasive feature of children's lives together; it was, for example, on display during the familiar practice of oral storytelling rounds. As people do across cultures, the children told stories about the remarkable and the unusual, sometimes performing the story with dramatic flair and thus wrapping others into their social space (Bauman, 2004; Ochs and Capps, 2001). One storyteller could engender others' stories; 'I hear you,' listeners seemed to say, 'and something like that happened to me.'

In the following oral vignette, Alicia takes her narrative cue from her peers, responding to the evolving talk; in turn, Odette takes narrative license with a plot element of Alicia's story – that of flying:

> Alicia, Odette, and Della are coloring a picture as part of a reading activity; the picture is captioned 'A cat scared of a bat.' As they color, they share stories of seeing bats, and then Odette recalls seeing birds in an odd place:
>
> Odette: Guess what? In preschool, there were some birds in the lunch room ... I seen some birds on my food, and they go, 'Peep peep peep.'
> Della: Guess what? I seen some birds in a store.
> Odette: Oh my goodness.
> Alicia: Me too [facing Odette]. They were way up on the ceiling 'Peep peep ...'. And they were–came flying down. I tried to catch it but it flew back up.
> Odette: (continuing her story by building on Alicia's) And then I was starting to fly, and I tried to catch one.

Peeping birds in schools and stores, flying birds and a flying child – when community participants take a discursive turn, their utterances borrow from and respond to the turns of others; that is, their turns are dialogically linked (Bakhtin, 1981).

During writing time, this oral responsiveness blended with graphic responsiveness: children responded orally and graphically to each other's drawn, dramatized, and written stories with some version of 'me too.' In this way, the narrative practice of storytelling rounds provided an avenue into 'writing a real story' in school. Thus, children did not necessarily have an individual writing topic but, rather, an evolving conversation and a play with ideas; individual productions could link together on a shared textual playground and then veer off.

In the kindergarten, this spontaneous linking of stories accounts for the writing episode immediately following Mrs Bee's admonition against writing about flying superheroes:

Now that the Spiderman talk is done, the children turn back to their work. Soon LaTrell has a story to tell:

LaTrell: I seen a balloon when I went on my–
Cici: I seen a air balloon! It was up in the sky.
LaTrell: It was the color blue. Yeah, it went all the way in the sky.
Cici: It was over by my day care.
    (raising voice) Ms. Bee, we seen the air balloon!
Della: Me too! I saw the air balloon.
    As 'Me too's arise from the room, Mrs Bee comments:
Mrs Bee: Everybody didn't see an air balloon now. ('I did"s can be heard all around.) Only the things you really did see.
    At his table, LaTrell draws a flying balloon.
LaTrell: I'm gonna make a air balloon.
Cici: I seen an air balloon. Red, yellow, different colors!

Now other children are making air balloons. Cici notes that she and LaTrell stand out among the crowd:
Cici: You all got one. Me and him got two.
LaTrell: I got two air balloons!

Soon, though, one of LaTrell's air balloons sprouts petals and becomes a flower, and another grows appendages and becomes him flying in the air, propelled by his mother:
LaTrell: This how I went up in the sky when I was a baby. My mommy throw me up in the sky. I couldn't come down. I didn't know I couldn't come down. A robot catched me.

In the end, children at LaTrell's table had drawn air balloons, in part because they had seen them or, perhaps, wanted to see them. And LaTrell, whose products were fluid, moved from flying air balloons to his own flying through the air, saved by a conveniently located robot. This was a true account of what was happening on his page, but not, one suspects, a true account of his early experiences. In a similar way children exchanged varied kinds of stories, including recurring ones of getting bitten by sharks in the lake, the pool, and even the bath tub!

Officially, if papers ended up with the same ideas, then a logical conclusion could be that the children had 'copied.' But the children did not copy in the official sense; they conversed, and they borrowed from their conversing. The observed collegiality seems similar to that reported by Matthews (1999), based on his studies of young children drawing together; across cultures, children's evolving productions were linked through their conversational topics and rhythms. They seemed attuned to the possibilities and constraints of the page and their peers. Thus, their symbol-making became a 'spatio-temporal theater of symbolic play' (1999: 9–10).

In short, storytelling among peers was a common social practice and a discursive resource, potentially contextualizing the children's entry into written language use. The children did get wrapped up in their own adventure, as did LaTrell in the above vignette, but there was an expectation of responsiveness, especially if one was with a close companion – a 'friend.'

This seemed to be the case one day when Alicia had been sitting across from her friend Ella during writing workshop. They had been chatting from time to time, especially about Alicia's rendition of TinkerBell (a Disney character). But Ella had become unusually quiet, which elicited this response from Alicia: 'Excuse me. Hello. Talk!' Talk to me, like you were doing, she seems to say. Do not ignore me. That is not what a 'good' child does. I am right here.

Through such talk, social expectations were built, relationships were sustained, and composing became a potential mediator of children's relations and practices; in this way, composing figured into the production of children's shared childhoods.

On the one hand, such imaginative play and social responsiveness can be viewed as basic to authorial action – children may compose in response to others' voices on a topic that appeals. This responsiveness can conceivably be channeled into more specific relations, like that between text performers and audience members (through classroom sharing times), authors and actors (through an 'Authors Theater' [Dyson, 1997] or a dramatizing of texts), or official collaborators (through joint writing on one page). On the other hand, such sociability, this linking of individual papers into a social networking of ideas and relations, can be viewed as simply unruly, even unethical – as copying!

Another potentially foundational participation mode, one strongly linked to ethics and, particularly, issues of reciprocity, representation, and inclusion, is that of complementary relations. In the next subsection, I consider its beginnings as captured in project data.

'What about me?': Reciprocity and inclusion

In complementary relations, children share a topic, but they also separate their roles as social players and, thus, as composers. Such relations are common in dramatic play, in which children take separate roles in order to enact a pretend world, for example, mothers and babies, superheroes and villains, or, a favorite of Mrs Bee's children, the feuding 'princess' and 'prince' of recess, whose gendered teams chased each other wildly about.

In nascent form in Mrs Bee's room, these relations could involve two or more children but only one child author; for example, Jamal felt he should be included in Coretta's text about 'friends' going to the mall. In more elaborately enacted relations, children's roles as players *and* as composers were contingent on each other's, shaped by the interactional moment, the pretend world, and societal ideologies (e.g., gender). Violations of expectations led to explicit corrections and, sometimes, hurt feelings.

The vignette below is from early in the school year. Alicia, who had been through kindergarten once already, knew about playing together on paper, and she was quite put out when Jamal did not respond appropriately, from her point of view.

Mrs Bee has just given a spirited lesson on the importance of independence and of each child thinking about their experiences and what they plan to write. The children now leave the classroom rug, where group lessons occur, and go off to their work tables.

Jamal, Alicia, and others at their table have been drawing and talking about mermaids. Jamal has made it clear that, on his paper, he is 'a mermaid, but I'm not a girl mermaid.'

Alicia has made a row of mermaids, and one, she announces to the table, is Jamal! She even has his 'J' underneath that mermaid. So now, she tells Jamal, he needs to put her and her name in his picture! But he does not. Alicia tries to show him how to write her name on his paper. But he grabs his paper away. Alicia complains loudly that Jamal doesn't want her in his picture! But he is not moved.

Jamal has a complaint of his own: Alicia has misrepresented his identity. Alicia's mermaids, like her usual people, all have circle heads out of which emanate roughly rectangular – sometimes more triangular – bodies. Although most have longer bodies than her people usually do, they are typical in having short arms and short legs. Jamal takes one look at her picture and is immediately aggrieved:

Jamal: Hey, you got me in a dress!
Alicia: No I didn't, no I didn't, no I didn't, no I didn't.
Jamal: I do have a dress on. That's me [the shorter 'mermaid' alongside the elongated swimming ones in Figure 27.1; that mermaid has a more triangular than rectangular body], and you gave me a dress.
Alicia: I'm not – this is not a dress ... That's boys' pants. Boys have pants with ties. (Of course, one might wonder if boy mermaids have pants with ties!)
Jamal: You gave me a dress though.

Jamal's own mermaids, like his people, were in the main composed of a single circle for body and head, with appendages (legs and arms). After talking with Alicia, he attempted to make a mermaid like hers,

Figure 27.1   Alicia's swimming mermaids

with a differentiated head and body. (He did not, however, give the mermaid a name, like 'Alicia.') As for Alicia, after this encounter, she abruptly changed her way of making people. She drew stick figures (no more bodies like 'dresses') and, when she needed to differentiate gender, she did so by drawing hair of differing lengths, a standard classroom practice.

Alicia's fix-it, grounded in a sense of reciprocal obligations for inclusion, led Jamal to a fix-it comment of his own about how she had represented him. The children's encounter revealed tensions in their sense of the ongoing social event and, moreover, in ideological positioning: the child declaring the self as a '*boy* mermaid' had differing sensitivities than the one who could adopt the usual gendered identity of 'mermaid.' This tension led to more deliberate use of 'organized material [symbolic] expression,' to borrow from Bakhtin's colleague Volosinov (1986: 84). They both needed ways to mark gender when it mattered – and it definitely mattered in mermaid play.

In such ways, children learn the cultural act of writing – of participating in the social and intellectual life around them through written language (Vygotsky, 1978). Children seem more likely to engage in such dialogic actions with their peers, rather than with their teachers, at least in part because they are closer in status, interests, and position in school.

The children in Mrs Bee's classroom were just beginning to situate written language in familiar practices and relations. Yet, even though their teacher, Mrs Bee, often enjoyed and chuckled at the children's efforts, there was *nothing* in the curriculum to suggest that children's use of written language was connected to their relations with others. In fact the blanket admonition against copying could lead the children to adopt a competitive, rather than a communicative, stance toward each other, as I explain in the final section on the ethics of school writing.

SELVES IN RELATIONSHIP: OFFICIAL AND UNOFFICIAL VIEWS OF COPYING

In the composing of individual experience or expression, copying others' ideas is 'illegal,' an act of stealing called 'plagiarism.' Indeed, one reason that writing, and play, influenced by popular culture is often officially discouraged is that it is viewed as mere imitation (Levin, 2003), despite the identity-fueled appropriation and the re-imagining and remixing it may entail (e.g., Dewayani, 2011; Dyson, 1997, 2003; Marsh, 2005; Newkirk, 2009; Pahl and Roswell, 2005). Addressing teachers of older students, particularly foreign students, Valentine (2006) argues that the ethical discourse that permeates discussions of plagiarism is a simple dichotomy – one does, or one does not, take another's idea. In her view, learning to be an effective writer – and a 'good student' who does not steal ideas – involves learning the complex discursive practices involved in relating one's own text to those of others.

My argument here is related but distinctive. Children engage in complex acts of authorship. Even when the official world imagines the lone individual, the writer alone with her or his thoughts, children may enact varied relations. They are colleagues and reciprocal participants in unofficial productions; they may deliberately coordinate their separate texts or even collaborate (although, in the studied classrooms, on different paper). Authorship itself is a social negotiation and not just between authors and anticipated addressees but potentially among multiple authors themselves (Dyson, 2010).

The media scholar Henry Jenkins argues that the burgeoning involvement of youth in popular culture has shifted 'the focus of literacy from one of individual expression to community involvement' (Jenkins, 2009: xiii; see also, for examples, Fisher, 2003; Kirkland and Jackson, 2009). Participation in literacy practices is thus supported by 'social skills developed through collaboration and networking' in playful, artistic contexts (Jenkins, 2009: xiii). Although Jenkins is discussing older children, in varied cultural and curricular contexts the youngest children may take advantage of time and space available for their agential infusion and social organization (e.g., Lisanza, 2011; Sahni, 2001).

The kindergarteners in Mrs Bee's room did such organizing, building on already familiar childhood relations and practices. The official curriculum, though, did not view social structures for composing as an aspect of what children should learn to name and to include in their repertoire of authorial choices and possibilities. What the official world was attempting to do, in effect, was to have the children rearrange their relationships to each other and to text production itself. The children, as it happens, found this a difficult lesson to learn.

'You're copying us': Copying and relationship

Neither Mrs Kay's nor Mrs Bee's children interpreted copying as a simple matter of individual dishonesty. Indeed, initially, the admonition against sharing 'ideas' did not even seem salient to the kindergarteners. 'So what?' LaTrell had said when Alicia accused his friend Ernest of 'copying' his snowman. By midyear, though, copying was viewed widely as an accusation – but usually only if the copying took place outside a peer relationship.

For example, a child copying another surreptitiously could be so accused (i.e., 'You're copying!'), unless that child had been told to copy by another aiming to help. 'Do it like this,' a child might say. To further illustrate, children playing together through writing might tell another child trying to join them that she/he could not play (i.e., she/he could not copy *them*). One day kindergarteners Tia, Charis, and Monique had been doing 'Shame, Shame, Shame,' a handclap game. Charis came up with the idea of writing about the game, and the other girls responded immediately:

Monique: Yeah! That's what we can do.
Charis: Come on! Let's get to work. Let's write *Shame*.

As they worked out the spelling, Tia said with great joy, 'This is fun!' But when the girls thought Vashon was going to write *Shame* too, Monique was quick to react: 'You can't write about [it], cause you copying!' Inherent in her comments was the notion that the topic belonged to a relationship – to the text-mediated activity of the three girl friends; Vashon could not join in.

'I got it first': Copying as competition

Near the end of the year, the children would sometimes appropriate the general admonition against copying, especially if Mrs Bee had just stressed that rule. Then the children would accuse others of copying as if they were telling them 'I got it [the topic] first.' That is, 'copying' was a matter

of who first claimed ownership of some entity (like snowmen), just as they claimed rights to any valued object that was not private property (e.g., a ball on the playground).

One day in May, the kindergarteners were to write their plans for the summer. The children at LaTrell's table had very similar plans. LaTrell began writing, and orally monitoring, the sentence 'I go to the park.' Cici started writing too and, in similar fashion, began a sentence about playing at the park. 'Me too, y'all!' said Precious joyfully. 'I like to play at the park!'

In the background, Mrs Bee could be heard telling children at another table not to copy off of anybody's paper.

'And Precious,' said LaTrell now. 'You can't write that 'cause I said that.'

'I said "I like to play at the park with my friends,"' noted Cici in a matter-of-fact voice.

'Actually,' piped up Ernest, 'I was going to write "I am going to the park."'

And so they all wrote about going to the park. No one copied anyone, although they did help each other with spelling. They all just happened to be planning to spend their summer playing at the park.

Ironically, when children appropriated the ethical rules of the official world – when they tried to have their very own individual *truth* – their texts were the least unique. Their inexperience as writers – and their emerging understanding of curricular demands for 'realness' – could reduce elaborate stories to simple statements of liking this or that and going here or there. This was especially so for LaTrell, who tried hard to be 'good.' The more he understood about what 'good' writers did, the less 'individual' his texts could become. So, LaTrell, the little boy who, as a baby, was saved by a well-placed robot, became just another child playing at the park.

LEARNING TO BE AN ETHICAL PARTICIPANT IN ONE'S WORLDS: THE 'GOOD' WRITER … COLLABORATOR … PEER … PARTICIPANT

Given the expectations of official schooling that children be 'good,' official practices aim to socialize children in ways that may change their very subjectivities, their affect-laden ways of experiencing school (Kulick and Schieffelin, 2004). When schools, be they traditional or seemingly 'progressive,' teach children that writing is only a set of skills or an individualistic, rather than a participative, act, they misrepresent the dialogic nature of writing practices and, moreover, marginalize childhoods themselves.

Children, like human beings generally, are searching for relationships and for meaning; cross culturally, they use talk and play to dramatize, narrate, make sense of, and have some control over what can be a very confusing world. This is, of course, not an exhaustive list of their discourse possibilities. When relevant to their intentions, children may tell about special happenings in their lives; they may report on unfairness, discuss what really happened in all kinds of stories, and on and on. Still, sitting with friends, a blank paper at hand, a guiding directive to 'compose a story,' children may venture forward interacting with paper and peers as dramas unfold.

Over time, building on what children do, teachers can help children name their ways of writing (e.g., fiction, nonfiction [Dyson, 1993]) and articulate authorial relationships as well (e.g., sometimes we write with a friend). If we do not support writing as part of the social and playful lives of children, we risk contributing to the early alienation of creative production from schooling (Nixon and Comber, 2005). This potential alientation has been documented most strikingly among teenagers (Willis, 1990), but children *and* youth are forging ahead outside of school in social networks oriented to participation in newly evolving (and sometimes virtual) communities (Paris and Kirkland, 2011; Marsh, 2011).

As their composing becomes socially situated in their lives together, child composers may confront issues of responsiveness, representation, and inclusiveness. Teachers' sensitivity to such issues matters because these issues matter; they are worthy of public discussion in an official classroom world that aims to support 'good" communicators who learn to respond to others in an ever-widening world. In the end, this seems the ultimate aim of educational efforts in contemporary language arts education: to support child communicators who, in increasingly disciplined (but still imaginative) ways, feel obligated, as did Pablo Neruda, to slip words through potential fences to others with whom they are making a world.

REFERENCES

Appiah, K. A. (2005). *The Ethics of Identity.* Princeton: Princeton University Press.

Bakhtin, M. (1981). 'Discourse in the novel', in C. Emerson and M. Holquist (eds), *The Dialogic Imagination: Four Essays by M. Bakhtin.* Austin: University of Texas Press. pp. 254–422.

Bakhtin, M. (1986). *Speech Genres and Other Late Essays.* Austin: University of Texas Press.

Bauman, R. (2004). *A World of Others' Words: Cross-Cultural Perspectives on Intertextuality.* Malden, MA: Blackwell.

Beresin, A. R. (2010). *Recess Battles: Playing, Fighting, and Storytelling*. Jackson, MS: University of Mississippi.

Boldt, G. M. (2009). 'Kyle and the basilisk: Understanding children's writing as play', *Language Arts*, 87: 9–17.

Calkins, L. and Mermelstein, L. (2003). *Launching the Writing Workshop*. Portsmouth, NH: Heinemann.

Cazden, C. (2001). *Classroom Discourse: The Language of Teaching and Learning* (2nd ed.). Portsmouth, NH: Heinemann.

Christianakis, M. (2010). '"I don't need your help!": Peer status, race, and gender during peer writing interactions'. *Journal of Literacy Research*, 42: 418–58.

Clark, K. and Holquist, M. (1984). *Mikhail Bakhtin*. Cambridge, MA: Harvard University Press.

Cooper, P. A. (2009). *The Classrooms all Young Children Need: Lessons in Teaching from Vivian Paley*. Chicago: University of Chicago Press.

Corsaro, W. (1985). *Friendship and Peer Culture in the Early Years*. Norwood, NJ: Ablex.

Corsaro, W. (2011). *The Sociology of Childhood* (3rd ed.). Thousand Oaks, CA: Pine Forge Press.

DeLoache, J. S. and Gottlieb, A. (2000). *A World of Babies: Imagined Childcare Guides for Seven Societies*. Cambridge: Cambridge University Press.

Dewayani, S. (2011). 'Stories of the intersection: Indonesian "street children" negotiating narratives at the intersection of society, childhood, and work', Unpublished doctoral dissertation, University of Illinois at Urbana-Champaign, IL.

Dyson, A. Haas (1985). 'Writing and the social lives of children', *Language Arts* 62: 632–39.

Dyson, A. Haas (1993). *Social Worlds of Children Learning to Write in an Urban Primary School*. New York: Teachers College Press.

Dyson, A. Haas. (1997). *Writing Superheroes: Contemporary Childhood, Popular Culture, and Classroom Literacy*. New York: Teachers College Press.

Dyson, A. Haas. (2003). *The Brothers and Sisters Learn to Write*. New York: Teachers College.

Dyson, A. Haas. (2006). 'On saying it right (write): "Fix-its" in the foundations of learning to write', *Research in the Teaching of English*, 41: 8–44.

Dyson, A. Haas. (2008a). 'Staying in the (curricular) lines: Practice constraints and possibilities in childhood writing', *Written Communication*, 25: 119–57.

Dyson, A. Haas. (2008b). 'The Pine Cone Wars: Studying writing in a community of children', *Language Arts*, 85: 305–15.

Dyson, A. Haas. (2010). 'Writing childhoods under construction: Revisioning "copying" in early childhood', *Journal of Early Childhood Literacy*, 10: 7–31.

Fisher, M. T. (2003). 'Open mics and open minds: Spoken word poetry in African Diaspora participatory literacy communities', *Harvard Educational Review*, 73: 362–89.

Gallas, K. (1992). 'When children take the chair: A study of sharing time in a primary classroom', *Language Arts*, 69: 172–82.

Genishi, C. and Dyson, A. Haas. (2009). *Children, Language, and Literacy: Diverse Learners in Diverse Times*. New York: Teachers College Press.

Hirsh-Pasek, K., Golinkoff, R. M., Berk, L. E., and Singer, D. G. (2009). *A Mandate for Playful Learning in Preschool: Presenting the Evidence*. New York: Oxford University Press.

James, A., Jenks, C., and Prout, A. (1998). *Theorizing Childhood*. New York: Teachers College Press.

Jenkins, H. (2009). *Confronting the Challenges of Participatory Culture: Media Education for the 21st Century*. Cambridge, MA: MIT Press.

Levin, D. E. (2003). 'Beyond banning war and superhero play: Meeting children's needs in violent times', *Young Children*, 58: 60–69.

Kirkland, D. and Jackson, A. (2009). '"We real cool": Toward a theory of Black masculine literacies', *Reading Research Quarterly*, 44: 278–97.

Kontovourki, S. and Siegel, M. (2009). 'Discipline and play within a mandated literacy curriculum', *Language Arts*, 87: 30–38.

Kulick, D. and Schieffelin, B. (2004). 'Language socialization', in A. Duranti (ed.), *A Companion to Linguistic Anthropology*. Oxford: Blackwell. pp. 349–68.

Lancy, D. F. (2007). 'Accounting for variability in mother/child play', *American Anthropologist*, 109: 273–84.

Lisanza, E. (2011). 'What does it mean to learn oral and written English language?: A case study of a rural Kenyan classroom', Unpublished doctoral dissertation, University of Illinois at Urbana-Champaign, IL.

Marsh, J. (2003). 'Early childhood literacy and popular culture', in N. Hall, J. Larson, and J. Marsh (eds), *Handbook of Early Childhood Literacy*. Los Angeles: Sage. pp. 112–25.

Marsh, J. (2005). 'Moving stories: Digital editing in the nursery', in J. Evans (ed.), *Literacy Moves On: Using Popular Culture New Technologies, and Critical Literacy in the Primary Classroom*. London: Fulton. pp. 31–47.

Marsh, J. (2011). 'Young children's literacy practices in a virtual world: Establishing an online interaction order', *Reading Research Quarterly*, 46: 101–18.

Matthews, J. (1999). *The Art of Childhood and Adolescence: The Construction of Meaning*. London: Falmer Press.

Moats, L. (2004). *Language Essentials for Teachers of Reading and Spelling*. Longmont, CO: Sopris West Educational Services.

Montgomery, H. (2009). *An Introduction to Childhood: Anthropological Perspectives on Children's Lives*. Malden, MA: Wiley-Blackwell.

Neruda, P. (2004). 'Poetry in childhood', in P.R. Loeb (ed.), *The Impossible Will Take a Little While*. New York: Basic Books. pp. 132–3.

Newkirk, T. (2009). *Holding on to Good Ideas in a Time of Bad Ones: Six Literacy Principles Worth Fighting For*. Portsmouth, NH: Heinemann.

Nixon, H. and Comber, B. (2005). 'Behind the scenes: Making movies in early years classrooms', in J. Marsh (ed.), *Popular Culture, New Media and Digital Literacy in Early Childhood*. London: Routledge. pp. 219–36.

Ochs, E. and Capps, L. (2001). *Living Narrative: Creating Lives in Everyday Storytelling*. Cambridge, MA: Harvard University Press.

Ochs, E. and Schieffelin, B. B. (2001). 'Language acquisition and socialization: Three developmental stories and their implications', in A. Duranti (ed.), *Linguistic Anthropology: A Reader*. Malden, MA: Blackwell. pp. 263–301.

Opie, I. (1993). *The People in the Playground*. Oxford: Oxford University Press.

Opie, I. and Opie, P. (1959). *The Lore and Language of School Children*. London: Oxford University Press.

Pahl, K. and Rowsell, J. (2005). *Literacy and Education*. London: Paul Chapman.

Paris, D. and Kirkland, D. (2011). '"The consciousness of the verbal artist": Understanding the vernacular literacies in digital and embodied spaces', in V. Kinloch (ed.), *Urban Literacies*. New York: Teachers College Press. pp. 177–94.

Prinsloo, M. (2004). 'Literacy is child's play: Making sense in Khwezi Park', *Language and Education*, 18: 291–314.

Qvortrup, J. (2005). 'Varieties of childhood', in J. Qvortrup (ed.), *Studies in Modern Childhood*. New York: Palgrave Macmillan. pp. 1–20.

Sahni, U. (2001). 'Children appropriating literacy: Empowerment pedagogy from young children's perspective', in B. Comber and A. Simpson (eds), *Negotiating Critical Literacies in Classrooms*. Mahwah, NJ: Lawrence Erlbaum Associates. pp. 19–35.

Salvio, P. M. and Boldt, G. M. (2009). '"A democracy tempered by the rate of exchange": Audit culture and the sell-out of progressive writing pedagogy', *English in Education*, 43: 113–28.

Smith, K. and Stock, P. (2003). 'Trends and issues in research in the teaching of the English Language Arts', in J. Flood, D. Lapp, J. Squire, and J. M. Jensen (eds), *Handbook of Research on Teaching the English Language Arts*. Mahwah, NJ: Lawrence Erlbaum Associates. pp. 114–30.

Smitherman, G. (1986). *Talkin and Testifyin: The Language of Black America*. Detroit, MI: Wayne State University Press.

Thorne, B. (1993). *Gender Play: Girls and Boys in School*. New Brunswick, NJ: Rutgers University Press.

Thorne, B. (2005). 'Unpacking school lunchtime: Structure, practice, and the negotiation of differences', in C. R. Cooper, C. T. G. Coll, W. T. Bartko, H. Davis, and C. Chatman (eds), *Developmental Pathways through Middle Childhood: Rethinking Contexts and Diversity as Resources*. Mahwah, NJ: Lawrence Erlbaum Associates. pp. 63–88.

Tobin, J. (1995). 'The irony of self-expression', *American Journal of Education*, 103: 233–58.

Tomasello, M. (2009). *Why we Cooperate*. Cambridge, MA: MIT Press.

Valentine, K. (2006). 'Plagiarism as literacy practice: recognizing and rethinking ethical binaries', *College Composition and Communication*, 58: 89–109.

Volosinov, V. N. (1986). *Marxism and the Philosophy of Language*. Tr. L. Matejka and I. R. Titunik. New York: Seminar Press.

Vygotsky, L. S. (1978). *Mind in Society*. Cambridge, MA: Harvard University Press.

Willis, P. (1990). *Common culture: Symbolic work at play in the everyday culture of the young*. Boulder, CO: Westview Press.

Wohlwend, K. (2008). 'Play as a literacy of possibilities: Expanding meanings in practices, materials, and spaces', *Language Arts*, 86(2): 127–36.

28

Talk and Discourse in Formal Learning Settings

Joanne Larson and Shira M. Peterson

Research on talk and discourse in educational settings broadly defined has been a topic of study for many years. We know a great deal about how the patterns of classroom talk shape participation (Cazden, 1988; Larson, 1999; McCarthey, 1994; Mehan, 1979), about the consequences of classroom discourse on learning and identity (Gee, 2004), and about the ways in which talk and discourse construct and are constructed by robust contexts for learning (Dyson, 1993; Gutierrez, Rymes, and Larson, 1995). Research on talk and discourse in early childhood literacy events has dealt with a wide variety of productive research issues that have significantly impacted early childhood education. While there is overlap and consensus in the research topics, underlying these research programmes are a number of diverse and often incompatible epistemological positions that shape the researchers' choice of method, conclusions, and recommendations for educational practice. In particular,

two theoretical issues shape the field of early childhood literacy research. The first concerns the nature of literacy. Street's (1995) distinction between ideological and autonomous conceptions of literacy is well known and has been broadly incorporated into literacy research and theory. Street posits a continuum between research that frames literacy as a neutral set of skills and research that understands literacy as a social practice. A second issue concerns the purpose or function of literacy. We argue that researchers fall along a continuum between viewing successful literacy outcomes as fixed, marked by the achievement of traditional notions of literacy success, and viewing literacy outcomes as fluid, characterized by emergent and multiple forms of collaboratively constructed meaning. Competing ideologies, in addition to being unproductive theoretically, have made it increasingly difficult for readers of the research to understand how to interpret research findings. The current diversity of positions has also discouraged researchers from reading across epistemological positions.

This chapter presents a theoretical framework for situating research on talk and discourse in formal learning contexts that combines the two continua of ideological versus autonomous and fixed versus fluid outcomes, resulting in a four-quadrant grid with which we analyse the literature. This theoretical heuristic provides a framework for our review of research that focuses on the social, cultural, historical, and political contexts of literacy learning in formal learning settings, which we identified as schools, preschools, churches, and both formal and family day care centres. The goal of locating research studies within their respective epistemological positions is to illuminate the underlying historical contexts that have shaped current research on language and literacy in early childhood.

We use the following definitions to guide our analysis of the literature. We define talk as social action in which interlocutors co-construct meaning in interaction in everyday activity (Duranti, 1997; Goodwin, 1990). Ochs defines discourse as a 'set of norms, preferences, and expectations relating linguistic structures to context, which speaker–hearers draw on and modify in producing and interpreting language in context' (1988: 8). This distinction between talk and discourse is echoed in Gee's (2010a) notion of 'little d' and 'big D' D/discourse. 'Discourse' with a 'big D' represents the various culturally organized ways of acting and being in the world, or 'forms of life', that are enacted, reproduced, or transformed through language in use, or what Gee calls discourse with a 'little d'. Our definitions of talk and discourse parallel the notion of literacy events and practices articulated in social

practice views of literacy. From this perspective, literacy events are the 'bits', or the social action pieces, that make up the more abstract literacy practices, or discourses, of formal learning settings in early childhood.

Additionally, we draw on definitions of discourse in critical discourse analysis to explore how discourse in local sites and in larger social structures constructs and positions human subjects (Foucault, 1972; Compton-Lilly and Graue, this volume; Luke, 1995). Critical discourse analysts acknowledge the dialectical relationship between discourse in use and the larger social structures, each constituting and transforming the other through social interactions (Fairclough, 1992). A critical discourse analysis perspective investigates the constitutive and constructive links between discourse in everyday interactions and the differential distribution of power and subjectivity in macro-level social structures (Luke, 1995).

ANALYTIC HEURISTIC

We use the four-part grid described earlier to organize and understand the various research perspectives that have been applied to the study of talk and discourse in early childhood literacy events (Heath, 1983). We want to emphasize that we mean this framework to be used as a fluid analytic heuristic and not as a rigid structure within which to hierarchically determine research orientations.

The first continuum represents varying ideological perspectives on the definition and nature of literacy. *Ideological models* define literacy as a social practice grounded in social, historical, cultural and political contexts of use and imbued in relations of power (Barton and Hamilton, 1998; Larson and Marsh, 2005; Street, 1995). In this view, the nature and meaning of literacy are constructed by and through the specific social practices of participants in particular cultural settings. In contrast, *autonomous models* define literacy as a unified set of neutral skills that can be applied across contexts (Street, 1995). Literacy is isolated as an independent variable or set of variables that imply standard cognitive and economic consequences. The autonomous definition of literacy is typically based on the essay text genre and generalized to apply to all contexts in which literacy is used. Until recently, nearly all of the research on talk in early childhood literacy events has been dominated by an autonomous view of literacy. Based in a traditional psychological paradigm, these studies treat talk as 'input' into the child's language acquisition system (Larson and Marsh, 2005). Correlational and causal models are used to trace the effects of talk on child outcomes, typically measured by standardized tests of language and literacy skills, administered in a laboratory setting.

An ideological view of literacy assumes that literacy is a set of social practices that are historically situated, highly dependent on shared cultural understandings, and inextricably linked to power relations in any setting (Irvine and Larson, 2007; Street, 1995). From this anthropological perspective, social and linguistic practices are mutually constituted within past and present power relations among people who write and read to accomplish social goals and for specific audiences. In this model, the context is constituted by local, culturally specific practices that outline who has access to learning to read and write which kinds of texts for which audiences and which purposes.

While the ideological/autonomous distinction has been widely discussed in the literacy research community, our second continuum has not received the same level of attention. This continuum represents differing views on the purpose or functions of literacy. We distinguish those approaches that view literacy outcomes as fixed (meaning is defined from an etic point of view) from those that view literacy outcomes as fluid (meaning is defined from an emic point of view). The fixed view of literacy outcomes is one that posits prespecified goals in the process of learning literacy. Whether defined as 'skills', 'competencies', or 'repertoires', these outcomes are determined *a priori*, deriving from the theoretical assumptions of the researchers. Typically, these outcomes are based on traditional notions of school-based literacy. In contrast to the fixed approach, in which 'schooled' types of literacy and meaning are privileged, the 'fluidly defined outcomes' approach takes a more relativistic stance towards meaning making, viewing both school- and home/community-based forms of meaning as collaborative 'forms of life' (Wittgenstein, 1958). In addition, the fluidly defined outcome approach emphasizes emergent meaning, rather than classifying meaning according to fixed categories. An emergent view sees meaning as continuously changing with context and interaction, rather than fitting into prespecified definitions. This perspective values the creative and non-standard forms of literacy that children produce in the process of meaning making. Figure 28.1 illustrates the quadrant structure of this heuristic.

In reviewing and analysing the literature, we used the following set of questions to guide the analysis: What is the definition of literacy? What is the implied or articulated learning outcome? What is the position of the learner in relation to text? What is the role of language in literacy

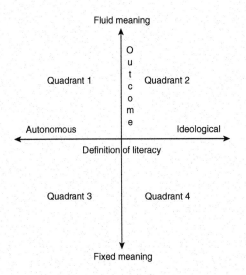

Figure 28.1 Framework for research perspectives on early talk and discourse

learning? What is the research methodology? How are talk and discourse defined? Given this handbook's definition of early years, we limited our review to studies of talk and discourse in formal learning settings with children 8 years old and younger. While we focus our review on current research studies, these studies are contextualized through their placement in one of the four quadrants in our grid, linking them historically to previous foundational research perspectives from which they arose.

QUADRANT 1: AUTONOMOUS, FLUID MEANING

The studies reviewed in quadrant 1 focus on teaching children the explicit process of becoming literate subjects and encouraging children to produce creative expressions within conventional, school-based texts. Researchers, both qualitative and quantitative, focus on the fluid construction of meaning as the academic outcome

of schooled literacy. Researchers view children's language and social interactions during writing activities as a window into children's understanding of reading and writing processes. In this quadrant, discourse is conceptualized as what Cazden (1988) has called a catalyst or scaffold for student learning. This perspective views discourse as a tool through which adults can effectively impart objectified knowledge to children. Because research in this quadrant draws on an autonomous model of literacy, reproduction logic or connections to macro social, cultural, and political processes are not typically examined.

The process model of literacy learning is a representative area of research in this quadrant. We categorized writing process work as using an autonomous definition of literacy because the explicit and implicit goal is to teach students school-based literacy competencies or academic literacy that is rooted in essayist text (Street, 1995). However, learning to write is understood to be a social process embedded in meaning making. Writing process researchers have made an invaluable contribution to our understanding of writing in the early years by making internal writing processes available to students through modelling and supporting children's multiple literacies. While the process approach to writing focuses on constructing personal meaning, it has been critiqued for its romanticized view of writing and writer's work as art (Willinsky, 1990). Lensmire (1994) has pointed out the potential risks of reproducing race, class, and gender inequities through unproblematized sharing of student writing in writers' workshops.

The work of Donald Graves (1983, 1991, 1994, 2001, 2004) serves as our case example of research on writing processes. Graves' (1983) research in *Writing: Teachers and Children at Work*, in which he examined the composing processes of 7-year-olds, and subsequent research examining writing development in early childhood helped to establish the process model of writing instruction in schools. The book itself is a descriptive, hands-on guide for teachers that clearly delineates how to create a studio-craft atmosphere in the classroom. Graves focuses on writing as a craft in which the goal is to build on children's natural desire to write. Children are seen as writers who need to be instructed to find their own processes for expression. Access to understanding these learning processes is gained through analysis of talk and interaction in classrooms and through examination of children's texts.

Lucy Calkins (1994, 2003) built on Graves' work in her research in early childhood classrooms while participating in the Teachers' College Writing Project. Like Graves, Calkins produced a practitioner's handbook outlining the hows of teaching writing to elementary school children that has become one of the guiding works for writing process teachers. She presents a detailed outline of children's writing development and offers explicit strategies for teaching preschool, kindergarten, and first- and second-grade children. Children are viewed as authors who learn to write when they see writing done for real purposes. The focus on audience, purpose, and conventions (defined as school-based notions of correctness) comes into play when making writing public. While the goal is to produce creative expression, the means is through conventional, school-based text, thereby meriting placement in quadrant 1.

Arguing that the primary concern of education is 'with enabling individual students both to contribute to society and to achieve their human potential ... just as important as the acquisition of productive skills for the marketplace' (Wells, 2001: 173), Wells' (2009) research presents analyses of talk in process-oriented literacy events in which knowledge is understood to be constructed in and through discourse. Donoahue (2001) examines the development of classroom community in her second-grade classroom. Through weekly class meetings designed to teach children speaking and listening skills that would facilitate community development, she found that children indeed felt a strong sense of community, enhancing their ability to work together during literacy activities. These researchers make the argument that the community skills revealed in this research are needed in the contemporary workplace.

A clear emphasis found among these studies was a focus on using children's spontaneous utterances as a valuable source of information about children's thinking as it is embedded in literate action (Dahl, 1993). In a study of Finnish kindergarten children's literacy development, Korkeamaki and Dreher (2000) examined how classroom discussions contributed to the development of children's spelling ability over time, finding that classroom discussions about letters and sounds allowed children to infer more specific understandings of the alphabetic principle. Analysis of student utterances revealed the students' metacognitive awareness of sound–symbol relationships, self-appraisal and self-management strategies, developmental patterns, text patterns, and the relationship of reading and writing (Dahl, 1993). The research illustrates that young children have a clear sense that text is meaningful and predictable and that they monitor their own understanding of written text. Thus, interaction around writing activity can provide information about children's internal processes (Daiute et al., 1993). For example, Jacobs (2004) found that young children's metacognition grew and developed as children talked about their thinking and strategies during writing activity.

Researchers in this quadrant argue that the writing and reading processes of 'real' authors and readers need to be made explicit for young children in classroom instruction through modelling and mini-lessons (Larson and Marsh, 2005). The goal is for students to understand the craft of writing as a means for meaningful personal expression. However, the definition of literacy remains grounded in autonomous, school-based literacy practices.

QUADRANT 2: IDEOLOGICAL, FLUID MEANING

Quadrant 2 is characterized by research focusing on how teachers and children can negotiate meaning in literacy events through incorporating children's literacy practices into the official curriculum in authentic ways, and in ways that do not simply colonize children's practices for the school's purposes. Researchers in this area stress the need for teachers to acknowledge the intertextuality of children's literacy understandings, and to validate the social worlds that they bring to the official school world (Dyson, 1993; Marsh, 2005; Wohlwend, 2008). Teachers must not only learn to appreciate their students' multiple ways of knowing about literacy, but also expand their own views of appropriate participation and ways of interacting with text, in order to allow for more meaningful types of learning (Larson, 2002) and to acknowledge the ways in which children negotiate social membership (Danby, 1996). Classrooms that capitalize on children's propensity towards participating in a community enable the creation of co-constructed forms of literacy knowledge (Gallas, 1994). Research in quadrant 2 also illustrates the ways that the dominant definition of literacy contributes to inscribing children's bodies with ways of talking and acting that serve to maintain power relations and result in curriculum as 'training to be trained' (Luke, 1992). Researchers have begun to take a more overt political stance by bringing poststructural analyses of discourse to early childhood literacy research and to focus on the production of knowledge by young children (Blaise, 2005a, 2005b; MacNaughton, 2005).

While approaches to literacy based on an autonomous model assume that literacy skills are context-independent, an ideological definition seeks to understand how literacy forms and practices have evolved to serve culturally specific purposes. In Street's conception of literacy as ideological, the cognitive processing of linguistic parts is wholly dependent on context because it takes place 'within cultural wholes and within structures of power' (1995: 161).

In an ideological model of literacy education, students would have opportunities to use reading and writing to access the world, not as objects of instruction, but as the subjects of meaning making (Coles, 1998; Edelsky, 1996; Freire and Macedo, 1987; Vasquez, 2004). Moreover, language is understood to mediate literacy learning as children actively participate in and are socialized into culturally organized activities (Cole, 1996; Duranti, 1997; Heath, 1983; Ochs, 1988; Rogoff, 1994, 2003, 2011). Some quadrant 2 researchers tend to define discourse in ways that align with Ochs' definition described earlier, or as what Cazden (1988) describes as reconceptualization/recontextualization. In this view, discourse enables learners to revise their conceptions based on previous experience and interactions with others. Other researchers draw from critical discourse analysis (Gee, 2010a, 2010b; Fairclough, 1992; Luke, 1995) to connect micro language and literacy practices to macro social, cultural, historical, and political processes. Grounded in anthropological theories of culture and language, most of the research in this quadrant uses ethnography, or other forms of ethnographic and qualitative methods, to study language and literacy practices in contexts of use.

Anne Dyson's ethnographic research in early childhood classrooms is our representative case example for this quadrant (Dyson, 1992, 1993, 1996, 1997a, 1997b, 1999, 2000, 2003). Dyson's research has provided the field with in-depth analyses of children's literacy practices. Starting from a sociocultural perspective on language learning, Dyson focuses on the social practices of children as they participate in meaningful literacy activities. Across her research, Dyson defines literacy as a social practice grounded in the social, cultural, historical, and political practices of children's communities. She focuses on the personal and social meanings children collaboratively and interactively construct in academic learning contexts. One of her major contributions to our understanding of children's literacy learning was the finding that school contexts typically separate the social and the academic in ways that inhibit the interactive potential of socially mediated learning.

In *Social Worlds of Children Learning to Write in an Urban Primary School* (1993), Dyson challenges the rigidity of school boundaries by examining the ways in which young children interactively negotiate their social and academic worlds. In the classrooms she studied, children negotiated the official classroom culture by mixing diverse genres and traditions on 'the classroom stage' (1993: 215). We learn about Jameel's boundary crossing as he made a home in school by bringing in cartoons as a legitimated writing genre. Lamar and Eugenie took 'curricular side roads' through peer talk during officially sanctioned activities. All the students and teachers Dyson worked with operated in what she calls a 'permeable curriculum' (1993: 38) that dialogically engages children's interest in the meaning, context, and complexity of social worlds.

Dyson expanded her analysis to include the ways in which children's and popular culture was incorporated into both oral and written classroom stories (Dyson, 1996, 1997a, 1997b, 1999, 2003). Children's identities were textually constructed as they took control of stories, placing themselves in superhero roles as they interpreted, analysed, compared and contrasted texts (Dyson, 1997a). Children's social goals were enacted through affiliating, resisting, and negotiating classroom social life as it shaped text. This negotiation of classroom texts in turn shaped classroom life. In sum, Dyson's point of interest is in the intertextual links between popular culture and academic culture seen in the talk and discourse of classroom interaction. She argues that pedagogy should help children extend the textual knowledge they bring to school into the official school world (Dyson, 2000).

Deborah Hicks and colleagues carry the argument Dyson makes to actively build on young children's language and literacy practices further. Hicks and Kanevsky (1992) use a sociocultural theoretical frame to analyse one first-grade African-American student's use of language within and across activity settings. They found that through his use of multiple modalities of language use – verbalization, writing, and drawing – the student came to assume an authorial voice, to use classic narrative themes, and to develop complex, fictional characters. In another study of an urban first-grade classroom, Hicks (1996) studied how two children reconstructed their understandings of popular superhero texts through talk and writing during journal activities. Children socially enacted meaning in their peer collaborations, creatively transforming the discourses of the classroom and the larger community. All of the research described in this quadrant thus far provides evidence of the utility of children's language and literacy practices and makes compelling arguments for actively using, not simple 'valuing', these resources in the early childhood curriculum.

Several studies we assigned to this quadrant examined competing ideologies of literacy between teachers and students and the resultant conflicts in literacy practices and meaning making that occurred. Like Dyson and Hicks, Rymes and Pash (2001) explore how the social lives of children mediate their participation in school literacy events. In their study of one second-language learner in a mainstream second-grade classroom, Rymes and Pash argue that the student's concern for maintaining his social identity as an 'ordinary' student sometimes conflicted with the teacher's academic goals for classroom literacy activities. The authors argue that teachers must be aware of how conflict between the various language games enacted in the classroom may limit students' academic learning.

Children bring multiple intertextual, multimodal understandings of language and literacy to school, even at the young ages examined in this volume; however, these practices are often not valued in school settings (Ballenger, 1996; Harris and Trezise, 1997; Sipe, 2000). Kliewer et al. (2004) used children's narratives to show that young children with significant disabilities were competent meaning makers despite ubiquitous deficit model perception of their literacy development. When students' practices are not valued or are actively dismissed, they become increasingly marginalized in the lessons and in classroom social life (Harris and Trezise, 1997; Larson and Irvine, 1999). Furthermore, young children's multiple literacy understandings tend to be acknowledged by the teacher only when they are consistent with the teacher's expectations. When this is not the case, children's responses are often misconstrued as 'misconceptions' (Harris and Trezise, 1997). Teachers who engage children's multiple literacies can enhance student participation and overall classroom experience. For example, Ballenger found that Haitian children's 'shadow curriculum' (1996: 318) provided them with nurturance and comfort in literacy activities, making them more motivated to learn. Wohlwend (2009a) examines young children's use of technology-mediated popular culture and games in early childhood to discuss the varying and complex ways young children build identities in play activities. Her work shows how young children write and rewrite messages constructed in merchandise to take up more authentic and powerful identity positions.

Constructing meaning across home and school provides another area of research that builds on the argument for understanding and using children's cultural, linguistic and literacy practices in the classroom. Drawing from anthropology, these studies seek to understand the fluid construction of meaning situated in local communities.

For example, Goodman (2000) argues that analysis of classroom discourse reveals students' and teachers' implicit understandings of text and particular beliefs and values that all classroom participants bring from home and other discourse communities. Understanding the multiple discourse communities that are at work in classrooms, then, becomes a key factor in the construction of the early childhood literacy curriculum.

Duranti et al. (1995) reconsider the relationship between home and school and between home and community in their comparison of literacy instruction in pastors' schools in Western Samoa and in a Samoan-American Sunday school in Los Angeles. In both communities, teachers instructed the children in the Samoan alphabet using an educational tool called the Pi Tautau. However, because of the differences in linguistic repertoires and identities of the students and teachers in the two settings, the two instructional activities had different meanings. The authors note the changing meaning of the Pi Tautau, originally used as an instrument of Westernization of Samoan culture by Protestant missionaries, but held up today as a powerful symbol of Samoan culture in the Samoan-American community.

Furthering the argument that children's socially and contextually situated understandings of literacy are necessary contributions to curriculum, Gallas (1992, 1994, 1997, 2001) contends that children should have the opportunity to acquire multiple discourses (literacies) in school and that discourse acquisition is the point at which educational equity occurs. Children acquire discourse through the bridging of the child's imaginative life with the world of school in authorship processes (Gallas, 2001). She argues strongly that a classroom should be a 'sharing community that privileges all kinds of talk and values every child's cultural membership' (1992: 173).

Gallas' (1994) contribution has been a careful examination of narrative as a source of knowledge for young children and as a vehicle for learning that makes children's thinking visible. In a study of her own first- and second-grade classrooms, Gallas analysed sharing time as a speech event to understand her role as a central figure in classroom talk. She implemented what she called a 'noninterventionist' (1994: 17) style during sharing time to explore what would happen if children became the primary audience or ratifiers of classroom discourse. She found that multiple language genres were constructed by the students and were used as an interactive social force that produced an ethic of social inclusion in the classroom community.

Examining how language is used in everyday classroom interactions as a starting point for examining equity of access to participation in literacy events, Larson's body of work (1995, 1997, 1999, 2002) focuses on language and literacy practices in early childhood classrooms and how those practices mediate literacy learning. Through microanalysis of talk and interaction using classroom participation frameworks (Goffman, 1981) as a unit of analysis, Larson articulates a range of ways in which young children participate in literacy events that includes traditional understandings of speaker–hearer dyads to more complex frameworks. In particular, Larson problematizes the conception of overhearer as a passive role in the participation framework and argues that overhearer participation is active and meaningful (Larson, 1995, 1997; Larson and Maier, 2000).

Not only can early childhood classrooms be places where students' language and literacy practices are excluded, they can also be places where reductionist literacy practices and unequal power relations are reproduced. Luke (1992) analysed classroom discourse in an Australian grade 1 classroom and offers a model of ideological transmission in which the body becomes a political object of literacy instruction. He argues that there is no monolithic dominant ideology of literacy that directly mediates ideological reproduction; rather school practices are a form of moral and political discipline. Teachers inscribe the body during routinized literacy events and lessons through the use of strict IRE (initiation, response, evaluation; Mehan, 1979) discourse patterns and directed group recitation, or what Luke calls 'training the mouth' (1992: 120). He claims that while so-called natural learning approaches acknowledge classroom events as being grounded in social context and are opposed to skill and drill instruction, they are still lacking in political theorization of classroom discourse and literacy learning in early childhood as a means of correct training. He concludes that the forms of cultural capital taught in school are not important for today's linguistic market; rather, they are solely for the purpose of discipline and promotion within the school institution. In other words, young children are 'training to be trained' (1992: 126). Williams' (2006) linguistic analysis of the social features of talk found that the domestic activity of book reading between adults and young children was recontextualized as a school literacy practice through pedagogic discourse.

Using critical discourse analysis, Luke (1995) and Luke et al. (1994) studied the reading and writing practices in four mixed Aboriginal/Islander and Anglo-Australian students in four first-grade classrooms. They found that basal reader texts and accompanying pictures constructed a subject position of monocultural, middle-class family life and gender roles that excluded the realities of the working class Aboriginal and Islander children. Group reading events following a round robin structure positioned students as characters in the text in ways that made their own sociocultural realities invisible. In writing events, the subjectivity of the child as gendered literate writer/author was constructed in classroom talk. The child 'is positioned to reproduce and naturalize particular forms of cultural logic and social identity under the guise of the transmission of particular cultural techniques of authorship' (Luke, 1995: 29).

In sum, the researchers in this quadrant argue strongly that, rather than continuing to devalue students' linguistic, cultural, and discursive practices and simply train them to be trained (Luke, 1992), schools need to understand more deeply how intentions, multiple approaches to text meaning, children's social worlds, and multiple discourses can be used as resources for curriculum. Specifically, understanding children's multiple interpretations of text (Sipe, 2000) and the multiple literacies children use to interpret and use text (MacGillivray, 1997; Wohlwend, 2009b) may begin to address issues of educational equity (Gallas, 1997). Finally, a critical discourse analysis perspective argues that examining the various subject positions established within and across texts reveals how power relations constitute and are constituted by texts (Luke, 1995).

QUADRANT 3: AUTONOMOUS, FIXED MEANING

Research in quadrant 3 is characterized by an autonomous model of literacy and an emphasis on the acquisition of a prespeci-fied set of school-specific literacy skills. Literacy is understood as a set of skills that children need to learn in order to succeed in school, in college, and in the world. The research in this quadrant is influenced to a large extent by traditional psychological theories of literacy development, which posit a developmental continuum in the cognitive and linguistic achievements nec-essary for literacy acquisition. Most stud-ies in this quadrant are characterized by quantitative methods, including scores on standardized tests of language and literacy and quantitative coding and analysis of naturalistic language.

Studies in this tradition often focus on giving children from 'disadvantaged' back-grounds (those from minority or impover-ished families, and native speakers of a language other than English) opportunities to develop the type of language and literacy skills that their home environment is thought to lack, in order to help them 'catch up' with their middle-class peers (Bereiter and Engelmann, 1966; Hart and Risley, 1995). This perspective highlights the differences between oral language and literacy, presuming that only certain types of oral language, which replicate some of the demands of literacy, are related to literacy development (Dickinson and Tabors, 2001). While many researchers in this quadrant focus on the social contexts in which children acquire such language and literacy skills, the skills themselves are not treated as contextualized or historical. Rather, traditionally defined literacy skills are accepted as important to children's suc-cess in school. This conception views lit-eracy knowledge as an objective commodity that is transmitted from the teacher to the student, whether it is through direct trans-mission (Bereiter and Engelmann, 1966) or scaffolding (Bruner, 1975).

Collectively, the research studies located in quadrant 3 point to the importance of particular oral language practices as pre-cursors for children's later literacy abili-ties. Researchers recommend that early childhood environments provide children with ample opportunities to engage in complex conversations with adults and peers across multiple content areas, includ-ing such 'extended discourse' forms as narratives, explanations, pretend play, and other forms of complex conversation (Dickinson and Tabors, 2001; French, 2004). The finding that not all children participate in these types of language practices at home leads to the recommen-dation that teachers engage 'disadvantaged' children more often in such practices.

The Home School Study of Language and Literacy, led by David Dickinson and Catherine Snow, is a representative case in this quadrant. The purpose of this large-scale study was to identify the lin-guistic features of children's home and classroom environments that predict their later literacy abilities, as measured by standardized tests of oral language and emergent literacy. Data were collected from home and school experiences of 64 children from low-income families over a period of 2 years, beginning when the children were 3 years old. The same chil-dren completed a battery of language and literacy measures in kindergarten called the SHELL–K (the School–Home Early Language and Literacy Battery–Kindergarten; Snow et al., 1995). These tasks were intended to measure the skills that support or relate to literacy acquisition. They included narrative production, picture description, formal definitions, superordinates, story com-prehension, emergent literacy (including writing concepts, letter recognition, story and print concepts, sounds in words, and environmental print), and receptive vocabulary as measured by the Peabody Picture Vocabulary Test (PPVT).

Of primary interest in this study is the use of 'extended discourse' in adult–child conversations. Extended discourse is characterized as talk that replicates some of the demands of literacy. It is defined in this study as 'talk that requires participants to develop understandings beyond the here and now and that requires the use of several utterances or turns to build a linguistic structure' (Dickinson and Tabors, 2001: 2). Examples given in the study are narratives, explanations, pretend talk, and other non-immediate talk. The concept of extended discourse has its roots in Bernstein's (1962) distinction between restricted and elaborated codes. Elaborated or extended language has also been variously characterized as cognitively challenging (Smith and Dickinson, 1994), disembedded (Wells, 1981), representational talk that is used to communicate information rather than control behaviour (Dickinson and Tabors, 2001), decontextualized (in which the audience is at a distance from the speaker, whether physically or socially: Snow, 1991), and explicit (talk that depends on linguistic, rather than contextual, cues to represent meaning). Previous research has suggested that experience with this type of language is related to children's later literacy abilities (Hart and Risley, 1995; Snow, 1983, 1987; Sulzby, 1985; Wells, 1981).

The results of the Home School Study demonstrated that several aspects of preschool teachers' language predicted children's scores on the kindergarten measures. These include low rates of teacher talk to child talk, using rare words in conversation with children, using a 'performance-oriented' book reading style rather than a 'didactic' style, using strategies to direct children's attention during large group time, extending children's comments in conversation, and engaging children in cognitively challenging, analytic, interactive conversations.

Furthermore, the analysis reveals that children's participation in extended discourse with teachers in preschool is a strong predictor of their language and literacy skills in kindergarten. A number of previous studies point to the fact that teachers' language in formal early childhood settings is rarely used for complex thinking purposes such as reasoning, predicting, and problem solving (Makin, 1994; Tizard and Hughes, 1984; Tough, 1977). Dickinson and Snow conclude from the Home Study findings that young children should be given opportunities in preschool to participate in the types of extended discourse forms identified in this study.

Other researchers in this quadrant have investigated teacher talk in early childhood formal learning environments as a predictor of children's acquisition of the oral language skills that are thought to precede literacy. While many studies have shown that expressive language ability is an important predictor of literacy, receptive language (the ability to take information from incoming language) is an often overlooked but equally important component of literacy. In a study of early childhood classrooms in Korea, French and Song (1998) found that Korean teachers support children's receptive language skills through extensive use of extended adult talk during large-group activities. Listening to long stretches of teacher talk about interesting, child-appropriate subjects gives children a basis to practise several preliteracy skills such as drawing inferences, making predictions, and interpreting new information (French and Song, 1998). Other researchers have identified contextual factors that affect teacher talk in preschools, including programme type (McGill-Franzen and Lanford, 1994), literacy instruments (Stahl and Yaden, 2004), and activity setting (Kontos, 1999; Mistry and Martini, 1993). In identifying predictive factors, Griffin et al., (2004) found that oral language tasks in narrative and expository texts at age 5 predicted reading comprehension at age 8. They concluded that young children need specific skills in expository texts to engender reading comprehension and writing competence at a later age. Similarly, Price van Kleeck, and Huberty (2009) found that higher rates of feedback utterances in expository text reading increased vocabulary diversity.

The ability to compose an oral narrative is highlighted by the research in this quadrant as an important component of children's literacy development (Dickinson and McCabe, 1991). The development of personal narratives in European North American children has been well documented (see McCabe and Peterson, 1991). Research with Japanese (Minami, 1995; Minami and McCabe, 1991) and Venezuelan (Shiro, 1995) preschool children have reported structural differences in the personal narratives of 4- and 5-year-olds. By age 5, children in these diverse countries typically develop an understanding of their culture's canonical narrative form. In addition to narrative, researchers have also identified explanation as an important oral language skill that predicts literacy success (Dickinson and Tabors, 2001). Peterson (2002) found that through participation in extended conversations with teachers, children in a science-based preschool programme made significant gains in their oral explanations for physical phenomena.

Many researchers in this quadrant emphasize that early childhood educators can give children opportunities to learn school-based forms of oral language through scaffolding (Bruner, 1975). Speidel (1993) found that comprehension reading lessons in a Hawaiian first-grade classroom (part of the Kamehameha Early Education Program, or KEEP) became opportunities for scaffolding children to use standard English forms. Researchers have also identified peer interaction as another way that children can learn to participate in school-based literacy practices. In one multiage (K–2) classroom, Stone and Christie (1996) found that 40 per cent of children's time in the sociodramatic play centre was engaged in school forms of literacy activities and that most of these activities were in collaborative interactions with an older or a younger child. The authors suggest that multiage classrooms have the potential to naturally foster 'communit[ies] of learners' (1996: 133) due to the children's wide range of literacy expertise.

When looking at potential transfer of first language literacy skills for English language learners (ELLs), Proctor, August, Carlo, and Snow (2006) found that instructional language strongly mediated oral language and reading proficiencies, while additive effects were only found for decoding skills. The authors conclude, however, that first language development is not a prerequisite for ELLs' English language comprehension. In a related study, Carlo et al. (2004) found that ELLs benefitted from specific instruction in word analysis and vocabulary instruction.

As a whole, researchers in quadrant 3 have argued that experience with school-based oral language practices is related to children's later success in school-based forms of literacy. Students who lack experience with such language and literacy forms are frequently disadvantaged when it comes to participating in school-based literacy practices and performance on standardized measures of literacy. The orientation in this quadrant to an autonomous view of literacy leads to suggestions for educational practices that are focused on the types of language and literacy typically expected of students in school. On the whole, these researchers agree that early childhood educators should give children ample opportunities to participate in extended discourse forms, including narratives, explanations, pretend talk, and other forms of complex conversation, in order to achieve successful school-based outcomes.

QUADRANT 4: IDEOLOGICAL, FIXED MEANING

Researchers in quadrant 4 subscribe to an ideological model of literacy, in which literacy practices are understood in cultural and historical context, yet their ultimate focus is on children's participation in school-based literacy practices. From this perspective, researchers problematize traditional definitions of literacy and school success, acknowledging that they represent only one of many types of literacy understandings based in cultural practices. However, they also recognize that the traditional definition of literacy is the one that carries the most political and ideological weight in mainstream cultures in the US, as well as in most Western nations (Delpit, 1988). An ideological approach views literacy knowledge as constructed through participation in literacy events, during which children appropriate cultural knowledge through language, participating in ways of talking and acting that are preferred by the cultural and social group in which the child lives (Gee, 2001). While

all of these types of literacy understandings are valuable to the child, children who are not familiar with school-based literacy practices are at a disadvantage in mainstream school settings and in a global capitalist workforce. Researchers in quadrant 4 advocate that school should provide children with opportunities to learn 'legitimate' forms of literacy, in order for them to become familiar with and appropriate the *cultural capital* (Bourdieu, 1977) of school-based ways of approaching literacy.

Like researchers in quadrant 3, those in quadrant 4 acknowledge that extended discourse forms as characterized by Snow and Dickinson are privileged in school settings, and children's facility with such forms predicts their acquisition of traditional literacy knowledge. However, researchers in quadrant 4 do not assume that this kind of school talk (Genishi and Fassler, 1999) is explicit and decontextualized in absolute terms. As Gee argues, school language is simply 'inexplicit and contextualized in a different way' (1999: 31). 'Schooled literacy' (Street, 1995) represents a particular set of social practices and a particular kind of language use that are considered the 'legitimate' form in schools. Researchers of this view focus on ways that teachers either expose or conceal their expectations for 'legitimate' literacy participation from children. Researchers in quadrant 4 urge teachers to integrate children's home discourse practices into the classroom. This approach acknowledges the diversity of language practices that children bring with them to school, and makes use of this knowledge through discourse that provides for reconceptualization/recontextualization (Cazden, 1988) in teaching children the 'legitimate' literacy practices of mainstream school culture. Both quantitative and qualitative research methods can be found in this quadrant.

For our case study in this quadrant, Shirley Brice Heath defines literacy events as 'occasions in which written language is integral to the nature of participants' interactions and their interpretive processes and strategies' (1982: 74). Heath proposes that ways of taking meaning from the printed word are interdependent with ways children learn to talk in social interactions, a view that challenges the validity of the oral–literate dichotomy. In her study of three communities in the Piedmont Carolinas (1982, 1983), Heath describes the ways in which families from different communities differ in their literacy practices with their children. While children in a white, middle-class community (Maintown) participate in ways of talking that are parallel to classroom interactions, children in a white, working-class community (Roadville) and in a black, working-class community (Trackton) experience language and literacy practices in ways that do not necessarily prepare them for what they find in the classroom.

Trackton children in particular score poorly on reading readiness tests, yet Heath observes that they excel at a variety of language abilities, such as analogy skills, which are not tapped in the school setting. Heath suggests that children who are not socialized to 'school talk' at home are at a considerable disadvantage when they enter school, due to the different expectations that teachers have of children's language. She argues that Roadville children need opportunities to practise new forms of discourse, and to learn distinctions in discourse strategies and structures, especially related to interactions with books. Trackton students need to learn to take meaning from books, to adapt their creative language abilities for use in learning to read, to recount factual events, and to learn the mainstream discourse appropriate to school.

Like Heath's work, the work of Sarah Michaels identifies ways that children's home experiences with literacy are devalued in school settings. Michaels' (1984, 1985) research on talk in early childhood classrooms focuses on the diverse literacy understandings that children bring to the classroom. She proposes that children's school success is hindered by teachers' evaluations, which are often unconsciously based on their discourse expectations of children. When asked to judge transcripts of children's sharing time narratives, white adults responded more positively to linear, 'topic centred' stories produced by most white children, while black adults responded positively to both 'topic centred' stories and 'topic associating' stories, used more often by black children (Michaels, 1984). Michaels argues that, while control over various language forms should be the ultimate goal, the focus of sharing time should be more concerned with allowing children to use the forms and strategies they are most familiar with in order to successfully express themselves. This attitude is prevalent among teachers participating in the structural equivalent of sharing time in Spanish classrooms, known as *la ronda* (Poveda, 2001). Instead of a lesson in discourse forms, *la ronda* is primarily seen as a means of socializing students into a moral community. Consequently, Spanish teachers have fewer expectations for children's discourse forms, are less intrusive in correcting children's stories, and allow for more individual differences in children's participation, including permitting students not to participate if they do not wish to.

Researchers in this quadrant focus on exposing the consequences of teachers' tacit expectations for children's participation. In a study of an elementary school in the Piedmont Carolinas, Edwards and

Davis (1997) found that the middle-class white teachers frequently judged their Appalachian and African-American students' answers to be off-topic when they were in fact 'mishearing' the children's language. Furthermore, the researchers found teachers' questions to be ambiguous in that they carried implicit expectations that were not clear in the language and were not made clear to the children. The authors reiterate Au's (1993) suggestion that teachers create 'culturally composite classrooms' where a diversity of languages is acknowledged.

Gregory's (1993) study of nine children in one urban, multilingual early childhood classroom in the UK revealed that the teacher blurred the boundaries between the text and her commentary on it. Successful children in this classroom 'ignore[d] the teacher's explicit instructions [to talk about what they think] ... and work[ed] within her implicit expectations of "getting the story"' (1993: 218), that is, adhering to the teacher's assumptions about what was relevant in the story. Gregory also found that children who were unsuccessful at participating in the reading activity were given less feedback about their performance than the successful children, hindering their future participation and achievement. Gregory argues that the 'legitimate' (school-based) interpretation of literacy is important for children's later school reading success (1993: 223). Teachers should become aware of their own expectations for children's participation in literacy events and encourage children's awareness of social practices surrounding literacy.

In sum, research in quadrant 4 deals with ways that educators can help children to participate in school-based literacy practices, while at the same time acknowledging and integrating the multiple language and literacy resources that children bring from home. By recognizing the differences in local conceptions of 'doing literacy', educators can more effectively teach children from various backgrounds the forms of cultural capital that are valued in school and in mainstream social institutions. Viewing school-based literacy through an ideological lens, researchers in this quadrant emphasize the importance of making explicit the multiple conceptions of literacy held by students, their families, teachers, schools, and mainstream society, so that children's literacy knowledge may be incorporated in the classroom as an important resource in children's overall literacy development.

CONCLUSIONS AND IMPLICATIONS FOR FUTURE RESEARCH

The research reviewed in this chapter represents four approaches to the study of talk and discourse related to children's literacy learning, falling within the two continua of ideological versus autonomous approaches to literacy and fluid versus fixed meaning outcomes. In reviewing the research on talk and discourse in formal early childhood settings, we noticed a number of trends across the studies. First, researchers tend not to read across ideological positions and as a result do not build on each other's work. This practice limits the potential advances we can make in the field. It is our recommendation that researchers take an ideological approach to the research and acknowledge multiple ways of knowing in the different research communities from which we approach the subject of talk and discourse. To do this, researchers must position themselves as critical readers of research and view individual studies as located within a historical, a social, and an ideological framework. This practice to a large extent depends upon researchers acknowledging their own assumptions in their research, which brings us to our second point.

In writing this review, it became clear that some researchers whom we placed on the autonomous side of the continuum are in fact beginning to draw from ideological models. We found that a number of researchers in quadrants 3 and 4 are focusing on the same issues as researchers in quadrants 1 and 2, although their research did not articulate the same ideological position. This phenomenon made placing researchers into a particular quadrant problematic, since it was not always obvious what ideological position the researchers actually held. The lesson that emerges from this analysis, then, is that researchers should ideally be explicit about acknowledging their theoretical assumptions so that their findings can be interpreted in light of their view of literacy and their focus on outcomes for educational practice. Furthermore, positioning in our chart should be understood to be more fluid than one-dimensional representations allow. Research positions are fluid and changing, largely depending on the research questions asked.

A third finding is that, in spite of the rhetoric of the reading wars, most of the research we examined was located in quadrant 2, indicating a growing appreciation of literacy as a social practice and talk as a means of fluid meaning making. Perhaps this distribution can be attributed to a lack of focus on classroom talk by researchers who are interested in school-based literacy skills.

Fourth, while we now know a good deal about how teachers and students use talk and discourse in the construction of literacy in the early school years, we know much less about the use of talk in the preschool years. We therefore identify a need for more research conducted in the various formal settings for the education of young children, such as church schools, day care centres, and family day care programmes. We argue for an increased focus on the kinds of talk that are occurring in preschool and day care settings, particularly where multimodal, technology mediated texts are in use.

Finally, we found that studies on talk and discourse in formal early childhood learning settings constitute a robust field of research, characterized by important research questions concerning the role of talk in young children's literacy learning and identity formation. In the future, we hope that researchers in this area begin to ask, and hopefully answer, some of the following important questions: How does talk mediate literacy learning in the digital age? What is the relationship between participation framework, literacy activity, and children's experiences in the construction of literacy knowledge when that knowledge is constructed in digital spaces? How do curriculum and pedagogy affect discourse interactions in literacy events and practices? How can future research move the field toward a more critical analysis of how young children are positioned as objects of literacy instruction in traditional literacy events?

REFERENCES

Au, K. (1993) *Literacy Instruction in Multicultural Settings*. New York: Harcourt Brace.

Ballenger, C. (1996) 'Learning the ABCs in a Haitian preschool: A teacher's story', *Language Arts*, 73: 317–23.

Barton, D. and Hamilton, M. (1998) *Local Literacies*. London: Routledge.

Bereiter, C. and Engelmann, S. (1966) *Teaching Disadvantaged Children in the Preschool.* Englewood Cliffs, NJ: Prentice Hall.

Bernstein, B. (1962) 'Social class, linguistic codes and grammatical elements', *Language and Speech*, 5: 31–46.

Blaise, M. (2005a) 'A feminist poststructuralist study of children "doing" gender in an urban kindergarten classroom', *Early Childhood Research Quarterly*, 20(1): 85–108.

Blaise, M. (2005b) *Playing it Straight: Uncovering Gender Discourses in the Early Childhood Classroom.* New York: Routledge.

Bourdieu, P. (1977) *Outline of a Theory of Practice.* Cambridge: Cambridge University Press.

Bruner, J.S. (1975) 'The ontogenesis of speech acts', *Journal of Child Language*, 2(1): 1–19.

Calkins, L. (1994) *The Art of Teaching Writing.* Portsmouth, NH: Heinemann.

Calkins, L. (2003) *The Nuts and Bolts of Teaching Writing.* Portsmouth, NH: Heinemann.

Carlo, M., August, D., McLaughlin, B., Snow, C., Dressler, C., Lippman, D., Lively, T., and White, C. (2004) 'Closing the gap: Addressing the vocabulary needs of English-language learners in bilingual and mainstream classrooms', *Reading Research Quarterly*, 39(2): 188–215.

Cazden, C. (1988) *Classroom Discourse: The Language of Teaching and Learning.* Portsmouth, NH: Heinemann.

Cole, M. (1996) *Cultural Psychology: A Once and Future Discipline.* Cambridge, MA: Harvard University Press.

Coles, G. (1998) *Reading Lessons: The Debate over Literacy.* New York: Hill and Wang.

Dahl, K.L. (1993) 'Children's spontaneous utterances during early reading and writing instruction in whole-language classrooms', *Journal of Reading Behavior*, 25(3): 279–94.

Daiute, C., Campbell, C., Griffin, T., Reddy, M., and Tivnan, T. (1993) 'Young authors' interactions with peers and a teacher: Toward a developmentally sensitive sociocultural literacy theory', in C. Daiute (ed.), *The Development of Literacy through Social Interaction.* San Francisco: Jossey Bass. pp. 41–63.

Danby, S. (1996) 'Constituting social membership: two readings of talk in an early childhood classroom', *Language and Education*, 10(2–3): 151–70.

Delpit, L. (1988) 'The silenced dialogue: power and pedagogy in educating other people's children', *Harvard Educational Review*, 58(3): 280–98.

Dickinson D.K. and McCabe, A. (1991) 'A social interactionist account of language and literacy development', in J. Kavanaugh (ed.), *The Language Continuum.* Parkton, MD: York pp. 1–40.

Dickinson, D.K. and Tabors, P.O. (eds) (2001) *Beginning Literacy with Language: Young Children Learning at Home and at School.* Baltimore, MD: Brookes.

Donoahue, Z. (2001) 'An examination of the development of classroom community through class meetings', in G. Wells (ed.), *Action, Talk, and Text: Learning and Teaching through Inquiry.* New York: Teachers College Press.

Duranti, A. (1997) *Linguistic Anthropology.* Cambridge: Cambridge University Press.

Duranti, A., Ochs, E., and Ta'ase, E.K. (1995) 'Change and tradition in literacy instruction in a Samoan American community', in B. McLaughlin, B. McLeod, and S. Dalton (eds), *Teaching for Success: Reforming Schools for Children from Culturally and Linguistically Diverse Backgrounds.* pp. 57–74.

Dyson, A.H. (1992) ' "Whistle for Willie", lost puppies, and cartoon dogs: The sociocultural dimensions of young children's composing', *Journal of Reading Behavior*, 24(4): 433–62.

Dyson, A.H. (1993) *Social Worlds of Children Learning to Write in an Urban Primary School.* New York: Teachers College Press.

Dyson, A.H. (1996) 'Cultural constellations and childhood identities: on Greek gods, cartoon heroes, and the social lives of schoolchildren', *Harvard Educational Review*, 66(3): 471–95.

Dyson, A.H. (1997a) 'Rewriting for, and by, the children: the social and ideological fate of a media miss in an urban classroom', *Written Communication*, 14(3): 275–312.

Dyson, A.H. (1997b) *Writing Superheroes: Contemporary Childhood, Popular Culture, and Classroom Literacy.* New York: Teachers College Press.

Dyson, A.H. (1999) 'Coach Bombay's kids learn to write: Children's appropriation of media material for school literacy', *Research in the Teaching of English*, 33(4): 367–402.

Dyson, A.H. (2000) 'On reframing children's words: The perils, promises, and pleasures of writing children', *Research in the Teaching of English*, 34(3): 352–67.

Dyson, A.H. (2003) *The Brothers and Sisters Learn to Write: Popular Literacies in Childhood and School Cultures.* New York: Teachers College Press.

Edelsky, C. (1996) *With Literacy and Justice for All: Rethinking the Social in Language and Education.* 2nd edn. Bristol, PA: Taylor and Francis.

Edwards, B. and Davis, B. (1997) 'Learning from classroom questions and answers: Teachers' uncertainties about children's language', *Journal of Literacy Research*, 29(4): 471–505.

Fairclough, N. (1992) *Discourse and Social Change*. Cambridge: Polity.

Foucault, M. (1972) *The Archaeology of Knowledge*. Tr. A. Sheridan Smith. Oxford: Blackwell.

Freire, P. and Macedo, D. (1987) *Literacy: Reading the Word and the World*. South Hadley, MA: Bergin and Garvey.

French, L. (2004) 'Science as the center of a coherent, integrated early childhood curriculum', *Early Childhood Research Quarterly*, 19(1): 138–49.

French, L. and Song, M. (1998) 'Developmentally appropriate teacher-directed approaches: Images from Korean kindergartens', *Journal of Curriculum Studies*, 30(4): 408–30.

Gallas, K. (1992) 'When the children take the chair: A study of sharing time in a primary classroom', *Language Arts*, 69: 172–82.

Gallas, K. (1994) *The Languages of Learning: How Children Talk, Write, Dance, Draw, and Sing their Understanding of the World*. New York: Teachers College Press.

Gallas, K. (1997) 'Story time as a magical act open only to the initiated: What some children don't know about power and may not find out', *Language Arts*, 74(4): 248–54.

Gallas, K. (2001) '"Look, Karen, I'm running like Jell-O": Imagination as a question, a topic, a tool for literacy research and learning', *Research in the Teaching of English*, 35(4): 457–92.

Gee, J. (2001) 'Reading, language abilities, and semiotic resources: Beyond limited perspectives on reading', in J. Larson (ed.), *Literacy as Snake Oil: Beyond the Quick Fix*. New York: Lang. pp. 7–26.

Gee, J. (2004) *Situated Language and Learning: A Critique of Traditional Schooling*. New York: Routledge.

Gee, J. (2010a) *An Introduction to Discourse Analysis: Theory and Method*. 3rd edn. New York: Routledge.

Gee. J. (2010b) *How to do Discourse Analysis: A Toolkit*. New York: Routledge.

Genishi, C. and Fassler, F. (1999) 'Oral language in the early childhood classroom: Building on diverse foundations', in C. Seefeldt (ed.), *The Early Childhood Curriculum: Current Findings in Theory and Practice*. 3rd edn. New York: Teachers College Press. pp. 54–83.

Goffman, E. (1981) *Forms of Talk*. Philadelphia: University of Pennsylvania Press.

Goodman, D.L. (2000) 'Becoming literate in an inner-city, whole language school'. Unpublished doctoral dissertation, Michigan State University.

Goodwin, M.H. (1990) *He-Said-She-Said: Talk as Social Organization among Black Children*. Bloomington, IN: Indiana University Press.

Graves, D. (1983) *Writing: Teachers and Children at Work*. Portsmouth, NH: Heinemann.

Graves, D. (1991) *Building a Literate Classroom*. Portsmouth, NH: Heinemann.

Graves, D. (1994) *A Fresh Look at Writing*. Portsmouth, NH: Heinemann.

Graves, D. (2001) *The Energy to Teach*. Portsmouth, NH: Heinemann.

Graves, D. (2004) *Teaching Day by Day: 100 Stories to Help You along the Way*. Portsmouth, NH: Heinemann.

Gregory, E. (1993) 'What counts as reading in the early years' classroom?', *British Journal of Educational Psychology*, 63: 214–30.

Griffin, T., Hemphill, L., Camp, L., and Wolf, D. (2004) 'Oral discourse in the preschool years and later literacy skills', *First Language*, 24(2): 123–47.

Gutierrez, K., Rymes, B., and Larson, J. (1995) 'Script, counterscript and underlife in the classroom: James Brown versus Brown v. The Board of Education', *Harvard Educational Review*, 65(3): 445–471.

Harris, P. and Trezise, J. (1997) 'Intertextuality and beginning reading instruction in the initial school years', *Journal of Australian Research in Early Childhood Education*, 1: 32–9.

Hart, B. and Risley, T.R. (1995) *Meaningful Differences in the Everyday Experience of Young American Children*. Baltimore, MD: Brookes.

Heath, S.B. (1982) 'What no bedtime story means: Narrative skills at home and school', *Language in Society*, 11: 49–76.

Heath, S.B. (1983) *Ways with Words: Language, Life, and Work in Communities and Classrooms*. Cambridge: Cambridge University Press.

Hicks, D. (1996) 'Contextual inquiries: A discourse-oriented study of classroom learning', in D. Hicks (ed.), *Discourse, Learning, and Schooling*. Cambridge: Cambridge University Press. pp. 104–41.

Hicks, D. and Kanevsky, R. (1992) 'Ninja Turtles and other superheroes: A case study of one literacy learner', *Linguistics and Education*, 4: 59–105.

Irvine, P.D. and Larson, J. (2007) 'Literacy packages in practice: Constructing academic disadvantage', in J. Larson (ed.), *Literacy as Snake Oil: Beyond the Quick Fix*. New York: Lang. pp. 49–72.

Jacobs, G. (2004). 'A classroom investigation of the growth of metacognitive awareness in kindergarten children through the writing process', *Early Childhood Education Journal*, 32(1): 17–23.

Kliewer, C., Fitzgerald, L., Meyer-Mork, J., Hartman, P., English-Sand, P., and Raschke, D. (2004) 'Citizenship for all in the literate community: An ethnography of young children with significant disabilities in inclusive early childhood settings', *Harvard Education Review*, 74(4): 373–403.

Kontos, S. (1999) 'Preschool teachers' talk, roles, and activity settings during free play', *Early Childhood Research Quarterly*, 14(3): 363–82.

Korkeamaki, R. and Dreher, M.J. (2000) 'Finnish kindergartners' literacy development in contextualized literacy episodes: A focus on spelling', *Journal of Literacy Research*, 32(3): 349–93.

Larson, J. (1995) 'Talk matters: The role of pivot in the distribution of literacy knowledge among novice writers', *Linguistics and Education*, 7: 277–302.

Larson, J. (1997) 'Indexing instruction: The social construction of the participation framework in kindergarten journal writing activity', *Discourse and Society*, 8(4): 501–21.

Larson, J. (1999) 'Analyzing participation frameworks in kindergarten writing activity: the role of over-hearer in learning to write', *Written Communication*, 16(2): 225–57.

Larson, J. (2002) 'Packaging process: Consequences of commodified pedagogy on students' participation in literacy events', *Journal of Early Childhood Literacy*, 2(1): 65–95.

Larson, J. and Irvine, P.D. (1999) '"We call him Dr King": Reciprocal distancing in urban classrooms', *Language Arts*, 76(5): 393–400.

Larson, J. and Maier, M. (2000) 'Co-authoring classroom texts: Shifting participant roles in writing activity', *Research in the Teaching of English*, 34: 468–98.

Larson, J. and Marsh, J. (2005) *Making Literacy Real: Theories and Practices for Learning and Teaching*. London: Sage.

Lensmire, T. (1994) *When Children Write: Critical Re-visions of the Writing Workshop*. New York: Teachers College Press.

Luke, A. (1992) 'The body literate: Discourse and inscription in early literacy training', *Linguistics and Education'*, 4: 107–29.

Luke, A. (1995) 'Text and discourse in education: An introduction to critical discourse analysis', *Review of Research in Education*, 21: 1–48.

Luke, A., Kale, J., Singh, M.G., Hill, T., and Daliri, F. (1994) 'Talking difference: Discourse on Aboriginal identity in grade one classrooms', in D. Corsen (ed.), *Discourse and Power in Educational Organizations*. Creskill, NJ: Hampton. pp. 211–24.

MacGillivray, L. (1997) '"I've seen you read": Reading strategies in a first-grade class', *Journal of Research in Childhood Education*, 11(2): 135–46.

MacNaughton, G. (2005) *Doing Foucault in Early Childhood Studies: Applying Poststructural Ideas*. New York: Routledge.

Makin, L. (1994) 'Quality talk in early childhood programs', *Journal for Australian Research in Early Childhood Education*, 1: 100–8.

Marsh, J. (2005) *Popular Culture, New Media and Digital Literacy in Early Childhood*. New York: Routledge.

McCabe, A. and Peterson, C. (1991) *Developing Narrative Structure*. Hillsdale, NJ: Erlbaum.

McCarthey, S. (1994) 'Authors, text, and talk: The internalization of dialogue from social interaction during writing', *Reading Research Quarterly*, 29(3): 200–31.

McGill-Franzen, A. and Lanford, C. (1994) 'Exposing the edge of the preschool curriculum: teachers' talk about text and children's literacy understandings', *Language Arts*, 71(4): 264–73.

Mehan, H. (1979) *Learning Lessons*. Cambridge, MA: Harvard University Press.

Michaels, S. (1984) 'Listening and responding: Hearing the logic in children's classroom narratives', *Theory into Practice*, 23(3): 218–24.

Michaels, S. (1985) 'Hearing the connections in children's oral and written discourse', *Journal of Education*, 167(1): 36–56.

Minami, M. (1995) 'Japanese preschool children's personal narratives: A sociolinguistic study'. Research report, US Department of Education.

Minami, M. and McCabe, A. (1991) '*Haiku* as a discourse regulation device: A stanza analysis of Japanese children's personal narratives', *Language in Society*, 20: 577–99.

Mistry, J. and Martini, M. (1993) 'Preschool activities as occasions for literate discourse', in R. Roberts (ed.), *Coming Home to Preschool: the Sociocultural Context of Early Education*. Norwood, NJ: Ablex. pp. 220–46.

Ochs, E. (1988) *Culture and Language Development: Language Socialization and Language Acquisition in a Samoan Village*. Cambridge: Cambridge University Press.

Peterson, S.M. (2002) 'Explanatory discourse in preschool science lessons'. Paper presented at the annual meeting of the American Educational Research Association, New Orleans, LA.

Poveda, D. (2001) '*La ronda* in a Spanish kindergarten classroom with a cross-cultural comparison to sharing time in the USA', *Anthropology and Education Quarterly*, 32(3): 301–25.

Price, L., van Kleeck, A., and Huberty, C. (2009) 'Talk during book sharing between parents and preschool children: A comparison between storybook and expository book conditions', *Reading Research Quarterly*, 44(2): 171–94.

Proctor, C., August, D., Carlo, M., and Snow, C. (2006) 'The intriguing role of Spanish language vocabulary knowledge in predicting English reading comprehension', *Journal of Educational Psychology*, 98(1): 159–69.

Rogoff, B. (1994) 'Developing understanding of the idea of communities of learners', *Mind, Culture, and Activity*, 1(4): 209–29.

Rogoff, B. (2003) *The Cultural Nature of Human Development*. New York: Oxford University Press.

Rogoff, B. (2011) *Developing Destinies: A Mayan Midwife and Town*. New York: Oxford University Press.

Rymes, B. and Pash, D. (2001) 'Questioning identity: The case of one second-language learner', *Anthropology and Education Quarterly*, 32(3): 276–300.

Shiro, M. (1995) 'Focus on research: Venezuelan preschoolers' oral narrative abilities', *Language Arts*, 72(7): 528–37.

Sipe, L.R. (2000) 'The construction of literary understanding by first and second graders in oral response to picture storybook read-alouds', *Reading Research Quarterly*, 35(2): 252–75.

Smith, M.W. and Dickinson, D.K. (1994) 'Describing oral language opportunities and environments in Head Start and other preschool classrooms', *Early Childhood Research Quarterly*, 9: 345–66.

Snow, C.E. (1983) 'Literacy and language: Relationships during the preschool years', *Harvard Educational Review*, 53: 165–89.

Snow, C.E. (1987) 'Beyond conversation: Second language learners' acquisition of description and explanation', in J. Lantolf and A. Labarca (eds), *Research in Second Language Learning: Focus on the Classroom*. Norwood, NJ: Ablex. pp. 3–16.

Snow, C. E. (1991) 'The theoretical basis for relationships between language and literacy in development', *Journal of Research in Childhood Education*, 6(1): 5–10.

Snow, C.E., Tabors, P., Nicholson, P., and Kurland, B. (1995) 'SHELL: A method for assessing oral language and early literacy skills in kindergarten and first grade children', *Journal of Research in Childhood Education*, 10(1): 37–48.

Speidel, G.E. (1993) 'The comprehension reading lesson as a setting for language apprenticeship', in R. Roberts (ed.), *Coming Home to Preschool: The Sociocultural Context of Early Education*. Norwood, NJ: Ablex. pp. 247–74.

Stahl, S. and Yaden, D. (2004) 'The development of literacy in preschool and primary grades: Work by the Center for the Improvement of Early Reading Achievement', *The Elementary School Journal*, 105(2): 141–65.

Stone, S.J. and Christie, J.F. (1996) 'Collaborative literacy learning during sociodramatic play in a multiage (K-2) primary classroom', *Journal of Research in Childhood Education*, 10(2): 123–33.

Street, B.V. (1995) *Social Literacies: Critical Approaches to Literacy in Development, Ethnography and Education*. New York: Longman.

Sulzby, E. (1985) 'Children's emergent reading of favorite storybooks: Developmental study', *Reading Research Quarterly*, 20(4): 458–81.

Tizard, B. and Hughes, M. (1984) *Young Children Learning*. Cambridge, MA: Harvard University Press.

Tough, J. (1977) 'Children and programmes: How shall we educate the young child?', in A. Davies (ed.), *Language and Learning in Early Childhood*. London: Heinemann.

Vasquez, V. (2004) *Negotiating Critical Literacies with Young Children*. Mahwah, NJ: Erlbaum.

Wells, G. (1981) 'Some antecedents of early educational attainment', *British Journal of Sociology of Education*, 2(2): 181–200.

Wells, G. (2001) *Action, Talk, and Text: Learning and Teaching through Inquiry*. New York: Teachers College Press.

Wells, G. (2009) *The Meaning Makers: Learning to Talk and Talking to Learn*. 2nd edn. Ontario, CA: Multilingual Matters.

Williams, G. (2006) 'The pedagogic device and the production of pedagogic discourse: A case example in early literacy education', in F. Christie (ed.). *Pedagogy and the Shaping of Consciousness: Linguistic and Social Process*. New York: Continuum. pp. 88–122.

Willinsky, J. (1990) *The New Literacy: Redefining Reading and Writing in the Schools*. New York: Routledge.

Wittgenstein, L. (1958) *Philosophical Investigations*. 2nd edn. G.E.M. Anscombe and R. Rhees (eds). Tr. G.E.M. Anscombe. Oxford: Blackwell.

Wohlwend, K.E. (2008) 'Play as a literacy of possibilities: Expanding meanings in practices, materials, and spaces', *Language Arts*, 86(2): 127–36.

Wohlwend, K. (2009a) 'Damsels in discourse: Girls consuming and producing identity texts through Disney Princess play', *Reading Research Quarterly*, 44(1): 57–83.

Wohlwend, K.E. (2009b). 'Early adopters: Playing new literacies and pretending new technologies in print-centric classrooms', *Journal of Early Childhood Literacy*, 9(2): 119–43.

29

Effective Literacy Teaching in the Early Years of School: A Review of Evidence

Kathy Hall

INTRODUCTION

This chapter explores the literature on effective literacy teaching in the early stages of schooling, where early years is defined as ranging from 5 to 8 years. The focus is not so much about the relative effectiveness of various teaching methods, instructional programmes, teaching materials, or the 'natural' development of literacy in young children as it is about what characterises teacher expertise in the intentional promotion of literacy in the early-years classroom.

There is now considerable agreement in the research field regarding how young children become literate (e.g., Roskos and Christie, 2001; Bissex, 1980; Bussis et al., 1985; Adams, 1991; Snow et al., 1998; Neuman, 2011; Olson and Torrance, 2009; Kamil et al., 2011; Flood et al., 2003), but this consensus does not extend to literacy pedagogy which still remains quite controversial (e.g., Raphael and Brock, 1998; Foorman et al., 1998; Taylor et al., 2000a; 2000b; Hall, 2002; Barrs et al., 2008; Teale et al., 2010; Harrison, 2010). What constitutes literacy is also contested, although it is increasingly recognised that while print literacy remains fundamental to becoming literate in the early years of school, literacy is now inescapably multimodal, requiring the integration of pictures, movies, written prose and electronic texts. There is a growing appreciation that, from the earliest stages of literacy learning, a broader set of skills around an increasing range of texts and technologies is important. However, the conceptualisation of literacy in this chapter is determined primarily by the available studies claiming to describe effective literacy teaching in the early years of school and this tends to still privilege print literacy.

The specific area of effective literacy teaching or expertise in the promotion of literacy, however 'effective' is understood, has a short history. Although reviews of instructional research exist (e.g., Hiebert and Raphael, 1996; Roehler and Duffy, 1996; Raphael and Brock, 1998) much of the available research up to the 1990s did not involve teachers who were defined as effective being observed teaching in classroom over long periods of time. In 1996 Pressley et al. reported a gap in the literature and in 1998 Wharton-McDonald et al., with particular reference to the early years, noted that '[t]here is a lack of systematic study of effective literacy teachers, a lack of understanding of their practices and perspectives' (1998: 102). However, since the 1990s several researchers have begun to determine what exemplary literacy teaching looks like and it is primarily this line of enquiry that is of particular interest here. As will be shown, within this line of study a shift is emerging which is directing researchers away from a focus on individual teachers and their practice in individual classrooms and towards schools as the unit of analysis. There is now a much greater concern with enabling teachers and schools to become effective, so improvement studies are tending to replace literacy teacher effectiveness studies.

While the chapter draws primarily on and foregrounds the body of research on effective literacy teachers and their teaching, it also draws on the more general scholarship on literacy teaching that provides theoretical and empirical insights in order to describe the role of teachers in fostering effective early-years literacy education. The empirical studies discussed in the review all bear on early-years classrooms even though several studies incorporated higher grades or classes in their design, in addition to early-years classes.

The organisation of the chapter reflects the kinds of questions that guided the initial search of the literature: What characterises the practices of effective early years' literacy teachers? How are these teachers distinguished from their less-expert colleagues? What perspectives appear to underpin their practices? What are the critical areas in need of further study?

CHARACTERISING EFFECTIVE EARLY-YEARS LITERACY TEACHING

The body of empirical research reviewed here derives mainly from the US, but also from the UK, Australia and to a lesser extent, New Zealand. The overarching message is that effective literacy teachers integrate two major aspects. What seems to be key is the integration and balancing of the learning of the codes of written language with uses and purposes of literacy that are meaningful to the learner (Knapp et al., 1995; Pressley et al., 1996, 2001; Wharton-McDonald et al., 1998; Pressley, 1998; Medwell et al., 1998; Morrow et al., 1999; Taylor et al., 1999, 2000a, 200b, 2005; Rankin-Erickson and Pressley, 2000; Block et al., 2002; Au, 1997; Tharp, 1982; Wilkinson and Townsend, 2000; Scott et al., 2009; Topping and Ferguson, 2005; Weber et al., 2009; Parr and Limbrick, 2010; Mazzoli and Gambrell, 2003; Hattie et al., 2005; Hiebert and Pearson, 2000; Louden et al., 2005a, 2005b; Au et al., 2005). On the one hand, they provide extensive opportunities for their pupils to read and respond to children's literature and to write for a variety of authentic purposes. On the other hand, they attend to the codes of written language – sound symbol correspondence, word recognition, spelling patterns, vocabulary, punctuation, grammar, and text structure.

The research of Michael Pressley and others

I will illustrate further with reference to the first significant series of studies in terms of scale and scope about effective early-literacy teaching. This US-based work was initiated and led by Michael Pressley in the mid-1990s, beginning with an interview survey of kindergarten, grade-1, and grade-2 teachers (Pressley et al., 1996). It proceeded to a more fine-grained, qualitative analysis of outstanding and more typical grade-1 teachers in New York. This research involved observational literacy assessments of pupils, in-depth teacher interviews, close class-room observations, and cross-case analyses of classrooms where achievement was high, i.e., in which the pupils were reading grade-level books, end-of-year writing was extended and mechanically sound relative to other first graders, and task involve-ment during literacy lessons was high (Wharton-McDonald et al., 1997, 1998). So the definition of 'effective' and 'outstand-ing' teaching here bears on pupils' high literacy achievement as revealed by their ability to read and write at a minimum at a level expected for their grade. It then tested the findings emerging from this ethnographic study in a national investiga-tion of effective teaching in five different areas of the US using a similar range of methodological data-gathering tech-niques and cross-case analysis methods, and involving 30 'outstanding' and 'more typical' teachers (Block and Pressley, 2000; Pressley et al., 2001).

These studies included mostly children from middle- to lower middle-income communities and incorporated pupils from a variety of ethnic backgrounds, but they appear not to have represented well the very lowest income groups, a point I will return to later. Exemplary teachers were nominated by supervisors according to pre-specified criteria, which prioritised their success in raising pupils' literacy achieve-ment levels. However, a major strength of this work is that such nominations were only the starting point and the research team's final samples were based on a subset of teachers whose pupils demonstrated con-sistently higher levels of achievement in reading, in writing, and task-engagement in literacy activities (Wharton-McDonald et al., 1998; Pressley et al., 2001). Researchers themselves assessed pupil achievement and on-task engagement using qualitative measures. For example, in the national study, teachers selected as most effective were ones where more than 90 per cent of their pupils were engaged in pro-ductive reading and writing more than 90 per cent of the time; where, by the end of the year during which they participated in the study, their pupils were reading picture books with several sentences per page; and where their pupils' written com-positions were coherent, quite well struc-tured, and several pages long. The outcomes from this series of studies are highly consistent, with the findings of the second study being confirmed by the more broadly-based third one. Moreover, findings from a survey of instructional practices of spe-cial education teachers nominated as effec-tive teachers of literacy (Rankin-Erickson and Pressley, 2000: 218) were 'strikingly similar' to the findings in Pressley et al. (1996) which was based on a sample of primary teachers nominated as outstanding. Taken together all these studies offer a consensus on what exemplary literacy teachers do in their classrooms and how they do it. In addition, the findings from one smaller-scale, qualitative study of the reading practices of four outstanding early years' teachers, nominated as effec-tive, in New Zealand are also in line with the US evidence (Wilkinson and Townsend, 2000).

Exemplary teachers offer a variety of literacy experiences to their pupils from partner reading, shared reading, independent reading and book choosing to explicit instruction using familiar and new texts, and from daily writing in journals and workshop settings to mini-lessons about the mechanics of writing based on children's needs. Guided reading lessons typically incorporate mini-lessons on phonics and phonemic awareness, the use of new and familiar text, the introduction and use of new vocabulary. These teachers show their pupils how to use a range of reading cues (graphophonic, picture, syntactic and semantic cues) in the context of ongoing reading and writing activity and explicit methods are used for the development of comprehension. The teaching of the mechanics of writing, such as punctuation, occurs in the context of real writing and teachers increasingly emphasise the process of writing such as planning and revising as pupils move from kindergarten to grade 2.

The most effective teachers consciously integrate the teaching of skills with authentic literacy experiences. Indeed integration, as already noted, would appear to be a salient feature of their practice. This means that pupils are encouraged to apply their literacy skills in a variety of reading and writing situations. Literacy for these teachers permeates the curriculum. Writing, for example, is integrated into content areas or other curriculum areas and also thoroughly integrated into reading. The books pupils read and the topics for writing are connected and there is much emphasis on oracy. The researchers conclude that the 'extremely strong presence of themes taught through cross-curricular connections was one of the most extraordinary characteristics of outstanding first-grade literacy instruction' (Morrow et al., 1999: 469).

The classrooms are organised for whole-group, small-group, paired, and one-to-one teaching. But perhaps more significantly, these teachers make extensive use of scaffolding whereby they tune into their learners' thinking, have a grasp, through careful monitoring, of their pupils' conceptions and misconceptions and then intervene with assistance as necessary. They demonstrate a keen awareness of their pupils' thinking and are able to intercede at just the right moment to ensure the acquisition of some skill or concept. They are expert in seizing the 'teachable moment' and they are not tightly bound by the planned lesson (Block and Pressley, 2000). Arguably, for this reason they are also especially adept at pitching pupils' work at what might be described as a level of 'easy difficulty' for individual pupils. The researchers noted, 'we observed time and time again the most effective teachers making sure that students were reading books just a little bit challenging for them' (Pressley et al., 2001: 47). They are experts at differentiating tasks according to pupil need. Similarly, Wilkinson and Townsend (2000) reported that their effective teachers continually sought opportunities to move students along a gradient of difficulty with an appropriate level of interactive support. What enabled the New Zealand teachers to achieve such a close fit between the tasks they set their pupils and their learning needs was a combination of their thorough knowledge about their learners (obtained through close observations and running records) and their extensive knowledge of children's literature and the texts that were generally in use in the classroom.

What distinguishes outstanding teachers from their more average colleagues is their ability to incorporate multiple goals into a single lesson – the researchers termed this 'instructional density' saying this was one of the most striking characteristics of practices in high-achievement classes (Wharton-McDonald et al., 1998). In contrast, these teachers' counterparts spend time on activities that are less cognitively complex and less literacy-relevant; their lessons are typically of a single teaching goal; and they do not deviate as much from their intended plan to seize an incidental learning opportunity.

The more effective teachers overtly model what they wish their pupils to do. For instance one teacher was observed writing on a chart how she had helped her mother prepare thanksgiving dinner before asking pupils to write about a time when they helped someone. Similarly, the effective teacher models comprehension by making predictions about what might be in the text that s/he reads to pupils, s/he identifies questions and major messages that the text suggests as the reading occurs (Morrow et al., 1999). Effective teachers also exhibit excellent classroom management, including the co-ordination of support and special teachers; they are well-planned; they carefully monitor their pupils' literacy activities, monitoring pupils, for example, as they write; they have well-established routines that children understand and work within; and pupils are expected to be self-regulated and independent (Pressley et al., 2001).

Research by Block et al. (2002) based in seven English-speaking countries sought to identify the qualities of teaching expertise that distinguished highly effective instruction at different grade levels. Highly effective kindergarten teachers, for instance, are described as 'masterful guardians, catching, cradling, and championing every child's discoveries about print'

(2002: 189). Interestingly, when their pupils do not learn in their initial attempt, these teachers repeat those literacy experiences again and again reusing the same text and context – unlike their counterparts at pre-school and grade 1 levels. Highly effective kindergarten teachers believe that frequent repetition enhances background knowledge and facilitates 'ah ah' connections with print. These teachers are described as having 'exceptional talents in creating classrooms that are inviting, print-rich, and home-like' (2002: 189). Highly effective first-grade teachers are expert 'reteachers' – they distinguish themselves in their ability to teach literacy all day, motivating pupils by varying the breadth, depth and speed of literacy lessons, teaching up to 20 different skills in a single hour.

What the literature, so far, shows is the complexity of excellent literacy teaching, that expertise involves the smooth interweaving of a whole host of elements, and that outstanding literacy teachers do not adhere to one particular method of teaching.

Research from the UK and Australia

UK-based research and more recent research from Australia on effective literacy teaching converge strongly with the above. Descriptive of the range of primary classrooms, and thus not only confined to early-years classrooms, the research commissioned by the Teacher Training Agency in England and carried out by Jane Medwell, David Wray, Louise Poulson and Richard Fox compared the teaching of a sample of teachers whose pupils made effective literacy gains with a more random, comparison (validation) sample of teachers whose pupils made less progress in reading (Medwell et al., 1998; Poulson et al., 2001;

Wray et al., 2001). The 'effective' teachers were chosen from a list of teachers recommended as effective by advisory staff. The key criterion used by the research team for their selection from this list was evidence of above-average learning gains in reading for their pupils. The research design incorporated questionnaires, close observations of and interviews with 26 teachers, and a quiz to test teachers' knowledge. It is worth pointing out that this research was carried out in England at a time when there was unprecedented central governmental interest in literacy pedagogy and a highly prescriptive framework for the promotion of literacy was being developed (Hall, 2001). The study conducted by William Louden and his colleagues (Louden et al., 2005a, 2005b) in Australia bears directly on the early years of school. Its aim was to identify teaching practices that lead to improved literacy outcomes for children. It adopted a sophisticated research design involving the initial identification of a random sample of some 2000 teachers, pupil assessments in literacy, the production of value added assessments of pupil achievement, the application of an observation schedule based on the research team's literature review of effective literacy teaching and how young children develop literacy, and in-depth multi-validation procedures based on qualitative and quantitative techniques. Categories of teachers, 'more effective', 'as effective' and 'less effective' were empirically established and their classroom practices and activities described in detail in relation to the themes they identified from their literature review, namely, participation, knowledge, orchestration, support, differentiation, and respect. This study is important because it did not begin with teachers who were nominated as effective, rather this was empirically established, and its focus was exclusively

early-years settings. As such, it addressed two key limitations identified by other narrative and systematic reviews of the field (Hall and Harding, 2003).

Effective literacy teachers in England generally seek to contextualise their teaching of language conventions to maximise its meaningfulness to pupils. This means that letter–sound correspondence, word recognition, and vocabulary, for example, are taught within the context of interacting with whole texts – often shared texts like 'big books'. Effective teachers are distinguished by their explicitness of the functions of what their pupils are learning in literacy and why what they are learning is necessary and useful for them. Other research (e.g., Hattie, 2005) confirms the significance of meaningfulness, integration of reading, writing, and oracy, and collaboration and sharing texts. Like the US work, and also based on observational evidence, Medwell et al. 1998 found that their effective teachers use short, regular teaching sessions to promote word recognition which involve them modelling to their pupils how sounds work. They use a wider range of texts than their validation colleagues. They tend to use grammar to describe language whereas their colleagues tend to use grammar to prescribe rules for the use of language.

They also adopt very clear assessment procedures involving focused observation and systematic record keeping. They are adept at differentiating the support they offer pupils during the completion of tasks. While effective teachers in England might set all pupils in the group or class the same task and expect them to achieve the same learning outcome, the more effective teachers offer struggling readers and writers more or different support to achieve this outcome. In the light of this, it is not surprising that more effective teachers are also more 'highly diagnostic' in their interpretations of their pupils' written work – they are better and quicker than their validation colleagues at offering explanations as to why children read or write as they do.

William Louden and his team confirmed much of the earlier findings. However, their analyses and findings bear some repetition not least because some of them are new and extend our understanding. For instance, one major finding was that the type of literacy activity on offer in early-years classrooms varied only slightly by teacher effectiveness. It seems that teachers, regardless of their effectiveness (which it will be recalled is based on their pupils' literacy achievements) engaged in more or less the same activities: shared book reading, phonics teaching, and the modelling of writing. But they found distinct differences in the effectiveness with which these activities were carried out. Features that distinguished the more effective and effective teachers included: attention and engagement, pace and metalanguage, and challenge. Mirroring the US and UK findings, the more effective and effective teachers were observed teaching word level knowledge and skills within a wider and applied context, e.g., within the reading of a shared book, a writing lesson, or a spelling lesson. What appeared to distinguish these teachers in this regard was their emphasis on making purposes clear and relevant to learners and their ability to bring in higher order and more meaningful and authentic features of language for their pupils. A further feature distinguishing these teachers was their greater emphasis on guided practice in a variety of contexts and their emphasis on the broader text-level aspects of language, especially comprehension. These teachers' clarity and precision in offering explanation to learners was a constant theme in their practice and this seems to have been critical in their effectiveness. Of importance also was their knowledge of their pupils' out-of-school lives and their willingness and ability to adapt the classroom literacy environment to their learners' lives beyond the school. In this way these teachers were able to maximise the participation of children in literacy activities since clarity and precision were aligned with the interests and passions of learners. As in other studies these teachers were found to use every minute well for learning and to offer timely and focused feedback.

Neither Louden et al.'s nor Medwell et al.'s research samples could be considered particularly representative of teachers working with pupils from ethnic minority groups or from areas of poverty – neither set out to be so, seeking instead to represent as well as possible the various contexts in their respective countries in which teachers work. However, some work, including more recent research, provides insights in this regard.

Research based on more diverse populations

Research conducted at the US government-funded, Center for the Improvement of Early Reading Achievement (CIERA) (Taylor et al., 1999, 2000a, 2000b; Taylor, 2000; Adler and Fisher, 2001; Hiebert and Pearson, 2000; Weber et al., 2009) and research by Knapp et al. (1995) is especially insightful. So too is the work of Parr and Limbrick (2010) in New Zealand on Maori populations and that of Topping and Ferguson (2005) on mostly low-income settings in Scotland. Although not as focused on what specifically characterises effective literacy teachers and their teaching, some studies of school effectiveness in urban areas of the US (e.g., Designs for Change, 1998) also provide insights about distinctive teacher practices that are especially relevant to success with low-income catchments and more ethnically diverse populations. The longitudinal work of Kathy Au in Hawaii (Au, 1997; Au and Carroll, 1997; Au et al., 2005), though again not specifically designed to explore effective teachers' practices, provides valuable insights into effective literacy teaching with minority ethnic groups while more recent work by Au, Taffy Raphael and others in both Hawaii and Chicago schools (e.g. 2005) represents a shift towards schools as opposed to individual teachers as the unit of analysis.

A national study of effective schools and accomplished teachers at CIERA sought to understand the practices of accomplished teachers in schools that were *beating the odds,* or more precisely, that were achieving unexpectedly high results (Taylor et al., 1999, 2000a, 2000b; Taylor and Pearson, 2002). Based on 14 high-achieving, high-poverty, inner-city schools and 70 teachers of kindergarten to grade 3 (i.e., 5–8-year-olds) this research used a range of quantitative and qualitative data gathering methods and cross-case analyses determining similarities and differences across settings, especially across effective and ineffective settings. Two teachers from each class, kindergarten to grade 3, were observed and achievements in reading (word recognition, accuracy, fluency and comprehension) were measured by the researchers at the beginning and end of the school year. Michael Knapp et al. (1995) investigated 140 'high-poverty', grades 1–6 classrooms across three US states also using a combination of qualitative and quantitative approaches including the testing of pupils. The mixed

method research by Topping and Ferguson (2005) focused on five highly effective teachers on the basis of a combination of their pupils' literacy achievements and expert nomination of expertise. Parr and Limbrick (2010) attended to writing rather than literacy in more broad terms and their research spanned the range of primary age pupils rather than just the early years. The results of these studies are largely consistent and in line with the other US and UK evidence, but some additional and specific insights merit some discussion and integration with the previous literature.

First, literacy is a priority for teachers in the most effective schools and the most accomplished teachers devote more time to reading activities (including independent reading and writing in response to reading) than the moderately and least effective schools (Taylor et al., 1999, 2000; Taylor and Pearson, 2002; Topping and Ferguson, 2005). Pupils of effective teachers read more and write extended texts about topics they care about. Creativity and self-expression are important. (Knapp et al., 1995; Parr and Limbrick, 2010). They spend more time on task and, apparently, enjoying what they do.

Second, accomplished teachers are distinguished from their counterparts in spending more time in small-group teaching which includes teacher-directed text activity, literature circles, and explicit teaching in phonics, comprehension and vocabulary. This is not altogether surprising when one considers the likelihood that the small-group context allows for activities to be personalised as well as differentiated or targeted more directly at pupils' needs, and for teaching to be repeated as needed so children can internalise and better understand. Previous research on early reading demonstrates that whole-class phonics instruction, for example, is not likely to be effective for the majority of children (Juel, 1994). In the CIERA study the greater time allotted to small-group teaching is a collaborative decision that is made at school level – could only be made at school level – by all four of the most effective schools (Adler and Fisher, 2001). This small-group work is characterised by regular, special education, and resource teachers working together to provide small-group teaching. Much like the effective small-group teaching in a New Zealand study by Wilkinson and Townsend, 2000, groups are similar-ability based, although the accomplished teachers in the study refer to it as 'instructional level grouping', the composition of which changes frequently in the light of assessments and continuous monitoring. Previous literacy research (e.g., Allington, 1983) shows that similar-ability grouping meant that those consigned to the lower ability groups were frequently given work that was low in cognitive demand. But in the CIERA study pupils in the lower 'instructional-level group spent as much time on higher-order activities as did average achievers' (Taylor et al., 2000b: 156). The authors point out the success of this strategy is down, not merely to the accomplished teachers, but to school culture, i.e., to the school-level decisions that led to flexible deployment of teaching staff together with a common assessment system that ensured flexible movement between groups. Indeed one of the substantive strengths of the CIERA study is its linkage of school and classroom effectiveness measures. What comes across from the evidence is that the classrooms of the most effective teachers are more discursive, conversational and dialogic places to be – one gets a sense of negotiation, tentativeness, and power-sharing, yet there is

explicitness, clarity about expectations, and a sense of security for children.

Third, the most effective teachers explicitly build on children's personal and cultural backgrounds and teachers in the most effective schools reach out more to communicate with and involve parents. This suggests a view of literacy that involves social and cultural interactions at home and at school, a view that recognises that some children have home cultures that differ from the culture of the school and that such cultural conflict may impede literacy learning (e.g., Hicks, 2001). The effective teachers' emphasis on the sociocultural aspect is in line with previous, longitudinal research in classrooms (Au, 1997), and in line with a perspective on literacy learning that does not separate cognitive and affective aspects (Hall, 2010). Au's earlier work, for example, demonstrated the benefits of bridging the gap between school and community literacies (Tharp, 1982). She has researched the Kamehameha Elementary Education Program (KEEP) in Hawaii for several decades. This is a programme based on Vygotskian theory and, more specifically, on the idea that pupils from diverse and poor neighbourhoods have rich funds of knowledge and community literacy practices. Its success suggests that a culturally-responsive curriculum is important for improving literacy among pupils who do not come from middle-class backgrounds – pupils whose home and community culture may not align with the traditional school culture of literacy.

The fourth insight is entirely in line with previous studies. While explicit word recognition strategies are taught in all schools, what distinguishes the most accomplished teachers is their additional 'coaching' of pupils (as opposed to telling or recitation which is more evident among the least accomplished teachers) in how to apply their word recognition skills to their everyday texts (Taylor et al., 2000b; Taylor and Pearson, 2002; Topping and Ferguson, 2005). A major distinguishing feature of the most successful first-grade teachers, Knapp et al. (1995: 74) claims, is that 'skills are taught as tools to be used immediately (or very soon) in the work of making sense of the printed page, not be mastered for their own sake without applications to the act of reading'. When skills are taught separately they are integrated into games and there is much emphasis on recognising learning patterns through rhyme and story.

A fifth insight concerns sharing purposes and success criteria with learners in a way they can understand. Timely feedback, formative assessment, and deep knowledge of learners as people with interests, intentions, and their own agendas were all highly related to high achievement and high motivation among the learners of the most accomplished teachers.

The consistency across the findings in all the studies reviewed permit their integration under three inter-related headings: curricular, organisational and pedagogical. Table 29.1 highlights the range of practices that distinguish the most effective literacy teachers. The effective literacy teacher is not someone who has a single identifying approach but rather is someone who weaves and interweaves several literacy goals and literacy practices through attending to a variety of curricular, organisational and pedagogical matters. Effective teachers appear to approximate to an 'apprenticeship' model (Rogoff, 2008; Sternberg, 2008). This model focuses on learning through guided participation, it highlights the role of experience and the significance of engaging in authentic practices alongside the more accomplished other; it also

highlights the role of adaptive expertise and the processes involved in expert performance. In this way learners are made sensitive to the details of expert performance. It also embeds knowledge, skills and strategies in their social and functional contexts. It is clear that outstanding literacy teachers in the early years of school build upon the variety of rich language-acquisition strategies that children have informally developed outside of school. They appear to act on the Hallidayan theory that meaning is the driving force in literacy growth. In other words it is from an understanding of what language does, semantically and pragmatically, that children learn its form, both syntactically and graphophonemically (Harste et al., 1994).

That effective teachers are adept at seizing the 'teachable moment', and that they closely observe and act on children's literate practices as they occur in a variety of classroom contexts suggest that they also draw on a kind of situated learning theory that emphasises the creation of learning contexts for which literacy can be used to meet the demands of a situation. In this view, activities create the context that stimulates learners to construct their own knowledge (Rogoff, 2008; Neuman and Roskos, 1997).

EFFECTIVE LITERACY TEACHERS PERSPECTIVES

A fuller understanding of expertise is facilitated through an examination of the thinking and perspectives they bring to bear on their decision-making in the literacy classroom. Some of the above studies together with other, smaller-scale studies shed light on this. Research conducted on effective teachers during the 1960s and 1970s focused almost exclusively on

Table 29.1 Distinguishing characteristics of the practices of effective literacy teachers

Curricular	• Their pupils read more and write more extended text
	• Their pupils read and write about what matters to them
	• Word recognition, vocabulary, spelling, comprehension and writing skills are explicitly taught through application
	• They teach their pupils multiple cues for word recognition
	• These teachers offer greater variety in literacy experience: partner reading, shared reading, independent reading, book choosing, explicit teaching using new and familiar texts; writing for a variety of purposes; collaborative writing but do so in a manner that always maintains a focus on meaningful purpose
Organisational	• Excellent class management, incorporating routines that support pupil independence, thorough planning, and strong emphasis on literacy-rich classroom environments, on specific feedback about progress, and on positive reinforcement
	• These teachers spend more time on cognitively-demanding and literacy-relevant tasks
	• They co-ordinate support staff to maximise curricular integrity and task differentiation according to pupil need
	• They provide organisational variety: small group teaching, pair work, one-to-one and whole-class teaching
	• They spend more time on teacher-directed, similar-ability, small-group work, the composition of which changes frequently due to careful monitoring
	• They establish close links with parents and community
Pedagogical	• Integration and balance: reading and writing are integrated by these teachers so pupils write in response to texts read; thematic approach is used to integrate the content areas; balance between reading good quality literature, writing for meaningful purposes and learning the conventions of print; literacy knowledge and skills are applied to real texts as they are learned
	• Teachers are aware of the experiences learners bring with them from their families and communities and their pedagogies link with this knowledge so there is explicit building on children's cultural backgrounds
	• Teachers model literate behaviour to make learning and thinking explicit for pupils
	• More extensive scaffolding of pupil learning and providing the right level of support, and monitoring and giving feedback as pupils complete tasks
	• More emphasis on self-regulation and pupil independence
	• Greater use of opportunistic/incidental teaching; instructional density, and multiple goals for a single lesson

the teacher behaviours in the classroom that related to pupil achievement (e.g., Rosenshine and Furst, 1973; Brophy, 1973; see Hoffman, 1991 for a review in relation to literacy). The largely behaviourist perspective underpinning that line of enquiry meant that little or no attention was paid to the teacher as critical decision-maker who comes to the act of teaching as agentic, intentional and with a perspective on what constitutes a good way to teach. The thinking underlying research since the 1990s, however, does consider the significance of the teachers' beliefs and knowledge and their reasoning behind their practices. This information is typically elicited through semi-structured interviewing, conversations about lessons just observed or about samples of their pupils work, although questionnaires have also been used (e.g., Poulson et al., 2001). In addition, since experts in a profession tend to have a privileged understanding of what they do and are able to give valid and accurate accounts of the decisions they make (Wharton-McDonald et al., 1998), highly competent literacy teachers are extremely well positioned to provide insights into the nature of effective teaching. Moreover, on the basis of the effective practices outlined already in this chapter it is possible to imply a theory of learning and teaching to which effective teachers appear to subscribe. I will return to this point in the Conclusion.

What additional insights then are available about outstanding early-years teachers' literacy practices? The first point to be made here is that the most effective teachers exhibit continuity between their pedagogical philosophies and their practices. Questionnaire and interview surveys designed to assess teachers' orientations to different literacy perspectives, found that there are differences in beliefs between effective teachers and less accomplished teachers (Poulson et al., 2001; Parr and Limbrick, 2010). First, the effective teachers of literacy show a higher level of consistency between their beliefs and choice of teaching activities. Effective teachers claim to be more committed to their pupils making sense of text, on authentic as opposed to decontextualised texts, on literacy processes, and on writing for a range of purposes. While all emphasise the importance of coming to grips with the technical aspects of literacy, the more effective teachers accord much more status to children recognising the purposes and functions of the literacy tasks they are set. Parr and Limbrick (2010) for instance found that interviews with their six highly accomplished teachers showed that they placed significantly greater value on sense of purpose, meaningfulness, the articulation of learning aims, and having learners appreciate the success criteria against which their work is judged. In this regard their teachers were keen to promote self-assessment and ability to reflect realistically on their own learning and achievements.

The most accomplished teachers hold consistently high expectations for *all* their pupils. They define all their pupils as capable of becoming successful readers and writers and their practices bear this out (Wharton-McDonald, 1998; Block and Pressley, 2000; Block et al., 2002; Taylor et al., 2000a, 2000b; Taylor and Pearson, 2002; Parr and Limbrick, 2010; Au et al., 2005; Wilkinson and Townsend, 2000). The New Zealand teachers, for example, are described as holding a developmental view of ability, a notion of ability as 'learnable' and incremental rather than innate or immutable. Effective teachers also exhibit a keen awareness of purpose. The most effective teachers are strikingly different from their less effective colleagues in their detailed descriptions of why their pupils were allocated specific tasks (e.g., Block and Pressley, 2000; Louden et al., 2005a, 2005b). They talk about their philosophies with reference to specific children. While typically teachers can 'talk the talk' in that they tend to be familiar with the latest literacy terminology, the most effective teachers go beyond general terms and general descriptions and apply their theoretical understanding to individual children. Formative assessment and ongoing monitoring of literacy success would appear to be the result of this way of thinking.

Effective teachers know they are effective. To exemplify, Block and Pressley (2000: 8–9) allocated themselves the highest possible ranking in meeting the needs of pupils with special literacy needs and they could also explain how their teaching contributed to pupils' literacy growth – they could cite, for example, 'what part of their actions, instructional program, or teaching repertoire had scaffolded the success of individual students'. The most effective teachers implicitly define their pupils as active, thinking, feeling sense-makers, rather than mere rememberers or forgetters. They implicitly define themselves as powerful enablers whose task it is to understand what their learners already know and can do in various literacy contexts, to recognise what motivates and engages them, and to extend their literacy repertoires by building on their strengths. Becoming literate is implicitly defined as becoming increasingly adept at using literacy to do things for purposes that are valued by them and within their communities. Effective teaching involves evidence-informed practices but crucially evidence not only about literacy learning *per se* but about actual children's literacy practices and experiences.

CONCLUSION

The research reviewed here demonstrates that effective literacy teaching in the early years of school is about far more than 'method'. Rather it is a complex mix of philosophy, method, teacher development and school culture. Effective teachers are clearly eclectic in their approach to literacy teaching and dichotomies such as phonics-oriented versus literature-based approaches seem not to be relevant to real-life contexts. The complexity of what effective literacy teachers do, which, to varying degrees, fits with what we know about the complexity of children's early learning about written language (e.g., Kamil et al., 2010; Neuman, 2011, Barrs et al., 2008; Adams, 1991; Snow et al., 1998; Roskos and Christie, 2001; Bussis et al., 1985; Kress, 1997; Dyson and Genishi, 1994) should lead us to question the validity of perspectives that seek to find a single best approach. The effective teaching of literacy cannot be packaged in teacher-proof scripts or prescriptive programmes on the assumption that 'one size fits all'.

Children benefit from a combination of teaching approaches to become successful readers and writers and effective teachers know and act on this. This conclusion is not only justified by the research on teacher effectiveness reviewed here, it is also confirmed by research that focuses on different pedagogical approaches to literacy development. To illustrate, Juel and Minden-Cupp (2001) demonstrated that when teachers use the same approach with all first-grade pupils, its impact differs according to the children's varying entry profile to that class. Those first-graders who already had considerable experience of and success in literacy activities benefited from an emphasis on real texts and good quality children's literature and were disadvantaged by an emphasis on phonics training. The opposite was the case for lower-achieving pupils in the first grade – they benefited from an emphasis on phonics training. Once pupils appreciate that print carries meaning and once they master some initial skills, it seems that more direct attention to specific reading strategies is timely. The point of this illustration is that children in kindergarten (or any year/grade) are not homogeneous and teachers have to base their teaching on a knowledge of their pupils' specific literacy strengths and weaknesses in order to maximise their effectiveness. This is what effective literacy teachers are adept at doing. They recognise the need for careful differentiation.

The CIERA research demonstrates that school and classroom factors interact to influence the quality of the child's literacy experience while the more recent CIERA work (Taylor et al., 2005) explores the nature of the relationship between school-level and classroom-level decision making about literacy pedagogy. Their focus is how knowledge about effective literacy development is translated into classroom practice. One assumption of this line of recent work is that there is now available sufficient understanding regarding what effective schools and teacher do to promote literacy success. The CIERA School Change Framework takes the school, as opposed to the classroom, as the unit of change and supports schools in looking at their own school data as well as externally set standards in order to improve practices. This work recognises the significance of school cultures and how individuals, whether students or teachers, matter and that interventions, policies and attempts to improve literacy achievement need to look at the collective as well the individual teacher. They show that in effective schools teachers plan and teach together and there is ongoing professional development linked to their school and to individual professional needs. Of crucial importance is the sharing of student work and assessment data, reflective dialogue with other colleagues in the school, all of which results in the 'deprivatisation of practice' (Cochran-Smith, 2011). This in turn supports shared understandings. In line with the developments noted in the *Handbook of Research on Reading* (Kamil et al., 2010) Taylor et al. demonstrate the significance of 'homegrown' literacy instruction as opposed top-down programmes which, recognising the irony, they say hinder meeting the legislative mandates to improve literacy standards.

Other researchers (Au et al., 2005) who also follow this logic show how a network of schools in Chicago and Hawaii have used a systematic approach – the Standards-Based Change (SBC) Process – to guide teachers in developing sustainable, high-quality literacy curricula designed to meet the specific needs of their diverse learners. Not dissimilar to the CIERA School Change Framework, the SBC process guides schools in implementing a system for improving student achievement through a focus on standards, but significantly it does this through professional development for teachers which guides them to creating their own solutions for raising students' literacy achievement as opposed to implementing a solution designed by outsiders. Their work shows how deep and lasting change involves significant collaboration and engagement on the part of teachers as a collective and that strong school leadership is vital to enable colleagues stay the course of curriculum and staff development.

This line of research and development work is beginning to show that the quality of classroom literacy teaching can be enormously enhanced through research-based intervention programmes that target actual school and teacher professional development. This work is certainly important and opportune, given the considerable consensus that exists within the research of literacy teacher effectiveness. It is likely that future studies (see Taylor et al., 2011) will continue to focus on processes of enabling schools to become more accomplished sites for literacy learning. In the near future this line of work is likely to seek to better understand how individual schools take responsibility for their own literacy curricula while mindful of the externally-set standards.

The existing studies on literacy teacher effectiveness imply a model of literacy that is still restricted largely to the interpretation and production of print. This brings me to the implicit theory of literacy and literacy acquisition underlying the studies of effectiveness reviewed in this chapter. Contemporary literacy practices suggest the need for pedagogic research that incorporates a fuller range of symbolic tools that are available to children to support meaning-making, drawing especially on popular culture and information technologies (Dyson, 1994; Marsh, 2008). Research on children's ways of using written language which demonstrates the non-linearity of literacy development offers new perspectives for policy and practice. Dyson, for example, views written language development within a broad context of children's development as symbolisers. She demonstrates how children's use of written language is interrelated in complex ways with their use of other media and with the relationships they form through interaction with other people. Viewing written language development as part of the child's developing symbolic repertoire and changing social relationships offers new ways of thinking about its development in the classroom. The talking, drawing, playing, storytelling and experiences with print and multimodal texts all provide resources which teachers and children can draw on to build new possibilities. Future research might usefully show how successful teachers and schools draw on and develop their learners' literacy capacities in relation to multimodal literacy.

In conclusion, it is arguable that the more accomplished teachers of literacy subscribe to a view of learning, learners, and knowledge that coincides with a sociocultural perspective (Lave, 1996; Wenger, 1998; Rogoff, 2008), while the more recent line of inquiry involving whole schools working together to improve literacy achievement seems firmly based on a sociocultural orientation to change, policy implementation and professional learning. Though not necessarily explicit in the various studies, learning is seen as being about participation and the opportunity to belong to a practice. Learners, like teachers themselves, are seen as agentic who come to activities with ideas, histories and feelings about their tasks and the relations they have with the people with whom they work. Knowledge, including what counts as literacy, is seen as dynamic and produced in interaction and enactment, while success in literacy is a matter of a collective and shared recognition of what is worth knowing and being able to do in a given situation. Becoming literate involves the transformation of a self, aligned with the transformation of the practices engaged in and valued in local and wider communities of learners.

REFERENCES

Adams, M.J. (1991) *Beginning to Read: Thinking and Learning about Print.* Cambridge, MA: MIT Press.

Adler, M.A. and Fisher, C.W. (2001) 'Early reading programs in high-poverty schools: A case study of beating the odds', *The Reading Teacher*, 54(6): 616–19.

Allington, R.L. (1983) 'The reading instruction provided readers of differing abilities', *Elementary School Journal*, 83: 548–59.

Au, K. (1997) 'A sociocultural model of reading instruction: The Kamehameha Elementary Education Program', in S.A. Stahl, *Instructional Models in Reading*. Mahwah, NJ: Erlbaum. pp. 181–202.

Au, K.H. (2008) 'Negotiating the slippery slope: School change and literacy achievement', *Journal of Literacy Research*, 37(3): 267–86.

Au, K. and Carroll, J. (1997) 'Improving literacy achievement through a constructivist approach: The KEEP demonstration classroom project', *The Elementary School Journal*, 97: 203–21.

Au, K., Raphael, T., and Mooney, K. (2005) 'Improving reading achievement in elementary schools: Guiding change in a time of standards', in S.B. Wepner and D.S. Strickland (eds), *The Administration and Supervision of Reading Programs*. 4th edn. New York: Teachers College Press.

Barrs, M., Pradl, G., Hall, K., and Dombey, H. (eds) (2008) 'Literacy as a complex activity', *Literacy*, 42 (whole issue).

Bissex, G.L. (1980) *Gnys at wrk: a child learns to write and read.* Cambridge, MA: Harvard University Press

Block, C.C. and Pressley, M. (2000) 'It's not scripted lessons but challenging and personalized interactions that distinguish effective from less effective primary classrooms', Paper presented at the National Reading Conference, Phoenix, December.

Block, C.C., Oakar, M., and Hurt, N. (2002) 'The expertise of literacy teachers: A continuum from preschool to grade 5', *Reading Research Quarterly*, 37(2): 178–206.

Brophy, J. (1973) 'Stability of teacher effectiveness', *American Educational Research Journal*, 10: 245–52.

Bussis, A., Chittenden, F., Amarel, M., and Klausner, E. (1985) *Inquiry into Meaning. An Investigation of Learning to Read*. Hillsdale, NJ: Erlbaum.

Cochran-Smith, M. (2011) *A Tale of Two Teachers: Learning to Teach Across the Professional Lifespan*. Keynote Address Teaching Council of Ireland Conference, Cork.

Designs for Change (1998) 'What makes these schools stand out: Chicago elementary schools with a seven-year trend of improved reading achievement', Chicago Public Schools http://www.dfc1.orghttp://www.designsforchange.org/pdfs/SOScomplete.pdf Accessed 9/5/2012

Dyson, A. H. (1998) Folk processes and media creatures: Reflections on popular culture for literacy educators *The Reading Teacher*, 51(5): 392–402.

Dyson, A.H. (1994) 'Viewpoints: the word and the world – reconceptualizing written language development or, do rainbows mean a lot to little girls?', in R.B. Ruddell, M.R. Ruddell, and H. Singer (eds), *Theoretical Models and Processes of Reading*. 4th edn. Delaware: International Reading Association. pp. 297–322.

Dyson, A.H. and Genishi, C. (eds) (1994) *The Need for Story: Cultural Diversity in Classroom and Community*. Urbana, IL: National Council of Teachers of English.

Flood, J., Lapp, D., Squire, J.R., and Jensen, J.M. (eds) (2003) *Handbook of Research on Teaching English Language Arts*. 2nd edn. Mahwah, NJ: LEA.

Foorman, B.R., Francis, D.J., Fletcher, J.M., and Mehta, P. (1998) 'The role of instruction in learning to read: Preventing reading failure in at-risk children', *Journal of Educational Psychology*, 90(1): 37–55.

Hall, K. (2001) An analysis of primary literacy policy in England using Barthes' notion of "readerly" and "writerly" texts', *Journal of Early Childhood Literacy*, 1(2): 153–65.

Hall, K. (2002) *Listening to Stephen read: Multiple Perspectives on Literacy*. Buckingham: Open University Press.

Hall, K. and Harding, A. (2003) 'A systematic review of effective literacy teaching in the 4 to 14 age range

of mainstream schooling', in *Research Evidence in Education Library*. London: EPPI-Centre, Social Science Research Unit, Institute of Education

Hall, K. (2010) Significant lines of research in reading pedagogy, in K. Hall, U. Goswami, C. Harrison, S. Ellis, and J. Soler (eds), *Interdisciplinary Perspectives on Learning to Read: Culture, Cognition and Pedagogy*. London: Routledge. pp. 1–16.

Harrison, C. (2010) 'Why do policy makers find the "simple view of reading" so attractive, and why do I find it so repugnant?', in K. Hall, U. Goswami, C. Harrison, S. Ellis, and J. Soler (eds), *Interdisciplinary Perspectives on Learning to Read: Culture, Cognition and Pedagogy*. London: Routledge. pp. 207–18.

Harste, J.C., Burke, C.L., and Woodward, V.A. (1994) 'Children's language and world: Initial encounters with print', in R.B. Ruddell, M.R. Ruddell, and H. Singer (eds), *Theoretical Models and Processes of Reading*. 4th edn. Delaware: International Reading Association. pp. 48–69.

Hattie, J.A. (2005) 'What is the nature of evidence that makes a difference to learning?', in *Research Conference 2005 Proceedings*. Camberwell, VIC: Australian Council for Educational Research. pp. 11–21. Available at: www.acer.edu.au

Hicks, D. (2001) 'Literacies and masculinities in the life of a young working-class boy', *Language Arts*, 78(3): 217–26.

Hiebert, E. and Pearson, D. (2000) 'Building on the past, bridging to the future: A research agenda for the centre for the improvement of early reading achievement', *Journal of Educational Research*, 93(3): 133–44.

Hiebert, E.H. and Raphael, T.E. (1996) 'Psychological perspectives on literacy and extensions to educational practice', D.C. Berliner and R.C. Calfree (eds), *Handbook of Educational Psychology*. New York: Macmillan. pp. 550–602.

Hoffman, J.V. (1991) 'Teacher and school effects in learning to read', in R. Barr, M.L. Kamil, P.B. Mosenthal, and P.D. Pearson (eds), *Handbook of Reading Research*. Vol. 2. New York: Longman. pp. 911–50.

Juel, C. (1994) *Learning to Read and Write in one Elementary School*. New York: Springer-Verlag.

Juel, C. and Minden-Cupp, C. (2001) 'Learning to read words: Linguistic units and instructional strategies', *Reading Research Quarterly*, 35(4): 458–93.

Kamil, L., Pearson, D.P., Moje E.B., and Afflerbach, P. (eds) (2010) *Handbook of Reading Research*. Vol. 4. New York: Routledge.

Knapp, M.S. and Associates (1995) *Teaching for Meaning in High-Poverty Classrooms*. New York: Teachers' College Press.

Kress, G. (1997) *Before Writing: Rethinking the Paths to Literacy*. London: Routledge.

Lave, J. (1996) 'Teaching, as learning, in practice', *Mind, Culture and Activity*, 3: 149–64.

Louden, W., Rohl, M., Barrat-Pugh, C., Brown, C., Cairney, T., Elderfield, J., House, H., Meiers, M., Rivaland, J., and Rowe, K.J. (2005a) *In Teachers' Hands: Effective Literacy Teaching Practices in the Early Years of Schooling*. Canberra: Australian Government Department of Education, Science and Training. Available at: http://www.dest.gov.au/sectors/school_education/publications_resources/profiles/

Louden, W., Rohl, M., Barrat-Pugh, C., Brown, C., Cairney, T., Elderfield, J., House, H., Meiers, M., Rivaland, J., and Rowe, K.J. (2005b) 'In teachers' hands: Effective literacy teaching practices in the early years of schooling', *Australian Journal of Language and Literacy*, 28(3): 173–252 (whole issue).

Marsh, J. (2008) 'Media literacy in the early years', in J. Marsh and E. Hallet (eds), *Desirable Literacies: Approaches to Language and Literacy in the Early Years*. 2nd edn. London: Sage. pp. 205–22.

Mazzoli, S. and Gambrell, L.B. (2003) 'Principles of best practice: Finding the common ground', in L.M. Morrow, L.B. Gambrell, and M. Pressley (eds), *Best Practices in Primary Instruction*. 2nd edn. New York: Guilford Press. pp. 9–21.

Medwell, J., Wray, D., Poulson, L., and Fox, R. (1998) *The Effective Teachers of Literacy Project*. Exeter: University of Exeter.

Morrow, L.M., Tracey, D.H., Woo, D.G., and Pressley, M. (1999) 'Characteristics of exemplary first-grade literacy instruction', *The Reading Teacher*, 52(5): 462–76.

Neuman, S.B. (ed.) (2011) *Handbook of Early Literacy Research*. New York: Guilford Press.

Neuman, S.B. and Roskos, K. (1997) 'Literacy knowledge in practice: Contexts of participation for young writers and readers', *Reading Research Quarterly*, 32(1): 10–32.

Olson, D. and Torrance, N. (eds) (2009) *The Cambridge Handbook of Literacy*. New York: Cambridge University Press.

Parr, J. and Limbrick, L. (2010) 'Contextualising practice: Hallmarks of effective teachers of writing', *Teaching and Teacher Education*, 26: 583–90.

Poulson, L., Avramidis, E., Fox, R., Medwell, J., and Wray, D. (2001) 'The theoretical beliefs of effective teachers of literacy: An exploratory study of orientations to literacy', *Research Papers in Education*, 16(3): 1–22.

Pressley, M. (1998) *Reading Instruction that Works: the Case for Balanced Teaching*. New York: Guilford Press.

Pressley, M., Rankin, J., and Yokoi, L. (1996) 'A survey of the instructional practices of outstanding primary-level literacy teachers', *Elementary School Journal*, 96: 363–84.

Pressley, M., Wharton-McDonald, R., Allington, R., Block, C.C., Morrow, L., Tracey, D., Baker, K., Brooks, G., Cronin, J., Nelson, E., and Woo, D. (2001) 'A study of effective first-grade literacy instruction', *Scientific Studies of Reading*, 5(1): 35–58.

Rankin-Erickson, J.L. and Pressley, M. (2000) 'A survey of instructional practices of special education teachers nominated as effective teachers of literacy', *Learning Disabilities Research and Practice*, 15(4): 206–25.

Raphael, T.R. and Brock, C.H. (1998) 'Instructional research in literacy: Changing paradigms', in C. Kinzer, D. Leu, and H. Hinchman (eds), *46th National Reading Conference Yearbook*. Chicago, IL: National Reading Conference.

Roehler, L.R. and Duffy, G.G. (1991) 'Teachers' instructional actions', in R. Barr, M.L. Kamil, P. Mosenthal, and P.D. Pearson (eds), *Handbook of Reading Research*. Vol. 2. Mahwah, NJ: Erlbaum. pp. 861–83.

Rogoff, B. (2008) 'Observing sociocultural activity on three planes', in K. Hall, P. Murphy, and J. Soler, J. (eds), *Pedagogy and Practice: Culture and Identities*. London: Sage.

Rosenshine, B. and Furst, N. (1973) 'The use of direct observation to study teaching', in R.M.W. Travers (ed.), *Second Handbook of Research on Teaching*. Chicago: Rand McNally. pp. 122–83.

Roskos, K. and Christie, J. (2001) 'Examining the play-literacy interface: A critical review and future directions', *Journal of Early Childhood Literacy*, 1(1): 59–89.

Sternberg, R.J. (2008) 'Abilities are forms of developing expertise', in P. Murphy and B. McCormick (eds), *Knowledge and Practice: Representations and Identities*. London: Sage. pp. 15–29.

Taylor, B.M. (2000) 'Highly accomplished primary grade teachers in effective schools', Paper presented at the National Reading Conference, Phoenix, December.

Taylor, B.M. and Pearson, P.D. (eds) (2002) *Teaching Reading: Effective Schools, Accomplished Teachers*. Mahwah, NJ: Erlbaum.

Taylor, B.M., Pearson, D.P., Clark, K.F., and Walpole, S. (1999) 'Effective schools/accomplished teachers', *The Reading Teacher*, 53(2): 156–9.

Taylor, B.M., Anderson, R.C., Au, K.H., and Raphael, T. (2000a) 'Discretion in the translation of research to policy: A case from beginning reading', *Educational Researcher*, 29(6): 16–26.

Taylor, B.M., Pearson, P.D., Clark, K., and Walpole, S. (2000b) 'Effective schools and accomplished teachers: Lessons about primary-grade reading instruction in low-income schools', *The Elementary School Journal*, 101(2): 121–65.

Taylor, B.M., Pearson, P.D., Peterson, D., and Rodriquez, M. (2005) 'The CIERA school change framework: An evidence based approach to professional development and school reading improvement', *Reading Research Quarterly*, 40: 1.

Taylor, B., Raphael, T., and Au, K. (2011) 'Reading and school reform', in M. Kamil, D. Pearson, E. Birr Moje, and P. Afflerbach (eds), *Handbook of Reading Research*. New York: Routledge. pp. 594–628.

Teale, W., Paciga, K., and Hoffman, J. (2010) 'What it takes in early schooling to have adolescents who are skilled and eager readers and writers', in K. Hall, U. Goswami, C. Harrison, S. Ellis, and J. Soler (eds), *Interdisciplinary Perspectives on Learning to Read: Culture, Cognition and Pedagogy*. London: Routledge. pp. 151–63.

Tharp, R.G. (1982) 'The effective instruction of comprehension: Results and description of the Kamehameha Early Education Program', *Reading Research Quarterly*, 17(4): 503–27.

Topping, K. and Ferguson, N. (2005) 'Effective literacy teaching behaviours', *Journal of Research in Reading*, 28(2): 125–43.

Weber, C., Raphael, T., and Goldman, S. (2009) 'Literacy coaches: Multiple issues, multiple roles, multiple approaches, *available at http://www.schoolriseusa.com/SRPublic/researcharticles/LiteracyCoaches.pdf*. Accessed 9/5/2012

Wenger, E. (1998) *Communities of Practice: Learning, Meaning, and Identity*. New York: Cambridge University Press.

Wharton-McDonald, R., Pressley, M., Rankin, J., Mistretta, J., Yokai, L., and Ettenberger, S. (1997) 'Effective primary-grades literacy instruction = balanced literacy instruction', *The Reading Teacher*, 50: 518–21.

Wharton-McDonald, R., Pressley, M., and Hampston, J.M. (1998) 'Literacy instruction in nine first-grade classrooms: Teacher characteristics and student achievement', *Elementary School Journal*, 99(2): 101–28.

Wilkinson, I.A., and Townsend, M.A. (2000) 'From Rata to Rimu: Grouping for instruction in best practice New Zealand classrooms', *The Reading Teacher*, 53(6): 460–71.

Wray, D., Medwell, J., Fox, R., and Poulson, L. (2001) 'The teaching practices of effective teachers of literacy', *Educational Review*, 52(1): 75–84.

30

Creating Positive Literacy Learning Environments in Early Childhood: Engaging Classrooms, Creating Lifelong Readers, Writers and Thinkers

Eithne Kennedy

I think deep in my brain ... I think all the while during my life. When I just get the best one, the best one for my story, I'll go yeah, I'll use that.

(Fergus, aged 6)

You think what the book is going to be called and then you think what people are going to be in it or is there going to be a dog in it or a haunted girl or a happy ending or maybe it doesn't work out in the end.

(Linda, aged 7)

I find I am learning as he's learning. It's actually broadened his outlook a little bit ... information things that you wouldn't even think about, say dinosaurs. (Parent, child Year 2)

(Kennedy, 2008)

As literacy educators what is it that we are after? Against what benchmark do we measure success? For me as a literacy educator, success would entail every child emerging from primary school as a confident, engaged reader, writer and independent thinker, with high expectations for themselves and their futures and the tools, persistence and confidence to achieve their highest aspirations and fullest potential regardless of their cultural or socio-economic background. For that to happen, we need to think deeply about how we conceptualise literacy, how we teaching literacy, how we organise our classrooms, what we prioritise in our classrooms and what messages either consciously or subconsciously we convey to children about what it means to be literate.

In the opening quotes above, we can hear the energy and voice of these young learners as they discuss their writing.

Fergus, we can see, has internalised some key messages about writing. Good writers write from their own experiences about which they can write more authentically. They dig deep into their reservoir of thoughts, feelings and life events to find a topic of real concern that has the possibility of reaching out and touching the universal chord in each of us. It is the pursuit of the single fingerprint which draws us back time and again to our favourite authors, poets, playwrights, songwriters and filmmakers. With Linda we can hear the vigour in her voice as she articulates how one goes about writing fiction; and can see that she has a very good understanding of how one creates an interesting story. In the final quote, we hear a parent note how reading has broadened her son's outlook and had an impact on her own learning. If I was the teacher in that classroom I would take satisfaction in the knowledge that I had facilitated a creative nurturing dynamic environment and all the more so given that these voices are those of children and families located in a high-poverty community, whom the research tells us are often performing well below their potential in literacy (Eivers et al., 2004; Gamse, Bloom, Kemple, and Jacob, 2008; DCSF, 2010).

When positive literacy environments are created in schools they can induct children into a life of reading and writing, which can spill out beyond the walls of the school and into children's homes and extended families, and in so doing create whole communities of readers and writers. How well are we doing on reaching this vision of every child a reader, a writer, a thinker? To what extent are we succeeding in creating the kinds of powerful positive literacy environments that can make a real difference to children's and families' literacy development? This chapter reflects on the research that gives us insights into how positive literacy environments can be successfully designed and implemented. The kinds of literacy resources and physical environments that are critical to the development of early literacy skills are considered. The kinds of literacy contexts and adult interactions that foster critical and creative literacy skills are explored. Also considered are some of the barriers and potential blocks that can work against the development of effective literacy environments including policy, home and school factors and teacher knowledge for literacy.

DEFINING LITERACY

A first concern in creating a positive literacy environment is considering what it means to be literate in the twenty-first century. For what we believe literacy to be influences how we shape our classrooms, how we use instructional time and the kinds of literacy materials and experiences we provide for our students. Current definitions of literacy espouse a broad and rich vision, acknowledging that literacy extends far beyond print-based text to include visual, spoken, multimodal and digital forms. A new early years' framework *Aistear* (National Council for Curriculum and Assessment, NCCA, 2009) recently introduced in Ireland, defines literacy as being:

> ... more than having the ability to read and write. It is about helping children to communicate with others and to make sense of the world. It includes oral and written language and other sign systems such as mathematics, art, sound, pictures, Braille, sign language and music. Literacy also acknowledges the nature of information communication technology, and many other forms of representation relevant to children including screen-based (electronic games, computers, the internet, television)
>
> (NCCA: 56)

This definition embraces a semiotic perspective which recognises the multiple modalities that young children utilise to communicate and represent their thinking and learning (Hill and Nichols, 2009; Bodrova and Leong, 2006). The Progress in International Reading Literacy Study (PIRLS) conducted with 4th grade pupils defines literacy as the:

> ability to understand and use those written language forms required by society and/or valued by the individual. Young readers can construct meaning from a variety of texts. They read to learn, to participate in communities of readers in school and in everyday life, and for enjoyment
> (Mullis, Martin, Kennedy, and Foy, 2007: 103)

The Programme for International Student Assessment (PISA) conducted with 15-year-olds by the Organisation for Economic Co-operation and Development (OECD) define literacy as 'understanding, using, and reflecting on written texts, in order to achieve one's goals, to develop one's knowledge and potential, and to participate in society' (OECD, 2010: 37).

In these definitions, we see an emphasis on literacy as a meaning-making and enjoyable activity which an individual chooses to engage in, in order to construct knowledge, to create, to communicate, to reflect, to empathise, to critique and to appreciate, within social communities of practice either within the ecology of the classroom or in the wider community. When literacy is conceptualised in this way, it is a tool for personal empowerment which can facilitate full participation in society and the fulfilment of personal goals. When schools truly embrace literacy in all its forms, they develop environments that recognise and value these dimensions of literacy and provide opportunities for children to develop the creative, emotional and aesthetic dimensions as well as the cognitive skills and strategies to be successful

readers, writers, thinkers and creators (Kennedy, in press). This view is consistent with an emergent literacy perspective which emphasises literacy as developing along a continuum and which includes the 'skills, knowledge and attitudes that are presumed to be developmental precursors to conventional forms of reading and writing' (Whitehurst and Lonigan, 1998: 849).

PROMOTING LEARNING THROUGH MOTIVATION, ENGAGEMENT, SELF-EFFICACY AND SELF-REGULATION

A wide and varied literature exists which has investigated the various dimensions of motivation, engagement, self-efficacy and self-regulation and their influence and impact on children's learning in general and more recently on children's literacy development. This body of research acknowledges that a concentration on cognitive skills alone such as those identified by the National Reading Panel (NRP; NICHHD, 2000) (phonological awareness, phonics, fluency, vocabulary, comprehension) is not enough to ensure development in literacy, rather affective factors are also powerful mediators of the learning process and of children's literacy development in particular.

Fredericks, Blumenfeld, and Paris (2004), in a timely review of the literature have argued for a broad definition in order to capture the range and complexity of the construct and to bring clarity to the field given that the terms motivation and engagement are often used interchangeably in the literature. From their reading of the literature, they see engagement as a meta-construct encompassing cognitive, emotional and behavioural elements, each of which plays an important role in learning. Behavioural engagement relates to the level of involvement and participation that a child devotes to a given task and includes the effort, concentration, persistence and interaction required to complete it successfully while emotional engagement refers to the response of the child to the task which can range from positive to negative (e.g., interested, excited, bored or anxious). Cognitive engagement has a number of dimensions which are also on a continuum from highly desirable to less desirable: motivation to learn which can be intrinsic or extrinsic; the setting of goals which can range from mastery goals to performance goals and the deployment or not of meta-cognitive strategies such as planning, rehearsing, monitoring and evaluating progress required to successfully achieve a goal. Drawing on socio-constructivist theories of learning, others have argued convincingly for the addition of a fourth element, 'social engagement', highlighting that learning is also mediated by the socio-cultural environment of the classroom (Lutz, Guthrie, and Davis, 2006). Engagement, then, is multi-dimensional and important for learning, but it is also influenced by other constructs such as expectancy-value (Eccles et al., 1983) and self-efficacy theory (Bandura, 1995). Bandura (1995: 2) defines self-efficacy as: 'beliefs in one's capabilities to organize and execute the courses of action required to manage prospective situations. Efficacy beliefs influence how people think, feel, motivate themselves and act.'

Thus, the value placed on a particular task, the attractiveness of the task and the kind of reward expected for engaging in it, as well as a person's perceived level of competency to complete it, dictate the level of engagement and persistence an individual may be willing to invest in it. It is clear that these constructs are key drivers of children's learning and can work synergistically to enhance or impede the development of the child as a learner who has 'developed expertise in a variety of areas, who can self-regulate his or her own learning and motivation and adjust accordingly, and who is able to perform to the best of his or her ability' (Rueda, 2011: 8). Rueda suggests that the success of the school in attaining the goal of every child an expert, engaged and self-regulated learner is contingent on three variables, each of which are of equal importance and each of which are influenced by the wider social and cultural context: 1) levels of teacher and student knowledge and skill; 2) teacher and student motivation; 3) organisational and contextual factors.

How then might these constructs be used in relation to literacy to ensure children develop the positive dispositions and habits of mind to become life-long readers, writers and creators? What principles are important for schools and educators to consider as they set about planning, designing and implementing literacy environments and classroom frameworks for effective stimulating literacy teaching and learning?

LITERACY PRACTICES FOR DEVELOPING ENGAGED LIFE-LONG READERS AND WRITERS

Research indicates a variety of ways in which educators can create a classroom environment which signals a value and priority on literacy and which fosters real engagement in literacy while simultaneously building literacy skills. As Roskos and Neuman (2003: 281) note, the 'features, organisational structures, props and materials influence the types, quality and complexity of activity for children'. Thus, it follows that we can optimise learning by considering carefully the physical arrangement of the room, the choice of resources and materials provided and the kinds of activities and pedagogies utilised.

Positive literacy environments in early years' settings

Access to books

Providing an up-to-date library filled with a wide range of genres matched to children's interests and stages of development is vital. In early-childhood classrooms, early studies such as that of Morrow and Weinstein (1986) found that when library corners were re-designed the frequency with which children chose to visit and use the library increased significantly. This occurred as a result of four changes to the space: 1) delineating the space and enlarging it to accommodate up to seven children; 2) providing comfortable chairs and private nooks with soft furnishings and within the space; 3) displaying books in ways that invited browsing; 4) providing additional props such as listening posts, and writing materials. More recent research also highlights the benefits of a defined literacy space in creating a sense of a literate community within the classroom e.g. Calkins (2003) advocates equipping the space with child-friendly book shelves, an armchair and soft furnishings such as lamps and cushions so that a homely, comfortable and inviting space is created where children and teacher can gather to have literary conversations about the books they are reading and the texts they are writing.

Play environments

Other researchers (Makin, 2003) have been concerned with setting up authentic play environments in early childhood classrooms (e.g., nurseries, child care centres and pre-kindergarten) which mirror real-life situations (e.g., a grocery [Hall, 1987]; a flower shop and a bank [Vukelich, 1991]; a veterinarian's surgery [Morrow, 1990]; an office, library and post-office [Neuman and Roskos, 1992]), and in providing a range of literacy props which would be used in these familiar settings (e.g., signage, labels, writing tools, books appropriate to the setting, cash register, receipts, instructions, withdrawal slips, forms, prescriptions) with a view to investigating their impact on children's engagement, interaction and, language and literacy development. Typically in these kinds of studies, children are observed prior to the intervention and pre- and post-data are compared. Results from this line of research indicate many positive effects including: increased frequency of literacy acts (pretend reading and writing), increased complexity in play as children moved from exploration to more mature play and increased mastery of language routines used in the setting. Bodrova and Leong (2006) outline the important signifiers of mature play as: 1) the child uses any object to signify a real object and uses gestures to represent actions (e.g., a stick as a horse); 2) ability to sustain the actions, speech and interactions associated with a role; 3) the ability to follow rules in relation to the play scenario and character; and 4) the integration of several themes sustained over several days or weeks. They voice a word of caution in relation to adding artefacts to the play environment, recommending that children have ample prior opportunity to gain experience by first taking on roles, exploring unstructured materials and engaging in extended language opportunities (Bodrova and Leong, 2006).

Those who espouse a Vygotskian perspective on play advocate making provision for make-believe play or socio-dramatic play to occur (Bodrova and Leong, 2006). According to Vygotsky, make-believe play is characterised by three main conditions: children create an imaginary situation, take on and act out roles, and follow the rules associated with the roles. He cited it as one of the social contexts for creating children's 'zone of proximal development (ZPD)' (Vygotsky, 1978: 74). Thus, it is a mechanism for 'propelling child development forward' (Bodrova, 2008: 359). In this view of play, the teacher creates flexible spaces and provides a range of materials which children can combine to signify objects or make their own literacy artefacts as they adopt roles within their imaginary play scenario either alone or with peers. In collaborative make-believe play, children are exercising power and agency and learning to consciously self-regulate and exercise restraint as they are called upon to use language in new and complex ways and to negotiate and compromise with peers within the confines of the roles and rules of the game (Roskos and Christie, 2007; Wood, 2009). Bodrova, analysing Vygotsky's theories, notes that:

> for children of preschool and kindergarten age, their mastery of academic skills is not as good a predictor of their later scholastic abilities as the quality of their play. In a four-year old's play one can observe higher levels of such abilities as attention, symbolizing, and problem solving than in other situations-one can actually see the child of tomorrow.
>
> (2008: 360)

In addition to supporting development of these higher mental functions critical for learning, make-believe play has been shown to impact positively on children's literacy in relation to oral language development, the development of meta-linguistic awareness, the development of the imagination and an understanding of the authentic purposes of reading and writing (Bodrova, 2008: 362–3). Research has also linked play and oral language development with later reading achievement (Dickinson and Tabors, 2001).

Adult interaction

Of course it is not a simple matter of planning a thoughtful and stimulating play environment and providing a range of material and supplies; what is also of critical importance is the interaction that occurs with a knowledgeable and responsive adult who can intervene and scaffold a child's learning within the play environment. Research has attempted to explore the nature of these interactions and to discover how children's development may be best supported (Morrow and Schickedanz, 2006). Interesting research conducted in Russia by Smirnova and Gudarev (2004, cited in Bodrova, 2008) presents evidence that the level of self-regulation of today's 7-year-olds is more like that of pre-schoolers in the 1940s. The decline was attributed to the reduction in quantity and quality of play in pre-schools and kindergartens. Vygotskians view play as a cultural–historical phenomenon, therefore changes in the socio-cultural context contribute to changes in children's level of play. Bodrova (2008), summarising research into changes in children's play experiences, notes a number of factors which affect the quality of play: the increase in adult-directed forms of children's learning and recreation, the increase in toys and games which limit children's imaginations, safety limits set by teachers and parents in relation to what children are allowed to do in play and the decrease in adult-mediation of make-believe play. Bodrova (2008) calls for high-quality pre-school programmes and cites research (Bodrova and Leong, 2001, 2003; Barnett et al., 2006) which indicates that intentional scaffolding in make-believe play should be encouraged and that when it is provided sensitively it can support the development of mature play, the characteristics of which have been outlined earlier. Adults can support children's play 'modelling, demonstrating skills, playing, talking, problem-setting and problem-solving, inventing with the child, engaging in shared thinking' (Wood, 2009) about how to use tools and materials to build knowledge.

Story book reading

While play is one way in which children develop literacy in authentic ways other methods include story book reading and discussion. With very young children educators can promote engagement and understanding by providing literacy props and toys related to the story for children to hold during the reading (Rowe, 2007). In her study of middle-class 2- and 3-year-olds, children were seen to look for and use these toys in subsequent re-readings of the story and in their own play scenarios. Rowe suggests that book-related dramatic play during this emergent stage of reading builds the kinds of reader responses of conventional readers: 'dramatic play may be seen not only as a context for reflecting on books, but also an important part of children's reading and response processes' (2007: 57). Shared reading practices that are dialogic in nature support children's oral language development, with positive effects found in relation to grammar, vocabulary knowledge and listening comprehension which in turn, correlate with later reading comprehension (NELP, 2008). Dialogic reading is more interactive than other forms of read-aloud and the adult intentionally involves the child in the story by asking questions about elements of the story and pictures and by modelling answers and helping children to expand their thinking. New vocabulary is best dealt with in playful and conversational ways with many opportunities to repeat and use the new words (Harris, Golinkoff, and Hirsch-Pasek, 2011). In this way, children are intellectually and linguistically challenged as educator and child co-construct meaning and respond to text. Dickinson and Tabors (2001) advocate a range of behaviours to maximise the benefit of dialogic reading which include previewing the book, encouraging predictions and personal connections to build empathy with characters, questioning motive and plot, encouraging an emotional response to text, encouraging children to ask questions and encouraging children to notice new words and to use them in conversation.

Emergent writing

Positive literacy environments in early childhood also include opportunities for children to express themselves through drawing, painting and other multi-modal responses. These are all forms of early writing as children express their thoughts and ideas and response to experiences by putting marks on paper in a way that conveys their inner thoughts and emotions. Providing choice and control over form of mark-making builds motivation and engagement and allows children to enhance the depth and richness of their ideas (Kress, 1997). Involving children in discussions about their drawings and mark making conveys the important message to them that writing, painting and drawing are primarily about communicating and meaning making. It is a useful strategy for understanding children's emergent writing (Hall, 2010). For Vygotsky, writing was a cultural tool to be used to communicate with others, the self and as a mental tool to clarify ideas. This in his view was the goal of instruction in writing: 'to teach a child written language and not writing the alphabet' (Vygotsky, 1983/1997: 147, cited in Bodrova, 2008). Further, it can be noted that for Vygotsky '...make believe play, drawing and writing can be viewed as different moments of written language ...' (1978: 116).

Impact of literacy environments

A longitudinal study in the UK, the Effective Pre-School and Primary Education project (EPPE) has been tracking the influence of emergent literacy environments (both home and pre-school) on children's literacy development at age 5, 7 and 11 (Sylva et al., 2011), recognising that the quality of the environment and socialisation of the child are important mediators of children's learning. Baseline data on children's cognitive and linguistic development was gathered (BAS-11 Verbal and Nonverbal skills), letter recognition and phonological awareness (Bryant and Bradley, 1985; National Curriculum Assessments in Years 2 and 6) as well as evidence on the quality of children's home literacy environment (HLE) measured through in-depth interviews with parents while the quality of preschool literacy environments was measured by the ECERS-R (Early Childhood Environment Rating Scale – Revised; Harms, Clifford, and Cryer, 2005) and ECERS-E (Early Childhood Environment Rating Scale – Extension; Sylva, et al., 2011). High-quality home literacy environments (being read to, painting and drawing, visiting the library, playing with letters/numbers, learning activities with letters/numbers/songs and poems) and a high-quality preschool environment (as measured by ECERS-R/ECERS-E) were found to provide children with a strong start to formal school with better code-related and oral language skills

and to have the strongest positive benefit to children's later literacy development in Year 6 (effect sizes [ES] = 0.61) while high-quality HLE were able to compensate for attendance at low-quality pre-schools (ES = 0.37) indicating the important influence of the home. The power and long-term effects of early environments are clearly demonstrated in this study but the challenge remains to make them a reality for all children.

Literacy practices in early primary school

As children move toward conventional literacy development the shape of the literacy environment changes accordingly in order to maximise motivation, engagement, self-efficacy and self-regulation. Positive literacy environments in kindergarten through third grade are developed within a balanced literacy framework which balances skills and strategy development within authentic literacy experiences such as guided and independent reading and writing within reading and writing workshops.

Access to books

High-quality literacy classrooms are immediately discernible upon entry and are 'suffused by literary richness' (Knapp et al., 1995), characterised by visual displays of children's learning and libraries filled with a diversity of reading materials (500 or more), including novels (e.g., realistic, fantasy, science-fiction, historical-fiction, adventure, classics, myths and legends, fairytales), informational texts, picture books, comics, graphic novels, poetry, encyclopaedias and reference material (Lipson, Mosenthal, Mekkelson, and Russ, 2004) at a variety of levels ranging from easy to challenging. Children need to be introduced to this wide range of books and encouraged to explore them and so begin to establish a literacy identity. They should be taught how to choose a 'just right book' (Calkins, 2001: 122) which reflects their interests and is within their ZPD (Vygotsky, 1978: 74). Gambrell (2007) recommends providing for 'bounded choice' by establishing browsing boxes for children which are colour coded according to difficulty level. Scaffolding of book choice is critical and communicates powerful messages to children that reading is about constructing meaning from text and not just about decoding words (Kennedy, 2009).

Culture of reading

Provision of books for independent reading is one thing; promoting a culture of reading both inside school and outside is another. This can be facilitated by providing time for daily independent reading in school, by providing a range of books for children to take home and by providing time for children to discuss their choices. Access to books and providing choice and control over reading material promotes curiosity and involvement in reading, which are characteristics of intrinsically motivated readers (Guthrie, 1996). Gambrell (1996) in a study designed to investigate the reading motivation of first, third and fifth graders noted that 80 per cent of children in that study reported that the books they enjoyed the most were the ones they had self-selected. Teachers can act as role models for children, sharing their reading preferences and leading children towards new genres and authors, thus widening their horizons (Cremin, Mottram, Collins, and Powell, 2008). Promoting reading for fun is a critical factor in encouraging children to develop a literacy history where they will weave literacy into their lives each and

every day and continue to build their literacy knowledge. For children who do not read, a Matthew effect (Stanovich, 1986) appears, as children who read avidly have more sophisticated vocabulary, syntax and comprehension than their peers who do not. They are intrinsically motivated, set their own mastery goals and have an appetite for challenge (Guthrie, McRae, and Lutz Klauda, 2007). They have a positive self-concept believing that they can be successful at the challenges they set for themselves so are more likely to persist and succeed and as a result their sense of self-efficacy grows. Recent PISA results (OECD, 2010) indicate that 42 per cent of 15-year-olds report never reading for fun and the difference in their scores on PISA compared to those who reported reading for an hour a day was large (100 point difference). Access to books is also a critical mediator as large achievement differences were also noted amongst children who had access to more than 500 books in the home compared to children who had access to fewer than 10 (100 points also), highlighting the importance of high-quality classroom libraries, particularly in schools located in areas of low socio-economic power where access to books may be problematic. Encouraging children to take books home in these contexts can make an important contribution to family literacy as children share books with siblings and parents. An infusion of books, explicit attention to reading materials and providing time for high-quality discussion creates an environment where reading is seen as a most desirable activity (Kennedy, 2008) and, as Knapp et al. (1995) noticed in their observations of high-poverty classrooms which promoted reading as a meaning-making activity, children were seen to be reading even when they should not have been.

Reading and writing workshops

As children grow in confidence, it is important to match them to books at an instructional level for small-group guided reading instruction, which they can read with a large degree of accuracy, fluency and expression. Successful experiences with print builds children's self-concept and allows them to 'integrate complex skills and strategies into an automatic, independent reading process' (Allington, 2002: 743). Introducing children to progressively more challenging reading material as the year advances 'ups the ante' (Pressley, Allington, Wharton-McDonald, Collins Block, and Mandel Morrow, 2001), helping children develop stamina and skills while providing optimal challenge; all of which are associated with high levels of engagement (Fredericks et al., 2004) and with the practices of effective teachers of literacy (see Hall, K., this volume). It is important that children have access to a wide range of fiction and informational texts within their guided reading workshops so that they have opportunities to build their knowledge of text structures (Goldman and Rakestraw, 2000), vocabulary and 'word-consciousness' (Neuman, 2011; Graves and Watts-Taft, 2002; Beck, McKeown, and Kucan, 2002) in order to build their power to respond to and create increasingly more complex texts.

Giving genuine control and autonomy to children to direct their learning enhances engagement (Jeffrey and Woods, 2003). Writing workshops (Graves, 1994; Calkins, 2003) facilitate this as children choose topics they are interested in writing about and so their sense of agency is fostered (Cremin and Myhill, 2011). Writing workshops provide opportunities for children to 'demonstrate their creativity, individuality, voice and verve' (Grainger, Goouch, and Lambirth, 2005: 1). As they mine their experiences for worthwhile topics, their sense of 'voice' (Graves, 1994) is nurtured, which in turn develops a positive self-concept. As Graves notes:

> voice is the imprint of ourselves on writing. It is the part of the writing that pushes the writing ahead, the dynamo in the process ... voice is the engine that sustains writers through the hard work of drafting and redrafting.

Within writing workshops children learn the craft of writing by apprenticing themselves to real authors, as teachers explicitly model and demonstrate techniques. They begin to notice 'rich, precise, interesting and inventive use of words' (Graves and Watts-Taft, 2002: 150) within their reading material and begin to see how important the apt use of language is for writing so that readers may visualise and connect with their written texts.

Interaction within workshops

Positive literacy environments are cultivated through the kinds of interaction that is prioritised within reading and writing workshops and which sends powerful messages to children about what it means to be a member of a literate community. When teachers prioritise high-level discussion of texts within literature circles (e.g., Daniels, 2002), inquiry-based learning groups (e.g., Guthrie, Wigfield, and Perencevich, 2004), and reciprocal teaching routines (Palinscar and Brown, 1984; Oczkus, 2003), children learn to transact with text from the outset and have opportunities to learn through language. They learn that reading is thinking work, thinking about the big ideas in the text, learning new vocabulary, discovering new ideas, building conceptual knowledge and, learning about what it is to be human.

Conversational structures are put in place to support 'reader response' (Rosenblatt, 1978) as children respond aesthetically and critically to a text learning to question, wonder, agree and disagree, critique, evaluate, synthesise, to give their own interpretation and to have the confidence to do so. Teachers who facilitate this kind of interaction are laying the foundations for the higher-order thinking skills so valued in the adult world: the inquiring mind, the critical evaluative mind, the synthesising mind and the creative mind (Kennedy, 2011). These kinds of conversations do not occur naturally and require teachers who can model and demonstrate the art of conversation, scaffolding high-level oral language discourse amongst children before expecting them to lead and guide discussions themselves (Shanahan et al., 2010; Mills and Jennings, 2011). Likewise in writing workshops, the social dimension of learning (Guthrie and Anderson, 1999; Allington, 2002) can be facilitated as children work to generate ideas, plan, draft, revise and publish. Opportunities for collaboration can be provided as children work together on texts which can be particularly helpful for the child who is reluctant to write. Teachers can respond to children and scaffold development by providing thoughtful feedback through daily conferences as children engage in the act of writing. Share sessions can be powerful motivators for children as they see and hear their peers' responses to their writing (Graves, 1994) and discover ways to hone their own scripts. As Guthrie and Anderson (1999: 36) note, 'when students can talk to each other about their writing, they learn an acute sense of audience and authorship'. These kinds of focused literary conversations are at the heart of reading and writing workshops and are particularly important experiences for children in high-poverty

schools, as research suggests children in these schools require explicit support in acquiring the 'literate style' of language required in school (Cregan, 2007). Drawing on socio-cultural theories of learning, responsive teachers are able to bridge the world of home and school (Feiler et al., 2007) and communicate to children that the 'funds of knowledge' (Gonzalez, Moll, and Amanti, 2005) they possess are important and useful. As Knapp et al. (1995: 92) in their study of the level of meaning-oriented instruction provided by teachers in high-poverty schools: 'the key factor was the degree to which teachers communicated to students that their home lives – however different those lives might be – were a respected, welcomed and valuable part of the classroom discourse, both written and otherwise'.

Another critical component of interaction in positive literacy environments is the manner in which skills and strategies are handled. Teachers carefully monitor children's reading and writing, teaching skills and strategies when children demonstrate a need and a readiness for them. Research indicates that using a gradual release of responsibility model (Pearson and Gallagher, 1983; Duke and Pearson, 2002) is an effective means of teaching skills, particularly reading comprehension strategies (Shanahan et al., 2010). By explaining why the strategy is important to learn, explicitly modelling the strategy in action through a think-aloud, providing guided and scaffolded practice in pairs and small groups, before moving to independent practice and finally guiding children to reflect on the learning and set goals for future use of the strategy, teachers are supporting children in developing metacognitive awareness to the conditional level (Paris, Lipson, and Wixson, 1994). This suggests that children are aware of the strategy (declarative knowledge), know how to carry it out (procedural knowledge), and most critically, know when and why a strategy is used (conditional knowledge), indicating a level of self-regulation in that they can choose when they will use the strategy. Teaching strategies to this level empowers children and builds their self-concept as they call upon and activate strategies as needed, to succeed at complex tasks when working independently. As Bandura points out 'successes build a robust belief in one's personal efficacy' (1995: 3). Strategy knowledge in reading comprehension, writing processes and word identification promotes academic independence and supports persistence and resilience and is of particular benefit to lower- achievers (Taylor, Pearson, Peterson, and Rodriguez, 2003; Knapp et al., 1995).

For creativity to flourish and deep excavation of texts to occur, blocks of time are needed to allow for what Csíkszentmihályi (1978, in Wigfield and Guthrie, 1997) calls 'flow experience' (Csíkszentmihályi, 1978: 3), a loss of awareness of time passing as one loses oneself in a story or become absorbed in a challenging task. This means that we must reconsider how we distribute and use time in the classroom. Research indicates that time is often wasted in classrooms, e.g., on managerial tasks or on isolated skills. Allington (2002) contends from his observations of classrooms, that in the more typical classrooms, the 90-minute block may only translate into 15 minutes of reading of whole texts, whereas in the classrooms of exemplary teachers children spend a lot of time reading connected text in a range of contexts, e.g., shared reading, guided reading or independent reading (see Hall, K., this volume).

Balancing skills and strategy with meaning-oriented approaches to literacy is a characteristic of the most effective teachers of literacy (see Hall, K., this volume), but most importantly it conveys very different messages to children about what it means to be literate. Skills and strategies embedded within authentic literacy activities as children engage in deep explorations of a text or spend time crafting and creating their own within writing workshops convey to children that reading and writing are ultimately meaning-making activities. In this environment skills and strategies are kept in perspective, are seen as tools to be mastered in order to read and create more complex texts. Teachers spend more time on unconstrained skills (Paris, 2005) which continue to develop across the life span (e.g., vocabulary, comprehension and writing) than on constrained skills (e.g., phonics and punctuation) which once mastered contribute little to further development. Unfortunately, this kind of instruction is not the norm, particularly for children who struggle with literacy or children attending high-poverty schools where unwittingly teachers can spend more time on discrete skills than on meaningful activities, since it is often the basic skills that children struggle with (Duke, 2001). This is despite evidence that a meaning-oriented approach is more effective (Knapp et al., 1995) and more intellectually challenging and engaging (Kennedy and Shiel, 2010).

Challenges and opportunities to establishing positive learning environments

Policy

In the literacy field, over the past 15 years or so there has been a major emphasis on educational reform in many countries including the US (No Child Left Behind, 2001, www.ed.gov/policy), the UK (National Literacy Strategy, Department for Education and Employment (DfEE), 1998) and Ireland (National Literacy and Numeracy Strategy, Department of Education and Skills (DES), 2011). Systematic reviews and meta-analyses of the research on literacy (NRP, NICHHD, 2000; Eurydice, 2011; Hall and Harding, 2003), and early literacy in particular (NELP, 2008; *What Works Clearinghouse Guide*; Shanahan et al., 2010; DfES, 2006), have identified essential skills and effective teaching practices which have influenced policy initiatives that have had and continue to have far-reaching implications for how literacy is conceptualised and taught. Policy directives can invite new ways of thinking and support positive change in the system or they may impede progress or have unintended consequences.

While meta-analyses have their place represent an important body of knowledge about what we know to be effective in literacy, they also have many limitations. For example, the kinds of studies that can be included in meta-analyses must meet strict guidelines in order to be included and so important studies may be overlooked because they do not employ an experimental design. In addition, some reports like the NRP (NICHHD, 2000) had a narrow research brief and did not examine vital elements of literacy such as motivation, engagement, parental involvement and the teaching of writing, each of which is pivotal to literacy development. More worryingly, meta-analyses drive policy and particular messages are conveyed as to what counts for literacy instruction, despite the narrow conceptualisation of literacy in some of these reports. The message is given, that high levels of literacy can be achieved by concentrating on a particular skill set or by utilising particular methodologies.

In reality, we know that literacy teaching is highly complex and what counts is how skills are mediated in particular classrooms according to the needs of particular children in environments that are intellectually stimulating. As acknowledged by the International Reading Association (IRA, 2000, 2010) there is no one best way of teaching literacy, rather what matters is that teachers have a deep content knowledge, a repertoire of pedagogical strategies and assessment tools and the knowledge to know when and how to combine them in ways that capitalise on children's motivation ensuring they reach their full literacy potential. Mandating scientifically-based programmes reduces literacy to a set of skills to be mastered and denies the complexity involved and is no guarantee of success. A review of No Child Left Behind (Gamse et al., 2008) illustrated that while time spent on the essential skills of literacy as identified by the NRP (phonemic awareness, phonics, fluency, vocabulary and comprehension) had increased, there was not a statistically significant rise in reading comprehension scores.

The mandate to teach in a scientific manner has now been extended to preschools through the dissemination of recent reports and has resulted in increased pressure on early childhood educators to begin teaching literacy skills at an ever earlier age and not surprisingly has led to fears of a reductionist approach to practice (Roskos and Christie, 2007: 83): 'a new science-based perspective on early learning is starting to erode play's curricular status, raising the possibility that play-based activities will be pushed aside in favour of more direct forms of instruction to address the new basics ...'.

This trend is not seen in all countries and Ireland is a case in point. In 2009, the NCCA published *Aistear* (an Irish word meaning journey), a new framework which adopts a play-based pedagogy for learning in the early years, centred around important themes in children's lives and has put in place a team of co-ordinators to deliver in-service training to teachers across the country to support them in making changes to their classroom frameworks. Since the publication of the NELP report (2008) which has been subject to much critique (Teale, Hoffman, and Paciga, 2010; Neuman, 2010; Pearson and Hiebert, 2010; Dickinson, Golinkoff and Hirsch-Pasek, 2010), particularly for its narrow focus and privileging of code-based knowledge, there have been calls in the literature for a more balanced or blended approach. As Neuman so aptly puts it:

> Through no fault of this panel, this report, could be the subject of much mischief. There will be people out there who will apply these skills like a laundry list of what they should teach. They'll work on alphabetic knowledge, phonological awareness, phonological memory, rapid naming of random letters, and digits and colours and objects and they will confidently argue that they are teaching children to read. But they are not. What they are doing is exposing children to a set of narrow, largely procedural skills and training them to recite, mimic and repeat nonsense or what appear to be meaningless at the time.
>
> (2010: 303)

Such a narrow focus on literacy skills limits children's opportunities to develop rich vocabulary, conceptual knowledge, creativity and imagination through engagement in meaningful authentic contexts responsive to their interests and stages of development. It will exacerbate rather than ameliorate the pervasive knowledge gap that already exists before children walk in the school door (Neuman, 2006; Neuman and Celano, 2006) and it also runs counter to the beliefs and practices of our most effective literacy teachers (see Hall, K., this volume).

Knowledge and practice

What can we do counter this 'basic skills conspiracy of good intentions' (Pearson and Hiebert, 2010: 292)? It would seem we need to find a way to build every teacher's knowledge of the stages of development in literacy and strengthen their understanding of the theoretical and philosophical underpinnings so they may critique the knowledge base and use it as the 'grounds for their actions' (Shulman, 1987: 13). We have a long road to travel, particularly in relation to early years' classrooms, as research indicates large variation in the quality of literacy environments (Dunn and Beach, 2007; Sylva et al., 2011) and instructional programmes (Neuman, 2011; Neuman and Dwyer, 2009; Sylva et al., 2011) with many less than optimal for establishing a firm foundation for literacy in these critical years. Finding the right path to building teacher knowledge, beliefs and practices is vital, as teachers are critical decision-makers (Hall, 2002) and powerful enablers who can transform outcomes for all children but especially those most at risk for literacy underachievement. Creating and maintaining high-quality responsive literacy environments is more demanding than the implementation of a basic skills approach and as such requires high levels of expertise. Professional development initiatives for teachers are showing promise and the most effective ones take a multi-faceted approach to enhancing teacher expertise (e.g., Biancarosa, Bryk, and Dexter, 2010; Gehsmann and Woodside-Jiron, 2005; Kennedy, 2008, 2010b; Neuman and Cunningham, 2009) and acknowledge the importance of building teacher understandings of what it is to be reader and a writer (Cremin, 2006; Cremin, Mottram, Collins, Powell, and Safford, 2009; Cremin and Myhill, 2011). They promote a collaborative inquiry-as-stance (Cochran-Smith and Lytle, 2009) approach within the school, supporting teachers on-site as they analyse children's needs, set goals, experiment with new approaches and monitor their effectiveness in relation to children's achievement and engagement. They are cognisant of teacher autonomy, creativity, and the cognitive and affective dimensions which are important mediators in building teacher agency and in sustaining change long after the professional development ends. Just as we expect teachers to differentiate in the classroom, so too must professional development be customised to teachers' needs taking into consideration their current stage of career, qualifications and level of in-service in-career.

CONCLUSION

How we conceptualise literacy, our beliefs about how literacy develops and the level of our professional knowledge about literacy are key influences on the kinds of literacy environments we create. Literacy environments are powerful mediators of children's learning and can work to either support or impede their literacy development. It is important that early childhood classrooms are print-rich, support children to engage in several forms of play including make-believe play, literacy-enriched play, interactive storybook reading and make provision for emergent writing to occur. Such environments are likely to lead children to notice print, to experiment with print in multimodal ways and to develop language skills with the added advantage of being more motivating for children.

When we view children as agentic and capable of constructing and co-constructing meaning we provide choice and autonomy for them and create environments that allow them to satisfy their curiosity, develop imagination and self-regulation. A knowledgeable and supportive adult who can observe and scaffold interactions without being too intrusive can maximise children's early literacy development, laying the foundations for successful conventional literacy to develop which can have long-term benefits for children's later literacy attainment (Sylva et al., 2011).

As children move on to develop more conventional forms of literacy we want to build their literacy stamina by providing opportunities for them to build the 'unconstrained skills' (Paris, 2005) in literacy, including vocabulary (oral and written), comprehension and writing (composition). We know that simply including these skills is not enough; how they are differentiated according to the needs and stage of development of children is critical and how they are mediated within classrooms is also vital. If we want children to weave literacy into each and every day throughout their lives that means getting the message out early that reading and writing are desirable activities worth doing each and every day. It means providing opportunities for children to develop the creative, emotional and aesthetic dimensions of literacy as well as the cognitive skills and strategies to be successful readers, writers, thinkers and creators. It means teaching in ways that make reading and writing irresistible, desirable, meaningful and sociable activities. It means teaching in ways that hook children in, building their creativity and agency and stirring their curiosity about the world. This would send out the powerful message to children that reading and writing are tools to be harnessed in pursuit of knowledge, in the pursuit of their own interests, hopes, and dreams and not just isolated skills to be mastered in a linear fashion. The current shift in policy towards a more skills-based approach to literacy militates against the enactment of such a pedagogy. When we allow basic skills to dominate what counts for literacy in our classrooms in effect we are perpetuating social inequality, since it is the higher-order skills that are valued and needed for success and fulfilment in adult life and which provide the purpose and passion for engagement in literacy activities. If education is to realise its promise of equity and access for all we need to provide the kinds of interventions that will support all early childhood educators in developing the knowledge and skills to provide high-quality literacy environments for all children.

REFERENCES

Allington, R.L. (2002). 'What I've learned about effective reading instruction from a decade of studying elementary classroom teachers', *Phi Delta Kappan*, 83(10): 740–7.

Bandura, A. (1995). 'Exercise of personal and collective efficacy in changing societies', in A. Bandura (ed.), *Self-efficacy in Changing Societies*. Cambridge, UK: Cambridge University Press.

Barnett, W.S., D.J. Yarosz, J. Thomas, and A. Hornbeck (2006). *Educational effectiveness of a Vygotskian approach to preschool education: A randomized trial*. Rutgers, NJ: National Institute for Early Education Research.

Beck, I.L., McKeown, M.G., and Kucan, L. (2002). *Bringing Words to Life: Robust Vocabulary Instruction*. New York: Guilford Press.

Biancarosa, G., Bryk, A.S., and Dexter, E.R. (2010). 'Assessing the value-added effects of literacy collaborative professional development on student learning', *Elementary School Journal*, 111(1): 7–34.

Bodrova, A. (2008). 'Make-believe play versus academic skills: A Vygotskian approach to today's dilemma', *European Early Childhood Education Research Journal*, 16(3): 357–69.

Bodrova, E. and Leong, D.J. (2006). 'Vygotskian perspectives on teaching and learning early literacy', in S. Neuman and D. Dickinson (eds), *Handbook of Early Literacy Research*. Vol. 2. New York: Guilford Press. pp. 243–68.

Bodrova, E., and Leong, D.J. (2003). 'Learning and development of preschool children from the Vygotskian perspective', in A. Kozulin, B. Gindis, V. Ageyev and S. Miller(eds), *Vygotsky's educational theory in cultural context*. New York: Cambridge University Press. pp. 156–76.

Bodrova, E., and Leong, D.J. (2001). *The tools of the mind project: A case study of implementing the Vygotskian approach in American early childhood and primary classrooms*. Geneva, Switzerland: International Bureau of Education, UNESCO.

Bryant, P. and Bradley, L. (1985). *Children's Reading Problems*. Oxford, UK: Blackwell.

Calkins, L. M. (1986). *The Art of Teaching Writing*. Portsmouth, NH: Heinemann.

Calkins, L. M. (2001). *The Art of Teaching Reading*. New York: Addison Wesley.

Calkins, L.M. (2003). *Units of study for primary writing: A yearlong curriculum*. Portsmouth, NH: FirstHand.

Cochran-Smith, M. and Lytle, S.L. (2009). *Inquiry as Stance. Practitioner Research for a New Generation*. New York: Teachers' College Press.

Cregan, A. (2007). *From Difference to Disadvantage: 'Talking Posh' Sociolinguistic Perspectives on the Context of Schooling in Ireland*. Dublin: Combat Poverty Agency.

Cremin, T. (2006). 'Creativity, uncertainty and discomfort: Teachers as writers', *Cambridge Journal of Education*, 36(3): 415–33.

Cremin, T. and Myhill, D. (2011). *Writing Voices: Creating Communities of Writers*. London: Routledge

Cremin, T, Mottram, M., Collins, F., and Powell, S. (2008). *Building Communities of Readers*. Leicester, UK: PNS/United Kingdom Literacy Association.

Cremin, T., Mottram, M., Collins, F., Powell, S., and Safford, K. (2009). 'Teachers as readers: Building communities of readers', *Literacy*, 43(1): 11–19.

Daniels, H. (2002). *Literature Circles: Voice and Choice in Book Clubs and Reading Groups* (2nd ed.). Portland, ME: Stenhouse.

DES (Department of Education and Skills) (2011). *Literacy and Numeracy for Learning and Life. The National Strategy to Improve Literacy and Numeracy among Children and Young People*. Dublin: Government Publications.

DCSF (Department for Children Schools and Families) (2010). *Statistical First Release: Attainment by Pupil Characteristics in England*. www.dcsf.gov.uk

DfEE (Department for Education and Employment) (1998). *The National Literacy Strategy: Framework for Teaching.* London: DfEE.

DfES (Department for Education and Skills) (2006). *Independent Review of the Teaching of Early Reading.* London: DfES.

Dickinson, D. and Tabors, P. (2001). *Beginning Literacy with Language: Young Children Learning at Home and at School.* Baltimore, MD: Paul Brooks Publishing.

Dickinson, D., Golinkoff, R.M., and Hirsch-Pasek, K. (2010). 'Speaking out for language: Why language is central for learning development. Comment on the NELP Report', *Educational Researcher*, 39(4): 505–30.

Duke, N.K. (2001). 'Print environments and experiences offered to first-grade students in very low- and very high-SES school districts', *Reading Research Quarterly*, 35(4): 456–7.

Duke, N.K. and Pearson, D.P. (2002). 'Effective practices for developing comprehension', in A.E. Farstrup and S.J. Samuels (eds), *What the Research has to Say about Reading Instruction* (3rd ed.), Newark, DE: International Reading Association. pp. 205–42.

Dunn, L. and Beach, S.A. (2007). 'Supporting play and literacy in early childhood programs: Promising practices and continuing challenges', in K.A. Roskos and J.F. Christie (eds), *Play and Literacy in Early Childhood: Research from Multiple Perspectives* (2nd ed.). New Jersey: Lawrence Erlbaum Associates. pp. 101–18.

Eccles, J., Adler, T.F., Futterman, R., Goff, S.B., Kaczala, C.M., Meece, J., and Midgely, C. (1983). 'Expectancies, values, and academic behaviours', in J.T. Spence (ed.), *Achievement and Achievement Motives.* San Francisco, CA: W.H. Freeman. pp. 75–146.

Elliott, C.D., Smith, P. and McCulloch, K. (1996). *British Ability Scales-II administration and scoring manual.* Windsor, Uk: nferNelson

Eivers, E., Shiel, G., and Shortt, S. (2004). *Reading literacy in disadvantaged primary schools.* Dublin: Educational Research Centre.

Eurydice (2011). *Teaching Reading in Europe: Contexts, Policies and Practices.* Brussels: Education, Audiovisual and Culture Executive Agency.

Feiler, A., Andrews, J., Greenhough, P., Hughes, M., Johnson, D., Scanlan, M., and Yee, W. C. (2007). *Improving Primary Literacy: Linking Home and School.* London: Routledge.

Fredericks, J.A., Blumenfeld, P.C., and Paris, A.H. (2004). 'School engagement: Potential of the concept, state of the evidence', *Review of Educational Research*, 74(1): 59–109.

Gambrell, L.B. (1996). 'Creating classrooms that foster reading motivation', *The Reading Teacher*, 50(1): 14–25.

Gambrell, L.B. (2007). 'Keynote address' Reading Association of Ireland Conference. Rathmines, Dublin.

Gamse, B.C., Bloom, H.S., Kemple, J.J., and Jacob, R.T. (2008). *Reading First Impact Study: Interim Report* (NCEE 2008-4016). Washington, DC: National Center for Education Evaluation and Regional Assistance, Institute of Education Sciences, US Department of Education.

Gehsmann, K.M. and Woodside-Jiron, H.W. (2005). 'Becoming more effective in the age of school accountability: A high-poverty school narrows the literacy achievement gap', in B. Maloch, J. Hoffman, D.L. Schallert, C.M. Fairbanks, and J. Worthy (eds), *Fifty-fourth Yearbook of the National Reading Conference.* Oak Creek, WI: National Reading Conference. pp. 182–97.

Goldman, S.R. and Rakestraw, J.A. Jr (2000). 'Structural aspects of constructing meaning from text', in M.L. Kamil, P.B. Mosenthal, P.D. Pearson, and R. Barr (eds), *Handbook of Reading Research.* Vol. 3. New York: Erlbaum. pp. 311–36.

Gonzalez, N., Moll, L., and Amanti, C. (2005). *Funds of Knowledge: Theorizing Practices in Households, Communities and Classrooms.* London: Erlbaum.

Grainger, T., Goouch, K., and Lambirth, A. (2005). *Creativity and Writing, Developing Voice and Verve in the Classroom.* Abingdon, UK: Routledge.

Graves, D. (1994). *A Fresh Look at Writing.* Portsmouth, NH: Heinemann.

Graves, M. and Watts-Taft, S.M. (2002). 'The place of word consciousness in a research-based vocabulary programme', in A.E. Farstrup and S.J. Samuels (eds), *What the Research has to say About Reading Instruction* (3rd ed.). Newark, DE: International Reading Association. pp. 140–165.

Guthrie, J.T. (1996). 'Educational contexts for engagement in literacy', *The Reading Teacher*, 46(6), 432–45.

Guthrie, J.T. Anderson, E. (1999). 'Engagement in reading: Processes of motivated, strategic, knowledgeable, social readers', in J.T. Guthrie and D.E. Alvermann (eds), *Engaged Reading: Processes, Practices, and Policy Implications.* New York: Teachers' College Press. pp. 17–45.

Guthrie, J.T., Wigfield, A., and Perencevich, K.C. (2004). *Motivating Reading Comprehension: Concept-Oriented Reading Instruction.* Mahwah, NJ: Erlbaum.

Guthrie, J.T., McRae, A., and Lutz Klauda, S. (2007). 'Contributions of concept-oriented reading instruction to knowledge about interventions for motivations in reading', *Educational Psychologist*, 42(4): 237–50.

Hall, N. (1987). *The Emergence of Literacy*. Portsmouth, NH: Heinemann.

Hall, E. (2010). Identity and young children's drawings: Power, agency, control and transformation. In P. Broadhead, J. Howard & E. Wood (eds), *Play and Learning in the Early Years*. London: Sage. pp. 95–111.

Hall, K. (2002). 'Effective literacy teaching in the early years of school: A review of the evidence', in N. Hall, J. Larson, and J. Marsh (eds). *Handbook of Early Childhood Literacy*. London: Sage. pp. 315–26.

Hall, K., and Harding, A. (2003). *A Systematic Review of the Effective Literacy Teaching in the 4-14 Age Range of Mainstream Schooling*. London: EPPI-Centre, Social Science Research Unit, Institute of Education.

Harms, T., Clifford, R., and Cryer, D. (2005). *Early Childhood Environmental Rating Scale – Revised Edition (ECERS-R)*. New York: Teachers' College Press.

Harris, J., Golinkoff, R., and Hirsch-Pasek, K. (2011). 'Lessons from the crib: How children really learn vocabulary', in S. Neumann and D. Dickinson (eds), *Handbook of Early Literacy Research*. Vol. 3. New York: Guilford Press. pp. 49–65.

Hill, S. and Nichols, S. (2009). 'Multiple pathways between home and school literacies', in A. Anning, J. Cullen, and M. Fleer, *Early Childhood Education, Society and Culture*. London: Sage. pp. 169–84.

IRA (International Reading Association) (2000). *Using Multiple Methods of Beginning Reading Instruction: A Position Statement of the International Reading Association*. Newark, DE: International Reading Association.

IRA (International Reading Association) (2010). *Standards for Reading Professionals. Revised 2010*. Newark, DE: International Reading Association.

Jeffrey, B. and Woods, P. (2003). *The Creative School: A Framework for Success, Quality and Effectiveness*. London: Routledge Falmer.

Kennedy, E. (2008). 'Improving literacy achievement in a disadvantaged primary school; Empowering classroom teachers through professional development', Unpublished doctoral dissertation, St Patrick's College/Dublin City University, Dublin.

Kennedy, E. (2009). 'Literacy in disadvantaged schools: Policy and implementation issues', Commissioned paper: National Economic and Social Forum: Research report no.39: Child Literacy and Social Inclusion: Policy and Implementation Issues.

Kennedy, E. (2010). 'Improving literacy achievement in a high-poverty school: Empowering classroom teachers through professional development', *Reading Research Quarterly*, 45(4) pp. 384–87: Newark, DE: International Reading Association.

Kennedy, E. (2011). 'Envisioning schools where literacy thrives', Keynote address and webcast. Irish National Teachers Organisation Annual Education Conference, Athlone. Ireland.

Kennedy, E. (in press). *Raising Literacy Achievement in High-Poverty Schools: An Evidence-Based Approach*. New York : Routledge.

Kennedy, E. and Shiel, G. (2010). 'Raising literacy levels with collaborative on-site professional development in an urban disadvantaged school', *The Reading Teacher*, 63(5): Special Themed Issue on Urban Education, Newark, DE: International Reading Association. pp. 373–383

Knapp, M.S. and Associates (1995) *Teaching for Meaning in High-Poverty Classrooms*. New York: Teachers' College Press.

Kress, G. (1997). *Before Writing: Rethinking the Road to Literacy*. New York: Routledge.

Lipson, M.Y., Mosenthal, J.H., Mekkelson, J., and Russ, B. (2004). 'Building knowledge and fashioning success one school at a time', *The Reading Teacher*, 57(6): 534–45.

Lutz, S.L., Guthrie, J.T., and Davis, M.H. (2006). *Scaffolding for Engagement in Learning: an Observational Study of Elementary School Reading Instruction*. Retrieved from www.cori.umd.edu, February 2011.

Makin, L. (2003). 'Creating positive literacy learning environments in early childhood', in N. Hall, J. Larson, and J. Marsh (eds), *Handbook of Early Childhood Research*. London: Sage. pp. 327–37.

Mills, H. and Jennings, L. (2011). 'Talking about talk: Reclaiming the value and power of literature circles', *The Reading Teacher*, 64(8): 590–8.

Morrow, L.M. (1990). 'Preparing the classroom environment to promote literacy during play', *Early Childhood Research Quarterly*, 5: 537–54.

Morrow, L. and Schickedanz, J. (2006). 'The relationship between socio-dramatic play and literacy development', in S. Neuman and D. Dickinson (eds), *Handbook of Early Literacy Research*. Vol. 2. New York: Guilford Press. pp. 269–80.

Morrow, L.M. and Weinstein, C.S. (1986). 'Encouraging voluntary reading: The impact of literature programmes on children's use of library corners', *Reading Research Quarterly*, 21: 330–46.

Mullis, I.V.S., Martin, M.O., Kennedy, A.M., and Foy, P. (2007). *IEA's Progress in International Reading Literacy Study in Primary School in 40 Countries.* Chestnut Hill, MA: TIMSS and PIRLS International Study Center, Boston College.

NCCA (National Council for Curriculum and Assessment) (2009) *Aistear: The Framework for Early Learning.* Dublin: NCCA.

NELP (National Early Literacy Panel) (2008). 'Developing early literacy: Report of the national early literacy panel. A scientific synthesis of early literacy development and implications for intervention'. Jessup, MD: National Institute for Literacy.

NICHHD (National Institute of Child Health and Human Development) (2000). 'Report of the National Reading Panel. Teaching children to read: An evidence-based assessment of the scientific research literature on reading and its implications for reading instruction. Reports of the subgroups'. (NIH Publication No. 00-4769). Washington, DC: US Government Printing Office.

Neuman, S. (2011). 'The challenges of teaching vocabulary in early education', in S. Neuman and D. Dickinson (eds), *Handbook of Early Childhood Literacy.* Vol.3. New York: Guilford Press. pp. 358–72.

Neuman, S. (2010). 'Lesson from my mother: Reflections on the National Early Literacy Panel Report', *Educational Researcher,* 39: 301–3.

Neuman, S.B. (2006). 'The knowledge gap: Implications for early education', in D.K. Dickinson and S.B. Neumann (eds), *Handbook for Early Literacy Research.* Vol. 2. London: Guilford. pp. 29–40.

Neuman, S.B. and Dwyer, J. (2009). 'Missing in action: Vocabulary instruction in pre-K', *Reading Teacher,* 62: 384–92.

Neuman, S. and Cunningham, L. (2009). 'The impact of professional development and coaching on early language and literacy instructional practices', *American Educational Research Journal,* 46: 532–66.

Neuman, S.B. and Celano, D. (2006). 'The knowledge gap: Implications of levelling the playing field for low-income and middle-income children' *Reading Research Quarterly,* 41(2): 176–201.

Neuman, S.B. and Roskos, K. (1992). 'Literacy objects as cultural tools: Effects on children's literacy behaviours in play', *Reading Research Quarterly,* 27: 202–25.

Oczkus, L.D. (2003). *Reciprocal Teaching at Work: Strategies for Improving Reading Comprehension.* Newark, DE: International Reading Association.

OECD (Organisation for Economic Co-operation and Development) (2010). *PISA Results: What students know and can do. Student performance in Reading, Mathematics and Science.* Vol. 1. Paris: OECD.

Palinscar, A.S. and Brown, A.L. (1984). 'Reciprocal teaching of comprehension fostering and monitoring activities', *Cognition and Instruction,* 1: 117–75.

Paris, S.G. (2005). 'Reinterpreting the development of reading skills', *Reading Research Quarterly,* 40(2): 184–202.

Paris, S.G., Lipson, M.Y., and Wixson, K.K. (1994). 'Becoming a strategic reader', in R.B. Ruddell, M.R. Ruddell, and H.S. Singer (eds), *Theoretical Models and Processes of Reading.* Newark, DA: International Reading Association. pp. 788–810.

Pearson, D.P. and Gallagher, M.C. (1983). 'The instruction of reading comprehension', *Contemporary Educational Psychology,* 8: 317–44.

Pearson, D.P. and Hiebert, E.H. (2010). 'National reports in literacy: Building a scientific base for practice and policy', *Educational Researcher,* 39: 286–94.

Pressley, M., Allington, R.L., Wharton-McDonald, R., Collins Block, C., and Mandel Morrow, L. (2001). *Learning to Read: Lessons from Exemplary First-Grade Classrooms.* New York: Guilford Press.

Rosenblatt, L.M. (1978). *The Reader, the Text, the Poem: The Transactional Theory of Literary Work.* Carbondale, IL: Southern Illinois University Press.

Roskos, J. and Christie, J.A. (2007). 'Play in the context of the new pre-school basics', in K.A. Roskos and J.F. Christie (eds), *Play and Literacy in Early Childhood: Research from Multiple Perspectives* (2nd ed.). New Jersey: Lawrence Erlbaum Associates. pp. 83–100.

Roskos, K. and Neuman, S.B. (2003). 'Environment and its influences for early literacy teaching and learning', in S.B. Neumann and D.K. Dickinson (eds), *Handbook of Early Literacy Research.* New York, London: Guilford Press. pp. 281–294.

Rowe, D. (2007). 'Bringing book to life: The role of book-related dramatic play in young children's literacy learning', in K.A. Roskos and J.F. Christie (eds), *Play and Literacy in Early Childhood: Research from Multiple Perspectives* (2nd ed.). New Jersey: Lawrence Erlbaum Associates. pp. 37–63.

Rueda, R. (2011). 'Cultural perspectives in reading', in M.L. Kamil, P.D. Pearson, E.B. Moje, and P.P. Afflerbach (eds), *Handbook of Reading Research.* Vol. 4. New York: Routledge.

Shanahan, T., Callison, K., Carriere, C., Duke, N.K., Pearson, P.D., Schatschneider, C., and Torgesen, J.

(2010). *Improving Reading Comprehension in Kindergarten Through 3rd Grade: A Practice Guide.* (NCEE 2010-4038). Washington, DC: National Center for Education Evaluation and Regional Assistance, Institute of Education.

Shulman, L.S. (1987). 'Knowledge and teaching: Foundations of the new reform', *Harvard Educational Review*, 57(1): 1–22.

Stanovich, K.E. (1986). 'Matthew effects in reading: Some consequences of individual differences in the acquisition of literacy', *Reading Research Quarterly*, 21(4): 360–407.

Sylva, C., Chan, L., Melhuish, E., Sammons, Siraj-Blatchford, I., and Taggart, B. (2011). 'Emergent literacy environments: Home and preschool influences', in S. Neuman, and D. Dickinson (eds), *Handbook of Early Childhood Literacy*. Vol. 3. New York: Guilford Press. pp. 97–117.

Taylor, B.M., Pearson P.D., Peterson, D.S., and Rodriguez, M.C. (2003). 'Reading growth in high-poverty classrooms: The influence of teacher practices that encourage cognitive engagement in literacy learning', *The Elementary School Journal*, 104(1): 3–28.

Teale, W.H., Hoffman, J.L., and Paciga, K.A. (2010). 'Where is NELP leading preschool literacy instruction? Potential positives and pitfalls', *Educational Researcher*, 39: 311–15.

Vukelich, C. (1991). 'Materials and modelling: Promoting literacy during play', in J.E. Christie (ed.), *Play and Early Literacy Development*. Albany, NY: SUNY Press. pp. 215–31.

Vygotsky, L. (1978). *Mind in Society: The Development of Higher Psychological Processes*. Cambridge, MA: Harvard University Press.

Whitehurst, G. and Lonigan, C. (1998). 'Child development and emergent literacy', *Child Development*, 69: 848–72.

Wigfield, A. and Guthrie, J.T. (1997). 'Relations of children's motivation for reading to the amount and breadth of their reading', *Journal of Educational Psychology*, 89(3): 420–32.

Wood, E. (2009). *Developing Play*. Podcast, NCCA: www.ncca.ie/aisteartoolkit

31

Towards Knowing Well and Doing Well: Assessment and Early Childhood Education

Sharon Murphy

In 1992, the following headline appeared in the health section of the *New York Times*: 'Study backs deep anesthesia for babies in surgery.' This newspaper article revealed that physicians generally did not administer pain-relieving medication to babies undergoing surgery even though they would routinely administer medication to adults. Two explanations were offered for this practice. Some physicians believed that babies would experience negative side-effects from the pain-relieving medications, while others believed that 'newborns did not feel pain the same way adults do' (*New York Times*, 1992). However, a research study reported in the newspaper article revealed that not only did babies experience pain during surgery, but, because they were not medicated for pain, babies actually experienced greater distress in surgery. The public outcry following the release of these research findings quickly brought an end to the medical practice of withholding pain relief from infants (CBC Radio, 2010).

What does a story about infant pain relief have to do with research on early childhood assessment? Like the medical practitioners of this story, early childhood practitioners engage in daily acts of assessment, of looking at a situation and assessing a course of action in relation to the persons within their care. Most often, when any of us think of professional practitioners engaging in acts of assessment, we assume that these professionals are operating from a basis of knowledge, but, as the newspaper article demonstrates, even in a profession considered to have strong scientific underpinnings, professional practitioners operate from a grounding of values which they use to manage or filter the knowledge and situations that they encounter in their daily practice.

This news story's importance is that it brings into sharp relief the use of values in assessments, a use that might not be as immediately transparent in a less provocative and more familiar example. Values, then, must be a starting point for any discussion of assessment.

VALUES, JUDGMENT AND DESIGN IN ASSESSMENT

Values consist of assumptions and beliefs.[1] Values form the basis of the stances we have towards what we see as knowledge and offer us a starting point for action in any one circumstance. When we engage in assessments, we make judgments as a result of assessments, we use judgment to design assessments, and, in turn, the design of assessments may affect the subsequent judgments we make (Murphy, 2003). These three elements – values, judgment and design – operate dynamically in any one assessment act. However, it is not enough to consider how assessments work but we must go beyond how assessments work to consider the larger question of what makes an assessment *good* or, at least, *good enough*. In essence, we must consider *how we know well* and *do well with what we know* (Murphy, 2009a,b).

This idea of knowing and doing well originates from Code's (1987, 2006) philosophical work on epistemic responsibility. Code starts from the position that 'most so-called knowledge is really well-warranted belief' (1987: 47) and sees what counts as knowledge as constantly shifting. Therefore, in making claims about anything, whether it be the status of a young child's literacy skills or Pluto's standing as a planet, our principal efforts must be directed towards the warrantability of the knowledge – the provision of evidence and argumentation to support a knowledge claim in relation to the context in which that knowledge claim is made. Situated warrantable knowledge claims are the order of the day for Code (1987, 2006) who sees ethics as central to this endeavour. She argues that 'in some sense, ethical responsibility is founded upon epistemic responsibility, even if it is not identifiable with it. One who has not been scrupulous in knowing cannot be scrupulous in doing' (Code, 1987: 95). If values, judgment, and design are dynamic within an assessment, this dynamic process must be governed by a responsibilist stance towards knowledge and the process of assessing.

Part of this responsibilist stance begins with understanding the basis of our own values. One place to start is with how we think about the learner's or student's knowledge. According to the philosopher, Immanuel Kant (1790/2005), judgment can be viewed as either determinative or reflective. Rømer (2003), who has translated Kant's concepts for the field of educational assessment, observes that 'a determining judgment subsumes a particular under an a priori and universal category' (2003: 323); an example might be the determinative judgment made as to whether the mark a child makes is or is not the letter 'A'. There is a normative formulation of 'A-ness' against which we judge past, present, and potential 'A's. Determinative judgments separate the learner's knowledge from the situation; assessment, within this viewpoint is oriented towards 'correction or feedback' (Rømer, 2003: 315). Determinative judgments answer the question, 'Does the phenomenon under scrutiny belong to a category or class and, if not, what work must be undertaken so that the learner produces marks that do belong?'.

A reflective judgment, on the other hand, is 'the assessment of phenomenon for which we have no general rule' (Rømer, 2003: 323). Reflective judgments cannot be oriented retrospectively towards established rules nor are they oriented towards the achievement of a standard, which itself is a kind of established rule; rather, reflective judgment 'is exactly defined by working within a "lack of rules"' (Rømer, 2003: 324). Reflective judgment results in a dialogue between the action a learner has engaged in to make something new within the learning nested within the epistemic community. So, for example, when a student writing about the death of a pet draws upon an understanding that marks are used in print to signify vocal intonation, and invents the 'sadlamation point' (Goodman, 2003), there is no prototypical sadlamation point to consider. Unless one reverts to a discussion of whether the sadlamation point is part of the culturally accepted family of punctuation marks, the sadlamation point cannot be judged against other sadlamation points but must considered in relation to its signification potential in the context of the literacy event. Reflective judgments focus on the questions, 'What sense do the learner and the teacher/assessor make of the phenomenon under scrutiny and what are the possibilities for action given the sense that is made?'. The emphasis is not on the normativity of the phenomenon but the usefulness and fertility of the phenomenon and the thinking it provokes in relation to the situation.

Values permeate not only the perspective of an assessor but are embedded in assessment design as instances of the values of their creators. The design, or the architecture of an assessment, shapes the epistemic potential of assessment. The premise of architecture, according to de Botton, is that 'we are, for better or for worse, different people in different places' (2006: 13). Buildings invite certain types of engagement through their sizes, shapes, colours and other architectural features. Similarly, assessments, by virtue of their design, define the ways in which knowledge is represented and, in doing so, allow for some representations of knowledge while disallowing others. *Every* assessment is marked by limitations in design because no design can serve all possible functions. All assessment designs, in that sense, are flawed; they offer a view of learning but they are also marked by a lack of completeness. Epistemically responsible assessment is based on the premise that both the potential *and* the lack or limits of assessment are foregrounded in thinking about assessments and their consequences.

PRINCIPLES OF EPISTEMICALLY RESPONSIBLE ASSESSMENT

A number of principles form the basis of epistemically responsible assessment. These principles, derived in part from the work of Rømer (2002, 2003) as well as Code (1987, 2006), are as follows:

1 Students in schools are engaged in representing their knowledge; in effect, their representations, in action and as a result of action, turn students' knowing into phenomenon for reflection, analysis and scrutiny, even when the phenomenon are processes as opposed to products.

2 Judgments of student representations of knowing may be determinative or reflective; the type of judgment made about a student's knowing may have consequences for the student.

3 Warrants for assessment should recognize the possibilities as well as the limitations of design in relation to the situation or circumstances of any one assessment activity. In particular, the representational possibilities for knowing offered by assessment designs should be acknowledged as limiting some representations while enabling others. Reasoned and reasonable warrants form the basis for thinking about the consequences of an assessment.

4 Those involved in assessment should warrant assessments in a manner that is reasonable in

relation to the practices of their own *epistemic locations*, and does not overextend the reach of the assessment; their 'judgments made in the different contexts of assessments should be made with reference to a particular community' (Rømer, 2002: 238). In essence, this principle requires that if one is operating within a specific epistemic community with its specific set of values, unless one is deliberately attempting to operate hybridically, then one should adhere to the principles espoused by that community.

5 Assessment developers and users should be attentive to their *ethical location* – assessors should not respond to competing interests (e.g., self-interest in relation to student success) but should give credit in a moral sense which respects the idea of 'how we *ought* to work with knowledge' (Italics added) (Rømer, 2002: 238).

6 Given the acknowledged complexity of assessment, those engaged in assessment within a community of practice, with their own vocabulary and ways of talking about assessment, should be open to being 'discontented by examining other vocabularies' from their own perspective; and they should look at their 'own vocabulary through the spectacles of the other' (Rømer, 2002: 239). This tripartite gaze may seem paradoxical given the requirement to adhere to the values of one's epistemic community; however, this gaze keeps the community of assessment practice open to new possibilities, and is governed by a responsibilist stance towards persons being assessed rather than to paradigm or self-interest.

Using values as the starting point, I will now turn to early childhood assessment with regard to its relationship to the broad categories of determinative or reflective judgment. I will also occasionally make reference to other principles of epistemically responsible assessment, but a full discussion of these principles is outside the scope of this chapter.

Unsurprisingly, because of the mediating influence of culture and context and the values embedded within cultures, tendencies towards determinative or reflective judgment in educational assessment seem to fall along cultural lines. Some countries

follow what Bennett (2005), in an OECD (Organisation for Economic Co-operation and Development) report on early childhood education, refers to as the pre-primary approach in which, not merely the early years in schools, but the years that precede them, are focused on a fairly narrow vision of the achievement of success in school. One description offered for such schools is as follows: 'high child/staff ratios ... well-trained educators but trained mainly in discipline-based, primary school methodologies; adult directed classrooms using predominantly direct instruction, question assessments and table-top reinforcement activities; intensive modeling generally of high quality; and a strong focus on early literacy and numeracy' (Bennett, 2005: 10). This type of educational environment leads towards assessments that are based upon determinative judgment.

Another group of countries envision broader goals with 'classrooms ... organized to facilitate movement and activity, child/staff ratios are correct; mixed age grouping is practiced; resources and materials are in plentiful supply ... a greater emphasis on play, with a wide choice of activities for children to engage in ...' (Bennett, 2005: 10).

Early childhood environments in this second group of countries replete with their social values will echo the same values in the assessments that are used within them. Such spaces are more likely to be associated with assessments based on reflective judgment or a hybrid of reflective and determinative judgment.

ASSESSMENTS INVOLVING DETERMINATIVE JUDGMENT

Throughout the world, a greater understanding of the importance of the early years (Maynard and Thomas, 2009) has coincided with worries about succeeding in the global knowledge economy (Hopmann, 2008). These two factors often combine to become a rationale for extending the practices associated with schooling into the early childhood and preschool years. Increased governance and oversight of early childhood education, in the form of the synchronized articulation of early childhood literacy assessment with the literacy assessment of schooling in general, accompanies such practices (Bennett, 2005; Brown, 2010; Invernizzi, Justice, Landrum, and Booker, 2004/2005; Roach, McGrath, Wixson, and Talapatra, 2010). Assessment within this pre-primary-school determinative approach has the following characteristics: 'Learning outcomes and assessment often required, at least on entry into primary school. Goals for the group are clearly defined. Graded assessment of each child with respect to pre-defined competences may be an important part of the teacher's role' (Bennett, 2005: 13).

Three different assessment types fall within those involving determinative judgments: 1) standardized testing, whether large in scale or individualized; 2) rubric-based assessments; and 3) assessments based on observational or developmental checklists. All use a normative comparator (whether based on statistical descriptions of the performance of other people or categorical descriptions of skills) to assess learning.

Standardized testing

In the United States in particular, routine standardized testing has found its way into some North American early childhood programs (e.g., Brown, 2007; Shute, 2009). Standardized testing is perhaps the example *par excellence* of determinative judgment in that:

1 Standardized testing attempts to create a *single context for assessment* by controlling as many factors in the environment as possible. This control can be such that it may be reasonable to ask whether the environment created within the standardized test condition resembles typical non-test literacy contexts. Further, the standardized testing literature in relation to schooling is filled with examples of standardized tests being an ill-fitted match to the curriculum of schools (e.g., Murphy, Shannon, Johnston, and Hansen, 1998).

2 The *concept of normativity* embedded within standardized testing is based on how any one instance of performance by a child on the test maps onto the performance of the norm group, a group that initially took the test and which was selected to meet specific criteria (Crocker and Algina, 1986). The determinative judgment, then, is twofold; it is both about making inferences about student knowledge and it is about the similarity of test participants to the group upon which the test was normed.

3 The *encoding mechanism* for encapsulating the standardized testing is numerical (Murphy, 2009b). Numbers suggest a degree of precision which is more illusion than reality in this particular kind of determinative judgment. Many have written on the problems inherent with such uses of numbers, ranging from philosophers (see, Hacking, 1990; Poovey, 1998) to educationists (e.g., Murphy et al., 1998) to popular commentators (Seife, 2010).

Kindergarten children in the United States are screened in areas such as phonological awareness, phonics, fluency, vocabulary and comprehension (Invernizzi et al., 2004/2005), and screening tools for emergent literacy development have been designed (e.g., Wilson and Lonigan, 2009). The choice of what areas to emphasize within these assessments is indicative of values about what is important in literacy learning. Context is considered of such limited significance that such tests are seen to be predictive of much performance on other tests. For instance, Adlof, Catts and Lee (2010) use the Woodcock Reading Mastery Test – Revised (described as assessing letter recognition and naming speed), and the Test of Language Development (described as assessing vocabulary and grammar phonological awareness) to predict eighth-grade reading impairments. Issues such as the particular nature of the tasks, the stability of young students' performances across short amounts of time, and children's responses to task situations are eclipsed by an interest in normative patterns and predictive relationships. Epistemic cautions about the limitations of tests (often found in technical manuals), the problems of separating subtests from the whole assessment battery (often cautioned against in discussions of validity in technical manuals), and other validity and reliability concerns are heard only by those willing to go the extra step of accessing background documentation and trying to figure out what that information means in relation to any current test participants.

Typically, the development of self-consciousness about the epistemic limitations of standardized tests is overwritten by the culture of practices focused on efficiency within educational contexts rather that the ideals introduced in tests and measurements statements for such professionals (Joint Committee on Testing Practices, 2004). Such practices routinely see subtests used as determinative (although test manuals suggest that uncoupling subtests from the test as a whole often impacts the subtest's validity and reliability), large-scale tests being used for inappropriate consequences despite warnings in technical documentation against such practices, and statistical assumptions being violated in relation to mapping sets of test participants onto normative tables. To some extent, part of the culture of standardized testing practices involves bypassing some principles of standardized testing while holding firm to others with the result that the practices associated with standardized testing sometimes are at best inscrutable and at worst epistemically and ethically flawed when viewed by expert practitioners (Joint Committee on Testing Practices, 2004).

Large-scale assessments based on rubrics

Another example of determinative assessment closely related to standardized testing can be found in large scale assessments based on rubrics (LSAR). LSAR, like standardized testing, typically create assessment situations that are unique to schooling.[2] A seeming advantage of LSAR is that the knowledge domains assessed are often asserted to be mapped onto the curriculum of the local, regional, or national body governing education. Unlike standardized tests which compare test-takers to each other, LSAR compare performances to prototypical exemplars by using rubrics or descriptions of desired qualities; such descriptions are often accompanied by an alphabetical or numerical label signifying a level of performance, which in turn is typically associated with a specific grade or age level. These rubrics may be developed by a team of educationists with expertise in the age group and area being assessed. The rubrics may or may not be representative of the values of the educationists in that most often arriving at agreements on rubrics may require compromises across value differences in order to generate the rubrics. The resultant prototypical exemplars along with the accompanying categorical or numerical labels exemplify determinative judgment in that a child's performance is mapped onto the descriptors, despite the ambiguities and situational specificities that might mitigate such performance mapping.

Unlike in standardized norm-referenced test culture, within LSAR there may be some explicit public consciousness of the entanglement of ethical and epistemological issues. Brown (2010), for example, describes one such situation that occurred in a United States context where stakeholders close to the assessment situation worried about whether the descriptors and examples were difficult enough:

> Principal White also questioned the rigor of the performance expectations. The principal stated, 'The rubric gives kids credit for doing things that basically anybody can do.' Principal White worried that the assessment tool would create problems for school personnel because their PreK students would be identified as being more prepared for the K-12 system than she believes they actually are.
>
> (2010: 148)

In such circumstances, the focus is not so much on either the epistemic location of the assessment, or the way the assessment is warranted but instead it is on what the assessment actually signifies, its potential and its lack. In this example, Principal White's worries about the reach of the assessment are actually worries about values, about the degree to which the committee's values map onto those of educational and school communities. The arguments made can be oblique and can avoid substantial discussion of how the assessment accomplishes its ends leaving one to wonder about the ethics of the types of decisions involved in LSAR. Even though such discussions make for greater transparency about values than found within standardized test development, more often than not, the epistemic and ethical locations of individuals in relation to such assessments are implied or left undiscussed.

The consequences of the school-based use of high stakes testing, whether norm-referenced or LSAR, are well documented (e.g., Firestone, Schorr, and Monfils, 2004; Hillocks, 2002; Madaus, Russell, and Higgins, 2009; Thomas, 2005; Valli, Croninger, Chambliss, Graeber, and Buese, 2008). Studies are emerging of the specific impact of LSAR on early-childhood classrooms. Consider, for instance, Wohlwend's (2008) study in which she observed how a kindergarten teacher's instructional decisions were influenced because she 'believed that writing samples would receive higher scores on the district writing rubric' if they included features 'addressed within the rubric descriptors' (2008: 53). Wohlwend (2008) observed that when values broader than those represented in the rubric were infused into the teachers pedagogical practices, the types of writing that were generated were qualitatively and quantitatively different, in positive directions, from those generated in rubric-driven instruction. Such studies raise significant questions about the weight of single assessment systems and the failure of recognizing the strengths and lacks of each individual assessment instrument.

Checklists and structured observation guides

Much assessment within early childhood classrooms occurs through observation. One form of structured observation can be found in the practice of using checklists of key behaviors; yet the examination of this type of assessment as a system of assessment practice does not receive much attention in the research literature. An example of a checklist assessment tool that has been around for several decades is the Bracken Basic Concept Scale. This scale itemizes basic concepts such as colour-name knowledge, number and letter identification, location (e.g., beside, on) which become an inventory of what a child 'knows.' The development of this scale is highly self-referential in that new forms build on older forms of the scale; in other words, despite the many iterations of the scale, the scale developer does not appear to be attentive to looking outward to other systems or ways of viewing young children's knowing to broaden the perspective of the scale. For instance, in a review of the comparability of state standards in early childhood across 50 states of the United States, Bracken and Crawford (2010) unabashedly make the Bracken Basic Concept Scale developed by the first author central in the comparability of state standards and legitimize the scale by referring to earlier versions of the scale rather than looking outward to the work of others.

Despite the determinative sensibility of a tool like the Bracken Basic Concept Scale, observational assessments are the place where assessments involving reflective judgment begin to emerge to the extent that some of these are more interested in understanding the activities of learners rather than categorizing them. In the field of literacy assessment observationally based protocols include: Clay's (2005) *An Observation of Early Literacy Achievement*, complete with specialized booklets, Owocki and Goodman's (2002) *Kidwatching: Documenting Children's Early Literacy Development*, and Goodman, Watson, and Burke's (2005) *Reading Miscue Inventory*. These mediated observational techniques typically include the observation of a focal child involved in a literacy engagement that is a simulation of a literacy activity one might experience in ordinary living – children are asked to handle a book to read or to write and observations/recordings of these experiences are made. As with many checklists, sometimes the activities embedded in something like Clay's (2005) 'concepts of print' are themselves a cataloguing or coding of

emergent literacy knowledge. Other times, as in Clay's (2005) running records or Goodman et al.'s (2005) miscue analysis, reading behaviours are coded using sociopsycholinguistic categories. However, both approaches to coding reading relate to normative patterns because coding occurs in relation to a text. Even so, Goodman et al. (2005) moves towards a hybridical stance in that the interest favours meaning making while Clay (2005) emphasizes accuracy.

Interestingly, less structured observation may also be determinative in nature. For example, Alasuutari and Karila (2010), in analysing how children are viewed in early childhood education in Finland, note that despite a rooting in traditional discourse, Finnish early childhood educators, in comparison to North Americans, are interested in broad views of children, but yet the idea of the child as an agent or the idea of the child's view of the world are absent. In these forms of observation, as with other determinative forms, the goal is not oriented towards dialogue and understanding but towards tradition, or, in other words, normativity.

All assessments involving determinative judgment embed normative formulations into the assessment protocols. Often these normative formulations are represented by the language of the assessment – the forms to complete, whether completed by teacher or by child. Assessments based on reflective judgment start from a place that is less structured and more open to the unanticipated.

ASSESSMENTS INVOLVING REFLECTIVE JUDGMENT

Escaping the discourse of determinative judgment is difficult. Nevertheless, calls for alternative visions have been made (e.g., Bagnato and Macy, 2010; Orellana and D'warte, 2010) and educators find themselves working hybridically in that they must implement prescribed assessments while working to develop alternatives (e.g., Bauer and Garcia, 2002). These hybridical conceptualizations of assessment can be found not merely in the work that teachers do, but in the policy documents that advise them (e.g., Dunphy, 2008; New Zealand Ministry of Education, 2009).

One example of assessment involving reflective judgment that has become known worldwide is that of the pedagogical documentation at the heart of early childhood education in Reggio Emilia, Italy. Assessments informed by pedagogical documentation's efforts to 'make learning visible' (Giudici, Rinaldi, and Krechevsky, 2001) are emerging within North American contexts as well as elsewhere (e.g., Buldu, 2010; Dahlberg, Moss, and Pence, 2007; Falk and Darling-Hammond, 2010; Forman, 2010; Krechevsky, Rivard, and Burton, 2010; MacDonald, 2007; Project Zero, 2006). These assessments (which involve capturing dialogue, images, and representations of the activity of children and representing the activity so that it becomes a recursive and expanding site of reflection and discourse) are more likely to be associated with flexible contexts which value not merely the child's autonomy but which value the child as a thinker.

Rinaldi (2001) perhaps best captures reflective nature of pedagogical documentation through the following questions posed for educators: 'How can we help children find the meaning of what they do, what they encounter, what they experience? And how can we do this for ourselves? These are questions of meaning

and the search for meaning (why? how? what?)' (2001: 79). Central to this effort is the 'capacity for listening and reciprocal expectations' (2001: 82). Images, notes, audio-recordings – the physical matter of pedagogical documentation – offer residues of the experience of learning and enable interpretive opportunities for child and adult. These interpretive opportunities may be marked by 'doubt and uncertainty' which become opportunities for conversation; 'in this space between the predictable and the unexpected. . . the communicative relationship between the children's and teachers' learning processes is constructed' (2001: 85).

The whole point of pedagogical documentation is to come up with an 'interpretive 'theory,' a narration that gives meaning to events and objects of the world' (Rinaldi, 2001: 79–80). The assessor who, in determinative assessment, stands somewhat apart from the work of learning to place value on it, is replaced by a child and adult who conjointly work to find value by theorizing and coming to understand the experiences gestured to in the documentation panels associated with pedagogical documentation.

Given the strong sensibility towards understanding and relationality, it is not surprising that within this framework there is an orientation towards 'knowing well and doing well.' One example of such an orientation can be found in Cheeseman and Robertson's (2006) reflections on the ethics involved in the process of pedagogical documentation with particular emphasis on children's rights of privacy and the protection of their intellectual property. These reflections focus on the decisions made in pedagogical documentation, the choices made of what to document and who to document, and the importance of treating children as one would wish to be treated oneself. As Sandra Cheesman says,

> We acknowledge that the experience is shared; however, the power of the adult can dominate here as decisions are made about how children's ideas are interpreted, questioned or represented within the documentation. I often wonder whether we steal from children – their ideas, their hypotheses, and their wisdom.
>
> (Cheesman and Robertson, 2006: 198–9)

That abducting the knowledge of children is the worry of an adult involved in pedagogical documentation illustrates how much of a demarcation there is between this assessment form and other forms, because of the presumption that children are knowledge makers rather than knowledge imitators.

Like other forms of educational assessment, values affect the choices made in pedagogical documentation; however, unlike other forms of assessment, reflection about the choices and the values that guide them are embedded into the pedagogical documentation process. This reflection reveals the fragility of the pedagogical documentation experience, a revelation that is not something to be hidden or spirited away in a technical manual or background paper, as is the practice in determinative assessment, but something to be reflected upon. For instance when Belinda Connerton, a teacher on staff at a child care centre for 3–5-year-olds in Sydney, Australia, considers her experience in pedagogical documentation she is conscious of the limitations of her early work and notes that at one point she spent time documenting longer and longer examples of engagements; she remarks that 'over time, I think I found the long examples became too predictable. . . I got to the point where I was looking for the deeper stories' (Connerton and Patterson,

2007: 100). Connerton goes on to describe examples that are derived from the here-and-now of children's experiences and that help them make sense of these experiences, examples such as the building and rebuilding of the Twin Towers following their destruction on September 11, 2001.

While pedagogical documentation reveals much about children's knowledge and their ability to use a variety of representational forms to display their knowledge; a focus on matters of the conventional representation of or the complexity of form, often the emphasis in determinative assessments or literacy, is only a focus if it is of interest to the child. So, for instance, when a child's representations in answer to a question like 'Can weaving make a horse?' (Miller, 2008: 126) show increasing sophistication in representing the horse anatomically, it is the child's reflection and the adult's careful listening and response to that reflection which drive the representational refinements of form. Literacy finds its way into pedagogical documentation as the tool for representation rather than as the object of representation – in other words, children use story, writing, and image to represent their curiosities about the world and their emerging understanding of questions around them. Literacy could become the focus of documentation panels but such a focus would be determined to relation to interest and drive of the participants. As such, in standards driven educational systems, pedagogical documentation may be used hybridically in that it can be mined for evidence of the benchmarks identified by school governance systems. However, if pedagogical documentation is used towards such ends, one must be mindful of maintaining the ethical relations established during the process of pedagogical documentation and perhaps a *post hoc* search of evidence of the benchmarks is the optimal way to proceed in such contexts.

CONCLUSION

I have argued elsewhere (Murphy, 2003) that the assessment tools determine the nature of the 'literacy' that one finds. For example, if one uses a multiple-choice test of sound-symbol relations and names that as literacy, then one finds the literacy one is looking for. I have also argued here and elsewhere (Murphy, 2003, 2009a, 2009b) that assessments are instantiations of values. Differences in values complicate the representations of literacy knowledge offered in different assessments; however, more often than not in early childhood assessments – whether standardized tests, LSAR, or some type of observational checklist-assessments in early childhood education (and in schooling in general) are determinative in nature. Determinative assessments – because they rely on the standards that are 'out there' agreed upon as a common good by governments, school districts, or sometimes simply created by someone who designed a checklist – can have the effect of distancing the early childhood educator from the actions of assessment. The educator does not have to think about the child so much as to assign the child's performance to a category, and quite often assessment instruments even do this for the educator; in such assessments, understanding becomes secondary to categorization.

Yet, I would argue that, like the physicians mentioned at the outset of this chapter, educators cannot operate from the presumption of the goodness of the instruments and practices at hand but must move towards nuanced work. The example of reflective assessment found in pedagogical documentation offers starting points for moving towards a different stance in assessment. The system we have in education inevitably will demand determinative assessment, but early childhood educators can move towards operating hybridically, towards understanding the what and the how behind children's thinking by listening to children's explanations of their representations of knowledge and by introducing provocations that allow children to demonstrate the kinds of thinking that lie behind their efforts to represent their world. When all is said and done, the child's intellectual life will be fostered, not by being numerically or lexically categorized, but by being stimulated and moved to action; if early childhood educators can achieve such an end, then their assessments will have accomplished much.

NOTES

1 For instance, an example of an assumption at work in the medical story would be that because adverse effects for pain-relieving medications were observed in some adults, then babies, who are so much smaller than adults, are likely to be more highly affected by such medications. The assumption is about a heightened sense of vulnerability among babies, perhaps because of their size or perhaps because of their newness in the world. Interestingly (and perhaps, paradoxically), the position of some physicians that babies did not experience much in the way of pain may result in the fact that young babies were valued as 'less than fully human' and therefore not susceptible to pain in the same way as full humans are.

2 In some countries, such the United States, it has been argued (e.g., Hanson, 1993) that the society itself is permeated with a testing mentality.

REFERENCES

Adlof, S.M., Catts, H.W., and Lee, J. (2010). 'Kindergarten predictors of second versus eighth grade reading comprehension impairments', *Journal of Learning Disabilities*, 43: 332–45.

Alasuutari, M. and Karila, K. (2010). 'Framing the picture of the child', *Children and Society*, 24: 100–111.

Bagnato, S.J. and Macy, M. (2010). 'Authentic assessment in action: A "R-E-A-L" solution', *NHSA Dialog*, 13(1): 42–45.

Bauer, E.B. and García, G. E. (2002). 'Lessons from a classroom teacher's use of alternative literacy assessment, *Research in the Teaching of English*, 36(4): 462–94.

Bennett, J. (2005). Curriculum issues in national policy-making, *European Early Childhood Education Research Journal*, 13(2): 5–23.

Bracken, B.A. and Crawford, E. (2010). 'Basic concepts in early childhood educational standards: A 50-state review', *Early Childhood Education Journal*, 37: 421–30.

Brown, D. (2007). 'High stakes testing arrives in kindergarten', *The Huffington Post*, 7 December. http://www.huffingtonpost.com/dan-brown/highstakes-testing-arrive_b_75806.html

Brown, C.P. (2010). 'Balancing the readiness equation in early childhood education reform', *Journal of Early Childhood Research*, 8(2): 133–60.

Buldu, M. (2010). 'Making learning visible in kindergarten classrooms: Pedagogical documentation as a formative assessment technique', *Teaching and Teacher Education*, 26: 1439–69.

CBC Radio (2010). *The Current. Pt. 3. Medical orthodoxy*. 20 September. http://www.cbc.ca/thecurrent/2010/#September%202010

Cheeseman, S. and Robertson, J. (2006). 'Unsure – private conversations publicly recorded', in A. Fleet, C. Patterson, and J. Robertson (eds), *Insights: Behind early childhood pedagogical documentation*. Castle Hill, New South Wales: Pademelon Press. pp. 191–204.

Clay, M. (2005). *An Observation of Early Literacy Achievement*. Portsmouth, NH: Heinemann.

Code, L. (1987). *Epistemic Responsibility*. London: University Press of New England.

Code, L. (2006). *Ecological Thinking: The Politics of Epistemic Location*. New York: Oxford University Press.

Connerton, B. and Patterson, C. (2007). 'Growing into documenting stories of war and secret places', in A. Fleet, C. Patterson, and J. Robertson (eds), *Insights: Behind Early Childhood Pedagogical Documentation*. Castle Hill, New South Wales: Pademelon Press. pp. 97–113.

Crocker, L. and Algina, J. (1986). *Introduction to Classical and Modern Test Theory*. New York: Holt, Rinehart, and Winston.

Dahlberg, G., Moss, P., and Pence, A. (2007). *Beyond Quality in Early Childhood Education and Care: Languages of Evaluation* (2nd ed.). London: Routledge.

de Botton, A. (2006). *The Architecture of Happiness*. Toronto: McLelland & Stewart.

Dunphy, E. (2008). *Aistear: Creatchuraclam na Luath-Óige/The early childhood curriculum Framework – Supporting Early Learning and Development through Formative Assessment: A Research Paper*. Dublin: National Council for Curriculum and Assessment.

Falk, B. and Darling-Hammond, L. (2010). 'Documentation and democratic education', *Theory into Practice*, 49(1): 72–81.

Forman, G. (2010). 'Documentation and accountability: The shift from numbers to indexed narratives', *Theory into Practice*, 49(1): 29–35.

Firestone, W.A., Schorr, R.Y., and Monfils, L.F. (eds) (2004). *The Ambiguity of Teaching to the Test: Standards, Assessment, and Educational Reform*. Mahwah, NJ: Erlbaum.

Giudici, C., Rinaldi, C., and Krechevsky, M. (eds) (2001). *Making Learning Visible: Children as Individual and Group Learners*. Cambridge, MA: Project Zero, Harvard Graduate School of Education.

Goodman, Y. (2003). *Valuing Language Study: Inquiry into Language for Elementary and Middle Schools*. Urbana, IL: National Council of Teachers of English.

Goodman, Y.M., Watson, D.J., and Burke, C.L. (2005). *Reading Miscue Inventory: From Evaluation to Instruction*. Katoneh, NY: Richard C. Owen.

Hacking, I. (1990). *The Taming of Chance*. Cambridge: Cambridge University Press.

Hanson, F.A. (1993). *Testing Testing: Social Consequences of the Examined Life*. Berkeley: University of California Press.

Hillocks, Jr, G. (2002). *The Testing Trap: How State Writing Assessments Control Learning*. New York: Teachers College Press.

Hopmann, S.T. (2008). 'No child, no school, no state left behind: Schooling in the age of accountability', *Journal of Curriculum Studies*, 40: 417–56.

Invernizzi, M., Justice, L., Landrum, T.J., and Booker, K. (2004/2005). 'Early literacy screening in kindergarten: Widespread implementation in Virginia', *Journal of Literacy Research*, 36(4): 479–500.

Joint Committee on Testing Practices (2004). *Code of Fair Testing Practices in Education*. Washington, DC: American Psychological Association.

Kant, I. (1790/2005). *Critique of Judgment*. New York: Barnes and Noble.

Krechevsky, M., Rivard, M., and Burton, F.R. (2010). 'Accountability in three realms: Making learning visible inside and outside the classroom', *Theory into Practice*, 49(1): 64–71.

MacDonald, M. (2007). 'Toward formative assessment: The use of pedagogical documentation in early elementary classrooms', *Early Childhood Research Quarterly*, 22: 232–42.

Madaus, G., Russell, M., and Higgins, J. (2009). *The Paradoxes of High Stakes Testing: How they Affect Students, Their Parents, Teachers, Principals, Schools, and Society*. Charlotte, NC: Information Age Publishing.

Maynard, T., and Thomas, N. (eds) (2009). *An Introduction to Early Childhood Studies* (2nd ed.). London: Sage.

Miller, M.J. (2008). 'Can you weave a horse? Kang as protagonist', in C.A. Wien (ed.), *Emergent Curriculum in the Primary Classroom: Interpreting the Reggio Emilia Approach in Schools*. New York: Teachers College Press. pp. 126–1443.

Murphy, S. (2003). 'Finding literacy: A review of the research on literacy assessment in early childhood education', in N. Hall, J. Larson, and J. Marsh (eds), *Handbook of Early Childhood Literacy*. London: Sage. pp. 369–78.

Murphy, S. (2009a). 'Knowing and doing well in the creation and interpretation of reading assessments: Towards epistemic responsibility', in P. Anders (ed.), *Defying Convention, Inventing the Future in Literacy Research and Practice: A Tribute to Ken and Yetta Goodman*. Mahwah, NJ: Erlbaum. pp. 173–87.

Murphy, S. (2009b). 'Matters of goodness: Knowing well and doing well in the assessment of critical thinking', in J. Sobocan and L. Groarke (eds), *Critical Thinking Education and Assessment: Can Higher Order Thinking be Tested?* London, ON: Althouse Press. pp. 331–9.

Murphy, S., with Shannon, P., Johnston, P., and Hansen, J. (1998). *Fragile Evidence: A Critique of Reading Assessment*. Mahwah, NJ: Lawrence Erlbaum.

New York Times (1992) Study backs deep anesthesia for babies in surgery. http://www.nytimes.com/1992/01/02/us/study-backs-deep-anesthesia-for-babies-in-surgery.html

New Zealand Ministry of Education (2009). *Kei Tua o te Pae/Assessment for Learning: Early Childhood Exemplar*. http://www.educate.ece.govt.nz/learning/curriculumAndLearning/Assessmentforlearning/KeiTuaotePae.aspx

Orellana, M.F. and D'warte, J. (2010). 'Recognizing different kinds of "head starts"', *Educational Researcher*, 39: 295–300.

Owocki, G. and Goodman, Y. (2002). *Kidwatching: Documenting Children's Early Literacy Development*. Portsmouth, NH: Heinemann.

Poovey, M. (1998). *A History of the Modern Fact: Problems of Knowledge in the Sciences Of Wealth And Society*. Chicago: University of Chicago Press.

Project Zero (2006). *Making Learning Visible: Understanding, Documenting and Supporting Individual and Group Learning*. http://pzweb.harvard.edu/mlv/ (Accessed 15 April, 2011).

Roach, A.T., McGrath, D., Wixson, C., and Talapatra, D. (2010). 'Aligning an early childhood assessment to state kindergarten content standards: Application of a nationally recognized alignment framework', *Education Measurement: Issues and Practice*, 29(1): 25–37.

Rinaldi, C. (2001). 'Documentation and assessment: What is the relationship?', in C. Giudici, C. Rinaldi, & M. Krechevsky (eds), *Making learning visible: Children as individual and group learners* Cambridge: Project Zero, Harvard Graduate School of Education.

Rømer, T.A. (2002). 'Situated learning and assessment', *Assessment and Evaluation in Higher Education*, 27(3): 233–41.

Rømer, T.A. (2003). 'Learning and assessment in postmodern education', *Educational Theory*, 53(3): 313–27.

Seife, C. (2010). *Proofiness: The Dark Arts Of Mathematical Deception*. New York: Viking.

Shute, N. (2009). 'Kindergarten tests and the importance of play', *U.S. News and World Report*, 7 April. http://health.usnews.com/health-news/blogs/on-parenting/2009/04/07/kindergarten-tests-and-the-importance-of-play.html

Thomas, R.M. (2005). *High Stakes Testing: Coping with Collateral Damage*. Mahwah, NJ: Erlbaum.

Valli, L., Croninger, R.G., Chambliss, M.J., Graeber, A.O., and Buese, D. (2008). *Test Driven: High-Stakes Accountability in Elementary Schools*. New York: Teachers College Press.

Wilson, S.B. and Lonigan, C.J. (2009). 'An evaluation of two emergent literacy screening tools for preschool children', *Annals of Dyslexia*, 59: 115–31.

Wohlwend, K. (2008). 'From "What did I write?" to "Is this Right?": Intention, convention, and accountability in early literacy', *The New Educator*, 4(1): 43–63.

32

Learning, Literacies and New Technologies: The Current Context and Future Possibilities

Cathy Burnett and Guy Merchant

INTRODUCTION

In its repeated questioning of models of natural development, childhood studies has increasingly turned attention to the ways in which social and cultural influences intervene from the very beginning (Gardner, 1991). Although interaction with adult caregivers and siblings may be of primary importance, early childhood is also very much concerned with the material artefacts to hand. To suggest that childhood is infused with technology may at first sound extreme, but when we consider the context of affluent and highly-digitized societies, it is not in fact an over-exaggeration of the current condition. Rather, digital technology must be factored in from the prenatal stage, when the first images of a baby are the scans displayed on computer screens and mobile phones, circulated to family and friends by email and via social networking sites. And of course, technology is there from birth, not only in the hands of parents and relatives but also in the service of health care professionals and others attending to the newly born.

We know relatively little about the ways in which the very young react to technology, but we can observe that most babies will look at television screens in the first few months (Rideout and Hammel, 2006), may well be shown a mobile phone as a pacifier (Oksman and Rautiainen, 2003), and that some of a baby's first toys will have digital components. Whilst views on the possible enriching or detrimental effects of growing up in such an environment are hotly debated (Plowman, McPake, and Stephen, 2010a), it does seem that childhood is highly technologised.

Regional, social and familial variations in ownership, access and use notwithstanding, learning with and learning about technology are undoubtedly important parts of growing up in the twenty-first century.

Literacy is deeply implicated in any consideration of technology and childhood, particularly since the rapid adoption of new practices in everyday life is closely tied up with meaning-making and communication, predominantly, although by no means exclusively, through the use of lettered representation. The proliferation of tweets, text messages, status updates and emails are potent contemporary reminders of this. Even very young children are part of a society in which these new forms of communication are taken for granted. But it is not simply the case that writing has 'gone digital' since, as many have observed, new communications are also multi-modal in character (see for example: Kress, 2010) and new technologies themselves involve new ways of being literate for young children (Hesse and Lane, 2003).

Despite such developments, reviews of technology and education have revealed a lack of evidence related to the impact of new technologies on literacy and learning (Stephen and Plowman, 2003; Andrews, 2004; Yelland, 2005). A major theme here is the scarcity of research focused on early childhood – systematic reviews have consistently failed to produce more than a handful of studies that could be seen as methodologically rigorous (Lankshear and Knobel, 2003; Burnett, 2009, 2010). Moreover, reviews of research spanning the last 50 years (Labbo and Reinking, 2003; Lankshear and Knobel, 2003; Merchant, 2007b; Burnett, 2010) have highlighted that the majority of studies

focus on using technology as a tool to support the development of the kinds of reading and writing associated with print literacy. There has been little work that explores children's reading, writing and interactions with digital texts. This scarcity may well be linked to a discomfort amongst practitioners and theorists with respect to the appropriateness of technology-use for very young children, seen by some as a distraction from more 'natural', 'healthy' and 'developmentally appropriate' activities (Miller, 2005). We see this in surveys of practitioners' views on the role of technology in the early years (Stephen and Plowman, 2003). Uncertainty about the place of digital literacy in the early years curriculum is further complicated through 'back to basics' discourses, particularly those that adopt a narrow definition of literacy and advocate simplified instructional practices. As Yelland observes: 'Paradoxically, the use of new technologies is discouraged by both those who advocate traditional play-based curricula, and those who want standardisation and the practice of defined (industrial) basic skills via clearly constructed and limited tasks.' (2010: 12).

The limited focus of research can also be linked to the predominance of cognitive models of reading, which have tended to position technology as a tool for literacy development as opposed to a medium for diverse literacy practices (Hassett, 2006). We see this in the multiplicity of studies that have explored the impact of software packages on specific aspects of children's literacy development (for example, Macaruso, Hook, and McCable, 2006; Chera and Wood, 2003). While such studies are valuable in supporting practitioners' evaluation of such resources, they do little to enable educationalists to understand the connections between children's digital lives within and outside educational settings, or to consider the processes or possibilities associated with new literacies.

In this chapter, we argue that there is an urgent need for more extensive and varied research relating to digital literacies in the early years. We begin by reviewing recent studies which have explored young children's engagement with digital texts in educational settings and summarise the insights gained from such work. Then we consider what can be learned from children's encounters with digital technologies at home and from the kinds of connections that children themselves seem to make between digital literacies in different domains. We use these insights to generate a series of recommendations for further research. In doing so, we note that literacy itself has become a contentious term, with some advocating a broad definition to include a wide array of meaning-making practices and others arguing for a narrower view which anchors literacy to lettered representation (Merchant, 2007a). In what follows, we adopt a broad definition of literacy, focusing in particular on meaning-making in technologically-enriched contexts.

NEW TEXTS AND TECHNOLOGIES IN EDUCATIONAL SETTINGS

We identify two groups of studies that have investigated young children's uses of digital texts in educational settings. The first includes work focused on using digital texts to support learning that is framed by conventional descriptions of print literacy. The second explores the possible role of digital texts in mediating new relationships to support more diverse kinds of learning.

Using digital texts to meet print literacy objectives

This first group of studies investigates how reading and writing in digital environments impacts on comprehension or composition. Beck and Fetherston (2003) note how opportunities to word-process their writing may motivate reluctant writers by relieving anxieties about their handwriting. This lends further support to the evidence cited by Clements and Sarama (2003: 13) who suggest that working on-screen can promote a 'fluid idea of the written word.' Other studies adopt more open-ended approaches, aiming to capture children's responses to particular opportunities and resources. Kuhlman, Everts Danielson, Campbell, and Topp (2005) describe a project where first graders were given handheld computers. They observed how children integrated these into their play. For some but not all, the use of handheld computers seemed to impact on motivation and on their engagement with planning activities that the teacher was trying to introduce to support their writing. Tancock and Segedy (2004) compared children's comprehension following readings of printed and online texts. Their work suggested that children were more motivated by the opportunity to search online but learned more from the printed texts.

Such studies, focusing on specific skills or tasks, locate the role of digital texts firmly within the dominant paradigm of print literacy: technology then is seen as a tool which may, or may not, enhance literacy learning. Others report studies which focused on embedding new technologies within more open-ended and project-based approaches. Voogt and McKenney (2007), for example, explore the use of Pictopal to support emergent reading and writing skills whilst Labbo, Eakle, and Montero (2002) explore the integration of digital photography within a language experience approach, encouraging children to take, select and annotate images of their activities. In these examples, working with images on screen helped children capture ideas and experience and use these as a stimulus for writing. They illustrate how digital texts can be used to support the writing process in motivating and enabling children to experiment with meaning. They also highlight the semiotic possibilities of digital texts and provide ways that these can be harnessed to engage children in the processes of composition and comprehension. This work suggests that digital environments can provide meaningful and motivating contexts for literacy development whilst drawing attention to the skills children need to operate within such environments.

Introducing new technologies may also result in unintended consequences. For example, Schiller and Tillett (2004) describe an action-research project through which 7–8-year-old children captured their perceptions of school – again using digital images. The authors note how relationships between teachers and learners seemed to shift as they worked together to learn how to use the new technologies. Pedagogy, in this context, became more aligned with enquiry-led approaches.

Using digital texts to mediate new relationships

The second group of studies explores the potential of new literacies to help generate new kinds of relationships or contexts for meaning-making through connecting children with one another and those outside the classroom. Teale and Gambrell (2007) describe a project in which email was used to mediate discussions about literature between young children and adult penpals. This seemed to have significant impact on children's attainment in reading, which Teale and Gambrell attribute both to the value of the online community and the opportunity to engage meaningfully with high-quality texts. In another study Pelletier, Reeve, and Halewood (2006) explored using a networked learning environment to enable 4-year-olds to post, review and comment on their own and others' photo-journals in order to explore how they might be involved in knowledge building. Such studies explore children's responses to planned interventions and offer models to educators looking for ways of using networked technologies within language and literacy provision. Like those in the previous section, these studies use new technologies to try to raise attainment in relation to specific literacy outcomes. However they do so by focusing on how new technologies may be used to mediate relationships within and beyond the classroom.

Two further studies locate the significance of technology in a different way. Rather than using digital texts as media for exploring a wider world, they are used to make connections between different domains of children's lives, addressing notions of identity and community. Auld (2007) describes a project which involved recording the telling of indigenous Australian stories as talking books for use by children at home. She recognises a number of cultural tensions inherent in the project but describes how, by being flexible with how computers were used, the sharing of these stories was accommodated within existing social practices.

In Taylor et al.'s (Taylor, Bernhard, Garg, and Cumins, 2008) project, technology was used to scan dual-language home-made books which captured 4–5-year-old children's home experience for sharing shared with the wider family. This was designed to highlight the significance of family members' multilingual literacy practices in children's ongoing literacy development, and to legitimise community practices. In so doing, they aimed to draw on family members' 'cultural' and 'linguistic capital' (2008: 270), in supporting their children's literacy development as a way of helping them to 'reconceptualise their literacy practice' (Taylor et al., 2008: 286).

Whereas the significance of new technologies in the previous section is seen in terms of semiotic affordances, the studies summarised in this section could be conceived of in spatial terms. Teale and Gambrell's study *expanded* the classroom, whilst Pelletier et al. argued that theirs provided a 'shared virtual space' (2006: 340) in which children were able to develop their ideas collaboratively. They noticed an impact on children's early reading and writing skills (relative to children who engaged in similar print-focused activity). Auld's (2007) and Taylor et al.'s studies seemed to shift classroom boundaries in other ways through creating new spaces which gave status to established but marginalised communities and identities.

Projects such as these illustrate how digital environments can be embedded in practice that builds on well-established principles of literacy provision. These are not 'digital literacy projects' but projects designed to enable children to engage with digital technologies alongside other texts and resources in meaningful contexts-much as children may do in their own lives. We could argue here that technology 'becomes invisible'. For those committed

to a socio-cultural perspective, such work may offer a welcome complement to the still growing literature on the impact of specific programmes on specific reading/ writing skills. At the same time, there is perhaps a danger that in naturalising the use of digital texts we miss some of their implications for literacy itself. Indeed, when such projects are evaluated, they tend to be done in ways that refer to well-established educational aims and objectives – relating to literacy skills or motivation, for example, or social relationships and self-esteem. In this way the skills, knowledge and possibilities associated with digital texts themselves may become just as invisible as the technologies which mediate them.

If we are to integrate digital literacies in ways that more effectively build on the new possibilities offered for meaning making through new media, we need to know more about the possibilities and challenges associated with children's engagement with digital texts and the skills and understandings associated with them. In beginning to address this, the following section draws on studies that have focused on young children's responses to and interactions with and around digital texts and technologies through looking beyond educational settings. First we consider studies that have documented children's experimentation in the home environment, and second those which have explored continuities and discontinuities between literacies in educational settings and homes.

YOUNG CHILDREN'S ENGAGEMENT WITH NEW TECHNOLOGIES AT HOME

Our understandings about young children's engagement with new technologies at home come from a group of small-scale, primarily qualitative studies that explore the nature of children's interactions with digital texts. Much of this work has highlighted the playfulness, agency and creativity of very young children. For example, Marsh's study of 2½–4-year-olds draws on interviews and observational data to describe how young children respond to technologies such as televisions, computer games and mobile phones (Marsh, 2004). Challenging notions that technology encourages passive engagement, the practices observed by Marsh and described in parental interviews show children engaged meaningfully with computer games drawing on 'emergent techno-literacy' supported by (often male) family members. These children were not simply learning operational skills but developing complex understandings about how people communicate using electronic media. The role that new technologies play in wider practices was also evident in the ways in which the children integrated these technologies in their play. As such, the children's 'techno-literacy practices' were often connected to multiple literacy events, as children drew not just on new technologies but on a wide range of communicative practices. Marsh's work highlights a number of themes that are reflected in other studies of young children's technology use: the significance of family members; children's recontextualisation of understandings; and their active engagement. Whilst these themes are interconnected, they are explored separately below, drawing on other exemplar studies.

Sharing expertise: the significance of family members

Various studies have explored how informal interactions with family members can support children's learning in the context of new technologies and the meaning-making practices that are involved. Davidson's (2009) analysis of one family's conversations around a computer highlight how such interactions upheld and re-worked social relationships in everyday life. Such opportunities seem to offer rich opportunities for learning: children are able to draw from both digital and print resources to explore interests, learn from the combined expertise of parents and siblings, and share or refine their own understandings. The value of this kind of shared activity is endorsed by Plowman, Stephen, and McPake (2010b) who contrast the 'guided interactions' that occurred around new technologies at home and those that took place in early-years settings. They found that children had a wider variety of opportunities to engage with technologies at home, and that they were often guided by family members who provided direct support for technology use as and when it was needed. Children also saw family members using new technologies and so became more aware of its potential and how it might be useful in particular contexts. This availability of support combined with models of purposeful use meant that children learned about 'the cultural roles of technology' (2010b: 105).

Other studies have explored how children may act as mentors to older relatives. For example Kenner, Ruby, Jessel, and Gregory (2008) explored how bilingual children and grandparents mentored one another as they engaged in computer activities, with children leading their older relations in navigating the computer whilst their relatives supported them in making meaning from the texts they found. Such studies highlight the significance of the social in both the use and development of understanding of new technologies.

Making sense of new technologies: re-contextualising understandings

In providing insights into how children negotiate understandings around computers with other family members, the studies cited above focus on the significance of events centred on technology – using the internet to search for information or working out how to send a text message. Other studies explore what children take from these encounters and how they make sense of them in other contexts, re-contextualising their understandings and experiences. Smith (2005), for example, explores how her daughter re-created both the form and content of a CD-ROM storybook drawing on objects and places in the home and through embodying elements of this herself. Similarly Pahl (2005) describes how three 6–7-year-olds used narratives and characters borrowed from console games as 'cultural resources' to create new texts such as videos, drawings and conversations. These studies highlight how children re-contextualise their experience and in doing so develop new concepts and find new spaces for identity play.

Meaning-making around digital texts: active engagement

In demonstrating how young children engage actively with and through digital texts, a small set of studies have explored children's linguistic experimentation. Mavers (2007) analysed the design choices – relating to grammar, punctuation and layout – made by a 6-year-old girl as she exchanged emails with her uncle. These innovations could be seen as transductions in that they may begin as attempts to translate a message into written form but then take on new dimensions as the affordances of the medium become apparent and this both enables child and uncle to

play out their relationship in new ways. In some senses, this sort of exchange is what Plowman et al. (2010b) describe as a 'distal' guided interaction – through his emails, the uncle provides a model for what is possible and gently scaffolds the child's communication. This is also a theme in Merchant's account of exchanging emails with young children as part of a school project (Merchant, 2005a). Here, children took up and innovated with the kinds of textual innovations Merchant introduced. His emails gave children permission to draw on conventions developed in out-of-school contexts and also offered them resources for meaning-making including linguistic structures and innovations such as emoticons, abbreviation and figurative language.

There are fewer studies which explore young children's screen-based meaning-making in non-formal contexts without an adult model. Whilst understandings about this are only just emerging, some studies have begun to trace and articulate patterns of meaning-making in digital texts. One such study is Marsh's analysis of young children's engagement with the Disney-owned virtual world, Club Penguin (Marsh, 2010). In a development of this work Marsh (2011) explores children's literacy practices in this environment and investigates how they managed relationships and exchanges. Drawing on Goffman's notion of social order she describes conventions that are developed and sustained in order to manage or avoid interaction with others in what initially seemed a chaotic environment.

This small group of studies illustrate how young children can participate in meaningful exchanges that are relevant to their current lives: making and negotiating meaning rather than developing skills to be used at some future date. Engaging with digital texts then is about 'being rather than becoming' literate (Mavers, 2007: 172). This meaning making, however, plays out in different spaces and is embedded in other social interventions – whether face-to-face with peers or family members or through on-screen interactions with familiar and unfamiliar others.

CONTINUITIES AND DISCONTINUITIES BETWEEN HOME AND EDUCATIONAL SETTINGS

Analyses of classroom interactions and literacy practices have explored how children draw on varied resources in enacting and transacting relationships and improvising within official and unofficial discourses as they author classroom texts (Dyson, 2008). In doing so, children often integrate or recontextualise learning from out-of-school literacies. It is perhaps unsurprising then that recent classroom studies have revealed how such improvisations often reflect children's engagement with *digital* texts. Wohlwend (2009), for example, describes how young children integrated digital literacies into their role play even though available resources were designed to promote print literacy. By using a plastic carrot to simulate a mobile phone, for example, children garnered available resources to serve their own interests and create classroom spaces that resonated with their lives outside the setting.

In Wohlwend's study, the open-ended role-play activity provided a space for children to improvise and 'reinscribe' classroom discourses (Wohlwend, 2009). Other studies illustrate how children may use their digital experience to serve their own purposes even within the context of closed tasks. Siegel, Kontorourki, Schmier,

and Ennquez (2008), for example, showed how one child, working with a friend, drew on her knowledge of digital texts to experiment with design as she composed texts on screen, chatting with her friend, for example, about favourite colours as they selected fonts. In doing so, she drew from her out-of-school experience to create social capital in the classroom even though these experiences were not acknowledged by the teacher.

Studies such as Siegel et al.'s illustrate how such activities occur even when they are not recognised in dominant discourses. In some cases teachers may be unaware of children's experiences, knowledge and skill. We see this in McTavish's (2009) case study of an 8-year-old boy, whose individualised and print-based school literacies contrasted with his multilingual, digital home literacies. Whilst these literacies sometimes crossed boundaries – for example, as he did homework in the dining room or used graphics from computer games in his school work – the skills and understandings he brought from home or the possible value of this to his identity as a learner went unrecognised in the classroom.

Of course these differences may play out in different ways for different children. Wolfe and Flewitt's (2010) multimodal analysis of young children's engagement with literacy in an early years setting demonstrates how digital technologies may diversify modalities for children's meaning-making whilst acknowledging that individual children will draw from these possibilities to varying degrees. To some extent a child's perceived success at school may be linked to her ability to recognise these different discourses and shift identities as she moves between them. For some children, such changing expectations, and the resources and possibilities associated with them, may have significant implications for how they see their reading and writing and their associated sense of confidence and competence. Levy (2009), for example, demonstrates how young children may develop identities as readers/ writers of digital texts at home which are incompatible with the readers/writers they are expected to be at school. She describes how such contrasts may impact negatively on some young children's chances; whilst children may engage meaningfully with multimodal screen-based texts at home, knowledge about meaning-making and the confidence associated with this may be undermined as they encounter 'schooled' approaches to literacy.

Taken together these studies highlight how children may negotiate shifts between the predominantly print literacy practices of school and the more diverse and often digitally mediated literacy practices they encounter in the rest of their lives. They demonstrate how children may do so in different ways, sometimes finding ways to draw on digital literacies within print-dominated educational settings, sometimes shifting between different kinds of literacies and sometimes facing feelings of failure due to the mismatch between the reading and writing they engage in at home and in educational settings.

IMPLICATIONS AND FUTURE DIRECTIONS FOR RESEARCH

When we consider the place of digital communication in everyday affairs and the growing significance of new technology in the lives of young children it is surprising how little empirical work focuses on new literacies in the early years. The dominance of developmental models that emphasise what is 'natural' or 'age-appropriate' may

all too readily combine with discourses that encourage a return to the basic skills of print literacy with the effect that digital literacy is often seen as something that older children do, and then only after the mastery of alphabetic skills. This is clearly not the case, as studies of home literacies are now beginning to show. Research that focuses on 'being' rather than 'becoming' literate begins to draw our attention to the place of new technology in the ecology of meaning-making which in itself provides a context for children's early learning. The interplay between active engagement, guided interaction and shared expertise in new kinds of meaning-making offers rich opportunities for future research.

The short history of research and development work in this field is characterised by an unhelpful polarization of what technology can do and what children can do. In part this appears to stem from a struggle to conceptualise new technologies and the literacy practices associated with them. Conceiving of new technology as a tool – a sophisticated teaching machine – tends to position children as passive recipients of skills and knowledge, irrespective of any perceived notions of 'interactivity'. Here technology is at best used to motivate children or to enrich traditional literacy practices and at worst it is pressed into the service of efficiently delivering the skills of print literacy. An alternative view is one which sees new technology as a gateway to new communicative spaces, and this, as we have seen, has proved more fruitful. To the extent that this view allows for a consideration of how young children are placed in new kinds of relationships through new meaning-making practices it has the potential to tap into the distinctive qualities of new literacies.

This underlines the pressing need to redefine what we mean by literacy and its role in play, creativity and in the wider communicative landscape of the early-years curriculum. Some innovative work has begun to explore this territory. For example, Marsh's (2006) work with 3- and 4-year-olds explores the creation of short animated films. She traced how children worked as designers and bricoleurs to create first paper-based storyboards and then simple animations using stop-frame animation. This work provides insights into how children approached composition and the understandings and intentions they seemed to bring to this, particularly in relation to the challenge of creating movement through the juxtaposition of a series of still images. Understanding how children engage in such multimodal interactions around texts (Taylor, 2006) may help us to learn more about young children's approaches to composition. Indeed, Marsh argues that there is a need to supplement knowledge of children's development as readers and writers of printed texts with knowledge of their involvement in broader 'communicative practices' (Marsh, 2006: 504). These analyses highlight the need to re-frame understandings about young children's literacy learning. Research-informed attempts to do so are scarce. One example is work by Merchant (2005b) which draws on analysis of observations in a children's centre in which he explored young children's interactions with a variety of technological tools, toys and applications. He uses this analysis to re-interpret Clay's *Concepts About Print* (Clay, 2000) in terms of writing on screen, drawing attention to the work that still needs to be undertaken in mapping what we understand by new literacies in the early years.

In this chapter, we have repeatedly drawn attention to the place of new technology in young children's lifeworlds and,

by implication, to the cultural and linguistic capital associated with digital literacy. However it is clear that inequities in access and meaning-making practices are as evident in digital worlds as they are in other domains of social life, even though they may be patterned differently. Whilst the concept of a digital divide masks much complexity (Selwyn, 2004), young children in home and school contexts are differentiated by their access to 'advantageous practice' (Greenhow and Robelia, 2009; Burnett and Merchant, 2011). This is true both within and between societies (Prinsloo, 2005) and points to the need for large-scale studies with the capacity to map the patterns of young children's engagement with new literacies across contexts. At the same time there is a need for research embedded in the particular contexts of family and institutional life that provides a more fine-grained analysis of young children's interactions with and around digital texts over time.

REFERENCES

Andrews, R. (ed.) (2004) *The Impact of ICT on Literacy Education*. London: Routledge Falmer.

Auld, G. (2007) 'Talking books for children's home use in a minority Indigenous Australian language context', *Australian Journal of Educational Technology*, 23(1): 48–67.

Beck, N. and Fetherston, T. (2003) 'The effects of incorporating a word processor into a year three writing program', *Information Technology in Childhood Education Annual*, 2003(1): 139–61.

Burnett, C. (2009) 'Research into literacy and technology in primary classrooms: An exploration of understandings generated by recent studies', *Journal of Research in Reading*, 31(1): 22–37.

Burnett, C. (2010) 'Technology and literacy in early childhood educational settings: A review of research', *Journal of Early Childhood Literacy*, 10(3): 247–70.

Burnett, C. and Merchant, G. (2011) 'Is there a space for critical literacy in the context of social media?',

English Teaching: Practice and Critique, 10(1): 41–57.

Chera, P. and Wood, C. (2003) 'Animated multimedia "talking books" can promote phonological awareness in children beginning to read', *Learning and Instruction*, 13(1): 33.

Clay, M. (2000) *Concepts About Print: What Have Children Learned About the Way We Print Language?* Portsmouth, NH: Heinemann.

Clements, D. and Sarama, J. (2003) 'Strip mining for gold: Research and policy in educational technology – a response to "Fools Gold"', *Educational Technology Review*, 11(1): 7–69.

Davidson, C. (2009) 'Young children's engagement with digital texts and literacies in the home: Pressing matters for the teaching of English in the early years of schooling', *English Teaching: Practice and Critique*, 8(3): 36–54.

Dyson, A.H. (2008) 'The Pine Cone Wars: Studying writing in a community of children', *Language Arts*, 85(4): 305–15.

Gardner, H. (1991) *The Unschooled Mind: How Children Think and How Schools Should Teach.* New York: Basic Books.

Greenhow, C. and Robelia, B. (2009) 'Informal learning and identity formation in online social networks', *Learning, Media and Technology*, 34(2): 119–40.

Hassett, D. (2006) 'Signs of the times: The governance of alphabetic print over "appropriate" and "natural" reading development', *Journal of Early Childhood Literacy*, 6(1): 77–103.

Hesse, P. and Lane, F. (2003) 'Media literacy starts young: An integrated curriculum approach', *Young Children*, 58(6): 20–6.

Kenner, C., Ruby, M., Jessel, J., and Gregory, E. (2008) 'Intergenerational learning events around the computer: A site for linguistc and cultural exchange', *Language and Education*, 22(4): 298–319.

Kress, G. (2010) *Multimodality: A Social Semiotic Approach to Contemporary Communication.* London: Routledge.

Kuhlman, W.D., Everts Danielson, K., Campbell, E.J., and Topp, N. (2005) 'Implementing handheld computers as tools for first-grade writers', *Computers in Schools*, 22(34): 173–85.

Labbo, D.L. and Reinking, D. (2003) 'Computers and early literacy education', in N. Hall, J. Larson, and J. Marsh (eds), *Handbook of Early Childhood Literacy*. London: Sage. pp. 338–54.

Labbo, L., Eakle, J., and Montero, M.K. (2002) 'Digital Language Experience Approach: Using digital photographs and software as a Language Experience Approach innovation', *Reading Online*, 5(8): 1–19.

Lankshear, C. and Knobel, M. (2003) 'New technologies in early childhood literacy research: A review of research', *Journal of Early Childhood Literacy*, 3(1): 59–82.

Levy, R. (2009) '"You have to understand words ... but not read them": Young children becoming readers in a digital age', *Journal of Research in Reading*, 32(1): 75–91.

Macaruso, P., Hook, P., and McCable, R.(2006) 'The efficacy of computer-based supplementary phonics programs for advancing reading skills in at-risk elementary students', *Journal of Research in Reading*, 29(2): 162–72.

Marsh, J. (2004) 'The techno-literacy practices of young children', *Journal of Early Childhood Research* 2(1): 51–66.

Marsh, J. (2006) 'Emergent media literacy: Digital animation in early childhood', *Language and Education*, 20(6): 493–506.

Marsh, J. (2010) 'Young children's play in online virtual worlds', *Journal of Early Childhood Research*, 8(1): 23–9.

Marsh, J. (2011) 'Young children's literacy practices in a virtual world: Establishing an online interaction order', *Reading Research Quarterly*, 46(2): 101–18.

Mavers, D. (2007) 'Semiotic resourcefulness: A young child's email exchange as design', *Journal of Early Childhood Literacy*, 7(2): 155–76.

McTavish, M. (2009) '"I get my facts from the internet": A case study of the teaching and learning of information literacy in in-school and out-of-school contexts', *Journal of Early Childhood Literacy*, 9(1): 3–28.

Merchant, G. (2005a) 'The Dagger of Doom and the Mighty Handbag: Exploring identity in children's on-screen writing', in J. Evans (ed.), *Literacy Moves On: Popular Culture, New Technologies and Critical Literacies in the Elementary Classroom.* Portsmouth, NH: Heinemann pp. 63–82.

Merchant, G. (2005b) 'Barbie meets Bob the Builder at the workstation: Learning to write on screen', in J. Marsh (ed.), *Popular Culture, New Media and Digital Literacy in Early Childhood*. London: Routledge. pp. 183–200.

Merchant, G. (2007a) 'Writing the future in the digital age', *Literacy*, 41(3): 119–28.

Merchant, G. (2007b) 'Digital writing in the early years', in D. Leu, J. Coiro, M. Knobel, and C. Lankshear, *The Handbook of Research on New Literacies.* New York: Lawrence Erlbaum.

Miller, E. (2005) 'Fighting technology for toddlers', *Education Digest*, 71(3): 55–8.

Oksman, V. and Rautiainen, P. (2003) '"Perhaps it is a body part"; how the mobile phone became an organic part of the everyday lives of Finnish children and teenagers', in J.E. Katz (ed.), *Machines that Become Us: the Social Context of Personal Communication Technology.* New Jersey: Transaction. pp. 293–311.

Pahl, K. (2005) 'Narrative spaces and multiple identities: Children's textual explorations of console games in home settings', in J. Marsh (ed.), *Popular Culture, New Media and Digital Literacy in Early Childhood.* London: Routledge. pp. 126–43.

Pelletier, J., Reeve, R., and Halewood, C. (2006) 'Young children's knowledge building and literacy development through knowledge forum', *Early Education and Development*, 17(3): 323–46.

Plowman, L., McPake, J., and Stephen C. (2010a) 'The technologisation of childhood? Young children and technology in the home', *Children & Society*, 24: 63–74.

Plowman, L., Stephen, C., and McPake, J. (2010b) 'Supporting children's learning with technology at home and in pre-school', *Research Papers in Education*, 25(1): 93–113.

Prinsloo, M. (2005) 'The new literacies as placed resources', *Perspectives in Education,* 23(4): 87–98.

Rideout, V.J., and Hammel, E. (2006). *The Media Family: Electronic Media in the Lives of Infants, Toddlers, Preschoolers and their Parents.* Menlo Park, CA: Kaiser Family Foundation.

Schiller, J. and Tillett, B.(2004) 'Using digital images with young children: Challenges of integration', *Early Child Development and Care*, 174(4): 401.

Selwyn, N. (2004) 'Reconsidering political and popular understandings of the digital divide', *New Media & Society*, 6(3): 341–62.

Siegel, M., Kontorourki, S., Schmier, S., and Ennquez, G. (2008) 'Literacy in motion: A case study of a shape-shifting kindergartener', *Language Arts*, 86(2): 89–98.

Smith, C. (2005) 'The CD-ROM game: A toddler engaged in computer-based play', in J. Marsh (ed.), *Popular Culture, New Media and Digital Literacy in Early Childhood.* London: Routledge. pp. 108–25.

Stephen, C. and Plowman, L. (2003) 'Information and communication technologies in pre-school settings: A review of the literature', *International Journal of Early Years Education*, 11(3): 224–34.

Tancock, S. and Segedy, J. (2004) 'A comparison of young children's technology-enhanced and traditional responses to texts: An action research project', *Journal of Research in Childhood Education*, 19(1): 58.

Taylor, R. (2006) 'Actions speak as loud as words; a multimodal analysis of boys' talk in the classroom', *English in Education*, 40(3): 66–82.

Taylor, L.K., Bernhard, J.K., Garg, S, and Cumins, J. (2008) 'Affirming plural belonging: Building on students' family-based cultural and linguistic capital through multiliteracies pedagogy' *Journal of Early Childhood Literacy*, 8(3): 269–294.

Teale, W. and Gambrell, L. (2007) 'Raising urban students' literacy achievement by engaging in authentic, challenging work', *Reading Teacher*, 60(8): 728–39.

Voogt, J. and McKenney, S. (2007) 'Using ICT to foster (pre)reading and writing skills in young children', *Computers in Schools*, 24(3/4): 83–94.

Wohlwend, K. (2009) 'Early adopters: Playing new literacies and pretending new technologies in print-centric classrooms', *Journal of Early Childhood Literacy*, 9(2): 117–40.

Wolfe, S. and Flewitt, R. (2010) 'New technologies, new multimodal practices and young children's metacognitive development', *Cambridge Journal of Education*, 40(4): 387–99.

Yelland, N. (2005) 'The future is now: A review of the literature on the use of computers in early childhood education (1994–2004)', *Association for the Advancement of Computing in Education Journal*, 13(3): 201–32.

Yelland, N. (2010) 'New technologies, playful experiences, and multimodal learning', in I.R. Berson and R.J. Berson (eds), *High-Tech Tots: Childhood in a Digital World.* Charlotte, NC: Information Age Publishing. pp. 5–22.

33

Critical Literacy in the Early Years: Emergence and Sustenance in an Age of Accountability

Barbara Comber

INTRODUCTION

The work of early childhood educators in facilitating young children's literacy acquisition has never received more attention than in the new millennium. Media hype about literacy crises, falling standards, teacher quality and government promises of minimum standards for all children have simultaneously increased the 'visibility' of literacy and the stakes for school performance. Indeed the last two decades could be seen as an age of pronouncements with respect to literacy, with politicians internationally promising to cure supposed low literacy with standardized tests and mandated programmes. As the rhetoric around literacy intensifies many late-capitalist economies are experiencing shifts that have increased the gaps between rich and poor, changed the very nature of work, and fundamentally altered the cultural mix of their populations. More and more children attending schools where English is the language of instruction speak it as a second or third language. Many children have experienced the effects of war, terrorism, migration and poverty. Many live in fractured, fragmented and changing families. Teacher populations are changing too. In some places aging teacher workforces mean that there is already a shortage of qualified teachers. Literacy is also changing as the impact of digital technologies on global and local communication, economies and knowledges begins to bite in everyday and working lives. It is challenging to think about how spaces for the emergence and sustenance of critical literacy in early childhood education might be created.

Critical literacy is a relative newcomer to early childhood educational discourse which has typically been dominated by developmental theory with its attendant assumptions of the naturally developing child and emergent literacy (Dyson and Genishi, 2009; Luke and Luke, 2001; Reid and Comber, 2002). Ideologies of child innocence and the 'goodness' of literacy permeate the field and infuse literacy curriculum and pedagogy. The child literacy learner is positioned as a maturing individual – a psychological subject – who grows and blossoms with the right conditions and support. Indeed this developmental discourse is central to the notion of 'readiness', a key word in early schooling and literacy, a yardstick by which some children are judged as ready to come to school and/or ready for reading and others not (Comber, 1999). Critical literacy, with its focus on power and language, has not been a force in early-childhood literacy education. Indeed critical literacy is often seen as most appropriate for older or more advanced students.

In this chapter I first introduce the concept of critical literacy. The next section focuses on research which addresses questions of power, language and representation in early-childhood literacy education. I then describe two case studies where ground-breaking early childhood educators explicitly set out to build and investigate critical literacies in their classrooms. Finally I summarize recent research and theory, and outline some challenges and questions for future work.

CRITICAL LITERACY: AN EVOLVING CONCEPT

The history of *critical literacy* is located more in adult and community sites (e.g.,

Freire, 1972; Kamler, 2001; Lankshear and McLaren, 1993; Wallace, 2001), middle- and high schools (e.g., Bigelow, 2001; Janks, 1993; Kinloch, 2011; Mellor, Patterson, and O'Neill, 1987; Searle, 1993; Zacher Pandya, 2012), rather than in early schooling. Paolo Freire is typically credited with its genesis and his phrase 'reading the word, reading the world' (Freire and Macedo, 1987) is emblematic of critical literacy internationally. Freire's insistence that literacy could and should position people to argue for their rights underpins much of the work of educators committed to critical literacy (Edelsky, 1999; Giroux, 1993; Lankshear, 1994; Luke, 2000; Powell, 1999). Defining critical literacy goes against its ethos of 'debate, dissonance and difference' (Luke and Freebody, 1997: 16), involving locally contingent, dynamic repertoires of practices (Kamler and Comber, 1996; Luke, 2000, 2012) negotiated in different situations (Comber and Simpson, 2001; Comber, 2001).

Critical literacy educators have drawn on perspectives from feminism, anti-racist education, critical discourse analysis, multiculturalism, theories of social justice and more. In the US for instance critical literacies have developed out of a politicized whole language approach, multiculturalism, cultural and critical theory. In the United Kingdom critical linguistics, cultural, literary and literacy studies influenced critical approaches to teaching English literacy. In South Africa a critical language awareness model based upon the work of Norman Fairclough (1992) and others has been a powerful catalyst for change particularly in secondary schools and tertiary institutions. Clearly this developed alongside anti-Apartheid political activism (Janks, 2010). And there are other histories in other places. There is not a single correct critical literacy (Kamler and Comber, 1996; Luke, 2012); rather it is an evolving contingent concept. While it would be worthwhile, a genealogy of critical literacy is beyond the scope of this chapter (but see Luke, 2012 and Janks, 2010). Luke and Freebody (1997: 1), whilst also underscoring the range of approaches, suggest critical literacy marks out: '[A] coalition of educational interests committed to engaging with the possibilities that the technologies of writing and other modes of inscription offer for social change, cultural diversity, economic equity and political enfranchisement.'

Critical literacy is an evolving repertoire of practices of analysis and interrogation which move between the micro features of texts and the macro conditions of institutions, focusing upon how relations of power work through these practices. In early childhood classrooms this often involves three key pedagogical moves (Comber, 2001a) – recognizing and mobilizing children's analytic resources (Dyson, 1997), examining existing texts (Baker and Davies, 1993; Harste and Leland, 2001), and offering children new discursive resources (O'Brien, 1994a, 1994b; Vasquez, 2001a, 2001b)

Freebody and Luke's (1990, 1997) model of reading incorporated four roles:

- code-breaker (How do I crack this?);
- text-participant (What does this mean?);
- text-user (What do I do with this, here and now?);
- text-analyst (What does this do to me?).

In later iterations of the model they renamed the roles as resources – coding, pragmatic, semantic and critical (Luke and Freebody, 1997) to reflect their sociological rather than psychological approach to literacy as assembling repertoires of practices. A social view of reading requires

that teachers give attention to the socio-political nature of their work and the non-neutrality of textual practices. They suggest that critical literacy practices might include:

- asking in whose interests particular texts work;
- examining multiple and conflicting texts;
- examining the historical and cultural contexts of discourses in texts;
- reading texts against one another;
- comparing the vocabularies and grammars of related texts;
- investigating how readers are positioned by the ideologies in texts;
- making multiple passes through texts.

Along with analysis, they included transforming and redesigning texts as part of critical literacy (Luke and Freebody, 1999). Similarly a critical orientation is applicable to visual, electronic texts and the hybrid multi-media and multi-modal texts of everyday life (Luke and Luke, 2001). In explaining the critical dimension of the model they emphasized that learners need to:

Critically analyse and transform texts by acting on knowledge that texts are not ideologically natural or neutral – that they represent particular points of view while silencing others and influence people's ideas – and that their designs and discourses can be critiqued and redesigned in novel and hybrid ways.

(Luke and Freebody, 1999)

Further, they argued that these dimensions of literacy need to be learnt together; that critical literacy is as important in early childhood as adult literacy or secondary English.

The four resources model of literacy acknowledges the dimensions of literacy with which early childhood educators are already familiar (code-breaking and understanding the text) and for which they are usually held responsible. Precisely because it is an inclusive approach to literacy, that does not discount the importance of any aspect of literate practice, 'the four resources model' makes critical literacy more attractive to teachers and policy makers to the extent that it was taken up in many Australian state curricula, and indeed resources were provided for teachers (e.g., Department for Education and Children's Services, 1995; Education Queensland, 2000).

POWER, LANGUAGE AND REPRESENTATION IN EARLY LITERACY LESSONS

Although the term critical literacy has only recently been taken up in early childhood education contexts, it has been clear for some time that addressing questions about power, language and representation was certainly possible in early childhood classrooms (Dyson, 1989, 1993, 1997). In an extensive series of ethnographic case studies over three decades in the US, Anne Haas Dyson showed that young, poor, urban children of colour could deal with the complexity of power relations and bring to bear multiple sophisticated representational resources in their classroom writing. Drawing theoretically on Bakhtin's notion of the dialogic nature of texts – 'in a world riddled with voices to talking to, past, and over each other' – Dyson (1993: 6) demonstrated that children employ 'sociocultural intelligence' (Dyson, 1993) in constructing texts that position them powerfully and productively in their classroom contexts.

Dyson argued that young children are not simply media dupes or TV sponges but that they selectively appropriate material from popular culture which they assemble anew with home language traditions and school genres. As young children compose

texts they simultaneously compose spaces for themselves in the world, often marked by irreverent play, jokes, songs and parodies, not always the serious display of scholarship – an effective method of contesting dominant discourses of the official realms of schooling and beyond. Dyson's extensive corpus provides more than ample evidence of young children and their teachers' capacities to engage with complex analyses of language as they produce their stories filled with characters grappling for power, influence and social effects. Along with other researchers of children's writing (Gilbert, 1989; Kamler, 1994; Lensmire, 1994) Dyson illustrated persuasively that gender, class and race impact strongly on children's writing and their responses to each other's writing. Her research showed that, when it comes to an analysis of language and power, young children have greatest investments in situations and texts that arise in their immediate social classroom worlds. The 'critical literacies' invented in the sites Dyson studied arose from the productive interplay of young children's social goals with the teachers' academic agenda.

Dyson demonstrated repeatedly how seriously we underestimate what children do intellectually and socially within the micro-politics of their everyday lives in classrooms.

In particular, her respect for young children's social agency and their appropriation and re-workings of popular cultural texts has informed international curriculum design and classroom based research in a range of very different early childhood settings (Kavanagh, 1997; O'Brien and Comber, 2000; Marsh, 2000, and this volume; Sahni, 2001; Vasquez, 2003).

Research which explicitly addresses social justice, multi-culturalism and/or anti-racism can be seen as a parallel movement to critical literacy in the sense that it contributed to the production of a discursive space, allowing educators to re-think their work in overtly political ways. The relationship between literacy and a politics of difference underlies critical literacy in theory and in practice. In the United States there has been a strong tradition of arguing for bilingual education as a key move in respecting minority children's identities and cultures (e.g., de la Luz Reyes, 2001; Moll, 2001). Internationally, socio-cultural literacy research has contested normative educational discourse by promoting respect for poor and culturally diverse communities by highlighting neighbourhood 'funds of knowledge' (Moll, Amanti, Neff, and Gonzalez, 1992), the 'resourcefulness' of families (McNaughton, 1995) and the children's use of syncretized (or blended) literacies (Gregory and Williams, 2000). Whilst these studies do not name their objectives as critical literacy they are directly concerned with the relationships between language, power and identity.

Research contesting the mainstream normative model of early literacy, with its insistence of mothers reading to children as the single and preferable readiness route to literacy (Carrington and Luke, 2002; Dixon, 2011; Panofsky, 2000), can be seen as making discursive space for different and culturally inclusive literacies that are part of a critical literacy agenda which operates beyond the individual teacher and classroom to change the discourses that pervade and delimit early literacy instruction. Similarly, research debunking deficit discourses about the poor is still needed to make inroads on the pervasiveness of blame and derision (Comber and Kamler, 2004; Freebody, 1992).

These discursive shifts with respect to normative models of early childhood development underpinned the early ground-breaking work of two teacher-researchers who invented critical and feminist approaches to re-designing early literacy curriculum – Jennifer O'Brien and Vivian Vasquez. Their work was important for demonstrating what could actually be accomplished with young children and opening up practice, policy and inquiry.

CRITICAL READING IN EARLY CHILDHOOD CLASSROOMS: STARTING WITH TEXTS

Jennifer O'Brien developed her approach to critical literacy in early childhood classrooms working with 5–8-year-old children in culturally diverse low to middle socio-economic communities in South Australia in the late eighties and early nineties. She was profoundly influenced by post-structuralist feminist theory, gender and literacy (e.g., Gilbert and Rowe, 1989) critical discourse analysis, and critiques of early childhood and progressive pedagogies. Such theories suggested that children's capacities were being under-estimated in literacy classrooms. In a series of studies O'Brien developed a pedagogy of critical literacy that made sense to and engaged young children. Working with feminist poststructuralist theory and critical literacy approaches developed for high-school students (Mellor et al., 1987; Janks, 1993) as her guide, plus the critiques of early childhood literacy and progressive pedagogies (Baker and Freebody, 1989) on her mind, O'Brien adapted, re-shaped and invented ways of examining texts with young children and assignments which positioned them as text analysts and researchers.

O'Brien believed that children learning to decode could take up analytical stances in relation to texts. Influenced by Dyson's ethnographic accounts of young children's grasp of power relations in their writing and also by Au and Mason's (1981) work indicating that the patterns of talk around text could be altered, she was confident that children had the capacities for critical literacy. O'Brien's main goal was that children question the social worlds constructed in texts. This meant children understanding that texts are constructed by authors and illustrators who make particular decisions about who and what to show and how, who and what not to show, about the scripts and actions different characters are given and so on. O'Brien's tasks drew attention to the craftedness of texts. For example, referring to contrasting versions of the Hansel and Gretel story she asked the children to consider both stepmother and the father:

> Draw the woman as you think Anthony Browne will draw her. Show her face and her clothes. Use a speech bubble to show what she says.
> Draw the man as you think Anthony Browne will draw him. Show his face and his clothes. Use a speech bubble to show what he says.
> (O'Brien and Comber, 2000: 159)

In this way she mobilized children's existing cultural knowledge about representations of women and men in texts. The commonalities and differences between children's predictions became the object of study. O'Brien attempted to increase children's awareness of the ways in which their reading practices were constructed. She took a similar approach with picture books, school reading series (both fact and fiction) and everyday texts (O'Brien, 2001a, 2001b) and she invited children to consider how texts position their readers. Referring to *My First Book of Knowledge* (Petty, 1990), O'Brien invited children to consider the content that adults include in such books: 'I wonder what Kate Petty

and the other people who produced this book decided to put in this book for you to read about'.

O'Brien positioned children as readers who could and should question the texts that were produced for them. As the children began to critically examine the text and to point out mistakes in the pictures, O'Brien broadened their inquiry and invited them to look at other factual texts in the school reading series to see if there were similar problems there: 'Let's look out for other examples of authors not taking the trouble to get things right for young readers'. In particular, they examined how 'science texts' designed for young readers construct knowledge. The children discovered that such texts contained many inaccuracies, a mixture of fact and fiction, and under-estimated what they already knew.

O'Brien invited learner readers to interrogate, to examine, and to compare other texts and their own knowledge, to dare to question the authority of the text. She frequently focused on the representation of the family or family members in children's literature, basal readers and everyday texts. She is perhaps best known for working with young children to deconstruct everyday texts, such as junk mail, using questions such as the following:

- Who are the important people (powerful, good, etc.) in the family created in this text?
- How do they behave?
- What kinds of words does the writer/illustrator think you should know about family members?
- Who are the unimportant people in this family?
- How can you tell they are less/more important for the writer/illustrator?
- How does this compare with your experience?
    (O'Brien and Comber, 2000: 164).

O'Brien's feminist stance meant that she focused a great deal on the ways in which men and women were depicted in textual families – as kings, queens, princesses, aunts, mothers and fathers and so on. Her work over several years with different groups of children, examining Mothers' Day catalogues and the wider cultural event of Mothers' Day (O'Brien, 1994a; Luke, O'Brien, and Comber, 1994) provided an accessible approach to introducing critical literacy to young children.

Luke, in analyzing this work with O'Brien and Comber, points out four key moves in critical text analysis, which are evident here (Luke et al., 1994):

1 Talk about the institutional conditions of production and interpretation;
2 Talk about the textual ideologies and discourses, silences and absences;
3 Discourse analysis of textual and linguistic techniques in relation to (1) and (2);
4 Strategic and tactical action with and/or against the text.

While O'Brien employed a planned approach to critical literacy such as the Mothers' Day unit, like most early-childhood teachers she worked with everyday events and incidental texts in the context in which they appeared (O'Brien, 1998). O'Brien's was a trailblazer in building, designing and documenting her innovations with critical reading practices. References to her work appear in many state department materials for teachers. In this chapter considerable space has been devoted to describing her actual framing of tasks and questions around specific texts and events because a major contribution of O'Brien's work is its customization of discourses of critical literacy for pedagogical work with young children. Few educators or researchers had grappled with such issues and indeed, this review suggests that only a limited amount of research focusing on the pedagogy of critical literacy in the early years has been done at this time.

O'Brien also conducted research in her classroom which addressed different children's responses to her critical literacy curriculum. She (O'Brien, 1994b) reported that there was a differential response to the disruptive feminist discourse she had made available, mainly along gender lines, with some girls taking up socially critical positions and transferring this approach into new texts and tasks. Indeed one young student even appropriated the discourse to the point where she explained that, 'It's written in our head'. This 7-year-old had understood O'Brien's point that texts follow culturally familiar storylines. Yet several boys in the class were less enthusiastic about her disruptive readings and did not take up these positions themselves. O'Brien research raises important questions about what young children do with discursive practices and ideological positions which are different to their own. This relates to what might be seen as the 'limits of English' (Patterson, 1997) or literacy teaching. Patterson suggests that advocates of critical literacy need to think about 'training' children in particular kinds of critical reading techniques and strategies – sets of capacities which they can bring to bear in particular situations, rather than ethical positions which we ask them to take up. O'Brien's research certainly demonstrated that young children could read critically. Sometimes some children resisted her invitations to do so. Questions about differential response, take up and transfer require further research.

CHILDREN'S CULTURAL AND SOCIAL QUESTIONS ABOUT EVERYDAY LIFE AS CURRICULUM

Vivian Vasquez was a kindergarten teacher working in a highly multi-cultural catholic school in Toronto when she first encountered O'Brien's classroom research, along with the theoretical resources of scholars such as Allan Luke, Carole Edelsky and other literacy educators in the early nineties. Vasquez decided to make her whole language pedagogy more overtly political, by taking up children's questions about justice in representational and schooling practices. Part of her strong justice standpoint grew from painful memories of her own school experiences in Canada as an immigrant child from the Philippines (Vasquez, 2001a, 2003).

Vasquez designed her critical literacy curriculum around children's issues, interests, questions and observations (Vasquez, 2001a). Often these focused around school and family life. For instance children raised questions about why as the youngest children in the school they were sometimes excluded from events and places (e.g., a school café), why they had to wait for certain privileges (e.g., receiving a sacrament), differences between men and women in various media representations (e.g., Canadian Mounted Police), people's rights to different cultural preferences and practices (e.g., vegetarianism, McDonalds), languages taught at school (e.g., Why French rather than Spanish or Chinese?).

Vasquez believed in making the curriculum and her research visible. She and the children collected and posted key artifacts and products of their work – transcripts of their conversations, covers of texts discussed, photographs, drawings, written responses and so on – on a wall (40 feet × 6 feet) of the classroom she had covered in paper. Children got to see what was recorded as significant and worth exploring. This, Vasquez described as the 'audit trail':

> Retracing thinking invites theorizing. As I constructed the audit trail, I began to think about using it as a tool for critical conversation with young children ... By the end of the school year, the audit trail had become a joint construction between teacher and children and a means of generating and reflecting on the classroom curriculum ... Each of the artifacts became a way for us to make visible the incidents that caused us to want to learn, the issues we had critical conversations about, and the action we took to resist being dominated and to reposition ourselves within our community. They became our demonstration of and our site for constructing critical curriculum for ourselves.
> (Vasquez, 2001b: 57–8)

Vasquez reported that over the school year children frequently referred to objects on the wall and re-visited earlier conversations. Topics raised and explored included fairness, gender, the media, the environment and, as Vasquez puts it, a range of questions about 'power and control'. Because the wall was visible to all, parents and guardians became involved. Children regularly polled their own class and others about school matters; they wrote a petition; they organized a Speaker's Corner; they conducted their own conference to which parents, and other children and teachers were invited. In short the children were inducted into the social use of literate practices in specific situations. Over time the children became questioners. While many parents were delighted by the children's engagement some teachers saw them as 'radical, rude and disrespectful' (Vasquez, 2001b: 59), because they questioned how things were. These children were clearly not performing normal kindergartner subjectivities. Vasquez's work made it clear that when young children begin to interrogate and research things that matter to them it is a continuously generative process – 'an incidental unfolding of social justice issues' (Vasquez, 2001a).

Reluctant to 'frontload' social justice topics selected by the teacher, Vasquez's approach was to work with the everyday issues that are often put to one side in classrooms or seen as disruptive. The repertoires of language and literacy practices she assisted young children to assemble – public speaking, letter writing, surveys, petitions – were goal-directed and situation-specific, inducting them in ways of making a difference through talk and writing (or attempting to!).

Whereas O'Brien tended to focus on questions of representation in texts, Vasquez emphasized writing, conversation and action within the classroom and school community 'grounding the curriculum in the lives of students' (Vasquez, 2001a: 211). Yet both these early-childhood teachers started with the everyday – either everyday texts or everyday life. Both examined school practices and texts. Both were committed to a political standpoint of social justice informed by feminist and critical multiculturalism. Both invited young children to become co-researchers and explore the secrets of institutional life and what is taken for granted in texts.

A number of researchers, especially in north America, have been inspired by the work of Vasquez and O'Brien, and have gone on to develop approaches with teacher-researchers which put children's concerns about justice at the centre of their curriculum, foster local social action, or explore social justice through engagement with texts (Cooper and White, 2006; Dozier, Johnston, and Rogers, 2006; Leland, Harste, and Huber, 2005; Lewison, Flint, and Van Sluys, 2002; Souto-Manning, 2009).

SUSTAINING A CRITICAL LITERACY AGENDA IN AN AGE OF ACCOUNTABILITY

Since the ground-breaking work of O'Brien and Vasquez, a number of early childhood researchers have investigated critical approaches to early literacy (Arthur, 2001; de La Luz Reyes, 2001; Jones Diaz, Beecher and Arthur, 2002; Leland et al., 2005; Lewison, Flint, and Van Sluys, 2002; Martello, 2001; Jones, Clarke, and Enriquez, 2010; Souto-Manning, 2009).

Some of the US-situated early critical literacy work has focused on generating social justice conversations through the use of well-chosen children's literature concerning themes such as racism, sexism and poverty (Leland et al., 2005; Leland and Harste, 2005; Souto-Manning, 2010). These researchers have typically worked through teacher education programmes to build the understandings and influence the practices of the teaching profession with respect to critical literacy.

There have been few full-scale practitioner accounts of critical literacy in early-childhood classrooms. However Souto-Manning's (2009, 2010) body of work applying a Freierian-inspired pedagogy demonstrates powerfully that even young children consider how inequality and oppression work in everyday life to exclude people from particular places or social practices. In an action research project with first-graders Bourke (2008) reports that learning to read fairy tales critically gradually impacted on his students who composed their own stories. However, he notes that the process of learning to interrogate texts critically and framing critical questions takes some time and elicits some awkward conversations when ideologically problematic readings are voiced. Both Souto-Manning and Bourke note the ways in which critical literacy pedagogy is always undertaken within wider social and educational institutions and discursive practices into which children are already inducted, namely competition, special education, good guys and bad guys and so on. The work that can be accomplished by individual classroom teachers and their students needs to be understood as situated within ongoing policy and practice regimes, which may well be contradictory.

Other researchers have focused on the ways in which a critical literacy approach can supplement other literacy pedagogies. For example Sandretto et al. (2006), working in New Zealand and informed by a multiliteracies approach, worked collaboratively with teacher-researchers to add critical literacy strategies to their broader guided-reading approach to the teaching of reading. Stephanie Jones and colleagues add to the design of a differentiated reading instruction through the use of Freebody and Luke's (1990) four resources heuristic and their own emphasis on the reader's identity.

Research in critical literacy remains comparatively rare in early childhood sites and perhaps is less visible in nations where it is not yet, or, is no longer, part of the authorized curriculum and where teacher autonomy and flexibility are limited (Dyson and Genishi, 2009). It may be as Luke (2000: 459) suggested that it's not whether governments bring critical literacy into state curriculum policy but rather a 'matter of government getting out of the way so that "critical literacies" can be invented in classrooms'. And of late governments have been less likely to get out of the way!

Paugh, Carey, King-Jackson, and Russell (2007) discussed the ways in which *No Child Left Behind* mandated for tight linear scripted curriculum predominated in the US context and produced ongoing surveillance of teachers through regimes of practice such as the literacy block. They reported on the ways teachers made space

for critical literacy beyond the literacy block by following children's leads in conversation into what the teachers called Choice Time. Further they explained how children were involved in communicating their complex learning directly to the parent community. Similarly, in the context of the Australian federal government having introduced high-stakes literacy and numeracy assessment, Comber and Nixon (2011) described the ways in which experienced critical literacy teachers are making spaces outside the time set aside for students to study English literacy, but working across the curriculum in design and technology and studies of society and environment. The importance of teachers being able to design and negotiate critical literacy curriculum in their own contexts is important. Zacher Pandya (2012) has identified the risks of standardized pre-packaged versions of critical literacy. In a study of the implementation of the 'Inquiry' component of *Open Court Reading*, she powerfully demonstrated the dangers of pre-scripted inquiry, which limits what can be asked and investigated. We still need to know a great deal more about what constitutes critical literacies in different early years classrooms and the extent to which the critical can or should be given priority (Hall, 1998) and to look systematically at what constitutes critical literacy in different nation states in relation to literacy policy and accountability frameworks (see special issue of *Theory into Practice*, 2012).

Yet we know from what has been done that young children can appreciate how relations of power are produced through textual practices. We know they can deal with questions of fairness and justice. However there is a great deal more that needs to be explored. The timing is right for some systematic studies of what critical literacy looks like in different communities and what different groups of children do with the critical discourses which are made available to them. We need to conduct micro-analyses of the ways different children participate in critical literacy curricula and what they take from that into their everyday literate practices. We need to look closely at the connections and overlap between critical media literacy, multimodal literacies and new e-literacies (Alvermann and Hagood, 2000; Kress, 2000; C. Luke, 1997; Myers, Hammett, and McKillop, 2000; Nixon, 2002) and critical literacy (see chapters by Kress and Mackey, this volume). We need to explore the relationship between the critical, the popular and the everyday (Comber, 2001a; Dyson, 1997; Janks, 2010; Marsh, 2000). Productive connections may be made with critical scientific literacy (Roth and Desautels, 2002) and place studies (Smith, 2002), where local action on and within the environment are stressed (Healy, 1998; Powell, 2001; Comber, Thomson, and Wells, 2001).

Recently Janks (2010), Janks and Vasquez (2011) and Luke (2012) have provided useful syntheses of critical literacy theory and practice and some directions for future exploration. Working in a highly multilingual context, Janks points out that students need to access, and acquire mastery with, academic language; to learn how to deconstruct dominant discourses; to use the diversity of their language and life experiences as productive resources for learning; and to produce their own multi-modal texts in order to generate new meanings. She argues that different models of critical literacy have emphasized different aspects of practice as fundamental – domination, access, diversity and design, yet her model stresses the interdependence of each of these principles. In an edited volume of

English Teaching: Practice and Critique, Janks and Vasquez (2011) argue new communication landscapes which allow for different forms of knowledge production thereby providing an impetus for critical literacy researchers and teachers to re-consider text production.

Luke (2012: 9) makes it clear that critical literacy must engage with new contemporary crises as they are constructed through various discourses, modes and media, such as the global economic meltdown, which will 'require a new vocabulary for dealing with print and digital attempts to describe, analyze and indeed, critique current economic structures, trends and phenomena'. It will also require serious exploration of the synergies between environmental studies, place-based pedagogies and critical pedagogy (Comber, Nixon, and Reid, 2007). Sustaining critical literacy will also require engaging with youth and community concerns and working across generations (Johnson and Rosario-Ramos, 2012), with the challenges and possibilities of policy framings (Zacher Pandya, 2012). This requires continual re-invention of critical literacies guided by ongoing analyses of the ways in language and power are implicated in the lived politics of everyday life experienced by particular people in particular places.

REFERENCES

Alvermann, D. and Hagood, M. (2000) 'Critical media literacy: Research, theory, and practice in "New Times"', *Journal of Educational Research*, 93(3): 193–205.

Arthur, L. (2001) 'Young children as critical consumers', *Australian Journal of Language and Literacy*, 24(3): 182–94.

Baker, C. and Davies, B. (1993) 'Literacy and gender in early childhood', in A. Luke and P. Gilbert (eds),

Literacy in Contexts: Australian Perspectives and Issues. St Leonards, New South Wales: Allen & Unwin. pp. 55–67.

Baker, C. and Freebody, P. (1989) *Children's First School Books: Introductions to the Culture of Literacy.* Oxford: Basil Blackwell.

Bigelow, B. (2001) 'On the road to cultural bias: A critique of the Oregon Trail CD-ROM', in B. Comber and A. Simpson (eds), *Negotiating Critical Literacies in Classrooms.* Mahwah, NJ/London: Lawrence Erlbaum Associates. pp. 109–30.

Bourke, R. (2008) 'First graders and fairy tales: One teacher's action research of critical literacy', *The Reading Teacher,* 62(4): 304–12.

Carrington, V. and Luke, A. (2002) 'Reading, homes and families: From postmodern to modern?', in A. van Kleeck, S. Stahl, and E. Bauer (eds), *On Reading Books to Children: Parents and Teachers.* Mahwah, NJ: Lawrence Erlbaum Associates. pp. 231–52.

Comber, B. (1999) 'Coming ready or not: What counts as early literacy!', *Language and Literacy Journal,* 1(1): http://www.langandlit.ualberta.ca/archives/vol11papers/coming.htm

Comber, B. (2001a) 'Critical literacy: Power and pleasure with language in the early years', *The Australian Journal of Language and Literacy,* 24(3): 168–81.

Comber, B. (2001b) 'Critical literacy and local action: Teacher knowledge and a "new" research agenda', in B. Comber and A. Simpson (eds), *Negotiating Critical Literacies in Classrooms.* Mahwah, NJ/London: Lawrence Erlbaum Associates. pp. 271–82.

Comber, B. and Kamler, B. (2004) 'Getting out of deficit: Pedagogies of reconnection', *Teaching Education,* 15(3), 293–310.

Comber, H. and Nixon, H. (2011) 'Critical reading comprehension in an era of accountability', *Australian Educational Researcher,* 38(2), 167–179.

Comber, B. and Simpson, A. (eds) (2001) *Negotiating Critical Literacies in Classrooms.* Mahwah, NJ/London: Lawrence Erlbaum Associates.

Comber, B., Thomson, P., with Wells, M. (2001) 'Critical literacy finds a "place": Writing and social action in a neighborhood school', *Elementary School Journal,* 101(4): 451–64.

Comber, B., Nixon, H., and Reid, J. (eds) (2007) *Literacies in Place: Teaching Environmental Communication.* Newtown, Sydney: Primary English Teaching Association.

Cooper, K. and White, R. (2006) 'Critical literacy in action: Action research in a grade three classroom', in K. Cooper and R. White (eds), *The Practical Critical Educator: Critical Inquiry and Educational Practice.* Dordrecht, the Netherlands: Springer. pp. 3–16.

de La Luz Reyes, M. (2001) 'Unleashing possibilities: Biliteracy in the primary grades', in M. de la Luz Reyes and J. Halcón (eds), *The Best for Our Children: Critical Perspectives on Literacy for Latino Students.* New York/London: Teachers College Press. pp. 96–121.

Department for Education and Children's Services (1995) *Texts: the Heart of the English Curriculum.* Adelaide: Department for Education and Children's Services.

Dixon, K. (2011) *Literacy, Power, and the Schooled Body: Learning in Time and Space.* New York/London: Routledge.

Dozier, C., Johnston, P., and Rogers, R. (2006) *Critical Literacy, Critical Teaching: Tools for Preparing Responsive Teachers.* New York/London: Teachers College Press.

Dyson, A.H. (1989) *Multiple Worlds of Child Writers: Friends Learning to Write.* New York: Teachers College Press.

Dyson, A.H. (1993) *Social Worlds of Children Learning to Write in an Urban Primary School.* New York: Teachers College Press.

Dyson, A.H. (1997) *Writing Superheroes: Contemporary Childhood, Popular Culture, and Classroom Literacy.* New York/London: Teachers College Press.

Dyson, A.H. and Genishi, C. (2009) *Children, Language and Literacy: Diverse Learners in Diverse Times.* New York/London: Teachers College Press and Washington, DC: National Association for the Education of Young Children.

Edelsky, C. (ed.) (1999) *Making Justice our Project: Teachers Working Towards Critical Whole Language Practice.* Urbana, IL: National Council of Teachers of English.

Education Queensland (2000) *Why Wait? A Way into Teaching Critical Literacies in the Early Years.* Brisbane: The State of Queensland (Department of Education).

Fairclough, N. (1992) *Discourse and Social Change.* Cambridge: Polity Press.

Freebody, P. (1992) 'Social class and reading', *Discourse,* 12(2): 68–84.

Freebody, P. and Luke, A. (1990) '"Literacies" programs: Debates and demands in cultural context', *Prospect: the Journal of Adult Migrant Education Programs,* 5(3): 7–16.

Freire, P. (1972) *Pedagogy of the Oppressed.* New York: Seabury.

Freire, P. and Macedo, D. (1987) *Literacy: Reading the Word and the World.* Westport, CN: Bergin & Garvey.

Gilbert, P. (1989) 'Student text as pedagogical text', in S. De Castell, A. Luke, and C. Luke (eds), *Language*

Authority and Criticism: Readings on the School Textbook. London: The Falmer Press. pp. 195–202.

Gilbert, P. and Rowe, K. (1989) *Gender, Literacy and the Classroom*. Carlton North, Victoria: Australian Reading Association.

Giroux, H. (1993) 'Literacy and the politics of difference', in C. Lankshear and P. McLaren (eds), *Critical Literacy: Politics, Praxis and the Postmodern*. Albany: State University of New York Press. pp. 367–77.

Gregory, E. and Williams, A. (2000) *City Literacies: Learning to Read Across Generations and Cultures*. London/New York: Routledge.

Hall, K. (1998) 'Critical literacy and the case for it in the early years of school', *Language, Culture and Curriculum*, 11(2) 183–94.

Harste, J. and Leland, C. (2001) 'That's not fair! Critical literacy as unlimited semiosis', *Australian Journal of Language and Literacy*, 24(3): 208–19.

Janks, H. (ed.) (1993) *Critical Language Awareness Series*. Johannesburg: Witwatersrand University Press and Hodder & Stoughton Educational.

Janks, H. (2010) *Literacy and Power*. New York/London: Routledge.

Janks, H. and Vasquez, V. (2011) 'Editorial: Critical literacy revisited: Writing as critique, *English Teaching; Practice and Critique*, 10(1): 1–6.

Johnson, L.R. and Rosario-Ramos, E.M. (2012). 'The role of educational institutions in the development of critical literacy and transformative action', *Theory into Practice*, 51(1): 49–56.

Johnson, E. and Vasudevan, L. (2012) 'Seeing and hearing students lived and embodied critical literacy practices', *Theory into Practice*, 51 (1), 34–41.

Jones, S., Clarke, L.W., and Enriquez, G. (2010) *The Reading Turn-Around: A Five-Part Framework for Differentiated Instruction*. New York/London: Teachers College Press.

Jones Diaz, C., Beecher, B., and Arthur, L. (2002) 'Children's worlds and critical literacy', in L. Makin and C. Jones Diaz (eds) *Literacies in Early Childhood: Challenging Views, Challenging Practice*. Sydney: MacLennan & Petty.

Kamler, B. (1994) 'Lessons about language and gender', *The Australian Journal of Language and Literacy*, 17(2): 129–38.

Kamler, B. (2001) *Relocating the Personal: A Critical Writing Pedagogy*. Albany: State University of New York Press.

Kamler, B. and Comber, B. (1996) 'Critical literacy: Not generic-not developmental-not another orthodoxy', *Changing Education*, 3(1): 1–9.

Kavanagh, K. (1997) *Texts on Television: School Literacies Through Viewing in the First Years of School*. Adelaide, South Australia: Department of Education and Children Services.

Kinloch, V. (ed.) (2011) *Urban Literacies: Critical Perspectives on Language, Learning, and Community*. New York/London: Teachers College Press.

Kress, G. (2000) 'Multimodality', in B. Cope and M. Kalantzis (eds), *Multiliteracies: Literacy Learning and the Design of Social Futures*. South Yarra, Victoria: Macmillan Publishers Australia. pp. 179–200.

Lankshear, C. (1994) *Critical Literacy*. Occasional paper No 3. Australian Curriculum Studies Association, Canberra.

Lankshear, C. and McLaren, P. (1993) *Critical Literacy: Politics, Praxis and the Postmodern*. Albany: State University of New York Press.

Lankshear, C., Bigum, C., Green, B., Wild, M., Morgan, W., Snyder, I., Durrant, C., Honan, E., and Murray, J. (1997) *Digital Rhetorics: Literacies and technologies in Education – Current Practices and Future Directions*. Canberra: Department of Employment, Education and Youth Affairs, Commonwealth of Australia.

Leland, C., and Harste, J. (2005) 'Doing what we want to become: Preparing new urban teachers', *Urban Education*, 40(1): 60–77.

Leland, C., Harste, J., and Huber, K. (2005) 'Out of the box: Critical literacy in a first-grade classroom', *Language Arts*, 82(4): 257–68.

Lensmire, T. (1994) *When Children Write: Critical Revisions of the Writing Workshop*. New York: Teachers College Press.

Lewison, M., Flint, A., and Van Sluys, K. (2002) 'Taking on critical literacy: The journey of newcomers and novices', *Language Arts*, 79(5): 382–92.

Luke, A. (2000) 'Critical literacy in Australia: A matter of context and standpoint', *Journal of Adolescent and Adult Literacy*, 43(5): 448–61.

Luke, A. (2012) 'Critical literacy: Foundational notes', *Theory into practice*, 51 (1), 4–11.

Luke, A. and Freebody, P. (1997) 'Critical literacy and the question of normativity: An introduction', in S. Muspratt, A. Luke, and P. Freebody (eds), *Constructing Critical Literacies: Teaching and Learning Textual Practice*. Sydney: Allen & Unwin. pp. 1–18.

Luke. A. and Freebody, P. (1999) 'Further notes on the four resources model', *Reading online*. http://www.readingonline.org/research/lukefreebody.html

Luke, A. and Luke, C. (2001) 'Adolescence lost/childhood regained: On early intervention and the emergence of the techno-subject', *Journal of Early Childhood Literacy*, 1(1): 91–120.

Luke, A., O'Brien, J., and Comber, B. (1994) 'Making community texts objects of study', *The Australian Journal of Language and Literacy*, 17(2): 139–49.

Luke, C. (1997) 'Media literacy and cultural studies', in S. Muspratt, A. Luke, and P. Freebody (eds), *Constructing Critical Literacies: Teaching and Learning Textual Practice.* Creskill, NJ: Hampton Press. pp. 19–50.

Marsh, J. (2000) '"But I want to fly too!": Girls and superhero play in the infant classroom', *Gender and Education*, 12(2): 209–20.

Martello, J. (2001) 'Drama: Ways into critical literacy in the early childhood years', *Australian Journal of Language and Literacy*, 24(3): 195–207.

McNaughton, S. (1995) *Patterns of Emergent Literacy.* Oxford: Oxford University Press.

Mellor, B., Patterson, A., and O'Neill, M. (1987) *Reading Stories.* Perth: Chalkface Press.

Moll, L. (2001) 'The diversity of schooling: A cultural-historical approach', in M. de La Luz Reyes and J. Halcon (eds), *The Best for our Children: Critical Perspectives on Literacy for Latino Students.* New York/London: Teachers College Press. pp. 13–28.

Moll, L., Amanti, C., Neff, D., and Gonzalez, N. (1992) 'Funds of knowledge for teaching: Using a qualitative approach to connect homes and classrooms', *Theory Into Practice*, 31(2): 132–41.

Myers, J., Hammett, R., and McKillop, M. (2000) 'Connecting, exploring, and exposing the self in hypermedia projects', in M. Gallego and S. Hollingsworth (eds), *What Counts as Literacy: Challenging the School Standard.* New York/London: Teachers College Press. pp. 85–105.

Nixon, H. (2002) 'Exploring the communicational webs of popular media culture in English language arts curriculum', in R.F. Hammett and B.R.C. Barrell (eds), *Digital Media, Cultural Studies and Technology* Calgary: Detselig of University of Calgary. pp. 113–35,

O'Brien, J. (1994a) 'Show mum you love her: Taking a new look at junk mail', *Reading*, 28(1): 43–6.

O'Brien, J. (1994b) 'It's written in our head: The possibilities and contradictions of a feminist post-structuralist discourse in a junior primary classroom', Unpublished Masters of Education Thesis, University of South Australia.

O'Brien, J. (1998) 'Experts in Smurfland', in M. Knobel and A. Healy (eds), *Critical Literacies in the Primary Classroom.* Newtown, New South Wales: Primary English Teaching Association. pp. 13–25.

O'Brien, J. (2001a) 'Children reading critically: A local history', in B. Comber and A. Simpson (eds),

Negotiating Critical Literacies in Classrooms. Mahwah, NJ/London: Lawrence Erlbaum Associates. pp. 41–60.

O'Brien, J. (2001b) '"I knew that already": How children's books limit inquiry', in S. Boran and B. Comber (eds), *Critiquing Whole Language and Classroom Inquiry.* Urbana, IL: Whole Language Umbrella and National Council of Teachers of English. pp. 142–68.

O'Brien, J. and Comber, B. (2000) 'Negotiating critical literacies with young children', in C. Barratt-Pugh and M. Rohl (eds), *Literacy Learning in the Early Years.* Crows Nest, New South Wales: Allen & Unwin. pp. 152–71.

Panofsky, C. (2000) 'Examining the research narrative in early literacy: The case of parent–child book-reading activity', in M. Gallego and S. Hollingsworth (eds), *What Counts as Literacy: Challenging The School Standard.* New York and London: Teachers College Press. pp. 190–212.

Patterson, A. (1997) 'Setting limits to English' in S. Muspratt, A. Luke, and P. Freebody. *Constructing Critical Literacies: Teaching and Learning Textual Practice.* Sydney: Allen & Unwin. pp. 335–353.

Paugh, P., Carey, J., King-Jackson, V., and Russell, S. (2007) 'Negotiating the literacy block: Constructing spaces for critical literacy in a high-stakes setting', *Language Arts*, 85(1): 31–42.

Petty, K. (1990) *My First Book of Knowledge.* London: Conran Octopus.

Powell, R. (1999) *Literacy as a Moral Imperative: Facing the Challenges of a Pluralistic Society.* Lanham, MD: Rowman & Littlefield Publishers.

Powell, R. (2001) 'Saving Black Mountain: The promise of critical literacy in a multicultural democracy', *The Reading Teacher*, 54(8): 772–81.

Reid, J. and Comber, B. (2002) 'Theoretical perspectives in early literacy education: Implications for practice', in L. Makin and C. Jones Diaz (eds), *Literacies in Early Childhood: Challenging Views, Challenging Practice*, Sydney Maclennan & Petty. pp. 15–34.

Roth, W.M. and Desautels, J. (eds) (2002) *Science Education as/for Sociopolitical Action.* New York: Peter Lang.

Sahni, U. (2001) 'Children appropriating literacy: Empowerment pedagogy from young children's perspective', in B. Comber and A. Simpson (eds), *Negotiating Critical Literacies in Classrooms.* Mahwah, NJ/London: Lawrence Erlbaum Associates. pp. 19–35.

Sandretto, S. and the Critical Literacy Research Team (2006) 'Extending guided reading with critical literacy', *SET: Research Information for Teachers*, 3: 23–8.

Searle, C. (1993) 'Words to a life-land: Literacy, the imagination, and Palestine', in C. Lankshear and P. McLaren (eds) *Critical Literacy: Politics, Praxis and the Postmodern.* Albany: State University of New York Press. pp. 167–91.

Smith, G.A. (2002) 'Place-based education: Learning to be where we are', *Phi Delta Kappan*, April: 584–94.

Souto-Manning, M. (2009) 'Negotiating culturally responsive pedagogy through multicultural children's literature: Towards critical democratic literacy practices in a first grade classroom', *Journal of Early Childhood Literacy*, 9(1): 50–74.

Souto-Manning, M. (2010) *Freire, Teaching, and Learning: Culture Circles Across Contexts.* New York: Peter Lang.

Vasquez, V. (2001a) 'Classroom inquiry into the incidental unfolding of social justice issues: Seeking out possibilities in the lives of learners', in S. Boran and B. Comber (eds), *Critiquing Whole Language and Classroom Inquiry.* Urbana, IL: Whole Language Umbrella and National Council of Teachers of English. pp. 200–15.

Vasquez, V. (2001b) 'Constructing a critical curriculum with young children', in B. Comber and A. Simpson (eds), *Negotiating Critical Literacies in Classrooms.* Mahwah, NJ/London: Lawrence Erlbaum Associates. pp. 55–66.

Vasquez, V. (2003) *Negotiating Critical Literacies with Young Children.* Mahwah, NJ/London: Lawrence Erlbaum Associates.

Wallace, C. (2001) 'Critical literacy in a second language classroom: Power and control', in B. Comber and A. Simpson (eds), *Negotiating Critical Literacies In Classrooms.* Mahwah, NJ/London: Lawrence Erlbaum Associates.

Zacher Pandya, J. (2012) Mandating and standardizing the teaching of critical literacy skills: A cautionary tale. *Theory into practice*, 51(1), 20–26.

PART 5

Researching Early Childhood Literacy

Methodologies in Research on Young Children and Literacy

David Bloome, Laurie Katz, Huili Hong,
Patricia May-Woods and Melissa Wilson

INTRODUCTION

In this chapter we ask what are the chronotopes underlying the methodological grammars employed in research on young children and literacy.[1] By chronotope we are referring to an implied ideology about how people move through time and space. Every research study has an implied chronotope(s) expressed through its methodological grammar (see Kamberelis and Dimitriadis, 2005).

We have borrowed the term chronotope from literary theory, specifically from Bakhtin (1981):

> We will give the name chronotope (literacy, 'time space') to the intrinsic connectedness of temporal and spatial relationships that are artistically expressed in literature ... [chronotope] expresses the inseparability of space and time ... In the literary artistic chronotope, spatial and temporal indicators are fused into one carefully thought-out, concrete whole. Time, as it were, thickens, takes on flesh, becomes artistically visible; likewise, space becomes charged and responsive to the movements of time, plot, and history. ... The chronotope as a formally constitutive category determines to a significant degree the image of man [sic] in literature as well. The image of man [sic] is always intrinsically chronotopic.
>
> (1981: 84–5)

If the 'image of man is always intrinsically chronotopic,' then research methodologies in the human sciences are necessarily arguments, explicitly or implicitly, about the nature of human beings in the world; that is, they are arguments about personhood. Personhood refers to the notion of the 'person' as an ideological field within a society (Bloome et al., 2005; Geertz, 1966, 1973; Kirkpatrick, 1983), including the attributes that are viewed as explicitly or implicitly defining the 'person' (cf., Egan-Robertson, 1998; Gergen and Davis, 1985; Shweder and Miller, 1985). More specifically, research methodological grammars are arguments first about what counts as knowledge of people; second, about what counts as language (including literacy);

and third, where and how people are located in space and time (where they have been and where they are going, their histories). We use these three dimensions (the nature of children, the nature of language/literacy, and locations) as heuristics to organize this chapter.[2]

In order to make visible underlying chronotopes, it is necessary to examine the methodological grammars of research studies. By methodological grammar we are referring to the components of a research study and their structural relationship (grammar) to each other; what some might call a research model. It is important to make a distinction between methodological grammar and the theory-method connection of a research study. Although researchers may explain the theoretical and ideological grounding of their research methods, such an explanation does not necessarily describe the components of a research study, its grammar, nor its underlying chronotope.

METHODOLOGICAL GRAMMARS AND THE NATURE OF CHILDREN

Methodological grammars in research on children and literacy vary in their underlying assumptions about the personhood of children. What can be known about children is constrained by how 'child' is conceptualized. Researchers construct the personhood of children through their assignment of attributes to the children in their research studies.

Child-attribute improvement methodological grammar

For example, consider the methodology shown in Figure 34.1, which we label the child-attribute improvement methodological grammar. The child is conceived as

having a series of attributes, some of which are potentially affected by a particular treatment or a set of events. The attributes are 'of' the child. The child may *have* these attributes to a greater or lesser degree. By defining reading and literacy skills as attributes of the child, one can ask whether the child has the skills or cognitive and linguistic abilities/processes of reading and writing. Defining literacy as an attribute of the child allows one to define the individual as a 'reader' or 'non-reader', as 'literate' or 'illiterate,' etc.; as such the attributes of literacy become part of a definition of the child's personhood.

Within the child-attribute improvement methodological grammar, the purpose of the intervention/treatment is to examine effects on one or more of the attributes that defines the child. The attributes may be measured by tests or predetermined criteria (quantitatively or qualitatively); the intervention may be simple or complex; and the relationship between the child attributes and the intervention may be viewed as mediated by other factors or not. Regardless, the unit of analysis is the child and particular attributes assigned to the personhood of the child.

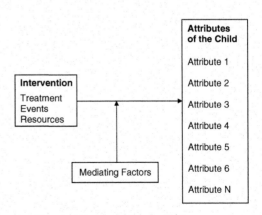

Figure 34.1 Child-attribute improvement methodological grammar

A study by Lonigan and Whitehurst (1998) of the effects of reading to children provides an illustration of child-attribute improvement methodological grammar. The children in their study were exposed to a series of events (various formulations of reading to the children) to examine the effect on the child's language/literacy skills. The chronotope underlying the methodology of the study is that as the child moves through time and space, the events change the person/child by increasing (or failing to increase) the person's/child's attributes, specifically the child's language/literacy attributes.

Although one could examine and debate the adequacy of the measures of the specified child attributes and the nature and accuracy of the descriptions of the interventions/treatments they experienced, regardless of the measurements and methods used, part of the meaningfulness of a study or a set of studies conducted in the field is in their underlying chronotope, in how it promulgates a conception of children moving through time and space and in how the chronotope defines change and personhood. In those studies involving a child-attribute improvement methodological grammar each child is conceived of as an individual unit (the children may have collective experiences but the underlying chronotope conceptualizes each child as experiencing the journey as if in isolation from others). The child experiences events (that is, things happen to the child, he/she does not create the events nor fundamentally change the events), and each child either acquires, increases, or fails to increase the targeted attributes.

A variation of the child-attribute improvement methodological grammar is shown in Figure 34.2 which we label the complex event-attribute improvement methodological grammar.

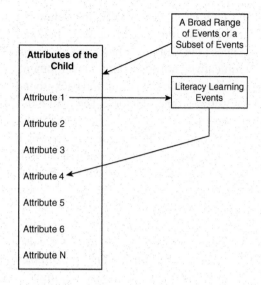

Figure 34.2 Complex event-attribute improvement methodological grammar

Studies that employ this methodological grammar frame attributes as influenced by multiple types of events rather than by a single type of event, and frame changes in one attribute or set of attributes as influencing the child's behavior in key events that then influences other attributes of the child. In brief, there is a complex and interactive view of the influence of events on attributes.

For example, in a study by Bus et al. (1997), young children's literacy skills were viewed as influenced indirectly by their affective relationships with their parents. A broad range of interactions with their parents were viewed as influencing children's attachment-security which was viewed as influencing children's literacy behaviors (their eagerness to explore books) which was viewed as influencing their literacy skills. Another example is provided by Craig and Washington's (2006) study of the literacy progress of African-American children who were speakers of African-American Vernacular English (AAVE). They assessed the degree to which the children spoke AAVE, the schooling and instruction they received, parental support, the children's language and communicative abilities and development, socio-economic status, cultural background as well as other factors. The children's literacy achievement was viewed as influenced indirectly by the degree to which the child was exposed to dominant forms of English (such as the dialect of English used in school instruction) and to code-switching practices which influenced the nature of their engagement in reading instruction activities that were positively related to success in reading and literacy achievement. Their findings highlight a key aspect of the underlying chronotope of the complex event-attribute improvement methodological grammar. Here, the 'deficient' attribute was not inherent to the child, nor the child's language, culture, socioeconomic status, family, race, etc. Rather, it was a function of the politics of racial dynamics that were played out with regard to language variation and schooling. This situation makes it advantageous for African-American children to be able to code-switch from AAVE to School English, and as such, code-switching becomes an attribute of the child.

The two chronotopes discussed above define personhood in terms of attributes the child has (and the degree to which the child has them). As a child moves through classroom lessons, the child experiences instruction that either does or does not improve pertinent attributes. The conception of the child in the complex event-attribute improvement methodological grammar is one in which the child acts on events in a way that defines the nature of events, at least in part. Both children and events are malleable and changing. Thus, the complex event-attribute improvement methodological grammar promulgates a

substantially different chronotope than the child-attribute improvement methodological grammar.

Child as meaning maker/language learner methodological grammar

A different chronotope underlies what we call child as meaning maker/language learner methodological grammar. Studies by Dyson (1989, 1997, 2003), Goodman and Wilde (1992), Wells (1981), and Yaden and Tardibuono (2004), for example, define the child as a meaning maker and language learner. They then ask what processes influence their meaning making and language learning, and how. By defining the child as a meaning maker and language learner such studies warrant a different methodological grammar and establish a different chronotope than the methodological grammars discussed previously. The child is seen as actively engaging in a journey through many different events that are influenced by the child's efforts and in turn influence the child. At issue in such studies is understanding the nature of the child as a meaning maker and language learner (by closely examining what the child does with language over time) and how the events in which the child participates affect the child's language learning (by closely examining how the child responds to what is happening) (see Figure 34.3).

For example, consider Dyson's studies (1989, 1997, 2003), in which children are defined as meaning makers and language learners who use a broad range of semiotic tools. Through careful observation and analysis of children in interaction with each other, their teachers, and others, over time and across a broad range of classroom situations (including journal writing, dramatic play, instructional conversations,

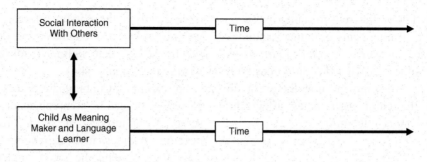

Figure 34.3   Child as meaning maker and language learner methodological grammar

free play, etc.) and non-classroom situations, as well as analysis of the texts, artifacts, and social events interactionally created, she asks what must constitute meaning making and language learning and what must constitute the nature of the social contexts of the meaning making and language learning.

The underlying chronotope in studies employing a child as meaning maker and language learner methodological grammar defines the child organically as a meaning maker and language learner who changes as he/she journeys through numerous events and contexts which she/he helps create. As the child evolves, the journey evolves. Children move through time and space making meaning and learning language, and they do so to the extent that the spaces they move through allow them to do so. The spaces they move through are not 'interventions' but opportunities for the child to engage in meaning making and language learning that is inherent in the nature of being human.

Goodman and Wilde (1992) provide an illustration. In their study, they document how children from the Tohono O'odham community manifest the same underlying meaning-making and language-learning processes as children from middle-class Anglo communities. Thus, the rhetorical aspect of their research is not only to illuminate the nature of literacy learning in classrooms over time, but to validate the conception of all children as meaning makers and language learners with regard to literacy learning.

Summary: methodological grammars and the nature of children

This section discussed three methodological grammars that are pertinent to studying the nature of children; 1) child-attribute improvement; 2) complex event-attribute improvement; and 3) child as meaning maker/language learner. In the child-attribute improvement methodological grammar, the child is conceived as having a series of attributes that are potentially affected as the child moves through a particular treatment or a set of events. The complex event-attribute improvement methodological grammar frames the child as having attributes *influenced* by multiple types of events; thus, changes in one attribute or set of attributes influence the child's behavior in key events and subsequently influence other attributes of the child. The child as meaning maker/ language learner methodological grammar doesn't define the child as having or not having a series of attribute, but conceives the child as an inherent meaning maker or language learner. This grammar examines the spaces in which the child journeys as opportunities for what the child does with language over time and how the events in which the child participates affect the child's language learning.

METHODOLOGICAL GRAMMARS AND THE LANGUAGE/LITERACY USED BY CHILDREN

The studies discussed in this section begin with establishing a definition of reading and/or literacy. Definitions of reading and literacy can be heuristically categorized as autonomous models or ideological models (cf., Street, 1984, 1995). An autonomous model assumes that reading and literacy consist of a distinct set of skills or cognitive processes that are relatively stable across situations and contexts. An ideological model assumes that reading and literacy are inherently multiple and consist of diverse social, cultural, political, economic, and psychological practices that vary across situations. How literacy is manifested in any particular situation depends largely on shared cultural norms (the cultural ideology) realized as social practices for the use of written language for such situations.

Autonomous models of literacy and methodological grammars

The underlying methodological grammars of research grounded in autonomous models of literacy begin with a definition of reading or writing as a thing (process) in and of itself, distinct from the child and from the context of use, and then ask, what factors facilitate the child's enactment of that definition (process). The methodological grammar of such studies

often involves the parsing of reading or writing into a set of cognitive and linguistic processes that define reading and writing (see Figure 34.4).

For example, Cunningham et al. (1999) parsed silent reading comprehension into a series of underlying skills in order to develop an assessment of reading. They sought to validate the set of underlying cognitive and linguistic processes through their association with various reading tasks.

Another approach to researching the cognitive and linguistic processes defining reading has been the manipulation of text factors (see Figure 34.5). By manipulating a text and carefully examining the responses of a reader, inferences can be made about the cognitive and linguistic processes that are assumed to have been present.

For example, Calhoon and Leslie (2002) investigated the influence of word frequency and rime neighborhood size on young children's ability to read target words embedded in a story the children read aloud. They studied the effect on children over time (3 years) as a way to explore the effect of texts on the process of learning to read defined as the acquisition of the various reading skills.

As shown in Figure 34.5, the relationship between the text and the cognitive processes involved in reading and writing may be mediated by a series of factors, including individual differences in children, and their background experiences, among others. For example, Cox et al. (1997) examined the effect of producing a text under two conditions (one associated with writing, the other associated with reading) on 4- and 5-year-old children who varied in their development as readers and writers in order to assess their ability to code-switch into a literate register. They defined a literate register as one involving particular types of textual cohesion

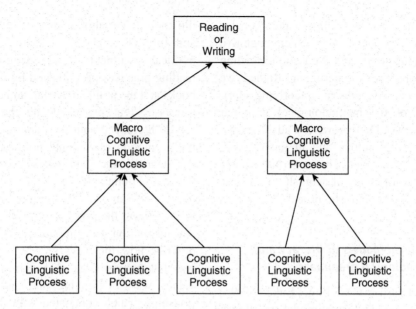

Figure 34.4   Literacy as a set of autonomous cognitive and linguistic processes methodological grammar

associated with conventional reading and writing. Their interest was in the mediating effect of income level and level of each child's development as an emergent reader/ writer on the cognitive and linguistic processes employed. They claimed that the effects of the various mediating factors were evidence of particular kinds of cognitive and linguistic processing.

Another set of studies has examined how the nature of a particular language affects the process of learning to read. Such studies include investigations of the transparency and depth of an orthography (e.g., Ellis et al., 2004), the morphological structure of a language (e.g., Verhoeven and Perfetti, 2003), the similarities and differences between a child's primary language and a different target language used in school reading instruction (e.g., Jimenez et al., 1996), among other language characteristics. Such studies have a methodological grammar similar to that of 'text manipulation' methodological grammars; but here variation is the nature of the language of the text.

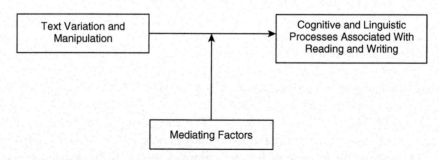

Figure 34.5   Text manipulation methodological grammar

For the purposes of this chapter, debates among researchers over which cognitive and linguistic processes constitute reading or writing are not pertinent. Rather, we are concerned with the underlying chronotope of the methodological grammar regardless of the researcher's advocacy for one set of cognitive and linguistic processes over another. The underlying chronotope is a journey of acquisition of those cognitive and linguistic processes.

Ideological models of literacy and methodological grammars

With regard to reading, Luke (1995) describes an ideological model as follows:

> ... there are no universal 'skills' of reading. Reading is a social practice, comprised of interpretive rules and events constructed and learned in institutions like schools and churches, families and work places. Implicit in ways of teaching reading are social theories – models of the social order, social power, and social change; models of the institutional everyday life; models of worker/employee relations; and ultimately models of how the literate worker and citizen should look and be. Simply put, reading instruction has always described and prescribed forms of life: of how Dick, Jane, and Spot should be and act as citizens and readers, and indeed of how migrants and workers, women and men, should be and act as citizens and readers.
>
> (1995: 97)

Here Luke emphasizes the diversity of literacy practices, their connection to social institutions, and their use as an agent of social, cultural, and political socialization. One goal has been to identify and describe a set of literacy practices, their connections to the social institutions from which they emanate, and the ways in which they foster particular configurations of culture, social relations, social identity, and power relations (see Figure 34.6).

Luke's (1988) study of reading textbooks in Canadian primary schools is one illustration. Through analysis of the texts and through analysis of historical and political documents, Luke identifies the reading practices promulgated by the textbooks and the political, social, and cultural processes that produced this particular set of literacy practices often related to the promotion of national political agendas. Duranti and Ochs (1986) examined the instructional practices and classroom events in a Samoan village school in order to investigate the potential impact of literacy instruction on Samoan culture. They describe how the ways in which reading was taught promulgated certain Western values, ways of thinking, and social relationships, which contrasted with those of traditional Samoan village culture. Fishman (1988) provides another illustration. She identifies and describes a set of literacy practices across various social institutions (e.g., family, school) within an Amish community showing how those literacy practices reflected cultural themes in Amish life.

Despite differences in specific methods employed, the studies here are similar in terms of methodological grammar. Luke describes how literacy practices are employed to enhance state control; Duranti and Ochs describe how literacy practices carry values, culturally specific ways of thinking, and social relationships; Fishman describes how literacy practices are employed to express a culture. The underlying chronotope of 'literacy practices as social practices of social institutions and community cultures' methodological grammar posits the child as moving through various adventures that define the child and define the child's relationship with others and with the world in which he/she lives. The adventures do not change (although they may be resisted). As the child moves through formal and informal instruction in

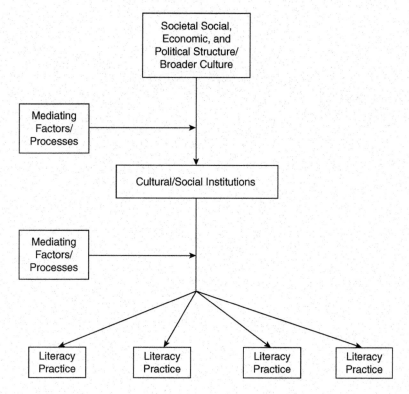

Figure 34.6   Literacy practices as social practices of social institutions and community cultures methodological grammar

the literacy practices of the social institutions of her/his society, the child is defined and positioned within society.

One issue of considerable importance in the methodological grammar of studies of literacy practices and events from an ideological model is how micro contexts (e.g., face-to-face interaction or analogous levels of social context) are embedded in and relate to macro social contexts (i.e., broader social, cultural, political and economic structures) (see Figure 34.7). In some studies, data at the micro level is examined in order to identify and detect more macro influences (e.g., Marsh, 2011); while in other studies attention is focused on how a particular macro structure (e.g., a national government policy) influences how literacy practices at the micro level

are played out (e.g., Pacheco, 2010; Willis, 2002).

It is important to note that the relationship between the social, cultural, economic, and political structure of a society, its social institutions, and its literacy practices, may be mediated by a series of factors. For example, people may resist the imposition of a particular set of literacy practices or transform them because the literacy practices are associated with the imposition of a dominant culture (e.g., Ogbu and Simons, 1998; Street, 1993) or limiting social identities (e.g., Wohlwend, 2009). For example, Manyak (2001) researched a first- and second-grade immersion English classroom in the United States in a state that had enacted laws that mandated language and literacy instruction

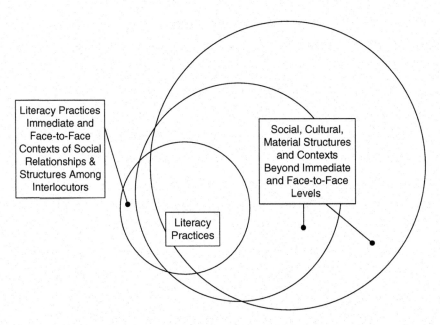

Figure 34.7   Literacy practices influencing and influenced by multiple levels of social contexts methodological grammar

and development only in English. Over time, the students and teacher resisted the limitation to English only and engaged in the daily classroom literacy practice of the Daily News in both English and Spanish. (See also Owodally, 2011, for similar example involving Mauritian Creole in a case study of a young children's education in a madrassah in Mauritius.) Similarly, Gutierrez et al. (2011) show how dual-language learners' literacy practices develop in the out of school location of *Las Redes*, a digital network. In this space, dual-language learners use their home languages and everyday English to write community letters, produce digital stories and communicate with *El Maga*, a mythical cyberwizard. Within this social and imaginative polylingual space (rather than an instructional classroom space), these students gain confidence in their English academic literacy practices. In another example, Wohlwend (2009) studied how

young girls take up the Disney Princess narratives and commercially gendered identities as represented in films, toys, and books. Wohlwend found that over time the girls produced counter-narratives that allowed them to go beyond the social limitations of the given gendered identities associated with the Disney Princess stories.

In a volume edited by Street (1993) there are a series of case studies of literacy practices where there is contact between two cultures or social institutions and there are differential power relations between them (one may be attempting to impose its culture and social structure on the other either directly or tacitly). Rather than starting with the dominating culture and its social institutions and examining the production of literacy practices, the case studies in Street (1993) begin with the literacy practices of people's everyday lives and examine how these literacy practices reflect a relationship with dominant social institutions, how people adapt the literacy practices of the dominant social institutions to their own needs and way of life, and how people produce literacy practices that eschew dominant social institutions (see Figure 34.8).

Similarly, Heath (1983, 2012) documents literacy practices in three communities and describes how differences in those literacy practices create boundaries and obstacles for some of the children, families, and communities in classrooms. Taylor (1983; Taylor and Dorsey-Gaines,1988) provides a series of case studies of literacy practices in families that document family literacy practices and their use to establish social relationships among family members and between the

Figure 34.8 Adopting and adapting literacy practices methodological grammar

family and other social institutions, such as the school. At issue in the studies by Heath and Taylor, among similar studies, is not just documentation of a range of literacy practices, but rather the social, cultural, economic, and political relationships among social institutions (such as family and school) and how literacy practices are employed within and across social institutions and various social contexts to define who and how people are (see also Gee, 1996, for a discussion of literacy practices and identity).

The chronotope underlying the 'adopting and adapting literacy practices' methodological grammar (Figure 34.8) involves a protagonist (as an individual or a collective) creatively acting on the adventures in which she/he/they find(s) herself/himself/themselves, the way forward based on the consequences of his/her/their creativity and on how others respond to that creativity.

In addition to describing diversity of literacy practices both within and across social institutions, another purpose of studies grounded in an ideological model of literacy has been to problematize taken-for-granted foundational concepts and assumptions associated with literacy. The methodological grammar of such studies often involves identification of a particular set of events combined with detailed microanalysis in order to make evident the problematic nature of a concept or assumption. On the surface, such studies may take the form of a case study (e.g., a case study of a child, a group, a classroom). However, at a deeper level, the methodological grammar involves setting up a dialectic between a given construct or assumption and data that warrants dissonance (see Figure 34.9).

For example, Poole (2008) conducted a case study of two readers in mixed-ability

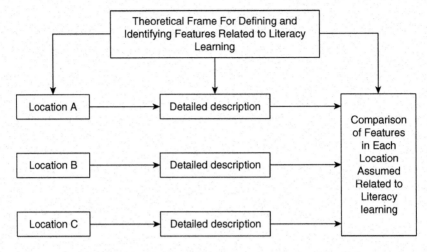

Figure 34.9   Comparative location methodological grammar

reading groups. The case study descriptions problematized the assumption that mixed-ability reading groups would not produce the same kind of stigmatizing effects for struggling readers associated with homogeneous-ability reading groups. Dyson (2010) problematizes the concept of 'copying' in a study of a kindergarten and a first-grade classroom. 'Copying' is not simply a low-level skill, but rather a complex social process involving collegiality, textual choreography, complementary authorial roles, and co-constructed dramas. Similarly, studies of learning to read by Bloome (1989), McDermott (1977; McDermott et al., 1978), and Trueba (1988), among others, problematize the construct of academic failure.

The underlying chronotope of the methodological grammars of these studies is one in which the times and places experienced by a child (or by a group of children) are ones that lead to what appears to be a 'natural' destination – often failure and marginalization. However, the 'natural' destination is problematized by the research showing that definitions of personhood associated with particular literacy practices (often the literacy practices of dominant social institutions) construct the journey and destination and give it meaning.

Summary: methodological grammars and the language/literacy used by children

This section discussed the methodological grammars and underlying chronotopes of research leading with conceptions of literacy used by children as autonomous and ideological. In the methodological grammar, 'literacy as a set of autonomous cognitive and linguistic processes', a distinct set of skills or cognitive processes is examined reflecting a specific definition of literacy. In the text-manipulation methodological grammar, a series of factors are mediated (e.g. instructional strategies, children's individual differences, family background, language of the text) in the relationship between the text and the cognitive processes involved in literacy. Ideological models of literacy assume that there are diverse literacy practices (and definitions of literacy) connected to social institutions and their use as an agent of social, cultural, and political socialization (Figure 34.6). Figure 34.7 reflects the interactions and influences between the micro and macro levels in how literacy practices are played out in each level. The chronotope underlying the adopting and adapting literacy practices methodological grammar shows/reveals how the protagonist is positioned and acts and reacts to the school literacy practices according to his/her relationships with family, community and dominant culture. The comparative-location methodological grammar allows the researcher to problematize the individual's literacy journey by making visible personhood in relation to particular literacy practices.

METHODOLOGICAL GRAMMARS AND LOCATIONS OF CHILDREN

Even if unacknowledged, every methodological grammar locates the child and the use of written language somewhere: in a classroom, a family, a research laboratory, a community, etc. At issue in this section are research methodologies whose grammar explicitly foregrounds the location of children. For heuristic purposes we distinguish between two sets of methodological grammars: 1) presage–process–product methodological grammars, and 2) situated methodological grammars.

Presage–process–product methodological grammars

We include three types of studies in this section: input–output methodological grammars, process–product methodological grammars, and process–process

methodological grammars. We note that many studies involve a combination of these three types (e.g., Morrison et al., 2005). The labeling of these three types of methodological grammars derives from Dunkin and Biddle's (1974) review of research on teaching, and Figure 34.10 is based on their model. After noting the lack of systematicity and rigor in studies of teaching, Dunkin and Biddle identified three sets of factors considered in classroom research: presage (or input) factors, process (or classroom) factors, and product (or output) factors. Then, they characterized studies based on whether they examined the relationship between input and output factors, process and product factors (what influence did what happened in the classroom have on outcomes), or process and other process factors (what influence did one aspect of the classroom have on other aspects of the classroom) (see Figure 34.10).

Input–output methodological grammar

Input–output studies examine the consequences of factors such as child background, family income, child age, teacher education, gender, amount of money spent by a district per child, formal instructional program, among other givens on outcome measures such as reading test scores, number of words read during recreational reading, teacher evaluation of student reading, reading strategy assessment. Input–output studies are often described as 'black-box' studies because attention is not paid to how the input factors are manifested in the classroom, only the outcomes are of concern. The underlying chronotope is that of a competition between literacy programs racing through an opaque space (see Figure 34.11). When the effectiveness of a set of input factors are compared, such

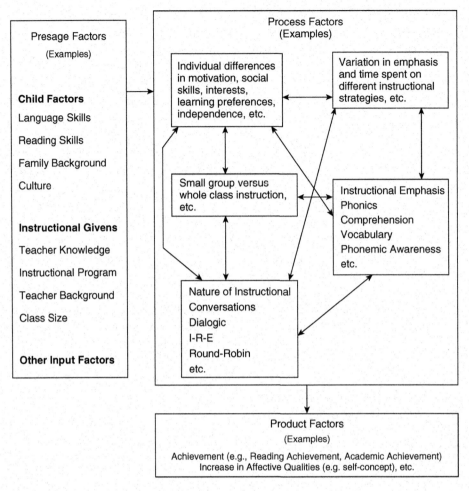

Figure 34.10   Presage–process–product methodological grammar (adapted from Dunkin and Biddle, 1974)

studies are referred to as 'horse-race' studies. Two or more locations (e.g., classroom environments or instructional programs) are described in detail and then compared in order to suggest that one will facilitate literacy learning better than the other. For convenience, we label studies that employ such a methodological grammar 'comparative location methodological grammars' (see Figure 34.11).

An example of an input–output study is Santa and Høien's (1999) study of the effects of an early intervention program called Early Steps. Santa and Høien compared the achievement of first-grade children who participated in the program with children who participated in no program. The children who participated in the program did better, especially those children who were at risk for reading failure. Similarly, Menon and Hiebert's (2005) examined the effectiveness of an instructional intervention called the 'little book curriculum' in facilitating the independent word-solving skills of first-grade readers. They compared the intervention

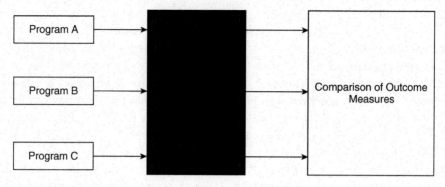

Figure 34.11   Comparative location methodological grammar

program with a comparison group using basal literature texts. The children in the intervention group scored higher on the outcome measures. In both the Santa and Høien study and the Menon and Hiebert study, the effectiveness of an input factor (an instructional program) is assessed in terms of an output (reading achievement scores); what happens in between the input and output may be assumed, briefly documented, or not considered at all – regardless such process factors are not in and of themselves of substantive issue.

One of the weaknesses associated with input–output studies is that they lack explanatory and descriptive power. One may know which instructional program (or other input variable) was associated with improved reading or writing achievement, but how it 'won the race' remains speculation. For example, Santa and Høien describe the theory behind the early-intervention program and its given components. Although they suggest that the achievement gains are the result of enactment of the theoretical constructs that guided the program and the design of the components, there is no direct data about the enactment of the program nor did the methodological grammar allow for

identification and examination of complexities and confounding factors.

A famous set of input–output studies of young children and reading instruction were the 'First-Grade Studies' (see Bond and Dykstra, 1964). The First-Grade Studies were conducted in the early 1960s and involved 17 research studies conducted across the United States. Although each study collected some similar data to allow comparison across sites, each study also varied depending on the goal of each study. For example, some studies compared the use of a basal reading series with the use of a basal reading series supplemented by additional phonics instruction. Another study compared the effects of a Language Experience instructional method with a basal reading instructional method. Another examined the consequences of amount and nature of teacher education on reading achievement; among other foci. Although almost all of the studies found that the researcher's favored instructional method produced better results, in brief and simplified, analysis conducted by Bond and Dykstra (1964) across the studies noted that instructional method *per se* was not related to outcome measures; rather, the quality and the commitment of the teacher was influential on outcomes. The findings reported by Bond and Dykstra have led to suspicion of the validity of 'horse-race' studies of instructional programs and methods. In brief, the methodological grammar of input–output studies is not viewed as providing sufficient explanatory power, or sufficient concern for researcher and educator bias, the complexity of mediating factors, the complexity of response to change (often any type of change will lead to improvement, a phenomenon known as the 'Hawthorne' factor; see Landsberger, 1958). Thus, input–output studies are critiqued for defining instructional programs and methods in terms of how they are supposed to be implemented rather than how they are actually enacted.

Process–product and process–process methodological grammars

The methodological grammar of process–product studies focuses on the relationship of various classroom processes to outcome measures such as reading achievement test scores (see Figure 34.12).

Classroom processes include such variables as academic engaged time, instructional strategies, teacher–student interaction, classroom organization, classroom management, and others. Such factors, either alone or in combination, are correlated with outcome measures. For example, Silverman and Crandall (2010) examined the relationship between particular instructional strategies and children's achievement of vocabulary knowledge. They found that particular instructional practices were related with higher vocabulary performance on their outcome measures.

Typically, process–product studies begin with an assumption of a relationship between a process factor(s) and an outcome, and measure each. The identification of

the process variable may be grounded in an *a priori* theory of classroom learning or it may be sought within the study itself (that is, the study asks the question 'What classroom processes are related to what outcomes?'). An example of the latter is a study by Dahl et al. (1999) that examined phonics instruction in whole-language classrooms. The study sought to identify what occurred and where it occurred (in which instructional activities) and correlated those findings with reading achievement gains for three student groups differentiated by their knowledge of phonics during pretesting.

Studies can be designed to include both an input–output component and a process–product component. For example, Leslie and Allen (1999) examined the difference in achievement for inner-city children between those who attended an early-literacy intervention project and those who did not; they also examined the relationship between classroom factors such as type of instruction received, number of times taught, number of core words taught, and reading achievement. Yaden et al. (2003), working with 4–5-year-old Spanish-speaking children, reported on the implementation of a 4-year, bilingual emergent literacy intervention at an inner-city childcare center. The intervention included daily emergent reading and writing activities, regular staff professional development activities and meetings with preschool teachers, and the operation of a parent lending library. The children who were enrolled in the intervention program gained higher scores in concepts about print test and outperformed English-as-second-language and native-English-speaking peers in standard achievement tests. Another example of a combined input–output and process–product study is Neuman's (1999) study of the impact on

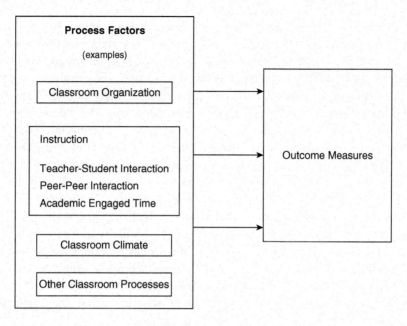

Figure 34.12   Process–product methodological grammar

childcare centers of a 'book flood'. The input variables were the books provided (as a quantity), teacher training in the use of storybooks, and the children's initial literacy level. Process variables included the physical environment of the classroom, teacher–child interactions, amount of storybook reading activity, access to books, and time spent in reading. Outcome measures of reading and literacy development were linked to classroom processes (access to books, storybook reading-aloud activities) as well as to input variables (the provision of books and teacher training).

Closely related to process–product methodological grammars are process–process ones. Process–process methodological grammars focus attention on how various classroom processes relate to each other. For example, Juel and Minden-Cupp (2000) studied four classrooms to examine which classroom processes influenced particular instructional strategies with regard to their success for specific students. Among the factors they examined were reading ability level of the child, instructional practices, the distribution of instructional strategies within the classroom (e.g., how much emphasis on vocabulary instruction versus phonemic awareness versus comprehension instruction), teacher modification and use of the instructional practices, and types of texts. At issue was how these variables influenced each other with regard to providing increased reading achievement for children.

An example of a study that employs a methodological grammar incorporating presage, process, and product structures is Justice et al. (2009). They investigated the effect of a classroom intervention on preschool students' print knowledge. Teachers in an experimental group and a control group both read the same storybooks to children with similar frequency. The experimental group of teachers was taught to use a particular set of techniques that called the children's attention to various types of print knowledge. Videotapes of the teachers while they were engaged in storybook reading were analyzed both to insure fidelity to the experimental instructional program as well as to explore the existence of other potential factors. At the end of a 9 month period, the students of the experimental group of teachers had higher scores on measures of print knowledge. In this study, the input factor was the professional development, the process factor was the particular instructional method of reading storybooks to children, and the product factor was the print knowledge scores.

The underlying chronotope of presage–process–product methodological grammars is that a child with particular characteristics moves through a series of experiences (adventures) that result in a change in an attribute of the child. In this sense, presage–process–product studies are similar to child-attribute improvement methodological grammars (see Figure 34.1) and complex event-attribute improvement methodological grammars (see Figure 34.2).

Summary: input–output, process–product and process–process methodological grammars

At issue in input–output, process–product, and process–process studies is how the chronotope defines those factors and events that influence the enactment of a given reading model. First, there is the issue of quantification. The quantification itself is a definition of the variable as is the isolation of the variable required in order to quantify it. That is, in order to count a phenomenon it has to have distinct and integral boundaries. Assigning boundaries makes a phenomenon a discrete entity (even if only for heuristic purposes) and involves the linguistic process of nominalization.

Nominalization refers to the process of transforming verbs (actions, processes, and states of being) into nouns.

A second issue related to presage–process–product methodological grammars concerns the complexity of how classroom (or non-classroom) reading and writing events evolve over time. The methodological grammar of input–output, process–product, and process–process studies requires reducing complexity in conceptualizing and codifying change in events. Similarly, the evolution of a reading practice over time, the potential distinct importance of a single event, and the particularities of a specific event are non sequitur given the methodological gramma

A third issue with presage–process–product methodological grammars concerns the centrality of speed and efficiency in achieving targeted reading and literacy outcomes. The underlying chronotope defines the purpose of classroom reading (or writing) instruction as speeding movement toward reading achievement. Such a monolithic definition of classroom events obviates aspects of classroom education associated with the hidden curriculum, enculturation, stability and change in societal structures, language socialization, the development of social competence, social and cultural identity, as well as the meaning of classroom events within themselves (for example, the importance of a literary experience within a classroom event as meaningful in its own right and not just for development of some future academic literacy skill).

Situated methodological grammars

Situated methodological grammars define people and their use of written language as part of a situation (cf., Gee, 1996, 2001, for a detailed discussion of literacy and young children as situated social practices). The situation can be a material/ physical/ geographical one (such as a house or a playground), an institutional one (such as a classroom or a family), an event (such as a reading instruction lesson), or some combination. Unlike the chronotope of adventure time in which the protagonists experience a series of situations, in situated methodological grammars there is no separation between the people and the situations within which they act.

The chronotope of situated methodologies' might be compared to the examination of a painting such as Claude Monet's *La Gare St-Lazare* (1877). The painting portrays the train station not through the presenting of endless and undifferentiated detail, but by creating impressions of the whole scene.[3] Although the situation is frozen in time and place, the painting nonetheless suggests an ongoing activity. It is the freezing of the situation that allows the depth of analysis and allows an

examination of the complexity and particularities of the situations and events in which people find themselves. In brief, the chronotope can be described as a 'freeze frame' (see Figure 34.13).

An example of a freeze-frame situated methodological grammar is Sipe's (2000) study of a class of first- and second-grade students. Although Sipe spent 8 months in the classroom and collected data over time, his analysis created a detailed freeze-frame view of the responses and interactions the children made to the books and stories they read. In so doing, Sipe was able to identify three types of literary impulses and differentiate five different types of responses and five different types of literary understanding as a means to reconceptualize and theorize literary understanding as a situated process in classrooms. That is, unlike the presage–process–product methodological grammars described earlier, which focused on antecedents to 'better' reading, the grammar of the methodology employed by Sipe

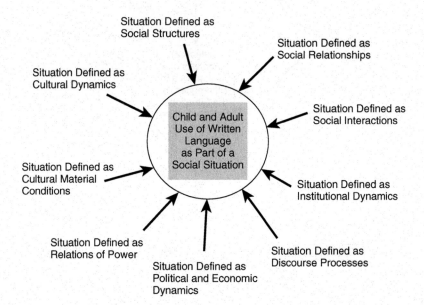

Figure 34.13 'Freeze-frame' situated methodological grammar

focused on theorizing and defining a phenomenon grounded in the lived experience of young children reading literature in that classroom. Although the grammar of the methodology does not allow for a generalized statement about what factors lead to increased literary understanding, the grammar of the methodology does allow for statements about what literary understanding may be and how it is situated in particular locations.

Cairney and Ashton (2002) employ a situated methodological grammar that involves multiple locations. In so doing, Cairney and Ashton use comparison to generate theoretical constructs about the nature of literacy within and across settings (which is conceptually the opposite of comparative location methodologies which use theoretical framing to define and order the relative value of multiple locations). Similarly, a study by Rogers (2002) examines the discursive practices of a mother and daughter around various literacy practices in family, community, and school settings. At issue is not just a match or mismatch in discursive practices between family and school contexts, but the social and cultural ideological commitments underlying the discourses defining social relationships and personhood. We label the methodological grammar underlying situated studies such as Cairney and Ashton's and Rogers' comparative situations theory-building methodological grammar (see Figure 34.14).

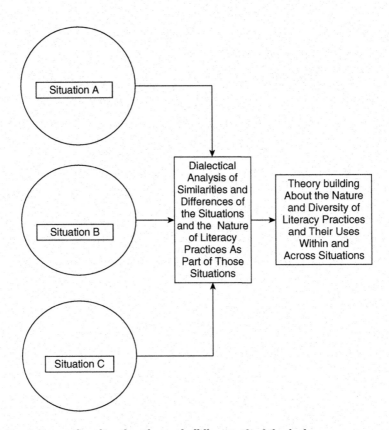

Figure 34.14   Comparative situation theory-building methodological grammar

The nature of the comparison involved in comparative situations theory-building methodological grammars frames the situation as the unit of analysis (as opposed to distinct literacy behaviors or the decontextualized individual). The comparison involves a dialectical process that results in a theoretical description of the nature and diversity of literacy practices as situated social phenomena. Although the data collection may have occurred over time, comparative situations theory-building methodological grammars present 'freeze frames' of multiple locations. This is the case in the Rainbird and Rowsell study (2011) where the authors present four case studies of the literacy 'home spaces' families provide for their preschool children. These descriptions provide information about how 'discourses of literacy, parental agency and learning needs intersect' in middle-class homes. Likewise, Nixon (2011) examines ways in which the nature of preschool literacy practices are designed and promoted through on-line commercial spaces as they are navigated and understood by families and caregivers. The underlying chronotope of situated methodological grammar depends on how the study is located. As children move back and forth across these social institutions they are a part of one location, then another, and what is at stake is how these locations affect and define each other.

Situated methodological grammars can be oriented to movement through time and space. The child (or children) and their uses of written language can be described as part of a set of evolving and changing situations. For example, consider Rowe's (2008) 9-month study of children writing in a preschool classroom. For the children, writing is not only an activity in which they engage but also a way in which they interact with others and thus it is a way in which they constitute community. Children's knowledge of writing practices is not located in their individual minds but socially negotiated and collectively constructed as those social practices and social events continue to evolve and change over time. Similarly, Reyes (2006) conducted a study of three 4-year-old children who were growing up bilingual and biliterate. Her research showed how the children developed their concepts and theories about both languages and their biliteracy competence through their interactions with peers and family members over time in a variety of situations. Yeager et al. (1998) conducted a study where the participation of children in one set of classroom literacy events was compared to a subsequent set of classroom literacy events later in the year and then again to another set later, and so on. The location (defined as a social context for participation) and the students (defined as part of the location) evolved over time. That is, who they were, what they were doing, where they were, and how all of this evolves and changes, is conceptualized as an organic whole. We label such a methodological grammar 'situated over time and space methodological grammar' (see Figure 34.15).

Another example of this methodological grammar and chronotope are studies conducted under the rubric of Language Socialization (cf., Duff and Hornberger, 2008; Ochs, 1988). The child is described as part of a set of situations over time in which the nature of the situation and the nature of the child's participation changes over time. Although the study may be organized around the case of a child, doing so is only a trope to enable the researcher to select a set of situations to describe. What is foregrounded is not the child and

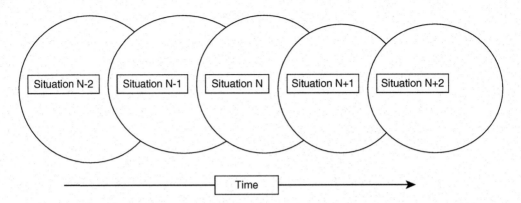

Figure 34.15   Situated over time and space methodological grammar

the child's attributes *per se*, but the ways in which a group, a family, a culture, an institution, a community, socialize a member to their ways of using written language over time. For example, Larson and Maier (2000) documented how a first-grade teacher socialized her students into the role of 'author' by engaging them in a series of activities in which she modeled what being an author involved and then required the children's collaboration with her as co-authors. Although attention is paid to the teacher and children, in studies like Larson and Maier's, the unit of analysis is not the child but the social locations/situations that make up the process of language socialization. Similarly, in a study by Moore (2008) of language socialization within Qur'anic schooling attention is paid to how interaction among teachers and students provides a way for the children to acquire the social practices of Qur'anic oralcy and literacy as a gradual transfer of responsibility for rendering the sacred text. Using the perspective of language socialization, Moore shows that becoming 'literate' involves not only acquiring the literacy practices for the rendering of text but also the taking up

of particular subjectivities of, by, and for participation as part of the 'situation' of Qur'anic literacy.

In these studies and their underlying chronotopes, personhood is a component of the situation or set of situations examined, but it does not exist separate from the situations and events. For example, Miller, Nemoianu and Dejong's (1986) study of early reading at home employs a methodological grammar that foregrounds the family as a unit of analysis. The children, their parents, siblings, etc., and their uses of written language are described as part of the family's everyday life, including the family's efforts at preparing their children for school. The families shared a neighborhood and a socioeconomic class. The methodological grammar allows Miller et al. to describe the literacy practices as an attribute of enculturation (as a family and class process) rather than an attribute of the child *per se*. The underlying chronotope focuses on the family as social institution as it creates and responds to a series of events at home, in the community, and in schools.

Whether research is conducted at the level of the family, the classroom, or schooling at a national level, etc., a key aspect of situated methodological grammars is often a comparative perspective (see Hymes, 1980, for discussion of the need for a comparative perspective). Unlike the 'horse-race' studies described earlier which compare two instructional programs to determine a 'winner', the purpose of comparison in situated methodological grammars is to reveal otherwise hidden issues and processes that can then

be used for either theory development or for more insightful future research (see Figure 34.16).

The comparisons may also be oriented to the relationship of the research to a particular audience or to power relations that exist both within and beyond the research study itself. For example, one can assume that the audience of a research study will bring their knowledge and their personal experience to the reading; the

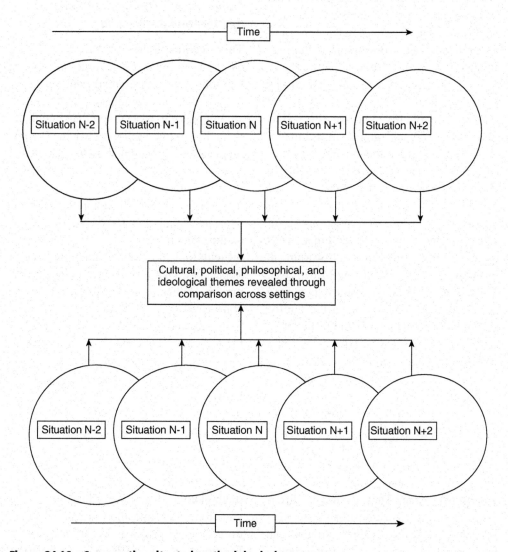

Figure 34.16   Comparative situated methodological grammar

comparison in the research study can be viewed, therefore, as a rhetorical tool for challenging and expanding the understandings that the reader has of the foreign situation and of the situation with which he/she is familiar. Alternatively, there may be an unequal power relationship between groups and the comparison embedded in the research may provide a way to challenge the rationale that underlies that power relationship. Thus, Miller et al.'s research implicitly challenges the assumption held by some people in the middle class (including some middle-class educators and researchers) that working-class families are deficit with regard to their concern and activity around their young children's learning to read.

Whether explicitly stated or not, a situated methodological grammar assumes a relationship between the situation or event analyzed (Situation N in Figure 34.16) and other situations and events (Situations N–1, N–2, N+1, N+2 in Figure 34.16) or some end goal. The relationship of situations and events to each other needs to be carefully considered and warranted. For example, in the study by Miller et al. there is an assumed relationship among the events of enculturation in the family, school, community, etc. In the Miller et al. study, situations were sampled as part of a whole, the whole being the child-rearing culture of the neighborhood and class.

Another approach has been to examine a particular type of situation over time. For example, Borko and Eisenhart (1987) studied the discourse used in instructional reading groups focusing on differences among high-, middle-, and low-ability reading groups over time. They examined differences in norms for using spoken and written language across reading groups, and how young children's ways of using spoken and written language within a reading group matched or did not match the norms for language use within the reading groups. Findings aside, their methodological grammar illustrates one principle for selecting the series of situations to be examined; namely, the nature of a particular set of reading practices over time and their consequences for defining children by positioning them within a social organization.

Summary: methodological grammars and location of the child

This section addressed the location of children within presage–process–product methodological grammars and situated methodological grammars. A difference among presage–process–product methodological grammars relate to whether or not input factors are studied as to their manifestation within the location of the study. Input factors that are not studied within the processes of the location *prima facie* lack an explanation for their relationship to the outcome measures, thus making it difficult to determine how the input factors impact or do not impact the outcome measures and other processes that ought to be considered.

In situated methodological grammars, the separation between input and outcome measures is not an issue in explanatory power because there is no separation between the children being studied and the processes of their location. The study of freeze-frames captures the complexity and particularities of the situations and events within a location during a child's journey within the studied location(s). Situated methodological grammars that emphasize situations over time allow attention to how events, social practices, social institutions, locations, and the people who are a part of them, evolve and change over time.

CONCLUSION

In this chapter we have focused attention on the methodological grammars and underlying chronotopes of methodologies used in research on young children and literacy. We have not attempted to be comprehensive in our coverage of studies, methodological grammars, or chronotopes. Nor do we claim that our analysis of methodological grammars or underlying chronotopes is the only analysis and interpretation possible. Rather, we only claim that it is one analysis and one interpretation. Our effort was aimed at foregrounding a rhetorical aspect of the methodological grammars of research on young children and literacy: underlying conceptions of how people move through time and space drive research methodologies, what counts as knowledge derived from research methodologies, and what counts as personhood. As an effort to make visible the underlying concepts, we examined three interrelated dimensions (the nature of children, their language/literacy uses, and their locations) of the arguments about children's personhood constructed in various chronotopes underlying methodological grammars. At issue in conducting research (and in reading research) is not just the rigor or validity of a research methodology, nor is it simply a matter of the trustworthiness of the findings. The meaning of a research study lies not only in the bits of knowledge produced, the questions asked, or in the topic studied, but in the methodological grammar employed, the underlying chronotope and the implied definition of personhood. Such recognition makes it possible to unpack hidden ideological assumptions and to generate new insights about the nature of inquiry and the nature of the accumulation of knowledge on young children and literacy.

When educators act on the basis of research, they need to reflect on the rhetorics of the methodological grammar and how those rhetorics construct a definition of the child and his/her personhood.

NOTES

1 In this chapter, we define literacy as reading and writing (regardless of material – paper, screen, etc.).

2 Although we have organized this chapter around the three dimensions described above, it is often difficult to separate these dimensions from each other and thus such distinctions should be viewed as heuristic.

3 See Van Maanen (1988) for an argument on the legitimacy and usefulness of impressionistic description in ethnographic research.

REFERENCES

Bakhtin, M. (1935/Tr. 1981). *The Dialogic Imagination.* Austin, TX: University of Texas Press.

Bloome, D. (1989). 'Beyond access: A sociolinguistic and ethnographic study of reading and writing in a culturally diverse middle school classroom', in D. Bloome (ed.), *Classrooms and Literacy.* Norwood, NJ: Ablex. pp. 53–104.

Bloome, D., Carter, S.P., Christian, B.M, Otto, S., and Shuart-Faris, N. (2005). *Discourse Analysis and the Study of Classroom Language and Literacy Events – A Microethnographic Perspective.* Mahwah, NJ: Lawrence Erlbaum.

Bond, G. and Dykstra, R. (1964). 'Report of a developmental program', conference on Coordination of Accepted Proposals for the Cooperative Research Program in First Grade Reading Instruction. Minneapolis: University of Minnesota.

Borko, H. and Eisenhart, M. (1987). 'Reading ability groups as literacy communities', in D. Bloome (ed.), *Classrooms and Literacy.* Norwood, NJ: Ablex. pp. 107–34.

Bus, A.G., Belsky, J., Ijzendoorn, M.H., and Crnic, K. (1997). 'Attachment and book reading patterns; A study of mothers, fathers, and their toddlers', *Early Childhood Research Quarterly*, 12: 81–98.

Cairney, T. and Ashton, J. (2002). 'Three families, multiple discourses: Parental roles, constructions of literacy and diversity of pedagogic practice', *Linguistics and Education*, 13(3): 303–45.

Calhoon, J.A. and Leslie, L. (2002). 'A longitudinal study of the effects of word frequency and rime-neighborhood size on beginning readers' rime reading accuracy in words and nonwords', *Journal of Literacy Research*, 34(1): 39–58.

Cox, B., Fang, Z., and Otto, B.W. (1997). 'Preschoolers' developing ownership of the literate register', *Reading Research Quarterly*, 32(1): 34–55.

Craig, H.K. and Washington, J.A. (2006). *Malik goes to School: Examining the Language Skills of African American Students from Preschool–5th Grade*. Mahwah, NJ: Lawrence Erlbaum.

Cunningham, J., Erickson, K., Spadorica, S., Koppenhaver, D., Cunningham, P., Yoder, D., and McKenna, M. (1999). 'Assessing decoding from an onset-rime perspective', *Journal of Literacy Research*, 31(4): 391–414.

Dahl, K., Scharer, P., Lawson, L., and Grogam, P. (1999). 'Phonics instruction and student achievement in whole language first grade classrooms', *Reading Research Quarterly*, 34(3): 312–41.

Duff, P. and Hornberger, N. (eds) (2008). Language socialization. Vol. 8, *Encyclopedia of Language and Education*. New York: Springer Reference. pp. 175–85.

Dunkin, M. and Biddle, B. (1974). *The Study of Teaching*. Washington, DC: University Press of America.

Duranti, A. and Ochs, E. (1986). 'Literacy instruction in a Samoan village', in B. Schieffelin and P. Gilmore (eds), *The Acquisition of Literacy; Ethnographic Perspectives*. Norwood, NJ: Ablex. pp. 213–32.

Dyson, A.H. (1989). *Multiple Words of Child Writers: Friends Learning to Write*. New York: Teachers College Press.

Dyson, A.H. (1997). *Writing Superheroes: Contemporary Childhood, Popular Culture, and Classroom Literacy*. New York: Teachers College Press.

Dyson, A.H. (2003). *The Brothers and Sisters Learn to Write: Popular Literacies in Childhood and School Cultures*. New York: Teachers College Press.

Dyson, A.H. (2010). 'Writing childhoods under construction: Re-visioning "copying" in early childhood'. *Journal of Early Childhood Literacy*, 10(1): 7–31.

Egan-Robertson, A. (1998). 'Learning about culture, language, and power: Understanding relationships among personhood, literacy practices, and intertextuality', *Journal of Literacy Research*, 30: 449–87.

Ellis, N.C., Natsume, M., Stavropoulou, K., Hoxhallari, L., Van Daal, V.P., Polyzoe, N., Tsipa, M., and Petalas, M. (2004). 'The effects of orthographic depth on learning to read alphabetic, syllabic, and logographic scripts', *Reading Research Quarterly*, 39(4): 438–68.

Fishman, A. (1988). *Amish Literacy: What and How it Means*. Portsmouth, NH: Heinemann.

Gee, J.P. (1996). *Social Linguistics and Literacies: Ideology in Discourses*. 2nd edn. London: Taylor & Francis.

Gee, J.P. (2001). 'A sociocultural perspective on early literacy development', in S. Neuman and D. Dickinson (eds), *Handbook of Early Literacy Research* . New York: Guilford Press. pp. 30–42.

Geertz, C. (1966). *Person, Time, and Conduct in Bali: An Essay in Cultural Analysis*. New Haven, CT: Yale University Press.

Geertz, C. (1973). *The Interpretation of Cultures: Selected Essays*. New York: Basic Books.

Gergen, K.J. and Davis, K.E. (eds) (1985). *The Social Construction of the Person*. New York: Springer-Verlag.

Goodman, Y. and Wilde, S. (1992). *Literacy Events in a Community of Young Writers*. New York: Teachers College Press.

Gutierrez, K., Bien, A., Selland, M., and Pierce, D. (2011). 'Polylingual and polycultural learning ecologies: Mediating emergent academic literacies for dual language learners', *Journal of Early Childhood Literacy*, 11(2): 232–61.

Heath, S. (1983). *Ways with Words*. Cambridge, UK: Cambridge University Press.

Heath, S. (2012). *Words at work and play: Three decades of family and community life*. Cambridge: UK: Cambridge University Press.

Hymes, D. (1980). *Language in Education: Ethnolinguistic Essays*. Washington, DC: Center for Applied Linguistics.

Jimenez, R.T., Garcia, G.E., and Pearson, D.P. (1996). 'The reading strategies of bilingual Latina/o students who are successful English readers: Opportunities and obstacles', *Reading Research Quarterly*, 31(1): 90–112.

Juel, C. and Minden-Cupp, C. (2000). 'Learning to read words: Linguistic units and instructional strategies', *Reading Research Quarterly*, 35(4): 458–92.

Justice, L., Kaderavek, J.N., Fan. X., Sofka, A., and Hunt, A. (2009). 'Accelerating preschoolers' early literacy development through classroom-based teacher-child storybook reading and explicit print referencing', *Language, Speech and Hearning Sciences in Schools*, 40: 67–85.

Kamberelis, G. and Dimitriadis, G. (2005). *On Qualitative Inquiry: Approaches to Language and*

Literacy Research. New York: Teachers College Press.

Kirkpatrick, J. (1983). *The Marquesan Notion of the Person.* Ann Arbor, MI: UMI Research Press.

Landsberger, H.A. (1958). *Hawthorne Revisited. Management and the Worker: Its Critics, and Developments in Human Relations in Industry.* New York: Cornell University Press.

Larson, J. and Maier, M. (2000). 'Co-authoring classroom texts: Shifting participant roles in writing activity', *Research in the Teaching of English,* 34(4): 468–98.

Leslie, L. and Allen, L. (1999). 'Factors that predict success in an early literacy intervention project', *Reading Research Quarterly,* 34(4): 404–25.

Lonigan, C.J., and Whitehurst, G. (1998). 'Relative efficiency of parent and teacher involvement in a shared-reading intervention for preschool children from low-income backgrounds', *Early Childhood Research Quarterly,* 13(2): 263–90.

Luke, A. (1988). *Literacy, Textbooks and Ideology.* New York: Falmer.

Luke, A. (1995). 'When basic skills and information processing just aren't enough: Rethinking reading in new times', *Teachers College Record,* 97(1): 95–115.

Manyak, P. (2001). 'Participation, hybridity, and carnival: A situated analysis of a dynamic literacy practice in a primary-grade English immersion class', *Journal of Literacy Research,* 33(3): 423–65.

Marsh, J. (2011). 'Young children's literacy practices in a virtual world: Establishing an online interaction order', *Reading Research Quarterly,* 46(2): 101–18.

McDermott, R. (1977). 'Social relations as contexts for learning in school', *Harvard Educational Review,* 47(2): 198–213.

McDermott, R.P., Gospodinoff, K., and Aron, J. (1978). 'Criteria for an ethnographically adequate description of concerted activities and their contexts', *Semiotics,* 24: 246–75.

Menon, S. and Hiebert, E.H. (2005). 'A comparison of first graders' reading with little books or literature-based basal anthologies', *Reading Research Quarterly,* 40(1): 12–38.

Miller, P., Nemoianu, A., and DeJong, J. (1986). 'Early reading at home: Its practice and meanings in a working class community', in B. Schieffelin and P. Gilmore (eds), *The Acquisition of Literacy; Ethnographic Perspectives.* Norwood, NJ: Ablex. pp. 3–15.

Moore, L. (2008). 'Body, text, and talk in Maroua Fulbe Qur'anic schooling', *Text & Talk,* 28(5): 643–65.

Morrison, F., Bachman, H.J., and Connor, C.M. (2005). *Improving Literacy in America.* New Haven: Yale University Press.

Neuman, S. (1999). 'Books make a difference: A study of access to literacy', *Reading Research Quarterly,* 34(3): 286–310.

Nixon, H. (2011). '"From bricks to clicks": Hybrid commercial spaces in the landscape of early literacy and learning', *Journal of Early Childhood Literacy,* 11(2): 114–40.

Ochs, E. (1988). *Culture and Language Development: Language Socialization and Language Acquisition in a Samoan Village.* New York: Cambridge University Press.

Ogbu, J. and Simons, H. (1998). 'Voluntary and involuntary minorities: A cultural-ecological theory of school performance and some implications for education', *Anthropology and Education Quarterly,* 29(2): 155–88.

Owodally, A. (2011). 'Multilingual language and literacy practices and social identities in Sunni madrassahs in Mauritius: A case study', *Reading Research Quarterly,* 46(2): 134–55.

Pacheco, M. (2010). 'English-Language learners' reading achievement: Dialectical relationships between policy and practices in meaning-making opportunities', *Reading Research Quarterly,* 45(3): 292–317.

Poole, D. (2008). 'Interactional differentiation in the mixed-ability group: A situated view of two struggling readers', *Reading Research Quarterly,* 43(3): 228–50.

Rainbird, S. and Rowsell, J. (2011). '"Literacy nooks": Geosemiotics and domains of literacy in home spaces', *Journal of Early Childhood Literacy,* 11(2): 214–31.

Reyes, I. (2006). 'Exploring connections between emergent biliteracy and bilingualism', *Journal of Early Childhood Literacy,* 6(3): 267–92.

Rogers, R. (2002). 'Between contexts: A critical discourse analysis of family literacy, discursive practices, and literate subjectivities', *Reading Research Quarterly,* 37(3): 248–77.

Rowe, D.W. (2008). 'Social contracts for writing: Negotiating shared understandings about text in the preschool years', *Reading Research Quarterly,* 43(1): 66–95.

Santa, C. and Høien, T. (1999). 'An assessment of Early Steps: A program for early intervention of reading problems', *Reading Research Quarterly,* 34(1): 54–79.

Shweder, R.A. and Miller, J.G. (1985). 'The social construction of the person: How is it possible?', in K.J. Gergen and K.E. Davis (eds), *The Social Construction of the Person*. New York: Springer-Verlag. pp. 41–69.

Silverman, R. and Crandall, J. (2010). 'Vocabulary practices in prekindergarten and kindergarten classrooms', *Reading Research Quarterly*, 45(3): 318–40.

Sipe, L. (2000). 'The construction of literary understanding by first and second graders in oral response to picture storybook read-alouds', *Reading Research Quarterly*, 35(2): 252–75.

Street, B. (1984). *Literacy in Theory and Practice*. New York: Cambridge University Press.

Street, B. (ed.) (1993). *Cross-cultural Approaches to Literacy*. Cambridge, UK: Cambridge University Press.

Street, B. (1995). *Social Literacies*. London: Longman.

Taylor, D. (1983). *Family Literacy*. Portsmouth, NH: Heinemann.

Taylor, D. and Dorsey-Gaines, C. (1988). *Growing up Literate*. Portsmouth, NH: Heinemann.

Trueba, H.T. (1988). 'English literacy acquisition: From cultural trauma to learning disabilities in minority students', *Linguistics and Education*, 1(2): 125–51.

Van Maanen, J. (1988). *Tales of the Field: On Writing Ethnography*. Chicago: University of Chicago Press.

Verhoeven, L. and Perfetti, C. (eds) (2003). 'Special issue on the role of morphology in learning to read', *Scientific Studies of Reading*, 7(3): 209–307.

Wells, G. (1981). *Learning through Interaction: The Study of language Development*. Cambridge, UK: Cambridge University Press.

Willis, A. (2002). 'Literacy at Calhoun Colored School 1892–1945', *Reading Research Quarterly*, 37(1): 8–44.

Wohlwend, K.E. (2009). 'Damsels in discourse: Girls consuming and producing identity texts through Disney princess play', *Reading Research Quarterly*, 44(1): 57–8.

Yaden, D.B. Jr and Tardibuono, J. (2004). 'The emergent writing development of urban, Latino preschoolers: Developmental perspectives and instructional environments for second-language learners', *Reading and Writing Quarterly*, 20: 29–62.

Yaden, D.B. Jr, Madrigal, P., and Tam, A. (2003). 'Access to books and beyond: Creating and learning from a book lending program for Latino families in the inner city', in G. Garcia (ed.), *English Learners: Reaching the Highest Level of English Literacy*. Newark, DE: International Reading Association. pp. 357–86.

Yeager, B., Floriani, A., and Green, J. (1998). 'Learning to see learning in the classroom', in A. Egan-Robertson and D. Bloome (eds), *Students as Researchers of Culture and Language in their own Communities*. Cresskill, NJ: Hampton Press. pp. 115–39.

Methodologies of Early Childhood Research

Marjorie Faulstich Orellana and Karisa Peer

INTRODUCTION

In this chapter we examine the methodologies that have been used to conduct early childhood literacy research during the past decade (2000–2010). In a comparative analysis of publications in five major literacy journals, we focus on general methodologies, considering how qualitative, quantitative, and mixed-methods researchers have addressed particular kinds of questions.

We begin by situating early childhood literacy within the broader field of literacy research, in order to examine whether or not *early* literacy studies in this time period follow the same general patterns employed in research with older youth. Then, focusing on the early childhood research articles, we identify the major kinds of research questions that have been asked in the field, and look within those categories at the kinds of research methods used to answer those questions. We took this approach because methods are so tightly linked to questions, and this allows us to see not just what *methods* are used in the field, but what kinds of questions are being asked. This further helps us to see gaps in the field.

Because the methods used in this large set of studies varied widely, and in many cases were underspecified, we concentrate on identifying general patterns in the design of the studies as well as in the methodologies deployed, rather than examining in detail the specific kinds of methods and analyses deployed in these studies. We look in more detail at a few of the studies that utilized more unique or innovative methodologies, because we believe these have great potential for moving the field forward in productive ways. We especially underscore the value of research that takes seriously children's perspectives on their own literacy experiences and that looks at literacy in contexts, situations, and relationships that have been neglected in the past. We conclude the chapter with reflections on what this methodological overview reveals about the current field of early childhood literacy, including its gaps and new directions, and provide recommendations for researchers who plan to conduct future studies in this diverse field.

METHODOLOGY FOR OUR REVIEW

We wanted to make sure that our review was comprehensive of the field, and so we began by identifying journals that possess the greatest 'face validity' for early childhood literacy. We selected the following five journals: *Reading Research Quarterly (RRQ), Journal of Literacy Research (JLR), Research in the Teaching of English (RTE), Journal of Early Childhood Literacy (JECL)*, and the *Australian Journal of Language and Literacy (AJLL)*. A significant amount of groundbreaking work in early childhood literacy research emanates from Australia and the UK; hence, we included the *JECL* and *AJLL* in our review of the literature; the rest of the journals are from the US. We surveyed the contents of the five journals from 2000 through the present, with two exceptions: *AJLL*, which only provides online access from 2002 and *JECL*, which began publication in 2001.

EARLY CHILDHOOD LITERACY RESEARCH

After selecting these journals, we purposefully looked at *all of the articles* published in them over the past decade, and selected articles that discussed children between the ages of 0 and 6, or kindergarten and below. There are different working definitions of 'early childhood' in the field; we selected this age range in order to delimit our search

to studies of children before they enter the primary grades, where literacy generally takes particular institutionally-defined forms.

Because our goal was to look at the *methodologies* employed in early childhood literacy studies, we used only the empirical studies located through our search. After removing the theoretical/conceptual papers, we identified all of the articles that were in peer-reviewed journals addressing literacy for children in this age group; there were approximately 123 studies that fit our criteria.

Expanding the search

We recognized that articles on early childhood research may also be published in journals that are not specifically dedicated to literacy. Therefore, we broadened our search to include non-literacy focused journals. We primarily utilized the ERIC (Education Resources Information Center) database, which is an index to journal articles on educational research and practice. ERIC allows access to the full text of most ERIC documents from 1996 to the present. We delimited our search to the most recent research, anchoring this broader search in the last 5 years (2005–2010). In our ERIC search, we used keyword searches which included the following combinations: (a) early childhood + literacy; (b) preschool + literacy; (c) kindergarten + literacy; (d) culture + early childhood + literacy; (e) kindergarten + culture + literacy; (f) preschool + culture + literacy.

This base search was supplemented with a search using googlescholar.com – an online, general access search engine. Our googlescholar search yielded many of the same articles we had already accessed through our ERIC search as well as our review of the five peer-reviewed journals, but it also surfaced several articles in non-literacy focused peer-reviewed journals (e.g., *The Educational Researcher*) that were pertinent to our survey of the field.

From this broader search (i.e., ERIC and googlescholar), we acquired an additional 99 studies that fit our selection criteria. In sum, between the studies we found in our broader search (*n*=99) and the studies that matched our criteria in the five aforementioned peer-reviewed journals (*n*=123), we identified a total of 222 studies for our survey of the early childhood literacy research field.

LITERACY RESEARCH METHODOLOGIES: QUANTITATIVE AND QUALITATIVE STUDIES

Our goal in this chapter was to address what methodologies have been used over the past decade in early childhood research articles. To begin, we took a broad overview of the methods used in the field of literacy research as a whole, and divided *all* of the articles we found in the five aforementioned peer-reviewed journals into qualitative, quantitative, and mixed methods. Table 35.1 presents this breakdown for each of the major literacy journals.

We then used this same breakdown for the articles that focused specifically on early childhood literacy research. Table 35.2 presents this overview of the five journals.

In our survey of the five aforementioned peer-reviewed journals, we found that the majority of empirical studies within the broader field of literacy (n=396) employed a qualitative methodology (see Table 35.1.) Similarly, when only looking at early childhood literacy studies in these same journals, a majority of the studies (n=79) utilized a qualitative research design. (See Table 35.2.) Similarly, when only looking at early childhood literacy studies in these same journals, 64 per cent of researchers utilized a qualitative research design. (See Table 35.2.) When comparing the broader field of literacy with *early* literacy research, the percentage of studies in the five peer-reviewed journals that took on a quantitative approach was fairly consistent (respectively 23 per cent and 24 per cent). For three of the journals (*RRQ*, *JECL*, and *AJLL*), the balance of qualitative to quantitative studies in early childhood literacy research was roughly consistent with the balance in the field as a whole. *Research in the Teaching of English,* not surprisingly, published very few articles focused on early childhood; the three studies it did publish were quantitative in nature. In the *Journal of Literacy Research* the majority

Table 35.1 Methodology of articles in five major peer-reviewed reading and writing journals (2000–2010)

Methodology/foci	RRQ	RTE	JLR	JECL	AJLL	Total articles (n)*
Qualitative	67	82	82	89	76	396
Quantitative	47	10	53	5	11	126
Mixed-methods	6	5	3	2	9	25

*Total articles (*n*) refers to the total number of studies in all five peer-reviewed journals that we surveyed in that category.

Table 35.2 Methodology of early childhood articles in five major peer-reviewed reading and writing journals (2000–2010)

Methodology/foci	RRQ	RTE	JLR	JECL	AJLL	Total articles (n)*
Qualitative	10	3	6	51	9	79
Quantitative	12	-	13	3	1	29
Mixed-methods	2	-	4	7	2	15

*Total articles (n) refers to the total number of studies in all five peer-reviewed journals that we surveyed in that category.

of all studies were qualitative in nature, but those focused on early childhood research were more than twice as likely to use quantitative methods as qualitative. Lastly, 12 per cent of the early childhood research articles used a mixed-method design; whereas, in the broader field of literacy, approximately five per cent of the studies that we surveyed employed mixed methods. Overall, mixed-methods appear to have been *least* utilized; yet, early literacy researchers seem to use this approach more so than in the larger field.

BEYOND THE QUALITATIVE/ QUANTITATIVE DIVIDE

After this broad overview, we wanted to look beyond the qualitative/quantitative divide, and think about the wide variety of methods that have been deployed in the field of early childhood literacy. Knowing that methods are driven by questions, we decided to sort the literature into the various kinds of questions that have been asked, and then to look at the methods that have been used to answer those questions. We sorted the studies into the following categories: those asking about children's literacy developmental processes; those focused on classroom literacy practices; those examining teachers' beliefs and practices; and those concerned with parents' beliefs and practices. Within the classroom-based articles, we found a number that analyzed children's drawings as literacy artifacts. There was some overlap in these categories, of course; we included the studies in multiple categories as appropriate in the discussion that follows.

Children's literacy development

Fifty-three of the articles that we analyzed focused principally on processes of early literacy development. (Other articles may have addressed literacy development, but we include in this count only those focused on describing developmental processes and/or predicting developmental outcomes.) These included large-scale studies examining patterned ways in which children's literacy developed over time, or correlations between early and later measures of literacy, as well as qualitative studies examining the literacy development of individuals or small groups of children.

Large data sets

Thirty-two of these articles involved large or relatively large data sets (i.e., >50 subjects). They tracked a number of measures of child literacy or 'pre-reading' skills as well as other factors that were assumed to predict literacy skills development, such as oral language skills, vocabulary, word recognition, story retelling, phonemic and phonological awareness, pseudo-word reading, spelling of words and pseudo-words, letter-name knowledge, sentence completion, and listening comprehension. These were measured by a battery of 'comprehensive' assessments such as the Dynamic Indicators of Basic Early Literacy Skills (DIBELS), the Test of Word Reading Efficiency (TOWRE), and the Peabody Picture Vocabulary Test (PPVT) as well as a wide range of other measures of discrete skills. Some researchers accompanied the child measures with measures of home and school literacy environments, garnered through interviews or structured observations, such as the Home Literacy Environment Questionaire (Hood et al., 2008). It was in this group of studies that we found the majority of the quantitative and mixed-method research designs.

Within this set of articles there was considerable variation in the populations studied, and the specific kinds of predictors of literacy development that were measured.

Boudreau (2005), for example, looked at the correlation between the language development of special-needs students with their emergent/early literacy development. Several other studies focused on the literacy development of young English learners and examined how oral language impacted this trajectory (e.g., Atwill, Blanchard, Christie, Gorin, and Garcia, 2010; Cardenas-Hagan, Carlson, and Pollard-Durodola, 2007). A unique study conducted by Laurent and Martinot (2009) explored bilingualism, asking whether it improved the metaphonological abilities of 50 pre-readers (30 monolingual French, 20 bilingual French–English). Another unique study looked at the relationship between African American preschoolers' use of African American English and their language and emergent literacy skills (Connor and Craig, 2006). Two studies (Oliver, Dale, and Plomin, 2005; Byrne et al., 2009) analyzed early literacy development in twins.

In virtually all cases 'development' was defined by growth in particular skills, as measured by changes in skills at particular time points, rather than in qualitative changes in ways of using literacy, talking about it, or engaging in literate practice. No researchers looked for *decreases* in particular skills. This may seem a strange point to make, but we want to suggest that it bears consideration, because some skills – such as the ability to speak a home language – may indeed be *lost* as children grow older. Lily Wong Fillmore made this argument in her (1991) paper, *When learning a second language means losing the first,* but her cautionary tale has not been examined empirically by developmentalists.

The developmental studies looked at the unfolding of general literacy skills along a pre-imagined developmental trajectory, or at the development of specific literacy skills, such as phonological sensitivity (Anthony, Lonigan, Driscoll, Phillips, and Burgess, 2003), with the aim of describing 'typical' developmental trajectories. A number of studies measured only child-level variables, looking for the relationship between early and later skills. Others looked at how either home factors or school factors influenced these trajectories; and some examined both. Lynch (2008), for example, tested children on their knowledge about print and correlated the results with reports parents provided on their children's home literacy practices. Connor, Son, Hindman, and Morrison (2005) considered both home and school factors as they related to children's vocabulary and early reading skills; the researchers used an ecological model to assess the distal and proximal sources of influence on students' learning.

We note that in studies considering both school and home factors, researchers' attention was generally drawn to how the practices of adults (most often teachers and mothers) influenced young children's literacy development. Children's *own* views of development, or actions they took to promote their own learning, were not explored in any depth. Such approaches might reveal things that cannot be seen using an adult-centric or teacher-centric stance. Similarly, we might understand literacy development in new ways if we looked beyond what teachers and parents do, and considered as well the influence of siblings or peers.

Qualitative studies of children's literacy development

Fifteen of the articles making claims about literacy development looked in depth at the developmental processes of case study children. The scope of these studies varied, with many involving close-up observations of single cases (e.g., Bauer,

2000; Harris, Fitzsimmons, and McKenzie, 2004; Martinez-Roldan and Malave, 2004; Mavers, 2007) or a small set of cases (Flewitt, Nind, and Payler, 2009; Kenner and Kress, 2003; Levy, 2008; Lysaker, 2006; Reyes, 2006; Rivalland, 2004; Stadler and Ward, 2005; Wilkinson, 2003). Some (e.g., Brooker and Siraj-Blatchford, 2002; Comber, 2004; Martello, 2004; Ranker, 2009) were drawn from larger ethnographies; others were case study research projects. Most of the studies relied on naturalistic observation. Many (e.g., Flewitt et al., 2009; Kenner and Kress, 2003; Lysaker, 2006; Martinez-Roldan and Malave, 2004; Ranker, 2009; Stadler and Ward, 2005) used video or audio data. Others (e.g., Brooker and Siraj-Blatchford, 2002; Comber, 2004; Harris, Fitzsimmons, and McKenzie, 2004; Martello, 2004; Wilkinson, 2003) supplemented their observations with interviews.

Approaches to analysis also varied considerably. For instance, Martinez-Roldan and Malave (2004) used critical discourse analysis (CDA). Mavers (2007) employed semiotic analysis. But more often than not – in these studies of child development as well as in much of the qualitative research we examined – researchers did not name particular analytic methods. Instead, they spoke more generally of 'coding' the data, looking for 'emergent themes,' or using general approaches to analysis such as the 'constant comparative' method. Some detailed how themes and codes were determined; but many did not.

Intervention studies

Finally, a group of studies (n=12) examined literacy development in the context of an intervention. The effects of the interventions were usually tested using some form of pre- and post-test. A few, such as Van Der Heyden, Snyder, Broussard, and Ramsdell (2007) and Lovelace and Stewart (2007) took repeated measures of children's development over a period of time during which the intervention was delivered. Most researchers utilized some kind of comparative groups; for example, Nicolson and Ng (2006) looked at the effects of phonemic awareness training on phonemic awareness scores, in contrast with the effects of dialogic reading. Pagani, Jalbert, Lapointe, and Hébert (2006), in a natural experiment, looked at the benefits of junior kindergarten for linguistic-minority 4-year-olds in comparison with their linguistic-minority peers from the same neighborhood. Landry and Smith (2006) conducted a quasi-experimental study of 370 Head Start classrooms that were randomly selected to receive an intervention targeting teachers' enhancement of language and literacy.

Some studies put particular measures in place to ensure or check the fidelity of the interventions; Connor and Craig (2006), for example, included videotaped classroom observations, which revealed considerable variability across the classrooms in their studies. Jackson et al. (2006) treated teaching practices as a mediating variable; they looked at how a professional development literacy workshop series affected teachers' practices and in turn their preschool students' literacy skills. Most of these studies involved quantitative analyses, most typically multiple hierarchical regression analyses. Zvoch, Letourneau, and Parker (2007) used multilevel growth models to examine children's literacy development in a study involving multi-site program implementation.

Classroom practices and processes

Observations of classroom literacy practices formed another large subset of these studies, with at least 26 studies involving naturalistic classroom observations, plus 14 that involved observations of some kind of classroom intervention. (We do not include in our count the studies focused on children's development that *included* classroom observations; we count here only ones that were uniquely and centrally concerned with classroom practices and processes.) Most of these used ethnographic methods, though some appeared to be more fully ethnographic than others, in the sense that they used multiple forms of data in a concerted attempt to access participants' 'emic' perspectives on classroom processes. Observations examined different aspects of classroom life, including the nature of the classroom environment as a support for literacy, classroom talk and interactions, and children's writing processes and written work.

The aspects of classroom practices that were studied varied widely; this is a methodological issue in that it determined the kinds of data that were gathered (such as fieldnotes based on observations; audiotapes of classroom talk; artifacts produced by students). Foci included attention to children's engagement in literacy through play (Gillen, 2002; Moon and Reifel, 2008; Wohlwend, 2008a, 2009); the kinds of intertextual connections that were made by children and teachers (Roache-Jameson, 2005); other kinds of interactions with texts (Bomer, 2003; Dombey, 2003; Moody, Justice, and Cabell, 2010); the relationship between children's classroom talk and their production of texts (Fisher, 2010); and the overall classroom environment (Inan, 2009). Pahl (2009), for example, examined the production of meaning across children's talk and multimodal texts (i.e., a panorama box environment that children created); she emphasized the importance of looking at improvised talk.

Levy (2008) and Feiler (2005) examined how children made connections between their home and school literacies. Silvers, Shorey, and Crafton (2010) analyzed young children's critical and multimodal literacies as students explored personal inquiries about Hurricane Katrina in New Orleans, LA.

Those focused on writing processes included studies of dictation and dramatization of original stories (Cooper, 2005), other approaches to supporting young children's writing (Bomer, 2003; Lysaker, Wheat, and Benson, 2010; Rowe and Neitzel, 2010; Wohlwend, 2008b), and peer-to-peer interactions during the writing process (Dyson, 2008, 2010). Other researchers studied artifacts produced by the children: their drawings (Brooks, 2005; Knight, 2008; Soundy and Drucker, 2010; Wohlwend, 2008a) and writing (e.g., Wohlwend, 2008b; Dyson, 2008, 2010). Wohlwend's (2008b) study analyzed writing samples produced by children working both before and after the teacher introduced peer sharing as a strategy, using 'constant comparative' method.

Those examining drawings primarily considered the *meanings* and/or *messages* that could be gleaned from children's drawings, as an incipient form of literacy, rather than the development of semiotic skills. Most related the drawings to other classroom practices. For instance, using ethnographic methods to study the classroom context, Hopperstad (2010) looked for the events that inspired children's drawings, and identified the different kinds of drawings that were thus produced. She examined how visual features in children's drawings carried ideational, interpersonal and textual meaning. Kendrick and McKay (2004) specifically looked at the types of literacy events that were portrayed in children's drawings, coding these for social settings, reading and writing practices and genres, as well as domains. In other words, they used children's drawings as a window into children's daily life literacy practices. This allowed the researchers to tap into children's perspectives in ways that other methods do not. All of these studies employed a qualitative approach. Most invoked some form of semiotic analysis (i.e., examining signs, lines, shapes, combinations and color) to assess the ways that preschool-aged children expressed their ideas through drawing.

The data that were gathered in classroom research included fieldnotes based on participant observation, children's drawings and writing, transcripts of videotaped or audiotaped classroom interactions, and interviews. Increasingly, researchers seem to be incorporating video data of classroom interactions (e.g., Bomer, 2003; Martinez-Roldan and Malave, 2004; Pramling and Carlsson, 2008; Wohlwend, 2008a). Some captured particular kinds of events on video and transcribed the data for discourse analysis. Martinez-Roldan and Malave (2004), for example, videotaped classroom literature discussions, and used information from their larger ethnography (including home visits and parent interviews) to make sense of children's talk, via CDA. But in most studies that utilized video data we found rather little discussion of how video data worked in concert with other data, such as the fieldworkers' own observations. We also found little discussion about decisions of where to place the cameras; when to turn them on and off; and; or how videos were analyzed beyond the analyses of the audiotaped data. Roberts et al., however, *did* offer an 'innovative method of transcription ... (that) captures each child's language, body posture, facial expressions and gestures, in relation to the visual image and game

sounds they are currently attending to' in their study of children's responses to electronic texts (2008: 242).

Most of the classroom-based research examined literacy within the context of the whole classroom, analyzing teaching practices and learning processes. Some tracked the activities of single children (e.g., Spencer, 2009) or small groups of children (e.g., Nichols, Nixon, and Rowsell, 2009) as they moved across different spaces in the classroom over time. Others compared different kinds of classroom contexts or observed classroom life under varied conditions. Only one of the school-based research articles that we uncovered in this time period looked at children operating in anything but official classroom space; Grugeon (2005) worked with student teachers to observe and record children's playground activities and to identify pedagogical connections.

Most researchers centered their analyses on what teachers or other adults did, how children responded, or what children appeared to learn, using adult-centric and teleological lenses. But some – perhaps *more* than in research with older youth – made concerted efforts to tap into children's perspectives, and approached their analyses from a decidedly child-centered stance. These were also the studies that used some of the most innovative methodological approaches.

Intervention studies

A few of the articles that centered on classroom processes examined the effects of interventions. This is in addition to the studies cited above under the developmental section, some of which included classroom observations. (The studies cited in that section were ultimately concerned with intervention effects on child development, and we distinguish them from ones that highlighted effects on *teaching* practices.) Hsieh, Hemmeter, and McCollum (2009), for example, looked at the impact of classroom coaching, and Neuman and Cunningham (2009) examined the effect of professional development as well as a yearlong coaching intervention on teachers' literacy practices. Marsh (2000) introduced the television program *Teletubbies* to two nurseries in England to see its motivating effect on young children's literacy.

Home literacy activities

Almost all of the studies that looked at children in anything but classroom settings worked with children in their homes. These involved a combination of naturalistic observations of parent–child interactions, a general overview of home literacy environments, and informal conversations with parents (e.g., Gillanders and Jimenez, 2004; Johnson, 2010; Li, 2010; Pahl, 2002). A few examined home literacy in specific domains or practices; for example Mavers (2007) deployed semiotic analysis to explore in depth one child's spontaneously initiated email exchanges with her uncle.

Other researchers used a more formal protocol for 'measuring' and cataloguing the home literacy environment. For example, Lopez (2005) created a phone interview survey as well as a Language, Literacy, and Culture Questionnaire, which included in-depth questions related to language use in the home; home literacy exposure and support; parents' attitudes, expectations and involvement in their child's school; and cultural influences on these factors. Neuman, Koh, and Dwyer (2008) reported on the *development* of a tool for measuring home language and literacy environments: the Literacy Environment Checklist and the Group/Family Observation and Provider

Interview. Neuman et al.'s (2008) article describes their methods for securing inter-rater reliability and the internal consistency of the measure.

As in the classroom studies, many of the home-based research seemed to assume an adult-centric and developmental stance, probing how parents shaped the literacy-learning environment and how that environment impacted children's learning. Mielonen and Paterson (2009), on the other hand, concentrated on children's activities – their uninterrupted play and its relation to literacy development. They gathered examples of reading and writing competence that was revealed in two 5-year-olds' social interactions. In addition to writing observational field notes the authors conducted informal ethnographic interviews using non-intrusive and developmentally appropriate *who, what, where, when*, and *why* questioning. They also analyzed the girls' journal reflections (sheets of paper that read, 'Today I …') and drawings. They evaluated attitude scales (pieces of paper that read, 'When I play I feel …') and asked the children to write how they felt. After the attitude scales, the girls were given a simple iconic rating scale that gave them the opportunity to 'rate' their experience in play. We highlight this study because it deployed innovative methods that were directly tailored to gain insight into young children's viewpoints and their experiences with literacy.

A few studies did not directly observe the home environment, but instead assessed it based on *interviews* (Downes, 2002; Lynch, 2008) or an 'interview survey' (Nutbrown and Hannon, 2003: 115). In Downes, Arthur, and Beecher's (2001) study, structured observations and discussions with eight preschool children (3–5 years) as well as 10 elementary school students (5–8 years) were conducted in a day care center and at a school while the children used a computer. Researchers held focus group discussions with parents and teachers of young children who regularly used computers at home and at their school, preschool or day care centre. Nutbrown and Hannon (2003) also pursued the perspectives of young children via interviews; they compared the reports that children whose parents had participated in a family literacy program provided about their home literacy activities with those of children who had not participated. They found modest differences, and used this to suggest that the impact of a family literacy program is detectable through children's viewpoints.

Yamada-Rice (2010) employed a particularly innovative approach to tapping into children's perspectives, asking 11 4-year-olds to take photographs of home multi-modal texts, and using the photos to elicit discussion with the children. Adhering to 'the belief that research for and about children should include their participation in the process and product,' Yamada-Rice then guided the children in publishing their photos as a book. A content analysis of the photos that the children took revealed how multi-modal media had penetrated the lives of young children, and parental surveys corroborated how children participated in multi-modal technological practices.

Reese and Goldenberg (2007) provided the only study of community language and literacy use that we found in this set of studies. Reese and Goldenberg base their claims on observations of the community context (including studies of the signage and other public print) as well as interviews with parents and children. By using the community as a unit of analysis, and focusing their observations there, they raise questions that rarely get addressed about variations in the ways communities – not just families – support literacy development.

Parent–child storybook reading practices

A fairly large subset of the articles we identified focused specifically on parent–child interactions during storybook reading – and in one case, those of grandparents and children (Gregory, Arju, Jessel, Kenner, and Ruby, 2007). Some of these studies involved naturalistic observations and/or were part of larger ethnographies of home language and literacy practices (e.g., Gregory et al., 2007; Morgan, 2005); others involved story-book reading under experimental conditions. Some coupled the observations with interviews and other means of assessing participants' perspectives, but the analyses centered on the nature of interactions in the observed activities. A few videotaped the interactions and transcribed them for discourse analysis. A variety of contexts and populations were studied, including a middle-class bilingual home (Kabuto, 2010); children with language delays (Woude and Barton, 2003); a Bengali immigrant family in East London (Gregory et al., 2007); and children from 'socioeconomically disadvantaged homes' (Morgan, 2005). A few studies attempted to sketch broader portraits of storybook reading practices among particular groups or in particular communities by using parent interviews (Nichols, 2000) or a survey (Raban and Nolan, 2005).

The experimental studies involved comparisons of the storybook reading practices and/or styles of different groups, or under different conditions. Hammer,

Nimmo, Cohen, Draheim, and Johnson (2005), for example, compared the book reading styles of African American and Puerto Rican mothers in a Head Start program. Vandermaas-Peeler, Nelson, Bumpass, and Sassine (2009) contrasted low-income and middle-class interactional styles under controlled circumstances in which parents were instructed to read two books to their children and then engage in a 15-minute play session. Rodriguez, Hines and Montiel (2009) examined low-income and middle-class Mexican mothers' interactive strategies under similarly controlled circumstances. Torr and Scott (2006) analyzed the reading practices of 12 mothers (half of whom were college educated) and 12 preschool teachers, as they read two different types of books (one narrative and one informational), keying in on how these adults explained unusual vocabulary. In another paper Torr (2004) used data from the same study to evaluate how children responded to these readings of different texts by different people.

Other researchers observed interactions across *different conditions.* Kaderavek and Pakulski (2007) compared the practices of the mothers of hearing-impaired children in storybook reading and in free play. Korat and Or (2010) assessed the reading of e-books versus print-books. They analyzed discourse initiated by the child as well as his/her responses to mother initiations as mothers read. Kim and Anderson (2008) also contrasted the reading of e-books versus print books, as mothers read to a 3-year-old versus a 7-year-old. Hindman et al. (2008) videotaped 130 children reading with parents and in their preschool classrooms.

Most of these researchers developed their own coding schemes, but a few used established protocols. Rodriguez et al.

(2009), for example, used the Adult/Child Interactive Reading Inventory to code their data. Hindman et al. (2008) coded the storybook reading for contextualized and decontextualized language relating to both meaning making and decoding. The results were integrated with a larger longitudinal study of children's literacy development. Quiroz, Snow, and Zhao (2010) similarly integrated their analyses of mother–child dyads sharing picture books with data from a larger longitudinal study to see how interactions predicted children's vocabulary development.

Parenting beliefs and practices

Six of the studies we identified examined parents' beliefs and practices related to literacy (Diaz, 2003; Chen and Harris, 2009; Hammer, Rodriguez, Lawrence, and Miccio, 2007; Nichols, 2002; Nichols et al., 2009; Peterson and Heywood, 2007); one of these (Peterson and Heywood, 2007) contrasted the perspectives of immigrant parents, principals and teachers. All utilized interviews or questionnaires, but these varied in their degree of formality, and the authors took quite different approaches to analysis. Nichols (2002) for example, analyzed parents' views using critical discourse analysis, to identify three distinct discourses about childhood. With her colleagues Nichols et al. (2009) then compared parents' beliefs with representations of parenting in commercial and government-produced texts. Hammer et al. (2007) used structured questionnaires administered by trained home visitors to collect information on specific beliefs and practices held by Puerto Rican mothers. They classified the practices as 'traditional' and 'progressive' and identified variations across the group.

Teachers' beliefs and practices

A comparable set of nine studies centered on *teachers'* beliefs and practices. (Many of the studies of child development and of classroom practices included attention to teaching practices, but we distinguish those from ones that focused only on teachers, and especially on their *beliefs*.) Hindman and Wasik (2008) used the Preschool Teacher Literacy Beliefs Questionnaire to illuminate beliefs that were shared by Head Start teachers as well as points of variability. Lim (2010) used 'Q-methodology' to identify four viewpoint groups among 30 preschool teachers, and possible teacher characteristics that correspond with the various viewpoints. Lim asserts that 'through factor analysis, Q-methodology is able to determine what is statistically different about various viewpoints, and to identify the number of common responses that are shared by a particular group of individuals' (2010: 216). Lim and Torr's (2008) study was exploratory work for the larger study reported by Lim; Lim and Torr report on the beliefs of eight teachers, garnered from interviews. Hill (2010) developed a case study of one teacher showing how she used teacher-research on children's multimodal funds of knowledge in her planning and assessment practices.

CONCLUSION

Our comprehensive overview of all early childhood literacy research published in the last decade in five key literacy journals, supplemented by a wider search of the field in the last 5 years, allows us to make a number of observations about patterns in the field, in terms of research design and methodologies, as well as to identify important gaps in the research.

We present our observations here, along with suggestions for future research.

First, we note the wide variety of methods used in the field. For the most part, researchers selected methods that were appropriate for the questions they were asking, rather than attempting to follow closely in any given methodological tradition. This was evident in *both* the qualitative and quantitative work, though there were some general *kinds* of methods that were specific to each (e.g., regression analyses or linear growth modeling of longitudinal data, and ethnographic approaches to analyzing processes and practices). These varieties of research help us to see beyond the qualitative/quantitative divide, and to recognize many, varied ways of mixing methods. In a way, the vast majority of the studies we examined mixed methods in some way, in that they combined different approaches to gathering data. But using the more standard meaning of 'mixed methods,' – i.e., the mixing of qualitative and quantitative methods – we note that although the percentage of mixed methods studies was relatively low (12 per cent), it was much higher than in the field of literacy writ large (5 per cent).

Studies using quantitative or mixed methods were focused principally on children's developmental processes, which seemed to be a central preoccupation of the field. The considerably larger number of mixed or quantitative studies in early childhood research, compared to literacy research writ large, seems due to the large number of studies that examined developmental processes. (Perhaps there is less interest in measuring the literacy growth of older youth, but we might wonder why this is so.)

The developmental research was 'mixed' in the sense that researchers studied discrete measures of children's growth in literacy skills (usually measured through a set of comprehensive assessments) while supplementing these quantitative assessments with qualitative measures of classroom contexts, home literacy environments, and parenting or teaching styles. We saw few that put equal emphasis on the quantitative and qualitative results. The qualitative measures in these studies were usually quite limited in scope. Research focused specifically on classroom processes, on the other hand, used principally qualitative methods, usually in an ethnographic approach to understanding classroom culture.

Importantly, the variations in methods that we have identified in this body of literature seem to reflect different conceptions of literacy, development, and socialization. Most of the developmental studies using quantitative or mixed methods treated literacy as an 'autonomous' (Street, 1995) set of cognitive skills that was presumed to follow a normative developmental trajectory and that functioned independently of other practices. Early literacy or pre-literacy skills were presumed to predict later literacy success, and the studies were designed to see just what skills had predictive value. The early literacy skills that were measured were based on conventional notions of literacy, like the 11 variables identified by the National Early Literacy Panel (2008), rather than the kinds of skills that children from non-dominant groups might be exposed to in their homes through family cultural practices.

Qualitative research set in homes and classrooms, on the other hand, treated literacy as a social and cultural practice, one that is cultivated by engaging in the practice in situated contexts. Development, if considered at all within this model, is not assumed to involve the unfolding of a normative trajectory, but to be shaped by particular contexts as well as beliefs and values. Implicitly, if not explicitly, these researchers adopted Street's 'ideological' notions of literacy (1995), focusing on the form and function of literacy as it is used in social and cultural contexts. These researchers also considered a wider range of literacy practices and skills than was the case in the quantitative studies.

Based on who was selected as the subjects of studies, it would seem that most researchers assume mothers and teachers to be the key agents for children's socialization into literate practices. Indeed, most research claiming to study *parents* looked only at *mothers'* literacy practices. Bauman and Wasserman (2010), in an important exception to this trend, looked specifically at a project designed to empower fathers to take a more active role in their children's preparation for school literacy. Only one study looked at the work that grandparents do (Gregory et al., 2007); and one focused on siblings' interactions (Gregory, 2001). This research focus is responsive to the communities under study, because grandparents and siblings arguably play an important role in child socialization in immigrant communities. All researchers of family literacy would do well to follow these researchers' approach, and attend to the influence of non-parental adults, siblings, cousins, or others on children's literate development.

Although the majority of researchers operated with 'parent-centric' or 'teacher-centric' lenses, there were certainly a number of researchers who made concerted efforts to examine children's viewpoints on their own experiences. Tapping into children's perspectives is a methodological challenge. It's not enough to collect children's writing, drawing and other work products; it is important to listen to how children talk about their own work. By giving kids cameras, for example, we can literally see what is salient to them, but rather than imposing an adult interpretation it is important to hear how kids make sense of their own photos. We applaud the efforts that researchers made to suspend their own interpretations and to listen carefully to children.

In pointing to the wide variety of methods, we are not suggesting that the field necessarily needs narrowing. Using varied methods allows for different kinds of insights into what is most certainly a complex and multi-dimensional phenomenon. At the same time, the field might benefit from a larger corpus of studies that use similar methodology to ask similar questions. By looking across similar studies set in different contexts or working with distinct populations, we might identify patterns that are not evident in single studies, and have a more comprehensive picture of early childhood literacy. This might help us to see varied pathways to literacy and a wider range of ways of supporting children's literacy growth.

In addition to broadening the scope of the field, we all might benefit from research that builds on what others have done. We especially suggest that researchers might learn from the more innovative approaches to tapping into young children's perspectives, since this is one of the most challenging aspects of working with this age group.

Finally, we want to identify what we see as a significant problem in the literature in terms of methodology: many of the studies *underspecified* their methodology. Data *gathering* methods were generally named, but approaches to data *analyses* were often not detailed, or were presented in superficial or very general ways. This is a problem that Smagorinsky (2008)

underscores; he calls on social science researchers to make the methods section the 'epicenter of research,' and to provide detailed accounts of how data get reduced (with particular attention to disconfirming or discrepant evidence), and then coded and/or analyzed. To view the methods section as the 'epicenter' of research is to recognize that methods are tightly linked to theoretical perspectives; that different methods are appropriate for answering different questions; and that the way data are represented matters, and thus should be explained as part of the analytical process. As Smagorinsky writes: 'Results need to be specifically linked to method so that it is clear to readers how results have been rendered from data and how the theoretical apparatus that motivates the study is realized in the way that the data are analyzed and then organized for presentation' (2008: 408). We echo Smagorinsky's call here, based on our assessment of the methods used in early childhood literacy research.

NOTE

1 For the purposes of this chapter, it is important to distinguish between *methods* and *methodology*. Methods are the *research practices* chosen by the researcher, such as particular kinds of qualitative, quantitative, or mixed methods; whereas, methodology addresses *theoretical questions* about the examination of research and how research is conducted. Renowned feminist and educational researcher Sandra Harding defines methodology as 'a *theory* and *analysis* of how research does and should proceed' (1987: 3).

REFERENCES

Anthony, J. L., Lonigan, C. J., Driscoll, K., Phillips, B. M., and Burgess, S. R. (2003). 'Phonological sensitivity: A quasi-parallel progression of word structure units and cognitive operations', *Reading Research Quarterly*, 38(4): 470–87.

Atwill, K., Blanchard, J., Christie, J., Gorin, J. S., and Garcia, H. S. (2010). 'English-language learners: Implications of limited vocabulary for cross-language transfer of phonemic awareness with kindergartners', *Journal of Hispanic Higher Education*, 9(2): 104–29.

Bauer, E. B. (2000). 'Code-switching during shared and independent reading: Lessons from a preschooler', *Research in the Teaching of English*, 35(1): 101–30.

Bauman, D. C. and Wasserman, K. B. (2010). 'Empowering fathers of disadvantaged preschoolers to take a more active role in preparing their children for literacy success at school', *Early Childhood Education Journal*, 37(5): 363–70.

Bomer, R. (2003). 'Things that make kids smart: A Vygotskian perspective on concrete tool use in primary literacy classrooms', *Journal of Early Childhood Literacy*, 3(3): 223–47.

Boudreau, D. (2005). 'Use of a parent questionnaire in emergent and early literacy assessment of preschool children', *Language, Speech, and Hearing Services in Schools*, 36: 33–47.

Brooker, L. and Siraj-Blatchford, J. (2002). '"Click on Miaow!": How children of three and four years experience the nursery computer', *Contemporary Issues in Early Childhood*, 3: 251–73.

Brooks, M. (2005). 'Drawing as a unique mental development tool for young children: Interpersonal and intrapersonal dialogues', *Contemporary Issues in Early Childhood*, 6(1): 80–91.

Byrne, B., Coventry, W. L., Olson, R. K., Samuelsson, S., Corley, R., Willcutt, E. G., et al. (2009). 'Genetic and environmental influences on aspects of literacy and language in early childhood: Continuity and change from preschool to grade 2', *Journal of Neurolinguistics*, 22: 219–36.

Cardenas-Hagan, E., Carlson, C. D., and Pollard-Durodola, S. D. (2007). 'The cross-linguistic transfer of early literacy skills: The role of initial L1 and L2 skills and language instruction', *Language, Speech, and Hearing Services in Schools*, 38: 249–59.

Chen, H. and Harris, P. (2009). 'Becoming school literate parents: An ESL perspective', *Australian Journal of Language and Literacy*, 32(2): 118–35.

Comber, B. (2004). 'Three little boys and their literacy trajectories', *Australian Journal of Language and Literacy*, 27(2): 114–27.

Connor, C. M. and Craig, H. K. (2006). 'African American preschoolers' language, emergent literacy skills, and use of African American English: A complex relation', *Journal of Speech, Language, and Hearing Research*, 49: 771–92.

Connor, C. M., Son, S. H., Hindman, A. H., and Morrison, F. J. (2005). 'Teacher qualifications, classroom practices, family characteristics, and preschool experience: Complex effects on first graders' vocabulary and early reading outcomes', *Journal of School Psychology*, 43: 343–75.

Cooper, P. M. (2005). 'Literacy learning and pedagogical purpose in Vivian Paley's "storytelling curriculum"', *Journal of Early Childhood Literacy*, 5(3): 229–51.

Diaz, C. J. (2003). 'Latino/a voices in Australia: Negotiating bilingual identity', *Contemporary Issues in Early Childhood*, 4(3): 314–36.

Dombey, H. (2003). 'Interactions between teachers, children, and texts in three primary classrooms in England', *Journal of Early Childhood Literacy*, 3(1): 37–58.

Downes, T. (2002). 'Children's and families' use of computers in Australian homes', *Contemporary Issues in Early Childhood*, 3(2): 182–96.

Downes, T., Arthur, L., and Beecher, B. (2001). 'Effective learning environments for young children using digital resources: An Australian perspective', *Information Technology in Childhood Education*, 1: 129–43.

Dyson, A. H. (2008). 'Staying in the (curricular) lines', *Written Communication*, 25(1): 119–59.

Dyson, A. H. (2010). 'Writing childhoods under construction: Re-visioning 'copying' in early childhood', *Journal of Early Childhood Literacy*, 10(1): 7–31.

Feiler, A. (2005). 'Linking home and school literacy in an inner city reception class', *Journal of Early Childhood Literacy*, 5(2): 131–49.

Fisher, R. (2010). 'Young writers' construction of agency', *Journal of Early Childhood Literacy*, 10(4): 410–29.

Flewitt, R., Nind, M., and Payler, J. (2009). '"If she's left with books she'll just eat them": Considering inclusive multimodal literacy practices', *Journal of Early Childhood Literacy*, 9(2): 211–33.

Gillanders, C. and Jimenez, R. T. (2004). 'Reaching for success: A close-up of Mexican immigrant parents in the USA who foster literacy success for their kindergarten children', *Journal of Early Childhood Literacy*, 4(3): 243–69.

Gillen, J. (2002). 'Moves in the territory of literacy? The telephone discourse of three- and four- year olds', *Journal of Early Childhood Literacy*, 2(1): 21–43.

Gregory, E. (2001). 'Sisters and brothers as language and literacy teachers: Synergy between siblings playing and working together', *Journal of Early Childhood Literacy*, 1(3): 301–22.

Gregory, E., Arju, T., Jessel, J., Kenner, C., and Ruby, M. (2007). 'Snow White in different guises: Interlingual and intercultural exchanges between grandparents and young children at home in East London', *Journal of Early Childhood Literacy*, 7(1): 5–25.

Grugeon, E. (2005). 'Listening to learning outside the classroom: Student teachers study playground literacies', *Literacy*, 39(1): 3–9.

Hammer, C. S., Nimmo, D., Cohen, R., Draheim, H. C., and Johnson, A. A. (2005). 'Book reading interactions between African American and Puerto Rican Head Start children and their mothers', *Journal of Early Childhood Literacy*, 5(3): 195–227.

Hammer, C. S., Rodriguez, B. L., Lawrence, F. R., and Miccio, A. W. (2007). 'Puerto Rican mothers' beliefs and home literacy practices', *Language, Speech, and Hearing Services in Schools*, 38: 216–24.

Harding, S. (1987). 'Is there a feminist method?', in S. Harding (ed.), *Feminism and Methodology*. Bloomington, IN: Indiana University Press. pp. 1–14.

Harris, P., Fitzsimmons, P., and McKenzie, B. (2004). 'Six words of writing, many layers of significance: An examination of writing as social practice in an early grade classroom', *Australian Journal of Language and Literacy*, 27(1): 27–45.

Hill, S. (2010). 'The millenium generation: Teacher-researchers exploring new forms of literacy', *Journal of Early Childhood Literacy*, 10(3): 314–40.

Hindman, A. H., Connor, C. M., Jewkes, A. M., and Morrison, F. J. (2008). 'Untangling the effects of shared book reading: Multiple factors and their associations with preschool literacy outcomes', *Early Childhood Research Quarterly*, 23: 330–50.

Hindman, A. H. and Wasik, B. A. (2008). 'Head Start teachers' beliefs about language and literacy instruction', *Early Childhood Education Journal*, 23(4): 479–92.

Hood, M., Conlon, E., & Andrews, G. (2008). 'Preschool home literacy practices and children's literacy development: A longitudinal analysis', *Journal of Educational Psychology*, 100(2): 252–271.

Hopperstad, M. H. (2010). 'Studying meaning in children's drawings', *Journal of Early Childhood Literacy*, 10(4): 430–52.

Hsieh, W. Y., Hemmeter, M. L., and McCollum, J. A. (2009). 'Using coaching to increase preschool teachers' use of emergent literacy teaching strategies', *Early Childhood Research Quarterly*, 24: 229–47.

Inan, H. Z. (2009). 'Understanding features of amiable environments that can nourish emergent literacy skills of preschoolers', *Australian Journal of Basic and Applied Sciences*, 3(3): 2510–8.

Jackson, B., Larzelere, R., St Clair, L., Corr, M., Fichter, C., and Egertson, H. (2006). 'The impact of HeadsUp! Reading on early childhood educators' literacy practices and preschool children's literacy skills', *Early Childhood Research Quarterly*, 21: 213–26.

Johnson, A. S. (2010). 'The Jones family's culture of literacy', *The Reading Teacher*, 64(1): 33–44.

Kabuto, B. (2010). 'Code-switching during parent-child reading interactions: Taking multiple theoretical perspectives', *Journal of Early Childhood Literacy*, 10(2): 131–57.

Kaderavek, J. N. and Pakulski, L. A. (2007). 'Mother-child story book interactions: Literacy orientation of pre-schoolers with hearing impairment', *Journal of Early Childhood Literacy*, 7(1): 49–72.

Kendrick, M. and McKay, R. (2004). 'Drawings as an alternative way of understanding young children's constructions of literacy', *Journal of Early Childhood Literacy*, 4(1): 109–28.

Kenner, C. and Kress, G. (2003). 'The multisemiotic resources of bilingual children', *Journal of Early Childhood Literacy*, 3(2): 179–202.

Kim, J. E. and Anderson, J. (2008). 'Mother–child shared reading with print and digital texts', *Journal of Early Childhood Literacy*, 8(2): 213–45.

Knight, L. (2008). 'Communication and transformation through collaboration: Rethinking drawing activities in early childhood', *Contemporary Issues in Early Childhood*, 9(4): 306–16.

Korat, O. and Or, T. (2010). 'How technology influences parent-child interaction: The case of e-book reading', *First Language*, 30(2): 139–54.

Landry, S. H. and Smith, K. E. (2006). 'The influence of parenting on emerging literacy skills', in D. K. Dickinson and S. B. Neuman (eds), *Handbook of Early Literacy Research*. New York: Guilford Press. pp. 135–48.

Laurent, A. and Martinot, C. (2009). 'Bilingualism and phonological segmentation of speech: The case of English-French pre-schoolers', *Journal of Early Childhood Literacy*, 9(1): 29–49.

Levy, R. (2008). '"Third spaces" are interesting places: Applying "third space theory" to nursery-aged children's constructions of themselves as readers', *Journal of Early Childhood Literacy*, 8(1): 43–66.

Li, G. (2010). 'Race, class, and schooling: Multicultural families doing the hard work of home literacy in America's inner city', *Reading and Writing Quarterly*, 26: 140–65.

Lim, C. (2010). 'Understanding Singaporean preschool teachers' beliefs about literacy development: Four different perspectives', *Teaching and Teacher Education*, 26: 215–24.

Lim, C. and Torr, J. (2008). 'Teaching literacy in English language in Singaporean preschools: Exploring teachers' beliefs about what works best', *Contemporary Issues in Early Childhood*, 9(2): 95–106.

Lopez, L. M. (2005). *A Look into the Homes of Spanish-speaking Preschool Children*. Somerville, MA: Cascadilla Press.

Lovelace, S. and Stewart, S. R. (2007). 'Increasing print awareness in preschoolers with language impairment using non-evocative print referencing', *Language, Speech, and Hearing Services in Schools*, 38: 16–30.

Lynch, J. (2008). 'Engagement with print: Low-income families and Head Start children', *Journal of Early Childhood Literacy*, 8(2): 151–75.

Lysaker, J. T. (2006). 'Young children's readings of wordless picture books: What's 'self' got to do with it?', *Journal of Early Childhood Literacy*, 6(1): 33–55.

Lysaker, J. T., Wheat, J., and Benson, E. (2010). 'Children's spontaneous play in Writer's Workshop', *Journal of Early Childhood Literacy*, 10(2): 209–29.

Marsh, J. (2000). 'Teletubby tales: Popular culture in the early years language and literacy curriculum', *Contemporary Issues in Early Childhood*, 1(2): 119–33.

Martello, J. (2004). 'Precompetence and trying to learn: Beginning writers talk about spelling', *Journal of Early Childhood Literacy*, 4(3): 271–89.

Martinez-Roldan, C. M. and Malave, G. (2004). 'Language ideologies mediating literacy and identity in bilingual contexts', *Journal of Early Childhood Literacy*, 4(2): 155–80.

Mavers, D. (2007). 'Semiotic resourcefulness: A young child's email exchange as design', *Journal of Early Childhood Literacy*, 7(2): 155–76.

Mielonen, A. M. and Paterson, W. (2009). 'Developing literacy through play', *Journal of Inquiry and Action in Education*, 3(1): 15–46.

Moody, A. K., Justice, L. M., and Cabell, S. Q. (2010). 'Electronic versus traditional storybooks: Relative influence on preschool children's engagement and communication', *Journal of Early Childhood Literacy*, 10(3): 294–313.

Moon, K. and Reifel, S. (2008). 'Play and literacy learning in a diverse language pre-kindergarten classroom', *Contemporary Issues in Early Childhood*, 9(1): 49–65.

Morgan, A. (2005). 'Shared reading interactions between mothers and pre-school children: Case studies of three dyads from a disadvantaged community', *Journal of Early Childhood Literacy*, 5(3): 279–304.

National Early Literacy Panel (2008). *Developing Early Literacy: Report of the National Early Literacy Panel*. Washington, DC: National Institute for Literacy.

Neuman, S. B. and Cunningham, L. (2009). 'The impact of professional development and coaching on early language and literacy instructional practices', *American Educational Research Journal*, 46(2): 532–66.

Neuman, S. B., Koh, S., and Dwyer, J. (2008). 'CHELLO: The Child/Home Environmental Language and Literacy Observation', *Early Childhood Research Quarterly*, 23, 159–72.

Nichols, S. (2000). 'Unsettling the bedtime story: Parents' reports of home literacy practices', *Contemporary Issues in Early Childhood*, 1(3): 315–28.

Nichols, S. (2002). 'Parents' construction of their children as gendered, literate subjects: A critical discourse analysis', *Journal of Early Childhood Literacy*, 2(2): 123–44.

Nichols, S., Nixon, H., and Roswell, J. (2009). 'The "good" parent in relation to early childhood literacy: Symbolic terrain and lived practice', *Literacy*, 43(2): 65–74.

Nicolson, T. and Ng, G. L. (2006). 'The case for teaching phonemic awareness and simple phonics to preschoolers', in R. M. Joshi and P. G. Aaron (eds), *Handbook of Orthography and Literacy*. Mahwah, NJ: Lawrence Erlbaum. pp. 637–48.

Nutbrown, C. and Hannon, P. (2003). 'Children's perspectives on family literacy: Methodological issues, findings and implications for practice', *Journal of Early Childhood Literacy*, 3(2): 115–45.

Oliver, B. R., Dale, P. S., and Plomin, R. (2005). 'Predicting literacy at age 7 from preliteracy at age 4', *Psychological Science*, 16(11): 861–5.

Pagani, L. S., Jalbert, J., Lapointe, P., and Hébert, M. (2006). 'Effects of junior kindergarten on emerging literacy in children from low-income and linguistic-minority families', *Early Childhood Education Journal*, 33(4): 209–15.

Pahl, K. (2002). 'Ephemera, mess and miscellaneous piles: Texts and practices in families', *Journal of Early Childhood Literacy*, 2(2): 145–66.

Pahl, K. (2009). 'Interactions, intersections, and improvisations: Studying the multimodal texts and classroom talk of six- to seven- year olds', *Journal of Early Childhood Literacy*, 9(2): 188–210.

Peterson, S. S. and Heywood, D. (2007). 'Contributions of families' linguistic, social, and cultural capital to minority-language children's literacy: Parents', teachers', and principals' perspectives', *The Canadian Modern Language Review*, 63(4): 517–38.

Pramling, N. and Carlsson, M. A. (2008). 'Rhyme and reason: Developing children's understanding of rhyme', *Contemporary Issues in Early Childhood*, 9(1): 14–26.

Quiroz, B. G., Snow, C. E., and Zhao, J. (2010). 'Vocabulary skills of Spanish-English bilinguals: Impact of mother-child language interactions and home language and literacy support', *International Journal of Bilingualism*, 14(4): 379–99.

Raban, B., and Nolan, A. (2005). 'Reading practices experienced by preschool children in disadvantaged areas', *Journal of Early Childhood Research*, 3(3): 289–98.

Ranker, J. (2009). 'Redesigning and transforming: A case study of the role of semiotic import in early composing processes', *Journal of Early Childhood Literacy*, 9(3): 319–47.

Reese, L. and Goldenberg, C. (2007). 'Community contexts for literacy development of Latina/o children: Contrasting case studies', *Anthropology and Education Quarterly*, 37(1): 42–61.

Reyes, I. (2006). 'Exploring connections between emergent biliteracy and bilingualism', *Journal of Early Childhood Literacy*, 6(3): 267–92.

Rivalland, J. (2004). 'Oral language development and access to school discourses', *Australian Journal of Language and Literacy*, 27(2): 142–58.

Roache-Jameson, S. (2005). 'Kindergarten connections: A study of intertextuality and its links with literacy in the kindergarten classroom', *Australian Journal of Language and Literacy*, 28(1): 48–66.

Roberts, T. A. (2008). 'Home storybook reading in primary or second language with preschool children: Evidence of equal effectiveness for second-language', *Reading Research Quarterly*, 43(2): 103–130.

Roberts, S., & Djonov, E. (2008). '"The mouse is not a toy": Young children's interactions with e-games', *Australian Journal of Language and Literacy*, 31(3): 242–259.

Rodriguez, B. L., Hines, R., and Montiel, M. (2009). 'Mexican American mothers of low and middle socioeconomic status: Communication behaviors and interactive strategies during shared book reading', *Language, Speech, and Hearing Services in Schools*, 40: 271–82.

Rowe, D. W. and Neitzel, C. (2010). 'Interest and agency in 2- and 3-year-olds' participation in emergent writing', *Reading Research Quarterly*, 45(2): 169–95.

Silvers, P., Shorey, M., and Crafton, L. (2010). 'Critical literacy in a primary multiliteracies classroom: The Hurricane Group', *Journal of Early Childhood Literacy*, 10(4): 379–409.

Smagorinsky, P. (2008). 'The method section as conceptual epicenter in constructing social science research reports', *Written Communication*, 25(3): 389–411.

Soundy, C. S. and Drucker, M. F. (2010). 'Picture partners: A co-creative journey into visual literacy', *Early Childhood Education Journal*, 37: 447–60.

Spencer, T. G. (2009). 'Complicating what it means to "struggle": One young child's experience with a mandated literacy initiative', *Contemporary Issues in Early Childhood*, 10(3): 218–31.

Stadler, M. A. and Ward, G. C. (2005). 'Supporting the narrative development of young children', *Early Childhood Education Journal*, 33(2): 73–80.

Street, B. (1995). *Social Literacies: Critical Approaches to Literacy in Development, Ethnography, and Education*. New York: Longman.

Torr, J. (2004). 'Talking about picture books: The influence of maternal education on four-year-old children's talk with mothers and pre-school teachers', *Journal of Early Childhood Literacy*, 4(2): 181–210.

Torr, J. and Scott, C. (2006). 'Learning "special words": Technical vocabulary in the talk of adults and preschoolers during shared reading', *Journal of Early Childhood Research*, 4(2): 153–67.

Van Der Heyden, A. M., Snyder, P. A., Broussard, C., and Ramsdell, K. (2007). 'Measuring response to early literacy intervention with preschoolers at risk. *Topics in Early Childhood Special Education*, 27(4): 232–49.

Vandermaas-Peeler, M., Nelson, J., Bumpass, C., and Sassine, B. (2009). 'Social contexts of development: Parent-child interactions during reading and play', *Journal of Early Childhood Literacy*, 9(3): 295–317.

Wilkinson, K. (2003). 'Children's favourite books', *Journal of Early Childhood Literacy*, 3(3): 275–301.

Wohlwend, K. E. (2008a). 'Kindergarten as nexus of practice: A mediated discourse analysis of reading, writing, play, and design in an early literacy apprenticeship', *Reading Research Quarterly*, 43(4): 332–34.

Wohlwend, K. E. (2008b). 'From "What did I write?" to "Is this right?": Intention, convention, and accountability in early literacy', *The New Educator*, 4: 43–63.

Wohlwend, K. E. (2009). 'Early adopters: Playing new literacies and pretending new technologies in print-centric classrooms', *Journal of Early Childhood Literacy*, 9(2): 117–40.

Wong Fillmore, L. (1991). 'When learning a second language means losing the first', *Early Childhood Research Quarterly*, 6: 323–46.

Woude, J. V. and Barton, E. (2003). 'Interactional sequences in shared book-reading between parents and children with histories of language delay', *Journal of Early Childhood Literacy*, 3(3): 249–73.

Yamada-Rice, D. (2010). 'Beyond words: An enquiry into children's home visual communication practices', *Journal of Early Childhood Literacy*, 10(3): 341–63.

Zvoch, K., Letourneau, L. E., and Parker, R. P. (2007). 'A multilevel multisite outcomes-by-implementation evaluation of an early childhood literacy model', *American Journal of Evaluation*, 28(2): 132–50.

Index

abbreviations 581
ABCDery method 468
Aboriginal communities 212, 286, 510
accent *see* pronunciation
access to books 97, 99, 137, 226, 282, 545, 548–9, 595–7
accountability 44, 83–4, 288, 347, 410, 413, 419
action possibilities 297
action-research projects 218, 374, 578, 595
Adams, M.J. 470
Adlof, S.M. 566
adolescents 10–11, 13, 44, 218
adult education 5, 123, 134, 195
adult literacy 26, 137, 196–9, 201–2, 204, 589
Adult Literacy Act 347
Adult Literacy and Basic Skills Unit (ALBSU) 196–7
Adult/Child Interactive Reading Inventory 643
advertising 82, 213, 289–90
advocacy 183–4, 612
African-American Vernacular English (AAVE) 607–8, 637
afterschool programmes 19, 123
agency 53, 176, 182–4, 186, 191, 215, 281, 391, 432, 491, 537, 555, 580, 590, 625
Ahlgrim-Delzell, L. 123
Aistear 542, 553–4
Alasuutari, M. 568
Albers, P. 302
Alexander, R. 298
Algeria 242, 244, 246
Allen, L. 620
Allen, S.E.M. 30–1
Allington, R. 390, 552
alliteration 119, 341
alphabet 23, 29–30, 65, 83–4, 119, 122, 153, 170, 255, 259, 323, 355, 369, 371, 381, 383–5, 387, 389, 392, 395, 427, 430, 456, 469, 505, 583
alphabetic systems 379, 428–9, 434, 449–50, 464–7
Amadeo, C. 391
Amanti, C. 11
Amazon.com 235–6
American Girls 87–8
American Indians 251–60
Americanization 18–19
Amish communities 612

An, R. 366
analogy 320, 384–5, 452, 458, 460–3, 515, 613
Anderson, A.B. 167
Anderson, D.R. 232
Anderson, E. 551
Anderson, J. 66–7, 375
Andrews, R. 391
Anning, A. 322
anthropology 8, 58, 97, 99, 106–7, 138, 251, 375, 503, 507–8
Apel, K. 472–3
Apes, W. 253
Appadurai, A. 208
Appiah, K. 486, 488
applied linguistics 58
apprenticeship 8, 63, 84, 297, 419, 532
apps 224
Aram, D. 430
Arbuthnot, M.H. 412
Argentina 242, 244, 246, 345
Arizpe, E. 398, 400
Aro, M. 385–6, 466
art 12, 300, 436
   see also drawing
Arthur, L. 641–2
artifactual literacies 263–76, 298, 409–10, 545, 639
Ashcroft, B. 24
Ashton, J. 624
assessment 116–19, 122–4, 165, 218, 405, 410, 413, 449, 464, 487, 525, 528, 531–2, 553, 561–2, 617, 645
   involving determinative judgment 564–8
   involving reflective judgment 568–71
   spelling assessment 469–70, 473–4
   values, judgment and design in 562–4
   see also testing
asset models 226–9
at-risk children 118–19, 139, 203, 354, 358, 461–2, 475, 487–8, 618
attention deficit disorder 143, 591
Au, K. 516, 530–1, 592
audio books 122, 125, 402, 578
Auerbach, E. 179, 182, 184, 188, 198
augmentative and alternative communication (AAC) devices 121, 126

Auld, G. 578–9
authoring *see* children's writing
authority 68, 71, 82, 118, 176, 191, 289, 341, 361, 418, 420, 592
    in family literacy scholarship 185–9
author's chair 64, 66
author's theater 64, 215, 494
authorship 10, 215, 375, 496, 509–10, 551
    see also children's writing
autism 119, 123
autonomous models 610–12, 645
avatars 90, 270, 417–18
    see also virtual worlds
Ayres, K. 121
Azerbaijan 242, 244, 246
Azuara, P. 105, 107, 283

Baby Einstein 230, 235
Baghban, M. 7, 324
Bahktin, M. 47
Bahrain 242, 244, 246
Baker, C. 370
Baker, L. 179, 182, 184
Bakhtin, M. 36, 87, 486, 490, 590, 605
Ballenger, C. 508
Bandura, A. 552
Barbie 46, 211, 263, 273
Barbie Girls 89, 146, 270, 417–18
Barnabus, E. 194
Barr, M. 331
Barth, R. 346
Barton, D. 279, 429
basalization 414–15
Basic Skills Agency 195, 197, 199
Basso, K.H. 255
Batman 490
Bauman, D.C. 645
Bear, D.R. 471, 473
Bearne, E. 41, 299–300
Beaulieu, D.L. 254
Beck, N. 577
bedtime stories 66, 143
    see also reading to children
Beecher, B. 641–2
behaviorism 5, 57, 70, 412, 468, 533
Behdad, A. 22
Bekman, S. 195
Belarus 242, 244, 246
Belgium 242, 244, 246
Bell, M. 188
Bell, V. 121
Bennett, J. 564
Bennett, K. 281
Bennett, W.J. 347
Benson, E. 438
Bernstein, B. 512
Bhatt, A. 365
Bhojwani, P. 41

Bible 29–30, 144, 167–8, 256, 259, 412
Bickham, D.S. 234, 238
Biddle, B. 617
Biklen, D. 126–7
bilingualism 12–13, 19, 26, 103–9, 122, 144, 148–9, 364, 366–70, 372, 374–6, 397, 579–80, 591, 620, 625, 637
    and children's writing 431, 434–5
    and community classes 161–3
    and family literacy 198, 204
    and popular culture 210–12
    and spelling 474
biliteracy 54, 69, 103–9, 364–5, 625
    and children's writing 434–5
    and community classes 162–3
    early encounters with 365–8
    processes involved in 368–73
    the task for educators 373–6
Bindman, M. 459–60
Birney, B.G. 402
birthday cards *see* greetings cards
Bissex, G. 7, 60, 331
Bjorkvall, A. 305, 440
Black, R.W. 89
Blackledge, A. 198
Block, C.C. 527, 534
blogging 81, 153
Bloodgood, J. 426, 454
Bloome, D. 616
Bloomsbury Publishing 19
Blue's Clues 230
Blumenfeld, P.C. 543–4
Blyton, E. 43
Bob the Builder 419
Boder, E. 464
Bodrova, E. 545–7
Boisvert, P. 121–2
Bolivia 171, 242, 244, 246
Bond, G. 619–20
book nooks 283, 545
book ownership *see* access to books
Borko, H. 628
Bosse, M. 463
Both-de Vries, A.C. 454
Boudreau, D. 637
Bourdieu, P. 217, 267, 304
Bourke, R. 595
Bovill, M. 233, 236
Bowman, J. 397
Bracaliello, C. 194
Bracken, B.A. 568
Bracken Basic Concept Scale 567–8
Bradley, L. 468
Braille 542
brain functioning 348–50
Brandt, D. 265, 275
Bratz 46, 264–5
Brayboy, B. 253

Brightman, A. 398
British Cohort Study 197
Brizius, J.A. 203–4
Brockmeier, J. 20
Brofenbrenner, U. 281
Brooks, G. 194–5, 198–9
Broussard, C. 638
Browder, D. 122–3
Brown, C.P. 567
Brown, G.D.A. 385
Brown, K.J. 473
Browne, A. 400, 592
Brubaker, R. 20
Bruchac, J. 259
Bruns, D. 123
Bryant, P. 459–60, 468
Buckingham, D. 229
Bulgaria 242, 244, 246
Bullen, E. 229–30
Bullock, R. 60
Bumpass, C. 643
Burgess, S.R. 180, 188–9
Burke, C. 12, 301, 453
Burke, C.L. 568
Burman, E. 23
Burnett, C. 13, 54, 151–2, 217, 219
Bus, A.G. 179, 186, 189, 402, 436, 454, 607
Bush, G.W. 346, 352, 360–1
Bynner, J. 197
Byrd, J. 253

Cain, C. 176
Cairney, T. 179, 183, 198, 624
calendars 267, 367, 374
Calhoon, J.A. 610
Calkins, L. 39, 505, 545
callouts 419–20
Cameroon 242, 244, 246
Camilli, G. 390
Campbell, E.J. 577
Caper, C. 178
capitalism 20, 25, 420, 514, 587
Caravolas, M. 463
Cardoso-Martins, C. 464–5
Carey, J. 596
Carlo, M. 513
Carpentieri, J. 194, 199
Carrington, V. 87, 289, 300
cartoons 66–7, 211–12, 235, 238, 319, 419
Casselman-Bell, M. 459
Catts, H.W. 566
causality 55, 177, 179, 185, 188–9, 349, 358, 396, 503
Cazden, C. 504, 506
CD-Roms 66–7, 152–3, 402, 581
Celano, D. 284
cell phones 36, 65–6, 89, 211, 214, 223–5, 227, 230,
        233, 235, 242–3, 301, 439, 575, 580, 582
    see also smartphones; text messaging

Center for the Improvement of Early Reading
        Achievement (CIERA) 529, 531, 535–6
Chall, J. 346
Chan, K. 285
Chan, L. 318
Chandler-Olcott, K. 127
chapter books 399, 403
checklists 567–8, 571
Cheeseman, S. 569–70
Cherland, M.R. 20, 23
Child Development Supplement (CDS) 99, 108–9
child selves 485–8
    and copying 496–8
    in official writing curricula 488–90
    in unofficial curricula 491–6
child-attribute improvement methodological grammar
        606–8
childhood studies 22–4, 147, 410–11, 487, 575
child-rearing practices 27–8, 30–1, 628
    see also parenting skills
children's writing 12, 40, 63, 148, 215, 288–9, 322,
        423–4, 455, 533, 541–2, 547–8, 550–2, 555,
        590, 625, 639, 645
    and child selves 485–98
    cognitive and sociocognitive perspectives on 424–9
    and culture 426, 430, 432–4, 437, 441
    and gender 39–42, 433
    and meaning making 436, 440
    and multimodality 435–41
    social semiotic perspectives on 432, 435–41
    sociocultural perspectives on 429–36
Chiong, C. 231
Choice Time 596
Chomsky, C. 60
Chomsky, N. 5, 57–8
Christie, J. 305, 513
chronotopes 605–9, 615, 617, 622–3, 625–6, 629
chunking 458, 461–3
civil rights 251, 254, 404
Clark, K. 486
class 9, 21, 31, 36–7, 67–8, 71, 88, 98, 111, 136, 139,
        142–6, 150, 192, 207, 213, 215, 217, 251, 396,
        492, 504, 510–11, 515–16, 531, 609, 625–6,
        628, 643
    and children's writing 430–1, 433
    and space and place 279, 283, 287
    and textbooks 410, 412, 414, 416
Clay, M. 6, 299, 331, 453–4, 568, 584
Clements, D. 577
Clinton, H. 360–1
Clinton, K. 265, 275
Club Penguin 89–90, 146, 270, 273, 417–18, 581
Code, L. 562
codeswitching 434, 608
cognitive capacity 21, 36, 53, 61, 64, 98, 102, 181,
        229, 289, 313–14, 375, 380, 388, 391, 412, 511,
        543–4, 548, 555, 610, 612, 616, 645
    and children's writing 432, 435, 441

cognitive psychology 5–6, 58
Cohen, R. 643
Cole, M. 63, 71, 104
collegiality 492–4
Collier, V. 375
colonialism 22–8, 30, 253, 258, 412
Comber, B. 99, 218, 266, 272–3, 593, 596
Comenius, J. 411
Committee on the Prevention of Reading Disabilities in
    Young Children 186–7
Common Core State Standards Initiative 53, 346, 361,
    415
Common Sense Media 224
communication technology see information and
    communication technology (ICT)
communities 9–10, 53–7, 59, 86–7, 97, 134, 139,
    141–2, 161–3, 210, 219, 258, 260, 317, 386,
    403, 485, 503, 506, 531, 533, 564, 579, 612,
    615, 617, 624–6, 642, 645
    and artifactual literacies 267, 269, 273–4
    and biliteracy 369, 374–6
    and children's writing 430, 434–5
    and critical literacy 591, 597
    and language socialization 68–70
    and space and place 284–6
    and textbooks 412, 415, 419
community classes 137, 161–72, 365, 367–9, 371, 517
competing victims syndrome 44–5
complementary schools see community classes
comprehension 52–3, 371, 390, 456, 513, 526, 530,
    533, 543, 547, 549, 552–3, 555, 565, 577, 618,
    621, 636
Comprehensive Adult Student Assessment System
    (CASAS) 201
Compton-Lilly, C. 69
computer games see video games
computers see digital technologies
Confucian educational traditions 409
Connerton, B. 570
Connor, C.M. 637–8
constructivism 177, 181, 183, 185, 187, 192, 544
    and policy-making 345, 351, 354
consumerism 284, 490
Cook, D. 88
Cook, S.J. 154
Cook-Gumperz, J. 68
Cooper, F. 20
Cope, B. 229
Copenhaver-Johnson, J. 397
coping strategies 107
copying 88, 320, 365, 461, 468, 470, 488–91, 494,
    496–8, 616
Correa, M. 464–5
Corsaro, W.A. 85
Costa Rica 242, 244, 246
Coulmas, F. 449–51
Council for Exceptional Children 124
Courage, M.L. 231–2
Courtade, G. 123

Cowan, K. 302
Crafton, L. 639
crafts 165, 272
Crago, H. 7
Crago, M. 7, 30–1
Craig, H.K. 607–8, 638
Craig, S.A. 456
Crandall, J. 620
Crawford, E. 568
creationism 351
creativity 67, 71, 216, 371, 391, 397, 530, 550–1, 555,
    580, 584
creolization 25, 30
crime 22, 100, 102, 110
critical discourse analysis 92, 138, 179–81, 502, 507,
    510, 588, 638
critical literacy 21, 272–4, 345, 587–8
    children's questions as curriculum 593–5
    critical indigenous literacies 251–60
    critical reading in early childhood classrooms 591–3
    and culture 588–9, 591, 593
    and curricula 591, 593–7
    and gender 45–7, 591, 593–5
    history of 588–90
    power, language and representation 590–1
    sustaining a critical literacy agenda in an age of
        accountability 595–7
critical race theory (CRT) 253
cross-cultural studies 47, 54, 56, 68–9, 91, 172, 315,
    488, 490, 492–3, 498
    see also multiculturalism
Cruickshank, K. 367
cultural psychology 8, 55–6, 136–7
culture 9, 18, 20, 28–9, 31, 42, 47, 53–5, 59–61, 68–9,
    92, 123, 139, 161, 170, 172, 192, 198, 207–8,
    212, 217, 258, 264, 315, 379, 489–93, 504,
    507–8, 514, 516, 531, 541, 547, 564, 578–9,
    584, 608, 612–14, 617–18, 622, 624, 626–7, 645
    and artifactual literacies 266, 269
    and biliteracy 364–6, 368, 370, 372, 374–5
    and children's writing 426, 430, 432–4, 437, 441
    and critical literacy 588–9, 591, 593
    and meaning making 330, 332, 336–7, 339, 397–8
    and multimodality 298–9, 306
    and play 80–92
    and space and place 279–80, 283
    and textbooks 410–12, 414, 416, 418–20
    see also cross-cultural studies; popular culture;
        sociocultural theory
Cummins, J. 370, 374–5, 415
Cunningham, J. 610
Cunningham, L. 641
curricula 21, 35, 41, 44, 46, 53, 83–5, 118, 122–3, 125,
    134–5, 152–5, 161, 165, 207, 213, 216–19, 375,
    386–7, 389–91, 404, 506, 508, 510, 517, 526,
    532–3, 536, 553, 565, 576, 588, 590
    and children's writing 439–40
    and critical literacy 591, 593–7
    and ethical issues 486–91, 496

and multimodality 299–301
and space and place 290–1
and textbooks 412–13
cyberspace *see* internet; virtual worlds

Dahl, K. 620
daily routines 120–1, 267
Dalton, L. 384–5
dancing 12, 146, 154, 166, 297, 300
Darling, S. 196
data collection methods 141, 182, 428, 463, 511, 525, 619, 625, 644, 646
Datta, M. 364, 368–70, 374
Davidson, C. 147, 150, 152, 580
Davies, B. 43
Davies, J. 320
Davis, B. 516
de Acosta, M. 144–5, 153
de Certeau, M. 89
de la Piedra, M. 366
Deacon, S.H. 459–60
Deacon, T.W. 323
deaf–blindness 120
Deavers, R.P. 385
DeBaryshe, B.D. 179, 182, 190
Declaration of the Rights of Indigenous Peoples 258
decoding 5, 40, 52, 237, 285, 296, 299, 305, 371–2, 388, 549, 591
and policy-making 352–3, 355, 358–9
deficit approach 195–6, 225–7, 230, 508
Dehyle, D. 254
Dejong, J. 626
Delgado-Gaitan, C. 179, 183–4, 189–90, 198
Deloache, J. 318
Demmert, W. 258
Denmark 242, 244, 246
Department for Children, Schools and Families (DCSF) 37, 46
Department for Education and Science (DES) 164
developmental delays 115
see also disabilities
Developmental Spelling Analysis 473
Devonshire, V. 428
Dewayani, S. 491
dialect 168, 232, 338, 427, 465, 502, 608, 615, 624–5
dialogic reading 547, 638
diaries *see* journals (diaries)
diasporas 25, 171
Diaz, E. 63
Diaz, R.M. 105
Dick and Jane 412, 414, 612
Dickinson, D. 511–12, 514, 547
diction 19, 340
dictionaries 4, 223, 330, 367, 448
Digital Beginnings 211, 214, 218
digital divide 584
digital literacies 41–2, 145, 213, 219, 320, 366, 435, 577–83, 597
digital natives 54, 300

digital technologies 13, 40–1, 65, 70, 80–2, 138–9, 142, 147, 151–4, 200, 209–11, 217, 235, 320, 366, 390, 409–10, 508, 517, 542, 575–7, 614
and artifactual literacies 264, 268
and children's writing 435, 438–41
continuities and discontinuities between home and educational settings 582–3
and critical literacy 587
e-books 66–7, 89, 218, 401–2, 405, 474, 476, 640, 643
in the home 579–83
implications for future research 583–4
and multimodality 295, 298–302, 305–6
new texts and technologies in educational settings 577–9
and play 89–90 *see also* video games
and space and place 282–4, 289–90
and textbooks 416–19
digraphs 414
diphthongs 414
disabilities 115–16, 143, 348–51, 405, 429, 508, 637, 643
early childhood intervention 119–24
future research 127–8
ladder to literacy 126–7
perspectives of professional organizations 124–6
at-risk children 118–19, 139, 203, 354, 358, 461–2, 475, 487–8, 618
themes of 'literate disconnection' 116–18
disadvantaged children *see* poverty; socioeconomic factors
discourse *see* talk and discourse
Disney 208, 226, 230, 253, 269, 365–6, 494
Disney Princesses 46, 87, 89, 211, 318, 614
Dissanayake, E. 323
Diva Starz dolls 87
Division for Early Childhood (DEC) 116, 123–4
Donaldson, L.E. 23–4
Donoahue, Z. 505
Dora the Explorer 269, 274
Doraemon 211
Dorsey-Gaines, C. 182, 184, 186, 188, 190
Douglas, K. 121
Downes, T. 641–2
Downing, J. 6
Doyle, J. 46
Draft Directive on the Education of Migrant Children 164
Draheim, H.C. 643
dramatic play 62, 64–5, 70, 80, 82, 84, 146, 397, 435–6, 438, 494, 513, 546–7, 608
drawing 12, 40, 64–6, 133, 148, 315, 317–25, 425, 435–6, 453, 537, 547–8, 581, 636, 639–40, 645
and artifactual literacies 265
and critical literacy 594
and ethical issues 487
and meaning making 333–6
and multimodality 297, 301–2
and space and place 282, 287–8
see also mark-making
Dreher, M.J. 505
dual language learners 105, 366, 614

dual language texts 371, 375, 579
Duke, N.K. 398, 401
Duncan, A. 361–2
Dunkin, M. 617
Dunst, C.J. 319
Duranti, A. 28–30, 69, 170, 612
DVDs 66, 149, 152, 223–4, 230–1, 233, 236, 238
   see also movies
Dwyer, J. 641
Dykstra, R. 619–20
Dynamic Indicators of Basic Early Literacy Skills
   (DIBELS) 636
Dynavox 126
dyslexia 348–51
Dyson, A.H. 41–3, 45, 47, 64, 84–6, 215–16, 237, 241,
   270, 331, 432–3, 435, 439–40, 507–8, 537, 590,
   592, 608–9, 616

Eakle, J. 578
Early, M. 305
early childhood literacy
   before the age of three 313–26
   artifactual literacies 263–76
   and disability 115–28
   and family literacy see family literacy
   and gender see gender
   history and emergence of 3–14, 56–60
   and play see play
   policy-making in 96–110
   and popular culture see popular culture
   postcolonial perspectives on 18–32
   and sociocultural theory 52–72
Early Learning Centre (ELC) 288
Early Literacy Skills Assessment 123
Early Reading First see Reading First
Early Years Learning Framework 300
East End Community School 164–5
e-books 66–7, 89, 218, 401–2, 405, 474, 476, 640, 643
Economic and Social Research Council (ESRC) 301
Edelsky, C. 594
Edmiston, B.W. 87
Education Resources Information Center (ERIC) 20,
   634–5
Edwards, B. 515–16
Edwards, V. 375
effective literacy teaching 523–32, 535–7, 554–5
   teachers' perspectives 532–5
Effective Pre-School and Primary Education (EPPE)
   project 548
efficiency–equity tradeoff 99–101
Egypt 242, 244, 246, 345
Ehri, L.C. 452, 455, 465
Eisenhart, M. 628
Eisner, E. 268
electronic books see e-books
Eliot, J. 256
e-literacies see digital literacies
Elson, R.M. 419

Elster, C.A. 399, 403
email 148, 152, 272, 290, 305, 418, 425, 439, 575–6,
   578, 581, 641
emergent literacy 7–8, 56–60, 72, 120, 122, 127, 134,
   136, 145, 149, 152, 186, 229, 299, 306, 424–5,
   431, 435, 511, 543, 548, 565, 568, 588, 620, 637
emoticons 581
emotions 47, 64, 88, 98, 215, 226, 252, 264, 269,
   547, 555
   emotional engagement 88, 302, 543–4
empowerment 24, 64, 184–5, 376, 543, 552
   see also power relations
encoding 296, 299, 372, 565
enculturation 9, 92, 144, 622, 626, 628
End User Licensing Agreements (EULAs) 90
Engblom, C. 305, 440
English language learners 56, 64, 99, 101, 104–6, 360,
   405, 437, 513
enjoyment see reading for pleasure
Ennquez, G. 582
epistemological racism 177
Erion, J. 194
Erskine, J.M. 385–6, 466
Estonia 242, 244
Etch-a-Sketch 271
e-texts see e-books
ethical issues 25, 87, 369, 412–13, 419, 485–98, 562,
   564, 566–7
   see also values
ethnicity 36, 56, 69–70, 97, 99, 111, 137, 139, 148–50,
   219, 252, 431, 491–2, 525, 530
   see also culture; race
ethnography 8–10, 21, 30–1, 38, 56, 59–61, 66–7, 70,
   84, 88–91, 137–8, 141–4, 146, 148–50, 154–5,
   166–7, 279, 301, 388, 404, 507, 525, 639–40,
   642, 645
   and artifactual literacies 266–7
   and biliteracy 365, 375
   and critical literacy 590, 592
   and ethical issues 487, 491
ethnoscapes 208
European Commission 199
European Union 164
Evans, M.A. 180, 188
Even Start 27, 123, 184, 199, 201–2
Everts Danielson, K. 577
everyday routines see daily routines
executive control 162–3
Exemplary Model of Early Reading Growth and
   Excellence (EMERGE) 118–19
experimental studies 56, 386, 428–9, 475, 638, 642

Facebook 225, 228, 233
Facetime 223, 226–8, 233, 235
Faircloth, S.C. 254
Fairclough, N. 588
fairness 42, 98, 100, 280, 487, 498, 594, 596
fairy tales 110, 142, 397, 400, 440, 548, 595

faith *see* religion
Falchi, L. 105
families *see* family literacy; home literacy environment
family literacy 9, 26–8, 54, 97–8, 106, 119, 122–4, 134,
    136–7, 142, 144, 149, 155, 161, 170, 542, 549,
    579–80, 592, 608, 615, 617, 624, 642, 645
  and children's writing 430–1
  epistemological assumptions in scholarship 175–92
  research issues in 194–204
  and space and place 281–2
  and textbooks 414–16
Family Literacy Demonstration Programmes 199
feedback 123, 470, 513, 516, 529, 532–3, 551, 562
Feiler, A. 639
Fein, S. 324
feminist research 35–6, 43, 45, 47, 138
  and critical literacy 588, 591–3, 595
  see also gender
feminization of literacy 37–8
Ferguson, N. 529–30
Fernandez, R. 21
Ferriero, E. 7, 322, 454, 465
Fetherston, T. 577
Fields, M.K. 473
fighting *see* violence
films *see* movies
financescapes 208
First-Grade Studies 619
Fisher, R. 432
Fishman, A. 612
five components of reading 52–3
Flesch, R. 346
Fletcher, M. 391
Flewitt, R. 13, 319–20, 582
Flores, B. 63
Flowers, C. 123
Fluck, M. 428
fluency 52–3, 543, 553, 565
folktales 208, 258–9, 279, 369, 491
food labels 133, 182, 210, 291
Foorman, B. 356
formative assessment 532, 534
Foster, S.A. 203–4
Fox, R. 527–9
Francis, B. 37, 47
Frederick, T. 302
Fredericks, J.A. 543–4
Freebody, P. 252, 596
Freeman, R. 100
Freeman, Y. 414
freeze frames 623–5
Freire, P. 588, 595
French, L. 512
Freppon, P. 358–60
Fresch, M.J. 473
Freud, S. 300
Frith, U. 455
frustration 143, 462, 472

Fryberg, S.A. 253–4
functional magnetic resonance imagery (fMRI) 348–9
funding 45, 96, 201, 361, 374, 390, 414
Furnes, B. 467

Gadsden, V. 179, 184, 188, 191
Galaburda, A. 348
Gallego, M. 21–2
Gallimore, R. 69
Gambrell, L.B. 405, 549, 578–9
Gamse, B. 184
Gandhi, L. 24
gangs 285
Ganske, K. 473
Garcia, E. 372
Garcia, O. 105
Gee, J.P. 71, 502, 514
gender 18, 21, 27, 35–6, 64, 99, 139, 141, 150, 192,
    215–16, 274, 302, 396, 412, 504, 510, 614, 617
  'under achievement' of boys 43–5
  and children's writing 39–42, 433
  counteracting stereotypes 42–3
  and critical literacy 45–7, 591, 593–5
  and ethical issues 492, 494–5
  and family literacy 197–8, 204
  and literacy in the home 36–8
  and play 37–9, 41, 64, 91
  postmodern analysis and critical literacy 45–7
Generating Principle 454
generation Z 54, 65–8
genre 42, 44, 67, 87, 239, 315, 320, 323, 376, 395,
    398–9, 403, 425–6, 545, 548–9, 590
gesture 81, 166, 170, 209, 267–8, 288, 295–8, 316, 318,
    321, 325, 342, 401, 405, 435–8, 545, 640
Gettinger, M. 119
Ghahremani-Ghajar, S. 375
Gibbons, P. 373
Gibbs, S. 123
Gibson, J. 297
Gieryn, T. 280
Gillborn, D. 177
Ginn 410
Ginsburg-Block, M. 194
Glissant, E. 25, 30
global positioning systems (GPS) 298
globalization 22, 140, 208, 284, 413, 416, 420, 433, 474
Goble, P. 260
Golden Books 415
Goldenberg, C. 642
Goldman, R. 197
González, N. 11
Good Start, Grow Smart 97
Goodman, K. 6, 351–2, 362, 414
Goodman, N. 316
Goodman, Y. 319, 568, 608–9
Google 147, 211, 235–6, 635
Gorman, E. 319
Gort, M. 372, 434

Goswami, U. 384–5, 391, 452, 468
government 18, 30, 44, 96, 145, 164–5, 391–2, 413–14,
  416, 528, 571, 587, 596, 613
  see also policy-making
gradual release of responsibility model 551
graffiti 284–5
Graham, S. 464, 473
grain size theory 384–9, 391, 427, 464
grammar 121, 239, 255, 302, 322, 330, 372, 390, 411,
  414, 439, 487–8, 524, 528, 547, 566, 581
Grande, S. 253
grapheme-phoneme recoding skills 358, 372–3, 381,
  384–6, 453–5, 470–1, 526, 532
Graves, D. 39, 504–5, 550
Gray, W.S. 412
Greece 242, 244, 246, 456
greetings cards 365–6
Gregory, E. 37, 86, 180, 189, 191, 317, 369, 372–4,
  516, 580
Griffin, P. 63
Griffin, T. 513
Grimes, S.M. 90
Gruenewald, D. 273
Grugeon, E. 640
guessing 461–2
guided reading 526, 550, 552, 596
Guthrie, J. 388, 551
Gutierrez, K.D. 106, 110, 298, 372, 614

Haas, A.M. 255
Habbo 417
Hakuta, K. 105
Halewood, C. 578–9
Hall, K. 550, 552, 554
Halliday, M. 296, 532
Hamilton, M. 429
Hammer, C.S. 642–3
Hanauer, D.I. 399, 403
Hancock, A. 366
Handsfield, L. 320
handwriting 323–4, 340, 366, 450, 577
Hanlen, W. 286
Hanley, J.R. 387
Hanline, M.F. 120
Hannon, P. 179, 182–4, 188–91, 194, 197, 642
Hanson, K.F. 232
Harcourt-Brace 410
Hardman, J. 376
Harper, H. 20, 23
Harris, R. 379
Harste, J. 12, 301, 317, 453
Harste, J.C. 435
Hawthorne factor 620
Headstart 59, 97, 191, 638
health 21, 30, 409, 561, 575
hearing impairments 119, 429, 643
Heath, S. B. 9, 68–9, 141–2, 145, 167, 179, 297, 515, 615
Hebert, M. 638

Hebrew classes 163–4
Hecht, S. 188
Heckman, J. 98–103, 106
Heller, M.F. 401
Hemmeter, M.L. 122–3, 641
Henderson, E. 458–9
heritage language schools *see* community classes
Hernandez, A. 285
heteroglossia 47
Hicks, D. 143, 145, 154, 507–8
hidden curriculum 35, 418, 622
Hiebert, E. 110, 618–19
Hildreth, G. 426
Hill, S. 301, 440, 644
Hindman, A.H. 637, 643–4
Hines, R. 643
Hirst, K. 198, 366
history 165, 253, 258–9, 298, 507, 514, 517
Hodge, B. 225
Hoffman, J. 391
Høien, T. 618–19
Holland, D. 176
Hollingsworth, S. 21–2
Holquist, M. 486
home literacy environment 8–9, 12, 32, 53–4, 57, 59,
  65, 67, 70, 102, 104, 107, 136, 139, 143–4, 148,
  152, 155, 188–9, 191, 217, 219, 314, 503, 508,
  511, 515, 531, 542, 548–9, 582–3, 625, 637,
  639–43, 645
  and artifactual literacies 263–4, 270–2
  and biliteracy 365, 369, 374
  and children's writing 427, 430–1
  and critical literacy 590
  daily routines 120–1, 267
  and digital technologies 579–83
  and gender 36–8, 42–3
  and language socialization 68–70
  and meaning making 403
  and multimodality 301
  and play 86–7
  and popular culture 209–14
  and space and place 279, 281–4
  and textbooks 410, 412, 414–17
  see also family literacy; out-of-school literacy
    practices
Home Literacy Environment Questionnaire 636
Home School Knowledge Exchange Project 218
Home School Study of Language and Literacy 511–12
home tuition 364, 366
homework 133, 153, 271, 366, 582
Hoole, C. 380
Hopi Cultural Preservation Office 258
Hopperstad, M.H. 639
Hoque, M.N. 164–5
horse-race studies 618–20, 627
Howe, M.L. 231–2
Hsieh, W.Y. 122–3, 641
Huberty, C. 513

Huey, E.B. 4
Hufnagel, K. 473
Huggan, G. 24
Hughes, C. 194
Hughes, M. 9, 455–6
Hull, G. 104, 140–1, 150
Hulme, C. 463
Hulme, P. 22
Hurdley, R. 264
Hussein, A. 164–5
Huxford, L. 391
hybridity 20, 24–31, 47, 54, 65, 67, 70, 290, 426,
    434, 568
hypertext 255, 398, 402

I Can Read series 415
identity 28, 53, 68, 70, 91, 138, 151, 215, 253, 306,
    318, 375, 507–8, 517, 549, 583, 591, 612, 622
  and artifactual literacies 266–8, 274
  and children's writing 432, 434
  and textbooks 412, 417
ideological models 612–17, 645
ideoscapes 208
illiteracy 5, 21–2, 27, 70–1, 375, 606
imagery 253–4, 348, 374, 403
Imagine It! reading series 415
immigrant communities 28, 69–70, 99, 101, 107, 122,
    161, 170, 184–5, 189, 208, 283, 474, 594,
    642–3, 645
imperialism 18, 24, 28, 212, 253
improvisation 90, 146, 148, 176, 305, 490, 492, 582, 639
indigenous communities 20, 29, 56, 177, 212, 286, 578
  critical indigenous literacies 251–60
individualism 122–3, 171, 215, 255, 346, 488–9, 498,
    565, 582
information and communication technology (ICT) 13,
    54, 300, 305, 537
  see also digital technologies
Ingold, T. 273
inner speech 62
input–output studies 617–20, 622
Institute of Medicine 102
intellectual property 251, 569
intergenerational programmes 134, 136, 213
  see also family literacy
International Reading Association (IRA) 116, 124,
    362, 553
internet 40, 65–7, 82, 142–3, 147, 152–3, 211, 214,
    219, 223, 234, 281, 290, 300, 350, 366–7, 375,
    398, 415, 417–19, 439
  see also virtual worlds
internet generation *see* digital natives; generation Z
intertextuality 87, 149, 209, 211–12, 236, 396–7,
    399–401, 419, 439, 492, 506–8, 639
interventions 137, 143, 416, 475, 536, 609, 618–20,
    638, 640–1
  adult-focused 122–4
  child-focused 120–2

intonation 296, 381, 563
Inuit children 30–1
invented spellings 60, 429, 454, 456, 464, 469–72
Invernizzi, M. 456
iPads 125–6, 211, 224, 231
iPods 65–6, 125, 214, 224
IQ 102, 348
  see also cognitive capacity

Jackson, B. 638
Jacobs, G. 506
Jalbert, J. 638
Janks, H. 597
Jeffords, J. 360
Jenkins, H. 418, 496
Jessel, J. 580
Jimenez, R.T. 286
Johnson, A. 397
Johnson, A.A. 643
Johnson, G.M. 214
John-Steiner, V. 60
Johnston, B. 256
Johnston, F.R. 472
Johnston, R. 390
Jones, S. 596
Jordan 19, 242, 244, 246
journals (academic) 3, 54, 124, 141, 342, 415,
    424, 633–5
journals (diaries) 108–9, 123, 399, 431, 470, 473, 508,
    526, 578, 608, 641, 644
Juel, C. 535, 621
junk mail 210, 592
Jurassic Park 149
Justice, L. 621

Kaderavek, J.N. 643
Kalantzis, M. 229
Kamehameha Early Education Program (KEEP) 513, 531
Kamii, C. 454–5
Kamler, B. 287, 289
Kanaris, A. 40
Kanevsky, R. 507–8
Kant, I. 562
Karila, K. 568
Karmiloff-Smith, A. 317–18
Kellogg, R. 323–4
Kendrick, M. 64, 639
Kennedy, E. 360–1
Kenner, C. 12–13, 198, 211, 317, 325, 342, 365, 367–8,
    371, 374, 434, 580
Kenway, J. 229–30
Kessler, B. 463
keyboards 65, 298, 302
Kim, J. 66–7
Kim, J.E. 643
Kim, Y. 465
Kindle 402
  see also e-books

King-Jackson, V. 596
Kinloch, V. 274
Kirby, J.R. 459
Kleifgen, J.A. 105
Kliewer, C. 116–17, 122, 126–7, 508
Klinger, C. 105
Kluth, P. 127
Knapp, M.S. 529–30, 532, 549, 551
Knobel, M. 299
Knudsen, E. 102–3
Koh, S. 641
Kondyli, M. 456
Kontovourki, S. 85, 438–9, 582
Korat, O. 431, 643
Korkeamaki, R. 505
Kozol, J. 21
Kress, G. 12, 36–7, 41, 151, 298–303, 306, 321–2, 342, 425, 434–5, 437
Kuhlman, W.D. 577
Kuhn, M.R. 402
Kuwait 19, 243, 245, 247
Kyle, D. 280

la ronda 515
Labbo, L. 321, 402, 578
Lachicotte, W. 176
ladder to literacy 126–7
Lancaster, L. 12, 302, 316, 318–19, 321–3, 332, 342, 436
Landerl, K. 384
Landis, D. 122
Landry, S.H. 638
Landsberger, H.A. 620
Langer, J.A. 399, 405
Langone, J. 121
language acquisition device (LAD) 57
Language Experience instructional method 619
Languages Review 165
Lanigan, R.L. 268
Lankshear, C. 299
Lapointe, P. 638
large scale assessments based on rubrics (LSAR) 566–7
Larson, J. 273, 332, 402, 626
Lass, B. 7
Latour, B. 265, 275
Latvia 243, 245, 247
Laurent, A. 637
layout 82, 295–6, 299, 302–3, 437, 581
Le Grand, J. 100–1
league tables 44
Leander, K. 153
Learning Literacy Together 201–2
Lee, J. 566
Lee, L. 89, 208, 305, 465
Lefebvre, H. 279–80
Lemos, L. 464–5
Lensmire, T. 504
Leong, D.J. 545
Leos, K. 258
Leslie, L. 610, 620

Letourneau, L.E. 638
letter identification 356, 427, 487, 511, 548, 566–7, 636
Letter Name strategies 455–6, 458, 462
letter-sound correspondence 104, 136, 355, 384, 389, 395, 450, 457, 463, 466, 468, 471, 528
Leuven Involvement Scale for Young Children 218
Levin, I. 427, 431, 436
Levy, R. 214, 217, 305, 583, 639
Lewis, D. 240
Li, G. 212
libraries 148, 153, 282, 284, 369, 414–15, 545, 549, 620
lifelong learning *see* adult education; professional development
lifelong readers and writers 544–55
Lim, C. 644
Limbrick, L. 529–30, 534
Lionnet, F. 25, 28
literacy crisis 97–9, 110, 347
literacy events 55, 137, 143–4, 213–14, 226, 389, 412–13, 429–30, 438, 485, 501–2, 516, 580
little book curriculum 618
Livingstone, S. 228–9, 233, 236
logographic systems 317, 371, 434, 450
logos 291, 301, 315, 323
Lomawaima, K.T. 256
Long, R. 454
Long, S. 86
Lonigan, C. 188, 607
Lopez, L.M. 641
Lopez-Robertson, J. 398
Louden, W. 528–9
Lovelace, S. 638
Low, D. 255
low-earning households *see* poverty; socioeconomic factors
Luke, A. 192, 252, 412, 510, 593–4, 596–7, 612
Luria, A. 322
Lynch, J. 430, 637
Lysaker, J. 438

MacGillivray, L. 39
Mackay, M. 325
Macmillan 410
MacNaughton, G. 47
magazines 211, 367, 416
'magic e' 385
Mahiri, J. 418
Mahn, H. 60
Maier, M. 626
Makin, L. 212–13
Malave, G. 638, 640
Malaysia 243, 245, 247
Mallett, M. 401
Maloch, B. 403
Manning, G. 454
Manning, M. 454–5
Manyak, P. 613–14
Manz, P.H. 194
maps 65, 298

marginalization 46, 86, 91, 99, 118, 135, 137–8, 150, 181, 426, 431, 488, 498, 508, 579, 616
Marinelli, S. 121
mark-making 314–18, 320, 322–5, 425–6, 547
Marsh, J. 13, 40, 42, 45, 84, 88, 90, 145–7, 152–3, 211, 214, 216–17, 237, 241, 264, 270, 273, 283, 285, 301, 315, 320, 332, 440, 580–1, 584, 641
Martens, P.A. 454
Martin, S. 281
Martinez, A. 39
Martinez, M. 399
Martinez-Roldan, C. 397, 638, 640
Martin-Jones, M. 365
Martino, W. 45
Martinot, C. 637
Martlew, M. 325
Marvin, C. 179, 186, 189, 191
Masny, D. 375
Mason, J. 592
Massey, D. 274, 280
Masterov 100
Masterson, J.J. 473
mathematics 100, 164–6, 300
    see also number systems
Matinez-Roldan, C. 398
Matthew effect 549
Matthews, J. 322, 493
Mavers, D. 148, 150, 152, 305, 332, 342, 439, 581, 638, 641
May, L. 404
Mayer, M. 415
Maynard, T. 39
McCardle, P. 258
McCloskey, D. 110
McCollum, J. 122–3, 641
McDermott, G. 260
McDermott, R.P. 10–11, 616
McDonald's 88, 208, 230, 291, 594
McGee, L.M. 469
McGraw-Hill 361, 415
McIntyre, M. 280, 286–7
McKay, R. 639
McKenney, S. 578
McNeal, J. 285
McPake, J. 580
McTavish, M. 143, 152–3, 290, 582
McWilliam, N. 374
Meade, C. 121
meaning making 12, 37, 46, 64, 67, 72, 81, 142, 144, 147–9, 154, 216, 232–3, 238, 241, 316–17, 322, 329–43, 395–405, 503, 506, 517, 537, 543, 549, 552, 576, 578
    and artifactual literacies 263, 265–6, 268–72, 274–6
    and children's writing 436, 440
    and culture 330, 332, 336–7, 339, 397–8
    and digital technologies 581–3
    and methodological grammar 608–10
    and multimodality 295–6, 298, 301–6
    and policy-making 345
    and space and place 286
media 46, 54, 65–8, 81–2, 89, 140, 149, 151, 154, 218, 269, 350–2, 391, 410, 416–20, 587, 590, 594, 597
mediascapes 208, 215, 285
mediation 8, 42, 54–6, 61–7, 70, 72, 92, 137, 275, 295, 298, 417, 546
Medwell, J. 527–9
Meek, M. 240, 387
Meier, D.R. 431
Meisels, S.J. 405
Mele-McCarthy, J. 258
memorization 144, 166–7, 301, 366, 455, 457, 468
Menon, S. 618–19
Mercer, N. 298
Merchant, G. 581, 584
metacognition 505–6, 551
metalinguistic awareness 62, 65–6, 105, 162, 371, 434, 456, 546
metaphors 85, 110, 126, 240, 280–1, 374, 485, 490
methodological grammars 605–6, 629
    and the language/literacy used by children 610–17
    and locations of children 617–28
    and the nature of children 606–10
    see also research methodologies
Michael, I. 380
Michaels, S. 515
Mielonen, A.M. 641
Mihesuah, D.A. 252
Millard, E. 40, 47
Miller, D. 264
Miller, P. 626, 628
Minden-Cupp, C. 535, 621
Minns, H. 365, 369
Mirenda, P. 186, 189, 191
Misson, R. 47, 218
mobile phones see cell phones
model of skill formation 98–9, 101–3, 106, 110
Moje, E. 20, 32
Mol, S.E. 194
Moll, L. 11, 69, 179, 182–4, 187, 190, 267
Monet, C. 623
monolingualism 23, 198, 372, 374, 388, 429, 433–4
Montenegro 243, 245, 247
Montero, M.K. 578
Montiel, M. 643
Moore, G. 280
Morais, J. 469
moral panic 13, 345
    see also ethical issues
Morgan, A. 197
Morocco 167, 243, 245, 247
morphology 324, 326, 427–8, 458–60, 464, 468, 611
Morrell, E. 274
Morris, D. 455–6, 471–3, 475
Morrison, F.J. 637
Morrow, L.M. 405, 545
Mor-Sommerfeld, A. 371
Mosely, M. 280, 287
Moses, A. 148–50, 153

Moss, G. 44–5, 342, 391
Mother-Child Education Foundation 198
mother–child relationship 8, 23, 30–1, 37, 66–7, 71, 88, 199, 591, 624, 643, 645
Mother-Tongue to English Teaching Project (MOTET) 164
motivation 40, 42, 44, 102, 216, 218, 238, 297, 301, 305, 350, 375–6, 388, 396–7, 508, 527, 532, 543–4, 549, 551, 553, 555, 577, 641
movies 66–7, 87–8, 144, 146, 208, 210–11, 217–18, 233–4, 374, 419, 439–40, 614
    see also DVDs
MTV 420
Mulhearn, G. 301
multiculturalism 177, 404, 590, 593
    and critical literacy 588, 595
    see also cross-cultural studies
multilingualism 23, 37, 65, 70, 86, 139, 166, 364, 366–8, 370–1, 375, 388, 516, 579, 582, 596–7
    and artifactual literacies 271
    and children's writing 430, 433–5
    and family literacy 198
    and popular culture 211
multimodality 37, 39, 41–2, 136, 138, 145, 151, 166, 185, 210, 214–15, 295–306, 417, 425, 508, 537, 542–3, 555, 576, 582–4, 639, 642
    and artifactual literacies 264–8, 273
    and children's writing 435–41
    and critical literacy 589, 597
    definition of 296–7
    and meaning making 342, 400, 402
    and play 297, 435, 438
    and sociocultural theory 296–8
    and space and place 282, 299
Murphy, S. 414
music 12, 66, 149, 297, 300, 402, 405, 436
    see also singing
myths 258–9

name writing 119, 133, 426–8
Napoleao, R.F. 465
Nasaw, D. 347
Nash, A. 195
nation building 251, 254, 257–8
National Association for the Education of Young Children (NAEYC) 116, 124
National Center for Family Literacy 203
National Child Development Study 196
National Committee on Reading 57
National Council for Mother Tongue Teaching (NCMTT) 164
National Curriculum 41
National Early Literacy Panel (NELP) 52–3, 109–10, 645
National Institute for Literacy 109
National Institute of Child and Human Development (NICHD) 352
National Literacy and Numeracy Strategy 553
National Literacy Strategy 41–2, 44, 390–1, 415, 553
National Literacy Trust 226

National Reading Panel (NRP) 52–3, 352–61, 389–90, 469, 543, 553
National Research Council 102
National Scientific Council 102
Native Americans *see* American Indians
neighborhoods *see* communities
Neitzel, C. 432
Nelson, J. 643
Nemoianu, A. 626
Neopets 417
Neruda, P. 485, 487, 498
Ness, M.K. 472
Neuman, S. 284, 402, 544–5, 554, 620–1, 641
neuropsychology 348
new literacy studies (NLS) 71, 140, 151, 217, 266, 320, 389, 391–2
New London Group (NLG) 388–9
New York Times 350–1, 561
New Yorker, The 225
New Zealand 135, 171, 243, 245, 247, 300, 376, 392, 412, 414, 524–6, 529, 531, 534, 596
newspapers 18–19, 84, 146, 367, 374, 561
Newsweek 351
Ng, G.L. 638
Nichols, S. 38, 99, 213, 288, 643
Nickse, R.S. 196
Nicktropolis 146
Nicolson, T. 638
Nimmo, D. 643
Nixon, H. 213, 274, 596, 625
No Child Left Behind (NCLB) 106, 346, 360–1, 390, 413, 553, 596
Nodelman, P. 332
nominalization 622
non-sequential approaches 105–6
nooks *see* book nooks
normativity 67, 69, 126, 138, 181, 216, 276, 562–3, 565–6, 568, 591, 645
number systems 61, 65, 170, 315, 317, 319, 548
    see also mathematics
Nunes, T. 318, 459–60
nursery rhymes 320
Nutbrown, C. 203, 642
Nye, C. 194

Obama, B. 346, 361–2
objectivism 177–8, 181, 185, 187, 190, 192
O'Brien, D. 20, 32
O'Brien, J. 591–5
Ochs, E. 28–30, 69, 502, 506, 612
O'deKirk, M. 123
Office for Standards in Education, Children's Services and Skills *see* OFSTED
OFSTED 43, 416
Okun, A. 99
Olsen, D.R. 20
Ong, W. 409, 419
ongoing professional development *see* professional development

onsets 382–4, 387, 452, 464, 468
opacity 25, 28
open education 346–7
Or, T. 643
Orellana, M.J. 36, 39, 47, 212, 285
Organisation for Economic Co-operation and Development (OECD) 543, 564
origins of writing 379
O'Rourke, M. 305
Orsolini, M. 453
orthographic consistency *see* spelling
Orwell, G. 20
Osberg, L. 99
Ostrosky, M. 122–3
Ouellette, G. 429, 470
Our Languages project 165
out-of-school literacy practices 133–55, 217, 263–4, 291, 374, 410, 426
   out-of-school schooling *see* community classes
overlapping waves model 460–1
Owocki, G. 568
Oyserman, D. 254

Pacton, S. 460
Pagani, L.S. 638
Pahl, K. 41, 46, 67, 145–8, 150, 180, 185, 189, 219, 264, 291, 304–5, 319–20, 322, 332, 342, 581, 639
Pakulski, L.A. 643
Paley, V. 84–5
Palinscar, A.S. 398
Pallotta-Charolli, M. 45
Panaleo, S. 400
Panel Study of Income Dynamics (PSID) 99, 108–9
Papandropoulou, I. 453
Pappas, C.C. 425
Paradise Lost 412
para-linguism 296
parallel talk 121
Paratore, J. 179, 186
Parent Empowerment through Family Literacy 199
parenting skills 26–8, 31, 58, 118, 183, 189–90, 195–6, 199, 258, 274, 281–2, 376, 419, 434, 533, 553, 575, 608, 620, 643, 645
Paris, A.H. 543–4
Pariser, D. 325
Parker, F.W. 346
Parker, R.P. 638
Parr, J. 529–30, 534
Parry, B. 217
Parsons, S. 197
Pash, D. 508
passive learning 10, 37, 39, 41, 43, 45, 63–4, 67, 144, 181–2, 184, 229, 238, 306, 317, 402, 509, 580, 583
Paterson, W. 641
Patrick, G. 4
Patterson, A. 593
Paugh, P. 596
Payton, S. 7

Peabody Individual Achievement Test 197
Peabody Picture Vocabulary Test (PPVT) 512, 636
Pearson, D. 110
pedagogic texts 419–20
peer assistance 44, 54, 126, 368–9
peer culture 85–6, 91, 216, 289, 433, 439, 491, 493, 497–8, 508, 551, 582, 639
Pelletier, J. 578–9
Perney, J. 455
Perry, K. 148–50, 153
Perry, M.D. 320–1, 325
Perry, P. 391
personhood 605–8, 624, 626, 629
Peru 171, 243, 245, 247
Peterson, S.M. 513
Petty, K. 592
Philippines 243, 245, 247
phonemic awareness 52–3, 64, 104, 121, 123, 126, 153, 455–6, 466, 468–9, 475, 526, 553, 618, 621, 636, 638
   and policy-making 353–5, 358
phonics 4, 52–3, 57, 339, 383–6, 389–91, 450, 454–5, 470, 526, 529–31, 535, 543, 553, 565, 618–20
   and policy-making 346–7, 350–2, 354–7, 360
   and spelling 462–3
   and textbooks 412–14
phonological awareness 52, 83, 118, 120, 349, 372, 387, 389, 391–2, 452, 459, 467–9, 475, 543, 548, 565–6, 636
   and children's writing 427–9
   in different languages 380–2
   phonological complexity 382–3
photo-journals 578
photoshopping 81
Pi Tautau 170
Piaget, J. 313–14, 317, 332, 453
Pictopal 578
picture books 28, 66, 240, 258, 282, 300, 342, 396, 398–9, 401–2, 404, 525, 548, 592, 643
   postmodern picture books 399–401
Piegan Institute 257
Pierce, C. 123
Pierce, P. 123
Piker, R.A. 405
Pink, S. 273
place-making 268, 274
plagiarism *see* copying
play 8, 80–3, 120, 145, 151, 492, 494, 537, 547, 554–5, 576–7, 584, 590, 641, 643
   directions for teaching and research 90–2
   environments for 545–6
   and ethical issues 486–8, 491
   and gender 37–9, 41, 64, 91
   and multimodality 297, 435, 438
   as pedagogy 404–5
   playing to be and belong 83–90
   and sociocultural theory 63–6, 70, 82
   and space and place 282–3, 289
   see also dramatic play; video games

PlayStation 226
Plowman, L. 212, 580–1
pluralism 25, 178, 251, 254, 299
podcasting 81
poetry 120, 164, 168, 340, 366, 374, 395, 403, 471,
    485, 548
Pokémon 68, 89, 148, 269, 273
policy-making 96–9, 109–10, 203–4, 300, 306,
    348–50, 353–62, 380, 388–92, 536, 552–6,
    590–1, 596, 613
  efficiency–equity tradeoff 99–101
  need for comprehensive conceptualizations 103–6
  proposed frameworks and methodologies 106–9
  skill formation 101–3
  and textbooks 410, 413–14, 416, 419
Pollo, T.C. 454
Poole, D. 615–16
poor children *see* low-earning households; poverty
popular culture 10, 41–2, 54, 67–8, 134, 138–9, 144,
    147–54, 218–19, 230, 301, 367, 496, 507–8,
    537, 590
  and artifactual literacies 269, 274, 276
  and children's writing 431, 439
  in the home 209–14
  and literacy 207–9
  parental attitudes to 212–13
  and schooling 214–18
  and space and place 282–4
  and textbooks 410, 417–18
Port, R. 380
Portecorvo, C. 453
positive literacy environments 541–56
postcolonialism 18–32, 140
postmodernism 43, 208
  and gender 45–7
  postmodern picture books 399–401
poststructuralism 45, 138, 591
Potter, B. 415
Poulson, L. 195, 527–9
poverty 27, 56, 58–9, 97–9, 107, 203, 530, 542, 549,
    551–2, 587, 595
  see also socioeconomic factors
Powell, R. 21–2
power relations 36, 47, 56, 70–2, 110, 136, 176, 191,
    215–16, 273–4, 297, 341, 376, 503, 510, 531,
    612, 614, 619, 627–8
  and children's writing 426, 429, 432
  and critical literacy 588–92, 594
  and meaning making 397–8
  and space and place 280–1, 286
  see also empowerment
PowerPoint 300
Prabhu, A. 24–5, 28
Pratt, R.H. 256
Pressley, M. 524–7, 534
Price, L. 513
primers 410–11
  see also textbooks
print awareness 83, 119, 133, 136

prison populations 21, 197–8
private speech 62
process–process studies 621–2
process–product studies 620–4
Proctor, P. 105
professional development 118–19, 122–3, 134, 194,
    203–4, 475, 536, 554–5, 620, 622, 638, 641
Programme for International Student Assessment
    (PISA) 44, 543
Progress in International Reading Literacy Study
    (PIRLS) 543
Project Headstart *see* Headstart
pronunciation 19, 99, 338, 449–50, 459
  see also dialect
pseudohomophones 384
pseudo-words 356, 463, 465–6, 636
psycholinguistics 5–6, 53, 58, 136, 151, 384–5, 412, 568
  see also grain size theory
psychology 4–6, 136, 154, 298, 332, 412, 426, 503, 589
  cognitive psychology 5–6, 58
  cultural psychology 8, 55–6, 136–7
Publishers Association 415
Puerto Rico 345
Pugh, A.J. 88, 91
punctuation 148, 239, 372, 414, 439, 524, 526, 552,
    563, 581
Puranik, C. 472
Purcell-Gates, V. 179, 185–7

Q-methodology 644
Qualitative Inventory of Word Knowledge
    (QIWK) 472–3
Quincy method 346
Quintero, E.P. 404
Quiroz, B.G. 643
Qur'anic classes 161–2, 165–6, 626

Rabinowitz, P.J. 239–41
race 21, 24, 27, 36, 42–3, 47, 56, 58–9, 69–70, 72, 88,
    97, 111, 139, 143, 177, 215, 219, 251–3, 504,
    507–16, 607–8, 637, 643
  and children's writing 426, 431, 433
  and critical literacy 588, 590, 595
  and ethical issues 486, 490, 492
  and meaning making 396–8
  and space and place 280, 287
  and textbooks 411–12
  see also ethnicity
Rainbird, S. 283, 625
Ramsdell, K. 638
RAND Corporation 18
randomized control trials (RCTs) 200–2
Ranker, J. 439
Rao, K. 121–2
Raphael, T. 530
rapid automatic naming (RAN) 467
Razfar, A. 54, 65–6, 298
Read, C. 6, 331, 427, 458–9, 464
reader-response theory 396

Reading Excellence Act 351–2
Reading First 53, 83, 97, 135, 346, 353, 360–1
reading for pleasure 19, 31, 41–2, 44, 549
Reading Rainbow 230
reading readiness 4–5, 52, 57–8, 122, 136, 551, 588
Reading Recovery 331, 471
reading to children 28, 66, 69, 97, 118, 133, 136, 143,
         161–2, 190, 224, 229, 237, 282, 304, 367, 548,
         591, 642–3
Reagan, R. 351
reciprocity 30, 61, 86–7, 180–1, 184, 358, 451, 456–7,
         461–2, 469, 491, 494–6, 550, 569
recitation 144, 166–7, 170, 264, 366, 468, 510, 531, 554
recoding 187, 381, 383–5
recorded books *see* audio books
Recurring Principle 454
reductionism 25, 97, 106, 510, 553
Reese, L. 69, 642
Reeve, R. 578–9
Reeves, C. 149
reflexivity 266, 315
Reformation 409, 411, 413
reforms 18–19, 45, 552
Reid, J. 6
Reid Lyon, G. 352
Relation 25–6
religion 29–30, 105, 138–9, 144, 150, 153, 164–6,
         170–1, 256, 259, 267, 271, 283, 351, 366,
         370–1, 374, 403, 409, 411–12, 418, 448, 502,
         517, 593–4
   faith classes *see* community classes
repetition 144, 166, 170, 233, 239, 527, 529
research methodologies 633–5, 644–6
   beyond the qualitative/quantitative divide 636–44
   quantitative and qualitative studies 635–6
   see also methodological grammars
Response to Intervention (RTI) 119
Reyes, I. 105, 107, 283, 434, 625
Reyes, L.V. 26–7
Reynolds, R.E. 461–2
rhyming 119–20, 143, 302, 348–9, 381–2, 384–5, 403,
         468–9, 471, 532
rhythm 300, 403
Richgels, D.J. 469–70
Rickard Liow, S.J. 465
rimes 382–5, 452, 463–4, 468, 610
Rinaldi, C. 569
Ritchey, K.D. 472
rites of passage 170, 267
Rittle-Johnson, B.R. 460–2
Ritzer, G. 208
Robbins, K. 171–2
Roberts, R. 316, 319, 321, 323
Roberts, T.A. 640
Robertson, J. 569
Robinson, M. 144–5
Rockhill, K. 21
Rodriguez, B.L. 643
Rodriguez-Brown, F.V. 198

Rogers, R. 179, 280, 287, 624
role models 43–4, 549
Rømer, T.A. 562
Rose, J. 384
Rosenblatt, L. 231–2, 388–9, 396
Rosenthal, J. 452, 455
Roser, N.L. 399
Roskos, K. 305, 544–5
Rosowsky, A. 372
Rothenberg, J. 346
Rowe, D. 12, 84, 288, 316, 319, 321, 431–2, 436, 547, 625
Rowsell, J. 46, 213, 283, 291, 332, 625
Ruby, M. 580
Rueda, R. 544
Russell, S. 596
Ryan, J. 301
Rymes, B. 508

safety 86–7, 89–90, 283, 315, 418, 546
Smagorinsky, P. 646
Samuelsson, S. 467
Sandretto, S. 596
Santa, C. 618–19
Saracho, O.N. 180
Sarama, J. 577
Sassine, B. 643
Savage, M. 210–12, 219
Save Our Schools movement 362
Sawyer, W. 390
Saxena, M. 367
scaffolding 8, 149, 372, 472, 504, 511, 513, 547, 549,
         551, 581
scanning 146, 301
Scheurich, J.J. 177
Schiller, J. 578
Schlagal, R. 472–3
Schmier, S. 582
Schneider, W. 384–5
Schultz, K. 104, 140–1, 150
Scollon, R. 70
Scooby Doo 274
Scott, A. 301
Scott, C. 643
Scott-Foresman 410
scribble 314, 425–6, 453
   see also mark-making
Scribner, S. 71
Searle, D. 455–6
Second World War 5, 189, 284
second-wave feminism *see* feminist research
Seed, P. 23
Segedy, J. 577
Seiter, E. 216
self-confidence 166, 200, 214, 376, 550, 583
self-efficacy 253, 543–4
self-regulation 62, 287, 527, 533, 543–4, 546, 548,
         552, 555
semantics 103, 163, 302, 339, 349, 366, 372–3, 425,
         434, 450, 453, 469, 526, 532, 589

semiotic theory 8, 11–13, 37, 40, 64, 81, 91, 138, 148, 151, 265, 315–17, 325, 332, 413, 543, 578–9, 608, 638–40
  and children's writing 432, 435–41
  and meaning making 330, 342
  and multimodality 296, 300, 306
  and space and place 281, 283
  and textbooks 410, 414, 419
Sénéchal, M. 179, 186, 194, 429, 470
Serafini, F. 401–2
Serbia 243, 245, 247
Serpell, R. 182
Sesame Street 230, 235, 415, 420
Seuss, Dr 415
sexism *see* gender
Seymour, P.H.K. 385–6, 466
Shakespeare, W. 208
Shankar, S. 264
Shannon, P. 97, 412, 414
Share, D.L. 466
Sharp, A.C. 428, 461–2
Sharp Corporation 234
Shaw, D. 188
Shaywitz, S.E. 348–51
Shegar, C. 149–50, 211
SHELL–K 511
Shine, S. 399
shoebox projects 218, 269, 272, 305
Shor, I. 347
Shorey, M. 639
show-and-tell 153, 155
Shuler, C. 231
siblings 31, 37, 86, 126, 136, 147, 152–3, 228, 265, 320, 366–7, 430, 549, 575, 580, 626, 637, 645
Siegel, M. 85, 438–9, 582
Siegler, R.S. 460–2
sight words 357, 455, 457
sign language 297, 542
signs 12, 40, 65–7, 265, 284, 302, 306, 316–17, 320–3, 330–3, 336–7, 339–40, 437, 439, 441
  see also semiotic theory
Silko, L.M. 259–60
Silverman, R. 105, 620
Silvers, P. 639
Sinatra, G.M. 461–2
Sinclair, H. 453
singing 64–5, 120, 146, 154, 165–7, 211, 214–15, 471, 548, 590
single-parent families 98, 137, 148
Sipe, L.R. 237, 396–8, 403–4, 471, 623–4
situated methodological grammars 622–8
Skaar, H. 40–1
Skinner, B. F. 5
Skinner, D. 176
Skouge, J. 121–2
Skype 211, 223, 228, 235
smartphones 223–4, 231, 233, 491
  see also cell phones
Smith, C. 581

Smith, F. 5–6, 37
Smith, K.E. 638
Smith, L.B. 322
Smith, P.H. 286
Sneddon, R. 371
Snow, C. 179, 186, 189, 191, 511–12, 514, 643
Snowling, M. 463
Snyder, P.A. 638
social constructivism 14, 23, 57–9, 72, 409, 434
social justice 45, 98, 273, 287, 588, 590, 594–5
social networking sites 81, 225, 228, 416, 418, 575–6
social sciences 21, 646
social security benefits 196
social semiotic theory *see* semiotic theory
social voice 432–3
socialization 35, 54, 56, 61, 71–2, 92, 288, 298, 329, 418, 491, 494, 496, 498, 506, 514, 537, 612, 617, 622
  language socialization 68–70, 625–6
sociocognitive processes 423–6, 441, 448
sociocultural theory 36, 52–6, 140, 142, 153, 208, 214, 380, 386–7, 389, 391, 396, 507, 510, 537, 544, 546, 551, 579, 587
  and children's writing 429–36
  and critical literacy 590–1
  historical context 56–60
  and the internet generation 65–8
  language socialization 68–70
  literacy as a socially mediated process 61–5
  and multimodality 296–8
  and play 63–6, 70, 82
  power relations and early literacy 70–2
  studies of early literacy 60–1
sociodramatic play *see* dramatic play
socioeconomic factors 9, 53, 56, 68, 97–8, 105, 138, 196, 284, 366, 401, 430, 485–8, 511, 525, 529–31, 541, 549, 608, 617, 626, 642
  and critical literacy 590–1
  and policy-making 355, 357
  and textbooks 410, 414
  see also poverty
sociolinguistics 8, 138, 414
Soja, E. 274, 280, 291
Sole, K.E. 24
Solsken, J. 37–8
Son, S.H. 637
Song, M. 512
Sonnenschein, S. 182
Sorsby, A. 325
sound–letter relationships 450, 463, 466–7, 505
Souto-Manning, M. 404, 595
sovereignty 253, 258
spaces 279–81, 299, 320
  community spaces 290–1
  connecting spaces 289–91
  domestic spaces 279, 281–4
  institutional spaces 286–9
Spain 243, 245, 247
Speaker's Corner 594

special-needs students *see* disabilities
Speidel, G.E. 513
spelling 60, 146, 148, 314, 338, 340, 355, 372,
       383–4, 386–7, 448–50, 467, 488, 497, 524,
       529, 533, 636
   and children's writing 425–6, 430, 434, 455
   developmental perspectives 457–64
   English as 'outlier' 465–8
   future research directions 474–6
   how children acquire early written language
       understandings 451–7
   instruction 468–73
   invented spellings 456, 470–2
   in other alphabetic languages 464–5
   retheorizing developmental trajectories 427–8
   spelling–reading connections 428–9
   and textbooks 411, 414
   see also writing systems
Spelling Sensitivity Score 473
Spiderman 211–12, 489–90, 493
Sponge Bob 269, 489
St. Pierre, R.G. 179, 201
standardized testing 57, 85, 138, 218, 359, 405, 412,
       414–16, 419, 503, 511, 565–6, 571, 587
Standards-Based Change (SBC) 536
status updates *see* social networking sites
Steedman, C. 207, 214–15
Steensel, R. 194
Stein, P. 332
Stellakis, N. 456
Stephen, C. 580
stereotypes 88, 216, 218
   American Indian stereotypes 252–3, 257
   disability stereotypes 115, 117
   gender stereotypes 42–3, 45
Stewart, S.R. 638
stickers 209, 271
Stoiber, K. 119
Stokes, S.J. 167
Stone, S.J. 513
storybook reading *see* reading to children
Street, B. 9, 71, 151, 264, 275, 314, 389, 392, 501, 506,
       614, 645
street children 491
Stuckey, J.E. 21
Styles, M. 398
subjectivism 25, 176–8, 181, 185, 188–92, 275, 498,
       502, 510, 594, 626
Sulzby, E. 314, 452
Summer, G. 123
Sunday Schools 167–8
Super Mario 68, 148
superheroes 149, 211–12, 216, 489–90, 493–4, 507–8
Superman 149, 490
super-rimes 382
supplementary schools *see* community classes
Sure Start 145
Swain, J. 201
Swann Report 164

Sweden 96, 243, 245, 247
Sweet, B. 351
Switzerland 243, 245, 247
syllables 381–2, 427, 454, 464–5, 467–8
symbol weavers 64, 436
symbols 12, 66–7, 230, 284, 286, 295–6, 298, 302, 306,
       314, 318–19, 323, 347, 349, 367, 449, 493, 524
syntax 103, 339–40, 353, 434, 453, 549

Tabors, P. 547
Taiwan 243, 245, 247, 345
talk and discourse 501–2, 537, 551
   analytic heuristic 502–4
   autonomous fixed meaning 510–14
   autonomous fluid meaning 504–6
   ideological fixed meaning 514–16
   ideological fluid meaning 506–10
   implications for future research 516–17
talking books *see* audio books
Tancock, S. 577
Tao, F. 180, 184
Tardibuono, J. 608
Tarr, H. 184
Taxel, J. 251
Taylor, B.M. 536
Taylor, D. 9, 179, 182, 184, 186, 188, 190, 194, 196,
       579, 615
Te Whariki 300
Teacher Rating of Language and Literacy 123
Teacher Training Agency 527–8
Teachers' College Writing Project 505
Teale, W.H. 319, 578–9
Teberosky, A. 7, 322, 454
technology *see* digital technologies
technoscapes 208
teenage pregnancy 102, 110
Teletubbies 230, 641
television 67–8, 109, 142–4, 146–50, 152, 154, 171–2,
       208–12, 214, 223–41, 244–7, 273, 282–3, 367,
       416, 439, 489, 575, 580, 590, 641
Test of Language Development 566
Test of Word Reading Efficiency (TOWRE) 636
testing 44, 57, 83–4, 97, 100, 197, 201, 218, 347,
       391, 405, 412–13, 415, 468, 487–8, 530,
       565–6, 606, 617
   and policy-making 353–4
   see also assessment; standardized testing
text messaging 36–7, 81, 576
textbooks 171, 345, 347, 368, 409–10
   and crossover into home reading 414–16
   from home reading to new technologies 416–19
   and the production of the modern reading child
       410–14
   from textbooks to pedagogic texts 419–20
Thelen, E. 322
Thomas, W. 375
Thomas the Tank Engine 88, 226, 269
Thornton, R. 255
Tiffin, H. 24

Tikly, L. 18
Tillett, B. 578
time diaries (TD) 108–9
TinkerBell 494
Tippeconnic, J.W. 254
Tizard, B. 9
Tohono O'odham community 609
Tolchinsky, L. 324
Tomasello, M. 322, 485
Topp, N. 577
Topping, K. 529–30
Torr, J. 643–4
Torres, M.N. 26–7
touch-screens 298
Tower, C. 401
Townsend, M.A. 526, 531
toys 7, 13, 37, 39, 46, 81–2, 86–8, 91–2, 144, 209–10,
    213–14, 219, 228, 231, 235–7, 264, 268–71,
    274–5, 282–4, 288, 304, 315, 336, 409–10, 414,
    419, 485, 490, 546–7, 575, 584, 614
trading cards 147–8, 209, 273
training to be trained 506, 510
transduction 302–3, 437, 581
Traveller communities 219
Treiman, R. 426, 459
Tripp, D. 225
triphthongs 340
Troia, G.A. 475
Trueba, H.T. 616
Tse, L. 376
Tucker, R. 364
Turkish Early Enrichment Project (TEEP) 195, 199
Turnbull, B. 144–5
TV see television
TV guides 210, 212
Tyner, K. 226

underprivileged children see socioeconomic factors
unfairness see fairness
United Nations 21, 258
Universal Design for Learning 125

Valentine, K. 496
values 4, 12, 29–31, 56, 59, 64, 68–9, 71, 80, 85, 101,
    124, 142, 195, 208, 216–17, 227, 252, 259, 268,
    283, 297–9, 351, 411–13, 429, 431, 433, 503,
    509, 561–7, 570–1, 612, 645
    see also ethical issues
Van Der Heyden, A.M. 638
van Kleeck, A. 513
Van Leeuwen, T. 41
Vandermaas-Peeler, M. 643
Vasquez, V. 21, 591, 593–5, 597
Verhoeven, L. 371, 375
Vernon-Feagans, L. 69
video games 66–8, 82, 88–9, 91, 142, 144, 146–9,
    152–4, 209–12, 214, 226, 233, 235, 288, 301,
    419–20, 439, 580–1
violence 40, 87, 98, 146, 217, 334, 489

virtual worlds 65, 81–2, 89–90, 146, 152, 211, 270,
    281, 416–18, 581
    see also avatars
vocabulary 29, 52–3, 64, 119–20, 182, 355, 390, 414,
    425, 455, 524, 526, 528, 530, 533, 543, 547,
    549–50, 552–5, 564–6, 618, 621, 636–7
Volk, D. 86, 144–5, 153
Volosinov, V.N. 490, 495
Voogt, J. 578
Vygotsky, L.S. 8, 60–4, 87, 91, 136, 151, 163, 178, 298,
    321, 331–2, 396, 531, 545–8

Wagner, D.A. 371
Walker, E. 391
Walking With Dinosaurs 149, 226
Wall Street Journal 352
Walsh, M. 301, 398, 402
War on Poverty 58
Warhammer 269
Washington, J.A. 607–8
Wasik, B.A. 644
Wasserman, K.B. 645
Watson, D.J. 568
Watson, J. 390
Webkinz 89–90
websites see internet
Weigel, D. 281
Weinberger, J. 282
Weinstein, C.S. 545
Wells, G. 9, 505, 608
Welsh Language Board 369
Weninger, C. 149–50, 211
Wertsch, J.V. 297–8
WH Smith 415
Wharton-McDonald, R. 524
Wheat, J. 438
Wheelock, E. 256
white supremacy see race
Whitehurst, G.J. 179, 607
whole-language 46, 345–7, 351, 354–8, 360, 413, 620
Widjaja, V. 465
Wigfield, A. 388
Wiggins, G. 53
Wikipedia 147
Wilde, S. 470, 608–9
Wilkinson, I.A. 526, 531
Wilkinson, K. 282
Williams, A. 189, 191, 317
Williams, C. 473
Williams, G. 510
Williams, R. 207, 267
Willis, P. 207
Wilson, A.C. 252
Winnie the Pooh 88
Winskel, H. 465
Within Word Pattern 456, 458–9, 462–3
Wohlwend, K.E. 46–7, 66, 214, 217, 265, 270, 274, 288,
    301, 320, 404, 438–9, 508, 567, 582, 614, 639
Wolf, D. 320–1, 325

Wolfe, S. 320, 582
Wollman-Bonilla, J.E. 431
Wong Fillmore, L. 637
Wood, C. 469
Woodcock Reading Mastery Test – Revised 566
Woodward, V. 12, 301, 453
word recognition 104, 146, 354–5, 412–14, 455, 465, 467, 471, 524, 528, 530–3, 552, 636
word searches 418
workshops 39, 183, 489, 494, 526, 550–2
World Bank 21
World War II *see* Second World War
Wray, D. 527–9
writing *see* children's writing
writing systems 466
    history and nature of 449–51
    how children acquire early written language understandings 451–7
Wyse, D. 391

Xu, S.H. 212

Yaden, D.B. 105, 608, 620
Yamada-Rice, D. 210, 217, 219, 285, 642
Yang, E. 54, 65–6
Yelland, N. 576
Yeung, C. 305
Young, K. 461
Young, L. 194
Young, M.D. 177
Young, R.J.C. 22, 24
YouTube 223, 225, 228, 233, 320

Zacher Pandya, J. 596
Zhao, J. 643
Ziegler, J.C. 384–5
Ziliak, S.T. 110
Zinsser, C. 167
zone of actual development (ZAD) 62
zone of proximal development (ZPD or Zoped) 62–3, 546, 549
Zutell, J. 456
Zvoch, K. 638